REVISED EDITION

College English:
the first year

J. HOOPER WISE · J. E. CONGLETON · ALTON C. MORRIS

University of Florida

JOHN C. HODGES

University of Tennessee

HARCOURT, BRACE AND COMPANY

New York

Drawing on cover is based on photograph taken in the Harvard Yard.

Copyright, 1941, 1943, 1946, 1947, 1951, 1952, © 1956
by Harcourt, Brace and Company, Inc.

B.3.56

PRINTED IN THE UNITED STATES OF AMERICA

CONTENTS

Book One · College Readings

part one *Essays and Articles*

THE NOVEL

DRAMA

POETRY

The Poet as Story Teller

The Poet as Singer

The Poet as Wit and Humorist

The Poet as Portrayer of Character

Book Two · Fundamentals of Speaking, Listening, and Writing

FOREWORD

Reading maketh a full man; conference a ready man; and writing an exact man.—BACON

Since reading and writing, speaking and listening are distinct but closely related aspects of the whole process of effective communication, this Revised Edition of *College English: The First Year*, like the First Edition, has been designed to offer a complete course in these four basic disciplines that go into making a *full, ready,* and *exact* man. Its economy and convenience are readily obvious: here are all the components of first-year English in one volume.

College English is divided into five parts: Parts I and II comprise Book One, "College Readings"; Parts III, IV, and V make up Book Two, "Fundamentals of Speaking, Listening, and Writing."

Part I, like its predecessors—*Essays for Better Reading,* 1940, *The Meaning in Reading,* 1943, 1947, and Part I of the First Edition—is designed primarily to improve skill in reading expository prose and to stimulate the student's interest in the mature thinking of our day. The essays and articles were chosen because they are timely but not narrowly dated, mature but within the understanding of the first-year student. These selections, if read thoughtfully, should provide valuable standards of writing and speaking. The essays in the special section "Language in Use," which have primarily a social and psychological approach, give the student a fuller understanding of the implications of the language processes and thereby improve his ability to read, write, listen, and speak.

Part II, an introduction to the study of literature, contains generous representations of each of the five major types of literature. The selections were chosen not because they represent an author, a period, a movement, or a nationality but because they are arresting and meaningful for the freshman reader and because they have genuine literary merit and lasting value.

Part III emphasizes the layman's need—personal, social, and professional—for proficiency in speaking and listening and presents the basic principles which will aid the student to speak and listen with greater effect.

Part IV illustrates the basic principles of composition through an examination of the major forms of discourse—exposition, argument, description, and narration.

Part V, the *Harbrace College Handbook,* Fourth Edition, is concerned with the mechanics of written English and the art of composition. It not only contains rules and illustrations drawn from the best modern usage but also presents certain rhetorical principles, which are supplemented by Part IV.

The *Exercise Manual,* accompanying the text, shares the inclusiveness of the text itself. The exercises are designed to make the preparation of assignments more thorough and informative for the student and to furnish the instructor with a convenient teaching device. Growing out of each essay and article are exercises that test for central idea, analyze the organization, and evaluate the supporting details, improve vocabulary, acquaint the students with some indispensable library reference works, and suggest subjects for talks and themes. The exercises for Part II—biography, short story, novel, drama, and poetry—not only check for ideas and content but also focus upon the work as literature, frequently giving special attention to its theme, feeling, tone, and intention. The *Manual* also contains exercises on speech, listening, and rhetoric, to enable the student to work out the ideas contained in Parts III and IV. And, lastly, it contains drills to accompany the *Handbook;* these drills emphasize the areas of written language where students have the greatest difficulties and where failure or incompetence would most seriously interfere with effective writing.

Eight essays in Part I comprise a special reading project. Suggestions for improving reading, directions for carrying out the project, tests on reading comprehension and rate, and a chart on which the student may record his progress have been included in the *Manual.*

College English does more than present in one volume the materials for a complete freshman English course; the various parts of the text complement one another, and the exercises are interrelated. For instance, Stephen Leacock's biography of Mark Twain adds interest and pleasure to the reading of *Huckleberry Finn;* some selections, like Van Wyck Brooks's "Helen Keller," Susanne K. Langer's "The Language Line," and Helen Keller's "The Story of My Life," enrich each other; some poems, like Matthew Arnold's "Dover Beach" and Arthur Hugh Clough's "Say Not the Struggle Nought Availeth," present opposing points of view. Frequent cross references in the exercises show the basic affinity of the various components of the text. If *College English* contains more than can be used in many freshman English courses, such abundance will allow each instructor considerable choice in the arrangement of his course and the opportunity to vary it from time to time to meet the needs of his students.

In such an extensive undertaking the editors have had to ask for much assistance. Though it is impossible to name everyone who has helped in one way or another in preparing this book, a few have given such substantial help that they are in a sense co-editors. We gratefully acknowledge their contributions. Our own colleagues to whom we are especially indebted are: Denver E. Baughan, Robert H. Bowers, Clarence Derrick, James R. Hodges, C. E. Mounts, David Stryker, Richard B. Vowles, and Biron H. Walker. And to Professor Francis X. Connolly, of Fordham University, we are indebted for the section entitled "A Preface to Writing."

part one

Essays and Articles

INTRODUCTION

The distinction between the essay and the article is one with which not everyone agrees, since today *essay* is used as a general term to include almost any piece of short nonfictional prose on a fairly compact or unified subject. Yet the distinction, properly made, is useful, for *essay* becomes more meaningful if its application is limited.

Both the essay and the article may be concerned with almost any sublunary subject—or even the moon itself, as Arthur Clarke's piece demonstrates. The writer may take for his subject man in general, or man in particular, or any of the ideas or concepts or beliefs of mankind. He may write about people or places or traditions or mountain climbing or college spirit or man's conscience. There is no limit to his subject, as may be seen by a glance at the great variety of topics covered in the few pieces in this section.

But in general the essay is concerned with man's beliefs, ideas, concepts, whereas the article is concerned with the transitory event, the ephemeral thought. Mr. Fischer's piece on American politics is an essay; Mr. Angell's discussion of baseball is an article.

A correlative distinction is the lasting quality of the essay in contrast to the brief life of the article. An essay and an article may at a given time be almost equally interesting and important. But the essay endures, it is read and reread in after years, whereas the article—no matter how effective—is soon forgotten. And usually we find, on further examination, that the essay is of a higher literary quality than the article; indeed, endurance in itself is an important touchstone of literary value.

Today the term *essay*, whose original meaning—an "attempt," *essai*—was demonstrated rather than defined by Montaigne and Bacon, the first so-called essayists, still retains something of its early significance, for essayists do not undertake to be exhaustive in the treatment of their subjects. Rather they propose, as John Morley has remarked, "to open questions, to indicate points, to suggest cases, to sketch outlines."

This Part also contains a few examples of a special type of article known as reportage. Reportage is documentary, factual literature that has the high interest and great insight typical of first-rate fiction. The subject matter of reportage, as exemplified by Berton Roueché's "A Game of Wild Indians" and Maurice Herzog's "The Third of June," is specific, recorded events, but events that are of wide, even universal, significance.

The essay is profoundly sensitive to social environment. Probably no form of written expression records the social, political, and cultural interests of an age more completely and more accurately. The essay had its beginning in an age that delighted in proverbial lore; the essays of Montaigne and Bacon reflect that taste. The periodical essays of the eighteenth century represent the wit, gossip, and learning that passed among men conversing in the coffee houses of Addison's and Steele's London. Today the essay, through its diversified subject matter, its proliferation of types, and the unlimited possibility it affords for men to speak their minds, not only reflects the complexity of modern life but also, in a larger sense, is a sounding board of men's aspirations and fears. The essay has maintained its popularity as a medium through which the layman as well as the professional writer may impart knowledge, opinion, and counsel. The modern essay, therefore, provides a valuable means by which men may be informed of the thinking, the conflicting opinions, and the achievements of the times.

ROBERT U. JAMESON *How to Stay in College*

Robert U. Jameson (1910-   ), teacher and student counselor, was educated at Harvard University. Following his graduation, he taught two years at The Rectory School, Pomfret, Connecticut. Since 1934 he has been teaching and counseling students at Haverford School, a Pennsylvania boys' preparatory school, where he heads the English Department. As reader for the College Entrance Board and as a grader of English examinations for the State Department, he has had ample opportunity to view the deficiencies of matriculating college freshmen.

During the summer of 1954 Mr. Jameson visited the officials in a large number of colleges and conducted an extensive correspondence with some of his former students who are now in college. Some of the findings of this investigation are reported in this essay, which discusses frankly and realistically the problems that first-year students inevitably face in adjusting themselves to academic life.

1. At least 2,500,000 young Americans are in college this fall. Of these, about 1,000,000 are freshmen. These figures are impressive; they seem to indicate that the ideal of a college-educated democracy is on the way to realization. Yet the unhappy fact is that more than a third of the men and women who enter college fail to graduate. Why?

2. To find the answer to this question, I have talked to deans and instructors in several colleges and to a large number of young men and women who have just finished their freshman year in colleges all across the United States. Some facts are clear.

3. Of those who drop out of college, some leave for financial reasons, and this is often tragic because these people in many cases do well in college before they have to leave. Some

HOW TO STAY IN COLLEGE: Reprinted, by permission of the author, from *The Saturday Evening Post*, October 2, 1954.

leave because of poor health. A few are drafted. Many leave for "personal" reasons—marriage, family mixups or just the realization that college is not the place for them.

4. But the principal concern of the colleges is the disappearance of students who should graduate, but who simply fail instead. Therefore the real question is this: Why do students fail in college?

5. Although they may state it differently, all college deans from coast to coast agree on one point: The major problem of the college freshman is that of adjusting to a new kind of life, in which he is expected to behave like an adult. The Assistant Dean of Freshmen at Yale, Harold B. Whiteman, Jr., calls this "the acquiring of self-discipline." Dr. J. W. Graham, Assistant Dean at Carnegie Tech, calls the same process "learning to think." Diogenes, among others, said simply "Know thyself." In one way or another, what happens

in the first year or two of college depends largely upon this one thing: Is the college student ready to grow up, to understand what college is?

6. What is college? By the end of this article, I believe that the question will be answered fairly. To begin with, here are some general statements about what college is. Robert B. Cox, Dean of Men at Duke University, says that his fervent wish is to be able some day to prove to an entering class that the freshman year is not Grade 13 in high school. Father Edward Dwyer, of Villanova College, says this: "I wish that it were possible for us to demonstrate that college is a place for adults, not an advanced school for children." And a young man who has just finished his first year at Princeton says this: "The most important problems facing a freshman are those of adjustment to a unique society, one totally different from high school."

7. Can college be defined?

8. In the first place, college is a place in which a person can learn how to learn. In school, boys and girls are taught something about how to pass courses in order to get a school diploma. Often enough they get the diploma at a certain age even with a record of failure. In college, on the other hand, these boys and girls are asked to learn to think, to meet complex intellectual problems and to handle these problems on their own. Intellectual independence, the first requisite of college, is often a distinct shock to a freshman.

9. An example of one college's method will perhaps make the point clearer. At The Carnegie Institute of Technology, English composition courses are quite unlike high-school courses. Students may be given several opposing points of view about a single topic and told to reach a logical, unbiased conclusion in a composition about this topic. The unwary freshman is thus faced with the necessity of using logic, of discarding personal prejudices and of writing carefully in order to prove to his instructor that he is capable of thinking through a problem. This "case-study" method is used in more than one freshman course in college.

10. Another course will present a student with the necessity of doing a large volume of reading and drawing conclusions from the

reading. Or an instructor may say something like this: "What happened in England during the first week of July, 1751?" The freshman who asks how to find out such things will probably be rewarded with an icy stare and a map showing where the college library is—no more.

11. How do freshmen react to situations like these? Unfortunately, many will react badly because the spoon feeding of the high school, the parents eager to help with homework, the teacher who leads classes by the nose are all missing. Now the human brain, perhaps the least-used muscle in the human body, has to start working on its own.

12. A student who has finished a year at Washington and Lee says this: "I have just begun to realize, at the end of a rough year, what college has to offer. I hope that next year I will do a better job." "In college," says a girl at Michigan, "you get nowhere until you grow up."

13. But no college dean or adviser can possibly walk up to a floundering freshman and say, "You will do all right as soon as you grow up." Instead, all colleges provide elaborate programs to introduce the college to the freshmen, to warn the young people about what is ahead.

14. When the 1,000,000 new freshmen arrive for Freshman Week at any of the nearly 2000 colleges in the land, they are put through a complicated and sometimes bewildering mill. They meet their roommates. They meet their advisers. They take placement tests and aptitude tests and reading tests and physical examinations. They meet the president. They are invited to buy the school paper, pennants, beer mugs, rugs, laundry service and everything else under the sun. They attend a football rally and chapel and a dance or two and a picnic and a number of meetings for indoctrination in the methods of study.

15. They are breezed through a very pleasant week—dizzying, perhaps, but new and different. They don't even have time to get homesick. That comes about two weeks later. Now, during this week, deans and advisers say many things which freshmen may, to their sorrow, ignore:

Start studying at once.
Get to know the library immediately.

Set up a schedule for yourself—revise it later, if necessary—to include both social and academic activities.

Join one or two extracurricular activities, but not every one in sight.

Get enough sleep.

Don't forget chapel.

Don't cut classes.

You're on your own; make the most of your independence. But if you get into trouble, see your adviser right away.

16. Then classes begin, and the realities of college are suddenly all too evident. The first theme is written; the first history test is taken; the first physics experiment is done. And the first blast comes from a teacher, who, unlike lovable old Mr. Chips at home in the high school, is apparently half devil and half dragon.

17. An angry English instructor throws a theme on the desk in front of the dean of admissions and says acidly, "Would you be good enough to tell me why this man, who is obviously an idiot, has been admitted to this college?"

18. A freshman hands in a paper two days late and wonders why he gets an E. Another is stymied by the fact that his edition of *King Lear* has no footnotes to explain the text. "How am I supposed to be able to understand this stuff?"

19. A freshman's reaction to failure is a clear indication of whether he is a child or an adult. The adult simply works harder. The child may get surly. He may blame the instructor, not realizing that it is he, not the instructor, who has failed. He may look for excuses to explain his failure—headaches, a loud-mouthed roommate, the radio across the hall.

20. Because the college is concerned about the student who is in trouble and wants to save him, elaborate counseling programs have been set up in every college. The counselors, or advisers, try first to find out why students fail and then try to correct the trouble.

21. Among the causes for freshman failure, certainly the most important is lack of adequate training in secondary school. Overworked and underpaid teachers are simply not finding it possible to condition many of their students for the rigors of college work, particularly in the one most important subject of all: English.

22. According to almost every administrative officer in the colleges, the average freshman is deficient in the basic skills of reading and composition. Poor reading is usually caused by lack of practice. The average student today simply does not read many books; consequently, when he has to face long and complicated reading assignments in college, he may find that he has to study forty or fifty hours a week to keep his head above water. Or he may throw up his hands, say the assignments are impossible and go to the movies. In the latter case he will probably be on probation before long.

23. Colleges all over the land are finding it necessary to establish reading clinics for the most seriously retarded readers. Yet the number of students who get clinical attention is usually limited because few colleges are rich enough to set up a really adequate reading center. The student who is in trouble here should, however, at least go over the problem with his adviser, who will be able to give sound advice about the art of studying.

24. A large number of young men and women, college Class of 1958, say that one of their most serious freshman-year mistakes was not seeing their advisers often enough.

25. If reading by freshmen is poor, composition is generally even worse. It is pathetic to see items like this in college catalogues: "English W-1. Remedial course in composition. M.W.F. 9. Required of students who show insufficient preparation for English A. Students who pass the course with an A or B receive two points credit. Others receive no credit and are required to take English A."

26. English W-1 and its counterparts in hundreds of colleges waste time doing high-school work while advanced work has to wait. But college students must be able to communicate an idea, whether in literature or physics. College advisers wish that all schools could somehow graduate all students with at least a rudimentary idea of what a good sentence is.

27. This description of poor preparation in English, which is commented on again and again in the colleges—a Harvard faculty report in 1898 made the complaint—is not intended to condemn the high-school English teachers of America. Nor is it to be understood that every freshman is poorly prepared. The ma-

jority of freshmen have been in classes so large that no teacher can be expected to assign a weekly theme, much less correct the theme and confer with every student about the paper. Thus the freshman is too often in trouble because of shortcomings which have nothing to do with his ability. Under the circumstances, the best advice for a high-school student may well be this: beginning two or three years before you go to college, work on English composition and read a lot of books. Otherwise you may have serious trouble in all your college work, even if you are going to study animal husbandry or mining engineering.

28. The next academic problem of the freshman year—and this applies to all students, whether or not they have specific subject-matter difficulty—is that of how to study and how much to study.

29. According to most college authorities, high-school graduates, not usually so coddled as private-school students, get at their work early but do not realize how much is demanded of them. Independent-school graduates are likely to coast during the first part of the freshman year, because much of what they are being taught is in some way a repetition of their prep-school work. Then they may fall into the habit of thinking that college is easy.

30. "Because of my excellent high-school preparation, I did not have to work very hard during the first term," writes a young man who had hard sledding at Cornell last year. "Most of the material was review, and I became over-confident, ending the term with a 74. When I began learning completely new material in the second term, I did not improve my study habits enough to maintain the standards set by the faculty. I learned how to study the hard way, by 'busting out.' If I had the year to do over, I would study regularly and keep up with assignments, even though the material was neither new nor interesting. I do not like summer school."

31. Every college adviser tells his advisees the same thing. Some listen. A hundred freshmen, at the end of the year, say the same thing: start to study at once. Don't get behind. "Boy, if I dropped a pencil in the lecture room, I missed a semester's work," said a Penn State Marine Corps veteran.

32. This "busting out," or flunking, by

well-prepared, intelligent students is what the Dean of Freshmen at Duke calls the "G-Factor." G stands for Goof, in the current slang use of the word. The bright boy who goofs is a very big headache to his college and a terrible waste of money, brains, effort and teaching. Obviously a number of these G-boys find themselves. What is tragic is that failure is the only way to show such a bright boy or girl that the college means business.

33. The jolt of failure sometimes produces results other than recovery. One common reaction is to blame the instructor. But no college adviser has much time for such an attitude. "I always tell characters like that," says a dean of a Southern college, "that I don't care what he thinks of the teacher. I tell him the library is right across the street. He can learn a lot there."

34. Or failure may bring a defeatist attitude, particularly to a student who has always done well in school. Colleges are on the watch for the defeatist, because they want to salvage at least something which the student has to offer, and they want also to keep him on an even keel emotionally. Deans, advisers, the college health service, coaches and others go into action. The student who fails to react to the collective wisdom of a group like this eventually will probably be dropped.

35. An additional cause of failure, other than lack of study, is, according to many college admissions officers, the insistence by families that their children shall do thus and so in college. There are several unfortunate kinds of family influence. On the one hand is the family which, because of tradition, thinks that only one college in the country is worth anything. Attending that college is therefore mandatory, even if the college and the boy or girl do not fit each other.

36. Much unhappiness can be caused in this way, and many transfers to other institutions are arranged every year for students who start off in the wrong place.

37. On the other hand is the family, not college-trained, which has laudable but often unrealistic hopes for a son or daughter: my son is going to be a doctor or an engineer; my daughter is going to be a nurse. In many instances these students become discouraged

easily, and many of them drop out when they realize that they are not college material.

38. This particular problem is one found more often in the large state universities than in the smaller colleges, whose admissions requirements are stricter, and in which the student's purposes are more closely investigated before he is admitted.

39. But academic failure is by no means the only cause of trouble in college. Since college life is a complete and complicated existence, failure often comes to the student who cannot preserve the important balance between his academic and his social life. Overemphasis on extracurricular activities, too much drinking, too much dating, too much fraternity activity—all of these will lead to trouble.

40. College, like life, is far too full of temptations. "My hardest job," says a bright young man, "was to take over where my parents left off—to learn to face facts: when you have to work, work; don't go to the movies." Another writes this way: "All people had to do was mention a party and I left the books."

41. In college, as in the world, the herd instinct is very strong. Offer cigars to a group of teen-agers and see what happens. (No youngster actually likes cigars.) If the first boy refuses, all may refuse. If the first accepts the gift, who will have the courage to refuse?

42. Eugene S. Wilson, Dean of Freshmen at Amherst College, has a very sound piece of advice. "The big job is to get students to be themselves. Most people don't dare to be a nobody; they must conform, be like everybody else. We try to tell our students that they should not be afraid to be good students—to study instead of holding a 'bull session.'" Or, to quote Emerson: "Whoso would be a man must be a nonconformist."

43. Activities in college are very attractive, and every student will miss a great deal if he stays completely away from them. From varsity football to the radio station, from intramural field hockey to folk dancing, there is something of interest to everyone on the campus. The problem is one of proportion.

44. Here are student comments:

"If I had the year to do over, I would say 'no' to all but one carefully chosen extracurricular activity." (Cornell)

"Athletics are good, but don't try to be a three-letter man. Actually, one sport is enough, due to the tremendous drain on one's studying time." (Princeton)

"If you don't have time for intercollegiate sports, get into the intramural program. That is enough exercise for anybody." (Amherst)

"Join some clubs, but don't stress them over classes." (Middlebury)

"Watch out for varsity athletics. Intramurals take less time." (Oklahoma)

45. Colleges vary considerably in their approach to extracurricular activities, to be sure —from the institution which has abolished intercollegiate sports to the one which provides scholarships for athletes. But all colleges agree that too much nonacademic exertion is certain to upset a student's normal balance.

46. Every freshman dean advises his charges to join a team or a club if it can be done without letting classwork suffer. Every dean also advises his charges not to join everything in sight. The wonderful independence of the freshman cannot be allowed to turn into license. One college simply advises its students to spend eight hours sleeping, eight hours in study and classes, and eight hours on everything else—as an average.

47. There are extracurricular activities which seem to help the student's over-all maturing in judgment and balance: the "cultural" clubs—music and dramatics—and, of increasing importance, religious activities. Nearly all campuses report an increasing awareness of the need for personal religion. This need, reflecting perhaps the uncertainty of the times, is filled by prayer groups and religious-discussion groups. Many colleges, like Dartmouth and the University of North Carolina, report increased activity on the part of the Christian Union and the Y.M.C.A., which carry on extensive social-work projects in the college and in the community. At Yale, among other groups, there is even a U. S. Grant Institute, which gives free tutoring to Negro children in New Haven. Ohio State University has every year a popular Religion in Life Week, organized by student church groups and presenting an imposing array of speakers and discussion leaders.

48. A serious social problem on most campuses is a three-way problem: drinking, dating and driving. These, or at least the first and

third, concern some colleges more than others. Most college freshmen can be realistic about drinking. Nearly all of them say: drink moderately, if at all; date on weekends only—otherwise marks suffer. One Wellesley girl thinks that learning to drink is as important as other types of education. But she drinks "rye and ginger (one)" only if her date drinks. And a young man at Middlebury makes this astute remark: "Being a big drinker doesn't make you popular or a big wheel on campus. Far from it. If anything, it hinders your chances of making lasting friends."

49. College authorities vary in their approach to the question of drinking, especially when college policy in the matter is not rigid. Big-city colleges like Columbia realistically accept the fact that no "prohibition" is possible on a campus surrounded by several dozen New York City taprooms. Many colleges urge the prosecution of bars which serve minors, and a number of such places have been closed —temporarily. Some colleges simply ban liquor from the campus and hope for the best. Still others put into their Campus Code the stipulation that drinking in public is not gentlemanly. And while all colleges will expel students who make public nuisances of themselves, nearly all are philosophical about the problem.

50. But when, as in the small-town college or the college in a "dry" county, driving and drinking are combined, administrations have a real problem. When students who want a drink have to go to the next county or even the next state, or when they have to go a distance for a date, they go by automobile. When alcohol is added, disaster sometimes occurs.

51. As to the automobile by itself—it is here to stay, whether colleges allow it or not. And it is a difficult problem for both college authorities and college students.

52. At Dartmouth, for instance, about half of the upperclassmen have cars. Hanover, New Hampshire, is a long way from girls, and on Friday there is a major exodus and too little weekend studying. Big-city colleges have another kind of problem. At Ohio State, for instance, students "need" cars to get to class. In order to pay for the upkeep of the automobile, large numbers of car owners get part-

time jobs which often use up so many hours that little time is left for study. Then academic failure appears just because of a car. Fathers are culprits in this thing too. They often give their college sons cars in order to maintain social status. Here again, maturity is what matters—even in father.

"Don't spend too much time with a car," one freshman says, "because it just costs too much." Sound advice.

53. Many colleges allow only juniors and seniors to drive cars. Others crack down when a student is in academic trouble. A few allow no cars at all. But in spite of the ban on cars at one college in the Philadelphia area, the dean shakes his head and says, "When our graduates die and go to heaven, the first thing they will say is, 'Where can I get a car?'"

54. Good advice to freshmen, agreed to by all sources, would surely be this: leave your car at home and for a year or two find out what college has to offer you, other than a parking lot. You are presumably in college for something besides automobile mechanics.

55. Indeed, what are the reasons why people are in college today? This is the big question, and the answers which college freshmen give to the question will indicate pretty clearly that there is an enormous amount of misunderstanding about what college is, what it means to students, what it can do for students. This last major item must be explored in some detail.

56. Some of the commonly accepted values of a college education are these:

One can join many clubs.
One can meet the right people.
One can continue a distinguished career in athletics.
One can stay out of the Army.
One can learn a business.
One can get a degree.
One can learn to be a research scholar.
One can prepare for a profession.
One can get a background of culture.
One can learn how to think.

57. The first five of these are unworthy or invalid objectives for the college student. Yet they exist, and they cause trouble. Overemphasis on social life—the first two in the list— has already been discussed, but the others need some attention.

58. It is no secret that the high pressure of interscholastic and intercollegiate athletics is itself responsible for confusion in the minds of many muscular young men. They have been coddled in school because they could throw passes accurately. Colleges bid for their services, often pay them well. Hence they expect to slide through colleges as athletes, and, in some colleges, they do just this. The coddling goes on, and the happy students move serenely to the Chicago Bears or the Detroit Tigers. Thus for some individuals there is no problem except that college education is perhaps an inaccurate description of what they have been doing.

59. But most colleges fortunately have a philosophy different from this. In most colleges, athletes must pass their courses or run the risk of probation and ineligibility. In these colleges much time is spent on the guidance of athletes in an attempt to keep the men on an even keel. At Columbia, for instance, nearly all of the coaches have professorial rank and attend faculty meetings, where athletic policy and academic problems are both discussed. The coaches are educators, and many of them are student counselors. Most colleges attempt to orient the student, athletically, by organizing an extensive intramural-sports program, which ordinarily enlists the support of most of the students in games for fun, not for dollars. The thoughtful freshman will put athletics into reasonable balance with his other activities.

60. Selective Service still looms large in young men's minds, for obvious reasons. But the draft is not nearly so strong an upsetting factor as it was even two or three years ago. Today, thanks to provisions in the Selective Service Act which temporarily defer most college students who stay out of academic trouble, "draft jitters" is a minor problem on most campuses.

61. What is more, ROTC programs are proving attractive and profitable to many young men, some of whom "find" themselves only while in the service and make a career of the Army or Navy. In some colleges, ROTC programs are compulsory for the first two years, then elective; in others they are elective all the way.

62. The freshman who has the option of electing or not electing ROTC may find himself in a quandary. His draft deferment is more certain if he joins. On the other hand, college deans point out that many freshmen are unhappy about joining because the quality of instruction in ROTC courses is often not so good as that in the academic courses which the student wants to take. The serious student may find Military Science and Tactics, to say nothing of drill, a waste of time.

63. The attitude of the administrations and advisers varies markedly, and the freshman should certainly listen to the advice which is apt for his college. At least one Eastern college advises freshmen not to enroll in ROTC. More than one dean is in favor of universal military training. Many others simply point out what the program has to offer and leave the decision up to the student. Advisers will probably have two main things to say: (1) Students who stay in the upper half of their class, scholastically, have a good chance of keeping their I-S classification until they graduate. And (2) students who go into ROTC and graduate with a commission will probably have a more enjoyable time when they do go into service.

64. And all college deans to whom I mentioned the matter are agreed on one final point about the draft. Students who worry most about being drafted are almost always those who are doing poor work and want something to blame for their failure. It is easy for the student failing two or three subjects to think that the international situation did it. Such men are often advised to drop out of college, do their stretch in the service and then come back to college. Service has a habit of making the immature grow up.

65. Many failures in college happen because freshmen think that college is a place in which to learn a trade or business. Having received high-school credit for typing, shorthand, automobile driving, band, and what not, they are chagrined to learn that college is not like that. Dean Whiteman, of Yale, says that students often complain about courses such as economics on the ground that these courses do not tell anyone how to run a business; they just teach theories. In much the same way, every college of engineering has on its hands a number of freshmen who are misfits at the start because they are not working with their hands, but are

exposed to English, history and psychology. A college course in electricity is not for the embryo television-repair man, who should go to trade school, not college.

66. Those who have this mistaken idea often drop out of the technical schools, where mortality is high anyway. In liberal-arts colleges, students more often than not can adjust themselves to the idea of a liberal education. But the adjustment is painful and often takes two or three years.

67. Colleges aim not to produce what Dr. J. W. Graham, of Carnegie Tech, calls the "complete technician," but instead a man whose education makes him able to fit a problem into its historical frame. Or, as a professor of chemistry in a small liberal-arts college puts it, "In three or four years all one can learn is that there are unsolved problems for research."

68. There are two real reasons for college education, and the two are actually the same stated differently: preparation for one of the professions, and acquisition of an idea of culture. Together, these two things mean the beginning of the development of the adult mind. Woodrow Wilson once said, "The object of a university is intellect."

69. Part of a circular given to each entering freshman at Columbia in 1953 reads as follows: "A liberal-arts education is one that aids the youth to grow into a mature, well-rounded individual who knows how to think objectively, to make the best use of his talents and to understand his responsibilities in a democratic society."

70. A liberal-arts education means, of course, a general education in which the humanities (literature, language, fine arts), the social sciences (history, economics, political science) and the natural sciences (chemistry, biology, physics) are about equally balanced.

71. During the war, emphasis in colleges lay in the turning out of people with the specific skills which a complicated war economy required. But today, all over the United States, the trend is returning to the kind of education described as the liberal arts. Even professional schools are now asking for students who have a broad academic background. For example, the Harvard Medical School does not require its candidates to have majored in science any more: some science, of course, but not just science. About a quarter of the curriculum at Carnegie Tech is made up of humanities courses. Massachusetts Institute of Technology has working arrangements with a number of small liberal-arts colleges under which students take "general-education" courses for two or three years and then transfer to M.I.T. for engineering.

72. Understanding the aims of the liberal-arts program in the American college is probably the hardest and also the most important job for the freshman today. Some freshmen— indeed, some graduate students—will never understand why general education is valuable. They may finish their course, but they will have wasted a lot of time and money. Some freshmen will drop out of college because, not understanding, they will simply fail their courses for lack of direction. Fortunately many freshmen will get the point and will come out of college with at least the beginning of a conception of what learning is.

73. If the freshman will take advantage of his adviser's experience, of his teachers' knowledge and of the wealth of his college library, and if he will study on his own, most of his minor adjustment problems will disappear. He will stop thinking of the college degree as a high-class work permit, a ticket of admission to this or that job. He will know that hard, analytical study is required in college. He will realize that liberal education means a good balance between academic, athletic and social life. And he will quite surely, out of his broad background, find a special interest to develop into a college major, even if it turns out to be an "impractical" field like Chinese, Indic philology or archaeology.

74. And the man or woman who finds out what education means has grown up. Surely the proof of the broad education which Americans can get if they want it is a deep understanding of how good that education can be.

ROGER W. HOLMES *What Every Freshman Should Know*

Roger Wellington Holmes (1905-   ) was born in Boston and educated at Harvard University, from which he has received four degrees. He has taught and lectured at Harvard, Amherst, and Smith, and since 1944 has been chairman of the Department of Philosophy at Mount Holyoke. He was awarded the Sheldon Traveling Fellowship in 1928, the Bowdoin Prize in 1933, and the *Atlantic Monthly* Prize in 1940. During World War II he was a member of the Signal Corps. He has written many articles for the *Atlantic Monthly* and the *American Mercury*, and three books, *The Idealism of Giovanni Gentile,* 1937, *The Rhyme of Reason,* 1939, and *Exercises in Reasoning,* 1940.

Though the early parts of this essay are iconoclastic and may be read with surprise by students and with consternation by professors, the last part is a clear statement of a positive educational philosophy. And the essay, taken as a whole, shows how a sound liberal education rises above "academic taradiddle."

1. I never face a class without wondering what would happen if students were not so docile. Why do you meet your professors and the academic taradiddle of college with such fear and respect? You are everywhere in chains because you accept a tradition about college work which at cost to you misrepresents its values and overestimates its importance. You remind me of the elephant chained to his stake at the circus. If the poor devil knew his own strength! And if you and your classmates but knew *yours!* The good things that might happen to our colleges if you would take matters into your own hands and pull up a few of the rotted stakes of academic tradition are worth dreaming about. Consider some confidential advice from one who would like to see you gain your freedom, who knows the weaknesses of academic life from the inside, and can give a few pointers on how to pull at those stakes.

2. One of the first things you are told is that you must study hard. But that is only half of the story. The other half is that beyond a certain point which is easily reached, the more you work the poorer the results. In my particular college you would be supposed to devote not more than fifteen hours a week to classes and another thirty to outside assignments. That means that you should be able to escape academic duties for one whole day each week and to take either the afternoon or the evening off almost every day. Work hard when you work. Mornings are the best times. But never work through both afternoon and evening. And take off part of Saturday and most of Sunday. Use three afternoons for exercise in the open air and three evenings for movies or concerts or plays or for that novel you want to read. Your college work will benefit.

3. You will be told that classes are the most important thing at college. Don't believe it. President Eliot of Harvard said that if he wished to found a college the first thing he would build would be a dormitory. If there were money left over, he would erect a library and fill it with books. And if he had money to burn he would hire a faculty and build a

WHAT EVERY FRESHMAN SHOULD KNOW: Reprinted, by permission of the author and the publisher, from *The American Mercury,* November, 1940.

classroom building. Those of us who are willing to remember find it easy to recollect that the most valuable things that happened to us in college usually happened in our dormitories, and most of them after midnight. We also recall with considerable pleasure the few occasions when we had the time and audacity to enter the college library and just browse among books utterly unconnected with our courses. Somehow we remember those books. We read them not because we had to, but because we wanted to. The difference is tremendous.

4. You will be told that marks are important. But they are a meager indication of a student's worth. Some day we shall have the courage to scuttle the whole marking system, and with it, I hope, will go that awful and meaningless sheepskin. Marks provide the outward and visible sign of the whole academic tradition. I wish every college student might come behind the scenes and watch his instructors doling out grades on papers and bluebooks. We have such curious foibles. The odds are definitely in favor of a paper read after rather than before dinner. A typewritten paper stands a better chance than one in longhand. And that factor of length! I know one student who got himself an A by sandwiching a dozen pages of economics notes into a long term-paper on Beethoven. It is a matter of record that given the same set of papers twice we will grade them differently. Given the same paper, moreover, various teachers will assign it grades ranging from D to A, even in mathematics. Some departments give as many as 40 per cent of their students A's, while others in the same institution allow only 5 per cent of the same students to get the highest marks.

5. You have probably been told that your academic record as an undergraduate will make or break your life. That simply is not so. Are you going into teaching? There is not a college president worth his salt who does not know that a Phi Beta Kappa key is small indication of your promise as a teacher. Are you going to professional school? Countless men and women with average grades as undergraduates have done brilliantly in professional school. And in getting jobs, it is what they have been able to do in professional school that counts. Are you going to seek work as

soon as you finish college? Letters of recommendation these days cover numerous items which have nothing to do with your academic achievement but are just as important. It would not be true to say that marks mean nothing, but if you will remember these facts every time you enter a classroom you will be on the right track.

6. Your professors form part of the academic taradiddle too. We stand on little raised platforms, the academic equivalents of the pedestal; we call ourselves "doctors" and smile with patient condescension when mistaken for medical men; we put high-sounding letters after our names; and we march in academic processions, clothed in magnificent medieval costumes. All in all we manage by such devices to convey the impression that we know what we are talking about. To be sure, we are not as pompous as some of our European colleagues in crime. Some of us even have the courage to sit on the same level and at the same seminar table with our students and listen to what they have to say. But it is not difficult to get the impression that your professors are founts of wisdom.

7. You will be told to take careful notes on their lectures and to commit those notes to memory. This whole business of note-taking is outmoded. Students started taking notes in the Middle Ages, before the printing press was invented. The student wrote his own books. Today, with large college libraries and with textbooks crowding and jostling one another for attention, the taking of notes is anachronistic. What you will do, if you are like the rest of the sheep, will be to produce pages and pages of notes, study them religiously for the examinations, then store them away. If you ever look at them again it will be simply to realize that the information they convey is far better presented in at least a dozen books immediately available, or that it is so thoroughly out of date that the notes are useless.

8. One of the major instruments of torture in collegiate education is the course examination. By this device the professor is enabled to discover how much of what he has said in class you have committed to memory. The night before the examination you cram the notes into your head. Next morning you enter a room heavy with the atmosphere of suspicion.

You leave all notes and books in the hall, and you write on questions the answers to which you will have forgotten within a week, answers which in ordinary life no one in his right mind would ask you to remember because the information is available in the reference books where it belongs. Either you are working under the honor system, an unwitting accessory to the hocus-pocus, or you are annoyed and upset by a proctor who marches around among the desks looking for trouble. The more you understand why you are in college, the less seriously you will take examinations. Some day you may even educate us to the point where we will compose tests which will measure your ability to use your knowledge with originality, rather than your ability to ape teacher. When that day arrives we shall let you bring notes, texts and even the *Encyclopædia Britannica* to examinations. And then you may take examinations seriously.

9. Now that you are in college and going to classes, pause long enough to ask yourself why *we* are teaching and *you* are learning. In spite of what you may have heard from us or your high school teachers or your parents, the answer is not that we know the final answers to the problems we are discussing. We are teaching because we have studied carefully subjects in which you are a beginner, and because we have had more worldly experience than you. But neither of these facts makes us omniscient. If the truth be known, there are those of you in our classes who are more intelligent than we are—who will outstrip us in our chosen fields. Question us. Doubt us. Raise objections. Make us think! Avoid us when we measure your achievement in terms of the proximity of your thinking to our own. Welcome us when we admit that we do not know the answers to your questions, when we help you to find your own answers, when we encourage you to consider views with which we do not agree.

10. Why are you going to college? Not to enhance your parents' social position; not to get high marks; not to get the ultimate answers, which not even *we* can furnish. To use our own professional jargon, you come to college to get a liberal education. We must admit that we do not altogether know what a liberal education is, but we have some fairly good ideas on the subject. We do not entirely follow these ideas. None of us, for example, believes that there is a magic in piling up a certain number of hour-credits. Yet, sixty credits and you get your diploma. And that diploma is supposed to admit you to the company of educated men and women. Why not fifty-five, or sixty-five? We do not know. Indeed if you pressed us we should have to admit that some students are liberally educated with thirty credits while others will not belong to the educated company if they take sixty times sixty hours of credit. Do not measure your education by simple arithmetic.

11. Elect your courses with care. If you go to a college which requires that you juggle five courses at once, you will do well to find one easy berth and sleep in it; otherwise you cannot do justice to the other four. This is a secret practice acceptable and accepted by all. But in general easy courses should be avoided simply because they are easy and do not give you your father's money's worth.

12. Do not select your courses with an eye to a specific job or type of occupation. More of you will make this mistake than not, and it is one of the most serious you can make. In the first place, we know at least that a liberal education involves a balance and harmony of interests. Secondly, your interests and talents are by no means fully appreciated or explored when you come to us. You do not want to wake up in your senior year and wish that you had not missed many important and interesting things. Thousands of seniors do.

13. When you come to college you are intellectually very young and have not yet learned to proceed safely or efficiently under your own intellectual power. You are what your environment and your elders have made you. Your ideas are not your own. The first thing you must learn is to stand on your own ideas. This is why you should not take us and our ideas too seriously. Broaden your horizon so that as you become more and more able to take care of yourself you will move intelligently. Do considerable mental visiting in your first years in college. Try to encounter the major points of view represented on the faculty and among the students. Entertain them the more seriously the more they differ from your own. You may return to your own,

but if you do it will be with greater tolerance and broader understanding.

14. You come to college to gain a liberal perspective. In gaining this perspective you must come to know the nature which surrounds and compels you, the society with which you must live and cooperate, the creative spirit which is your heritage, and the tools of language and of thought. To express it in this specific manner is helpful. It suggests certain intellectual virtues which you must possess before you can be considered an educated man or woman. This does not mean that there are particular courses which can alone provide you with these virtues. Do not take a course solely for its specific content.

15. For example, we have said that you must come to know the natural world. This does not mean that you must study physics *and* chemistry *and* astronomy *and* geology. It means that you must acquire the scientific attitude, understand the atmosphere and significance of the exact sciences, know their fundamental assumptions, their key concepts, their major contributions. And the same is true of the biological sciences. A course in botany *or* zoology *or* physiology *or* psychology is enough to give you an understanding of the important aspects of biology. You have not time for them all. But one is essential. Far too many are ignorant of the biological forces affecting human conduct. You should get into the laboratory while you are in college, and you should work in both the exact and the biological sciences.

16. You want also to know the society with which you must live and cooperate. And one of the ways in which you want to know it is the historical. You must be historically minded. You must recognize the importance of the past for the present. Man learns by experience, and history is social experience. Greek, Roman, European, American history—you cannot study them all, *but* you can become historically minded. And you can become socially minded in your view of the present world. Economic, social and political forces have your world in their grips. You must study these forces, measure them, evaluate them.

17. Our heritage in the field of the arts has always been recognized as liberalizing. Not so

much need to urge you here. Most of the greatest interpretation of human living is to be found in painting, sculpture, music and literature. What are some of the things which the great creative geniuses have told us about ourselves? What are modern artists trying to do? You must find out these things, not just that you may go to museums and concerts, but that you may *want* to go to museums and concerts. Elect some art or music, for pleasure, but also to increase your knowledge. Also, get a full and enthusiastic knowledge of the literature of your mother tongue. You will have discovered a source of wisdom, good taste and pleasure. Such studies need no recommendation.

18. Finally, you must come to understand the tools of language and of thought. And here urging is necessary. You ought to know another language, ancient or modern, inflected or non-inflected, so well that you dream in it. Such knowledge gives a far better understanding of your own tongue, both as a tool and as an art, than you could otherwise obtain. And you will have open to you another literature. Furthermore, you should be conversant with the structures and powers of thought as an intellectual tool, and you should be willing to examine fundamental assumptions. Mathematics, logic and philosophy are helpful here. You may think them difficult, but do not avoid them altogether.

19. If you will examine this program for the enlarging of your intellectual horizon you will see that it involves some eight subjects spread throughout the departments of your college. It is a program which you can complete in your freshman and sophomore years and one which you should carry through in order that you may be equipped intellectually to proceed to the second part of your college education. It will give you necessary breadth.

20. But you must also specialize, when the foundation has been laid. You must do this not because specialization will prepare you for a specific job, but because a certain degree of specialization is the second essential of true intellectual endeavor. Without specialization your college work is in danger of becoming that thin veneer of "culture" which we all recognize as superficial. And now you will find the faculty more cooperative. We are

specialists and we like to encourage specialization. But still be on your guard, for we shall mislead you by overemphasizing the importance of our particular little corners of learning. The important matter is not *what* you specialize in, but that you specialize. Specialization for its own sake, that is my point. If you are going on to graduate work you will find the overwhelming advice of graduate school faculties to be that you specialize in *anything but* your subject of graduate study. If you are going into medicine, you might major in history. If you will be a lawyer, major in art or music.

21. Even your specialization should be carefully planned. In the first place, it will probably be advisable for you to do advanced work in each of the four major fields of study: natural science; social science; art and literature; and language, mathematics or philosophy. If you studied chemistry as a freshman, you might go on to more advanced chemistry and take elementary astronomy or geology as allied work. In short, in each major field in which you took two elementary courses as an underclassman, you should follow one elementary course into advanced work and at the same time gain some knowledge in an allied field.

22. But this will take only half of your time as an upperclassman. You should devote the other half of your last two years to intensive specialization in one subject in which you have the greatest interest and for which you have shown marked talent. Perhaps you have found history the most absorbing of subjects. Good! Go on in it. Devote half of your junior and senior years to history. Show that you can work intensively on the details of your chosen major, manipulate these details correctly, and fit them into a comprehensive picture of the whole. But remember—though your teachers will work against you here—remember that you are studying primarily for the sake of the intensive specialization and not of the history. Your roommate is getting the same thing from majoring in mathematics or English literature.

23. When you have avoided the Scylla of heterogeneous meanderings among elementary facts and concepts and the Charybdis of a study so narrow that you are ignorant of what is going on outside your own little corner of interest, you will have intellectual balance and perspective. Do not take us as your models. We represent a special world and we are an academic people. You are going into a broader world and a non-academic environment. Make us realize that our interests and understandings should spread into every field. Make us see that our students are at least as important as the subjects we teach. Make us understand that marks and examinations are mere administrative conveniences to be taken far less seriously than we take them. In short, insist that we get together as a unified organization and provide you with a liberal education. Strength to you! If you will do these things you will be performing a service to us and to yourselves.

G. GADDIS SMITH *Lo, the Old College Spirit*

G. Gaddis Smith (1932-   ) received his A.B. degree from Yale in 1954 and began working on his M.A. degree in the Department of History. He has published a number of articles and short stories in college periodicals and was chairman of the *Yale News*, "the oldest college daily."

In "Lo, the Old College Spirit" a mature student writes from firsthand observation about a new kind of college spirit, found especially in some of the older Eastern colleges, which is radically different from that of a generation ago.

1. It is customary these days, midway between the football season and class reunions, for many college alumni who have long since reached what used to be called the age of discretion to wave a tattered school pennant rather dispiritedly and complain that the old college spirit has disappeared. At first glance, a number of things would seem to bear out this fretful observation: dwindling attendance figures at intercollegiate sports in recent years, almost silent cheering sections for most college teams, and the general impression that Master Youngblood has turned into Mr. Sobersides.

2. What has happened in college if headlong enthusiasm is as rare as charged, if old grads see nothing left of it but nostalgia, and undergrads view any errant manifestation of it with wonder? Is today's student a humorless, apathetic cog in a lifeless community, or is he a quiet, mature individual not given to flamboyance and exhibitionism of the do-or-die-for-dear-old-Rutgers type?

3. The old grad who remembers his hip flask and raccoon coat and bewails the spiritlessness of today should join with the superficial critic who called this generation "silent." At least the two can comfort each other. Today's college student has more genuine spirit and a better sense of humor than his father or his grandfather. He doesn't make as much

noise and he doesn't lavish as much narrow attention on athletics and boyish pranks because his spirit goes deeper and means more to the school he loves.

4. Humor is one of the best indicators of how a generation really thinks. Let's see what sort of thing is considered humorous in college today:

An Amherst junior succeeded in planting a story in the local newspaper to the effect that two campus buildings were moving towards each other because of a geologic fault and would collide in 500 years.

Yale's 130-pound football manager, no football player, was sent in to catch a pass for the final extra point against Harvard. "It stinks," said the Harvard captain, but he was in the minority; even Harvard men admitted it was pretty funny.

Former Governor Dever of Massachusetts was "kidnapped" by a bogus Harvard political group. He spoke for two hours before an attentive but fake audience while the real audience waited impatiently in a near-by hall.

5. Compare these stunts with those of the past: cows in dormitories, greased railroad tracks, mysterious snowballs (and other missiles) sent flying from atop some tower, head-shaving raids on unsuspecting freshmen. Compare the two and you will see a pattern. The college sense of humor today is more subtle and restrained. It makes fun of the times and does not depend merely on a situation.

LO, THE OLD COLLEGE SPIRIT: Reprinted, by permission of the author and the publisher, from the *New York Times Magazine*, January 17, 1954.

Twenty-five years ago the humor was as slap-stick and obvious as the era itself.

6. In the football stands, where the old grad still likes best to cavort, the undergraduate of today may appear overly dignified, but he enjoys his football just the same. Unlike some of the alumni, he knows that only a game and not the honor and reputation of his school is being fought for on the field. Some criticize him for not always knowing the cheers. (At Yale last fall, a small band of Boy Scouts out-yelled the entire student cheering section.) But his spirit is more spontaneous. As a rooter, he likes nothing better than to mimic his elders. One of Harvard's favorite cheers is known as the "angry murmur"; it's often used after a questionable decision by a referee.

7. Traditional college bravado has been re-placed by a quiet thing which one might call "summer spirit." During the winter it is un-necessary to boast long and loud of your loy-alty—that is taken for granted. But in the sum-mer you do not think of an all-conquering football team. (The chances are that you've won.) You think proudly of your school as a mother of educated men. Since the war, at least in the liberal arts institutions of the East, the college student has placed the emphasis of his spirit increasingly on first things, on education for a free society and not on sports for meaningless prestige.

8. This was put another way by a Princeton graduate of the class of '04 who remarked that "the decrease in effusive demonstration has been replaced by a deeper pride in the university and a personal interest in her per-manent welfare."

9. Wildly hysterical torchlight snake dances and rah-rah coaches left the campus with the Stutz Bearcat or not long thereafter. Gone, too, from most colleges are many of the cus-toms and traditions of the past: bonfires, tug-of-war battles and wrestling between classes, freshman beanies, hazing, and so on. The change is obvious. The reasons are complex mixtures of the good and the bad, the trivial and the significant.

10. Today's undergraduate has almost no leisure time; his existence has been accurately described as "lurching from crisis to crisis." On top of a far more time-consuming academic schedule has been piled an amazing prolifera-tion of extracurricular activity. Instead of spending half the day in unhurried conver-sation, smoking a pipe and sipping beer, the average college man of the mid-twentieth cen-tury wants to do things: compete strenuously in intramural sports if he is not varsity ma-terial, edit a newspaper or magazine, engage in dramatics or sing with the glee club. Every day he is launching new enterprises, inventing new schemes. There is no time to think about college-spirit traditions—much less learn and practice them.

11. The Ivy League colleges, to mention one instance, have undergone a tremendous so-cial revolution in regard to the opposite sex. When the legendary Dink Stover came to Yale in 1911 a wise upper classman advised: "And another thing: no fooling around women; that isn't done here—that'll queer you absolutely." And Stover echoed his generation by replying, "Of course." Twenty years later the shrill cry of "Fire!" still resounded through the dormitories of Yale whenever a female appeared in the courtyard. An alumnus re-marked recently that "gals were as scarce as Indians" in his day, except at the one or two big football games.

12. What a change has taken place! Harvard and Radcliffe form virtually one co-educa-tional institution. It has been suggested, half seriously, that Yale merge with Connecticut College for Women. More than half the un-dergraduates in the Ivy League schools have at least one date a week. The natural result of this collegiate discovery of women is an almost total abandonment of the stag folderol that once was such an integral part of the mani-festation of college spirit. No one wants to stay in Princeton or New Haven over a week-end when he can be in Northampton or Poughkeepsie.

13. Other reasons are of a more serious nature. Leading the list is the general appre-hension about the state of the world. A senior at Hamilton College wrote me recently: "A liberal-arts education is supposed to make one inquire into the nature of things and form value judgments. Let's assume that it is suc-cessful. For a student who has benefited by that education, it is terribly difficult to get

overly worked up about any football team, defeated or undefeated. As such a student, I am just too conscious of the real problems of the world. Things are a little too gray; in some ways they seem to be about as messed up as they can be. And most guys feel that problems can't be solved on a grassy field 100 yards long."

14. This increased awareness of the world is evident everywhere you look in college. One of the first things which most alumni notice when they return to college is the great number of students who daily read a metropolitan newspaper. "When I was in college," said one alumnus, "I didn't read a newspaper from September to June. We just didn't care what was happening in the world."

15. The terrific competition for places in each freshman class at almost every college and university (Yale, Harvard, and Princeton can accept only about one-fourth of all those who apply for admission) has had a direct effect on college spirit in the old style. The energetic alumnus who now enrolls his new-born son for the class of 1975 has little assurance that the boy eventually will be accepted.

16. As I. Q.'s go up, the rich boys find that more and more poor boys are displacing them. The result is a simultaneous diluting of old family college ties—the best defenders of outmoded tradition—and the acceptance of a broader and more balanced social system. This process was speeded immediately after the Second World War by the return of veterans who found they had no taste for social snobbery. After fighting side by side with Negro and Jew, they discovered that both groups were just as acceptable as white Protestants. Throughout the East, this opened the way to social equality (often symbolized by fraternity membership) for those who had sometimes been excluded.

17. Finally, there is the great educational awakening going on throughout the country. You can see this in the concrete terms of ambitious new experiments and you can sense it in the bull sessions where today's undergraduates are constantly questioning the purpose and content of what they study. Someone will say: "I don't want to be like my

father. He went through college and graduated as an uneducated man. All he did learn was useless facts which he forgot overnight." And others will agree. No longer is the "gentleman's 70" a fashionable mark, or a safe one, with draft boards scanning every report card and graduate schools demanding far more than mediocrity. The well-rounded scholar is more respected today than the one-sided athlete.

18. The old spirit is altered—no one will deny that. And altered with it are some things of value: the spontaneous lack of reserve, the boundless enthusiasm, and, often, the fun. It is hard to make an exact definition of the college spirit of today, for it is in an awkward state of transition.

19. Many undergraduates, like their fathers, still long for the days of Dink Stover. They wish that Frank Merriwell were more than a ghost that flitted quietly along the side-lines once or twice during the football season. These people are uneasy. They would prefer to paint statues and derail trolley cars. (Incidentally, the symbolic death blow to the old Yale football spirit occurred some five years ago when the last open trolley car made its last round trip to the Bowl.)

20. Because of a handful of collegiate dinosaurs, the new spirit is far from a perfect fit. It is a bit pretentious, it is condescending, it is too often coldly stone-faced. The reaction against the childish antics of the Twenties is occasionally so extreme that some never learn to have fun.

21. However, the oil of time will smooth all that. Already the broad outlines of the new college spirit are apparent. It is a spirit which, I feel, will not stop at the colleges, but will spread through all of the present generation. I apologize for ending on what may be a too-serious note, but the new spirit has serious implications and three chief qualities:

(1) It will be soundly "conservative" in the best meaning of the word. Mere change will not be confused with genuine reform. Conclusions will be tested with sound principles; tradition, per se, will not be embellished with false sanctity.

(2) It will be a spirit of faith. Our fathers went to college in an era of starry-eyed op-

timism. They had no faith because there seemed to be no need for faith. Now our fathers are disillusioned. They are also confused. That's why they impute their disillusionment to us. The present college generation, on the other hand, is living in a time when supreme faith is essential. That faith is now growing and with it grows the belief that the world's problems are fundamentally problems of religion and morals.

(3) It will be a spirit of leadership. Confused by transition and overwhelmed by the tidal waves of war, the new spirit has not had a real chance to develop. Now it is stronger, more sure of its direction. Soon it will produce leaders.

JAMES L. MURSELL *The Miracle of Learning*

James Lockhart Mursell (1893-   ), an Englishman who received his undergraduate degree from the University of Queensland, Australia, came to America in 1915. Three years later he received a Ph.D. from Harvard University and subsequently studied at Union Theological Seminary and Columbia University. He was Director of the Research and Library Department of the Interchurch World Movement in 1919-20, taught at Lake Erie College, 1921-23, and at Appleton College, 1923-35, before joining the staff of Teachers College, Columbia University, where he is now professor of education. Among the many books he has written, two of his most recent are *Developmental Teaching*, 1949, and *Psychology for Modern Education*, 1952.

In "The Miracle of Learning," Professor Mursell, writing about an area of knowledge in which much is yet to be discovered, describes the wonders of the learning process and its abiding satisfactions.

I

1. Recent years have cast a glamour over the doings of the abnormal mind which I, for one, am constrained to deplore. Ever since Freud's *Psychopathology of Everyday Life* set the wild echoes flying, the unconscious, the libido, the censor, suppressed sexual desires, organ inferiority, and sublimation have been words of power and wonder. And for many people psychology has figured as the drama of an uncanny realm of portents, the tale of how

> The wild man took his weary way
> To his strange and lonely pump.

THE MIRACLE OF LEARNING: Reprinted, with slight changes made with the approval of the author, by permission, from *The Atlantic Monthly*, June 1935. Copyright 1935, by The Atlantic Monthly Company, Boston 16, Massachusetts.

2. All this pageantry and hurly-burly has distracted us from a range of phenomena not only far better attested, but also, I believe, far more truly amazing and deeply significant. These are the everyday phenomena of the learning process. To the discerning eye nothing is more fascinating and marvelous than the way in which the mind advances from weakness to power, from vagueness to precision, from halting clumsiness to refined accuracy, from the limited to the embracing view. Just because these things are so familiar we take them as commonplace. Yet, compared with the combinations of popular psychopathology, they are true drama contrasted with melodrama. In psychology the seemingly commonplace is the truly wonderful. Here, to paraphrase the saying of Kipling, the true romance indeed "brings up the five-fifteen"

and too often goes "all unseen." Whenever we manage to learn anything, no matter how simple or how complex, a miracle has been achieved.

II

3. Speak of learning to most people and they think you are talking of something dull and humdrum. They have a vision of some patient creature endlessly repeating a string of digits or a series of nonsense words, or grinding away at a stupid physical coördination. But quite another picture should come before us. The story of Newton and the apple, apocryphal or no, is the archetype of all human learning. A flash of insight coordinates a great mass of material; a new pattern of ideas is born; a crystallization of things held in solution is achieved. Learning is not a routine, but a drama. Archimedes running naked from the bath with shouts of εὕρηκα [I have found (it).] is the type of the successful learner.

4. We quite wrongly assume that repetition is the key and cause of learning. This is probably the chief reason why we think it humdrum and commonplace. But the process depends on something utterly different—the wooing and incidence of the creative moment, the making of something not there before. Indeed, it should be evident that repetition cannot in the least explain learning.

5. Consider how the business starts. You are perhaps—Heaven help you—learning to play golf. You go out on the practice tee with fifty balls and proceed to swat them toward the waiting caddy. How many will go at all where you want to put them? Let us be generous and say ten. Ten successes—forty dubs. If the repetition formula is correct, how do you ever improve your game? Why don't you merely learn to dub, and dub more and more adequately as time goes on?

6. An experimental problem was set up in the laboratory which could be approached in 1024 different ways. Of these, 1023 were wrong and led to failure; one was right. And yet the right way was learned, and the wrong ways discarded. Ten hundred and twenty-three chances for practice to make imperfect, yet perfection arrived. Why?

7. A psychologist found that he was developing a persistent bad habit in his typewriting. He constantly wrote "the" as "h-t-e." Being a good behaviorist and a sensible person, he took himself firmly in hand and practiced a great many "t-h-e's." It did no good; still the mistake hung on. Then he had a thought: he deliberately practiced "h-t-e"—and the difficulty evaporated. Practice worked in reverse. He learned the thing he didn't practice. Why?

8. So far from its being true that we learn by repetition or by doing, repetition is absolutely incapable of accounting for learning. When I start a new piece on the piano I *can't* play it; when I first try to write poetry I find I *can't* write it; when I undertake to drive my initial golf ball I *can't* drive it. The thing is simply not there at all. What sense is there in telling me that I learn to do something by continually doing it when I can't do it anyhow? Consider a child learning to speak English. Can he speak English or not? Yes or no? Clearly no! Then on what is he practicing? Surely not on the English language. How could he?

9. Repetition cannot in the least explain the beginnings of any job of learning, simply because the thing to be learned is always something new, not something already there. No more can it explain the development and continuation of the process. One of the oldest though still among the best experiments on this subject dealt with learning to send and receive the Morse Code on the telegraph instrument. The first job of the pupil was to master the separate letters. This took a long time, but finally he had it. Still for a long while he made no progress. He knew the letters, but the higher speeds and higher masteries were far beyond him. He plodded over an interminable plateau. Then, on a propitious day, he suddenly began to write *words* —whole words all together. Again a long pause in progress—then suddenly entire phrases.

10. Now notice this—the mastery of the letters grew no better. Far down the line it was already as good as it ever could be. For progress an entirely new integration must come in. Whence did it come? From the letters? How could it? Apparently out of the everywhere!

11. An enormous amount of our learning

shows this mysterious and creative rhythm. The first time I drive a car I glance anxiously hither and yon, and take all sorts of pains with the levers; I stall my engine at the traffic lights, and go in the ditch to avoid another vehicle when there is plenty of room. Later on I notice only a few things in the shifting traffic pattern and am hardly aware of the car's mechanism—and I am fairly safe. The beginning golfer thinks of twenty matters with keen anxiety—and tops the ball. Ben Hogan steps up with only one thing in his mind's eye, but that one thing perfectly clear, and the ball sails two hundred and fifty yards down the fairway. The wretch "unaccustomed to public speaking" memorizes every word, forgets half of them, and looks, sounds, and feels subhuman. Sir Winston Churchill faces an audience, seemingly with little or no preparation, and achieves a triumph. How do these changes come about? What makes us stop being anxious about many things, and fashion a new and more excellent way? Whence this new pattern of attention and behavior?

12. Of course, in our easy fashion, we say that the routines have become "automatic," through repetition. But this misses the whole point. Automatic routines never created first-rate skill. One may know every rule of grammar perfectly without being able to write good style—though style is simply applied grammar. One may be as familiar with the Morse letters as one ever can be, and still remain bad at sending and worse at receiving. Wherever the secret is to be found, it is not here. Macaulay could read a page in the time most of us need for a sentence, but did he know the alphabet better than you or I? Superior controls, more effective patterns of behavior, new directions of the attention, must emerge, or there is no improvement. And, just because these things are brand-new, they cannot be what we are practicing.

13. If repetition were really the key to learning, then the more we repeated anything the better we should learn it. But this is very often not the case. A group of children practiced a certain simple skill for eighteen days; then half of them went on practicing for seventy-six days longer, after which the others, who in the meantime had done nothing,

joined them; and within ten days there was no difference at all between the two halves of the group. Overlearning persistently refuses to behave in a common-sense way. It is a broken reed, a fickle and dangerous device. The everlasting plodder may be defeating his own ends.

14. Learning is precisely not the wearing down of a pathway in the nervous system, the repetitive establishment of a routine. So far from being the formation of habit, it requires a breach with established ways of doing and thinking, and the substitution of better ways. Improvement is in the truest and most accurate sense a creative process. Long ago Plato perceived this. How, he asked himself, can anything absolutely new come into our minds? It seems to whenever we learn, whenever we recombine our ideas or improve our skills. He found this impossible, and replied that indeed we never learn anything, but only recollect what is already implicitly known. Here, as so often happens, our most recent science confirms the insight of that profound mind, and we are confronted in this latter day with something amazingly akin to the ancient doctrine of ἀνάμνησις [recollection].

III

15. To invoke Plato's doctrine of reincarnation as an explanation of learning, and to say that whenever we seem to learn a new thing we merely recapture the visions of a previous existence, would certainly strike us as a counsel of scientific despair. But psychology has not yet really done very much better in the way of an ultimate account. Still, one consideration of major importance stands out in recent research: learning appears to be a function of the will.

16. Two groups were put to work at memorizing the same material. They both made the same number of repetitions. The first group was told to learn with an intent permanently to retain the material; no such instructions were given to the second. Five minutes after practice, no difference to amount to anything was discernible; both knew the stuff about equally well. Yet a fortnight later the first group showed an indisputable superiority. Once again two groups were put to work at learning. One was stimulated by powerful

motives, among them a money reward; the others just drilled. It was found that the first group completed the job in half the number of repetitions required by the latter. A very ingenious experiment was devised in which the subjects had to solve complex puzzles—to learn a type of thinking, that is to say. The crux of success was found to be the presence of a strong determination, a certain dynamic, attacking attitude of mind. It is not plodding, it is not routine, that builds the new structure, apparently out of nothing. Will is the creative force. Without the will to learn there is no learning. And when the will is feeble and confused, learning lags.

17. Notice that the master key is not the wish but the will to learn. The will must be pointed and organized. We must endeavor not merely to improve in general, but to learn just these things for just this purpose. We must have a clear-cut goal, a limited objective. A bunch of carrots must often be dangled before the donkey's nose.

18. Frequently we need to hire a teacher to do the dangling. And he earns his pay by choosing the right carrots and dangling them with the proper skill. Whether we put ourselves under another person or do our own teaching, a very large part of the art consists in establishing the proper goals of effort, in showing us what we ought to work for, and how to work for it. Socrates called himself a midwife of ideas, and the task of all worthwhile teaching is to hasten and assure the coming of the creative moment of improvement.

19. Now there are clumsy and stupid and also wise and skillful ways of organizing the will to learn. For instance, it has been experimentally established that to blame the learner for failure, to bully and scold and nag, is thoroughly bad. We know that if a teacher really wishes to direct the dynamics of learning, rather than just to release his own pent-up Uticas, the worst possible thing he can do is to indulge in sarcasm. All such procedures tend to disintegrate, confuse, and stultify the learner's will. They make for chaos, not cosmos; they amount to saying *fiat obscurum* [let there be darkness] rather than *fiat lux* [let there be light]. The encouragement of success, the appreciation of effort—these are the things

that pay. Suspect any teacher who deals habitually in the coin of condemnation; and if you teach with yourself as pupil, do not, as you value your progress, be daunted by failure.

20. Some curious discoveries have been made concerning the incentives which help learning most. For instance, a great many things are learned most rapidly and surely in the company of other learners rather than alone. This is true not only of physical but also of many mental skills, such as memorizing or solving problems or doing sums. The mere sight of others busy points up the will to learn. Again, one of the surest ways of getting a job of learning well and quickly done is to offer a dime for its completion. Perhaps the ideal school of the future will have a treasury of dimes for inspirational purposes! Hypnotism has been tried as an aid to learning, with uncertain results, though students at Cambridge hypnotized the night before an examination and instructed to remember excelled themselves next day in their papers. Another and more normal way of directing the will is to arrange a situation where we become aware of our success or lack of it. In financial drives a common stimulus is the big thermometer which shows the steady rise of the fund. The same sort of thing should be provided for the learner—a record in which he sees his own progress, and knows whether he is moving, and how fast.

21. The will to learn seems capable of triumphing over the most astonishing obstacles. It can triumph over fatigue. There is abundant evidence that one can go on and on with the most exacting mental tasks with astonishingly little decline in efficiency. Even after a job of work has become acutely distasteful, it still remains possible to go on doing it well. Indeed, the suggestion has been made in highly responsible quarters that there is no such thing as mental fatigue at all, in the sense of sheer literal inability to produce any more results as a consequence of continuous work. What we usually call mental fatigue is commonly a combination of tired eyes, an aching back, and a violent wish to do something else. When we want to stop we salve our consciences by saying that we can't continue.

22. Again, the will to learn can triumph over age. Few psychological dogmas have been

more easily swallowed than the notion that we learn best when we are young; but it is entirely unsubstantiated by ascertained fact. We assume it to be true, not because we are aware of any proof, but merely because we have been told many times that it is so, and because to believe it comports so well with the besetting laziness and timidity of mankind. On the contrary, however, there is excellent reason to hold that a man of thirty, forty, or even fifty can learn nearly anything better than he could when he was fifteen. To many readers this may seem heresy so violent that I hasten to bulwark myself behind authority. Professor E. L. Thorndike, in his book, *Adult Learning,* has brought together all the investigations ever made on learning at advanced ages. He finds no scintilla of evidence for the notion that children learn better than adults because of the flexibility of their muscles or the plasticity of their minds. A child of ten can acquire almost any technique better than when he was six. A man in his thirties or forties can acquire almost anything quite as well as he could in his teens—and probably better. This applies even to learning a new language. As far as the psychological processes themselves go, it would be better to attend school between the ages of twenty and thirty-two than between the ages of six and eighteen. The only difficulty would be that of earning a living.

23. Why, then, do so many adults give up learning new things? Here is the point for our discussion. They stop learning because of a subtle but fatal disintegration of the will to learn. To begin something new at an elementary level seems to them queer, even shameful. The cares of life enmesh them. Or, like E. F. Benson's *Lucia,* they begin to feel a little *vecchio* [old]. The feeling, not the fact, is the poison. All such resignations, despairs, and distastes are the death of that creative impulse which is the heart of learning. They are not among the inevitabilities of life; we yield ourselves to them "through the weakness of our own feeble wills."

24. The only obstacle which can definitely defeat the will to learn is stupidity. And this is natural enough, because stupidity is the inability to take a situation apart, and to recognize the key logs of the jam. This means an

obliteration of all goals, a breakdown of organization. The wish to learn may be strongly felt, but it takes planning and direction to transmute the wish into effective will.

25. Stupidity not only varies in degree; also it is of many kinds. For instance, there is the specific or limited stupidity which afflicts even the most brilliant. The learning studies have continually revealed a factor which most of us can recognize only too painfully well in ourselves. This is called "the persistence of error." One experiment required learners to disentangle wire puzzles—labyrinths of wire on which hung a key detachable by obscure manipulations. Time and again a worker would get the key up into one corner where it could not possibly be detached, and fumble and twist with the persistence of an insect on a windowpane. Often the director would stop and give aid. He would point out the hopelessness of the blind alley, and suggest that a new plan be tried. The worker would cordially agree, and the director would walk off. Five minutes later he would find the worker back at the old place, knitting his brows, pursing his lips, and sticking to the old error, which he knew to be an error.

26. This kind of stupidity victimizes all of us. Why do I continually misspell certain words, so that I have an actual vocabulary of spelling errors? Why do I make the same grammatical mistake in Latin again and again? Why can't I see at once what it means to organize a piece of writing? Why did Newton have to wait for inspiration till he saw the apple fall? The answer is our inveterate tendency to get into ruts. So far removed is the essence of learning from becoming routinized that, when this happens to us, learning stops. To continue we have to jolt ourselves out of the rut, to try out alternatives, to overcome a limited and specific stupidity which, like a paralysis, can frustrate and render nugatory the will to learn. To put it otherwise, we are all strongly subject to mental cramp. When the great genius breaks with the past, and achieves a profoundly original and significant regrouping of experience, we exclaim: "Inspiration!" We should do better to call it learning.

27. Then there is a more general stupidity, which is the failure to see how a principle or

procedure perfectly well known applies in circumstances that are new and strange. A problem in algebra was given to 1200 people. Simple tests proved that 1000 or more of them knew every operation required to solve it, but only about 300 got the solution. Why? They could not apply what they knew. Is this unusual? Well, try this one on yourself. What are the factors of $(x - y)$? Do you say there are none? This was the answer of a group of graduate students to whom the test was given. But don't you recall that $(x^2 - y^2) = (x + y)$ $(x - y)$? So did they. Then why didn't they see that $(x - y) = (x^{1/2} + y^{1/2}) (x^{1/2} - y^{1/2})$? Just stupidity—just a failure to see the point.

28. Then there is universal stupidity, universal limitation. It is said that a monkey cannot learn to unwrap a cord wound twice round a stick. The situation is too complex for him. For us it is simple and obvious. But you and I can never learn to solve at a glance the puzzle of a tangled fishline. Perhaps to a superhuman intelligence that would be as simple as the monkey's problem seems to us.

29. A girl in the sixth grade was given the following problem: "Joseph rode on a merry-go-round twelve times. Each time cost him three cents. How much did he pay for all his rides?" She utterly failed to solve it. Questioned as to her methods of work, she replied, "If there are lots of numbers, I add. If there are only two numbers with lots of parts [digits], I subtract. But if there are just two numbers and one littler than the other, it is hard; I divide if they come out even, but if they don't I multiply." You smile? Perhaps the high gods smile also when you yourself find something a little troublesome with differential equations or the theory of functions. Your wish to learn may vault as high as heaven. Your effective will to learn is limited by the complexity of the pattern your mind can grasp.

30. So critically important is the organized, directed will that its regular effect is to diminish, and sometimes greatly to diminish, the amount of effort needed to achieve a goal. Investigation has shown many times that students in school who do the best work also do the least studying. When a girl in college bitterly complains that her roommate works only for a day or two before exams and pulls A's and B's, while she studies till her eyes drop out and can only get C's and D's, she is having quite an ordinary experience. Though she may not know it, she is the victim of one of the common disabilities of human nature. Quality, not quantity, counts. Not the number of repetitions, but the intelligent will, is the crux of learning. In one university 348 students were divided into three groups of decreasing intelligence. The best group had an average mark of 86, and studied 23 hours in a normal week; the next best had a mark of 80, and studied 30 hours; the lowest group had a mark of 76, and studied 49 hours. Surely this reveals much concerning the conditions of human achievement.

IV

31. Learning is a fateful process. There is good reason to hold that, once a person has learned anything, he is permanently and irrevocably changed. We may doubt the dogma of the psychoanalysts that no impression is ever forgotten. It seems too sweeping; universal negatives are hard to prove. But all the facts seem to point away from what I might call the desert-sand theory of learning. This is the view that practice imprints certain traces, and that the moment it ceases the sand begins to drift in, till at last everything is utterly erased.

32. A certain psychologist memorized a number of selections of prose and verse. He banished them from his mind, and stowed the clippings away in a file for five years. When he turned his thoughts to them again, he could remember hardly a word. He had a friend read them to him, mixed in with many other selections, and he could not even tell which were the ones he had learned. This seems like almost utter loss. But then he undertook to learn them once again, and he found he could do so in about half the time it had taken him originally. Everything seemed gone, yet something very permanent remained.

33. Similar results have been obtained with physical skills. When Paderewski returned to the piano after many years, all the world wondered at the reconstitution of his technique. Wonderful, to be sure, yet a marvel familiar enough in the experimental psychology of learning. We often think that swimming and

dancing belong to a small group of special skills, because we do not seem to lose them over long intervals without practice. As a matter of fact, this is the rule rather than the exception. The refinements of technique, to be sure, are not immediately there,—this is true also of swimming and dancing,—but the basic adjustment, the basic structure embedded in the personality, which is far more important than the refinements and nuances, remains at our service.

34. Even when we think at first that we have forgotten something, this may not be the case at all. In a certain experiment the subjects were asked to recite poems learned some time ago. Their efforts were very imperfect. Then they were urged to try hard, to do their best, to reconstruct what seemed lost, to take their time. And more and more was steadily recovered. This may, perhaps, seem rather commonplace, except in so far as an everyday experience is subjected to experimental verification. Yet to the reflective mind such salvagings from some strange limbo have an uncanny look. What is it that we lose? What is it that we keep? Why should the directed will be able to hook so many fish swimming in the psychic depths?

35. As a matter of fact, what we call forgetting is less an affair of sheer loss than of confusion. Details become mixed; fact and fancy intertwine with one another. The material is not ready on the instant, but apparently it is still there.

36. One of the most curious features of our mental life is the quantity of undocumented material we carry about with us. We know—or think we know—all sorts of things. Yet of how we came to know them we have not the vestige of an idea. If we were asked to give chapter and verse, we could not do it. A prosecuting attorney would have us very much at his mercy. Still we are perfectly confident, sure that we are right. The fact seems to be that we are capable of learning a great deal incidentally, by just "picking it up." An experiment was set up in which adult pupils learned a special and complex multiplication table. Some of them memorized the table first, and then did sums with it; others started with the sums, referred to the table for each operation, but never memorized it. These latter came to know and independently to use the table better and with less effort than the former. They had just "picked it up." They would be quite sure, for instance, that 7×29 is 203, but exactly how they had acquired the knowledge they were unaware. A great many of our most valuable items of knowledge and skill are acquired in this way, without documentation or conscious reference—incidentally acquired, that is. The sources of the item are buried in oblivion; the structure of thought and action remains.

37. If the reader wishes to catch the true feel of the learning process, let him try the following simple and not unprofitable experiment. Let him take a poem of a hundred lines or more. Let him read it through once in the morning and once in the evening, day after day. At first nothing much in the way of learning seems to take place. One reads the poem, and forgets almost all of it. But suddenly there arrives a time when one becomes aware that one knows the poem, that one could start at the beginning and recite along to the end. Contrast this with the businesslike process of learning perfectly ten lines each day. How dutiful and practical it seems! Something attempted, something done, to earn a night's repose. Yet if one pursues the ten-line method one will learn the poem more slowly and less well than by the procedure which seems utterly unbusinesslike, and which at first appears to yield no results at all. The point is that what we call learning a poem is not grinding it bit by bit into our tissues. Learning the poem means creating it as a living structure in our minds.

V

38. The considerations just adduced help us to understand the extraordinary subtlety of the learning process, and its pervasive influence upon human destiny. It is a good many years now since William James, in words of insinuating eloquence, implored teachers to build all learning upon native instinct. Today the position we would take seems almost the inverse of his. For it appears that most of those impulsive tendencies which seem so much a part of us that we think they must be inborn

are indeed the products of learning. Here is no school-bound process, but a force ramifying through all the affairs of life. We learn our hopes and fears, our ambitions and dreads, our loves and hates, our interests and distastes, and we do it so naturally that we are hardly more aware of what is happening to us than of the beating of our hearts.

39. Why does one man shine as an executive, another as a salesman, another as a soldier, another as a mathematician, another as a musician? The answer which leaps first to our minds is: Because they were born so. But such a view finds little in psychological investigation to substantiate it. Many a careful search has been made to isolate special innate abilities, but in the main such attempts have drawn blank. What usually emerges is not the difference in the abilities of mathematician, executive, musician, soldier, sailor, tinker, and tailor, but their extraordinary similarity. Great achievement in any field requires just about the same basic equipment. Almost we seem constrained to believe that there is no such thing as innate musical ability, or executive ability, or legal ability, or mathematical ability. Even the great genius seems to be, in the first instance, simply a high-grade human being, capable of developing in many directions, and not in one alone. He gains his special slant through learning, and the fact that he often acquires it very young may be accounted for by the subtle, pervasive, yet conquering power of a will to learn which

is often aroused by influences that escape ordinary observation. Versatility, rather than specialization, is nature's gift to man. Learning cashes the blank check of native versatility in the name of some special achievement; and it may come about so easily and so fast that we call the special achievement the handiwork of nature too.

40. Yet in a sense we should be right. The products of learning are themselves products of nature. They are not artifacts or tricks. We only think they are when we think of learning as an affair of schoolrooms, dull books, dry routines. When we see a Kramer on the court, a Hogan on the green, a Menuhin with his violin, an Einstein solving a problem, an O'Neill writing a play, we are not beholding the artificial tricks of a very superior trained animal. Such virtuosity is a manifestation of human nature at the very topmost peak of realization. Everything works together, perfectly and without impediment. The whole personality is mobilized, integrated, expressing its essential nature in the triumphant act. In learning their skills these men learned to be natural, to be themselves in fullest measure.

41. Just as plants are shaped and tinted by the soil and climate, so are men moulded by the climate of ideas and expectations in which they live. The process of such shaping is what we call learning. And learning is the familiar miracle which creates out of the raw material of nature the finished product called humanity.

JOHN SLOAN DICKEY *Conscience and the Undergraduate*

John Sloan Dickey (1907-   ), president of Dartmouth College, graduated from Dartmouth in 1929 and from the Harvard Law School three years later. He has practiced law, served in the State Department, and taught foreign affairs. Under his administration, Dartmouth has introduced a required course for seniors called "Great Issues," which deals with vital national and international problems in the modern world. A basic assumption behind the Great Issues program is that students profit more from such a course after they have acquired the maturity and knowledge of three years of college experience.

At the beginning of the essay, President Dickey refers to an American youth "driving a hundred and sixty big white horses across the scenes of an increasingly open society." What is this driver like? Does he know where he is going? If not, can he be helped to obtain a sense of direction?

I

The American male at the peak of his physical powers and appetites, driving a hundred and sixty big white horses across the scenes of an increasingly open society, with weekend money in his pocket and with little prior exposure to trouble and tragedy, personifies an "accident going out to happen." He is not always a college undergraduate, and not all undergraduates are trouble-prone, but I am sure that any close observer of the campus will agree that there is no more vulnerable human combination than an undergraduate.

The college undergraduate is a lot of things —many of them as familiar, predictable, and responsive as the bounce of a basketball, and others as startling (and occasionally as disastrous) as the bad bounce of a football. But it is important to keep in mind that he is an undergraduate because he lives and works within a specific context—the purposes of his college. The focus of that total experience which we call "going to college" is the day-to-day relationship between the undergraduate as a person and the college as an institutional embodiment of other people's purposes. This relationship is not easily probed.

There are those who tell us that the basic trouble with the liberal arts college is that it really has no purpose. In this suspicious view, such institutions are guilty of engaging in a gigantic shell game swindle where "there ain't any pea" under any of the shells.

Without attempting here the impossibility of conclusive proof, I suggest that the American liberal arts college (including the church colleges) can find a significant, even unique, mission in the duality of its historic purpose: to see men made whole in *both* competence and conscience. Is there any other institution

CONSCIENCE AND THE UNDERGRADUATE: Reprinted, by permission of the author and the publisher, from *The Atlantic Monthly*, April 1955. Copyright 1955 by The Atlantic Monthly Company, Boston 16, Massachusetts.

at the highest level of organized educational activity that is committed explicitly by its history and by its program to these twin goals?

This is not to say that our great professional and technical institutions or the graduate schools of arts and sciences are something less than the liberal arts college, but rather that they have set themselves a different task—the mission of developing a special competence. Nor am I unaware that these institutions and the liberal arts colleges are borrowing more and more from each other and may be moving toward each other in approaching a closer integration of all higher education. But my point is that the historic liberal arts college has had a *unique* mission and that this mission has reality and validity today.

There is almost no form or field of learning that does not multiply a man's power economically, socially, politically, or physically. This is commonplace because the creation of competence at every level of education is commonplace. We could hardly stop it if we would. The appetite of self-interest will keep enough of us hungry for ever larger portions of competence. It is the job of the college to keep competence civilized.

There are many problems and shortcomings in the business of educating for competence. Mostly they are the problems of any dynamic enterprise: how to do it better, how to do more. These "how to do" problems trouble the liberal arts colleges as well as the professional and technical schools; and, up to a point, I am glad they do, although some fear that for a liberal arts college any concern of this kind is the shortest route to perdition. I have no interest in seeing the liberal arts college become too precious for the man who hungers for competence. He greatly needs the tempering of liberal education; and in turn such an undergraduate, whether he is heading for medicine, law, engineering, business, or some other field, by the very fact that he is headed somewhere brings a healthy reality and vigor to the work of the college. Too many men in a college who think they know just what they want can make liberal education too narrowly purposeful. But in order to have the abrasiveness that the "practical" fellows bring to the campus, I am prepared to take my chances on this danger and the exasperating troubles it breeds.

The risk seems to me worth taking because I am increasingly persuaded that the cause of liberal education will not be overrun by vocationalism if the college holds to its birthright and remains committed as a matter of purpose to serious concern with the issues of conscience. A concern for the choice of good and the rejection of evil in an institution of liberal learning quickens all humanistic studies and prevents our increasing reliance on the physical and social sciences from smothering those intuitive insights which both produce and spring from goodness in a man.

A moral purpose exists for its own sake or it is nothing. I have no thought of propping it up here with extraneous arguments. I merely offer the observation that there seems to be a significant natural affinity between the liberating arts and an educational enterprise committed to the dual pursuit of competence and conscience. You might call it reciprocal invigoration.

To create the power of competence without creating a corresponding sense of moral direction to guide the use of that power is bad education.

II

This is the point in the story where most college catalogue statements of high purpose end, leaving the blissful impression that the undergraduate and the moral purpose of his college once met will live happily together ever afterward. There are more reasons why this is not so than I understand; but, in fairness to the undergraduate and to the task the liberal arts college has set itself, there are certain things which ought to be taken into account before he and the modern college are assumed to be hopelessly immoral and faithless.

Consider the raw material on which the college seeks to work a moral purpose. The undergraduate begins as a boy and leaves as a man. Between the ages of seventeen and

twenty-two he crosses the last dramatic threshold of personal growth. As a freshman he is sure all things are known or knowable; as a senior he wonders. I have never known a freshman who sensed the humorous ambiguity in the advice given a city-bound daughter by her mountaineer father: "When in doubt, Nell, do right." On the other hand, the sophistication of the senior is wonderfully caught in the reply of one of them to my tirade on respect for facts: "Sir, the only trouble with facts is that there are so many of them."

In adult life there are new adjustments to be made, new troubles to be met, and wisdom to be learned, but instead of four there are fifty years or more for learning the ways of goodness and creating the works of love. And to put it very mildly, adult learning is not handicapped by the fact that it takes place on the ebb tide of a man's physical appetites and power.

The undergraduate on the other hand must make his peace with the moral purposes of an institution during four hectic years when his appetites and powers are at flood tide and before he has had much, if any, experience with what can happen. The lack of intimate personal acquaintance with trouble and tragedy is not, of course, a condition peculiar to modern youth, but it is the impression of many of us that most undergraduates today have seen far less of these things than had their grandfathers or even many of their fathers at the same age. Again there are many reasons—among them the rising standard of living, the lack of hard times or widespread business failures in the last ten years, and the growing urbanization, or sub-urbanization, of the population that heavily patronizes the liberal arts college.

The farm or small-town home where the whole family shared the troubles and uncertainties of life at all three meals, seven days a week, provided an earlier exposure to the rough edges of life than does a suburban childhood topped perhaps by years away at boarding school. The fact that life has narrow margins also comes earlier in the story for most rural boys. This is not a lament for the good old days and it is not an appraisal of our many contemporary advantages; but before we apply the standards of yesterday to the undergraduate of today, we ought to remember that some basic things in his pre-college experience are very different.

I shall forgo here any attempt to compare the pre-college church background of today's youth with yesterday's, but I do want to mention one more changing reality that seems to me to have a very sharp bearing on the undergraduate's readiness for the deep spiritual insights of humility, compassion, and faith. Today's freshman was only seven at the end of World War II and he was too young for Korea. He brings to college a very dim and impersonal notion of death.

It is increasingly probable that he comes to college without having known the immeasurable grief which falls on a boy with the death of a parent, a brother, a sister, or of a grandparent living in the same household. The terror of diphtheria epidemics is unknown to him; he is rarely wrenched from college by the death of a father. Modern medicine pushes death further and further up the years, both for those who go and those who stay. In a time when each young family goes off to its own home, when hospitalization of the sick increasingly takes illness and death out of the home, and when the practice of holding funerals in the home has almost passed, young people know little of shared suffering and are kept at arm's length from the crush of death. How many boys now coming to college have lived day in and day out with a grandparent dying on the parlor sofa?

You may well say, with me, "Thank God for this." But can we doubt that deep personal experience with the reality that every life ends and that, with all our knowing, there are earthly bounds beyond which there is no knowing—can we doubt that these are the ingredients out of which honest humility, compassion, and faith become personal to the human self? An undergraduate who has not yet known these things in his own life can sometimes borrow from the total store of human woe and joy, and by using the tools of the intellect he can begin to lay out a pattern of belief for himself, but it will be a sharper etching after the bite of life's acid is on it.

Moreover, one of the very tools he must use can cause an undergraduate to feel that the liberal arts college is at war with itself, and that there is an irreconcilable contradiction between its approach to competence and its approach to conscience. The name of that tool is doubt. The tool of doubt is simply indispensable to the fashioning of the kind of critical mind that does the daily intellectual work of the world. Any fact, any assumption, any theory, that has not been tested by the diamond-pointed drill of doubt is at best a doubtful thing. Almost every good teacher at some point takes the calculated risk of pressing this tool into the hands of his undergraduate students. Most of them learn to handle and respect it as a tool, but there are always some who, for a time at least, insist on treating doubt as an end in itself. Likewise, I think, many undergraduates go through a phase of being genuinely perplexed because the use of doubt does not produce uniformly satisfying results in all situations.

III

Today's undergraduate—and for that matter today's college teacher—is not much interested in the type of science versus religion wrestling match that drew so well on many campuses in the twenties. He is quite willing to leave that argument where it fell of its own futility. You can, of course, hear almost anything on any campus if you listen long enough, but generally the questions today seem more manageable: What is science? How far can it reach? Are different religions compatible? Is religion really livable? Is it "for me"? And, as always, there is the large, relatively silent sector of opinion which believes in letting your mind alone about such things. For these fellows the religious practice or indifference of their fathers is good enough.

I am often asked whether there is not greater interest in religion on the campus today than during the pre-war period. Such judgments are at best imprecise, but so far as I can judge, the answer is yes. On our campus we see such intensified interest in the classroom, the chapel, and the Christian Union. Student attendance and activity in the local churches have sharply increased. This manifestation of growing religious interest on the campus undoubtedly reflects in part what is happening throughout American society, but

I am sure there is also in it a factor indigenous to the college.

Even though there is no great debate between science and religion as competing absolutes on the campus today, a goodly percentage of freshmen and sophomores can be counted on to keep their parents harried about religious matters. It has ever been thus, and I feel certain that so long as disciplined doubt is one of the mind's tools it will always be thus—at least until the last apprenticeship has been served in these workshops of the mind. This seems to me healthy as well as inevitable, and I commend those who need reassurance to President William Jewett Tucker, who, after a lifetime of preaching and teaching, wrote: "The doubting mind always seemed to me a part of the believing mind." The understanding of such paradox is the fruit of full maturity, rarely, if ever, within the reach of any undergraduate.

Whatever the reason, an undergraduate often hesitates to accept moral and spiritual commitments that seem to him to limit his free-wheeling maneuverability of either body or soul. I respect and value this instinct as a reaction to unexamined dogma. However, I think I also know something of its perverse possibilities as a subterfuge for an unwillingness to examine, and as a form of chronic immaturity. These are ancient foes of education; they are hard to live with even when you are paid to do it, and they are harder to cure.

The undergraduate of the days before yesterday was not quite all that as an alumnus he now thinks he was, but as a general thing he probably was ready to commit himself earlier and more rigidly on moral and spiritual issues. He personally often felt the need of such commitment earlier, and such commitments fell right into the general pattern of his family and community life. Any commitment comes easier if everyone is doing it. Whatever the reasons, for some time now, not everybody is doing it, and as a consequence today's undergraduate feels very much more on his own in working his way through these things. Working out such commitments on your own builds self-reliance. It is, however, difficult, even dangerous, and it certainly takes more time. It is a lonely business and today's

undergraduate is often more lonely than he admits or we realize.

But nothing could be more foolish and unjust than to assume that today's undergraduate does not respond positively and in distinctive ways to a moral challenge. Within the reality of his experience he is ready, willing, and able to come to grips with issues of conscience which in other days were largely left to his elders. During the past ten years I have watched our post-war undergraduates face up to problems of conscience in passing hard disciplinary judgments on fellow students, in taking their own measure on the issues of racial discrimination and the honor system, and in meeting the easy-to-duck challenges of such things as the campus community chest, the needs of DP students, and the unadvertised troubles of some hard-pressed North countryman in the outlying community. It is no false bravery to say that having watched both his doing of these things and his contagion for trouble, I am prepared to take my chances with the kind of world the undergraduate creates when he works at it.

And he does work at it. It is a common thing for our undergraduate committee handling the investigation and recommendations on disciplinary cases to sit into the early morning hours of the night. There is no duty on a modern campus more distasteful to an undergraduate than sitting in judgment on the shortcomings of his peers. He is keenly aware that "but for the grace of God, there go I" and he probably still retains a strong trace of the American schoolboy's loyalty to the group as against the authority of the school. And yet I have never known an outgoing undergraduate judiciary chairman whose capacity for both compassion and just judgment was not admired, indeed envied, by students and faculty alike.

Recently this committee sat until 2 A.M. considering whether to recommend the dismissal from college of a boy who had gotten himself into serious trouble. It was a hard case all around, and it was only after an independent investigation, a hearing of the boy, and lengthy deliberation that the committee finally decided the interests of the college required dismissal of the student. Before he went to bed that night the undergraduate chairman on his own initiative called on the boy's parents at the Inn to report the decision and to give them the kind of explanation he would have wanted his parents to get if he were being dismissed. This is more than responsibility; this is conscience.

It is not the leaders alone who measure up. On things such as racial discrimination and compulsory military service every man must face himself as well as the nation and his Maker. Today's undergraduate has no choice about going or not going into the armed forces. He must go, but his attitude in going is important. At Dartmouth, we who have worked with all our seniors in the Great Issues Course know that today's senior goes into the service of his country understanding far more than did his father or grandfather why he does so. He knows why it is all so necessary and yet so unnecessary. He puts two or three years of his life into what he is told needs to be done without becoming embittered, without retreating either to "know-nothingism" or pacifism, and with a growing awareness of the role of conscience in all his doing.

An undergraduate generation capable of coming to terms with itself and its elders on the issues of man's brotherhood is surely capable in the course of a lifetime of coming to terms with the universe as children of God.

IV

Is today's college as well prepared as it should be to meet these needs of conscience? When it comes to commitments, the independent college itself has a problem. It has a long history of fighting clear of doctrinal commitments and for good reasons. Yet a college cannot take its problems of purpose seriously without venturing into some form of institutional commitment. The early American colleges were generally very clear about their commitment to a moral and religious purpose. For several hundred years the primacy of this purpose was both attested and served by three constitutional elements in the life of these colleges: (1) the tradition of preacher presidents, (2) a curriculum heavy with religion and moral doctrine, and (3) compulsory church and chapel. I refer to these elements as "constitutional" because for a

long period, above and beyond men, their influence permeated all that these institutions were and did. But, as with other mortal constitutional forms, they proved susceptible of amendment and not as permanent as they had seemed to earlier generations. Certainly it is a rare thing today to find any college, except those institutions which are integral parts of a church, where the moral purpose of higher education continues to be attested by this triad of constitutional witnesses.

The time has passed on most campuses for arguing the merits of these changes; they are done and in the main they were in response to serious weaknesses and real needs. There is little or no prospect that any of these elements could be re-established intact today. Many do believe that college chapel in some form still has a future. I hope so and I should personally be sorry to see it abandoned or weakened on those campuses where it still exists even though in greatly modified form from the rigors and requirements of yesterday.

The deeper significance of these traditions has become apparent only as we begin to be aware that with the passing of these constitutional elements from the campus, the college's concern for conscience was left without tangible, pervasive, and enduring witness. Nothing comparable was substituted for the outmoded agencies, and this gap in the context of purpose remains an uncorrected weakness on most undergraduate campuses today. This seems to me to be clear unless we are ready to say either (1) that the college's historic commitment to furthering the moral and spiritual growth of an undergraduate truly ceased with the passing of these particular witnesses, or (2) that in serving this purpose we can rely exclusively on the ebb and flow of its awareness in individual teachers and administrators rather than on the more traditional combination of men plus the prod of institutional form and purpose. Either of these seems to me bad education.

The challenge of this problem is to get beyond words. In an effort to be concretely responsive we have done three things at Dartmouth:—

First, the Board of Trustees has formally affirmed that the College's "moral and spiritual purpose springs from a belief in the existence of good and evil, from faith in the ability of men to choose between them and from a sense of duty to advance the good."

Secondly, the Trustees by the same resolution established an independent endowment within the College to be known as the William Jewett Tucker Foundation for the specific purpose of supporting and furthering in all ways and in all areas the moral and spiritual work of the College.

Thirdly, the Trustees have created a new position of pervasive scope, to be known as the Dean of the Tucker Foundation, the occupant of which will have the campus as well as the chapel for his province.

The Tucker Foundation takes its aim and scope from the outlook of Dr. Tucker, Dartmouth's last preacher president and one of the greatest, who at the turn of the century spoke thus in the College chapel:—

I make no closing plea for any formal religion, but I do plead now as always for the religious spirit. . . . Seek, I pray you, moral distinction. Be not content with the commonplace in character any more than with the commonplace in ambition or intellectual attainment. Do not expect that you will make any lasting or very strong impression on the world through intellectual power without the use of an equal amount of conscience and heart.

There are no panaceas in education and I claim no patentable novelty for the individual features of the Tucker Foundation. Taken together, however, I wonder if they do not add up to an approach that is genuinely responsive to the problem of keeping conscience to the fore as an indispensable ingredient of an education that can commit a man to a better life as he liberates himself from a lesser one.

Here on the side of conscience in the broadest and firmest terms is an explicit commitment of purpose. So long as our society places

its bet on the power of free men to choose their destiny, such a commitment will be relevant. It is built low to the ground but it looks up, and I should think that it had a good chance to remain resilient and meaningful under well-nigh any future circumstance. Here also is a store of material resources which, joined with the avowal of purpose, will stand as a tangible reminder to the students, teachers, alumni, presidents, and trustees of tomorrow that they are committed to the work of righteousness and that it is their task to fashion tools appropriate to their day. Finally, here in the deanship of the Tucker Foundation is a position of both scope and prestige which, while rooted in the religious spirit, could open to its occupant the kind of intimate but wide-ranging relationship to the campus that our highly departmentalized colleges so badly need. Incidentally, such a representative-at-large might well accomplish some of the college-wide missions the preacher presidents were able to perform in their day which a present-day college president is kept from doing because of his amphibious existence, half on and half off the campus.

Up to now I have spoken of competence and conscience as if they were the twain that never get closer than the opposite sides of that ubiquitous thing called "and." This cleavage is not the reality either on or off the campus. It is the mixture that counts, and among our other blessings I rate very highly the fact that in the liberal arts college neither competence nor conscience is taken straight. Rather, it is the human interplay between these two poles of purpose that gives liberal education its orientation to the light and brings to the undergraduate grown a man those liberating and civilizing qualities men never quite define nor ever quite deny.

PEOPLE AND PLACES

PAUL HORGAN *Pages from a Rio Grande Notebook*

Paul Horgan (1903-   ) was born in Buffalo, but his family moved to Albuquerque when he was fifteen. He was educated at the New Mexico Military Institute, where he later became librarian and assistant to the president. He won the Harper Prize Novel Competition in 1933 and was a Guggenheim Fellow in 1947-48. During World War II he was on active duty and was awarded the Legion of Merit, as Chief of the Army Information Branch of the United States Department of War.

Besides a large number of essays and stories, Mr. Horgan has written more than a dozen books. Since several of them are centered around the great river, he has been called, with considerable accuracy and justice, the Herodotus of the Rio Grande. His magnum opus is the two-volume, Pulitzer-Prize-winning *Great River: The Rio Grande in North American History,* 1954.

Mr. Horgan's writings about the Rio Grande are obviously a labor of love. While writing *Great River,* he traveled the river's full length of 1,800 miles three times and made dozens and dozens of trips to check facts, often going 100 miles to clear up a footnote. "Pages from a Rio Grande Notebook" are excerpts from Mr. Horgan's first working notebooks, tracing the Rio Grande's life through the seasons and the miles from the Rockies to the Gulf of Mexico.

1. It is born of winter, this river, in the longest season of cold in the United States. The source mountains in the Colorado Rockies are hard and wild. The air is thin and at such altitude subject to swift, crystalline changes of condition which may bring blue darkness in midday, and yield snow during nine months of the year.

2. Past monstrous peaks of ragged lifeless rock, clouds tear and roll from wall to wall up in the sky. Wind cries there much of the time, and when the atmosphere is overcharged with electricity, the cut and flare of lightning,

the trundle and bounce of thunder after its valley-sharpened crash seem to require new senses, capacities, to be wholly heard.

3. The river's course—here as in its whole career—widens and narrows by turns. Where it is narrow, the slopes are dark, the stream is shadowed all day but for a little while at noon, when straight fingers of sunlight reach down through the forest. The stream is clear and icy, going rapidly over polished brown speckled stones. They remind us of something. At a glance the diamond water going over its stony bed makes the image of the fish it carries—the same speckled colors, the same watery flicker, the same half-lights of reflection and golden flecks. In and out of leaf

shadow, protected by the dazzle of moving water, the trout in plain sight is safe because he and his river are so close in likeness.

4. The Rio Grande towns in Colorado—Del Norte, Monte Vista, Alamosa—are pleasant young communities whose life in each place parallels the railroad tracks for a mile or two. About twenty miles southeast of Alamosa the first sign of Spanish adobe culture appears in a little village—Los Sauses, with houses built of earth, under grand cottonwoods, on a gentle slope above the river, encircled by fine hills. This scene made of slow water, bounteous tree, earthen brick and irrigated field is like a symbolic image of much that is to follow as the river goes south. It is the kind of cell of family, primal want and basic sustenance made visible from which, down-river, grew clusters of kinsmen, and then of neighbors, and then of material defendants, and then of parishioners, and then of descendants, in turn, until a village became a town which became a city, all originally and even now dependent upon the Rio Grande for life.

5. Over the three communities of Taos—the pueblo, the middle commercial town, and the old Ranchos—there is a piercing sweet illimitable clarity of light and sky. Sounds carry, meadow larks, mocking birds, black birds have returned. Over the long plain breathes the wind, sharply sweet and already warmed, disturbing nothing but the senses. Space is so great, vision is so plain, air is so clear that human activities can be seen from afar. Small figures like humanity in Brueghel go about their tasks. Earthen buildings go up. Carts travel. Winter rubble is cleared off the fields and out of the acequias. Furrows are seeded. Out in the sage brush of Taos plain, where the old road winds toward the canyon, tiny newborn lambs take fright and scamper before the gusty sand devils whipped up by the darting wind. Flocks move more slowly than cloud shadows. Shepherds sit on a modern culvert and watch what the road brings. The valor and pity of men and women in their renewed use of a corner of the earth is as much a part of spring as everything else.

6. Above Albuquerque begins the lyric grace of the river in its richest passage of the pastoral life. Where life is fed by water, the landscape here recalls the opulence and grandeur and occasional vistas of order in the image of classical country painted by Nicholas Poussin, who left so many celebrations of grove and meadow, shady leaf and column of light, reflecting stream and stepped mountain and composed bodies. There is more than a reminder here, there is a real likeness. It is a likeness of grace and plenty in the midst of dramatic nature; nourishment in the desert; bounty summoned by the most ancient of agricultural rites out of the most inscrutable of antiquities; cool for the heated, slaking for the parched, food for the hungry, rest for the weary, ease for the eye blinded in the unimpeded sun.

7. Up to now, going south, when you looked across the river, you knew exactly how things were on the other side—just more United States of America. But at El Paso with the new concept of a boundary between nations, things are no longer the same on the opposite bank. It is another country, with another people, and with other ways. Many manners and customs have remained common to both sides of the Rio Grande since the time a little over a century ago when the river was not a frontier—when in fact both its banks and all its courses were Spanish or Mexican. But in the United States, subject to a more powerful energy in a more technical society, such survivals remain as exotic, quaint, or commercially glamorous; while in Mexico the same expressions are sincere and not self-conscious. From El Paso southeastward, every United States town has its Mexican counterpart across the river. Commerce, appetite and corruption draw them together. Language, national boundary and law keep them apart. The river itself is hardly an obstacle anywhere, for it can be waded for most of the year, whatever else its common uses may be.

8. Seventy miles below El Paso, mountains reach in on both sides of the Rio Grande and present to it another of its many obstacles; but the stream bed passes between them and continues upon its depleted way. The river is dying. The desert finally seems ready to triumph over it and drink out of sight the last crawling trickles of the flow that was born in the Colorado Rockies.

9. And so it would, but relief and replenishment are on their way from another mountain system lying deep in Mexico, where the Rio Conchos with its major tributary the Rio San Pedro courses northeastward to join the Rio Grande at an altitude of 2,400 feet a few miles above the old Texas town of Presidio. With it comes new power for the river, to create dramatic, and even melodramatic, phases of its career, in the accomplishment of water over rock, as demonstrated by the vast implausibilities of the earth features of the Big Bend.

10. At Presidio the replenished river fashions another of those green and easy valleys which, as at Alamosa, Espanola, Algodones, Albuquerque, Belen and Mesilla, lie on ancient fertile flats of old river bottoms between gravel terraces and outlying mountains. After the bare and voracious desert in which it nearly died, the river brings again willows and cottonwoods, lilac mountains and attendant clouds, blue sky and emerald green fields and pink sand, with a sweetness in the air made from all these together.

11. Summer is a long season here, after the harsh, bitter wind storms of spring, with their abrasive white dust that flies out of rocky arroyos to the north, casting a steel-blue obscurity across the sun.

12. Previously the river has always been accompanied by mountains, near or far; but they lay generally parallel to its course. Now in the Big Bend the river encounters mountains in a new and extraordinary way; for they lie, chain after chain of them, directly across its way as though to impede and divert it and deny it passage to the sea. But the pull of the sea is stronger than rock, and the river was here before the mountains, and as they rose, in slowness beyond time, it cut its way against and through them.

13. Born in mountains, and cradled by them, and then opposed by them, the Rio Grande has always been within sight of them. But below the Big Bend they start to fall away. If you can say so, now as the river goes southeastward, mountains are getting lost, like beads of a string which has broken so the ones at the end rest separate without apparent

connection with each other until finally there are no more.

14. Autumn is the seasonal analogy of age; and now in autumn, and here approaching the sea, the river shows its age most plainly. In its last phase with less than two feet a mile to drop, it flows slowly, making bend after bend of wide loops. Built by the drag of silt the river banks rise above the surrounding country. Everywhere are signs of former river beds which finally became too shallow and too elevated to retain the river in storm time. The river broke over, making new courses. The older ones grew grass and softened their contours. Everywhere is the green growth of semitropical climate.

15. The citrus, palm, garden aspect of the lower valley land begins to merge east of Brownsville into white sand and salt grass, through which the Rio Grande twists from side to side, mild and nearly exhausted. Dunes accompany it and migrate with the wind. Sometimes hurricanes formed in the West Indies slash inland over the delta. But it is too late for weather to create much downstream change in the Rio Grande in its last wandering miles.

16. There is evidence of marsh life. The river banks in places are hardly an inch or two above the flow. Water fowl attend—cranes, herons, geese, ducks, curlews, plover, sandpipers. The light of the sky continuously fades and brightens according to sea clouds that hardly form but hang low and filmy, as white as the wilderness of sand on which they make glistening shadows. Salt marshes and lagoons rest like misted mirrors among the low hollows bounded by dunes. The wasted flood plain is running out with the continent.

17. Isolated, depleted, heavy with suspended soil, the river widens gradually to a thousand feet and leaves the dunes between low shelves of sandy beach littered with driftwood that is polished to silver by wind and sun, or blackened by saturation. Through a waste of sand, misty air and silence, in the presence of no human concern, having come more than eighteen hundred miles from mountains nearly three miles high, the Rio Grande at last enters the Gulf of Mexico and the sea.

VAN WYCK BROOKS *Helen Keller*

Van Wyck Brooks (1886-   ), biographer, critic, and literary historian, was educated at Harvard. He began his professional career as a teacher and later became a member of a publishing firm. Since 1920 he has devoted his time mostly to writing biographies and critical and social studies of American authors. To date he has written more than twenty books, excluding his several translations of French authors. His biographies of Mark Twain (1920), Henry James (1925), and Emerson (1932) were popular but not nearly so widely read as his three volumes of literary history—*The Flowering of New England (1815-1865)*, 1936; *New England: Indian Summer (1865-1915)*, 1940; and *The World of Washington Irving*, 1944. More recently he has written *The Times of Melville and Whitman*, 1947; *The Confident Years (1885-1915)*, 1951; and *Scenes and Portraits: Memories of Childhood and Youth*, 1954.

At present he lives in Westport, Connecticut, where he is a neighbor of Helen Keller. From this unique perspective, he has written an intimate portrait of Miss Keller.

I

1. When I was in St. Augustine, Florida, in the winter of 1932, Helen Keller appeared at the Cathedral Lyceum, and I went to see and hear her there, drawn by curiosity, such as one feels for any world-famous person. For Helen Keller was not only famous but she had been so from the age of ten, when she had sat on Edward Everett Hale's knee and Queen Victoria asked Phillips Brooks about her. A ship was named after her in 1890, and, while Oliver Wendell Holmes had published a letter of hers in one of his books, she had visited Whittier in his house on the Merrimac river. President Grover Cleveland had received her in the White House, as other presidents were to do in after years, and Mark Twain had said that the two most interesting characters of the nineteenth century were, quite simply, Napoleon and Helen Keller. Yet there she was in St. Augustine, still young, in 1932, and here she continues to be twenty-two years later.

HELEN KELLER: Reprinted, by permission of the author, from *Harper's Magazine*, May 1954.

2. I remember one phrase she uttered then, interpreted by her companion (for, never having heard her own voice, her speech was turbid): a phrase referring to the subway in New York that "opened its jaws like a great beast," which struck me at the moment as reminiscent of the prophets in the Bible. I was not aware then how steeped she was in the language of the Bible, which I later heard her expound with Biblical scholars; nor did I know how familiar she was, literally, with the jaws of beasts, for she had once stroked a lion's mouth. The lion, it is true, was young and well fed in advance, but nevertheless she entered its cage boldly; for her "teacher," as she always called Anne Sullivan, the extraordinary woman who developed her mind, wished her to meet experiences of every sort.

3. The daughter of a Confederate officer, Miss Keller was born on an Alabama farm and knew cows, mules, and horses from her earliest childhood; they had eaten apples from her hand and never harmed her; and her teacher, feeling that she should know wild animals as well, introduced her early to the zoo of a circus. She shook hands with a bear, she patted

a leopard, she was lifted up to feel the ears of a giraffe. She encouraged elephants to wind their trunks about her neck and big snakes wrapped their coils about her, so that Helen Keller, for this reason partly, grew up without fear, and she has remained both physically and morally fearless. The only animals she has not touched are the panther and the tiger, for the tiger is "wanton," as I once heard her say, an appropriate word but characteristic of a mind that has been fed from books instead of the give-and-take of everyday talk.

4. At that time I knew little of Helen Keller's life and mind, and I could not have guessed that a few years later I was to be her neighbor, seeing her often. My old friend the sculptor Jo Davidson brought us together, just as her own feeling for sculpture had drawn her to Jo Davidson, because Helen Keller "saw" with her hands. She has "ten eyes for sculpture," as Professor Gaetano Salvemini said when, in 1950, she visited Florence, and he arranged for her to see Michelangelo's Medici tombs and the sculpture of Donatello in the Bargello. Salvemini had movable scaffolds set up so that she could pass her hands over the Medici heads and St. John the Baptist, the figures of Night and Day and the Madonna and Child; and our friend Jo, who was present, said he had never seen these sculptures before as when he watched her hands wandering over the forms. She peered as it were into every crevice and the subtlest modulations, exclaiming with pleasure as she divined the open mouth of the singing youth and murmuring over the suckling infant, "Innocent greed!" She had quoted in *The World I Live In* a saying of Ghiberti about some sculptured figure he had seen in Rome, that "its most exquisite beauties could not be discovered by the sight but only by the touch of the hand passed over it." To how much else and to how many others her "seeing hand" has led her first or last! It has been her passport to the world outside her.

5. For the world in which she lives herself is built of touch-sensations, devoid of physical color and devoid of sound, and she has written much about the hand by which she lives and which takes the place of the hearing and sight of others. Exploring the faces of her friends and people whom she has just met, she reads them as if she were clairvoyant, and she can

distinguish the Yankee twang and the Southern drawl she has never heard by touching two or three spots on the throats of the speakers.

6. She says that hands are quite as easy to recognize as faces and reveal the secrets of the character more openly, in fact, and she can tell from hands at once whether people have large natures or whether they have only "dormouse valor." In the soft smooth roundness of certain hands, especially of the rich who have never known toil, she feels a certain chaos of the undeveloped; and, in her land of darkness and silence, she can feel with her own hands the beautiful, the strong, the weak, the comic.

7. She had early learned geography from maps that her teacher made out of clay or sand on the banks of the Tennessee river, feeling mountains and valleys and following the course of other rivers, and she relates in *The Story of My Life* how, in 1893, she virtually saw with her fingers the World's Fair in Chicago. It is true that the inventor of the telephone, Alexander Graham Bell, one of her early admirers, was there with her and described to her some of the sights in the deaf-and-dumb "system," but he had arranged for her to touch all the objects in the bazaars, the relics of ancient Mexico, the Viking ship. She had taken in with her finger tips the Arabian Nights of the fair as she had learned to read from the raised letters of Braille.

8. It is natural that Helen Keller has dwelt at length in her books on the hand by which alone the blind are able to see. She very early dedicated her own life to the cause of the education of the blind—doubly handicapped as she was and the only one so handicapped who has ever become a thoroughly well-educated person. (The only possible exception is Robert Smithdas, who graduated from St. John's University in 1952.) Because she was handicapped, because two of her senses were cut off, nature augmented her three remaining senses, not the sense of touch alone but the sense of taste and the sense of smell, which others regard, she says, as a "fallen angel."

9. In her these are all exceptionally acute and alert. She tells in her *Journal* how in London, passing through a gate, she knew at once by the smell of burning leaves, with the smell of

the grass, that she was in Green Park, and she says she can always distinguish Fifth Avenue from humbler New York streets by the odors issuing from the doors as she walks past. She knows the cosmetics that women are using and the kind of coffee they are roasting within and whether they use candles and burn soft coal or wood, just as she recognized St. Louis from the smell of the breweries miles away and Peoria from the smell of the whisky stills. "Listening" with her feet, she says, in a hotel dining-room, she knows the moods and characters of people who walk past her, whether they are firm or indecisive, active or lazy, careless, timid, weary, angry, or sad; and she will exclaim, "What lovely white lilacs!", knowing they are white by touch or smell, for in texture and perfume white lilacs differ from purple. Sometimes, hearing her say these things, I have thought of Edward Sheldon, my blind friend who remarked to Cornelia Otis Skinner, "Your hair is dark, isn't it? I can tell from your voice." Helen Keller, who cannot hear voices, feels vibrations. When an orchestra plays, she follows the music waves along the floor; and, detecting on her desk upstairs the vibration of the bell from the pantry below, she answers with a shuffle of the feet, "Coming down!"

10. All this gave rise in early years to legends of a "wonder girl" that always annoyed Helen Keller—for she is the embodiment of humor and simple good sense—as well as to rumors in Europe that she was the last word in "American bluff," which led to various efforts to discredit and expose her. The girl who had "found the Blue Bird," as Maeterlinck put it, was said never to be tired or discouraged or sad, and all sorts of supernatural faculties were attributed to her, especially the gift of making uncanny predictions.

11. But, while Anne Sullivan took pains to keep her from being a prodigy, and no one found anything to expose, it was impossible to conceal the fact that she had a remarkable mind and even perhaps a still more remarkable will. Speaking of this, Emma Goldman said she proved that the human will had "an almost illimitable power"; and what could one say of an intellect as handicapped as hers that, at eighteen, carried her so far in so many directions? If she did not master, she learned much

of geometry, algebra, physics, with botany, zoology, and the philosophy that she knew well, while she wrote good letters in French, as later she spoke German, reading Latin too when she went to college. Unable to hear lectures or take notes, she graduated with honors at Radcliffe, where she wrote her autobiography in the class of Mr. Copeland, the famous "Copey" who said she showed that she could write better, in some of her work, than any other man or woman he had had as a pupil.

12. It was Anne Sullivan who had invented the methods of connecting mind with mind that made all this possible, of course—and that seemed to be "superhuman," as Einstein remarked; although Helen all but outstripped her perceptive teacher and retained all that she took in. Few of the required books were printed for the blind, and she had to have whole books spelled into her hand, while, always examining, observing, reflecting, surrounded by darkness and silence, she wrote that she found music and brightness within. Through all her thoughts flashed what she supposed was color. With her native traits of pluck and courage, energy, tenacity, she was tough-minded and independent also, and her only fear was of writing something that she had been told or that she had read, something that was not out of her own life and mind.

II

13. This was the girl who had evolved from the headstrong child whom Anne Sullivan had found in Alabama and whom she had taken at the age of eight to the Perkins Institution in Boston where Helen afterward visited off and on. There she encountered Laura Bridgman, the first deaf-and-dumb person who had ever been taught to communicate with her fellow-creatures, Dr. Howe's celebrated pupil whom Dickens had written about and who was a contrast indeed to the "young colt" Helen. Laura Bridgman was shocked, in fact, by her impulsive movements and rebuked her for being too forward, robust as she was, while the statue-like motionless Laura, with her cool hands, struck Helen as like a flower that has grown in the shade.

14. A much more interesting personality, and ruddily healthy from the start, Helen her-

self was to grow up fond of sports, riding a horse and a bicycle tandem, playing cards and chess and all but completely self-reliant. Moreover, she was never guarded from the knowledge of evil, and, fully informed as she always was about the seamy sides of life, the mind that she developed was realistic. Nothing could have been more tonic than Helen Keller's bringing up, under the guidance of Anne Sullivan, on the farm in Alabama. They read and studied out of doors on the river-bank, in the woods, in the fields, in the shade, as Helen remembered, of a wild tulip tree, and the fragrance of the mimosa blossoms, the pine needles, and the grapes were blended with all her early lessons. She learned about the sun and rain, and how birds build their nests, about squirrels, frogs, wild flowers, rabbits, and insects; and, as it came back to her, everything that sang or bloomed, buzzed or hummed was part of her education.

15. It might have been supposed, meanwhile, that the Perkins Institution also influenced Helen in various ways, for she carried through life what seemed to be the stamp of the reformist mind that the great Dr. Howe represented. An old Yankee abolitionist, Samuel Gridley Howe was concerned for all the desolate and all the oppressed, and Helen has written with the same indignation and grief about lynching and anti-Semitism and the case of Sacco and Vanzetti. Usually on the unpopular side, and for years a follower of Debs, she was almost a social outcast in certain circles when Mark Twain, who hated injustice —and was a special friend of hers—said there were worse things than being blind. It was worse to have eyes and not to see. Helen liked Mark Twain all the better because, as she wrote in *Midstream,* he did not temper his words to suit feminine ears, because "his talk was fragrant with tobacco and flamboyant with profanity," while, with his tender heart, he matched her tough mind. It pleased her when, bidding her good night, he said she would find in the bathroom not only Bourbon and Scotch but plenty of cigars.

16. Helen's realism, along with her social imagination, developed in her the planetary mind, so that on her tours to help the blind in all the six continents she has read in every country the signs of the times. With an out-

look that was molded more or less by Emerson and Whitman, along with the New Church doctrines that are her religion—for she was early convinced by Swedenborg's writings—she has become a world citizen who stands for the real America that public men so often misrepresent. She has understood Japan and Greece and especially perhaps the Bible lands, Egypt, Lebanon, Syria, Israel, where she has lectured at universities from Cairo to Jerusalem and where new schools for the blind have risen as she passed. Reaching out to meet the minds of all sorts and conditions of men, she comprehends their needs and aspirations, so that she is a true spokesman of our multiracial country that is already a vestibule of the coming "one world."

III

17. Now it happens that, living myself in Connecticut, not far from Helen Keller, I have taken a few notes about her in recent years, jotting down chance remarks of hers and other memoranda, comments that from time to time she has suggested. I offer some of these, unconnected as they are, as follows:

September 1944
Helen has been out picking blueberries today. She has only to touch them to know when they are ripe.
The paths and garden at her house are all so perfectly kept that I exclaimed over them. Helen does it. In summer she is up at five every morning, edging the driveway and the paths. She asks Herbert [Herbert Haas, who drives the car and runs the house] what she should do next. Then she weeds the flower beds. She distinguishes by touch between the flowers and the weeds.

Helen comes to dinner, bringing her checkerboard for a little game.
I had happened on a poem "To Helen Keller" by Edmund Clarence Stedman, published in 1888, fifty-seven years ago. Richard Watson Gilder also addressed a poem to her, and both these poets had written sonnets and odes to Lincoln at the time of his death. Now, halfway through another century, Helen looks at times, and even very often, like a young girl. How many poems were written to her by Robert Frost and others in the good old days when poetry was still "public."

Dinner with Helen and Salvemini at Professor Robert Pfeiffer's. Our Florentine hostess Mrs.

Pfeiffer played an Italian song. Helen stood by with her left hand on the piano top, waving her right hand, keeping time. In this way she knows by heart Beethoven's "Ninth Symphony" and recognizes many other compositions.

Someone asked her how she tells the difference between day and night. "Oh," she said, "in the day the air is lighter, odors are lighter, and there is more motion and more vibration in the atmosphere. At night there is less vibration; the air is dense and one feels less motion in things."

With Helen and Polly Thomson [Anne Sullivan's successor] in New York, at a small political meeting in the Hotel Astor. Maury Maverick was with us, just back from England, marveling over the work of the English surgeons in the war. Vice-President Truman had come up from Washington to make a short speech, and we were all introduced to him. Later Helen said, "He has an open hand. There are no crooks in his fingers." She grasps character instantly. Truman was deeply touched by Helen. He was in tears when she spoke to him.

September 1945

Today, more than usually, an air of Scotland pervades Helen's house. In the first place, it is called Arcan Ridge after an old farmhouse in the Scottish Highlands, and Polly Thomson, who has been with Helen since 1914, speaks with a livelier than ever Scottish accent. But this evening William Allan Neilson comes to dinner, the president of Smith College who was one of Helen's professors at Radcliffe and learned the manual alphabet to talk with her there. (He was one of my old professors at Harvard too, and now he is the only person living who, meeting me, aged sixty, invariably addresses me as "Boy.") Neilson still speaks broad Scots, almost every word with "hair on it," as Rudolph Ruzicka said of another Scotsman.

After dinner the talk fell on Scottish songs. Helen went upstairs to her study—for she knows her way perfectly about the house—and brought down a two-volume collection of Scottish songs in Braille which the publishers in Edinburgh had sent her. She read the table of contents with her fingers rapidly, found a song she wanted, turned the pages and read it out to us—a Highland "wail from Skye," as Polly put it.

With Helen and Polly to the harvest festival at the Jewish Theological Seminary far uptown in New York. Midday meal in the Sukkah, the festival tent set up in the quadrangle. The walls were hung with all the fruits of the season, or all the fruits of the Holy Land that are mentioned in the Bible. We sat with the president of the

Seminary, Dr. Louis Finkelstein, and the famous Hebrew scholar, Dr. Saul Lieberman. For a moment I thought of the New Testament scene in the Temple at Jerusalem, for Helen surprised these great Jewish doctors with her knowledge of the Bible. I remembered what she wrote in *Midstream:* she had read her Braille Bible so often that in many places the dots had been rubbed off.

Listening to the Hebrew grace with her fingers on Dr. Finkelstein's lips, she said, "It is like the voice of the Lord upon many waters, the Lord of Glory, thundering."

Then she said, "The Bible is the only book that reaches up to the times in which we live. It speaks knowingly of the sun, the skies, the sea, and the beauty of distant stars. . . . There are no differences in men. Differences are only as the variation in shadows cast by the sun."

After lunch we rode down town in a Broadway bus to the Grand Central Station. Helen likes to feel the crowd around her. Suddenly she said, "There is a painter in the bus." I looked around and, sure enough, there was a house painter sitting in a corner at the other end of the bus, twenty feet away.

July 1946

Dinner at Helen's. She is ready for any adventure. We talked about the gypsies and Conrad Bercovici, and I told her how Bercovici had taken me through the East Side one night where the gypsies were camping out in the cellars of old warehouses. Obliged to come into the city so that their children could go to school, they lived in these abandoned cellars just as they lived on the road in summer. They even set up tents and built campfires on the concrete floors, while their young women told fortunes on the streets.

In Polly's hand Helen's fingers rippled with excitement. She asked me to remind Bercovici of his promise to take her through the East Side and show her the gypsies.

October 1949

Helen comes to dinner. . . . One of our friends asked Helen how she had come to understand abstractions. She said she had found that good apples were sweet and that there were also bad apples that were bitter. Then she learned to think of the sweetness and bitterness apart from the apples. She grasped the idea of sweetness and bitterness in themselves. Sir Alfred Zimmern, at dinner with us, my friend since the days when he wrote *The Greek Commonwealth* forty years ago, listening to Helen, exclaimed, "She is exactly following the method of Plato's dialogues." And indeed her words and their rhythm were Platonic.

The fact is that Helen has a philosophic mind.

She relates in her little book *My Religion* how, when she was twelve or so, she suddenly said to her teacher, "I have been in Athens." She meant, of course, in imagination, for she had been reading about Greece, but observe what followed in her thinking. She instantly perceived that the "realness" of her mind was independent of conditions of place and body, that she had vividly seen and felt a place thousands of miles away precisely because she had a mind. How else could one explain this being "in Athens"? From that moment, she continued, "Deafness and blindness were of no real account. They were to be <u>relegated</u> to the outer circle of my life."

Is not that real philosophy, the life of reason?

Christmas 1951

Helen has a way of bursting out with the most surprising remarks at table. Today she was full of Thucydides and the Peloponnesian war, about which she had been reading this Christmas morning. "What a stupid war!—the stupidest war in history," she said, shaking her head in mournful disapproval. She had been brooding and grieving over this war, which destroyed the democracy of Athens. For the rest, she was sure there was nothing about war that Thucydides did not know.

The other day she burst out about a certain Evelyn Cheesman, an English <u>entomologist</u> who had written wonderful things, she said, about insects. Helen had read her in one of the Braille magazines, no doubt—whether English, American, French, or German, for Helen reads them all.

Polly took her up. "What's this, Helen? Who is this Evelyn Cheesman?" Polly likes to tease her, and she is sometimes severe with her. For instance, if Helen makes a mistake in typewriting one of her letters Polly makes her copy the page again. (Usually Helen's typing is like an expert stenographer's, but the other day there were a few dim lines in one of her letters and she added this postscript: "Polly says the writing of this machine doesn't please her critical eye. My apologies. H.K.")

To return to the lady entomologist, Helen is charmingly eager about these shining new bits of knowledge. She has the earnest innocence of a ten-year-old child. Often, on the other hand, she speaks like an <u>oracle,</u> or, as one might say, an Asiatic sage. In spite of her incessant work, much of her life is still spent in solitary meditation, alone in the dark with her own thoughts, or with the Bible or the classics; and, as she lives in her way as the old prophets lived in the desert, many of her words inspire a kind of reverential wonder. She naturally uses archaic and poetic expressions of the sort that children pick up in their reading, words that are seldom heard in the ordinary talk that she only

hears when the ever-alert Polly passes it on to her.

(I must add, what all their friends know, that Polly is in her way as extraordinary a person as Helen. Without her vitality and her diplomatic sense what could Helen do in her journeys about the world? And what inexhaustible buoyancy both of them have! I have seen them together on a midnight train, when everyone else was asleep, smiling and chatting like birds on a branch in the morning.)

June 1953

Helen is seventy-three years old today. She lives much in eternity and much in history, but she only lives in time when she is able to keep up with the news. This week she returned from a two-months' absence in South America, and she has not had a moment yet to catch up with the newspapers and magazines. Unable to talk politics, she talks at table about Pepys's Diary, which our host Stuart Grummon is reading. She fishes up two or three facts about Pepys that I had forgotten or never knew, remembered from her own reading twenty years ago.

What variety there is in her mind! She is interested in everything. One day she recalled to me the dancing of La Argentina, though how she conceived of this so well I cannot imagine. Another day she quoted at length from a poem by Robinson Jeffers, who once told me he had seen Helen's name in the register of a hotel in the Orkney Islands. And what happy phrases come to her mind. Some children spelled words into her hand and she said their small fingers were like "the wild flowers of conversation."

18. About Helen Keller, it seems to me, William James uttered the last word when he wrote, "The sum of it is that you are a *blessing*"; a verdict that has been ratified in hundreds of hospitals throughout the world where she has all but raised the dead. Some day the story will be told of the miracles she has performed, or what would have passed for miracles in less case-hardened ages, when the blind have opened inward eyes and really seen life for the first time after Helen Keller has walked and talked with them.

19. How many, meanwhile, may have thought of her while reading the colonel's soliloquy at the end of Arthur Koestler's *The Age of Longing*, observing that American women are all too busy "playing bridge" to be "cut out for the part of martyrs and saints. . . . American womanhood," the colonel went on,

"has produced no Maid of Orleans, no Rosa Luxembourgs or Madame Curies, no Brontës or Florence Nightingales or Krupskayas," and one might add that it seldom produces anyone as rash as various people who generalize about it. For how many types there are in our teeming population! One might easily suggest a list to set beside the list this fictional colonel has drawn from three or four countries. The names of Jane Addams and Emily Dickinson would appear somewhere on such a list, and I dare say that for not a few the name of Helen Keller would figure as leading all the rest.

VIRGINIA WOOLF *Beau Brummell*

Virginia Woolf (1882-1941), daughter of the versatile Sir Leslie Stephen, was born in London and educated at home, in her father's magnificent library. Here she met such literary figures as Hardy, Stevenson, Ruskin, Bryce, Morley, and Meredith. In 1912 she married Leonard Sidney Woolf, a leader of the Labor Party and a writer on economic problems, and their home in Bloomsbury became the gathering place of a brilliant literary coterie. Mrs. Woolf published several collections of literary essays, best known of which are *The Common Reader*, 1925, and *The Second Common Reader*, 1932. Her most popular and significant books, however, are two novels—*Mrs. Dalloway*, 1925, and *To the Lighthouse*, 1927. In these particularly, through her minute exploration of human thinking, she established her position as a dominant influence in the development of the modern novel.

George Bryan Brummell, the subject of Virginia Woolf's biographical essay, was born in 1778, the son of William Brummell, private secretary to Lord North. He was very popular at Eton, where he was known as "Buck" Brummell, and during his short stay at Oxford he developed a reputation for wit and was presented to the Prince of Wales (later George IV). Because of his friendship with the prince and the fastidiousness of his dress, the "Buck" was changed to "Beau," and he became conspicuous in the society of the day. But so great were his living expenses and so heavy his gambling debts that he quickly squandered a legacy of about £30,000, and, his tongue proving too sharp even for the Prince Regent, he fled to France in 1816 to escape both debtors and revilers. For a while he was consul at Caen but soon lost the post in the course of his rapid deterioration. He died at the charitable asylum of Bon Sauveur at Caen in 1840.

1. When Cowper, in the seclusion of Olney, was roused to anger by the thought of the Duchess of Devonshire and predicted a time when "instead of a girdle there will be a rent, and instead of beauty, baldness," he was acknowledging the power of the lady whom he

BEAU BRUMMELL: From *The Second Common Reader* by Virginia Woolf, copyright 1932, by Harcourt, Brace and Company, Inc.

thought so despicable. Why, otherwise, should she haunt the damp solitudes of Olney? Why should the rustle of her silken skirts disturb those gloomy meditations? Undoubtedly the Duchess was a good haunter. Long after those words were written, when she was dead and buried beneath a tinsel coronet, her ghost mounted the stairs of a very different dwelling-place. An old man was sitting in his armchair at Caen. The door opened, and the servant announced, "The Duchess of Devonshire." Beau Brummell at once rose, went to the door and made a bow that would have graced the Court of St. James's. Only, unfortunately, there was nobody there. The cold air blew up the staircase of an inn. The Duchess was long dead, and Beau Brummell, in his old age and imbecility, was dreaming that he was back in London again giving a party. Cowper's curse had come true for both of them. The Duchess lay in her shroud, and Brummell, whose clothes had been the envy of kings, had now only one pair of much-mended trousers, which he hid as best he could under a tattered cloak. As for his hair, that had been shaved by order of the doctor.

2. But though Cowper's sour predictions had thus come to pass, both the Duchess and the dandy might claim that they had had their day. They had been great figures in their time. Of the two, perhaps Brummell might boast the more miraculous career. He had no advantage of birth, and but little of fortune. His grandfather had let rooms in St. James's Street. He had only a moderate capital of thirty thousand pounds to begin with, and his beauty, of figure rather than of face, was marred by a broken nose. Yet without a single noble, important, or valuable action to his credit he cuts a figure; he stands for a symbol; his ghost walks among us still. The reason for this eminence is now a little difficult to determine. Skill of hand and nicety of judgment were his, of course, otherwise he would not have brought the art of tying neck-cloths to perfection. The story is, perhaps, too well known—how he drew his head far back and sunk his chin slowly down so that the cloth wrinkled in perfect symmetry, or if one wrinkle were too deep or too shallow, the cloth was thrown into a basket and the attempt renewed, while the Prince of Wales sat, hour after hour, watching. Yet skill of hand and nicety of judgment were not enough. Brummell owed his ascendency to some curious combination of wit, of taste, of insolence, of independence—for he was never a toady—which it were too heavy handed to call a philosophy of life, but served the purpose. At any rate, ever since he was the most popular boy at Eton coolly jesting when they were for throw-

ing a bargee into the river, "My good fellows, don't send him into the river; the man is evidently in a high state of perspiration, and it almost amounts to a certainty that he will catch cold," he floated buoyantly and gaily and without apparent effort to the top of whatever society he found himself among. Even when he was a captain in the Tenth Hussars and so scandalously inattentive to duty that he only knew his troop by "the very large blue nose" of one of the men, he was liked and tolerated. When he resigned his commission, for the regiment was to be sent to Manchester—and "I really could not go—think, your Royal Highness, Manchester!"—he had only to set up house in Chesterfield Street to become the head of the most jealous and exclusive society of his time. For example, he was at Almack's one night talking to Lord ——. The Duchess of —— was there, escorting her young daughter, Lady Louisa. The Duchess caught sight of Mr. Brummell, and at once warned her daughter that if that gentleman near the door came and spoke to them she was to be careful to impress him favourably, "for," and she sank her voice to a whisper, "he is the celebrated Mr. Brummell." Lady Louisa might well have wondered why a Mr. Brummell was celebrated, and why a Duke's daughter need take care to impress a Mr. Brummell. And then directly he began to move towards them the reason of her mother's warning became apparent. The grace of his carriage was so astonishing; his bows were so exquisite. Everybody looked overdressed or badly dressed—some, indeed, looked positively dirty beside him. His clothes seemed to melt into each other with the perfection of their cut and the quiet harmony of their colour. Without a single point of emphasis everything was distinguished—from his bow to the way he opened his snuff-box, with his left hand invariably. He was the personification of freshness and cleanliness and order. One could well believe that he had his chair brought into his dressing-room and was deposited at Almack's without letting a puff of wind disturb his curls or a spot of mud stain his shoes. When he actually spoke to her, Lady Louisa would be at first enchanted—no one was more agreeable, more amusing, had a manner that was more flattering and enticing—and then she would be puzzled. It was quite possible that before the evening was out he would ask her to marry him, and yet his manner of doing it was such that the most ingenuous débutante could not believe that he meant it seriously. His odd grey eyes seemed to contradict his lips; they had a look in them which made the sincerity of his compliments very doubtful. And then he said very cutting things about other people. They were not exactly witty; they were certainly not profound; but they were so skilful, so adroit—they had a twist in them which made them slip into the mind and stay there when more important phrases were forgotten. He had downed the Regent himself with his dexterous "Who's your fat friend?" and his method was the same with humbler people who snubbed him or bored him. "Why, what could I do, my good fellow, but cut the connection? I discovered that Lady Mary actually ate cabbage!"—so he explained to a friend his failure to marry a lady. And, again, when some dull citizen pestered him about his tour to the North, "Which of the lakes do I admire?" he asked his valet. "Windermere, sir." "Ah, yes—Windermere, so it is—Windermere." That was his style, flickering, sneering, hovering on the verge of insolence, skimming the edge of nonsense, but always keeping within some curious mean, so that one knew the false Brummell story from the true by its exaggeration. Brummell could never have said, "Wales, ring the bell," any more than he could have worn a brightly coloured waistcoat or a glaring necktie. That "certain exquisite propriety" which Lord Byron remarked in his dress, stamped his whole being, and made him appear cool, refined, and debonair among the gentlemen who talked only of sport, which Brummell detested, and smelt of the stable, which Brummell never visited. Lady Louisa might well be on tenter-hooks to impress Mr. Brummell favourably. Mr. Brummell's good opinion was of the utmost important in the world of Lady Louisa.

3. And unless that world fell into ruins his rule seemed assured. Handsome, heartless, and cynical, the Beau seemed invulnerable. His taste was impeccable, his health admirable; and his figure as fine as ever. His rule had lasted many years and survived many vicissitudes. The French Revolution had passed over his head without disordering a single hair. Empires had risen and fallen while he experimented with the crease of a neck-cloth and criticised the cut of a coat. Now the battle of Waterloo had been fought and peace had come. The battle left him untouched: it was the peace that undid him. For some time past he had been winning and losing at the gaming-tables. Harriette Wilson had heard that he was ruined, and then, not without disappointment, that he was safe again. Now, with the armies disbanded, there was let loose upon London a horde of rough, ill-mannered men who had been fighting all those years and were determined to enjoy themselves. They flooded the gaming-houses. They played very high. Brummell was forced into competition. He lost and won and vowed never to play again, and then he did play again. At last his remaining ten thousand pounds was gone. He borrowed until he could borrow no more. And finally, to crown the loss of so many thousands, he lost the six-penny-bit with a hole in it which had always brought him good luck. He gave it by mistake to a hackney coachman: that rascal Rothschild got hold of it, he said, and that was the end of his luck. Such was his own account of the affair—other people put a less innocent interpretation on the matter. At any rate there came a day, 16th May 1816, to be precise—it was a day upon which everything was precise—when he dined alone off a cold fowl and a bottle of claret at Watier's, attended the opera, and then took coach for Dover. He drove rapidly all through the night and reached Calais the day after. He never set foot in England again.

4. And now a curious process of disintegration set in. The peculiar and highly artificial society of London had acted as a preservative; it had kept him in being; it had concentrated him into one single gem. Now that the pressure was removed, the odds and ends, so trifling separately, so brilliant in combination, which had made up the being of the Beau, fell asunder and revealed what lay beneath. At first his lustre seemed undiminished. His old friends crossed the water to see him and made a point of standing him a dinner and leaving a little present behind them at his banker's. He held his usual levee at his lodgings; he spent the usual hours washing and dressing;

he rubbed his teeth with a red root, tweezed out hairs with a silver tweezer, tied his cravat to admiration, and issued at four precisely as perfectly equipped as if the Rue Royale had been St. James's Street and the Prince himself had hung upon his arm. But the Rue Royale was not St. James's Street; the old French Countess who spat on the floor was not the Duchess of Devonshire; the good bourgeois who pressed him to dine off goose at four was not Lord Alvanley; and though he soon won for himself the title of Roi de Calais, and was known to workmen as "George, ring the bell," the praise was gross, the society coarse, and the amusements of Calais very slender. The Beau had to fall back upon the resources of his own mind. These might have been considerable. According to Lady Hester Stanhope, he might have been, had he chosen, a very clever man; and when she told him so, the Beau admitted that he had wasted his talents because a dandy's way of life was the only one "which could place him in a prominent light, and enable him to separate himself from the ordinary herd of men, whom he held in considerable contempt." That way of life allowed of verse-making—his verses, called "The Butterfly's Funeral," were much admired; and of singing, and of some dexterity with the pencil. But now, when the summer days were so long and so empty, he found that such accomplishments hardly served to while away the time. He tried to occupy himself with writing his memoirs; he bought a screen and spent hours pasting it with pictures of great men and beautiful ladies whose virtues and frailties were symbolised by hyenas, by wasps, by profusions of cupids, fitted together with extraordinary skill; he collected Buhl furniture; he wrote letters in a curiously elegant and elaborate style to ladies. But these occupations palled. The resources of his mind had been whittled away in the course of years; now they failed him. And then the crumbling process went a little farther, and another organ was laid bare —the heart. He who had played at love all these years and kept so adroitly beyond the range of passion, now made violent advances to girls who were young enough to be his daughters. He wrote such passionate letters to Mademoiselle Ellen of Caen that she did not know whether to laugh or to be angry.

She was angry, and the Beau, who had tyrannised over the daughters of Dukes, prostrated himself before her in despair. But it was too late—the heart after all these years was not a very engaging object even to a simple country girl, and he seems at last to have lavished his affections upon animals. He mourned his terrier Vick for three weeks; he had a friendship with a mouse; he became the champion of all the neglected cats and starving dogs in Caen. Indeed, he said to a lady that if a man and a dog were drowning in the same pond he would prefer to save the dog—if, that is, there were nobody looking. But he was still persuaded that everybody was looking; and his immense regard for appearances gave him a certain stoical endurance. Thus, when paralysis struck him at dinner he left the table without a sign; sunk deep in debt as he was, he still picked his way over the cobbles on the points of his toes to preserve his shoes, and when the terrible day came and he was thrown into prison he won the admiration of murderers and thieves by appearing among them as cool and courteous as if about to pay a morning call. But if he were to continue to act his part, it was essential that he should be supported—he must have a sufficiency of boot polish, gallons of eau-de-Cologne, and three changes of linen every day. His expenditure upon these items was enormous. Generous as his old friends were, and persistently as he supplicated them, there came a time when they could be squeezed no longer. It was decreed that he was to content himself with one change of linen daily, and his allowance was to admit of necessaries only. But how could a Brummell exist upon necessaries only? The demand was absurd. Soon afterwards he showed his sense of the gravity of the situation by mounting a black silk neck-cloth. Black silk neck-cloths had always been his aversion. It was a signal of despair, a sign that the end was in sight. After that everything that had supported him and kept him in being dissolved. His self-respect vanished. He would dine with any one who would pay the bill. His memory weakened and he told the same story over and over again till even the burghers of Caen were bored. Then his manners degenerated. His extreme cleanliness lapsed into carelessness, and then into positive filth. People objected to his presence in the dining-room of the hotel. Then his mind went—he thought that the Duchess of Devonshire was coming up the stairs when it was only the wind. At last but one passion remained intact among the crumbled débris of so many—an immense greed. To buy Rheims biscuits he sacrificed the greatest treasure that remained to him—he sold his snuffbox. And then nothing was left but a heap of disagreeables, a mass of corruption, a senile and disgusting old man fit only for the charity of nuns and the protection of an asylum. There the clergyman begged him to pray. " 'I do try,' he said, but he added something which made me doubt whether he understood me." Certainly, he would try; for the clergyman wished it and he had always been polite. He had been polite to thieves and to duchesses and to God himself. But it was no use trying

any longer. He could believe in nothing now except a hot fire, sweet biscuits and another cup of coffee if he asked for it. And so there was nothing for it but that the Beau who had been compact of grace and sweetness should be shuffled into the grave like any other ill-dressed, ill-bred, unneeded old man. Still, one must remember that Byron, in his moments of dandyism, "always pronounced the name of Brummell with a mingled emotion of respect and jealousy."

[Note.—Mr. Berry of St. James's Street has courteously drawn my attention to the fact that Beau Brummell certainly visited England in 1822. He came to the famous wine-shop on 26th July 1822 and was weighed as usual. His weight was then 10 stones 13 pounds. On the previous occasion, 6th July 1815, his weight was 12 stones 10 pounds. Mr. Berry adds that there is no record of his coming after 1822.]

E. B. WHITE *Here Is New York*

Elwyn Brooks White (1899-   ) is a humorist, familiar essayist, and poet. He was born in New York State and educated at Cornell University. After having served as a private in the Army in World War I, he became a reporter on the Seattle *Times*, later a production assistant in a New York advertising agency, and then a special contributor to the *New Yorker* and to *Harper's Magazine*. He is best known for his publications in the *New Yorker* and his "One Man's Meat" department in *Harper's* (from 1938 to 1943). He has also published several books and many articles.

Whether writing poems, essays, humorous pieces, or a psychological analysis of a city, Mr. White invests his work with the feeling of an extraordinarily sensitive and alert person, a person whose judgments, though quietly propounded, stem from a carefully reasoned attitude toward life in general. His style is notably figurative ("reaching for the sun"), rhythmical ("the tidal restlessness of the city"), allusive ("the intimation of mortality"), and epigrammatic ("Prosperity creates its bread lines, the same as depression").

1. On any person who desires such queer prizes, New York will bestow the gift of loneliness and the gift of privacy. It is this largest

HERE IS NEW YORK: Reprinted by permission of the publisher, Harper and Brothers. Copyright, 1949, by The Curtis Publishing Company.

that accounts for the presence within the city's walls of a considerable section of the population; for the residents of Manhattan are to a large extent strangers who have pulled up stakes somewhere and come to town, seeking sanctuary or fulfillment or some greater or lesser grail. The capacity to make such dubious gifts is a mysterious quality of New York. It can destroy an individual, or it can fulfill him, depending a good deal on luck. No one should come to New York to live unless he is willing to be lucky.

2. New York is the <u>concentrate</u> of art and commerce and sport and religion and entertainment and finance, bringing to a single compact arena the gladiator, the evangelist, the promoter, the actor, the trader and the merchant. It carries on its lapel the unexpungeable odor of the long past, so that no matter where you sit in New York you feel the vibrations of great times and tall deeds, of queer people and events and undertakings. I am sitting at the moment in a stifling hotel room in 90-degree heat, half-way down an air shaft, in midtown. No air moves in or out of the room, yet I am curiously affected by <u>emanations</u> from the immediate surroundings. I am twenty-two blocks from where Rudolph Valentino lay in state, eight blocks from where Nathan Hale was executed, five blocks from the publisher's office where Ernest Hemingway hit Max Eastman on the nose, four miles from where Walt Whitman sat sweating out editorials for the Brooklyn Eagle, thirty-four blocks from the street Willa Cather lived in when she came to New York to write books about Nebraska, one block from where Marceline used to clown on the boards of the Hippodrome, thirty-six blocks from the spot where the historian Joe Gould kicked a radio to pieces in full view of the public, thirteen blocks from where Harry Thaw shot Stanford White, five blocks from where I used to usher at the Metropolitan Opera and only a hundred and twelve blocks from the spot where Clarence Day the Elder was washed of his sins in the Church of the Epiphany (I could continue this list indefinitely); and for that matter I am probably occupying the very room that any number of exalted and somewise memorable characters sat in, some of them on hot, breathless afternoons, lonely and private and full of their own sense of emanations from without.

3. When I went down to lunch a few minutes ago I noticed that the man sitting next to me (about eighteen inches away along the wall) was Fred Stone. The eighteen inches were both the connection and the separation that New York provides for its inhabitants. My only connection with Fred Stone was that I saw him in *The Wizard of Oz* around the beginning of the century. But our waiter felt the same stimulus from being close to a man from Oz, and after Mr. Stone left the room the waiter told me that when he (the waiter) was a young man just arrived in this country and before he could understand a word of English, he had taken his girl for their first theater date to *The Wizard of Oz*. It was a wonderful show, the waiter recalled—a man of straw, a man of tin. Wonderful! (And still only eighteen inches away.) "Mr. Stone is a very hearty eater," said the waiter thoughtfully, content with this fragile participation in destiny, this link with Oz.

4. New York blends the gift of privacy with the excitement of participation; and better than most dense communities it succeeds in insulating the individual (if he wants it, and almost everybody wants or needs it) against all enormous and violent and wonderful events that are taking place every minute. Since I have been sitting in this <u>miasmic</u> air shaft, a good many rather splashy events have occurred in town. A man shot and killed his wife in a fit of jealousy. It caused no stir outside his block and got only small mention in the papers. I did not attend. Since my arrival, the greatest air show ever staged in all the world took place in town. I didn't attend and neither did most of the eight million other inhabitants, although they say there was quite a crowd. I didn't even hear any planes except a couple of westbound commercial airliners that habitually use this air shaft to fly over. The biggest ocean-going ships on the North Atlantic arrived and departed. I didn't notice them and neither did most other New Yorkers. I am told this is the greatest seaport in the world, with six hundred and fifty miles of water front, and ships calling here from many exotic lands, but the only boat I've happened to notice since my arrival was a small <u>sloop</u> tacking out of the East River night before last on the ebb tide when I was walking across the Brooklyn Bridge. I heard the *Queen Mary* blow one midnight, though, and the sound carried the whole history of departure and longing and loss. The Lions have been in con-

vention. I've seen not one Lion. A friend of mine saw one and told me about him. (He was lame, and was wearing a bolero.) At the ballgrounds and horse parks the greatest sporting spectacles have been enacted. I saw no ballplayer, no race horse. The governor came to town. I heard the siren scream, but that was all there was to that—an eighteen-inch margin again. A man was killed by a falling cornice. I was not a party to the tragedy, and again the inches counted heavily.

5. I mention these merely to show that New York is peculiarly constructed to absorb almost anything that comes along (whether a thousand-foot liner out of the East or a twenty-thousand-man convention out of the West) without inflicting the event on its inhabitants; so that every event is, in a sense, optional, and the inhabitant is in the happy position of being able to choose his spectacle and so conserve his soul. In most metropolises, small and large, the choice is often not with the individual at all. He is thrown to the Lions. The Lions are overwhelming; the event is unavoidable. A cornice falls, and it hits every citizen on the head, every last man in town. I sometimes think that the only event that hits every New Yorker on the head is the annual St. Patrick's Day parade, which is fairly penetrating—the Irish are a hard race to tune out, there are 500,000 of them in residence, and they have the police force right in the family.

6. The quality in New York that insulates its inhabitants from life may simply weaken them as individuals. Perhaps it is healthier to live in a community where, when a cornice falls, you feel the blow; where, when the governor passes, you see at any rate his hat.

7. I am not defending New York in this regard. Many of its settlers are probably here merely to escape, not face, reality. But whatever it means, it is a rather rare gift, and I believe it has a positive effect on the creative capacities of New Yorkers—for creation is in part merely the business of forgoing the great and small distractions.

8. Although New York often imparts a feeling of great forlornness or forsakenness, it seldom seems dead or unresourceful; and you always feel that either by shifting your location ten blocks or by reducing your fortune by five dollars you can experience rejuvenation.

Many people who have no real independence of spirit depend on the city's tremendous variety and sources of excitement for spiritual sustenance and maintenance of morale. In the country there are a few chances of sudden rejuvenation—a shift in weather, perhaps, or something arriving in the mail. But in New York the chances are endless. I think that although many persons are here from some excess of spirit (which caused them to break away from their small town), some, too, are here from a deficiency of spirit, who find in New York a protection, or an easy substitution.

9. There are roughly three New Yorks. There is, first, the New York of the man or woman who was born here, who takes the city for granted and accepts its size and its turbulence as natural and inevitable. Second, there is the New York of the commuter—the city that is devoured by locusts each day and spat out each night. Third, there is the New York of the person who was born somewhere else and came to New York in quest of something. Of these three trembling cities the greatest is the last—the city of final destination, the city that is a goal. It is this third city that accounts for New York's highstrung disposition, its poetical deportment, its dedication to the arts, and its incomparable achievements. Commuters give the city its tidal restlessness; natives give it solidity and continuity; but the settlers give it passion. And whether it is a farmer arriving from Italy to set up a small grocery store in a slum, or a young girl arriving from a small town in Mississippi to escape the indignity of being observed by her neighbors, or a boy arriving from the Corn Belt with a manuscript in his suitcase and a pain in his heart, it makes no difference: each embraces New York with the intense excitement of first love, each absorbs New York with the fresh eyes of an adventurer, each generates heat and light to dwarf the Consolidated Edison Company.

10. The commuter is the queerest bird of all. The suburb he inhabits has no essential vitality of its own and is a mere roost where he comes at day's end to go to sleep. Except in rare cases, the man who lives in Mamaroneck or Little Neck or Teaneck, and works in New York, discovers nothing much about the city except the time of arrival and departure of

trains and buses, and the path to a quick lunch. He is desk-bound, and has never, idly roaming in the gloaming, stumbled suddenly on Belvedere Tower in the Park, seen the ramparts rise sheer from the water of the pond, and the boys along the shore fishing for minnows, girls stretched out negligently on the shelves of the rocks; he has never come suddenly on anything at all in New York as a loiterer, because he has had no time between trains. He has fished in Manhattan's wallet and dug out coins, but has never listened to Manhattan's breathing, never awakened to its morning, never dropped off to sleep in its night. About 400,000 men and women come charging onto the Island each week-day morning, out of the mouths of tubes and tunnels. Not many among them have ever spent a drowsy afternoon in the great rustling oaken silence of the reading room of the Public Library, with the book elevator (like an old water wheel) spewing out books onto the trays. They tend their furnaces in Westchester and in Jersey, but have never seen the furnaces of the Bowery, the fires that burn in oil drums on zero winter nights. They may work in the financial district downtown and never see the extravagant plantings of Rockefeller Center—the daffodils and grape hyacinths and birches and the flags trimmed to the wind on a fine morning in spring. Or they may work in a midtown office and may let a whole year swing round without sighting Governors Island from the sea wall. The commuter dies with tremendous mileage to his credit, but he is no rover. His entrances and exits are more devious than those in a prairie-dog village; and he calmly plays bridge while buried in the mud at the bottom of the East River. The Long Island Rail Road alone carried forty million commuters last year; but many of them were the same fellow retracing his steps.

11. The terrain of New York is such that a resident sometimes travels farther, in the end, than a commuter. Irving Berlin's journey from Cherry Street in the lower East Side to an apartment uptown was through an alley and was only three or four miles in length; but it was like going three times around the world.

12. A poem compresses much in a small space and adds music, thus heightening its meaning. The city is like poetry: it compresses all life, all races and breeds, into a small island and adds music and the accompaniment of internal engines. The island of Manhattan is without any doubt the greatest human concentrate on earth, the poem whose magic is comprehensible to millions of permanent residents but whose full meaning will always remain illusive. At the feet of the tallest and plushiest offices lie the crummiest slums. The genteel mysteries housed in the Riverside Church are only a few blocks from the voodoo charms of Harlem. The merchant princes, riding to Wall Street in their limousines down the East River Drive, pass within a few hundred yards of the gypsy kings; but the princes do not know they are passing kings, and the kings are not up yet anyway—they live a more leisurely life than the princes and get drunk more consistently.

13. New York is nothing like Paris; it is nothing like London; and it is not Spokane multiplied by sixty, or Detroit multiplied by four. It is by all odds the loftiest of cities. It even managed to reach the highest point in the sky at the lowest moment of the depression. The Empire State Building shot 1250 feet into the air when it was madness to put out as much as six inches of new growth. (The building has a mooring mast that no dirigible has ever tied to; it employs a man to flush toilets in slack times; it has been hit by an airplane in a fog, struck countless times by lightning, and been jumped off of by so many unhappy people that pedestrians instinctively quicken step when passing Fifth Avenue and 34th Street.)

14. Manhattan has been compelled to expand skyward because of the absence of any other direction in which to grow. This, more than any other thing, is responsible for its physical majesty. It is to the nation what the white church spire is to the village—the visible symbol of aspiration and faith, the white plume saying that the way is up. The summer traveler swings in over Hell Gate Bridge and from the window of his sleeping car as it glides above the pigeon lofts and back yards of Queens looks southwest to where the morning light first strikes the steel peaks of midtown, and he sees its upward thrust unmistakable: the great walls and towers rising, the smoke rising, the heat not yet rising, the hopes and

ferments of so many awakening millions rising —this vigorous spear that presses heaven hard.

15. It is a miracle that New York works at all. The whole thing is implausible. Every time the residents brush their teeth, millions of gallons of water must be drawn from the Catskills and the hills of Westchester. When a young man in Manhattan writes a letter to his girl in Brooklyn, the love message gets blown to her through a pneumatic tube— *pfft*—just like that. The subterranean system of telephone cables, power lines, steam pipes, gas mains and sewer pipes is reason enough to abandon the island to the gods and the weevils. Every time an incision is made in the pavement, the noisy surgeons expose ganglia that are tangled beyond belief. By rights New York should have destroyed itself long ago, from panic or fire or rioting or failure of some vital supply line in its circulatory system or from some deep labyrinthine short circuit. Long ago the city should have experienced an insoluble traffic snarl at some impossible bottleneck. It should have perished of hunger when food lines failed for a few days. It should have been wiped out by a plague starting in its slums or carried in by ships' rats. It should have been overwhelmed by the sea that licks at it on every side. The workers in its myriad cells should have succumbed to nerves, from the fearful pall of smoke-fog that drifts over every few days from Jersey, blotting out all light at noon and leaving the high offices suspended, men groping and depressed, and the sense of world's end. It should have been touched in the head by the August heat and gone off its rocker.

16. Mass hysteria is a terrible force, yet New Yorkers seem always to escape it by some tiny margin: they sit in stalled subways without claustrophobia, they extricate themselves from panic situations by some lucky wisecrack, they meet confusion and congestion with patience and grit—a sort of perpetual muddling through. Every facility is inadequate—the hospitals and schools and playgrounds are overcrowded, the express highways are feverish, the unimproved highways and bridges are bottlenecks; there is not enough air and not enough light, and there is usually either too much heat or too little. But the city makes up for its hazards and its deficiencies by supplying its citizens with massive doses of a supplementary vitamin—the sense of belonging to something unique, cosmopolitan, mighty and unparalleled.

17. To an outlander a stay in New York can be and often is a series of small embarrassments and discomforts and disappointments: not understanding the waiter, not being able to distinguish between a sucker joint and a friendly saloon, riding the wrong subway, being slapped down by a bus driver for asking an innocent question, enduring sleepless nights when the street noises fill the bedroom. Tourists make for New York, particularly in summertime—they swarm all over the Statue of Liberty (where many a resident of the town has never set foot), they invade the Automat, visit radio studios, St. Patrick's Cathedral, and they window shop. Mostly they have a pretty good time. But sometimes in New York you run across the disillusioned—a young couple who are obviously visitors, newlyweds perhaps, for whom the bright dream has vanished. The place has been too much for them; they sit languishing in a cheap restaurant over a speechless meal.

18. The oft-quoted thumbnail sketch of New York is, of course: "It's a wonderful place, but I'd hate to live there." I have an idea that people from villages and small towns, people accustomed to the convenience and the friendliness of neighborhood over-the-fence living, are unaware that life in New York follows the neighborhood pattern. The city is literally a composite of tens of thousands of tiny neighborhood units. There are, of course, the big districts and big units: Chelsea and Murray Hill and Gramercy (which are residential units), Harlem (a racial unit), Greenwich Village (a unit dedicated to the arts and other matters), and there is Radio City (a commercial development), Peter Cooper Village (a housing unit), the Medical Center (a sickness unit) and many other sections each of which has some distinguishing characteristic. But the curious thing about New York is that each large geographical unit is composed of countless small neighborhoods. Each neighborhood is virtually self-sufficient. Usually it is no more than two or three blocks long and a couple of blocks wide. Each area is a city within a city within a city. Thus, no

matter where you live in New York, you will find within a block or two a grocery store, a barbershop, a newsstand and shoeshine shack, an ice-coal-and-wood cellar (where you write your order on a pad outside as you walk by), a dry cleaner, a laundry, a delicatessen (beer and sandwiches delivered at any hour to your door), a flower shop, an undertaker's parlor, a movie house, a radio-repair shop, a stationer, a haberdasher, a tailor, a drugstore, a garage, a tearoom, a saloon, a hardware store, a liquor store, a shoe-repair shop. Every block or two, in most residential sections of New York, is a little main street. A man starts for work in the morning and before he has gone two hundred yards he has completed half a dozen missions: bought a paper, left a pair of shoes to be soled, picked up a pack of cigarettes, ordered a bottle of whisky to be dispatched in the opposite direction against his home-coming, written a message to the unseen forces of the wood cellar, and notified the dry cleaner that a pair of trousers awaits call. Homeward bound eight hours later, he buys a bunch of pussy willows, a Mazda bulb, a drink, a shine—all between the corner where he steps off the bus and his apartment. So complete is each neighborhood, and so strong the sense of neighborhood, that many a New Yorker spends a lifetime within the confines of an area smaller than a country village. Let him walk two blocks from his corner and he is in a strange land and will feel uneasy till he gets back.

19. Storekeepers are particularly conscious of neighborhood boundary lines. A woman friend of mine moved recently from one apartment to another, a distance of three blocks. When she turned up, the day after the move, at the same grocer's that she had patronized for years, the proprietor was in ecstasy—almost in tears—at seeing her. "I was afraid," he said, "now that you've moved away I wouldn't be seeing you any more." To him, *away* was three blocks, or about seven hundred and fifty feet.

20. I am, at the moment of writing this, living not as a neighborhood man in New York but as a transient, or vagrant, in from the country for a few days. Summertime is a good time to re-examine New York and to receive again the gift of privacy, the jewel of loneliness. In summer the city contains (except for tourists) only die-hards and authentic characters. No casual, spotty dwellers are around, only the real article. And the town has a somewhat relaxed air, and one can lie in a loincloth, gasping and remembering things.

21. I've been remembering what it felt like as a young man to live in the same town with giants. When I first arrived in New York my personal giants were a dozen or so columnists and critics and poets whose names appeared regularly in the papers. I burned with a low steady fever just because I was on the same island with Don Marquis, Heywood Broun, Christopher Morley, Franklin P. Adams, Robert C. Benchley, Frank Sullivan, Dorothy Parker, Alexander Woollcott, Ring Lardner and Stephen Vincent Benét. I would hang around the corner of Chambers Street and Broadway, thinking: "Somewhere in that building is the typewriter that Archy the cockroach jumps on at night." New York hardly gave me a living at that period, but it sustained me. I used to walk quickly past the house in West 13th Street between Sixth and Seventh where F.P.A. lived, and the block seemed to tremble under my feet—the way Park Avenue trembles when a train leaves Grand Central. This excitation (nearness of giants) is a continuing thing. The city is always full of young worshipful beginners—young actors, young aspiring poets, ballerinas, painters, reporters, singers—each depending on his own brand of tonic to stay alive, each with his own stable of giants.

22. New York provides not only a continuing excitation but also a spectacle that is continuing. I wander around, re-examining this spectacle, hoping that I can put it on paper. It is Saturday, toward the end of the afternoon. I turn through West 48th Street. From the open windows of the drum and saxophone parlors come the listless sounds of musical instruction, monstrous insect noises in the brooding field of summer. The Cort Theater is disgorging its matinee audience. Suddenly the whole block is filled with the mighty voice of a street singer. He approaches, looking for an audience, a large, cheerful Negro with grand-opera contours, strolling with head thrown back, filling the canyon with uninhibited song. He carries a long cane as his sole prop, and is tidily but casually dressed—slacks,

PLACES

seersucker jacket, a book showing in his pocket.

23. This is perfect artistic timing; the audience from the Cort, where *The Respectful Prostitute* is playing, has just received a lesson in race relations and is in a mood to improve the condition of the black race as speedily as possible. Coins (mostly quarters) rattle to the street, and a few minutes of minstrelsy improves the condition of one Negro by about eight dollars. If he does as well as this at every performance, he has a living right there. New York is the city of opportunity, they say. Even the mounted cop, clumping along on his nag a few minutes later, scans the gutter carefully for dropped silver, like a bird watching for spilt grain.

24. It is seven o'clock and I re-examine an ex-speakeasy in East 53rd Street, with dinner in mind. A thin crowd, a summer-night buzz of fans interrupted by an occasional drink being shaken at the small bar. It is dark in here (the proprietor sees no reason for boosting his light bill just because liquor laws have changed). How dark, how pleasing; and how miraculously beautiful the murals showing Italian lake scenes—probably executed by a cousin of the owner. The owner himself mixes. The fans intone the prayer for cool salvation. From the next booth drifts the conversation of radio executives; from the green salad comes the little taste of garlic. Behind me (eighteen inches again) a young intellectual is trying to persuade a girl to come live with him and be his love. She has her guard up, but he is extremely reasonable, careful not to overplay his hand. A combination of intellectual companionship and sexuality is what they have to offer each other, he feels. In the mirror over the bar I can see the ritual of the second drink. Then he has to go to the men's room and she has to go to the ladies' room, and when they return, the argument has lost its tone. And the fan takes over again, and the heat and the relaxed air and the memory of so many good little dinners in so many good little illegal places, with the theme of love, the sound of ventilation, the brief medicinal illusion of gin.

25. Another hot night I stop off at the Goldman Band concert in the Mall in Central Park. The people seated on the benches fanned out in front of the band shell are attentive, appreciative. In the trees the night wind stirs, bringing the leaves to life, endowing them with speech; the electric lights illuminate the green branches from the under side, translating them into a new language. Overhead a plane passes dreamily, its running lights winking. On the bench directly in front of me, a boy sits with his arm around his girl; they are proud of each other and are swathed in music. The cornetist steps forward for a solo, begins, "Drink to me only with thine eyes. . . ." In the wide, warm night the horn is startlingly pure and magical. Then from the North River another horn solo begins—the *Queen Mary* announcing her intentions. She is not on key; she is a half tone off. The trumpeter in the bandstand never flinches. The horns quarrel savagely, but no one minds having the intimation of travel injected into the pledge of love. "I leave," sobs Mary. "And I will pledge with mine," sighs the trumpeter. Along the asphalt paths strollers pass to and fro; they behave considerately, respecting the musical atmosphere. Popsicles are moving well. In the warm grass beyond the fence, forms wriggle in the shadows, and the skirts of the girls approaching on the Mall are ballooned by the breeze, and their bare shoulders catch the lamplight. "Drink to me only with thine eyes." It is a magical occasion, and it's all free.

26. On week ends in summer the town empties. I visit my office on a Saturday afternoon. No phone rings, no one feeds the hungry *In*-baskets, no one disturbs the papers; it is a building of the dead, a time of awesome suspension. The whole city is honeycombed with abandoned cells—a jail that has been effectively broken. Occasionally from somewhere in the building a night bell rings, summoning the elevator—a special fire-alarm ring. This is the pit of loneliness, in an office on a summer Saturday. I stand at the window and look down at the batteries and batteries of offices across the way, recalling how the thing looks in winter twilight when everything is going full blast, every cell lighted, and how you can see in pantomime the puppets fumbling with their slips of paper (but you don't hear the rustle), see them pick up their phone (but you don't hear the ring), see the noiseless, ceaseless

moving about of so many passers of pieces of paper: New York, the capital of memoranda, in touch with Calcutta, in touch with Reykjavik, and always fooling with something.

27. In the café of the Lafayette, the regulars sit and talk. It is busy yet peaceful. Nursing a drink, I stare through the west windows at the Manufacturers Trust Company and at the red brick fronts on the north side of Ninth Street, watching the red turning slowly to purple as the light dwindles. Brick buildings have a way of turning color at the end of the day, the way a red rose turns bluish as it wilts. The café is a sanctuary. The waiters are ageless and they change not. Nothing has been modernized. Notre Dame stands guard in its travel poster. The coffee is strong and full of chicory, and good.

28. Walk the Bowery under the El at night and all you feel is a sort of cold guilt. Touched for a dime, you try to drop the coin and not touch the hand, because the hand is dirty; you try to avoid the glance, because the glance accuses. This is not so much personal menace as universal—the cold menace of unresolved human suffering and poverty and the advanced stages of the disease alcoholism. On a summer night the drunks sleep in the open. The sidewalk is a free bed, and there are no lice. Pedestrians step along and over and around the still forms as though walking on a battlefield among the dead. In doorways, on the steps of the savings bank, the bums lie sleeping it off. Standing sentinel at each sleeper's head is the empty bottle from which he drained his release. Wedged in the crook of his arm is the paper bag containing his things. The glib barker on the sight-seeing bus tells his passengers that this is the "street of lost souls," but the Bowery does not think of itself as lost; it meets its peculiar problem in its own way—plenty of gin mills, plenty of flophouses, plenty of indifference, and always, at the end of the line, Bellevue.

29. A block or two east and the atmosphere changes sharply. In the slums are poverty and bad housing, but with them the reassuring sobriety and safety of family life. I head east along Rivington. All is cheerful and filthy and crowded. Small shops overflow onto the sidewalk, leaving only half the normal width for passers-by. In the unshaded lights gleam

watermelons and lingerie. Families have fled the hot rooms upstairs and have found relief on the pavement. They sit on orange crates, smoking, relaxed, congenial. This is the nightly garden party of the vast Lower East Side—and on the whole they are more agreeable-looking hot-weather groups than some you see in bright canvas deck chairs on green lawns in country circumstances. It is folksy here with the smell of warm flesh and squashed fruit and fly-bitten filth in the gutter, and cooking.

30. At the corner of Lewis, in the playground behind the wire fence, an open-air dance is going on—some sort of neighborhood affair, probably designed to combat delinquency. Women push baby carriages in and out among the dancers, as though to exhibit what dancing leads to at last. Overhead, like banners decorating a cotillion hall, stream the pants and bras from the pulley lines. The music stops, and a beautiful Italian girl takes a brush from her handbag and stands under the street light brushing her long blue-black hair till it shines. The cop in the patrol car watches sullenly.

31. The Consolidated Edison Company says there are eight million people in the five boroughs of New York, and the company is in a position to know. As in every dense community, virtually all races, all religions, all nationalities are represented. Population figures are shifty—they change almost as fast as one can break them down. It is safe to say that about two million of New York's eight million are Jews—roughly one in four. Among this two million who are Jewish are, of course, a great many nationalities—Russian, German, Rumanian, Austrian, and so forth. The Urban League of Greater New York estimates that the number of Negroes in New York is about 700,000. Of these, about 500,000 live in Harlem, a district that extends northward from 110th Street. The Negro population has increased rapidly in the last few years. There are half again as many Negroes in New York today as there were in 1940. There are about 230,000 Puerto Ricans living in New York. There are half a million Irish, half a million Germans. There are 900,000 Russians, 150,000 English, 400,000 Poles, and there are quantities of Finns and Czechs and Swedes and Danes

and Norwegians and Latvians and Belgians and Welsh and Greeks, and even Dutch, who have been here from away back. It is very hard to say how many Chinese there are. Officially there are 12,000, but there are many Chinese who are in New York illegally and who don't like census takers.

32. The collision and the intermingling of these millions of foreign-born people representing so many races, creeds and nationalities make New York a permanent exhibit of the phenomenon of one world. The citizens of New York are tolerant not only from disposition but from necessity. The city has to be tolerant, otherwise it would explode in a radio-active cloud of hate and rancor and bigotry. If the people were to depart even briefly from the peace of cosmopolitan intercourse, the town would blow up higher than a kite. In New York smolders every race problem there is, but the noticeable thing is not the problem but the inviolate truce. Harlem is a city in itself, and being a city Harlem symbolizes segregation; yet Negro life in New York lacks the more conspicuous elements of Jim Crowism. Negroes ride subways and buses on terms of equality with whites, but they have not yet found that same equality in hotels and restaurants. Professionally, Negroes get on well in the theater, in music, in art and in literature; but in many fields of employment the going is tough. The Jim Crow principle lives chiefly in the housing rules and customs. Private owners of dwellings legally can, and do, exclude Negroes. Under a recent city ordinance, however, apartment buildings that are financed with public moneys or that receive any tax exemption must accept tenants without regard to race, color or religion.

33. To a New Yorker the city is both changeless and changing. In many respects it neither looks nor feels the way it did twenty-five years ago. The elevated railways have been pulled down, all but the Third Avenue. An old-timer walking up Sixth past the Jefferson Market jail misses the railroad, misses its sound, its spotted shade, its little aerial stations, and the tremor of the thing. Broadway has changed in aspect. It used to have a discernible bony structure beneath its loud bright surface; but the signs are so enormous now, the buildings and shops and hotels have largely disappeared under the neon lights and letters and the frozen-custard façade. Broadway is a custard street with no frame supporting it. In Greenwich Village the light is thinning: big apartments have come in, bordering the Square, and the bars are mirrored and chromed. But there are still in the Village the lingering traces of poesy, Mexican glass, hammered brass, batik, lamps made of whisky bottles, first novels made of fresh memories—the old Village with its alleys and ratty one-room rents catering to the erratic needs of those whose hearts are young and gay.

34. Grand Central has become honky-tonk, with its extradimensional advertising displays and its tendency to adopt the tactics of a travel broker. I practically lived in Grand Central Terminal at one period (it has all the conveniences and I had no other place to stay) and the great hall always seemed to me one of the more inspiring interiors in New York, until Lastex and Coca-Cola got into the temple.

35. All over town the great mansions are in decline. Schwab's house facing the Hudson on Riverside is gone. Gould's house on Fifth Avenue is an antique shop. Morgan's house on Madison Avenue is a church administration office. What was once the Fahnestock house is now Random House. Rich men nowadays don't live in houses; they live in the attics of big apartment buildings and plant trees on the setbacks, hundreds of feet above the street.

36. There are fewer newspapers than there used to be, thanks somewhat to the late Frank Munsey. One misses the *Globe,* the *Mail,* the *Herald;* and to many a New Yorker life has never seemed the same since the *World* took the count.

37. Police now ride in radio prowl cars instead of gumshoeing around the block swinging their sticks. A ride in the subway costs ten cents, and the seats are apt to be dark green instead of straw yellow. Men go to saloons to gaze at televised events instead of to think long thoughts. It is all very disconcerting. Even parades have changed some. The last triumphal military procession in Manhattan simply filled the city with an ominous and terrible rumble of heavy tanks.

38. The slums are gradually giving way to

the lofty housing projects—high in stature, high in purpose, low in rent. There are a couple of dozens of these new developments scattered around; each is a city in itself (one of them in the Bronx accommodates 12,000 families), sky acreage hitherto untilled, lifting people far above the street, standardizing their sanitary life, giving them some place to sit other than an orange crate. Federal money, state money, city money and private money have flowed into these projects. Banks and insurance companies are in back of some of them. Architects have turned the buildings slightly on their bases, to catch more light. In some of them, rents are as low as eight dollars a room. Thousands of new units are still needed and will eventually be built, but New York never quite catches up with itself, is never in equilibrium. In flush times the population mushrooms and the new dwellings sprout from the rock. Come bad times and the population scatters and the lofts are abandoned and the landlord withers and dies.

39. New York has changed in tempo and in temper during the years I have known it. There is greater tension, increased irritability. You encounter it in many places, in many faces. The normal frustrations of modern life are here multiplied and amplified—a single run of a crosstown bus contains, for the driver, enough frustration and annoyance to carry him over the edge of sanity: the light that changes always an instant too soon, the passenger that bangs on the shut door, the truck that blocks the only opening, the coin that slips to the floor, the question asked at the wrong moment. There is greater tension and there is greater speed. Taxis roll faster than they rolled ten years ago—and they were rolling fast then. Hackmen used to drive with verve; now they sometimes seem to drive with desperation, toward the ultimate tip. On the West Side Highway, approaching the city, the motorist is swept along in a trance—a sort of fever of inescapable motion, goaded from behind, hemmed in on either side, a mere chip in a millrace.

40. The city has never been so uncomfortable, so crowded, so tense. Money has been plentiful and New York has responded. Restaurants are hard to get into; businessmen stand in line for a Schrafft's luncheon as

meekly as idle men used to stand in soup lines. (Prosperity creates its bread lines, the same as depression.) The lunch hour in Manhattan has been shoved ahead half an hour, to 12:00 or 12:30, in the hopes of beating the crowd to a table. Everyone is a little emptier at quitting time than he used to be. Apartments are festooned with No Vacancy signs. There is standing-room-only in Fifth Avenue buses, which once reserved a seat for every paying guest. The old double-deckers are disappearing—people don't ride just for the fun of it any more.

41. At certain hours on certain days it is almost impossible to find an empty taxi and there is a great deal of chasing around after them. You grab a handle and open the door, and find that some other citizen is entering from the other side. Doormen grow rich blowing their whistles for cabs; and some doormen belong to no door at all—merely wander about through the streets, opening cabs for people as they happen to find them. By comparison with other less hectic days, the city is uncomfortable and inconvenient; but New Yorkers temperamentally do not crave comfort and convenience—if they did they would live elsewhere.

42. The subtlest change in New York is something people don't speak much about but that is in everyone's mind. The city, for the first time in its long history, is destructible. A single flight of planes no bigger than a wedge of geese can quickly end this island fantasy, burn the towers, crumble the bridges, turn the underground passages into lethal chambers, cremate the millions. The intimation of mortality is part of New York now: in the sound of jets overhead, in the black headlines of the latest edition.

43. All dwellers in cities must live with the stubborn fact of annihilation; in New York the fact is somewhat more concentrated because of the concentration of the city itself, and because, of all targets, New York has a certain clear priority. In the mind of whatever perverted dreamer might loose the lightning, New York must hold a steady, irresistible charm.

44. It used to be that the Statue of Liberty was the signpost that proclaimed New York and translated it for all the world. Today

Liberty shares the role with Death. Along the East River, from the razed slaughterhouses of Turtle Bay, as though in a race with the spectral flight of planes, men are carving out the permanent headquarters of the United Nations—the greatest housing project of them all. In its stride, New York takes on one more interior city, to shelter, this time, all governments, and to clear the slum called war. New York is not a capital city—it is not a national capital or a state capital. But it is by way of becoming the capital of the world. The buildings, as conceived by architects, will be cigar boxes set on end. Traffic will flow in a new tunnel under First Avenue. Forty-seventh Street will be widened (and if my guess is any good, trucks will appear late at night to plant tall trees surreptitiously, their roots to mingle with the intestines of the town). Once again the city will absorb, almost without showing any sign of it, a congress of visitors. It has already shown itself capable of stashing away the United Nations—a great many of the delegates have been around town during the past couple of years, and the citizenry has hardly caught a glimpse of their coattails or their black Homburgs.

45. This race—this race between the destroying planes and the struggling Parliament of Man—it sticks in all our heads. The city at last perfectly illustrates both the universal dilemma and the general solution, this riddle in steel and stone is at once the perfect target and the perfect demonstration of nonviolence, of racial brotherhood, this lofty target scraping the skies and meeting the destroying planes halfway, home of all people and all nations, capital of everything, housing the deliberations by which the planes are to be stayed and their errand forestalled.

46. A block or two west of the new City of Man in Turtle Bay there is an old willow tree that presides over an interior garden. It is a battered tree, long suffering and much climbed, held together by strands of wire but beloved of those who know it. In a way it symbolizes the city: life under difficulties, growth against odds, sap-rise in the midst of concrete, and the steady reaching for the sun. Whenever I look at it nowadays, and feel the cold shadow of the planes, I think: "This must be saved, this particular thing, this very tree." If it were to go, all would go—this city, this mischievous and marvelous monument which not to look upon would be like death.

GERALD CARSON *A Man of Many Parts*

Gerald Carson (1899-   ) was for many years an advertising copy writer. From 1940 to 1951 he was a business executive in New York City. He has now retired from business and devotes himself to writing.

While searching for the material for *The Old Country Store,* 1954, from which the following selection is taken, Mr. Carson actually found a few stores with old counters and coffee grinders still intact, visited the museum stores maintained by various historical organizations, sought out old-timers who had "kept store," and talked with descendants of rural merchants.

Many tributes have been paid to the contribution to American life made by the old

A MAN OF MANY PARTS: From *The Old Country Store* by Gerald Carson. Reprinted by permission of the publisher. Copyright 1954 by Oxford University Press, Inc.

country doctor, the lawyer, and the preacher, whose special places in the community may be understood from many appreciative and sympathetic accounts. The keeper of the general store, though he existed by the hundreds of thousands, has never received his due as a leader and as a civilizing influence. One might speculate about this. Being a merchant was not a learned occupation, and there were all kinds of merchants, some quite temporary. It was not hard to get into the business of running a store, as one Michigan wit used to remark; it was just hard to *stay* in.

Many men of low capacity or unstable temperament tried their hand at a store, as they did at farming, trapping, lumbering, or fighting. When a store failed to prosper, and creditors outnumbered debtors, the owner could take shelter under lenient bankruptcy laws, or skedaddle "over the hill" as did Denton Offut, Lincoln's employer at New Salem, and many another.

Yet if we were to cut a profile of the really successful country merchant, we should find ourselves charactering a very flexible, a very versatile and durable man, with astonishing skills and accomplishments, and a considerable knowledge of the world. The whole complex of buying and selling presented many more difficulties than the merchandising of the twentieth century. His knowledge of his community was minute and intimate, his contact with it more continuous than that of the doctors, the lawyers, or the clergy. His store was the necessary core of crossroads life, the best hope that the spot might some day grow into a town.

The country merchant's opportunities to become a judge of men were exceptional. As salesman, middleman, issuer of credit, banker, supplier of necessities and some luxuries, as shipper of farm crops and local manufactures, the country trader had contacts with all his neighbors and with the larger commercial world. As a cash buyer he was in the market at all times, his policy, "Cash given for anything he can make money by." As a seller of store goods he was willing to take his pay in "anything eatable, drinkable, wearable, or burnable, at fair prices." In many instances the more prosperous merchants took on outside activities, not as a necessary supplement to their incomes, as did the petty storekeeper who cut hair or did cobbling as a side line, but as employment for capital or energies not needed in their store business. Some, when in funds, speculated in wheat or in Western lands.

Others underwrote a lumbering operation in the wintertime, made a turn in shingles, bought and shipped hemlock bark to the tanyards. William Battel, father and son, two generations of storekeepers in the town of Torrington, Connecticut, "had also a manufactory of potash," as did many others.

Stephen Thacher, as industrious a Maine man as ever came down the pike, not only kept at his dwelling "a large stock of all goods usually found in a country store," but also found time to be postmaster, judge of the probate court, raise Merino sheep, and keep an "Academical school, with thirty scholars." The local power-site, with its mill, frequently belonged to the owner of the general store. In a region of older, more mature communities such as southern New England, with an easy access to distant markets and large centers of population, the country dealer took on some of the characteristics of the city merchant, shipping provisions himself in the coastwise trade, collecting goods of local manufacture, and trading them on his own account with New York, Virginia, the Carolinas, and even the West Indies. Following the opportunities of the changing times, the merchants along the seaboard often gave up retail trade for the newer industrial enterprises requiring larger aggregations of capital and the corporate structure—canals, railroads, banking, insurance, and manufacturing.

The store owner enjoyed a favored position because he had the opportunity of constantly enlarging his frame of reference. There was, perhaps, no other rural citizen, living within a radius of ten to twenty miles of the store, who touched life at as many different places as the retailer. Through the necessity of disposing of the country produce that he took in from his customers, the trader had connections with commission dealers in distant cities. He traveled regularly once or twice a year to one of the commercial capitals on the strenuous business of filling out his broken assortment of goods with new merchandise. He was in touch with stage lines, freight forwarders, knew steamboat or coasting captains, money brokers, and brushed up against men of large affairs among the importers and jobbing houses in the cities. He wrote and received letters when both were uncommon experiences.

Though not a man of professional education, the merchant somehow acquired as he went along a good knowledge of business law, especially the law of contracts, of mortgages and promissory notes, of partnerships and bankruptcy, of fraud, of agent and principal, and of those troublesome matters of consignment, common carrier, and insurance which are apt to arise when a boatload of flour sinks at the Falls of the Ohio. Farmers who "forgot my specs" turned to the merchant on those momentous occasions when they had to write a business letter. He had the necessaries, a quire of writing paper, a well of ink, blotting sand, and his thoughts flowed as the farmers' could not from the tip of a goose quill. When death came to a customer of the old store and his will was read, the trader turned out like as not to be the executor. This was so true that a generation later the old safe was usually found to contain more old wills, letters of administration, and accountings of estates than anything else.

The merchant of the stagecoach era, wrote one of the few of the genus to try his hand at describing his own class, "is a general *locum tenens*, the agent of everybody! And familiar with every transaction in his neighborhood. He is a counselor without license, and yet invariably consulted, not only in matters of business, but in domestic affairs. Parents ask his opinion before giving their consent to their daughters' marriages; and he is always invited to the weddings. He furnishes the nuptial garments for both bride and groom, and his taste is both consulted and adopted. Every item of news, not only local, but from a distance—as he is frequently the postmaster, and the only subscriber to the newspaper— has general dissemination from his establishment, as from a common center; and thither all resort, at least once a week, both for goods and for intelligence."

During long winter days and evenings trade was slow. Many account books show as few as six or eight customers in a whole day. This was the country dealer's opportunity to improve his mind. He had the time and, since he did a small stationery business, he often had a few books around—Parson Weems' *Life of Washington, Pilgrim's Progress*, histories of Greece and Rome, some of the English poets. There was the Bible, too, and works devoted to its interpretation; tough octavo sermons, bound in calf, today's stickers on the shelves of antique shops and old bookstores, corners scuffed, the pages foxed, backstrap torn from much handling. They seem dull enough reading to us, but it was stimulating fare to our hardy ancestors, who enjoyed honing their minds on theological argument. Thus the country merchant acquired a local reputation as "a great reader" and as a well-posted man.

If a man wished to give himself an extension course in some vocational subject there were handbooks on the mercantile life, such as J. Montefiore's *The American Trader's Compendium*, books on agriculture, in case he had a farm, and ready-reckoners which would tell him how to find the capacity of bins and boxes, how to calculate interest for an odd number of days, and how many bushels of West India salt made a ton. There was an extensive literature on herb medicines, such as Wilkinson's *Family Medical Practise;* and the ambitious clerk poring over his law book is fixed in our minds as a symbol of the national faith that you cannot keep a good man down. The image is, of course, of the lanky frame of Abe Lincoln, extended along the rough counter of the Berry-Lincoln store in New Salem, the future President's nose deep in the *Illinois General Statutes*—which Berry owned, being the constable—or in Blackstone's *Commentaries*, which Lincoln found at the bottom of an "empty" barrel, bought to accommodate a "mover."

The store often acted as a subscription depot for popular magazines, the newspapers of the nearest city or the little weekly sheet with "patent insides" which was published in the nearest town. The store owner's contacts with the weekly *Argus* or *County Clarion* were close and frequent, as an occasional buyer of circulars and printing, as an advertiser announcing the arrival of seasonal goods, and sometimes as country correspondent sending in the news from his neck of the woods. "Most of the mails have been carried on horseback, and it is quite uncertain about your getting the paper today," an editor in Taunton, Massachusetts, wrote to a general store down the line, adding that money and news were scarce, but that there was "snow in abundance."

Equipped by his natural endowments, by experience with men, polished—somewhat—by reading and reflections, strategically situated with the local world revolving around him, the country storekeeper was pushed forward by all these circumstances as a leader in the affairs of the church, school, and town, the lodge or the militia. If there was a school teacher to be hired, the merchant was apt to shoulder the burden of the correspondence, satisfying himself about the prospective teacher's moral character, his ability to teach reading, writing, and arithmetic up to the rule of three. He had to be sure also that the new teacher could deal firmly with those twin problems of rural pedagogy, the big and the backward. He had to wade patiently through letters of application, such as this:

"The subscriber makes a tender of his services to the inhabitants of the second school district in Swansea as a teacher for the term of three months to commence on Monday the 3rd inst. And he assures those who may think proper to intrust their children to his care, that if the most strenuous exertions on his part can prevent it, their confidence shall not be misplaced. Hoping by assiduous application and unremitting attention to ensure the patronage and meet the approbation of his employers—Jos. D. NICHOLS."

The storekeeper, who was often required to diagnose a consumption or prescribe a good medicine for all-around use by the whole family, was also expected to know how to extract beans from small boys' noses. If he was musically inclined, he might lead the Silver Cornet Band. The merchant was the natural custodian of the madstone, if the township was so fortunate as to possess one. What is a madstone? When a small, hard object lodged in a deer's stomach, it was sometimes surrounded by a calcium deposit to form a smooth, round "stone," the madstone, which made the deer twice as hard to kill, it was said, as the ordinary kind. The virtue of the stone was that when applied to the bite of a dog, it told whether or not the dog was mad. If the stone would not adhere, the dog did not have rabies. If the dog was infected, or in cases of snake bite, spider bite, or bee stings, the madstone

was popularly believed to bring relief and drive out the poison.

At election time the candidates were thick as blackbirds around the store. Here, too, the tax collector set up for business, announcing, "Taxes are now due and payable . . . bring last Year's receipts." The electoral rolls were often deposited at the general store, along with the school trustee book. The back room was the polling place, where the voters gathered to select a supervisor, town clerk, justice of the peace, assessors and collectors, commissioners of highways, inspectors of election, overseers of the poor, hogreeves, and constables. The country merchant was often also the town clerk, or treasurer, his cubicle, safe, and store books suggesting his fitness, no doubt, for clerkly tasks. Often the merchant was deep in politics, holding various offices through the years, rising enough in the esteem of his constituency to go from some humble office such as hogreeve to sit for a term in the state legislature; and for years afterward there would be some people who would point him out and say, "You wouldn't think that man had been in the legislature, would you?"

In states having the grand jury system, the merchant, if his name was drawn, was almost certain to be appointed by the judge to act as foreman. He would swear with one hand upraised, the other upon the courtroom Bible, that he would diligently inquire and true presentment make, that he would keep his own counsel, that of his fellows, and of the people of his state, that he would present no person from envy, hatred, or malice; nor leave anyone unpresented through fear, favor, affection, or reward, or hope thereof, but that he would present all things truly as they came to his knowledge.

The rural trader was a hustler, often a lover of gossip and a sort of walking newspaper. Yet he sometimes sat silent at his books, lost in work or, like other men, in the vagaries of his imagination. A man with executive gifts, he managed his own affairs and those entrusted to him by others as well as any man could have done in his place. Looked upon as "well-to-do," his sympathies generally with the moneyed classes, he regularly disregarded his own interest in supplying the needs of those who could not pay. Often sharp in a trade, the merchant usually headed the list in supporting church, lodge, or any movement for a public improvement. He knew as well as the town physician or pastor the sins and secret griefs of his customers, their ills, aberrations, and follies. Like the doctor and pastor he discreetly kept his own counsel, and without the restraints of church discipline or the Hippocratic oath. He was spry as a cricket, tougher'n green elm, well-meaning on the whole—a man who in a less favored situation might hope to see hard service and die a sergeant. Plato, who in his ideal Republic assigned the role of shopkeeper to the weak and unfit, would have found the country traders a tough set if he had been able to visit the American republic.

MAX BLACK *The Uses of Language*

Max Black (1909-   ) was born in Russia and educated at the University of Göttingen, Germany, at Cambridge, and at the University of London, where for several years he was a member of the faculty. In America he has taught at Columbia University and at the University of Illinois, and since 1946 he has been professor of philosophy at Cornell University.

Professor Black has served as co-editor of the *Journal of Symbolic Logic* and of the *Philosophical Review* and as associate editor of the periodical *Philosophy of Science*. Among his books are *The Nature of Mathematics*, 1933, *Language and Philosophy*, 1949, and *Critical Thinking*, 1946, 1952, from which the following selection is taken.

In every tongue the speaker labours under great inconveniences, especially on abstract questions, both from the paucity, obscurity, and ambiguity of the words, on the one hand, and from his own misapprehensions, and imperfect acquaintance with them, on the other.
—George Campbell, 1776.

I. INTRODUCTION

1. Ever since men began to reflect critically upon their own thinking, the wisest of them have been acutely aware of the imperfections of the language in which their thought must be expressed. The greatest of the Greek philosophers often returned to this theme, and centuries later we find Francis Bacon echoing the ancient complaint and listing "false notions" generated by the "common tongue" as one of the main hindrances to the advancement of knowledge. Every important advance in science and scholarship has required a re-

form in terminology. Thinkers, as ingenious as they were public-spirited, have labored to invent artificial languages, systems of notations, and a bewildering tangle of other symbolic aids to accurate thinking. Yet after thousands of years of criticism and improvement, the chorus of complaint continues, and experts insist today, more emphatically than ever, on the importance of critical study of language and its relation to thought. The brave new science of "semantics," though still in swaddling clothes, already has many interesting results to its credit, and its many enthusiastic followers are actively exploring its implications for logic, aesthetics, education, psychiatry, and other subjects.

2. Philosophy of language, for all its importance, is too intricate a subject to be fully discussed in an elementary introduction to "critical thinking." We shall therefore not attempt a systematic account of the nature of language and its relation to the objects of thought. Nevertheless, our dealings with specimens of actual reasoning have shown us the importance of attention to the lan-

guage in which ideas are expressed; since ideas are communicated in language, criticism of thought must also be criticism of its vehicle. We shall undertake the relatively modest task of developing just so much theory of language (or "semantics") as will be useful in criticizing the types of reasoning we are most likely to encounter. . . .

II. THE COMPLEXITY OF LANGUAGE

3. When we read a sentence, or understand conversation, we are responding to **signs**. It is characteristic of a sign that a person who understands it is led to attend to *something other than the sign itself;* the headline "HURRICANE DUE TOMORROW," considered as an object in its own right, is a mere string of ink blotches; it is a sign for the reader because it leads him to think of things quite other than printer's ink—the approaching storm, the precautions that need to be taken, and so forth.

4. Signs need not be *linguistic.* A herd of animals taking flight on hearing a warning cry from a sentinel, a man entering a dining room at the sound of a gong, a doctor diagnosing the visible symptoms of a disease, a spider set in motion by a twitch of its web, are all interpreting signs. These examples also illustrate the point that quite primitive organisms can interpret non-linguistic signs.

5. If such instances of elementary sign-interpretation are contrasted with the processes of reading a book, hearing a speech, or otherwise responding to complex uses of language, a number of important points of difference may be noticed.

(1) *Linguistic signs are artificial, while the simplest kinds of non-linguistic signs are natural.*

6. If a flash of lightning causes me to expect a clap of thunder, it is because the two kinds of event normally occur together; but the presence of pepper in a can would not result in the appearance of the word "pepper" on the can *but for human intervention*. Men have to agree that certain noises and marks shall cause interpreters to attend to certain other objects (their "meanings") before there can be *language*. We notice, however, that some non-linguistic signals (such as the cones hoisted to warn of the approach of a storm) can also be artificial.

7. Let us agree to use the word **signal** as an abbreviation for the phrase "the simplest kind of sign." (This agrees fairly well with the customary meaning of the word "signal.")

(2) *Response to signals is stereotyped and undifferentiated, while response to linguistic signs is variable and complex.*

8. The presence of a dog will cause a cat to bristle with anticipatory fear, but a man's response to the remark "a lion has escaped from the circus" will vary with circumstances. The spoken sentence is constructed out of *component signs* (the words) arranged in a conventional *order,* and the man responds to the components and to their arrangement as well as to the sentence as a whole. He is able to understand an isolated word (such as the word "lion" appearing alone on a sheet of paper); and he can interpret a sentence *he has never seen before,* if it is composed of known words in a known arrangement. The natural signals to which animals respond always occur in association with the things to which they refer. But the users of a *language* have learned to deploy and re-deploy linguistic signs in an endless variety of sign situations; they can therefore anticipate novelty and respond to situations of radically new types.

(3) *Signals normally serve a single purpose, while linguistic signs tend to serve a number of different purposes simultaneously.*

9. The spoor of a wild animal may tell the skilful hunter a great deal about the beast that made it, yet consider how much more is conveyed to the sensitive listener by even the most trivial remark. If we hear a stranger say "I've missed that train again!" we may learn something about a train, but we may sometimes learn even more about the speaker— that she is annoyed, is not disposed to be friendly, is in a hurry to go somewhere, and was educated in the Middle West! Nor is this an exceptional case. Because men and women express their feelings and attitudes as well as their beliefs by means of language, all talk conveys information about much more than its ostensible subject. And because language is a social product, the result of interaction between persons sharing common purposes, any individual utterance also conveys information about the *community of language users* to which the speaker belongs.

10. These three differences between fully developed language and the simplest kinds of non-linguistic signs give us but a glimpse of the full complexity of language. No doubt they are differences of degree, and "The metaphysician," as Anatole France said, "has only the perfected cry of monkeys and dogs with which to construct the system of the World." Yet the differences are important: we shall find that failure to be aware of them, and to appreciate some of their consequences is responsible for much fallacious reasoning.

III. THE MANY PURPOSES SERVED BY LANGUAGE

11. Any spoken utterance will usually express feelings, attitudes, desires, and beliefs, and will convey information (either true or false) about the speaker and other objects. But there is such a tremendous variety of human transactions in which language is used, that the appropriate response to a particular utterance may vary widely according to the circumstances of its use. Everybody understands that the spoken words "Pass down the bus, please" are primarily intended to cause the passengers to move and are not said for the purpose of giving information about the conductor; and it is equally obvious that the remark "This bus is over-loaded" is an *assertion,* not a request or command, even though it, too, causes the passengers to move. When we contrast "assertions" with "questions," "requests," "commands," "exclamations," or "prayers," we are recognizing *different ways in which language can be used.* Such crude distinctions, however, hardly begin to do justice to the variety of different uses of language.

12. In order to see how variable the correct response to language may be, let us examine the following two utterances, *both of which are "statements":*

(1) "A body immersed in a fluid is acted upon by an upward force equal in magnitude to the weight of the fluid displaced." (From a text.)

(2) "The apples were falling like great drops of dew to bruise themselves an exit from themselves." (D. H. Lawrence.)

13. The first statement makes a certain *claim* concerning the behavior of solid bodies and fluids: it is intended to produce in us (the readers) a definite belief that can be tested and confirmed by actual observation of the weight of bodies immersed in a fluid. If observation proved that the belief does not accord with the facts, we should be justified in calling the writer a liar. In formulating a supposition to be tested against experience in this way, we are behaving in the way intended by the scientist who made the statement. Since the statement (1) was used in order to produce such beliefs and testing procedures, our interpretation was *appropriate.*

14. It would, of course, be absurdly inappropriate to interpret the second statement in similar fashion. Only a very stupid reader would ask "What apples is he talking about? How big are the drops of dew? How can an apple *make an exit from itself?*" Such questions are stupid because the poet has no intention of producing beliefs that could be tested in a manner appropriate to a scientific statement. And to call him a liar because his statement could not be confirmed in the laboratory would serve only to reveal our own misunderstanding of what poetry "is all about." For the poet's intention, here as elsewhere, is to embody and communicate an aesthetic experience in words that will give pleasure as well as insight.

15. And there are many other ways in which language can be used. Consider, for instance, these words, which might be spoken by any departing guest to his hostess:

(3) "Thank you for a nice party—we've had a wonderful time."

Sometimes the guest has had anything but a pleasant time,[1] but he is not on that account to be regarded as dishonest. To insist that "a really truthful person" would, if necessary, say "Good-bye, I've had a very dull and uncomfortable time," would be to repeat the mistake that occurs when poetry is treated as if it were science. A formula of polite thanks is not intended, or understood, as a factual claim (nor as a snatch of poetry). Questions of truth and falsity are no more applicable to such *ceremonial* uses of language than they are to a handshake.

[1] The actress, Beatrice Lillie, is reported to have made the parting remark: "Don't think I haven't had a wonderful time—because I haven't!"

16. The moral of such examples is that *all intelligent criticism of any instance of language in use must begin with understanding of the motives and purposes of the speaker in that situation.* Unfortunately, the type of case that causes trouble in practice is that in which the kind of use made of language is not as transparently clear as in our examples. Language is often used to *conceal* motives and purposes, and human motives and purposes are notoriously mixed. One and the same utterance may convey factual information (true or false), embody aesthetic insight, express social conformity, or do a number of other things *all at the same time.* For this reason, any attempt to isolate "pure" types of language uses (such as "scientific," "poetic," "ceremonial," and so on) would be of little help to us. In the next two sections we formulate distinctions applying, in varying degree, to *all* uses of language.

IV. SOME WORKING DISTINCTIONS

17. *Personal and impersonal aspects of utterance.* We have already said that any utterance normally gives some information about the speaker himself, as well as other matters. Let us, therefore, refer to the **personal** and **impersonal aspects** of an utterance. By the first term we shall mean the information given about the speaker, and more especially about the attitudes, feelings, and wishes that caused him to make the utterance; by the second, whatever other information may be conveyed by the utterance. The personal aspects may be further divided into **expressive** and **dynamic** aspects. The utterance is expressive insofar as it is caused by the speaker's feelings or attitudes, *without any desired effect on a hearer.* An involuntary cry of pain or joy is markedly expressive in this sense. The utterance is dynamic insofar as it is caused by the speaker's desire to produce actions or other effects in a hearer; a command or a question is markedly dynamic in this sense. Actual utterances vary widely in the relative importance of their expressive, dynamic, and impersonal aspects.

18. *Statement and suggestion.* No human speaker explicitly symbolizes all that he conveys to the hearer; we must constantly "read between the lines." One important consequence of this has already been mentioned.

A speaker very rarely says: "I want you to feel that I am a thoroughly likable person of the sort you can trust; I am not much interested in tariffs (or whatever it may be) except insofar as some knowledge of this subject is necessary to persuade you to trust me." Such devastating frankness would be self-defeating, but many a speaker talks in such a way as to convey the same impression. Intelligent understanding of the utterance requires an awareness of much more than is "said in so many words." The *general setting* of the utterance (whether it is predominantly "scientific" or "poetic," intended to produce approval, result in actions, and so on) is not usually symbolized explicitly.

19. Let us examine a striking instance of "reading between the lines." In answering a letter not long ago, a certain Senator began his reply with the words "My dear Wop"—an action that led to considerable indignation on the part of his correspondent and many of the lady's sympathizers. Furious letters were written to Congress and the newspapers, and the Senator's action was denounced at meetings of protest as "undemocratic" and "un-American."

20. Why all this fuss about three words? A foreigner, not thoroughly familiar with the subtleties of the American language, would find on enquiry, that "Wop" means about the same as "Italian" or "person of Italian origin." "Well, well," he might wonder, in his naïve way, "is it so insulting to an American to be accused of having Italian ancestors?" The answer, of course, is that "Wop" is a term of powerful *abuse*, conventionally used as a way of expressing a high degree of contempt for the person addressed. The three words might be expanded in some such way as this: "Madam, the usual rules of politeness require me to use the words 'My dear so-and-so.' I show my contempt for you and your opinions by refusing even to call you by your name. I am pretty sure that you can't be an American; I suspect that you are of Italian origin; and I regard Italians in general as inferior and degenerate."

21. Yet the abusive Senator did not *say* all this "in so many words"—even though much of it is quite clearly understood by his readers. Offense is properly taken at the insulting

suggestions of the utterance, rather than at its explicitly formulated content.

22. The unformulated implications and suggestions of an utterance are not always abusive. Often we convey feelings of approval, enjoyment, or appreciation by gesture, tone of voice, and choice of words. The means employed are so flexible and variable that usually we are hardly aware of them, even while constantly responding to their influence. A large part of the information conveyed by utterance is *suggested, not stated.*

23. When a purported fact, a wish, a judgment of value, and so forth, are conveyed by means of a symbol conventionally used for that purpose we shall say the fact, wish, and so on, has been **stated**; when information is conveyed by means not conventionally reserved for that purpose we shall say that that information has been **suggested**. Thus, a **statement** is an explicitly formulated assertion, command, desire, judgment, and so forth, while a **suggestion** is conveyed, though not explicitly formulated. (It is, however, hard to draw a sharp line between suggestion and statement, as here defined. Sometimes, of course, there can be no doubt at all that an important part of a given utterance has been suggested, though not explicitly symbolized. The man who asks "When did you start smoking so heavily?" has not *actually* said "You are smoking heavily.")

24. All human languages rely, to an astonishing degree, on what is understood, though not said "in so many words." It has been reported of the Eskimos that "Their phrases are as sober as their faces. A gleam in an Eskimo's eye tells you more than half a dozen of our sentences concerning desire, repugnance, or another emotion. Each Eskimo's word is like that gleam: it suggests at once what has happened and what is to come. . . ." (Gontran de Poncins, *Kabloona*, page 247.) The more articulate languages of Western civilization, though not as suggestive as those of the Eskimo, still retain enormous suggestive power.

25. *Emotive and neutral language.* Among the most effective suggestions conveyed in human utterance are those expressive of the speaker's *feelings* (and especially feelings of approval or disapproval). Not only *feelings* are conveyed by suggestion: Any statement about "impersonal" matters of fact makes use of tacit assumptions, which are suggested, not stated. Nevertheless, the uses of suggestion to communicate the nature of a speaker's feelings are particularly important, for the following reasons:

(1) Suggested feelings concerning a person or object can powerfully influence people's opinions. To call a man a "Red" is already to turn an audience against him; to call him a "dirty Red," in certain contexts, is practically to condemn him outright. Such "name calling" is usually more successful than explicit statement or reasoned argument.

(2) Feelings, especially strong feelings, concerning a person or object spontaneously find expression in the use of "satisfying" symbols. (All praise and abuse tend to become poetic.) An angry man tends to *show* his anger rather than talk *about* it: thus the means by which he expresses his feelings will be a suggestion, not a statement. In general, suggestion is a very "natural" way of conveying a feeling.

26. Much attention has accordingly been given, in recent times, to the use of those signs that particularly lend themselves to the expression and communication of feelings. Such symbols are termed **emotive,** and are contrasted with **neutral** symbols. An emotive word, then, is one expressive of strong feelings (especially of approval or disapproval) on the part of the speaker. The use of emotive words has a tendency to produce similar feelings in the hearer.

27. The English language has a few words reserved for the expression of feeling and used for no other purpose—exclamations like "Shame!" "Hurrah!" "Encore!" While these words are highly emotive according to our definition, they express very generalized feelings. For this reason (and because they are so seldom used in discourse) they have negligible influence in determining people's views concerning *specific* topics.

28. If an advertiser wants to predispose the man in the street in favor of his product, he will probably adopt more subtle means to recommend it. Suppose he is selling a dentifrice consisting of powdered beef bone (an actual case): the slogan "Hurrah for powdered beef bone!" is unlikely to enlist many customers for the new product, even though re-

peated thousands of times in newspaper advertisements and on the radio. For the words "powdered beef bone" have suggestions that are unfavorable to the advertiser's purpose: we have all seen raw bones, and we are led to think of an unappetizing mess of blood-stained splinters, not at all the sort of stuff we would choose for cleaning the teeth. How much better then from the advertiser's standpoint to label the product "Numin" (the name actually chosen). Instead of the *negative* emotive force of "powdered beef bone," we have a *positive* emotive appeal of the substitute term, "Numin." For the latter has a scientific flavor, as of some new vitamin, and can therefore be relied upon to attract the man in the street.

29. The device used in this instance to stimulate a favorable reaction to a certain object (the dentifrice) consists in *the choice of a name having agreeable associations.* The English language is very rich in words approximately equivalent in *explicit* meaning, while markedly divergent in their emotive associations and suggestions.

30. The terms "government official," "bureaucrat," and "public servant" have much the same explicit meaning, yet the first is neutral, the second abusive, and the last honorific. "Liquidation of the opposition" sounds a great deal more agreeable than "torture and murder of the minority." A man may "talk eloquently" or "jabber"; a statesman may "have the gift of compromise" or be a "slippery trimmer"; a friend is "understandably confused," an enemy "has gone a bit off his noodle"; all these examples were in a single newspaper editorial.

31. The list of examples could be indefinitely extended, for nearly all the words we use are colored with some shade of respect or contempt, and every notion can be so worded as to make its subject seem either admirable or ridiculous.

32. The expression and influence of attitudes by means of such highly emotive words as those we have cited should be too obvious to escape notice. *But these cases are not exceptional.* The view that only in "propaganda" and abuse is language used emotively is none the less profoundly mistaken for being widely held. We must insist, to the contrary, that language is *normally* used to express attitudes

and exert influence as well as to convey explicit statement; it is as much of an exception for language to be "uncolored" or neutral as for matter to be without odor.

33. Since the emotive and suggestive influence of language is so strong, we must take account of it in our general program of establishing principles and standards of right thinking. (If, on the other hand, we were to neglect these aspects of language, and pay attention only to what is explicitly stated in neutral terms, we should be behaving like a pilot who refused to take account of any part of an iceberg that was not visible above the water.) By discussing a concrete example in detail, we shall now illustrate the types of critical procedure that are appropriate.

V. ANALYSIS OF A SPECIMEN OF HIGHLY EMOTIVE WRITING

34. A recent newspaper editorial opened with this sentence:

(A) "A fabulously rich playboy, who got tired of his ponies, got the idea that he would like to repudiate the free enterprise that privileged his grandfather to endow him with so many million dollars he could never hope to count them."

This passage tells us a good deal more about the editorial writer (or his employer) than about the millionaire who is the target of his abuse. Yet the passage does contain a little *impersonal* information (true or false), and the first step in analysis is to make this context explicit. An experienced journalist who happened to read (A) would immediately "discount" much of what was said. What this probably means, he might comment, is:

(B) The rich man in question is supporting federal control of industry.

After the invective of (A), this partial translation appears insipid. Clearly the writer had little interest in conveying the information expressed by (B).

35. We proceed, therefore, to identify the *emotive suggestions* of the original passage. A convenient way of doing this is to begin by picking out (say by underlining) all the words and phrases that make a notable contribution to the total impression intended. After this has been done, we try to state ex-

plicitly the nature of the suggestion conveyed in each case. Proceeding in this fashion, we get the following analysis:

LANGUAGE USED	SUGGESTION CONVEYED
playboy, ponies	X (the man in question) is an idler and gambler
fabulously rich	X is excessively wealthy
so many million dollars he could never hope to count them	
got tired of	X is irresponsible—
got the idea	makes decisions for no
would like to repudiate	good reason
privileged	X has received special
endow	and unearned favors

36. It will be seen that these suggestions reinforce each other in painting the picture of a most unattractive character. The malice of the writer's intention is obvious when the various suggestions are combined in a single explicit statement, in some such fashion as this:

(C) The man in question is an idle gambler, who has far more money than he deserves and is now irresponsibly using the vast financial power that he did nothing to earn.

37. This last statement, if made explicitly, might well be libelous and expose its author to a legal suit for damages. Yet even so it would probably be less effective than the hints and innuendoes of the original passage (A). In all such cases the rule holds that the outspoken accusation is less dangerous than the whispered calumny.

38. A good way of neutralizing the suggestive power of the original passage is to replace the crucial emotive terms and phrases by others having *opposite emotive tendency* (but approximately the same explicit content). In this way we get the following substitute for (A):

(D) A very wealthy American sportsman has decided to oppose the system of unregulated commercial trading that enabled his grandfather to leave him his large fortune.

(You would do well to compare versions A and D very carefully, in order to decide for yourself whether the latter can be regarded as a "fair translation" of the former.)

39. It still remains for us to determine whether the suggestions contained in the original passage (and explicitly formulated in C) are to be regarded as justified. *We must guard carefully against assuming that the implicit suggestions of an utterance can be automatically rejected without further examination, just because they are suggested and not explicitly stated.* Such an assumption would be grossly mistaken, for there are many occasions on which the expression of our feelings is perfectly justified.

40. We take as a second instance of highly emotive language a passage from one of Garrison's addresses to the public:

"I am aware that many object to the severity of my language; but is there not cause for severity? I will be as harsh as truth, and as uncompromising as justice. On this subject, I do not wish to think, or speak, or write, with moderation; No! no! Tell a man whose house is on fire to give a moderate alarm; tell him to moderately rescue his wife from the hands of the ravisher; tell the mother to gradually extricate her babe from the fire into which it has fallen; But urge me not to use moderation in a cause like the present. I am in earnest—I will not equivocate—I will not retreat a single inch,— AND I WILL BE HEARD."

41. This is the language of a man laboring under strong emotions, conveyed in words well fitted to communicate indignation. Shall we say he is wrong to have the feelings or to attempt to communicate them? Or that he ought to resort to the pallid and ineffective use of "neutral" language? Surely not. But to grant the right of Garrison or anybody else to express feelings and attitudes towards a subject by the most effective means he can find at hand is a very different thing from admitting without further examination that the specific emotion or attitude is justified. The suggestions of eloquence, rhetoric or poetry, insofar as they consist of claims that might be true or false, must submit to enquiries into their evidence, general credibility, consistency; if their moving appeals to our feelings are justified, they should survive such examination without detriment or loss of eloquence.

42. Returning to our original example, then, we must ask *what evidence* is provided

for the claim formulated in (C). In this particular instance, the answer is quickly given: for *no reasons at all* are brought forward in support of the scurrilous accusation. Even while we admit the editorial writer's general privilege of accusing his subject of idleness, irresponsibility, and so forth, in the manner he has chosen, we must object strenuously that in the case at issue his accusation is presented as a bare assertion, destitute of any supporting evidence in its favor. Our summing up of the value of passage (A) might take some such form as this: "The passage is intended to arouse prejudice against its subject, by representing him as idle, irresponsible, and undeservedly wealthy. It appeals successfully to the reader's presumed dislike of these qualities. But it offers no particle of evidence in support of its hostile contention."

VI. SOME SUGGESTED RULES OF PROCEDURE

43. The painstaking analysis illustrated in the last section will be too elaborate for everyday use—life is too short for us to be always ferreting out the full emotive implications of what we read and hear. It is nevertheless of much value as a training in critical awareness of the suggestive overtones of human utterance to perform a few such exercises in great detail. When this is done, the following suggestions for procedure may be helpful:

(1) *Begin by reading the passage slowly, carefully, and calmly several times, noting any points in the utterance that seem to deserve further examination.* [The reader will pardon this insistence on so elementary and obvious a point. Experience shows that once the excitement of the chase has been aroused, there is a tendency to "discover" sinister or profound implications in a passage, *before even reading it with any degree of attention!*]

(2) *State the general intention and context of the utterance.* [E.g., "This is a report of a new scientific discovery made to an audience thoroughly familiar with the general background, and made by a man who is trying to suppress all that is personal in the circumstances he is describing." Or "This is an advertisement whose main object is to arouse curiosity concerning a mysteriously labelled new product; it is designed to appeal especially to women to make them more receptive to later 'follow-ups.'" It is useful also to try to determine *the evidence used in arriving at this verdict concerning the general nature of the symbolic situation.*]

(3) *Extract the words and phrases in the passage that are particularly effective in conveying the desired suggestion.* [Crude instances of this, such as those discussed in the last section, are easily detected. More subtle suggestion, *e.g.,* those due to the general style of a passage, may easily escape notice. It is an excellent practice here, as throughout this training, to compare one's results with those of others working independently on the same passage. Hunting down the reasons for disagreement will often bring to light unsuspected resources of the language used.]

(4) *Make the suggestions of each word explicit, and combine the partial suggestions in a single statement.* [This has been illustrated by the analysis of preceding version (C) above. You will soon find, on trial, that the suggestions of a word or phrase can be made explicit only in a rough and approximate way. Paraphrasing the implicit content largely neutralizes its emotive influence. Instead of extracting the implicit content in this way, a useful variation is to rewrite the original passage *reversing the emotive effect of the critical terms,* as illustrated in statement (D) above.]

(5) *Formulate, in neutral language, the impersonal content of the original passage.* [The products of steps 4 and 5 should together approximate in informative content to the original passage.]

(6) *Determine the evidence in favor of the original passage, as now elaborated. . . .*

WILLIAM H. WHYTE, JR., and the Editors of *Fortune*
The Language of Business

William H. Whyte, Jr. (1917-   ), has been assistant managing editor of the magazine *Fortune* since 1951. He was educated at Princeton University, and during World War II he served in the United States Marine Corps through the Guadalcanal campaign. After his discharge from the service in 1945 with the rank of captain, he began writing about various aspects of American life, particularly about businessmen, who, he thinks, fail to talk intelligibly either to one another or to the public.

Is Anybody Listening?, 1952, from which "The Language of Business" is taken, is an inquiry into the American business mind and its techniques of communication. This essay, which in tone and approach is representative of the eleven in the volume, is a barbed yet frequently humorous analysis of "businessese," a jargon described by the authors as fumbling and meaningless.

Mr. Whyte's collaborators in *Is Anybody Listening?* are the editors of *Fortune*. This staff of scholars, journalists, and writers have developed a collaborative technique of journalistic writing in which many staff members make suggestions and conduct the necessary research for each article but leave the actual composition largely to one person. The resulting product is well written, unusually informative, and reliable in its conclusions.

1. In line with his great new interest in communication, the businessman has been taking quite a close look at his language. It is not, he fears, up to the job. Some businessmen, in fact, have gone so far as to assert that the pomposity of management prose is the "root ill of our communication troubles." While that may be an overexcited judgment, management's surveys have demonstrated that a large amount of its language has been not only incomprehensible to the people it is trying to reach, but enormously expensive in money, time, and misunderstanding as well. "It is high time the American businessman discovered the English language—it would be

THE LANGUAGE OF BUSINESS: From *Is Anybody Listening?* by William H. Whyte, Jr., and the Editors of *Fortune*. Published by Simon and Schuster; copyright 1950 by Time, Inc. A longer version of this essay originally appeared under the same title in the November 1950 issue of *Fortune* magazine. Reprinted by permission of the author.

very useful to him" . . . "We've turned our offices into paper mills" . . . "We love curt clear correspondence—but damned few of us know how to write it." Everywhere the chorus of self-flagellation is growing.

2. The activity stirred up by this scrutiny has been impressive. Over a third of the country's top corporations, we found, have set up some kind of formal program; executives have been setting up "writing clinics" to scour management copy, staging correspondence-improvement courses, holding school in conference and public-speaking techniques, and, at the very least, peppering subordinates with "For-God's-sake-won't-you-people-learn-to-use-English-around-here" memos.

3. The crusade is more than a nine-to-five concern. To judge by recent book sales, businessmen are reading more "practical" English and vocabulary-building books than ever before. In growing numbers they are taking ad-

vantage of the extra-curricular courses offered them by business and civic associations, and, sometimes, setting up their own. In one notable instance, at Bridgeport, Connecticut, an informal group of businessmen became so absorbed in the problem that they chipped in and hired a Yale professor to teach them how to address groups and conduct meetings.

4. The target of all this is that infamous jargon, which, for want of a better term, can be called businessese. While the English that is to replace it has some rather extraordinary qualities itself, businessese is certainly ready for an overhaul. Its signal characteristic, as the reader and all other critics of businessese will recognize, is its uniformity. Almost invariably, businessese is marked by the heavy use of the passive construction. Nobody ever *does* anything. Things *happen*—and the author of the action is only barely implied. Thus, one does not refer to something, reference is made to; similarly, while prices may rise, nobody *raises* them. To be sure, in businessese there is not quite the same anonymity as is found in federal prose, for "I" and "we" do appear often. Except when the news to be relayed is good, however, there is no mistaking that the "I" and "we" are merely a convenient fiction and that the real author isn't a person at all but that great mystic force known as the corporation.

5. Except for a few special expressions, its vocabulary is everywhere quite the same. Midwesterners are likely to dispute the latter point ("It is characteristic of us, as opposed to the Easterner," says one, "to be concise and to the point"), but a reading of approximately 500,000 words of business prose indicates no striking differences—in the Midwest or anywhere else. Moreover, when executives expound on the subject, their views coincide remarkably on the matter of pet peeves (principally: "please be advised," "in reference to yours of . . . ," "we wish to draw attention," "to acknowledge your letter"). The phrases of businessese are everywhere so uniform, in fact, that stenographers have a full set of shorthand symbols for them.

6. Because of this uniformity, defenders of businessese can argue that it doesn't make for misunderstanding. After all, everybody knows the symbols, and, furthermore, wouldn't a lot of people be offended by the terseness of more concise wording? There is something to this theory. Since businessese generally is twice as wordy as plain English, however, the theory is rather expensive to uphold. By the use of regular English the cost of the average letter—commonly estimated at 75 cents to $1—can be cut by about 20 cents. For a firm emitting a million letters a year, this could mean an annual saving of $200,000. Probably it would be even greater; for, by the calculations of correspondence specialist Richard Morris, roughly 15 per cent of the letters currently being written wouldn't be necessary at all if the preceding correspondence had been in regular English in the first place.

7. Where do the terms of businessese come from? Most, of course, are hand-me-downs from former generations of businessmen, but many are the fruit of other jargons. A businessman who castigates government bureaucrats, for example, is at the same time apt to be activating, expediting, implementing, effectuating, optimizing, minimizing, and maximizing—and at all levels and echelons within the framework of broad policy areas. Similarly, though he pokes fun at the long-hairs and the social scientists, he is beginning to speak knowingly of projective techniques, social dynamics, depth interviewing, and sometime soon, if he keeps up at this rate, he will probably appropriate the hallmark of the sound sociological paper, "insightful." Businessese, in fact, has very nearly become the great common meeting ground of the jargons.

8. Why do people who in private talk so pungently often write so pompously? There are many reasons: tradition, the demands of time, carelessness, the conservative influence of the secretary. But above all is the simple matter of status. Theorem: the less established the status of a person, the more his dependence on jargon. Examine the man who has just graduated from pecking out his own letters to declaiming them to a secretary and you are likely to have a man hopelessly intoxicated with the rhythm of businessese. Conversely, if you come across a blunt yes or no in a letter, you don't need to glance further to grasp that the author feels pretty firm in his chair.

9. The application of euphemism, a favored

device of businessese, further illustrates this status principle. Take the field of selling. At the top of the ladder you will find a great many people in it: *sales* managers, vice presidents for *sales,* etc. As you go down the ranks, however, it becomes difficult to find people in this line of work. Field underwriters, estate planners, merchandising apprentices, social engineers, distribution analysts, and representatives of one kind or another, yes. But *salesmen*? Rarely.

10. Not only does businessese confer status, it protects it as well, for it is ideally adapted to buck passing and hedging. "All you have to remember," one executive says, "is the one basis which characterizes all such intracommunication: let the language be ambiguous enough that if the job be successfully carried out, all credit can be claimed, and if not, a technical alibi be found in the text itself."

11. For this purpose there is a regular subglossary of businessese. Most notable terms: "in the process of," "at this time," "under consideration," "in the not-too-distant future," "company policy," and, when one is unable to explain something properly, "obviously." People who have to submit periodic reports to their superiors are particularly dependent on such terms—salesmen, for example, would have a hard time if they couldn't report of some prospects that they were "very impressed." ("I am allergic to that word," says one sales manager. "It results in so few orders.")

12. The full application of businessese to hedging occurs when more than two heads are put to work on a problem. As the members of top management sit around the table, a relatively simple policy statement is introduced for discussion. This is kicked around a bit, as the saying goes, for though it certainly is a fine statement, couldn't agree with it more, there are just a few little angles and suggestions that maybe ought to be noted. Thereupon each executive, much as a baseball captain grasps a bat in choosing up sides, adds his qualification, until finally the original statement has been at once pointed up, toned down, given more dignity, made more forceful, altered to anticipate possible objections, concretized, amended, and resolved. Now no longer a mere statement but a philosophy, or

collection of philosophies, it is turned over to the Public Relations Department to give to the waiting public. There is nothing, as so many people say, quite like what you get when everybody on the team works together.

13. Now with almost every use of the cliché and stereotype mentioned so far, a better case could be made out for the use of simple, unhackneyed English. It is a mistake, however, to be too rigorously critical on this score. Since the symbols of language convey emotion as well as communicate facts and ideas, many a prefabricated phrase has become inextricably tied with certain emotional responses. This infuriates the semanticists—"intensional thinking" is their cuss word for it—but a good part of business has been built on it.

14. Like many another occupation, business is governed by a ritual as rigid as the steps of the ballet, and while the efficient executive makes fun of all this, he has the good sense to know when to put it to use himself. The dinner for the retiring employee, for example, As short-story writers have so often pointed out, it is often pure dissimulation. But what if the toastmaster were to dispense with the timeworn expressions and thus tacitly concede what everyone knows to be nothing less than the truth: that old Charlie has been getting in everybody's hair for the last fifteen years and it'll be wonderful to see him go. Everyone, Charlie's worst enemies included, would be shocked, morale would suffer, and the usefulness of the executive to the organization would be lessened.

15. So with the interoffice memo about the man being horizontally promoted to some branch office. Again the ceremonial is unvarying: pillar of strength . . . larger responsibilities . . . Ed's invaluable experience in this field makes him the logical . . . know the whole staff will join me in wishing Ed good luck in his new job . . . Nobody is fooled in the slightest, of course, but what could have been a disagreeable, and for Ed a shattering, experience is smoothed over by the blessed analgesic of businessese. There is *something* of a case, then, for timeworn expressions. It needs no further making.

16. So far, it is on the elimination of businessese that business has been concentrating in its better-English campaign. This is proper

enough work. Unfortunately, however, there is an accompanying prose development that has gone comparatively unnoticed. Yet of the two it may well be the more important. For what is now appearing in business prose with as much frequency as businessese, is something even worse—its exact opposite.

17. It could be called *reverse* gobbledegook. Where the traditional jargon is multisyllabic, long-winded, and passive, it is filled with short, terse words; its sentences are short and the construction of them so much more active than passive that exclamation marks are as frequent as periods. Heavy on personification, homely analogies, and a rigid glossary of hard-hitting words, it lends a powerful straight-from-the-shoulder effect to ambiguity and equivocation. It is English that is on the beam, English with its feet on the ground; to borrow the description of one of its proponents, it is "shirt-sleeve" English. To date, it has been applied chiefly to the language of the banquet and conference table, but it is creeping into the written language at an alarming rate. . . .

18. To give a clearer idea of its anatomy, we have taken 200 business speeches and made a systematic count of the expressions and constructions most common to them. Put together in loose fashion, the sixty most characteristic expressions add up to the following composite address. It is *not* a parody. As a matter of fact, one executive who had planned to borrow it as a humorous preface to a speech of his own very properly got cold feet at the last moment; the audience was so conditioned to the expressions, he feared, that it might easily break into premature applause. The chances are strong that it would have; and at this very moment, undoubtedly, somewhere in the U.S. the following words, in some arrangement or another, are bringing automatic nods of assent.

Cooperation—An Opportunity and a Challenge

An Address

19. It is a pleasure and a privilege to be here with you today. These great annual meetings are always an inspiration to me, and doubly so today. After that glowing introduction by our toastmaster I must confess, how-

ever, that I'd like to turn the tables and tell a little story on Chuck. When I say it's about the nineteenth hole and a certain gentleman whose baritone was cracked, those of you who were at the Atlanta conference last year will know what I mean. But I won't tell it. Chuck Forbes is too good a friend of mine and, seriously, I know full well we all realize what a tower of strength his yeoman service has been to the association in these trying times.

20. Yes, gentlemen, trying times. So you'll pardon me if I cast aside the glib reverberation of glittering generalities and the soothing syrup of sugar-coated platitudes and put it to you the only way I can: straight English. WE'RE LOSING THE BATTLE!

21. From every corner the people are being weaned from the doctrines of the Founding Fathers. They are being detoured from the high-speed highways of progress by the utopian highwaymen.

22. Now, the man in the street is a pretty savvy fellow. Don't sell him short. Joe Doakes may be fooled for a while, but in the end he wants no part of the mumbo jumbo the global saboteurs are trying to sell him. After all, he is an American.

But he has to be told.

AND WE'RE NOT TELLING HIM!

23. Now let me say that I do not wish to turn the clock back. None of us does. All forward-looking businessmen see themselves as partners in a team in which the worker is a full-fledged member. I regard our employees as our greatest business asset, and I am sure, mindful as I am of the towering potentials of purposeful energy in this group of clear-sighted leaders, that, in the final analysis, it is the rock foundation of your policies too.

24. But the team can't put the ball across for a first down just by wishing it. The guards and the tackles can't do their job if the quarterback doesn't let them in on the play. And we, the quarterbacks, are muffing the ball.

25. How are we to go over for a touchdown? My friends, this is the $64 question. I don't know the answers. I am just a plain-spoken businessman. I am not a soothsayer. I have no secret crystal ball. But I do know one thing: before we round the curve into the home-stretch we have a job to do. It will not be easy. I offer no panaceas or nostrums. Instead,

I would like to suggest that the real key to our problem lies in the application of the three E's.

What are the three E's?

ENTERPRISE! ENDEAVOR! EFFORT!

26. Each and every one of us must appoint himself a salesman—yes, a missionary, if you will—and get out and do some real grass-roots selling. And when we hit the dirt, let's not forget the customers—the greatest asset any business has.

27. Now, much has been done already. But let's not fool ourselves: the surface, as our chairman has so wisely said, has hardly been scratched. The program is still in its infancy. So let me give it to you straight from the shoulder. The full implementation, gentlemen, depends on *us*.

28. So let's get on the beam! In cracker-barrel fashion, let's get down to earth. In good plain talk the man in the street can understand, let's remind Joe Doakes that the best helping hand he will ever find is the one at the end of his own shirt sleeve.

We have the know-how.

WITH SIGHTS SET HIGH, LET'S GO OVER THE TOP!

29. As the swelling torrent of this kind of thing is demonstrating, the less you have to say the more emphatically you can say it with reverse gobbledegook. In addition to using the hard-hitting expressions, you have simply to call attention as frequently as possible to the fact that these expressions are being used. A sure warning of its onrush, accordingly, is a prefatory announcement by the speaker that he is not going to beat around the bush, pull any punches, pussyfoot, use two-dollar words, or the like. The rest is inevitable. The expressions of reverse gobbledegook have now become so predictable that an audience would be sharply awakened were a single one of them altered by the omission of so much as a word. (One of these days a clever speaker is going to capitalize on this. "Gentlemen," he will say, with a meaningful pause, "I offer a panacea.")

30. As a result, reverse gobbledegook can be self-defeating; that is, since its whole effect lies in the dynamic quality the words convey, their constant use tends to neutralize them.

This can be overcome, however, by adding strengtheners—so that, in a very real sense of the word, it cannot be overemphasized that you sincerely and unquestionably meant what you said in the first place.

31. Like written businessese, a reverse gobbledegook also confers status. For this purpose, it provides a sort of slang that, skillfully applied—particularly at the conference table—will impart to the user an appearance of saviness, cooniness, and general know-how. Want to mark yourself as a comer in the advertising field? Speak, then, of fun stories, sweet guys, the hard sell, straw men you set up to back into, and points you can hang your hat on.[1] For each field you will find a subglossary, and, common to all of them, such universal terms as "play it by ear," "the pitch," "the deal," and the many expressions built on the suffix "wise." ("Budget-wise, Al, the pitch shapes up like this . . .")

32. Another characteristic of reverse gobbledegook is its dependence on analogy and metaphor. During a single banquet you may find business problems equated with an airplane, a broad highway, a boat being rocked, a river, a riverbank, a stream, a bridge, a train, a three-legged stool, and, sometimes, three or four of these things at once—in which case the passage is generally summed up with something like "It's as simple as that," or "That's all there is to the problem." (From a recent speech: "So business enterprise of America is trying to hone a sales force into the cutting edge of an economy and there is a virus running rampant in the flock. Security-mindedness is a log across the stream when it comes to developing the optimistic salesman outlook.")

[1] Other current advertising favorites: "let's pull all the stops out on this one"; "let's noodle this one"; "let's sneak the message across"; "we'll touch all bases on this one"; "means absolutely nothing to the lay mind"; "we'll get a plus value on this one"; "it was quite a hassle"; "let's not hassle over this." Journalists laugh and laugh at this sort of thing. Just why, it is difficult to say, except possibly that being less inventive, they prefer to hang on to the old expressions rather than coin new ones. Terms now nearing the end of the run (including some of *Fortune's*): ambivalence, dichotomy, schizophrenic, "two hours and four martinis [beers, etc.] later"; "it's as difficult [easy, etc.] as it is complex [difficult, etc.]"; "their profits [feelings, etc.] are showing."

33. Outstanding is the great American football analogy. No figure of speech is a tenth as seductive to the businessman. Just why this should be so—baseball, curiously, is much less used—is generally explained by its adaptability to all sorts of situations. Furthermore, the football analogy is *satisfying*. It is bounded by two goal lines and is thus finite. There is always a solution. And that is what makes it so often treacherous.

34. Analogy and metaphor can be insidiously attractive as substitutes for thought. They are not, of course, when fleetingly used, when, as H. W. Fowler puts it (in *Modern English Usage*), they "flash out for the length of a line or so and are gone." But this is rarely the case in reverse gobbledegook. The user starts innocuously enough; his policy is *like* a thingamajig in one respect. But only the stanchest mind can resist the analogy further. Before long he is entwined, and unconsciously adopts the premise that *his* policy *is* a thingamajig. The language, in short, has molded thinking—and the results can be a good bit more serious than a poor speech.

35. The mishaps of one consumer-goods corporation illustrate this hazard. Not so long ago, the men who owned the company were casting about for a Goal. Up to then it had been money. But now they had acquired a lot of it, they were getting on in years, and anyway it didn't sound good. And so, on this enlightened-goal problem, the Chief fell to pondering at the conference table. When you get right down to it, the company was just like a big football team. You don't win unless you have a good team, do you? You could say that again. Well, before he gets a good team, what does the coach have to do? Very simple. He has to go out and find good players. Just thinking out loud, mind you, but wasn't the big job then to get the right recruits?

36. Almost automatically, this was mimeographed as the company's rationale—"The Touchdown Play" it was called—and before long executives were spending almost as much time on the new trainees as they were on their regular jobs, and when they weren't doing this, they were scouring the colleges for more. Everything went swimmingly; the policy was soon the wonder of the merchandising world; the top executives were suffused with a sense of enlightenment, and the place was jammed with eager young men.

37. In only one respect did the analogy break down. A year later practically all of the competition came out with a new product embodying a notable technical advance. Our company didn't. It was still getting the team ready.

38. The wellsprings of reverse gobbledegook are many. In part, it is explainable as a venial by-product of the businessman's enthusiastic revulsion against businessese. In an equal part, it is probably due also to the laziness of some of the public relations men who compose the speeches. Reverse gobbledegook is universal to any topic—and whatever its disadvantages, it cannot put anyone out on a limb. . . .

SUSANNE K. LANGER *The Language Line*

Susanne K. Langer (1895-   ), a New Yorker by birth, was educated at Radcliffe College, where she received both undergraduate and graduate degrees, and later taught for fifteen years as a tutor in philosophy. She has taught logic, esthetics, and other courses in philosophy at leading universities, including the University of Delaware, New York University, and Columbia. In 1952 she joined the faculty of the University of Washington.

Among Mrs. Langer's writings are *The Practice of Philosophy*, 1930, *Introduction to Symbolic Logic*, 1937, *Philosophy in a New Key*, 1942, and *Feeling and Form*, 1953. Already established as an authority in the field of symbolic logic, she has turned in her most recent book to esthetics, presenting the concept that art is the creation of significant forms symbolic of human feeling.

This selection, excerpted from a longer article, "The Lord of Creation," which appeared in *Fortune*, deals with man's use of symbols as the characteristic that establishes the line of demarcation between him and other animals.

1. The trait that sets human mentality apart from every other is its preoccupation with symbols, with images and names that *mean* things, rather than with things themselves. This trait may have been a mere sport of nature once upon a time. Certain creatures do develop tricks and interests that seem biologically unimportant. Pack rats, for instance, and some birds of the crow family take a capricious pleasure in bright objects and carry away such things for which they have, presumably, no earthly use. Perhaps man's tendency to see certain forms as *images,* to hear certain sounds not only as signals but as expressive tones, and to be excited by sunset colors or starlight, was originally just a peculiar sensitivity in a rather highly developed brain. But whatever its cause, the ultimate destiny of this trait was momentous; for all human activity is based on the appreciation and use of symbols. Language, religion, mathematics, all learning, all science and supersti-

THE LANGUAGE LINE: From *The Lord of Creation* by Susanne K. Langer. Reprinted from the January 1944 issue of *Fortune* magazine by special permission of the Editors; copyright 1944 Time Inc.

tion, even right and wrong, are products of symbolic expression rather than direct experience. Our commonest words, such as "house" and "red" and "walking," are symbols; the pyramids of Egypt and the mysterious circles of Stonehenge are symbols; so are dominions and empires and astronomical universes. We live in a mind-made world, where the things of prime importance are images or words that embody ideas and feelings and attitudes.

2. The animal mind is like a telephone exchange; it receives stimuli from outside through the sense organs and sends out appropriate responses through the nerves that govern muscles, glands, and other parts of the body. The organism is constantly interacting with its surroundings, receiving messages and acting on the new state of affairs that the messages signify.

3. But the human mind is not a simple transmitter like a telephone exchange. It is more like a great projector; for instead of merely mediating between an event in the outer world and a creature's responsive action, it transforms or, if you will, distorts the event into an image to be looked at, retained, and

contemplated. For the images of things that we remember are not exact and faithful transcriptions even of our actual sense impressions. They are made as much by what we think as by what we see. It is a well-known fact that if you ask several people the size of the moon's disk as they look at it, their estimates will vary from the area of a dime to that of a barrel top. Like a magic lantern, the mind projects its ideas of things on the screen of what we call "memory"; but like all projections, these ideas are transformations of actual things. They are, in fact, *symbols* of reality, not pieces of it.

4. A symbol is not the same thing as a sign; that is a fact that psychologists and philosophers often overlook. All intelligent animals use signs; so do we. To them as well as to us sounds and smells and motions are signs of food, danger, the presence of other beings, or of rain or storm. Furthermore, some animals not only attend to signs but produce them for the benefit of others. Dogs bark at the door to be let in; rabbits thump to call each other; the cooing of doves and the growl of a wolf defending his kill are unequivocal signs of feelings and intentions to be reckoned with by other creatures.

5. We use signs just as animals do, though with considerably more elaboration. We stop at red lights and go on green; we answer calls and bells, watch the sky for coming storms, read trouble or promise or anger in each other's eyes. That is animal intelligence raised to the human level. Those of us who are dog lovers can probably all tell wonderful stories of how high our dogs have sometimes risen in the scale of clever sign interpretation and sign using.

6. A sign is anything that announces the existence or the imminence of some event, the presence of a thing or a person, or a change in a state of affairs. There are signs of the weather, signs of danger, signs of future good or evil, signs of what the past has been. In every case a sign is closely bound up with something to be noted or expected in experience. It is always a part of the situation to which it refers, though the reference may be remote in space and time. Insofar as we are led to note or expect the signified event we are making correct use of a sign. This is the

essence of rational behavior, which animals show in varying degrees. It is entirely realistic, being closely bound up with the actual objective course of history—learned by experience, and cashed in or voided by further experience.

7. If man had kept to the straight and narrow path of sign using, he would be like the other animals, though perhaps a little brighter. He would not talk, but grunt and gesticulate and point. He would make his wishes known, give warnings, perhaps develop a social system like that of bees and ants, with such a wonderful efficiency of communal enterprise that all men would have plenty to eat, warm apartments—all exactly alike and perfectly convenient—to live in, and everybody could and would sit in the sun or by the fire, as the climate demanded, not talking but just basking, with every want satisfied, most of his life. The young would romp and make love, the old would sleep, the middle-aged would do the routine work almost unconsciously and eat a great deal. But that would be the life of a social, superintelligent, purely sign-using animal.

8. To us who are human, it does not sound very glorious. We want to go places and do things, own all sorts of gadgets that we do not absolutely need, and when we sit down to take it easy we want to talk. Rights and property, social position, special talents and virtues, and above all our ideas, are what we live for. We have gone off on a tangent that takes us far away from the mere biological cycle that animal generations accomplish; and that is because we can use not only signs but symbols.

9. A symbol differs from a sign in that it does not announce the presence of the object, the being, condition, or whatnot, which is its meaning, but merely *brings this thing to mind*. It is not a mere "substitute sign" to which we react as though it were the object itself. The fact is that our reaction to hearing a person's name is quite different from our reaction to the person himself. There are certain rare cases where a symbol stands directly for its meaning: in religious experience, for instance, the Host is not only a symbol but a Presence. But symbols in the ordinary sense are not mystic. They are the same sort of thing that ordinary signs are; only they do not call our attention to something necessarily present or

to be physically dealt with—they call up merely a conception of the thing they "mean."

10. The difference between a sign and a symbol is, in brief, that a sign causes us to think or act *in face of* the thing signified, whereas a symbol causes us to think *about* the thing symbolized. Therein lies the great importance of symbolism for human life, its power to make this life so different from any other animal biography that generations of men have found it incredible to suppose that they were of purely zoological origin. A sign is always embedded in reality, in a present that emerges from the actual past and stretches to the future; but a symbol may be divorced from reality altogether. It may refer to what is *not* the case, to a mere idea, a figment, a dream. It serves, therefore, to liberate thought from the immediate stimuli of a physically present world; and that liberation marks the essential difference between human and non-human mentality. Animals think, but they think *of* and *at* things; men think primarily *about* things. Words, pictures, and memory images are symbols that may be combined and varied in a thousand ways. The result is a symbolic structure whose meaning is a complex of all their respective meanings, and this kaleidoscope of *ideas* is the typical product of the human brain that we call the "stream of thought."

11. The process of transforming all direct experience into imagery or into that supreme mode of symbolic expression, language, has so completely taken possession of the human mind that it is not only a special talent but a dominant, organic need. All our sense impressions leave their traces in our memory not only as signs disposing our practical reactions in the future but also as symbols, images representing our *ideas* of things; and the tendency to manipulate ideas, to combine and abstract, mix and extend them by playing with symbols, is man's outstanding characteristic. It seems to be what his brain most naturally and spontaneously does. Therefore his primitive mental function is not judging reality, but *dreaming his desires.*

12. Dreaming is apparently a basic function of human brains, for it is free and unexhausting like our metabolism, heartbeat, and breath. It is easier to dream than not to dream, as it is easier to breathe than to refrain from breathing. The symbolic character of dreams is fairly well established. Symbol mongering, on this ineffectual, uncritical level, seems to be instinctive, the fulfillment of an elementary need rather than the purposeful exercise of a high and difficult talent.

13. The special power of man's mind rests on the evolution of this special activity, not on any transcendently high development of animal intelligence. We are not immeasurably higher than other animals; we are different. We have a biological need and with it a biological gift that they do not share.

14. Because man has not only the ability but the constant need of *conceiving* what has happened to him, what surrounds him, what is demanded of him—in short, of symbolizing nature, himself, and his hopes and fears—he has a constant and crying need of *expression.* What he cannot express, he cannot conceive; what he cannot conceive is chaos, and fills him with terror.

15. If we bear in mind this all-important craving for expression we get a new picture of man's behavior; for from this trait spring his powers and his weaknesses. The process of symbolic transformation that all our experiences undergo is nothing more nor less than the process of *conception,* which underlies the human faculties of abstraction and imagination.

16. When we are faced with a strange or difficult situation, we cannot react directly, as other creatures do, with flight, aggression, or any such simple instinctive pattern. Our whole reaction depends on how we manage to conceive the situation—whether we cast it in a definite dramatic form, whether we see it as a disaster, a challenge, a fulfillment of doom, or a fiat of the Divine Will. In words or dreamlike images, in artistic or religious or even in cynical form, we must *construe* the events of life. There is great virtue in the figure of speech, "I can *make* nothing of it," to express a failure to understand something. Thought and memory are processes of *making* the thought content and the memory image; the pattern of our ideas is given by the symbols through which we express them. And in the course of manipulating those symbols we inevitably distort the original experience, as

we abstract certain features of it, embroider and reinforce those features with other ideas, until the conception we project on the screen of memory is quite different from anything in our real history.

17. Conception is a necessary and elementary process; what we do with our conceptions is another story. That is the entire history of human culture—of intelligence and morality, folly and superstition, ritual, language, and the arts—all the phenomena that set man apart from, and above, the rest of the animal kingdom. As the religious mind has to make all human history a drama of sin and salvation in order to define its own moral attitudes, so a scientist wrestles with the mere presentation of "the facts" before he can reason about them. The process of *envisaging* facts, values, hopes, and fears underlies our whole behavior pattern; and this process is reflected in the evolution of an extraordinary phenomenon found always, and only, in human societies— the phenomenon of language.

18. Language is the highest and most amazing achievement of the symbolistic human mind. The power it bestows is almost inestimable, for without it anything properly called "thought" is impossible. The birth of language is the dawn of humanity. The line between man and beast—between the highest ape and the lowest savage—is the language line. Whether the primitive Neanderthal man was anthropoid or human depends less on his cranial capacity, his upright posture, or even his use of tools and fire, than on one issue we shall probably never be able to settle—whether or not he spoke.

19. In all physical traits and practical responses, such as skills and visual judgments, we can find a certain continuity between animal and human mentality. Sign using is an ever evolving, ever improving function throughout the whole animal kingdom, from the lowly worm that shrinks into his hole at the sound of an approaching foot, to the dog obeying his master's command, and even to the learned scientist who watches the movements of an index needle.

20. This continuity of the sign-using talent has led psychologists to the belief that language is evolved from the vocal expressions, grunts and coos and cries, whereby animals vent their feelings or signal their fellows; that man has elaborated this sort of communion to the point where it makes a perfect exchange of ideas possible.

21. I do not believe that this doctrine of the origin of language is correct. The essence of language is symbolic, not signific; we use it first and most vitally to formulate and hold ideas in our own minds. Conception, not social control, is its first and foremost benefit.

22. Watch a young child that is just learning to speak play with a toy; he says the name of the object, e.g.: "Horsey! horsey! horsey!" over and over again, looks at the object, moves it, always saying the name to himself or to the world at large. It is quite a time before he talks to anyone in particular; he talks first of all to himself. This is his way of forming and fixing the *conception* of the object in his mind, and around this conception all his knowledge of it grows. *Names* are the essence of language; for the *name* is what abstracts the conception of the horse from the horse itself, and lets the mere idea recur at the speaking of the name. This permits the conception gathered from one horse experience to be exemplified again by another instance of a horse, so that the notion embodied in the name is a general notion.

23. To this end, the baby uses a word long before he *asks for* the object; when he wants his horsey he is likely to cry and fret, because he is reacting to an actual environment, not forming ideas. He uses the animal language of *signs* for his wants; talking is still a purely symbolic process—its practical value has not really impressed him yet.

24. Language need not be vocal; it may be purely visual, like written language, or even tactual, like the deaf-mute system of speech; but it *must be denotative*. The sounds, intended or unintended, whereby animals communicate do not constitute a language, because they are signs, not names. They never fall into an organic pattern, a meaningful syntax of even the most rudimentary sort, as all language seems to do with a sort of driving necessity. That is because signs refer to actual situations, in which things have obvious relations to each other that require only to be noted; but symbols refer to ideas, which are not physically there for inspection, so their

connections and features have to be represented. This gives all true language a natural tendency toward growth and development, which seems almost like a life of its own. Languages are not invented; they grow with our need for expression.

25. In contrast, animal "speech" never has a structure. It is merely an emotional response. Apes may greet their ration of yams with a shout of "Nga!" But they do not say "Nga" between meals. If they could *talk about* their yams instead of just saluting them, they would be the most primitive men instead of the most anthropoid of beasts. They would have ideas, and tell each other things true or false, rational or irrational; they would make plans and invent laws and sing their own praises, as men do.

ALBERT H. MARCKWARDT *What Is Good English?*

Albert Henry Marckwardt (1903-   ) was educated at the University of Michigan, where he was awarded a doctorate in 1934. Long a member of the Michigan faculty and now professor of English, Professor Marckwardt has become one of the leading students of language. He is highly successful as author, scholar, lecturer, consultant, and teacher. Among his books are *Scribner Handbook of English*, 1940, and *Introduction to the English Language*, 1942. Since 1940 he has been director of the Linguistic Atlas of the North Central States.

In language, as in art, ethics, philosophy, and religion, people are continually seeking an ultimate standard. In this brief talk, Professor Marckwardt clearly sets forth the doctrine of usage, which today is generally accepted by students of linguistics.

Editorials are written about every phase of it. Teachers are deluged with letters asking them to referee disputes over it. Even our statesmen have manifested a consistent interest in the problem—both Benjamin Franklin and Theodore Roosevelt tried to reform our spelling. As far as the schools are concerned, everyone generally agrees upon one point: Good English should be successfully taught. But when it comes to deciding what is not Good English, there are almost as many points of view as there are persons to hold them.

In all this diversity, two diametrically opposed attitudes may be discerned. At one extreme are those who look to the conventional rules of grammar, to dictionaries, to lists of

frequently mispronounced words as absolute authorities. This attitude of dependence upon authority, since it implies a belief that a language may arrive at and maintain a relatively static condition—that it may be kept pure— is usually spoken of as *purism*. Little more need be said about this point of view for most of us are quite familiar with it. We have all met it somewhere, in the schools or out.

During the last twenty-five years, however, there have been indications of a change of attitude toward the question of Good English and its teaching, both in the schools and among the most competent linguists in the country. There has been formulated what may be called for want of a more accurate term a "liberal" attitude toward language, which is directly in opposition to many of the tenets and practices of the purists. As in the case of any liberal movement, this one has been accompanied by much misunderstanding as to its aims and methods. There are abroad sinister rumors that "anything you hear is right," and dire forebodings of future generations whose verbs and nouns will not agree.

It is most important, I believe, to the general success of the English language program in our schools, to clear away some of the erroneous conceptions which have sprung up in connection with linguistic liberalism. This may best be accomplished by pointing out, first of all, how and why this change in attitude came about; second, by defining the standards of Good English which the liberal grammarians uphold; and finally, by pointing out certain ideas and attitudes which they do not put forward. The limitations of space necessitate my treating only one aspect of this broad question, namely grammar in its more restricted sense; although what I have to say may be applied in most cases to problems of pronunciation and vocabulary as well.

To explain the rise of the liberal attitude toward a standard of Good English, we must examine briefly the history of the rules which are to be found in the school grammars of today. These rules, for the most part, originated with certain English grammarians of the eighteenth century—notably William Ward, Robert Lowth, and James Buchanan. These men were not as interested in reflecting and codifying the actual spoken English of their time as in setting up an ideal language for their own and future generations to strive to master. This ideal language was based in part upon the rules of Latin grammar—for the eighteenth century was an age which revered the classics—and in part upon what seemed to be a rational arrangement for a language—for the eighteenth century was also an age of reason.

In the two hundred years which have elapsed since the formulation of these rules, the study of language has progressed remarkably, and we have learned much concerning this aspect of human behavior. The early nineteenth century was marked by a tremendous growth in our knowledge of the history of both ancient and modern languages.

The grammarians of the eighteenth century assumed that language was static, that it might reach and be kept at a state of perfec-

tion. In the nineteenth century we learned to apply the evolutionary concept to language as well as to botany and zoology. We came to see that language is not stationary, that it is in a state of continuous development, that standards which may hold good for one century are not necessarily applicable to another.

Along with our increased knowledge of the history of the English language and the conception of language as an evolving organism, came the realization that many of the rules of so-called correct English did not reflect actual speech habits; that they set up standards which were not only absent from spoken English but, more than this, were virtually foreign to the genius of the language.

In 1927, the late Professor S. A. Leonard, together with Professor H. Y. Moffat, began to study this problem. They selected from typical school text-books then in use 102 expressions condemned as incorrect; they submitted these to a jury composed of twenty-six eminent linguists and a similar number of authors, editors, business executives, teachers of English and of speech—about 225 all told. This jury was asked to rate the 102 condemned expressions as acceptable, questionable, or illiterate. It is possible to give only a few of the results of the survey here, but it was found that more than 40 of the 102 expressions usually condemned in the school texts were considered acceptable by over 75 per cent of the linguists, and many others were held by them to be matters of divided usage.

Among the expressions condemned by the text-books and accepted by the jury were: "This is a man I used to know," "That will be all right," "You had better stop that foolishness." The first of these omits the relative pronoun; the second used the term "all right" to which some grammars object; in the third the locution "had better" is at times condemned by text-books as a colloquialism. All of them are obviously in current use today.

It is interesting to read what an eminent British linguist, Professor J. H. G. Grattan, has said on this same subject. He writes, "The attitude of the American schools is, so far as the English language is concerned, ultra-conservative. Eighteenth century ideas of correctness are not yet dead in the United States. Indeed, by American standards, many idiomatic usages long sanctioned in Great Britain are still bad grammar."

When it became apparent that the rules of many of the school grammars prescribed something that was not idiomatic English, the question immediately arose: If the rules of the grammars cannot be held to constitute a valid standard of Good English, what standard can be set up in its place? This is, it will be recalled, the second of the three questions which were raised before.

The liberal grammarians answer in the following manner: The history of most modern languages shows that from generation to generation, and from century to century, there has been in existence an accepted or received standard form of that language—English, French, or whatever it may be; and that that standard form has been based upon the speech of the class and section of the country which was politically, economically, and culturally dominant at the time.

London English, just one of many English dialects, became the standard speech of England chiefly because the city of London rose to a position of prime importance in the affairs of the English-speaking people. The same was true of the language of the Ile de France and of the Kingdom of Castile. If this is generally the case, why should we not consider as the standard of present-day English that speech which is in actual use by the large group who is carrying on the affairs of the English-speaking people? An attitude of this kind is usually spoken of as a doctrine of usage.

In connection with such a doctrine or standard, one problem arises. Suppose the usage of this dominant group is not wholly in agreement on all points? Suppose some of its members occasionally use a split infinitive while others do not? What then is to be our guiding principle?

Here again we may have recourse to our knowledge of the history of our language. Since it is possible to examine with some accuracy the forms of the English language during the last thousand years, such a study will indicate that certain inflectional and syntactical traits have been constantly expanding and developing, while others have been disappearing. If it is possible from an examina-

tion of what has gone on in the past to make a reasonable prediction as to what will come about in the future—and we assume this with most of the studies we undertake—then, in the case of a divided usage, let us choose that form or construction which seems to be in accord with the developing tendencies or patterns of the English language.

To return to the problem of a split infinitive. Since a careful examination of the English of the last five hundred years shows such a construction to have been in constant use, and to have arisen from a desire to speak English naturally and clearly, the least we can do is to allow it equal rank with the alternative construction; to favor it when it seems better to perform the function of communicating the idea involved; and to rule it out when it does not express the thought as clearly.

Unfortunately a number of misconceptions have arisen in connection with such a proposed standard of usage. Uninformed people frequently ask if such a doctrine means that any sort of English that may be heard on the street is Good English. If an expression is used, no matter where or by whom, must it then necessarily be correct? The answer is no. The doctrine of usage does not legalize the language of the gutter, for the language of the gutter is not the English which is apt to prevail as Standard Spoken English. It is perfectly true that upon occasion certain expressions and certain modes of pronunciation have spread from one social class to another, frequently from a higher to a lower, and at times from a lower to a higher. The broad *a* sound in such words as *past* and *half*, now considered to be ultra-refined by many speakers, is a case in point; for in the late eighteenth and early nineteenth centuries it was, as a dictionary of the time puts it, "the sound used by the vulgar but not the polite and learned world." But these occasional cross currents do not justify an acceptance of wholly uncultivated speech as a norm. By virtue of the historical principles upon which the liberal grammarians proceed, they are still committed to the speech of the people who direct the affairs of the community as a standard. On the other hand since the English-speaking countries are democratic in character, the limitation of the speech standard to the narrowest top layer of the social order is also precluded.

The second aspect of the doctrine of usage which frequently troubles people to whom the idea is somewhat new is the fear that the lack of strict and ironclad rules will lead to eventual disintegration. Again history shows such fears to be unfounded. It has been pointed out that rules for the speaking of correct English date chiefly from the beginning of the eighteenth century. They have existed only two hundred years of the fifteen hundred since the Angles and Saxons first came to the British Isles. Accordingly when English is considered in the light of its millennium of existence as a separate language, one is inclined to feel that the rules have had relatively little effect in either hindering or accelerating the main trends of development.

Moreover, we can never be too sure as to just what is meant by disintegration of a language, which innovations are bad and which are good. As one eminent linguist has written, "To the conservative grammarian all change is decay. Although he knows well that an old house often has to be torn down in part or as a whole in order that it may be rebuilt to suit modern conditions, he never sees the constructive forces at work in the destruction of old grammatical forms. He is fond of mourning over the loss of the subjunctive and the present slovenly use of the indicative. He hasn't the slightest insight into the fine constructive work of the last centuries in rebuilding the subjunctive."

At present the greatest need confronting those who are entrusted with the teaching of our language in the schools is for new textbooks which describe accurately the language of those now carrying on the affairs of the English-speaking people, particularly grammars which will record the forms and syntax of present-day American English. A most significant beginning in this direction has already been made by the National Council of Teachers of English who, in November 1932, sponsored the publication of *Current English Usage*. This volume is in reality a continuation of the survey mentioned above, begun by Professors Leonard and Moffat, a survey which has for its purpose a codification of the usages of present-day English, and which proceeds upon the theory that it is the principal function of the grammarian to describe the language as it exists rather than to prescribe a state of perfection for it.

I can close in no more appropriate manner than to quote from Miss Ruth Mary Weeks' introduction to this forward-looking work. She writes, "Language is a living thing and the greatest law of life and growth is change. Dictionaries, grammars, books of rhetoric are not eternal statutes handed down from heaven like the tables of Mosaic law. They are history, not dogma; description, not command—description of the changing speech habits of the mass of men.

"As our speech changes, so do dictionaries and grammars change; so must they change if we are to prepare our students to speak the language of their own time, or to secure from the better speech of our own day reinforcement of our teaching."

J. Y. COUSTEAU *Menfish*

Jacques Yves Cousteau (1910-   ) is an inventor, naval captain, traveler, and oceanographer. Born in France, he attended American secondary schools and has traveled extensively in America. At present, while on leave from his duties as an officer in the French Navy, he is in command of an extensive five-year marine-research expedition, whose purpose is to study oceanography by means of the newly invented Cousteau-Girardot submarine cinecamera. He and his associate, Frédéric Dumas, the chief diver of the expedition, have explored a vast new frontier beneath the sea's surface.

   The Silent World, from which "Menfish" has been taken, is an exciting account of fantastic underwater adventures through sunken galleys and caverns filled with sharks, mantas, and moray eels. Such explorations have been made possible only through the invention of the aqualung, the first use of which Cousteau describes in this article.

1. One morning in June, 1943, I went to the railway station at Bandol on the French Riviera and received a wooden case expressed from Paris. In it was a new and promising device, the result of years of struggle and dreams, an automatic compressed-air diving lung conceived by Émile Gagnan and myself. I rushed it to Villa Barry where my diving comrades, Philippe Tailliez and Frédéric Dumas waited. No children ever opened a Christmas present with more excitement than ours when we unpacked the first "aqualung." If it worked, diving could be revolutionized.

2. We found an assembly of three moderate-sized cylinders of compressed air, linked to an air regulator the size of an alarm clock. From the regulator there extended two tubes, joining on a mouthpiece. With this equipment

MENFISH: From *The Silent World* by J. Y. Cousteau with Frédéric Dumas. Copyright, 1953, by Harper and Brothers.

harnessed to the back, a watertight glass mask over the eyes and nose, and rubber foot fins, we intended to make unencumbered flights in the depths of the sea.

3. We hurried to a sheltered cove which would conceal our activity from curious bathers and Italian occupation troops. I checked the air pressure. The bottles contained air condensed to one hundred and fifty times atmospheric pressure. It was difficult to contain my excitement and discuss calmly the plan of the first dive. Dumas, the best goggle diver in France, would stay on shore keeping warm and rested, ready to dive to my aid, if necessary. My wife, Simone, would swim out on the surface with a schnorkel breathing tube and watch me through her submerged mask. If she signaled anything had gone wrong, Dumas could dive to me in seconds. "Didi," as he was known on the Riviera, could skin dive to sixty feet.

4. My friends harnessed the three-cylinder block on my back with the regulator riding at the nape of my neck and the hoses looped over my head. I spat on the inside of my shatterproof glass mask and rinsed it in the surf, so that mist would not form inside. I molded the soft rubber flanges of the mask tightly over forehead and cheekbones. I fitted the mouthpiece under my lips and gripped the nodules between my teeth. A vent the size of a paper clip was to pass my inhalations and exhalations beneath the sea. Staggering under the fifty-pound apparatus, I walked with a Charlie Chaplin waddle into the sea.

5. The diving lung was designed to be slightly buoyant. I reclined in the chilly water to estimate my compliance with Archimedes' principle that a solid body immersed in liquid is buoyed up by a force equal to the weight of the liquid displaced. Dumas justified me with Archimedes by attaching seven pounds of lead to my belt. I sank gently to the sand. I breathed sweet effortless air. There was a faint whistle when I inhaled and a light rippling sound of bubbles when I breathed out. The regulator was adjusting pressure precisely to my needs.

6. I looked into the sea with the same sense of trespass that I have felt on every dive. A modest canyon opened below, full of dark green weeds, black sea urchins and small flower-like white algae. Fingerlings browsed in the scene. The sand sloped down into a clear blue infinity. The sun struck so brightly I had to squint. My arms hanging at my sides, I kicked the fins languidly and traveled down, gaining speed, watching the beach reeling past. I stopped kicking and the momentum carried me on a fabulous glide. When I stopped, I slowly emptied my lungs and held my breath. The diminished volume of my body decreased the lifting force of water, and I sank dreamily down. I inhaled a great chestful and retained it. I rose toward the surface.

7. My human lungs had a new role to play, that of a sensitive ballasting system. I took normal breaths in a slow rhythm, bowed my head and swam smoothly down to thirty feet. I felt no increasing water pressure, which at that depth is twice that of the surface. The aqualung automatically fed me increased compressed air to meet the new pressure layer.

Through the fragile human lung linings this counter-pressure was being transmitted to the blood stream and instantly spread throughout the incompressible body. My brain received no subjective news of the pressure. I was at ease, except for a pain in the middle ear and sinus cavities. I swallowed as one does in a landing airplane to open my Eustachian tubes and healed the pain. (I did not wear ear plugs, a dangerous practice when under water. Ear plugs would have trapped a pocket of air between them and the eardrums. Pressure building up in the Eustachian tubes would have forced my eardrums outward, eventually to the bursting point.)

8. I reached the bottom in a state of transport. A school of silvery sars (goat bream), round and flat as saucers, swam in a rocky chaos. I looked up and saw the surface shining like a defective mirror. In the center of the looking glass was the trim silhouette of Simone, reduced to a doll. I waved. The doll waved at me.

9. I became fascinated with my exhalations. The bubbles swelled on the way up through lighter pressure layers, but were peculiarly flattened like mushroom caps by their eager push against the medium. I conceived the importance bubbles were to have for us in the dives to come. As long as air boiled on the surface all was well below. If the bubbles disappeared there would be anxiety, emergency measures, despair. They roared out of the regulator and kept me company. I felt less alone.

10. I swam across the rocks and compared myself favorably with the sars. To swim fishlike, horizontally, was the logical method in a medium eight hundred times denser than air. To halt and hang attached to nothing, no lines or air pipe to the surface, was a dream. At night I had often had visions of flying by extending my arms as wings. Now I flew without wings. (Since that first aqualung flight, I have never had a dream of flying.)

11. I thought of the helmet diver arriving where I was on his ponderous boots and struggling to walk a few yards, obsessed with his umbilici and his head imprisoned in copper. On skin dives I had seen him leaning dangerously forward to make a step, clamped in heavier pressure at the ankles than the head,

a cripple in an alien land. From this day forward we would swim across miles of country no man had known, free and level, with our flesh feeling what the fish scales know.

12. I experimented with all possible maneuvers of the aqualung—loops, somersaults and barrel rolls. I stood upside down on one finger and burst out laughing, a shrill distorted laugh. Nothing I did altered the automatic rhythm of air. Delivered from gravity and buoyancy I flew around in space.

13. I could attain almost two knots' speed, without using my arms. I soared vertically and passed my own bubbles. I went down to sixty feet. We had been there many times without breathing aids, but we did not know what happened below that boundary. How far could we go with this strange device?

14. Fifteen minutes had passed since I left the little cove. The regulator lisped in a steady cadence in the ten-fathom layer and I could spend an hour there on my air supply. I determined to stay as long as I could stand the chill. Here were tantalizing crevices we had been obliged to pass fleetingly before. I swam inch-by-inch into a dark narrow tunnel, scraping my chest on the floor and ringing the air tanks on the ceiling. In such situations a man is of two minds. One urges him on toward mystery and the other reminds him that he is a creature with good sense that can keep him alive, if he will use it. I bounced against the ceiling. I'd used one-third of my air and was getting lighter. My brain complained that this foolishness might sever my air hoses. I turned over and hung on my back.

15. The roof of the cave was thronged with lobsters. They stood there like great flies on a ceiling. Their heads and antennae were pointed toward the cave entrance. I breathed lesser lungfuls to keep my chest from touching them. Above water was occupied, ill-fed France. I thought of the hundreds of calories a diver loses in cold water. I selected a pair of one-pound lobsters and carefully plucked them from the roof, without touching their stinging spines. I carried them toward the surface.

16. Simone had been floating, watching my bubbles wherever I went. She swam down toward me. I handed her the lobsters and went down again as she surfaced. She came up under a rock which bore a torpid Provençal citizen with a fishing pole. He saw a blonde girl emerge from the combers with lobsters wriggling in her hands. She said, "Could you please watch these for me?" and put them on the rock. The fisherman dropped his pole.

17. Simone made five more surface dives to take lobsters from me and carry them to the rock. I surfaced in the cove, out of the fisherman's sight. Simone claimed her lobster swarm. She said, "Keep one for yourself, monsieur. They are very easy to catch if you do as I did."

18. Lunching on the treasures of the dive, Tailliez and Dumas questioned me on every detail. We reveled in plans for the aqualung. Tailliez penciled the tablecloth and announced that each yard of depth we claimed in the sea would open to mankind three hundred thousand cubic kilometers of living space. Tailliez, Dumas and I had come a long way together. We had been eight years in the sea as goggle divers. Our new key to the hidden world promised wonders.

ARTHUR C. CLARKE *Weekend on the Moon*

Arthur Charles Clarke (1917-   ), a native of England, seems to have spent little of his imaginative life on terra firma. He has traveled through outer space in such books as *Exploration of the Moon*, 1954, and *Earthlight*, 1955, and down under the sea in the article "Undersea Holiday," *Holiday*, August 1954. "We are just beginning," he says, "to open up two great frontiers, space and ocean. They make the earth very small potatoes."

Although "Weekend on the Moon" may seem to be, and no doubt is, an example of bold extrapolation from known facts, it makes fresh and interesting use of some of the discoveries of physics and astronomy.

1. Just a hundred years ago, back in 1986, the first men landed on the Moon, and the age of space flight began. During the last few years, it must be admitted, the glamour of more romantic places like Mars and Venus has diverted attention from our satellite. Perhaps it's so close we tend to take it for granted, just as no New Yorker bothers to go to the top of Transplanet Tower to see how his city looks from half a mile up. Moreover, until very recently few people went to the Moon unless they were scientists or technicians on official business.

2. Two things have changed this. Now that the necessary facilities exist, the Lunar Commission is encouraging a limited tourist trade, though for the present it will be restricted to the Earthward face of the Moon. The second factor, of course, is the establishment of Pasteur City, which is likely to have a profound effect on medical research and even, ultimately, on human society.

3. Looking back on it from our vantage point, it is obvious that the first landing on the Moon was an anticlimax. Everyone had been expecting it for almost half a century: it had been the theme of countless books and movies, and rockets had been getting closer and closer for twenty years before the final

WEEKEND ON THE MOON: Reprinted by permission of the author. From *Holiday* magazine, February 1955.

touchdown was made. Moreover, no one had expected to find very much on the Moon. It was the general impression through most of the 20th Century that the Moon was completely dead and unchanging—a cosmic slag heap of interest only to geologists and astronomers. It might be useful as an observatory and a fueling stop on the road to the planets, but otherwise it was a valueless piece of real estate.

4. Let's see how accurate that first impression was. Imagine you're aboard the passenger ship *Archimedes* as it drops down toward the rugged lunar landscape. The journey from Space Station One, just outside the Earth's atmosphere, has taken less than ten hours. At one time it required almost five days, but now that atomic propulsion has been perfected, fuel economy is no longer a prime consideration and the crossing can be made at much higher speeds.

5. No matter how many times you do it, a landing on the Moon is an awe-inspiring experience, totally different from the long glide through the upper atmospheres of planets like Earth or Mars. The lunar landing must be made by rockets alone at the end of an interminable fall that is only checked when you are within a hundred miles of the jagged, pockmarked landscape. Then the rockets flare

into life, and your returning weight forces you down into your seat. Through the observation window (if you're lucky enough to be near one) you see the white-hot pillar of flame that is checking your headlong fall. The squat and stubby *Archimedes* looks like a giant spider as it descends, outthrust landing legs spread to take up the shock of impact.

6. Touchdown itself is indicated only by the final cessation of thrust, and a ringing silence inside the ship as the rockets die. Then there is a curious, heaving motion as the long hydraulic cylinders in the undercarriage absorb the ship's momentum. It lasts for less than a second, but if the landing has been badly off the vertical you'll think you're aboard a boat in a choppy sea. Luckily it doesn't last long enough for anyone to be seasick.

7. Within seconds of touchdown, the spaceport vehicles are clustering round the ship. Besides the specialized servicing trucks, there is a large pressurized bus fitted with an accordionlike tube which will be coupled up to the airlock of the *Archimedes*. When the connection is made, you walk through this tube into the bus without bothering about a spacesuit. And the bus will take you straight into the pressure dome which houses the administration section of the port.

8. The first question everybody asks when they arrive on the Moon is, "Where are the mountains?" For hours you have seen those great peaks coming closer and closer. You have watched the crater walls rise around you until the summits seem to tower above the falling ship. And then, when the flurry of dust and flame has died away, the *Archimedes* stands on a rocky plain, with only a few low hills in sight. Though you are in the center of a mountain-fringed plain, the steep curve of the Moon's surface has hidden the surrounding heights from view. It takes some time to get used to this nearness of the horizon; remember, the Moon is only a quarter the size of Earth.

9. The *Archimedes* lands in the *Sinus Medii* —a small plain at the exact center of the Moon's visible face. This region is of enormous geological interest, for it is surrounded by crevasses up to a hundred miles long. Digging down through these gigantic fissures, men have been able to penetrate far into the Moon's crust and hence the area is one of great mining activity. Though no sound can exist where there is no atmosphere to carry it, you sometimes feel the ground shake as blasting charges are let off round the colossal canyon known as the Hyginus Cleft.

10. *Sinus Medii* means Central Bay. Though of course there is no free water on the Moon, such terms as bay, sea, ocean and lake were used by the early astronomers and have stuck so thoroughly that no one can change them now. To make matters more confusing to newcomers, the Latin and English versions are used indiscriminately. It may take you some time to realize, for example, that *Palus Somnii* is the same place as the Dream Marsh. There have been several attempts to tidy up lunar nomenclature, but nothing has come of them and we're stuck with the five-hundred-year-old names. Luckily the Moon's other side, which of course was never seen until the first rockets started to land there, isn't littered with remnants of medieval astrology. The great formations there have been named after famous men of more modern times, so don't be surprised to encounter Einstein, Churchill, Rutherford, Sibelius, Roosevelt, each a crater more than a hundred miles across.

11. The *Sinus Medii* is not only the main space port on this side of the Moon, but also the center for surface transport. All long-distance travel is by monorail, for the Moon is an ideal place for this type of locomotion. There's no air resistance, so speeds of five hundred miles an hour can be reached with little difficulty. And the low gravity greatly eases the construction problem, for the single rail need only be supported at wide intervals and bridges can have enormous spans.

12. So come aboard the northbound track to Pasteur City, in the great walled (or mountain ringed) plain of Plato, and take a ride over the most spectacular scenery on the Moon. We'll leave in darkness, a few hours after the beginning of the long lunar night.

13. The monorail car holds about fifty passengers, and is controlled automatically. Because its weight is too light to give good traction, the driving wheels grip the rail on either side, like pincers, under the pressure of powerful springs.

14. The terminal itself resembles a station

on Earth: there are the usual lines of track, the announcements of departures and arrivals. When everyone has come aboard, the car is sealed and slides through double doors into a huge airlock. You feel the throb of giant pumps as the chamber is evacuated, then the outer door opens and there is a surge of acceleration as the monorail's electric motors speed you out of the terminal, on to the surface of the Moon.

15. If you're lucky, you may see a take-off as you skirt the edge of the space port. A night launching from the Moon is an unforgettable sight. Its utter soundlessness somehow adds to the effect. The ship ascends in a cloud of dust blasted up from the plain, a cloud within which the jets will burn like incredibly brilliant suns. As the dust falls behind, the blue-white glare floods the landscape with a light fiercer even than that of noon. It ebbs away as the ship dwindles against the stars, and suddenly winks out of existence as the departing vessel reaches escape velocity and cuts its drive.

16. For the first few hundred miles of your trip to Pasteur City, the monorail runs over relatively flat country as it heads northeast. Though the sun has set, the landscape is brilliantly illuminated by the Earth, just passing its first quarter but already giving a dozen times as much light as the full Moon does to the terrestrial scene. It's a cold light, an arctic radiance that gives not an atom of heat, for it is tinged with the blues and greens of Earth's oceans and clouds. It sparkles from the polar caps that are too dazzling, even across a quarter of a million miles of space, for the unprotected eye. It's hard to believe that this freezing luminosity really comes from a world of warmth and life.

17. There's an observation room at the front of the car, curtained off from the light of the main cabin. Unless you're a seasoned, blasé traveler, you'll spend most of your time here, watching the lunar landscape racing past. Ahead of you the single rail, supported by pillars disquietingly far apart, is now running almost due east. Here's another paradox to bother you: on the Moon the sun sets in the east, not the west.

18. The monorail is losing speed as it climbs up out of the shadowed lowlands. At any moment now, you'll overtake the sun. The line of darkness moves so slowly here that a running man could almost keep abreast of it, and could hold the sun balanced on the horizon as long as he could maintain his speed.

19. On your left (that's the north) the broken land falls away in a series of layers as if, a billion years ago, the lava welling up from the Moon's molten heart had solidified in successive, weakening waves. It's a scene that chills the soul, yet there are spots on Earth as bleak as this. The Badlands of Arizona are equally desolate and the upper slopes of Everest are still more hostile, for though the temperature here is two hundred degrees below zero, at least there is no eternal, ravening wind.

20. Suddenly the cliff on the right comes to an abrupt halt as if a monstrous chisel has sliced it off the surface of the Moon. You can see all the way around to the north, and there, marching across the sky in flaming glory, are the peaks of the Apennines, incandescent in the last rays of the hidden sun. The abrupt blaze of light almost blinds you, and you have to shield your eyes from the glare until you can safely face it. When you look again, the transformation is complete. The stars, which until a moment ago had filled the sky, have vanished. Your contracted pupils can no longer see them. Even the glowing Earth now seems no more than a feeble patch of phosphorescence. The glare from the sunlit mountains, still fifty miles away, has eclipsed all other sources of light.

21. The peaks float in the sky, fantastic pyramids of flame. They seem to have no more connection with the ground beneath them than do the clouds that hover round a sunset on Earth. The line of shadow is so sharp, the lower slopes of the mountains so lost in utter darkness, that only the burning summits have any real existence. It will be hours yet before the last of those proud peaks slips back into the shadow of the Moon and surrenders to the night.

22. The Apennines are the finest range on this side of the Moon. Those summits tower more than twenty thousand feet above the plain and seem an impassable barrier. But twenty thousand feet on the Moon is equivalent to less than four thousand feet on Earth

in the effort required to negotiate them, and it is possible to ascend vertiginous inclines with impunity. The monorail weaves and climbs through spectacular passes, then drops down the northern slopes into the vast plain of the *Mare Imbrium,* the Sea of Rains. As you descend into the lowlands, the sun, which your speed has magically conjured up from night, sinks again below the edge of the Moon. There is little more to see until you reach Pasteur. You might as well go back into the cabin and join your fellow passengers.

23. You'll catch your first glimpse of the city as you descend the inner ramparts of Plato, the superb walled plain on the northern border of the *Mare Imbrium.* It is strange to think that Man built his first extraterrestrial cities on distant Mars, not on his nearest neighbor in space. But the incentive was greater, the technical problems less. Now that these problems have been overcome, we can expect to see many more cities on the Moon.

24. The first lunar bases were entirely underground and many of them still are. By digging a few feet into the interior the four-hundred-degree temperature change between day and night can be avoided. The first colonists were also nervous about meteors, and decided to take no chances against bombardment from space.

25. We know now that meteors are no more common on the Moon than they are on Earth. For the Moon has an atmosphere. True, it's a million times less dense than ours, but because of the lower gravity of the Moon it extends much farther into space. As far as breathing it is concerned, you might just as well be in a vacuum, but this tenuous envelope has two very important practical uses. It is a first-class meteor screen, and it provides an ionosphere like that on Earth, reflecting radio waves round the curve of the planet, so that long-distance communication is possible.

26. Pasteur City consists of a dozen pressure domes, linked together by airlocks, a few miles from the north wall of Plato. One of the domes is transparent, so that the residents can watch the pageant of the changing heavens, can see the long dawn break above the mountains and can watch the seasons come and go on the world to which they will never return.

27. Yet it is quite wrong to think of Pasteur City as a home for convalescents like the space-station hospitals circling Earth. Almost all its twenty thousand inhabitants live normal, unrestricted lives. But they could do so only here, where they weigh no more than thirty pounds and the strain on hearts and muscles is correspondingly reduced.

28. Like all great advances in medical science, the founding of Pasteur City has opened new and unsuspected frontiers. If people suffering from chronic heart disease can live out their normal span under the Moon's low gravity, what will be the expectation of an ordinary, healthy man? No one talks too much about this, but there's an air of suppressed excitement among the doctors studying the matter. Some of them have been heard to say that old age can now be postponed until far into the second century. If this is true, and the technical problems of supporting a large lunar population can be overcome, we can expect some interesting social changes.

29. Pasteur should be an ideal center for the tourist trade when this gets into high gear, for the *Mare Imbrium* is one of the most beautiful regions of the Moon. The city itself still lacks many luxuries, since the effort to become self-supporting has absorbed most of its energy. Oxygen and water have to be extracted from the lunar rocks in which, luckily, they are fairly common. Food is produced under acres of glass in the huge hydroponic farms, where nutrient solutions flow through pressurized tubes during the fourteen days of continuous sunlight. It is surprising how tasty some of the foods are, but don't ask for steaks or chops.

30. In Pasteur City you encounter a practical problem that won't have bothered you greatly elsewhere. At the space port in the *Sinus Medii,* and on the monorail trip, you were in fairly cramped surroundings and couldn't perform those athletic feats that were given so much emphasis by the earlier writers about the Moon. It's not very practical, for instance, to jump twenty feet high when the ceiling is only a yard above your head. But in Pasteur City, under the domes, you have your first real opportunity to show off.

31. Well, take it easy. Don't go up until you are sure you know how to come down. It's too easy to turn over in flight and land on your

head, which will damage you just as much as it would on Earth at the same impact velocity.

32. Should you wear one of those lead belts which are recommended for visitors during their first few days on the Moon? Try one, by all means, if you feel it may save you from injury through carelessness. But there's a difficulty, which many people overlook, about loading yourself down with lead. Whereas *weight* on the Moon is reduced to a sixth, *inertia* remains exactly the same. The hundred-pound lead belt will help keep you on the ground and will be no burden when you are standing still. But as soon as you try to start or stop or change direction, it will feel exactly what it is—a hundred pounds of lead!

33. Personally, I think the best thing is to accept your weight for what it is, and learn to reduce muscular effort accordingly. Your first attempts to take strides of normal length will look somewhat prissy and mincing, but you'll soon get used to it.

34. You haven't come all the way to the Moon to look at other human beings, and you'll want to spend as much time as possible outside the city. So let's investigate transportation possibilities. Short-range lunar transport is carried out by tractors—pressurized vehicles with large balloon tires and caterpillar treads that can negotiate any ground not actually vertical. (Even that limitation is not always true, for tractors have often hauled themselves up perpendicular cliffs with their power winches.) They are virtually space ships on wheels and prospectors often live in the larger ones for weeks.

35. Rockets are hardly practical for prospecting, so the detailed examination of the Moon has depended almost entirely on these tough little vehicles. Some have now been turned into observation cars, and are already carrying sight-seers from Pasteur City. The most popular trips are those along the foothills of the Alps, and over the Pole to the hidden face of the Moon.

36. Of course the scenery on the Moon's other face is of just the same general type as on the visible side, but there's a mystery and glamour about going into territory which no human eye had ever seen until little more than a lifetime ago.

37. The Alpine excursion runs south from Plato to the great mountain of Pico, rearing eight thousand feet above the plain. It now stands in splendid isolation, but was once part of a mighty crater wall destroyed by volcanic action when the Moon was young.

38. From Pico the tractor swings west for two hundred miles until it comes to Mount Blanc, the great sentinel standing guard at the entrance to the extraordinary Alpine Valley. This weird valley formation, eighty miles long, slices through the Alps like a railroad cutting, and even now we do not know exactly how it was caused. Entering it is like driving into the Grand Canyon, except that *this* cleft is almost perfectly straight and was certainly not produced by the action of water.

39. If you are an expert mountaineer, and sign the necessary indemnities, you may be allowed to try your skill on some of the Alpine peaks. At first, your reduced weight will seem a great advantage and so it is, since you can easily lift yourself with one arm. But low gravity can also induce carelessness. A sixty-foot fall on the Moon is as dangerous as a ten-foot one on Earth—more dangerous, in fact, since there is always the risk of damaging your space suit. Although these suits have now reached a high degree of perfection (they are practically foolproof, and can keep a man alive for twenty-four hours), no one claims that they are exactly comfortable, and they prevent free and unimpeded movement. With all your equipment, your Earth weight when you start climbing will be about fifty pounds.

40. One surprising fact about lunar mountains is that, on the whole, they are not so steep as those on Earth. Because of the absence of weathering, however, they are angular and jagged. There have been no winds or rains to soften their contours. The complete absence of snow or ice removes one major obstacle to climbing, and when all factors are taken into account lunar mountaineering, despite its risks, is no more suicidal a pursuit than its terrestrial equivalent.

41. From the region around Pasteur City, the Earth hangs low in the southern sky, its continents clearly visible and its blanket of atmosphere forming a luminous haze around its edge. It hangs so close to the horizon that

you expect it to set at any moment, and it will be a long time before you get used to the idea that it will always be there, fixed in the lunar sky. The sun and stars rise and set, taking two weeks of earth time to cross from horizon to horizon; but Earth remains forever motionless, apart from a slight swaying back and forth caused by the fact that the Moon's orbital motion is not perfectly regular. The only change Earth shows is that of phase, as it waxes to full and wanes to a threadlike crescent. After a while, you will be able to tell the time of lunar day by that great clock hanging there against the stars.

42. The stars will give you another surprise. Even today, people tell you that on the Moon you can see Sun and stars in the sky at once. It's a statement that is both true and false. If you look directly at the sun, you won't see anything else for a long time, and you'll be lucky not to damage your eyes. During the daytime on the Moon, if you are out in the open, the glare from the rocks demands the use of sunglasses, and your pupils will be fully contracted. Consequently, though the stars *are* shining in the sky, you won't be able to see them and everything will be black overhead. (Remember, it is because of the Earth's dense atmosphere that the sky looks blue from that planet.) If you want to look at the stars, step into the shadow of a convenient rock and shield your eyes from all the glare around you.

43. Then, as your vision adapts itself and your pupils enlarge, you'll see the stars come out. First there will be the bright, familiar constellations, then the legions of their faint companions, until at last the whole sky seems packed with glowing dust. All those countless points of light will be shining with a steady, unvarying radiance, none will twinkle or scintillate as they do on the clearest nights on Earth. Now you will understand why all the great observatories are on the Moon. You will realize that, until he had climbed above the atmosphere of his own planet, no man had ever really seen the stars.

44. Though it was known long before the first landings that the conquest of the Moon would revolutionize astronomy, few people believed that biologists would find anything of interest on our satellite. Yet as far back as the beginning of the 20th Century, evidence had been accumulating that plant life existed around certain craters. There had been curious changes of shading and variable patches of darkness that were hard to explain in any other way.

45. The explanation was correct. The mistake was in assuming that any lunar plants would be primitive, when a little thought would have shown that the reverse must be the case. Conditions on the Moon are so severe that only very advanced and sophisticated types of plant can exist there. The primitive, unspecialized forms died out aeons ago. Most of the existing vegetation is found in the neighborhood of the great lunar clefts, such as the Herodotus Valley, for traces of carbon dioxide, water vapor and sulphur dioxide occasionally gush out of these fissures, sometimes producing short-lived mists that are visible from Earth. These precious gases are eagerly trapped by the slender, cactuslike plants. They are absorbed through systems of pores and tubes which are virtually air compressors. You can cause great excitement among the plants by deliberately spilling some air from your suit. Then the multitudes of pores will start frantically opening and closing.

46. The lunar plants have another ingenious trick which allows them to trap sunlight without losing water vapor. Their upper parts are studded with tiny "windows" of horny material, transparent to light but impenetrable to gases. Oddly enough, exactly the same technique has been worked out independently by certain plants in the dry African deserts, where in some respects conditions are not so very different from those on the Moon.

47. Incidentally, no one has yet found any practical use for these plants. They contain too much sulphur to be edible, but when we have learned more about them they may teach us how to grow our own crops on the unprotected lunar surface—obviously a matter of great practical importance.

48. Is there any evidence of *animal,* as opposed to plant, life on the Moon? It's true that much of the Moon's 15,000,000 square miles of highly contorted terrain is still unexplored, and there may yet be some surprises in store for us. But it is most unlikely that animal life will be found among them. Though biologists

have had a lot of fun imagining creatures that could live under lunar conditions, so far none has obliged by making an appearance.

49. One must not be greedy. The Moon has already turned out to be a much more valuable and interesting place than the first pioneers expected. The millions that have been sunk into it are beginning to pay off in terms of knowledge (from the observatories and vacuum labs), of raw materials (from the mines and refueling stations) and of human happiness (from Pasteur City). There were some who feared that when we reached the Queen of Night, her romance and mystery would be destroyed. They need not have worried. We may roof the lunar craters, spread our cities across the dusty seas, build our farms on the sunward slopes of the mountains. We will not change the essential nature of the Moon. She watched life emerge from the steaming oceans of the dawn, she saw Man embark on the conquest of his own world and, a little later, the conquest of space itself. She will still be watching, drawing the tides beneath her, when our descendants have spread so far from home that few could say in what region of the sky lies the ancestral planet Earth.

BERTON ROUECHÉ *A Game of Wild Indians*

Berton Roueché (1911-   ) is a staff writer for the *New Yorker* magazine. Before joining the *New Yorker*, he worked as a reporter on various newspapers, including the Kansas City *Star* and the St. Louis *Post-Dispatch*.

Mr. Roueché has written three books: the first, *Black Weather*, 1945, is a psychological horror story; the second, *Greener Grass and Some People Who Found It*, 1948, is a collection of *New Yorker* articles, mostly on rural subjects. "A Game of Wild Indians" is taken from *Eleven Blue Men and Other Narratives of Medical Detection*, 1954. For two of these stories, "A Pig from Jersey" and "The Fog," Mr. Roueché won a Lasker Foundation Award for medical reporting.

1. During the second week in August, 1946, an elderly man, a middle-aged woman, and a boy of ten dragged themselves, singly and painfully, into the Presbyterian Hospital, in the Washington Heights section of Manhattan, where their trouble was unhesitatingly identified as typhoid fever. This diagnosis was soon confirmed by laboratory analysis, and on Thursday morning, August 15th, a report of the outbreak was dutifully telephoned to the Department of Health. It was received and recorded there, in accordance with the routine in all alarms of an epidemiological nature, by a clerk in the Bureau of Preventable Diseases

A GAME OF WILD INDIANS: From *Eleven Blue Men* by Berton Roueché, by permission of Little, Brown and Company. Copyright 1952, by Berton Roueché. This article originally appeared in the *New Yorker*.

named Beatrice Gamso. Miss Gamso is a low-strung woman and she has spent some thirty callousing years in the Health Department, but the news gave her a turn. She sat for an instant with her eyes on her notes. Then, steadying herself with a practiced hand, she swung around to her typewriter and set briskly about dispatching copies of the report to all administrative officers of the Department. Within an hour, a reliable investigator from the Bureau was on his way to Washington Heights. He was presently followed by one of his colleagues, a Department public-health nurse, several agents from the Bureau of Food and Drugs, and an inspector from the Bureau of Sanitary Engineering.

2. Typhoid fever was among the last of the massive pestilential fevers to yield to the prob-

ings of medical science, but its capitulation has been complete. It is wholly transparent now. Its clinical manifestations (a distinctive rash and a tender spleen, a fiery fever and a languid pulse, and nausea, diarrhea, and nose-bleed), its cause (a bacillus known as *Eber-thella typhosa*), and its means of transmission have all been clearly established. Typhoid is invariably conveyed by food or drink contaminated with the excreta of its victims. Ordinarily, it is spread by someone who is ignorant, at least momentarily, of his morbid condition. One reason for such unawareness is that for the first several days typhoid fever tends to be disarmingly mild and indistinguishable from the countless fleeting malaises that dog the human race. Another is that nearly five per cent of the cases become typhoid carriers, continuing indefinitely to harbor a lively colony of typhoid bacilli in their systems. The existence of typhoid carriers was discovered by a group of German hygienists in 1907. Typhoid Mary Mallon, a housemaid and cook who was the stubborn cause of a total of fifty-three cases in and around New York City a generation ago, is, of course, the most celebrated of these hapless menaces. About seventy per cent, by some unexplained physiological fortuity, are women. The names of three hundred and eighty local carriers are currently on active file in the Bureau of Preventable Diseases. They are called on regularly by public-health nurses and are permanently enjoined from any employment that involves the handling of food. More than a third of all the cases that occur here are traced to local carriers but, because of the vigilance of the Health Department, rarely to recorded carriers; new ones keep turning up. Most of the rest of the cases are of unknown or out-of-town origin. A few are attributable to the products of polluted waters (clams and oysters and various greens).

3. The surveillance of carriers is one of several innovations that in little more than a generation have forced typhoid fever into an abrupt tractability throughout most of the Western world. The others include certain refinements in diagnostic technique, the institution of public-health measures requiring the chlorination of city-supplied water and proscribing the sale of unpasteurized milk, and the development of an immunizing vaccine. Since late in the nineteenth century, the local incidence of typhoid fever has dropped from five or six thousand cases a year to fewer than fifty, and it is very possible that it may soon be as rare as smallpox. Banishment has not, however, materially impaired the vigor of *Eberthella typhosa*. Typhoid fever is still a cruel and withering affliction. It is always rambunctious, generally prolonged, and often fatal. It is also one of the most explosive of communicable diseases. The month in which it is most volcanic is August.

4. The investigator who led the sprint to Washington Heights that August morning in 1946 was Dr. Harold T. Fuerst, an epidemiologist, and he and Dr. Ottavio J. Pellitteri, another epidemiologist, handled most of the medical inquiry. One afternoon, when I was down at the Bureau, they told me about the case. Miss Gamso sat at a desk nearby, and I noticed after a moment that she was following the conversation with rapt attention. Her interest, it turned out, was entirely understandable. Typhoid-fever investigations are frequently tedious, but they are seldom protracted. It is not unusual for a team of experienced operatives to descry the source of an outbreak in a couple of days. Some cases have been riddled in an afternoon. The root of the trouble on Washington Heights eluded detection for almost two weeks, and it is probable that but for Miss Gamso it would never have been detected at all.

5. "I got to Presbyterian around eleven," Dr. Fuerst told me. "I found a staff man I knew, and he led me up to the patients. It was typhoid, all right. Not that I'd doubted it, but it's routine to take a look. And they were in bad shape—too miserable to talk. One—the woman—was barely conscious. I decided to let the questioning go for the time being. At least until I'd seen their histories. A clerk in the office of the medical superintendent dug them out for me. Pretty skimpy—name, age, sex, occupation, and address, and a few clinical notations. About all I got at a glance was that they weren't members of the same family. I'd hoped, naturally, that they would be. That would have nicely limited the scope of the investigation. Then I noticed something interesting. They weren't a family, but they had

a little more in common than just typhoid. For one thing, they were by way of being neighbors. One of them lived at 502 West 180th Street, another at 501 West 178th Street, and the third at 285 Audubon Avenue, just around the corner from where it runs through the five-hundred block of West 179th Street. Another thing was their surnames. They were different, but they weren't dissimilar. All three were of Armenian origin. Well, Washington Heights has an Armenian colony—very small and very clannish. I began to feel pretty good. I didn't doubt for a minute that the three of them knew each other. Quite possibly they were friends. If so, it was reasonable to suppose that they might recently have shared a meal. It wasn't very likely, of course, that they had been the only ones to share it. Ten-year-old boys don't usually go out to meals without their parents. Maybe there had been a dozen in on it. It could even have been some sort of national feast. Or a church picnic. Picnic food is an ideal breeding ground for the typhoid organism. It can't stand cooking, but it thrives in raw stuff—ice cream and mayonnaise and so on. And if a carrier had happened to have a hand in the arrangements . . . I decided we'd do well to check and see if there was an Armenian carrier on our list."

6. "We found one, all right," Dr. Pellitteri said. "A widow named Christos—she died a year or two ago—who lived on West 178th Street."

7. "To be sure, we had only three cases," Dr. Fuerst went on. "But I didn't let that bother me. I've never known an outbreak of typhoid in which everybody who was exposed got sick. There are always a certain number who escape. They either don't eat whatever it is that's contaminated or they have a natural or an acquired immunity. Moreover, the incubation period in typhoid—the time it takes for the bug to catch hold—varies with the individual. Ten days is about the average, but it can run anywhere from three to thirty. In other words, maybe we had seen only the vanguard. There might be more to come. So in the absence of anything better, the Armenian link looked pretty good. I called the Bureau and told Bill Birnkrant—he was acting director at the time—what I thought, and he seemed to think the same. He said he'd start

somebody checking. I went back upstairs for another try at the patients."

8. "That's when the rest of us began to come into the picture," Dr. Pellitteri said. "My job was the recent social life of the Armenian colony. Ida Matthews, a public-health nurse, took the carrier angle. Neither of us had much luck. The file listed twelve carriers in Washington Heights. As I remember, the only Armenian was Mrs. Christos. At any rate, the nurse picked her first. I remember running into Miss Matthews somewhere on Audubon toward the end of that first afternoon. She told me what progress she had made. None. Mrs. Christos was old and sick, and hadn't been out of her apartment for a month. Miss Matthews said there was no reason to doubt the woman's word, as she had a good reputation at the Department—very coöperative, obeyed all the rules. Miss Matthews was feeling pretty gloomy. She'd had high hopes. Well, I knew how she felt. I'd hit nothing but dead ends myself. Our patients didn't seem to be friends. Apparently, they just knew each other. The priest at the Gregorian church in the neighborhood—Holy Cross Armenian Apostolic, on West 187th Street—knew of no recent feasts or festivals. He hadn't heard of any unusual amount of illness in the parish, either. No mysterious chills and fevers. And the Armenian doctors in the neighborhood said the same. They had seen nothing that resembled typhoid except the cases we already had. Before I gave up for the day, I even got in touch with an Armenian girl who used to work at the Department. The only thing I could think of at the moment was a check of the Armenian restaurants. When I mentioned that, she burst out laughing. It seems Armenians don't frequent Armenian restaurants. They prefer home cooking."

9. "I got Pellitteri's report the next morning," Dr. Fuerst said. "And Miss Matthews'." I was back at the hospital, and when I called Birnkrant, he gave me the gist of them. I can't say I was greatly surprised. To tell the truth, I was relieved. The Armenian picnic I'd hypothesized the day before would have created a real mess. Because the hospital had reported two new cases. Two women. They lived at 500 West 178th Street and 611 West 180th Street, but they weren't Armenians. One was Italian.

The other was plain American. So we were right back where we started. Only, now we had five cases instead of three, and nothing to tie them together but the fact that they all lived in the same neighborhood. And had the same brand of typhoid. There are around a dozen different strains, you know, which sometimes complicates matters. About the only thing Birnkrant and I could be sure of was that the feast theory—any kind of common gathering—was out. I'd had a word with the new patients. They had never even heard of each other. So the link had to be indirect. That gave us a number of possibilities. The source of infection could be water—either drinking water or a swimming pool. Or it could be commercial ice. Or milk. Or food. Drinking water was a job for Sanitary Engineering. The others, at the moment, were up to us—meaning Pellitteri and me. They were all four conceivable. Even ice. You can find a precedent for anything and everything in the literature on typhoid. But just one was probable. That was food. Some food that is sold already prepared—like potato salad or frozen custard—or one that is usually eaten raw. All we had to do was find out what it was, and where they got it, and how it got that way. Birnkrant and I figured out the area involved. It came to roughly four square blocks. I don't know if you know that part of Washington Heights. It's no prairie. Every building is a big apartment house, and the ground floors of most are stores. At least a fourth have something to do with food."

10. "I was in the office when Fuerst called," Dr. Pellitteri said. "Before he hung up, I got on the phone and we made the necessary arrangements about questioning the patients and their families—who was to see who. Then I took off. I wasn't too pessimistic. The odds were against a quick answer, but you never know. It was just possible that they all bought from the same store. Well, as it happened, they did. In a way. The trouble was it wasn't one store. It was practically all of them. Fuerst had the same experience. We ended up at the office that evening with a list as long as my arm—half a dozen fruit-and-vegetable stands, four or five groceries, a market that sold clams, and an assortment of ice-cream parlors and confectioneries and delicatessens. Moreover, we couldn't even be sure the list included the right store. Most people have very strange memories. They forget and they imagine. You've got to assume that most of the information they give you may be either incomplete or inaccurate, or both. But there *was* a right store—we knew that. Sanitary Engineering had eliminated drinking water, and we had been able to rule out swimming and milk and ice. Only one of the group ever went swimming, all but one family had electric refrigerators, and none of them had drunk unpasteurized milk. It had to be contaminated food from a store. That much was certain."

11. "It was also certain that we had to have some help," Dr. Fuerst said. "Pellitteri and I could have handled a couple of stores. Or even, at a pinch, three or four. But a dozen or more—it would take us weeks. Let me give you an idea what an investigation like that involves. You don't just walk in the store and gaze around. You more or less take it apart. Every item of food that could conceivably cause trouble is examined, the physical setup is inspected for possible violations of the Sanitary Code, and all employees and their families are interviewed and specimens taken for laboratory analysis. So we needed help, and, of course, we got it. Birnkrant had a conference with the Commissioner the next morning and they talked it over, and the result was an engineer and another nurse and a fine big team from Food and Drugs. Very gratifying."

12. "And Miss Matthews," Dr. Pellitteri said. "We had her back again. She had finally finished with her carriers. They were all like the first. None had violated any of the rules."

13. "As expected," Dr. Fuerst said. "The average carrier is pretty coöperative. Well, that was Saturday. By Monday, we had made a certain amount of progress. We hadn't found anything yet, but the field was narrowing down. And all of a sudden we got a little nibble. It came from a confectionery called Pop's, on 178th Street, around noon. Pop's had been well up on our list. They sold ice cream made on the premises, and the place was a neighborhood favorite. Which meant it got a very thorough going over. But we were about ready to cross it off—everything was in good shape, including the help—when it developed that the place had just changed hands. Pop

had sold out a week before, and he and his wife, who'd helped him run it, were on the way to California. Needless to say, Pop's went back on the list, and at the top. Also, somebody did some quick checking. Pop and his wife were driving, and their plan was to spend a few days with friends in Indianapolis. That gave us a chance. We called Birnkrant and he called Indianapolis—the State Health Department. They were extremely interested. Naturally. They said they'd let us know."

14. Dr. Fuerst lighted a cigarette. "Then we got a jolt," he said. "Several, in fact. The first was a call from the hospital. Four new cases. That brought the total up to nine. But it didn't stay there long. Tuesday night, it went to ten. I don't mind saying that set us back on our heels. Ten cases of typhoid fever in less than a week in one little corner of the city is almost unheard of in this day and age. The average annual incidence for the whole of Washington Heights is hardly half a case. That wasn't the worst of it, though. The real blow was that tenth case. I'll call him Jones. Jones didn't fit in. The four Monday cases, like the three Armenians and the Italian and the American, all lived in that one four-block area. Jones didn't. He lived on 176th Street, but way over west, almost on Riverside Drive. An entirely different neighborhood. I had a word with Jones the first thing Wednesday morning. I remember he worked for the post office. That's about all I learned. He hardly knew where he was. When I left the hospital, I called on his wife. She wasn't much help, either. She did all the family marketing, she told me, and she did it all within a block or two of home. That was that. She was very definite. On the other hand, there was Mr. Jones. He had typhoid, which doesn't just happen, and it was the same strain as all the rest. So either it was a very strange coincidence or she was too upset to think. My preference, until proved otherwise, was the latter. I found a phone, and called Birnkrant and gave him the latest news. He had some news for me. Indianapolis had called. They had located Pop and his wife and made the usual tests. The results were negative."

15. "I don't know which was the most discouraging," Dr. Pellitteri said. "Jones, I guess. He meant more work—a whole new string of stores to check. Pop had been ninety per cent hope. He merely aroused suspicion. He ran a popular place, he sold homemade ice cream, and when the epidemic broke, he pulled out. Or so it appeared from where we stood. It hurt to lose him. Unlikely or not, he had been a possibility—the first specific lead of any kind that we had been able to find in a week of mighty hard work. During the next few days, it began to look more and more like the last. Until Friday evening. Friday evening we got a very excited call from the laboratory. It was about a batch of specimens we had submitted that morning for analysis. One of them was positive for *E. typhosa*. The man's name doesn't matter. It didn't even then. What did matter was his occupation. He was the proprietor of a little frozen-custard shop—now extinct—that I'll call the Jupiter. The location was interesting, too. It was a trifle outside our area, but still accessible, and a nice, easy walk from the Joneses'. Food and Drugs put an embargo on the Jupiter that night. The next morning, we began to take it apart."

16. "I missed that," Dr. Fuerst said. "I spent Saturday at the hospital. It was quite a day. We averaged a case an hour. I'm not exaggerating. When I finally left, the count was nine. Nine brand-new cases. A couple of hours later, one more turned up. That made twenty, all told. Fortunately, that was the end. Twenty was the grand total. But, of course, we didn't know that then. There was no reason to believe they wouldn't just keep coming."

17. "The rest of us had the same kind of day," Dr. Pellitteri said. "Very disagreeable. There was the owner of the Jupiter—poor devil. You can imagine the state he was in. All of a sudden, he was out of business and a public menace. He didn't even know what a typhoid carrier was. He had to be calmed down and instructed. That was the beginning. It got worse. First of all, the Jupiter was as clean as a whistle. We closed it up—had to, under the circumstances—and embargoed the stock, but we didn't find anything. That was peculiar. I can't explain it even now. He was either just naturally careful or lucky. While that was going on, we went back to the patients and questioned them again. Did they know the Jupiter? Were they customers? Did they ever buy anything there? We got one yes.

The rest said no. Emphatically. If there had been a few more yeses—even three or four—we might have wondered. But they couldn't all be mistaken. So the Jupiter lead began to look pretty wobbly. Then the laboratory finished it off. They had a type report on the Jupiter organism. It wasn't the *E. typhosa* we were looking for. It was one of the other strains. That may have been some consolation to Mr. Jupiter. At least, he didn't have an epidemic on his conscience. But it left us uncomfortably close to the end of our rope. We had only a handful of stores still to check. If we didn't find the answer there, we were stumped. We didn't. We crossed off the last possibility on Tuesday morning, August 27th. It was Number Eighty. We'd examined eighty stores and something like a thousand people, and all we had to show for it was a new carrier."

18. "Well, that was something," Dr. Fuerst said. "Even if it was beside the point. But we also had another consolation. None of the patients had died. None was going to. They were all making excellent progress."

19. "That's true enough," Dr. Pellitteri said. "But we couldn't claim much credit for that." He paused, and shifted around in his chair. "About all we can take any credit for is Miss Gamso, here." He smiled. "Miss Gamso saved the day. She got inspired."

20. Miss Gamso gave me a placid look. "I don't know about inspired," she said. "It was more like annoyed. I heard them talking—Dr. Birnkrant, and these two, and all the rest of them—and I read the reports, and the days went by and they didn't seem to be getting anywhere. That's unusual. So it was irritating. It's hard to explain, but I got to thinking about that carrier Mrs. Christos. There were two things about her. She lived with a son-in-law who was a known food handler. He was a baker by trade. Also, where she lived was right in the middle of everything—519 West 178th Street. That's just off Audubon. And Audubon is the street where practically all our cases did most of their shopping. Well, there was one store in particular—a fruit-and-vegetable market called Tony's—on almost everybody's list. The address was 261 Audubon Avenue. Then I really got a brainstorm. It was right after lunch on Tuesday, August 27th. I picked up the telephone and called the bureau that

registers house numbers at the Borough President's office, and I asked them one question. Did 519 West 178th Street and 261 Audubon Avenue happen by any chance to be the same building? They asked me why I wanted to know. I wasn't talking, though. I just said was it, in a nice way, and the man finally said he'd see. When he came back, I was right. They were one and the same. I was so excited I thought I'd burst. Dr. Pellitteri was sitting right where he is now. He was the first person I saw, so I marched straight over and told him. He kind of stared at me. He had the funniest expression." Miss Gamso smiled a gentle smile. "I think he thought I'd gone crazy."

21. "I wouldn't say that," Dr. Pellitteri said. "I'll admit, however, that I didn't quite see the connection. We'd been all over Tony's—it was almost our first stop—and there was no earthly reason to question Miss Matthews' report on Mrs. Christos. The fact that they occupied the same building was news to me. To all of us, as I recall. But what if they did? Miss Gamso thought it was significant or suspicious or something. The point escaped me. When she mentioned the son-in-law, though, I began to get a little more interested. We knew him, of course—anybody who lives with a carrier is a potential cause of trouble—and checked on him regularly. But it was just possible that since our last checkup he had become infected. That happens. And although we hadn't found him working in any of the stores, he could have come and gone a couple of weeks before we started our investigation. At any rate, it was worth looking into. Almost anything was, by then. I went up that afternoon. I walked past Tony's on the way to 519. There wasn't any doubt about their being in the same building. Tony's is gone now, like Mrs. Christos, but the way it was then, his front door was about three steps from the corner, and around the corner about three more steps was the entrance to the apartments above. The Christos flat was on the fifth floor—Apartment 53. Mrs. Christos and her son-in-law were both at home. They let me in and that's about all. I can't say they were either one delighted to see me. Or very helpful. She couldn't add anything to what she had already told Miss Matthews. The son-in-law hardly opened his mouth. His last regular job, he said, had been

in January, in a cafeteria over in Astoria. Since then, he'd done nothing but odd jobs. He wouldn't say what, when, or where. I couldn't completely blame him. He was afraid that if we got to questioning any of his former employers, they'd never take him on again. When I saw how it was, I arranged for a specimen and, for the moment, let it go at that. There was no point in getting rough until we knew for sure. I told him to sit tight. If he was positive, I'd be back in a hurry. I got the report the next day. He wasn't. He was as harmless as I am. But by then it didn't matter. By that time, it was all over. To tell the truth, I had the answer before I ever left the building."

22. Dr. Pellitteri shook his head. "I walked right into it," he said. "It was mostly pure luck. What happened was this. On the way out, I ran into the superintendent—an elderly woman. I was feeling two ways about the son-in-law—half sympathetic and half suspicious. It occurred to me that the superintendent might have some idea where he'd been working the past few weeks. So I stopped and asked. She was a sour old girl. She didn't know and didn't care. She had her own troubles. They were the tenants, mainly. She backed me into a corner and proceeded to unload. The children were the worst, she said—especially the boys. Always thinking up some new devilment. For example, she said, just a few weeks ago, toward the end of July, there was a gang of them up on the roof playing wild Indians. Before she could chase them off, they'd stuffed some sticks down one of the plumbing vent pipes. The result was a stoppage. The soil pipe serving one whole tier of apartments blocked and sprang a leak, and the bathroom of the bottom apartment was a nice mess. I hadn't been paying much attention until then. But at that point— Well, to put it mildly, I was fascinated. Also, I began to ask some questions. I wanted to know just what bathroom had flooded. The answer was Apartment 23. What were the other apartments in that tier? They were 33, 43, and 53. What was underneath Apartment 23? A store—Tony's Market, on the corner. Then I asked for a telephone. Birnkrant's reaction was about what you'd expect. Pretty soon, a team from Sanitary Engineering arrived. They supplied the details and the proof. Tony stored his fruits and vegetables in a big wooden walk-in refrigerator at the rear of his store. When Sanitary Engineering pulled off the top, they found the soil pipe straight overhead. The leak had been repaired almost a month before, but the sawdust insulation in the refrigerator roof was still damp from the waste that had soaked through. It wasn't Tony's fault. He hadn't known. It wasn't anybody's fault. It was just one of those things. So that was that."

23. "Not entirely," Dr. Fuerst said. "There was still Jones to account for. It wasn't necessary. The thing was settled. But I was curious. I had a talk with him the next day. We talked and talked. And in the end, he remembered. He was a night walker. Every evening after dinner, he went out for a walk. He walked all over Washington Heights, and usually, somewhere along the line, he stopped and bought something to eat. It was generally a piece of fruit. As I say, he finally remembered. One night, near the end of July, he was walking down Audubon and he came to a fruit stand and he bought an apple. On the way home, he ate it."

JOHN M. CONLY *Toscanini Records the Ninth*

John M. Conly (1913-   ), who studied at the University of Rochester and Columbia University with the intention of becoming a history teacher, is now editor of *High Fidelity*, a magazine for music listeners, and music columnist for the *Atlantic Monthly*.

As one of eight listeners privileged to be present in Carnegie Hall while Toscanini was recording Beethoven's Ninth Symphony, Mr. Conly eloquently describes what the exacting performance meant to the conductor, the musicians, and the technicians. Moreover, he presents a dramatic portrait of the personality of the octogenarian conductor.

I

1. On March 31, 1952, something happened for which music lovers around the world had been waiting, none too patiently, for a quarter century. Arturo Toscanini, eighty-five years and six days old, walked into Carnegie Hall to put on RCA Victor records his incandescent interpretation of Beethoven's Ninth Symphony.

2. Patently he had rededicated himself all anew to the score, after fifty years' acquaintance with it. Each note sounded as if it might have been written the day before. As he played, there grew in the minds of his listeners the inescapable conviction that they never really had heard the symphony until now. Quite possibly they hadn't; quite possibly nobody had.

3. Ludwig van Beethoven started work on the Ninth in 1817, his forty-seventh year. His deafness was approaching totality. He lived in utter, self-imposed loneliness and in untended squalor. His music was earning ever decreasing understanding and popularity. To undertake six years of labor on the most ambitious work he ever had planned, he had no possible motive but one. This was enough: it was the unshakable conviction (correct, of course) that

the world of the future would take his music to its heart.

4. This conviction has mystified some of his biographers, but needlessly. Beethoven well knew his own achievements. Beginning in 1805, with the *Eroica* symphony, he had released into the world what almost amounted to a new language. Wordless but potent, infinitely flexible, it reached directly to the core of noble drama deep in every human mind. For fifty minutes, the listener to the *Eroica* symphony *is* the hero in surging combat, *is* the mourning public, *is* the sane rebuilder in a civilization set free. Beethoven in his own time had seen the idiom take root. In later days it would dominate all Western instrumental music, from the Brahms First to the film score for *Walk East on Beacon*.

5. Unappreciated, Beethoven was cut off from his own time. But he knew the idiom as the future would understand it. He went to work for the future, showing in the process how terribly he had needed the language he launched; he had such a great deal to say. There was only one thing he had not foreseen.

6. For at least half the century and a quarter after his death, Western civilization was to be dominated by a philosophy which valued tangibility and describability to the exclusion of all other qualities. Music's function was to amuse, to titillate, and nothing more. Music with pretensions beyond this was regarded

with actual hostility, particularly in the English-speaking portions of the world. This is not to say that such music was not performed. It was, but largely by and for a sort of oppressed minority of aesthetes. Many of these, it must be suspected, were vessels too frail to contain the enormous emotions of the Ninth Symphony. For here the deaf and tortured Beethoven had dug to the most painful deeps of his own soul, past the terror of death and the shadow of meaninglessness, to deal as best he could with the biggest question he knew—what it means to be a human being, what it takes to be a good one.

7. To perform his essential part in this great communication, Toscanini arrived a little before two o'clock, Monday, March 31, at the stage entrance to Carnegie Hall. He was accompanied by his son and manager, Walter Toscanini, and driven in a black custom Cadillac (New York license 10-T-1) by Luigi Gaddoni, chauffeur and general factotum to the Toscanini household. It was a fine, crisp spring afternoon.

8. The other 191 parties to the venture had preceded him. At ten in the morning, in an RCA panel truck, came Henry Richel, a genial ex-Viennese, and Ray Hall, a powerful, soft-spoken young Negro, escorting the specially designed tape recorders which they were to operate for the session's nine tense hours. Next to appear was Lewis Layton, a Victor recording technician for twenty-six years, to install the mixing amplifier and the microphones which would feed it music. The heavy equipment had to be lugged up a narrow flight of stairs to the monitor room, a cubicle above and to the left of the stage. For utmost clarity, which Toscanini demands, two very sensitive microphones, of an all-directional variety, were mounted over the stage itself. To supply balance and perspective, these were supported by three velocity, or ribbon-type, microphones hung in wedge formation back in the empty hall. When all the equipment was in order, Albert Pulley, RCA Victor's chief recording engineer, joined his crew and double-checked everything. Pulley is a quiet, gray-haired man whose twenty-five years with Victor (fourteen in his present job) have given him an imperturbability which verges on the supernatural, and which he frequently needs.

9. Next to show up, after lunchtime, were Richard Mohr, RCA Victor's Red Seal (classical) artist-and-repertory manager, and his assistant, Jack Pfeiffer. Both are urbane, scholarly young men whom Mohr describes as frustrated musicians. Normally only one of them attends a session, but the Ninth was something special. Both wore horn-rimmed spectacles and bore scores, which they laid on the table beside Layton's amplifier with its VU (volume unit) meter and the monitor loud-speaker through which they would follow the performance. Toscanini is fanatically insistent that every instrument be heard in its part; if any passage is in doubt, it is best that he be warned at once—otherwise his irreversible veto may come down on the whole recording later.

10. The musicians, when they arrived, were gayer than the technical staff, partly because they had been through all this two days earlier, when Toscanini had broadcast the Ninth over the NBC network. They might have been less gay had they known he had gone home thereafter fuming with dissatisfaction and had refused even to listen to the tapes of the broadcast, but they didn't. The hundred men of the NBC Symphony Orchestra, reinforced by two extra horns and extra stands of strings in each section, tossed their coats into the front row seats and tuned up. The eighty singers of the RCA Victor Chorale listened to last-minute directions from their leader, young Robert Shaw, who always manages to look like a very large, worried, very bright child. The four vocal soloists, who were to join the chorus in the finale, based on Schiller's *Hymn to Joy*, came in last, looking fit but apprehensive. They were Eileen Farrell, soprano, Nan Merriman, contralto, Jan Peerce, tenor, and Norman Scott, bass. No singer is ever confident about the Ninth. Beethoven had long been deaf when he wrote it, and apparently had forgotten the limitations of the human voice. At best it is a twenty-minute ordeal. With Toscanini on the podium, it can be a full hour of absolute torture. Only the veteran Peerce had the nerve to wisecrack: "Who's afraid of *him?*" looking over his shoulder in mock panic.

11. Toscanini mounted the steps (five) into the hall and the stairs (thirteen) to his dressing room. He is extremely myopic; to judge from

the way he looks at his watch, his clear vision must extend all of three inches beyond his nose. However, he detests wearing glasses and he is gifted with a fantastic memory. He has memorized every set of stairs he uses—as well as every score he has conducted, and a few he hasn't—and he doesn't like to be helped. He walks alone. This, together with the fact that he has a bad knee, the result of an accident two years ago, adds a unique dramatic quality to his presence anywhere. Each time he walks down a stairs (he also avoids handrails) the suspense is almost intolerable.

"Orchestra ready," came Dick Mohr's very businesslike voice from the loud-speaker on the stage wall, "Maestro coming down."

II

12. Toscanini is barely over five feet tall, though his head is large and leonine; and he looks even smaller in his working clothes, which consist of a black alpaca jacket, buttoned to the neck, gray striped trousers, and black, elastic-sided Italian shoes. Just the same, and any of the eight onlookers in Carnegie that day can attest this, the whole huge, dim auditorium seemed to tingle with almost physical tension when he walked on the stage. Nor did the feeling abate when the music began. Toscanini first conducted the Ninth in Milan almost exactly fifty years earlier, and he had played it many times since. Once, when he was a mere eighty-one, he had said, "I think that is the best I can do." Now, from the first baton stroke onward, he was proving beyond doubt that he could do better.

13. As Toscanini recording sessions go, both Pulley and Mohr contend, this was not a tough one, considering the difficulty and importance of the music. Nevertheless, when it was done, more than three hours of music had been put on tape. The symphony itself, at Toscanini's tempi, lasts about an hour and five minutes. Thus, on the average, he had recorded each portion three times. The entire job took nine hours. It had been scheduled for seven, in two sessions, but Toscanini ran over and required a two-hour session Tuesday night.

14. He began with the last movement, so that the chorus, recruited to double strength for the broadcast and the recording, might be done with and disband. Once, running through the orchestral introduction, he displayed an interesting device. Toscanini is not, as Beethoven was not, a man of words. In a pregnant passage, wherein the low-voiced strings invoke the theme of the final hymn to joy, he could not get the proper accent from the bass fiddles. He did not attempt to explain what he wanted. He had the cellos play their part alone, while he, in a series of stentorian grunts, illustrated what he wanted from the basses. The next playing, they gave it to him. The following morning he performed the same service for the finale of the first movement. In that instance, the whole string section soloed in a fateful, swelling undercurrent while Arturo Toscanini impersonated the brasses and tympani, shouting and stamping out the notes with a volume almost alarming from a man so small and so old. The hall echoed nobly.

15. There was seldom any doubt about who, on the stage, was working the hardest. The recording was made in "takes," each seven to eight minutes long, partly to fit 45 rpm record sides. Often a take would be played back. The orchestra would rest, but Toscanini would conduct all over again, measuring his intent against what came out of the loudspeaker. He was patient. Occasionally he asked the men to "play musically, musically, not stupidly." But there were no tantrums—not even when the triangle player came in a bar too soon, nor when Jan Peerce unaccountably blew his lines. He spared no one, however. Just before the final choral variation, there is a long, sublime, but terribly taxing round for vocal quartet. He put the soloists through it eight times running. In the last two attempts, Miss Farrell's voice simply died. Toscanini finally let them go, and the chorus cheered them as they left.

16. In the half-hour breaks, Toscanini trudged up to his dressing room, took off his steaming jacket, and donned a terry-cloth robe. He drank a little fruit juice or chewed Italian licorice drops. At the very last break, at ten-thirty Tuesday night, he didn't even bother to go up. He stood on the podium, passing out licorice drops and reminiscences to his fiddlers, who crowded fondly around. Walter Toscanini looked down at the stage

through the control-room window and said softly, "Where do you get all that energy, old fellow?" Everyone upstairs was on the verge of exhaustion. It was at that juncture that Toscanini, having made the fourth, first, second, and third movements in triplicate, decided to make the finale of the first movement once more, just to be on the safe side. Then he repeated the first two takes of the fourth.

17. Finally he called it a day, cheerily bade his players good night, and mounted to his dressing room for a glass of champagne. When Gaddoni drove him away it was nearly midnight, and he felt fine.

III

18. What makes this not less amazing is that, between September 28 and March 31, in addition to a full schedule of weekly broadcasts, Toscanini had played twenty recording dates. Among the works taped were five Beethoven symphonies, the First (which will be paired on LP with the Ninth, filling out the fourth record side), Second, Fourth, Sixth, and Seventh; the Brahms First, Second, and Fourth; Wagnerian selections including the *Liebestod* and *Lohengrin* preludes, and works by Donizetti, Weber, Prokofiev, Elgar (the *Enigma* Variations), Respighi, Franck, Cherubini, and Richard Strauss. Not all have the Maestro's approval for release, which is not easily come by. In the past, Toscanini was not, to put it mildly, well disposed toward records as a musical medium. That this is no longer the case can be credited in no small part to the unstinting, if unsung, efforts of Walter Toscanini.

19. Walter Toscanini is a middle-sized, graying man with a quick wit, who used to be good at soccer, book publishing, and bibliography. More recently he has become good at photography, artist management, and audio engineering. He is an unspecialized intellectual of a type too rarely found: he has not the slightest trepidation about tackling technical problems. With all this, he is also very much like a man who has been given, ready or not, the custody of the Holy Grail, and he bears his responsibility very well.

20. It occurred to him, some time ago, that the Maestro might release recordings more readily if he could hear them better; so he acquired a high-powered tuner-amplifier and a variety of handsomely cabineted loudspeakers. However, the latter had been designed for ordinary living rooms, not for the baronial hall, at least fifty feet square and nearly as high, in the Toscanini home near Riverdale, New York. The Maestro likes to hear his music as he hears it on the podium, not remote. Walter experimented tirelessly. At one time he had sixteen public-address speakers, mounted in four corner cabinets, going at once. At that point, fortunately, he became friends with David Sarser, a young violinist in the NBC Symphony who is also known to all high-fidelity enthusiasts as co-inventor of the Musician's Amplifier, the *ne plus ultra* of fine home-music equipment.

21. Sarser became almost a fixture at the Villa Paulina, the Toscanini house, and at once its other fixtures began to multiply as only high-fidelity equipment can. Now the corner of the Maestro's hall is graced by an Altec Lansing 820-A system, an awesome combination of two huge bass cones and a theater-type treble horn. In the Maestro's studio upstairs, the sanctum sanctorum of musical America, is a smaller, coaxial Altec speaker in a cabinet specially designed by William Shrader, Washington audio engineer, incorporating a spiral, bass-boosting exponential horn. In the basement, where Walter has converted a quasi-Byzantine billiard room into a sound laboratory, are a magnificent Ampex console tape recorder, several Sarser amplifiers, monitor speakers, and three precision turntables, with Audak and General Electric phono pickups.

22. Toscanini is very proud of his equipment and, without doubt, it has softened him on the whole subject of recording. When Jack Pfeiffer went to Riverdale with test tapes of the Ninth, a few days after the session, the Maestro kept him five hours listening, but readily gave an okay to two movements, pieced from various takes. Mohr went up later with the rest, and Toscanini was more than merely tolerant. Hearing the adagio movement, he wept briefly, at Beethoven's vision, and said: "It is so beautiful . . . like the Twenty-first Canto of Dante . . . where all is flowers and light, light, light!"

23. Of course, not all was flowers and light, even after that. Toscanini has learned to distrust recording procedure from beginning to end, and is never absolutely satisfied with his own judgment. For nearly a month, before the Maestro went vacationing to Italy, Walter labored in his electronic dungeon, playing tape after tape to satisfy his father's doubts. Walter ruefully claims to be a self-made masochist. He works always in the hope that any fault the Maestro finds will be blamed on him or his cherished equipment, not on the performance or the recording. When the Maestro came back, there were test disk-pressings and more hazards. He has a fine sense of pitch and a phenomenal sense of tempo. A test disk played at $33\frac{4}{9}$ revolutions per minute, instead of $33\frac{1}{3}$, will send him raging to the piano to prove that it is off key. Fortunately, Walter recently got a variable-speed turntable, able to compensate for such variations.

24. This Ninth, judged as a recording from the test pressings, is very good—certainly by far the best cutting of the work made yet. Like all Toscanini recordings, it features crystalline clarity; there is no attempt at mellowness. This is not the work of engineers; Toscanini actually makes the orchestra sound that way in the concert hall. It is wide in tonal range; according to Albert Pulley it encompasses from 30 to 13,000 cycles per second. Every instrument is heard, but in good perspective. The treatment is ideal for the Ninth, wherein the whole dramatic impact is contained in the structure and dynamics of the music. The last movement, employing the chorus, seems to be recorded at a slightly lower level than the others in the long-playing version, possibly to economize on groove room and allow it to fit on one record side. This is a minor matter, easily corrected by a twist of the volume control.

25. Why, after fifty years of playing the Ninth but refusing to record it, Toscanini elected to make it this year is anyone's guess. Dick Mohr says, "We asked him to," but he had been asked before. At any rate, he acquiesced. A month before the recording date, he dug out scores of the symphony and spent hours with them at the piano. He asked Walter to play recordings of it—not only transcriptions of his own performances, but interpretations by Bruno Walter, Stokowski, Weingartner, and Ormandy. He listened while, over his head, from the balcony at the sunny end of the hall, his forty-three canaries twittered in their cages.

26. There may be some bearing in what he said to a friend several years ago, as reported by Howard Taubman in his biography, *The Maestro* (Simon and Schuster, 1951): "The Ninth is difficult. Sometimes the chorus is not good. The soloists are seldom good. Sometimes the orchestra is not good. Sometimes I am no good. You know, I still don't understand the first movement." On Monday and Tuesday, March 31 and April 1, nearly everyone was good, but particularly the conductor. And at eleven o'clock Tuesday morning he put down his baton and told his orchestra: "I think we know now how the first movement goes."

27. How it goes, it would be idle to try to tell in words, except to liken it to a bombshell, or to quote sundry sample listeners, whose invariant reaction was: "That is the greatest piece of music ever written." It can be said, however, that at last the giant symphony really hangs together, from its first ominous note to its last massed cry for human brotherhood.

28. Toscanini would not like to have this called Toscanini's Beethoven Ninth. He considers such proprietorial terminology presumptuous, but he needn't worry. For some time hence, this is going to be called *the* Beethoven Ninth.

MAURICE HERZOG *Annapurna—The Third of June*

Maurice Herzog (1919-   ), industrial engineer and mountain climber, was born in Lyons, France, of a family devoted to mountain climbing. Following his education at the University of Lyons and the University of Paris, he was employed as an industrial engineer for a French associate of the B. F. Goodrich Company. During World War II he served three years in the artillery before transferring to the Alpine Corps. For his war service he was awarded the *Croix de guerre*.

In 1950 Herzog led a team of French mountain climbers on an assault upon Annapurna, a 26,493-foot mountain of the Himalayan chain in Central Nepal. The expedition proceeded in three stages: first, locating and exploring the approaches to Annapurna (since this particular mountain had never been climbed and little was known about it); second, the assault on the summit, as reported in the article that follows; and third, the hazardous, near-tragic downward retreat.

The difficulties the climbers had in attaining the summit, great as they were, do not compare with those which followed the successful climb. Herzog and his companion Lachenal suffered frozen feet which became gangrenous. They had to endure amputations under most primitive conditions on the frozen slopes of the mountain. Both men had to be carried down the steep mountainside on the backs of their comrades, in one instance by men who were themselves suffering from snow-blindness. As a result of losing his gloves, Herzog's hands were frozen and he lost most of his fingers. The fact that Herzog and Lachenal finally reached the bottom alive is a tribute to their tenacity and the courageous loyalty of their comrades. In 1952 Herzog, who had been depressed because he had believed that he would never again experience the exhilaration of mountain climbing, proved his indomitable will by climbing the Matterhorn in spite of being crippled.

Why do men climb mountains? Herzog says:

"Perhaps it is pride that makes men risk their lives to conquer the mountains; perhaps it is extreme curiosity, the compulsion to know all, to have touched everything. Perhaps in their efforts the mountaineers represent mankind, which has increased its power over nature for centuries but which has a feeling of uncertainty and uneasiness, so long as this point on the roof of the world flaunts its independence."

The complete account of the French Himalayan expedition is recounted in Herzog's book *Annapurna*, 1952.

On the third of June, 1950, the first light of dawn found us still clinging to the tent poles at Camp V. Gradually the wind abated, and with daylight, died away altogether. I made desperate attempts to push back the soft, icy stuff which stifled me, but every moment became an act of heroism. My mental powers were numbed: thinking was an effort, and we did not exchange a single word.

What a repellent place it was! To everyone who reached it, Camp V became one of the worst memories of their lives. We had only one thought—to get away. We should have waited for the first rays of the sun, but at half-past five we felt we couldn't stick it any longer.

"Let's go, Biscante," I muttered. "Can't stay here a minute longer."

"Yes, let's go," repeated Lachenal.

Which of us would have the energy to make tea? Although our minds worked slowly we were quite able to envisage all the movements that would be necessary—and neither of us could face up to it. It couldn't be helped—we would just have to go without. It was quite hard enough work to get ourselves and our boots out of our sleeping-bags—and the boots were frozen stiff so that we got them on only with the greatest difficulty. Every movement made us terribly breathless. We felt as if we were being stifled. Our gaiters were stiff as a board, and I succeeded in lacing mine up; Lachenal couldn't manage his.

"No need for the rope, eh, Biscante?"

"No need," replied Lachenal laconically.

That was two pounds saved. I pushed a tube of condensed milk, some nougat and a pair of socks into my sack; one never knew, the socks might come in useful—they might even do as Balaclavas. For the time being I stuffed them with first-aid equipment. The camera was loaded with a black and white film; I had a color film in reserve. I pulled the movie-camera out from the bottom of my sleeping-bag, wound it up and tried letting it run without film. There was a little click, then it stopped and jammed.

"Bad luck after bringing it so far," said Lachenal.

In spite of our photographer Ichac's precautions taken to lubricate it with special grease, the intense cold, even inside the sleep-

ing-bag, had frozen it. I left it at the camp rather sadly: I had looked forward to taking it to the top. I had used it up to 24,600 feet.

We went outside and put on our crampons, which we kept on all day. We wore as many clothes as possible; our sacks were very light. At six o'clock we started off. It was brilliantly fine, but also very cold. Our super-lightweight crampons bit deep into the steep slopes of ice and hard snow up which lay the first stage of our climb.

Later the slope became slightly less steep and more uniform. Sometimes the hard crust bore our weight, but at others we broke through and sank into soft powder snow which made progress exhausting. We took turns in making the track and often stopped without any word having passed between us. Each of us lived in a closed and private world of his own. I was suspicious of my mental processes; my mind was working very slowly and I was perfectly aware of the low state of my intelligence. It was easiest just to stick to one thought at a time—safest, too. The cold was penetrating; for all our special eiderdown clothing we felt as if we'd nothing on. Whenever we halted, we stamped our feet hard. Lachenal went as far as to take off one boot which was a bit tight; he was in terror of frostbite.

"I don't want to be like Lambert," he said. Raymond Lambert, a Geneva guide, had to have all his toes amputated after an eventful climb during which he got his feet frostbitten.[1] While Lachenal rubbed himself hard, I looked at the summits all around us; already we overtopped them all except the distant Dhaulagiri. The complicated structure of these mountains, with which our many laborious explorations had made us familiar, was now spread out plainly at our feet.

The going was incredibly exhausting, and every step was a struggle of mind over matter. We came out into the sunlight, and by way of marking the occasion made yet another halt. Lachenal continued to complain of his feet. "I can't feel anything. I think I'm beginning to get frostbite." And once again he undid his boot.

[1] In May 1952 Lambert, with the Sherpa Ang-Tsering, reached 28,215 feet on Mount Everest, possibly the highest point yet attained. (Translators' note.)

I began to be seriously worried. I realized very well the risk we were running; I knew from experience how insidiously and quickly frostbite can set in if one is not extremely careful. Nor was Lachenal under any illusions. "We're in danger of having frozen feet. Do you think it's worth it?"

This was most disturbing. It was my responsibility as leader to think of the others. There was no doubt about frostbite being a very real danger. Did Annapurna justify such risks? That was the question I asked myself; it continued to worry me.

Lachenal had laced his boots up again, and once more we continued to force our way through the exhausting snow. The whole of the Sickle glacier was now in view, bathed in light. We still had a long way to go to cross it, and then there was that rock band—would we find a gap in it?

My feet, like Lachenal's, were very cold and I continued to wriggle my toes, even when we were moving. I could not feel them, but that was nothing new in the mountains, and if I kept on moving them it would keep the circulation going.

Lachenal appeared to me as a sort of specter —he was alone in his world, I in mine. But— and this was odd enough—any effort was slightly *less* exhausting than lower down. Perhaps it was hope lending us wings. Even through dark glasses the snow was blinding— the sun beating straight down on the ice. We looked down upon precipitous ridges which dropped away into space, and upon tiny glaciers far, far below. Familiar peaks soared arrow-like into the sky. Suddenly Lachenal grabbed me:

"If I go back, what will you do?"

A whole sequence of pictures flashed through my head: the days of marching in sweltering heat, the hard pitches we had overcome, the tremendous efforts we had all made to lay siege to the mountain, the daily heroism of all my friends in establishing the camps. Now we were nearing our goal. In an hour or two, perhaps, victory would be ours. Must we give up? Impossible! My whole being revolted against the idea. I had made up my mind, irrevocably. Today we were consecrating an ideal, and no sacrifice was too great. I heard my voice clearly:

"I should go on by myself."

I would go alone. If he wished to go down it was not for me to stop him. He must make his own choice freely.

"Then I'll follow you."

The die was cast. I was no longer anxious. Nothing could stop us now from getting to the top. The psychological atmosphere changed with these few words, and we went forward now as brothers.

I felt as though I were plunging into something new and quite abnormal. I had the strangest and most vivid impressions, such as I had never before known in the mountains. There was something unnatural in the way I saw Lachenal and everything around us. I smiled to myself at the paltriness of our efforts, for I could stand apart and watch myself making these efforts. But all sense of exertion was gone, as though there were no longer any gravity. This diaphanous landscape, this quintessence of purity—these were not the mountains I knew: they were the mountains of my dreams.

The snow, sprinkled over every rock and gleaming in the sun, was of a radiant beauty that touched me to the heart. I had never seen such complete transparency, and I was living in a world of crystal. Sounds were indistinct, the atmosphere like cotton wool.

An astonishing happiness welled up in me, but I could not define it. Everything was so new, so utterly unprecedented. It was not in the least like anything I had known in the Alps, where one feels buoyed up by the presence of others—by people of whom one is vaguely aware, or even by the dwellings one can see in the far distance.

This was quite different. An enormous gulf was between me and the world. This was a different universe—withered, desert, lifeless; a fantastic universe where the presence of man was not foreseen, perhaps not desired. We were braving an interdict, overstepping a boundary, and yet we had no fear as we continued upward. I thought of the famous ladder of St. Theresa of Avila. Something clutched at my heart.

Did Lachenal share these feelings? The summit ridge drew nearer, and we reached the foot of the ultimate rock band. The slope was very steep and the snow interspersed with rocks.

"Couloir!"

A finger pointed. The whispered word from one to another indicated the key to the rocks—the last line of defense.

"What luck!"

The couloir up the rocks though steep was feasible.

The sky was a deep sapphire blue. With a great effort we edged over to the right, avoiding the rocks; we preferred to keep to the snow on account of our crampons and it was not long before we set foot in the couloir. It was fairly steep, and we had a minute's hesitation. Should we have enough strength left to overcome this final obstacle?

Fortunately the snow was hard, and by kicking steps we were able to manage, thanks to our crampons. A false move would have been fatal. There was no need to make handholds—our axes, driven in as far as possible, served us for an anchor.

Lachenal went splendidly. What a wonderful contrast to the early days! It was a hard struggle here, but he kept going. Lifting our eyes occasionally from the slope, we saw the couloir opening out on to . . . well, we didn't quite know, probably a ridge. But where was the top—left or right? Stopping at every step, leaning on our axes we tried to recover our breath and to calm down our racing hearts, which were thumping as though they would burst. We knew we were there now—that nothing could stop us. No need to exchange looks—each of us would have read the same determination in the other's eyes. A slight détour to the left, a few rocks to avoid. We dragged ourselves up. Could we possibly be there?

Yes!

A fierce and savage wind tore at us.

We were on top of Annapurna! 8,075 meters, 26,493 feet.

Our hearts overflowed with an unspeakable happiness.

"If only the others could know . . ."

If only everyone could know!

The summit was a corniced crest of ice, and the precipices on the far side which plunged vertically down beneath us were terrifying, unfathomable. There could be few other mountains in the world like this. Clouds floated halfway down, concealing the gentle, fertile valley of Pokhara, 23,000 feet below. Above us there was nothing!

Our mission was accomplished. But at the same time we had accomplished something infinitely greater. How wonderful life would now become! What an inconceivable experience it is to attain one's ideal and, at the very same moment, to fulfill oneself. I was stirred to the depths of my being. Never had I felt happiness like this—so intense and yet so pure. That brown rock, the highest of them all, that ridge of ice—were these the goals of a lifetime? Or were they rather, the limits of man's pride?

"Well, what about going down?"

Lachenal shook me. What were his own feelings? Did he simply think he had finished another climb, as in the Alps? Did he think one could just go down again like that, with nothing more to it?

"One minute, I must take some photographs."

"Hurry up!"

I fumbled feverishly in my sack, pulled out the camera, took out the little French flag which was right at the bottom, and the pennants. Useless gestures, no doubt, but something more than symbols—eloquent tokens of affection and goodwill. I tied the strips of material—stained by sweat and by the food in the sacks—to the shaft of my ice-axe, the only flagstaff at hand. Then I focused my camera on Lachenal.

"Now, will you take me?"

"Hand it over—hurry up!" said Lachenal.

He took several pictures and then handed me back the camera. I loaded a color film and we repeated the process to be certain of bringing back records to be cherished in the future.

"Are you mad?" asked Lachenal. "We haven't a minute to lose: we must go down at once."

And in fact a glance round showed me that the weather was no longer gloriously fine as it had been in the morning. Lachenal was becoming impatient.

"We must go down!"

He was right. His was the reaction of the mountaineer who knows his own domain. But I just could not accustom myself to the idea that we had won our victory. It seemed inconceivable that we should have trodden those summit snows.

It was impossible to build a cairn; there were no stones; everything was frozen. Lachenal stamped his feet; he felt them freezing. I felt mine freezing too, but paid little attention. The highest mountain to be climbed by man lay under our feet! The names of our predecessors on these heights raced through my mind: Mummery, Mallory and Irvine, Bauer, Welzenbach, Tilman, Shipton. How many of them were dead—how many had found on these mountains what, to them, was the finest end of all?

My joy was touched with humility. It was not just one party that had climbed Annapurna today, but a whole expedition. I thought of all the others in the camps perched on the slopes at our feet, and I knew it was because of their efforts and their sacrifices that we had succeeded. There are times when the most complicated actions are suddenly summed up, distilled, and strike you with illuminating clarity: so it was with this irresistible upward surge which had landed us two here.

Pictures passed through my mind—the Chamonix valley, where I had spent the most marvelous moments of my childhood; Mont Blanc, which so tremendously impressed me! I was a child when I first saw "the Mont Blanc people" coming home, and to me there was a queer look about them; a strange light shone in their eyes.

"Come on, straight down," called Lachenal.

He had already done up his sack and started going down. I took out my pocket aneroid: 8,500 meters. I smiled. I swallowed a little condensed milk and left the tube behind—the only trace of our passage. I did up my sack, put on my gloves and my glasses, seized my ice-axe; one look around and I, too, hurried down the slope. Before disappearing into the couloir I gave one last look at the summit which would henceforth be all our joy and all our consolation.

Lachenal was already far below; he had reached the foot of the couloir. I hurried down in his tracks. I went as fast as I could, but it was dangerous going. At every step one had to take care that the snow did not break away beneath one's weight. Lachenal, going faster than I thought he was capable of, was now on the long traverse. It was my turn to cross the

area of mixed rock and snow. At last I reached the foot of the rock-band. I had hurried and I was out of breath. I undid my sack. What had I been going to do? I couldn't say.

"My gloves!"

Before I had time to bend over, I saw them slide and roll. They went further and further straight down the slope. I remained where I was, quite stunned. I watched them rolling down slowly, with no appearance of stopping. The movement of those gloves was engraved in my sight as something irredeemable, against which I was powerless. The consequences might be most serious. What was I to do?

"Quickly, down to Camp V."

Rebuffat and Terray would be there. My concern dissolved like magic. I now had a fixed objective again: to reach the camp. Never for a minute did it occur to me to use as gloves the socks which I always carry in reserve for just such a mishap as this.

On I went, trying to catch up with Lachenal. It had been two o'clock when we reached the summit; we had started out at six in the morning, but I had to admit that I had lost all sense of time. I felt as if I were running, whereas in actual fact I was walking normally, perhaps rather slowly, and I had to keep stopping to get my breath. The sky was now covered with clouds, everything had become gray and dirty-looking. An icy wind sprang up, boding no good. We must push on! But where was Lachenal? I spotted him a couple of hundred yards away, looking as if he was never going to stop. And I had thought he was in indifferent form!

The clouds grew thicker and came right down over us; the wind blew stronger, but I did not suffer from the cold. Perhaps the descent had restored my circulation. Should I be able to find the tents in the mist? I watched the rib ending in the beak-like point which overlooked the camp. It was gradually swallowed up by the clouds, but I was able to make out the spearhead rib lower down. If the mist should thicken I would make straight for that rib and follow it down, and in this way I should be bound to come upon the tent.

Lachenal disappeared from time to time, and then the mist was so thick that I lost sight of him altogether. I kept going at the same speed, as fast as my breathing would allow.

The slope was now steeper; a few patches of bare ice followed the smooth stretches of snow. A good sign—I was nearing the camp. How difficult to find one's way in thick mist! I kept the course which I had set by the steepest angle of the slope. The ground was broken; with my crampons I went straight down walls of bare ice. There were some patches ahead—a few more steps. It was the camp all right, but there were *two tents!*

So Rebuffat and Terray had come up. What a mercy! I should be able to tell them that we had been successful, that we were returning from the top. How thrilled they would be!

I got there, dropping down from above. The platform had been extended, and the two tents were facing each other. I tripped over one of the guy-ropes of the first tent; there was movement inside, they had heard me. Rebuffat and Terray put their heads out.

"We've made it. We're back from Annapurna!"

WINSTON CHURCHILL *Painting as a Pastime*

Sir Winston Leonard Spencer Churchill (1874-   ) is a man of great versatility—statesman, soldier, historian, and biographer. Among his many books is his six-volume history, *The Second World War*, which he completed in 1953 while he was still Prime Minister of Great Britain and for which he received the Nobel Prize for literature.

In spite of his unusually active and strenuous life, Sir Winston has found time to pursue several hobbies, among which bricklaying and painting are special favorites. His interest in painting began in 1915, when he was forced out of his position as First Lord of the Admiralty and needed a challenging occupation for his leisure time. Sir Winston has completed some three hundred canvases, painted in nearly every section of the British Isles, in France, Africa, Switzerland, Spain, Portugal, in the Rocky Mountains region of the United States, and in Miami, Florida.

For men and women in search of a relief from daily cares, Sir Winston's essay presents a convincing brief for hobbies in general and painting in particular and, to the uninitiated, offers suggestions as well as encouragement.

1. Many remedies are suggested for the avoidance of worry and mental overstrain by persons who, over prolonged periods, have to bear exceptional responsibilities and discharge duties upon a very large scale. Some advise exercise, and others, repose. Some counsel travel, and others, retreat. Some praise solitude, and others, gaiety. No doubt all these may play their part according to the individual temperament. But the element which is constant and common in all of them is Change.

2. Change is the master key. A man can wear out a particular part of his mind by continually using it and tiring it, just in the

PAINTING AS A PASTIME: Reprinted from *Amid These Storms* by Winston Churchill; copyright 1932 by Charles Scribner's Sons; used by permission of the publishers.

same way as he can wear out his elbows of his coat. There is, however, this difference between the living cells of the brain and inanimate articles: one cannot mend the frayed elbows of a coat by rubbing the sleeves or shoulders; but the tired parts of the mind can be rested and strengthened, not merely by rest, but by using other parts. It is not enough merely to switch off the lights which play upon the main and ordinary field of interest; a new field of interest must be illuminated. It is no use saying to the tired "mental muscles" —if one may coin such an expression—"I will give you a good rest," "I will go for a long walk," or "I will lie down and think of nothing." The mind keeps busy just the same. If it has been weighing and measuring, it goes on weighing and measuring. If it has been worrying, it goes on worrying. It is only when new cells are called into activity, when new stars become the lords of the ascendant, that relief, repose, refreshment are afforded.

3. A gifted American psychologist has said, "Worry is a spasm of the emotion; the mind catches hold of something and will not let it go." It is useless to argue with the mind in this condition. The stronger the will, the more futile the task. One can only gently insinuate something else into its convulsive grasp. And if this something else is rightly chosen, if it is really attended by the illumination of another field of interest, gradually, and often quite swiftly, the old undue grip relaxes and the process of recuperation and repair begins.

4. The cultivation of a hobby and new forms of interest is therefore a policy of first importance to a public man. But this is not a business that can be undertaken in a day or swiftly improvised by a mere command of the will. The growth of alternative mental interests is a long process. The seeds must be carefully chosen; they must fall on good ground; they must be sedulously tended, if the vivifying fruits are to be at hand when needed.

5. To be really happy and really safe, one ought to have at least two or three hobbies, and they must all be real. It is no use starting late in life to say: "I will take an interest in this or that." Such an attempt only aggravates the strain of mental effort. A man may acquire great knowledge of topics unconnected with his daily work, and yet hardly get any benefit or relief. It is no use doing what you like; you have got to like what you do. Broadly speaking, human beings may be divided into three classes: those who are toiled to death, those who are worried to death, and those who are bored to death. It is no use offering the manual labourer, tired out with a hard week's sweat and effort, the chance of playing a game of football or baseball on Saturday afternoon. It is no use inviting the politician or the professional or business man, who has been working or worrying about serious things for six days, to work or worry about trifling things at the week-end.

6. As for the unfortunate people who can command everything they want, who can gratify every caprice and lay their hands on almost every object of desire—for them a new pleasure, a new excitement is only an additional satiation. In vain they rush frantically round from place to place, trying to escape from avenging boredom by mere clatter and motion. For them discipline in one form or another is the most hopeful path.

7. It may also be said that rational, industrious, useful human beings are divided into two classes: first, those whose work is work and whose pleasure is pleasure; and secondly, those whose work and pleasure are one. Of these the former are the majority. They have their compensations. The long hours in the office or the factory bring with them as their reward, not only the means of sustenance, but a keen appetite for pleasure even in its simplest and most modest forms. But Fortune's favoured children belong to the second class. Their life is a natural harmony. For them the working hours are never long enough. Each day is a holiday, and ordinary holidays when they come are grudged as enforced interruptions in an absorbing vocation. Yet to both classes the need of an alternative outlook, of a change of atmosphere, of a diversion of effort, is essential. Indeed, it may well be that those whose work is their pleasure are those who most need the means of banishing it at intervals from their minds.

8. The most common form of diversion is reading. In that vast and varied field millions find their mental comfort. Nothing makes a man more reverent than a library. "A few books," which was Lord Morley's definition of anything under five thousand, may give a sense of comfort and even of complacency. But a day in a library, even of modest dimensions, quickly dispels these illusory sensations. As you browse about, taking down book after book from the shelves and contemplating the vast, infinitely varied store of knowledge and wisdom which the human race has accumulated and preserved, pride, even in its most innocent forms, is chased from the heart by feelings of awe not untinged with sadness. As one surveys the mighty array of sages, saints, historians, scientists, poets and philosophers whose treasures one will never be able to admire—still less enjoy—the brief tenure of our existence here dominates mind and spirit.

9. Think of all the wonderful tales that have been told, and well told, which you will never know. Think of all the searching inquiries into matters of great consequence which you will never pursue. Think of all the delighting or disturbing ideas that you will never share. Think of the mighty labours which have been accomplished for your service, but of which you will never reap the harvest. But from this melancholy there also comes a calm. The bitter sweets of a pious despair melt into an agreeable sense of compulsory resignation from which we turn with renewed zest to the lighter vanities of life. . . .

10. But reading and book-love in all their forms suffer from one serious defect: they are too nearly akin to the ordinary daily round of the brain-worker to give that element of change and contrast essential to real relief. To restore psychic equilibrium we should call into use those parts of the mind which direct both eye and hand. Many men have found great advantage in practising a handicraft for pleasure. Joinery, chemistry, book-binding, even brick-laying—if one were interested in them and skilful at them—would give a real relief to the over-tired brain. But, best of all and easiest to procure are sketching and painting in all their forms. I consider myself very lucky that late in life I have been able to develop this new taste and pastime. Painting came to my rescue in a most trying time, and I shall venture in the pages that follow to express the gratitude I feel.

11. Painting is a companion with whom one may hope to walk a great part of life's journey,

"Age cannot wither her nor custom stale
    Her infinite variety."

One by one the more vigorous sports and exacting games fall away. Exceptional exertions are purchased only by a more pronounced and more prolonged fatigue. Muscles may relax, and feet and hands slow down; the nerve of youth and manhood may become less trusty. But painting is a friend who makes no undue demands, excites to no exhausting pursuits, keeps faithful pace even with feeble steps, and holds her canvas as a screen between us and the envious eyes of Time or the surly advance of Decrepitude.

12. Happy are the painters, for they shall not be lonely. Light and colour, peace and hope, will keep them company to the end, or almost to the end, of the day.

13. To have reached the age of forty without ever handling a brush or fiddling with a pencil, to have regarded with mature eye the painting of pictures of any kind as a mystery, to have stood agape before the chalk of the pavement artist, and then suddenly to find oneself plunged in the middle of a new and intense form of interest and action with paints and palettes and canvases, and not to be discouraged by results, is an astonishing and enriching experience. I hope it may be shared by others. I should be glad if these lines induced others to try the experiment which I have tried, and if some at least were to find themselves dowered with an absorbing new amusement delightful to themselves, and at any rate not violently harmful to man or beast.

14. I hope this is modest enough: because there is no subject on which I feel more humble or yet at the same time more natural. I do not presume to explain how to paint, but only how to get enjoyment. Do not turn the superior eye of critical passivity upon these efforts. Buy a paint-box and have a try. If you need something to occupy your leisure, to divert your mind from the daily round, to illuminate your holidays, do not be too ready to believe that you cannot find what you want here. Even at the advanced age of forty! It would be a sad pity to shuffle or scramble along through one's playtime with golf and bridge, pottering, loitering, shifting from one heel to the other, wondering what on earth to do—as perhaps is the fate of some unhappy beings—when all the while, if you only knew, there is close at hand a wonderful new world of thought and craft, a sunlit garden gleaming with light and colour of which you have the key in your waistcoat-pocket. Inexpensive independence, a mobile and perennial pleasure apparatus, new mental food and exercise, the old harmonies and symmetries in an entirely different language, an added interest to every common scene, an occupation for every idle hour, an unceasing voyage of entrancing discovery—these are high prizes. Make quite sure they are not yours. After all, if you try,

and fail, there is not much harm done. The nursery will grab what the studio has rejected. And then you can always go out and kill some animal, humiliate some rival on the links, or despoil some friend across the green table. You will not be worse off in any way. In fact you will be better off. You will know "beyond a peradventure," to quote a phrase disagreeably reminiscent, that that is really what you were meant to do in your hours of relaxation.

15. But if, on the contrary, you are inclined —late in life though it be—to reconnoitre a foreign sphere of limitless extent, then be persuaded that the first quality that is needed is Audacity. There really is no time for the deliberate approach. Two years of drawing-lessons, three years of copying woodcuts, five years of plaster casts—these are for the young. They have enough to bear. And this thorough grounding is for those who, hearing the call in the morning of their days, are able to make painting their paramount lifelong vocation. The truth and beauty of line and form which by the slightest touch or twist of the brush a real artist imparts to every feature of his design must be founded on long, hard, persevering apprenticeship and a practice so habitual that it has become instinctive. We must not be too ambitious. We cannot aspire to master-pieces. We may content ourselves with a joy ride in a paint-box. And for this Audacity is the only ticket.

16. I shall now relate my personal experience. When I left the Admiralty at the end of May, 1915, I still remained a member of the Cabinet and of the War Council. In this position I knew everything and could do nothing. The change from the intense executive activities of each day's work at the Admiralty to the narrowly measured duties of a counsellor left me gasping. Like a sea-beast fished up from the depths, or a diver too suddenly hoisted, my veins threatened to burst from the fall in pressure. I had great anxiety and no means of relieving it; I had vehement convictions and small power to give effect to them. I had to watch the unhappy casting-away of great opportunities, and the feeble execution of plans which I had launched and in which I heartily believed. I had long hours of utterly unwonted leisure in which to contemplate the frightful unfolding of the War. At a moment when every fibre of my being was inflamed to action, I was forced to remain a spectator of the tragedy, placed cruelly in a front seat. And then it was that the Muse of Painting came to my rescue—out of charity and out of chivalry, because after all she had nothing to do with me—and said, "Are these toys any good to you? They amuse some people."

17. Some experiments one Sunday in the country with the children's paint-box led me to procure the next morning a complete outfit for painting in oils.

18. Having bought the colours, an easel, and a canvas, the next step was *to begin*. But what a step to take! The palette gleamed with beads of colour; fair and white rose the canvas; the empty brush hung poised, heavy with destiny, irresolute in the air. My hand seemed arrested by a silent veto. But after all the sky on this occasion was unquestionably blue, and a pale blue at that. There could be no doubt that blue paint mixed with white should be put on the top part of the canvas. One really does not need to have had an artist's training to see that. It is a starting-point open to all. So very gingerly I mixed a little blue paint on the palette with a very small brush, and then with infinite precaution made a mark about as big as a bean upon the affronted snow-white shield. It was a challenge, a deliberate challenge; but so subdued, so halting, indeed so cataleptic, that it deserved no response. At that moment the loud approaching sound of a motor-car was heard in the drive. From this chariot there stepped swiftly and lightly none other than the gifted wife of Sir John Lavery. "Painting! But what are you hesitating about? Let me have a brush —the big one." Splash into the turpentine, wallop into the blue and the white, frantic flourish on the palette—clean no longer—and then several large, fierce strokes and slashes of blue on the absolutely cowering canvas. Anyone could see that it could not hit back. No evil fate avenged the jaunty violence. The canvas grinned in helplessness before me. The spell was broken. The sickly inhibitions rolled away. I seized the largest brush and fell upon my victim with Berserk fury. I have never felt any awe of a canvas since.

19. Everyone knows the feelings with which

one stands shivering on a spring-board, the shock when a friendly foe steals up behind and hurls you into the flood, and the ardent glow which thrills you as you emerge breathless from the plunge.

20. This beginning with Audacity, or being thrown into the middle of it, is already a very great part of the art of painting. But there is more in it than that.

> La peinture à l'huile
> Est bien difficile,
> Mais c'est beaucoup plus beau
> Que la peinture à l'eau.

I write no word in disparagement of watercolours. But there really is nothing like oils. You have a medium at your disposal which offers real power, if you can only find out how to use it. Moreover, it is easier to get a certain distance along the road by its means than by water-colour. First of all, you can correct mistakes much more easily. One sweep of the palette-knife "lifts" the blood and tears of a morning from the canvas and enables a fresh start to be made; indeed the canvas is all the better for past impressions. Secondly, you can approach your problem from any direction. You need not build downwards awkwardly from white paper to your darkest dark. You may strike where you please, beginning if you will with a moderate central arrangement of middle tones, and then hurling in the extremes when the psychological moment comes. Lastly, the pigment itself is such nice stuff to handle (if it does not retaliate). You can build it on layer after layer if you like. You can keep on experimenting. You can change your plan to meet the exigencies of time or weather. And always remember you can scrape it all away.

21. Just to paint is great fun. The colours are lovely to look at and delicious to squeeze out. Matching them, however crudely, with what you see is fascinating and absolutely absorbing. Try it if you have not done so—before you die. As one slowly begins to escape from the difficulties of choosing the right colours and laying them on in the right places and in the right way, wider considerations come into view. One begins to see, for instance, that painting a picture is like fighting a battle; and trying to paint a picture is, I suppose, like

trying to fight a battle. It is, if anything, more exciting than fighting it successfully. But the principle is the same. It is the same kind of problem as unfolding a long, sustained, interlocked argument. It is a proposition which, whether of few or numberless parts, is commanded by a single unity of conception. And we think—though I cannot tell—that painting a great picture must require an intellect on the grand scale. There must be that all-embracing view which presents the beginning and the end, the whole and each part, as one instantaneous impression retentively and untiringly held in the mind. When we look at the larger Turners—canvases yards wide and tall—and observe that they are all done in one piece and represent one single second of time, and that every innumerable detail, however small, however distant, however subordinate, is set forth naturally and in its true proportion and relation, without effort, without failure, we must feel in the presence of an intellectual manifestation the equal in quality and intensity of the finest achievements of warlike action, of forensic argument, or of scientific or philosophical adjudication.

22. In all battles two things are usually required of the Commander-in-Chief: to make a good plan for his army and, secondly, to keep a strong reserve. Both these are also obligatory upon the painter. To make a plan, thorough reconnaissance of the country where the battle is to be fought is needed. Its fields, its mountains, its rivers, its bridges, its trees, its flowers, its atmosphere—all require and repay attentive observation from a special point of view. One is quite astonished to find how many things there are in the landscape, and in every object in it, one never noticed before. And this is a tremendous new pleasure and interest which invest every walk or drive with an added object. So many colours on the hillside, each different in shadow and in sunlight; such brilliant reflections in the pool, each a key lower than what they repeat; such lovely lights gilding or silvering surface or outline, all tinted exquisitely with pale colour, rose, orange, green, or violet. I found myself instinctively as I walked noting the tint and character of a leaf, the dreamy, purple shades of mountains, the exquisite lacery of winter branches, the dim, pale silhouettes of far

horizons. And I had lived for over forty years without ever noticing any of them except in a general way, as one might look at a crowd and say, "What a lot of people!"

23. I think this heightened sense of observation of Nature is one of the chief delights that have come to me through trying to paint. No doubt many people who are lovers of art have acquired it in a high degree without actually practising. But I expect that nothing will make one observe more quickly or more thoroughly than having to face the difficulty of representing the thing observed. And mind you, if you do observe accurately and with refinement, and if you do record what you have seen with tolerable correspondence, the result follows on the canvas with startling obedience. Even if only four or five main features are seized and truly recorded, these by themselves will carry a lot of ill-success or half-success. Answer five big questions out of all the hundreds in the examination paper correctly and well, and though you may not win a prize, at any rate you will not be absolutely ploughed.

24. But in order to make his plan, the General must not only reconnoitre the battleground, he must also study the achievements of the great Captains of the past. He must bring the observations he has collected in the field into comparison with the treatment of similar incidents by famous chiefs. Then the galleries of Europe take on a new—and to me at least a severely practical—interest. "This, then, is how —— painted a cataract. Exactly, and there is that same light I noticed last week in the waterfall at ——." And so on. You see the difficulty that baffled you yesterday; and you see how easily it has been overcome by a great or even by a skilful painter. Not only is your observation of Nature sensibly improved and developed, but you look at the masterpieces of art with an analysing and a comprehending eye.

25. The whole world is open with all its treasures. The simplest objects have their beauty. Every garden presents innumerable fascinating problems. Every land, every parish, has its own tale to tell. And there are many lands differing from each other in countless ways, and each presenting delicious variants of colour, light, form, and definition. Obviously, then, armed with a paint-box, one cannot be bored, one cannot be left at a loose end, one cannot "have several days on one's hands." Good gracious! what there is to admire and how little time there is to see it in! For the first time one begins to envy Methuselah. No doubt he made a very indifferent use of his opportunities.

26. But it is in the use and withholding of their reserves that the great Commanders have generally excelled. After all, when once the last reserve has been thrown in, the Commander's part is played. If that does not win the battle, he has nothing else to give. The event must be left to luck and to the fighting troops. But these last, in the absence of high direction, are apt to get into sad confusion, all mixed together in a nasty mess, without order or plan—and consequently without effect. Mere masses count no more. The largest brush, the brightest colours, cannot even make an impression. The pictorial battlefield becomes a sea of mud mercifully veiled by the fog of war. It is evident there has been a serious defeat. Even though the General plunges in himself and emerges bespattered, as he sometimes does, he will not retrieve the day.

27. In painting, the reserves consist in Proportion or Relation. And it is here that the art of the painter marches along the road which is traversed by all the great harmonies in thought. At one side of the palette there is white, at the other black; and neither is ever used "neat." Between these two rigid limits all the action must lie, all the power required must be generated. Black and white themselves, placed in juxtaposition, make no great impression; and yet they are the most that you can do in pure contrast. It is wonderful—after one has tried and failed often—to see how easily and surely the true artist is able to produce every effect of light and shade, of sunshine and shadow, of distance or nearness, simply by expressing justly the relations between the different planes and surfaces with which he is dealing. We think that this is founded upon a sense of proportion, trained no doubt by practice, but which in its essence is a frigid manifestation of mental power and size. We think that the same mind's eye that can justly survey and appraise and prescribe beforehand the values of a truly great picture

in one all-embracing regard, in one flash of simultaneous and homogeneous comprehension, would also with a certain acquaintance with the special technique be able to pronounce with sureness upon any other high activity of the human intellect. This was certainly true of the great Italians.

28. I have written in this way to show how varied are the delights which may be gained by those who enter hopefully and thoughtfully upon the pathway of painting; how enriched they will be in their daily vision, how fortified in their independence, how happy in their leisure. Whether you feel that your soul is pleased by the conception or contemplation of harmonies, or that your mind is stimulated by the aspect of magnificent problems, or whether you are content to find fun in trying to observe and depict the jolly things you see, the vistas of possibility are limited only by the shortness of life. Every day you may make progress. Every step may be fruitful. Yet there will stretch out before you an ever-lengthening, ever-ascending, ever-improving path. You know you will never get to the end of the journey. But this, so far from discouraging, only adds to the joy and glory of the climb.

29. Try it, then, before it is too late and before you mock at me. Try it while there is time to overcome the preliminary difficulties. Learn enough of the language in your prime to open this new literature to your age. Plant a garden in which you can sit when digging days are done. It may be only a small garden, but you will see it grow. Year by year it will bloom and ripen. Year by year it will be better cultivated. The weeds will be cast out. The fruit-trees will be pruned and trained. The flowers will bloom in more beautiful combinations. There will be sunshine there even in the winter-time, and cool shade, and the play of shadow on the pathway in the shining days of June.

30. I must say I like bright colours. I agree with Ruskin in his denunciation of that school of painting who "eat slate-pencil and chalk, and assure everybody that they are nicer and purer than strawberries and plums." I cannot pretend to feel impartial about the colours. I rejoice with the brilliant ones, and am genuinely sorry for the poor browns. When I get to heaven I mean to spend a considerable por-

tion of my first million years in painting, and so get to the bottom of the subject. But then I shall require a still gayer palette than I get here below. I expect orange and vermilion will be the darkest, dullest colours upon it, and beyond them there will be a whole range of wonderful new colours which will delight the celestial eye. . . .

31. It would be interesting if some real authority investigated carefully the part which memory plays in painting. We look at the object with an intent regard, then at the palette, and thirdly at the canvas. The canvas receives a message dispatched usually a few seconds before from the natural object. But it has come through a post-office en route. It has been transmitted in code. It has been turned from light into paint. It reaches the canvas a cryptogram. Not until it has been placed in its correct relation to everything else that is on the canvas can it be deciphered, is its meaning apparent, is it translated once again from mere pigment into light. And the light this time is not of Nature but of Art. The whole of this considerable process is carried through on the wings or the wheels of memory. In most cases we think it is the wings—airy and quick like a butterfly from flower to flower. But all heavy traffic and all that has to go a long journey must travel on wheels.

32. In painting in the open air the sequence of actions is so rapid that the process of translation into and out of pigment may seem to be unconscious. But all the greatest landscapes have been painted indoors, and often long after the first impressions were gathered. In a dim cellar the Dutch or Italian master recreated the gleaming ice of a Netherlands carnival or the lustrous sunshine of Venice or the Campagna. Here, then, is required a formidable memory of the visual kind. Not only do we develop our powers of observation, but also those of carrying the record—of carrying it through an extraneous medium and of reproducing it, hours, days, or even months after the scene has vanished or the sunlight died. . . .

33. There is no better exercise for the would-be artist than to study and devour a picture, and then, without looking at it again, to attempt the next day to reproduce it. Nothing can more exactly measure the prog-

ress both of observation and memory. It is still harder to compose out of many separate, well-retained impressions, aided though they be by sketches and colour notes, a new, complete conception. But this is the only way in which great landscapes have been painted —or can be painted. The size of the canvas alone precludes its being handled out of doors. The fleeting light imposes a rigid time-limit. The same light never returns. One cannot go back day after day without the picture getting stale. The painter must choose between a rapid impression, fresh and warm and living, but probably deserving only of a short life, and the cold, profound, intense effort of memory, knowledge, and will-power, prolonged perhaps for weeks, from which a masterpiece can alone result. It is much better not to fret too much about the latter. Leave to the masters of art trained by a lifetime of devotion the wonderful process of picture-building and picture-creation. Go out into the sunlight and be happy with what you see.

34. Painting is complete as a distraction. I know of nothing which, without exhausting the body, more entirely absorbs the mind. Whatever the worries of the hour or the threats of the future, once the picture has begun to flow along, there is no room for them in the mental screen. They pass out into shadow and darkness. All one's mental light, such as it is, becomes concentrated on the task. Time stands respectfully aside, and it is only after many hesitations that luncheon knocks gruffly at the door. When I have had to stand up on parade, or even, I regret to say, in church, for half an hour at a time, I have always felt that the erect position is not natural to man, has only been painfully acquired, and is only with fatigue and difficulty maintained. But no one who is fond of painting finds the slightest inconvenience, as long as the interest holds, in standing to paint for three or four hours at a stretch.

35. Lastly, let me say a word on painting as a spur to travel. There is really nothing like it. Every day and all day is provided with its expedition and its occupation—cheap, attainable, innocent, absorbing, recuperative. The vain racket of the tourist gives place to the calm enjoyment of the philosopher, intensified by an enthralling sense of action and endeavour. Every country where the sun shines and every district in it, has a theme of its own. The lights, the atmosphere, the aspect, the spirit, are all different; but each has its native charm. Even if you are only a poor painter you can feel the influence of the scene, guiding your brush, selecting the tubes you squeeze on to the palette. Even if you cannot portray it as you see it, you feel it, you know it, and you admire it for ever. When people rush about Europe in the train from one glittering centre of work or pleasure to another, passing—at enormous expense—through a series of mammoth hotels and blatant carnivals, they little know what they are missing, and how cheaply priceless things can be obtained. The painter wanders and loiters contentedly from place to place, always on the lookout for some brilliant butterfly of a picture which can be caught and set up and carried safely home.

36. Now I am learning to like painting even on dull days. But in my hot youth I demanded sunshine. Sir William Orpen advised me to visit Avignon on account of its wonderful light, and certainly there is no more delightful center for a would-be painter's activities: then Egypt, fierce and brilliant, presenting in infinite variety the single triplex theme of the Nile, the desert, and the sun; or Palestine, a land of rare beauty—the beauty of the turquoise and the opal—which well deserves the attention of some real artist, and has never been portrayed to the extent that is its due. And what of India? Who has ever interpreted its lurid splendours? But after all, if only the sun will shine, one does not need to go beyond one's own country. There is nothing more intense than the burnished steel and gold of a Highland stream; and at the beginning and close of almost every day the Thames displays to the citizens of London glories and delights which one must travel far to rival.

ERNEST HEMINGWAY *On the Blue Water*

Ernest Hemingway (1898-   ) is an ardent sportsman. As a spectator he enjoys bullfighting, the sport he commemorated in *Death in the Afternoon*, 1932; as a participant he favors big-game hunting, the subject of *The Green Hills of Africa*, 1935, and deep-sea fishing, which he describes in the article below.

In all these sports, the elements of danger and adventure seem to attract Hemingway and provide his literary inspiration. Indeed, many times in his life Hemingway has sought out dangerous situations and used his personal experiences in his creative writing. He served as an ambulance driver in World War I, out of which experience he wrote *A Farewell to Arms*, 1929. When the Spanish Civil War broke out in 1936, he went to Spain and remained there during much of that turbulent period, which furnished the setting of *For Whom the Bell Tolls*, 1940. His most recent book, *The Old Man and the Sea*, 1952, is, like this essay, a story of deep-sea fishing. He was awarded the Nobel Prize in 1954.

Although Mr. Hemingway now lives in Cuba, he also has a home in Key West, Florida. Vice-president of the International Game Fish Association, he has contributed many rare specimens of deep-sea life to various museums and is proud that a scorpion fish, the *neomerinthe hemingwayi*, has been named for him.

1. Certainly there is no hunting like the hunting of man and those who have hunted armed men long enough and liked it, never really care for anything else thereafter. You will meet them doing various things with resolve, but their interest rarely holds because after the other thing ordinary life is as flat as the taste of wine when the taste buds have been burned off your tongue. Wine, when your tongue has been burned clean with lye and water, feels like puddle water in your mouth, while mustard feels like axle-grease, and you can smell crisp, fried bacon, but when you taste it, there is only a feeling of crinkly lard.

2. You can learn about this matter of the tongue by coming into the kitchen of a villa on the Riviera late at night and taking a drink from what should be a bottle of Evian

ON THE BLUE WATER: From *Esquire*, April 1936. Reprinted by permission of Esquire, Inc., and the author.

water and which turns out to be *Eau de Javel,* a concentrated lye product used for cleaning sinks. The taste buds on your tongue, if burned off by *Eau de Javel,* will begin to function again after about a week. At what rate other things regenerate one does not know, since you lose track of friends and the things one could learn in a week were mostly learned a long time ago.

3. The other night I was talking with a good friend to whom all hunting is dull except elephant hunting. To him there is no sport in anything unless there is great danger and, if the danger is not enough, he will increase it for his own satisfaction. A hunting companion of his had told me how this friend was not satisfied with the risk of ordinary elephant hunting but would, if possible, have the elephants driven, or turned, so he could take them head-on, so it was a choice of killing them with the difficult frontal shot as

they came, trumpeting, with their ears spread, or having them run over him. This is to elephant hunting what the German cult of suicide climbing is to ordinary mountaineering, and I suppose it is, in a way, an attempt to approximate the old hunting of the armed man who is hunting you.

4. This friend was speaking of elephant hunting and urging me to hunt elephant, as he said that once you took it up no other hunting would mean anything to you. I was arguing that I enjoyed all hunting and shooting, any sort I could get, and had no desire to wipe this capacity for enjoyment out with the *Eau de Javel* of the old elephant coming straight at you with his trunk up and his ears spread.

5. "Of course you like that big fishing too," he said rather sadly. "Frankly, I can't see where the excitement is in that."

"You'd think it was marvelous if the fish shot at you with Tommy guns or jumped back and forth through the cockpit with swords on the ends of their noses."

"Don't be silly," he said. "But frankly I don't see where the thrill is."

"Look at so and so," I said. "He's an elephant hunter and this last year he's gone fishing for big fish and he's goofy about it. He must get a kick out of it or he wouldn't do it."

"Yes," my friend said. "There must be something about it but I can't see it. Tell me where you get a thrill out of it."

"I'll try to write it in a piece sometime," I told him.

"I wish you would," he said. "Because you people are sensible on other subjects. Moderately sensible I mean."

"I'll write it."

6. In the first place, the Gulf Stream and the other great ocean currents are the last wild country there is left. Once you are out of sight of land and of the other boats you are more alone than you can ever be hunting and the sea is the same as it has been since before men ever went on it in boats. In a season fishing you will see it oily flat as the becalmed galleons saw it while they drifted to the westward; white-capped with a fresh breeze as they saw it running with the trades; and in high, rolling blue hills the tops blow-

ing off them like snow as they were punished by it, so that sometimes you will see three great hills of water with your fish jumping from the top of the farthest one and if you tried to make a turn to go with him without picking your chance, one of those breaking crests would roar down in on you with a thousand tons of water and you would hunt no more elephants, Richard, my lad.

7. There is no danger from the fish, but anyone who goes on the sea the year around in a small power boat does not seek danger. You may be absolutely sure that in a year you will have it without seeking, so you try always to avoid it all you can.

8. Because the Gulf Stream is an unexploited country, only the very fringe of it ever being fished, and then only at a dozen places in thousands of miles of current, no one knows what fish live in it, or how great size they reach or what age, or even what kinds of fish and animals live in it at different depths. When you are drifting, out of sight of land, fishing four lines, sixty, eighty, one hundred and one hundred fifty fathoms down, in water that is seven hundred fathoms deep you never know what may take the small tuna that you use for bait, and every time the line starts to run off the reel, slowly first, then with a scream of the click as the rod bends and you feel it double and the huge weight of the friction of the line rushing through that depth of water while you pump and reel, pump and reel, pump and reel, trying to get the belly out of the line before the fish jumps, there is always a thrill that needs no danger to make it real. It may be a marlin that will jump high and clear off to your right and then go off in a series of leaps, throwing a splash like a speedboat in a sea as you shout for the boat to turn with him watching the line melting off the reel before the boat can get around. Or it may be a broadbill that will show wagging his great broadsword. Or it may be some fish that you will never see at all that will head straight out to the northwest like a submerged submarine and never show and at the end of five hours the angler has a straightened-out hook. There is always a feeling of excitement when a fish takes hold when you are drifting deep.

9. In hunting you know what you are after and the top you can get is an elephant. But who can say what you will hook sometime when drifting in a hundred and fifty fathoms in the Gulf Stream? There are probably marlin and swordfish to which the fish we have seen caught are pygmies; and every time a fish takes the bait drifting you have a feeling perhaps you are hooked to one of these.

10. Carlos, our Cuban mate, who is fifty-three years old and has been fishing for marlin since he went in the bow of a skiff with his father when he was seven, was fishing drifting deep one time when he hooked a white marlin. The fish jumped twice and then sounded and when he sounded suddenly Carlos felt a great weight and he could not hold the line which went out and down and down irresistibly until the fish had taken out over a hundred and fifty fathoms. Carlos says it felt as heavy and solid as though he were hooked to the bottom of the sea. Then suddenly the strain was loosened but he could feel the weight of his original fish and pulled it up stone dead. Some toothless fish like a swordfish or marlin had closed his jaws across the middle of the eighty-pound white marlin and squeezed it and held it so that every bit of the insides of the fish had been crushed out while the huge fish moved off with the eighty-pound fish in its mouth. Finally it let go. What size of a fish would that be? I thought it might be a giant squid but Carlos said there were no sucker marks on the fish and that it showed plainly the shape of the marlin's mouth where he had crushed it.

11. Another time an old man fishing alone in a skiff out of Cabañas hooked a great marlin that, on the heavy sashcord handline, pulled the skiff far out to sea. Two days later the old man was picked up by fishermen sixty miles to the eastward, the head and forward part of the marlin lashed alongside. What was left of the fish, less than half, weighed eight hundred pounds. The old man had stayed with him a day, a night, a day and another night while the fish swam deep and pulled the boat. When he had come up the old man had pulled the boat up on him and harpooned him. Lashed alongside the sharks had hit him and the old man had fought them out alone in the Gulf Stream in a skiff, clubbing them, stabbing at them, lunging at them with an oar until he was exhausted and the sharks had eaten all that they could hold. He was crying in the boat when the fishermen picked him up, half crazy from his loss, and the sharks were still circling the boat.

12. But what is the excitement in catching them from a launch? It comes from the fact that they are strange and wild things of unbelievable speed and power and a beauty, in the water and leaping, that is indescribable, which you would never see if you did not fish for them, and to which you are suddenly harnessed so that you feel their speed, their force and their savage power as intimately as if you were riding a bucking horse. For half an hour, an hour, or five hours, you are fastened to the fish as much as he is fastened to you and you tame him and break him the way a wild horse is broken and finally lead him to the boat. For pride and because the fish is worth plenty of money in the Havana market, you gaff him at the boat and bring him on board, but the having him in the boat isn't the excitement; it is while you are fighting him that is the fun. If the fish is hooked in the bony part of the mouth I am sure the hook hurts him no more than the harness hurts the angler. A large fish when he is hooked often does not feel the hook at all and will swim toward the boat, unconcerned, to take another bait. At other times he will swim away deep, completely unconscious of the hook, and it is when he feels himself held and pressure exerted to turn him, that he knows something is wrong and starts to make his fight. Unless he is hooked where it hurts he makes his fight not against the pain of the hook, but against being captured and if, when he is out of sight, you figure what he is doing, in what direction he is pulling when deep down, and why, you can convince him and bring him to the boat by the same system you break a wild horse. It is not necessary to kill him, or even completely exhaust him to bring him to the boat.

13. To kill a fish that fights deep you pull against the direction he wants to go until he is worn out and dies. It takes hours and when the fish dies the sharks are liable to get him before the angler can raise him to the top. To catch such a fish quickly you figure by trying

to hold him absolutely, which direction he is working (a sounding fish is going in the direction the line slants in the water when you have put enough pressure on the drag so the line would break if you held it any tighter); then get ahead of him on that direction and he can be brought to the boat without killing him. You do not tow him or pull him with the motor boat; you use the engine to shift your position just as you would walk up or down stream with a salmon. A fish is caught most surely from a small boat such as a dory since the angler can shut down on his drag and simply let the fish pull the boat. Towing the boat will kill him in time. But the most satisfaction is to dominate and convince the fish and bring him intact in everything but spirit to the boat as rapidly as possible.

14. "Very instructive," says the friend. "But where does the thrill come in?"

15. The thrill comes when you are standing at the wheel drinking a cold bottle of beer and watching the outriggers jump the baits so they look like small live tuna leaping along and then behind one you see a long dark shadow wing up and then a big spear thrust out followed by an eye and head and dorsal fin and the tuna jumps with the wave and he's missed it.

16. "Marlin," Carlos yells from the top of the house and stamps his feet up and down, the signal that a fish is raised. He swarms down to the wheel and you go back to where the rod rests in its socket and there comes the shadow again, fast as the shadow of a plane moving over the water, and the spear, head, fin and shoulders smash out of water and you hear the click the closepin makes as the line pulls out and the long bight of line whishes through the water as the fish turns and as you hold the rod, you feel it double and the butt kicks you in the belly as you come back hard and feel his weight, as you strike him again and again, and again.

17. Then the heavy rod arcing out toward the fish, and the reel in a band-saw zinging scream, the marlin leaps clear and long, silver in the sun, long, round as a hogshead and banded with lavender stripes and, when he goes into the water, it throws a column of spray like a shell lighting.

18. Then he comes out again, and the spray roars, and again, then the line feels slack and out he bursts headed across and in, then jumps wildly twice more, seeming to hang high and stiff in the air before falling to throw the column of water and you can see the hook in the corner of his jaw.

19. Then in a series of jumps like a greyhound he heads to the northwest and standing up, you follow him in the boat, the line taut as a banjo string and little drops coming from it until you finally get the belly of it clear of that friction against the water and have a straight pull out toward the fish.

20. And all the time Carlos is shouting, "Oh, God the bread of my children! Oh look at the bread of my children! Joseph and Mary look at the bread of my children jump! There it goes the bread of my children! He'll never stop the bread the bread the bread of my children!"

21. This striped marlin jumped, in a straight line to the northwest, fifty-three times, and every time he went out it was a sight to make your heart stand still. Then he sounded and I said to Carlos, "Get me the harness. Now I've got to pull him up the bread of your children."

22. "I couldn't stand to see it," he says. "Like a filled pocketbook jumping. He can't go down deep now. He's caught too much air jumping."

"Like a race horse over obstacles," Julio says. "Is the harness all right? Do you want water?"

"No." Then kidding Carlos, "What's this about the bread of your children?"

"He always says that," says Julio. "You should hear him curse me when we would lose one in the skiff."

"What will the bread of your children weigh?" I ask with mouth dry, the harness taut across shoulders, the rod a flexible prolongation of the sinew, the pulling ache of arms, the sweat salty in my eyes.

"Four hundred and fifty," says Carlos.

"Never," says Julio.

"Thou and thy never," says Carlos. "The fish of another always weighs nothing to thee."

"Three seventy-five," Julio raises his estimate. "Not a pound more."

23. Carlos says something unprintable and Julio comes up to four hundred.

24. The fish is nearly whipped now and the dead ache is out of raising him, and then, while lifting, I feel something slip. It holds for an instant and then the line is slack.

"He's gone," I say and unbuckle the harness.

"The bread of your children," Julio says to Carlos.

25. "Yes," Carlos says. "Yes. Joke and no joke yes. *El pan de mis hijos.* Three hundred and fifty pounds at ten cents a pound. How many days does a man work for that in the winter? How cold is it at three o'clock in the morning on all those days? And the fog and the rain in a norther. Every time he jumps the hook cutting the hole a little bigger in his jaw. Ay how he could jump. How he could jump!"

"The bread of your children," says Julio.

"Don't talk about that any more," says Carlos.

26. No it is not elephant hunting. But we get a kick out of it. When you have a family and children, your family, or my family, or the family of Carlos, you do not have to look for danger. There is always plenty of danger when you have a family.

27. And after a while the danger of others is the only danger and there is no end to it nor any pleasure in it nor does it help to think about it.

28. But there is great pleasure in being on the sea, in the unknown wild suddenness of a great fish; in his life and death which he lives for you in an hour while your strength is harnessed to his; and there is satisfaction in conquering this thing which rules the sea it lives in.

29. Then in the morning of the day after you have caught a good fish, when the man who carried him to the market in a handcart brings the long roll of heavy silver dollars wrapped in a newspaper on board it is very satisfactory money. It really feels like money.

30. "There's the bread of your children," you say to Carlos.

"In the time of the dance of the millions," he says, "a fish like that was worth two hundred dollars. Now it is thirty. On the other hand a fisherman never starves. The sea is very rich."

"And the fisherman always poor."

"No. Look at you. You are rich."

"Like hell," you say. "And the longer I fish the poorer I'll be. I'll end up fishing with you for the market in a dinghy."

"That I never believe," says Carlos devoutly. "But look. That fishing in a dinghy is very interesting. You would like it."

"I'll look forward to it," you say.

"What we need for prosperity is a war," Carlos says. "In the time of the war with Spain and in the last war the fishermen were actually rich."

"All right," you say. "If we have a war you get the dinghy ready."

ROGER ANGELL *Baseball—The Perfect Game*

Roger Angell (1920-   ) was associate editor of the GI magazine *Brief* during World War II. Since 1946 he has been connected with the Curtis Publishing Company and is now senior editor of *Holiday*.

For the past ten years Mr. Angell has also been one of the leading contributors to *Holiday* —he has written columns, departments, and some thirty-five articles ranging in subject matter from African drumming to Paris night clubs. He has also written many stories for the *New Yorker*.

In "Baseball—The Perfect Game," Mr. Angell not only gives an informative explanation of the game but also accounts for its widespread—almost universal—appeal.

1. Everyone talks about baseball.

2. "Baseball?" a man said to me at a cocktail party last summer. "Baseball?" he repeated in a loud, angry voice. "I despise it. I loathe baseball. What a bore, what a criminal waste of time to spend even five minutes of one's day reading or talking about a boys' game played by hired hands. It's a mark of our childishness that we pay so much attention to it. I hate baseball!" And he looked fiercely around the room over his glass, a rebel unafraid.

3. In the same week last summer I attended a dinner party where I heard two new Americans, a Swedish-born oceanographer and a Hungarian-born magazine editor, deep in a serious conversation. They were discussing what was wrong with the Giants' infield. And later I had lunch with a friend just back from an international convention in Venice. He told me he had been introduced to a Japanese delegate there and that the man's first question had been: "How do you think the Yankees' pitching is going to hold up this year?"

4. Baseball is everybody's game, still the American pastime. Baseball preoccupies us, fascinates us, excites us, charms us, lulls us, bores us, and otherwise takes up more of our time and attention from late winter to early autumn than all other sports put together.

BASEBALL—THE PERFECT GAME: Reprinted by permission of the author, from *Holiday*, May, 1954.

Whether or not we ever get to the ball park, whether or not we even care for the game, we are all, in a sense, in attendance. More than a sport, baseball is an environment, a condition of our warm-weather existence.

5. All through the summer in my suburban house, life goes on, on hot weekend afternoons and on steamy evenings, against a backdrop of baseball-by-radio, to the cry of cicada and Mel Allen, to the noise of double-play and thrush and Stan Musial and lawn mower, all intermingled in a summer sound. I am not *listening* to the ball game, not really, but I am there; part of me, at least, is following the game. And so are millions of Americans, many of them not even within earshot of a radio. Late one night last summer in New York, my cab stopped for a red light on a crosstown street. Beside me, in a parked limousine, a Negro chauffeur was sprawled out behind the wheel, his feet on the dashboard and his eyes closed, apparently asleep. There was a faint running murmur from his radio. My driver listened for a moment and then asked, "They score yet?" The dead man stirred, opened one eye and said "Nah." The light changed, we moved on. But the link was there; the exchange of four words had been enough to establish the three of us—hackie, chauffeur and passenger—as fans sitting side by side at the same far-off ball game.

6. So widespread is this phenomenon, this disease of the half-cocked ear, this bemused preoccupation with the doings of eighteen athletes on a distant playground, that it is truly inescapable. . . . I stop at a crowded gas station in a little coastal Maine village on Route U.S. 1. Cars from four different states are being serviced, drivers are stretching and drinking Cokes, the pumps ring and grind, and the Red Sox are behind, 5-2, in the seventh. The attendant handles the hose to my car and we both watch the wavering gas fumes ascend in the hot air, but his heart is in Boston and it is broken. . . . Again in New York, I am walking down Lexington Avenue in midafternoon. Just as I pass a bar there are shouts and laughter from the friendly darkness within. A man comes out adjusting his straw hat and blinking at the light, and falls into step beside me. "Campy just parked one!" he tells me, happily shaking his head. "Two on in the fifth. How *about* that guy!" . . . And in the morning subway, still cool and pleasant before the heat of the day, I sit beside the secretary in her crisp linen dress and across from the businessman in his fresh seersucker and from the window washer with his pail, and in our *Times* and *News* and *Mirror* and *Herald-Tribune* we all search out the cryptic, all-American news: BROOKS COP PAIR . . . YANKS LOSE . . . PHILS ROUT MAGLIE. . . .

7. What is behind this, anyway? What is this lure of baseball, this entranced national fascination with a rather simple game played by a few score well-paid professionals? One thing is certain to anyone who knows the game of baseball and who has pondered how strong a grip it has on every level of our society: this is *not* simply childishness, not just an escapist American obsession with youth and a pastime of youth. It is much more than that. It is a complicated and wonderful set of circumstances, accidents and inventions, involving the nature of Americans and the nature of the game itself.

8. I am a baseball fan (which is short, of course, for fanatic), a lifelong fan, and I know that the fan loves the game on many levels and for many reasons. Simplest of all these reasons, perhaps, is one which applies only to men— self-identification. To a foreigner seeing the game for the first time, baseball appears not only hard to understand but incredibly difficult to play. Yet oddly enough it is a game which almost any reasonably well-co-ordinated boy of ten can pick up in a single summer, at least to the point where he can enjoy himself vastly. As a consequence, and in spite of a thirty-year shrinkage of the space available for ball fields and the conversion of thousands of good diamonds into city streets and parking lots and drive-in theaters and gas stations, baseball remains a tremendously popular *participant* sport, almost entirely among the young. Men don't play much baseball after they leave school or college, mostly because of the difficulty involved in getting eighteen adult males in reasonably good condition together at the same time. But the fan can never forget that he has played, and every time he sees a big-league third baseman dig a ball out of the dirt and whip it over to first just in time to beat the runner, he himself is making the same play; every time Ed Mathews swings at a curve, he himself is swinging. The more baseball a fan has played, the more he gets out of watching the game from the stands. Nobody who has ever spent a sweaty afternoon on a high-school field trying to learn the complexities of the cutoff play, nobody who has ever felt the sharp joy of punching the ball behind a base runner on a hit-and-run play, will ever see the same play executed in Yankee Stadium without feeling a proprietary thrill.

9. This feeling of identification and remembered prowess is often carried further, into direct self-comparison with a big-league player. Every male fan has moments of this; a man in my office had a bad attack of it last spring, shortly after the season opened. He and a co-worker were challenging each other, in an off moment, to identify notable batting styles. They were using a long ruler for a bat. My friend knocked the imaginary dirt off his imaginary spikes, took a left-handed stance, bat held high, and said, "American Leaguer."

10. The other considered briefly and said, "Johnny Mize."

11. "Oh, no," my friend said. "*Here's* Mize," and he cocked his head over the plate. "No, watch me swing the top of the bat around— it's Gehrig." And then, smiling a little but half

seriously, he said: "My own batting style is just like Mize's, though. And we're the same age. This might be my last year, but I'd be a terror, an absolute terror, in the pinches." He wadded up a piece of paper, tossed it in the air and lashed it over his desk—a natural pull hitter.

12. Next to self-identification, the most elementary form of fandom is hometown pride— the simple joy of seeing your own St. Louis (or Detroit or Toledo or Elmwood) team whale the stuffings out of Chicago (or Washington or Kansas City or Parkersville). Actually, a fan's loyalty to his team is not always so simple: often it is a profound and mysterious affair, established early in life. It survives distance and time, which explains why there are plenty of fans who will turn out to cheer the Chicago White Sox when they appear in Detroit's Briggs Stadium, and why a man can live in Seattle, Washington, and still eat his heart out daily over the doings of the Cincinnati Redlegs.

13. Me, I am a New York resident and a Yankee fan. I am a Giants fan, too, but I *hate* the Dodgers; I would like to see the Dodgers lose 154 straight games some year. So great has been the success of the Yankees recently (the team has won five straight world championships) that owning up to being a Yankee fan today is like admitting to being a majority stockholder in General Motors, and just as likely to win you popular affection and sympathy for your problems. Yet I come by it honestly: I adopted the Yankees in 1930, when I was ten years old and the Yankees comparatively adolescent and unopulent. I saw Lefty Gomez pitch his first game in the Stadium; I remember when Frank Crosetti came up from the minors with a kid second baseman named Jack Saltzgaver; I remember when Crosetti gave way to another rookie, Phil Rizzuto, who came up with Jerry Priddy. (Both Crosetti and Rizzuto, of course, went on to baseball immortality as Yankee shortstops.) These memories are like those of a sentimental old woman toward her family: they establish the fan's blood relationship to his team and give him the right to glory in its triumphs and despair over its failures.

14. I have the same memories concerning the Giants, yet my feeling for the Giants is nothing like my feeling for the Yankees. I admire the Yankees extravagantly; I *know* they are the best; I will bet on them every time to win a big game or a big series, and they almost never let me down. Over the years, they have given me immeasurable satisfaction, excitement and pride. Yet there is, let it be admitted, something a little sterile about admiring the best. Backing a sure thing is rewarding but it lacks kicks. As a Giant fan, however, I hope for the best, expect the worst, and never, never lack for kicks.

15. The Giants aggravate me, dismay me, embarrass me, but when they win, they fill me with a rare and wonderful joy. When they whip the Dodgers my cup runs over.

16. I mention these opposite feelings toward my two teams because I believe that most ball fans have similar split emotions. As believers in good baseball and in success and bigness in general, they cannot help but respect the best and winningest team of all, just as they cannot help but admire the best pitcher or the best hitter. But at the same instant, they can entertain a sharp desire to see the balloon pricked, the champion thrown down. They are delighted when a last-place club beats the Yanks, when an obscure pitcher strikes out Ted Williams. This is a large part of the appeal of the game, because in baseball the hero is always on the spot and frequently fails horribly, and the underdog team or the kid player has endless opportunities and often comes through spectacularly.

17. And the true fan, the knowing fan, suffers from another interesting split in his loyalty: he is capable of objectively admiring good baseball and subjectively rooting for his home team at one and the same time. These two devotions come into painful conflict frequently at the ball park and result in the most admirable and pathetic cry to be heard from any sports fan: "Come on, ya bum!"

18. Baseball has not been quite the same for me since Joe DiMaggio retired. Joe was my boy, my nonpareil, my hero. From his first days in the majors to his last, I followed his every move, turned first to his name in the box scores, and sopped up every word I could read

about him. I saw him win games with his bat and with his arm. I suffered with him through his slumps, held my breath for fifty-six straight games during his unmatched hitting streak in 1941. I watched him play ball in Hawaii during the war, where we both were GI's.

19. I remember the time, in June of 1949, when DiMaggio returned to the Yankee line-up after having missed the whole first third of the campaign with a serious ailment. There were grave doubts about him, stories that he was all washed up. It was a big series, too, a battle for first place with the tough Red Sox at Fenway Park. All DiMaggio did was to hit four home runs during the three games; the Yankees swept the series and went on to win the pennant.

20. DiMaggio, although personally a cold, restrained, almost disdainful man, had the knack which almost all great stars have shared —the ability of making his every move on the field seem distinctive and exciting. To this moment, I can see his exact stance at the plate —feet planted wide apart, bat held high— remember the way he stood in center field with his hands on his knees, how he raced across the outfield with huge, easy strides, and how he rounded first base after a hit. Not once did I see him look hurried or graceless. I was there the last time he came up to bat in the major leagues—in the eighth inning of the last game of the 1951 World Series. He hadn't yet announced his retirement, but almost everyone knew that this would be the last time they would see him play. And as usual, he didn't disappoint us. He lined a long, clean hit to the right center-field wall and pulled into second base standing up. While the applause and cheers roared around him, he stood there as he always had, his hands on his hips, his head cocked to one side, studying his shoetops.

21. Possibly I am getting crotchety or sentimental, but it seems to me that the major leagues today are suffering from an unfortunate shortage of true stars—of men of the caliber of DiMaggio, Ruth, Cobb, Gehrig, Sisler, Dizzy Dean, Hubbell, Johnson, Hornsby, Mathewson, Frisch, Speaker, Alexander, Waddell. All of these men were not only magnificent ballplayers but they had that other quality, that aura of distinction and excitement, that distinguishes the true star. Such

men have never been numerous, but in the past there have almost always been five or six of them active in the majors at the same time, plus a larger assortment—men like Heilmann, Cochrane, Simmons, Hartnett, Greenberg, the Waners, Bob Meusel, Rabbit Maranville—who were almost equally talented. Today, out of all the active big leaguers, most experts would rank only Ted Williams and Stan Musial and perhaps Bob Feller in the very first rank and would have a hard time picking another four or five in the second group. And even a man like Musial, who has won the National League batting crown six times, lacks that extra dimension, that spark that kindles the imagination. On the field and off, he appears to be exactly what he is—not a hero, but an extremely likable, pleasant man who is extremely good at his profession.

22. This is not a plea for more roughnecks in baseball, but only a complaint against uniformity. More and more, there is a flattening out of differences, and off the field most ballplayers now look and act like suburban householders instead of like giants. There is a reason for this, of course; they *are* suburban householders. Better pay and better working conditions have made big-leaguers prosperous and respectable. No one can legitimately complain against such a gain, yet the fan still longs for an occasional gangly, country-boy rookie like those immortalized by Ring Lardner, for a scrapper like Frisch, for a hater like Cobb, for a likable loudmouth like Dean, and for an outright baseball god like Babe Ruth.

23. Most of all, perhaps, he longs for the screwballs—the weird and hilarious assortment of real eccentrics and simple extroverts who used to be drawn to the game and who are the subjects of most of the baseball yarns which the fan treasures.

24. Screwballs like Smead Jolley, for instance. Jolley, according to a story told by Red Smith, never could learn to play the outfield for the Boston Red Sox. Finally, in desperation and in order to keep his potent bat in the line-up, he was tried as a catcher. Jolley at this time was beginning to get bald and his wife always warned him to keep his hat firmly on so that the fans wouldn't see his thinning locks. Jolley got along fine as a catcher for an inning or two, but then a batter sent up a

high twisting foul, almost directly over home plate. Jolley whipped off his mask to follow the ball, and then suddenly realized that his cap had come off too.

25. Frantically he clapped his catcher's glove over his head with both hands and shouted to his wife in the stands, "I got it, Mary!" He then turned to the astonished third baseman and announced, "It's all yours, guinea."

26. Babe Herman of the Dodgers was another screwball who could hit but who never mastered the simplest aspects of fielding. Herman was the subject of so many fantastic yarns that he finally decided to complain. He cornered a sportswriter in a hotel lobby and seriously demanded that the reporters cease circulating such tall tales about him. "I'm no nut," he said. The reporter promised to do his best, whereupon Herman thanked him, pulled a lighted cigar from his pants pocket, and walked off puffing clouds of smoke. Herman's odd reputation was almost matched by an American League pitcher, Cletus Elwood ("Boots") Poffenberger, who once, while riding in a New York subway train, decided to take the kinks out of his pitching arm and managed to get his hand entangled in the moving blades of an overhead fan. Then there was Flint Rhem, the Cardinals' pitcher of an earlier day, who was excessively fond of the bottle. Rhem once vanished from the team for several days, missed his pitching turn, and was slapped with a heavy fine. On his return, rather the worse for wear, he did not deny he had been drinking. But he claimed, with great vehemence, that he had been kidnaped by gangsters and *forced* to drink the stuff.

27. Perhaps the last legitimate screwball was a muscular and cheerful second-stringer with the Giants a few years ago named Danny Gardella. Gardella did everything (he ended up suing all of organized baseball), but perhaps his wildest caper came on the day when he decided to frighten his roommate, a peaceable Cuban named Nap Reyes. Gardella picked an argument with Reyes, who was shaving in the bathroom, and brought it to a quick climax. Reyes, hearing an unaccustomed silence, walked into the bedroom and discovered a "suicide note" on the dresser, blaming the act

on Reyes. Frantically Reyes rushed to the open window and found his roommate joyfully giggling while he hung by his finger tips ten stories above the sidewalk.

28. If ballplayers today are monotonously alike and more sophisticated than they used to be, one of the causes is radio and television. The big-league ballplayer is now in range of the TV eye every moment he is on the field and therefore unlikely to cut up or indulge a crazy whim; instead, he is worrying about his appearance and often staging his "battles" or complaints for the benefit of the camera.

29. What is even more deadening is the odd passion radio announcers have for reducing every ballplayer to the same respectable, dull level by describing them *all* as level-headed, quiet-spoken, home-loving, friendly good fellows.

30. All big leaguers appear on TV and radio interview shows now, and all have fallen into this insipid pattern. Certainly none of them nowadays would be so gauche or full of gusto as to make the mistake Babe Ruth made on a radio program once. Imitating the sound of a pitched ball hitting a glove, he slammed his fist into his leather windbreaker and then blanched. "Jesus!" he exclaimed to several thousand fascinated listeners, "I broke the God-damned cigars!"

31. In spite of their shortcomings, radio and television have been responsible for creating uncounted millions of new and knowing fans (including a large proportion of women), many of whom have never been near a ball park. These fans, as well as the long-timers, are insatiable for information about their sport. They read everything they can get their hands on about their team, their players.

32. As a result, every big-league game (and there are 16 teams playing 154 games each, every year) gets as much coverage as a good murder case and more than the average Congressional hearing. Western Union transmitted 494,664 words after the first game of last year's World Series. Nor does the spate of newspaper baseball writing stop in the winter. Winter, to the really devoted fan, is the time to catch up on records and to read about *next* year.

33. Ball fans have memories which enable them to astonish or bore their friends with

Hornsby's 1924 batting average and with the line-up of George Stallings' 1914 Braves. I'm pretty rusty now but, a few years ago, a friend and I often passed a happy evening trying to stick each other with questions like: "What was Kiki Cuyler's real first name?" and "What hitter holds the lifetime strike-out record?" and "What was the only game played where all the players of one team ended up with the same batting averages that they started with?" (The answers, for the curious, are: Hazen Cuyler; Babe Ruth, with 1330 whiffs; the no-hit game which Bob Feller pitched against the White Sox on the first day of the 1940 season, when all the White Sox players started and finished with .000 averages.)

34. Even more rewarding to the passionate fan are his own memories, the stories he can tell of great plays and great moments he has shared at the ball park. I don't think I have ever attended more than a dozen big-league games in a single season. I have never seen a no-hit game (although I saw a pitcher come within two outs of one last summer) or a triple play. Yet so remarkable is this game, so frequently does it produce moments of wild excitement, and so vivid is the action of a ball field, that I can remember with utter clarity a few plays which took place five, ten and even twenty years ago. Any ball fan can do the same.

35. I remember, for instance, a play in a wild Yankees-Senators doubleheader in 1933 when the two teams were struggling for the pennant. The Yankees were at bat and during a rally had put Lou Gehrig on second base and Dixie Walker, later to become a star with the Dodgers, on first. One out. Gehrig nursing a sore leg. The hitter blasted a long double to center field. Walker took off with the hit, Gehrig waited to see if it would be caught. Thus by the time Gehrig had hobbled around third, Walker was right at his heels, the two of them rushing for the plate. The relay came in beautifully from the outfield, and the catcher, taking the ball on one hop, tagged Gehrig out as he slid in front of him and spun around in time to tag Walker skidding past behind him. It was a double play, one of the oddest of all time. The Yankees lost the doubleheader and, subsequently, the pennant.

36. I saw Mickey Owen drop that ninth-inning third strike in the 1941 World Series game that would have won the game for the Dodgers; instead, the Yankees scored four runs with two out and won it. I saw, in August of 1951, the greatest throw from the outfield I will ever see. In a tight, seesaw ball game between the Dodgers and the Giants, the Dodgers had Billy Cox standing on third base with one out. The batter sent a drive to deep right center field. Willie Mays, the Giants' rookie center fielder, running at top speed, managed to spear the ball, and Cox took off for the plate. Still in full flight to his left, Mays turned completely around in the air and cut loose his right-handed throw *with his back to the plate*. The ball came in on a great curve from the outfield, straight into the catcher's glove, in time to nab Cox for a double play. The Dodgers lost the game, the Giants won to keep their sixteen-game winning streak alive.

37. Eventually, in the ninth inning of the final play-off game at the end of the regular season, Bobby Thomson hit that homer which beat the Dodgers out of the 1951 flag. Incredible? Sure, but this is baseball.

38. In the end, you always get back to this, back to the game itself. The extraordinary appeal of baseball, its astonishing hold on vast adult sections of this nation, may be disparaged, deplored, dismissed or accounted for with dozens of simple or intellectual explanations. But in the last analysis, it is not the spectacle of the game, not its unplanned aesthetics, not the self-identification nor the hero worship, not the capitalistic aspects of the sport nor the democratic aspects, not its pleasant summer setting nor home-town pride which make baseball so popular. It is the game itself.

39. Baseball, you see, is probably the greatest team sport ever developed. Every fan or near-fan should occasionally remind himself of this fact and take the time to analyze the game again. He will be astonished. Familiarity with baseball only increases his wonder.

40. Start with the ball. A baseball is a lovely thing, a perfect object for a man's hand. You can get a good grip on it, and it is the right weight to throw. A softball, by contrast, is too big and a tennis ball is too light—wind will affect a thrown tennis ball and you can ruin your arm throwing it. A baseball thrown by

a big-league pitcher travels close to a hundred miles an hour and can be, *must* be, controlled to within a fraction of an inch of its intended destination, sixty and a half feet away. By some miracle, the batter decides whether or not to swing at this hurtling object and, again miraculously, often does hit it. Hard. A batted baseball can move at a speed sufficient to knock a full-grown third baseman staggering, just from the impact of it on his glove. Its speed implacably reveals the skill and courage of the infielder. If a shortstop charges a ground ball which is hopping in front of him, he will be able to make his play to first. If he hesitates, even for an instant, or steps back, remembering that the ball can jump up and sock him in the teeth, it will zip past him or throw him off balance so that he will not catch the base runner.

41. Baseball, it has often been pointed out, is a game of exquisite distances. Yet it is more than that. The distance from base to base, the consistency of the ball, the kind of wood in the bat, the strength and speed of the average (not the super-strong or extra large) man—all these have been taken into account down to a fraction of an ounce and tenth of a second. Thus is the double play made possible—that highly skilled maneuver of lightning co-operation between a scrambling shortstop, a leaping, dodging second baseman and a straining first baseman, who can, *if the play is perfectly done,* just manage to beat the runner at first, usually by a matter of six inches or so and all in the space of less than five seconds.

42. Described this way, the double play sounds like a super-feat, which a team might be lucky to pull off two or three times in a season. Yet it is an everyday event, and if a big-league infield messes up the play, the fans will berate the players unmercifully. In baseball, the miracle—the double play, the peg from outfield to catcher, the hit-and-run, the squeeze play—is taken for granted, is the rule rather than the exception. Baseball, as practiced in the big leagues, is an incredibly difficult sport. It is much more demanding than football, for example. Every year, the best college football players graduate right to big-league professional football teams. Yet very few college baseball players go straight to the majors; they simply are not good enough. And

for the same reason, college and high-school and even semiprofessional baseball is a dull and sloppy sport by contrast with the tight, near-perfect artistry of the big-league game.

43. Unknowing people, new to the game, often complain that "nothing happens" in a baseball game. Innings pass, the teams change sides, yet no one scores or appears to come close to it. This, of course, is far from the truth. It is only the fantastic, almost contemptuous ease with which a big-league team completes the routine plays that makes it appear, when a good pitcher is working, that it will never be scored on. Yet disaster, as every player and every fan knows, waits on every pitch and can descend with appalling violence and speed. A pitcher can be working beautifully after six perfect innings and then find himself, in the space of four minutes, on his way to the showers. A scratch hit, a bit of bad luck, an adverse call on a close pitch and a hit ball which just eludes the fingers of a racing outfielder, and the pitcher is done, his team defeated. Here, in its purest form, is the drama, the perfection of baseball. Action and tragedy, defeat and triumph are suddenly enacted, against a background of apparent safety and invulnerability. A good baseball game, in those innings of mounting tension before the break and the sudden coming of excitement, can be fondly described, as Red Smith described a World Series game last fall, as "fine entertainment, splendidly close and dull and dragging. . . ."

44. The more you analyze this dull, splendid game, the more wonderful it becomes. Nothing in baseball is left to chance, nothing is slipshod. Although baseball is played outdoors, in an area so large that the contestants are dwarfed, every movement in a game can be and is measured against a standard of absolute perfection. If a base runner gets on base, it is because he has either cleanly earned it, with a hit, or else because somebody has made a mistake—an error or a walk. And this is written down, records are kept; someone is blamed or credited for every play. The scoring of a run requires an even greater break in the defensive pattern; it cannot happen by accident. You can sacrifice a runner to second base and then (if you are foolish enough) to third base, but

you cannot then sacrifice him home, because there are exactly three bases and three outs. Against this rigidly confining background of the rules and of precisely apportioned responsibility, anything as free and as suddenly conclusive as a solidly hit triple with the bases loaded is unbelievably exciting to see.

45. The exactitude of the game is responsible for its endless statistics; the skill of a player can be precisely measured in his batting average, his runs batted in, his earned-run average, and so forth. This all-pervading neatness in what should be, by appearances, a sprawling, disjointed game, extends everywhere on the playing field. Almost never is there a baseball play which cannot be instantly seen and understood by everyone in the park; almost never does the baseball fan have to ask "What happened?" It is no accident that the basic rules of baseball have stood unchanged for a half century, while the regulations governing such sports as football, hockey, basketball and boxing have been altered again and again in an effort to make them clearer or more appealing or more exciting. No, baseball stands alone. As much as any sport can be perfect, it is perfect.

46. And finally, as if this were not enough, the league system, the business of baseball, works too. (To everyone's amazement.) The business side of baseball is as slipshod as the game itself is neat. It is capitalism gone berserk, monopoly on horseback. Ballplayers are sold, swapped and resold like shares of cheap stock under a system which brings out the very worst in acquisitiveness and suspicion on the parts of the owners and which many people suspect is totally illegal. Yet it works. Sixteen big-league teams end up every year with players who are so close in ability to each other that every team has an almost even chance against its opponent in every game. So close are the top teams that a pennant race is not usually determined until late in September, five months and 140 to 150-odd games after the start of the season. Incredible as it may seem, the Brooklyn Dodgers recently went through three whole seasons and the greater part of a fourth—611 consecutive games—before they played a game which could not be termed crucial. In 1949, they won the National League championship in the tenth inning of the final game of the season. In 1950, they lost it in the tenth inning of the final game. In 1951, they lost it in the ninth inning of the third playoff game, after tying in the fourteenth inning of the last game of the regular 154-game season. Only on September 25 of 1952, after they clinched that year's pennant, a few days before the end, could they (and the rest of the nation) relax for a moment.

47. Is it any wonder then that baseball managers frequently worry themselves into the hospital with the thought that a single inconsequential April decision of theirs can mean the loss of millions of dollars in September? Is it any wonder that the players, grown professionals, can turn into scuffling, snarling animals on the hot, sun-baked August infields, as the pennant scramble moves toward its climax? Is it any wonder that such childishness as home-town pride and hero worship grips great segments of the population of America and that adults will pay well for the right to sit under a broiling midsummer sun on hard seats in order to scream and pray over the flight of a ball? Is it any wonder that to those of us—those millions of us—who love the game, baseball will *always* remain the only game, the sport of our hearts' content?

HAROLD W. STOKE *College Athletics*

Harold Walter Stoke (1903-   ) discusses intercollegiate athletics from a wide background of experience. He studied at Marion College, the University of Southern California, and Johns Hopkins University. He has taught history and political science at Berea College, the University of Nebraska, the University of Tennessee, the University of Pennsylvania, and the University of Wisconsin. After serving as president of the University of New Hampshire and later as president of Louisiana State University, he became dean of the graduate school of the University of Washington. More recently he has become dean of the Graduate School of Arts and Sciences of New York University.

There are few who will contest the assertion that in many colleges athletics is a big business. But regarding the implications of this fact—for good or evil—opinions vary. If one accepts Dean Stoke's basic premise, however, the solution to long-standing problems becomes obvious and easy.

I

On the morning of December 7, 1951, in the General Sessions Court in New York City, fourteen tall young men stood before Judge Saul S. Streit. The scene was the climax of the notorious basketball scandals in which players had been convicted of receiving bribes from professional gamblers for throwing basketball games in Madison Square Garden. The judge was stern, but for the culprits he tempered justice. Jail sentences and fines were few and light. Judge Streit then looked over the heads of the defendants and hurled angry words at the colleges and universities they represented. He charged that these institutions had so far forgotten their educational mission and had so overemphasized athletics that they themselves had made this scene in his courtroom all but inevitable.

Addressing himself to the colleges, Judge Streit demanded immediate and drastic reforms. Among these were the restoration of athletic responsibilities to faculties and to the

academic administrative authorities; the revitalization of the National Collegiate Athletic Association; the establishment of an amateur code and of a capable, well-financed policing authority.

While there was some dismay (if little surprise) in university circles at the basketball scandals, there was genuine puzzlement about the judge's suggestions for reform. The point that had escaped him was that all his proposals had been tried for years—uniformly without success. If Judge Streit and the countless educators who have tackled this problem had asked themselves why Bradley University, Kentucky, New York University, North Carolina State, or any other university should ever play basketball in Madison Square Garden, they would have started on a line of inquiry which would have brought about a better understanding. Obviously it was no educational interest that brought the teams there, no huge concentration of alumni, no essential training program. It wasn't wholly a matter of money. They were there in response to a far more complex and subtle compulsion: to assist their schools as a part of the system of American higher education to carry out that system's latest and growing responsibility—namely, to provide public entertainment.

In our American society the need for entertainment is an inevitable consequence of the changing conditions of our lives—the lengthening life span, the shorter work week, speed and mobility, industrialization and prosperity. These changes create social vacuums, and for filling social vacuums the American system of education—and particularly higher education—is one of the most efficient devices ever invented. It is flexible, highly varied, and in touch with virtually the entire population; furthermore, it is characterized by a genuine spirit of service. It is manned by aggressive and accommodating people; it is suffused with a thoroughly practical philosophy. Hence, to its already great and growing array of services—its teaching, research, adult education, military training, and general public service—it has added another, public entertainment. This responsibility has been accepted in some instances eagerly, in some instances reluctantly, but nonetheless accepted. Drama, music, radio, and television widen the educational as well as the entertainment services of the universities; wherever these touch the public they possess more of the characteristics of entertainment than of education. Yet of all the instrumentalities which universities have for entertaining the public, the most effective is athletics.

What educational institutions thus far have not seen is that the responsibility for supplying public entertainment is a responsibility different in kind from those they have previously performed. The failure to understand this fact has led to endless strain in the management of athletics, to bewilderment among educators and the public, and even to outright scandal. Conceived as education, athletics is inexplicable, corrupting, and uncontrollable; as public entertainment, and even as public entertainment to be provided by educational institutions, athletics becomes comprehensible and manageable.

The most essential distinction between athletics and education lies in the institution's own interest in the athlete as distinguished from its interest in its other students. Universities attract students in order to teach them what they do not already know; they recruit athletes only when they are already proficient. Students are educated for something which will be useful to them and to society after graduation; athletes are required to spend their time on activities the usefulness of which disappears upon graduation or soon thereafter. Universities exist to do what they can for students; athletes are recruited for what they can do for the universities. This makes the operation of the athletic program in which recruited players are used basically different from any educational interest of colleges and universities.

The fundamental distinctions between athletics and education are somewhat obscured by several arguments frequently heard. The first is that athletics has "educational values." This is the familiar "character building," "team spirit," "sportsmanship" argument. Anyone who knows the actual operations of athletics will admit that such values could be realized far better if athletics were handled as recreation and physical education. The second argument is that many fine athletes make fine scholastic records—implying that there must not, after all, be any conflict between athletics and education. Again the answer can be short. Big-time athletics requires 20 to 28 hours per week of its devotees, aside from the time spent away from the campus; hence it is bound to detract from an athlete's education. But how can an impoverished athlete get a chance at a college education? I'll answer that question with another: Is he any more entitled to it than anyone else?

II

College athletics *is* public entertainment. Last year football audiences numbered 40 million, and now basketball is outstripping football in attendance. It is estimated that the public pays $100 million a year to the colleges for admission tickets, and television has added enormously to the number of spectators and to the revenue. Public interest as measured in publicity, newspaper coverage, and attention is far beyond that given to any educational activity. In no major school does the attention given to the appointment of a president compare with that given to the appointment of a coach, and the general public can name many more coaches than presidents.

The organization of this public entertainment is intricate. Most of the larger colleges and universities, private and public, are organized into athletic conferences managed by highly paid commissioners. Through them, complicated athletic schedules are worked out with all the finesse of the international bargaining table, and considerations of finance, publicity, the prospective careers of coaches and even of presidents, are balanced in equations which would baffle electronic computers. Stadiums, field houses, and playing fields are constructed with the entertainment-seeking public primarily in mind. At the time the Yale Bowl was built it would have seated the entire adult population of New Haven, while Michigan could have put twice the population of Ann Arbor into its stadium. The University of Southern California and the University of California at Los Angeles are big schools, but even they would scarcely need the Memorial Stadium for their students and faculty. Obviously the real underwriters of bonds which build athletic plants are not students, but the public. Many an athletic director caught in a squeeze of high costs and inadequate gate receipts wishes to heaven he had all of the student tickets to sell to the people willing to pay more for them.

The same force lies back of the other features of athletics—the numerous and high-priced coaching specialists, the elaborate half-time shows, the colorful bands (supported almost as completely by scholarships as are the athletes and for the same purpose), the frolicsome majorettes, the carefully planned and executed spontaneous student rallies and demonstrations, the food, drink, and program concessions. None of these could possibly serve any educational purpose for which a college or university exists, but they are wonderful aids to public entertainment.

Perhaps most significant of all is the fact that the rules of the games themselves are now constructed and reconstructed with their entertainment value uppermost. Like dramatic coaches and directors bringing into being a Broadway production, the coaches and athletic directors gather each year to adjust the rules of football and basketball for the purpose of heightening the dramatic and enter-tainment value. The substitution rule, who may run with the ball, what may be allowed to happen within the ten-yard line or within the last four minutes, the nature of the penalties, and, currently, the one- or two-platoon system in football are matters which are governed by their effect upon the entertainment and upon the welfare of the enterprise. In basketball, the rules have been changed to encourage high scoring, constant running and action, alternate chances at scoring in order to provide the murderously exciting finishes which now characterize the game. Revisions are made each year only after the most elaborate study and consideration and with a wariness which would do credit to the fuse workers in a munitions factory.

Consider the Bowl games. They are important influences on athletic policies and at the same time irrefutable evidence that athletics, so far as the Bowls are concerned, have no educational significance whatsoever. So far as I know, no one seriously claims that they do.

All of the Bowls for obvious reasons are located in the South or in winter vacation areas. They are immensely successful business promotions; there is nothing about them remotely related to education. As one man put it: "Rose Bowl, Sugar Bowl, Orange Bowl—all are gravy bowls!" A half-million people saw the games in the eight major bowls last January 1, and it is estimated 70 million more heard them on radio or saw them on television. Receipts were almost $2.5 million. The distribution of the money follows a kind of formula in each conference—a large percentage to each school participating in the Bowl, a smaller percentage to each school in the conference and to the conference treasury itself. A more subtle formula to ensure support for Bowl games could hardly be devised. Participation in one of the Big Four Bowls—Rose, Sugar, Cotton, and Orange—may bring each participating school as much as $125,000. Everyone profits—except the players, whose amateur status has thus far confined them to such grubby rewards as gifts of gold watches, blankets, free tickets which can be scalped, sometimes a little cash—the last usually secretly. Under pressure from the players and perhaps from a sense of institutional guilt at the indefensible exploitation, the rewards to players are improving, but they still are far below the A.S.C.A.P. and Equity pay scales for big-time entertainers.

III

How is all this to be made compatible with the nation's educational system? Most troubles arise from the failure of colleges to see that in supplying public entertainment they have embarked upon an operation which is different from their educational functions—and one that requires different management. Colleges have acted as if athletics were merely an extension of student recreation. Since athletes come from the same high schools as other students, are about the same age, and do get a kind of education, it has been assumed that the academic regulations applicable to the general run of students should also apply to athletes. We overlook completely the different reasons for which each is there. Hence schools have prescribed the same formal academic requirements for both the athlete and the nonathlete —a minimum number of hours must be taken, a certain number of courses must be passed, systematic progress, however slow, must be made toward a degree, and a host of other regulations must be followed.

Yet athletics, like a corrosive acid, has eaten through every academic regulation—to the great frustration, bewilderment, and cynicism of the educational community. It has defeated faculties, forced the resignations of presidents, wrecked coaches, and undercut the support of institutions where the efforts to apply academic regulations have been insistent. Where such regulations have been successfully applied they have all but killed the athletic programs, or put them in abeyance, as at New York University, Fordham, or Pittsburgh, until a more "understanding" attitude permits revival. There are, of course, many schools— Oberlin, Swarthmore, Haverford, Bowdoin, to name a few—that attract little attention from the entertainment-seeking public because they make little attempt to supply public entertainment.

The truth is that the appetite of the public cannot be satisfied by the quality of entertainment which can be provided by athletics governed by academic regulations. Consequently, at institutions which are meeting the public's demands, academic regulations must be ignored, compromised, or eliminated. Admission requirements for athletes have become less formidable than they used to be, and usually an arrangement can be made for the boys to make up high school deficiencies. The requirements as to courses, progress toward degrees, and even grades can generally be met by either a flexible elective system or the "tailored curriculum" leading to a highly specialized "degree" in which many hours of handball, swimming, and coaching can be included. Where this does not suffice, every athletic department of any size provides at its own expense counseling and tutoring service for any of its men likely to get into trouble. Not all athletes need these negations of educational regulations, but the point is that when required the negations must be available. How compelling the necessity is can be estimated by the situations which come to light when these compromises are not sufficient—the wholesale cheating at West Point, the alteration of records at William and Mary, special examinations, and countless other devices involving various degrees of accommodation or even fraud and misdemeanor. No matter what the regulation, if it prevents athletics from supplying the public entertainment for which it exists, a way around must be found. This has been the fate which has uniformly attended the regulative efforts of faculties, administrators, code committees, accrediting associations, and even the N.C.A.A. itself.

Why should this conflict be so irreconcilable? There are many reasons, but perhaps the most compelling is that adequate entertainment can only be provided by winning teams. No amount of gushy sentiment about "playing the game" will conceal the fact that the public wants its teams to win. Victory is a part of the total titillation. If the public can't have it from one source it will transfer its loyalties and money to some other. Chick Meehan filled Yankee Stadium with football fans roaring for N.Y.U., but when de-emphasis came, N.Y.U. found that 6000 was a good crowd to watch it play Fordham, the archrival. "When Michigan loses, someone has to pay" may be a slogan at Ann Arbor, but it sums up the attitude of all schools with athletic entertainment programs.

This means that to supply the entertainment, the schools must get the entertainers.

The recruitment of players is the key to most of the athletic anxieties of college presidents, the desperation of coaches, the pressure of alumni, and the activities of outside influences, business and otherwise. A chain reaction of undesirable consequences follows. The school must get the player, and the best one; the player knows this, and the bidding starts. Sometimes negotiations are carried on by a parent or other relative in order that the player may be technically free of all non-amateur bargains; otherwise he becomes a part of a corrupt bargain about which, if questions arise, he must lie or forever keep silent. Gradually the "board, room, and tuition" formula —plus a little extra, if necessary—has won acceptance. Sometimes the myth of employment persists as the justification for such payments, but it is now generally acknowledged to be a myth. The effort to limit the number of such scholarships is actually an effort to equalize competition between schools. The conferences often set a limit—but there are ways around it, the junior college "farm system" for one.

The bidding, of course, is highest for the best. In this field rumor is rife. There is the cartoon of the coach who angrily turns to one of his players and says: "Jones, you're through! Turn in your suit and your convertible." The deal may have a hundred variations, from a pledge to help the ambitious athlete on through medical school to assistance to various relatives. My own experience leads me to believe that the bizarre bargain is less frequent than educators and the public think, but is crucial nonetheless. One or two stars can transform a team into a winner and are worth what they cost. Schools bargain with all kinds of appeals—the prestige of the Ivy League may appeal to the boy from the Middle West; religious affiliation may take a boy to Notre Dame; the lavish dormitory facilities for athletes may tip the scales for Louisiana State or Texas. Most conferences have rules which prevent an athlete who has signed with one school from leaving it to join another, even though he later discovers the immense advantages of the second school. Conferences resent scouts from outside their territory, yet raiding is universal. By a dozen devices high school coaches are encouraged to become feeders for particular colleges and universities, sometimes by the flattering appointment to a coaching school staff, support for a bigger job, or even cash. Thus the web of recruitment is widespread, subtle, and effective.

The services of the American educational system in the field of public entertainment cannot be taken lightly—least of all by the educational institutions themselves. It may not be an ideal use of an educational institution to supply public entertainment, but the public interest exists; and for the institutions, either the necessity or the willingness to supply it also exists. The schools which would like to refuse will be compelled to supply it to keep up with their willing rivals. Their only choice is whether they will manage the entertainment in such a way as to prevent damage to themselves as educational institutions—damage which the present methods certainly entail. These methods frequently create financial obligations which imperil educational development because they have contractual priority over educational budgets. Those who recruit players and the players who are recruited are too often corrupted not because of the bargains they strike, but because the bargains are in violation of pledges all have agreed to uphold. Influences outside universities are encouraged to seek control of educational operations—influences which are seldom willing to confine their interests to athletics. Athletics requires an atmosphere of academic accommodation to its necessities, to the great cynicism of faculties and students. It has bred a kind of humiliating schizophrenia in educational administrators who are compelled to defend with platitudes what they do not believe or to keep an uneasy silence. It has created a kind of amused tolerance toward institutions on the part of the very public which buys the entertainment—a tolerance which says that whatever the virtues and respectability of higher education on all other scores, it must be given the privilege of this secret sin.

IV

At the risk of scornful disagreement let me outline how, it seems to me, the great strain in our educational institutions can be reduced. The first and most crucial step is purely intellectual: to make the admission, both inside and outside the universities, that our programs of intercollegiate athletics are operated primarily as public entertainment and not as educational responsibilities. This will lay a foundation for entirely new solutions to the problem.

With the acceptance of this concept most of the undesirable stresses and strains will begin to disappear. Athletics—that is, *winning* athletics—now becomes a legitimate university operation. Recruiting becomes not only legal but justifiable. To get the best athletes becomes not only understandable but commendable in exactly the same way that one seeks for excellence in any department of the university. One gives the athlete what the resources will allow—just as Illinois offers the graduate assistant in history or chemistry what it can to attract the best. No one thinks the less of Illinois because it can outbid Montana for graduate students. In short, athletic practices which are not at all appropriate to "educational" activities become acceptable and legitimate as parts of a program of public entertainment.

The same principle clarifies the position and character of the coaching staff. Let it be the best that can be obtained, as large and specialized as the situation requires. Let it be freed to meet its obligations without the moral strain imposed by the necessity to circumvent impossible requirements. The financial situation likewise becomes manageable. Since athletics is to be managed as entertainment, it need not in logic or in fact be a charge on the educational budget; and just as no educational institution expects to support itself from athletics, so athletics should not expect to be a charge on education. Self-support for athletics as public entertainment is at once a financial liberation and a restraint.

And why should there be concern about the academic record of a young man who comes to a university primarily to play on a team and whom the university has brought for exactly that purpose? I submit that nothing is lost by relieving all athletes of the obligation to meet academic requirements, if they cannot or do not wish to do so. Let us be courageous enough to admit that the university's interest in them is that they be good athletes, not that they be good students. It is the insistence that they be

students which creates the problem both for the faculty and for the athletic managers, and to the detriment of both. Of course, if a boy wishes to be a student as well as an athlete, by all means encourage him, but in that case the fact that he is an athlete need not enter into his status as a student any more than his grades as a student should be made to affect his effectiveness as an athlete. The athlete will then for the first time be on a par with every other student who works his way through school. His academic progress will be exactly proportional to the time and interest he has beyond the demands of his employment.

What if the athlete has no interest whatsoever in his further education? A team entirely made up of professionals is not the solution for the colleges. The best solution is a prescription of academic work suited to the tastes and talents of the athlete but with the clear understanding by professors and athletes alike that the record as a student will be neither a hindrance nor a help to athletic success.

What! someone says. Have unbridled bidding for athletes? No eligibility rules? No discipline? By no means—but let these things arise, as they will, from athletic and not from academic sources and necessities. Let eligibility rules be drawn and enforced by those who are most concerned about them—the athletic managements—not by faculties. Who can be counted on to expose infractions of eligibility rules? Opponents! Every roster of players is exchanged between coaches—why should a faculty committee bother? Who is hurt if the ineligible player plays? The opposition! Who is the best insurance that he won't? The opposition! No, faculties and administrators have gratuitously assumed a lot of unnecessary burdens—and to what purpose or to what effect it is hard to see.

The relinquishment of formal academic—not institutional—control over athletics will have very substantial advantages both for athletics and for education. The first is the restoration of institutional and personal integrity. Gone will be the necessity to keep up the pretense that at the present time suffuses the discussion of athletics as a part of an educational program. The establishment of single-mindedness will be the greatest advantage, for educational institutions are basically devoted to intellectual honesty. Such honesty will free athletics as well as education from the schizophrenia from which they both now suffer.

A very valuable outcome will also be the dissipation of the sentimentality which currently surrounds college athletics in the mind of the public. This myth is carefully preserved not for its truth but for its utility. Listen to any major coach talk about his team and you will see how little such sentimentality is justified. He refers to his "material," not to boys; he discusses weakness at end and tackle and backfield, completely oblivious of the feelings of his men. There is not a player whom he will not instantly displace if he can get a better one. One of the most unhappy tasks that athletic managements must perform is to get rid of players to whom scholarships have been given—commitments made—but who can't

quite make the grade on the field. Perhaps the public which sees the universities as operating departments of public entertainment and sees athletes as assistants in the department will come to think of the whole matter a little differently—to the great relief of everyone concerned.

When doctors find that a given treatment results in no improvement, they re-examine their diagnosis; when scientists find that experiments produce no anticipated results, they revise their basic hypothesis. Educators now find that what was once the recreation of students in school has been transformed into a responsibility of the educational system to supply the public with entertainment. It is essential that educators carry through a fundamental revision of concepts of athletic management appropriate to this transformation.

SCIENCE AND TECHNOLOGY

I. I. RABI *Faith in Science*

Isidor Isaac Rabi (1898-   ), Higgins Professor of Physics at Columbia University, was born in Austria and was brought to America in his infancy. After attending Cornell and Columbia Universities he did postgraduate work at several European universities. He served as a member of the General Advisory Committee for the United States Atomic Energy Commission and was awarded the Nobel Prize in 1944 for his work in nuclear physics.

For scientists, Professor Rabi feels, the unknown is full of interest and promise, and the scientific tradition should help man to renew and reaffirm his faith. Although the references in the opening paragraphs may have lost some of their pointedness, the central idea of the essay remains relevant and important to our society.

1. Mankind is puny and feeble under the heavens as long as it is ignorant. It is ignorant in so far as it is self-limited by dogma, custom, and most of all by fear—fear of the unknown. To science the unknown is a problem full of interest and promise; in fact science derives its sustenance from the unknown; all the good things have come from that inexhaustible realm. But without the light of science the unknown is a menace to be avoided by taboo or propitiated by incantation and sacrifice. The scientific tradition rests first of all on a faith in mankind, in the ability of humans to understand, and ultimately, within certain limits, which are in the nature of things, to control, the environment in which we live in all its aspects: physical, biological, and social.

2. This optimistic faith has always permeated and energized the American way of life. The scientific tradition should help us to renew and reaffirm our faith. In recent years, however, ominous symptoms of moral hypochondria have disturbed the develop-

FAITH IN SCIENCE: Reprinted, by permission of the author, from *The Atlantic Monthly*, January 1951. Copyright, 1951, by the Atlantic Monthly Company.

ment of our institutions. Under the threat of impending conflict with the Russian empire some sections of the public have reacted with blind, irrational fear. The action of Congress in overriding the presidential veto of the anti-Communist bill and the arrogant dismissal of a large number of professors by the regents of the University of California are the newest examples of what I would call moral hypochondria. A healthy awareness of grave danger should lead to clear, considered, decisive action. Hysterical fear results in the setting up of taboos around emotionally charged words and symbols. The real objective, security for the free development of our institutions, becomes hazy and possibly perverted when panic takes over.

3. The greatest enemy of the scientific tradition is superstition. By superstition I do not mean merely a belief in goblins, gremlins, and the malevolent power of Friday the 13th. The superstition which is completely incompatible with the scientific tradition usually comes as a plausible system of ideas founded on premises which defy exact formulation. They may be words without a definite meaning or infer-

ences from events inexactly described or unique and nonrepetitive.

4. An attempt to study a superstition in an external, objective fashion usually encounters emotional and often physical opposition from its proponents. Mankind seems to have a genius for the invention of superstition. As science advances, superstition makes more and more use of the terminology of science; it becomes in fact a parody of the scientific method, a deft mixture of the true and the false, which often has a fatal fascination.

5. The best examples of this sort of thing can probably be found within the realm of the Soviets. The whole Nazi movement in Germany was founded on this kind of superstition. Superstitions arise everywhere and there is no force which can hope to combat them successfully except science.

6. Even science itself has not been wholly free from superstition. Science strives for understanding, but how can one distinguish understanding from mere plausibility? The scientific tradition, although affirmative in spirit, polices itself by a profound skepticism. There are many examples where scientists have made mistakes, where they have been fooled or have fooled themselves. However, all their work passes under the scrutiny of friendly but skeptical minds.

7. Individual authority no longer possesses any force in the scientific tradition. No scientist, however great his renown, can mislead his fellow scientists for longer than it takes to check his observations or verify his conclusions and their consequences. Whether the individual scientist acknowledges his error or not is of little consequence as long as the tradition is kept pure. Controversy and polemic are now outmoded forms of scientific publication except possibly within the Soviet Union. Even there the appeal is hardly meant for fellow scientists.

8. I dwell on this point not only to show something of the reason for the great authority of established scientific doctrine, but also to indicate the way of life of science when it is free. If some of the customs and tradition of science could be transferred to the halls of our Congress or the United Nations, how beautiful life could become.

9. It is a truism to say that the application of science to technology is the basis of modern life in the United States. I refer not only to the products in everyday use, from the automobile parked in the street to the detergent in the kitchen, but more to the living social integration of our economy. Cut a relatively few electric power lines and the larger gasoline pipes which cross the country from west to east and south to north and keep them cut for a while. The effect on the life of the country would be like a thumb on the windpipe of a baby. Even the proud independent farmer would be unable to cultivate his acres without gasoline. His horses are gone and his wife is not inured to pulling the plow.

10. The development of new means of communication, production, transportation, and control have not merely added new possibilities to an existing way of living: they have so altered our basic patterns of organization that national life as of today would be impossible without them. We consider ourselves exponents of individualism and free enterprise, and national planning is on the whole unpopular. Yet we live under a degree of integration of social effort comparable to that of the cells in our bodies. I doubt very much whether we would have dared to build a social structure which is so vulnerable to attack from without, and to social disorganization from within, if it were actually planned from the very beginning.

11. On the other hand, if we consider the assimilation of science into our way of thought we find that our general public—and even our educated public—is as ignorant of science as a healthy Hottentot is of physiology. We are like the city boy who likes milk but is afraid of cows.

12. It is one of the paradoxes of our age that our general public, our lawmakers, our molders of public opinion, novelists, columnists, labor leaders, and administrators, have not devoted themselves more to understanding this force which is shaping our present and our future. Wise decisions in which science is involved cannot be reached merely by consulting experts. The very aims and ideals which condition these decisions come from the intellectual and spiritual background of the people who are in positions of responsibility. These ideals come from within and are

a part of the culture of the nation. We do not ask an expert to tell us what should be our heart's desire. We only ask him how it is to be attained.

13. Barring war or other catastrophe our standard of living, and therefore our dependence on science, will increase rather than decrease. Even if our population were decentralized, our dependence on science would not be lessened, but rather increased, if we wish to maintain and better our standards of health and comfort. Is it not folly to believe that a complex organism like our society, dependent as it is on science for its lifeblood and development, can continue to be managed properly by people whose education is not imbued with the living tradition of science, who have never experienced the influence of a scientific discipline?

14. For what science has to offer, and for what the country needs, a mere interest in the so-called scientific method, without specific knowledge of some part of some science, is as devoid of content as moral principle without moral action.

15. Over and above our lives as citizens, we also live our lives as individuals. What has science to offer as a guide to conduct and to the enrichment of one's inner life?

16. Fundamental to the existence of science is a body of established facts which come either from observation of nature in the raw, so to speak, or from experiment. Without facts we have no science. Facts are to the scientist what words are to the poet. The scientist has a love of facts, even isolated facts, similar to the poet's love of words. But a collection of facts is not science any more than a dictionary is poetry. Around his facts the scientist weaves a logical pattern or theory which gives the facts meaning, order, and significance. For example, no one can look at a brilliant night sky without emotion, but the realization that the earth and planets move in great orbits according to simple laws gives proportion and significance to this experience.

17. Theory may be qualitative and descriptive like Darwin's theory of the origin of species, or quantitative, exact, and mathematical in form like Newton's theory of the motions of planets. In both cases the theory goes far beyond the facts because it has unforeseen consequences which can be applied to new facts or be tested by experiment.

18. A scientific theory is not a discovery of a law of nature in the sense of a discovery of a mine or the end result of a treasure hunt or a statute that has been hidden in an obscure volume. It is a free creation of the human mind. It becomes a guide to new discovery and a way of looking at the world—which gives it meaning.

19. A successful theory goes far beyond the facts which it was made to fit. Newton in his laws of motion and theory of universal gravitation essentially created a universe which seemed to have the same properties as the existing universe. But it is hardly to be expected that the creation of a finite human mind would duplicate existing nature in every respect. The history of science indicates that it can't be done. Newton's theory has given place to Einstein's theory of relativity and gravitation. The Darwinian theory has been greatly modified by the geneticists.

20. The great scientific theories enable us to project our knowledge to enormous distances in time and space. They enable us to penetrate below the surface to the interior of the atom, or to the operation of our bodies and our minds. They are tremendously strong and beautiful structures, the fruit of the labors of many generations. Yet they are man-made and contingent. New discoveries and insights may modify them or even overthrow them entirely. However, what was good in them is never lost, but is taken over in the new theory in a different context. In this respect the scientist is the most conservative of men.

21. More than anything else, science requires for its progress opportunity for free, untrammeled, creative activity. The scientist must follow his thought and his data wherever they may lead. A new and fundamental scientific idea is always strange and uncomfortable to established doctrine and must have complete freedom in its development; otherwise it may be strangled at birth. Ever since the time of Galileo the progress of science has continued without a break and at an accelerated rate in spite of war, revolution, and persecution. However, this progress has not always been in the same country. When science faltered in Italy,

it began to bloom in England and Holland, then in France and Germany. Now that scientific progress is unfortunately slowing down in Europe, science in the United States after an incredibly long period of quiescence has burst out with tremendous vigor.

22. The great contributions to science in any country have usually come during or close to a period of great vigor in other fields, in periods of optimism, expansion, and revolutionary creative activity. In England it was right after the Elizabethan period. Newton's great contributions came within fifty years after the death of Shakespeare. The other great period in British science was between the Napoleonic Wars and the First World War. It was also a period of great poetry. In the United States the giant figure of Benjamin Franklin had no equal down to the most recent times; his period also produced the greatest statesmen in our history.

23. I do not wish to imply any necessary causal connection between important achievement in different fields of activity, but no one will deny that certain intellectual, moral, and spiritual climates are more conducive to creative activity than others. No one can deny that the continuity of a living tradition can be broken by the murder, exile, or ostracism of its chief exponents, or that a culture which is sterile can be kept so indefinitely by rigorous police action which prevents the intrusion of alien ideas. We have seen all too many examples of the self-preservation of sterility in recent years.

24. Fortunately for the scientific tradition it carries with it many gifts, some of which are more practical than spiritual, and therefore it has never lacked a new home when the time came to move. Science has never become localized in any place or in any culture. It is merely human and universal. French science and German science, Russian, English, Japanese, and American, do not exist separately as does poetry or some other arts such as law and government. They all speak the same universal language of science and say the same things when they have something to say. When another mode is imposed from without, science either quietly dies or goes away, leaving the field to the charlatan and pseudoscientist.

25. What then are our conclusions? What does the tradition of science teach us?

26. It teaches us moderation and tolerance of ideas, not because of lack of faith in one's own belief, but because every view is subject to change and every truth we know is only partial. The strange thought or custom may still be valid.

27. It teaches coöperation not only among people of the same kind, but also of the most diverse origins and cultures. Science is the most successful coöperative effort in the history of mankind.

28. Science inspires us with a feeling of hopefulness and of infinite possibility. The road ahead may be invisible but the tradition of science has shown that the human spirit applied in the tradition of science will find a way toward the objective. Science shows that it is possible to foresee and to plan and that we can take the future into our own hands if we rid ourselves of prejudice and superstition.

29. The tradition of science teaches us that no vested interests in institutions or systems of thought should escape continual re-examination merely because they have existed and have been successful. On the other hand it also teaches us to conserve what is operative and useful.

30. Science teaches us self-discipline. One must continually look for the mote in one's own eye. The history of science shows that it is always there.

31. These lessons can be multiplied to cover almost the entire range of human activity, because science is itself a contemporaneous living thing made by men for man's edification and entertainment.

32. I will close with one last point. Science is fun even for the amateur. Every scientist is himself an amateur in another field of science which is not his specialty, but the spirit is the same. Science is a game that is inspiring and refreshing. The playing field is the universe itself. The stakes are high, because you must put down all your preconceived ideas and habits of thought. The rewards are great because you find a home in the world, a home you have made for yourself.

RALPH ROSS *The Social Consequences of Science*

Ralph Gilbert Ross (1911-   ) is chairman of the humanities program at the University of Minnesota. Although he is primarily a philosopher, he has taught world literature and political theory and has been a member of the editorial board of the *Bulletin of the Institute of Social Studies*. He has contributed to numerous journals, among them the *Journal of Philosophy, Ethics, New Republic,* the *Partisan Review,* and the *Public Opinion Quarterly.* He is the author of *Skepticism and Dogma,* 1940, and co-author of *An Introduction to Contemporary Society,* 1957, from which the following excerpt is taken.

After reviewing the rapid progress of technology during the past century and a half and describing its effects on our society, Professor Ross raises some provocative questions: How can man, liberated from slavery by the machine, prevent the machine from making him subhuman, as does slavery itself? What role should the social scientist play in society, what sort of influence does he want to have, and how can he have that influence under contemporary conditions?

CONSEQUENCES OF TECHNOLOGY

1. For good or ill, the rate of social change is constantly being accelerated. Every decade seems to contain more changes than the half century before it and these changes are, to an enormous extent, the results of modern invention: the electric light, the telephone, wireless, radio, television, propeller-driven aircraft, jet aircraft, atomic energy. Of course, to get these society had to approve research, and to use them it had to be receptive to technological innovation. But granted these conditions, which surely characterize our society, technology has a pervasive influence on our lives.

2. Although technology is the most obvious social consequence of contemporary science, it is not the only one. Acceptance of science fosters a pragmatic and engineering attitude which leads to the manipulation of the environment, physical and social, for the deliberate attainment of ends. This attitude has probably weakened religious belief and the

THE SOCIAL CONSEQUENCES OF SCIENCE: From *An Introduction to Contemporary Society* by Ernest van den Haag and Ralph Ross, Harcourt, Brace and Company. Inc., 1957.

acceptance of many traditional values. It has also led to a cult of the pseudoscientific, which nurtures irrationality.

3. Technology has become part of us in a more intimate way than the scientific outlook has. Life is much more comfortable, and physical mobility is increasing with the greatest rapidity. Within the last hundred and fifty years there has been more technological change in Europe and America than there was for a thousand years before. The chief form of conveyance at the beginning of the nineteenth century was the horse or horse-drawn carriage, exactly as it was in ancient Rome or, for that matter, among the Mongolian hordes of the Steppes. Agriculture was conducted essentially as it had been on the farms of the Middle Ages. Oil and wax still lit houses at night. Communication was so slow that Andrew Jackson and his troops fought the battle of New Orleans months after the War of 1812 had been officially ended by treaty. Roads and dams were not nearly so good as those the Romans used to construct; neither was plumbing.

4. In these hundred and fifty years applied

science in the form of medicine, higher standards of living, and sanitation, has been a factor in increasing population and extending the individual life span. Whereas the total population of the world in 1800 is estimated at one billion ninety-eight million, demographic figures for the year 2000, only two hundred years later, estimate the population of China alone at one billion. The population of the United States at the end of 1800 was only three-quarters as great as the population of New York City today. (Of course, immigration was a factor in America's growth.) Surely this immense increase has contributed to the intensity of pressures felt, especially by the urban population, in our day.

5. Not only are there more of us, but we are older. On the average, the life span in the United States is sixty-eight years; in 1800 it was about thirty-five years. Countries that are technologically backward, especially crowded ones, are far behind our standards of longevity, even behind our standards as of 1800. Life-expectancy in India, for example, is about twenty-eight years. A tremendous infant mortality accounts largely for this low figure, but even when an Indian survives infancy, his life span is less than that of Americans taken as a whole. Further, women outlive men by as much as five years in all European and American countries, but Indian women do not live as long as Indian men; the primitive conditions of their work and the sheer amount of it take a great toll.

6. Law, industry, and social mores are affected by the increased average age of our population. Either people must be allowed to work to a later age than before, or they become a financial burden for many years on their children—or, through pensions and social security, on business and government. The tax structure is being revised to meet this new expenditure, and businesses are changing their retirement rules, but there is another problem which cannot be met so directly: what are retired people to do with their leisure time? This is part of the general problem of increased leisure brought about for all age groups by more money and fewer working hours. The entertainment industries have boomed in consequence; Florida, California, and Arizona have new settlers of advanced

years; and adult education has become a major part of American education.

7. What is still not clear is the effect of this ever growing age group on political attitudes and social customs. Obviously, there are new interests to be served by social security plans, and so there is some movement toward a welfare state. But what about public attitudes toward war and peace, freedom, initiative and personal security, love and marriage, when the public is composed of age groups in a different numerical proportion than ever before? Is such a public more "liberal" or more "conservative"? Is it partly responsible for the changes in the political climate of the last decade? These are important questions for the social sciences. When we have some answers to particular questions like these, we may also have the outline of an ongoing trend.

8. Technology is also responsible for an enormous physical mobility and for an increase in the social mobility inherent in our system. Although the airplane is the most dramatic symbol of the revolution in transportation, it is the automobile that has so far affected our lives most. Sociologists and novelists have given us a picture of the alteration in family life brought about by the automobile: the drives on week ends, the dating and courtship patterns of adolescents, the roadside motel. We are a nation on wheels and we move about restlessly.

9. Physical and social mobility have, to some extent, grown together. As it gets easier for labor to move and be moved our economy grows more flexible and opportunities for advancement that depend on physical movement are more readily seized. Innovation, especially in the form of laborsaving devices, releases workers from one job and creates a demand for them in others which may be geographically distant. To move to a new locale in order to profit economically is also to give up friends and to break the ties of community that are often the source of emotional stability and happiness.

10. The premium placed on innovation raises the level of aspiration and this in turn yields more innovation. To many Americans there seems no end to this process; and since the prospect of constant technological advance

fits so well with other beliefs—the optimism of democratic and egalitarian attitudes and a religious notion of the perfectibility of man—it bolsters a basic social myth, progress.

11. For the moment, the belief in progress is countered by fear of world destruction. We seem to alternate between dread of a future shattered by deadly atomic weapons and hope of a future which combines H. G. Wells with Buck Rogers: prosperity for everybody, almost all work done by the machine, spaceships traveling on schedule through the planetary system, a world which is really a vision of New York City developed in mechanization and made universal.

12. Yet the greater dangers are probably not in the prospects of destruction but in the future we hope for, and many of them already exist. Many traditional values of American life —self-improvement, advancement by merit, the possibility that every man will reach the top, novelty, adventure, and excitement—can be realized today in terms of technological advance as they were once in terms of the frontier. But there is now an enormous price to pay in insecurity and anxiety. The greater the rate of change, the more difficult it is to adjust to the new situation; and the more we emphasize the future, the less we remember the past. If every day brings something new, yesterday was little preparation for it. Competition may yield progress, but it also yields insecurity and the fear of failure, and novelty and adventure are not easy to reconcile with stability and peace. An ever changing and exciting society is likely to be full of restless people, living frantically in a pursuit of success and approval, having no time for contentment, regarding serenity as an antique or medieval ideal.

13. A peculiar tragedy of our time is the split between life and work, a division made more extreme by the machine. Tending the machine for seven or eight hours a day is the lot of many of us,[1] and it is work that is properly called "mechanical," work in which we ourselves behave as though we were machines, and in which little is asked of us except a

[1] Not only of "workers," but of the white-collar tenders of typewriters, calculators, check-writing machines, etc.

monotonous, machinelike accuracy. It is an old story that the age of the craftsman is behind us. On the modern assembly line, men are not able to carry through the making of a product from its inception to its completion, garnering the satisfaction of creativity. Rather, they work constantly at a single operation, usually not knowing what precedes or succeeds it. At its worst, the task of the machine tender is the task of the robot; and only when the worker of the machine returns to his home after his day's labor does he begin his real life. Creativity, which was once the birthright of every craftsman, is now limited to the designer in the drafting room. A life in which basic interests extend to work is usually led only by the artist, the scientist, the entrepreneur, sometimes the physician, lawyer, and teacher. The machine has liberated us from actual slavery; it is one of our greatest problems to see that it does not, like slavery, make us subhuman.

CONSEQUENCES OF THE SCIENTIFIC OUTLOOK

14. The scientific outlook, both of method and conclusion, has become part of our image of ourselves and our place in the world. Looking first at the effect of the conclusions of science, we find that chemistry, physics, and physiology have helped create the belief that man is a machine, more complicated perhaps than the machines he creates, but of the same general type. Astronomy and biology have yielded new perspectives on man's place in nature; the newly discovered vastness of the physical universe leads man to see himself as a parasite clinging to a tiny ball in a corner of one of the smaller galactic systems.[2]

15. It is a commonplace that the medieval view was that this is an earth-centered universe in which all physical things were made for man. But it is worth quoting Anatole France's description of that world in The Garden of Epicurus.

We have some trouble in picturing the state of mind of a man of olden times who firmly believed that the earth was the center of the world and that

[2] The effect of this perspective on older religious views of man is dramatized by Wilbur Daniel Steele in a short story, "The Man Who Saw Through Heaven." See The Best Stories of Wilbur Daniel Steele, Doubleday, 1946.

all the stars turned round it. He felt under his feet the souls of the damned writhing in flames, and perhaps he had seen with his own eyes and smelled with his own nostrils the sulphurous fumes of Hell escaping from some fissures in the rocks. Lifting his head he contemplated the twelve spheres, that of the elements, containing the air and fire, then the spheres of the Moon, of Mercury, of Venus, which Dante visited on Good Friday of the year 1300, then those of the Sun, of Mars, of Jupiter, and of Saturn, then the incorruptible firmament from which the stars were hung like lamps. Beyond, his mind's eye discerned the Ninth Heaven to which saints were rapt, the Primum Mobile or Crystalline, and finally the Empyrean, abode of the blessed, toward which, he firmly hoped, after his death two angels robed in white would bear away, as it were a little child, his soul washed in baptism and perfumed with the oil of the last sacraments. In those days God had no other children than men, and all his creation was ordered in a fashion at once childlike and poetic, like an immense cathedral. Thus imagined, the universe was so simple that it was represented in its entirety with its true shape and motions in certain great painted clocks run by machinery.

We are done with the twelve heavens and the planets under which men were born lucky or unlucky, jovial or saturnine. The solid vault of the firmament is shattered. Our eye and our thought plunge into the infinite abysses of heaven. Beyond the planets we discover no longer the Empyrean of the elect and the angels, but a hundred million rolling suns, escorted by their cortege of obscure satellites invisible to us. In the midst of this infinity of worlds our own sun is but a bubble of gas and our earth but a drop of mud. . . .

16. What is seldom perceived about the medieval world view is that because it was God who had created and sustained the universe and man in this fashion, man—though the center of the *physical* universe—was weak and dependent in his more important capacity as a *spiritual* being. The universe was physically man-centered because it was spiritually God-centered. But modern science removes man from the center only as a physical creature in a physical world. Even if no place is found for the soul, the intelligence, which discovered and formulated the laws of science, takes credit for having worked the transformation by which man was removed from the center of things. We may be tiny, unimportant creatures, but it is we who know it and we who say so. The universe dwarfs man's body but is

plumbed from end to end by man's mind. Indeed, we will call a statement true only if it can be verified by man's methods and senses. Once again, as for the ancient Greek sophists, "man is the measure of all things." He has taken himself from the physical center of the universe, where medieval man had placed him, and put himself in the spiritual center where medieval man placed God.

17. Instead of humility resulting from this change in physical conception, as many scientists expected, man became arrogant. As some of Dostoevski's characters say, if there is no God, then man is God; or as Nietzsche's Zarathustra put it, since God is dead we must prepare the way for the Man-God.

18. The methods of science have perhaps affected our outlook less than the picture of the world implicit in scientific conclusions. To be sure, there may be a more widespread demand today than ever before for evidence of a sort science would accept, and a skepticism about knowledge that is not scientific. But we tend to replace beliefs we have come to doubt with others no less dubious and often much more dangerous. Belief in religion is replaced by religious devotion to political belief and redemption in heaven by redemption on earth. And we are often naïve when we most want to be "scientific" about the views we have inherited. We think that we are no longer entitled to once cherished beliefs and biases which cannot be supported by scientific information. Yet all that an inability to find scientific warrant for our beliefs means is that they cannot be accepted in the body of science, or that our rationalizations are poor. It does not follow that the beliefs should be abandoned—that religious people, for example, are obligated to become atheists or agnostics, or that we should regard moral virtues, like honesty, as matters of taste.

19. Science has perhaps had its greatest effect on man's outlook indirectly, through technology. This is an age of machines and gadgets, and they stand between us and the simple essentials of daily life. Between the housewife and the dirty floors, dirty dishes, and dirty clothes are the vacuum cleaner, the dishwasher, and the automatic washing machine. For a long time now, the abattoir, the butcher, and the grocer have stood between

the city dweller and his food, but today the picture magazine, the comic strip, and the digest have come between man and his books. The enormous rate of literacy—but literacy without real education—yields a mass market for the great industries of "popular culture," which create our entertainment in patterns as rigid as if they were stamped out by machine.

20. In contrast, the arts are always individual and unstereotyped. They have not become "scientific," whatever that might mean for art, but they have been influenced to the extent of expressing the values of an age that seemed characteristically scientific and technical. In some artists the idea of a technical age was relatively simple. They wrote poems about bridges (the highly talented American poet Hart Crane is a good example) and factories and skyscrapers. They tried to express the spirit of the age by painting pictures of machines and writing music that gave the quality of steel mills and subways. A minor Russian composer, Mosolov, made a popular success with an orchestral composition called *Iron Foundry*, which celebrated the factory and its workers. Jazz music was discovered as art because its tempo had the frantic urgency of modern life. In other artists particular physical aspects of a "scientific" or machine society dominated. The sharp, geometrical outline of machines—exaggerated, to be sure—was a model that exerted great influence on modern abstract painting; and the beauty of steel scaffoldings and turning wheels was a byword in the 1920's. The French painter Fernand Leger, for example, went from machines to abstractions in his canvases.

21. The reaction against both science and technology in the arts has more recently been the rule. For some artists there is a dedication to older values and traditional wisdom which, they feel, it is the mission of art to save. This is the belief of T. S. Eliot and most of his followers, many of whom first accepted this technical age and then rebelled against it. Other artists have tried to escape the consequences of one sort of science (physical) by fleeing to another (psychological). Psychoanalysis has inspired painting that is said to be a direct expression of the subconscious, as in the work of surrealists like Salvador Dali. In a more extreme art, even the shapes and forms of

the external world are absent—note the work of a school called "abstract expressionism." And there is an insistence on being self-taught [3] because, it is said, formal study inhibits creativity and is essentially technical, like the world that is being rejected.

22. Perhaps the most obvious influence of science and technology on social behavior is the growth of social engineering, the manipulation of specific environments to effect desired changes. Applications of penology and child psychology are good examples. As we have overcome beliefs that all criminals are possessed by demons, or that criminality is inherited, or that particular physical types are inclined to crime, we have become more willing to clear slum areas and to try to reform prisoners, to socialize them properly, by changing prisons and reformatories. Much child psychology is ridiculed, often justifiably, when it is applied, but when we compare the rearing of children today with that of the past, we can only be grateful for the change.

23. Group relations is another sphere of social engineering. How large a part the spread of social science has played in curing one of the dread sores of American life, the lynching of Negroes in the South, we cannot tell. But religion and old-fashioned moral education were surely strongest when lynchings were at their numerical height, so they can claim no credit. The Supreme Court decision on segregation in the schools, whether right or wrong, was avowedly based on documents of sociology and social psychology presented by the plaintiffs.

24. But there has been at least as much foolishness as rationality engendered by the way in which the layman understands science and acknowledges its prestige. People are prone to find new superstitions when they give up old ones, and today it is fashionable to call current superstitions "scientific." A generation ago thousands of Americans responded to the new psychology by treating a Frenchman named Coué as a hero. They applied his principle of cure through suggestion by staring at themselves in the mirror as they repeated twenty times in succession: "Every day, in

[3] Ben Jonson said that the man who boasts he is self-taught had a fool for his master.

every way, I am getting better and better." At the moment, reverence for science is often exhibited by well-fed people in comfortable financial circumstances who consume a cupful of unnecessary vitamin pills every twenty-four hours.

25. Even where the attitudes of science have taken deeper root, as they have among engineers, they sometimes lead to strangely unscientific beliefs, of which we can cite an interesting political example. In America during the post-1929 depression, a group that were led by engineers and that called themselves Technocrats had a brief moment of popularity. The Technocrats proposed to solve all economic and social problems by the application of engineering methods. They promised an average family income of $20,000 a year and painted a future of abundance and leisure in a "scientific" society. Yet if asked their stand on international relations, political democracy, or racial minorities, they replied only that these matters were irrelevant. The Technocrats still exist but their numbers have understandably dwindled.

26. Perhaps what underlies these follies is the disparity between the riches of the technical environment we use with such aplomb and the poverty of our knowledge of the laws, the methods, and the meaning of the science on which the techniques are based. For too many of us, the latest applications of scientific genius are so many miracles that pass understanding. This is an age in which members of a primitive tribe which has never seen a bicycle can be brought to a modern capital in a jet plane. Their astonishment and fright would be amusing and pathetic. But are we, except for being used to mechanical din and movement and the operation of gadgets, any better off? How many of us can explain what happens when a light switch is snapped and a bulb lights, beyond saying, "The current went on"? Most of us are, so far as knowledge of science is concerned, simply barbarians accustomed to machines.

27. Yet this, the press assures us, is a scientific age. And in two obvious ways the press is right. The artifacts that surround us, that we use daily and unthinkingly, are amazingly different from the artifacts of fifty, even twenty, years ago. Secondly, science and the scientist

have become symbols of authority, most powerful to those for whom they are as miraculous as the hypostatic union of the spirit and body of Christ. For the sake of our argument, it may be worth reminding ourselves of what educated people have pointed out almost *ad nauseum*. In the advertisements we see daily, men in white jackets (laboratory scientists? physicians? the advertisement does not tell) inform us that these cigarettes are milder, that toothpaste makes teeth whiter, shoes with arch supports end flat feet, and a mouthwash poured on the scalp cures dandruff. Women must wear the right brassières or they will die virgin, lonely, and ashamed. Love potions are sold everywhere but they are no longer imbibed: the ubiquitous white-jacketed man tells women to dab it on the skin and wait for the odor to overpower some male. This is the age of the expert; and the expert in white sells products not just for their imagined merits but by haunts and bogeys.

28. One result of this authoritative assault on our eyes and ears is a concern with externals that is both foolish and frightening. The mechanical, the trivial, the incidental are treated as if they were focal. Women attend "charm schools" and men take courses in winning friends and influencing people, secure in the belief that "salesmanship" alone will make their way in the world. And they are often right, for the judges of their wares are as much interested in externals as they are.

29. Another result is a change in our attitude toward "necessities." Although princes and industrial magnates of fifty years ago did without them, almost every American today assumes that life cannot be sustained without refrigerators, radios, and television sets. As for the telephone and the automobile, their absence would reduce life to the level of savagery.

30. The concept of "necessities" has varied through history with the standard of living, but the greatest change came with the fruits of the Industrial Revolution. Not only have we become accustomed to a standard of living that is comparatively very high but we are quickly dissatisfied if we do not maintain the new standard, and even dissatisfied if we do not improve on it. This psychological conversion of every gain into a necessity is fostered

by the doctrine of progress, which leads us to believe that we *should* have more all the time. It is no cause for thanksgiving when we get more, but it is a cause for complaint when we don't.

31. To round out our discussion of the social consequences of science, it is necessary to mention the change that has come from governmental support of science, especially of physics. Basic research is now fostered by the federal government through the National Science Foundation, a policy that would have horrified scientists a few years ago, because they feared control of science by government, as it would have horrified many large business groups who would have regarded it as a waste of the taxpayers' money. Similarly, universities now accept government contracts for their science faculties, although some federal control of the flow of scientific information is an obvious consequence.

32. The ideal of a free movement of scientific information throughout the world has

been seriously eroded. Sir Humphry Davy, a British physicist and chemist of the early nineteenth century, was invited by the French Academy of Sciences to deliver a lecture in Paris while France was at war with England. Equivalent action today would be treason. The national welfare in the atomic age takes precedence over many of the older ideals of the international scientific community.

33. The social scientist, too, is in a new situation. . . . Although exchange of information with his colleagues is not limited so much for the social scientist as for the natural scientist, some social research may be classified as secret: morale problems of soldiers under battle conditions, responses of civilian populations to saturation bombing, etc. But the major problem is an atmosphere of some hostility to public discussion of controversial social issues. The social scientist must ask himself what role he should play in society, what sort of influence he wants to have, and how he can have that influence under contemporary conditions.

ROBERT JUNGK *A Bit of Hell*

Robert Jungk (1913-   ) spent an adventurous youth working against the Nazi government of his native Germany. When only nineteen he was arrested for anti-Nazi activity but was later released and fled the country. Two years later he returned to Germany illegally to work for an underground press. Forced to flee Germany again, he went to Czechoslovakia, then to Paris, and finally to Switzerland, all the while engaging in anti-Nazi activities.

In 1947 Mr. Jungk came to the United States as correspondent for the Swiss press. He remained here until 1953, and in these six years accumulated the material for *Tomorrow Is Already Here*, a dramatic interpretation of the scientific miracles which are being performed in America. Mr. Jungk's picture of the atomic age is perhaps too horrific. As Herbert Agar says in his preface, ". . . so far, thank heaven, these facts are all entangled with happier aspects of our past and present—and thus they are ameliorated." Nevertheless, the facts and their implications are worth considering.

1. "Don't pick up anything you see lying in the street or in the fields," the Richland parents, who are employed by the Hanford Plutonium Works, tell their children. "Absolutely nothing, do you understand?"

2. And to underline their prohibition they tell the story of the White Man.

"Once there was a watchman from Richland who found a tool while going his rounds and picked it up and brought it home although it didn't belong to him," the story opens. "It wasn't till the next morning that he noticed that his hands had become contaminated by alpha rays and he ran in fright to H.I. Division. Then the doctors and the watchman's superiors began to dither and to make a great uproar. They drove at once to the little house where he lived with his wife and children, to get back the tool as quickly as possible. But the contagion in it had already spread everywhere: Not only the watchman and his family

had to go to the hospital but also the whole house was sick. So the White Men with the black rubber masks had to be called. They ordered the beds, tables, chairs, pillows and in fact everything that could be moved to be taken away and burned. Then they had the paint scraped from the walls, the floors torn up and the kitchen stove dismantled. For everything, everything had been poisoned. . . . And if you're disobedient, the White Man will come to us too and take all the toys away with him, and the bedroom, the dining room, the kitchen and perhaps the whole house. . . ."

3. The story of the White Man is no cautionary tale invented for pedagogical purposes. It really happened in May, 1951. There are sheaves of documents relating to it in the archives of the Atomic Energy Commission and of General Electric which, under a mandate from the state, administers the atomic factories of the U.S.A.[1] The incident itself

A BIT OF HELL: From *Tomorrow Is Already Here* by Robert Jungk. Reprinted by permission of Simon and Schuster, Inc. Copyright, 1954, by Robert Jungk.

[1] More accurately, General Electric operates the plants at Hanford, Washington, not all the atomic factories in the country [Ed. note].

could not be suppressed. Too many people in the neighborhood of the "poisoned house" knew about it. Only the watchman's name was kept secret. It was not wished that his children should be treated like pariahs at school, that the shops should refuse to deal with his wife because they did not want to receive money from her hand, that he himself should be avoided as one who has the plague. For his nearest neighbors had already done all that to him. Only when he moved from Richland to Kennewick, its sister town, where nobody knew of his mishap, was he able to live in peace again.

4. One cannot take the neighbors' alarm greatly amiss. In Richland, the brand-new, spotlessly clean town of thirty thousand inhabitants, built at the close of the war for the employees of the atomic factory twelve to twenty-five miles away, fear of contagion through the invisible radioactive particles and rays amounts to an obsession.

5. In public and continually repeated courses everyone who comes to live in Richland learns the atomic age's alphabet of fear:

Alpha rays. Positive charged helium nucleuses emanating out of the atom. Cannot penetrate the skin but can do great damage if they enter the body through small open places.

Beta rays. Electrons. Slight power of penetration. Penetrate about a third of an inch through the skin. Great danger of burns.

Gamma rays. Can penetrate from the outside deep into the body. Weaker in the mass than other forms of rays but the most difficult to ward off by protective measures because of their strong penetrative power.

Neutrons. Danger! Harmful in the highest degree. According to speed they penetrate different depths into the tissue. In the case of strong radiation internal organs are paralyzed.

6. The force of the threat is matched by the strength of the defense against it. Dr. Compton, head of the scientific armaments development in the Second World War, stated before the Special Committee of the Senate: "The atomic energy program involves by far the most dangerous production process ever undertaken by man." In 1942 some of the American atomic experts still believed it would be practically impossible to protect the workers

in the atomic industry, then existing only on paper, against the rays produced by nuclear fission. Until then there had been altogether about three pounds of radium in human possession. Now in the nuclear burners literally millions of pounds of radioactive material of widely different varieties were generated by the influence of the atom demolisher. The scientists saw clearly that enormous quantities of life-menacing rays were being generated as by-products of nuclear fission. Safety measures of such scope and severity had to be taken as had never before been remotely necessary in the protection of industrial health.

7. The geographical location of the Hanford area, where the various divisions of the plutonium works are housed, fulfills the safety requirements. In the dry, barren inland desert of Washington State in the remote Northwest of the United States, an area of nearly six hundred square miles was enclosed. Pasco, Kennewick and Richland, which are gradually growing together into one town, lie eight to twelve miles from the entrance to the factory grounds, and twenty-five to forty miles from the windowless, gray cement, fortresslike block in which the actual process of the transformation of uranium ore into the artificial element plutonium (Pu 239) takes place.

8. For miles after entering the segregated area one sees nothing different from the other side of the barrier: dry ground overgrown with dusty sagebrush, a few frightened prairie dogs scurrying before automobiles, the railway to the factory guarded by soldiers of the Fifth Army and, finally, on the distant horizon, the metal chimneys, pencil thin, painted in the same dull camouflage colors as the first warehouses which now come into view. The constantly reappearing placards, a sinister variety of the loud advertising posters to be seen along normal American roads, are a reminder, as one approaches, of the particular nature of the spot. "SILENCE MEANS SAFETY," they warn.

9. But that is only the beginning. Inside the works the admonitions follow you step by step:

DANGER! STAY OUTSIDE. FLOOR HEAVILY CONTAMINATED, or

DANGER! RADIOACTIVE RAYS, or

DANGER! HIGH NEUTRONIC FLUX

The posters exhort:

PUT ON RUBBER SHOES! CONTAMINATION BEYOND
   THIS POINT, or
DO NOT FORGET GLOVES! HOT REGION, or
TIE ON MASK! AIR UNCLEAN

The posters direct:

CONTAMINATED GLASSWARE! SWITCH ON THE
   COUNTER BEFORE USE, or
DANGER OF RADIATION! SEE THAT GLASS IS FILLED
   WITH WATER, or
SHOULD ANYTHING BE SPILLED:
   (1) HOLD YOUR BREATH
   (2) LEAVE THE ROOM AND LOCK
   (3) IMMEDIATELY NOTIFY THE HEALTH DE-
       PARTMENT

10. Next to the warnings is always the special symbol signifying danger: three purple
radial segments arranged round a dark point.

11. These lists which hang in all the halls,
passages, work and observation rooms of the
Hanford Works are only a few voices in the
unceasing chorus of warnings against the invisible poisoned rays.

12. There are the dosimeters which look
like fountain pens and change color when the
bearer has been too long exposed to radiation.
Danger when green turns to yellow. High time
to leave the workroom when yellow changes to
orange. There are the brooches with a self-
developing film which darkens, rings whose
inset turns black, water taps which tell by
their paint whether they are cool, warm, semi-
hot or hot. Mechanical sniffers emit screaming
sounds when the air becomes too strongly saturated with harmful particles. A man who
enters the most dangerous regions is put into
fantastic disguises and must feel his way with
a long staff to whose tip a Geiger tube is
fastened.

13. Countless are the measures against radioactivity. Sharp chemical soaps and fluids
attack the remains of radiation on the clothes
or hair. A chronic scrubbing, brushing and
washing goes on. As in a bad dream one tries
to scour away an invisible spot, a stain which
one is never quite sure of having removed. For
no one can as yet say with certainty whether
the effects of the work with radiating elements
may not appear years hence. Monthly as well

as special half-yearly and yearly blood and
secretion tests must be made by the Health
Division on every employee of the Hanford
Works. How many tiny particles may have
entered the circulatory system, the liver, the
gall, kidneys or spleen? Have the lymphatic
glands suffered, is the spinal cord affected?
How high is the number of white blood cor-
puscles? Are there deposits in the bone tissue?
These examinations are obligatory and unceasing.

14. To work under such conditions a man
must be fearless. But he may neither belong
to the phlegmatic group, who often appear to
advantage in dangerous situations through
lack of temperament, nor may he take the
considerable risks of his occupation too
lightly. Here again, as with the jet pilots, a
man of quiet, even temperament is sought, the
intermediate type possessing neither too much
nor too little initiative and imagination.

15. A man newly entering the army of
nearly a thousand workers in the Hanford
area is given, before ever he sets eyes on one
of the factories, a four weeks' course of instruction by lectures and educational films. Here he
is taught that because of the dangers of radiation he will often work more fussily and
slowly than he has been accustomed to doing.
He learns that he will presumably never lay
his own eyes upon the dangerous material with
which he works, that he may approach the
infected caps, screws and other machine parts,
if at all, only with special tools a yard long.
But above all, the new man will make the
acquaintance of his guardian angel who will
never leave his side for more than two or three
hours during his working time in the plutonium factory. This is the H.I. man in white,
employee of the Hanford Health Instrument
Division, which is responsible for the protection of health in the factory. To every four
persons occupied in the "hot regions" of the
works there is at least one health guardian.
He takes many tests a day to find out whether
any of his protégés may have received more
than the biologically assimilable dose of rays,
and places a precise dossier before each individual entrusted to him, in which day by day,
week by week, the current data relating to his
health are entered. If, in the H.I. man's opinion, a worker who has done a particularly "hot

job"—such as a repair or the removal of radio-active waste—has received too high a dose of dangerous rays, he can send him home on his own responsibility for the rest of the working shift or, under certain conditions, even for several days.

16. When the atomic worker, John P. Bryant, comes to the factory in the morning he is handed at the entrance two ionic chambers in pocket form, known as "pencils," and his personal brooch containing a small bit of film sensitive to rays. First of all he goes into the canteen to deposit his lunch, which he has brought along from Richland. There are no kitchens here because for reasons of safety no food may be cooked or served within the Hanford Area. Although the dining hall is far from the atomic ovens, in a "clean region," the tables are inspected at half-hourly intervals with Geiger counters for the possible presence of beta or gamma radiation, or with the portable alpha-radiation counter, known as "Poppy"; for the most feared and dangerous form of poisoning is the penetration of small particles into the stomach and intestines during the intake of food.

17. Now Mr. Bryant goes to the dressing room where he leaves his own clothes, and daily finds in his locker fresh underwear, socks, cleaned overalls, working shoes painted yellow on the tips and heels, a tight-fitting head covering, cellophane-wrapped gloves and protective goggles. Now he crosses the white line which divides the clean zone from the intermediate zone. Here, at the end of his working period, he will take off his strange uniform to step naked into the shower room watched by inspectors and equipped with special disinfectant soaps. At present the worker does not pause in the intermediate zone but proceeds directly to the hot region whose photoelectric door opens automatically before him.

18. Now he is standing in a high, bare, windowless room known as "the canyon," and waiting for his H.I. man who will make the first control tests of the morning upon him. No sooner is this accomplished than the foreman fetches him and brings him to his place of work. The colleague who has been on the night shift gives him a friendly glance through protective goggles. The men who relieve one another cannot even exchange a friendly slap

on the shoulder. The predecessor shows the newcomer the logbook of the atomic furnace in which the exact reading of the various measuring implements is recorded at regular intervals. Then John P. Bryant remains alone before a high wall without door or crevice but full of dial plates, pressure gauges, scales on whose finely marked graph paper curves are drawn in variously colored inks. Now for a few hours the worker will control the implements for control, supervise the instruments for supervision, will from time to time press buttons, turn wheels or move levers through which, behind the wall many yards thick, radioactive material is being mixed, receptacles emptied, uranium cartridges introduced and expelled.

19. There, behind the mighty shield, rages an inferno of radioactive rays. To encounter them for a matter of seconds would mean certain, even if creeping, death. Through a loud-speaker attached to a microphone connected inward, John P. Bryant can tell that something is really going on beyond the bare silent wall. Sometimes it sounds like the chirping of crickets in the summer meadows which now seem infinitely far away.

20. At ten-twenty-one during the morning shift John P. Bryant is conscious of something amiss in his atomic oven. The instrumental slate pencil on his vibration gauge has crossed the red danger line, the loud-speaker is sending an entirely new melody out of the interior of the burner. It is as though the cricket had associated himself with another animal, as though his little metal tongue were whetting itself angrily against metal teeth.

21. Bryant immediately notifies the overseer, who after brief inspection applies to Technical Division 200. Canyon 7 of Group S begins to fill with people. Engineers have hastened to the spot. A number of H.I. men are standing in readiness. Bryant's white guardian angel wishes to take radiation measurements on him at once and leads him quickly away. Meanwhile the organization's chain reaction is set going. Word is passed to the emergency Station at Richland which, in case of an improbable but not impossible explosion, would take charge of the rescue work. Twelve minutes later the signal to stop work resounds through the cement gorges of the

canyon. The plant, which operates uninterruptedly day and night, weekdays, Sundays and holidays, must be closed for repairs.

22. Occasional repairs to the machinery are as inevitable in the Hanford Plutonium Works as in other factories, even though here in the construction of reservoirs, supply lines and mixing apparatus, care was taken to use particularly resistant material. A group of new resistant metals such as titanium, germanium and zirconium has been intensively developed in the United States with a particular view to their employment in atomic installations. For in the realm of radioactive danger the replacement of a malfunctioning part becomes an endlessly awkward, timewasting and dangerous operation.

23. It is totally impossible for a human being, however strong his protective clothing, to enter the atomic furnace. The defective part must therefore be unscrewed by a remotely controlled grasping implement and then brought to a sealed region especially prepared for these occasions.

24. The preparation of this repair place, which must lie as close as possible to the site of the damage, is the first task of a small special group. It erects provisional walls of leaden tiles, provides for the installation of strong light fittings and spreads a layer of removable artificial material over the floor which will thereby be protected from contamination. It is on this spot that the remotely controlled grasping tool will lay the faulty piece.

25. This grasping implement, doomed to remain forever behind the thick walls of the furnaces because of its hopeless radioactivity, is a sort of robot whom the plutonium workers have named "Sweet Hot Dolly." She does not look in the least as the layman tends to picture a robot. Robots—and there are thousands of these mechanical slaves in the U.S.A. today, equipped with subhuman intelligence but often superhuman sense and memory organs— seldom appear in forms resembling the human body. Their creators do not care to make them in their own image; at most they bear a likeness to an organ overdeveloped to serve a purpose. Thus there are robots who are all eye, others who are all ear; that is, their seeing or hearing capacity, untrammeled by considerations of proportion to other organs, is super-

dimensional. Dolly, for instance, is all hand and arm. She requires only a small brain which needs to obey the fairly simple directions of the wireless controller, but on the other hand, her ability to touch, feel, hold and carry things is above the average. Earlier types of Dolly could make only straightforward motions, the new types can copy and combine all seven fundamental movements of the human hand.

26. The master of Sweet Hot Dolly, sitting in his cabin protected from radioactivity, begins to direct his creature into the interior of the atomic furnace. As he touches the button of the televisor and the picture flares up, he can see the robot's massive white painted body in the jungle of pipes, boilers, valves and levers behind the thick wall of lead and cement. Now he begins to move the lever, which has been placed on his left, and immediately this movement transmits itself across a distance of over a hundred yards to Dolly's left arm. She gropes in the gray metal labyrinth, she hesitates at a certain point. Her twitching movement conveys itself back to the lever in her master's hermetically closed berth. Without a doubt her sensitive electronic "feeling system" has discovered an irregularity, a fractured place in the organs of the oven. The master switches on a second television screen, puts on a pair of special glasses and now obtains by the combination of the two televisors a single three-dimensional, solid-looking picture on which a fresh white break in a transmission box is plainly recognizable.

27. Now the robot hand begins to work. It flexes its joints, it takes hold of the machine part with its unbelievably dexterous fingers, loosens it, detaches it, is holding it. Dolly is guided through the long walk in the interior of the furnace to a precise spot. For a split second the heavy protective wall soundlessly opens a crack, lets out the object brought by Dolly and falls shut again. The defective part is now lying on the repair place in the sealed region.

28. The repair crew is standing ready. They are four mechanics, a foreman and naturally an H.I. man. They were chosen not only for their abilities but above all on account of their health records. Only workers whose total dose of radiation since they came to Hanford

is reasonably slight can be appointed for such a job, in which overradiation is unavoidable even if only for a brief period.

29. Two members of the repair crew remain at the entrance to the sealed region. They are the reserves. Wearing double white overalls, two pairs of gloves, high rubber boots, tight-fitting head coverings and masks to which oxygen is being conveyed from their own reservoirs, the four men now stand before the defective, highly radioactive part.

30. In view of the great danger inherent in the repair work, it would be simpler to do away with the whole damaged part and replace it by a new one. This does not happen because a "bit of hell," once it is outside the oven, is not so easy to get rid of. Its transport to the radioactive refuse pit would involve far greater difficulties than its repair. If a damaged part can really not be mended, it must be quickly walled in on the spot. All over the hot zone of the Hanford Works one sees here and there in a room, without any regular arrangement, little molehills of leaden tiles, like prehistoric tombs. The all-too-living atom particles and rays are beating against the walls; it will be thousands of years before they lose their fatal power.

31. In the case of the transmission box of atomic oven 7, the operation proceeds normally. With instruments mounted on long pliers, the two fitters succeed in mending the breach. But, stop! When the work is nearly completed and probably not more than two or three minutes would be needed to finish the job, the H.I. man gives two of the three masked figures a nod meaning: stop at once. Almost reluctantly the two workers leave the sealed region. Something in them refuses to believe in what is unseeable and unfeelable. But they are sufficiently experienced to know that their H.I. guardian angel has sent them away in their own interest, that just the additional fraction of a second needed to bring the job to completion might suffice to cause great damage to their health. The two reserve men move in immediately and finish the work of their predecessors.

32. A whistle announces the successful termination of the operation. Only when everyone has moved to safety will Sweet Hot Dolly reach out from within the furnace for the

mended part and fetch it back into the atomic purgatory. The sirens sound: Section S, one of the six great units of the Hanford establishment, begins to work again.

33. Not far from Richland I was shown a quietly grazing flock of sheep. These, it seems, are plutonium tasters. As long as they keep well people need have no fear. For just as distrustful despots used to have their nourishment tasted first by a slave for fear of poisoning, so the health guardians of atomic factories send experimental animals on ahead to test whether the filtered but still, under certain atmospheric conditions, dangerous waste gases may not continue doing biological harm.

34. On the day when I saw the animals they were bustling about happily. The A.E.C. could write in its logbook: "The quantity of radiation in the atmosphere surrounding the Hanford area is slighter today than in the city of Denver, exposed to space radiation by its greater height above sea level."

35. The safety system stretches well beyond the immediate vicinity of the factory grounds. Mobile control stations with radiological testers take daily measurements within a circumference of one hundred and twenty miles. They concern themselves particularly with the danger of contamination which threatens the mighty Columbia River, part of whose water is used for the cooling of the atomic ovens. Not only is this water detained in special basins and chemically treated until it is only feebly radioactive, but the seaweed, driftwood and fishes, in which radioactivity may have gathered, are also systematically examined.

36. Most strongly supervised of all are the "burial grounds" in which radioactive refuse is interred. These are dismal squares in the desert surrounded by red painted cement stakes. Each is under the care of a "burial operator," an atomic cemetery custodian, and is serviced by heavily masked workers.

37. Here, in long deep graves are buried the contaminated objects made of solid materials, such as receptacles, cans, metal caps, under a layer of earth a yard thick. Fluid refuse goes from the factory through subterranean pipes directly into deep underground tanks. These atomic graves increase in dimensions year by year. They provide the Atomic Energy Com-

mission with more headaches than any other phase of its activity.

38. For the materials buried here in the northwest inland desert will outlive us, the generation who have freed them through nuclear fission, by thousands, in part even by millions, of years before they lose their life-destroying power. Therefore the graveyards must be marked so clearly and durably that each succeeding generation will know to shun them. Woe if the knowledge of the exact position of these poisoned zones were to be lost in the course of time!

39. But there is also the danger that the "buried" in the Hanford graveyard may not be lying as quiet as their custodians wish. It is possible, even probable, that the radioactive poisons may be gradually working their way through the subsoil water and conceivably even through the layers of earth to regions not yet contaminated. A constant supervision of the entire geological substructure not only during our lifetime but increasingly during the lives of our grandchildren, great-grandchildren and more remote descendants is therefore indispensable. All other attempts at "removal of waste" through encasement in cement blocks which were sunk into the sea, interspersion with certain forms of bacteria and seaweed, mixture with special sorts of loam, have so far shown themselves uncertain and not particularly promising. There has even been some thought of the possibility later on of shooting the bits of refuse with rockets out of our atmosphere into space. Only in this way, it is said, shall we be truly rid of them.

40. "In the long run," a research worker at one of the Hanford laboratories said to me, "this problem seems weightier to me than the question of atomic-weapon control. For even if the powers were finally to agree and an atomic war should never be fought, the fact still remains that by splitting the atom we have released life-destroying forces into the world with which the future will have to deal. With each century it will be more difficult to control the mounting quantity of atomic waste. Everything made by man has faded, fallen into ruin or rotted within measurable time. For the first time we have produced something by our own interference with nature which if not eternal, is, by our measures, nearly eternal. A dangerous inheritance which may far outlive all our other creations, a bit of near-eternity: a bit of hell."

RACHEL L. CARSON *The Birth of an Island*

Rachel Louise Carson (1907-   ) was educated at Pennsylvania College for Women and at Johns Hopkins University. She has been a research scholar at the Woods Hole Marine Biological Laboratory, biologist for the United States Bureau of Fisheries, and is now editor-in-chief for the United States Wildlife Service.

Nearly all of her writings, from her first book, *Under the Sea-Wind*, 1941, to *The Edge of the Sea*, 1955, have been about aquatic life. Miss Carson has won many awards and prizes. For "The Birth of an Island," which appeared in the *Yale Review*, she received the Westinghouse Award "for the best piece of scientific writing to appear in a magazine" in 1950. This selection later became a part of *The Sea Around Us*, which won the 1952 National Book Award for nonfiction.

1. Millions of years ago, a volcano built a mountain on the floor of the Atlantic. In eruption after eruption, it pushed up a great pile of volcanic rock, until it had accumulated a mass a hundred miles across at its base, reaching upward towards the surface of the sea. Finally its cone emerged as an island with an area of about 200 square miles. Thousands of years passed, and thousands of thousands. Eventually the waves of the Atlantic cut down the cone and reduced it to a shoal—all of it, that is, but a small fragment which remained above water. This fragment we know as Bermuda.

2. With variations, the life story of Bermuda has been repeated by almost every one of the islands that interrupt the watery expanses of the oceans far from land. For these isolated islands in the sea are fundamentally different from the continents. The major land masses and the ocean basins are today much as they have been throughout the greater part of geologic time. But islands are ephemeral, created today, destroyed tomorrow. With few exceptions, they are the result of the violent, explosive, earth-shaking eruptions of submarine volcanoes, working perhaps for millions of years to achieve their end. It is one of the paradoxes in the ways of earth and sea that a process seemingly so destructive, so catastrophic in nature, can result in an act of creation.

3. Islands have always fascinated the human mind. Perhaps it is the instinctive response of man, the land animal, welcoming a brief intrusion of earth in the vast, overwhelming expanse of sea. Here in a great ocean basin, a thousand miles from the nearest continent, with fathoms of water under our vessel, we come upon an island. Our imaginations can follow its slopes down through darkening waters to where it rests on the sea floor. We wonder why and how it arose here in the midst of the ocean.

4. The birth of a volcanic island is an event marked by prolonged and violent travail, the forces of the earth striving to create, and all the forces of the sea opposing. The sea floor, where an island begins, is probably nowhere more than about fifty miles thick—a thin covering over the vast bulk of the earth. In it are deep cracks and fissures, the results of unequal cooling and shrinkage in past ages. Along such lines of weakness the molten lava from the earth's interior presses up, and finally bursts

THE BIRTH OF AN ISLAND: From *The Sea Around Us* by Rachel L. Carson. Copyright 1951 by Rachel L. Carson. Reprinted by permission of Oxford University Press, Inc.

forth into the sea. But the eruption of a submarine volcano is different from one on the earth's surface, where through an open crater the lava, molten rocks, gases, and other ejecta are hurled into the air. Here on the bottom of the ocean the volcano has resisting it all the weight of the ocean water above it. Despite the immense pressures of two or three miles of sea water, the new volcanic cone builds upward towards the surface, in flow after flow of lava. Once within reach of the waves, its soft ash and tuff are violently attacked, and for a long period the potential island may remain a shoal, unable to emerge. But, eventually, in new eruptions, the cone is pushed up into the air and a rampart of hardened lava is built against the attacks of the waves.

5. Navigators' charts are marked with numerous recently discovered submarine mountains. Many are the submerged remnants of the islands of a geologic yesterday. On the same charts appear islands that emerged from the sea at least fifty million years ago, others that arose within our own memory, and undersea mountains that may be the islands of tomorrow, forming, unseen, on the floor of the ocean at this moment.

6. For the sea is by no means done with submarine eruptions; they occur fairly often, sometimes detected only by instruments; sometimes obvious to the most casual observer. Ships in volcanic zones may suddenly find themselves in violently disturbed water. There are heavy discharges of steam. The sea appears to bubble or boil in a furious turbulence. Fountains spring from its surface. Floating up from the deep, hidden places of the actual eruption come the bodies of fishes and other deep-sea creatures, and quantities of volcanic ash and pumice.

7. One of the youngest of the large volcanic islands of the world is Ascension in the South Atlantic. As the only piece of dry land between the hump of Brazil and the bulge of Africa, Ascension became known during the Second World War to every American airman crossing the South Atlantic. It is a forbidding mass of cinders, in which the vents of no less than forty extinct volcanoes can be counted. It has not always been so barren, for its slopes have yielded the fossil remains of trees. What happened to the forests no one knows, for the first men to explore the island, about the year 1500, found it treeless, and today it has no natural greenness except on its highest peak.

8. In modern times we have never seen the birth of an island as large as Ascension. But now and then there is a report of a small island appearing where none was before. Perhaps a month, a year, or five years later, the island has disappeared into the sea again. These are the little, stillborn islands, doomed to only a brief emergence above the sea.

9. About 1830 such an island suddenly appeared in the Mediterranean between Sicily and the coast of Africa, rising from 100-fathom depths after there had been signs of volcanic activity in the area. It was little more than a black cinder pile, perhaps 200 feet high. Waves, wind, and rain attacked it. Its soft and porous materials were easily eroded; its substance was rapidly eaten away and it sank beneath the sea. Now it is a shoal, marked on the charts as Graham's Reef.

10. Falcon Island, the tip of a volcano projecting above the Pacific nearly two thousand miles east of Australia, suddenly disappeared in 1913. Thirteen years later, after violent eruptions in the vicinity, it as suddenly rose again above the surface and remained as a physical bit of the British Empire until 1949. Then it was reported by the Colonial Under-Secretary to be missing once more.

11. Almost from the moment of its creation, a volcanic island is foredoomed to destruction. It has in itself the seeds of its own dissolution, for new explosions, or landslides of the soft soil, may violently accelerate its disintegration. Whether the destruction of an island comes quickly or only after long ages of geologic time may also depend on external forces: the rains that wear away the loftiest of land mountains, the sea, even man himself.

12. South Trinidad, a group of volcanic peaks lying about 700 miles east of the coast of Brazil, is an example of an island that has been sculptured into bizarre forms through centuries of weathering—an island in which the signs of dissolution are clearly apparent. E. F. Knight wrote in 1907 that Trinidad "is rotten throughout, its substance has been disintegrated by volcanic fires and by the action of water, so that it is everywhere tumbling to

pieces." During an interval of nine years that elapsed between Knight's visits, a whole mountainside had collapsed in a great landslide of broken rocks and volcanic debris.

13. Sometimes the disintegration takes abrupt and violent form. The greatest explosion of historic time was the evisceration of the island of Krakatoa. In 1680 there had been a premonitory eruption on this small island in Sunda Strait, between Java and Sumatra in the Netherlands Indies. Two hundred years later came a series of earthquakes. In the spring of 1883, smoke and steam began to ascend from fissures in the volcanic cone. The ground became noticeably warm, and warning rumblings and hissings came from the volcano. Then, on August 27, Krakatoa literally exploded. In an appalling series of eruptions that occupied two days, the whole northern half of the cone was carried away. The sudden inrush of ocean water added the fury of superheated steam to the cauldron. When finally the inferno of white-hot lava, molten rock, steam, and smoke had subsided, the island that had stood 1,400 feet above the sea had become a cavity a thousand feet below sea level. Only along one edge of the former crater did a remnant of the island remain.

14. Krakatoa, in its destruction, became known to the entire world. The eruption gave rise to a hundred-foot wave that wiped out villages along the Strait and killed people to the number of tens of thousands. The wave was felt along the shores of the Indian Ocean and at Cape Horn; rounding the Cape into the Atlantic, it sped northward and retained its identity even as far as the English Channel. The sound of the explosions was heard in the Philippine Islands, in Australia, and on the Island of Madagascar, nearly 3,000 miles away. And clouds of volcanic dust, the pulverized rock that had been torn from the heart of Krakatoa, ascended into the stratosphere and were carried around the globe, providing a series of spectacular sunsets in every country of the world for nearly a year.

15. Although its dramatic passing was the most violent eruption that modern man has witnessed, Krakatoa seems to have come into being as the result of an even greater one. There is evidence that an immense volcano once stood where the waters of Sunda Strait

now lie. In some remote period a titanic explosion blew it away, leaving only its base represented by a broken ring of islands. The largest of these was Krakatoa, which, in its own destruction, carried away what was left of the original crater ring. But in 1929 a new volcanic island arose in this place, Anak Krakatoa—child of Krakatoa.

16. Subterranean fires and deep unrest disturb the whole area occupied by the Aleutians. The islands themselves are the peaks of a thousand-mile chain of undersea mountains of which volcanic action was the chief architect. The geologic structure of the ridge is little known, but it rises abruptly from oceanic depths of about a mile on one side and two miles on the other. Apparently this long narrow ridge indicates a deep fracture of the earth's crust. On many of the islands volcanoes are now active, or only temporarily quiescent. In the short history of modern navigation in this region, it has often happened that a new island has been reported, but perhaps as soon as the next year it had disappeared.

17. The small island of Bogoslof, since it was first observed in 1796, has altered its shape and position several times and has even disappeared completely, only to emerge again. The original island was a mass of black rock, sculptured into fantastic, towerlike shapes. Explorers and sealers coming upon it in the fog were reminded of a castle and named it Castle Rock. At the present time there are left only one or two pinnacles of the castle, a long spit of black rocks where sea lions haul out, and a cluster of higher rocks resounding with the cries of thousands of sea birds. Each time the parent volcano erupts, as it has done at least half a dozen times since men have been observing it, new masses of steaming rocks emerge from the heated waters, some to reach enormous heights before they are destroyed in fresh explosions.

18. One of the few exceptions to the almost universal rule that oceanic islands have a volcanic origin seems to be the remarkable and fascinating group known as St. Paul's Rocks. Lying in the open Atlantic between Brazil and Africa, they are an obstruction thrust up from the floor of the ocean into the midst of the racing equatorial current, a mass against which the seas, that have rolled a thousand

miles unhindered, break in sudden violence. The entire cluster of rocks covers not more than a quarter of a mile, running in a curved line like a horseshoe. The highest rock is no more than sixty feet above the sea; spray wets it to the summit. Abruptly the rocks dip under water and slope steeply down into great depths. Geologists since the time of Darwin have puzzled over their origin, though it is generally agreed that they are composed of material like that of the sea floor itself. In some remote period, inconceivable stresses in the earth's crust must have pushed a solid rock mass upward more than two miles.

19. So bare and desolate that not even a lichen grows on them, St. Paul's Rocks would seem one of the most unpromising places in the world to look for a spider, spinning its web in arachnidan hope of snaring passing insects. Yet Darwin found spiders when he visited the Rocks in 1833, and forty years later the naturalists of *H.M.S. Challenger* also reported them, busy at their web-spinning. A few insects are there, too, some as parasites on the sea birds, of which three species nest on the rocks. One of the insects is a small brown moth which lives on feathers. This very nearly completes the inventory of the inhabitants of St. Paul's Rocks, except for the grotesque crabs that swarm over the islets, living chiefly on the flying fishes brought by the birds to their young.

20. St. Paul's Rocks are not alone in having an extraordinary assortment of inhabitants, for the fauna and flora of oceanic islands are amazingly different from those of the continents. The pattern of island life is peculiar and significant. Aside from forms recently introduced by man, islands remote from the continents are never inhabited by any land mammals, except sometimes the one mammal that has learned to fly—the bat. There are never any frogs, salamanders, or other amphibians. Of reptiles, there may be a few snakes, lizards, and turtles, but the more remote the island from a major land mass, the fewer reptiles there are, and the really isolated islands have none. There are usually a few species of land birds, some insects, some spiders. So remote an island as Tristan de Cunha in the South Atlantic, 1,500 miles from the nearest continent, has no land animals but

these: three species of land birds, a few insects, and several small snails.

21. With so selective a list, it is hard to see how, as some biologists believe, the islands could have been colonized by migration across land bridges, even if there were good evidence for the existence of the bridges. The very animals which are missing from the islands are the ones that would have had to come dryshod, over the hypothetical bridges. The plants and animals which we find on oceanic islands, on the other hand, are the ones that could have come by wind or water. As an alternative, then, we must suppose that the stocking of the islands has been accomplished by the strangest migration in earth's history— a migration that began long before man appeared on earth and still continues, a migration that seems more like a series of cosmic accidents than an orderly process of nature.

22. We can only guess how long after its emergence from the sea an oceanic island may lie uninhabited. Certainly in its original state it is a land bare, harsh, and repelling beyond human endurance. No living thing moves over the slopes of its volcanic hills; no plants cover its naked lava fields. But little by little, riding in on the winds, drifting in on the currents, or rafting in on logs, floating brush, or trees, the plants and animals that are to colonize the island arrive from the distant continents.

23. So deliberate, so unhurried, so inexorable are the ways of nature that the stocking of an island may require thousands or millions of years. It may be that no more than half a dozen times in all these eons does a particular form, such as a tortoise, make a successful landing upon its shores. To wonder impatiently why man is not a constant witness of such arrivals is to fail to understand the majestic pace of the process.

24. Yet we have occasional glimpses of the method. Natural rafts of uprooted trees and matted vegetation have frequently been seen adrift at sea, more than a thousand miles off the mouths of great tropical rivers like the Congo, the Ganges, the Amazon, and the Orinoco. Such rafts could easily carry an assortment of insect, reptile, or mollusk passengers. Some of the involuntary passengers might be able to withstand long weeks at sea;

others would die during the first stages of the journey. Probably the ones best adapted for travel by raft are the wood-boring insects, which, of all the insect tribe, are most commonly found on oceanic islands. The poorest raft travellers must be the mammals. But even a mammal might cover short inter-island distances. A few days after the explosion of Krakatoa, a small monkey was found floating on some drifting timber in Sunda Strait. She had been terribly burned, but was rescued and survived the experience.

25. No less than the water, the winds and the air currents play their part in bringing inhabitants to the islands. The upper atmosphere, even during the ages before man entered it in his machines, was a place of congested traffic. Thousands of feet above the earth, the air is crowded with living creatures, drifting, flying, gliding, ballooning, or involuntarily swirling along on the high winds. Discovery of this rich aerial plankton had to wait until man himself had found means to make physical invasion of these regions. With special nets and traps, scientists have now collected from the upper atmosphere many of the forms which inhabit oceanic islands. Spiders, whose almost invariable presence on these islands is an intriguing problem, have been captured nearly three miles above the earth's surface. Airmen have passed through great numbers of the white, silken filaments of spiders' "parachutes" at heights of two to three miles. Many living insects have been taken at altitudes of 6,000 to 16,000 feet, and with wind velocities reaching 45 miles an hour. At such heights and on such strong winds, they might well have been carried hundreds of miles. Seeds have been collected at altitudes up to 5,000 feet. Among those commonly taken are members of the Composite family, typical of ocean islands.

26. An interesting point about transport of living plants and animals by wind is the fact that in the upper layers of the earth's atmosphere the winds do not necessarily blow in the same direction as they do on the earth's surface. The trade winds are notably shallow, so that a man standing on the cliffs of St. Helena, a thousand feet above the sea, is above these winds, though they blow with great force below him. Once drawn into the upper air, insects, seeds, and the like can easily be carried in a direction contrary to that of the winds prevailing at island level.

27. The wide-ranging birds that visit islands of the ocean in migration may also have a good deal to do with the distribution of plants, and perhaps even of some insects and minute land shells. From a ball of mud taken from a bird's plumage, Charles Darwin raised eighty-two separate plants, belonging to five distinct species. Many plant seeds have hooks or prickles, ideal for attachment to feathers. Birds also distribute plants by ingestion of seeds. Such birds as the Pacific golden plover, which annually flies from the mainland of Alaska to the Hawaiian Islands and even beyond, probably figure in many riddles of plant distribution on islands.

28. The catastrophe of Krakatoa gave naturalists a perfect opportunity to observe the colonization of an island. With most of the island itself destroyed, and the remnant covered with a deep layer of lava and ash that remained hot for weeks, Krakatoa, after the explosive eruptions of 1883, was, from a biological standpoint, a new volcanic island. As soon as it was possible to visit it, scientists searched for signs of life, although it was hard to imagine how any living thing could have survived. Not a single plant or animal could be found. It was not until nine months after the eruption that the naturalist Cotteau was able to report: "I only discovered one microscopic spider—only one. This strange pioneer of the renovation was busy spinning its web." Since there were no insects on the island, the web-spinning of the bold little spider presumably was in vain, and except for a few blades of grass, practically nothing lived on Krakatoa for a quarter of a century. Then the colonists began to arrive—a few mammals in 1908; a number of birds, lizards, and snakes; various mollusks, insects, and earth worms. Ninety percent of Krakatoa's new inhabitants, Dutch scientists found, were forms that could have arrived by air.

29. Isolated from the great mass of life on the continents, with no opportunity for the crossbreeding which tends to preserve the average, to eliminate the new and unusual, island life has developed in a remarkable manner, and nature has excelled in the crea-

tion of strange and wonderful forms. As though to prove her incredible versatility, almost every island has developed species which are endemic, that is, they are peculiar to it alone and are duplicated nowhere else on earth.

30. It was in the pages of earth's history written on the lava fields of the Galapagos that young Charles Darwin read the message of the origin of species. Observing their strange plants and animals—giant tortoises, amazing black lizards that hunted their food in the surf, sea lions, birds in extraordinary variety—he was struck by their vague similarity to mainland species of South and Central America, yet haunted by the differences, differences that distinguished them not only from the mainland species but from those on other islands of the archipelago. Years later he was to write in reminiscence: "Both in space and time, we seem to be brought somewhat nearer to that great fact—that mystery of mysteries—the first appearance of new beings on earth."

31. Of the "new beings" evolved on islands, some of the most striking examples have been birds. In some remote age before there were men, a small, pigeon-like bird found its way to the island of Mauritius, in the Indian Ocean. By processes of change at which we can only guess, this bird lost the power of flight, developed short, stout legs, and grew larger until it reached the size of a modern turkey. Such was the origin of the fabulous dodo, which did not long survive the advent of man on Mauritius. New Zealand was the sole home of the moas, ostrich-like birds of which one species stood twelve feet high. Moas had roamed New Zealand from the early part of the Tertiary; those that remained when the Maoris arrived soon died out.

32. Besides the dodo and the moas, other island forms have tended to become large. Perhaps the Galapagos tortoise became a giant after its arrival on the islands, although fossil remains on the continents cast doubt on this. The loss of wing use and even of the wings themselves (the moas had none) are common results of insular life. Insects on small, windswept islands tend to lose the power of flight. The Galapagos Islands have a flightless cormorant. There have been at least fourteen

species of flightless rails in the islands of the Pacific alone.

33. One of the most interesting and engaging characteristics of island species is their extraordinary tameness, a lack of sophistication in dealing with the human race which even the bitter teachings of experience do not quickly alter. When Robert Cushman Murphy visited the Island of South Trinidad in 1913 with a party from the brig *Daisy*, terns alighted on the heads of the men in the whaleboat and peered inquiringly into their faces. On Laysan, the albatrosses (whose habits include wonderful ceremonial dances) allowed naturalists to walk among their colonies, and responded with grave bows to similar polite greetings from the visitors. When the British ornithologist David Lack visited the Galapagos Islands, a century after Darwin, he found that the hawks allowed themselves to be touched, and the flycatchers tried to remove hair from the heads of the men for nesting material. "It is a curious pleasure," he wrote, "to have the birds of the wilderness settling upon one's shoulders, and the pleasure could be much less rare were man less destructive."

34. But man, unhappily, has written one of his blackest records as a destroyer on the oceanic islands. He has seldom set foot on an island without bringing about disastrous changes. He has destroyed environments by cutting, clearing, and burning; he has brought with him as a chance associate the nefarious rat; and almost invariably he has turned loose upon the islands a whole Noah's Ark of goats, hogs, cattle, dogs, cats, and other nonnative animals, as well as plants. Upon species after species of island life, the black night of extinction has fallen.

35. In all the world of living things, it is doubtful whether there is a more delicately balanced relationship than that of island life to its environment. This environment is a remarkably uniform one. In the midst of a great ocean, ruled by currents and winds that rarely shift their courses, climate changes little. There are few natural enemies, perhaps none at all. The harsh struggle for existence that is the normal lot of continental life is softened on the islands. When this gentle pattern of life is abruptly changed, the island creatures

have little ability to make the adjustments necessary to survival.

36. Ernst Mayr tells of a steamer wrecked off Lord Howe Island east of Australia in 1918. Its rats swam ashore. In two years they had so nearly exterminated the native birds that an islander wrote: "This paradise of birds has become a wilderness, and the quietness of death reigns where all was melody."

37. On Tristan de Cunha, nearly all of the unique land birds that had evolved there in the course of the ages were exterminated by the hogs and the rats. The native fauna of the island of Tahiti is losing ground against the horde of alien species that man has introduced. The Hawaiian Islands, which have lost their native plants and animals faster than almost any other area in the world, are a classic example of the results of interfering with natural balances. Certain relationships of animal to plant, and of plant to soil, had grown up through the centuries. When man came in and rudely disturbed this balance, he set off a whole series of chain reactions.

38. Vancouver brought cattle and goats to the Hawaiian Islands, and the resulting damage to forests and other vegetation was enormous. Many plant introductions were as bad. A plant known as the pamakani was brought in many years ago, according to report, by a Captain Makee for his beautiful gardens on the island of Maui. The pamakani, which has light, windborne seeds, quickly escaped from the Captain's gardens, ruined the pasture lands on Maui, and proceeded to hop from island to island. The CCC boys once were put to work to clear it out of the Honouliuli Forest Reserve, but as fast as they destroyed it, the seeds of new plants arrived on the wind. Lantana was another plant brought in as an ornamental species. Now it covers thousands of acres with a thorny, scrambling growth—despite large sums of money spent to import parasitic insects to control it.

39. There was once a society in Hawaii for the special purpose of introducing exotic birds. Today when you go to the islands, instead of the exquisite native birds that greeted Captain Cook, you see mynahs from India, cardinals from the United States or Brazil, skylarks from Europe, and titmice from Japan. Most of the original bird life has been wiped

out, and to find its fugitive remnants you would have to search assiduously in the most remote hills.

40. Some of the island species have, at best, the most tenuous hold on life. The Laysan teal is found nowhere in the world but on the small island of Laysan. Even on this island it occurs only on one end, where there is a seepage of fresh water. Probably the total population of this species does not exceed fifty individuals. Destruction of the small swampy bit of land that is its home, or the introduction of a hostile or competing species, could easily snap the slender thread of life.

41. Most of man's habitual tampering with nature's balance by introducing exotic species has been done in ignorance of the fatal chain of events that would follow. But in modern times, at least, we might profit by history. About the year 1513, the Portuguese introduced goats on the recently discovered island of St. Helena, which had developed a magnificent forest of gumwood, ebony, and brazilwood. By 1560 or thereabouts, the goats had so multiplied that they wandered over the islands by the thousand, in flocks a mile long. They trampled the young trees and ate the seedlings. By this time the colonists had begun to cut and burn the forests, so that it is hard to say whether men or goats were the more responsible for their destruction. But of the result there is no doubt. By the early 1800's the forests were gone, and the naturalist Alfred Wallace later described this once beautiful, forest-clad volcanic island as a "rocky desert" in which the fugitive remnants of the original flora persisted only in the most inaccessible peaks and crater ridges.

42. When the astronomer Halley visited the islands of the Atlantic about 1700, he put a few goats ashore on South Trinidad. This time, without the further aid of man, the work of deforestation proceeded so rapidly as to be nearly completed within the century. Today Trinidad's slopes are the place of a ghost forest, strewn with the fallen and decaying trunks of long-dead trees; its soft volcanic soils, no longer held by the interlacing roots, are sliding away into the sea.

43. One of the most interesting of the Pacific islands was Laysan, one of the far out-

riders of the Hawaiian chain, a tiny scrap of soil. It once supported a forest of sandalwood and fanleaf palms, and had five species of land birds, all peculiar to the island. One of them was the Laysan rail, a charming, gnome-like creature no more than six inches high, with wings that seemed too small (and were never used as wings), and feet that seemed too large, and a voice like distant, tinkling bells. About 1887, the captain of a visiting ship moved some of the rails to Midway, about three hundred miles to the west, establishing a second colony. It seemed a fortunate move, for soon thereafter rabbits were introduced on Laysan. Within a quarter of a century, the rabbits had killed off the vegetation of the tiny island, reduced it to a sandy desert, and all but exterminated themselves. As for the rails, the devastation of their island was fatal, and the last native rail died about 1924.

44. Perhaps the Laysan colony could later have been restored from the Midway group had not tragedy struck there also. During the war in the Pacific, rats went ashore from ships and landing craft on island after island. They invaded Midway in 1943. The adult rails were slaughtered. The eggs were eaten, and the young birds killed. The world's last Laysan rail was seen in 1944.

45. The tragedy of the oceanic islands lies in the uniqueness, the irreplaceability of the species they have developed, by the slow processes of the ages. In a reasonable world men would have treated these islands as precious possessions, as natural museums filled with beautiful and curious works of creation, valuable beyond price because nowhere in the world are they duplicated. W. H. Hudson's lament for the birds of the Argentine pampas might even more truly have been spoken of the islands: "The beautiful has vanished and returns not."

PHILIP WYLIE *Science Has Spoiled My Supper*

Philip Wylie (1902-   ), who was born at Beverly, Massachusetts, received his college education at Princeton University. His father was a Congregational minister, and his mother was a writer of popular fiction. In his varied writing career he has been press agent, staff writer of the *New Yorker*, script writer for Paramount Pictures and Metro-Goldwyn-Mayer, newspaper columnist, magazine contributor, and editor for the publishing house Farrar and Rinehart. He has written a large number of books, perhaps the best known of which is *Generation of Vipers*, 1942, a relentless castigation of American manners and morals. One of his more recent books is *Denizens of the Deep: True Tales of Deep-Sea Fishing*, 1953.

Mr. Wylie, it has been said, often writes in "a state of high anger." In this essay, with his characteristic fervor, he attacks science and technology for their standardization of our food which has resulted in emphasis upon quantity at the expense of quality.

I

I am a fan for Science. My education is scientific and I have, in one field, contributed a monograph to a scientific journal. Science, to my mind, is applied honesty, the one reliable means we have to find out truth. That is why, when error is committed in the name of Science, I feel the way a man would if his favorite uncle had taken to drink.

Over the years, I have come to feel that way about what science has done to food. I agree that America can set as good a table as any nation in the world. I agree that our food is nutritious and that the diet of most of us is well-balanced. What America eats is handsomely packaged; it is usually clean and pure; it is excellently preserved. The only trouble with it is this: year by year it grows less good to eat. It appeals increasingly to the eye. But who eats with his eyes? Almost everything used to taste better when I was a kid. For quite a long time I thought that observation was merely another index of advancing age. But

some years ago I married a girl whose mother is an expert cook of the kind called "old-fashioned." This gifted woman's daughter (my wife) was taught her mother's venerable skills. The mother lives in the country and still plants an old-fashioned garden. She still buys dairy products from the neighbors and, in so far as possible, she uses the same materials her mother and grandmother did—to prepare meals that are superior. They are just as good, in this Year of Grace, as I recall them from my courtship. After eating for a while at the table of my mother-in-law, it is sad to go back to eating with my friends—even the alleged "good cooks" among them. And it is a gruesome experience to have meals at the best big-city restaurants.

Take cheese, for instance. Here and there, in big cities, small stores and delicatessens specialize in cheese. At such places, one can buy at least some of the first-rate cheeses that we used to eat—such as those we had with pie and in macaroni. The latter were sharp but not too sharp. They were a little crumbly. We called them American cheeses, or even rat cheese; actually, they were Cheddars. Long ago, this cheese began to be supplanted by a material called "cheese foods." Some cheese foods and "processed" cheese are fairly edible; but not one comes within miles of the old kinds—for flavor.

A grocer used to be very fussy about his cheese. Cheddar was made and sold by hundreds of little factories. Representatives of the factories had particular customers, and cheese was prepared by hand to suit the grocers, who knew precisely what their patrons wanted in rat cheese, pie cheese, American and other cheeses. Some liked them sharper; some liked them yellower; some liked anise seeds in cheese, or caraway.

What happened? Science—or what is called science—stepped in. The old-fashioned cheeses didn't ship well enough. They crumbled, became moldy, dried out. "Scientific" tests disclosed that a great majority of the people will buy a less-good-tasting cheese if that's all they can get. "Scientific marketing" then took effect. Its motto is "Give the people the least quality they'll stand for." In food, as in many other things, the "scientific marketers" regard quality as secondary so long as they can sell most persons anyhow; what they are after is "durability" or "shippability."

It is not possible to make the very best cheese in vast quantities at a low average cost. "Scientific sampling" got in its statistically nasty work. It was found that the largest number of people will buy something that is bland and rather tasteless. Those who prefer a product of a pronounced and individualistic flavor have a variety of preferences. Nobody is altogether pleased by bland foodstuff, in other words; but nobody is very violently put off. The result is that a "reason" has been found for turning out zillions of packages of something that will "do" for nearly all and isn't even imagined to be superlatively good by a single soul!

Economics entered. It is possible to turn out in quantity a bland, impersonal, practically imperishable substance more or less resembling, say, cheese—at lower cost than cheese. Chain groceries shut out the independent stores and "standardization" became a principal means of cutting costs.

Imitations also came into the cheese business. There are American duplications of most of the celebrated European cheeses, mass-produced and cheaper by far than the imports. They would cause European food-lovers to gag or guffaw—but generally the imitations are all that's available in the supermarkets. People buy them and eat them.

Perhaps you don't like cheese—so the fact that decent cheese is hardly ever served in America any more, or used in cooking, doesn't matter to you. Well, take bread. There has been (and still is) something of a hullabaloo about bread. In fact, in the last few years, a few big bakeries have taken to making a fairly good imitation of real bread. It costs much more than what is nowadays called bread, but it is edible. Most persons, however, now eat as "bread" a substance so full of chemicals and so barren of cereals that it approaches a synthetic.

Most bakers are interested mainly in how a loaf of bread looks. They are concerned with how little stuff they can put in it—to get how much money. They are deeply interested in using chemicals that will keep bread from molding, make it seem "fresh" for the longest possible time, and so render it marketable and shippable. They have been at this monkey-shine for a generation. Today a loaf of "bread" looks deceptively real; but it is made from heaven knows what and it resembles, as food, a solidified bubble bath. Some months ago I bought a loaf of the stuff and, experimentally, began pressing it together, like an accordion. With a little effort, I squeezed the whole loaf to a length of about one inch!

Yesterday, at the home of my mother-in-law, I ate with country-churned butter and home-canned wild strawberry jam several slices of actual bread, the same thing we used to have every day at home. People who have eaten actual bread will know what I mean. They will know that the material commonly called bread is not even related to real bread, except in name.

II

For years, I couldn't figure out what had happened to vegetables. I knew, of course, that most vegetables, to be enjoyed in their full deliciousness, must be picked fresh and cooked at once. I knew that vegetables cannot be overcooked and remain even edible, in the best sense. They cannot stand on the stove. That set of facts makes it impossible, of course, for any American restaurant—or, indeed, any city-dweller separated from supply by more than a few hours—to have decent fresh vegetables. The Parisians manage by getting their vegetables picked at dawn and rushed in farmers' carts to market, where no middleman or marketman delays produce on its way to the pot.

Our vegetables, however, come to us through a long chain of command. There are merchants of several sorts—wholesalers before the retailers, commission men, and so on—with the result that what were once edible products become, in transit, mere wilted leaves and withered tubers.

Homes and restaurants do what they can with this stuff—which my mother-in-law would discard on the spot. I have long thought that the famed blindfold test for cigarettes should be applied to city vegetables. For I am sure that if you puréed them and ate them blindfolded, you couldn't tell the beans from the peas, the turnips from the squash, the Brussels sprouts from the broccoli.

It is only lately that I have found how much science has had to do with this reduction of noble victuals to pottage. Here the science of genetics is involved. Agronomists and the like have taken to breeding all sorts of vegetables and fruits—changing their original nature. This sounds wonderful and often is insane. For the scientists have not as a rule taken any interest whatsoever in the taste of the things they've tampered with!

What they've done is to develop "improved" strains of things for every purpose but eating. They work out, say, peas that will ripen all at once. The farmer can then harvest his peas and thresh them and be done with them. It is extremely profitable because it is efficient. What matter if such peas taste like boiled paper wads?

Geneticists have gone crazy over such "opportunities." They've developed string beans that are straight instead of curved, and all one length. This makes them easier to pack in cans, even if, when eating them, you can't tell them from tender string. Ripening time and identity of size and shape are, nowadays, more important in carrots than the fact that they taste like carrots. Personally, I don't care if they hybridize onions till they are as big as

your head and come up through the snow; but, in doing so, they are producing onions that only vaguely and feebly remind you of onions. We are getting some varieties, in fact, that have less flavor than the water off last week's leeks. Yet, if people don't eat onions because they taste like onions, what in the name of Luther Burbank do they eat them for?

The women's magazines are about one third dedicated to clothes, one third to mild comment on sex, and the other third to recipes and pictures of handsome salads, desserts, and main courses. "Institutes" exist to experiment and tell housewives how to cook attractive meals and how to turn leftovers into works of art. The food thus pictured looks like famous paintings of still life. The only trouble is it's tasteless. It leaves appetite unquenched and merely serves to stave off famine.

I wonder if this blandness of our diet doesn't explain why so many of us are overweight and even dangerously so. When things had flavor, we knew what we were eating all the while—and it satisfied us. A teaspoonful of my mother-in-law's wild strawberry jam will not just provide a gastronome's ecstasy: it will entirely satisfy your jam desire. But, of the average tinned or glass-packed strawberry jam, you need half a cupful to get the idea of what you're eating. A slice of my mother-in-law's apple pie will satiate you far better than a whole bakery pie.

That thought is worthy of investigation—of genuine scientific investigation. It is merely a hypothesis, so far, and my own. But people—and their ancestors—have been eating according to flavor for upwards of a billion years. The need to satisfy the sense of taste may be innate and important. When food is merely a pretty cascade of viands, with the texture of boiled cardboard and the flavor of library paste, it may be the instinct of *genus homo* to go on eating in the unconscious hope of finally satisfying the ageless craving of the frustrated taste buds. In the days when good-tasting food was the rule in the American home, obesity wasn't such a national curse.

How can you feel you've eaten if you haven't tasted, and fully enjoyed tasting? Why (since science is ever so ready to answer the beck and call of mankind) don't people who want to reduce merely give up eating and get the nourishment they must have in measured doses shot into their arms at hospitals? One ready answer to that question suggests that my theory of overeating is sound: people like to taste! In eating, they try to satisfy that like. The scientific war against deliciousness has been stepped up enormously in the last decade. Some infernal genius found a way to make biscuit batter keep. Housewives began to buy this premixed stuff. It saved work, of course. But any normally intelligent person can learn, in a short period, how to prepare superb baking powder biscuits. I can make better biscuits, myself, than can be made from patent batters. Yet soon after this fiasco became an American staple, it was discovered that a half-baked substitute for all sorts of breads, pastries, rolls, and the like could be mass-manufactured, frozen—and sold for polishing off in the home oven. None of these two-stage creations is as good as even a fair sample of the thing it imitates. A man of taste, who had eaten one of my wife's cinnamon buns, might use the premixed sort to throw at starlings—but not to eat! Cake mixes, too, come ready-prepared—like cement and not much better-tasting compared with true cake.

It is, however, "deep-freezing" that has really rung down the curtain on American cookery. Nothing is improved by the process. I have yet to taste a deep-frozen victual that measures up, in flavor, to the fresh, unfrosted original. And most foods, cooked or uncooked, are destroyed in the deep freeze for all people of sense and sensibility. Vegetables with crisp and crackling texture emerge as mush, slippery and stringy as hair nets simmered in Vaseline. The essential oils that make peas peas—and cabbage cabbage—must undergo fission and fusion in freezers. Anyhow, they vanish. Some meats turn to leather. Others to wood pulp. Everything, pretty much, tastes like the mosses of tundra, dug up in midwinter. Even the appearance changes, oftentimes. Handsome comestibles you put down in the summer come out looking very much like the corpses of woolly mammoths recovered from the last Ice Age.

Of course, all this scientific "food handling" tends to save money. It certainly preserves food longer. It reduces work at home. But these facts, and especially the last, imply that the first purpose of living is to avoid work—at home, anyhow.

Without thinking, we are making an important confession about ourselves as a nation. We are abandoning quality—even, to some extent, the quality of people. The "best" is becoming too good for us. We are suckling ourselves on machine-made mediocrity. It is bad for our souls, our minds, and our digestion. It is the way our wiser and calmer forebears fed, not people, but hogs: as much as possible and as fast as possible, with no standard of quality.

The Germans say, *"Mann ist was er isst—* Man is what he eats." If this be true, the people of the U.S.A. are well on their way to becoming a faceless mob of mediocrities, of robots. And if we apply to other attributes the criteria we apply these days to appetite, that is what would happen! We would not want bright children any more; we'd merely want them to look bright—and get through school fast. We wouldn't be interested in beautiful women—just a good paint job. And we'd be opposed to the most precious quality of man: his individuality, his differentness from the mob.

There are some people—sociologists and psychologists among them—who say that is exactly what we Americans are doing, are becoming. Mass man, they say, is on the increase. Conformity, standardization, similarity—all on a cheap and vulgar level—are replacing the great American ideas of colorful liberty and dignified individualism. If this is so, the process may well begin, like most human behavior, in the home—in those homes where a good meal has been replaced by something-to-eat-in-a-hurry. By something not very good to eat, prepared by a mother without very much to do, for a family that doesn't feel it amounts to much anyhow.

I call, here, for rebellion.

WORKING AND LIVING TOGETHER

MARGARET MEAD *Each Family in a Home of Its Own*

Margaret Mead (1901-   ), anthropologist, was born into an academic family. Her father was a professor of economics at the University of Pennsylvania, her mother a sociologist, and her grandmother a pioneer in child psychology. Dr. Mead was educated at DePauw University, Barnard College, and Columbia University. Soon after her first field trip to Samoa, she accepted a position with the American Museum of Natural History, where she is now a curator of ethnology. She is married to Gregory Bateson, an English anthropologist, and has one daughter. Among her books are *Coming of Age in Samoa*, 1928, *Sex and Temperament in Three Primitive Societies*, 1935, and *Male and Female*, 1949, from which the following selection is taken.

The problems presented in the following article are not remote from the lives of college freshmen. If they are not facing them now as sons and daughters, they will eventually face them as husbands and wives.

1. The belief that every family should have a home of its own seems like a truism to which almost every American would assent without further thought. Most Americans also accept the fact that we have a housing shortage as the consequences of a failure to build in the thirties and during World War II, and of discrepancies between housing costs and wages that should somehow be reconciled. But it is important to realize that the word "family" has come to mean fewer and fewer people, the number of families has steadily increased, and so the need for housing units as distinguished from living-space has also increased by leaps and bounds. Although Southern Senators may occasionally argue against some piece of legislation for women, claiming that women's place

is in the home, most legislators yield, at least nominally, to the question, "Whose home?" Women's place in the United States is no longer in the home, and her exclusion from a right that has been hers in most societies is part of our belief that every family should have its own home—with only one woman in it. Furthermore, each family should consist only of a husband, a wife, and minor children. . . .

2. Marriage is a state towards which young Americans are propelled, and within which American women, educated to be energetic and active, try to live out the desires that have both been encouraged and muffled in them as children. Although there are other cultures in which women dominate the home more, America is conspicuous for the extent to which women have set the style of the home. This may be referred to a variety of background events: to the way in which the realm of the

aesthetic was left to women during pioneer days, to the emphasis on work for every one which meant that men were too tired to spend much of their effort on the home; and, very importantly, to the division of labour among non-English-speaking immigrants. When immigrants came to this country, the husband set to work to make a living, the wife to find out how to live, and this division between making a living and a way of life, one as man's field, the other as woman's, has been intensified. Our patterns of urban life, with its highly developed transportation systems which mean that fewer and fewer men ever come home to lunch, are also one of the supporting factors in the situation. As more schools are consolidated and the distance from home is increased, and as school-lunches develop, the home with school-age children is deserted all day long, while Mother is free to study the magazines and rearrange the living-room or her knowledge of world peace or the community's school system, in between answering the telephone, waiting for the laundry-man, and doing the next errand.

3. So it falls to the lot of women to design the way of life of the family, consulting her husband on major issues only, simply because that is her job. Into it, during the early days of marriage and motherhood she pours all the energy that comes from a healthy well-fed active childhood. If she has had a good education and is trained for some outside work, or even possibly for a career, even more if she was successful before marriage, there is likely to be an extra bit of emphasis in the way she manages her home and her children, in her insistence on what a good mother and what a good wife she is. Sometimes she can even say frankly: "Yes, I know my child is old enough to go to school alone, but I still take her. After all, that is my justification for staying home." More often, without any articulate comment on her doubt as to whether home-making really is a full-time job, she simply puts more effort into her complex day. Here the same standards apply that apply to her husband: like him, she also must succeed, must make good, must meet higher and higher standards.

4. When we analyze the task of home-making in the United States to-day, in the home that is celebrated in the pages of the women's magazines and assumed in the carefully unspecific radio serials, we find some very curious contradictions. The well-equipped home—towards which all the advertisements are pointed—is a home in which everything can be done more quickly and more effortlessly, clothes get white in no time, irons press almost without your noticing it, the extra attachment on the vacuum cleaner will even brush the backs of your books, the new silver-polish keeps your silver looking like new. In fact, the American woman, and the American woman's husband, who does not escape the advertisements even if he misses the radio serials, are told how fortunate, modern, and leisurely she can be—if she simply equips her house properly. There really seems to have been a period—back in the twenties, when domestic servants were still relatively available—when a married woman who had a goodly supply of gadgets, and at least one servant, did get quite a little time to play bridge. Her image lingers on in the avid comments of professional women over fifty who still see the home-maker as having a wicked amount of leisure—especially when contrasted with the life led by the woman who must both work and discharge all the duties of the home-maker, as so many American women do, not by choice but by necessity. There was a time also when in the first fine flush of laundries and bakeries, milk deliveries and canned goods, ready-made clothes and dry-cleaning, it did look as if American life was being enormously simplified. A vacuum cleaner was a great addition to a home that kept the standards of a carpet-sweeper and a broom, laundries were a godsend to a household whose routine of sheet-changing was geared to the old-fashioned wash-tub, and bakeries to homes in which the making of bread had dominated one whole day. But just as our new medical palliatives are creating new vulnerabilities and new disease states, so the new equipment has led not to more leisure, more time to play with the baby, more time to curl up and read by an open fire, or to help with the PTA, but has merely combined with other trends in making the life of the American home-maker not easier, but more exacting. Most urban-living women do not realize that, as the Bryn Mawr report shows, housekeeping activities con-

sumed 60.55 hours a week in a typical farm family, 78.35 in urban households in cities under 100,000, and 80.57 in households in cities of over 100,000. This was in pre-war days, and in a world that has been moving steadily towards a forty-hour week on the job.

5. Perhaps the most significant word in family relationships that has been invented for a very long time is the word "sitter"—the extra person who must come into the family and sit whenever the two parents go out of it together. The modern wife and mother lives alone, with a husband who comes home in the evening, and children, who as little children are on her hands twenty-four hours out of twenty-four, in a house that she is expected to run with the efficiency of a factory—for hasn't she a washing-machine and a vacuum cleaner?—and from which a great number of the compensations that once went with being a home-maker have been removed. Except in rural areas, she no longer produces, in the sense of preserving and pickling and canning. She has no orgies of house-cleaning twice a year. She doesn't give the sort of party where she is admired because of the heaps of food that she has ostentatiously prepared, but instead she is admired just in proportion to the way she "looks as if it had taken her no time at all." As our factories move towards the ideal of eliminating human labour, our home ideals have paralleled them; the successful home-maker to-day should always look as if she had neither done any work nor would have to do any; she should produce a finished effect effortlessly, even if she has to spend all day Saturday rehearsing the way in which she will serve an effortless Sunday-morning breakfast. The creativity that is expected of her is a creativity of management of an assembly-line, not of materials lovingly fashioned into food and clothes for children. She shops, she markets, she chooses, she transports, she integrates, she co-ordinates, she fits little bits of time together so as "to get through the week," and her proudest boast often has to be "It was a good week. Nothing went wrong."

6. The average young American woman is very cheerful over these tasks. They are a drain on her nervous energy rather than on her physical strength, time-consuming rather than back-breaking; in her incredibly clean and polished home, her kitchen where the handle of the egg-beater matches the step-ladder in colour, she moves lightly, producing the miracle dishes that will make her husband and children happy and strong. Two things mar her happiness, however: the fear that even though she never has any time, she is not perhaps doing a full-time job, and the fact that although she, like her brother, was taught that the right to choose a job is every American's sacred right, she doesn't feel that she chose this one. She chose wifehood and motherhood, but she did not necessarily choose to "keep house." That, in the phrasing of contemporary America, is thrust upon her because she is a woman; it is not a full status to be proudly chosen, but a duty that one cannot avoid and still find happiness in marriage. Women who have jobs ask her what she is doing and she says, "Nothing," or, "Just keeping house." Eighty hours a week of work, a sitter perhaps one evening a week, great loneliness as she rushes through the work that no other woman now shares, with an eye on the children as they play, hurrying so as to look "fresh and rested" when her husband comes home.

7. As we have narrowed the home, excluded from it the grandmother, the unmarried sister, the unmarried daughter, and—as part of the same process of repudiating any sharing of a home with another adult—the domestic servant has vanished, we have multiplied the number of homes in which the whole life of the family has to be integrated each day, meals cooked, lunches packed, children bathed, doors locked, dogs walked, cats put out, food ordered, washing-machines set in motion, flowers sent to the sick, birthday-cakes baked, pocket-money sorted, mechanical refrigerators defrosted. Where one large pot of coffee once served a household of ten or twelve, there are three or four small pots to be made and watched and washed and polished. Each home has been reduced to the bare essentials—to barer essentials than most primitive people would consider possible. Only one woman's hands to feed the baby, answer the telephone, turn off the gas under the pot that is boiling over, soothe the older child who has broken a toy, and open both doors at once. She is a nutritionist, a child psychologist, an engineer, a production manager, an expert buyer, all in one. Her husband sees her as free to plan her

own time, and envies her; she sees him as having regular hours, and envies him. To the degree to which they also see each other as the same kind of people, with the same tastes and the same preferences, each is to a degree dissatisfied and inclined to be impatient with the other's discontent.

8. It is not new in history that men and women have misunderstood each other's roles or envied each other, but the significant aspect of the American scene is that there is a discrepancy between the way we bring up boys and girls—each to choose both a job and a marriage partner—and then stylize housekeeping as a price the girl pays without stylizing the job as the price the boy pays. Men are trained to want a job in a mill, or a mine, on a farm, in an office, on a newspaper, or on a ship as a sign of their maleness, their success, and to want a wife and children to crown that success; but women to-day are not given the same clear career line—to want an apartment, or a semi-detached house, or a farm-house, or a walk-up, or some other kind of home, as their job. The American woman wants a husband, yes, children, yes, a home of her own—yes indeed, it's intolerable to live with other people! But housekeeping—she isn't sure she wouldn't rather "do something" after she gets married. A great proportion of men would like a different job—to have at least better pay, or higher status, or different working-conditions—but they are not asked to face the seeming discrepancy between being reared for a choice and reared to think that success matters, and also that love matters and that everyone should marry, and yet not be able to feel that the mate one chooses and the job one does after marriage are independent. It is as if a man were to make a set of plans for his life—to be an accountant, or a lawyer, or a pilot—and then have to add, "Unless of course, I marry." "Why?" you ask. "Because then I'll have to be a farmer. It's better for the children, you know."

9. It is not that we have found any good substitute for the association between home-making and motherhood. Good nurseries and schools can put children into good settings for many hours a day, settings that are often better than the small family where two bitter little rivals may otherwise spend hours quarrelling

and traumatizing each other. Freezers and frozen-food services and pressure cookers make it possible to prepare meals without long hours beside a watched pot. Hospitals do care for the very ill. But the task of integrating the lives of little children, even with the help of nursery-schools, kindergarten, and playgrounds, remains a full-time charge on some woman's time. If one woman leaves the home to work, part time or full time, another woman must replace her unless the children are to suffer. The nursery-school is no answer for the child with a cold, or the child who has been exposed to some contagious disease that it has not contracted. American women have become steadily more independent, more enterprising, more efficient, less willing to be merely part of some on-going operation, more insistent that when they do paid work, they work on a strictly professional basis, with part of their personality only, and that when they keep house they must be completely in control. But the price of this autonomy has risen also. It is almost as if the pioneer dream, which led Europeans of all sorts of backgrounds to become the independent American farmer, who could turn his hand to anything—and which survives to-day in the perennial nostalgia for a chicken-farm, or a business where one is one's own boss—had been transferred to the women, who live it out in their homes, but without the full pleasure of feeling that this is the job as well as the husband, the routine as well as the children, that they chose.

10. The intensity with which the American woman with children tends to her task of home-making includes innumerable excursions out of the home, as consumer, as transportation officer of the family, as responsible citizen who must protect the environment in which her children grow up by working for better schools, better play-grounds, better public-health regulations. To the old puritan vigour of the pioneer woman is now added a recognition that the modern isolated home, just because it is so isolated, is also terribly dependent upon the community. The functions that no one woman in a home by herself can possibly discharge must somehow be organized in the community around her, and even so, mothers cannot get sick. When they do, there are no adequate ordinary social ways

of meeting this major emergency in the lives of their children. But however actively a married woman with small children takes responsibility for community work, still her life is centred in, her time filled by, her home, but principally by the children. She may importune her husband to take her out, she may complain loudly of the loneliness and the boredom of housework, but she does not complain that she has nothing to do.

11. It is all the harder for the mother of adolescent children when the break comes, when the children leave home for school or jobs and her task is over. Every social pressure to which she is subjected tells her that she should not spoil her children's lives, that she should let them lead their own lives, that she should make them independent and self-sufficient. Yet the more faithfully she obeys these injunctions, the more she is working herself out of a job. Some day, while she is still a young woman, she will have to face a breakfast-table with only one face across it, her husband's, and she will be alone, quite alone, in a home of their own. She is out of a job; her main justification, the work for which she "gave up everything," is gone, and yet there are still two, possibly three, meals a day to get, the door to be answered, the house to be cleaned. But there are only dishes for two and floors do not need to be polished so often when there are no children's feet to track them up. She isn't completely out of a job, but she is on the shelf, kicked upstairs, given one of those placebos by which large organizations whose employees have tenure try to disguise from the employee who is still too young to be retired the fact that he ought to be. This domestic crisis is of course much more difficult if it occurs at and is reinforced by the hormonal instability and emotional fears that surround the menopause, and combine unjustified fear of the loss of physical desire with the necessary recognition of the end of reproductivity. For married American women who have had children, the fear of loss of attractiveness and the fear of becoming emotionally unstable outweigh worries about the end of reproductivity, for they have had the one or two or three children that validate their marriages and, at least consciously, do not want more.

12. Meanwhile the father has been facing difficulties of his own. His role in the maturation of his children, especially in the maturation of his son, is to be the friendly ally of the boy, to help him cut free from his mother's apron-strings. To the extent that he sympathizes with and facilitates his son's growing desires for a job and a girl, he is a good father. He must pooh-pooh the mother's anxieties, back the boy up in minor escapades, be fraternally understanding. But to the extent that he does this he runs several risks. He relives, at least in imagination, his own budding freedom as a young adult, the freedom that he traded in so young, so willingly, for the continuous unremitting work that has kept his marriage going. Remembering, he may begin to feel that he has never really lived, that he settled down too early. This feeling may be all the stronger if it comes at a time when he realizes that further advancement in job or profession is unlikely. As long as the gradient of his life was rising, he was spurred on by the great rewards that Americans find in success. But now it will rise no further, he will instead in many cases have to work simply to hold his place, a dispiriting thought. Helping his son escape from his mother further identifies his wife for him as one from whom he has, after all, never properly escaped himself into the pleasant byways of irresponsible dalliance. Seeing his wife through his son's eyes, and through the eyes of his son's friends, he discovers a new impatience with her, as the representative of finished, self-satisfied achievement. Here he is, only in middle age, and his life is over—no new love, no new fields to conquer, only emptiness ahead. So while he is not out of a job—indeed he may often be at the height of his work-strength—the very nature of the life-cycle in America is such that he feels like an old man. He may have to fight very hard to resist the impulse to break away from it all, and he may develop serious health disturbances and die prematurely.

13. Superficially, the problem that faces the middle-aged couple in the home of their own is that the mother's main life-task is done while she is strong and well, and she must now find some other channel for her energies and still keep her life adjusted to the habits and needs of a husband who has lived terribly closely with her in that little self-contained

home, while that husband's life-task is still going full tilt. But because of the great emphasis on Youth, because Youth is the period to which both sexes look back and age holds so few rewards, both face a deeper crisis of disappointment. This crisis may be further intensified if there are deaths of aged parents to be faced, with all the complications of the disposition of a surviving parent, long months of illness, sales of houses and furniture, all of which exacerbate the conflict about growing older. Every step of this process is made more acute by the insistence that each married couple should be self-sufficient, because many such couples have forgotten how. Yet they cannot look forward to combined homes with their married children, or with their widowed or unmarried siblings. Deeply dependent upon each other in every way, they have often become so just to the extent that the marriage is a good marriage. They have become so much like a single person that, like most individuals in America, they feel the need of others to complete themselves, to reassure them that they are good, to rid them of the self-searching that comes from being left alone and the self-reproach that attends condemning others to aloneness.

14. There are emerging solutions to this crisis when the children leave home. Some couples attempt a last child, for which there are even affectionate slang phrases—"little postscript," "little frost blossom"—that change the tone of the old folk-phrase "change-of-life baby." To have such a child is one way of facing the extent to which the woman's life in that home, and the marriage itself, has centred on the children. The most familiar solution is for women to make much of the independence for which they have openly yearned during the time they were tied down and go in for some active voluntary work, or even go back to the work they did before they were married. But in this event they face new hazards, especially if they have lived successfully through the instabilities of the menopause. Free of their major previous responsibilities, with twenty good years ahead of them,

such women may start out on a gradient that rises steeply as they become involved in community activities or the delights of a job from which they have had a long vacation. And as it is the gradient that matters so much in America, their enthusiastic new spurt may contrast sharply with their husbands' unhappy acceptance of a plateau. A daughter's marriage and permitted absorption in grandchildren may mute the wife's energetic attitude towards her new activities, but that involves a severe problem for the husband who has to face the fact that he is a grandfather. In a country that gives so few rewards to age, who wants to be a grandfather? The woman of his unlicensed day-dreams is still a slim girl in her teens, now younger than his married daughter, who with each step that she takes towards maturity puts him more definitely out of the running.

15. Increasingly, the more aware middle-aged couples are treating this period seriously, assaying their personal as well as their material resources, and directing their plans not towards some dim and unhoped-for retirement, but towards the next twenty years. To the extent that both are able to re-plan their lives together, they make of the crisis a step forward rather than a step back. It is probable that society will recognize this period as a period in which professional counselling is needed as much as in adolescence. For each married couple alone in a home of their own is exposed to pressures and difficulties unknown in differently organized societies. And expressive of the shifting cycle of responsibility, the young married sons and daughters sit in their own small homes and try to decide what to do about Father and Mother. This is a question that is not answered by their all taking a house together, but by finding the parents something they can be interested in. Ideally, they will readjust their lives, live independently of their children except for grave emergencies, act as sitters, which means they go in as their children go out, and finally retire to a cottage in Florida, where their children piously hope they will have a lot of friends of their own age.

GILBERT SELDES *Radio, TV, and the Common Man*

Gilbert Seldes (1893-   ) was born in Alliance, New Jersey, in a Utopian colony started by his father. After graduating from Harvard College, he began his journalistic career as a music critic for the Philadelphia *Evening Ledger*. In 1937, after twenty years of newspaper and editorial work, Mr. Seldes became director of television programs for the Columbia Broadcasting System. Among his books are *The Seven Lively Arts*, 1924, *The Great Audience*, 1950, and *Writing for Television*, 1952. Under the pseudonym of Foster Johns, he also writes mystery stories.

Mr. Seldes has established himself as one of the foremost authorities on mass media—newspapers, magazines, radio, television, and movies. In *The Great Audience* and in many articles, he has asked some important questions: What are the reasons for the present content of the mass media? Do the mass media reflect the taste of the majority of Americans? Are those directing the mass media ignoring the needs of certain segments of their potential audience?

1. In the Thirty Years' War between the broadcasters and their critics the heavy battalions and God—as represented by the public—have been on the broadcasters' side. If television hadn't revived some ancient misgivings and made some early blunders, serious criticism of the broadcasting industry might have disappeared entirely; the critics had become fretful and ineffective, and the broadcasters—who had been occasionally apologetic—were so secure in public favor that they showed few symptoms of the guilt complex that had haunted them in their earlier phases. As far as the public was concerned the critics were asking irrelevant questions, withholding praise where it was clearly due, and setting themselves up as the enemy of whatever was popular. The coming of television gives the critics a second chance to ask the right questions and thereby arrive at a useful relation to the industry.

RADIO, TV, AND THE COMMON MAN: Reprinted from *Is the Common Man Too Common? An Informal Survey of Our Cultural Resources and What We Are Doing About Them*, by Joseph Wood Krutch and others; copyright 1954, by University of Oklahoma Press. Reprinted by permission.

2. The question being asked by *The Saturday Review* is one of the right ones. It is part of a general inquiry into the relation between the communicative arts and the public, and as it applies to broadcasting it can be put in simple terms: Is it true, as has often been said, that the broadcasters underestimate the taste, intelligence, and maturity of the public? Are the masses ahead of the media?

3. Oversimplified like this, the question is also overloaded. The critics are asking the broadcasters, "How much longer do you intend to go on beating your wives?" and the broadcasters' answer is usually a combination of "We aren't legally married" and "They love it."

4. Obviously you can't discuss the relationship between broadcasters and audience until you know what an audience is. If you dig down to the bedrock on which the industry is founded, these solid facts become apparent: (1) an audience is what the sponsor buys; (2) an audience is what the broadcasters deliver; (3) an audience is a measurable fraction of *the* audience; (4) all the fractional audiences put together fall short of being "the public." Not at all apparent, but confirmed by experience,

is the hypothesis that audiences are created by broadcasting.

5. The fundamental attitudes toward audiences are all simple. Broadcasters (including sponsors) attempt to satisfy the current wants of large sections of the total audience; critics assert that the people making up these audiences have other interests and curiosities, perhaps not intense enough to be called wants, but legitimate; they also assert that the definite wants of smaller, but sizable, audiences should also be satisfied. And the Government, representing us as the third party in the discussion, licenses broadcasters to operate "in the public interest," which transcends all partial interests and is greater than their sum. It is, for instance, in the public interest that a vast number of citizens should be alert and intelligent enough to meet the successive crises of the world today, and it is therefore against the public interest if broadcasting fails to contribute to our awareness of problems and our capacity to solve them. But the individual broadcaster can be and usually is absolved of this responsibility.

6. The fact that an audience is a commodity to be bought and sold is usually concealed, because technically sponsors buy "time on the air." But both the jargon of the trade and some recent rulings of the FCC indicate that what is actually bought is the time and attention given by the audience. To attract sponsors broadcasters often promise to *build* an audience for the time-period he has chosen, and there is ample evidence that audiences have been prevented from coming into existence. The hypothesis stated above can be expanded: audiences are created by broadcasts and exist only at those times and in those places that the broadcasters want them to exist.

7. This is the central fact about broadcasting, because it is the central fact about the audience, but its implications are so grave that I think some proof must be brought forward. There's a lot of it.

8. Several years ago CBS issued an effective promotion piece called "Our Sixty-ninth-Most-Popular-Program"; it pointed out that, although 68 other programs on the network had higher ratings, "Invitation to Learning" still had an impressive audience of over a million

listeners. At about the same time (according to FCC records) "Invitation to Learning" was being heard on only 39 CBS stations; 97 other affiliates of the network did *not* carry the program. No proof exists that any significant number of people in these 97 other cities demanded to hear "Invitation to Learning," but commonsense rejects the idea that *nobody* in 97 average cities wouldn't be glad to hear a program that a millon people in 39 other cities listened to with pleasure. That an audience in the 97 cities did not come into being was simply because the creative act, making the program available, was not performed.

9. The same thing has happened on other networks and with all kinds of programs. Thus 216 Mutual stations did not carry a round-table discussion and only 40 did; a Labor for Victory program during the war was taken by 35 NBC stations, refused by 104; and so on. We do not yet have comparable data for television, but the principle is the same.

10. Parallel and opposite is the case of symphonic music. The precarious lives of great orchestras in pre-radio days, their constant "drives" for endowment funds, indicate that at most a few hundred thousand musical individuals actively wanted to hear the classics. This hardly constituted a demand by broadcasting standards. It is a matter of record that when William S. Paley proposed to broadcast the concerts of the New York Philharmonic-Symphony he knew that an audience for them did not exist and declared his intention of creating one. He was successful; eventually the Philharmonic even acquired a sponsor, and its audience was at one time estimated at about ten million. The demand is so intense that an attempt to broadcast the concerts by transcription, at various hours, brought violent objections and was abandoned after a single season.

11. The effect of symphonic broadcasts and other musical programs on concert-going and the sale of classical records—some $50,000,000 a year spent on the first and 40 per cent of all record sales for the latter—are in a sense secondary proofs of the creative power of broadcasting. The primary effect is radio's own audience. In creating this audience sponsors were unable to afford the long pull; they paid for orchestral music but withdrew support

after a short time, so that it required a network with all its resources (and the happy coincidence of unsold time on the air) to sustain the programs long enough to let the audience form, to let enough people know that they didn't dislike "long-hair" music as much as they thought they did. Again, considering broadcasting only, and not cultural effects, it should be noted that the significance of this entire episode lies not in the fact that the music was good and serious, but that the broadcasters offered all kinds of music, widening the area of choice; if the prevalent mode had been classical and the broadcasters had created an audience for hot music, the moral would still be the same: audiences are created by programs.

12. There is a more significant but less spectacular case in which the broadcasters acted in the public interest far ahead of public demand. They began to supply international news and commentary of a high order in the 1930's, at a time when the people at large preferred not to be troubled by such matters, a period of marked self-absorption in domestic affairs and strong isolationism. These programs were unsponsored for many years and almost without exception they demanded real mental activity on the part of the listener to match the alert intelligence of the correspondents abroad. These broadcasts were a specific case of giving the public what the public ought to have—and no damned nonsense about what the public wants; and I believe that the high level of emotional stability of the American people after Pearl Harbor is largely due to the creation of an audience, of substantial size, aware of the international situation. This is one of the most honorable services radio has rendered to our country, and I think the industry ought to be proud of it, without reservation.

13. But the industry does make a reservation, in principle. It cannot accept the Paley principle of creative broadcasting because of the responsibility that principle implies. For you cannot logically say, "We created the audience for great music and for the discussion of public affairs, but in the case of neurotic daytime serials and sadistic murder playlets we weren't creative at all, we were merely satisfy-

ing a demand that already existed." Demand is generalized and diffuse—for entertainment, for thrills, for vicarious sadness, for laughs; it can be satisfied by programs of different types and different qualities; and only after these programs have been offered is there any demand for them. Supply comes first in this business and creates its own demand.

14. A few months ago *Time* published a letter from a reader in Nigeria which gives a perfect, though extreme, instance of this principle. The writer said: "In the Gold Coast one movie owner possesses only two features, 'King Kong' and 'The Mark of Zorro.' . . . On Mondays, Tuesdays, and Fridays he has packed them in for years with the former; [the other three weekdays he shows the latter] . . . On Sundays there is always a surefire double feature—'King Kong' and 'The Mark of Zorro.' " I submit that this enterprising exhibitor began by satisfying an unspecific demand for entertainment, then created an audience for a specific kind of entertainment, and finally prevented an audience for any other kind of entertainment from coming into existence.

15. Our mass media, the movies as well as radio and television, offer a greater variety of entertainments, but they are for the most part aimed at the same intellectual level and call for the same emotional responses, the level and the responses being relatively low. The challenge to the mind comes infrequently, and we are being conditioned to make frequent emotional responses of low intensity—the quick nervous reaction to melodrama and the quick laugh at everything else. If material cannot be adapted to give the thrill or the laugh, it is thrown out. A spectacular instance of this occurred recently in the Ford anniversary show, where the entire story of life in the United States in the past half century was reduced to vaudeville, the violent strikes of the 1920's being presented as part of a jocular newsreel, the Depression in a ballet, and the revolution of the New Deal, being intractable, omitted entirely. It was a very successful program, and its success is part of the conditioning process which I call creative, by which the audience is persuaded that it is getting all it can ever want.

16. Statistical evidence exists that actually the audience—the public, to be more accurate —wants more. I place few bets on the automatic answer given to researchers, "Yes, we would like more serious programs on the air," because, for one thing, some of the respondents call quiz shows educational and because this "want" is a pious aspiration as diffused and uncertain as what the broadcasters say they get from the public. Yet it is noteworthy that *all* the researches point in the same direction: people at every level of education, in significant numbers, do imply some dissatisfaction with the programs they are getting, and among these there are ten million people, not habitual book readers, not college graduates, who consistently ask for programs of a higher intellectual content. (Book readers and college graduates make the same request twice as often, but they are numerically less important. All these figures come from studies made for the industry.)

17. Direct corroborative evidence comes from the report of the FM stations; the Lowell Institute station in Boston, wholly educational, has a constantly increasing audience of unswerving loyalty; and the University of Michigan, broadcasting at unfavorable hours, within a small area, has an audience for its TV programs large enough to indicate that the same programs transmitted at good hours over a national network would attract a sponsorable audience.

18. The evidence favorable to the broadcasters (in music, for instance) and the unfavorable evidence (the prevalence of third-rate crime programs, let us say) come together at this point. If the broadcasters accept their social responsibility, they can continue to pile up huge profits without corrupting the taste and undermining the mental activity of the audience. Sponsors, agencies, packagers, stations, and networks taken together have created the kinds of wants they could satisfy, and while broadcasting has not lost audiences—as the movies have—by repeating the sure thing over and over again, there have always been vast untouched segments of the public. (At the time the two major networks were offering daytime serials all day long and protesting that women wouldn't listen to anything else 76 per

cent of all women who had radios in such a city as Boston were simply not listening; within a few years it was discovered that women would listen to many other kinds of programs.) It takes time, intelligence, and conviction to face the simple mathematical fact that 1 is not the only common denominator of 4 and 8 and 16 and 64. The broadcasters have ratings which prove to their satisfaction that a sufficient number of separate individuals watch each of the 100 or more programs of violence on television every week, but that is no proof of public demand for so many of these programs and it certainly is not proof that other kinds of programs would not build up equally satisfactory audiences.

19. The huge costs of television production have introduced a new element. The pure sustaining program of radio, experimental and not intended for sale, has disappeared, and the status of television may now be described as "commercialism mitigated by Foundations." "American Inventory" (Sloan) and "Omnibus" (Ford) are essentially comparable to network sustaining programs in radio, and all the networks and many stations are bringing in inexpensive programs from museums and universities with or without special endowments or other funds for broadcasting. Broadcasters have been glad to shift the burden of costs for such programs. Provided a sufficient number of them continue on the air, it doesn't matter to the public who pays the bill.

20. Other developments also point to the same ill-defined feeling that commercial broadcasting alone cannot satisfy all the legitimate wants of the public. Grand opera has been "narrowcast" into theatres, the audience paying admission, and there are a dozen plans to handle plays in a similar way. And while pay-as-you-go transmission of movies is more an economic move than a social one, it adds another variant from the standard commercial system. "Omnibus," the most successful of the experiments, makes the point of divergence particularly clear. It seems to assume that the usual commercial sponsor is not bound by any social duty to take long risks, to keep a program running until its audience forms; the program is therefore produced (as all radio programs were in the beginning) without ref-

erence to or interference from the sponsor, but is made available for sponsorship on these terms. Doing what neither the network nor the sponsor can do, such a program signifies that an area outside their capacities must be cultivated if television is to be satisfactory, not only to particular audiences, but to the public as a whole.

21. We know, in sum, that the broadcasting business has been ahead of the public as well as behind it. We know that better programs often fail to get support. One reason for this is that the better programs are often conceived as something totally different from good programs—the rhetorical documentaries of Norman Corwin, for instance—and not, as they should be, as a constant improvement in the quality of programs already proved acceptable. Another reason is that the volume and velocity of the average program surfeits the appetite and makes it progressively less likely that a keener taste will develop.

22. It is at this point that the broadcasters share responsibility with other manipulators of the public. They dodge it by the ancient excuse of giving the public what it wants, conceiving the public as a mass with tastes already formed. Once they admit that the media can raise or lower the public taste, in the very act of satisfying the public demand, they will come closer to their function, which is defined legally as operating in the public interest, and which, morally, does not insist on raising the public taste but demands, as a minimum, that the public be given every opportunity to find its own level of taste by having access to the best as well as to the mean—which, in this case, is far from golden.

RALPH J. BUNCHE *The Road to Peace*

Ralph Johnson Bunche (1904-   ), Under Secretary of the United Nations, was educated at the University of California and at Harvard University. He took post-doctoral work in anthropology and colonial policy at Northwestern University, the London School of Economics, and the University of Capetown. He has taught at the University of California and at Howard University.

Dr. Bunche has held a score or more of important assignments with various organizations and commissions, including the Institute of Race Relations, the International Labor Conference, the Office of Strategic Services, and the State Department.

In 1945 he was a delegate to the San Francisco conference at which the charter of the United Nations was drawn up; as a personal representative of the Secretary General, he accompanied Count Bernadotte, the United Nations mediator, to Palestine and subsequently became acting mediator when Bernadotte was assassinated. He was awarded the Spingarn Medal by the National Association for the Advancement of Colored People in 1949 and the Nobel Peace Prize in 1950 for successfully concluding the truce between the Israelis and Arabs.

In "The Road to Peace," an address delivered in 1954 in Madison Square Garden in New York before the annual convention of National Education Association, Dr. Bunche speaks authoritatively concerning the work, ideals, and future of the United Nations.

1. It is an honor and a very great pleasure to participate in the program of this 92nd Annual Convention of the National Education Association of the United States and to greet you who represent more than half a million members of one of the most vital if not the most vital of all the professions in the land. If you will pardon me for injecting a personal note, I would like to say that having started my career as a teacher and having spent fifteen years in the classroom, there is no company with which I experience more warm fellow-feeling than with teachers. I can truthfully say that those years in the academic fold were the most satisfying, rewarding, and in many ways the most challenging of my working life, and I often feel a deep nostalgia for the profession and a longing to get back into

THE ROAD TO PEACE: Reprinted, by permission of the author and the publisher, from *Vital Speeches*, August 15, 1954.

teaching harness. I might add, though I need hardly say it to this audience, that the reward of the teacher, as I early discovered, had to be far more in spiritual and subjective than in material things. I gather, however, that since my teaching days there has been some progress even in this regard, although the teacher's monetary compensation can probably never be commensurate with the importance of the service rendered to the society.

2. In the long view there can be scarcely any necessity more pressing in a democracy than the provision of an adequate corps of well-qualified teachers for education at every level. This is the greatest insurance democracy can offer to the development and the future of its youth, and thus to its own perpetuation. It is seriously disturbing, therefore, to contemplate teacher shortages, lagging in teacher recruitment and in replenishment of teacher supply.

3. As we have developed on these shores the

greatest democracy in human history, so have we developed the most impressive and, I believe, the most effective educational system in the world. The two clearly go hand in hand. Our American educational process has been geared to training the American citizen not only how to do but also how to understand—to know the reasons for things. Its general design, however uncertainly at times and places, has been to help us all learn how, as good beings and good citizens, to lead the good life. As Aristotle observed, goodness and wisdom are inseparable. If democracy is to be dynamic and forward-reaching, as it must be to flourish, it must constantly exert every effort to insure that all of its citizens are as good and wise as possible, that they achieve the maximum development of their mental capacities, and that they acquire an intellectual grasp of the aims of life in a democratic society and the means of achieving them.

4. It is of the very life blood of democracy that there be freedom to seek the truth through knowledge. The inquiring mind, indeed the boldly inquiring mind, persistent intellectual curiosity, the testing of every thesis and dogma against fact and reason are the working tools of free men and of the democratic educational process. It will be fatal to our way of life (and it is the best way of life ever devised for men and women who treasure freedom and dignity) should our educational process ever become shackled by the bonds of conformity of thought induced by fear, perverted by bigoted anti-intellectualism, or lose through intimidation its zest for knowledge and truth.

5. The horizon of the good citizen—the good citizen must be informed and comprehending—in our society has vastly widened. It has become a world horizon. Our nation's interest and responsibility have become worldwide in scope. The world has grown smaller through the miracles of modern transportation and communications. It grows even more interdependent though there are some who insist upon closing their eyes to the inevitable. Members of the family of nations must therefore, in their own interest, develop increasing mutual concern for the well-being of each other's peoples. Thus the field of responsible interest and active concern of the individual citizen correspondingly widens. One must know so much more, be alert to and informed about so much more, to be a good citizen today than was required in those days not so far removed when the world beyond our borders seemed to be of only casual concern to us. Today all thoughtful Americans know this is no longer the case and can never again be the case. The struggle to preserve freedom against aggressive communism is world-embracing. The quest for peace and security is a universal concern. Our friends, our concepts of the rights and dignity and worth of the individual, our system of free enterprise, all that goes with our way of life, are intimately related to and affected by daily events occurring in parts of the world formerly but no longer remote—in Korea, in Indo-China, in Africa.

6. The times in which we live—times which are dominated by the stark realization of the incalculable destructive power of the weapons of fission and fusion—are worrisome, tense, and dangerous. I would not for a moment minimize the insecurity and the danger. There seems to be no limit to the destructive possibilities of the weapons which the genius of man can now devise. Indeed, it becomes increasingly difficult for the human mind to grasp the frightful magnitude of the destructive potential of modern devices of war. In consequence, war can no longer be regarded, as in the past, as another tragic chapter in human history. Now war might well be the final chapter in the history of the civilization which mankind has so laboriously cultivated over the centuries.

7. But to view the hydrogen bomb as signalling the end of the world serves only to induce panic and to nourish the ambitions of the reckless ones who seek power through exploitation of fear. In the calm view, the new weapons are the logical end of the concept of total war in this scientific age. If reason prevails, the hydrogen bomb may yet prove to be the decisive deterrent to war as peoples the world over increasingly realize that another world war and the survival of civilization are irreconcilable. Despite all anxiety there is a great and exciting challenge in these days—to governments, peoples, and individuals.

8. I hold steadfastly to a reasoned and, I believe, reasonable optimism. For I am con-

vinced that the future is by no means hopeless if we refuse to surrender to despair and defeatism; if we do not lose faith in ourselves, in our fellow-men and in our way of life; and if each citizen has a true appreciation of the vital role of the individual in the unfolding of events, domestic and international, and cultivates the will to make the indispensable contribution which each of us in our daily living can make toward ensuring a future for ourselves and all humanity in which peace, freedom, human dignity and moral values will be secure.

9. Too many of us, I fear, are today inclined to sit back in resignation and assume that the determination of the future of the world is something beyond our influence, if not our ken, and that there is little we can do other than to anxiously wait and see what the statesmen and the diplomats may achieve in our behalf. Civilization and progress would not have come to this continent had our forbears adopted such attitudes when confronted with formidable dangers. They faced danger and an uncertain future with individual initiative, resolution, and limitless courage. We could do with more of the sturdy stuff that carried the pioneers across this land—their indomitable, fearless spirit, their stout hearts, and above all, their confidence in themselves and in each other.

10. Resignation, despair, and indifference are certainly costly and would prove to be fatal attitudes in contemporary times. The individual citizen has a highly responsible role to play in the shaping of international as well as of domestic history. Building a better world, digging out the roots of war, laying secure foundations for peace, must depend in the final analysis on the attitudes and efforts of people. The structure must rest on the shoulders of each of us and can be no more solid and sturdy than we the citizenry prove to be alert, informed, and determined, and above all, understanding of each other.

11. The freedom which through our history has been so hard won can be preserved against the sinister onslaughts of totalitarianism for ourselves and for all other peoples in the world who cherish it only if the citizens of America are prepared to pay the cost and make the sacrifices required. This involves much more than providing the fighting men for the armed forces and reluctantly paying taxes. Under our democratic system, which is responsive to the will of the people, the nation and our government can be strong only if our people are strong in their unity, their comprehension of world events and forces, their understanding and tolerance to other peoples even though their ways and views may differ from our own, their patience and emotional restraint, their devotion to our traditional ideals, and their determination to protect our way of life from all attacks upon it, whether from within or without.

12. It follows, therefore, that in these perilous times every effort in every American community—in the schools, churches and organizations, and in the homes—to bind our people more closely together, to promote understanding of all peoples, to make our democracy work better for all Americans irrespective of creed or race, strengthens the nation, elevates its international prestige, and reinforces the causes of peace and freedom in the world. In truth, every time any one of us finds his heart big enough to accept and treat his neighbor as a brother, an important contribution is made toward a better, a freer, and a more peaceful world.

13. In passing, it may be said that there would appear to be cause these days for some special concern on the subject of unity. Divisive forces are at work in the society, emotions are played upon, fear is sown, increasingly we become suspicious of each other, harsh accusations are hurled back and forth. All of this in my humble view can only serve to disrupt and seriously weaken us at the very moment—indeed, the most crucial moment in our entire history—when our maximum strength, unity, and self-confidence are imperatively demanded.

14. There is a facet of our strength as people which, I believe, is too little emphasized and recognized. Throughout the world, and even among ourselves, we Americans are noted for our material strength and our materialistic ways. That our material resources are vast, that we are materialistic-minded, that we love machines and gadgets, is undoubted. But what of our rich spiritual resources which in fact are our greatest? For behind our spec-

tacular material development, behind our matchless assembly lines, our ingenious machines, the bounteous harvests of our rich soil and vast fields, our tremendous over-all wealth, is the simple but deep spiritual quality of the American people. Here, I think, is to be found the true dynamic of our society and the seed-soil of our remarkable growth.

15. For the American people are a people who are humble before their Maker, who have deep reservoirs of faith, who believe in each other and in the essential goodness of man, who stand for fair play and justice, who live by the moral law. These are qualities of strength that transcend all material things, even the hydrogen bomb, and will ensure the success of our leadership and the preservation in the world of those principles of freedom and justice which we hold more dear than life itself.

16. It is our spiritual strength and our hard sense upon which we must rely to combat the cynicism which begins to run rampant in the society, resulting in a deterioration of moral values, a disregard for truth and principle, and a resignation to the inevitability of the catastrophe of war. This cynicism, which corrupts and corrodes our moral strength, can be countered only as we have firm faith in ourselves, in the essential worth and goodness of man, in our national destiny, and in the Supreme Being.

17. The general insecurity and anxiety of the times, which are exploited by the cynics both amateur and professional—and amongst us these days there are far too many of both varieties—have caused many well-meaning people to find questions in their minds about the efficiency and effectiveness of the United Nations, if not the entire effort toward international cooperation and collective security. There has been much disillusionment about the United Nations, not without some justification. For it has weaknesses and has suffered failures. But what alternative is there? What course of action might better serve peace and human advancement? Since peoples and nations have serious differences, is there any surer means of resolving them than to bring the conflicting nations together in the effort to bridge the gaps between them by full and frank discussion? It is often said in criticism

that there is too much talking at the United Nations. Perhaps so, but nevertheless we believe, and I hold rightly, that endless talking, no matter how aggravating, is far better than even a little shooting. And experience has convincingly demonstrated that so long as nations can be kept talking at the council tables about their differences there is always the possibility that the attempt to shoot those differences out can be stopped or averted.

18. It is never easy. But it should never be assumed that peace can be won easily or cheaply. It is enough, it seems to me, if it can be won honorably and without sacrifice of principle.

19. In my view, despite all its faults there is today no greater force for social justice and understanding among peoples throughout the world, and therefore for peace, than the United Nations, nor has there ever been. From its very beginning, the United Nations recognized that secure peace in the world required an effort far wider and deeper than preventing and stopping specific wars. Secure peace is a matter of digging out the political, economic, and social roots of war; of building firm political, economic, and psychological foundations; of reaching the hearts and minds of people; of cultivating peoples' understanding of each other and their mutual trust and regard; of dissipating fears and suspicions and bigotries in the relations among nations and peoples; of promoting mankind's continual progress toward a more abundant and a more just life for all.

20. Day in and day out the United Nations and the Specialized Agencies in alliance with it are directing their limited resources toward these ends in the vital interest of all of us. Progress in many directions is excruciatingly slow; these are tremendous tasks and the obstacles often appear insurmountable; there are frustrations and failures; but progress, even in the turbulence of the sharply divided post-war world, has been and is being made and, I feel confident, will continue to be made.

21. You have heard very much about the United Nations this week and there is probably very little about it that has been left unsaid. It will suffice, therefore, only to underscore a few points on which there is too often misunderstanding.

22. First, there are those who fear or who claim to fear that the United Nations is too strong. There are many more, I believe, who fear it is too weak. To the former it is necessary to say only that the United Nations is a voluntary association of fully independent nations; its Charter is a treaty between sovereign national governments; the decisions of the United Nations have authority only insofar as they represent the consensus of world opinion, that "decent respect to the opinions of mankind" to which our own Declaration of Independence refers. This, however, is a force and an authority which should not be underestimated. The United Nations cannot draft a soldier or command one unless a sovereign nation voluntarily provides him, as in Korea; cannot assess a sou in taxes; cannot pass a law. Still, solely on the basis of its moral authority, the United Nations has scored many achievements, exercises great influence, has restrained and controlled many conflict situations, and in Korea has been responsible for the first collective intervention to repulse aggression in history.

23. Secondly, the United Nations is not a "world government," or a government of supra-national authority in any sense. There is, in the minds of many, a persistent mental image of the U.N. as a government possibly because its Charter is regarded as similar to a written constitution and its organs appear to debate and vote in the manner of legislatures. But in fact and in practical operation the United Nations has no legislative or executive authority. It adopts resolutions, not laws; it issues recommendations, not decrees. Its Charter is not a constitution in any traditional sense, but rather a statement of goals and principles to guide the conduct of the nations voluntarily associated in it in international affairs.

24. Thirdly, the United Nations represents a world community which thus far, at least, is only in embryo. It is the response to the compelling need for an unceasing, organized effort towards the creation of such a community based on law. In recognition of this fact, President Eisenhower has described the United Nations as a "sheer necessity" and Prime Minister Winston Churchill has said of it: "The vast majority of all the peoples, wherever they may dwell, desire above all things to earn their daily bread in peace. To establish conditions under which they can do this, and to provide deterrents against aggression, are duties confided by the heart's desire to the United Nations. Our first duty is to aid this instrument loyally and faithfully in its task." I think it incontrovertible that if we did not already have the United Nations in these desperate times the world would urgently set about to create it as its chief means of self-preservation.

25. Fourthly, it is ironical, to say the least, that the United Nations should be regarded as a "problem," since it is strongly endorsed by President Eisenhower and his administration as it was by the previous administration, since the United States is a leading and very active member of the organization, and since the United Nations continues to be a corner stone of American foreign policy. But unfortunately, many of us, and teachers especially, become painfully aware that in the minds of some of our fellow-citizens the United Nations and its affiliated Specialized Agencies, is not only a problem, it is a highly controversial subject which teachers should shun in the classroom, unless, I presume, they denounce it. That this should be so with regard to the United Nations which only nine years ago was dedicated on these American shores, with such great enthusiasm to the unchallengeable ends of world peace and human advancement is a tragic expression of the confusion, fear, and rampant cynicism of the times in which we live.

26. My confidence and hope in the ability of the United Nations to succeed in its historic mission of peace, which must depend so fundamentally on the spirit and attitudes of peoples as expressed through their governments, is fortified by my knowledge that people can bow to reason, have big hearts, nurture a deep concern for each other's welfare, and though widely diversified in origin develop fellow-feeling. I have seen too many evidences of man's capacity for good deeds to be pessimistic on this count.

27. For example, I have spent much time in the troubled Near East, where the Palestine issue has stirred emotions and animosities mightily. Even in the frightening atmosphere of 1947-49, when Arab and Jew were locked in

grim warfare, I witnessed many evidences of man's innate ability to be compassionate toward his fellow-man. I have seen Jewish doctors and nurses of the Hadassah Hospital in Jerusalem attend Arab patients in that hospital with most tender solicitude. I have seen, in 1948, in the midst of the war, Arab Legion troops lining the road between Tel-Aviv and Jerusalem, daily watch unarmed convoys of indispensable food and medical supplies for the beleaguered civilian Jews of Jerusalem pass through their lines unmolested. I have seen in the Hotel des Roses at Rhodes the head of the Israeli Delegation, sharing, in deep compassion, the sorrow of the Arab Delegate at the word he had just received of the loss of his entire family in Jordan in a tragic accident at his home. As I walked into the Arab's room to express my own sorrow, I saw there in silent mourning, not an Arab and a Jew, but only two sorrowful men, who though enemies yesterday were bound together today in a warm bond of human brotherhood by the stark tragedy which had befallen one of them. I have seen, at Christmas time, Arab and Israeli commanders open their tense military lines in order that Christian civilians might pass through to worship at Bethlehem. In this age of increasing cynicism it is always warming and reassuring to have one's faith in people reinforced by concrete examples of human good will.

28. People managing to live together, to respect each other, and to help each other along is the fundamental lesson which mankind everywhere must somehow learn if world peace and progress are to be assured. If all too slowly, the lesson, I think, is being learned. The cultural gulfs between continents are being gradually narrowed. At the United Nations, the common denominator of all people is not infrequently found, the universal language of human aspiration toward peace, freedom and the better life is constantly spoken and becomes more widely understood. The differences are great and the process is not rapid. Granted the fierce emotions, the political and other difficulties, the way must and, I believe with patience and persistence, may well be found to bridge the gaps between populations now unfriendly—as, for example, Arab and Jew in the Near East, the peoples of Indo-China, of Korea North and South, of West and East.

29. There may never be perfection in the relations among people or in the operation of the mechanisms of democracy. But in democracy the gap between ideal and practice must be constantly narrowed. For democracy to prosper, or even to live, it must ever be dynamic. It must move forward toward the goals of greater freedom, better life, fuller dignity for the people it serves. Any backward step, any encroachment upon the rights of democracy's citizens, any violation of the dignity of the individual, any retreat in the well-being of the people, strikes at the virility of the ideal and retards the course of human progress.

30. We in America not only have democracy, but we have built it on unique foundations—a union of peoples more diversified in origin than any other society has ever known. From the beginning of our history, we have been diversified, culturally and racially. It has been a great human experiment which has been launched and conducted on our American shores and plains—perhaps the greatest and most challenging in the history of human society. We have set out here to demonstrate that peoples of all racial strains, of all colors, creeds, and cultures, of widely varying background, can be accepted as equals, can learn to live and work and play together and become a firm unity by the force and attraction of noble ideals mutually shared—the dignity and worth of the individual, the equality of all men, and the conception of the state as the democratic expression and the servant of free men and women. We have made remarkable progress along that course and have developed our great national strength and unity on that solid foundation. We are still building, still perfecting our democracy, and in some aspects of our life at a greatly accelerated pace. In the field of race relations, for example, there has been more progress in the last decade than in all the years before. As I travel about I see the signs of it everywhere.

31. The recent unanimous decision of the Supreme Court against segregation in the public schools marks a momentous forward step in the onward march of democracy. Our churches, too, are moving forward on the race-

relations front, although it continues ironical that between 10 and 1 on Sunday mornings democracy in worship is so little observed in all of our communities.

32. In the course of our great experiment, we have learned that it is not necessary to eradicate differences, to achieve a single human pattern, in order to enjoy democracy or to attain national unity. Rather, we have found that it is only necessary for people to change their attitudes and superstitions about differences, and that this can be done and is being done. Indeed, we know that differences of race, religion, and culture actually enrich the society. There is nothing, surely, in the entire realm of human activity so inspired or inspiring as free men of all races and religions bound together by the stimulus of common interests, objectives, and ideals.

33. The vision of a world in which all peoples will live together in peace and brotherhood may be far from realization, but it remains the noblest ideal of human existence. It is the ideal of all the great religions. It is the ideal which the United Nations embraces. Today it assumes a significance more impera-

tive than ever known. For the instruments of destruction now available to war make of mankind's ability to approach this ideal in his day-to-day relationships the decisive challenge. It is a blunt challenge—learn to live together or perish together.

34. Let me repeat—in meeting this challenge, and it can be met, the individual bears a crucial responsibility. It is, after all, in the understanding, the attitudes, the enlightened self-interest of the peoples of the world that the riddle of the future is locked. As we have hope, as we maintain faith and confidence in ourselves and in our fellow-men, as we heed reason and live by the good that is in our hearts, we contribute mightily to that security of the future, that peaceful and better world, toward which all mankind aspires.

35. The surest beacon, always, is good will among men. Here lies the sole road to peace on earth. May we travel along it with sure faith and confidence. Those who are privileged to teach the young can do much to ensure that this road will be travelled. But only if teachers are kept free, unregimented, and unafraid.

GEORGE ORWELL *Shooting an Elephant*

George Orwell (1903-50), whose real name was Eric Blair, was a British novelist, essayist, and satirist. He was born in Bengal, India, and after four years at Eton (1917-21) served for five years with the Indian Imperial Police in Burma (1922-27). His life in Burma is the background for the following essay. During the 1930's, Orwell spent several years in Paris writing fiction and one year in Spain fighting in the Civil War, in which he was badly wounded.

To the end of his life Orwell's favorite reading was Shakespeare, Swift, Fielding, Dickens, Charles Reade, Samuel Butler, Zola, Flaubert, Joyce, Eliot, D. H. Lawrence, and especially Maugham. Like some of these writers, Orwell was primarily satirical in his reactions to human experience and behavior. He was the author of many books, among which are *Animal Farm*, 1945, *Nineteen Eighty-Four*, 1949, *Shooting an Elephant*, 1950, *Homage to Catalonia*, 1952, and *Such, Such Were the Joys*, 1953, the last two published posthumously.

1. In Moulmein, in Lower Burma, I was hated by large numbers of people—the only time in my life that I have been important enough for this to happen to me. I was sub-divisional police officer of the town, and in an aimless, petty kind of way anti-European feeling was very bitter. No one had the guts to raise a riot, but if a European woman went through the bazaars alone somebody would probably spit betel juice over her dress. As a police officer I was an obvious target and was baited whenever it seemed safe to do so. When a nimble Burman tripped me up on the football field and the referee (another Burman) looked the other way, the crowd yelled with hideous laughter. This happened more than once. In the end the sneering yellow faces of young men that met me everywhere, the insults hooted after me when I was at a safe distance, got badly on my nerves. The young Buddhist priests were the worst of all. There were several thousands of them in the town and none of them seemed to have anything to do except stand on street corners and jeer at Europeans.

2. All this was perplexing and upsetting. For at that time I had already made up my mind that imperialism was an evil thing and the sooner I chucked up my job and got out of it the better. Theoretically—and secretly, of course—I was all for the Burmese and all against their oppressors, the British. As for the job I was doing, I hated it more bitterly than I can perhaps make clear. In a job like that you see the dirty work of Empire at close quarters. The wretched prisoners huddling in the stinking cages of the lock-ups, the grey, cowed faces of the long-term convicts, the scarred buttocks of the men who had been flogged with bamboos—all these oppressed me with an intolerable sense of guilt. But I could get nothing into perspective. I was young and ill-educated and I had had to think out my problems in the utter silence that is imposed on every Englishman in the East. I did not even know that the British Empire is dying, still less did I know that it is a great deal better than the younger empires that are going to supplant it. All I knew was that I was stuck between my hatred of the empire I served and

my rage against the evil-spirited little beasts who tried to make my job impossible. With one part of my mind I thought of the British Raj as an unbreakable tyranny, as something clamped down, in *saecula saeculorum,* upon the will of prostrate peoples; with another part I thought that the greatest joy in the world would be to drive a bayonet into a Buddhist priest's guts. Feelings like these are the normal by-products of imperialism; ask any Anglo-Indian official, if you can catch him off duty.

3. One day something happened which in a roundabout way was enlightening. It was a tiny incident in itself, but it gave me a better glimpse than I had had before of the real nature of imperialism—the real motives for which despotic governments act. Early one morning the sub-inspector at a police station the other end of the town rang me up on the 'phone and said that an elephant was ravaging the bazaar. Would I please come and do something about it? I did not know what I could do, but I wanted to see what was happening and I got on to a pony and started out. I took my rifle, an old .44 Winchester and much too small to kill an elephant, but I thought the noise might be useful *in terrorem.* Various Burmans stopped me on the way and told me about the elephant's doings. It was not, of course, a wild elephant, but a tame one which had gone "must." It had been chained up, as tame elephants always are when their attack of "must" is due, but on the previous night it had broken its chain and escaped. Its mahout, the only person who could manage it when it was in that state, had set out in pursuit, but had taken the wrong direction and was now twelve hours' journey away, and in the morning the elephant had suddenly reappeared in the town. The Burmese population had no weapons and were quite helpless against it. It had already destroyed somebody's bamboo hut, killed a cow and raided some fruit-stalls and devoured the stock; also it had met the municipal rubbish van and, when the driver jumped out and took to his heels, had turned the van over and inflicted violences upon it.

4. The Burmese sub-inspector and some Indian constables were waiting for me in the quarter where the elephant had been seen. It was a very poor quarter, a labyrinth of squalid bamboo huts, thatched with palm-leaf, winding all over a steep hillside. I remember that it was a cloudy, stuffy morning at the beginning of the rains. We began questioning the people as to where the elephant had gone and, as usual, failed to get any definite information. That is invariably the case in the East; a story always sounds clear enough at a distance, but the nearer you get to the scene of events the vaguer it becomes. Some of the people said that the elephant had gone in one direction, some said that he had gone in another, some professed not even to have heard of any elephant. I had almost made up my mind that the whole story was a pack of lies, when we heard yells a little distance away. There was a loud, scandalized cry of "Go away, child! Go away this instant!" and an old woman with a switch in her hand came round the corner of a hut, violently shooing away a crowd of naked children. Some more women followed, clicking their tongues and exclaiming; evidently there was something that the children ought not to have seen. I rounded the hut and saw a man's dead body sprawling in the mud. He was an Indian, a black Dravidian coolie, almost naked, and he could not have been dead many minutes. The people said that the elephant had come suddenly upon him round the corner of the hut, caught him with its trunk, put its foot on his back and ground him into the earth. This was the rainy season and the ground was soft, and his face had scored a trench a foot deep and a couple of yards long. He was lying on his belly with arms crucified and head sharply twisted to one side. His face was coated with mud, the eyes wide open, the teeth bared and grinning with an expression of unendurable agony. (Never tell me, by the way, that the dead look peaceful. Most of the corpses I have seen looked devilish.) The friction of the great beast's foot had stripped the skin from his back as neatly as one skins a rabbit. As soon as I saw the dead man I sent an orderly to a friend's house nearby to borrow an elephant rifle. I had already sent back the pony, not wanting it to go mad with fright and throw me if it smelt the elephant.

5. The orderly came back in a few minutes with a rifle and five cartridges, and meanwhile some Burmans had arrived and told us that

the elephant was in the paddy fields below, only a few hundred yards away. As I started forward practically the whole population of the quarter flocked out of the houses and followed me. They had seen the rifle and were all shouting excitedly that I was going to shoot the elephant. They had not shown much interest in the elephant when he was merely ravaging their homes, but it was different now that he was going to be shot. It was a bit of fun to them, as it would be to an English crowd; besides they wanted the meat. It made me vaguely uneasy. I had no intention of shooting the elephant—I had merely sent for the rifle to defend myself if necessary—and it is always unnerving to have a crowd following you. I marched down the hill, looking and feeling a fool, with the rifle over my shoulder and an ever-growing army of people jostling at my heels. At the bottom, when you got away from the huts, there was a metalled road and beyond that a miry waste of paddy fields a thousand yards across, not yet ploughed but soggy from the first rains and dotted with coarse grass. The elephant was standing eight yards from the road, his left side towards us. He took not the slightest notice of the crowd's approach. He was tearing up bunches of grass, beating them against his knees to clean them and stuffing them into his mouth.

6. I had halted on the road. As soon as I saw the elephant I knew with perfect certainty that I ought not to shoot him. It is a serious matter to shoot a working elephant—it is comparable to destroying a huge and costly piece of machinery—and obviously one ought not to do it if it can possibly be avoided. And at that distance, peacefully eating, the elephant looked no more dangerous than a cow. I thought then and I think now that his attack of "must" was already passing off; in which case he would merely wander harmlessly about until the mahout came back and caught him. Moreover, I did not in the least want to shoot him. I decided that I would watch him for a little while to make sure that he did not turn savage again, and then go home.

7. But at that moment I glanced round at the crowd that had followed me. It was an immense crowd, two thousand at the least and growing every minute. It blocked the road for a long distance on either side. I looked at the sea of yellow faces above the garish clothes—faces all happy and excited over this bit of fun, all certain that the elephant was going to be shot. They were watching me as they would watch a conjurer about to perform a trick. They did not like me, but with the magical rifle in my hands I was momentarily worth watching. And suddenly I realized that I should have to shoot the elephant after all. The people expected it of me and I had got to do it; I could feel their two thousand wills pressing me forward, irresistibly. And it was at this moment, as I stood there with the rifle in my hands, that I first grasped the hollowness, the futility of the white man's dominion in the East. Here was I, the white man with his gun, standing in front of the unarmed native crowd—seemingly the leading actor of the piece; but in reality I was only an absurd puppet pushed to and fro by the will of those yellow faces behind. I perceived in this moment that when the white man turns tyrant it is his own freedom that he destroys. He becomes a sort of hollow, posing dummy, the conventionalized figure of a sahib. For it is the condition of his rule that he shall spend his life in trying to impress the "natives," and so in every crisis he has got to do what the "natives" expect of him. He wears a mask, and his face grows to fit it. I had got to shoot the elephant. I had committed myself to doing it when I sent for the rifle. A sahib has got to act like a sahib; he has got to appear resolute, to know his own mind and do definite things. To come all that way, rifle in hand, with two thousand people marching at my heels, and then to trail feebly away, having done nothing—no, that was impossible. The crowd would laugh at me. And my whole life, every white man's life in the East, was one long struggle not to be laughed at.

8. But I did not want to shoot the elephant. I watched him beating his bunch of grass against his knees, with that preoccupied grandmotherly air that elephants have. It seemed to me that it would be murder to shoot him. At that age I was not squeamish about killing animals, but I had never shot an elephant and never wanted to. (Somehow it always seems worse to kill a *large* animal.) Besides, there was the beast's owner to be considered. Alive, the elephant was worth at least a hundred

pounds; dead, he would only be worth the value of his tusks, five pounds, possibly. But I had got to act quickly. I turned to some experienced-looking Burmans who had been there when we arrived, and asked them how the elephant had been behaving. They all said the same thing: he took no notice of you if you left him alone, but he might charge if you went too close to him.

9. It was perfectly clear to me what I ought to do. I ought to walk up to within, say, twenty-five yards of the elephant and test his behavior. If he charged, I could shoot; if he took no notice of me, it would be safe to leave him until the mahout came back. But also I knew that I was going to do no such thing. I was a poor shot with a rifle and the ground was soft mud into which one would sink at every step. If the elephant charged and I missed him, I should have about as much chance as a toad under a steam-roller. But even then I was not thinking particularly of my own skin, only of the watchful yellow faces behind. For at that moment, with the crowd watching me, I was not afraid in the ordinary sense, as I would have been if I had been alone. A white man mustn't be frightened in front of "natives"; and so, in general, he isn't frightened. The sole thought in my mind was that if anything went wrong those two thousand Burmans would see me pursued, caught, trampled on and reduced to a grinning corpse like that Indian up the hill. And if that happened it was quite probable that some of them would laugh. That would never do. There was only one alternative. I shoved the cartridges into the magazine and lay down on the road to get a better aim.

10. The crowd grew very still, and a deep, low, happy sigh, as of people who see the theatre curtain go up at last, breathed from innumerable throats. They were going to have their bit of fun after all. The rifle was a beautiful German thing with cross-hair sights. I did not then know that in shooting an elephant one would shoot to cut an imaginary bar running from ear-hole to ear-hole. I ought, therefore, as the elephant was sideways on, to have aimed straight at his ear-hole; actually I aimed several inches in front of this, thinking the brain would be further forward.

11. When I pulled the trigger I did not hear the bang or feel the kick—one never does when a shot goes home—but I heard the devilish roar of glee that went up from the crowd. In that instant, in too short a time, one would have thought, even for the bullet to get there, a mysterious, terrible change had come over the elephant. He neither stirred nor fell, but every line of his body had altered. He looked suddenly stricken, shrunken, immensely old, as though the frightful impact of the bullet had paralysed him without knocking him down. At last, after what seemed a long time —it might have been five seconds, I dare say— he sagged flabbily to his knees. His mouth slobbered. An enormous senility seemed to have settled upon him. One could have imagined him thousands of years old. I fired again into the same spot. At the second shot he did not collapse but climbed with desperate slowness to his feet and stood weakly upright, with legs sagging and head drooping. I fired a third time. That was the shot that did for him. You could see the agony of it jolt his whole body and knock the last remnant of strength from his legs. But in falling he seemed for a moment to rise, for as his hind legs collapsed beneath him he seemed to tower upward like a huge rock toppling, his trunk reaching skyward like a tree. He trumpeted, for the first and only time. And then down he came, his belly towards me, with a crash that seemed to shake the ground even where I lay.

12. I got up. The Burmans were already racing past me across the mud. It was obvious that the elephant would never rise again, but he was not dead. He was breathing very rhythmically with long rattling gasps, his great mound of a side painfully rising and falling. His mouth was wide open—I could see far down into caverns of pale pink throat. I waited a long time for him to die, but his breathing did not weaken. Finally I fired my two remaining shots into the spot where I thought his heart must be. The thick blood welled out of him like red velvet, but still he did not die. His body did not even jerk when the shots hit him, the tortured breathing continued without a pause. He was dying, very slowly and in great agony, but in some world remote from me where not even a bullet could damage him further. I felt that I had got to put an end to that dreadful noise. It seemed

dreadful to see the great beast lying there, powerless to move and yet powerless to die, and not even to be able to finish him. I sent back for my small rifle and poured shot after shot into his heart and down his throat. They seemed to make no impression. The tortured gasps continued as steadily as the ticking of a clock.

13. In the end I could not stand it any longer and went away. I heard later that it took him half an hour to die. Burmans were bringing dahs and baskets even before I left, and I was told they had stripped his body almost to the bones by the afternoon.

14. Afterwards, of course, there were endless discussions about the shooting of the elephant.

The owner was furious, but he was only an Indian and could do nothing. Besides, legally I had done the right thing, for a mad elephant has to be killed, like a mad dog, if its owner fails to control it. Among the Europeans opinion was divided. The older men said I was right, the younger men said it was a damn shame to shoot an elephant for killing a coolie, because an elephant was worth more than any damn Coringhee coolie. And afterwards I was very glad that the coolie had been killed; it put me legally in the right and it gave me a sufficient pretext for shooting the elephant. I often wondered whether any of the others grasped that I had done it solely to avoid looking a fool.

HARRY C. MESERVE *The New Piety*

Harry C. Meserve (1914-   ), a graduate of Haverford College and of the Harvard Divinity School, has been minister of the First Unitarian Church of San Francisco since 1949. For two terms he has served as a member of the Board of Directors of the American Unitarian Association, and for three years was chairman of the editorial board of the *Christian Register*. In 1955 he made a tour of the Near East as a member of the American Christian Palestine Committee. Because of his leadership in his church and his brilliant preaching he has attained a wide reputation as a religious spokesman.

There are signs today that the American people are experiencing a religious revival. How deep, Mr. Meserve asks, do some of the current popular pieties go, and is there not convincing evidence of another kind of religious revival that is both more general and more important?

I

Is there a revival of religion in America today? Many signs suggest it. Books dealing with frankly religious themes appear high on the best-seller lists. Movies on Biblical and religious subjects are popular box-office attractions. Gospel songs sung by crooners and swing quartets can frequently be heard on radio and

THE NEW PIETY: Reprinted, by permission of the author, from *The Atlantic Monthly*, June 1955. Copyright, 1955, the Atlantic Monthly Company, Boston 16, Massachusetts.

television. Popular mass-circulation magazines seem to include articles on religion more frequently than they used to. Bishop Sheen, Billy Graham, and Norman Vincent Peale each number their adherents and admirers in the thousands if not the millions.

Church membership and attendance are definitely up in almost all churches. Skepticism is no longer smart. Faith is fashionable. Each Saturday night the newspapers announce that the President and Mrs. Eisenhower plan to attend church on Sunday. Each Monday morning the papers announce that they did in fact do so. The Assembly of the World Council of Churches at Evanston, Illinois, last summer received more extended publicity coverage than any other religious event in the history of our country. Even Jane Russell, not hitherto noted as a theologian, recently announced that she had found God to be "a livin' doll." Cabinet meetings open with prayer. We pledge allegiance to the flag as "one nation under God" where before we were merely "one nation indivisible." A new stamp issue proclaims what our coinage has traditionally proclaimed: "In God we trust." These and many other signs point toward some kind of stirring of renewed interest in religion.

All in all, it is certainly true that religion is receiving a better press today and far more general attention and respect than it has had in many years.

But there is a real question as to what kind of religion is being revived in the new piety. Is it a discovery of a deep ethical faith and of the resources of courage and strength which can enable us to meet the severe challenges of this time? Or is it a more or less superficial interest in certain outward signs and gestures without the deep inward changes of mind and spirit which always mark a revival of genuine religion?

The new piety takes various forms. One of them is the peace of mind, peace of soul variety. Anxiety is one of the major characteristics of our time. Millions of people have left behind the "faith of our fathers" and have found little or nothing to put in its place. These are the spiritually displaced persons of the modern world. They are aware of a deep anxiety about their own meaning as persons and about the meaning of life as a whole. They are aware of a great need for reassurance and for self-confidence.

There can be no doubt whatsoever that their anxiety is real and justified and that their need and hunger are sincere. But what does the new piety of peace of mind and soul offer them? It says in effect: "Everything is really all right. It is you who are out of tune with the Infinite. If you can just get right with God, coöperate with Him, get Him on your side, so to speak, then the things you want and have striven for so far with such disappoint-

ment can be yours. Your anxieties will be relieved. Your frustrations will be removed and you will be on the way to success and happiness."

In this form of the new piety, religion appears as a means to an end. It justifies itself because it is useful to us in getting the things that we want and adjusting ourselves to the world. It helps us to "stop worrying and start living" or to get that promotion or to smooth out that unpleasant situation in our personal relationships.

All these things are undoubtedly good and necessary. But the interpretation of religion as primarily a means to getting the things that we want belongs in the realm of magic. Primitive religions do make this emphasis. But the more mature and highly developed religions have insisted for centuries that the best and truest experiences of religion come when a person has given up asking "What do I require of God?" and learned to ask humbly "What does God require of me?"

Peace of mind, self-confidence, courage, strength, and faith are all precious spiritual gifts. All of us want and need more of them than we have. But if there is one consistent lesson of our historic religious tradition, both in Judaism and in Christianity, it is that these gifts come as by-products of our sincere and humble commitment to the task of doing justly, loving mercy, and walking humbly with our God.

It is a strange and persistent paradox of man's religious experience that his peace of mind and his courage and strength lie on the other side of his faithful commitment to purposes and ends larger and more durable than his personal destiny and so worthy of his loyalty that he is able to give himself to them come what may. Jesus stated this paradox in two arresting passages: "Come unto me all ye that labor and are heavy-laden, and I will give you rest. Take my yoke upon you, and learn of me." That is to say, take up something of my labors; and in them, mysteriously you will find the rest which you could not find elsewhere. Again, in even more familiar words: "Whoever will save his life shall lose it and whoever will lose his life, for my sake, shall find it."

The new piety of peace of mind and soul, in

spite of the fact that it is helping many people to adjust themselves better to life and to the world as it is, must also come to terms with that aspect of religion which is concerned with man's efforts to transform himself and the world in the direction of what ought to be.

A gospel of smooth adjustment to the world as it is, with all its mediocrity and evil, leaves out that austere side of religious experience in which we see ourselves as pilgrims and pioneers, the creators of the colony of heaven in the wilderness of the world that is. The religious person at his best is never wholly content with himself and at peace with the world, for he knows how far he falls short of what he ought to be and can be. There is a positive and healthy tension between what is and what ought to be that forbids complacency and incites to action. We are admonished by St. Paul not to be conformed to this world, but to be transformed by the renewing of our minds that we may prove what is the good and acceptable and perfect will of God.

In so far as the new piety of peace of mind and soul permits us to forget or ignore the transforming task of religion, it is failing to offer a revival of individual conscience and ethical social concern. Remove these elements from religion and what is left is a palliative, a pain-killer, but not a healer and a restorer of courage and strength. The stern lesson of religion through the ages is: no peace of mind without adventurous thought and faith; no comfort without bold commitment to something better than the world that is; no abiding joy and security without loyalty to the best.

II

A second form of the new piety is the patriotic type. The intensity of the struggle with communism in recent years has led many to believe that since communism is dogmatically atheistic in its philosophy, those who are opposed to communism must be dogmatically theistic. From here it is not a long step to the point where we make belief in God a test of a proper hatred of communism. And from this point one proceeds quickly to the assumption that God is not the Father of all mankind but the peculiar protector of the chosen people against the rest of the world. By this process we reduce our idea of God to the level of the fierce tribal deity of the early Old Testament. We make Him into "an angry man, hating half the world." He becomes a sort of Big Brother upon whom we call for aid in our struggle. We assume His sanction and aid for whatever we propose to do since He is on our side.

Now there are many sound reasons for opposing communism, and the person who today can see no differences of ethical value between the ways of communism and the ways of democracy has certainly lost his power to discriminate between relative good and evil; but the tendency to think of God as the Big Brother destroys a higher and nobler vision of God which has been one of the best contributions of Judaeo-Christian faith. God is not the guarantor of any particular nation's destinies. As the prophets of Israel and Jesus after them insisted, God stands for that power of truth and justice and righteousness and love before which all men and all nations are judged. The very foundation of an ethical view of the world is the realization that "God is no respecter of persons, but in every nation he that feareth him and worketh righteousness is accepted with him." We may trust that in our struggles we are on God's side. But it is presumptuous and untrue to insist that God must back us up whatever we do.

We do not become a better or more religious people because the name of God is engraved on our stamps and coinage, or even by adding the words "under God" to the pledge of allegiance to the flag. We shall not survive as a nation by trusting that God will turn out to be our Big Brother in the conflict with our enemies. We become worthy to survive and to draw on the strength of God in the measure that our personal attitudes and our policies and actions as a nation genuinely reflect something of the divine justice, mercy, and love.

In so far as the new piety of patriotism permits us to forget this austere truth, it weakens our moral fiber as a people, degrades the idea of God, and points backward in time toward the primitive superstition and tribalism which the Hebrew prophets fought to overcome 2500 years ago. If we as a nation are truly under God, we will know ourselves as under the divine judgment, called to penitence and challenged to reveal in history a more universal justice, a wider compassion, and a more patient and long-suffering love than any nation has yet shown.

A third form of the new piety might be called the emotional shock treatment type. We live in anxious, desperate times and nobody can blame us if we are hungry for a sense of assurance and certainty which we cannot find. The temptation is always upon us to escape from the severe disciplines of reason, from the effort to think things through to some sort of sensible conclusion, from the tensions of doubt and questioning, from the challenges which make faith an adventure involving risk and the possibility of failure. Piety of the emotional shock treatment type offers a way out of all this. It calls on us to abandon thought, to ridicule reason, to acknowledge the complete helplessness and incompetence of our minds and by an act of desire and will to throw ourselves on the mercy of God and accept a scheme of supernatural salvation.

The prospect is in many ways alluring. No man who has attempted to think his way through the great problems of life can fail to regard with humility the vast gap between the reach of the human mind and the size of the mystery which surrounds and includes it. No one knows better than the thinker that reason is not enough, and that all human thought is at last defeated by the stubborn mysteries of life. But to the appeal of those who offer the emotional shock treatment, he can only reply that the abandonment of thought is not enough either. It would doubtless be a great relief to feel oneself "safe in the arms of Jesus." The vast crowds, the skillful modern techniques of presentation, the repetitive dogmatic assertions, are emotionally stirring and satisfying. But the thoughtful religious person cannot get out of his head the great command which says: "Thou shalt love the Lord thy God with all thy mind"—the heart and soul and strength along with, not instead of, the mind.

While the piety of emotional shock treatment may well induce a vigorous, positive response and even a deep desire to live a new life, it does not show much evidence as yet of aiding the growth of the whole person into an intelligent devotion to higher ethical and spiritual values, which is the only true revival of the religious spirit. In the midst of all the crowds, the floodlights, the techniques, the yelling and the general excitement, the earthquake, wind, and fire, a still, small voice whispers to the consciences of thoughtful men: "What doth the Lord require of thee but to do justly and to love mercy and to walk humbly with thy God?" And the words of Jesus set the standard of judgment: "By their fruits, ye shall know them."

It may be that a necessary part of a revival of genuine religion is to be found in the piety of emotional shock treatment, just as necessary parts are also found in the piety of peace of mind and of patriotism, but in themselves these three types of religious revival are not enough.

The piety of patriotism, now in danger of losing itself in the very nationalism which is threatening to plunge the world into total war, must grow up until it dares confront us with a vision of God who is the God of all mankind and a humanity made up of many peoples and nations all precious in His sight. Any smaller idea of God simply dooms us to the tribal conflicts and hatreds from which we have been trying to escape for centuries.

The piety of peace of mind and soul must grow up until its priests and adherents dare present it as something more than psychotherapy with a religious tinge and smooth adjustment to the world as it is. Somehow it must arouse in men not only the longing for comfort and peace but a vision of themselves as they long to be and of the cleaner world they can help to make. Something of the ancient prophetic and apostolic fire needs to be rekindled in the piety of peace of mind so that its adherents can move out of the vicious circle of their own neurotic fears and anxieties and seek their peace of mind in bold commitment to the effort to do something of God's will on earth.

The piety of emotional shock treatment will have to face the fact that religion is something more than emotional shock treatments, necessary and important as these may sometimes be. Religion is also the steady, sober search for intellectual and emotional integrity, for wholeness and harmony of mind and heart, and for the expression of this wholeness in patient, intelligent effort to realize, in the world as it is, the best possible ethical ideals and policies.

If these changes can take place in the prevailing popular pieties, there is at least a chance that our age may indeed witness an authentic revival of the religious spirit which could save us and our children from the prospect of continual frustration and anxiety and the ever-present dread of total destruction.

III

Meantime, there is another evidence of the possible existence of a religious revival which seems to me both more general and more important than any of the prevailing popular pieties. There has been a slow and subtle change in the mood of thought and feeling with which people approach religion. This has been due to the collapse of certain illusions by which many people lived until quite recently. There were in the 1930's hosts of people whose interest in religion centered in it as a means to social and political reform. Their real faith was that social and political reforms were ends in themselves and that religion could be a powerful aid in bringing about the necessary changes.

One meets this attitude today far less often than one used to. It is not that the concern for social change has decreased. Rather the problem is now seen by many in larger dimensions. The reformation of society, the idea of the kingdom of God on earth, is seen to be not merely a matter of laws, commissions, organizations, and programs. It is also a matter of man's spiritual orientation, his knowledge of himself, his faith in his own powers, his feeling of belonging not only to the human community but to some deeper and more enduring community of faith and meaning which was before he was and will be after he is gone. There has been an unmistakable revival of interest in what we used to call "personal religion" as distinguished from "social religion" or "the social gospel." This revival is healthy in that it recognizes the roots of faith and hope from which all significant action springs and is a sincere search for a better understanding of those roots as they exist and influence the lives of individuals.

A second evidence seems to me to exist in the widespread abandonment of what might be called the negative dogmatisms. One meets some people today who are frankly cynical and many who are skeptical as to religious faith. But there are few of these who are happy about it or proud of it. The smugness has gone out of cynicism and the skeptics are asking the questions which will lead at length to affirmation of some kind. One meets few atheists, though many agnostics. But the agnosticism is humble and open rather than self-satisfied. Whereas the agnostic of yesterday appears to have enjoyed his condition, the agnostic of today would like to be convinced of some positive content in religion, if such a thing is possible. He knows that it is frivolous to confront the ultimate issues of life as if he were not really concerned with them. He does care about the meaning of life and he would like to know more.

Disillusioned with force, with politics, and with science as saviors, man today searches within himself for hints of those foundations of truth and justice and love on which his thought and action must be based if his power is to be put in the service of justice, his politics redeemed from triviality and corruption, his science devoted to the enrichment of life.

"Man," said Albert Schweitzer when he accepted the Nobel Prize for Peace, "has today become superman because of the power for good or evil which science has placed in his hands. But the superman suffers from a fatal imperfection in his spirit. He is not elevated to that level of superhuman reason which must correspond to the possession of superhuman force."

Perhaps the single greatest factor which makes for a genuine religious revival today is the fact that men everywhere are becoming aware of this terrible truth and are uneasy about it. It is in this uneasiness and restlessness that the search for higher values, the search for God, can begin. Insofar as the new pieties of peace of mind and soul, of patriotism, and of emotional shock treatment are deepened and enlarged enough to aid men in this search, they will be of help in bringing about a general revival of authentic religion. Certainly they should not be condemned out of hand, however distasteful they may be. But neither should they be blindly accepted and approved.

For if they are, they may divert our attention from the most important need. That need is: the reorientation of the human spirit so that man sees himself as a child of the Universal God, conceived in dignity and in freedom, sharing a common humanity with all men the world over, answerable to abiding values of truth, justice, and love, in the service of which he finds himself and the things which belong to his peace.

THE AMERICAN TRADITION

LEE STROUT WHITE *Farewell, My Lovely!*

The reader will search in vain for a writer named Lee Strout White. This vivacious tribute was written by two individuals, Richard Lee Strout and E. B. White. Richard Lee Strout (1898-   ) was educated at Harvard University. He began his newspaper work in England with the Sheffield *Independent,* and was later a reporter for the Boston *Post.* In 1921 he joined the *Christian Science Monitor* and since 1925 has been with its Washington Bureau. One of the leading journalists of our day, Mr. Strout also publishes in the *Reader's Digest,* the *New Republic,* and other magazines. (A biographical sketch of E. B. White appears in the headnote to "Here Is New York.")

E. B. White has probably contributed more to the preservation of the familiar essay than any other American writer. Underlying his light-hearted style and his good-natured satire are a serious-ness of purpose, increasingly evident since World War II, and a quiet idealism, suggesting courage, honesty, and sympathy. In this essay he and Mr. Strout have given perfect expression to a subject admirably suited to the essay form. No "institution" is historically more significant or more thoroughly indigenous to the United States than the Model T. As these writers say, ". . . the old Ford practically was the American scene."

1. I see by the new Sears Roebuck catalogue that it is still possible to buy an axle for a 1909 Model T Ford, but I am not deceived. The great days have faded, the end is in sight. Only one page in the current catalogue is devoted to parts and accessories for the Model T; yet everyone remembers springtimes when the Ford gadget section was larger than men's clothing, almost as large as household furnishings. The last Model T was built in 1927, and the car is fading from what scholars call the American scene—which is an under-statement, because to a few million people who grew up with it, the old Ford practically *was* the American scene.

2. It was the miracle God had wrought.

And it was patently the sort of thing that could only happen once. Mechanically un-canny, it was like nothing that had ever come to the world before. Flourishing industries rose and fell with it. As a vehicle, it was hard-working, commonplace, heroic; and it often seemed to transmit those qualities to the persons who rode in it. My own genera-tion identifies it with Youth, with its gaudy, irretrievable excitements; before it fades into the mist, I would like to pay it the tribute of the sigh that is not a sob, and set down ran-dom entries in a shape somewhat less cumber-some than a Sears Roebuck catalogue.

3. The Model T was distinguished from all other makes of cars by the fact that its trans-mission was of a type known as planetary—which was half metaphysics, half sheer fric-tion. Engineers accepted the word "planetary"

FAREWELL, MY LOVELY!: By permission. Copyright, 1936, The New Yorker Magazine, Inc. Published under the title *Farewell to Model T* by G. P. Putnam.

in its epicyclic sense, but I was always conscious that it also meant "wandering," "erratic." Because of the peculiar nature of this planetary element, there was always, in Model T, a certain dull rapport between engine and wheels, and even when the car was in a state known as neutral, it trembled with a deep imperative and tended to inch forward. There was never a moment when the bands were not faintly egging the machine on. In this respect it was like a horse, rolling the bit on its tongue, and country people brought to it the same technique they used with draft animals.

4. Its most remarkable quality was its rate of acceleration. In its palmy days the Model T could take off faster than anything on the road. The reason was simple. To get under way, you simply hooked the third finger of the right hand around a lever on the steering column, pulled down hard, and shoved your left foot forcibly against the low-speed pedal. These were simple, positive motions; the car responded by lunging forward with a roar. After a few seconds of this turmoil, you took your toe off the pedal, eased up a mite on the throttle, and the car, possessed of only two forward speeds, catapulted directly into high with a series of ugly jerks and was off on its glorious errand. The abruptness of this departure was never equalled in other cars of the period. The human leg was (and still is) incapable of letting in a clutch with anything like the forthright abandon that used to send Model T on its way. Letting in a clutch is a negative, hesitant motion, depending on delicate nervous control; pushing down the Ford pedal was a simple, country motion—an expansive act, which came as natural as kicking an old door to make it budge.

5. The driver of the old Model T was a man enthroned. The car, with top up, stood seven feet high. The driver sat on top of the gas tank, brooding it with his own body. When he wanted gasoline, he alighted, along with everything else in the front seat; the seat was pulled off, the metal cap unscrewed, and a wooden stick thrust down to sound the liquid in the well. There were always a couple of these sounding sticks kicking around in the ratty sub-cushion regions of a flivver. Refuelling was more of a social function then, because the driver had to unbend, whether he

wanted to or not. Directly in front of the driver was the windshield—high, uncompromisingly erect. Nobody talked about air resistance, and the four cylinders pushed the car through the atmosphere with a simple disregard of physical law.

6. There was this about a Model T: the purchaser never regarded his purchase as a complete, finished product. When you bought a Ford, you figured you had a start—a vibrant, spirited framework to which could be screwed an almost limitless assortment of decorative and functional hardware. Driving away from the agency, hugging the new wheel between your knees, you were already full of creative worry. A Ford was born naked as a baby, and a flourishing industry grew up out of correcting its rare deficiencies and combating its fascinating diseases. Those were the great days of lily-painting. I have been looking at some old Sears Roebuck catalogues, and they bring everything back so clear.

7. First you bought a Ruby Safety Reflector for the rear, so that your posterior would glow in another car's brilliance. Then you invested thirty-nine cents in some radiator Moto Wings, a popular ornament which gave the Pegasus touch to the machine and did something godlike to the owner. For nine cents you bought a fan-belt guide to keep the belt from slipping off the pulley.

8. You bought a radiator compound to stop leaks. This was as much a part of everybody's equipment as aspirin tablets are of a medicine cabinet. You bought special oil to prevent chattering, a clamp-on dash light, a patching outfit, a tool box which you bolted to the running board, a sun visor, a steering-column brace to keep the column rigid, and a set of emergency containers for gas, oil, and water—three thin, disc-like cans which reposed in a case on the running board during long, important journeys—red for gas, gray for water, green for oil. It was only a beginning. After the car was about a year old, steps were taken to check the alarming disintegration (Model T was full of tumors, but they were benign.) A set of anti-rattlers (98¢) was a popular panacea. You hooked them on to the gas and spark rods, to the brake pull rod, and to the steering-rod connections. Hood silencers, of black rubber. were applied to the fluttering hood.

Shock-absorbers and snubbers gave "complete relaxation." Some people bought rubber pedal pads, to fit over the standard metal pedals. (I didn't like these, I remember.) Persons of a suspicious or pugnacious turn of mind bought a rear-view mirror; but most Model T owners weren't worried by what was coming from behind because they would soon enough see it out in front. They rode in a state of cheerful catalepsy. Quite a large mutinous clique among Ford owners went over to a foot accelerator (you could buy one and screw it to the floor board), but there was a certain madness in these people, because the Model T, just as she stood, had a choice of three foot pedals to push, and there were plenty of moments when both feet were occupied in the routine performance of duty and when the only way to speed up the engine was with the hand throttle.

9. Gadget bred gadget. Owners not only bought ready-made gadgets, they invented gadgets to meet special needs. I myself drove my car directly from the agency to the blacksmith's, and had the smith affix two enormous iron brackets to the port running board to support an army trunk.

10. People who owned closed models builded along different lines: they bought ball grip handles for opening doors, window anti-rattlers, and deluxe flower vases of the cut-glass antisplash type. People with delicate sensibilities garnished their car with a device called the Donna Lee Automobile Disseminator—a porous vase guaranteed, according to Sears, to fill the car with a "faint clean odor of lavender." The gap between open cars and closed cars was not as great then as it is now: for $11.95, Sears Roebuck converted your touring car into a sedan and you went forth renewed. One agreeable quality of the old Fords was that they had no bumpers, and their fenders softened and wilted with the years and permitted the driver to squeeze in and out of tight places.

11. Tires were 30 x 3½, cost about twelve dollars, and punctured readily. Everybody carried a Jiffy patching set, with a nutmeg grater to roughen the tube before the goo was spread on. Everybody was capable of putting on a patch, expected to have to, and did have to.

12. During my association with Model T's, self-starters were not a prevalent accessory. They were expensive and under suspicion. Your car came equipped with a serviceable crank, and the first thing you learned was how to Get Results. It was a special trick, and until you learned it (usually from another Ford owner, but sometimes by a period of appalling experimentation) you might as well have been winding up an awning. The trick was to leave the ignition switch off, proceed to the animal's head, pull the choke (which was a little wire protruding through the radiator), and give the crank two or three nonchalant upward lifts. Then, whistling as though thinking about something else, you would saunter back to the driver's cabin, turn the ignition on, return to the crank, and this time, catching it on the down stroke, give it a quick spin with plenty of That. If this procedure was followed, the engine almost always responded—first with a few scattered explosions, then with a tumultuous gunfire, which you checked by racing around to the driver's seat and retarding the throttle. Often, if the emergency brake hadn't been pulled all the way back, the car advanced on you the instant the first explosion occurred and you would hold it back by leaning your weight against it. I can still feel my old Ford nuzzling me at the curb, as though looking for an apple in my pocket.

13. The lore and legend that governed the Ford were boundless. Owners had their own theories about everything; they discussed mutual problems in that wise, infinitely resourceful way old women discuss rheumatism. Exact knowledge was pretty scarce, and often proved less effective than superstition. Dropping a camphor ball into the gas tank was a popular expedient; it seemed to have a tonic effect on both man and machine. There wasn't much to base exact knowledge on. The Ford driver flew blind. He didn't know the temperature of his engine, the speed of his car, the amount of his fuel, or the pressure of his oil (the old Ford lubricated itself by what was amiably described as the "splash system"). A speedometer cost money and was an extra, like a windshield-wiper. The dashboard of the early models was bare save for an ignition key; later models, grown effete, boasted an ammeter

which pulsated alarmingly with the throbbing of the car. Under the dash was a box of coils, with vibrators which you adjusted, or thought you adjusted. Whatever the driver learned of his motor, he learned not through instruments but through sudden developments. I remember that the timer was one of the vital organs about which there was ample doctrine. When everything else had been checked, you "had a look" at the timer. It was an extravagantly odd little device, simple in construction, mysterious in function. It contained a roller, held by a spring, and there were four contact points on the inside of the case against which, many people believed, the roller rolled. I have had a timer apart on a sick Ford many times, but I never really knew what I was up to—I was just showing off before God. There were almost as many schools of thought as there were timers. Some people, when things went wrong, just clenched their teeth and gave the timer a smart crack with a wrench. Other people opened it up and blew on it. There was a school that held that the timer needed large amounts of oil; they fixed it by frequent baptism. And there was a school that was positive it was meant to run dry as a bone; these people were continually taking it off and wiping it. I remember once spitting into a timer; not in anger, but in a spirit of research. You see, the Model T driver moved in the realm of metaphysics. He believed his car could be hexed.

14. One reason the Ford anatomy was never reduced to an exact science was that, having "fixed" it, the owner couldn't honestly claim that the treatment had brought about the cure. There were too many authenticated cases of Fords fixing themselves—restored naturally to health after a short rest. Farmers soon discovered this, and it fitted nicely with their draft-horse philosophy: "Let 'er cool off and she'll snap into it again."

15. A Ford owner had Number One Bearing constantly in mind. This bearing, being at the front end of the motor, was the one that always burned out, because the oil didn't reach it when the car was climbing hills. (That's what I was always told, anyway.) The oil used to recede and leave Number One dry as a clam flat; you had to watch that bearing like a hawk. It was like a weak heart—you could hear it start knocking, and that was when you stopped and let her cool off. Try as you would to keep the oil supply right, in the end Number One always went out. "Number One Bearing burned out on me and I had to have her replaced," you would say, wisely; and your companions always had a lot to tell about how to pamper Number One to keep her alive.

16. Sprinkled not too liberally among the millions of amateur witch doctors who drove Fords and applied their own abominable cures were the heaven-sent mechanics who could really make the car talk. These professionals turned up in undreamed-of spots. One time, on the banks of the Columbia River in Washington, I heard the rear end go out of my Model T when I was trying to whip it up a steep incline onto the deck of a ferry. Something snapped; the car slid backward into the mud. It seemed to me like the end of the trail. But the captain of the ferry, observing the withered remnant, spoke up.

17. "What's got her?" he asked.

"I guess it's the rear end," I replied, listlessly. The captain leaned over the rail and stared. Then I saw that there was a hunger in his eyes that set him off from other men.

"Tell you what," he said, carelessly, trying to cover up his eagerness, "let's pull the son of a bitch up onto the boat, and I'll help you fix her while we're going back and forth on the river."

18. We did just this. All that day I plied between the towns of Pasco and Kennewick, while the skipper (who had once worked in a Ford garage) directed the amazing work of resetting the bones of my car.

19. Springtime in the heyday of the Model T was a delirious season. Owning a car was still a major excitement, roads were still wonderful and bad. The Fords were obviously conceived in madness: any car which was capable of going from forward into reverse without any perceptible mechanical hiatus was bound to be a mighty challenging thing to the human imagination. Boys used to veer them off the highway into a level pasture and run wild with them, as though they were cutting up with a girl. Most everybody used the reverse pedal quite as much as the regular foot brake—it distributed the wear over the bands

and wore them all down evenly. That was the big trick, to wear all the bands down evenly, so that the final chattering would be total and the whole unit scream for renewal.

20. The days were golden, the nights were dim and strange. I still recall with trembling those loud, nocturnal crises when you drew up to a signpost and raced the engine so the lights would be bright enough to read destinations by. I have never been really planetary since. I suppose it's time to say good-bye. Farewell, my lovely!

CARL SANDBURG *Lincoln Speaks at Gettysburg*

Carl Sandburg (1876-   ) has gained wide recognition as an American poet and biographer. He has received many literary awards, chief among them the Pulitzer Prize in 1940 and again in 1951. His literary career has been devoted to poetry, to the singing and collecting of folk songs, and to writing a monumental biography of Abraham Lincoln, in six volumes. The first two volumes entitled *The Prairie Years* were published in 1926; the last four volumes, *The War Years*, appeared in 1936. In 1939 (with Paul M. Angle) he published *Mary Lincoln, Wife and Widow*. In 1953 Sandburg brought out a volume of autobiography, *Always the Young Strangers*, and in 1954, a one-volume condensation of the Lincoln biography.

All Carl Sandburg's writing has its setting in the United States. Time and again it reflects his awareness and appreciation of the milieu out of which American heroes come. "Lincoln Speaks at Gettysburg" shows this keen perceptiveness.

1. A printed invitation came to Lincoln's hands notifying him that on Thursday, November 19, 1863, exercises would be held for the dedication of a National Soldiers' Cemetery at Gettysburg. The same circular invitation had been mailed to Senators, Congressmen, the governors of Northern States, members of the Cabinet, by the commission of Pennsylvanians who had organized a corporation through which Maine, New Hampshire, Vermont, Massachusetts, Rhode Island, Maryland, Connecticut, New York, New Jersey, Pennsylvania, Delaware, West Virginia, Ohio, Indiana, Illinois, Michigan, Wisconsin, and Minnesota were to share the cost of a decent burying-ground for the dust and bones of the Union and Confederate dead.

2. In the helpless onrush of the war, it was

LINCOLN SPEAKS AT GETTYSBURG: From *Abraham Lincoln: The War Years* by Carl Sandburg, copyright, 1939, by Harcourt, Brace and Company, Inc.

known, too many of the fallen had lain as neglected cadavers rotting in the open fields or thrust into so shallow a resting-place that a common farm plow caught in their bones. Now by order of Governor Curtin of Pennsylvania seventeen acres had been purchased on Cemetery Hill, where the Union center stood its colors on the second and third of July, and plots of soil had been allotted each State for its graves.

3. The sacred and delicate duties of orator of the day had fallen on Edward Everett. An eminent cultural figure, perhaps foremost of all distinguished American classical orators, he was born in 1794, had been United States Senator, Governor of Massachusetts, member of Congress, Secretary of State under Fillmore, Minister to Great Britain, Phi Beta Kappa poet at Harvard, professor of Greek at Harvard, president of Harvard. His reputation as a public speaker began in the Brattle Street

Unitarian Church of Boston. Two volumes of his orations published in 1850 held eighty-one addresses, two more volumes issued in 1859 collected one hundred and five speeches. His lecture on Washington, delivered a hundred and twenty-two times in three years, had in 1859 brought a fund of $58,000, which he gave to the purchase and maintenance of Mount Vernon as a permanent shrine. Other Everett lectures had realized more than $90,000 for charity causes. . . . No ordinary trafficker in politics, Everett had in 1860 run for Vice-President on the Bell-Everett ticket of the Constitutional Union party, receiving the electoral votes of Virginia, Kentucky, and Tennessee. . . .

4. Serene, suave, handsomely venerable in his sixty-ninth year, a prominent specimen of Northern upper-class distinction, Everett was a natural choice of the Pennsylvania commissioners, who sought an orator for a solemn national occasion. When in September they notified him that the date of the occasion would be October 23, he replied that he would need more time for preparation, and the dedication was postponed till November 19.

5. Lincoln meanwhile, in reply to the printed circular invitation, sent word to the commissioners that he would be present at the ceremonies. This made it necessary for the commissioners to consider whether the President should be asked to deliver an address when present. Clark E. Carr of Galesburg, Illinois, representing his State on the Board of Commissioners, noted that the decision of the Board to invite Lincoln to speak was an afterthought. "The question was raised as to his ability to speak upon such a grave and solemn occasion. . . . Besides, it was said that, with his important duties and responsibilities, he could not possibly have the leisure to prepare an address. . . . In answer . . . it was urged that he himself, better than any one else, could determine as to these questions, and that, if he were invited to speak, he was sure to do what, under the circumstances, would be right and proper."

6. And so on November 2 David Wills of Gettysburg, as the special agent of Governor Curtin and also acting for the several States, by letter informed Lincoln that the several States having soldiers in the Army of the

Potomac who were killed, or had since died at hospitals in the vicinity, had procured grounds for a cemetery and proper burial of their dead. "These grounds will be consecrated and set apart to this sacred purpose by appropriate ceremonies on Thursday, the 19th instant. I am authorized by the Governors of the various States to invite you to be present and participate in these ceremonies, which will doubtless be very imposing and solemnly impressive. It is the desire that after the oration, you, as Chief Executive of the nation, formally set apart these grounds to their sacred use by a few appropriate remarks."

7. Mr. Wills proceeded farther as to the solemnity of the occasion, and when Lincoln had finished reading the letter he understood definitely that the event called for no humor and that a long speech was not expected from him. "The invitation," wrote Clark E. Carr, "was not settled upon and sent to Mr. Lincoln until the second of November, more than six weeks after Mr. Everett had been invited to speak, and but little more than two weeks before the exercises were held." . . .

8. Benjamin B. French, officer in charge of buildings in Washington, introduced the Honorable Edward Everett, orator of the day, who rose, bowed low to Lincoln, saying, "Mr. President." Lincoln responded, "Mr. Everett."

9. The orator of the day then stood in silence before a crowd that stretched to limits that would test his voice. Beyond and around were the wheat fields, the meadows, the peach orchards, long slopes of land, and five and seven miles farther the contemplative blue ridge of a low mountain range. His eyes could sweep them as he faced the audience. He had taken note of it in his prepared and rehearsed address. "Overlooking these broad fields now reposing from the labors of the waning year, the mighty Alleghenies dimly towering before us, the graves of our brethren beneath our feet, it is with hesitation that I raise my poor voice to break the eloquent silence of God and Nature. But the duty to which you have called me must be performed;—grant me, I pray you, your indulgence and your sympathy." Everett proceeded, "It was appointed by law in Athens," and gave an extended sketch of the manner in which the Greeks cared for their dead who fell in battle. He

spoke of the citizens assembled to consecrate the day. "As my eye ranges over the fields whose sods were so lately moistened by the blood of gallant and loyal men, I feel, as never before, how truly it was said of old that it is sweet and becoming to die for one's country."

10. Northern cities would have been trampled in conquest but for "those who sleep beneath our feet," said the orator. He gave an outline of how the war began, traversed decisive features of the three days' battle at Gettysburg, discussed the doctrine of state sovereignty and denounced it, drew parallels from European history, and came to peroration quoting Pericles on dead patriots: "The whole earth is the sepulchre of illustrious men." The men of nineteen sister States had stood side by side on the perilous ridges. "Seminary Ridge, the Peach-Orchard, Cemetery, Culp, and Wolf Hill, Round Top, Little Round Top, humble names, henceforward dear and famous,—no lapse of time, no distance of space, shall cause you to be forgotten." He had spoken for an hour and fifty-seven minutes, some said a trifle over two hours, repeating almost word for word an address that occupied nearly two newspaper pages, as he had written it and as it had gone in advance sheets to many newspapers.

11. Everett came to his closing sentence without a faltering voice: "Down to the latest period of recorded time, in the glorious annals of our common country there will be no brighter page than that which relates THE BATTLES OF GETTYSBURG." It was the effort of his life and embodied the perfections of the school of oratory in which he had spent his career. His erect form and sturdy shoulders, his white hair and flung-back head at dramatic points, his voice, his poise, and chiefly some quality of inside good heartedness, held most of his audience to him, though the people in the front rows had taken their seats three hours before his oration closed.

12. The Baltimore Glee Club sang an ode written for the occasion by Benjamin B. French, who had introduced Everett to the audience. The poets Longfellow, Bryant, Whittier, Lowell, George Boker, had been requested but none found time to respond with a piece to be set to music. The two closing verses of the ode by French immedi-

ately preceded the introduction of the President to the audience:

Great God in Heaven!
Shall all this sacred blood be shed?
Shall we thus mourn our glorious dead?
Oh, shall the end be wrath and woe,
The knell of Freedom's overthrow,
   A country riven?

It will not be!
We trust, O God! thy gracious power
To aid us in our darkest hour.
This be our prayer—"O Father! save
A people's freedom from its grave.
   All praise to Thee!"

13. Having read Everett's address, Lincoln knew when the moment drew near for him to speak. He took out his own manuscript from a coat pocket, put on his steel-bowed glasses, stirred in his chair, looked over the manuscript, and put it back in his pocket. The Baltimore Glee Club finished. The specially chosen Ward Hill Lamon rose and spoke the words "The President of the United States," who rose, and holding in one hand the two sheets of paper at which he occasionally glanced, delivered the address in his high-pitched and clear-carrying voice. The *Cincinnati Commercial* reporter wrote, "The President rises slowly, draws from his pocket a paper, and, when commotion subsides, in a sharp, unmusical treble voice, reads the brief and pithy remarks." Hay wrote in his diary, "The President, in a firm, free way, with more grace than is his wont, said his half dozen words of consecration." Charles Hale of the *Boston Advertiser,* also officially representing Governor Andrew of Massachusetts, had notebook and pencil in hand, took down the slow-spoken words of the President, as follows:

Fourscore and seven years ago, our fathers brought forth upon this continent a new nation, conceived in liberty and dedicated to the proposition that all men are created equal.

Now we are engaged in a great civil war, testing whether that nation—or any nation, so conceived and so dedicated—can long endure.

We are met on a great battle-field of that war. We are met to dedicate a portion of it as the final resting place of those who have given their lives that that nation might live.

It is altogether fitting and proper that we should do this.

But, in a larger sense, we cannot dedicate, we cannot consecrate, we cannot hallow, this ground. The brave men, living and dead, who struggled here, have consecrated it, far above our power to add or to detract.

The world will very little note nor long remember what we say here; but it can never forget what they did here.

It is for us, the living, rather, to be dedicated, here, to the unfinished work that they have thus far so nobly carried on. It is rather for us to be here dedicated to the great task remaining before us; that from these honored dead we take increased devotion to that cause for which they here gave the last full measure of devotion; that we here highly resolve that these dead shall not have died in vain; that the nation shall, under God, have a new birth of freedom, and that government of the people, by the people, for the people, shall not perish from the earth.

14. . . . The *New York Tribune* and many other newspapers indicated "[Applause.]" at five places in the address and "[Long continued applause.]" at the end. The applause, however, according to most of the responsible witnesses, was formal and perfunctory, a tribute to the occasion, to the high office, to the array of important men of the nation on the platform, by persons who had sat as an audience for three hours. Ten sentences had been spoken in five minutes, and some were surprised that it should end before the orator had really begun to get his outdoor voice.

15. A photographer had made ready to record a great historic moment, had bustled about with his dry plates, his black box on a tripod, and before he had his head under the hood for an exposure, the President had said "by the people, for the people" and the nick of time was past for a photograph.

16. The *New York Times* reporter gave his summary of the program by writing: "The opening prayer by Reverend Mr. Stockton was touching and beautiful, and produced quite as much effect upon the audience as the classic sentences of the orator of the day. President Lincoln's address was delivered in a clear loud tone of voice, which could be distinctly heard at the extreme limits of the large assemblage. It was delivered (or rather read from a sheet of paper which the speaker held in his hand) in a very deliberate manner, with strong emphasis, and with a most businesslike air."

17. The *Philadelphia Press* man, John Russell Young, privately felt that Everett's speech was the performance of a great actor whose art was too evident, that it was "beautiful but cold as ice." The *New York Times* man noted: "Even while Mr. Everett was delivering his splendid oration, there were as many people wandering about the fields, made memorable by the fierce struggles of July, as stood around the stand listening to his eloquent periods. They seem to have considered, with President Lincoln, that it was not what was *said* here, but what was *done* here, that deserved their attention. . . . In wandering about these battlefields, one is astonished and indignant to find at almost every step of his progress the carcasses of dead horses which breed pestilence in the atmosphere. I am told that more than a score of deaths have resulted from this neglect in the village of Gettysburg the past summer; in the house in which I was compelled to seek lodgings, there are now two boys sick with typhoid fever attributed to this cause. Within a stone's throw of the whitewashed hut occupied as the headquarters of General Meade, I counted yesterday no less than ten carcasses of dead horses, lying on the ground where they were struck by the shells of the enemy."

18. The audience had expected, as the printed program stipulated, "Dedicatory Remarks, by the President of the United States." No eloquence was promised. Where eloquence is in flow the orator must have time to get tuned up, to expatiate and expand while building toward his climaxes, it was supposed. The *New York Tribune* man and other like observers merely reported the words of the address with the one preceding sentence: "The dedicatory remarks were then delivered by the President." These reporters felt no urge to inform their readers about how Lincoln stood, what he did with his hands, how he moved, vocalized, or whether he emphasized or subdued any parts of the address. Strictly, no address as such was on the program from him. He was down for just a few perfunctory "dedicatory remarks."

19. According to Lamon, Lincoln himself felt that about all he had given the audience

was ordinary garden-variety dedicatory remarks, for Lamon wrote that Lincoln told
him just after delivering the speech that he
had regret over not having prepared it with
greater care. "Lamon, that speech won't *scour*.
It is a flat failure and the people are disappointed." On the farms where Lincoln grew
up as a boy when wet soil stuck to the mold
board of a plow they said it didn't "scour."

20. The near-by *Patriot and Union* of Har-
risburg took its fling: "The President succeeded on this occasion because he acted without sense and without constraint in a pano-
rama that was gotten up more for the benefit of his party than for the glory of the
nation and the honor of the dead. . . . We
pass over the silly remarks of the President;
for the credit of the nation we are willing
that the veil of oblivion shall be dropped over
them and that they shall no more be repeated
or thought of."

21. The *Chicago Times* held that "Mr. Lincoln did most foully traduce the motives of
the men who were slain at Gettysburg" in his
reference to "a new birth of freedom," the
Times saying, "They gave their lives to maintain the old government, and the only Constitution and Union." He had perverted history, misstated the cause for which they died,
and with "ignorant rudeness" insulted the
memory of the dead, the *Times* alleged:
"Readers will not have failed to observe the
exceeding bad taste which characterized the
remarks of the President and Secretary of
State at the dedication of the soldiers' cemetery at Gettysburg. The cheek of every American must tingle with shame as he reads the
silly, flat, and dish-watery utterances of the
man who has to be pointed out to intelligent
foreigners as the President of the United
States. And neither he nor Seward could refrain, even on that solemn occasion, from
spouting their odious abolition doctrines. The
readers of THE TIMES ought to know, too, that
the valorous President did not dare to make
this little journey to Gettysburg without being escorted by a bodyguard of soldiers. For
the first time in the history of the country,
the President of the United States, in traveling through a part of his dominions, on a
peaceful, even a religious mission, had to be
escorted by a bodyguard of soldiers . . . it

was fear for his own personal safety which
led the President to go escorted as any other
military despot might go." In the pronounce-
ment of a funeral sermon Mr. Lincoln had
intruded an "offensive exhibition of boorish-
ness and vulgarity," had alluded to tribal differences that an Indian orator eulogizing dead
warriors would have omitted, "which he knew
would excite unnecessarily the bitter prejudices of his hearers." Therefore the *Chicago
Times* would inquire, "Is Mr. Lincoln less
refined than a savage?"

22. A Confederate outburst of war propaganda related to Lincoln and the Gettysburg
exercises was set forth in a *Richmond Examiner* editorial, and probably written by its
editor, Edward A. Pollard, taking a day off
from his merciless and occasionally wild-eyed
criticism of President Jefferson Davis of the
Confederacy. And the *Chicago Times,* which
seldom let a day pass without curses on
Lincoln for his alleged suppression of free
speech and a free press, reprinted in full the
long editorial from the *Examiner.* "The dramatic exhibition at Gettysburg is in thorough
keeping with Yankee character, suited to the
usual dignity of their chosen chief," ran part
of the editorial scorn. "Stage play, studied attitudes, and effective points were carefully
elaborated and presented to the world as the
honest outpourings of a nation's heart. In
spite of shoddy contracts, of universal corruption, and cruel thirst for southern blood, these
people have ideas . . . have read of them in
books . . . and determined accordingly to
have a grand imitation of them. . . . Mr.
Everett was equal to the occasion. He 'took
down his Thucydides,' and fancied himself a
Pericles commemorating the illustrious dead.
The music, the eloquence, the bottled tears
and hermetically sealed grief, prepared for the
occasion, were all properly brought out in
honor of the heroes, whom they crimp in Ireland, inveigle in Germany, or hunt down in
the streets of New York.

23. "So far the play was strictly classic. To
suit the general public, however, a little ad-
mixture of the more irregular romantic drama
was allowed. A vein of comedy was permitted
to mingle with the deep pathos of the piece.
This singular novelty, and deviation from
classic propriety, was heightened by assigning

this part to the chief personage. Kings are usually made to speak in the magniloquent language supposed to be suited to their elevated position. On the present occasion Lincoln acted the clown."

24. This was in the customary tone of the *Chicago Times* and relished by its supporting readers. Its rival, the *Chicago Tribune,* however, had a reporter who telegraphed (unless some editor who read the address added his own independent opinion) a sentence: "The dedicatory remarks of President Lincoln will live among the annals of man."

25. The *Cincinnati Gazette* reporter added after the text of the address, "That this was the right thing in the right place, and a perfect thing in every respect, was the universal encomium."

26. The American correspondent of the London *Times* wrote that "the ceremony was rendered ludicrous by some of the sallies of that poor President Lincoln. . . . Anything more dull and commonplace it would not be easy to produce."

27. Count Gurowski, the only man ever mentioned by Lincoln to Lamon as his possible assassin, wrote in a diary, "Lincoln spoke, with one eye to a future platform and to re-election."

28. The *Philadelphia Evening Bulletin* said thousands who would not read the elaborate oration of Mr. Everett would read the President's few words "and not many will do it without a moistening of the eye and a swelling of the heart." The *Detroit Advertiser and Tribune* said Mr. Everett had nobly told the story of the battle, "but he who wants to take in the very spirit of the day, catch the unstudied pathos that animates a sincere but simple-minded man, will turn from the stately periods of the professed orator to the brief speech of the President." The *Providence Journal* reminded readers of the saying that the hardest thing in the world is to make a good five-minute speech: "We know not where to look for a more admirable speech than the brief one which the President made at the close of Mr. Everett's oration. . . . Could the most elaborate and splendid oration be more beautiful, more touching, more inspiring, than those thrilling words of the President? They had in our humble judg-

ment the charm and power of the very highest eloquence."

29. Later men were to find that Robert Toombs of Georgia had in 1850 opened a speech: "Sixty years ago our fathers joined together to form a more perfect Union and to establish justice. . . . We have now met to put that government on trial. . . . In my judgment the verdict is such as to give hope to the friends of liberty throughout the world."

30. Lincoln had spoken of an idea, a proposition, a concept, worth dying for, which brought from a Richmond newspaper a countering question and answer, "For what are we fighting? An abstraction."

31. The *Springfield Republican* had veered from its first opinion that Lincoln was honest but "a Simple Susan." Its comment ran: "Surpassingly fine as Mr. Everett's oration was in the Gettysburg consecration, the rhetorical honors of the occasion were won by President Lincoln. His little speech is a perfect gem; deep in feeling, compact in thought and expression, and tasteful and elegant in every word and comma. Then it has the merit of unexpectedness in its verbal perfection and beauty. We had grown so accustomed to homely and imperfect phrase in his productions that we had come to think it was the law of his utterance. But this shows he can talk handsomely as well as act sensibly. Turn back and read it over, it will repay study as a model speech. Strong feelings and a large brain were its parents—a little painstaking its *accoucheur.*"

32. That scribbler of curious touch who signed himself "The Lounger" in *Harper's Weekly* inquired why the ceremony at Gettysburg was one of the most striking events of the war. "There are grave-yards enough in the land—what is Virginia but a cemetery?— and the brave who have died for us in this fierce war consecrate the soil from the ocean to the Mississippi. But there is peculiar significance in the field of Gettysburg, for there 'thus far' was thundered to the rebellion. . . . The President and the Cabinet were there, with famous soldiers and civilians. The oration by Mr. Everett was smooth and cold. . . . The few words of the President were from the heart to the heart. They can not be read,

even, without kindling emotion. 'The world will little note nor long remember what we say here, but it can never forget what they did here.' It was as simple and felicitous and earnest a word as was ever spoken. . . . Among the Governors present was Horatio Seymour. He came to honor the dead of Gettysburg. But when they were dying he stood in New York sneeringly asking where was the victory promised for the Fourth of July? These men were winning that victory, and dying for us all; and now he mourns, *ex-officio,* over their graves."

33. Everett's opinion of the speech he heard Lincoln deliver was written in a note to Lincoln the next day and was more than mere courtesy: "I should be glad if I could flatter myself that I came as near to the central idea of the occasion in two hours as you did in two minutes." Lincoln's immediate reply was: "In our respective parts yesterday, you could not have been excused to make a short address, nor I a long one. I am pleased to know that, in your judgment, the little I did say was not entirely a failure."

34. At Everett's request Lincoln wrote with pen and ink a copy of his Gettysburg Address, which manuscript was auctioned at a Sanitary Fair in New York for the benefit of soldiers. At the request of George Bancroft, the historian, he wrote another copy for a Soldiers' and Sailors' Fair at Baltimore. He wrote still another to be lithographed as a facsimile in a publication, *Autographed Leaves of Our Country's Authors.* For Mr. Wills, his host at Gettysburg, he wrote another. The first draft, written in Washington, and the second one, held while delivering it, went into John Hay's hands to be eventually presented to the Library of Congress.

35. After the ceremonies at Gettysburg Lincoln lunched with Governor Curtin, Mr. Everett, and others at the Wills home, held a reception that had not been planned, handshaking nearly an hour, looking gloomy and listless but brightening sometimes as a small boy or girl came in line, and stopping one tall man for remarks as to just how high up he reached. At five o'clock he attended a patriotic meeting in the Presbyterian church, walking arm-in-arm with old John Burns, and listening to an address by Lieutenant Governor-

elect Anderson of Ohio. At six-thirty he was on the departing Washington train. In the dining-car his secretary John Hay ate with Simon Cameron and Wayne MacVeagh. Hay had thought Cameron and MacVeagh hated each other, but he noted: "I was more than usually struck by the intimate, jovial relations that existed between men that hate and detest each other as cordially as do these Pennsylvania politicians."

36. The ride to Washington took until midnight. Lincoln was weary, talked little, stretched out on one of the side seats in the drawing-room and had a wet towel laid across his eyes and forehead.

37. He had stood that day, the world's foremost spokesman of popular government, saying that democracy was yet worth fighting for. He had spoken as one in mist who might head on deeper yet into mist. He incarnated the assurances and pretenses of popular government, implied that it could and might perish from the earth. What he meant by "a new birth of freedom" for the nation could have a thousand interpretations. The taller riddles of democracy stood up out of the address. It had the dream touch of vast and furious events epitomized for any foreteller to read what was to come. He did not assume that the drafted soldiers, substitutes, and bounty-paid privates had died willingly under Lee's shot and shell, in deliberate consecration of themselves to the Union cause. His cadences sang the ancient song that where there is freedom men have fought and sacrificed for it, and that freedom is worth men's dying for. For the first time since he became President he had on a dramatic occasion declaimed, howsoever it might be read, Jefferson's proposition which had been a slogan of the Revolutionary War—"All men are created equal"—leaving no other inference than that he regarded the Negro slave as a man. His outwardly smooth sentences were inside of them gnarled and tough with the enigmas of the American experiment.

38. Back at Gettysburg the blue haze of the Cumberland Mountains had dimmed till it was a blur in a nocturne. The moon was up and fell with a bland golden benevolence on the new-made graves of soldiers, on the sepulchers of old settlers, on the horse car-

casses of which the onrush of war had not yet permitted removal. The *New York Herald* man walked amid them and ended the story he sent his paper: "The air, the trees, the graves are silent. Even the relic hunters are gone now. And the soldiers here never wake to the sound of reveille."

39. In many a country cottage over the land, a tall old clock in a quiet corner told time in a tick-tock deliberation. Whether the orchard branches hung with pink-spray blossoms or icicles of sleet, whether the outside news was seedtime or harvest, rain or drouth, births or deaths, the swing of the pendulum was right and left and right and left in a tick-tock deliberation.

40. The face and dial of the clock had known the eyes of a boy who listened to its tick-tock and learned to read its minute and hour hands. And the boy had seen years measured off by the swinging pendulum, and grown to man size, had gone away. And the people in the cottage knew that the clock would stand there and the boy never again come into the room and look at the clock with the query, "What is the time?"

41. In a row of graves of the Unidentified the boy would sleep long in the dedicated final resting-place at Gettysburg. Why he had gone away and why he would never come back had roots in some mystery of flags and drums, of national fate in which individuals sink as in a deep sea, of men swallowed and vanished in a man-made storm of smoke and steel.

42. The mystery deepened and moved with ancient music and inviolable consolation because a solemn Man of Authority had stood at the graves of the Unidentified and spoken the words "We cannot consecrate—we cannot hallow—this ground. The brave men, living and dead, who struggled here, have consecrated it far above our poor power to add or detract. . . . From these honored dead we take increased devotion to that cause for which they gave the last full measure of devotion."

43. To the backward and forward pendulum swing of a tall old clock in a quiet corner they might read those cadenced words while outside the windows the first flurry of snow blew across the orchard and down over the meadow, the beginnings of winter in a gun-metal gloaming to be later arched with a star-flung sky.

FREDERICK LEWIS ALLEN · *The Spirit of the Times*

Frederick Lewis Allen (1890-1954), who was educated at Groton and at Harvard, began his publishing career in 1914 as assistant editor of the *Atlantic Monthly*, became managing editor of the *Century* magazine in 1916, and in 1923 went to *Harper's Magazine*, of which he was editor from 1941 until his retirement in 1953. Mr. Allen's profound interest in American culture and education, which is apparent in this essay, led him to serve as secretary of the Harvard Corporation from 1919 until 1923 and as a trustee of Bennington College from 1937 until 1944. Among Mr. Allen's books are *Only Yesterday*, 1931, *The Lords of Creation*, 1935, *I Remember Distinctly*, 1947, and *The Big Change*, 1952.

Mr. Allen's writing deals almost entirely with American culture. In the following selection, taken from *The Big Change*, the author assesses contemporary American ethical and esthetic values and concludes that the United States has a fair chance of becoming the Greece rather than the Carthage of the twentieth century.

I

1. The late President A. Lawrence Lowell of Harvard was an extempore speaker so brilliant that he could go to a public dinner quite without notes, listen to three preliminary speakers, and then, rising to speak himself, comment aptly on the remarks of those who had preceded him and lead easily into an eloquent peroration of his own. His favorite peroration dealt with the difference between two ancient civilizations, each of them rich and flourishing—Greece and Carthage. One of these, he would say, lives on in men's memories, influences all of us today; the other left no imprint on the ages to follow it. For Carthage, by contrast with Greece, had a purely commercial civilization in which there was little respect for learning, philosophy, or the arts. "Is America in danger of becoming a Carthage?" Lowell would ask—and then he would launch into an exposition of the enduring importance of universities.

THE SPIRIT OF THE TIMES: From *The Big Change* by Frederick Lewis Allen. Reprinted by permission of Harper and Brothers. Copyright. 1952, by Frederick Lewis Allen.

2. There are a great many people today, there have been a great many people throughout American history, who have in effect called the United States a Carthage. There are those who argue that during the past half-century, despite the spread of good living among its people, it has been headed in the Carthaginian direction; has been producing a mass culture in which religion and philosophy languish, the arts are smothered by the barbarian demands of mass entertainment, freedom is constricted by the dead weight of mass opinion, and the life of the spirit wanes. There are millions in Europe, for instance, to whom contemporary American culture, as they understand it, is no culture at all; to whom the typical American is a man of money, a crude, loud fellow who knows no values but mechanical and commercial ones. And there are Americans aplenty, old and young, who say that achievement in the realm of the mind and spirit has become ominously more difficult in recent years, and that our technological and economic triumphs are barren because they have brought us no inner peace.

3. Some of the charges against contempo-

rary American culture one may perhaps be permitted to discount in advance. Thus one may discount the laments, by people with twenty thousand a year, that other people whose incomes have risen from two thousand to four are becoming demoralized by material success; or the nostalgia of those who, when they compare past with present, are obviously matching their own youth in pleasantly sheltered circumstances with the conditions and behavior of a much more inclusive group today. One may also point out a persistently recurring error in European appraisals of the American people: many Europeans, being accustomed to thinking of men and women who travel freely and spend amply as members of an elite, have a tendency to compare certain undeniably crude, harsh, and unimaginative visitors from the States with fellow-countrymen of theirs whose social discipline has been quite different—who belong, in European terms, to another class entirely. It is extraordinarily hard for many people, both here and abroad, to adjust themselves to the fact that the prime characteristic of the American scene is a broadening of opportunity, and that the first fruits of a broadening of opportunity may not be a lowered voice and a suitable deference toward unfamiliar customs.

4. So let us begin by giving the floor to a man who may be relied upon not to slip into these pitfalls, yet who nevertheless takes a hard view of what the past half-century has done to his country.

5. In his introduction to the book *Twentieth Century Unlimited*[1] Bruce Bliven says that in his opinion "the most significant fact about the changes in the past half-century" has been "the alteration in the moral climate from one of overwhelming optimism to one which comes pretty close to despair.

6. "Half a century ago," continues Mr. Bliven, "mankind, and especially the American section of mankind, was firmly entrenched in the theory that this is the best of all possible worlds and getting better by the minute. . . . There was a kindly God in the heavens, whose chief concern was the welfare, happiness, and

[1] Bruce Bliven, *Twentieth Century Unlimited*. Philadelphia: J. B. Lippincott Company, 1950; pp. 11, 12, and 13.

continuous improvement of mankind, though his ways were often inscrutable."

7. Today, says Mr. Bliven, we have lost faith and are "frightened to death"—of war, atom bombs, and the looming prospect of a general brutalization and deterioration of the human species.

8. Have we, then, become since 1900 a comparatively irreligious and rudderless people?

9. Church statistics do not help us far toward an answer to this question. They show steady gains in membership for most church groups, roughly comparable to the gain in population; but they are suspect because of a very human tendency to keep on the rolls people who never go to church any more except for weddings and funerals, and there is no way of knowing whether the compilers of church statistics have become more or less scrupulous in the past few decades. My own definite impression is that during the first thirty or forty years of the half-century there was a pretty steady drift away from church attendance and from a feeling of identification with the church and its creed and institutions, at least on the part of well-to-do Americans (except perhaps among the Roman Catholics, who were under an exceptionally rigid discipline). It became customary among larger and larger numbers of the solid citizenry of the land to sleep late on Sunday morning and then grapple with the increasing poundage of the Sunday paper, or have a 10:30 appointment at the first tee, or drive over to the Joneses' for midday cocktails, or pack the family into the car for a jaunt to the shore or the hills. I myself, making many week-end visits every year over several decades, noted that as time went on it was less and less likely that my host would ask on Saturday evening what guests were planning to go to church the next morning; that by the nineteen-twenties or -thirties it was generally assumed that none would be. And although the households in which I visited may not have been representative, they at least were of more or less the same types throughout this whole period. Today I should imagine that in the heavy out-of-town traffic on a Friday afternoon there are not many people who will be inside a church on Sunday morning.

10. It has been my further observation that

during at least the first thirty and perhaps the first forty years of the century there was an equally steady drift away from a sense of identification with the faiths for which the churches stood. Among some people there was a feeling that science, and in particular the doctrine of evolution, left no room for the old-time God, and that it was exceedingly hard to imagine any sort of God who was reconcilable with what science was demonstrating and would at the same time be at home in the local church. Among others there was a rising moral impatience with an institution which seemed to pay too much attention to the necessity of being unspotted by such alleged vices as drinking, smoking, cardplaying, and Sunday golfing, and too little to human brotherhood; the churches, or many of them, made a resolute effort to meet this criticism by becoming complex institutions dedicated to social service and the social gospel, with schools, classes, women's auxiliaries, young people's groups, sports, and theatricals, but not many of them held their whole congregation—at least on Sunday morning. Still others felt that the clergy were too deferential to wealthy parishioners of dubious civic virtue, or too isolated from the main currents of life. Among many there was a vague sense that the churches represented an old-fashioned way of living and thinking and that modern-minded people were outgrowing their influence. And as the feeling of compulsion to be among the church-goers and church-workers weakened, there were naturally many to whom the automobile or the country club or the beach or an eleven o'clock breakfast was simply too agreeable to pass up.

11. Whether or not this drift away from formal religion is still the prevailing tide, there was manifest during the nineteen-forties a counter-movement. In many men and women it took no more definite form than an uneasy conviction that in times of stress and anxiety there was something missing from their lives: they wished they had something to tie to, some faith that would give them a measure of inner peace and security. The appearance on the best-seller lists in recent years of such books as *The Robe, The Cardinal, Peace of Mind,* and *The Seven Storey Mountain* has indicated a widespread hunger and curiosity.

Some have returned to the churches—or entered them for the first time. In families here and there one has noted a curious reversal: parents who had abandoned the church in a mood of rebellion against outworn ecclesiastical customs have found their children in turn rebelling against what seemed to them the parents' outworn pagan customs. The Catholic Church in particular has made many converts, some of them counterrebels of this sort, and has spectacularly served as a haven for ex-Communists who have swung all the way from one set of disciplinary bonds to another. Whether the incoming tide is yet stronger than the outgoing one, or what the later drift may be, is still anybody's guess; but at least there is a confusion in the flow of religious feeling and habit.

12. Meanwhile, in quantities of families, the abandonment of church allegiance has deprived the children of an occasionally effective teacher of decent behavior. Some parents have been able to fill the vacuum themselves; others have not, and have become dismayed that their young not only do not recognize Bible quotations but have somehow missed out on acquiring a clear-cut moral code. There are other parents whose conscientious study of psychological principles, including the Freudian, and whose somewhat imperfect digestion of the ideas of progressive educators have so filled them with uncertainty as to what moral teachings to deliver and whether any sort of discipline might not damage young spirits that these young spirits have become—at least for the time being—brats of a singular offensiveness. And even if there have always been brats in the world, it has been easy for observers of such families to conclude that moral behavior is indeed deteriorating, and that basketball scandals and football scandals and teen-age holdup gangs and official corruption in Washington are all signs of a widespread ethical decay.

13. This conclusion is of doubtful validity, I am convinced. There has probably never been a generation some members of which did not wonder whether the next generation was not bound for hell in a handcar. It may be argued that at the mid-century the *manners* of many teen-agers have suffered from their mothers' and fathers' disbelief in stern meas-

ures; but that their *ethical standards* are inferior to those of their predecessors seems to me doubtful indeed. As for today's adults, there are undoubtedly many whose lack of connection with organized religion has left them without any secure principles; but as I think of the people I have actually known over a long period of time, I detect no general deterioration of the conscience: those I see today do a good many things that their grandparents would have considered improper, but few things that they would have regarded as paltry or mean. And there has been taking place among these people, and in the country at large, a change of attitude that I am convinced is of great importance. During the half-century the ancient question, "Who is my neighbor?" has been receiving a broader and broader answer.

14. There are still ladies and gentlemen who feel that they are of the elect, and that the masses of their fellow-countrymen are of negligible importance; but their snobbery is today less complacently assured, more defiant, than in the days when Society was a word to conjure with. The insect on the leaf is less often found "proclaiming on the too much life among his hungry brothers in the dust." There are still business executives with an inflated sense of their own value in the scheme of things, but the "studied insolence" which Mark Sullivan noted among the coal operators of 1902 when confronted by the union representatives and the President of the United States, and which magnates often displayed on the witness stand in those days, is no longer to be seen (except perhaps among such underworld gentry as Mr. Frank Costello). People who today look at what were originally the servants' quarters in an old mansion, or even in a swank apartment of the 1920 vintage, are shocked at their meagerness: is it possible, they ask themselves, that decent men and women could have had such disregard for the human needs of men and women living cheek by jowl with them?

15. The concept of the national income, the idea of measuring the distribution of this income, the idea of the national economy as an entity affected by the economic behavior of every one of us, the very widespread interest in surveying sociologically the status of this

and that group of Americans the country over, in the conviction that their fortunes are interdependent with ours: all these have developed during this half-century. The ideal of equality of educational opportunity never before commanded such general acceptance. In recent years there has been a marked shift of attitudes toward our most disadvantaged group, the Negroes, and no less noticeably in the South than elsewhere. One notes a widespread gain in group tact, as when the Hospital for the Ruptured and Crippled is renamed the Hospital for Special Surgery, and the Association for Improving the Condition of the Poor becomes the Community Service Society. The concept of responsibility to the general public has become more and more widespread among the managers of pivotal businesses. The amount of time which individual men and women give to good works in the broadest sense—including church work, volunteer hospital work, parent-teacher associations, the Boy Scouts, the Red Cross, the League of Women Voters, local symphony orchestras, the World Federalists, the American Legion, the service activities of Rotary, and so on endlessly—is in its total incalculable. (There are communities, I am told, where the number of people who engage in money-raising for the churches is larger than the number of churchgoers.) In sum, our sense of public obligation has expanded.

16. The change has had its amusing aspects. There comes to one's mind Anne Cleveland's cartoon of a Vassar girl dining with her parents and exclaiming, "How can I explain the position of organized labor to Father when you keep passing me chocolate sauce?" One thinks of a banker's daughter of one's acquaintance, who in her first job was much more deeply interested in the plight of the file clerk whom she regarded as underpaid, than in helping the company make money. And of the receipt by Dr. Ralph Bunche in June 1951 of no less than thirteen honorary degrees in rapid succession, the singular unanimity of his choice by so many institutions undoubtedly reflecting in part a delight at finding an unexceptional opportunity to pay tribute to a Negro.

17. That the change should meet, here and there, with heated resistance, is likewise nat-

ural. The democratic ideal imposes a great strain upon the tolerance and understanding of humankind. So we find a conscious and active anti-Semitism invading many a suburban community which once took satisfaction in its homogeneity and now finds it can no longer live to itself; or a savage anti-Negro feeling rising in an industrial town in which Negroes were formerly few and far between. And here one should add a footnote about the behavior of our armed forces abroad. For a variety of not easily defined reasons—including undoubtedly the traditionally proletarian position of the foreign-language-speaking immigrant in the United States—there is an obscure feeling among a great many Americans that the acceptance of the principle of human dignity stops at the water's edge: that a man who would be fiercely concerned over an apparent injustice to a fellow-private in the American Army may be rude to Arabs, manhandle Koreans, and cheat Germans, and not lose status thereby—and this, perhaps, at the very moment when his representatives in Congress are appropriating billions for the aid of the very sorts of people of whom he is so scornful.

18. Yet in spite of these adverse facts there has been, I am convinced, an increasing overall acceptance in America of what Dr. Frank Tannenbaum has called "the commitment to equality . . . spiritual equality." Whether, as Walter H. Wheeler, Jr., has suggested, we may be "depleting and living off inherited spiritual capital" is far from certain. Yet at any rate this may be said: If we as a people do not obey the first and great commandment as numerously and fervently as we used to, at least we have been doing fairly well with the second.

II

19. We come now to another question to which the answer must be even more two-sided and uncertain. Does the spread of American prosperity threaten quality? Are we achieving a mass of second-rate education, second-rate culture, second-rate thinking, and squeezing out the first-rate?

20. The charge that we are indeed doing this comes in deafening volume. To quote no less a sage than T. S. Eliot: "We can assert with some confidence that our own period is one of decline; that the standards of culture are lower than they were fifty years ago; and that the evidences of this decline are visible in every department of human activity." And if this seems a rather general indictment, without special reference to the United States, it may be added that Mr. Eliot has given abundant evidence that he is out of sympathy with the American trend, preferring as he does a "graded society" in which "the lower class still exists."

21. One could pile up a mountain of quotations by critics of the American drift, playing the changes upon the two notions that, according to C. Hartley Grattan's article in the November 1951 number of *Harper's,* account for the *Katzenjammer* of American writers today: "(1) a feeling . . . that the values by which men have lived these many years are today in an advanced state of decomposition, with no replacements in sight; and (2) that whatever a man's private values may be, he cannot expect in any case consistently to act on them successfully because the individual is, in the present-day world, at the mercy of ever more oppressive and arbitrary institutions." In other words, that the man of original bent—the writer, painter, musician, architect, philosopher, or intellectual or spiritual pioneer or maverick of any sort—not only faces what Eugene O'Neill called the "sickness of today," which in Lloyd Morris's phrasing has "resulted from the death of the old God and the failure of science and materialism to give any satisfactory new one," but must also confront a world in which the biggest rewards for literary creation go to manufacturers of sexy costume romances; in which the Broadway theater, after a glorious period of fresh creation in the nineteen-twenties, is almost in the discard, having succumbed to the high cost of featherbedding labor and the competition of the movies; in which the movies in their turn, after a generation of richly recompensing those who could attract audiences by the millions and stifling those whose productions had doubtful box-office value, are succumbing to television; in which the highest television acclaim goes to Milton Berle rather than to Burr Tillstrom; and in which the poet finds his market well-nigh gone. One might sum up the charge in another way by saying that the dynamic logic of mass production, while serving

admirably to bring us good automobiles and good nylons, enforces mediocrity on the market for intellectual wares.

22. This is a very severe charge. But there are a number of matters to be considered and weighed before one is ready for judgment upon it.

23. One is the fact that those who have most eloquently lamented the hard plight of the man or woman of creative talent have chiefly been writers, and more especially *avant-garde* writers and their more appreciative critics, and that the position occupied by these people has been a somewhat special one.

24. During the years immediately preceding World War I the inventors and innovators in American literature were in no such prevailing mood of dismay. On the contrary, they were having a high old time. In Chicago, such men as Vachel Lindsay, Edgar Lee Masters, Sherwood Anderson, Ring Lardner, and Carl Sandburg were experimenting with gusto and confidence. In New York, the young Bohemians of Greenwich Village were hotly and rambunctiously enamored of a great variety of unorthodoxies, ranging from free verse, imagism, postimpressionism, cubism, and the realism of the "Ashcan School" of art to woman's suffrage, socialism, and communism (of an innocently idealistic variety compared with what later developed in Moscow). When Alfred Stieglitz preached modern art at "291," when the Armory Show was staged in 1913, when Max Eastman and John Reed crusaded for labor, when Floyd Dell talked about the liberation of literature, they saw before them a bright new world in which progress would in due course bring triumph to their wild notions.

25. But the war brought an immense disillusionment. And the prevailing mood shifted.

26. The novelists of the Lost Generation concentrated their attention upon the meannesses and cruelties of contemporary life, and often their keynote was one of despair. Mencken led a chorus of scoffers at American vulgarity and sentimentality, not indignantly but cynically; when asked why he continued to live in a land in which he found so little to revere, he asked, "Why do men go to zoos?" Sinclair Lewis lampooned Main Street and George F. Babbitt; Scott Fitzgerald under-

scored the baseness of respectable folk who went to Jay Gatsby's lavish parties and then deserted him in his hour of need. And many of the *avant-garde* and their admirers and imitators went to Paris, where Gertrude Stein said that "the future is not important any more," and Hemingway's characters in *The Sun Also Rises* acted as if it were not. But in a world without hope one could still cherish art, the one thing left that was worth while, keeping it aloof from politics and business; and one could particularly cherish that art which it was most difficult for the vulgarians of politics and business to comprehend. To these refugees from twentieth-century America, "difficulty itself became a primary virtue," as Van Wyck Brooks has remarked: they paid special homage to the aristocratic elaborations of Henry James, the subtleties of the recluse Marcel Proust, the scholarly allusiveness of Eliot, and the linguistic puzzles of Joyce. And a pattern was set, quite different from the pattern of 1910. To have a literary conscience was to take a bleak view of American life, human life in general, and the way the world was going; and also of the ability of any readers but a few to understand and appreciate true literary excellence.

27. This credo was to prove astonishingly durable. During the nineteen-thirties it had to contend with another emotional force. The economy had broken down, revolution was in the wind (or so it seemed to many at the time), and many writers felt a generous urge to condemn the cruelty of capitalism to "one-third of a nation" and to espouse the cause of embattled labor. Thus they abandoned hopelessness for militancy. There was an outpouring of proletarian novels by writers whose firsthand knowledge of factory workers was highly limited. Yet even among many of the writers and critics who were most valiant in support of the common man there remained a conviction that the man of sensibility and integrity must inevitably write in terms intelligible only to the very uncommon man; and we beheld the diverting spectacle of authors and students of advanced composition returning from mass meetings held on behalf of sharecroppers and Okies to pore over the sacred texts of Henry James, who would have been oblivious to

sharecroppers, and Eliot, who was certainly out of tune with the Okies.

28. During the war the impulse to defend labor turned into an impulse to defend the GI against the military brass. The older impulse to depict the world as a dismal place turned into an impulse to show how brutal men at war could be (including, often, the very GI who was supposed to engage the reader's sympathy); and the belief that quality was bound to go unappreciated by all but a very few turned into a general pessimism over the future of culture that seemed almost to welcome defeat for any sort of excellence.

29. "It is a source of continual astonishment to me," wrote W. H. Auden in this magazine in 1948, "that the nation which has the world-wide reputation of being the most optimistic, the most gregarious, and the freest on earth should see itself through the eyes of its most sensitive members as a society of helpless victims, shady characters, and displaced persons. . . . In novel after novel one encounters heroes without honor or history; heroes who succumb so monotonously to temptation that they cannot truly be said to be tempted at all; heroes who, even if they are successful in a worldly sense, remain nevertheless but the passive recipients of good fortune; heroes whose sole moral virtue is a stoic endurance of pain and disaster."

30. Could it be that such novelists have been following a fashion set longer ago than they realize? That the reason why sales of novels in very recent years have been disappointing is that, as Mr. Grattan has suggested, "contemporary writers appear to have given up before contemporary readers are ready to do so," and that perhaps the readers are today ahead of the writers? That the continuing notion among many advanced writers that only difficult writing is good writing has led them to pay too little attention to the art of communication? And that a sort of contagion of defeatism among literary folk today should lead one to accept with a certain reserve their unhappy conclusions concerning the state of American culture?

31. Let us note their laments and look a little further.

III

32. One who has worked for a great many years for a magazine which nowadays can pay its authors no more than it did a decade ago, because it has to pay its typographers and shipping men so much more, is not likely to be complacent about the lot of the man of letters today. Nor is one who has felt he was waging a steady uphill fight on behalf of what he perhaps fondly considered distinguished journalism—uphill because there were constantly appearing new magazines aimed at readers by the millions, and because advertisers tended to want to reach those millions—likely to be complacent about the conditions of literary institutions. It seems to me undeniable that the great success of the mass-circulation magazines and the rise of the staff-written magazines have between them made life harder for the free-lance author who lacks the popular touch and who will not do pot-boiling, or cannot do it successfully, and who has no other assured source of income. But then he almost never has had things very easy financially. And there is this to be said: one reason why magazines with severely high standards find the going difficult is that they have no monopoly on material of high quality, for during the past few decades an increasing amount of such material has been finding a place in the mass periodicals. (For a couple of random examples, let me cite Winston Churchill's memoirs, appearing in *Life,* and Faulkner's short stories, coming out in the *Saturday Evening Post.*) Furthermore, the number of writers of talent who make good incomes by writing for the mass magazines without the sacrifice of an iota of their integrity is much larger than one might assume from the talk of the *avant-gardists.* The picture is a mixed one.

33. So too with regard to books. The market for the output of the "original" publishers, meaning those who sell newly-written books at standard prices, chiefly through the bookstores, is somewhat larger than before the war, but it is manifest that price increases, reflecting high labor cost, have been deterring buyers. The share of a few very successful writers in the total revenue of authors increases; and it becomes more difficult than it

used to be for those whose books are not likely to sell more than a few thousand copies (these include nearly all poets) to get their work accepted. Yet here again the situation is not as black as it has been painted. I agree with Bernard DeVoto that no book really worth publishing fails of publication by some unit of a very diversified industry; and I would add that while there is trash on the best-seller lists, most of the books which reach those lofty positions, with very pleasant results for their authors' pocketbooks, are among the best of their time.

34. And there is more to it than this. For there are also numerous book clubs, at least two of which—the Book-of-the-Month Club and the Literary Guild—sell books by the hundreds of thousands each month. There are the quarterly Condensed Books brought out by the *Reader's Digest*—four or five novels or non-fiction books condensed in one volume—which, launched in 1950, were selling by early 1952 at the rate of more than a million apiece. And there are the paper-bound reprint houses, whose volumes, priced at 25 or 35 cents for the newsstand and drugstore trade, are bought in phenomenal lots. In the year 1950 the total was no less than 214 million; in 1951 the figure had jumped to 231 million.

35. Two-thirds or more of these paper-bound books, to be sure, were novels or mysteries—thus falling into classifications too inclusive to be reassuring as to the public taste —and some were rubbish by any tolerable standard (the publishers of such wares having learned, as one cynic has put it, that you can sell almost anything adorned on the cover with a picture connoting sex or violence, or preferably both, as in a picture of a luscious girl getting her dress ripped off by a gunman). But consider these sales figures (as of January 1952) for a few paper-bound books: Tennessee Williams' *A Streetcar Named Desire,* over half a million; George Orwell's *Nineteen Eighty-four,* over three-quarters of a million; Ruth Benedict's *Patterns of Culture,* 400,000; and— to cite an incontrovertibly classical example —a translation of *The Odyssey* (with an abstract cover design), 350,000. And remember that these sales, which are above and beyond book-club sales and regular bookstore sales, have been achieved in a nation of avid magazine readers. It is true that the financial returns to the author from such low-priced books are meager: he gets less revenue from a million of them than from 20,000 sold at standard prices. Nevertheless there is an interesting phenomenon here. There is a big American market for good writing if it and the price are within easy reach.

36. Let us look at the market for art. The painter of today faces two great difficulties. The first is that his work is offered to the public at high prices (if he can get any price at all) because he can sell only his original work, to one collector or institution, and cannot dispose of thousands at a time; and collectors with money are scarce. The second is that the abler young painters of the day have mostly swung all the way to the abstract, which to most potential buyers is pretty incomprehensible. Yet the signs of interest among the public are striking. Forbes Watson is authority for the statement that there were more sales of paintings in the nineteen-forties than in all the previous history of the United States; that in the year 1948 there were a hundred exhibitions of American art in American museums; and that the total attendance at art exhibitions that year was over 50 million. One should also take note of the greatly enlarged number of local museums; of the lively promotion of an interest in art by many universities and colleges; the rising sale of reproductions, in book form and otherwise; and the recent sharp increase in the number of Sunday amateur dabblers with a paintbrush. Sales of artists' materials had a tenfold increase between 1939 and 1949. The suspicion comes over one that there is something stirring here, too, and that the plight of the contemporary artist, like the plight of the contemporary writer, may be partly due to the fact that the market for his output may not yet be geared to the potential demand.

37. We turn to music—and confront an astonishing spectacle.

38. In 1900 there were only a handful of symphony orchestras in the country; by May 1951 there were 659 "symphonic groups"— including 52 professional, 343 community, 231 college, and a scattering of miscellaneous amateur groups. Fifteen hundred American cities and towns now support annual series of con-

certs. Summer music festivals attract audiences which would have been unimaginable even thirty years ago. To quote Cecil Smith in *Twentieth Century Unlimited,* "The dollar-hungry countries of Europe are setting up music festivals by the dozen, not to give American tourists the music they would not hear at home, but to make sure they do not stay at home because of the lack of music in Europe. The programs at Edinburgh, Strasbourg, Amsterdam, Florence, and Aix-en-Provence are designed as competition for Tanglewood, Bethlehem, Ravinia, the Cincinnati Zoo, and the Hollywood Bowl." Mr. Smith cites further facts of interest: that the Austin, Texas, symphony recently took over a drive-in movie for outdoor summer concerts; that Kentucky hill people come in their bare feet when the Louisville Orchestra plays in Berea; and that "an all-Stravinsky program, conducted by the composer, strikes Urbana, Illinois, as a perfectly normal attraction."

39. During the nineteen-twenties the phonograph record business was threatened with virtual extinction by the rise of radio. But presently radio began giving millions upon millions of Americans such a variety of music—popular, jazz, and classical—in such quantity, year after year, that a good many of these people began to want to hear music on their own terms, and the record business went into a prolonged and phenomenal boom. The expansion was accelerated by the wild vogue of jazz, whose more serious votaries soon learned that if you were to become a really serious student of what Benny Goodman and Duke Ellington were producing, you must collect old recordings and become a connoisseur of Handy, Beiderbecke, and Armstrong. By the middle and late nineteen-forties, young people who in earlier years would have gone off dancing of an evening were finding that it was very agreeable to sit on the floor and listen to a record-player, with a few bottles of beer to wash the music down. Many people whose taste in books and in art was very limited were not only becoming able to identify the most famous symphonies by their first few notes, but were developing a pride in their acquaintance with the works of Bach's obscure contemporaries, and in their connoisseurship of the comparative merits of recordings by various orchestras. A very rough estimate of the sales of records during the year 1951, made by *Billboard* magazine, put the grand total at some 190 million—more than one for every man, woman, and child in the United States—and the total sale of records in the "classical" category at perhaps 10 to 15 per cent of that 190 million: let us say something like twenty to thirty million classical records. To give a single example: as many as 20,000 sets of Wanda Landowska's harpsichord recordings of the Goldberg Variations were sold in the first three months after they were issued. And a shrewd student of American culture tells me that as he goes about the United States he keeps being told, in place after place, "Our town is sort of unusual. I suppose the most exciting thing, to us, that's going on here isn't anything in business but the way we've put over our symphony orchestra (or our string quartet, or our community chorus)."

40. Verily, as one looks about the field of the arts, the picture is confused. Here is an incredible boom in public interest in music, along with expanding audiences for the ballet, old-style and new-style. Here is the Broadway theater almost ready for the Pulmotor—and local civic theaters and college theaters in what looks like a promising adolescence. Here are the movies, beloved by millions (and berated by highbrow critics) for decades, losing audiences little by little to television, which has not yet outgrown a preposterous crudity. Here is architecture, which has outgrown its earlier imitation of old European styles and is producing superb industrial buildings along with highly experimental and sometimes absurd modern residences—while the peripheries of our great cities, whether New York or Chicago or St. Louis or Los Angeles, display to the bus traveler from airport to town almost no trace of the handiwork of any architects at all. Here are lovely (if monotonous) motor parkways—and along the other main highways a succession of roadtown eyesores—garages, tourist courts, filling stations, billboards, junk dealers, and more billboards—which make the motor parkways seem, by contrast, like avenues for escapists.

41. Is not the truth of the situation perhaps something like this: Here is a great nation

which is conducting an unprecedented experiment. It has made an incredible number of people, previously quite unsophisticated and alien to art or contemptuous of it, prosperous by any previous standard known to man. These multitudes offer a huge market for him who would sell them equipment or entertainment that they can understand and enjoy. Let us say it in italics: *This is something new: there has never been anything like it before.*

42. The job before those Americans who would like to see the United States a Greece rather than a Carthage is to try to develop, alongside the media of entertainment and equipment which satisfy these people's present needs, others which will satisfy more exacting tastes and will be on hand for them when they are ready for more rewarding fare. The problem is an economic one as well as an artistic

one. Whether it can be solved is still anybody's guess. But in a day when, despite the discouragement of many literati, much of the best writing in the world is being done in the United States; when the impoverishment of foreign institutions of learning has made American universities no mere followers on the road of learning, but leaders despite themselves, attracting students from many continents; and when, willy nilly, a burden of responsibility for the cultural condition of the world rests heavily upon America, it should do us good to look at the army of music-lovers that we have produced. For if this is what auspicious economic conditions can bring in the area of one of the great arts, possibly the miracle may be effected elsewhere too, and the all-American culture may prove to have been, not the enemy of excellence, but its seed-bed.

JOHN FISCHER *The Unwritten Rules of American Politics*

John Fischer (1910-   ), beginning when he was only eighteen, worked as a reporter for several papers in the Southwest. In 1933-35 he represented the United Press in England and Germany while studying at Oxford University as a Rhodes Scholar. Upon his return to America in 1935, he was for a time connected with the Associated Press in Washington. He joined *Harper's Magazine* in 1944, and he is now editor. He is also editor-in-chief of general books for Harper and Brothers.

The article which follows is based on a speech which, apropos the 1948 elections, Mr. Fischer made at the Heritage of English-Speaking Peoples' Conference at Kenyon College in 1947. It was originally published in *Harper's Magazine* and reprinted with revisions in *Harper's Magazine Reader*, 1953. It is still today a pertinent, pragmatic commentary on American political parties.

I

1. Every now and then somebody comes up with the idea that the party system in American politics is absurd because our two great parties don't stand for clearly contrasting principles, and that we would be better off if we had a conservative party and a radical or lib-

eral party. It is a persuasive argument, especially for well-meaning people who have not had much first-hand experience in politics. You have probably heard it; it runs something like this:

2. "Both of the traditional American parties are outrageous frauds. Neither the Republicans nor the Democrats have any fundamental principles or ideology. They do not even have a program. In every campaign the platforms

of both parties are simply collections of noble generalities, muffled in the vaguest possible language; and in each case the two platforms are very nearly identical.

3. "Obviously, then, both parties are merely machines for grabbing power and distributing favors. In their lust for office they are quite willing to make a deal with anybody who can deliver a sizable block of votes. As a result, each party has become an outlandish cluster of local machines and special interest groups which have nothing in common except a craving for the public trough.

4. "This kind of political system"—so the argument runs—"is clearly meaningless. A man of high principles can never hope to accomplish anything through the old parties, because they are not interested in principle. Moreover, the whole arrangement is so illogical that it affronts every intelligent citizen.

5. "We ought to separate the sheep from the goats—to herd all the progressives on one side of the fence and all the conservatives on the other. Then politics really will have some meaning; every campaign can be fought over clearly defined issues. The Europeans, who are more sophisticated politically than we simple Americans, discovered this long ago, and in each of their countries they have arranged a neat political spectrum running from Left to Right."

6. This argument pops up with special urgency whenever a third party appears—Theodore Roosevelt's in 1912, Robert LaFollette's in 1924, or Henry Wallace's in 1948. And it sounds so plausible—at least on the surface—that many people have wondered why these splinter parties have always dwindled away after the election was over. Indeed, many veteran third-party enthusiasts have been able to account for their failure only by assuming a perverse and rock-headed stupidity among the American electorate.

7. There is, however, another possible explanation for the stubborn durability of our seemingly illogical two-party system; that it is more vigorous, more deeply rooted, and far better suited to our own peculiar needs than any European system would be; that it involves a more complex and subtle conception than the crude blacks and whites of the European ideological parties. There is considerable

evidence, it seems to me, that our system—in spite of certain dangerous weaknesses—has on the whole worked out more successfully than the European.

8. Perhaps it is the very subtlety of the American political tradition which is responsible for the almost universal misunderstanding of it abroad. Every practicing American politician grasps its principles by instinct; if he does not, he soon retires into some less demanding profession. Moreover, the overwhelming majority of citizens have a sound working knowledge of the system, which they apply every day of their lives—though many of them might have a hard time putting that knowledge into words. There are almost no foreigners, however, (except perhaps D. W. Brogan) who really understand the underlying theory. Even the editors of the London *Economist*—probably the most brilliant and well-informed group of journalists practicing anywhere today—display their bewilderment week after week. To them, and to virtually all other European observers, our whole political scene looks arbitrary, irrational, and dangerous.

9. Another reason for this misunderstanding lies in the fact that surprisingly little has been written about the rules of American politics during our generation. The newspapers, textbooks, and learned journals are running over with discussions of tactics and mechanics—but no one, so far as I know, has bothered to trace out the basic tradition for a good many years.

10. In fact, the most useful discussion of this tradition which I have come across is the work of John C. Calhoun, published nearly a century ago. Today of course he is an almost forgotten figure, and many people take it for granted that his views were discredited for good by the Civil War. I know of only one writer—Peter F. Drucker—who has paid much attention to him in recent years. It was he who described Calhoun's ideas as "a major if not the only key to the understanding of what is specifically and uniquely American in our political system"; and I am indebted to Mr. Drucker for much of the case set forth here.

11. Calhoun summed up his political thought in what he called the Doctrine of the

Concurrent Majority. He saw the United States as a nation of tremendous and frightening diversity—a collection of many different climates, races, cultures, religions, and economic patterns. He saw the constant tension among all these special interests, and he realized that the central problem of American politics was to find some way of holding these conflicting groups together.

12. It could not be done by force; no one group was strong enough to impose its will on all the others. The goal could be achieved only by compromise—and no real compromise could be possible if any threat of coercion lurked behind the door. Therefore, Calhoun reasoned, every vital decision in American life would have to be adopted by a "concurrent majority"—by which he meant, in effect, a unanimous agreement of all interested parties. No decision which affected the interests of the slaveholders, he argued, should be taken without their consent; and by implication he would have given a similar veto to every other special interest, whether it be labor, management, the Catholic church, old-age pensioners, the silver miners, or the corn-growers of the Middle West.

13. Under the goad of the slavery issue, Calhoun was driven to state his doctrine in an extreme and unworkable form. If every sectional interest had been given the explicit, legal veto power which he called for, the government obviously would have been paralyzed. (That, in fact, is precisely what seems to be happening today in the United Nations.) It is the very essence of the idea of "concurrent majority" that it cannot be made legal and official. It can operate effectively only as an informal, highly elastic, and generally accepted understanding.

14. Moreover, government by concurrent majority can exist only when no one power is strong enough to dominate completely, *and then only when all of the contending interest groups recognize and abide by certain rules of the game.*

15. These rules are the fundamental bond of unity in American political life. They can be summed up as a habit of extraordinary toleration, plus "equality" in the peculiar American meaning of that term which cannot be translated into any other language, even

into the English of Great Britain. Under these rules every group tacitly binds itself to tolerate the interests and opinions of every other group. It must not try to impose its views on others, nor can it press its own special interests to the point where they seriously endanger the interests of other groups or of the nation as a whole.

16. Furthermore, each group must exercise its implied veto with responsibility and discretion; and in times of great emergency it must forsake its veto right altogether. It dare not be intransigent or doctrinaire. It must make every conceivable effort to compromise, relying on its veto only as a last resort. For if any player wields this weapon recklessly, the game will break up—or all the other players will turn on him in anger, suspend the rules for the time being, and maul those very interests he is trying so desperately to protect. That was what happened in 1860, when the followers of Calhoun carried his doctrine to an unbearable extreme. Much the same thing, on a less violent scale, happened to American business interests in 1933 and to the labor unions in 1947.

17. This is the somewhat elusive sense, it seems to me, in which Calhoun's theory has been adopted by the American people. But elusive and subtle as it may be, it remains the basic rule of the game of politics in this country—and in this country alone. Nothing comparable exists in any other nation, although the British, in a different way, have applied their own rules of responsibility and self-restraint.

18. It is a rule which operates unofficially and entirely outside the Constitution—but it has given us a method by which all the official and Constitutional organs of government can be made to work. It also provides a means of selecting leaders on all levels of our political life, for hammering out policies, and for organizing and managing the conquest of political power.

II

19. The way in which this tradition works in practice can be observed most easily in Congress. Anyone who has ever tried to push through a piece of legislation quickly discovers that the basic units of organization on Capitol Hill are not the parties, but the so-called blocs,

which are familiar to everyone who reads a newspaper. There are dozens of them—the farm bloc, the silver bloc, the friends of labor, the business group, the isolationists, the public power bloc—and they all cut across party lines.

20. They are loosely organized and pretty blurred at the edges, so that every Congressman belongs at different times to several different blocs. Each of them represents a special interest group. Each of them ordinarily works hand-in-hand with that group's Washington lobby. In passing, it might be noted that these lobbies are by no means the cancerous growth which is sometimes pictured in civics textbooks. They have become an indispensable part of the political machine—the accepted channel through which American citizens make their wishes known and play their day-to-day role in the process of government. Nor is their influence measured solely by the size of the bankrolls and propaganda apparatus which they have at their disposal. Some of the smallest and poorest lobbies often are more effective than their well-heeled rivals. For example, Russell Smith, the one-man lobby of the Farmers Union, was largely responsible for conceiving and nursing through Congress the Employment Act of 1946, one of the most far-reaching measures adopted since the war.

21. Now it is an unwritten but firm rule of Congress that no important bloc shall ever be voted down—under normal circumstances—on any matter which touches its own vital interests. Each of them, in other words, has a tacit right of veto on legislation in which it is primarily concerned. The ultimate expression of this right is the institution—uniquely American—of the filibuster in the Senate. Recently it has acquired a bad name among liberals because the Southern conservatives have used it ruthlessly to fight off civil rights legislation and protect white supremacy. Not so long ago, however, the filibuster was the stoutest weapon of such men as Norris and the LaFollettes in defending many a progressive cause.

22. Naturally no bloc wants to exercise its veto power except when it is absolutely forced to—for this is a negative power, and one which is always subject to retaliation. Positive power to influence legislation, on the other hand, can be gained only by conciliation, compromise, and endless horse-trading.

23. The farm bloc, for instance, normally needs no outside aid to halt the passage of a hostile bill. As a last resort, three or four strong-lunged statesmen from the corn belt can always filibuster it to death in the Senate. If the bloc wants to put through a measure to support agricultural prices, however, it can succeed only by enlisting the help of other powerful special interest groups. Consequently, it must always be careful not to antagonize any potential ally by a reckless use of the veto; and it must be willing to pay for such help by throwing its support from time to time behind legislation sought by the labor bloc, the National Association of Manufacturers, or the school-teachers' lobby.

24. The classic alliance of this sort was formed in the early days of the New Deal, when most of the Roosevelt legislation was shoved onto the statute books by a temporary coalition of the farm bloc and urban labor, occasionally reinforced by such minor allies as the public power group and spokesmen for the northern Negroes. Mr. Roosevelt's political genius rested largely on his ability to put together a program which would offer something to each of these groups without fatally antagonizing any of them, and then to time the presentation of each bill so that he would always retain enough bargaining power to line up a Congressional majority. It also was necessary for him to avoid the veto of the business group, which viewed much of this legislation as a barbarous assault upon its privileges; and for this purpose he employed another traditional technique, which we shall examine a little later.

25. This process of trading blocs of votes is generally known as log-rolling, and frequently it is deplored by the more innocent type of reformer. Such pious disapproval has no effect whatever on any practicing politician. He knows that log-rolling is a sensible and reasonably fair device, and that without it Congress could scarcely operate at all.

26. In fact, Congress gradually has developed a formal apparatus—the committee system—which is designed to make the log-rolling process as smooth and efficient as possible. There is no parallel system anywhere; the

committees of Parliament and of the Continental legislative bodies work in an entirely different way.

27. Obviously the main business of Congress —the hammering out of a series of compromises between many special interest groups— cannot be conducted satisfactorily on the floor of the House or Senate. The meetings there are too large and far too public for such delicate negotiations. Moreover, every speech delivered on the floor must be aimed primarily at the voters back home, and not at the other members in the chamber. Therefore, Congress —especially the House—does nearly all its work in the closed sessions of its various committees, simply because the committee room is the only place where it is possible to arrange a compromise acceptable to all major interests affected.

28. For this reason, it is a matter of considerable importance to get a bill before the proper committee. Each committee serves as a forum for a particular cluster of special interests, and the assignment of a bill to a specific committee often decides which interest groups shall be recognized officially as affected by the measure and therefore entitled to a hand in its drafting. "Who is to have standing before the committee" is the technical term, and it is this decision that frequently decides the fate of the legislation.

III

29. Calhoun's principles of the concurrent majority and of sectional compromise operate just as powerfully, though sometimes less obviously, in every other American political institution. Our cabinet, for example, is the only one in the world where the members are charged by law with the representation of special interests—labor, agriculture, commerce, and so on. In other countries, each agency of government is at least presumed to act for the nation as a whole; here most agencies are expected to behave as servants for one interest or another. The Veterans' Administration, to cite the most familiar case, is frankly intended to look out for Our Boys; the Maritime Board is to look out for the shipping industry; the National Labor Relations Board, as originally established under the Wagner Act, was explicitly intended to build up the bargaining power of the unions.

30. Even within a single department, separate agencies are sometimes set up to represent conflicting interests. Thus in the Department of Agriculture under the New Deal the old Triple-A became primarily an instrument of the large-scale commercial farmers, as represented by their lobby, the Farm Bureau Federation; while the Farm Security Administration went to bat for the tenants, the farm laborers, and the little subsistence farmers, as represented by the Farmers Union.

31. This is one reason why federal agencies often struggle so bitterly against each other, and why the position of the administration as a whole on any question can be determined only after a long period of inter-bureau squabbling and compromise. Anyone who was in Washington during the war will remember how these goings-on always confused and alarmed our British allies.

32. Calhoun's laws also govern the selection of virtually every candidate for public office. The mystery of "eligibility" which has eluded most foreign observers simply means that a candidate must not be unacceptable to any important special interest group—a negative rather than a positive qualification. A notorious case of this process at work was the selection of Mr. Truman as the Democrats' Vice Presidential candidate in 1944. As Edward J. Flynn, the Boss of the Bronx, has pointed out in his memoirs, Truman was the one man "who would hurt . . . least" as Roosevelt's running mate. Many stronger men were disqualified, Flynn explained, by the tacit veto of one sectional interest or another. Wallace was unacceptable to the business men and to many local party machines. Byrnes was distasteful to the Catholics, the Negroes, and organized labor. Rayburn came from the wrong part of the country. Truman, however, came from a border state, his labor record was good, he had not antagonized the conservatives, and—as Flynn put it—"he had never made any 'racial' remarks. He just dropped into the slot."

33. The same kind of considerations govern the selection of candidates right down to the county, city, and precinct levels. Flynn, one of the most successful political operators of our time, explained in some detail the complicated

job of making up a ticket in his own domain. Each of the main population groups in the Bronx—Italians, Jews, and Irish Catholics— must be properly represented on the list of nominees, and so must each of the main geographical divisions. The result was a ticket which sounded like the roster of the Brooklyn Dodgers: Loreto, Delagi, Lyman, Joseph, Lyons, and Foley.

34. Comparable traditions govern the internal political life of the American Legion, the Federation of Women's Clubs, university student bodies, labor unions, Rotary Clubs, and the thousands of other quasi-political institutions which are so characteristic of our society and which give us such a rich fabric of spontaneous local government.

35. The stronghold of Calhoun's doctrine, however, is the American party—the wonder and despair of foreigners who cannot fit it into any of their concepts of political life.

36. The purpose of European parties is, of course, to divide men of different ideologies into coherent and disciplined organizations. The historic role of the American party, on the other hand, is not to divide but to unite. That task was imposed by simple necessity. If a division into ideological parties had been attempted, in addition to all the other centrifugal forces in this country, it very probably would have proved impossible to hold the nation together. The Founding Fathers understood this thoroughly; hence Washington's warning against "factions."

37. Indeed, on the one occasion when we did develop two ideological parties, squarely opposing each other on an issue of principle, the result was civil war. Fortunately, that was our last large-scale experiment with a third party formed on an ideological basis—for in its early days that is just what the Republican party was.

38. Its radical wing, led by such men as Thaddeus Stevens, Seward, and Chase, made a determined and skillful effort to substitute principles for interests as the foundations of American political life. Even within their own party, however, they were opposed by such practical politicians as Lincoln and Johnson —men who distrusted fanaticism in any form— and by the end of the Reconstruction period

the experiment had been abandoned. American politics then swung back into its normal path and has never veered far away from it since. Although Calhoun's cause was defeated, his political theory came through the Civil War stronger than ever.

39. The result is that the American party has no permanent program and no fixed aim, except to win elections. Its one purpose is to unite the largest possible number of divergent interest groups in the pursuit of power. Its unity is one of compromise, not of dogma. It must—if it hopes to succeed—appeal to considerable numbers on both the left and the right, to rich and poor, Protestant and Catholic, farmer and industrial worker, native and foreign born.

40. It must be ready to bid for the support of any group that can deliver a sizable chunk of votes, accepting that group's program with whatever modifications may be necessary to reconcile the other members of the party. If sun worship, or Existentialism, or the nationalization of industry should ever attract any significant following in this country, you can be sure that both parties would soon whip up a plank designed to win it over.

41. This ability to absorb new ideas (along with the enthusiasts behind them) and to mold them into a shape acceptable to the party's standpatters is, perhaps, the chief measure of vitality in the party's leadership. Such ideas almost never germinate within the party itself. They are stolen—very often from third parties.

42. Indeed, the historic function of third parties has been to sprout new issues, nurse them along until they have gathered a body of supporters worth stealing, and then to turn them over (often reluctantly) to the major parties. A glance at the old platforms of the Populists, the Bull Moosers, and the Socialists will show what an astonishingly high percentage of their once-radical notions have been purloined by both Republicans and Democrats—and enacted into law. Thus the income tax, child-labor laws, minimum wages, regulation of railroads and utilities, and old-age pensions have all become part of the American Way of Life.

43. While each major party must always stand alert to grab a promising new issue, it

also must be careful never to scare off any of the big, established interest groups. For as soon as it alienates any one of them, it finds itself in a state of crisis.

44. During the nineteen-thirties and -forties the Republicans lost much of their standing as a truly national party because they had made themselves unacceptable to labor. Similarly, the Democrats, during the middle stage of the New Deal, incurred the wrath of the business interests. Ever since Mr. Truman was plumped into the White House, the Democratic leadership has struggled desperately—though rather ineptly—to regain the confidence of business men without at the same time driving organized labor out of the ranks. It probably would be safe to predict that if the Republican party is to regain a long period of health, it must make an equally vigorous effort to win back the confidence of labor. For the permanent veto of any major element in American society means political death—as the ghosts of the Federalists and Whigs can testify.

IV

45. The weaknesses of the American political system are obvious—much more obvious, in fact, than its virtues. These weaknesses have been so sharply criticized for the past hundred years, by a procession of able analysts ranging from Walter Bagehot to Thomas K. Finletter, that it is hardly necessary to mention them here. It is enough to note that most of the criticism has been aimed at two major flaws.

46. First, it is apparent that the doctrine of the concurrent majority is a negative one—a principle of inaction. A strong government, capable of rapid and decisive action, is difficult to achieve under a system which forbids it to do anything until virtually everybody acquiesces. In times of crisis, a dangerously long period of debate and compromise usually is necessary before any administration can carry out the drastic measures needed. The depression of the early thirties, the crisis in foreign policy which ended only with Pearl Harbor, the crisis of the Marshall program all illustrate this recurring problem.

47. This same characteristic of our system gives undue weight to the small but well-organized pressure group—especially when it is fighting *against* something. Hence a few power

companies were able to block for twenty years the sensible use of the Muscle Shoals dam which eventually became the nucleus of TVA, and—in alliance with the railroads, rail unions, and Eastern port interests—they are still holding up development of the St. Lawrence Waterway. An even more flagrant example is the silver bloc, representing only a tiny fraction of the American people. It has been looting the Treasury for a generation by a series of outrageous silver subsidy and purchase laws.

48. The negative character of our political rules also makes it uncommonly difficult for us to choose a President. Many of our outstanding political operatives—notably those who serve in the Senate—are virtually barred from a Presidential nomination because they are forced to get on record on too many issues. Inevitably they offend some important interest group, and therefore become "unavailable." Governors, who can keep their mouths shut on most national issues, have a much better chance to reach the White House. Moreover, the very qualities of caution and inoffensiveness which make a good candidate—Harding and Coolidge come most readily to mind—are likely to make a bad President.

49. An even more serious flaw in our scheme of politics is the difficulty in finding anybody to speak for the country as a whole. Calhoun would have argued that the national interest is merely the sum of all the various special interests, and therefore needs no spokesmen of its own—but in this case he clearly was wrong.

50. In practice, we tend to settle sectional and class conflicts at the expense of the nation as a whole—with results painful to all of us. The labor troubles in the spring of 1946, for instance, could be settled only on a basis acceptable to *both* labor and management: that is, on the basis of higher wages *plus* higher prices. The upshot was an inflationary spiral which damaged everybody. Countless other instances, from soil erosion to the rash of billboards along our highways, bear witness to the American tendency to neglect matters which are "only" of national interest, and therefore are left without a recognized sponsor.

51. Over the generations we have developed a series of practices and institutions which

partly remedy these weaknesses, although we are still far from a complete cure. One such development has been the gradual strengthening of the Presidency as against Congress. As the only man elected by all the people, the President inevitably has had to take over many of the policy-making and leadership functions which the Founding Fathers originally assigned to the legislators. This meant, of course, that he could no longer behave merely as an obedient executor of the will of Congress, but was forced into increasingly frequent conflicts with Capitol Hill.

52. Today we have come to recognize that this conflict is one of the most important obligations of the Presidency. No really strong executive tries to avoid it—he accepts it as an essential part of his job. If he simply tries to placate the pressure groups which speak through Congress, history writes him down as a failure. For it is his duty to enlist the support of many minorities for measures rooted in the national interest, reaching beyond their own immediate concern—and, if necessary, to stand up against the ravening minorities for the interest of the whole.

53. In recent times this particular part of the President's job has been made easier by the growth of the Theory of Temporary Emergencies. All of us—or nearly all—have come around to admitting that in time of emergency special interest groups must forego their right of veto. As a result, the President often is tempted to scare up an emergency to secure legislation which could not be passed under any other pretext. Thus, most of the New Deal bills were introduced as "temporary emergency measures," although they were clearly intended to be permanent from the very first; for in no other way could Mr. Roosevelt avoid the veto of the business interests.

54. Again, in 1939 the threat of war enabled the President to push through much legislation which would have been impossible under normal circumstances.

V

55. Because we have been so preoccupied with trying to patch up the flaws in our system, we have often overlooked its unique elements of strength. The chief of these is its ability to minimize conflict—not by suppressing the conflicting forces, but by absorbing and utilizing them. The result is a society which is both free and reasonably stable—a government which is as strong and effective as most dictatorships, but which can still adapt itself to social change.

56. The way in which the American political organism tames down the extremists of both the left and right is always fascinating to watch. Either party normally is willing to embrace any group or movement which can deliver votes—but in return it requires these groups to adjust their programs to fit the traditions, beliefs, and prejudices of the majority of the people. The fanatics, the implacable radicals cannot hope to get to first base in American politics until they abandon their fanaticism and learn the habits of conciliation. As a consequence, it is almost impossible for political movements here to become entirely irresponsible and to draw strength from the kind of demagogic obstruction which has nurtured both Communist and Fascist movements abroad.

57. The same process which gentles down the extremists also prods along the political laggards. As long as it is in a state of health, each American party has a conservative and a liberal wing. Sometimes one is dominant, sometimes the other—but even when the conservative element is most powerful, it must reckon with the left-wingers in its own family. At the moment the Republican party certainly is in one of its more conservative phases; yet it contains such men as Senators Morse, Aiken, Flanders, and Tobey, who are at least as progressive as most of the old New Dealers. They, and their counterparts in the Democratic party, exert a steady tug to the left which prevents either party from lapsing into complete reaction.

58. The strength of this tug is indicated by the fact that the major New Deal reforms have now been almost universally accepted. In the mid-thirties, many leading Republicans, plus many conservative Democrats, were hell-bent on wiping out social security, TVA, SEC, minimum-wage laws, rural electrification, and all the other dread innovations of the New Deal. Today no Presidential aspirant would dare suggest the repeal of a single one of them. In this country there simply is no place for a hard

core of irreconcilable reactionaries, comparable to those political groups in France which have never yet accepted the reforms of the French Revolution.

59. This American tendency to push extremists of both the left and right toward a middle position has enabled us, so far, to escape class warfare. This is no small achievement for any political system; for class warfare cannot be tolerated by a modern industrial society. If it seriously threatens, it is bound to be suppressed by some form of totalitarianism, as it has been in Germany, Spain, Italy, Russia, and most of Eastern Europe.

60. In fact, suppression might be termed the normal method of settling conflicts in continental Europe, where parties traditionally have been drawn up along ideological battle lines. Every political campaign becomes a religious crusade; each party is fanatically convinced that it and it alone has truth by the tail; each party is certain that its opponents not only are wrong, but wicked. If the sacred ideology is to be established beyond challenge, no heresy can be tolerated. Therefore it becomes a duty not only to defeat the enemy at the polls, but to wipe him out. Any suggestion of compromise must be rejected as treason and betrayal of the true faith. The party must be disciplined like an army, and if it cannot win by other means it must be ready to take up arms in deadly fact.

61. Under this kind of political system the best that can be hoped for is a prolonged deadlock between parties which are too numerous and weak to exterminate one another. The classic example is prewar France, where six revolutions or near-revolutions broke out within a century, where cabinets fell every weekend, and no government could ever become strong enough to govern effectively. The more usual outcome is a complete victory for one ideology or another, after a brief period of electioneering, turmoil, and fighting in the streets; then comes the liquidation of the defeated.

62. Because this sort of ideological politics is so foreign to our native tradition, neither Socialists, Communists, nor Fascists have ever been accepted as normal parties. So long as that tradition retains its very considerable vitality, it seems to me unlikely that any third party founded on an ideological basis can take root. The notion of a ruthless and unlimited class struggle, the concept of a master race, a fascist élite, or a proletariat which is entitled to impose its will on all others—these are ideas which are incompatible with the main current of American political life. The uncompromising ideologist, of whatever faith, appears in our eyes peculiarly "un-American," simply because he cannot recognize the rule of the concurrent majority, nor can he accept the rules of mutual toleration which are necessary to make it work. Unless he forsakes his ideology, he cannot even understand that basic principle of American politics which was perhaps best expressed by Judge Learned Hand: "The spirit of liberty is the spirit which is not too sure that it is right."

T. V. SMITH *The Double Discipline of Democracy*

Thomas Vernor Smith (1890-   ), philosopher, statesman, author, and lecturer, has taught at Texas Christian University, the University of Texas, and the University of Chicago. He is now Maxwell Professor of Citizenship and Philosophy at Syracuse University, where in 1948 he was honored by a T. V. Smith Day. His position at Syracuse is known as the Three-P Professorship because he is a professor of poetry, politics, and philosophy. Teacher and author of more than a dozen books and co-author of nearly as many more, Professor Smith has also served in the Illinois state legislature, as a Representative in the Seventy-sixth Congress, and since World War II as a member of United States educational missions in Italy, Germany, and Japan.

In "The Double Discipline of Democracy" Professor Smith discusses the two general kinds of discipline—external and internal—and the two kinds of internal discipline—emotional and intellectual—which enable the citizens of a democracy to adjust to the actual while continuing to strive for the ideal.

I

No thoughtful person supposes that any government can survive, much less prosper, without a well disciplined citizenry. But there are two types of discipline, and of the superior type two kinds. There is the discipline of means, external in type and capable of being inflicted upon men, a type inherent in totalitarian régimes. But there is, too, the discipline of ends, internal in type, difficult if not impossible to inflict, but highly rewarding of choice. It is this difference in disciplines which gives birth to the two ideologies at awful odds today.

To make the matter concrete, consider American experience in trying to purify Italian education of Fascism and subsequently in seeking to re-educate highly gifted German prisoners of war in preparation for ruling Germany after the late invasion. These German prisoners were carefully chosen from volunteers, and were entirely devoted to the enterprise. Under high secrecy and in favorable

THE DOUBLE DISCIPLINE OF DEMOCRACY: Reprinted, by permission of the author and the publisher, from the *Virginia Quarterly Review*, Winter 1951.

isolation all went swimmingly well in their political reorientation until we American officers came to the crux of education.

Then there would come a time—a day almost predictable with successive groups—when the spokesman of these well "disciplined" Germans would arise in small group discussions and say substantially this:

"Sir, you have been showing us that democracy is pluralistic in its culture, and so must be undogmatic in its ideology."

"Yes."

"You have told us that to run a society democratically we must be ready to meet any and all our opponents half way."

"Right."

"But now, Sir, if we understand you, you are suggesting that we must come to terms with our enemies *even when we are right and they are wrong.*"

"Yes?"

"But, Sir, we cannot go this far. We Germans have character, and that means to us that we cannot compromise with those who are wrong."

Here they stuck, stuck almost to a man; and

we had to chalk off the inner failure of what, outwardly regarded, was a phenomenal success. The imposition of outer discipline had acquired a beachhead in their consciences. This "internalized authority" made it impossible for them to disclose to themselves what Justice Holmes once described as his happiest discovery: that he was not God. With the Germans the obstruction to democracy took the form of a dogmatic conviction of spiritual superiority. With the Italians it had previously manifested itself as fear, reflecting itself in inner bankruptcy, even after the form of outer authority had crumpled.

I shall never forget the look of amazement and helplessness on the faces of a group of Sicilian elementary schoolteachers when I made to them with American enthusiasm a certain pedagogical suggestion.

Before the Allied Control Commission had been able to get out of the Italian textbooks the rankest of Fascist propaganda, orders came down to re-open the schools, so as at least to keep the children off the streets and out of the way of our heavy movements of troops and supplies to the fighting front. But what were the teachers to teach while awaiting safe textbooks? My suggestion to them was that for the time being they do what I supposed every good elementary teacher had often longed to do: just keep the children out of mischief, direct their play, and teach them spontaneously whatever the teachers knew to be decent and helpful!

"But what do you want us to teach them?"

That is, a new "authority" must supplant the old before they could teach at all! It dawned on me slowly, watching their faces and listening to their pleas for directives, what was the real evil of Fascism: it had bankrupted all inner reliance. They were afraid to teach at all; indeed had nothing to give from within. Authority from without at length disintegrates all integrity within, until all is inner emptiness from the dominance of externalism. To the authoritarian, democracy must itself become authoritative before it can begin to mean freedom. And, sad truth, even purified textbooks could not be used by moral bankrupts until we had issued, with the text, manuals of instruction telling how to teach what was prescribed to be taught. At whatever level

external discipline operates, it leaves in its wake psychological impoverishment and moral bankruptcy.

II

Inner discipline, however, which is peculiarly democratic, is of two kinds: emotional and intellectual.

On the emotional side, the discipline that is democratic boils down to something very simple but not for that reason easy: the ability to *stand alone*. Only he can be a good democrat who, when he calls upon himself, finds somebody at home. Only he who finds this company within does not have to rely upon the crowd for support (whether operating as fear or as unreasoned pride in tradition). He is his own crowd: crowds collect around the man who himself needs no crowd for support. The incapacity to stand alone has in all ages led men into the camp of one symbol of authority after another. The temerity of loneliness we also know. We show our acquaintance with it in democratic societies by becoming chronic "joiners." The man who does not find his company at home has to join up with somebody in order to feel himself to be anybody. Our wise commandant used to try to strengthen our departing German prisoners for their ordeal by assuring them that even in their subsequent solitude they would not be alone: all decent men would be standing with them. The ideal democrat is one so emotionally disciplined that he can cheerfully stand by himself, and the actual democrat approaches this ideal as he values and enhances this moral self-sufficiency. How difficult this is, however, is indicated from of old by Aristotle's oft-quoted remark that the man who prefers solitude is either "a god or a brute."

Now the democrat need not prefer solitude; he has only to be able to abide it: to contain his loneliness when self-sufficiency becomes the *sine qua non* of self-respect. The only thing which will lessen the moral necessity to stand alone is increase of one's capacity to do so upon demand. Mussolini rode to power because of the absence of an adequate number of Italians who could stand alone against his nervous initial pretensions. Hitler's sadism grew great because of the lack of a sufficient number of Germans who would stand forth to make the early suffering of the Jews their cause.

Such initial obstacles to tyranny do not have to be numerous, but only initial and adamant, to prevent tyranny from growing great upon its own audacious exercise. Courage to stand alone for decency is an impregnable "cell" of virtue; and such cells can be few in proportion as they are opportune and self-sufficient.

As Justice Brandeis has said, "the dearest of all American rights is the right to be let alone." Recognizing from the beginning that without a solid core of this moral individualism there could be no sound society, our fathers obtruded, justified, and defended this legacy, man's *right* to be alone. But the enunciation of the rights does not of itself make easy the practice of solitude or effective the duty at times to stand quite by oneself. The right is one thing, a thing constitutionally bequeathed; the ability to stand is another thing, a thing gained only through discipline. It is a difficult discipline, the duty to live up to the sacred right. He has begun the hardening of himself to the discipline who exacts of himself that he must have a better reason for joining an organization than the fact that he has no good reason for not joining.

The contrary philosophy, all too prevalent today, that "shared" values are somehow more precious than individual sacredness, hides its shame behind a shibboleth of co-operation. Pragmatism, starting with William James' stalwart individualism, has degenerated through "progressive education" and the gospel of "shared" values into the opposite of James' conviction, into a sort of Christian communalism. This is the reason why liberals, especially Christian liberals, are the easy marks they sometimes are for the Communistic cult of "comradeship." Note, in high quarters, John Dewey's telltale dictum: "That vital impulses . . . are capable of extending themselves in the character of daydreaming and building castles in the air is *unfortunately* true." Observe particularly the tragic emphasis upon the word I have italicized, carrying, as it does, the sad implication that individual values get their worth from being shared. Where is art, that citadel of individualism, to get its inception if not in the *fortunate* fact of independence from both the world and the crowd? Character which is built upon the topsy-turvy notion that privacy is invidious is not likely to stand foursquare.

Now of course there is a place for shared values; co-operation has its value in the good life. But co-operation between bad men, when achieved, makes evil worse. The only thing that will make value shared more valuable still is the antecedent condition that there be value there before the sharing. It takes men to co-operate; automata cannot. Evils shared become, through newly acquired strength, more evil still; and goods shared are the better if and only if they were good to begin with.

In simple truth, any value that is shared becomes ordinarily not more but less ideal. The reason for this axiological declension is that we have to make accommodation with others in the art of sharing; and the resultant, as one sees in politics, partakes of compromise and illustrates an ideal less pure than the ideal which anticipates the sharing. It is not "unfortunate," as Dewey indicates, but is the supremely fortunate thing about human life, that our "vital impulses" can and do save their purity through the "escapism" of reverie and the solitude of artistic creation. It is not that compromise is bad: it is good as an alternative to worse, but it is bad as the alternative to the better. Politics and education must, for a fact, be done by men together, but with the resultant lessening of the quality of the value involved. Art, on the other hand, is what man does to please himself: it issues from the citadel of separateness. The poet speaks for all artists:

> The soul selects her own society,
> Then shuts the door;
> On her divine majority
> Obtrude no more.

We recognize this value priority of the inner self, to which Emily Dickinson thus repairs, by elevating to the top of our concern in both ethics and religion "the private conscience." Whitehead, the philosopher, has gone so far as to define religion as "what one does with his solitariness." And whatever the exaggeration in his remark, there is indeed this unshared, and even to any high degree unsharable, foundation to every public religion; else religion itself becomes but the empty shell of formalism.

This private aspect of value is its very core. No tyrant knows an enemy so implacable as stolid separateness on the part of citizens. Solitariness requires stamina, but also imparts stamina. "No," spoken in time and with emphasis, is the only insurance men have against the tyranny of the one, the tyranny of the minority, or even the tyranny of the majority. This capacity to stand alone feeds upon the company which one finds within, upon his own "choir invisible." Solitude is not emptiness, save to those who worship externalism; it is fullness, fullness to such as have life within. No man has begun to live, for no man has tasted of the creative life, who cannot be somebody without associating himself with anybody. Nowhere else does man approach perfection, and in no other manner does he get the stamina to make co-operation itself a good.

Justice Holmes knew, as few Americans have known, the emotional nature and the outer cost of democracy. "Only when [you] have worked alone," he says ". . . will you have achieved. Thus only can you gain the secret isolated joy of the thinker, who knows that, a hundred years after he is dead and forgotten, men who never heard of him will be moving to the measure of his thought. . . . Only thus . . . can you say that you have lived, and be ready for the end." How many "joiners," upon that showing, die without ever having lived at all! No man is prepared to live who has not already made his bargain of honor with death.

Among our spiritually great, then, Brandeis gives us to see how central is this sacred right to be alone. Emerson gives us to know the penalty of that right's reversion. Holmes gives us stoic grace to glimpse the self-reward which attends the duty accepted. A poet is required— and she is at hand in Emily Dickinson's practice of the presence of privacy—to show the right real, the incapacity empty, and the realization of the right immortal.

> Mine by the right of the white election!
> Mine by the royal seal!
> Mine by the sign in the scarlet prison
> Bars cannot conceal!
> Mine, here in vision and in veto!
> Mine, by the grave's repeal
> Titled, confirmed,—delirious charter!
> Mine, while the ages steal!

III

Such is the first mode of the discipline required by democracy, the emotional maturity which enables one to stand alone. The second mode is like unto it, though more intellectual in its reaches. The distinction between the emotional and the intellectual is, admittedly, without any absolute difference. No wise man is concerned exclusively, as C. Day Lewis phrases it, with

> . . . Truth that's grown
> Exhausted haggling for its own
> And speaks without desire.

There is, nevertheless, wisdom in the distinction, if it be not pushed beyond the actual difference. The logic of democracy implies the ability to stand alone; but it consists of the capacity, when so standing, to refrain from action which is predicated wholly upon private insight. This is hardship added to difficulty. Private insight has its rights, as well as its undisputed glory, but among the former is not the right to proceed directly from vision to collective action.

That there is a demand so to proceed is indubitable. So urgent is the impulsion, indeed, that it will hardly be resisted by those who do not find the positive reward of solitude in contemplation of the ideal itself. The logic of this urgency which for most men attends vision must now be spelled out. The mind will be restrained from debasing itself to a mere pragmatic instrument only by being convinced of the looseness of its own logic. We shall, therefore, delineate, in a rough way, the several rungs of the ladder which leads from ideals to collective action, even down to the extreme form known as politics.

We begin at the top with the vision of Good, or maybe of the Beautiful, or possibly of the Holy. At first this vision is what is commonly called imaginary, but it is not for that reason any the less "real." The vision, however, does project itself as an obligation. From having seen what would be better than what is, then, we infer that something ought *to be done*, in recognition of the first obligation that the imaginary ought *to be*, in addition to being imagined. The next rung of the logic-ladder is that what ought to be done, ought to be done by some man. And the fourth and final step is identification of the "somebody" with *this* body: in short, *I* ought to do something to make more actual the ideal that is already real in its imagined perfection.

It will be felt, no doubt, that there is a certain indignity toward obligation offered by this analytic dissection. And this indignity is admitted. It can be justified, if at all, only by its fruits. It is very hard to bring the mind to its senses as touching the dire consequences of its own impetuosity. The ordinary approach is to educate, or to re-educate, the emotions of men so that they will not feel shamefully right in doing the most shameful things. The fanatic, some wise wag has remarked, is only the man who does what God would do if God had all the facts. The most honorable way to get at the heart of a thinker is through his head. Paying that deference, we propose to disclose to the mind of the idealist how disjointed, how emotion-ridden, is his logic.

Take, for instance, the first step, the inference that because something is seen in vision it ought to be realized out of vision. No strict logician could make that inference authoritative. What might follow from imagination is merely its own autonomy: its right to be left alone in its glory. Is it not conceivably enough to be imagined, without having *to be* in some other way than in this finest of fashions? I do not present this as proved; I only assert that more than this is far from being proved.

The logic gets looser as we proceed. The second rung is weak, the third weaker, and the fourth weakest of all. The second inference is that something ought to be *done* about what ought to *be* other than imaginary. By what necessity do we infer obligation of action from mere oughtness of being? That we are animals before we are spirits is true enough; and as animals we of course like to hop around. Perhaps we even ought to hop around, to be chronically active. Children at least seem to thrive upon aimless activity. "The boy," Herbert Hoover has declared, "is an animal who takes exercise upon every possible occasion." But we are speaking of mature men and of the high spiritual fact of obligation. How tight is the logic that infers that something ought to be done, just because something ideal is and is real in an imaginary mode of being? Does

one need argument to see that that notion itself is an assumption rather than a cogent inference?

What, rather, would follow from ideal existence is this: that what is ideal ought to be in the way that it is. But the third rung is worse than the second: *somebody* ought to do something. If this means some human being, it is certainly wide of the proved mark. Maybe it is God who ought to do something, if something ought to be done. Even the devil is not to be ruled out of the orbit of our reference, for in most of the great religions, and certainly in ours, these two supernatural gentlemen have always divided certain responsibilities between them. Maybe, then, the devil is the person pointed to in this general obligation to act. The matter dealt with is so high and wide that some supernatural reference seems a more appropriate suggestion. And yet we can see how presumptuous our logic has become when we begin to order God and the devil around, out of the heat of our felt obligation.

It is, however, the final rung of this logic-ladder that is really rotted. Fortunate that it is at the groundward end of our ladder; else would all idealists break their necks on that step. How can it follow that *I* am the "fall guy" of the cosmos, that I must do something of such high emprise, even if it be granted that somebody, even some human body, ought to do it? This is stretching my personal obligation entirely beyond my poor capacities. I cannot do everything. If I undertake to do something toward the improvement of all the imperfections I see in the universe, is it not clear that I will get nothing at all done—nothing, that is, save to wreck myself on presumptuous undertakings? This is what Justice Holmes had in mind, in our previous reference, when he thanked God for the day that he discovered that he himself was not God. Liberals who make their logic-ladder reach all the way to the political ground on which they stand, become professional "joiners" and never do anything save help the wheels to go round, including the wheels in their heads. Lucky if they escape gastric ulcers or the final melodrama of suicide. It is morbid, and leads to ultimate presumption, for men to confuse themselves with God.

This is not to make light of the predicament of the sensitive, the overly-conscientious, man or woman; nor is it to cast discredit upon the uses of logic in the guidance of life. But it must be clear that this logic of impetuosity is worse than no logic at all. Every step downward toward action is taken by means of prompting more emotional than intellectual. The trouble with such logic is that it is not logical enough: it is illicit, inconsequential, and utterly undependable. To decide what one ought to do, ought ever to do, requires taste, natural piety, a strategy of succession, and integrity in the sequences. Action is arduous and is not subject directly to ideal considerations. The best that the mind can do here is to see the limitations inherent in its purity.

If we start more modestly, then, from the bottom, our first assumption would be that nobody owes a duty to do anything that is impossible for him to do. Even allowing a certain ambiguity in the statement, it is clear that it relieves man of a great load of responsibility, and eventually of guilt. Man isn't God; his powers are quite limited, and, worst of all, the time allowed him to exert his little powers is finite. Even of the things which appeal to him, man must make austere and wise choice lest he fritter away the little time he has, in jumping on the horse of his wild desires or his equally quixotic aspirations, and riding off in all directions all the time.

IV

Already we have limited man's obligation to act by his abilities; now we must limit obligation also by his choices. His third limitation brings us back to democratic discipline, from which we have never really strayed save to beguile the illogical mind. The other limitations will not become effective without an unwonted amount of discipline, but this third requirement is the more exacting. Man's obligation to do is limited by other men's obligations to do, or in the event by their desires not to be done in by him. Suppose my obligation as a citizen to effect industrial justice leads me toward the Taft-Hartley philosophy (or equally well toward the philosophy of its predecessor or successor on the political calendar). I have of course a clear vision of ideal Justice; I feel that the vision ought to materialize. I feel that something ought to be done to this end, be done by somebody, be done, in short, by me. What follows from all these feelings?

Nothing follows democratically, unless and until a majority of my fellow-men can be persuaded to this view of the matter. This is a big job; unbelievably complicated, unutterably trying, and almost intolerably long. What holds me to my original obligation throughout? The discipline known as patience, persistence, character. But what holds me to the democratic obligation of using the majority rule? Discipline, too; but this time in a peculiar sense the discipline of character, involving both thought and feeling. I have to feel right toward my fellow-men before I can harness my impetuosity to the yoke of their consent. If my conscience gets the best of my sympathy, I will override them on the presumption that they are either too stupid to know what is just or too corrupt to want justice to prevail over their self-interest. If this logic of presumption gets the best of my reasonableness, I will disturb the balance between action and contemplation by trying to take the kingdom of the ideal by violence.

This is of course the root trouble with the Communists. Dispensing with politics and liquidating all the politicians, as the "state withers away," they look for an end in which pure justice will automatically arise and will maintain itself without the use of any adverse means. This end is so purely romantic that it can be furthered only by romantic means. Pure violence must implement pure vision, for it is surely clear that nothing else will; and is it not also clear that we must have as the principle of our collectivity what has been glimpsed as the pure principle of our privacy?

Their means can become more reasonable only as their end gets better reasoned. Their rigorous logic is not rigorous enough to adapt the means that are actual to imaginary ends that are possible in the field of action. If they treated imagination with more respect than to insist upon actualizing it all, they could improve the actual by principles resident in its own progression. Lacking the inner discipline to do all this, they drug themselves and deaden the world by a discipline which, save to the few, is purely external.

v

This returns us to contemplation as our human polestar. Pure perfection is demonstrable only in imagination. It may exist elsewhere, but we always disturb the unity of our faith by the differences that arise in our interpretation of the faith. But who is to deny to any man what he sees, or says that he sees, in the solitude of his own soul? Nothing is made worse for anybody by his vision; everything is made better for him. In privacy alone does perfection thrive undisputed; and privacy is the one thing we can allow with impunity. Democratic discipline is what makes possible this final allowance. Democracy is private containment of the private, majority adjudication of the public.

This discipline becomes operative, however, only in men who find enough in their own private domain of perfection so that they can, in their enjoyment of it, allow others to be left alone. Empty men must somehow always inflict their emptiness. Full men alone can rejoice in their fullness. Emotional discipline and intellectual discipline come eventually, then, to the same thing; for they are two only initially. They come to this: that men must find in their own inner lives something which is good in itself before they can know what is good for others. When they have found this in themselves, they can believe other-rewarding what they have found self-rewarding.

Disciplined to such inner reliance, citizens may, dispensing with all ladders and at last with impetuosity itself, find their way from the ideal without breaking their own hearts, and may find ways and means toward the ideal without breaking other men's heads.

part two

Introduction to Literature

A PREFATORY NOTE

The chief purpose of the study of literature is to intensify one's awareness of the quality and variety of human experience. A literary work therefore possesses greatness by virtue of the power it is able to exert, through means peculiar to it as a form of art, over the imaginative life of attentive readers. It may range in complexity from a simple expression of personal emotion ("Stopping by Woods on a Snowy Evening") to the complex and accumulative force of a Shakespearean tragedy. But however modest or grand in scope a poem, or play, or novel may be, its full realization cannot be achieved without the active and eager participation of the reader. The person who has read many books with understanding has shared in many lives, vividly different from one another, and has added richness and perspective to his sum total of experience—to the outer and inner events of his own life.

Experience, it is said, is a costly teacher. Direct experience is of course desirable, despite its cost, but not all our experience can or need be acquired directly. It is possible to avoid disaster, for instance, and yet lay hold upon the quality of character which disaster sometimes gives. The imaginative projection of ourselves into the consciousness of others, through literature, yields experiences that would be too strenuous to endure without hazard in actual life, and yet still can chasten and humanize us, bringing us to a better understanding of ourselves and others. The range of such vicarious experiences is surprisingly large and varied—from the outrageous to the sublime—but they are most meaningful to the reader when they complement his actual experiences. Rostand's *Cyrano de Bergerac* comes home to the woman who has found that no degree of physical charm will compensate for a dull mind, and Edmund Waller's "Go, Lovely Rose" touches nearer the core of a man who has already felt the transient brush of beauty and learned the inevitability of its departure.

But literature, however closely allied to actual experience, is not exactly a reproduction or transcript of happenings, feelings, and scenes. That is, literature is not so much like a photograph of life as it is like a series of portraits, or interpretations. Life is so filled and crowded with details as to seem nearly chaotic to most of us at times, but each work of literature is a selection of such details as can be combined to suggest a coherent impression of life. The artist does not give us masses of unassimilated

knowledge. He imposes form upon the materials he uses and through this form suggests meaning. Organization is what gives us this sense of meaning. Test the truth of
this statement by analyzing any one of the stories in the group of short stories in this
text; how little, in the way of details—of description or character or action—the author
actually gives us, how much he suggests or implies.

The central importance of this selection and organization of materials is especially
well illustrated by the short story, because within its brief limits the author must select and organize his material with unusual care and skill. For example, when Irwin
Shaw, in "The Dry Rock," wants to show how difficult it is for a person of humble
means and circumstances to receive the minimum amount of justice and respect which
every individual deserves, he chooses only two principal characters, a cab driver and an
ill-mannered young man; centers the action about a single traffic accident; places the
story in a fast-moving city. But selectivity goes beyond the simple limitation of character and incident; it involves also the choice of these personalities and events that
will most economically and richly convey the theme of the story.

The meaning that emerges from organization and selection in any work of literature cannot be adequately conveyed in a summary. To perceive the full quality of the
experience interpreted, we have to become sensitively aware of every part and relationship; and the comprehension we finally achieve will depend in part on the scope
of our own consciousness. As one contemporary critic has suggested, the effect of a
work of art on the consciousness of various readers is like the effect of pebbles falling
into pools of water: the ripples always move out to the far edge of the pool, but some
pools are larger than others.

Literature appeals to both mind and heart. Therefore our whole being is involved
in the response to it. Sometimes full comprehension of a poem or of an experience
comes in a flash of illumination which enlarges our consciousness and lifts us to a
different plane of being. Robert Frost records such an incident in the following lines:

> The way a crow
> Shook down on me
> The dust of snow
> From a hemlock tree
>
> Has given my heart
> A change of mood
> And saved some part
> Of a day I had rued.[1]

The sudden illumination here spoken of yields a deep understanding, an unusual insight, a discovery. No doubt all of us have such moments of poetic insight when past
knowledge and present awareness come to focus upon a single point of understanding:
these are among our most memorable experiences. Readers of imaginative literature
may share these moments with artists. This is reading at its best—creative reading,
building and enriching the mind.

[1] "Dust of Snow" from *New Hampshire* by Robert Frost. Copyright, 1923, by Henry Holt and Company, Inc. Copyright, 1951, by Robert Frost. Reprinted by permission of the publishers.

BIOGRAPHY

INTRODUCTION

(mythical)

conveying personality

Biography, which is simply the story of a man's life, has taken many forms. Today we think of a biography as being an entirely factual prose narrative. But the word has not always been so precisely used.

The earliest biographers were probably those minstrels who praised the deeds of heroes in extemporaneous song. As a hero's exploits increased—in fact or in imagination—the songs grew in length and number, until at last the total reached epic proportions. Such, for instance, was the genesis of our most ancient epics, the *Iliad* and the *Odyssey*. Almost as ancient, and strictly speaking more biographical, are the accounts of the lives of the prophets in the Old Testament.

The earliest example of the carefully wrought, formal type of biography was Plutarch's *Parallel Lives*, written in the first century A.D., which presented in a series of contrasting pairs the lives of a number of famous Greeks and Romans. Plutarch's chief concern was with men as types of moral excellence or moral weakness, rather than as individuals endowed with complex personal characteristics.

During the centuries of development between Plutarch's *Lives* and the biography as we know it today, biographical writing took many forms, including miraculous lives of the saints and a multitude of chronicle accounts of kings and conquerors. The compelling motives in these biographical endeavors were largely didactic or commemorative. In the sixteenth and seventeenth centuries, however, a greater degree of curiosity about how other people thought and lived was reflected in such experiments in biographical writing as prefatory biographical essays, character sketches, printed funeral sermons, letters, and diaries. In short, emphasis was placed on the historical rather than the ethical motive, and more attention was given to the individual as a secular being.

The next stage in the development of biography centers around two prominent eighteenth-century writers—Samuel Johnson and James Boswell. Johnson insisted that the whole truth be given about a man: "If a man is to write *A Panegyrick,* he may keep vices out of sight; but if he professes to write *A Life,* he must write it as it was." James Boswell followed this dictum of his master and in consequence established for biography a permanent place as a type of literature. In *The Life of Samuel Johnson,* one of the most fascinating books in all of English literature, Boswell captured Johnson's individuality, wit, wisdom, and arrogance. As a work of art, Boswell's masterpiece possesses charm, realism, psychological analysis, and force far surpassing that of any of its predecessors.

The spirit of scientific accuracy and the respect for exhaustive scholarly research that characterized the late nineteenth century resulted in long, detailed biographies of the "life and times" type. These not only recounted the events of a man's life but used that life as a center around which to organize a history of the times in which the character lived. As a consequence, nineteenth-century biographies are of great scope: Lockhart's life of his father-in-law, Sir Walter Scott, was first published in ten volumes; Froude's *Life of Carlyle,* in four volumes; Forster's *Life of Dickens,* in three volumes.

Among modern readers biographical writing competes keenly in popularity with other types of literature. Recent biographers have drawn heavily from modern psychology for method in character analysis and from drama and the short story for techniques of presenting their subjects. Emphasis centers around character and personality. A person's shortcomings and follies, his merits and his virtues—all are displayed with equal exactitude. Modern biography, notable for its clever, crisp, and highly readable style, at its best combines Plutarch's effective use of anecdotes, Boswell's skill in character analysis and ability to reproduce vivid conversation, and the scientific demand for truth and factual accuracy which marked the nineteenth-century taste.

Every scantling of information or clue to character found in letters, journals, diaries, conversations of friends or enemies, published works, and magazine articles becomes the substance of biography. It has been said that Lytton Strachey, the eminent English biographer, read and studied a roomful of books and other printed matter in order to write his two-hundred-page life of Queen Victoria.

Autobiographical writing has followed a course paralleling that of biography, with ever closer attention to the selection of significant detail and a refreshing liveliness of style. Experimentation in autobiographical writing started when man first began keeping a record of his life in memoirs, diaries, letters, and chronicles. As a division of literature, however, the early eighteenth century marks the first use of the word *autobiography* to describe a narrative with the writer's life constituting the central framework of the story. Autobiography as a literary form is perhaps as popular today as biography, though not as extensively written. Helen Keller's account of her early life, one of the biographical selections in this text, is an excerpt from her *Story of My Life,* which sketches the manner in which the whole mystery of language was revealed to her.

The biographical selections, Stephen Leacock's *Mark Twain* and Samuel Eliot Morison's "The Young Man Washington," and the two biographical essays in Part I, Van Wyck Brooks's "Helen Keller" and Virginia Woolf's "Beau Brummel," are revealing accounts of four illustrious persons. The enjoyment of these biographies will be heightened if the reader observes closely the choice of illustrative detail—detail that not only gives literary or historical perspective but also presents the subjects as human beings endowed with traits of genius of differing kinds. So it is with all good biography: in reading it, one broadens his store of factual knowledge, gains an understanding of human behavior, comes intimately to know important people, and finds history personalized.

STEPHEN LEACOCK *Mark Twain*

Stephen Leacock (1869-1944), economist, teacher, biographer, and humorist, was born in Swan Moor, Hampshire, England, of parents who emigrated to Canada in 1876. He was educated at the Universities of Toronto and Chicago. From 1908 until 1936, he served as head of the Department of Economics and Political Science at McGill University in Montreal.

To Americans Stephen Leacock is known primarily as a humorist, and he has achieved a reputation among some critics as "the most popular humorist in America since Mark Twain." But he is more than a writer of humor. His versatility is evident in a sampling of his titles: *Elements of Political Science*, 1906; *Nonsense Novels*, 1911; *Lincoln Frees the Slaves*, 1934; *Humor: Its Theory and Technique*, 1935; *Montreal, Seaport and City*, 1942; *How to Write*, 1943. His first sustained attempt at biography, a life of Mark Twain, appeared in 1932. It is a readable book, interesting without being sensational, factual without being prosaic. In 1933, Leacock published *Charles Dickens*, the life of another man whom he held in high esteem.

CONTENTS

I. CHILDHOOD AND YOUTH— MARK TWAIN AS TOM SAWYER, 1835-1857

The name of Mark Twain stands for American humour. More than that of any other writer, more than all names together, his name

MARK TWAIN by Stephen Leacock. Copyright, 1933, D. Appleton & Company. Reprinted by permission of the publishers, Appleton-Century-Crofts, Inc.

conveys the idea of American humour. For two generations his reputation and his fame have been carried all over the world with this connotation. He has become, as it were, an idea, a sort of abstraction, comparable to John Bull who represents England, or Sherlock Holmes who signifies an inexorable chain of logic.

The name, as all the world knows, is only a pen-name, selected after the conceited fashion of the day and taken from the river-calls of the Mississippi pilots. But its apt and easy sound rapidly obliterated the clumsy name of the writer who wore it. Samuel Langhorne Clemens died to the world, or rather, never lived for it. "Mark Twain" became a household word for millions and came to signify not merely a particular person but an idea. Thus, side by side with Mr. Clemens, who is dead, there grew an imaginary person, Mark Twain, who became a legend and is living still.

American humour rose on the horizon of the nineteenth century as one of the undisputed national products of the new republic. Of American literature there was much doubt in Europe; of American honesty, much more; of American manners, more still. But American humour found a place alongside of German philosophy, Italian music, French wine, and British banking. No one denied its peculiar excellence and its distinctive national stamp.

Now Mark Twain did not create American humour nor the peculiar philosophy of life on which it rests. Before him were the Major Dowlings and the Sam Slicks, and in his own day the Petroleum Nasebys and the Orpheus C. Kerrs and others now resting as quietly as they do. But in the retrospect of retreating years nearly all the work of these sinks into insignificant dreariness or into a mere juggle of words, cheap and ephemeral. The name of only one contemporary, Artemus Ward, may be set in a higher light. Yet all that Ward ever wrote in words, as apart from his quaint and pathetic personality, is but a fragment. If Mark Twain did not create American humour, he at least took it over and made something of it. He did for it what Shakespeare did for the English drama, and what Milton did for Hell. He "put it on the map." He shaped it into a form of thought, a way of looking at things, and hence a mode or kind of literature.

Not that Mark Twain did all this consciously. A deliberate humorist, seeking his effect, is as tiresome as a conscientious clown working by the week. His humour lay in his point of view, his angle of vision and the truth with which he conveyed it. This often enabled people quite suddenly to see things as they are, and not as they had supposed them to be —a process which creates the peculiar sense of personal triumph which we call humour. The savage shout of exultation modified down to our gurgling laugh greets the overthrow of the thing as it was. Mark Twain achieved this effect not by trying to be funny, but by trying to tell the truth. No one really knew what the German Kaiser was like till Mark Twain dined with him. No one really *saw* the painted works of the old masters till Mark Twain took a look at them. The absurd multiplicity of the saints was never appreciated till Mark Twain counted them by the gross. The futility of making Egyptian mummies was never realized till he measured them by the cord as firewood. People who had tried in vain to rise to the dummy figures and the sentimental un-

reality of Tennyson's *Idylls of the King* got set straight on chivalry and all its works when they read *A Connecticut Yankee in King Arthur's Court.* "The boys went grailing," says the Yankee, in reference to the pursuit of the Holy Grail by the Knights of the Round Table. "The boys went grailing." Why not?

Readers who had tried in vain to feel impressed and reverent over Tennyson's impossible creations felt an infinite relief in seeing them reduced to this familiar footing. Thus in a score of books and in a thousand of anecdotes and phrases there was conveyed to the world something and somebody which it knew as Mark Twain.

All the rest of the man, the other aspects of his mind and personality, was left out of count. The flaming enthusiasms, the fierce elemental passion against tyranny, against monarchy, against hell, against the God of the Bible—all this was, and is, either unknown or forgotten. It has to be. The composite picture, filled in line by line, would leave a new person to be called Samuel L. Clemens. The "Mark Twain" of the legend would crumble into dust.

In any case, Mark Twain only half-expressed himself. Of the things nearest to his mind he spoke but low or spoke not at all. He would have liked to curse England for the Boer War, to curse America for the Philippine conquest, to curse the Roman Catholic Church for its past, and the Czar of Russia for his present. Instinct told him that had he done so, the Mark Twain legend that had filled the world would pass away. The kindly humorist, with a corn-cob pipe would also be a rebel, an atheist, an anti-clerical.

So it was that Mark Twain's nearest and dearest thoughts were spoken only in a murmur, and the world laughed, thinking this some new absurdity; or were left unspoken, and the world never knew; or were published after he was dead, when no one could catch him. The kindly conspiracy was played out to the end.

It is better that it should be so. It leaves the legendary Mark Twain and his work and his humour as one of the great things of nineteenth-century America.

American he certainly was. He had the advantage, or disadvantage, of being brought up solely in his own country, remote from its coasts, with no contact with the outside world, in the days when America was still America. He lived, and died, before the motion picture had flickered the whole world with similarity, and before rapid transport had enabled every country to live on the tourists of all the others. His childhood was spent in an isolation from the outside world now beyond all conception. Nor was the isolation much relieved by mental contact. Like Shakespeare and Dickens, young Sam Clemens had little school and no college. He thus acquired that peculiar sharpness of mind which comes from not going to school, and that power of independent thought obtained by not entering college. It was this youthful setting which enabled him to become what he was.

Here are some of the essential facts about his early life which need to be mentioned even in a biography.

Samuel Langhorne Clemens was born on the thirtieth of November in 1835 in a frontier settlement which he himself called the "almost invisible village of Florida, Monroe County, Missouri." His father and mother were people as impoverished and as undistinguished as one could wish. Both came of plain pioneer stock, the father originally from Virginia, the mother from Kentucky. Mark Twain's father, John Clemens, seems to have been a kindly but shiftless person, succeeding at nothing, but dreaming always of a wonderful future. At intervals in an impoverished youth he had picked up an education and for a time attended a frontier law school. But he turned his hand to store-keeping, to housebuilding, to anything; and his mind to dreaming. He and his wife Jane went and settled in the mountain wilderness of East Tennessee. The older brothers and sisters of the family, "the first crop of children," were born there. Then John Clemens, with the restlessness of the frontiersman, moved from one habitat to another, and presently passed on to the new State of Missouri just beginning its existence. But he had meantime managed to raise four hundred dollars and with it to buy a vast tract of land, of about a hundred thousand acres. For the rest of his life the elder Clemens was inspired by visions of his Tennessee land and what it would mean for the future of his descendants. These dreams he passed on to his descendants as their chief legacy.

The Tennessee land contained great forests of yellow pine, beds of oil, deposits of coal and iron and copper, an El Dorado of wealth as we see it now. But in those days the timber was unsaleable for lack of transport, coal was unusable, and petroleum a mere curiosity of the marshes. Yet Clemens managed, with a wrench, to pay his five dollars a year in taxes, and dreamed of wealth to come. After his death the land was muddled away and parted with for next to nothing, till the last ten thousand acres were sold in 1894 for two hundred dollars. But the inspiration of the Tennessee land served as the background of *The Gilded Age* and helped to fashion the cheery optimism of Colonel Sellers; converted into literature and the drama it earned a fortune.

Side by side with the legend of the Tennessee land and the golden future still to come went another family legend, a very frequent one with impoverished families of unknown origin in America. This was the tradition of noble descent from a collateral branch of a great English family. Mark Twain's mother, being a Lampton of Kentucky, could be converted by the mere change of a letter into a Lambton of the noble family of the earldom of Durham. The Clemenses, with a similar twist, could descend from or ascend to Geoffrey Clement, the regicide judge of Oliver Cromwell's day. But there is no need to linger over the Clemenses' claim to noble birth. It is shared by all of us in North America who can give no exact account of our remote origin. At any rate it served, along with the Tennessee dream, as the basis of the story to be called *The American Claimant*.

The Clemens family left the log village of Florida when little Sam was not yet four years old (1839). But his connection with the locality did not end there. An uncle and aunt and cousins lived on a farm about four miles from Florida, and he spent some part of every year there till he was twelve years old. Many of his most vital impressions and many of his fondest recollections centred around this Missouri farm. Even in old age he could recall "the solemn twilight and mystery of the deep woods, the earthy smell, the faint odours of the wild flowers, the sheen of rain-washed foliage, the rattling clatter of drops when the wind shook the trees, the far-off hammering of wood-peckers and the muffled drumming of wood pheasants in the remoteness of the forest." Beyond the woods again was "the prairie and its loneliness and peace with a vast hawk hanging motionless in the sky."

From the setting and surrounding of this farm of his uncle was drawn much of Mark Twain's literary inspiration. Here was "Uncle Daniel," a middle-aged Negro slave, converted later into "Nigger Jim" of *Huckleberry Finn*. Indeed the whole farm, as Mark Twain himself explains in his autobiography, was adopted into the story; his uncle, John Quarles, becomes "Silas Phelps," and the farm is moved, uncle, aunt and all, down to Arkansas. "It was all of six hundred miles," he tells us proudly, "but it was no trouble. It was not a very large farm—five hundred acres, perhaps —but I could have done it if it had been twice as large."

Note how typical of Mark Twain's humour, on its mechanical side, is this wilful confusion between the form of words and the facts conveyed.

But though the Missouri farm supplied many of his fondest recollections in later life, the real boyhood home of Sam Clemens was the little town of Hannibal on the Missouri side of the Mississippi River. It was a "steamboat town," half-asleep and half-awake, with slavery drudging in the sunlit streets, and manufacture trying to start into life, and with the great river and the river steamers as its glory.

Here John Clemens settled as a "merchant," that is, kept store, with a random pursuit of the law. His election (as in Florida) to be a local justice of the peace kept alive his title of "judge." But the circumstances of the family drifted and oscillated between a respectable competence and poverty, till the untimely death of the judge made poverty an anchorage.

Hannibal was a slave town in a slave state, with the daily sight and use and custom of slavery as a part and parcel of its life accepted and unquestioned. This was before the time when the soil was torn and riven with the Kansas-Nebraska quarrel, and before yet the ground trembled with the approaching conflict. The aspect of slavery was as familiar to that generation as the aspect of slums and pauperism to the generation that followed it. And it passed with as little protest. It was part of life as people knew it, and it drew its sanction, or at least its apology, from the fact that it was there.

It was scarcely possible for an unschooled boy of a Missouri village to surpass in outlook the people among whom he lived. Mark Twain himself has told later in his autobiography, in a chapter written in the middle 'nineties, how "natural" slavery had seemed fifty years before.

"In my school days," he writes, "I had no aversion to slavery. I was not aware that there was anything wrong about it. No one arraigned it in my hearing; the local papers said nothing against it; the local pulpit taught us that God approved it, that it was a holy thing, and that the doubter need only look in the Bible if he wished to settle his mind."

Yet he never liked slavery, never accepted it. It ran counter to the simple principles of right and wrong, of equality and fairness, on which his mentality was based. Mark Twain always tried to think in elementary terms, to reduce everything to a plain elementary form and to judge it so. By this process much of his humour was formed, and all of his philosophy. He knew nothing of relativity, of things right in one place and wrong in another, righteous in one day and wicked in another. Into such a code slavery could not be made to fit.

Not that Mark Twain ever came out as a champion or a protagonist against slavery. He never came out as a champion or protagonist against anything—or never for long. The mental fatigue of being a champion was contrary to the spirit of his genius. There are in his books none of the fierce diatribes of Charles Dickens against the "American institution." But he grew to dislike it, and then to hate even the memory of it, and the references to it in his books are all the more scathing from this matter-of-fact realism.

Readers of *Huckleberry Finn* will recall the passage where Huck is accounting for his turning up at the Arkansas farm.

"It was the grounding of the steamer," he

explains to Aunt Sally, *"that kept us back. We blowed out a cylinder head."*

"Good gracious, anybody hurt?"

"No'm. Killed a nigger."

"Well, it's lucky; because sometimes people do get hurt."

Pages of argument and volumes of history could not say more than this.

But the real feature of the life of little Sam Clemens and his playmates and fellow-citizens in Hannibal was the Mississippi River. It flowed past the town in a majestic stream, a mile wide from Missouri to the Illinois shore, coming from the unknown wilderness of the North and moving on to the infinite distance of the Gulf of Mexico. What the sea is to the English children of the Channel coast, the Mississippi was to the children of the river towns of the Middle West.

These were the great days of the river. The railroad was still unknown in the West, the high-road non-existent, the motor-car and the aeroplane mere dreams of the scientist. Transport was all by water, and on the Mississippi and its great tributaries there was developed a system of passenger steamboat navigation, unique in all the world. Mark Twain himself has described in numberless passages in his *Life on the Mississippi* and in *Tom Sawyer* and *Huckleberry Finn* the glories of the Mississippi steamboat.

Till his father died, little Samuel Langhorne Clemens lived in Hannibal somewhere between affluence and poverty, unaware of either. He had his full share of the careless happiness of childhood, and the fine, free adventure of boyhood on the frontier. There was the river, and the islands, the forests beyond, and above all, the great cave under the river bluff below the town. Sam Clemens was Tom Sawyer, and the adventurous fun of his childhood has passed into the world's literature.

Of education he had but little. Till he was twelve years old he attended school in his native town. He learned to "read and write and cipher," as the phrase was, with a little elementary geography and history. Beyond that, nothing. High school he never saw; college he never knew. Nearly all that he acquired he picked up for himself. He seems to have carried in himself a native desire for information, in particular for facts and figures, which was perhaps increased and strengthened by the early cessation of his schooling. In the preface to one of his books (*Roughing It*), he tells us that "information stewed out of him naturally like the precious attar of roses from the otter." This may or may not have been true. But, at any rate, information all through his life "stewed *into* him." He was fond of facts and figures, guidebooks and statistics. He liked to calculate how many feet and inches there would be in a "light year," and such things as that.

There seem, indeed, to be two distinct means by which a man of native genius may succeed in life. The one is by receiving a sound and complete education; the other by not getting any at all. It is likely that if Mark Twain had attended college and learned to rehearse the wisdom of other men and to repeat the standardized judgments of the past, he would have been badly damaged by the process. It is the crowning triumph of his life that Oxford in his old age should have awarded him its honorary degree, doctor of literature. But if he had ever earned and received its B.A., it would probably have knocked all the "Mark Twain" out of him.

When John Clemens died, school ended for his son and work began. He had a brother, Orion Clemens, ten years older than himself, who had already taken up the trade of a printer. Sam followed his example, became a printer's apprentice "for his board and clothes," and for ten years—from 1847 till 1857—followed the trade. As far as the record goes, these seem to be the dreariest and least significant years of his life. He worked at first as an apprentice in his home town, then assisted his brother Orion (in 1850), in getting out a sheet called the *Hannibal Journal*. He even contributed two sketches to the *Saturday Evening Post* of Philadelphia; they were accepted without pay and never identified. In 1853 he set out to see the world, printing as he saw it; worked on the *Evening News* in St. Louis; then visited New York and Philadelphia, working in both places; and so after two years back to join his brother in Keokuk (Iowa), printing still.

There is but little surviving intimate account of this youthful period of Mark Twain's life. A few letters sent to his family from New York and elsewhere have been preserved. They seem to differ in nothing from any other letters written by any young man who had come to New York from the Far West and describes to the home folk such marvels of the Latting Observatory, "height about 280 feet," and the Croton Aqueduct, "which could supply every family in New York with a hundred barrels of water a day." Among such touches of rustic wonder one looks in vain for the signs of emerging genius. Yet at least they reflect industrious days of hard work at the printer's case, and long evenings spent in devouring books from the free printers' library. Meantime he is saving up money so that he may take his mother for a trip to Kentucky next spring. "Tell ma," he writes, "that my promises are faithfully kept." The "promises" referred to a pledge which his mother had imposed, one might say inflicted, on him in the formula, "I do solemnly swear that I will not throw a card or drink a drop of liquor while I am gone."

Thus early in Mark Twain's life there entered a conflict between his natural ideas of conduct and belief and the pietistic code which he accepted from those he loved—his mother, his wife, his domestic circle. This conflict has been called by one of his most interesting critics the "ordeal" of his life. It never left him, and he carried it, so to speak, beyond the grave in the works that he wrote for publication when he should be dead. Mark Twain never really believed in the creed and the code of those who dictated to him. But he preferred, as it were, to accept it and then to rebel against it. His was that characteristic American attitude, at least for the America of his day, of alternating between prayer and profanity, emotional belief and iconoclastic denial, asceticism and a spree, hard work and a bust, cold water and raw rum—with nowhere a happy medium, an accepted path and way. Out of this national phase of development has sprung much of the legislation of the United States, and most of the worst of it. Mark Twain was in this, as in all else, a true American.

The sturdy and robust intelligence of young Sam Clemens need not have fortified itself with an oath against the temptations of a king

on cardboard. On the other hand, the fact remains that young Sam Clemens the printer lived straight and worked hard, and kept adding every day to his knowledge of the Croton Aqueduct and the Latting Observatory. No doubt he was not very distinguishable from other young printers also not "throwing" a card. Jumping on and off the water waggon, getting religion and losing it, swearing off cards and swearing on again, are favourite American performances, unknown to older and duller civilizations.

But the printer's trade was not destined to claim young Sam Clemens as its own, nor the cities of the East to contain his spirit. There seems to have been in him a certain restlessness calling him afar. As nearly as the boy could interpret it, the call was for South America—at that time a vague, almost fabulous land of gold-mines and revolutions. To get to the Amazon—his proposed destination —he left his job at Cincinnati (whither he had wandered again from Keokuk) and took ship on the river steamer *Paul Jones,* which brought him as far as New Orleans. Beyond that, fortune showed no means of attaining the Amazon. But in return it threw in his way, as he wandered about the levee and the wharves of New Orleans, an opportunity that he had coveted in vain for years—the chance to become a pilot's apprentice on the great river. With that the first period of Mark Twain's career—his servitude as a printer—came to an end, and gave place to the open life of the river and the Far West that was to fashion his genius and inspire his thought.

II. LIFE ON THE MISSISSIPPI, 1857-1861

When the youthful Sam Clemens turned his back on printing to follow his fortune on the river and in the West, he may be said, in a modern overworked phrase, to have "found himself." Put very simply, he turned into Mark Twain.

It was the West, the river and the prairie, the Nevada desert and the Rocky Mountains and the sunlit shores of the Pacific, and with it the new civilization of the West, raw but virile, that nurtured the genius that never could have blossomed in a New York boarding-house or a Philadelphia printing-room.

The West made Mark Twain. All that he wrote has its basis there. It supplies the point of view, the "eye of innocence," with which he was able later on to look upon Europe. His western life began on the Mississippi River. It resumed the play of childhood, broken ten years before.

Readers of the book that was published later as *Life on the Mississippi* do not need to be reminded of the romance, the interest and the humours of Mark Twain's pilot days. He has told the story so well that no one can follow him. The fascination of the river steamers, the pomp and luxury with which they seemed to glitter in an age of ox-waggons, mules, frame-houses and log churches, make the position of the pilot, seated sky-high in the pilot-house, almost one of majesty. Mark Twain, as a young man, had no higher ambition than to go on the river as a pilot. No doubt, in the dull hours of trying to set "10,000 ems of type a day," he often dreamed himself just such a sky-high pilot, the envy of mankind. In vain he had often sought an opening. And now by chance fate threw it in his way when he was stranded in New Orleans looking vainly towards South America. Chance threw him into the company of one Mr. Horace Bixby, a famous pilot of his day, and afterwards his lifelong friend. He agreed with the young man to "teach him the Mississippi River from New Orleans to St. Louis" for the sum of five hundred dollars chargeable against his future wages.

Mark Twain records how he "entered on the small enterprise of 'learning' twelve or thirteen hundred miles of the Mississippi River" with easy confidence, and records how he felt disillusioned, appalled and hopeless to find that he must know the river not only by day but in total darkness, not only upwards but downwards, not only at high water but at any water; must learn to follow all the shifts of sand-bars and snags, and that, too, at a day when the Mississippi bore neither buoys nor lights to indicate its tortuous channels. "If my ears hear aright," he reflected, in the course of his early instruction, "I have not only to get the names of all the towns and islands and bends, but I must get up a warm personal acquaintance with every old snag and one-limbed cotton-wood and obscure wood-pile

that ornaments the banks of this river for twelve hundred miles!"

What is more, he did it. Within eighteen months he got his licence; before the job ended (with the Civil War) he was second to few on the river. His knowledge of the great river and his abiding feeling for it became part of his life and the inspiration, as in the pages of *Huckleberry Finn,* of the finest of his work.

From his Mississippi days Samuel Clemens also carried away his pen-name of Mark Twain, which presently nullified the work of his godfather's and godmother's.

The origin of the *nom de plume* runs thus: "Mark Twain" is the pilot's designation for two fathoms of water. Now it happened that there was in Sam Clemens's pilot days an ancient and experienced pilot, a Captain Sellers, who sometimes contributed to the New Orleans papers little bits of wisdom and forecast about the river, as crude in form as they were valuable in fact. These contributions to the press were signed "Mark Twain." Clemens, still something of a journalist at heart, wrote a little burlesque of his senior's prophecies which called forth a laugh that echoed up the Mississippi—and incidentally broke old Sellers's heart with its ridicule. Young Clemens learned for ever a lesson in the cruelty of "fun," and seldom sinned again. But later on, when Sellers was dead and beyond injury, he annexed the pen-name for himself.

Mark Twain's pilot days were ended by the outbreak of the Civil War and the blockade of the river. He succeeded in getting north from New Orleans to his own State on the last boat that got up the river (January 1861). The part he took at the opening of the war was unheroic if not inglorious. He enlisted, as a Confederate, in some sort of irregular band which professed to be cavalry. Their aim was to "liberate the soil of Missouri"—from what, it was not clearly understood.

But Mark Twain dropped out of the conflict almost at once and saw nothing of warfare. He himself has narrated the episode with that characteristic mixture of fact and exaggeration which baffles foreign readers in all his "western" books, in his sketch called *A Campaign That Failed.*

But the truth is that his heart was not in

the Civil War on either side. His common sense showed him that the war, in spite of the urgent denials of President Lincoln and the rest, had something to do with slavery. He could not fight to maintain *that*. But he was equally far from being a "Yankee." His brief sojourn as a youth at New York and Philadelphia was that of a stranger in a strange land. Of New England and its traditions of liberty, piety, intolerance and "culture" he as yet knew nothing at all; nor ever sympathized with it later. His heart was neither in the North nor the South, but in the new West.

Thither he decided to go. His older brother, Orion Clemens, had contrived to secure an appointment as secretary of the new territory of Nevada. Sam Clemens offered to go along with his brother as "private secretary to the secretary," an office which he himself describes as a "unique sinecure," there being "nothing to do and no salary." Indeed, it was Sam Clemens's savings as a pilot which financed the journey to the West, his brother Orion being invited by the United States, as was Mr. Pickwick by the Pickwick Club, to travel at his own expense.

These, of course, were the days of the rise of the American West, from a vast untraversed wilderness to an El Dorado of gold and silver. The gold discoveries in California had started the "forty-niners" on the trail. In the decade following, a flock of prospectors found their way into the mountains and disclosed the fabulous wealth of silver-bearing loads of the district of the Carson Valley, a part of the Mormon territory of Utah. It was the organization of this district as the territory of Nevada which gave to the two Clemens brothers the opportunity of taking part in the western movement. To get to Nevada they must go overland by the stage. There was as yet no railway across the continent, nor was there till some years after the Civil War. To reach California one might make the stormy voyage around Cape Horn; or choose the dangerous Isthmus route, by Panama or Nicaragua; or the stage route over the prairies and mountains. For Nevada the stage route—only seventeen hundred miles!—was the obvious choice.

Behold, then, the Clemens brothers mounting the coach at St. Jo, Missouri, climbing up on the mail-sacks to bid farewell to warfare in the East and seek peace among the savages.

III. ROUGHING IT IN THE WEST, 1861-1866

Orion Clemens, secretary for the territory of Nevada, and his brother Sam, ex-pilot and retired Confederate soldier, set out from St. Jo for Carson City, Nevada, on the 26th of July 1861. Before them was seventeen hundred miles of prairie, mountain and desert, and nineteen days of glorious transit.

Mark Twain, in his book called *Roughing It,* has recalled in his own way his experience of the journey. There is no doubt of the exhilaration, the excitement, the thrill of it. But his account of it, like all his western books, is a standing perplexity to many of his British admirers. Where do the facts end and the lies begin? How much is statistical fact and how much is sheer exuberant exaggeration? For instance, is there, asks the reader, such an animal as the "Jackass Rabbit"? Is it true that such an animal sits and "thinks about its sins," and then moves off so fast that "long after he is out of sight you can hear him whizz"? Many British readers have felt that this is open to doubt.

Or take the account of the Mormon Settlement at Salt Lake. Is it really true that Brigham Young looked round to find one of his children and then gave up and said, "I thought I would have known the little cub again, but I don't"? Seems a little hard to believe, doesn't it? Or again, is the water in the Humbolt county so full of alkali that it is like lye? or the water in Lake Tahoe so clear that one can see through eighty feet of it? or is there a "washoe" wind which upsets stagecoaches and which blows so hard in Carson City as to account for the prevalence of so many bald-headed people, and which is described as a "soaring dust drift about the size of the United States"?

In this wonderland of marvel and adventure the American reader easily finds his way. He knows by instinct that Mark Twain did *not* hear the same story told about Horace Greeley four hundred and eighty-four times; and he knows, on the other hand, that the claims staked out on the Ophir mine *were* worth four thousand dollars a foot; and that

Mark and his friends *were* caught at night in a snowstorm and *did* actually give themselves up for lost and huddle to sleep in the snow, waking to find a hotel forty-five feet away. But he does not believe the story, told in another connection, of the group of congressmen snowbound on a western train, driven at last to cannibalism and making their choice of successive victims with the proper forms of legislative procedure. One is reminded of poor John Bright's perplexity over hearing Mark Twain's contemporary, Artemus Ward, lecture in London. "Many of the young man's statements," he said, "appear overdrawn and open to question." Mark Twain himself has humorously explained this western method of his narration. "I speak," he says in the *Innocents Abroad,* "of the north shore of Lake Tahoe, where one can count the scales on a trout at a depth of a hundred and eighty feet. I have tried to get this statement off at par here [he is writing from Europe], but with no success; so I have been obliged to negotiate it at fifty per cent discount. At this rate I find some takers; perhaps the reader will receive it on the same terms, ninety feet instead of a hundred and eighty." What is one to make of this? It seems to be giving the reader "what the traffic will bear."

But though overdrawn in the single statement, Mark Twain's western writings give in their entirety a wonderful and fascinating picture of the new land of hope. It has all passed away so long ago and the country changed so completely that perhaps the fascination is all the greater. "Where once the silent prairie saw the Indian and the scout, the Swede with alcoholic breath sets rows of cabbage out,"—so has a later songster chronicled the passing of frontier west.

Mark Twain's western life lasted in all some five and a half years. From his sinecure duties as secretary he turned to mining, caught for a time the fever of the day, and once only missed a fortune by quitting his washing-out of pay dirt a few bucketsful too soon. By a natural and easy transition he turned to journalism. These were the palmy days of the little local paper, favoured by isolation, springing up as easily as mushrooms and cultivated by hand. Such papers were the natural ground for local jests and squibs, and the practical

jokes and hoaxes which passed for fun with the people of eighty years ago.

Sam Clemens, working as a surface miner, began contributing a little to a paper called the *Territorial Enterprise,* published by Joe Goodman at Virginia City. The editor—who was also the proprietor—was struck by the quality of the sketches, and sent to the writer a proposal to join in the editorship at a salary of twenty-five dollars a week. Clemens dropped the pick and shovel, walked a hundred and thirty miles to take over the job, and with that stepped into a new life.

At the time when Sam Clemens abandoned mining and betook himself definitely to journalism (August 1862), he was twenty-six years old. He was a robust-looking young man with a mop of sandy hair turning to auburn and a blue eye filled with life and intelligence. In his infancy he had been a puny child, but the outdoor life of farm and bush and river had done its work and had presently endowed him with that deep-seated energy and vital power which is the birthright of the frontiersman.

As a young and rising pilot he had liked to make himself in point of dress a mirror of fashion. As a miner he did the exact opposite, outdoing his fellows in the careless roughness of his dress and the lazy slouch of his walk. He possessed, and accentuated by use, a slow and drawling speech. In short, he tried to make himself a "character," and succeeded to the full measure of his wish. A large part of his popularity and his local reputation in his Nevada days sprang from the attraction of this easy and careless manner and appearance. Second nature though it became, there was beneath it an eager and a restless mind, filled in his mining days with the fever of the search for gold, dreaming of fortune. At times even his robust health broke under the strain of the intensity of his pursuit of fortune.

But the outside world saw nothing of this. By nature easy and optimistic, on the surface at least, he enjoyed at this time all the careless exuberance of the morning of life, while his easy disposition and his peculiar cast of thought and drollery of speech endeared him to those about him. Many of the friends he made at this time he made for life, such as

Horace Bixby his pilot-master, Joe Goodman and Steve Gillis of the *Enterprise*.

By disposition Mark Twain was peaceful rather than belligerent. He lived in a rough world among rough men, with untamed Indians, desperadoes and outlaws as part of the environment of a western life. Under such circumstances no one could venture to be timorous, but Mark was at least not looking for a fight. He himself has described his feelings on finding himself in close contact with Slade, the most notorious "bad man" and "dead shot" of the West—afterwards to be hanged by the Vigilantes of Montana. Slade was at that time in charge of one of the eating-places of the Overland Company. "He was about to take some coffee," says the author of *Roughing It,* "when he saw that my cup was empty. He politely offered to fill it, but although I wanted it, I politely declined. I was afraid he had not killed anybody that morning and might be needing diversion."

Never was man more happily cast in his lot than young Sam Clemens when he joined the *Territorial Enterprise.* If he had become a reporter on the staff of an ordinary paper, he would have sickened rapidly at the drudgery of the task, the circumscribed round of duty, the necessity of carrying out the commands and ideas of other men. In fact, he did so sicken of it when later he held such a position as a reporter in San Francisco, and even as an editor and part-proprietor in Buffalo. But the *Enterprise* was an entirely different matter. The public of the roaring mining settlements cared nothing about foreign dispatches and world politics. Even the sound of the great war tearing the soil of the continent came faintly across the intervening two thousand miles. What the readers wanted was local stuff—news of robberies, scraps, lucky finds— and above all, such was the mood of the time and place, local "fun" about "local" characters, personal touches, practical jokes, lies, and interchange of sarcastic "cracks" between rival papers. For all this stuff "Mark Twain" and his fellows were given a free hand. They wrote what they felt like writing; they were not so much "reporters" as "minstrels." Looking back now on the surviving fragments of what Mark Twain wrote then, we can see emerging in it the outline of a clear and beautiful style,

we can see already a striking power of phrase to convey the sights and sounds of nature. But we could hardly see all this except in the light of what happened after. In and of themselves Mark Twain's western sketches are of no account. Here, for example, is the *Petrified Man,* which set the camp in a roar because they appreciated it as the "crack" at the local coroner who was supposed to hold an inquest over a body turned to rock centuries ago. But the story got somehow into the eastern papers as a fact, and that to the western mind was funnier still. The people in the West at that time seemed to have been moved to Homeric laughter every time they told a huge lie and got someone to believe it. Here again is *My Bloody Massacre,* as entirely imaginary as the *Petrified Man,* but meant as a slap against a California mining company. The terrific joke lay in the fact that the "Massacre" was committed—in the story— at a place where it couldn't have happened. The eastern papers, not knowing the locality, copied the story as an item of crime, at which the West slapped Mark on the back and roared again.

Into such life and such work the character of Sam Clemens fitted as into a mould. His skits and "take-offs" and "write-ups" became the delight of the territory. When he presently went to Carson City to "write up" the legislature, he became about as important as the legislature itself and far more popular.

This may well have been the happiest time of Mark Twain's life. He and his fellow-minstrels led a roaring life, painting the town red, drinking imported champagne at the French restaurant, playing cards all night and practical jokes all day. Into their midst one day blew the young man Charles F. Browne (Artemus Ward), for whom the world still has a smile and a tear. He was of the same stamp and kind as Clemens, but his feet were already higher on the ladder of success. He was "lecturing" in his own droll way, about anything or nothing, making money, touching Heaven and raising Hell. He "caught on" instantly to Mark Twain, not as a local "cut-up," but as a real genius—urged him to strike out, to come East, to conquer the world.

There is something in the life of a new and roaring settlement—a mining town, a boom town—cut off from the rest of the world, which intensifies local interest, local character, and local personality. All men seem giants. All character is exceptional. All jokes become a roar. All lives appear intense. All episodes become Homeric and historic. Read, if one will, the history of early San Francisco or talk with the surviving old-timers of the Manitoba boom.

Such was the setting supplied for Mark Twain by the environment of Virginia City. "Mark Twain" he was now by deliberate designation. The name was first signed to an *Enterprise* article of February 2, 1863. Henceforth he was Mark for the West.

The merry journalistic life at Virginia City was ended in a duel, the outcome of some particularly insulting jokes. How serious or how comic the duel was, Heaven only knows. The account given in *Roughing It* is at least, like all else in that great work, partly true. But the new Territory in a moral moment had passed a law against duelling, and Mark Twain had to "skip out." He skipped to San Francisco. There he got a real place as a real reporter on the *Call*, a job which soon put the iron into his soul. It was no part of his nature to work at a routine task in a routine way. The management of the *Call* soon found him listless and careless in his work and "let him go." But he stayed on in San Francisco for a while—according to his own account, a poor outcast mendicant on the fringe of want. But this is only a legend, the western lie reasserting itself. In reality he never lacked the means of support; he wrote daily "letters" for his old paper, the *Enterprise,* and did some "pieces" for the *Californian Magazine,* and did very well. More than that, he was thrown in with Bret Harte and the group of young men whose genius was ripening under the favouring isolation of the Pacific Coast.

But again his journalism got him into trouble. His letters to the Virginia City *Enterprise* denouncing municipal corruption in San Francisco hurt the feelings of the city police. They decided to make it hot for him. On which Mark Twain again skipped out, this time to the hills. Here he found refuge at the mining camp of Jim Gillis, the "truthful James" of Bret Harte, a brother of the Steve Gillis of Nevada. Here and in the near-by Calaveras County Mark Twain spent the rainy winter of 1864-65, scratching round for surface gold and listening to the endless yarns of the miners in the bar-room of Angel's Camp (see Bret Harte for *Abner Dean of Angel's*). Here was a solemn jackass who used to repeat to the point of weariness a solemn story about a frog—a jumping frog into which someone put shot to shut it out in what the Germans would call a frog-jump-money-bet-competition, and the English an "open frog jump." Mark Twain wrote up the story and sent it to New York for Artemus Ward's funny book. It missed the book, drifted into a newspaper, and became the famous *Jumping Frog* —vastly admired by those who haven't read it. But long before the *Jumping Frog* had found its way into print, its author had thrown down pick and shovel (missing a snug little fortune by one bucketful of dirt) and drifted back to San Francisco.

Here then was Mark Twain at the age of thirty, the period of his western life drawing to a close, his career of success about to begin. His biographers have greatly exaggerated the amount of his achievement at this period. His western success as a journalist and a wit was purely local. A few of his "pieces" had drifted into the eastern papers, but the world at large had never heard of him.

Indeed, nothing that he had written was of any real value. The *Jumping Frog* he himself declared to be "a villainous backwoods sketch," and he was just about right. We are told that when it appeared in the New York press it set all America in a roar. This is nonsense. Even the America of 1865 did not roar so easily as that. The legend rests on the phrase of a California correspondent in New York who sent home items to a home paper, and is merely the kind of legend that grows up round the life-story of a great man. The truth is that Mark Twain was practically unknown, and deserved to be.

But now things changed. A San Francisco newspaper offered the young man a job as a special correspondent to go forth and "write up" the Sandwich Islands, in those days (1865) an unknown paradise, lost in the Pacific. Mark Twain undertook the task and carried it out with wonderful success; saw, traversed, explored, and described the islands as no one else could have done; and sent also to his paper, by a piece of journalistic good luck, the first news of a disaster at sea—a "scoop" of the first magnitude. His Sandwich Islands letters attracted great attention in California. They well deserved it. Apart from any incidental humour, they reveal that power of vivid description, that marvellous facility in conveying the sights and sounds in nature, which henceforth constitutes one of the distinctive charms of Mark Twain's work. He returned to San Francisco in a blaze of glory.

The blaze was rapidly turned to a conflagration. His friends persuaded him to give a lecture on his Sandwich Islands trip. This was new. Until now Mark had spoken a few times "for fun" and made a burlesque speech or two on Carson City politics. But to attempt to talk for *money*—for a dollar a seat in a big public place—to be *"funny"* on a platform at a set hour, was as new and exciting as it was terrifying. His friends shoved him to it and took the biggest theatre in town. Mark advertised that the *"doors open at seven o'clock. The trouble begins at eight o'clock,"* and in due course found himself thrust out before the lights, a huge manuscript in his hand, to receive a welcoming roar of applause that must be repaid in services. An hour or so later, when he ended his talk that had been carried along in billows of laughter, he left the platform with his head among the clouds, and on it a golden crown (October 2, 1866).

This was the beginning of his success as a lecturer, unrivalled except by that of his senior contemporary, Charles Dickens. The lecture on the Sandwich Islands was carried around the State of California and repeated in theatres, in halls, and on improvised platforms in mining camps, amid a continuous roar of laughter.

Mark Twain was now "started" in earnest. He dreamed of wider fields—of a trip around the world. Alexander the Great wanted to conquer the world, Mark Twain wanted to write it up. He determined to follow the rising star of his success, to reverse the advice of Horace Greeley to his contemporaries and to "go East." He made a rough-and-ready arrangement with the *Alta* newspaper for sending them letters from somewhere or anywhere, then set off on the steamship *America*

on December 15, 1866, to reach the east of the Isthmus route, and landed in New York on January 11, 1867. The Innocent was abroad.

IV. INNOCENTS ABROAD AND AT HOME, 1867-1870

When Mark Twain landed in New York in January of 1867, he had in his mind an idea of travelling round the world and writing letters about it. But he was still a little vague as to how to begin. He started writing "letters" from New York to the *Alta* of San Francisco, made a trip to the Mississippi to see his mother at St. Louis, visited his native town of Hannibal, made arrangements about publishing a book of sketches, and then opportunity came to him, just as it should, at the opportune moment.

He learned that the luxurious paddle-wheel steamer *Quaker City* would leave New York on an excursion trip across the Atlantic to the Mediterranean and the Holy Land. The ship would be "provided with every necessary comfort, including library and musical instruments"; it would carry "an experienced physician"; it would proceed—but it is unnecessary to give further details. All the world knows of the *Quaker City* and its cargo of Innocents Abroad.

Mark Twain leaped at the chance. He proposed to the proprietors of the *Alta* that he should go on the excursion. They accepted the offer, forwarded his passage money, and promised him twenty dollars a letter for his correspondence.

To the elation caused by this prospect there was added just before he sailed the satisfaction of another laurel in his new crown of success. His friend, "Governor Frank Fuller"—governor once of Utah and hence "Governor" for ever—was in New York. He insisted that Mark should lecture; prophesied fame and a fortune, took the Cooper Institute and advertised "a serio-humorous lecture concerning Kanakadom," by "Mark Twain" (there was no Mr. Clemens any more). At the last moment it began to seem clear, to the lecturer's horror, that nobody was coming. Mark Twain as yet was not worth fifty cents. A great flood of free tickets was sent to all the school teachers within range. The lecture was given in a hall crowded to capacity, to an audience suffocated with laughter. Financially the lecture was a failure: it cost $500; the receipts were $300. The generous "Governor" made good the deficit. "It's all right, Mark," he said; "the fortune didn't come, but the fame has arrived."

And on June 8, 1867, in the glow of a new notoriety, Mark Twain sailed as one of the "lions" of the *Quaker City*.

The sea voyage, as judged by our pampered standards of today, was dingy and drab enough. The paddle-wheel steamer, luxurious in 1867, would seem cramped and dim today; the speed a crawl. The passenger list contained a high percentage of ministers of the Gospel, spinsters and teachers, whose moral worth is out of proportion to their value as fun. In these days when all the women are young enough to dance, and all the girls are old enough to drink, the "Innocents" seem a pretty dusty crowd. "Debates" in the evening in the saloon seem poor stuff in an age of jazz music and radio. But after all, they had with them the unregenerate American bar, that covered a multitude of sins, and was worth more than a floating palace, dry.

The excursionists "did" the Continent, from Paris to the Crimea, with Asia to the Holy Land and Africa to the pyramids. They got their money's worth. Without Mark Twain they would have been only a set of spectacled American tourists, thumbing their guidebooks, and trying to admire Giotto and remember when Vermicelli lived. Mark Twain waved over them the magic wand of inspired genius, and turned them into the merry group of Innocents Abroad, whose pilgrimage is part of history. The letters which he sent home to the *Alta* in California and to the *Tribune* in New York reached the public this time—east, west, and everywhere—and deserved to. When the boat returned to America (November 19, 1867), Mark Twain stepped off the *Quaker City* a celebrity. He had gone away a lamb—or at best a western mustang—he came back a lion.

Success greeted him on his return like a tidal wave. All of a sudden, it seemed, the American nation knew him and acclaimed him. His success was not as sudden, as sweeping and as phenomenal as that of Dickens after the *Pickwick Papers*. But it was second only to it. And it had in it the same ingredient of personal affection. The public took Mark to its heart, as England had taken young "Boz"; and with an added feeling of national pride unknown and unnecessary in the case of Dickens. Here was, at last, an *American* author. The Longfellows and the Hawthornes and the Fenimore Coopers had written English literature in America. Here at last was a man who wrote American literature, and wrote it in and on Europe. The publication of the *Innocents Abroad* was the first step in the Americanization of Europe now reaching its climax.

No wonder success came in a flood. A lecture bureau offered him a contract for eighteen nights at a hundred dollars a night. A western senator wanted him as literary secretary. The New York *Tribune* put him on their staff. All of the papers—the *Tribune,* the *Herald,* the San Francisco *Alta,* the Chicago press, the magazines, wanted letters and articles. And meanwhile his first book, *The Celebrated Jumping Frog of Calaveras County and Other Sketches,* which had appeared (May 1, 1867) just before the *Quaker City* left, was on the market and selling.

Bigger things were to come.

In Hartford, Connecticut, was a sagacious and wide-minded publisher, Elisha Bliss of the American Publishing Company. He saw at once the mine of humour, and of gold, in Mark Twain's work. He proposed to bring out the *Quaker City* letters as a book of travel. It was Mark Twain's visits to Hartford to consult with Bliss that made his first connection with that town—presently to be his home—and his friendship with the Reverend "Joe" Twitchell, henceforth his closest associate. The book arrangements, generous enough, were soon made.

Then came a hitch. The *Alta* people, having paid for the *Quaker City* trip and paid for the letters that described it, had got the idea in their heads that the literary material was theirs, and proposed to publish it. Hearing this, Mark Twain was consumed with fury at "the *Alta* thieves." It is unfortunate how often in his literary life Mark Twain felt that he was being cheated by a pack of rogues, and how many were the associations and friendships shattered thereby. Like most geniuses, he alternated in his view of his work between utter despair and absolute conceit. He was thus inclined to be first grateful to people for helping him, then angry with them for cheating him.

In the case of the *Alta,* he did an amazing but a wise thing. Letters and telegraphs could serve no purpose. He decided to "see the thieves face to face," set off for California (1868)—by sea, via Aspinwall. Once on the spot he easily persuaded the *Alta* people—noble fellows now and not thieves—to let go their claims. He only stayed long enough in San Francisco to deliver a lecture on the *Quaker City* trip—a pandemonium of success. Then on July 2, 1868, he made, at a dinner, a speech of farewell to the wonderland of the West, which he never saw again.

Back in New York (July 28, 1868), he picked up again the golden thread of success. The ensuing season was spent in getting his new book ready and in a triumphant lecture tour of the cities of the East. His lecture was called "A Vandal Abroad." He floated from place to place on a rising tide of national admiration. Money rolled in a flood. The season, his first on the platform, netted him $8000 in some sixty nights. Mr. Paine, his matchless biographer, quotes for us a contemporary journalist's impression at the time.

"Mark Twain is a man of medium height, about five feet ten, sparsely built, with dark reddish-brown hair and moustache. His features are fair, his eyes keen and twinkling. He dresses in scrupulous evening attire. In lecturing he hangs about the desk, leaning on it, or flirting around the corners of it, then marching or counter-marching in the rear of it. He seldom casts a glance at his manuscript."

Strangely enough, at this period, even with the exceptional success that had crowned his lecturing and the literary reputation, if not fame, that his writing had brought, Mark Twain did not yet think of himself as an author, or contemplate writing as his profession. He looked on himself as a journalist, a newspaperman, and his mind still ran rather in terms of a flow of "funny pieces" than the creation of a masterpiece. Indeed, up to this time, America took him still as a "funny man," not an author, and he followed, as we all do, the estimate of his fellows. He therefore looked about for a newspaper opening, bought with his accumulated surplus (one won't say "savings"; he never saved) a share in the Buffalo *Express,* and sat down at the editorial desk (August 14, 1869). He proposed evidently to use the desk in the old Nevada fashion, for he announced to his readers, "I shall not often meddle with politics because we have a political editor who is already excellent and only needs to serve a term or two in the penitentiary to be perfect. I shall not write any poetry unless I conceive a spite against the subscribers."

This cheerful form of editing, combined with lecturing and writing sketches for the *Galaxy* magazine in New York, kept him at work for the year 1869.

But meantime a new inspiration to effort and a greater happiness than fame had come into Mark Twain's life. He had met the girl who was to be his wife, he had entered on that lifelong devotion which only ended at the grave. Among the pilgrims of the *Quaker City* had been a young man from Elmira, New York, by name Charlie Langdon. One day (it was in the Bay of Smyrna) Langdon showed to his friend Clemens a beautiful little miniature of his beloved sister Olivia Langdon. As with David Copperfield and Dora, it was all over. Mark Twain fell so deeply in love that he never again came to the surface.

A month or so after the return of the pilgrims, the Langdons were in New York and young Charlie invited his celebrated friend to dine with them at the old St. Nicholas Hotel. There Mark Twain saw and loved at sight the girl of his day-dreams. After dinner they went to Steinway Hall to hear a lecture by the world-famous Charles Dickens, now on his second American tour (the first was twenty-six years before) and carrying all before him —including the remnants of his own strength and life—in the tumult of his success. It is strange to think of Mark Twain, seated beside his frail little sweetheart—she was that to his mind already—listening to Dickens's impassioned rendering of the storm scene in *David Copperfield.*

The dinner party was followed by a call,

and a little later by an invitation to visit the family at Elmira; also by Mark Twain "dropping in" during a lecture tour. In fact, it was soon clear that this impetuous young man was "courting Livy." Knowing a celebrity is one thing; letting him "court Livy" is another.

For Olivia Langdon was in complete contrast to her dynamic lover. She was as delicate as he was robust, as devout as he was sceptical, as orthodox as he was unconventional. For years, in consequence of a fall, she had been an invalid. Then she had been healed, through a sort of miracle, by a faith-healer. It left her with a deep sense of religious faith, that any doubt or irreverence wounded to the heart. But marriages are made in heaven—or were, in that Victorian age. To obtain the hand of Livy Langdon young Mr. Clemens, after the fashion of the time, must obtain the consent of her father and the approval of all her family. Now the Langdons were well-to-do people of the merchant class, orthodox, conventional, devout. To them, Mark Twain, arriving in a queer suit of clothes, with a shock of red hair, a piercing eye, an intensity of intelligence masked with a drawling speech, was an arresting personality. He appeared as an uncouth genius, an uncut diamond, a dynamo. About him was the aureole of celebrity, somewhat dazzling to plain people. But it is one thing to feel flattered in having an uncut diamond or a dynamo in the parlour. It is another thing to give to it your fragile, innocent daughter. The more so as young Charlie Langdon must have known that the dynamo had a profane tongue, or worse, and a mind sceptical to the verge of sin.

Hence the courtship met, if not with opposition from the family, at least with a certain inertia. But love, as Mr. Robert Benchley has said, conquers all. Mr. Jarvis Langdon, shrewd after his degree, forgave the young lover and gave the family consent to an engagement that was announced on February 4, 1869. Nor did he do things by halves. Without the knowledge of his prospective son-in-law he bought and furnished a house in Buffalo (472 Delaware Avenue) and turned it over as a fairy gift for the wedding day (February 2, 1870).

Behold then Samuel L. Clemens—now become for everybody Mark Twain, the great American humorist—the rough days of his western life put behind him, settled down at number 472 Delaware Avenue, Buffalo, trying hard to be respectable. Here he lives the model life of a family man, joins in morning prayer and listens as best he can to the daily reading of the Scriptures. More than that, he even makes desperate efforts to give up smoking.

He has his wife at his side, his desk at his elbow, and the world at his feet. After all, what does tobacco matter? Let's have another chapter of Deuteronomy.

V. THE FLOOD-TIDE OF SUCCESS, 1870-1877

On Mark Twain's wedding day his publishers handed him a cheque for $4000, as his royalty for three months' sale of the *Innocents Abroad*. The book was a success from the start; over 30,000 copies (at three dollars and a half) were sold in five months. The sales never stopped. We are told by those who know, that the *Innocents Abroad* is still the most widely sold travel book there is. The money received was the beginning of the phenomenal returns of Mark Twain's writings and plays and lectures. They should have made him a rich man. They never did. All his life he moved with a dark shadow of debt just behind him; always about to emerge into the sunshine of unbounded wealth, and never reaching it. In the end the shadow covered all the horizon; but as yet it was only a small dark cloud in a clear sky.

The book, *The Innocents Abroad, or the New Pilgrims' Progress,* deserves all its success. It could not be written again. The time has passed. Travel is too common, the world too completely unified, to leave room for Innocents. Everybody has been everywhere—at least through the magic door of the moving-picture house. But in those days world-travel was still new. The book was read for its wonderful pictures of foreign scenery and foreign cities and queer foreign people; it was read for the intense light in which it revealed the past—the monuments, the art, the catacombs, the history of Europe. It was read by Americans for its intense scorn of the bygone tyranny of the old world. But more than for all these reasons put together (and multiplied), it was read because it was "funny."

The first day out at sea, with the sea-sick old gentleman murmuring "Oh my!"—the Italian guide being rebuked in the matter of Christopher Columbus—the sheer burlesque thrown in to "modernize" the gladiatorial fights of Rome—these things remain in the mind of readers for a lifetime. It is an amazing book, that seldom flags and never stops, undisfigured as yet by the prolixity that grew into Mark Twain's later writing—the garrulousness of self-assured old age.

It is the point of view that appeals. The book represents Europe as seen from the Rocky Mountains, Rome as interpreted from Carson City. Mark Twain in all his life and work saw only two things, Western America and Europe. Of the East (meaning the Eastern States) he was unaware. He lived in it, worked in it, and died in it, but he never saw it. The East was just his audience. A good actor never sees them.

The success of the *Innocents Abroad* not only reached over America but spread to England. Indeed it was in England that Mark Twain was first recognized as an "author," as a man of literary genius, by people of taste and cultivation. In America he was the delight of the uncultivated West; to the "culture" of New England he was still regarded as an amusing western "cut-up," not to be classed, of course, with the solemn Emersons and the dignified Longfellows. Thus ever does enthroned dullness guard its sovereignty.

Seated thus in his new chair in Buffalo, Mark Twain planned all sorts of literary projects. It is amazing, from now on, how much he planned and never started; how much he started and never finished; how much he finished and threw away. He projected a six-hundred-page book on the cruise of Noah's Ark—presumably a monumental piece of funny irreverence. All through his life he never realized that people who read the Bible don't want it made fun of, and people who don't read the Bible don't see any fun to make of it.

He planned and executed a cheerful article on *God, Ancient and Modern.* "The sole solicitude of the God of the Bible," so he wrote, "was about a handful of truculent nomads. He worried and fretted over them in a peculiarly and distractingly human way. One day he coaxed and petted them beyond their due, the next he harried and lashed them beyond their deserts. He sulked, he cursed, he raged, he grieved, according to his mood and the circumstances . . . when the fury was on him, he was blind to all reason—he not only slaughtered the offender, but even his harmless little children and his cattle."

This is the real Mark Twain—elemental, defiant.

His wife would not let him publish the article. It was suppressed as one of the first victims of the new "censorship." Mark Twain's biographers are fond of telling us that after his marriage his wife became censor and the editor of his work. He himself says so, with affectionate gratitude, in the preface to his *Joan of Arc* twenty-five years later. For all that he wrote henceforth Olivia Clemens, "Livy," became his critic and his censor, cutting away what was wrong, and schooling him into culture. Nothing must be printed unless "Livy" gave it her approval.

Put very simply, this means that what he wrote must fit into the frame of what was thought "nice" in Elmira, N. Y., in 1870; that he mustn't write awful words like God damn! —though he may write d—n (with a stroke), provided that it is in a half-playful way and put into the mouth of a churchgoing character. He mustn't write about nasty things except in a nice way. Crime must be lighted up into melodrama—as Mr. Dickens did it. Love must sigh and languish—but keep its clothes on (Mark would have said, keep its pants on). Death itself may be as melodramatic as the drunkard's fate, as poignant as the death of little Paul, but it must be "respectable"— and never wander out of sight of the loving pastor, the kindly old clergyman, or the "stern minister" to whose business it belongs. Thus the whole of literature must be "stewed" in respectability before being served.

These were the fetters and this was the editing imposed upon Mark Twain. His marriage with Livy Langdon was from the first day such a beautiful romance, her love for him so tender and so cherishing, and his for her so instant and so undying, that the voice of the critic must be subdued. To those who love Mark Twain's work the memory of his sweet wife is sacred. Yet one cannot but wonder and question at her influence on her husband's work and the history of American letters.

To her influence was presently added that of the Reverend Joe Twitchell of Hartford—henceforth "Joe" to Mark, a muscular Christian of Mark's own age, a veteran chaplain of the Civil War—and an all-round good fellow. Mark Twain loved him with the love of the sceptic for the man who can believe something, the love of the brilliant man for the slow, of the erratic for the immovable. From now on, "Joe," in the intervals of preaching and expounding the Bible, undertook to help "Livy" to show Mark Twain what nice people ought to write and what not. When presently there was added the influence of Mr. Howells of the *Atlantic Monthly*, Mark Twain enjoyed such all-round support that the wonder is that he ever wrote at all.

Yet let it be noticed that all the basis and background of his work was and remained the Mississippi and the West, and Europe as seen therefrom; from his setting in Elmira, nothing; from his life and surrounding in Buffalo, nothing; from Hartford, nothing. There was as much to see on Delaware Avenue, Buffalo, as on Main Street in Carson City, Nevada; as much of light and shadow in Hartford as in Angel's Camp. But he had no eyes to see. To get vision he must shut his eyes and look across the prairies and the mountains to the sunset over the Golden Gate. Such was the genesis of *Tom Sawyer* and *Roughing It* and *Huckleberry Finn* and *Life on the Mississippi* and all the splendid work that he wrote in the years that followed his return from Europe. That the love of his wife and the happiness of his home helped him to work is beyond doubt. But to think that she and Joe Twitchell schooled him to write is childish. Mark Twain taught himself to write, just as he had taught himself everything since he was twelve years old.

But if Mark Twain, as a creative genius, wore fetters, it is only fair to remember that they were those of his day and age. This "Victorian" period of the late nineteenth century, for all its splendid courage in the field, its industrial force and its unsurpassed literature, was, in art and morals, a namby-pamby age. Nothing must be said or drawn or written that was not "respectable." Books, journals

and pictures must be suited to a Kensington drawing-room or a Boston boarding-house. "Damn" was a wicked word, and a "leg" was called a "limb." Characters in books who swore must say, "by Heaven!" or "by the Foul Fiend!" but not "Jesus Christ!" Consider the little clergyman, Lewis Carroll, blinking in the daylight when he emerged from Wonderland into society, and thinking "damn" terribly wicked and Gilbert and Sullivan's *Pinafore* hopelessly coarse. After all, if "Livy" and "Joe" and Mr. Howells put fetters on Mark Twain's hand, it was only a chain which most of his contemporaries wore as they worked. Some felt it, but others scarcely knew it was there. Dickens was never bothered by it, for he himself was eminently respectable. What he wanted to denounce and to satirize was the Court of Chancery, the Guardians of the Poor, and the Circumlocution Offices of the British Government. And that is respectable. But he had no wish to satirize God Almighty, to question whether Hell is just and the Bible "bunk." The things that Mark Twain wanted to write would have horrified Charles Dickens. As the editor of *Household Words* he could have found no place for them. Hence it was that Mark Twain, as his literary work passed from mere diversion to a great reality, found himself in a dilemma. He wanted to write of things which his loving "censors" told him he mustn't talk about; and he wanted to use words and phrases which his loving censors told him "nice" people didn't use. And his faith in their views was as naïve and as touching as the respect of Nigger Jim for white people. In reality he was a giant who towered over their heads. He should have brushed aside their censorship with a kiss and a laugh. The tradition that Howells and the Rev. Twitchell and Mrs. Clemens "made" Mark Twain is sheer nonsense. They did their loving best to ruin his work—and failed; that's all. By good luck *Huckleberry Finn*, afterwards excluded from more than one puritanical library, got past the censors, or nearly so. The manuscript was read aloud in the family circle, and the merry laughter of the children disarmed the censorship. In any case, neither Mrs. Clemens nor the other associates seemed to have realized the scope and reach of the book; nor apparently did Mark Twain himself. Even at that, many things were cut out or altered.

As a sample of how the language of the natural Huckleberry Finn was "improved" by Mrs. Clemens, take a passage from the concluding chapter of *Tom Sawyer*. Mark Twain made Huck say (in speaking of his benefactress, the widow Douglas): "She makes me git up at the same time every morning, she makes me wash . . . *they comb me all to hell.*" Mrs. Clemens changed this to: "*They comb me all to thunder.*" In other words, she changed what Huck would have said and must have said, which is exquisite, to a stupid phrase which neither Huck nor anyone else would have said. "She guarded his work sacredly," said his biographer. She did indeed.

Apart from his studies on Noah's Ark and God, Mark Twain, in his Buffalo days (1870), brought out a comic autobiography of himself—so funny, or so silly, that he presently bought in and destroyed the plates. This is not the fragmentary "Autobiography" of later years.

The Buffalo life lasted less than two years. Apart from the raptures of honeymoon days, it was not altogether a success. Mark Twain sat uneasily in the luxurious editorial chair that proved more rigid than a stool in Nevada. He sold out his share in the paper, at a loss; henceforth he began to dream of publishing, not editing.

Moreover, the Clemenses took no root in Buffalo, caring little for social life; and the shadow of death fell as on their family when Livy's father died in August of 1871. The death of a dear friend of his wife in their house itself, the premature arrival of a feeble little son (Langdon Clemens, November 7, 1870), whose days seemed numbered before they were begun, somehow turned the sunlight of the fairy house into gloom.

Mark Twain moved away to Hartford, attracted by the charm of an old-world town, the culture of the environment and companionship of his new friend Joe Twitchell. The cloud of debt that fringed the sunlight of his opulence followed him from Buffalo. To drive it away he took to lecturing, a thing he had already learned to hate. "I am not going to lecture any more for ever," he had written from Buffalo to Redpath, his manager.

"Count me out." But it was to be a quarter-century yet before he could count himself out of it. Life at Hartford seems to have been, from the beginning, as pleasant and natural as that in Buffalo was gloomy and ill-set. Mark Twain enjoyed the sense of being admitted—even if somewhat reluctantly—to the cultivated life of New England; he enjoyed his association with Twitchell, their endless walks and one-sided conversations. More than all, he appreciated the friendship and sympathy of W. D. Howells, for whose *Atlantic Monthly* he now became a contributor. His first offering was the article called *A True Story* (November 1874), to be followed by the papers on *Old Times on the Mississippi* (January to July 1875), which later became a book, and by many other sketches in the ensuing five years. Mark Twain, wisely or foolishly, took Howells for his mentor; and him at least he never cast aside.

In August of 1872 he made a journey to England, as sudden as the California trip to the *Alta* "thieves." This was inspired by the idea of getting after a new pack of thieves—the copyright pirates. For most of his life Mark Twain, like Charles Dickens, was obsessed with the copyright question, for which the present volume has neither space nor interest to spare. For both of them it was like King Charles's head to Mr. Dick in *David Copperfield*—it wouldn't keep out of things. But it worked differently. Dickens came out to America to be entertained like a prince and made a row about copyright. Mark Twain went over to England to make a row about copyright and was entertained like a prince—and forgot about it.

His reception was indeed overwhelming. Here, at last, he was treated at his true worth —as a real author, not as a western "cut-up." Authors vied to meet him. Dickens, alas! was gone (June 1870), but Tom Hood, Charles Reade, Charles Kingsley and a hundred others vied in doing him reverence. His visit was a series of dinners and entertainments. He had no time to get mad over copyright; no time to write anything or do anything. He did indeed plan a book on England (the Innocents, one recalls, had not visited it), designed to put it in its place. But nothing happened. In November he was back in America, a bigger figure than ever. "When I yell again for less than five hundred dollars," he had written to Redpath, "I'll be pretty hungry." Being hungry presently, he lectured twice in New York at six hundred and fifty dollars a night—a great sum in those days.

His life was too busy and too full to be bothered with lecturing. His new book, *Roughing It,* that he had begun at Buffalo, had come out (1872). He had invented—or rather recalled—a boy called Tom Sawyer, whose adventures he was trying to shape. He was busy with a book called *The Gilded Age,* done in collaboration with Charles Dudley Warner, which appeared in 1873, as imperfect as all collaborations are. But it contains the priceless character of Colonel Sellers, whose impecunious life was illuminated by a rainbow and bounded by a mirage.

More than all was his increasing interest in his home and his family circle. The little boy had faded out of life (June 2, 1872), but the place he might have filled was taken by a garland of little girls who grew up to be the idols of their father's heart. Susie Clemens, of marvellous and tragic memory, came first (March 1872); then Clara, renamed "Bay" for family purposes, and as the third, Jean (Jane Lampton), born in July 1880. It was as if fate decided to throw to Mark Twain's lot all that can be given—success, fame, affluence, a loving wife, and a babbling nursery. To frame such happiness, homes must be provided. He acquired two—always since connected with his life and memory. The one was the house at Hartford (on Farmington Avenue), largely designed by himself. Its special feature was the famous billiard-room on the top floor, henceforth its owner's sanctum. The game of billiards was an abiding passion with Mark Twain, as with so many successful men from the West. The crooked cues and the bounding cushions of the mining camp and the saloon had got in their deadly work. No recovery was possible.

The home at Hartford alternated with a summer home at Quarry Farm, a beautiful hillside country house just outside of Elmira. Mrs. Crane, Livy's sister, who owned the place, built for Mark a quaint little study with eight sides to it, looking far away in all directions. Mr. Paine compares it to a Mississippi pilot-house—an added attraction for its occupant. Such were the gifts which fortune showered upon Mark Twain—to remove them one by one: for affluence, poverty; for the warmth of love and affection nothing but the cold dignity of despair that knows no consolation that may conquer death.

But as yet all that was far away. Mark Twain was busy and happy beyond the common lot—on the verge (he knew it) of princely opulence—millions; and in his mind a book, a real book, not letters and scraps of journalism, but a book about a boy whom he remembered (better than all the world) called Tom Sawyer. On this boy he pondered like Gibbon over ancient Rome.

Around this boy he had already (in 1872) attempted to construct a play. But in Mark Twain's crowded, busy, happy and talkative life, with lectures to give, billiards to play, children arriving, and visitors coming and going, it took time to finish things. In fact, another triumphal progress in England intervened before "Tom" came to light. This time Mrs. Clemens accompanied her illustrious husband and could measure for herself the estimate they made of him abroad. From London they went on to Scotland, where a friendship was formed with John Brown (of *Rab and his Friends*) which was kept warm till that good old man's death. Most important of all, Mark Twain lectured in London (October 13, 1873). The announcement of the lecture is typically British, very unlike the San Francisco "trouble will begin at eight." "Mr. George Dolby," it declared, "begs to announce that Mr. Mark Twain will deliver a lecture of a humorous character on Monday evening next and *repeat it in the same place on Tuesday, Wednesday, Thursday and Friday.*" There is something brutally matter-of-fact in the promise of "repeating it in the same place."

But the lecture and all its repetitions were the wildest of successes. The London press was washed from its moorings in the flood of admiration. Mark Twain became a hero—a legend—a glory. Strange how mankind loves to create heroes—something greater than our poor mean selves—and of the heroes a legend. Such became Mark Twain.

The Clemenses were back in America in January of 1874. Mark Twain got *Tom Sawyer* finished, and it came out in December of 1876. Its success was immediate, complete and continuous. For such people as remained who had never heard of Mark Twain he was now "the man who wrote *Tom Sawyer*."

Tom Sawyer is a world-famous book, and the boy Tom a world celebrity. The book did not make Mark Twain's reputation. That had been done by the *Innocents Abroad*. But it clinched it. The publication of the *Adventures of Tom Sawyer* definitely established the position and reputation of Mark Twain as the great American humorist; so much so that few people realized that the book is on a lower plane altogether than the later *Huckleberry Finn*, which grew out of it. Indeed, *Tom Sawyer* owes some of its success to its very simplicity. It makes no great demand upon the intellect; anybody can read it. The famous story of how Tom Sawyer was set to white-wash the fence as a punishment, and by pre-tending that it was a treat got the other boys to pay for the privilege of whitewashing, is as simple and as wide in its appeal as any folk-lore. It is like the mediaeval stories of the "smartness" of Reynard the Fox. It strikes the familiar note of the clever hero who out-wits stupidity and defeats brute force. Tom Sawyer was a "smart" boy. Indeed, by a sort of general consensus he is supposed to be *the* boy, the typical boy, and parents who put the strap to their own Tom Sawyers chuckle with indulgent laughter over the escapades of the imaginary Tom.

But there is more in the book than all that. Its background of the vast moving river and the wilderness, the romance of the steamboat, the gloomy terror of the great cave, though but lightly sketched in the book *Tom Sawyer*, contains the same appeal—the appealing maj-esty of nature—which was to become an out-standing feature of the book *Huckleberry Finn*. Threaded through it is a really exciting story, painted in crude elemental colours. Tom Sawyer and his friend Huckleberry Finn, out on a night exploit, witness the robbing of a corpse from a grave by a young doctor and two hired body-snatchers. The crude details are all there—the graveyard, midnight, moon-light, terror. Of the body-snatchers, one is "Indian Joe," murderer and "bad man," the other the village drunkard. There is a quar-

rel at the graveside. Indian Joe stabs the young doctor dead, and Tom and Huck, having seen more than enough, flee in terror. The murder is fastened on the town drunkard, whose knife is found beside the dead body. Tom and Huck, in deadly fear of Indian Joe, keep an agonized silence. Then at last they speak out in a melo-dramatic scene at the murder trial of the drunkard. Indian Joe leaps through the court-room window and escapes, a fugitive from the law. He hides in the great cave in the river bluff. Weeks later Tom and a little girl com-panion Becky, lost in the cave and almost ex-piring, see the flickering light of a candle and the form of Indian Joe, groping in the darkness. The children are rescued. Only weeks later do they learn that the rescuers have barred and sealed the entrance to the cavern. Tom Sawyer's exclamation to Becky's father, *"Oh, judge, Indian Joe's in the cave!"* remains in the memory of thousands of read-ers as one of the sensations of literature.

Yet, all in all, the book is far below *Huckle-berry Finn*. Mark Twain, in writing *Tom Sawyer*, was unconsciously groping his way towards the broader canvas and the fuller meaning of the later book. *Tom Sawyer* as a book is full of obvious faults. The stage ef-fects are too elementary, too obvious; they belong to the class of the melodrama and the stock villain and the heroine who requested to be "unhanded"—in other words, the regular working apparatus of nineteenth-century popular literature. Tom Sawyer himself may be a "smart boy," but he runs dangerously close to being a "smart Aleck." Yet with all its faults the book went round the world and carried the name of Mark Twain into all the languages of civilization.

VI. MARK TWAIN AS A NATIONAL ASSET, 1877-1894

The period between the publication of *Tom Sawyer* and the time when he was over-whelmed by financial disaster shows Mark Twain at the height of his success, his literary reputation, his affluence, his domestic happi-ness. His name had become a household word in America. He had grown to be a sort of national asset. Men quoted his stories, his latest sayings, and much that he never said. His lecture trips were a triumphant progress;

his books flooded the country in sales that widened like ripples over a pond. His pictured face, with the shock of hair that turned from red to grey and from grey to white, with the Missouri corn-cob pipe to give it character, was as familiar to the public as those of Washington and Lincoln and Grant. Most of all, he had earned, as he had deserved, the affection of his fellowmen.

Nor was his fame confined within national limits. Mark Twain had become a citizen of the world, and his time in these ensuing years of affluence and achievement was divided between two continents. His reputation in England, his London lectures, his London dinner speeches, the wide sales of his books in Great Britain, may be said to have helped much in renewing the national sympathy of nations that had drifted apart in the ominous days of the Civil War. English people realized that, after all, America was the place that Mark Twain came from; it couldn't be so rotten.

In explaining the activities of Mark Twain's life during his prime, let it be remembered that he was perpetually busy, not only with things that came to completion, but with things that never did, or proved to be failures and were abandoned. A good deal of his time after *Tom Sawyer* was put into a play called *Ah Sin,* done in collaboration with his old friend Bret Harte. It was played in the National Theatre at Washington (May 7, 1877), tried out in New York and died of inanition. The only tangible result of the enterprise was to end the friendship of two old friends.

Following that came a trip to Bermuda with Twitchell largely done *incognito,* Mark now falling back on a privilege confined to royalty and the criminal class.

All the next summer (1877) he was busy with the idea of a story in which a little child of the people changes places with a king's son —but the story had to wait three years for its completion as *The Prince and the Pauper.* There was another idea of the same period which he started and threw aside as of no great value—a sort of wandering tale about Huckleberry Finn, who had already appeared as the satellite of Tom Sawyer. This, the greatest idea that he ever had, Mark Twain seems to have valued little. "I like it only tolerably well," he said, "and I may burn the manuscript when it is done." For years the "Huck" book lay around as neglected as Huck himself. But let the curious compare the author's fulsome praise of his *Joan of Arc.*

But Huckleberry Finn and much else had to wait while Mark Twain and his family sailed away on a sort of grand tour of Europe. They left in April of 1878, visited Germany, passed down to Italy, where they visited in especial Venice and Florence and Rome; then back to Germany to winter in Munich; then came Paris, England (in August of 1879), and home to America (September 3, 1879). It was in the earlier part of the tour that Mark Twain took his walking tour in Germany and Switzerland with Twitchell, immortalized as *A Tramp Abroad,* in which Twitchell is cast for the part of "Harris." It goes without saying that the book is not as good as the *Innocents.* No one can be born twice. But the book is the real thing, and parts of it are inimitable: the vividness of the word-pictures, the tourists, the waiters, the Alpine climbing, the incidents of history, the excursions into facts and, above all, the play of an interesting mind that illuminates everything that it touches. Mark Twain could do this kind of thing as no one else.

Here begins also his inexhaustible interest in the German language, a source of mingled wonder, fascination and annoyance. The family set themselves to learn German. Having had no schooling, linguistic study was a novelty to Mark Twain. He could take as much fun out of the interminable German nouns and the inverted sentences as a schoolboy out of a parody of Latin. Later on, in his *King Arthur* book, when he wants words to use as magic spells he finds them in such glorious compounds as *Constantinopolitanischerdudelsackmachersgesellschaft,* a much more imposing compound than the humble English— Bagpipe Manufacturers Company of Constantinople.

It would be as tedious as it would be purposeless to follow all the comings and goings of Mark Twain and his family in the years that followed their return from Europe. Among the more notable peregrinations was a trip to the Mississippi, down the river from St. Louis to New Orleans and up again to

St. Paul. Mark renewed his experiences as a pilot, fraternized again with Horace Bixby, dropped in at Hannibal for three days to see the boys and girls—in short, the return of the hero, enjoyed as much as it was earned.

The trip helped him to prepare, from his *Atlantic* articles, his work *Life on the Mississippi*—his pilot life already recounted—which appeared in 1883. It was published partly at his own expense and risk—the beginning of the new finance that was to ruin him. But he had got into his head that the previous publishers had been cheating him—like the *Alta* thieves and the copyright pirates. As literature, the book ranks high; as a commercial venture, low. "It cost me fifty thousand dollars to make," so its author said. He was dealing in big sums now.

Other episodes of the period were Mark Twain's brief pilgrimages to Canada. They were made to "acquire copyright," a sort of purification necessary under the existing law, but they turned into social and public triumphs. There was a great dinner at Montreal (1880), and on the next trip (1883) an invitation to stay at Rideau Hall, Ottawa, where resided the Marquis of Lorne and his wife, the Princess Louise, daughter of Queen Victoria. Mr. Paine, the biographer, writes of this: "It is a good deal like a fairy tale . . . the bare-footed boy of Hannibal who had become a printer, a pilot, a rough-handed miner, being summoned by royalty as one of America's foremost men of letters."

It takes an American democrat to see these things in their proper light.

Meantime *The Prince and the Pauper* had already appeared (1880), meeting with a reception in which approval mingled with disappointment. It is told that a certain great classical scholar of the eighteenth century said to Alexander Pope, when his *Iliad and Odyssey* appeared, "It's a very pretty poem, Mr. Pope, but it is not Homer." Many readers felt this way about *The Prince and the Pauper;* it was a very pretty story, but *it wasn't Mark Twain;* at least not the Mark Twain who made frogs jump and conducted innocents abroad. In other words, *it wasn't funny* (except in lapses). Its author could have answered the indictment by saying that it wasn't meant to be, and could have drawn attention to the beauty

of description of old London and its bridges.

Human nature being as discontented as it is, "funny" writers are never content with their cap and bells. They would like to write sermons. From this time on Mark Twain showed a desire to redeem himself from the charge of being "funny." As a result we have *The Prince and the Pauper* and, later on, *Joan of Arc,* which—whatever they may be—are not Mark Twain. There are books that he wrote in which he tried to be Mark Twain and failed; such as *Tom Sawyer Abroad or Pudd'nhead Wilson,* a Mississippi story of 1892, at best an attempt to recapture a tune also sung. But in the historical books he is trying to do something else altogether.

For serious historical writing he was not fitted. His view of the present is like a photograph; his view of the past is made of fierce lights and shadows thrown by firelight on a dark wall. His history is too elemental: for King read tyrant; for priest read bigot; for justice read torture; and for anything called Louis read putrefaction. Mark Twain was too much impressed by the cruelty, the bigotry and the tyranny of the past to see it in its true light. Strange that a man writing in the days of the Homestead strikes and the Haymarket riots, with hideous lynchings in the South, murder walking the streets in Chicago, and on the horizon the tyranny of the prohibitionist, the gangster, the hi-jacker and the racketeer, could see so little to regret in the vanished past.

But when Mark Twain turned from the Thames of 1550 to the Mississippi of 1850, that was another story. The appearance in print of the *Adventures of Huckleberry Finn* marks the highest reach of his achievement.

All the world has read the story of the ragged little outcast, Huckleberry Finn, floating down the Mississippi on a raft, his companion the runaway Nigger Jim. Every reader has felt the wonderful charm of the scenery and setting—the broad flood of the river, the islands tangled with wild vines, the sand-bars and the current swirling past the sunken snags: the stillness of the night with voices coming from the lumber rafts far over the water: the fascination of the passing steamboat, its lighted windows and its trail sparks breaking the black night; and then the dawn and the sun clearing the mist from the waters.

The writer seems to have groped his way into the book like a treasure-seeker. It opens to a wrong start—Tom Sawyer and his boy-chums and pirate games—that would never have gone far. Then it drifts to Huck Finn and his drunken, dissolute, unkempt father, "pap" ("His hair was long and tangled and greasy, and hung down, and you could see his eyes shining through like he was behind vines"); Huck a prisoner in a hut in the hands of the drunkard; his escape; the raft; the finding of Nigger Jim, and with that we float away on the bosom of the river. There are tragic episodes of the river, the feud, the murder, the false claim of the inheritance, the bag of money in the coffin. The story pushes hard against burlesque here and there, as when the raft is invaded by the down-and-out bummers, the "King" and the "Duke." Artistically it almost breaks here—yet oddly enough this is the very part that readers who care nothing for art like best—the sheer roaring fun of it. The Duke getting ready a performance to be given in passing a town and fur-bishing up his recollections of Shakespeare in the form of—"*To be or not to be; that is the bare bodkin,*" is as typically and triumphantly Mark Twain as anything he ever wrote.

In the end the raft floats to Arkansas; Huck is cast up at Silas Phelps's farm and Tom Sawyer gets back into the book—and spoils it. As soon as he comes all the depth of meaning, all the breadth of the picture is lost. It is just backyard stuff—the kind of thing they make "comic strips" of.

But the bulk of the book is marvellous. The vision of American institutions—above all, of slavery—as seen through the unsullied mind of little Huck; the pathos and charm of the Negro race shining through the soul of Nigger Jim—the western scene, the frontier people—it is the epic of a vanished America.

Strange that anyone could imagine that such a book as *Joan of Arc*—conventional, imitative, unnatural—could compare with this. Yet Mark Twain supposed it far superior, and the pundits and stodges, belly-heavy with culture, all agreed. Yet there are those, there must be, who considered the *Adventures of Huckleberry Finn* the greatest book ever written in America.

An outstanding feature of the book is that it is American literature. Whatever the works of Washington Irving and Fenimore Cooper and Longfellow were, there is no doubt about *Huckleberry Finn*. Every now and then the dispute breaks out in the colleges and spills over into the press as to what *American* literature was and is, and when it began. Like all controversies, the dispute is bottomless and involves a hopeless number of definitions of terms. But by American literature in the proper sense we ought to mean literature written in an American way, with an American turn of language and an American cast of thought. The test is that it couldn't have been written anywhere else. When we read the books of O. Henry we know that they were not written in England; they couldn't have been. Longfellow may have written about America, but the form of his language and his thought was the same as that of his English contemporaries. He shared in their heritage, and added to the common stock. Judged in this sense—in order to make the point clear and rob it of all venom—there is as yet no Canadian literature, though many books have been written in Canada, including some very bad ones.

But *Huckleberry Finn* was triumphantly obvious and undeniably American.

But the writing of books and of incidental sketches for the *Atlantic,* and presently for the *Century, Harper's,* and other magazines, was only the chief part and by no means the whole of Mark Twain's activity during these busy years. There were dinners and banquets and reunions to attend, with speeches to make. There was, alas, an increasing interest in the business of publishing. His earlier books were published by canvass and subscription, with a royalty to the author, who took no risk. The cost of sale under this system is high, the royalty low (five to seven per cent was fair enough), but Mark Twain felt that he could improve on this. He first took half the risk and half the profits, then presently launched into the publishing business itself. It seems that many authors feel a desire to be publishers, just as an English butler wants to run a public house and an American bar-tender aspires—or used to, when he existed—to "keep hotel." The results are usually unfortunate.

So it was to be in this instance. But for the time all was optimism and rosy calculation worthy of Colonel Sellers.

Another feature of this period was lecturing, including a notable tour in the season of 1884-1885 managed by the admirable Major J. B. Pond, of worthy and illustrious memory, and carried out with George W. Cable as partner on the platform.

The lectures were a huge success for all except Mark Twain, to whom they were a mere labour of necessity.

The truth is that Mark Twain never liked lecturing. Indeed, apart from the initial joys of triumph, he grew to abominate it. Nearly all lecturers hate lecturing, whether from nervousness of appearing in public, on account of need of working up a fixed emotion at a fixed hour, or because of the fatigues of travel or the effort demanded by social entertainment. No one likes lecturing except those who can't do it. A dull lecturer enjoys his own performance immensely.

Mark Twain hated lecturing for all the above reasons—even nervousness, in the sense of nervous intensity. And he added a special reason of his own, that he felt as if lecturing to make people laugh turned him into a buffoon. This, of course, was sheer ingratitude. But he wanted to be a man of letters, a philosopher, a character—he didn't want to be a comic man. "Oh, Cable!" he moaned to his lecture-mate one night, "I am demeaning myself. I am allowing myself to be a mere buffoon. It's ghastly. I can't endure it any longer." No doubt he was contrasting himself with the solemn little Cable, who didn't smoke, drank water, read the Bible in the hotel bedroom, and drew tears from the audience.

In other words, Mark Twain wanted it both ways, coming and going. He wanted to have the world laugh when he said the "reports of his death had been grossly exaggerated," he wanted to write a comic account of Noah's Ark and a comic life of Adam, he wanted to set King Arthur's knights to playing baseball —but he didn't want to take the consequences and have people think him "funny"; or rather, he wanted them to understand that he was also—as he was—a man of intense and passionate ideals, capable of righteous indignation against iniquity. About this the mass of the public cared nothing at all. Mark Twain to them was Mark Twain. That was all. When he said that he was a Chinese "Boxer"—meaning that the Chinese nationalists were right— they laughed. "Have you heard Mark Twain's latest?" they said.

Even more successful than his public lectures, if that were possible, were Mark Twain's after-dinner speeches. Here, of course, he was entirely himself. Here he could exploit to the full the natural drollery of his speech, the peculiar drawl, the assumption of innocence— all those arts and artifices which swept his auditors away on billows of tumultuous laughter. After-dinner speaking in those unredeemed days was an easier art in America than now. Indeed, the contrast of those days with the gloomy "banquet" of today is pathetic. Today the auditors sit in silence, their surreptitious cocktail, of three hours before, dead within them, chewing fiercely at celery and listening to an hour's talk on such a thing as the Chicago Drainage Canal. But in those evil days a banquet was a real banquet. The audience came from the bar to the banquet, and gravitated from the banquet to the bar. Swimming in champagne in a haze of blue smoke they wanted fun, not information. And Mark Twain could give it to them as no one else could.

These years were the great years of Mark Twain's public lecturing, in which he easily eclipsed all those who preceded and followed him. The only exception was Charles Dickens, whose crowded houses and breathless audiences at least equalled those of the great American humorist. But Dickens was different; his towering fame was the background; he "read," not lectured, though with intense dramatic effect and magnetic personal contact. What the audience saw was not Dickens but his characters—the death-bed of the dying child, the fury of the murderer Sykes, and the Homeric courtroom of Bardell versus Pickwick. What Mark Twain's audience saw was Mark Twain; what the audience heard was Mark Twain—not Tom Sawyer, nor Huck Finn, but Mark Twain. His thought and feeling, by the magic of his method, carried across.

Which was the higher art and which the lower, it is needless to enquire.

Many of the dinner speeches, such as that at the great Army dinner at Chicago (1879), became historic. For the rest of their lives those present recalled and magnified the wonder of Mark Twain. Once, once only, the magic failed utterly and dismally. One may recall, as an irony of personal history, Mark Twain's greatest after-dinner success (done with a third-rate joke at the end of a speech of no merit), and his great and ignominious failure with a prepared speech that was as funny as it was subtle, accidentally derailed in transit. The great success was the dinner given in honour of General Grant by the Army of the Tennessee at Chicago on November 13, 1879. Grant was there, and Sherman and Sheridan and a galaxy of great soldiers. Colonel Robert Ingersoll carried the audience away in a real speech of patriotic oratory; and there was the usual tiresome speaker (still unhanged among us) who began for a minute and spoke for an hour. Mark Twain rose at 2 A.M. to talk not on the Ladies, as invited, but on the Babies. "We haven't all the good fortune to be ladies," he said in opening, "we haven't all been generals or poets or statesmen; but when the toast works down to the babies—*we stand on common ground.*" We are told that the speaker "had to stop to let the tornado roar of laughter go by." The concluding paragraph of the speech is the most quoted part of all Mark Twain's oratory. It runs:

"And now in his cradle somewhere under the flag the future illustrious commander-in-chief of the American armies is so little burdened with his approaching grandeur and responsibilities as to be giving his whole strategic mind at this moment to find out some way to get his own big toe into his mouth, an achievement to which (meaning no disrespect) the illustrious guest of the evening also turned his attention some fifty-six years ago—"

Here Mark Twain paused. What followed is thus related by his incomparable biographer Mr. Paine:

"The vast crowd had a chill of fear. After all, he seemed likely to overdo it, to spoil it with a cheap joke at the end. He waited long enough to let the silence become absolute, until the tension was painful, and then . . . *'and if the child is but the father of the man,*

there are mighty few who will doubt that he succeeded.'

"The house came down with a crash."

Now let us admit that a joke cannot be fully appreciated without the voice, the mood, the occasion; let us admit also that it is historically interesting to think of such a distinguished audience swept away on a gale of laughter. But after all, what does the joke amount to? Nothing much, and they had to wait for it. But the reader may judge for himself.

The other occasion is equally historic—memorable in its utter and awful failure. For the time it crushed Mark Twain with a dead weight of despair. The scene was the dinner given on December 17, 1877, by the staff of the *Atlantic* to the aged poet Whittier on his seventieth birthday. Present were Whittier himself, and Longfellow and Emerson and Holmes and all the great literary lights of Boston, the Magi of the East, refulgent with their own genius and consuming their own smoke. Mark Twain shouldn't have given a damn for them, but he did. Longfellow was there and old Emerson—too deaf to hear—and others too stuffed to listen. But Mark Twain was afraid of them. In their eyes and in his own he was not in their class. They were "authors," real ones; he was just a rough, cheap westerner. So he prepared a speech line by line and word by word. It was a delightful piece of burlesque—picturing three old "bummers" arriving at a western mining camp and spouting poetry. One "bum" impersonated Longfellow, one Holmes, and one Emerson—the parody of their work was to show that. But the speech went wrong. The audience caught on to the "bums," but not to the parody—old men are slow in such things. There was a frozen silence. The speaker's "inferiority complex" (though he never lived to hear of it) seized him. His own face turned to misery. The speech ended. The old men shuffled into their coats. It was all over.

Next day Mark Twain wrote agonized letters of apology. He wanted to resign everything, to quit everything, to give up everything—not to be Mark Twain any more. His despair was as fierce as his hopes had been eager. Years after, he read the speech again, and again sank into a pit of despair. Years after that, he read it again, and the light broke in and he felt that it was glorious. So it was. If he had given that speech to the students of Yale and Harvard instead of the stuffy old men in Boston, it would have taken the roof off.

The mention of General Grant and the famous Grant dinner at Chicago recalls one of the outstanding episodes of Mark Twain's life in the hey-day of his success—his marvellous rescue of Grant and his family from ruin.

A grateful nation had made the hero of Appomattox its president. It has a way of doing so. It is said that the Chinese, in the days of the Empire, used to select by examination their highest scholars and make them generals. The Americans select their highest generals and make them presidents. Of Grant's presidency there is no need to speak here. After his time expired he was induced to go into Wall Street business, or rather to lend his name as a cover for business of which he understood absolutely nothing. The colossal success of the fraudulent Ward was followed by catastrophic failure and the imprisonment of Ward, and carried down with it the fortune, and worse still the reputation, of General Grant. There he was—ruined—saved only from legal prosecution by national sympathy and by the fact that he was already stricken with a disease destined to prove fatal.

In his adversity he turned to the idea of living by his pen—of fighting over again with ink and compasses the battles won by the sword. A leading magazine offered him what they thought a handsome sum for articles on his campaigns; a publishing firm were willing to bring out a book of memoirs of his life. But the whole plan, in scope and in prospective return, was on a modest scale. At this point Mark Twain "butted in." He saw the idea of Grant's memoirs with the eyes of Colonel Sellers! What! Offer the General a mere five hundred dollars for an article on the battle of Shiloh! What! Talk of ten thousand copies of a book from such a hand! "General" (the words are actual), "a book telling the story of your life and battles should sell not less than a quarter of a million, perhaps twice that!" And a little later, in a further discussion of the subject, "General, I have my cheque-book with me. I will draw you now a cheque for twenty-five thousand dollars as an advance royalty!"

And just for once the Colonel Sellers vision was absolutely correct.

Mark Twain had had a certain connection already, one might say friendship, with General Grant. Once, long before, he had visited him when President, and had relieved the awkwardness of the meeting by saying, "Mr. President, I am embarrassed, are you?" Grant treasured the remark as a man without humour keeps an old joke. Afterwards came the famous dinner and other casual meetings.

Mark Twain did not "butt in" in any offensive sense to steal the business of other publishers. He offered them a field they wouldn't take, and when it was clear, occupied it himself for his own publishing firm, Webster and Company. He set the General to work dictating his memoirs, watched over him, encouraged, cheered him to it. Grant, stricken as he was, worked stubbornly on. All the best in the man shone on in his stubborn fight against approaching death. When the cancer in his throat reached the point where dictation was impossible, he took a pencil and wrote on, firmly, stubbornly, as if his pencil were an iron point against paper. He won out. There came a day when he laid aside the pencil; the *Personal Memoirs of General Grant* were ended. Three days later (July 23, 1885) the world learned that General Grant was dead.

Grant had written with the plain simplicity of one not looking for style or effect, but setting down what he had to say for its own sake, without a wasted word. So wrote Xenophon and Julius Caesar.

But the vast success of the *Memoirs* was not solely due to the national interest in the narration, the national appeal of the circumstances, or the plain soldierly writing of the General. It owed much to the energy and boldness of Mark Twain, the fearless disregard of expense with which the enterprise was launched, the skill with which it was carried through.

Before Grant died he had the satisfaction of knowing that his name and his family were saved. After he was dead the royalties paid to his widow ran to nearly four hundred and fifty thousand dollars!

After the great Grant episode comes as a landmark the publication of *A Connecticut Yankee in King Arthur's Court*. It appeared in December 1889, but it had been long in thought and preparation. Ever since he had first visited England, Mark Twain had wanted to write a book about English institutions. The plan was originally killed by kindness, but refused to stay dead. It revived in his mind. He carried it about with him, and by 1866, in his new Hartford home, he began the felicitous book with the happy title in which his England was encompassed. The writing was interrupted by the composition of sketches and articles, by dinners and speeches, and by the receipt of honorary degrees (such as the Yale Master of Arts in 1888), but it never stopped till it culminated in the issue of the book by Webster and Company, the author's own publishing house.

To many of us who are old enough to remember most of Mark Twain's works from the time of their appearance, there is a certain list which seemed then and seem now the real Mark Twain. The rest don't matter. The list includes *Roughing It, Life on the Mississippi, The Innocents Abroad, Tom Sawyer* (a little grudgingly), *The Adventures of Huckleberry Finn*, and, most certainly and beyond controversy, *A Connecticut Yankee*. We don't need to care what the critics say; we can recall the sheer unadulterated joy of that first perusal.

The story is based thus:

A Connecticut Yankee, a factory boss, skilled in all mechanical arts, is "put to sleep" by a crack on the head with a crowbar from an employee. He wakes up to find himself—not forward in time as most Utopians are, but backward. He is lying on a grassy bank in the woodland country of King Arthur's England. To him approaches a knight in "old time iron armour from head to heel."

"*Fair sir, will ye joust?*" asks the knight.

"*Will I which?*" says the Yankee.

And with that the tale is on. The Yankee, about to be put to death, recalls the fact that an eclipse happened that very year and day, and "puts out" the sun. This beats out Merlin and makes the Yankee a magician. He rules King Arthur's England; introduces machinery, fights the superstitions of the church, the cruelty of the law, the brutality of the strong —only to meet disaster at the end.

It is a strange and wonderful tale, and carries with it not only a story but a meaning. By and through his Yankee Mark Twain is denouncing all the things that he hated— hereditary power, the church, aristocracy, privilege, superstition. He is able, under the guise of humour, to give vent to the fierce elemental ideas of justice and right and equality, hatred of oppression and religious persecution, by which he was inspired. In other books this could only be incidental—a word, a phrase, a quoted speech. Here it was the whole book.

It was no wonder that such a book called forth plenty of criticism, even of denunciation; no wonder that many of Mark Twain's English admirers turned their backs on him. The book seemed to challenge this. In the first place, from the point of view of the historian, if taken seriously, it is contemptible. The date of the story is fixed by a solar eclipse which is part of its machinery as the year 528 A.D. The time is that of King Arthur. But the author has lumped into it in an indistinguishable mass the manners and customs of ten centuries, all the tyrannies of all the countries he ever heard of (except America)—the Dark Ages, the Middle Ages, the Old Régime in France; all the aristocracies of Europe, with especial reference to the English, past and present; with this, and running all through it, is a denunciation, by name, of the Roman Catholic Church.

Witness, for example, the following typical quotations:

"*It was pitiful for a person born in a wholesome free atmosphere to listen to their humble and hearty outpourings of loyalty towards their king and church and nobility; as if they had any more occasion to love and honour king and church and noble than a slave has to love and honour the lash. . . .*"

"*Before the day of the church's supremacy in the world, men were men and held their heads up.*"

"*Any established church is an established crime, an established slave pen.*"

"A privileged class, an aristocracy, is but a band of slave-holders under another name."

Now of course it is not really the fictitious Yankee speaking here, but the author himself. The voice is Yankee but the hand is from Missouri.

Such criticism of England, past and present, from a citizen of the American Republic, was a little too much like a child of light reproving the children of darkness. Against the tyranny of aristocracy could be set the rising tyranny of the trust; the criminals and bandits of King Arthur's time (whenever it was) were soon to be overmatched by the gangsters of the United States; against the power of the church stood the social tyranny of Puritanical America; denunciations of slavery came ill from a writer brought up in a slave-holding family in the greatest slave state the world ever saw, and the rack and stake of the Middle Ages could be paralleled in the hell-fires of the southern lynchers.

At best it was Satan rebuking sin, the pot calling the kettle black. Underneath was the insult that Mark Twain really thought America a far superior place to England, a fact of which the next generation were not so assured. But the delusion of American freedom died hard.

Yet real lovers of Mark Twain's work, those who understand it, will "wipe all that out." When the *Yankee* book appeared, it was read by thousands with sheer unadulterated joy from cover to cover; by thousands who didn't care a rush for historical accuracy, and were as willing to fuse all the centuries together as the author was. To such readers the burlesque of chivalry was a delight; it was glorious to think of King Arthur's knights set to play baseball and to ride round with advertising boards instead of hunting the Holy Grail. The reader threw off the dead weight of literary reverence and roared at the fun of it. And the denunciation of cruelty and tyranny, and the triumph of machine-power, the revolver against the knight on horseback—all that was equally thrilling. It didn't matter where the tyranny was or when it was; the reader had a notion that the institutions of dark ages were dark indeed, and exulted in their overthrow.

These readers were right. The *Yankee* is

the most "artistic" of all Mark Twain's works; the burlesque the most unbroken, the theme the most continuous and consistent. The book *Huckleberry Finn* is imperfect as art when it breaks or nearly breaks into burlesque; in other books the burlesque is imperfect when it breaks into sentiment. The *Yankee* is a complete artistic conception, carried unbroken to a finish. Such faults as it has, in the technique of humour, lie elsewhere. Mark Twain never could convey the idea of prolixity except by getting prolix; to convey the idea of an interminable speech, he makes one; as witness the talk of Alisande in the tale and many of his characters elsewhere. Art should do better than that.

One may pass over with but little comment the other writings and the other achievements of Mark Twain, from the time between the appearance of the *Yankee* and his financial disasters of four years later. All through this period, and long before it, he had been reading intermittently about Joan of Arc, and presently working on a book about her. There was a family trip to Europe again in 1891-92 (France, Germany, Switzerland). To the family themselves the trip was chiefly memorable for its happiness. But to students of Mark Twain's work and life it is memorable for his famous dinner with the Kaiser and what he thought of that exalted potentate.

During that winter in Berlin, Mark Twain and his family saw more of "high society" than at any time of their lives. They were entertained as leading celebrities of the day in diplomatic and aristocratic circles at a time when European nobility enjoyed its last and its brightest lustre. Highest of all honours for Mark Twain was an invitation to dine at the royal table of the "young" German Emperor.

It is difficult for us, even for those of us whose memory carries back to it, to reconstruct the setting and surrounding of the past before the downfall of Europe: the pomp and majesty of kingship; the resplendent glory of unbroken militarism; the ancestral pride of nobility, the authority and dignity of the church and the stability of established society. The gap between all that and bankrupt nations, labour democracies, red revolutions, and the threatened collapse of our civilization, is as great as that between the majestic vassal of God, William the Second, and an old man with a half-withered arm sawing wood at Doorn. Anyone *now* can see the real figure of the Kaiser; Mark Twain could see it then.

He dined as one of a large company as a guest of the Kaiser on February 20, 1892. Afterwards he wrote down (for himself) his impressions of the Emperor and his entourage, the silent dinner, the monologue conversations, the rigid questions and the rigid answers, the utter suppression of everyone except the sovereign himself. He recorded how he alone in all that obeisant company had the hardihood to venture a few original observations, with the result of universal consternation and discomfort. Years later, he related the incidents, from his notes, to his biographer for publication after his death.

Very different was a meeting a little later (in the following summer), at Nauheim, with the Prince of Wales (Edward VII.). This was as jovial and informal as the "Kaiser-contakt" had been rigid and conventional. The two walked up and down arm in arm, the Prince joking with Mark about a reference he had made to His Highness in one of his books. The "royal memory," whether coached or not, worked its usual charm.

Meantime publishing went on in America. There was the book, *The American Claimant*, with a play made out of it, that brought in a lot of money. Then there was a new Tom Sawyer story published in *St. Nicholas* in 1893-1894, and later as a book. It was called *Tom Sawyer Abroad*, and is interesting only as illustrating the failures of genius. In this story Tom and Huck and Nigger Jim start off in a (highly) dirigible balloon, cross the Atlantic, and "fool around" the Sahara Desert. The whole setting is about as unconvincing and pointless as if we had a sequel story in which, let us say, Sherlock Holmes becomes a country clergyman, or Mr. Pickwick joins the army and heads a cavalry charge in the Crimean War. Another sequel, *Tom Sawyer, Detective*, is a little happier, the scene at any rate being laid where it belongs.

And all this time, though he didn't realize it, Mark Twain's fortunes were moving towards disaster, like swift-flowing water moving silently towards a cataract.

One pauses a moment before contemplating the shipwreck of a happiness that was never again restored, to dwell upon the completeness of it. It was not only in the world's goods and in the world's applause that Mark Twain was blessed. There was added to it the felicity of his private life. His abiding love for his sweet wife was only a part of the happy domestic and family relations with which his life was blessed throughout. His father, indeed, was little more than a memory, albeit a cherished one. For his mother, Jane Clemens,—the "Aunt Polly" of Tom Sawyer—he bore a constant affection and a deep respect, even after he ceased to obey her precepts and "touched" liquor and "threw" cards. He sent her money as soon and as often as he had any to send.

After he left home he seldom saw his mother, though in his pilot days he once took her for a trip down the river to New Orleans.

Later on, after her son's marriage and his rise to eminence, Jane Clemens came east with her daughter Pamela (Mrs. Moffatt), and lived for a while in Fredonia (N. Y.), but she moved west again to make her home with her oldest son Orion at Keokuk. There Mark Twain and his wife and children visited her in the summer of 1886. There she died in her eighty-eighth year in the summer of 1890, while her son was at the height of his success. All her later life was filled with pride over his achievements.

Orion Clemens, older than Sam by ten years and in his later life supported by his brother's bounty, was, in a way, nearer to Mark Twain, more sympathetic, than anyone else in the world. Orion was a sort of queer double of Sam, with the one quality of success left out. He was a printer who failed at printing (he hated to charge money for it), a writer who couldn't write, an inventor who didn't invent and a promoter who couldn't promote anything. But he felt himself always on the threshold of success and on the brink of fortune. After his return from the West, he lived, in the earthly sense, chiefly in Keokuk, Iowa, but in the real sense in a world of dreams. He wrote, at his brother's suggestion, a vast autobiography, pathetic in its record of failure. In his old age he was found one morning seated in the kitchen, his head upon the table—dead. Beside him were pens and paper; no doubt he had thought of something wonderful to write.

Mark Twain has paid a full tribute to his brother Orion in his autobiography. Among other things he says:

"Innumerable were Orion's projects for paying off his debts to me. These projects extended straight through the succeeding thirty years, but in every case they failed. During all those thirty years Orion's well-established honesty kept him in offices of trust where other people's money had to be taken care of, but where no salary was paid. He was treasurer of all the benevolent institutions; he took care of the money and other property of widows and orphans; he never lost a cent for anybody, and never made one for himself.

"Every time he changed his religion the church of his new faith was glad to get him; made him treasurer at once, and at once he stopped the graft and the leaks in that church.

"He exhibited a faculty of changing his political complexion that was a marvel to the whole community. One morning he was a Republican, and upon invitation he agreed to make a campaign speech at the Republican mass meeting that night. He prepared the speech. After luncheon he became a Democrat, and agreed to write a score of exciting mottoes to be painted upon the transparencies which the Democrats would carry in their torchlight procession that night. He wrote these shouting Democratic mottoes during the afternoon, and they occupied so much of his time that it was night before he had a chance to change his politics again; so he actually made a rousing Republican campaign speech in the open air while his Democratic transparencies passed by in front of him, to the joy of every witness present."

May the earth lie lightly on such a man.

In addition to Orion, his sister Pamela meant much in Mark Twain's life. Her little boy was christened after him as "Samuel." But it was when his own marriage was blessed with children that Mark Twain's domestic happiness received its final crown. His first child, it is true (Langdon Clemens, born November 7, 1870), was a delicate child and passed like an early flower (June 2, 1872). But the little girls who followed (Susie, 1872, Clara, 1874, and Jean, 1880) became the de-

light of their parents' life. Mrs. Clemens was a model mother—giving the children her time, her care, her teaching, her love, and Mark was an ideal father, romping with the children, playing games with them, acting with them, and spoiling them all he could— a proper division of parental labour. The little Susie, in especial, was a child of exception, destined, it would have seemed, for great things. She wrote a part of a "biography" of her father as quaint and interesting as her father's own work.

"Papa," she writes, "doesn't like to go to church at all, why, I never understood, until just now. He told us the other day that he couldn't bear to hear anyone talk but himself, but that he could listen to himself talk for hours without getting tired; of course he said this in joke, but no doubt it was founded on truth."

For the intense happiness of such affections Mark Twain was destined later on to pay the full price. For him each break in the circle must come as a cruel blow, beyond consolation, without hope, cruel, final.

Such a time was approaching.

VII. DISASTER, 1894-1900

It might have been thought that throughout the years of literary success Mark Twain was moving up from poverty to a competence, from a competence to wealth, from wealth to affluence. So indeed he thought himself. Books, plays and lectures were bringing in a stream of money, that at times ran in a flood. The colossal success of the Grant *Memoirs* seemed to open a boundless horizon. Shrewd investment, as the investor saw it, would multiply every dollar that was saved. There was no limit but the sky.

Of course, there was a stream of money going out in the other direction. The beautiful house in Hartford sopped up money as beautiful houses do. When its owner bought some adjacent land from his neighbour, his neighbour "stung" him as adjacent neighbours do. Then there was the cost of entertainment. Mark Twain never wanted to go to other people's houses, but he wanted everybody to come to his. This is an expensive taste. The dinners, the visits, the company went on without end.

Still, an income that runs to a hundred thousand dollars a year will stand a lot of strain. And Mark Twain carried with him the comfortable feeling that after spending a lot of money—say, twenty or thirty thousand a year—in keeping things going he was still able every year to "salt away" great sums of money that would guarantee the future against disaster. He felt this all the more because he knew that he had a progressive and inventive turn of mind, and was a man who could forecast the money that was going to be made of new inventions, new ideas. For instance, a large slice of his earlier savings went into a "steam generator." This was a marvellous mechanism calculated to save ninety per cent of the fuel, if it had ever generated anything. It never did. Thirty-two thousand dollars went into a "steam pulley" that didn't pull, and was followed by twenty-five invested under the sea in a marine telegraph. It never came up. Then there was the "Kaola-type"— a new process of engraving by means of which fifty thousand dollars was placed on a smooth sheet of steel coated with China clay and left there. At times Mark Twain showed what he thought to be his hard-headed business caution. A young man called Graham Bell offered him what he describes as "a whole hatful" of shares in a new ingenious sort of toy called a "telephone." But he was not to be caught with *that*.

Meantime ordinary profits had grown to look too small, ordinary gains too paltry. A hundred dollars was only fit to light a cigar with, a thousand too small to save. What was needed was something with "millions in it." In other words, Mark Twain having invented, or drawn, the character of Colonel Sellers, had turned into Sellers himself; brought up on the "Tennessee land" and the lost earldom of Durham and the Esmeralda mine, he ran true to form and became Colonel Sellers, James Lampton and the Earl of Durham all in one. It was as if a Greek Fate, a Destiny of Necessity, had doomed him for disaster.

All this ran along for years.

But the chief agent in his undoing was a wonderful invention, a "machine" calculated to revolutionize all the trade of printing, publishing and book-making. This was no less than a machine that would set type, would replace the laborious toil of the compositor by the dexterous and unerring work of mechanical power. Mark Twain had been a printer. He saw what this would mean. He realized that the dreamy young inventor James Paige had got hold of something that would turn the world upside down. All that was needed was to link up with Paige a man of keen business sense, a man with practical experience, a man commanding capital and bold enough to use it, in other words himself.

The calculations made were staggering, were super-Sellers. Such a machine (when Paige had it absolutely complete; it takes time to get a big thing like that just right) would be an indispensable necessity for all the newspapers in all the languages in all the world, and for all the magazines and book-printing of all nations everywhere. Multiply these by the circulation of the papers and the sales of the books, and remember that even in its earliest form the machine could work against four men—millions in it? no, billions.

Mark Twain had heard of the machine about 1880, had put in three thousand dollars just for luck; then later more; then determined to limit his stake in it to thirty thousand dollars; then plunged in on a neck-or-nothing contract that could eat up money as fast as he could save it. All through the years of his great success—the days of Huck Finn and General Grant and the Yankee— Paige was tinkering at the machine, perfecting it, and Clemens pouring money down an endless pipe. He never realized that other machines might "get there" first; he saw, as a printer, what a revolution a "linotype" would make; he didn't see that other revolutionists might step in ahead.

And with that went in these same years the publishing business. Mark Twain by this time was a publisher, the firm of Webster and Company being virtually owned by him, and managed by "Charlie" Webster, a man as visionary as himself and united to his family by marriage with a niece. Any optimism that Mark Twain lacked, Webster supplied. The resounding success of the Grant *Memoirs* had given the firm a universal éclat. Other war memoirs followed, a whole *Library of Humour* was planned. As the greatest undertaking of all, the firm brought out, by subscription sale, a magnificent *Life of Pope Leo the Thirteenth*. Here was an enterprise indeed! As Clemens saw it, this would make the 300,000 copies of the *Personal Memoirs of General Grant* look like a mere handful. This would be read by every living Roman Catholic; put the number of these at, say, 250,000,000, translate the book into every language, sell it on the average of, say, three dollars, and what do you get? Something pretty substantial! These are not Mark Twain's words, but they represent his state of mind. Charlie Webster took a run over to Italy and had a talk with the aged Leo. He carried with him a copy of the Grant book—bound in gold it was to be, but Mark Twain's friends dissuaded him; Webster talked in millions! The poor old pontiff was swept away. He gave his blessing to the work and begged Father O'Reilly, who was to write him up, somewhat pathetically, just to "tell the truth, tell the truth." As from a pope to a priest these are strong words. "We in Italy cannot comprehend such things," said Leo to Charlie. Neither they could in America, so it presently seemed. In short, "Mark" and "Charlie" had overlooked the fact that millions and millions of Roman Catholics couldn't read, and if they did, they wouldn't read the life of the pope, and that a pope doesn't have a "life" anyway, and they haven't got three dollars if he had.

So presently the magnificent *Life of Pope Leo* dragged along, beside the war memoirs and the humour library, with the increasing deficit of Webster and Company. Then came the hard times, the attempt to raise money in a falling market, the machine, the machine! that never could get down—and then right ahead in plain sight the prospect of disaster, ruin, bankruptcy, like breakers under the bow of a ship.

During these years, 1892, 1893 and 1894, Mark Twain rushed back and forward from Europe to America. He dashed across in June 1892; Paige and Webster recharged him with optimism, and in two weeks he was off again for Europe. *Pudd'nhead Wilson* was ready to be issued, and *The American Claimant* was already published; the hard times hit the sales (and in any case the book was not the real thing), but the house kept going. By April of 1893 Mark Twain was back in America, rushing to Chicago to see Paige, then in May, reassured, but devoured with anxiety, off to Genoa. That summer he was back again. The end was getting near.

One friend he found on the brink of his disaster—Henry H. Rogers of the Standard Oil Company. The name of that corporation in those days had an evil sound, but to Mark Twain, H. H. Rogers was and remained one of the noblest men in the world. All his life Rogers had read and admired Mark Twain's works. He met him now and played for him the part that Mark Twain had played for General Grant. He gathered in his firm hands the tangled threads of the humorist's enterprises and unravelled the disorder; marked with the eye of business genius the assets that lay in the skein, ready to be rewoven. Then with his back against the wall he faced the creditors, who stood, some reluctant and some ravenous, ready to spring. But even Rogers could not prevent the inevitable. Mark Twain, back in France (May 1894), where his wife remained, returned to America.

Then came the crash. Charles L. Webster and Company went bankrupt on April 18, 1894. Rogers, acting for Mark Twain, got a settlement with the creditors at fifty cents on the dollar for the hundred thousand dollars of debt that carried the firm down. Mark Twain was ruined.

One needs to reflect for a moment to realize the extent of disaster. Mark Twain was almost sixty years old. He must begin all over again. He had thought himself affluent beyond the common lot. He had now nothing; less than nothing. He had supposed that henceforth he could use his pen as he would wish to, writing for writing's sake—about such things, for example, as the life of Joan of Arc, about which he had dreamed for years. He had thought himself done and finished for ever with lecturing; he must pick up that weary task where he had left it off. Old and tired and wearying already of the world, he must assume the mantle of youth, the mask of merriment. He must pretend to be Mark Twain.

Nothing in his life became him better than the way he faced his adversity. He would have nothing to do with the fifty cents on the dollar; give him time, he would pay it all. When the news of his ruin reached the world there was at once talk of a national subscription to pay his debts. He would not hear of it; not while he could work; to people brought up to rough it on the frontier in the West, public charity was too much like the county poorhouse.

But the public sympathy counted for much. Letters and telegrams flowed in, cheques which he refused to take, but which touched his heart, and letters from some of the creditors waiving their claims indefinitely till he was ready to pay them. Most of all, from his wife, still in France, there came messages of love and encouragement; he wrote back with undaunted courage: "A burden has been lifted from me and I am blithe inside . . . except when I think of you, dear heart . . . for I seem to see you grieving and ashamed. There is temporary defeat, but no dishonour; we will march again."

Oddly enough, in one corner of his mind was one sunlit spot filled with hope. The machine! For even now Rogers, who knew everything, still thought it might work, and Paige was still perfecting it.

So within a few weeks Mark Twain was over again in France with his family, settled down at Étretat on the Normandy coast, filled with new hopes and busy at what he felt was the real work of his life, a presentation of the career of Joan of Arc. At Étretat and at Paris, while his business affairs were being straightened out, Paige continuing his perfecting, and the enthusiastic Major Pond organizing a world lecture tour, he completed his *Joan*— for which, perhaps, as a child of adversity, he had a greater affection than for any other of his books.

Authors are notoriously perverse creatures. They are apt to repudiate their noblest offspring; Conan Doyle hated to be always thought of as the author of *Sherlock Holmes;* he felt himself to be a historical novelist, and grew to hate Sherlock. Lord Macaulay thought himself a poet, and Sir Isaac Newton, very probably, imagined himself a humorist. So did Mark Twain turn from the roaring fun of *Roughing It* and the *Innocents* to cherish the sorrows of the martyred Joan.

Joan of Arc was finished in Paris in January 1895 (before the lecture tour started), and published as a serial in *Harper's* that year. The writer withheld his name, for fear that the signature of "Mark Twain" would give a false turn to the reader. The *Personal Recollections of Joan of Arc* were published as if a translation from an actual memoir written by the Sieur de Conte, a supposed contemporary and companion of the Maid of Orleans. But this thin pretence broke down. Such a literary secret could perhaps be kept in Shakespeare's time, but not in ours; and in any case the Sieur de Conte, when he philosophizes, talks rather like Nigger Jim. The leading critics and biographers have joined in ranking the book high. In its author's own opinion, expressed deliberately in writing, it is counted as his greatest work. When it came out as a book he dedicated it proudly to his wife "in grateful recognition of her twenty-five years of valued service as my literary adviser and editor." It seems presumption to express a contrary opinion. The actual story of Joan of Arc is of course a tragedy of the ages; no imaginable picture can surpass that of a beautiful and inspired girl, saving her country in arms, and dying in the flames of martyrdom. But because Joan is great it doesn't follow that Mark Twain's book about Joan is great. One very simple test of a book is whether people read it and whether they read it for its own sake; because they want to read it, or for some other reason, such as the vainglory of culture, the author's reputation, or by the attraction of the subject which the title professes to treat. Another excellent test of a book is whether the reader finishes it. It may be doubted by the sceptical whether the book *Joan of Arc* passes these tests. How many have said of it, "a sweet thing," "a beautiful thing," and left the beautiful thing unfinished. We recall how Mr. Pickwick listened to a story read out loud at Dingley Dell with his eyes closed as in an ecstasy of appreciation. No doubt he woke up at the end and said, "a sweet thing."

Those of us old enough to recall the appearance of *Tom Sawyer* and *Huckleberry Finn* and the *Yankee* and such, and the sheer joy of reading them without knowing or caring about critical judgment, cultural value and literary conversation, will remember that there was no such thing with the *Joan of Arc* book. The comment of the plain reader was, "Hell! it isn't funny!" What he meant was, it isn't Mark Twain; of course, it wasn't meant to be. But unfortunately it is Mark Twain whenever it gets prosy. Mark Twain, in *Is Shakespeare Dead?*", has scoffed at those who try to write in the words and technique of a trade and calling which they do not know. He shows that Captain Marryat and Richard Dana could write like sailors because they *were* sailors, and Shakespeare couldn't because he wasn't. Mark Twain gets intense fun out of Shakespeare's *Tempest* storm, where the captain says, *"Fall to it, yarely, or we run ourselves to ground; bestir; bestir!"* And the boatswain answers, *"Heigh! my hearts! Cheerly, cheerly, my hearts! Yare, yare!"* "That will do for the present," says Mark, in comment, "let us yare a little now, for a change." But compare the author himself as the Sieur de Conte, when he says of the fighting outside of Orleans: *"We had a long tough piece of work before us, but we carried it through before night, Joan keeping us hard at it. . . . Everybody was tired out with this long day's hard work."* Picturesque, isn't it? But is this mediaeval hand-to-hand fighting or setting ten thousand ems of type? Pretty exhausting, evidently, this mediaeval combat. A man deserves his supper after it.

Shakespeare on the deck of a ship "has nothing on this."

What is more, all the Sieur de Conte's knights and squires seem somehow to come from Missouri or Illinois. He says that Catherine Boucher belonged to Orleans, France, yet somehow she seemed to suggest Keokuk, Iowa. Even Joan and her enemies and her judges sound like a book of quotations. In fine, Mark Twain should have been content to remain Mark Twain, if he could face the ignominy of being a "funny" writer and live it down.

He was under the impression that he had "spent twelve years of preparation on this book." But as the years from 1883 to 1895 saw also the writing of *Huckleberry Finn, A Connecticut Yankee, The American Claimant, Tom Sawyer Abroad, Pudd'nhead Wilson,* a great quantity of sketches published and otherwise, a vast series of lectures all over the map, two or three trips to Europe, social life in floods of hospitality, billiards night and day, and company without end—the researches into the Middle Ages could not have been so very exacting. Mark Twain, who had never been to college, had no notion of the long slow labour of a Gibbon, or the devoted hours of a college historian buried in book-dust, invisible for years. In flat contradiction of real authorities, let it be stated here that *Joan of Arc,* apart from the elevated subject, is about as good or as bad as dozens of historical romances written at the time, but never could have made a great reputation, nor sustained it. Mark Twain's *Joan* floats down the stream of time held up by the humble arms of *Huckleberry Finn* and *A Connecticut Yankee.*

But meantime, while *Joan* was running in *Harper's,* Mark Twain had sailed back to America, where Major Pond had already arranged his round-the-world lecture tour. It was to cover a western trip across America, then Australia, India, South Africa, and thence to England and home. Anyone who realizes how tired Mark Twain was of lecturing, of posing as a celebrity, of forcing new sayings and old jokes, may imagine with what weariness of soul he looked towards this prospect.

Yet he went at it bravely enough. He wrote to his young friend and admirer, Rudyard Kipling, to meet him in India, where he would arrive "riding on his Ayah," and then, like the man in the ballad, set his face towards the West. The chain of lectures was delivered in midsummer heat from Cleveland out to Vancouver. There he took ship (August 1895) for Australia, busy on board with his notes for the book that should recall the world trip. In Australia, lectures, receptions, honours; in India the same; in South Africa the same. Political opinions, nationalities, conflicts made no difference; for all the world he was Mark Twain; all the world knew and appreciated the nobility of his present purpose. He travelled the length and breadth of India; was entertained everywhere by officials, by rajahs, by society. He was in South Africa and saw Johannesburg and Pretoria just after the Jameson Raid, with the Uitlanders still in jail and the world still humming with speculation. Then back to England in July of

1896. There he expected to greet again his daughter Susie, who had stayed behind at college in America. But fate was not done with Mark Twain yet. Instead of the rapturous meeting there came the ominous news of illness, and then of his child's death (August 18, 1896).

The blow fell with cruel force. Beside this the financial disaster seemed as nothing. From this, and the successive bereavements that followed, Mark Twain never recovered.

But his work he bravely carried to completion. His world tour presently appeared as a book (1897) under the happy title, *Following the Equator*. There is no need to discuss its literary merit; of course it is not the *Innocents Abroad*. But the marvel is that under such circumstances the book was done so well. Such as it is, no one else could have done it. There is as ever the same instinct in finding what is interesting, and the same queer "innocence" of the eye that by looking at things crooked gets them straight. In the case of South Africa, the book is of still greater interest. Its comments, written as between the Jameson Raid of New Year 1895-96 and the War of October 1899, and written without a knowledge of the sequel of the things described, show an unusual insight. Take the calculation—Mark Twain, one recalls, was great on calculation—made as a sort of comic statistics—that at the usual rate of casualties as between Boers and Britons at Majuba and elsewhere, Dr. Jameson would have needed 240,000 men for his raid! This was meant to be as funny as the calculations of the saints and the mummies in the *Innocents Abroad*. In the light of the Boer War it is just a ghastly prophecy.

Mark Twain did not return to America with his book. He lingered on in Europe. He spent the first winter in London (1896-97); then moved about, spending a summer in Switzerland and two winters in Vienna (1897-98, 1898-99), with an Austrian country summer in between. In Austria he seems to have found a new fatherland, a second country—or, counting England, a third. In the Austrian capital especially he enjoyed a peculiar prestige. Mr. Paine tells us that his rooms at the Metropole Hotel were something like a court. Even on the street the people knew his strik-

ing figure and loved to honour him. "Herr Mark Twain" was one of the celebrities of Vienna. Better still, money was coming in again fast. His new industry did not flag. There were articles in *Harper's*, the *Cosmopolitan* and the *Century*. *Pudd'nhead Wilson* had been published in 1894 by his first publisher, the American Publishing Company. It was accompanied by *Tom Sawyer Abroad* and followed by *Tom Sawyer, Detective*. The cloud of debt was lifting. The horizon was clearing again. The "machine," indeed, had finally gone on the scrap-heap, but financially the turn of the tide had come.

But the days were saddened by new bereavements. To Vienna came the news of Orion's death (December 11, 1897). It was as if a part of Mark Twain's own life had gone. Then came the death of his old coloured butler George, a part of his Hartford home, whose loss added to the increasing loneliness. Worst of all, his little girl Jean, who had accompanied her father and mother on their wanderings, was developing an epileptic illness that struck fear into her parents' hearts.

The family left Vienna and went to London for special treatment for Jean, and from there, on the same quest, to Sweden for the summer. It was partly Jean's illness, and partly ailments of his own, that turned Mark Twain's mind to thoughts of medicine, to osteopathy, to mental treatment by Christian Science and to the bypaths and mysteries of the healing art. For a time he took a terrific interest in a new food—some sort of harmless mess of concentrated milk which he wished to see the whole world adopt. For anyone brought up in the West, the patent medicine habit dies hard. The last days of the European sojourn were spent in London, and the last summer at a charming country house (Dollis Hill House) in the suburbs. The English had long since ceased to harbour any resentment for *A Connecticut Yankee*. The life in London was one continual offer of honours and entertainments. But he longed for home. Then at last, the exile ended, he could set his feet on the home trail. With his daughter's health improved, if not restored, with the burden of debt cleared and paid, dollar for dollar, Mark Twain in the autumn of 1900 said farewell to the tumults and tyrannies of beknighted Europe and stepped again into the free atmosphere of America (in a New York Customs House) on October 15, 1900.

He was back home. His work was done. His "career" was ended.

VIII. THE EVENING OF A LONG DAY, 1900-1910

Mark Twain's return to America in the autumn of 1900, with the cloud of debt lifted and ease and affluence assured, may be said to mark the end of his active career. His work was done. There was no further need for him to seek celebrity; the national reception which greeted him on his return, the affection which surrounded him, the legend which had grown about his personality, these things could be brought to no higher point. Moreover, he was sixty-five years old. His literary work was done. The rest of his life—for he lived for nearly ten years more—was only an epilogue. It was a long evening after the day's work.

Even now he did not settle down to a single place and home. He established himself first in a furnished house (14 West Tenth Street) in New York. But in the last ten years of his life, as between the ages of sixty-five and seventy-four, Mark Twain moved about more and lived in more homes than most people do in their whole lifetime. The migratory habit had become a part of his existence. The mere enumeration of his continued change of place is staggering to sedentary people of a fixed abode. In the summer after his return (that of 1901) he and his family occupied a "cabin" on Saranac Lake in the Adirondacks, with a trip to Elmira and a yachting cruise from New England to Nova Scotia with Henry Rogers. There followed a winter (1901-2) in a new home at Riverdale, a Hudson River suburb of New York. In the summer following there came a trip to the West to pick up a degree at Missouri, with five days at Hannibal, and then a summer residence at York Harbor, Maine. There was a second winter at Riverdale (1902-3), and then a summer, the last one, at Elmira. The Hartford house had been sold; that home and its associations were gone for ever. The next winter there was a new European tour for the sake of Mrs. Clemens's failing health. It was spent at Florence, and there on the fifth of June 1904 the deepest

of all shadows fell over Mark Twain's life, with the loss of his first and last love.

Henceforth, he still had his daughters, Jean almost to the end, and Clara, alone of the family to survive him. After the homecoming to America they lived out the summer in a cottage at Tyrringham, and the winter following in New York City, at 21 Fifth Avenue. The next summer was spent in the village of Dublin in New Hampshire, and again a winter in New York, with a second summer (1906) at Dublin. But the winter following saw a trip to Bermuda, and the summer after that— contrary to all Mark Twain's own expectations—a new voyage across the Atlantic. He had thought that nothing could again induce him to cross the sea. But the award of the honorary degree of Doctor of Literature by the University of Oxford could not be refused. With the degree went entertainment and honours in London—the final and crowning proof of England's admiration and affection for the great American.

After his return home there came another trip to Bermuda, and then, in June 1908, the entry into a new and specially built home at Redding—a beautiful country place for which Mark Twain had given general directions— especially for billiards—but which he never saw until he moved in. The place presently acquired the name of "Stormfield," after his latest character in fiction. The next winter saw another visit to Bermuda, from which he returned in April of the ensuing year to Stormfield, where he died on April 21, 1910.

It would be without purpose to indicate in detail all the varied happenings of these last ten years. There were occasions of special honour, such as the granting of degrees from Yale and from Missouri, the great dinner in New York in 1902, for Mark Twain's sixty-seventh birthday, and the famous banquet given by the Lotos Club in 1908 after his return from the crowning honours of Oxford. One such special occasion was the final and farewell lecture given in Carnegie Hall, New York, April 6, 1906, for a public charity, a *nunc dimittis* after a long servitude.

Nor is it of much use to deal at full length with all the varied and random writing of the last ten years, a part of it reserved for publication till after the writer's death. The truth is that what Mark Twain wrote after 1900 is chiefly interesting because Mark Twain wrote it. Yet even to this there are brilliant exceptions.

Students of Mark Twain's work will be inclined to agree that it can be divided into various categories. There is a part of it which represents The Great Humorist, drawing our spontaneous laughter from the contrasts, the follies, and the incongruity of life. Here the casts of thought and the form of the words vie in excellence. The form of thought consists in bringing to bear an absolutely open and "innocent" point of view on things already valued and prejudged and showing them as they are. The form of words consists in making terms and phrases take on a new and sudden meaning, obvious when found, but findable only by the same process of "innocent" application. For both these things— the power of vision and the innocence of expression—Mark Twain has never been surpassed. The works that bear this stamp fully indented and fall into this class are pre-eminently the ones indicated in an earlier chapter—*Life on the Mississippi, Roughing It, The Innocents Abroad, Tom Sawyer, Huckleberry Finn,* and the *Yankee.* This is all that Mark Twain ever need have written.

Alongside of these are works intended to be in the same strain, but failing in their aim— such as *Pudd'nhead Wilson, The American Claimant, Tom Sawyer Abroad. The Gilded Age* is a mixed product, to place where one will. Close to these are the vast gargantuan burlesques planned but not finished, such as the huge *Noah's Ark* that was to have been, and a lot of fragmentary sketches. It was always possible with Mark Twain for prolixity to destroy excellence, for exaggerations to reach the point of being meaningless.

Quite different are the stories in which Mark Twain laid aside the cap and bells of the humorist to assume, in whole or in part, the character of the romantic novelist. These are *The Prince and the Pauper* and, more than anything, *Joan of Arc. De gustibus non est disputandum,* but it may be humbly suggested that the praise awarded by the cultured to these books was not accompanied by the enjoyment of the uncultured public.

But quite different from all such work was what Mark Twain wrote not as humour but as invective, not as amusement but as denunciation, not for writing's sake but for the sake of a public cause, a public idea, for liberty, for humanity. Here he only used his matchless power of phrase, his matchless touch of humour—as a weapon to destroy, a hammer to drive home a blow.

Such illumination as was shed from his old age was exactly in this field: the denunciation of war and conquest, of England in South Africa, of Europe in China, of his own republic in the Philippines; the discussion, pointed and controversial, but not altogether hostile, of the power and meaning of Christian Science; the discussion, brilliant in spite of prolixity, of who was Shakespeare; and, most of all, the discussion of heaven and hell, of God and the devil, of man and immortality, in terms not known in the Sunday School at Hannibal, Missouri, in 1850.

In such work as this, after humour for its own sake was gone, and romance had simmered into sentimentality, Mark Twain was still a master.

One pauses a moment to consider some of it.

On Shakespeare one must not linger. The ashes of controversy fan too soon into a flame. But in the opinion of many unqualified people Mark Twain's *Is Shakespeare Dead?* is the best piece of Shakespearian criticism ever attempted. He proves conclusively that Shakespeare was not Shakespeare.

But his writings on peace and war, conquest and imperialism, merit a longer mention.

It was just in this closing period of Mark Twain's life, just at the turn of the century, that the "imperialism" of the white race, gathering for a generation, reached its culmination. These were the days of the "white man's burden," of the partition of Africa, the "opening-up" of China, and the "strangling" of Persia. There was the South African War, the European armed force in China; there was "red rubber" on the Amazon and on the Congo, and there was the American occupation of the Philippine Islands. It is impossible here to discuss the good and bad of this movement. Some of the best people in the world were in favour of it; and some of the best against it. Perhaps it was destiny, perhaps it wasn't. In any case, it is long since replaced by vast upheavals of nations and of classes that have destroyed the world in which it stood. The white man has burdens of his own now.

But at the time, to many of the outgoing generation, especially in America, the whole thing seemed, as it did to Mark Twain, a reversion to barbarism, the substitution of brute force for justice, of slavery for liberty.

There was the Boer War. Mark Twain himself had written (in *Following the Equator*) of rights and wrongs in South Africa, and had stated with great emphasis the case of the Uitlanders against the Kruger government. But the spectacle of the two little republics being overwhelmed by the sheer brute power of an associated Empire, fighting overmatched but without surrender, was more than he could stand. He could not, he the Mark Twain of the legend and the corn-cob pipe, speak out. Yet it was hard for him to be silent. He told his friends that he was writing bitter articles "in his head" about it. He did write at least one article, meaning to publish it, unsigned, in the London *Times.* But he withdrew it. He could not face the storm of obloquy and denunciation that would have replaced the affection of a nation. He tried to persuade himself. "Even if wrong—and she is wrong—England must be upheld." So he wrote to Howells, "he is an enemy of the human race who shall speak against her now." This is bunk, and he knew it.

His feelings were similar towards the Philippines conquest. Mark Twain was an American of the older covenant for whom the Monroe Doctrine worked both ways. "Apparently," so he wrote, but not for publication, "we are not proposing to set the Filipinos free and give their islands to them; and apparently we are not proposing to hang the priests and confiscate their property. If these things are so, the war out there has no interest for me."

Of China and the Boxers and the missionaries and so forth, Mark Twain could speak more freely. He had nothing but admiration for the labours of the real missionary, facing poverty, hardship, exile and barbarous death to extend God's Kingdom on earth. But for the other kind of missionary, living in com-

fort, accompanied by gunboats and protected by punitive expeditions—the advance guard of European rapacity—he had nothing but horror and contempt. Those who share his feelings may read with joy and comfort the fierce invective of the article *To the Person Sitting in Darkness,* published by the *North American* in February 1901, and since included in his book.

As with the missionaries, so—and much more so—with King Leopold and the Congo. See the pamphlet, *King Leopold's Soliloquy,* written by Mark Twain and circulated by the Congo Reform Association. Official Belgium now undertakes the augean task of whitewashing the former king. We may therefore be content with quoting, without comment, what Mark Twain wrote as a proposed epitaph for the King of the Belgians. "Here under this gilded tomb lies rotting the body of one the smell of whose name may still offend the nostrils of men ages upon ages after all the Caesars and Washingtons and Napoleons shall have ceased to be praised or blamed and been forgotten—Leopold of Belgium."

It is a sweet thought, nicely expressed.

For the present purpose bygone sins and dead-and-gone issues do not count. But the point is that in reading these invectives against injustice one is in contact with Mark Twain as vitally as in reading the smiling pages of the *Innocents Abroad.*

An interesting side-issue is found in Mark Twain's queer obsession with Christian Science. On this he wrote various articles (in the *Cosmopolitan* and the *North American,* 1899-1903), and ended by wasting a whole book on it. He had taken it into his head that Christian Science was about to envelop the world; that it was going to get all the money and all the world there is—over-ride all political parties, churches, corporations and governments, and dominate mankind.

Quite evidently Mark Twain didn't know what he himself thought about Christian Science. He was fascinated with its mental healing, with its dismissal of pain. But he denounced Mrs. Eddy as a liar and a humbug, who didn't write her own books because she couldn't. Mark Twain's whole attitude was a sort of obsession. He could not see that

Christian Science would come and go, like all other cults and creeds—lose its first hard outline, its combative enthusiasm, and become—respectable; in other words, just a way of "going to church," which is for many people an instinct and a necessity. "Christian Scientists" who call in doctors become like Methodists who dance and Presbyterians who don't go to hell. Mark Twain needn't have worried. His book, *Christian Science* (1907), sounds now like attacking a grass-bird with a cannon.

But chief in interest in all of these later writings are the ones that are meant to deal with fundamental issues of God and man, heaven and hell, the Bible and the sinner. Here, for example, is *Captain Stormfield's Visit to Heaven*. It relates, on a vast cosmic scale, of size and space and number, how Captain Stormfield—a sea-captain character lifted out of one of Mark Twain's California voyages—was taken up to heaven and what he saw. It is meant to show that people couldn't *really* play the harp all day. They'd get sick of it. They couldn't really sit and wear golden crowns all day. They'd get bored with it. Such a book from the point of view of the Hannibal Sunday School class of 1850 would be bold and wicked beyond words, fascinating indeed, but apt to land the reader in hell. To the ordinary reader of today it is as pointless as it is prosy. Perhaps a divinity student might find it an amusing skit.

In other words, Mark Twain was like Don Quixote tilting against windmills. He had been brought up amongst simple frontier people, slaves, western desperadoes and bad men. None of these people ever question the Scripture. All are willing to admit that the world was made in six days, or less, that Joshua stopped the sun, and that the proof of the existence of miracles is that one happened last year in Wyoming.

In *Captain Stormfield* and *What Is Man?* (1906) and in *The Mysterious Stranger,* published after his death, Mark Twain is attacking forms of literalism long since passed away among people of any enlightenment. Mark Twain could never forgive the "God of the Bible" for his cruelty to man, his eternal sentence to hell, his creation of pain and sorrow that man might suffer.

But if no such God ever existed, why worry about him?

Such thoughts and such angers Mark Twain carried in his intimate mind all his life. He wrote them into notes, into scraps, into odd fancies in his books. When Huck Finn says, "All right, I'll *go to hell*," that is Mark Twain defying God. Some of this writing was published in his lifetime, some printed privately (like *What Is Man?*), and some had to wait till the loving censorship that held it back was gone. And some of it he laid aside to be published after his death, when no one could "get after" him.

That time was approaching.

Mark Twain had gone to Bermuda in the autumn of 1909, but, with characteristic restlessness, sailed home again to spend the Christmas holidays with Jean, who had stayed home at Stormfield. Clara, the other daughter, whose voice and whose musical talent were the delight of her father, had married, had become Mrs. Gabrilowitch, and was abroad. There was only Jean.

On the day before Christmas, in the midst of her busy and loving preparation of the Christmas tree, Jean was suddenly stricken dead. On Christmas night her body was carried away to be buried beside her mother at Elmira. "From my windows," wrote her father, "I saw the hearse and the carriages wind along the road and gradually grow vague and spectral in the falling snow, and presently disappear. Jean had gone out of my life and would not come back any more."

Next day there was a great storm of driving snow. He looked out on it. "They are burying her now at Elmira," he said. "Jean always loved to see a storm like this." For Mark Twain this was the end.

He had not long to wait. In January of 1910 he went back to Bermuda, writing home cheerfully enough to Howells and the Mr. Paine who had for years past been preparing his biography, and to his daughter Clara. But he was a stricken man. There was trouble with his heart and he had lost the will to live. Each of us, it seems, lives, as apart from accidents, as long as we want to, but the time comes when we don't want to. So it was with Mark Twain. When the time came to leave Bermuda he was failing rapidly. They carried him on board the ship and so, two days later, to the shore, and then on by train and carriage to Stormfield. He gathered strength to step from the carriage across the threshold, and from there Paine and others carried him upstairs to his bed. This was on April 14. Meantime his daughter Clara was hurrying home, arriving a day or so after they brought her father there. The end came, just with the sunset, on the evening of April 21, 1910. His last words were, "Good-bye," and then, "if we meet—" and then silence. Mark Twain was gone.

His body was buried at Elmira beside the graves of his wife and daughter.

HELEN KELLER *The Story of My Life*

Helen Adams Keller (1880-   ) was a blind, deaf-mute child, having been stricken with scarlet fever at the age of nineteen months. Despite her handicaps, she learned to talk and received her B.A. with honors from Radcliffe in 1904; she has written many books, and has lectured and traveled on behalf of the deaf and blind in countries throughout the world. After World War II she visited veterans' hospitals, assisting the handicapped to see and hear with inner eyes and ears.

The Story of My Life, which was published while Helen Keller was in college and from which the following three chapters are taken, is an autobiography in which she describes how through the sympathetic and ingenious teaching of Anne Sullivan the mystery of language was revealed to her. Her other works—*The World I Live In,* 1908; *The Song of the Stone Wall,* 1910; *Out of the Dark,* 1913; *My Religion,* 1927; *Midstream—My Later Life,* 1930; *Peace at Eventide,* 1932; *Helen Keller in Scotland,* 1933; *Helen Keller's Journal,* 1938; and *Let Us Have Faith,* 1940—tell the story of a world citizen and reveal the personality of one of the great women of the twentieth century.

I

The most important day I remember in all my life is the one on which my teacher, Anne Mansfield Sullivan, came to me. I am filled with wonder when I consider the immeasurable contrast between the two lives which it connects. It was the third of March, 1887, three months before I was seven years old.

On the afternoon of that eventful day, I stood on the porch, dumb, expectant. I guessed vaguely from my mother's signs and from the hurrying to and fro in the house that something unusual was about to happen, so I went to the door and waited on the steps. The afternoon sun penetrated the mass of honeysuckle that covered the porch, and fell on my upturned face. My fingers lingered almost unconsciously on the familiar leaves and blossoms which had just come forth to greet the sweet southern spring. I did not know what the future held of marvel or surprise for me. Anger and bitterness had preyed

upon me continually for weeks and a deep languor had succeeded this passionate struggle.

Have you ever been at sea in a dense fog, when it seemed as if a tangible white darkness shut you in, and the great ship, tense and anxious, groped her way toward the shore with plummet and sounding-line, and you waited with beating heart for something to happen? I was like that ship before my education began, only I was without compass or sounding-line, and had no way of knowing how near the harbour was. "Light! give me light!" was the wordless cry of my soul, and the light of love shone on me in that very hour.

I felt approaching footsteps. I stretched out my hand as I supposed to my mother. Someone took it, and I was caught up and held close in the arms of her who had come to reveal all things to me, and, more than all things else, to love me.

The morning after my teacher came she led me into her room and gave me a doll. The little blind children at the Perkins Institution had sent it and Laura Bridgman had dressed it; but I did not know this until afterward. When I had played with it a little while, Miss Sullivan slowly spelled into my hand the word "d-o-l-l." I was at once interested in this finger play and tried to imitate it. When I finally succeeded in making the letters correctly I was flushed with childish pleasure and pride. Running downstairs to my mother I held up my hand and made the letters for doll. I did not know that I was spelling a word or even that words existed; I was simply making my fingers go in monkey-like imitation. In the days that followed I learned to spell in this uncomprehending way a great many words, among them *pin, hat, cup,* and a few verbs like *sit, stand* and *walk.* But my teacher had been with me several weeks before I understood that everything has a name.

One day, while I was playing with my new doll, Miss Sullivan put my big rag doll into my lap also, spelled "d-o-l-l" and tried to make me understand that "d-o-l-l" applied to both. Earlier in the day we had had a tussle over the words "m-u-g" and "w-a-t-e-r." Miss Sullivan had tried to impress it upon me that "m-u-g" is *mug* and that "w-a-t-e-r" is *water,* but I persisted in confounding the two. In despair she had dropped the subject for the time, only to renew it at the first opportunity. I became impatient at her repeated attempts and, seizing the new doll, I dashed it upon the floor. I was keenly delighted when I felt the fragments of the broken doll at my feet. Neither sorrow nor regret followed my passionate outburst. I had not loved the doll. In the still, dark world in which I lived there was no strong sentiment or tenderness. I felt my teacher sweep the fragments to one side of the hearth, and I had a sense of satisfaction that the cause of my discomfort was removed. She brought me my hat, and I knew I was going out into the warm sunshine. This thought, if a wordless sensation may be called a thought, made me hop and skip with pleasure.

We walked down the path to the well-house, attracted by the fragrance of the honeysuckle with which it was covered. Someone was drawing water and my teacher placed my hand under the spout. As the cool stream gushed over one hand she spelled into the other the word *water,* first slowly then rapidly. I stood still, my whole attention fixed upon the motions of her fingers. Suddenly I felt a misty consciousness as of something forgotten—a thrill of returning thought; and somehow the mystery of language was revealed to me. I knew then that "w-a-t-e-r" meant the wonderful cool something that was flowing over my hand. That living word awakened my soul, gave it light, hope, joy, set it free! There were barriers still, it is true, but barriers that could in time be swept away.

I left the well-house eager to learn. Everything had a name, and each name gave birth to a new thought. As we returned to the house every object which I touched seemed to quiver with life. That was because I saw everything with the strange, new sight that had come to me. On entering the door I remembered the doll I had broken. I felt my way to the hearth and picked up the pieces. I tried vainly to put them together. Then my eyes filled with tears; for I realized what I had done, and for the first time I felt repentance and sorrow.

I learned a great many new words that day. I do not remember what they all were; but I do know that *mother, father, sister, teacher* were among them—words that were to make the world blossom for me, "like Aaron's rod, with flowers." It would have been difficult to find a happier child than I was as I lay in my crib at the close of that eventful day and lived over the joys it had brought me, and for the first time longed for a new day to come.

II

I had now the key to all language, and I was eager to learn to use it. Children who hear acquire language without any particular effort; the words that fall from others' lips they catch on the wing, as it were, delightedly, while the little deaf child must trap them by a slow and often painful process. But whatever the process, the result is wonderful. Gradually from naming an object we advance step by step until we have traversed the vast distance between our first stammered syllable and the sweep of thought in a line of Shakespeare.

At first, when my teacher told me about a

new thing I asked very few questions. My ideas were vague, and my vocabulary was inadequate; but as my knowledge of things grew, and I learned more and more words, my field of inquiry broadened, and I would return again and again to the same subject, eager for further information. Sometimes a new word revived an image that some earlier experience had engraved on my brain.

I remember the morning that I first asked the meaning of the word, "love." This was before I knew many words. I had found a few early violets in the garden and brought them to my teacher. She tried to kiss me; but at that time I did not like to have anyone kiss me except my mother. Miss Sullivan put her arm gently round me and spelled into my hand, "I love Helen."

"What is love?" I asked.

She drew me closer to her and said, "It is here," pointing to my heart, whose beats I was conscious of for the first time. Her words puzzled me very much because I did not then understand anything unless I touched it.

I smelt the violets in her hand and asked, half in words, half in signs, a question which meant, "Is love the sweetness of flowers?"

"No," said my teacher.

Again I thought. The warm sun was shining on us.

"Is this not love?" I asked, pointing in the direction from which the heat came. "Is this not love?"

It seemed to me that there could be nothing more beautiful than the sun, whose warmth makes all things grow. But Miss Sullivan shook her head, and I was greatly puzzled and disappointed. I thought it strange that my teacher could not show me love.

A day or two afterward I was stringing beads of different sizes in symmetrical groups—two large beads, three small ones, and so on. I had made many mistakes, and Miss Sullivan had pointed them out again and again with gentle patience. Finally I noticed a very obvious error in the sequence and for an instant I concentrated my attention on the lesson and tried to think how I should have arranged the beads. Miss Sullivan touched my forehead and spelled with decided emphasis, "Think."

In a flash I knew that the word was the name of the process that was going on in my head. This was my first conscious perception of an abstract idea.

For a long time I was still—I was not thinking of the beads in my lap, but trying to find a meaning for "love" in the light of this new idea. The sun had been under a cloud all day, and there had been brief showers; but suddenly the sun broke forth in all its southern splendour.

Again I asked my teacher, "Is this not love?"

"Love is something like the clouds that were in the sky before the sun came out," she replied. Then in simpler words than these, which at that time I could not have understood, she explained: "You cannot touch the clouds, you know, but you feel the rain and know how glad the flowers and the thirsty earth are to have it after a hot day. You cannot touch love either; but you feel the sweetness that it pours into everything. Without love you would not be happy or want to play."

The beautiful truth burst upon my mind—I felt that there were invisible lines stretched between my spirit and the spirits of others.

From the beginning of my education Miss Sullivan made it a practice to speak to me as she would speak to any hearing child; the only difference was that she spelled the sentences into my hand instead of speaking them. If I did not know the words and idioms necessary to express my thoughts she supplied them, even suggesting conversation when I was unable to keep up my end of the dialogue.

This process was continued for several years: for the deaf child does not learn in a month, or even in two or three years, the numberless idioms and expressions used in the simplest daily intercourse. The little hearing child learns these from constant repetition and imitation. The conversation he hears in his home stimulates his mind and suggests topics and calls forth the spontaneous expression of his own thoughts. This natural exchange of ideas is denied to the deaf child. My teacher, realizing this, determined to supply the kinds of stimulus I lacked. This she did by repeating to me as far as possible, verbatim, what she heard, and by showing me how I could take part in the conversation. But it was a long time before I ventured to take the initiative, and still longer before I could find something appropriate to say at the right time.

The deaf and the blind find it very difficult to acquire the amenities of conversation. How much more this difficulty must be augmented in the case of those who are both deaf and blind! They cannot distinguish the tone of the voice, or, without assistance, go up and down the gamut of tones that give significance to words; nor can they watch the expression of the speaker's face, and a look is often the very soul of what one says.

III

It was in the spring of 1890 that I learned to speak. The impulse to utter audible sounds had always been strong within me. I used to make noises, keeping one hand on my throat while the other hand felt the movements of my lips. I was pleased with anything that made a noise and liked to feel the cat purr and the dog bark. I also liked to keep my hand on a singer's throat, or on a piano when it was being played. Before I lost my sight and hearing, I was fast learning to talk, but after my illness it was found that I had ceased to speak because I could not hear. I used to sit in my mother's lap all day long and keep my hands on her face because it amused me to feel the motions of her lips; and I moved my lips, too, although I had forgotten what talking was. My friends say that I laughed and cried naturally, and for a while I made many sounds and word-elements, not because they were a means of communication, but because the need of exercising my vocal organs was imperative. There was, however, one word the meaning of which I still remembered, *water*. I pronounced it "wa-wa." Even this became less and less intelligible until the time when Miss Sullivan began to teach me. I stopped using it only after I had learned to spell the word on my fingers.

I had known for a long time that the people about me used a method of communication different from mine; and even before I knew that a deaf child could be taught to speak, I was conscious of dissatisfaction with the means of communication I already possessed. One who is entirely dependent upon the manual alphabet has always a sense of restraint, of narrowness. This feeling began to agitate me with a vexing, forward-reaching sense of a lack that should be filled. My thoughts would often rise and beat up like birds against the wind; and I persisted in using my lips and voice. Friends tried to discourage this tendency, fearing lest it would lead to disappointment. But I persisted, and an accident soon occurred which resulted in the breaking down of this great barrier—I heard the story of Ragnhild Kaata.

In 1890 Mrs. Lamson, who had been one of Laura Bridgman's teachers, and who had just returned from a visit to Norway and Sweden, came to see me, and told me of Ragnhild Kaata, a deaf and blind girl in Norway who had actually been taught to speak. Mrs. Lamson had scarcely finished telling me about this girl's success before I was on fire with eagerness. I resolved that I, too, would learn to speak. I would not rest satisfied until my teacher took me, for advice and assistance, to Miss Sarah Fuller, principal of the Horace Mann School. This lovely, sweet-natured lady offered to teach me herself, and we began the twenty-sixth of March, 1890.

Miss Fuller's method was this: she passed my hand lightly over her face, and let me feel the position of her tongue and lips when she made a sound. I was eager to imitate every motion and in an hour had learned six elements of speech: M, P, A, S, T, I. Miss Fuller gave me eleven lessons in all. I shall never forget the surprise and delight I felt when I uttered my first connected sentence, "It is warm." True, they were broken and stammering syllables; but they were human speech. My soul, conscious of new strength, came out of bondage, and was reaching through those broken symbols of speech to all knowledge and all faith.

No deaf child who has earnestly tried to speak the words which he has never heard—to come out of the prison of silence, where no tone of love, no song of bird, no strain of music ever pierces the stillness—can forget the thrill of surprise, the joy of discovery which came over him when he uttered his first word. Only such a one can appreciate the eagerness with which I talked to my toys, to stones, trees, birds and dumb animals, or the delight I felt when at my call Mildred ran to me or my dogs obeyed my commands. It is an unspeakable boon to me to be able to speak in winged words that need no interpretation. As I talked, happy thoughts fluttered up out of my words that might perhaps have struggled in vain to escape my fingers.

But it must not be supposed that I could really talk in this short time. I had learned only the elements of speech. Miss Fuller and Miss Sullivan could understand me, but most people would not have understood one word in a hundred. Nor is it true that, after I had learned these elements, I did the rest of the work myself. But for Miss Sullivan's genius, untiring perseverance and devotion, I could not have progressed as far as I have toward natural speech. In the first place, I laboured night and day before I could be understood even by my most intimate friends; in the second place, I needed Miss Sullivan's assistance constantly in my efforts to articulate each sound clearly and to combine all sounds in a thousand ways. Even now she calls my attention every day to mispronounced words.

All teachers of the deaf know what this means, and only they can at all appreciate the peculiar difficulties with which I had to contend. In reading my teacher's lips I was wholly dependent on my fingers. I had to use the sense of touch in catching the vibrations of the throat, the movements of the mouth and the expression of the face; and often this sense was at fault. In such cases I was forced to repeat the words or sentences, sometimes for hours, until I felt the proper ring in my own voice. My work was practice, practice, practice. Discouragement and weariness cast me down frequently; but the next moment the thought that I should soon be at home and show my loved ones what I had accomplished, spurred me on, and I eagerly looked forward to their pleasure in my achievement.

"My little sister will understand me now," was a thought stronger than all obstacles. I used to repeat ecstatically, "I am not dumb now." I could not be despondent while I anticipated the delight of talking to my mother and reading her responses from her lips. It astonished me to find how much easier it is to talk than to spell with the fingers, and I discarded the manual alphabet as a medium of communication on my part; but Miss Sullivan and a few friends still use it in speaking to me, for it is more convenient and more rapid than lip-reading.

Just here, perhaps, I had better explain our use of the manual alphabet, which seems to puzzle people who do not know us. One who reads or talks to me spells with his hand, using the single-hand manual alphabet generally employed by the deaf. I place my hand on the hand of the speaker so lightly as not to impede its movements. The position of the hand is as easy to feel as it is to see. I do not feel each letter any more than you see each letter separately when you read. Constant practice makes the fingers very flexible, and some of my friends spell rapidly—about as fast as an expert writes on a typewriter. The mere spelling is, of course, no more a conscious act than it is in writing.

When I had made speech my own, I could not wait to go home. At last the happiest of happy moments arrived. I had made my homeward journey, talking constantly to Miss Sullivan, not for the sake of talking, but determined to improve to the last minute. Almost before I knew it, the train stopped at the Tuscumbia station, and there on the platform stood the whole family. My eyes fill with tears now as I think how my mother pressed me close to her, speechless and trembling with delight, taking in every syllable that I spoke, while little Mildred seized my free hand and kissed it and danced, and my father expressed his pride and affection in a big silence. It was as if Isaiah's prophecy had been fulfilled in me, "The mountains and the hills shall break forth before you into singing, and all the trees of the field shall clap their hands!"

SAMUEL ELIOT MORISON *The Young Man Washington*

Samuel Eliot Morison (1887-   ), a native of Boston, was educated at Harvard, Oxford, and the École des Sciences Politiques, Paris. Beginning his teaching career at the University of California, he subsequently joined the staff at Harvard, where he has been instructor, lecturer, and professor of history since 1915. In 1922-25, he held the Harold Vyvyan Harmsworth Professorship of American History at Oxford. Professor Morison, following his service in World War I, participated in several peace conferences. In World War II he was appointed historian of United States Naval Operations, with the rank of lieutenant commander, and retired in 1951 as a rear admiral.

Professor Morison has had wide popularity as a teacher, lecturer, and historian. Among his many books are the *Oxford History of the United States*, 1927, the five-volume *Tercentennial History of Harvard University*, 1936, the magnificent biography of Columbus, *Admiral of the Ocean Sea*, 1942, for which he was awarded a Pulitzer Prize, and the eight-volume *History of United States Naval Operations in World War II*, Volume VIII of which appeared in 1953. In 1949 Professor Morison was awarded the Columbia University Bancroft Prize.

"The Young Man Washington," presented as a lecture in commemoration of the George Washington Bicentennial Celebration, traces the steps of the "father of his country" from his boyhood years until the year he became a full colonel, at the age of twenty-seven. In this brief biographical sketch Professor Morison clears away some of the myths about Washington and shows how, by the strictest self-discipline, a man of considerable but not extraordinary talent became the first citizen of his day.

Washington is the last person you would ever suspect of having been a young man, with all the bright hopes and black despairs to which young men are subject. In American folklore he is known only as a child or a general or an old, old man: priggish hero of the cherry-tree episode, commander-in-chief, or the Father of his Country, writing a farewell address. By some freak of fate, Stuart's "Athenaeum" portrait of an ideal and imposing, but solemn and weary, Washington at the age of sixty-four has become the most popular. This year it has been reproduced as the "official" portrait, and placed in every school in the country; so we may expect that new generations of American school-children will be brought up with the idea that Washington was a solemn old bore. If only Charles Willson

Peale's portrait of him as a handsome and gallant soldier could have been used instead! Or one of the charming miniatures that shows him as a young man exulting in his strength! His older biographers, too, have conspired to create the legend; and the recent efforts to "popularize" Washington have taken the unfortunate line of trying to make him out something that he was not: a churchman, politician, engineer, business man, realtor, or even "traveling man." These attempts to degrade a hero to a "go-getter," an aristocrat to a vulgarian, remind one of the epitaph that Aristotle wished to have carved on the tomb of Plato: *Hic jacet homo, quem non licet, non decet, impiis vel ignorantibus laudare* ("Here lies a man whom it is neither permissible nor proper for the irreverent or the ignorant to *praise*").

Perhaps it is not the fault of the painters and biographers that we think of Washington as an old man, but because his outstanding

debunking - someone & built up as being good — then his weaknesses
character assassination - character portrayed as good & brought up
white washing - person portrayed as bad & then attempt is made to have him good
attempt to show him as bad

qualities—wisdom, poise, and serenity—are not the qualities usually associated with youth. He seemed to have absorbed, wrote Emerson, "all the serenity of America, and left none for his restless, rickety, hysterical countrymen." The Comte de Chastellux, one of the French officers in the war, said that Washington's most characteristic feature was balance: "the perfect harmony existing between the physical and moral attributes of which he is made up." Yet Gilbert Stuart, after painting his first portrait of Washington, said that "all his features were indicative of the most ungovernable passions, and had he been born in the forests, it was his opinion that he would have been the fiercest man among the savage tribes." Both men were right. Washington's qualities were so balanced that his talents, which were great but nothing extraordinary, were more effective in the long run than those of greater generals like Napoleon, or of bolder and more original statesmen like Hamilton and Jefferson. Yet as a young man Washington was impatient and passionate, eager for glory in war, wealth in land, and success in love. Even in maturity his fierce temper would sometimes get the better of him. In Cambridge, at his headquarters in the Craigie House, he once became so exasperated at the squabbling of drunken soldiers in the front yard that, forgetting the dignity of a general, he rushed forth and "laid out" a few of the brawlers with his own fists; and then, much relieved, returned to his study. Under great provocation he would break out with a torrent of Olympian oaths that terrified the younger men on his staff. Tobias Lear, the smooth young Harvard graduate who became Washington's private secretary, admitted that the most dreadful experience in his life was hearing the General swear!

It was only through the severest self-discipline that Washington attained his characteristic poise and serenity. Discipline is not a popular word nowadays, for we associate it with schoolmasters, drill-sergeants, and dictators; and it was certainly not discipline of that sort that made the passionate young Washington into an effective man. His discipline came in a very small part from parents, masters, or superiors; and in no respect from institutions. It came from environment, from a philosophy of life that he imbibed at an impressionable age; but most of all from his own will. He

apprehended the great truth that man can only be free through mastery of himself. Instead of allowing his passions to spend themselves, he restrained them. Instead of indulging himself in a life of pleasure,—for which he had ample means at the age of twenty,—he placed duty first. In fact he followed exactly that course of conduct which, according to the secondhand popularizers of Freud, makes a person "thwarted," "inhibited," and "repressed." Yet Washington became a liberated, successful, and serene man. . . .

Whence came this impulse to self-discipline? We can find nothing to account for it in the little we know of Washington's heredity. His family was gentle but undistinguished. George knew little of his forbears and cared less, although he used the family coat of arms. Lawrence Washington, sometime Fellow of Brasenose College, Oxford, was ejected from his living by the Roundheads as a "malignant Royalist." His son John came to Virginia by way of Barbados as mate of a tobacco-ship, settled there, and became an Indian fighter, so undisciplined as to embarrass the Governor of Virginia as much as the Indians. His son Lawrence, father of Augustine, George's father, earned a competence in the merchant marine and settled down to planting. Love of the land was a trait which all Washingtons had in common: they might seek wealth at sea or glory in war, but happiness they found only in the work and sport that came from owning and cultivating land.

Usually the Washingtons married their social betters, but the second marriage of George's father was an exception. Mary Ball, the mother of Washington, has been the object of much sentimental writing; but the cold record of her own and her sons' letters shows her to have been grasping, querulous, and vulgar. She was a selfish and exacting mother, whom most of her children avoided as soon and as early as they could; to whom they did their duty, but rendered little love. It was this sainted mother of Washington who opposed almost everything that he did for the public good, who wished his sense of duty to end with his duty to her, who pestered him in his campaigns by complaining letters, and who at a dark moment of the Revolutionary War increased his anxieties by strident complaints of neglect and starvation. Yet for one thing

Americans may well be grateful to Mary Ball: her selfishness lost George an opportunity to become midshipman in the Royal Navy, a school whence few Americans emerged other than as loyal subjects of the King.

There is only one other subject connected with Washington upon which there has been more false sentiment, misrepresentation, and mendacity than on that of his mother, and that is his religion. Washington's religion was that of an eighteenth-century gentleman. Baptized in the Church of England, he attended service occasionally as a young man, and more regularly in middle age, as one of the duties of his station. He believed in God: the eighteenth-century Supreme Being, a Divine Philosopher who ruled all things for the best. He was certain of a Providence in the affairs of men. By the same token, he was completely tolerant of other people's beliefs, more so than the American democracy of today; for in a letter to the Swedenborgian church of Baltimore he wrote, "In this enlightened age and in the land of equal liberty it is our boast that a man's religious tenets will not forfeit the protection of the law, nor deprive him of the right of attaining and holding the highest offices that are known in the United States." But Washington never became an active member of any Christian church. Even after his marriage to a devout churchwoman, and when as President of the United States the eyes of all men were upon him, he never joined Martha in the beautiful and comfortable sacrament of the body and blood of Christ. The story of the "prayer at Valley Forge" is pure fable, and "George Washington's Prayer" is a pious fabrication. Christianity had little or no part in that discipline which made Washington more humble and gentle than any of the great captains, less proud and ambitious than most of the statesmen who have proclaimed themselves disciples of the Nazarene. His inspiration, as we shall see, came from an entirely different source.

Washington gained little discipline from book-learning; but like all young Virginians of the day he led an active outdoor life which gave him a magnificent physique. When fully grown he stood a little over six feet, and weighed from 175 to 200 pounds. Broad-shouldered and straight-backed, he carried his head erect and his chin up, and showed a good leg

on horseback. There is no reason to doubt the tradition of his prowess at running, leaping, wrestling, and horsemanship. The handling of horses, in which Washington was skilled at an early age, is one of the best means of discipline that a youngster can have: for he who cannot control himself can never handle a spirited horse; and for the same reason fox-hunting on horseback, which was Washington's favorite sport, is the making or the breaking of a courageous and considerate gentleman. George may not have actually thrown a dollar across the Rappahannock (though as one elderly punster remarked, "a dollar went farther in those days!"); but his amazing physical vitality is proved by an incident of his reconnaissance to the Ohio. At the close of December, 1753, he and the scout Christopher Gist attempted to cross the river just above the site of Pittsburgh, on a raft of their own making. The river was full of floating ice, and George, while trying to shove the raft away from an ice-floe with his setting-pole, fell overboard, but managed to climb aboard again. They were forced to land on an island and spend the night there without fire or dry clothing. Gist, the professional woodsman, who had not been in the water, froze all his fingers and some of his toes; but Washington suffered no ill effects from the exposure. For that, his healthy Virginia boyhood may be thanked.

His formal education was scanty. The colonial colleges provided a classical discipline more severe and selective than that of their successors,—for higher education had to become painless in America before it could be popular,—but George had none of these "advantages." There were no means to prepare him for William and Mary, the college of the Virginia gentry; his father died when he was eleven years old; and his only schoolmasters were chosen haphazardly, as was natural for a younger son in a land-poor family. Endowed with the blood and the instincts of a gentleman, he was not given a gentleman's education, as he became painfully aware when at adolescence he went to live with his half-brother at Mount Vernon.

In modern phrase, George was "parked" on the estate which would one day be his. Evidently there had been some sort of family consultation about what to do with him; and Lawrence good-naturedly offered to take him in hand, if only to get him away from the exigent mother. Lawrence Washington, his father's principal heir and hope, had been sent to England for his schooling, had served under Admiral Vernon in the War of Jenkins's Ear, and had inherited the bulk of his father's property, to the exclusion of George and the four younger brothers and sisters. The proximity of Mount Vernon to the vast estates of the Fairfax family in the Northern Neck of Virginia gave Lawrence his opportunity. He married a Fairfax, and was admitted to the gay charmed circle of the First Families of Virginia. He was already a well-established gentleman of thirty when his hobble-de-hoy half-brother came to stay.

George was then a tall, gangling lad of sixteen years, with enormous hands and feet that were continually getting in his way. Young girls giggled when he entered a room, and burst out laughing at his awkward attempts to court them. He was conscious that he did not "belong," and made every effort to improve his manners. About three years before, a schoolmaster had made him copy out 110 "Rules of Civility" from a famous handbook by one Hawkins—a popular guide to good manners already a century and a half old; and George was probably glad to have this manuscript manual of social etiquette ready to consult. One of the most touching and human pictures of Washington is that of the overgrown schoolboy solemnly conning old Hawkins's warnings against scratching oneself at table, picking one's teeth with a fork, or cracking fleas in company, lest he commit serious "breaks" in the houses of the great.

These problems of social behavior no doubt occupied considerable space in Washington's adolescent thoughts. But he was also preparing to be a man of action. At school he had cared only for mathematics. He procured books, progressed farther than his schoolmaster could take him, and so qualified to be surveyor to Lord Fairfax. This great gentleman and landowner had much surveying to be done in the Shenandoah Valley, and it was difficult to find men with enough mathematics to qualify as surveyors, or with sufficient sobriety to run a line straight and see a job through. So George at sixteen earned as Lord Fairfax's surveyor the high salary of a doubloon (about $7.50) a day, most of which

he saved up and invested in land. For he had early decided that in the fresh lands of the Virginian Valley and the West lay the road to position, competence, and happiness. His personality as well as his excellent surveying earned him the friendship of the Fairfaxes, liberal and intelligent gentlemen; and this, as we shall see, was of first importance in Washington's moral and intellectual development.

That friendship, not the doubloon a day, was the first and most fortunate gain from his surveying job; the second was the contact which it gave young Washington with frontiersmen, with Indians, and with that great teacher of self-reliance, the wilderness. He had the advantage of a discipline that few of us can get today. We are born in crowded cities, and attend crowded schools and colleges; we take our pleasure along crowded highways and in crowded places of amusement; we are tempted to assert ourselves by voice rather than deed, to advertise, to watch the clock, escape responsibility, and leave decisions to others. But a hungry woodsman could not afford to lose patience with a deer he was trying to shoot, or with a trout he was trying to catch; and it did not help him much to "bawl out" an Indian. If you cannot discipline yourself to quiet and caution in the wilderness, you won't get far; and if you make the wrong decision in woods infested with savages, you will probably have no opportunity to make another. What our New England forbears learned from the sea—that tough old nurse who plays no favorites and suffers no weaklings—Washington learned from the wilderness.

His life from sixteen to twenty was not all spent on forest trails. This was the golden age of the Old Dominion, the fifteen years from 1740 to the French and Indian War. The old roughness and crudeness were passing away. Peace reigned over the land, high prices ruled for tobacco, immigrants were pouring into the back country; the traditional Virginia of Thackeray and Vachel Lindsay—"Land of the gauntlet and the glove"—came into being. Living in Virginia at that time was like riding on the sparkling crest of a great wave just before it breaks and spreads into dull, shallow pools. At Mount Vernon, on the verge of the wilderness, you felt the zest of sharp contrasts, and received the discipline that comes from life. On the one side were mansion houses where young Washington could learn manners and philosophy from gentlefolk. He took part in all the sports and pastimes of his social equals: dancing and card-playing and flirting with the girls. When visiting a town like Williamsburg he never missed a show; and later as President he was a patron of the new American drama. He loved gunning, fox-hunting, horse-racing, and all the gentleman's field sports of the day; he bet small sums at cards, and larger sums on the ponies—and was a good loser. He liked to make an impression by fine new clothes, and by riding unruly steeds when girls were looking on; for though a graceful figure on horseback he was ungainly afoot. He belonged to clubs of men who dined at taverns and drank like gentlemen; that is to say, they drank as much wine as they could hold without getting drunk—the opposite of modern drinking, the object of which appears to be to get "as drunk as a lord" on as little liquor as possible. Tobacco, curiously enough, made George's head swim; but he learned to smoke the peace-pipe with Indians when necessary without disgracing himself.

On the other side of Mount Vernon were log cabins, and all the crude elements of American life: Scotch and "Pennsylvania Dutch," and other poor whites who as insubordinate soldiers would prove the severest test of Washington's indefatigable patience, and proof of his power over men. The incidents of roughing it, such as the "one thread bear blanket with double its weight of vermin, such as lice, fleas, etc.," which he records in the journal of his first surveying trip, were not very pleasant at first, but he took it all with good humor and good sportsmanship. A little town called Alexandria sprang up about a tobacco warehouse and wharf, and young Washington made the first survey of it. A Masonic Lodge was formed at Fredericksburg, and George, who was a good "joiner," became brother to all the rising journalists and lawyers of the northern colonies. The deep Potomac flowed past Mount Vernon, bearing ships of heavy burthen to the Chesapeake and overseas; you sent your orders to England every year with your tobacco, and ships returned with the latest modes and manners, books and gazettes, and letters full of coffee-house gossip. London did not seem very far away, and young George confessed in a letter that he hoped to visit that "gay Matrapolis" before long.

It was probably just as well that he did not visit London, for he had the best and purest English tradition in Virginia. When Washington was in his later teens, just when a young man is fumbling for a philosophy of life, he came into intimate contact with several members of the Fairfax family. They were of that eighteenth-century Whig gentry which conformed outwardly to Christianity, but derived their real inspiration from Marcus Aurelius, Plutarch, and the Stoic philosophers. Thomas, sixth Lord Fairfax, was a nobleman devoted to "Revolution Principles"—the "Glorious Revolution" of 1688, in which his father had taken an active part. Of the same line was that General Lord Fairfax, commander-in-chief of the New Model Army, who of all great soldiers in English history most resembles Washington. The ideal of this family was a noble simplicity of living, and a calm acceptance of life: duty to the Commonwealth, generosity to fellow-men, unfaltering courage and enduring virtue; in a word, the Stoic philosophy which overlaps Christian ethics more than any other discipline of the ancients. A Stoic never evaded life: he faced it. A Stoic never avoided responsibility: he accepted it. A Stoic not only believed in liberty: he practiced it.

It is not necessary to suppose that young Washington read much Stoic philosophy, for he was no great reader at any time; but he must have absorbed it from constant social intercourse with the Fairfaxes of Belvoir, neighbors whom he saw constantly. At Belvoir lived George William Fairfax, eight years Washington's senior, and his companion in surveying expeditions. Anne, the widow of Lawrence Washington, was Fairfax's sister, and Sally, the lady with whom George Washington was so happy—and so miserable—as to fall in love, was his wife. Books were there, if he wanted them. North's Plutarch was in every gentleman's library, and it was Plutarch who wrote the popular life of Cato, Washington's favorite character in history—not crabbed Cato the Censor, but Cato of pent-up Utica. At the age of seventeen, Washington himself owned an outline, in English, of the principal Dialogues of Seneca the younger, "sharpest of all the Stoicks." The mere chapter headings are the moral axioms that Washington followed through life:

A Sensual Life is a Miserable Life
Hope and Fear are the Bane of Human Life
An Honest Man can never be outdone in Courtesy
A Good man can never be Miserable, nor a Wicked man Happy
The Contempt of Death makes all the Miseries of Life Easy to us

And of the many passages that young Washington evidently took to heart, one may select this:

No man is born wise: but Wisdom and Virtue require a Tutor; though we can easily learn to be Vicious without a Master. It is Philosophy that gives us a Veneration for God; a Charity for our Neighbor; that teaches us our Duty to Heaven, and Exhorts us to an Agreement one with another. It unmasks things that are terrible to us, asswages our Lusts, refutes our Errors, restrains our Luxury, Reproves our avarice, and works strangely on tender Natures.

Washington read Addison's tragedy *Cato* in company with his beloved; and if they did not act it together in private theatricals, George expressed the wish that they might. At Valley Forge, when the morale of the army needed a stimulus, Washington caused *Cato* to be performed, and attended the performance. It was his favorite play, written, as Pope's prologue says,

To make mankind in conscious virtue bold,
Live o'er each scene, and be what they behold.

Portius, Cato's son, whose "steddy temper"

Can look on guilt, rebellion, fraud, and Caesar
In the calm lights of mild Philosophy

declares (I, ii, 40-45):

I'll animate the soldiers' drooping courage
With love of freedom, and contempt of Life:
I'll thunder in their ears their country's cause
And try to rouse up all that's Roman in 'em.
'Tis not in Mortals to Command Success
But we'll do more, Sempronius, we'll Deserve it.

These last two lines sound the note that runs through all Washington's correspondence in the dark hours of the Revolutionary struggle;

and these same lines are almost the only literary quotations found in the vast body of Washington's writings. Many years after, when perplexed and wearied by the political squabbles of his presidency and longing to retire to Mount Vernon, Washington quoted the last lines of Cato's advice to Portius (IV, iv, 146-154):

Let me advise thee to retreat betimes
To thy paternal seat, the Sabine field,
Where the great Censor toil'd with his own hands,
And all our frugal Ancestors were blest
In humble virtues, and a rural life.
There live retired, pray for the peace of Rome:
Content thy self to be obscurely good.
When vice prevails, and impious men bear sway,
The post of honour is a private station.

From his camp with General Forbes's army in the wilderness Washington wrote to Sally Fairfax, September 25, 1758:

I should think our time more agreeably spent, believe me, in playing a part in Cato with the Company you mention, and myself doubly happy in being the Juba to such a Marcia as you must make.

Marcia was the worthy daughter of Cato, and Juba her lover, the young Numidian prince to whom Syphax says

You have not read mankind, your youth admires
The throws and swellings of a Roman soul
Cato's bold flights, th' extravagance of Virtue

To which Juba replies (II, iv, 49-58):

              Turn up thy eyes to Cato!
There may's thou see to what a godlike height
The Roman virtues lift up mortal man,
While good, and just, and anxious for his friends,
He's still severely bent against himself;
Renouncing sleep, and rest, and food, and ease,
He strives with thirst and hunger, toil and heat;
And when his fortune sets before him all
The pomps and pleasures that his soul can wish,
His rigid virtue will accept of none.

Given this combination—a young man of innate noble qualities, seeking a philosophy of life, thrown in contact during his most impressionable years with a great gentleman whom he admired, a young gentleman who was his best friend, and a young lady whom he loved, all three steeped in the Stoical tradition—and what would you expect? Can it be a mere coincidence that this characterization of the Emperor Antoninus Pius by his adopted son Marcus Aurelius, the imperial Stoic, so perfectly fits the character of Washington?

Take heed lest thou become a Caesar indeed; lest the purple stain thy soul. For such things have been. Then keep thyself simple, good, pure, and serious; a friend to justice and the fear of God; kindly, affectionate, and strong to do the right. Reverence Heaven and succour man. Life is short; and earthly existence yields but one harvest, holiness of character and altruism of action. Be in everything a true disciple of Antoninus. Emulate his constancy in all rational activity, his unvarying equability, his purity, his cheerfulness of countenance, his sweetness, his contempt for notoriety, and his eagerness to come at the root of the matter.

Remember how he would never dismiss any subject until he had gained a clear insight into it and grasped it thoroughly; how he bore with the injustice of his detractors and never retorted in kind; how he did nothing in haste, turned a deaf ear to the professional tale-bearers, and showed himself an acute judge of characters and actions, devoid of all reproachfulness, timidity, suspiciousness, and sophistry; how easily he was satisfied,—for instance, with lodging, bed, clothing, food, and servants,— how fond of work and how patient; capable, thanks to his frugal diet, of remaining at his post from morning till night, having apparently subjected even the operations of nature to his will; firm and constant in friendship, tolerant of the most outspoken criticism of his opinions, delighted if any one could make a better suggestion than himself, and, finally, deeply religious without any trace of superstition.

When Washington was twenty years old, his brother Lawrence died. George, next heir by their father's will, stepped into his place as proprietor of Mount Vernon. At this stage of his life, George did not greatly enjoy the exacting task of running a great plantation; he thirsted for glory in war. But he soon began to enlarge and improve his holdings, and in the end came to love the land as nothing else. Late in life, when the First Citizen of the World, he wrote, "How much more delightful is the task of making improvements on the earth than all the vain-glory which can be acquired from ravaging it by the most uninterrupted career of conquests." And again, "To see plants rise from the earth and flourish by the superior skill and bounty of the la-

borer fills a contemplative mind with ideas which are more easy to be conceived than expressed." That was the way with all Washington's ideas: they were more easily conceived and executed than expressed on paper. Ideas did not interest him, nor was he interested in himself. Hence the disappointing matter-of-fact objectiveness of his letters and diaries.

Nevertheless, it is clear from Washington's diaries that farming was a great factor in his discipline. For the lot of a Virginia planter was not as romance has colored it. Slaves had to be driven, or they ate out your substance; overseers watched, or they slacked and stole; accounts rigidly balanced, or you became poorer every year. There were droughts, and insect pests, and strange maladies among the cattle. Washington's life at Mount Vernon was one of constant experiment, unremitting labor, unwearying patience. It was a continual war against human error, insect enemies, and tradition. He might provide improved flails and a clean threshing floor in his new barns; when his back was turned the overseer would have the wheat out in the yard, to be trod into the muck by the cattle. His books prove that he was an eager and bold experimenter in that "new husbandry" of which Coke of Norfolk was the great exponent. There were slave blacksmiths, carpenters, and bricklayers; a cider press and a still-house, where excellent corn and rye whisky was made, and sold in barrels made by the slaves from plantation oak. Herring and shad fisheries in the Potomac provided food for the slaves; a grist-mill turned Washington's improved strain of wheat into flour, which was taken to market in his own schooner, which he could handle like a downeast skipper. Indeed, it is in his husbandry that we can earliest discern those qualities that made Washington the first soldier and statesman of America. As landed proprietor no less than as commander-in-chief, he showed executive ability, the power of planning for a distant end, and a capacity for taking infinite pains. Neither drought nor defeat could turn him from a course that he discerned to be proper and right; but in farming as in war he learned from failure, and grew in stature from loss and adversity.

Not long after inheriting Mount Vernon,

Washington had opportunity to test what his brother had taught him of military tactics and the practice of arms. Drilling and tactics, like surveying, were a projection of Washington's mathematical mind; like every born strategist he could see moving troops in his mind's eye, march and deploy them and calculate the time to a minute. He devoured accounts of Frederick's campaigns, and doubtless dreamt of directing a great battle on a grassy plain—a terrain he was destined never to find in this shaggy country. As one of the first landowners in the county, at twenty he was commissioned major of militia. He then asked for and obtained the post of adjutant of militia for the county. The settlement of his brother's affairs brought him into contact with Governor Dinwiddie, a shrewd Scot who knew a dependable young man when he saw one; and from this came his first great opportunity.

At twenty-one he was sent on a highly confidential and difficult thousand-mile reconnaissance through the back country from western Virginia to the Ohio, and almost to the shores of Lake Erie. This young man just past his majority showed a caution in wilderness work, a diplomatic skill in dealing with Indians, and a courteous firmness in dealing with French commanders that would have done credit to a man twice his age. But on his next mission, one notes with a feeling of relief, youthful impetuosity prevailed. Unmindful that one must always let the enemy make the first aggression, our young lieutenant-colonel fired the shot that began the Seven Years' War.

A phrase of the young soldier's blithe letter to his younger brother: "I heard the bullets whistle, and believe me, there is something charming in the sound," got into the papers, and gave sophisticated London a good laugh. Even George the Second heard it and remarked, "He would not say so, if he had been used to hear many." That time would come soon enough. Washington's shot in the silent wilderness brought the French and Indians buzzing about his ears. He retired to Fort Necessity, which he had caused to be built in a large meadow, hoping to tempt the enemy to a pitched battle. But the enemy was so inconsiderate! He swarmed about the fort in such numbers that Washington was lucky

to be allowed to capitulate and go home; for this was one of those wars that was not yet a war—it was not declared till two years after the fighting began. The enemy was so superior in numbers that nobody blamed Washington; and when General Braddock arrived with an army of regulars, he invited the young frontier leader to accompany his expedition into the wilderness.

There is no need here to repeat the tale of Braddock's defeat, except to say that the general's stupidity and the colonel's part in saving what could be saved have both been exaggerated. Parkman wrote in his classic *Montcalm and Wolfe*, "Braddock has been charged with marching blindly into an ambuscade; but it was not so. There was no ambuscade; and had there been one, he would have found it." That is the truth of the matter; and whilst Washington's behavior was creditable in every respect, he did not save Braddock's army; the French and Indians were simply too busy despoiling the dead and wounded, to pursue.

Shortly after Washington reached Alexandria, the annual electoral campaign began for members of the Virginia Assembly. In a political dispute the Colonel said something insulting to a quick-tempered little fellow named Payne, who promptly knocked him down with a hickory stick. Soldiers rushed up to avenge Washington, who recovered just in time to tell them he was not hurt, and could take care of himself, thank you! The next day he wrote to Payne requesting an interview at a tavern. The little man arrived, expecting a demand for an apology, or a challenge. Instead, Washington apologized for his insult which had provoked the blow, hoped that Payne was satisfied, and offered his hand. Some of Washington's biographers cannot imagine or understand such conduct. One of them brackets this episode with the cherry-tree yarn as "stories so silly and so foolishly impossible that they do not deserve an instant's consideration." Another explains Washington's conduct as a result of his defeat at Fort Necessity: "Washington was crushed into such meekness at this time that . . . instead of retaliating or challenging the fellow to a duel, he apologized." But the incident, which has been well substantiated, occurred after Braddock's defeat, not Washington's; and it was due to Stoical magnanimity, not Christian meekness. "It is the Part of a Great Mind to despise Injuries," says Seneca the younger, in the L'Estrange translation that Washington owned. The Payne affair was merely an early instance of what Washington was doing all his life: admitting he was wrong when he was convinced he was in the wrong, and doing the handsome thing in a gentlemanly manner. A man who took that attitude became impregnable to attack by politicians or anyone else. For a young man of twenty-three to take it, meant that he had firm hold of a great philosophy.

During the next two years, Washington had charge of the frontier defenses of Virginia, and a chain of thirty garrisoned stockades which followed the Shenandoah Valley and its outer bulwarks from Winchester to the North Carolina line. In the execution of this command he showed a prodigious physical activity, often riding thirty miles a day for several days over wilderness trails. His letters show a youthful touchiness about rank and recognition; he sorely tried the patience of Governor Dinwiddie, who, to Washington's evident surprise, accepted a proffered resignation; but he was soon reappointed and took a leading part in General Forbes's expedition against Fort Duquesne. It was merely to settle a question of precedence that Washington undertook a long journey to interview Governor Shirley, the commander-in-chief at Boston. One aide and two servants, clad in new London liveries of the Washington colors and mounted on horses with the Washington arms embroidered on their housings, accompanied their Colonel; for Washington had a young man's natural love of showing off. He stopped with great folk on the way and gave generous tips to their servants; he enjoyed seeing Bostonians gape at the servants in scarlet and white livery— somewhat soiled by travel to be sure, although they had stopped in New York long enough to have everything cleaned, and the Colonel had two new uniforms made in Boston. But Washington never made the mistake of wearing splendid clothes on the wrong occasion. In the French and Indian war he wore a plain neutral-colored uniform instead of British scarlet, and dressed his men as frontiersmen, in buckskin and moccasins, so that they carried no superfluous weight and offered no mark to the Indians.

As a young officer he often became impatient with the frontier folk—their short-sighted selfishness in refusing to unite under his command, their lack of discipline and liability to panic, and the American militiaman's propensity to offer unwanted advice and sulk if it were not taken. But he found something to like in them as he did in all men, and learned to work with and through them. Militia deserted Washington as they deserted other officers, despite the flogging of sundry and the hanging of a few to encourage the rest. Here is plenty of material for a disparaging biographer to describe Washington as a military martinet who had not even the merit of a notable victory; and some of the "debunkers," who have never known what it is to command troops, have said just that. A sufficient reply to them, as well as striking proof of the amazing confidence, even veneration, which Washington inspired at an early age, is the "Humble Address" of the twenty-seven officers of his regiment, beseeching him to withdraw his resignation:

Sir,

We, your most obedient and affectionate Officers, beg leave to express our great Concern, at the disagreeable News we have received of your Determination to resign the Command of that Corps, in which we have under you long served. . . .

In our earliest Infancy you took us under your Tuition, train'd us up in the Practice of that Discipline, which alone can constitute good Troops, from the punctual Observance of which you never suffer'd the least Deviation.

Your steady adherence to impartial Justice, your quick Discernment and invariable Regard to Merit, . . . first heighten'd our natural Emulation, and our Desire to excel. . . .

Judge then, how sensibly we must be Affected with the loss of such an excellent Commander, such a sincere Friend, and so affable a Companion. . . .

It gives us an additional Sorrow, when we reflect, to find, our unhappy Country will receive a loss, no less irreparable, than ourselves. Where will it meet a Man so experienc'd in military affairs? One so renown'd for Patriotism, Courage and Conduct? Who has so great knowledge of the Enemy we have to deal with? Who so well acquainted with their Situation and Strength? Who so much respected by the Soldiery? Who in short so able to support the military Character of Virginia? . . .

We with the greatest Deference, presume to entreat you to suspend those Thoughts [of resigning] for another Year. . . . In you we place the most implicit Confidence. Your Presence only will cause a steady Firmness and Vigor to actuate in every Breast, despising the greatest Dangers, and thinking light of Toils and Hardships, while led on by the Man we know and Love. . . .

Fully persuaded of this, we beg Leave to assure you, that as you have hitherto been the actuating Soul of the whole Corps, we shall at all times pay the most invariable Regard to your Will and Pleasure, and will always be happy to demonstrate by our Actions, with how much Respect and Esteem we are,

Sir,

Your most affectionate

Fort Loudoun   and most obedient

Decr 31st 1758   humble Servants

[Twenty-seven signatures]

There stands the young man Washington, reflected in the hearts of his fellows. As one reads this youthfully sincere composition of the officers' mess at Fort Loudoun, one imagines it addressed to a grizzled veteran of many wars, a white-whiskered colonel of fifty. Colonel Washington was just twenty-six.

A farewell to arms, Washington was determined it must be. Fort Duquesne was won, and his presence at the front was no longer needed. Virginia, the colony which had received the first shock of the war, could justly count on British regulars and the northern colonies to carry it to a glorious conclusion on the Plains of Abraham.

In four years Washington had learned much from war. He found it necessary to discipline himself before he could handle men. He had learned that the interminable boredom of drill, arguing about supplies, and begging for transportation was ill rewarded by the music of whistling bullets; that war was simply hard, beastly work. The sufferings of the border people, the bloody shambles on the Monongahela, the frozen evidence of torture on the road to Fort Duquesne, cured his youthful appetite for glory, completely. When Washington again drew his sword, in 1775, it was with great reluctance, and only because he believed, like Cato (II, v, 85):

The hand of fate is over us, and Heaven
Exacts severity from all our thoughts.
It is not now a time to talk of aught
But chains, or conquest; liberty, or death.

Nor was Washington one to be rushed off his feet by every gust of war propaganda. Twice, as President of the United States, he courageously resisted popular clamor for war, and cheerfully sacrificed his popularity to preserve peace with England.

From one woman he learned perhaps as much as from war. Sally Cary, his fair tutor in Stoicism and the great love of his life, was eighteen and married to his friend and neighbor George William Fairfax, when at sixteen he first met her. Beautiful, intelligent, and of gentle birth, Mrs. Fairfax took a more than sisterly interest in the callow young surveyor; and as near neighbors they saw much of each other. Cryptic jottings in his diary for 1748 show that he was already far gone in love. His pathetic letter to her from Fort Necessity in 1755, begging for a reply to "make me happy as the day is long," gives a human note in the midst of his businesslike military correspondence. No letters from her to him have been preserved, but from the tone of his replies I gather that Sally was somewhat more of a tease than befitted Cato's daughter. Whatever her sentiments may have been toward him, Washington's letters leave no doubt that he was passionately in love with her; yet gentlemanly standards were then such that while her husband lived she could never be his wife, much less his mistress. What anguish he must have suffered, any young man can imagine. It was a situation that schooled the young soldier-lover in manners, moderation, and restraint—a test case of his Stoical philosophy. His solution was notable for its common sense: when on a hurried visit to Williamsburg in the spring of 1758, to procure clothes for his ragged soldiers, he met, wooed, and won a housewifely little widow of twenty-seven named Martha Custis. She wanted a manager for her property and a stepfather for her children; he needed a housekeeper for Mount Vernon. It was a *mariage de convenance* that developed into a marriage of affection. But Martha well knew that she was not George's first or greatest love, nor he hers.

Twenty-five years later, when Mrs. Fairfax was a poor and childless widow in London, crushing the memories of her Virginia springtime in her heart, there came a letter from Washington. The First Citizen of the World writes that the crowded events of the quarter-century since they parted have not eradicated "from my mind the recollection of those happy moments, the happiest of my life, which I enjoyed in your company." Martha Washington enclosed a letter under the same cover, in order to show that she, too, understood.

Let us neither distort nor exaggerate this relation, the most beautiful thing in Washington's life. Washington saw no visions of Sally Fairfax in the battle-smoke. He did not regard himself as her knightly champion, or any such romantic nonsense; Walter Scott had not yet revived the age of chivalry. Women occupied a small part in Washington's thoughts, as in those of most men of action. No more than Cato did he indulge in worry or bitter thoughts about his ill fortune in love. Suppose, however, Washington had turned out a failure or shown some fault of character at a critical moment, instead of superbly meeting every test. Every yapping biographer of the last decade would have blamed the three members of this blameless triangle. Since he turned out otherwise, we can hardly fail to credit both women with an important share in the formation of Washington's character. And who will deny that Washington attained his nearly perfect balance and serenity, not through self-indulgence but through restraint?

What of other women?—a subject which cannot be shirked in any honest account of the young man Washington. Many of you must have heard, in club or smoking-car gossip, the story of that so-called letter of Washington inviting someone to Mount Vernon, and setting forth the charms of a certain slave-girl. No investigator has ever managed to see this letter, or even found a person who has seen it. The nearest we get is to the man who knows a man who has seen it—but that man for some peculiar reason is always sick, dead, or non-existent when you look for him, or else he refers you to another man, who knows the man, who knows the man that has it. Mr. John C. Fitzpatrick, who has spent much time on the trail of the seductive if mythical octoroon of Mount Vernon, believes that all stories of this sort were started by a spurious sentence in a letter from Benjamin Harrison to Washington during the war, which was intercepted by the British and printed in England. Fortunately the original, a plain letter of military information, has been preserved. But when it was given out for publication to the *Gentleman's Magazine* (of all places), the editor interpolated a jocularly bawdy description of "pretty little Kate the washer-woman's daughter," whose charms the commander-in-chief was invited to share. Of similar origin are the stories of Washington's illegitimate children. Of course one cannot prove a negative to every rumor. I can only state my opinion that, in view of the fact that Washington fell deeply in love at sixteen, and remained in love with the same lady until his marriage, and maintained a reputation for faithfulness under pitiless publicity, he led the life of a Christian gentleman.

Plutarch wrote of Cato, "He had not taken to public life, like some others, casually or automatically or for the sake of fame or personal advantage. He chose it because it was the function proper to a good man." That was why Washington got himself elected in 1758 to the Virginia Assembly, an office proper to a gentleman of his station. He had no gift for speaking or for wirepulling; he showed no talent or desire for political leadership. But he learned at first hand the strange behavior of *homo sapiens* in legislative assemblies. Everyone marvels at the long-suffering patience shown by Washington in his dealings with Congress during the war; few remember that he had been for many years a burgess of Virginia, and for several months a member of the very Congress to which he was responsible.

So at twenty-seven George Washington was not only a veteran colonel who had won the confidence and affection of his men, but a member of the Virginia Assembly, a great landowner, and a husband. His youth was over, and he had the means for a life of ease and competence; but the high example of antique virtue would not let him ignore another call to duty. When it came, his unruly nature had been disciplined by the land and the wilderness, by philosophy and a noble woman, and by his own indomitable will, to become a fit instrument for a great cause. There were other colonial soldiers in 1775 who from better opportunity had gained more glory in the last war than he; but there was none who inspired so much confidence as this silent, capable man of forty-three. So that when the political needs of the moment required a Virginian, there was no question but that Colonel Washington should be commander-in-chief.

If he had failed, historians would have blamed the Continental Congress for a political appointment of a provincial colonel with an indifferent war record. If he had failed, the American Revolution would have been something worse than futile—a Rebellion of '98 that would have soured the American charac-

ter, made us another Ireland, with a long and distressful struggle for freedom ahead. If, like so many leaders of revolutions, he had merely achieved a personal triumph, or inoculated his country with ambition for glory, the world would have suffered from his success. His country could and almost did fail Washington; but Washington could not fail his country, or disappoint the expectations of his kind. A simple gentleman of Virginia with no extraordinary talents had so disciplined himself that he could lead an insubordinate and divided people into ordered liberty and enduring union.

THE SHORT STORY

INTRODUCTION

The art of story telling is doubtless older than the records of civilization. Even the so-called modern short story, which was the latest of the major literary types to evolve, has an ancient lineage. Perhaps the oldest and most direct ancestor of the short story is the *anecdote*—an illustrative story, straight to the point. The ancient *parable* and *fable*, starkly brief narratives used to enforce some moral or spiritual truth, anticipate the severe brevity and unity of some short stories written today. With the Middle Ages came such types as the *exemplum*, a brief story used to support the text of a sermon, and the *ballad*, folk verse centered about a dramatic episode. During the sixteenth, seventeenth, and eighteenth centuries numerous forerunners of the short story appeared, such as the *sketch*, and the *tale*—loosely constructed prose narratives, not so compact, intense, and comprehensive as the short story. Though these early narratives sometimes bear close resemblance to the modern short story, few, if any, of them exemplify its specialized artistry.

THE DEVELOPMENT OF THE SHORT STORY. The short story as it is known today began with Nathaniel Hawthorne and Edgar Allan Poe. The first typical story of each of these writers was published in 1835—Poe's "Berenice" and Hawthorne's "The Ambitious Guest." Though it now seems naïve, Poe's horror story demonstrated its author's mastery of a new type of narrative. Poe's characters may be strange, the action of his plots far removed from ordinary experience, and his scenes fantastic, but everything in his stories is subordinate to narrative suspense and emotional effect.

Hawthorne's stories are as closely knit and unified as Poe's. But Hawthorne, unlike Poe, is primarily a moralist, and his constant focus on a moral problem—selfishness, pride, ambition—is usually the unifying factor of his story. It was this quality in his work that caused Poe, when reviewing the *Twice-Told Tales* in 1842, to observe:

A skillful literary artist has constructed a tale. If wise, he has not fashioned his thoughts to accommodate his incidents; but having conceived, with deliberate care, a certain unique or single effect to be wrought out, he then invents such incidents—he then combines such events as may best aid him in establishing this preconceived effect. If his very initial sentence tend not to the outbringing of this effect, then he has failed in his first step. In the whole composition there should be no word written, of which the tendency, direct or indirect, is not to the one pre-established design.

This celebrated passage is now generally considered the first significant definition of the type. And, along with an earlier stricture in the same essay—a story must not be so long that it "cannot be read at one sitting"—Poe's phrase "a certain unique or single effect" remains, with remarkable accuracy, the hallmark of the short story even today. By 1842, then, Hawthorne and Poe had isolated and defined the essential characteristics of the short story—brevity, unity, intensity. Forty years later an American critic, Brander Matthews, rephrased Poe's definition and supplied a label: the short story, called the "Short-story" (spelled with a hyphen) "to emphasize the distinction between the Short-story and the story which is merely short." In the meantime, two other American writers had made significant contributions to this literary form: Bret Harte, with his stories of early life in California, started a vogue of local color stories, and Henry James produced the first of his long series of peculiarly modern psychological investigations of the human mind and heart.

Later developments of the short story remain for the most part within the limits set by these writers and critics. One must not, however, overlook the far-reaching effect on the American short story of two foreign writers, Guy de Maupassant and Anton Chekhov. Maupassant showed remarkable ingenuity in inventing means to gain dramatic compression and considerable boldness in relentlessly subordinating everything to a central effect. The structural neatness of countless "plotted" stories owes, ultimately, something to Maupassant's technique. Chekhov's practice of presenting a segment of life, objective and seemingly plotless yet highly suggestive and penetrating, has been another influence on the short story—perhaps second to none in recent years. Many writers agree with Chekhov that life poses questions but has no answers for them. The artist, they believe, is therefore obliged only to give a unified impression of some part of life.

The major development in the short story in recent decades, in fact, has been the work of a group of writers sometimes called the Impressionistic School. The great masters from which this group descended are, in addition to Chekhov and James, Gustave Flaubert, Stephen Crane, and James Joyce. Some of the best known of the more recent members of the group are Katherine Mansfield, D. H. Lawrence, and Frank O'Connor in Great Britain and Sherwood Anderson, Ernest Hemingway, and William Faulkner in the United States. All of these writers seem to think (in James's phrase) that fiction should present "a direct impression of life."

The flowering of the short story was one of the principal literary events of the first half of the twentieth century, especially in the United States, where the rapid growth of periodicals and the tempo and pressure of American life have provided special inducements. Scores of writers have discovered dynamic materials in the isolated communities and forgotten backwoods, the humdrum towns, the congested cities; they have presented the lost generation, the gangster, the neglected artist, the immigrant, the lingering pioneer; they have written about Harlem, Chicago, Winesburg, the Prairies, the Appalachian Mountains, the Deep South.

THE ART OF THE SHORT STORY. An awareness of the essential characteristics already pointed out—brevity, unity, intensity—increases the reader's understanding and enjoyment of a short story. In addition, some knowledge of the specialized techniques by which these qualities are produced makes communication between writer and reader more satisfying.

Scene. In all forms of fiction, from the longest novel to the shortest short story, the basic elements are the same: scene, character, and action. The least important is scene, which in most instances merely "sets the stage" and, because of the premium on space in the short story, is handled as quickly as possible. Yet in some stories the scene is of basic importance—in "The Open Boat," for example, where the sea becomes the central force in the men's existence. And many of the most eminent authors (Chekhov, Faulkner, Hemingway) make scene contribute to the intensity of the story. Notice, for instance, how summarily Hemingway treats scene in "A Clean, Well-Lighted Place," and yet how central that element is to the whole story.

Character. The primary concern of most authors is character: "Take care of character," Galsworthy said; "action and dialogue will take care of themselves." Theme and meaning evolve from the interrelation between a character and the circumstances of his life. Yet there is in the short story neither time nor space to show development or disintegration; this is the province of the novel. Furthermore, the focus is usually on one character; other characters are portrayed only in complementary detail. In the Hemingway story, for instance, the main character is the older waiter. The other characters serve only to emphasize his personality and predicament. In most stories the main character is easily discovered. If the reader identifies the main character early in the story, he will more accurately understand the intricate relationships among the characters and consequently gain a fuller appreciation of what they do and say.

Action. For many readers action is the most important element of fiction. In fact the success of some stories—"Taste," for example—depends primarily on an ingenious plot. Yet many of the best short story writers today often minimize action, lest it destroy that delicate balance of all the elements on which their total achievement depends. Still, everyone agrees that some plot is indispensable. But the action by which plot is developed must, in the short story, be limited to a critical moment in the life of the chief character. His whole life history cannot be told; that again is the province of the novel. The essential of plot is conflict; it alone causes tension and creates suspense. The conflict may be of various kinds: an inner conflict (as in "A Clean, Well-Lighted Place"), a conflict between two persons (as in "The Catbird Seat"), a conflict between the characters and their surroundings (as in "The Open Boat"). Ordinarily the action follows a definite pattern. It begins with the *incentive moment* (first point of conflict), develops through a series of entanglements (*complication*), reaches a peak of intensity (*climax*), and becomes disentangled in the *resolution.* Though it would hardly be wise to graph the action of a story, fixing precisely the incentive moment, the climax, and the moment of last suspense, it is helpful, even in casual reading, to note the beginning of the conflict, to follow the increasing tension to the highest point of interest, and to watch the suspense subside and come to rest.

Scene, character, and plot are combined into a continuum of existence, an illusion of reality, so that the reader willingly suspends disbelief and enters into the experience of the story. In working the elements into a pattern of continuous experience, the writer makes use chiefly of two techniques—summary and drama (sometimes referred to as the "long view" and the "short view"). If he decides to hurry over a certain part of the story, he simply describes or summarizes what happens. But those parts which are crucial he presents in vivid detail. It is then that the characters usually break into dialogue. Thus by using the long view the author can economize, and by using the short view, he can gain the intensity that marks the short story.

The elements of scene, character, and plot may be discovered by analyzing a story, but they are in reality inseparable; and the art of the short story in no small degree depends on the skill of the writer in making all of them illuminate the theme of the story. Furthermore, the action of the story itself must be related to the life that existed before the story began and will continue to exist after the story ends. It is the relation between the specific action of the story and this enveloping action that affords the shock of discovery in the resolution and gives the story meaning.

Though the major devices which constitute the art of the short story concern the handling of the basic elements of scene, character, and action, there are a few special techniques which are of particular importance to the reader.

Beginning and Ending. Since the short story presents only a fragment of experience, the writer employs a special technique in handling the beginning and ending of his story, in order to give the reader a feeling that the story is a part of continuous life. Often he begins and ends his story with a sentence or phrase that will refer to the enveloping action. In "The Dry Rock," for instance, the background of the story is the strenuous life in a modern city, in which there is no time for "principle." The story begins with the remark, "We're late." The story ends immediately after describing Tarloff, the mistreated cab driver, whose efforts to defend his personal dignity are stranded on "the dry rock of principle," as he disappears in the noise and confusion of the city traffic.

Point of View. In writing or in reading a short story, an important consideration is point of view; that is, through whose eyes the story is seen. There are five rather widely used points of view: the *omniscient* point of view (as in "The Man Jones"), in which the author knows everything, even the minds of his characters, and can see the action from every angle; the *first person* point of view (as in Marjorie Kinnan Rawlings' "Cocks Must Crow"), in which the author speaks as one of the characters (usually as the protagonist); the *third person* point of view (as in "Birthday Party"), in which someone outside the story is the narrator; the *central intelligence* (as in "The Dry Rock"), in which the story is presented as seen through the eyes of one of the characters though related as by an omniscient narrator; and the *scenic* (as in "A Clean, Well-Lighted Place"), in which the narrator is effaced and the story is presented almost entirely through dialogue, as in a play. These narrative methods vary chiefly in two respects—the amount of freedom they allow and the degree of directness they permit. For the writer, fixing on point of view is of utmost importance, since, if he is to realize the full value of his material, he must choose a convenient position from which to tell the story. For the reader, an awareness of point of view is also highly important, for once he has discovered through whose eyes he is to see what happens, the story unfolds more easily and can be more readily interpreted.

Language. In the modern short story, language is a critical component—hardly less decisive than in poetry. Since a story is built around a particular isolated experience, the language in which it is set down must suggest the quality of that experience: the language must be incisive, suggestive, and alert. In a well-written story, one need not read beyond the first few sentences to find words that reveal its unique quality. Since so much of a short story is often presented dramatically, the language of dialogue is of particular importance. Perhaps no modern writer excels William Faulkner in writing dialogue full of meaningful cadence and rhythm. In "Spotted Horses," for example, when Mrs. Armstid sees that her husband is about to buy a worthless horse from the Texas stranger and the swindler Flem Snopes, she says, "He hain't no more despair than to buy one of them things. And us not five dollars ahead of the pore house, he hain't no more despair." In context, which includes some vivid descriptive detail, this remark reveals, with poetic accuracy, the character and role of Mrs. Armstid, which are a significant part of the story.

Ethical Insight. To many readers the highest test of fiction is ethical insight into the world of universal and ideal truth. Modern short stories may still depend on adventure, but not necessarily on the adventure of action in strange and dangerous places. They may be concerned with adventure in understanding human nature—complex and contradictory, amusing and surprising, comic and tragic. As we have said, theme is developed by showing how the limited action of the story is related to the enveloping action of its background in life. It is the struggle between these two forces that constitutes the main tension, the resolution of which makes the point of the story.

In order for a writer to attain the unity required of a successful short story, his feeling toward scene, character, action, and theme must be consistent. Since a short story is usually read at one sitting, and since the focus is so narrow, a writer must be extraordinarily skillful in utilizing every potential of his materials. It was, indeed, this central point of the art of the short story with which Poe was concerned when he observed that a "skillful literary artist" conceives "with deliberate care, a certain unique or single effect to be wrought out."

IRWIN SHAW *The Dry Rock*

Irwin Shaw (1913-   ) lives in New York City, where he was born and educated. His various experiences—as tutor, typist, library helper, clerk, factory worker, truck driver, writer of radio scripts and screen plays, semi-professional football player, and soldier—have given him an abundance of firsthand material for his plays and stories. Among his best-known works are the play *Bury the Dead,* 1936, a short story collection, *Welcome to the City,* 1942, and *The Young Lions,* 1948, by some considered one of the finest novels to come out of World War II. Shaw has been represented in nearly every volume of *Best American Short Stories* since 1939, and in 1944 he received the O. Henry Memorial Award for his story "Walking Wounded." Another collection of his stories was published in 1950 under the title *Mixed Company.*

Few stories are easier to read and interpret than "The Dry Rock." The setting is familiar, the characters are distinctly drawn and set in opposition, and the theme is explicit. Yet Mr. Shaw has clothed the framework with such life-like details—images, action, speech—that his story is remarkably convincing and effective.

"We're late," Helen said, as the cab stopped at a light. "We're twenty minutes late." She looked at her husband accusingly.

"All right," Fitzsimmons said. "I couldn't help it. The work was on the desk and it had to . . ."

"This is the one dinner party of the year I didn't want to be late for," Helen said. "So naturally . . ."

The cab started and was halfway across the street when the Ford sedan roared into it, twisting, with a crashing and scraping of metal, a high mournful scream of brakes, the tinkling of glass. The cab shook a little, then subsided.

The cabby, a little gray man, turned and looked back, worriedly. "Everybody is all right?" he asked nervously.

"Everybody is fine," Helen said bitterly, pulling at her cape to get it straight again after the jolting.

THE DRY ROCK: From *Welcome to the City* by Irwin Shaw, copyright 1941 by Irwin Shaw. Published originally in *The New Yorker.* Reprinted by permission of Random House, Inc.

"No damage done," said Fitzsimmons, smiling reassuringly at the cabby, who looked very frightened.

"I am happy to hear that," the cabby said. He got out of his car and stood looking sadly at his fender, now thoroughly crumpled, and his headlight, now without a lens. The door of the Ford opened and its driver sprang out. He was a large young man with a light gray hat. He glanced hurriedly at the cab.

"Why don't yuh watch where the hell yer goin'?" he asked harshly.

"The light was in my favor," said the cabby. He was a small man of fifty, in a cap and a ragged coat, and he spoke with a heavy accent. "It turned green and I started across. I would like your license, Mister."

"What for?" the man in the gray hat shouted. "Yer load's all right. Get on yer way. No harm done." He started back to his car.

The cabby gently put his hand on the young man's arm. "Excuse me, friend," he said. "It is a five-dollar job, at least. I would like to see your license."

The young man pulled his arm away, glared at the cabby. "Aaah," he said and swung. His fist made a loud surprising noise against the cabby's nose. The old man sat down slowly on the running board of his cab, holding his head wearily in his hands. The young man in the gray hat stood over him, bent over, fists still clenched. "Didn't I tell yuh no harm was done?" he shouted. "Why didn't yuh lissen t'me? I got a good mind to . . ."

"Now, see here," Fitzsimmons said, opening the rear door and stepping out.

"What d'*you* want?" The young man turned and snarled at Fitzsimmons, his fists held higher. "Who asked for *you*?"

"I saw the whole thing," Fitzsimmons began, "and I don't think you . . ."

"Aaah," snarled the young man. "Dry up."

"Claude," Helen called. "Claude, keep out of this."

"Claude," the young man repeated balefully. "Dry up, Claude."

"Are you all right?" Fitzsimmons asked, bending over the cabby, who still sat reflectively on the running board, his head down, his old and swollen cap hiding his face, blood trickling down his clothes.

"I'm all right," the cabby said wearily. He stood up, looked wonderingly at the young man. "Now, my friend, you force me to make trouble. Police!" he called, loudly. "*Police!*"

"Say, lissen," the man in the gray hat shouted. "What the hell do yuh need to call the cops for? Hey, cut it out!"

"*Police!*" the old cabby shouted calmly, but with fervor deep in his voice. "Police!"

"I ought to give it to yuh good." The young man shook his fist under the cabby's nose. He jumped around nervously. "This is a small matter," he shouted, "nobody needs the cops!"

"Police!" called the cabby.

"Claude," Helen put her head out the window. "Let's get out of here and let the two gentlemen settle this any way they please."

"I apologize!" The young man held the cabby by his lapels with both large hands, shook him, to emphasize his apology. "Excuse me. I'm sorry. Stop yelling police, for God's sake!"

"I'm going to have you locked up," the cabby said. He stood there, slowly drying the blood off his shabby coat with his cap. His hair was gray, but long and full, like a musician's. He had a big head for his little shoulders, and a sad, lined little face and he looked older than fifty, to Fitzsimmons, and very poor, neglected, badly nourished. "You have committed a crime," the cabby said, "and there is a punishment for it."

"Will yuh talk to him?" The young man turned savagely to Fitzsimmons. "Will yuh tell him I'm sorry?"

"It's entirely up to him," Fitzsimmons said.

"We're a half hour late," Helen announced bitterly. "The perfect dinner guest."

"It's not enough to be sorry," said the cab driver. "*Police . . .*"

"Say, lissen, Bud," the young man said, his voice quick and confidential, "what's yer name?"

"Leopold Tarloff," the cabby said. "I have been driving a cab on the streets of New York for twenty years and everybody thinks just because you're a cab driver they can do whatever they want to you."

"Lissen, Leopold." The young man pushed his light gray hat far back on his head. "Let's be sensible. I hit yer cab. All right. I hit you. All right."

"What's all right about it?" Tarloff asked.

"What I mean is, I admit it, I confess I did it, that's what I mean. All right." The young man grabbed Tarloff's short ragged arms as he spoke, intensely. "Why the fuss? It happens every day. Police are unnecessary. I'll tell yuh what I'll do with yuh, Leopold. Five dollars, yuh say, for the fender. All right. And for the bloody nose, another pound. What do yuh say? Everybody is satisfied. Yuh've made yerself a fiver on the transaction; these good people go to their party without no more delay."

Tarloff shook his arms free from the huge hands of the man in the gray hat. He put his head back and ran his fingers through his thick hair and spoke coldly. "I don't want to hear another word. I have never been so insulted in my whole life."

The young man stepped back, his arms wide, palms up wonderingly. "I insult him!" He turned to Fitzsimmons. "Did you hear me insult this party?" he asked.

"Claude!" Helen called. "Are we going to sit here all night?"

"A man steps up and hits me in the nose," Tarloff said. "He thinks he makes everything all right with five dollars. He is mistaken. Not with five hundred dollars."

"How much d'yuh think a clap in the puss is worth?" the young man growled. "Who d'yuh think y'are—Joe Louis?"

"Not ten thousand dollars," Tarloff said, on the surface calm, but quivering underneath. "Not for twenty thousand dollars. My dignity."

"His dignity!" the young man whispered. "For Christ's sake!"

"What do you want to do?" Fitzsimmons asked, conscious of Helen glooming in the rear seat of the cab.

"I would like to take him to the station house and make a complaint," Tarloff said. "You would have to come with me, if you'd be so kind. What is your opinion on the matter?"

"Will yuh tell him the cops are not a necessity!" the young man said hoarsely. "Will yuh tell the bastidd?"

"Claude!" called Helen.

"It's up to you," Fitzsimmons said, looking with what he hoped was an impartial, judicious expression at Tarloff, hoping he wouldn't have to waste any more time. "You do what you think you ought to do."

Tarloff smiled, showing three yellow teeth in the front of his small and childlike mouth, curved and red and surprising in the lined and weatherbeaten old hackie's face. "Thank you very much," he said. "I am glad to see you agree with me."

Fitzsimmons sighed.

"Yer drivin' me crazy!" the young man shouted at Tarloff. "Yer makin' life impossible!"

"To you," Tarloff said with dignity, "I talk from now on only in a court of law. That's my last word."

The young man stood there, breathing heavily, his fists clenching and unclenching, his pale gray hat shining in the light of a street lamp. A policeman turned the corner, walking in a leisurely and abstracted manner, his eyes on the legs of a girl across the street. Fitzsimmons went over to him. "Officer," he said, "there's a little job for you over here." The policeman regretfully took his eyes off

the girl's legs and sighed and walked slowly over to where the two cars were still nestling against each other.

"What are yuh?" the young man was asking Tarloff, when Fitzsimmons came up with the policeman. "Yuh don't act like an American citizen. What are yuh?"

"I'm a Russian," Tarloff said. "But I'm in the country twenty-five years now, I know what the rights of an individual are."

"Yeah," said the young man hopelessly. "Yeah . . ."

The Fitzsimmonses drove silently to the police station in the cab, with Tarloff driving slowly and carefully, though with hands that shook on the wheel. The policeman drove with the young man in the young man's Ford. Fitzsimmons saw the Ford stop at a cigar store and the young man jump out and go into the store, into a telephone booth.

"For three months," Helen said, as they drove, "I've been trying to get Adele Lowrie to invite us to dinner. Now we've finally managed it. Perhaps we ought to call her and invite the whole party down to night court."

"It isn't night court," Fitzsimmons said patiently. "It's a police station. And I think you might take it a little better. After all, the poor old man has no one else to speak up for him."

"Leopold Tarloff," Helen said. "It sounds impossible. Leopold Tarloff. Leopold Tarloff."

They sat in silence until Tarloff stopped the cab in front of the police station and opened the door for them. The Ford with the policeman and the young man drove up right behind them and they all went in together.

There were some people up in front of the desk lieutenant, a dejected-looking man with long mustaches and a loud, blonde woman who kept saying that the man had threatened her with a baseball bat three times that evening. Two Negroes with bloody bandages around their heads were waiting, too.

"It will take some time," said the policeman. "There are two cases ahead of you. My name is Kraus."

"Oh, my," said Helen.

"You'd better call Adele," Fitzsimmons said. "Tell her not to hold dinner for us."

Helen held her hand out gloomily for nickels.

"I'm sorry," Tarloff said anxiously, "to interrupt your plans for the evening."

"Perfectly all right," Fitzsimmons said, trying to screen his wife's face from Tarloff by bending over to search for the nickels in his pocket.

Helen went off, disdainfully holding her long formal skirt up with her hand, as she walked down the spit- and butt-marked corridor of the police station toward a pay telephone. Fitzsimmons reflectively watched her elegant back retreat down the hallway.

"I am tired," Tarloff said. "I think I will have to sit down, if you will excuse me." He sat on the floor, looking up with a frail apologetic smile on his red face worn by wind and rain and traffic-policemen. Fitzsimmons suddenly felt like crying, watching the old man sitting there among the spit and cigarette butts, on the floor against the wall, with his cap off and his great bush of musician's gray hair giving the lie to the tired, weathered face below it.

Four men threw open the outside doors and walked into the police station with certainty and authority. They all wore the same light-gray hats with the huge flat brims. The young man who had hit Tarloff greeted them guardedly. "I'm glad you're here, Pidgear," he said to the man who, by some subtle mixture of stance and clothing, of lift of eyebrow and droop of mouth, announced himself as leader.

They talked swiftly and quietly in a corner.

"A Russian!" Pidgear's voice rang out angrily. "There are 10,000 cab drivers in the metropolitan area, you have to pick a Russian to punch in the nose!"

"I'm excitable!" the young man yelled. "Can I help it if I'm excitable? My father was the same way; it's a family characteristic."

"Go tell that to the Russian," Pidgear said. He went over to one of the three men who had come in with him, a large man who needed a shave and whose collar was open at the throat, as though no collar could be bought large enough to go all the way around that neck. The large man nodded, went over to Tarloff, still sitting patiently against the wall.

"You speak Russian?" the man with the open collar said to Tarloff.

"Yes, sir," Tarloff said.

The large man sat down slowly beside him, gripped Tarloff's knee confidentially in his tremendous hairy hand, spoke excitedly, winningly, in Russian.

Pidgear and the young man who had hit Tarloff came over to Fitzsimmons, leaving the two other men in the gray hats, small, dark men with shining eyes, who just stood at the door and looked hotly on.

"My name is Pidgear," the man said to Fitzsimmons, who by now was impressed with the beautiful efficiency of the system that had been put into motion by the young driver of the Ford—an obviously legal mind like Pidgear, a man who spoke Russian, and two intense men with gray hats standing on call just to see justice done, and all collected in the space of fifteen minutes. "Alton Pidgear," the man said, smiling professionally at Fitzsimmons. "I represent Mr. Rusk."

"Yeah," said the young man.

"My name is Fitzsimmons."

"Frankly, Mr. Fitzsimmons," Pidgear said, "I would like to see you get Mr. Tarloff to call this whole thing off. It's an embarrassing affair for all concerned; nobody stands to gain anything by pressing it."

Helen came back and Fitzsimmons saw by the expression on her face that she wasn't happy. "They're at the soup by now," she said loudly to Fitzsimmons. "Adele said for us to take all the time we want, they're getting along fine."

"Mr. Rusk is willing to make a handsome offer," Pidgear said. "Five dollars for the car, five dollars for the nose . . ."

"Go out to dinner with your husband," Helen muttered, "and you wind up in a telephone booth in a police station. 'Excuse me for being late, darling, but I'm calling from the 8th Precinct, this is our night for street-fighting.'"

"Sssh, Helen, please," Fitzsimmons said. He hadn't eaten since nine that morning and his stomach was growling with hunger.

"It was all a mistake," Pidgear said smoothly. "A natural mistake. Why should the man be stubborn? He is being reimbursed for everything, isn't he? I wish you would talk to him, Mr. Fitzsimmons; we don't want to keep you from your social engagements. Undoubtedly," Pidgear said, eyeing their evening clothes respectfully, "you and the madam were going to an important dinner party. It would be too bad to spoil an important dinner party for a little thing like this. Why, this whole affair is niggling," he said, waving his hand in front of Fitzsimmons' face. "Absolutely niggling."

Fitzsimmons looked over to where Tarloff and the other Russian were sitting on the floor. From Tarloff's face and gestures, even though he was talking in deepest Russian, Fitzsimmons could tell Tarloff was still as firm as ever. Fitzsimmons looked closely at Rusk, who was standing looking at Tarloff through narrow, baleful eyes.

"Why're you so anxious?" Fitzsimmons asked.

Rusk's eyes clouded over and his throat throbbed against his collar with rage. "I don't want to appear in court!" he yelled. "I don't want the whole goddamn business to start all over again, investigation, lawyers, fingerprints . . ."

Pidgear punched him savagely in the ribs, his fist going a short distance, but with great violence.

"Why don't you buy time on the National Broadcasting System?" Pidgear asked. "Make an address, coast to coast!"

Rusk glared murderously for a moment at Pidgear, then leaned over toward Fitzsimmons, pointing a large blunt finger at him. "Do I have to put my finger in your mouth?" he whispered hoarsely.

"What does he mean by that?" Helen asked loudly. "Put his finger in your mouth? Why should he put his finger in your mouth?"

Rusk looked at her with complete hatred, turned, too full for words, and stalked away, with Pidgear after him. The two little men in the gray hats watched the room without moving.

"Claude?" Helen began.

"Obviously," Fitzsimmons said, his voice low, "Mr. Rusk isn't anxious for anyone to look at his fingerprints. He's happier this way."

"You picked a fine night!" Helen shook her head sadly. "Why can't we just pick up and get out of here?"

Rusk, with Pidgear at his side, strode back. He stopped in front of the Fitzsimmonses.

"I'm a family man," he said, trying to sound like one. "I ask yuh as a favor. Talk to the Russian."

"I had to go to Bergdorf Goodman," Helen said, too deep in her own troubles to bother with Rusk, "to get a gown to spend the evening in a police station. 'Mrs. Claude Fitzsimmons was lovely last night in blue velvet and silver fox at Officer Kraus's reception at the 8th Precinct. Other guests were the well-known Leopold Tarloff, and the Messrs. Pidgear and Rusk, in gray hats. Other guests included the Russian Ambassador and two leading Italian artillerymen, also in gray hats.' "

Pidgear laughed politely. "Your wife is a very witty woman," he said.

"Yes," said Fitzsimmons, wondering why he'd married her.

"Will yuh for Christ's sake ask?" Rusk demanded. "Can it hurt yuh?"

"We're willing to do our part," Pidgear said. "We even brought down a Russian to talk to him and clear up any little points in his own language. No effort is too great."

Fitzsimmons' stomach growled loudly. "Haven't eaten all day," he said, embarrassed.

"That's what happens," Pidgear said. "Naturally."

"Yeah," said Rusk.

"Perhaps I should go out and get you a malted milk," Helen suggested coldly.

Fitzsimmons went over to where Tarloff was sitting with the other Russian. The others followed him.

"Are you sure, Mr. Tarloff," Fitzsimmons said, "that you still want to prosecute?"

"Yes," Tarloff said promptly.

"Ten dollars," Rusk said. "I offer yuh ten dollars. Can a man do more?"

"Money is not the object." With his cap Tarloff patted his nose which was still bleeding slowly and had swelled enormously, making Tarloff look lopsided and monstrous.

"What's the object?" Rusk asked.

"The object, Mr. Rusk, is principle."

"You talk to him," Rusk said to Fitzsimmons.

"All right," Officer Kraus said, "you can go up there now."

They all filed up in front of the lieutenant sitting high at his desk.

Tarloff told his story, the accident, the wanton punch in the nose.

"It's true," Pidgear said, "that there was an accident, that there was a slight scuffle after by mistake. But the man isn't hurt. A little swelling in the region of the nose. No more." He pointed dramatically to Tarloff.

"Physically," Tarloff said, clutching his cap, talking with difficulty because his nose was clogged, "physically that's true. I am not badly hurt. But in a mental sense . . ." He shrugged. "I have suffered an injury."

"Mr. Rusk is offering the amount of ten dollars," Pidgear said. "Also, he apologizes; he's sorry."

The lieutenant looked wearily down at Rusk. "Are you sorry?" he asked.

"I'm sorry," said Rusk, raising his right hand. "On the Bible, I swear I'm sorry."

"Mr. Tarloff," the lieutenant said, "if you wish to press charges, there are certain steps you will have to take. A deposition will have to be taken. Have you got witnesses?"

"Here," Tarloff said with a shy smile at the Fitzsimmonses.

"They will have to be present," the lieutenant said sleepily.

"Oh, God," Helen said.

"A warrant will have to be sworn out, there must be a hearing, at which the witnesses must also be present . . ."

"Oh, God," Helen said.

"Then the trial," said the lieutenant.

"Oh, God!" Helen said loudly.

"The question is, Mr. Tarloff," said the lieutenant, yawning, "are you willing to go through all that trouble?"

"The fact is," Tarloff said unhappily, "he hit me in the head without provocation. He is guilty of a crime on my person. He insulted me. He did me an injustice. The law exists for such things. One individual is not to be hit by another individual in the streets of the city without legal punishment." Tarloff was using his hands to try to get everyone, the Fitzsimmonses, the lieutenant, Pidgear, to understand. "There is a principle. The dignity of the human body. Justice. For a bad act a man suffers. It's an important thing . . ."

"I'm excitable," Rusk shouted. "If yuh want, yuh can hit me in the head."

"That is not the idea," Tarloff said.

"The man is sorry," the lieutenant said, wiping his eyes, "he is offering you the sum of ten dollars; it will be a long, hard job to bring this man to trial; it will cost a lot of the taxpayers' money; you are bothering these good people here who have other things to do. What is the sense in it, Mr. Tarloff?"

Tarloff scraped his feet slowly on the dirty floor, looked sadly, hopefully, at Fitzsimmons. Fitzsimmons looked at his wife, who was glaring at Tarloff, tapping her foot sharply again and again. Fitzsimmons looked back at Tarloff, standing there, before the high desk, small, in his ragged coat and wild gray hair, his little worn face twisted and grotesque with the swollen nose, his eyes lost and appealing. Fitzsimmons shrugged sadly. Tarloff drooped inside his old coat, shook his head wearily, shrugged, deserted once and for all before the lieutenant's desk, on the dry rock of principle.

"O.K.," he said.

"Here." Rusk brought the ten-dollar bill out with magical speed.

Tarloff pushed it away. "Get out of here," he said, without looking up.

No one talked all the way to Adele Lowrie's house. Tarloff opened the door and sat, looking straight ahead, while they got out. Helen went to the door of the house and rang. Silently, Fitzsimmons offered Tarloff the fare. Tarloff shook his head. "You have been very good," he said. "Forget it."

Fitzsimmons put the money away slowly.

"Claude!" Helen called. "The door's open."

Fitzsimmons hated his wife, suddenly, without turning to look at her. He put out his hand and Tarloff shook it wearily.

"I'm awfully sorry," Fitzsimmons said. "I wish I . . ."

Tarloff shrugged. "That's all right," he said. "I understand." His face, in the shabby light of the cab, worn and old and battered by the streets of the city, was a deep well of sorrow. "There is no time. Principle." He laughed, shrugged. "Today there is no time for anything."

He shifted gears and the taxi moved slowly off, its motor grinding noisily.

"Claude!" Helen called.

"Oh, shut up!" Fitzsimmons said as he turned and walked into Adele Lowrie's house.

FRANCES GRAY PATTON *The Man Jones*

Frances Gray Patton (1906-   ) was born in Raleigh, North Carolina, of a long line of North Carolinians. She was educated at Trinity College, now Duke University, and at the University of North Carolina. While at the University, she became active in the newly organized Carolina Playmakers and wrote the play which was given at the opening of the Playmakers' Theater in 1925. Mrs. Patton did not publish her first story until 1945. Since then, however, she has become a favorite writer for the *New Yorker*, in which many of her stories have appeared. Some of these were collected and published in 1951 under the title, *The Finer Things of Life*. Her first novel, *Good Morning, Miss Dove*, the story of an American schoolteacher, was published in 1954.

Her husband, Lewis Patton, is professor of English at Duke University. The Pattons have one son and twin daughters. One may well surmise that in "The Man Jones," as well as in some of her other stories, Mrs. Patton has drawn on her own experience for her authentic and sensitive observations of young people and of academic life.

James Manigault Jones (who kept quiet about his middle name and was known to his college acquaintances as Jim or, when they were feeling high-flown and literary, as Eternity) paid a visit to Wendell Dormitory during the short interval between his lunch and his two-o'clock zoology-lab period. He carried a bunch of jonquils bought from a street-corner peddler—a poor, crop-legged man with hard-leather pads on his kneecaps—and as he entered the building he felt suddenly furtive, partly because he thought he must look foolish clutching those "flowers that bloom in the spring, tra-la" and partly because he suspected he was out of bounds. He hesitated in the vestibule, of half a mind to toss the jonquils in the trash can and retreat before anybody saw him. But he rose above that timid impulse. He started for the stairs, trying not to notice how his footsteps echoed in the empty corridor.

Early that morning, Jim and the rest of

THE MAN JONES: Reprinted by permission of Dodd, Mead & Company, from *A Piece of Luck* by Frances Gray Patton. © 1956 by Frances Gray Patton. Originally published in *The New Yorker*.

the boys had cleared out of Wendell, the main freshman dormitory at Amity College; in their wake, a crew of charwomen had arrived to make Wendell fit to receive a host of delicate visitors—the girls who were coming to the prom. The women had worked with a furious thoroughness that suggested contempt for the gross habits of the dormitory's regular inmates, scrubbing and polishing as if the place were far dirtier than it actually was. Now, in the purged, anomalous atmosphere, Jim had a fleeting illusion of being somewhere else. All this—the odors of soap and wax and furniture oil, the drone of a vacuum sweeper, and the rhythmic slipslap of a wet mop on the stairs—was like spring-cleaning week at home. He caught himself listening for his mother to call, "Is that you, Mannie boy? Will you take the kitchen screens in the back yard and squirt the hose on them before you settle down?" He frowned. He was too easily reminded of home, he thought, and it was abnormal to see a resemblance between anything here at Amity—this suave Eastern college, this "civilized oasis"—and Apex City, Georgia.

He picked his way up the stairs, walking

on his toes to avoid tracking the still damp marble. On the first landing, he saw a stringy woman lift a pail of water and begin toiling toward the second floor.

"Here. Let me have that," Jim said. He snatched the bucket from the woman's hand and ran lightly up the half flight. "This where you want it, Ma'am?" (He could have kicked himself for letting that "Ma'am" slip out.)

The woman nodded. "That was real nice of you," she said. "They's not many students as thoughtful as that. Thank you." Her sallow, equine face grew soft with the expression of maternal approval that older women, to Jim's discomfiture, were likely to bestow upon him. "Thank you, *sir!*"

"You bet," said Jim.

"A bokay for your lady?"

"These?" Jim said. "Oh, they're just something I bought from a cripple"—he was miserably certain that the scrubwoman knew he had bought them because he'd remembered how his mother put fresh flowers in the guest room—"and now I've got to do something with 'em."

"That was a Christian act," the woman said. "And they'll make your room look like a home away from home."

"I figured they'd brighten it up," Jim said. "It's pretty austere, you know." He yearned to get away—to make sure the room was all right, to indulge in lonely fantasies about the marvellous girl who was soon to occupy it—but he didn't know how to. It seemed rude to leave while the woman wanted to talk.

"The little things in life make the big difference," she said. "You tell your mama for me she raised a true Southern gentleman."

Jim felt himself blush, and knew that his heightened color gave him a heightened bloom of youth and innocence. He was a long-legged boy, with curly brown hair and pink cheeks. He looked like some mother's darling—which, indeed, he was—but, with a smile he hoped was a leer, he said, "She'll be surprised to hear *that!*"

"She prob'ly knows," the woman said. "I guess there ain't much a mother's heart don't know about her son." She plunged her mop into her pail, swished it, and plopped it down

with a wet, slimy sound. "You don't happen to be Jones, do you? Room 202?"

"The man in person," said Jim.

"A special delivery come for you. I slipped it under your door."

"A special delivery? For *me?*" Jim's bowels constricted. The letter, he was agonizingly sure, could be from no one but Barbara. From Barbara, breaking her date for the dance. And it seemed to him that he wasn't really surprised—that all week he had known such a letter was bound to come.

"I hope you ain't stood up," the woman said, leaning on her mop and regarding Jim with mournful eyes. "With the bokay and all, that would be a crime."

Her sympathy was a mirror. In it Jim saw reflected the image of what he feared was his true self. Not an Amity man—cool, civilized, capable of taking such things as freshman proms and the vagaries of girls with cynical undismay—but a skinny kid from the Bible Belt. A nice Sunday-school boy with yellow flowers in his fist. A boy who addressed a scrubwoman as "Ma'am" and blubbered into her bucket when somebody "went and hurt his Southern pride." In that drowning moment of self-realization, all that sustained Jim was the conviction, recently acquired from converse with a junior who was majoring in psychology, that self-realization, per se, was good. To view oneself objectively, ruthlessly—it was only thus that one gained insight into one's motivations and detached them from false values formed in infancy or even *in utero.* But to become aware of one's own hideous ignominy was one thing; to show it to a woman with a mop was another.

Jim cocked his left eyebrow—a muscular discipline that he practiced constantly. "There are plenty more fish in the sea," he said. His remark lacked urbanity, he knew—it was a disgruntled boast that one heard frequently in the Owl Drugstore in Apex City—but it had to serve. With a magnificent try at nonchalance, he sauntered down the long, quiet hall to Room 202.

Jim had met Barbara a week before, when he attended a dance at Hannah Benson, a small but reputedly sophisticated college for women. He had attended the function, with

-e- diminutive suffix - added to names. Make it little. Janie, Billie. *(Hemingway)*

heavy misgivings, on the bid of a girl named Earline Fitch—a girl who had grown up next door to him and who had beaten him out by a slim academic margin for the position of high-school valedictorian. He had nothing against Earline—he was even fond of her, in an old-time's-sake sort of way—but he did not care to establish a public connection with her here in the East.

Earline was a big, bouncy, uncomplicated girl who poked you in the ribs to make sure you got the point of her jokes. She had a passion for food, and a passion, very like in character, for what she called ideas. "I can't get the McCarthy problem off my chest," she would declare, her carrying voice soaring above the sound of the juke box at the Owl. "I can't bear to think he honestly represents the deep-down spiritual calibre of the average American." At a moonlight picnic, when the other couples had wandered off into the shade of the pine woods, she would remain sitting in full lunar glare beside Jim (somehow, he was usually paired off with Earline) and would say, less softly than the whippoorwills, "Now take salvation through faith—here's my slant on it. . . ." Her strong white teeth would glisten just as they did when they were about to seize upon a king-sized hamburger, succulent with chopped pickle and mustard. Worse still, she called Jim—and would always call him—by the humiliating abbreviation of his middle name. She called him Mannie.

Jim's immediate impulse had been to decline the invitation with emphasis. In the end, however, he had decided to accept it for two cogent, if disparate, reasons. First, he had wished not to embarrass his mother, who was a close friend of Mrs. Fitch's; second, he was aware that at Amity, where Earline's qualities were mercifully unknown, it wouldn't sound bad to say he had a date up at Benson. So he had gone to the dance, frozen-faced and wary, and there he had met the girl whom he'd always known he was fated to meet someday. (Jim, for all his determination to treat himself ruthlessly, nursed no morbid doubts as to Fate's tender preoccupation with his felicity.) He had assumed that the meeting would occur at some distant point in time when, as a key man in the diplomatic service,

a novelist on safari in Africa, or, perhaps, a psychiatrist long since beyond astonishment, he would be more than equal to it. Certainly he had never considered Earline Fitch as a probable instrument of destiny. But Fate moved in her own sweet way! *proportunably*

The visit to Benson had not begun auspiciously. The train had run late, and Jim had procured his supper from a vender. (A sorry meal it had been, consisting of a carton of milk and a dry sandwich; its sole virtue, Jim had thought morosely, was that it saved him from having to watch Earline eat.) Arriving, hungry and pessimistic, he'd had just time to change his clothes in the village's one dinky hotel before joining Earline at her dormitory.

"Mannie Jones! You're a sight for sore eyes!" Earline cried, bursting into the reception room almost immediately after he had sat down to wait for her. She had on a ballooning sky-blue taffeta dress (the one in which she had delivered the valedictory), and it made her appear larger than life and crude-colored, like the blonde on the Holsum Bakery calendar in the Joneses' kitchen. Showing her teeth, she advanced across the carpet. Jim stepped back and bumped into a floor lamp.   *crude-colored*

"That's right! Break up the furniture!" Earline exclaimed, catching the lamp before it toppled. She grasped Jim's hand and ground its bones together. "Gee! Seeing you makes me feel like I'm back in good old Apex City!"

Jim retrieved his hand. "You're looking fit," he said.

"I keep fit," Earline said. "I'm on the house hockey team and I never skip my daily dozens at the gym. Notice my tummy." She slapped it. "Flat as a board. *Mens sana in corpore sano!*"

"Good going," said Jim.

"Listen, Mannie," Earline said. "I'm sick about tonight. This is an old-fashioned card dance, and I gave four numbers to Jane Sadler, one of the keenest girls in our class. She's here on a Religious Ed. scholarship, like me."

"She is?" said Jim.

"You and Jane would have hit it off like ham and eggs. I told her how you were an Eagle Scout and how you'd won the Kiwanis medal for your oration on crime prevention, and she was wild to meet you. But this morning she woke up all broken out!"

(flash back & ahead)

place where you keep ammunition in a ship—

"Too bad," said Jim.

"Well, not too bad, one way you look at it," Earline said knowledgeably. "It's German measles, and, of course, it's good to get that over with before you get pregnant."

"I guess it is," Jim agreed quickly. Hoping to forestall a detailed lecture upon obstetrical hazards, he added gallantly, "Anyhow, it gives me four more dances with you."

"Well, no, it doesn't," Earline said. "I'd already promised those four to some other folks for their dates. So I got Jane's roommate, Barbara Davis, to pinch-hit."

"Much wrong with Barbara?"

"Not much," Earline said. "But she's not your type. Not very eager, you know. She wasn't even planning to come tonight. Said she preferred dances on men's campuses, where she had no responsibility! Though I must admit she was nice about filling in for Jane."

Jim's spirits, though scarcely bleeding for the loss of the eager Jane, were depressed by this juggling of partners. It was typical of the confusion—the absence of savoir-faire—that he had expected from Earline.

"Shall we shove off?" Earline said. "On with the dance, let joy be unrefined!" She jabbed her elbow into Jim's ribs. "Huh, Mannie?"

Jim made no attempt to smile. "Where do I call a cab?" he inquired.

Earline hooted. "What kind of gold-digger do you take me for? A walk in the nippy air will tune up our blood pressure."

Before long, fox-trotting with Earline in the crowded ballroom, Jim understood why she had wanted a preliminary workout. Earline was a person in whom physical exercise excited the instinct for competition.

"I believe you're winded," she said to Jim when the orchestra had stopped playing. "Relax!"

"Shall we sit the next one out?" Jim asked.

"Oh, the next belongs to Barbara," she told him. "Here she is, Johnny-on-the-spot, to claim you now." She grabbed Jim by the arm and spun him around. "Barbara Davis. Mannie Jones."

Barbara was a slightly built girl, five feet three or so in height, with quiet, regular features, a pale complexion, and very soft, shiny brown hair, which hung just clear of her shoulders. In broad day, with his faculties collected, Jim would have thought her pretty; in the dim light of festivity, dizzy from Earline's whirls and gallops, he saw her as the pure, incarnate principle of beauty. She stood so still. She was so undemanding. Her lips were curved in a half smile, amiable but aloof. Everything about her—her fragile white shoulders, the hollow at the base of her clavicle, the way she tilted her head, and even her dress, which was made of some foamy black stuff with pink shimmering through it —seemed serene and poised, and veiled in the filmy mystery of dream. She was, in brief, notably unlike Earline Fitch.

Barbara did not struggle for supremacy in the dance. Leaning on Jim's chest ("Light as a leaf on the wind," he thought), she seemed to float with him to the time of the music. She did not chatter, but by dint of direct questioning Jim learned something about her. She was from New York—"the city, not the suburbs." (Jim sneered with disdain at commuters' families, skulking in New Jersey.) She would like to live in Paris someday —or maybe Rome or Vienna. She guessed she was a gypsy at heart. (Jim decided definitely on foreign diplomacy instead of medicine.) She had never been to Amity (her tone implied familiarity with Yale, Princeton, Dartmouth, and the Service Academies), but she understood it was steeped in tradition. A civilized oasis, she said.

"Would you come down to my class prom next Friday?" Jim asked. He was shocked by the temerity of his question, blurted out bluntly, with no civilized prelude.

Barbara said why, yes, she'd love to come if he really meant it. "Only," she added, "you'll have to tell me your name. I can't very well call you what Earline did when she introduced us!" She began to laugh, noiselessly but uncontrollably, so that she was obliged, for a moment, to hide her face against his waistcoat.

"What did she call me?" asked Jim with death in his heart.

"She called you 'the man Jones'!" Barbara told him. She choked, and began to laugh again. "That's what she said—'Barbara Davis. The man Jones'!"

"Is that what she said? I never listen to

poor Earline," said Jim. "My name's Jim."

"I like Jim," Barbara said. "It's a virile name. Last summer, I saw this revival of an old movie called 'Lord Jim.' It was a scream in parts—you know how those old movies are —but Ronald Colman was wonderful. I knew you reminded me of somebody."

And now, Jim thought, as he approached Room 202, Barbara wasn't coming! Well, why should she? Why should a girl with the Ivy League at her feet climb on the smelly local train they called the Hedgehopper and ride for three hours, stopping at every wide place in the road, to attend a freshman dance with a boy from the upcountry of Georgia. It was out of sheer kindness—the reluctance to give pain—that she'd agreed to come in the first place. (He had read somewhere that beautiful women were invariably kind, frequently to their undoing!) Her letter would be kind, too. It would say that she had a cold, or a quiz to study for, or maybe that her family wanted her home for some special party at the Stork Club or "21."

He was not angry with Barbara. She was remote from human anger, like a classic myth. He was angry, and disgusted, with himself. He recalled several rich phrases in which he had described the girl's charms to his friends, and several optimistic hints as to the favorable light in which she regarded him. He remembered the government bond that his uncle had sent him on his eighteenth birthday, which he'd cashed to defray the expenses of the week-end; the new white dinner coat hanging in his locker at the gym; the orchid, selected and paid for, at the florist's; the table for two reserved at the Stromboli Tavern and the tip he'd added to the cover charge as tacit insurance against the management's querying his age when he ordered drinks. The thought of all that elaborate preparation for what should have been, to a young man of reasonable sang-froid, a routine occasion was mortifying to Jim. Like the charwoman's pity, it flayed him. It put his sentiment for Barbara into a mawkish category, along with his uncomfortable memories of the time he had stayed after school and cleaned the blackboards in order to be alone with a buxom teacher named Miss Myrtle Stubbs. (He had

picked jonquils for Miss Myrtle—early February ones that bloomed in the sheltered corner of the dining-room ell—and his mother had fitted a lace-paper doily around their stems to make them look like a valentine.) Jim winced. He opened his door.

The letter lay on a strip of bare floor between sill and rug. Against the dark wood, the white envelope looked as bleak as an old, bleached bone. But as Jim, sweating, forced himself to stoop for it, he saw that it could scarcely contain a message of doom. It was postmarked Apex City and addressed, in the sloping, Palmer-method hand of his mother, to Mr. J. Manigault Jones!

Relief did not come to Jim by degrees, as it comes to timeworn people who must absorb it gradually into veins long torpid with chronic anxiety. It hit him full force, flooding him with a lovely, sanguine warmth. (He had a nebulous vision of Barbara. She sat, leaning toward him, at a small table illumined by a single candle. Something glittered, like a spangle of stars, in her hair. As she gazed languorously at him above a crystal cocktail glass, the orchid he'd sent her rose and fell on her breast. He saw himself, in his white coat, guiding her through an intricate maze of dancers; over the shoulders of their commonplace partners his jealous classmates eyed him with respect.) He tossed the letter, unopened, upon the dresser. Humming a few bars from "Some Enchanted Evening," he went into the adjoining bathroom, where he arranged the jonquils in his toothbrush glass.

He returned to the bedroom. He set the flowers upon the night table beside "War and Peace," a volume of poems by Ogden Nash, and the current issue of *Holiday*—an assortment that spelled, he felt, a catholic and unimpeachable taste in literature. He stood back and surveyed the room. It was a single room, narrow and utilitarian. Without the Varga girls that he'd removed from the walls, lest they strike Barbara as a display of naïveté, it had, Jim fancied, a monkish aspect. But it was clean. Its bed was smoothly made. Its general effect could be called civilized.

Jim tried to imagine how that room—that celibate cell—would look after the dance. He conjured up a vague, intoxicating impression of diaphanous garments flung over a chair and of a girl's gently curving form swelling the covers on the bed. The girl's face was indistinct, but her hair made a shadowy mist on the pillow, and one shoulder—bare except for a wisp of black lace—was visible above the blanket. "Are you warm enough?" Jim whispered.

The scene changed. Years had passed. Jim sat in a closed compartment on a train that sped through the wine country of France. He was hard and lean. His eyes were shrewd. In his briefcase reposed the record—in code, of course—of an investigation that would point the way to international peace for a generation. His papers were complete save for one scrap of information. One missing link. And he would get that. He always got what he wanted.

Or did he? Had he? He was a lonely man.

The door of the compartment opened. A cold thrill shot along Jim's nerves, but his hand remained so steady that the long ash on the end of his cigar was undisturbed. Silently as a shadow, a woman entered the compartment. She was veiled, and wrapped in exotic furs. She tossed a fine linen handkerchief upon Jim's knee. Its monogram, Jim saw at a glance, provided the clue; it was the missing link.

"Do you not know me?" the woman asked. She spoke with the faint foreign accent of the expatriate, but the timbre of her voice was familiar. It took Jim back, back, back. Dance music. Spring. A handful of simple golden flowers. He laid down his cigar. He rose and lifted the veil that hid the face of his visitor. It was a face that showed the ravages of passion and danger, but its bones had stayed beautiful. Its lips were curved in the old half smile. "Well, Lord Jim," said Barbara. She closed the door. She snapped off the light. "We are no longer children, Lord Jim!"

The clock in the tower of Amity College Library struck the half hour.

"Whew!" Jim said. He moved to the looking glass above the dresser, half expecting to find his own face marked by the ravages of life. Observing that it was still round and sleek, he sucked in his cheeks to encourage in himself a lean-jawed look. Then, with a start of alarm, he saw his mother's neglected

letter. Why had she sent it special delivery? Was something wrong at home?

He ripped open the envelope and drew out a folded sheet of paper, inscribed closely on both sides. A five-dollar bill—an old, soft bill that wouldn't crackle and advertise its presence—lay in the fold. "Gosh!" Jim said, with the feeling of unworthiness that his mother's small attentions always gave him. He pictured her fingers as they'd smoothed the bill and as, immediately afterward, they'd seized a pencil to jot down "$5" under "Miscellaneous" in a black leather account book. He read her letter.

"Dear Mannie," she began. Jim stiffened. He had told his mother, as tactfully as he could, that he deplored being called Mannie —that it sounded babyish, like "Sonny" or "Bud"—but she had never been willing to see his point. It was short for a distinguished name, she had argued. His Manigault ancestor had been a Huguenot, a man who had sacrificed advantage to principle. It was a name to revere. Take it easy, Jim advised himself. She's too old to learn new tricks. She means well. She sent you five dollars. He began again:

DEAR MANNIE:

This is just a line to let you know I'm thinking of you on the eve of your first big college dance and that I'll be with you in spirit, enjoying the sound of revelry by night. Earline wrote her mother that you'd asked a mighty pretty Benson girl to be your partner. Naturally, I'm a trifle disappointed that you didn't ask Earline [Jim groaned], because I've always liked the way your wholesome friendship with her expressed itself in work as well as play. You were pals on the debating platform as well as in the swimming pool. And then it *would* have been polite after she made the first move. I'm afraid the Fitches may be wounded. [To hell with the Fitches, thought Jim.] Earline doesn't think this girl—Barbara, isn't she?—is quite your intellectual or spiritual equal, but then Earline can't judge for you ["You're damn right she can't!" said Jim out loud], and I know you could never be ensnared by mere physical appeal. I'm thankful we discussed the mating instinct long ago [I merely asked the girl to a *dance,* Jim thought indignantly], and I'll always cherish the recollection of the clear-eyed way you looked at me after we had everything straight and said, "Biology is as neat as algebra, isn't it?" I hope you'll never forget that, either.

Would that I could, thought Jim. The "frank discussion" to which his mother referred had taken place three years before, when he was only fifteen, but every wretched word of it haunted his memory. He had been setting out for a Hi-Y hay ride—Earline Fitch was his date—when his mother had urged him to sit down and have "an intimate little chat" with her. He recalled the scene objectively now—a plump, earnest woman in a Boston rocker, and a blob of a boy, *himself*, sitting pigeon-toed on the edge of a Victorian love seat—but not so objectively that he failed to recover a sense of being trapped. His hands, resting on his knees, had seemed limp and heavy and grossly oversized; his mother, in her determination not to whisper, had spoken more loudly than usual. She had begun by asking Jim if he had noticed that his voice was changing and if he recognized that change as Nature's way of telling him he was growing into manhood. She had gone on to say, in a booming voice, that she'd heard that some boys and girls, being uninstructed and confused by their budding instincts, didn't always conduct themselves sensibly in a truck full of hay—with the chaperon, no doubt, sitting up front with the driver. She wished Mannie to be forewarned, so that if the proximity of Earline's young body should give him a queer sensation, he would know what it was. He mustn't be frightened, though. The desire to mate was a healthy, holy thing, so long as it was controlled.

Glassy-eyed with chagrin, Jim had known that he had to say something—and something in his mother's vein—before he could escape. With the algebraic analogy he had bought his freedom. He was morally certain that his fatuous remark had been widely quoted in P.-T. A circles; also, it had effectively nipped Jim's incipient interest in higher mathematics.

Forgive me for clucking [the letter continued]. I know you're a man now and I want you to make your own independent decisions. Maybe you can ask Earline another time. I hope the enclosure will ease the strain on your allowance. With love always,

MAMA

Jim put the bill into his wallet. It would take more than five dollars, he reflected wryly, to ease his strain. Amity wasn't like Apex City, where a girl was satisfied with a drive-in movie and a bag of popcorn. But he'd eke out. He'd heard some of the fellows say you could sell your blood to the hospital for fifty bucks a quart.

The library clock struck the third quarter. Jim went into the bathroom. He tore his mother's letter into fine fragments and flushed it down the toilet.

Jauntily, he walked along the hall, descended the gleaming stairs, and left the building. The cleaning woman, in a brown hat and coat, was leaving, too.

"You look like your news warn't so bad," she said.

"Everything's rosy," said Jim. "Just a spot of dough from home."

At the moment, he meant what he said. But as he loped down the path that led to the Zoology Building, Jim realized that the true substance of the letter had not gone down the drain. It stayed in his consciousness and smirked at him. Its moralistic baby talk—such expressions as "wholesome friendship" and "mere physical appeal"—reduced the daring of the imagination to childish grandiosity. He would never, he was now persuaded, seem distinguished to a girl like Barbara Davis. He would never smoke an expensive cigar as he was borne through the wine country of France, or do anything beyond the ordinary. He would finish college (possibly with a B average), serve his time in the Army, and go back to Apex City and sell real estate. He would marry a local girl. (But *not* Earline!) He would lead, like other men, a life "of quiet desperation."

Yet only a short time before, the future had been his particular peach. And his mother had put a blight on it!

Jim's parents had been middle-aged when he was born. His father had died shortly thereafter, leaving his son's upbringing to his widow. He could not have left it in more consecrated hands. Mrs. Jones was a wonderful mother. (All Apex City said so, and until recently Jim had not dreamed that anyone would question the consensus.) Self-reliance, she had claimed, was her desire for her son, and she had consistently refused to weaken that quality by acts of overprotection. Other toddlers, when they skinned their knees, were gathered to maternal bosoms, there to howl against cosmic injustice; all little Jim got from Mrs. Jones was a cheerful "Upsy-daisy" and a stinging dab of iodine. Later, when problems of personal conduct arose, Jim was refused the support of hard-and-fast rules. On such matters as church attendance, playing marbles for keeps, and reading comic books, Jim was told to think things out and be guided by his conscience. (That his conscience generally led him down paths that Mrs. Jones approved had seemed a happy accident.) When he began, now and then, to take the car out at night, his mother never sat up for him. Turning in to the driveway after a Scout meeting or a school party, Jim often saw her lighted bedroom window go dark; next morning she would say, "I slept like a log, Mannie. I didn't hear you come in."

That transparent lie had always touched Jim, but when, in a nostalgic, confidential mood, he had related it to his friend the psychology major, he had regretted doing so.

"Why did she wish to deceive you?" the psychology major asked.

"To keep me from knowing she worried," Jim replied, surprised by his friend's obtuseness. "To make me independent."

"Not to render your chains invisible? Not to deprive you of the incentive to rebel?" the psychology major suggested.

"Ahhh, baloney!" Jim retorted. "I was just a kid. Naturally, she worried."

"If it was natural, why was she ashamed?"

"She wasn't ashamed," said Jim.

"No. Your insight tells you that much," the other student said, slowly and significantly. "She wasn't ashamed, but she was making goddam sure *you'd* be ashamed if you ever stayed out late—tomcatting in the red clay hills of Georgia."

"For Christ's sake!" Jim scoffed, hoping the oath did not sound as unaccustomed as it was. "I told you I was just a kid."

"Well, unless you want to remain a kid, you'd better get wise. You're in danger. You'd better make your break while there's time. Ruthlessly."

"You don't know my mother," Jim told him. "If she wanted me chained, why did she help me leave home? Why did she send me to college"—he checked himself; he had been about to say "up North," the way they did in Apex City—"in the East?"

"Any number of reasons. Guilt. Prestige." The psychology major shrugged. Then he whistled, as if in pain. "But, boy, the light going off in the upstairs window—that was practically Machiavellian!"

Jim had laughed. The notion of his innocent mother employing a fine Italian hand had been plain funny.

Now, beneath the budding elms of Amity, Jim was not inclined to mirth. His friend had not exaggerated. He *was* in danger. " 'Ah want y'all to make y'all's own independent decisions,' " he muttered between his teeth, with a contemptuous distortion of his mother's Southern accent and diction. " 'Maybe y'all kin ask Uhline another time!' " He knew he had to act.

He cut across the sprouting turf of the quadrangle and went to the post office, where he bought a stamped airmail envelope. Then he went to the college snack bar. He bought a milk shake, took it to an empty booth, sat down, and opened his loose-leaf notebook. He furrowed his brow. (Anyone seeing him would think him too deeply absorbed in scholarship to brook interruption.) After a while, when his anger had crystallized into sentences, he took his fountain pen (a Lifetime Sheaffer that his mother had given him when he won the Kiwanis medal) and started writing.

My dear Mother [he wrote, making his letters dark and vertical]: Thank you for the enclosure. Your generosity was unnecessary but not unappreciated. The big dance, as you put it, does not seem overwhelming to me. I expect, however, that it will prove diverting. Miss Davis, who is to be my guest, is from a prominent family in New York City—not the suburbs. She is not intimate with Earline Fitch nor does she care to be. She would be amazed to know that she had been discussed by Mrs. Fitch. I shall have to ask you not to bandy the names of my friends around the neighborhood. Who I take to a dance is absolutely none of the Fitches' business. It is the business of nobody but myself and the other party involved. After mature consideration, I trust you will see that at my age any other state of affairs would lack valid reality.

In the future please address your letters to James M. Jones. Here in the East pedigrees are taken for granted and unusual middle names are not impressive.

Aff'y,

JIM

Jim lit a cigarette. He pictured his mother reading his communication. She looked older than she had at Christmas, and lonelier, like a patient woman on a Mother's Day card. Her face wore a blank, puzzled expression.

I'd better soften it, Jim thought. He added a postscript: "'I must be cruel in order to be kind.'"

But the quotation, apt as it was, didn't seem to help much. It would not console his mother; it would only persuade her that her son had gone crazy. Why, she was liable to get right into her car—the old green Chevrolet that Jim had learned to drive in—and come straight to Amity. He could see her driving down the main street, sitting very straight and wearing the fierce, dedicated expression that she always wore in the face of illness. "Could any of you gentlemen direct me to Wendell?" she would call out to a group of students on the sidewalk. "I'm looking for Mannie Jones."

Jim tore the sheet from his notebook, crumpled it into a ball, placed it in his ashtray, and struck a match to it. He would have to do the thing over again a different way, he thought, as he watched the little conflagration flare and die out. He must say exactly what he'd said, but in his mother's native language.

This time, Jim wrote slowly. Now and again, he paused, trying out phrases in his mind and often shuddering as he set them down on paper. Short though his letter was, its composition consumed the better part of two hours.

Dear Mama [he wrote]: Pardon this notebook paper. I'm in the snack bar guzzling a malted to rebuild my tissues after a day of intellectual (?) labor. It was swell of you to send me the fiver and I can really use it! The prom is going to be terrific. We've got Buzz King's orchestra—Buzz used to play trombone with Guy Lombardo—and at intermission we'll have strawberry punch and homemade cookies served by the wives of the profs on the Freshman Advisory Council. My date is an awfully nice girl, a real slick chick, named Barbara Davis. She's from New York. The city, not

the suburbs. She's a better dancer than Earline. She lets me lead.

And now I have to say something I reckon most mothers couldn't take. But you and I have always been frank so I know you won't be hurt. It's this, Mama. Please stop being inquisitive about my date-life. You see, I've reached a stage in my development where I need to achieve emotional independence. Even if I make mistakes. Do you remember how it was when I first started driving the car? Other guys came home and found their families sitting up for them, ready to put them through the third degree. But you never did. Gee, I felt proud when I found the house dark and you asleep. I knew you trusted me. Well, that's what I can use now, Mama. Not questions. Not advice. Just *Trust* that's too big for words.

Jim read over what he had written. It was ghastly. It reminded him of articles concerning the problems of adolescence that appeared in the women's magazines, which his mother read and often left (by design, perhaps?) in the bathroom. It was no less priggish—and infinitely less polished—than what he had said before the Hi-Y hay ride. But, as he had been obliged to escape then, so he was obliged now. His mother would understand this letter. What was more, she would respect it. She would let him alone.

"Your loving son," Jim wrote. He sighed. He might as well go whole hog. "Manigault," he signed himself. Sadly, with the air of a poet forced to speak the vernacular of the masses, he folded the sheet of paper and put it into the stamped envelope, which he addressed and slid in his inside coat pocket.

A freshman stopped at the booth. "Missed you in lab," he said.

"I wasn't in the mood," said Jim.

"Hell, neither was I, but with this shindig tonight I couldn't afford a makeup. Sometimes I wonder if women are worth it."

"My ma sent me a little extra dough," said Jim.

The boy looked impressed. "My people have hearts of stone," he said. "Your girl come yet? Mine was due on the bus an hour ago but I guess she's wending her own sweet way to Wendell. She's my brother-in-law's kid sister."

"Mine's coming on the four-twenty," Jim said. "The Hedgehopper." As he spoke, he realized that, with the lab period over, it must be close to four. He rose, stretched, and feigned a yawn. "I'd better get along over to the depot."

Jim arrived at the station a few minutes before the train was due. In the waiting room, two of his classmates sat, half reclining, on the wooden bench. Their eyes were closed; their legs, looking boneless and bored, were thrust far into the public passageway. Jim considered taking a place beside them, but an unwelcome twinge of honesty deterred him. The fashionable ennui that to most of his friends (so he thought) was as natural as skin would never be more than a thin, protective glaze on him. It was safe to assume that neither of those boys had just written home begging his mother to trust him!

Jim went out onto the open-air platform and paced up and down. A switch engine was backing and filling on the track. The fireman lifted a hand in salute to Jim; Jim lifted a hand to the fireman, as he'd done a hundred times, waiting at the grade crossing in the center of Apex City. He was glad that only a baggage porter observed his small-town gesture.

In the distance, a diesel engine grunted.

"There she blows," the porter said.

"On time, for a change," Jim said with an air of indifference.

A bell clanged. The Hedgehopper, a comical little train composed of a converted steam engine and a short string of antiquated coaches, charged into the station and shook itself to a stop.

The two boys emerged from the waiting room. "Pawing the earth, Jones?" one of them said.

"That's right," said Jim. Panic chilled him. Suppose she hadn't come. But there she was, alighting from the last coach!

She wore a tan coat, and a long plaid scarf hung around her neck. She looked much younger than she had at Benson. She gave the curious impression, which Jim took as spurious, of being scared. But her hair was the same. Her hair and the way she stood—stiller than most girls, with her chin raised a little.

Jim hurried to her. "Hello, Barbara," he said. He had meant to say something cleverer than that.

"Hello, Jim," said Barbara. Her voice sounded relieved. She smiled in a broad, shy, delighted way that made her face look plump. "Lord Jim!"

"Were you afraid you wouldn't know me?"

"That you wouldn't know me!"

"Never fear," Jim said. "This your bag?"

"Yes," Barbara said. "Only—listen, Jim. It's utterly ridic, but I promised my mother I'd mail her this the second I got here." She handed Jim a postcard upon which the single word "Safe" was written in a dark, vertical, sarcastic-looking hand. "I can't imagine what dire thing she thought could happen to me on the Hedgehopper!"

"I guess people in cities get the habit of being cautious," Jim said. "Just wait where you are."

He sprinted to the railway post box. He dropped Barbara's card through the slot and was about to follow it with his own letter when he was pierced by a shaft of sweet and humorous tenderness for his mother. The manifestations of her nervous love that had sickened and seemed to threaten him earlier were now clothed in natural dignity. They were universal foibles, common to all parents —even to those who chose to dwell in the heart of a metropolis. He stuffed the letter back in his pocket.

He was filled with a heady and perfectly wonderful sense of buoyancy. The evening lay ahead, bright with orchids, with candle flame at the Stromboli, and with the agreeable envy of friends. Beyond the evening, the world—his peach—hung suspended from a golden bough, ripening, ready to drop at the proper moment into the palm of his outstretched hand.

(Conflict intro 2 persons)

JAMES THURBER *The Catbird Seat*

Simple ... template ... Intrusts only ... doing his job ... to thought ... out.

James Thurber (1894-   ), born in Columbus, Ohio, and educated at Ohio State University, began his literary career in newspaper work. From 1926 to 1933, he was managing editor of the *New Yorker*, to which he still frequently contributes drawings and stories. Some of his best-known books are *Is Sex Necessary?* (in collaboration with E. B. White), 1929, a parody of books on sex education; *My Life and Hard Times*, 1933, an "autobiography"; *The Thurber Carnival*, 1945, a collection of his best work to date; *The Beast in Me, and Other Animals*, 1948; and *Thurber Country*, 1953. In 1940 he collaborated with Elliott Nugent, who had been a fellow student at Ohio State, on *The Male Animal*, a comedy about university life. Thurber has also written a number of whimsical fairy tales for children and adults which contain acute comments on present-day life.

The psychological and moral commentaries in Thurber's drawings and stories and the originality of his plots have made him one of the leading American humorists and satirists. In "The Catbird Seat" one will recognize two Thurber types—the assertive, demoniac female and the meek, downtrodden male.

Mr. Martin bought the pack of Camels on Monday night in the most crowded cigar store on Broadway. It was theatre time and seven or eight men were buying cigarettes. The clerk didn't even glance at Mr. Martin, who put the pack in his overcoat pocket and went out. If any of the staff at F & S had seen him buy the cigarettes, they would have been astonished, for it was generally known that Mr. Martin did not smoke, and never had. No one saw him.

It was just a week to the day since Mr. Martin had decided to rub out Mrs. Ulgine Barrows. The term "rub out" pleased him because it suggested nothing more than the correction of an error—in this case an error of Mr. Fitweiler. Mr. Martin had spent each night of the past week working out his plan and examining it. As he walked home now he went over it again. For the hundredth time

he resented the element of imprecision, the margin of guesswork that entered into the business. The project as he had worked it out was casual and bold, the risks were considerable. Something might go wrong anywhere along the line. And therein lay the cunning of his scheme. No one would ever see in it the cautious, painstaking hand of Erwin Martin, head of the filing department at F & S, of whom Mr. Fitweiler had once said, "Man is fallible but Martin isn't." No one would see his hand, that is, unless it were caught in the act.

Sitting in his apartment, drinking a glass of milk, Mr. Martin reviewed his case against Mrs. Ulgine Barrows, as he had every night for seven nights. He began at the beginning. Her quacking voice and braying laugh had first profaned the halls of F & S on March 7, 1941 (Mr. Martin had a head for dates). Old Roberts, the personnel chief, had introduced her as the newly appointed special adviser to the president of the firm, Mr. Fitweiler. The woman had appalled Mr. Martin instantly, but he hadn't shown it. He had given her his dry hand, a look of studious concentration, and a faint smile. "Well," she had said, looking at the papers on his desk, "are you lifting the oxcart out of the ditch?" As Mr. Martin recalled that moment, over his milk, he squirmed slightly. He must keep his mind on her crimes as special adviser, not on her peccadillos as a personality. This he found difficult to do, in spite of entering an objection and sustaining it. The faults of the woman as a woman kept chattering on in his mind like an unruly witness. She had, for almost two years now, baited him. In the halls, in the elevator, even in his own office, into which she romped now and then like a circus horse, she was constantly shouting these silly questions at him. "Are you lifting the oxcart out of the ditch? Are you tearing up the pea patch? Are you hollering down the rain barrel? Are you scraping around the bottom of the pickle barrel? Are you sitting in the catbird seat?"

It was Joey Hart, one of Mr. Martin's two assistants, who had explained what the gibberish meant. "She must be a Dodger fan," he had said. "Red Barber announces the Dodger games over the radio and he uses those expressions—picked 'em up down South." Joey had gone on to explain one or two. "Tearing up the pea patch" meant going on a rampage; "sitting in the catbird seat" meant sitting pretty, like a batter with three balls and no strikes on him. Mr. Martin dismissed all this with an effort. It had been annoying, it had driven him near to distraction, but he was too solid a man to be moved to murder by anything so childish. It was fortunate, he reflected as he passed on to the important charges against Mrs. Barrows, that he had stood up under it so well. He had maintained always an outward appearance of polite tolerance. "Why, I even believe you like the woman," Miss Paird, his other assistant, had once said to him. He had simply smiled.

A gavel rapped in Mr. Martin's mind and the case proper was resumed. Mrs. Ulgine Barrows stood charged with willful, blatant, and persistent attempts to destroy the efficiency and system of F & S. It was competent, material, and relevant to review her advent and rise to power. Mr. Martin had got the story from Miss Paird, who seemed always able to find things out. According to her, Mrs. Barrows had met Mr. Fitweiler at a party, where she had rescued him from the embraces of a powerfully built drunken man who had mistaken the president of F & S for a famous retired Middle Western football coach. She had led him to a sofa and somehow worked upon him a monstrous magic. The aging gentleman had jumped to the conclusion there and then that this was a woman of singular attainments, equipped to bring out the best in him and in the firm. A week later he had introduced her into F & S as his special adviser. On that day confusion got its foot in the door. After Miss Tyson, Mr. Brundage, and Mr. Bartlett had been fired and Mr. Munson had taken his hat and stalked out, mailing in his resignation later, old Roberts had been emboldened to speak to Mr. Fitweiler. He mentioned that Mr. Munson's department had been "a little disrupted" and hadn't they perhaps better resume the old system there? Mr. Fitweiler had said certainly not. He had the greatest faith in Mrs. Barrows' ideas. "They require a little seasoning, a little seasoning, is all," he had added. Mr. Roberts had given it up. Mr. Martin reviewed in detail all the changes wrought by Mrs. Barrows. She had begun chipping at the cornices of the firm's edifice and now she was swinging at the foundation stones with a pickaxe.

Mr. Martin came now, in his summing up, to the afternoon of Monday, November 2, 1942—just one week ago. On that day, at 3 P.M., Mrs. Barrows had bounced into his office. "Boo!" she had yelled. "Are you scraping around the bottom of the pickle barrel?" Mr. Martin had looked at her from under his green eyeshade, saying nothing. She had begun to wander about the office, taking it in with her great, popping eyes. "Do you really need *all* these filing cabinets?" she had demanded suddenly. Mr. Martin's heart had jumped. "Each of these files," he had said, keeping his voice even, "plays an indispensable part in the system of F & S." She had brayed at him, "Well, don't tear up the pea patch!" and gone to the door. From there she had bawled, "But you sure have got a lot of fine scrap in here!" Mr. Martin could no longer doubt that the finger was on his beloved department. Her pickaxe was on the upswing, poised for the first blow. It had not come yet; he had received no blue memo from the enchanted Mr. Fitweiler bearing nonsensical instructions deriving from the obscene woman. But there was no doubt in Mr. Martin's mind that one would be forthcoming. He must act quickly. Already a precious week had gone by. Mr. Martin stood up in his living room, still holding his milk glass. "Gentlemen of the jury," he said to himself, "I demand the death penalty for this horrible person."

The next day Mr. Martin followed his routine, as usual. He polished his glasses more often and once sharpened an already sharp pencil, but not even Miss Paird noticed. Only once did he catch sight of his victim; she swept past him in the hall with a patronizing "Hi!" At five-thirty he walked home, as usual, and had a glass of milk, as usual. He had never drunk anything stronger in his life—unless you could count ginger ale. The late Sam Schlosser, the S of F & S, had praised Mr. Martin at a staff meeting several years before for his temperate habits. "Our most efficient worker neither drinks nor smokes," he had said. "The results speak for themselves." Mr. Fitweiler had sat by, nodding approval.

Mr. Martin was still thinking about that red-letter day as he walked over to the Schrafft's on Fifth Avenue near Forty-Sixth Street. He got there, as he always did, at eight o'clock. He finished his dinner and the financial page of the *Sun* at a quarter to nine, as he always did. It was his custom after dinner to take a walk. This time he walked down Fifth Avenue at a casual pace. His gloved hands felt moist and warm, his forehead cold. He transferred the Camels from his overcoat to a jacket pocket. He wondered, as he did so, if they did not represent an unnecessary note of strain. Mrs. Barrows smoked only Luckies. It was his idea to puff a few puffs on a Camel (after the rubbing-out), stub it out in the ashtray holding her lipstick-stained Luckies, and thus drag a small red herring across the trail. Perhaps it was not a good idea. It would take time. He might even choke, too loudly.

Mr. Martin had never seen the house on West Twelfth Street where Mrs. Barrows lived, but he had a clear enough picture of it. Fortunately, she had bragged to everybody about her ducky first-floor apartment in the perfectly darling three-story red brick. There would be no doorman or other attendants; just the tenants of the second and third floors. As he walked along, Mr. Martin realized that he would get there before nine-thirty. He had considered walking north on Fifth Avenue from Schrafft's to a point from which it would take him until ten o'clock to reach the house. At that hour people were less likely to be coming in or going out. But the procedure would have made an awkward loop in the straight thread of his casualness, and he had abandoned it. It was impossible to figure when people would be entering or leaving the house, anyway. There was a great risk at any hour. If he ran into anybody, he would simply have to place the rubbing-out of Ulgine Barrows in the inactive file forever. The same thing would hold true if there were someone in her apartment. In that case he would just say that he had been passing by, recognized her charming house, and thought to drop in.

It was eighteen minutes after nine when Mr. Martin turned into Twelfth Street. A man passed him, and a man and a woman, talking. There was no one within fifty paces when he came to the house, halfway down the block. He was up the steps and in the small vestibule in no time, pressing the bell under the card that said "Mrs. Ulgine Barrows." When the clicking in the lock started, he jumped forward against the door. He got inside fast, closing the door behind him. A bulb in a lantern hung from the hall ceiling on a chain seemed to give a monstrously bright light. There was nobody on the stair, which went up ahead of him along the left wall. A door opened down the hall in the wall on the right. He went toward it swiftly, on tiptoe.

"Well, for God's sake, look who's here!" bawled Mrs. Barrows, and her braying laugh rang out like the report of a shotgun. He rushed past her like a football tackle, bumping her. "Hey, quit shoving!" she said, closing the door behind them. They were in her living room, which seemed to Mr. Martin to be lighted by a hundred lamps. "What's after you?" she said. "You're as jumpy as a goat." He found he was unable to speak. His heart was wheezing in his throat. "I—yes," he finally brought out. She was jabbering and laughing as she started to help him off with his coat. "No, no," he said. "I'll put it here." He took it off and put it on a chair near the door. "Your hat and gloves, too," she said. "You're in a lady's house." He put his hat on top of the coat. Mrs. Barrows seemed larger than he had thought. He kept his gloves on. "I was passing by," he said. "I recognized— Is there anyone here?" She laughed louder than ever. "No," she said, "we're all alone. You're as white as a sheet, you funny man. Whatever *has* come over you? I'll mix you a toddy." She started toward a door across the room. "Scotch-and-soda be all right? But say, you don't drink, do you?" She turned and gave him her amused look. Mr. Martin pulled himself together. "Scotch-and-soda will be all right," he heard himself say. He could hear her laughing in the kitchen.

Mr. Martin looked quickly around the living room for the weapon. He had counted on finding one there. There were andirons and a poker and something in a corner that looked like an Indian club. None of them would do. It couldn't be that way. He began to pace around. He came to a desk. On it lay a metal paper knife with an ornate handle. Would it be sharp enough? He reached for it and knocked over a small brass jar. Stamps spilled out of it and it fell to the floor with a clatter. "Hey," Mrs. Barrows yelled from the kitchen, "are you tearing up the pea patch?" Mr. Martin gave a strange laugh. Picking up the knife, he tried its point against his left wrist. It was blunt. It wouldn't do.

When Mrs. Barrows reappeared, carrying two highballs, Mr. Martin, standing there with his gloves on, became acutely conscious of the fantasy he had wrought. Cigarettes in his pocket, a drink prepared for him—it was all too grossly improbable. It was more than that; it was impossible. Somewhere in the back of his mind a vague idea stirred, sprouted. "For heaven's sake, take off those gloves," said Mrs. Barrows. "I always wear them in the house," said Mr. Martin. The

idea began to bloom, strange and wonderful. She put the glasses on a coffee table in front of a sofa and sat on the sofa. "Come over here, you odd little man," she said. Mr. Martin went over and sat beside her. It was difficult getting a cigarette out of the pack of Camels, but he managed it. She held a match for him, laughing. "Well," she said, handing him his drink, "this is perfectly marvellous. You with a drink and a cigarette."

Mr. Martin puffed, not too awkwardly, and took a gulp of the highball. "I drink and smoke all the time," he said. He clinked his glass against hers. "Here's nuts to that old windbag, Fitweiler," he said, and gulped again. The stuff tasted awful, but he made no grimace. "Really, Mr. Martin," she said, her voice and posture changing, "you are insulting our employer." Mrs. Barrows was now all special adviser to the president. "I am preparing a bomb," said Mr. Martin, "which will blow the old goat higher than hell." He had only had a little of the drink, which was not strong. It couldn't be that. "Do you take dope or something?" Mrs. Barrows asked coldly. "Heroin," said Mr. Martin. "I'll be coked to the gills when I bump that old buzzard off." "Mr. Martin!" she shouted, getting to her feet. "That will be all of that. You must go at once." Mr. Martin took another swallow of his drink. He tapped his cigarette out in the ashtray and put the pack of Camels on the coffee table. Then he got up. She stood glaring at him. He walked over and put on his hat and coat. "Not a word about this," he said, and laid an index finger against his lips. All Mrs. Barrows could bring out was "Really!" Mr. Martin put his hand on the doorknob. "I'm sitting in the catbird seat," he said. He stuck his tongue out at her and left. Nobody saw him go.

Mr. Martin got to his apartment, walking, well before eleven. No one saw him go in. He had two glasses of milk after brushing his teeth, and he felt elated. It wasn't tipsiness, because he hadn't been tipsy. Anyway, the walk had worn off all effects of the whiskey. He got in bed and read a magazine for a while. He was asleep before midnight.

Mr. Martin got to the office at eight-thirty the next morning, as usual. At a quarter to nine, Ulgine Barrows, who had never before arrived at work before ten, swept into his office. "I'm reporting to Mr. Fitweiler now!" she shouted. "If he turns you over to the police, it's no more than you deserve!" Mr. Martin gave her a look of shocked surprise. "I beg your pardon?" he said. Mrs. Barrows snorted and bounced out of the room, leaving Miss Paird and Joey Hart staring after her. "What's the matter with that old devil now?" asked Miss Paird. "I have no idea," said Mr. Martin, resuming his work. The other two looked at him and then at each other. Miss Paird got up and went out. She walked slowly past the closed door of Mr. Fitweiler's office. Mrs. Barrows was yelling inside, but she was not braying. Miss Paird could not hear what the woman was saying. She went back to her desk.

Forty-five minutes later, Mrs. Barrows left the president's office and went into her own, shutting the door. It wasn't until half an hour later that Mr. Fitweiler sent for Mr. Martin. The head of the filing department, neat, quiet, attentive, stood in front of the old man's desk. Mr. Fitweiler was pale and nervous. He took his glasses off and twiddled them. He made a small, bruffing sound in his throat. "Martin," he said, "you have been with us more than twenty years." "Twenty-two, sir," said Mr. Martin. "In that time," pursued the president, "your work and your—uh—manner have been exemplary." "I trust so, sir," said Mr. Martin. "I have understood, Martin," said Mr. Fitweiler, "that you have never taken a drink or smoked." "That is correct, sir," said Mr. Martin. "Ah, yes." Mr. Fitweiler polished his glasses. "You may describe what you did after leaving the office yesterday, Martin," he said. Mr. Martin allowed less than a second for his bewildered pause. "Certainly, sir," he said. "I walked home. Then I went to Schrafft's for dinner. Afterward I walked home again. I went to bed early, sir, and read a magazine for a while. I was asleep before eleven." "Ah, yes," said Mr. Fitweiler again. He was silent for a moment, searching for the proper words to say to the head of the filing department. "Mrs. Barrows," he said finally, "Mrs. Barrows has worked hard, Martin, very hard. It grieves me to report that she has suffered a severe breakdown. It has taken the form of a perse-

cution complex accompanied by distressing hallucinations." "I am very sorry, sir," said Mr. Martin. "Mrs. Barrows is under the delusion," continued Mr. Fitweiler, "that you visited her last evening and behaved yourself in an—uh—unseemly manner." He raised his hand to silence Mr. Martin's little pained outcry. "It is the nature of these psychological diseases," Mr. Fitweiler said, "to fix upon the least likely and most innocent party as the—uh—source of persecution. These matters are not for the lay mind to grasp, Martin. I've just had my psychiatrist, Doctor Fitch, on the phone. He would not, of course, commit himself, but he made enough generalizations to substantiate my suspicions. I suggested to Mrs. Barrows, when she had completed her—uh—story to me this morning, that she visit Doctor Fitch, for I suspected a condition at once. She flew, I regret to say, into a rage, and demanded—uh—requested that I call you on the carpet. You may not know, Martin, but Mrs. Barrows had planned a reorganization of your department—subject to my approval, of course, subject to my approval. This brought you, rather than anyone else, to her mind—but again that is a phenomenon for Doctor Fitch and not for us. So, Martin, I am afraid Mrs. Barrows' usefulness here is at an end." "I am dreadfully sorry, sir," said Mr. Martin.

It was at this point that the door to the office blew open with the suddenness of a gas-main explosion and Mrs. Barrows catapulted through it. "Is the little rat denying it?" she screamed. "He can't get away with that!" Mr. Martin got up and moved discreetly to a point beside Mr. Fitweiler's chair. "You drank and smoked at my apartment," she bawled at Mr. Martin, "and you know it! You called Mr. Fitweiler an old windbag and said you were going to blow him up when you got coked to the gills on your heroin!" She stopped yelling to catch her breath and a new glint came into her popping eyes. "If you weren't such a drab, ordinary little man," she said, "I'd think you'd planned it all. Sticking your tongue out, saying you were sitting in the catbird seat, because you thought no one would believe me when I told it! My God, it's really too perfect!" She brayed loudly and hysterically, and the fury was on her again. She glared at Mr. Fitweiler. "Can't you see how he has tricked us, you old fool? Can't you see his little game?" But Mr. Fitweiler had been surreptitiously pressing all the buttons under the top of his desk and employees of F & S began pouring into the room. "Stockton," said Mr. Fitweiler, "you and Fishbein will take Mrs. Barrows to her home. Mrs. Powell, you will go with them." Stockton, who had played a little football in high school, blocked Mrs. Barrows as she made for Mr. Martin. It took him and Fishbein together to force her out of the door into the hall, crowded with stenographers and office boys. She was still screaming imprecations at

Mr. Martin, tangled and contradictory imprecations. The hubbub finally died out down the corridor.

"I regret that this has happened," said Mr. Fitweiler. "I shall ask you to dismiss it from your mind, Martin." "Yes, sir," said Mr. Martin, anticipating his chief's "That will be all" by moving to the door. "I will dismiss it." He went out and shut the door, and his step was light and quick in the hall. When he entered his department he had slowed down to his customary gait, and he walked quietly across the room to the W20 file, wearing a look of studious concentration.

BRYAN MACMAHON *The Lion-Tamer*

Bryan MacMahon (1909-   ) was born in Listowel, Ireland, and educated in the local schools and St. Patrick's College (Dublin). He was first recognized by Frank O'Connor as a poet, but, like many another writer, he soon turned to prose. In 1945 *The Bell*, an Irish literary magazine, awarded him a short-story prize for "The Good Dead in the Green Hills." As master of the National School in Listowel, he has learned much about the fishermen, farmers, and townspeople of County Kerry. "Our wonderful back gate," he says of his home near sea and market place, "opened on an exciting world." In this world one will look in vain for "the big bow-wow stuff" that makes the headlines of the metropolitan dailies.

MacMahon's interest in big dramas in little settings is exemplified in "The Lion-Tamer."

As I entered the public-house I saw the man eyeing me through the meshes of froth on the side of his uptilted glass. He was seated by the fire. It is a characteristic of the older public-houses in the smaller villages that the bar itself is half bar, half kitchen. The fire was burning brightly in the old range and strata of underclothing were drying on the bars above it. The publican gave me the glare such persons reserve for strangers. I ordered a bottle of stout and threw him a casual remark about the weather. As he gave me the

THE LION-TAMER: From the book *The Lion-Tamer and Other Stories.* Copyright, 1949, by Bryan Mac-Mahon. Published by E. P. Dutton and Co., Inc.

drink his face thawed into friendliness and he ordered me to pull over to the fire.

I did so and found myself opposite the man who had scrutinized me on my entrance; by this time he had placed his glass on the tiles at the side of the range and was balancing himself on the two hind legs of his chair. His prim eyes were on my every movement. I sat down opposite him and as his eyes dropped preparatory to taking up his drink, I appraised him as thoroughly as I could in the small span of time allowed me: he had a pale boyish face with the pimples of belated adolescence upon it; his nose was pointed to make his profile a shallow isosceles triangle with the vertex on the tip of his nose. A thing that struck me about him was his boyishness— his immaturity. I put his age at twenty-two or -three at the outside.

I am gregarious and convivial to a degree considered alarming by my friends. At that moment I was pining for company. The fact that my business in the village had been finished late in the afternoon necessitated my staying in the place overnight, and, according as one grows older, the prospect of spending a night out of one's home is by no means relished. I timed my imbibing so that the young man opposite me and myself should finish our drinks together. Then I was quick to offer to buy him a drink. His refusal came with the unexpectedness of a slap. "I prefer to buy my own drinks!" he said. This type of brusque unequivocal refusal is rare in country parts. I accepted defeat, rankling not a little under the brutal and un-Irish nature of it. Just as I had begun to spin myself a cocoon of outraged reserve, his explanation was offered, and I was impressed by the rare directness of it: "A custom I learned in England," he said. "Treating is abominable—neither fair to the treater nor the treated. When two are drinking together it is impossible to have an odd number of drinks, and that is a limitation I can never accept. Nevertheless I am grateful to you for having asked me." All this came with the aplomb of one three times his senior in age. I called for my own drink; he called for his. I paid for mine; he paid for his. It struck me as unusual that the publican seemed to consider this arrangement entirely normal.

I was tempted to hang some cloth on the conversational peg of England. When I did so he spoke fluently and authoritatively of the Midland cities. I had spent six months in Birmingham, and each observation of his regarding that city struck me as objective, terse and accurate. As he continued speaking I found myself compelled to renew my respect for him. Before long we were chatting brightly but restrainedly. Putting a man at his job is an old trick of conversation; so I indicated vaguely the nature of my business in the village. He rose to the bait with alacrity. Taking a sip out of his glass he sucked in his lips and laid down his drink with a good deal of cere-

mony. Then he said: "What would you say my occupation was?" Followed the usual chit-chat and mock-surprise. First, "You a native of this place?" ("Yes.") "Hmmm! Teacher?" ("No.") "Insurance Agent? Machinist? Student? Home Assistance Officer?" (We both laughed.) "Sacristan? Clerk of Works? Engineer?" The answer was always no.

"I give up," I said.

He sipped his drink with quiet triumph. "As a matter of fact I don't blame you in the least. I could have given you a thousand guesses and you'd never have got it."

"But that isn't telling me what you are!"

"I'm a lion-tamer," he said, "the only Irish-born lion-tamer there is."

I lifted my drink to my mouth and threw him a glance which must have spelled incredulity with a capital I.

He was quick to resent the fact that, in my own mind, I was calling him a liar. "If you doubt my word," he snapped, "I shall ask our friend O'Donoghue." He swivelled in his chair to ask the publican to bear witness for him, but Mr. O'Donoghue had vanished into the back premises from whence the clinking of bottles came to our ears.

I hastened to reassure him that I fully believed him. "You look so young," I said in extenuation of my fault.

"Young as I am, I've seen a good deal of life and have travelled more than my share."

There came a slight hiatus in the flow of our speech. I thought he seemed inclined to bear away from the absorbing subject of lion-taming. I hurried after him and, conversationally speaking, caught him by the coat-tails.

"How on earth, I ask, did you manage to become a lion-tamer?"

In lieu of response he took a packet of cigarettes from his pocket, extracted one and tamped it deftly on his knee. He did not offer me a cigarette.

"The story does me little credit," he began. "For my part of it I had always wanted to be a doctor. But my black friend here on the hob" (here he indicated his drink) "and his wee yellow brother said no to my dreams of medicine." I noted his lapse into the vernacular.

A pause. A smile flickered on his lips—it

was distressing to see one so young smile so bitterly. "I ran away with the circus one night after a row with the stepmother. Ever hear of Vaughan's? Not a top-notcher, but a good, honest little show as shows go. Vaughan's wife would have made a good sub. for the Fat Lady, only the old man never featured freaks. I remember a guy trying to sell the Boss a calf with six legs, but the Boss told him take the thing away. 'You'll gain two on the quarters of veal if you kill it,' the old man said.

"I found the tober hard graft. Taking down the Big Top of a wet night with your soaked pants clinging to your thighs was no picnic. I remember driving a wagon in the procession through the town—dressed as a cowboy I was—and my belly was back to my back with the hunger. Aye, and I had to turn every second minute to take a bite out of a raw turnip. I used chew it as strongly as I could to make the crowd believe I was chewing tobacco. Yes, and driving all night and trying to sleep on a pile of junk with the wind cutting through the slats in the wagon and every rut in the road rattling a panful of marbles on the floor of your skull. Right hard graft it was. But, by hell, I stuck it!

"The Boss saw I was frailer and finer than the ordinary run, aye, and that I had one hell of a tooth for the milk of the black cow. So he put me in charge of the cat—cleaning out from her and so on. The cat had four kittens, and this was the act: the cage was divided into two compartments and at every performance the trainer—he was an Edinburgh man—went into the cage and put them through their paces. First he went into the empty box. Then the four kittens were poked or coaxed out a small hole and McIvor put them up on four little stools—one in each corner of the box. When they were sitting pretty her ladyship was let out through a bigger slide and the tamer's job was to get her sitting on a big stool in the middle as if the whole cat family were posing for their photograph. The old lady was a sour old strap. During the performance three or four of us had to stand guard outside the bars with crowbars and poles ready to prise herself and Andy apart if she should take it into her head to maul him.

"I spent a few months cleaning out from

Minnie. At times she had all the tricks of a real cat. I used stop and laugh at the way she'd stretch herself out and scrape at the wood just like your own pussy scraping the table leg. Maybe she'd get humorous and play with the cubs with those quick flicks that we see so often in the household edition. A lioness is only a Tab seen through a telescope. But frost played Molly Bawn to her and when hard weather came she was like a red devil out of hell.

"Andy McIvor was a tyrant of tyrants. He had realized his indispensability. Lion-tamers aren't two a penny, you know. The trade isn't listed in 'Careers for Your Children.' Most of the tamers come from European zoos and a few from England and Scotland. Whenever Andy had a row with the Boss, the Boss would be the first to pipe down. If he didn't do this the Missus would send for Andy and palaver him. Andy was inclined to go on the booze—not with me though: he considered me his inferior. The first portent of Andy's intention of hitting the bottle was his donning of a gold signet ring. The sight of that ring on his finger early in the morning was enough to set the whole show on edge. He commemorated obscure festivals and obscurer anniversaries. On a few occasions he went into the cage paralytic drunk and called the cat a cowardly old so-and-so. Except for one rip on his arm he always got away with it. The others believed that he was immune because he carried a certain kind of herb in his pocket, the smell of which the cat loved. But I doubt it. I've watched him hundreds of times and he had only the four legs of a chair and a whip between him and the Jordan-box. His prat was a kind of continual hissing, the rhythm of which I was never able to pick up, no matter how hard I tried.

"Things went from bad to worse with Andy. The man became insufferable. 'Three lion-tamers in this blasted country,' he'd say, 'one tied up with—(here he named a rival circus), one crippled with arthritis in Derry City, and the third is mysel'. Three of us in this blasted country. Pss. . . . Which of you fellows is willin' to go in to the cat? Eh?'

"One night just before a show was due to commence Andy was brought back stone dead corpsed drunk. The Boss was fit to be tied.

The wife began to cry. When the time came for Andy to go on, the Boss pulled a fast one on the audience. He pitched a big yarn about the lion-tamer's arm being mauled and turning septic and that he craved the indulgence of his patrons. The country boys didn't like it a bit. They had planked their good money on the offchance of seeing a man mangled. They boohed, hooted and blackguarded. Country boys are like greyhounds: they get all their courage when they are in the pack, especially if the pack happens to meet in darkness. But the Boss had all this mapped out. He made himself heard above the noise and offered £100 to any man who would go into the cage and stay there with the cat for two minutes. That corked their bottle. No one stirred. We had one of our own lads placed in the crowd. He was there to size up the situation and was to get in first if any country fellow made a move. Suddenly there was a jostling match among the crowd around the door of the tent. Then we saw that a big fellow who seemed to be half drunk was being pushed forward into the ring. Our man waited for a split second to see if the country boy was in earnest about going in. Then he jumped in and beat the yokel to the draw. The country boy looked nowhere and was pushed back into the people.

"The Boss began his patter. First he asked our man if he was willing to go in, and receiving a good gulp in reply he disclaimed all responsibility on behalf of the management of the Circus. Then 'Are you married? Address of your nearest relative?' and a word of advice, 'Young man, in the cage make every move deliberate, nothing hasty, you understand?' The Boss took out his wallet, smacked it with the palm of his hand and stated that it contained £100 in £5 notes. After which he extracted his watch and bade the challenger to move in. Our man took off his cap, wiped the sweat off his face with it, swallowed his Adam's apple a few times, looked around wildly and finally moved towards the cage. There was a deadly silence. But the Boss had his head well screwed on. He had it all squared up with the two Civic Guards at the flap that if any country boy was idiot enough to risk going into the cage he was to be prevented from doing so. So at the tensest mo-

ment of the fake drama, the local Sergeant stepped forward, clicked his fingers and raised a legal hand at the sham adventurer. Immediately the pantomime warmed up; the Boss shrugged his shoulders in a gesture of impotence; the crowd went wild, our man grew truculent and was inclined to assert his constitutional rights to commit suicide if he so wished. Then at the height of the hubbub the Boss held up his hand for silence, drew a fiver from his wallet and handed it to the challenger, shook hands with him and made a magnificent speech congratulating him on his indomitable courage. The crowd liked this better than ever and cheered the hero as he resumed his seat. It was a first-class stunt thought up on the spur of the moment without any rehearsal. It worked so well that the Boss was inclined to keep it up and work it now and again—once, say, in each county, but when it was broached to a sober Andy he spurned the suggestion and said, 'By hell he'd be made a monkey of by no mon!'

"It was in Ennistymon in Clare that Andy McIvor walked out of the show for good and glory. When the Missus came out of the living-wagon after the evening performance she saw the Boss and Andy rolling over on the ground. Vaughan was no daw in a rough-and-tumble and he chawed a neat semicircle out of Andy's ear. It's surprising all the blood that can come out of a man's ear. Like a tap spouting red ink it was. The Missus started to holler like hell. Gathering her breath she'd shriek down to nothing. Then again she'd swell like an insulted hatching-hen—all with the dint of gathering her screech. The ponies grew restive in the long tent. We closed in to separate the pair of them. Andy was frothing at the mouth and his ear was a show to God and the world. The Boss had a big beard of blood after the bite. Andy bucked about with three of us clinging to his back; the Boss stripped his red teeth like a butcher's dog; the Missus went off in a dead weakness. The village lads watched us from a huge stupefied circle. As Andy calmed down he shrieked perdition and punishment on us all. He called us all Irish this and Irish that and Irish th' other thing. He said we were for the Boss. Indeed that was no lie for him; it was the Boss who was paying us, not Andy.

"Finally Vaughan was dragged into his wagon, and his Missus, who was prone on the grass, was slapped back to consciousness. Soon the Boss and the Missus were at it hot and heavy. In the heel of the hunt Mrs. Vaughan broke down and began to cry. In the meantime Andy had packed his bag and put on his signet ring; he cursed us all squarely as he departed. A bus was going the road—Andy hailed it and went away. The Circus was minus its lion-tamer.

"About six o'clock that evening I was in the harness-wagon when the Missus came up. 'Is he gone, Tim?' she asked. 'Aye, ma'am, gone by bus,' I answered. 'Good riddance!' she says. 'There's as good fish in the sea as was ever caught.' With that she eyed me shrewdly. Then, 'Come down, Tim, I want to talk to you.' I came down. Then, 'Take me down to the town, Tim. I want a drink.' With that she took my arm. The woman was huge and would persist in wearing a fur coat. Going out the gate I could feel the eyes of all the other chaps burning holes in my back. The vision of the Missus waltzing out arm-in-arm with a circus hand had no precedent in circus etiquette.

"When we got to a pub the Missus started to drink gin while I stuck to honest porter. But after a while she started to throw whiskey down me. 'You're out of the ordinary run, Tim,' she said, 'and I've been on to the Boss to give you your chance.'

"'My chance, ma'am?'

"'Aye, your chance, Tim.'

"Fuddled as I was, I started to put two and two together. I narrowed my eyes on her pneumatic side-face. 'This fat ould heap,' says I to myself, 'is aimin' to get me chawed up by the cat.' But she kept feeding me whiskey till she blunted the edge of my bitterness. Then I considered, 'Maybe I'm wrongin' the decent woman: maybe she *does* want me to go ahead in the world.'

"'Three of them in all Ireland,' she primed, 'one with th' other crowd, a good man—even though he's on the wrong side of the fence—one in the City of Derry an' he crippled with rheumatism . . .'

"'Arthritis, ma'am,' says I.

"'Arthritis,' says she. 'And the third you know. A beast! A sot! A toper! A swiller!

He'll never hold a job as long as he lives. None of the three are Irishmen,' she added regretfully.

"I sang dumb.

"'Ah,' says she with an authentic Genevan sigh, 'Ireland produced a great poet in Tommy Moore, a great greyhound in Master Magrath and a great boxer in John L. But Ireland never produced a lion-tamer. Ah, the pity of it!'

"There wasn't a sinner in the bar but the two of us, yet she leaned across to me conspiratorially and gave me the biggest wink I have ever seen. 'Dave got a letter from Ringling,' she whispers. 'Ringling and Dave are just like that,' with this she put one fat finger on top of the other. '"Dave," says he in the letter, "I could do with a first-class cat-man. Can you help me?"' After she had let this sink home in me, 'I like you, Tim. I like everything about you. I like the way you clean out the cat's cage. I'm going to see you get your chance!'

"When we got back, the band—our moth-eaten band—was playing in the Big Top. I was drunk but I was well able to put my legs under me. Dimly I saw a knot of people around the ticketwagon. The slide hadn't gone up as yet. The Boss came against us with question-mark written all over his face. 'Dave,' says the Missus, 'did I ever in my life cross you?'

"'Never!' says he.

"'Well,' says she, 'don't deny me my request. You've got to give Timmy Moran here his chance to see what he's able to do with the cats!'

"'I'm a man of quick decisions,' says the Boss. 'We'll bill you as Moranni. Wash your face in cold water. Get into that fellow's wagon. Pull up the duds on you and lie down until I call you.'

"Jacko and Drumshambo came from nowhere and took me in hand. They led me to the lion-tamer's wagon, dragged the togs on me, then heaved me into the bunk and left me.

"When I awoke I was perished with the cold. The two boys were pummelling hell out of me. I heard the band playing and listened to the machine-gun fire of handclapping breaking across the music. When the applause ceased the stentorian voice of the Boss boomed out in a build-up for the aerobats Vivo and Vivienne.

"Jacko and Drumshambo were working on me with a sponge and cold water. 'Snap out of it, Timothy,' they said, and slapped and splashed me as seconds pummel a fighter who is all but out on his feet. Then a voice spoke from the misty oblong of the caravan door: through gritted eyes I saw what looked like an up-ended sperm whale standing on the steps of the wagon. 'Twas the Missus, and whatever it was she was wearing it gave her the genuine sheen of something huge out of the ocean. She kept whispering 'Tim, Tim,' in a quavering voice. I fuddled out under the stars. The Boss bustled around from the back-flap. At first he was agitated, but on appreciating that I was actually erect, his agitation subsided. 'Come on,' says he, then, 'Don't let the cat see your face—and keep crouched. 'Tis a living cinch, I tell you! And always remember that we're there with the crowbars. And as soon as ever you see the cat and the four kittens sitting pretty, give your bow and get out. Above all, don't forget to make your bow!'

"When, with my trembling retinue, I got inside the tent, Vivienne was down on the strip waiting for Vivo to come down out of the air. I saw her sequins glittering though my eyes were the eyes of a dullard. There she stood with her Little Jack Horner pose until eventually Vivo thudded to the mat beside her.

"I put my nose sideways and upwards and searched the air for the odour of lion. Receiving it, I felt my face grow haggard. Hitherto that smell had connoted but a repugnant chore; now for me it had become charged with a novel deadliness.

"'The Great Moranni . . . jaws of death . . . dangers of this amazing feat . . . accentuated (the Boss always pivoted on this word) . . . by the fact . . . female of the species . . . cubs . . . defensive instincts of the lioness . . . African home . . . movement not wholly in harmony . . . intrepid Moranni . . . limb from limb . . . Ladies . . . gentlemen . . . privilege and pride . . . the Great Moranni!'

"All the small noises of the circus ceased.

I felt myself being propelled forward to make my bow. God forgive me, I did my level best to bounce out gaily with my hands up at 'Ou-la-la-la' and my crop flashing down to slap commandingly on my high boots. Uppermost in my mind was an access of retrospective appreciation of Andy McIvor. Roar after roar came from a circle that was studded with a thousand smoky blobs.

"The cage had been moved up to the verge of the outer ring. I turned to it. Jacko gave me a short, light iron bar and Drumshambo held out the chair. ''Tis as easy as pie,' said Jacko. Dirty Dan was there with a long iron pole. 'You poor so-and-so,' he said. Dirty Dan and I were old foes. I got up those steps, bent and went into the empty compartment. The Boss began to bark: now and again he gave an agonized look across his shoulder at me. I found the apprehension in his voice contagious. I got a squint at the Missus who was quivering like a bladder of lard in a hot corner. When the Boss had finished, the drummer picked up the thread of the tension and began to send his eerie peas hopping on the skin of the kettle-drum. This was designed to get the customers down, but, God's truth, it affected no one more than it did the Great Moranni. Iron poles clanged on the cage-bars as the men poked out the cubs through the smaller opening. It seemed to me that the cubs' heads had come together on the rim of a wheel and that the wheel had begun to spin violently. I blinked my way out of that spasm. I was fairly familiar with this routine, and after a good deal of tugging and hauling I got the four of them on their stools. The band pleaded for applause, got it, nourished it, fattened it, then killed it abruptly.

"Two things had begun to bother me: Number one, which of the poles clattering on the bars belonged to Dirty Dan? Number two, what was the jabber Andy carried on to Minnie when she came out? All I could think of was 'Allez-oop!' and that would have been acro-jabber, only any acros. I knew said 'Huppie!' or 'Hup!' Still, in a pinch I reckoned 'Allez-oop' better than nothing.

"As the big slide came across—in pardon to you—I began to retch off my stomach. But I had the presence of mind of half turning my back on the people who at this moment must have been closely watching the cat. The whiskey—subtly altered by my stomach-juices —began to dribble down my chin and neck. Some of it leaked out of my nose as out of a poteen-still. I felt so weak and banjaxed that I didn't give two hoots in hell whether it was on my leg or my hand that the lioness began to chew. Minnie came stalking out. Once again my tongue filled my mouth and I was racked by the second spasm of vomit. Through my tears I saw the four cubs eyeing their Ma's dinner. I grew conscious of voices nursing and cursing me alternately. I palmed away my dribbles and feebly raised the chair to shield me from the cat. She came padding towards me. I backed away from her. She put her nose to the retched whiskey and turned away without appearing to register any reaction except an ominous boredom. She looked at the kittens; then yawped ill-temperedly in my direction. The iron poles poked in through the bars. Which was Dirty Dan's? —that was the one that would let her in to me. I woke up, gathered my courage, crept towards her and started saying 'H..ss!' and 'Allez-oop!' in an endeavour to get her up on the centre stool. First she backed away from me; then she stopped and walked towards me. All the while I was hissing like a goose. I peeped from behind the chair at her face and I knew by it that she was itching to maul me. Just then one of the cubs put a trial paw towards the floor of the cage. I put down my hand and bundled her up again. The movement, simple as it was, made me sweat like a bull. As I was straightening myself my knees began to knock. Up to this I had thought that one's knees knocking was a figure of speech, but if anyone tells you that it's not a physical fact, you can call him a liar and quote me as your authority. Then I got a brainwave. I began to scrape the seat of the perch with one leg of my chair. The lioness put her nose to the point of scraping, so I brought my scraping to the offside of the seat from her and her inquisitive nose pursued it. I lowered the chair and scraped on the floor on my side of the seat. I'm blessed to God if she didn't jump up on the stool to view the situation as a whole. Immediately I pronged her with all four legs of the chair and put her sitting down.

"The deed was done! The kettle-drums rattled up and up and on and on. In barged the trumpets and brought the crowd to the peak of the huzza. The place swirled around me—cubs and lionesses and stools in that infernal wheel. My nostrils were assaulted by the fumes of whiskey and the unconquerable odour of lion-dung. Somebody called on me to bow. I backed against the side of the cage; my knees buckled while I gave the crowd as much of my profile as I could afford without even once taking my eyes off her ladyship. Again the applause backed up like a suddenly dammed river. I heard the gate clang open behind me. Inch by precious inch I retreated until my buttocks found the aperture: then the lads dragged me to the ground. I can't remember whether I took a second bow or not. Then the clowns spun out in cartwheels of colour and the feed banged in with his bright patter.

"The Boss and the Missus were there to congratulate me. Pride was flowing down off the pair of them. 'Leave it there!' said himself, extending his hand. 'At last Ireland can boast that she has a lion-tamer.'

"I stayed with Vaughan's for two seasons and, believe you me, before I was finished I could cuff that old cat across the ear. Like all women, she was contrary now and again: once she gave me the hooks in a little place in North Tipp., nothing worth talking about, but still . . ." Here the young man made as if to tug his shirt over the back of his belt and show me scars and weals, but on my counterfeiting squeamishness he desisted.

"I left Vaughan's to start on my own—on a small scale, you know. I picked up a performing bear dirt-cheap from a chap in Dublin and ran a Pick-and-Win joint for three months, making as much money in that time at that racket as I had made in my whole circus career."

A clock struck. "Oho!" said my friend, glancing up. He finished his drink hurriedly and bade good-night to myself and the publican. I ordered a nightcap. The publican put his elbows on the counter and nodded towards the door through which the story-teller had gone. I saw pride lighting in his eyes.

"Isn't he good?" he asked.

"Damn good!" I agreed.

"What was it?"

"Eh?"

"It wasn't the Lizard in the Cardinal's Pocket?" The man's eyes pipped in anticipation of tiny triumph.

"Eh? No, no."

"Nor the time he operated on his mother for appendicitis?"

"No, no."

"Let me think. Don't tell me. Was it the Litter of Elk-Hounds he sold in Cruft's?"

"He said he was a lion-tamer," I faltered.

The publican grew solemn; then wan. Suddenly he brightened in parochial pride. "Blast me if I ever heard that one before." Then, ominously, "Isn't he able to put them together well?"

"Never heard better," I said.

The publican cupped his face in his palms. "What gave him the lead to that one?" He ruminated for a moment. Then his face splintered into the joy of discovery. "Blast me if it isn't Miss Evans's cats!"

"Miss Evans's cats?"

"Aye! he's feeding them while she's away. He must have a lead. Cats—lions, see? The Lizard story—he got the lead of that from a kid who brought a frog to school in his handkerchief. Once they took him as far as the Falls of Doonass on a Confraternity excursion and he came back with a grand story about Niagara. I'd say the Niagara story is his best. That's all we have in this place, him and the Caves": here he dismissed the hamlet with a gesture. "The caves are about a mile up the hill—spikes comin' up out of the floor and more hanging down from the ceiling. There's a big name for them. Would you remember what it is?"

"Stalagmites and stalactites," I said.

He repeated the words, savouring them. Then, "The Caves are damn good, too." I pondered on the shade of meaning latent in the addendum "too."

I finished my drink, bade the publican good-night and walked up the village towards the tiny hotel. The night was still and frosty with a wealth of stars above. I heard the crunch-crunch of two Guards' boots on the gravelled path a hundred yards behind me. Lemon lamp-light glowed in a few houses, on the side of the street. On my right-hand side the bulk of the hill was clear against the northern sky. The place where the hotel stood was at the higher end of the street, and when I got to the top of the little eminence I looked back on the twenty or thirty mongrel houses in the village. Odd to consider, I pondered, that after all these years it is in this shabby insignificant hollow in Ireland the reincarnated spirit of Munchausen has found flesh fit to cover its shade.

ROALD DAHL *Taste*

Roald Dahl (1916-   ) was born in South Wales of Norwegian parents. He, his four sisters, and his brother were raised by his mother after his father's early death. At eighteen, he declined his mother's offer to send him to Oxford and joined the Shell Oil Company in London. After four years' training, he was sent to Dar-es-salaam in Arabia. During the war he was in the R.A.F. and saw action in the Libyan desert, then in Greece, where he was severely wounded. When he recovered, he fought the Vichy French in Syria. Finally he had to leave the R.A.F., because of old injuries, and in 1942 he was sent to Washington as an assistant air attaché to the British Embassy.

While in Washington he began to write short stories. The first twelve, all about flying, appeared in American magazines and were published in 1946 under the title *Over to You.* *Someone Like You,* a collection of stories, some of which had previously appeared in the *New Yorker, Collier's,* and *Harper's,* was published in 1953. In 1955, *The Honeys,* his first play, was produced in New York. Since he began writing, he has lived alternately in England and America.

Mr. Dahl invites comparison with O. Henry. Long on plot, short on character, he is an adroit craftsman. He knows how to make the unlikely seem probable. As *Time* magazine points out, "He builds long bridges of suspense, then skillfully carries his stories across to his predetermined point."

There were six of us to dinner that night at Mike Schofield's house in London: Mike and his wife and daughter, my wife and I, and a man called Richard Pratt.

Richard Pratt was a famous gourmet. He was president of a small society known as the Epicures, and each month he circulated privately to its members a pamphlet on food and wines. He organized dinners where sumptuous dishes and rare wines were served. He refused to smoke for fear of harming his palate, and when discussing a wine, he had a curious, rather droll habit of referring to it as though it were a living being. "A prudent wine," he would say, "rather diffident and evasive, but quite prudent." Or, "a good-

humored wine, benevolent and cheerful—slightly obscene, perhaps, but nonetheless good-humored."

I had been to dinner at Mike's twice before when Richard Pratt was there, and on each occasion Mike and his wife had gone out of their way to produce a special meal for the famous gourmet. And this one, clearly, was to be no exception. The moment we entered the dining room, I could see that the table was laid for a feast. The tall candles, the yellow roses, the quantity of shining silver, the three wineglasses to each person, and above all, the faint scent of roasting meat from the kitchen brought the first warm oozings of saliva to my mouth.

As we sat down, I remembered that on both Richard Pratt's previous visits Mike had played a little betting game with him over the claret, challenging him to name its breed

TASTE: Reprinted from *Someone Like You* by Roald Dahl, by permission of Alfred A. Knopf, Inc. Copyright 1951, 1953 by Roald Dahl, originally published in *The New Yorker.*

and its vintage. Pratt had replied that that should not be too difficult provided it was one of the great years. Mike had then bet him a case of the wine in question that he could not do it. Pratt had accepted, and had won both times. Tonight I felt sure that the little game would be played over again, for Mike was quite willing to lose the bet in order to prove that his wine was good enough to be recognized, and Pratt, for his part, seemed to take a grave, restrained pleasure in displaying his knowledge.

The meal began with a plate of whitebait, fried very crisp in butter, and to go with it there was a Moselle. Mike got up and poured the wine himself, and when he sat down again, I could see that he was watching Richard Pratt. He had set the bottle in front of me so that I could read the label. It said, "Geierslay Ohligsberg, 1945." He leaned over and whispered to me that Geierslay was a tiny village in the Moselle, almost unknown outside Germany. He said that this wine we were drinking was something unusual, that the output of the vineyard was so small that it was almost impossible for a stranger to get any of it. He had visited Geierslay personally the previous summer in order to obtain the few dozen bottles that they had finally allowed him to have.

"I doubt anyone else in the country has any of it at the moment," he said. I saw him glance again at Richard Pratt. "Great thing about Moselle," he continued, raising his voice, "it's the perfect wine to serve before a claret. A lot of people serve a Rhine wine instead, but that's because they don't know any better. A Rhine wine will kill a delicate claret, you know that? It's barbaric to serve a Rhine before a claret. But a Moselle—ah!—a Moselle is exactly right."

Mike Schofield was an amiable, middle-aged man. But he was a stock-broker. To be precise, he was a jobber in the stock market, and like a number of his kind, he seemed to be somewhat embarrassed, almost ashamed to find that he had made so much money with so slight a talent. In his heart he knew that he was not really much more than a book-maker—an unctuous, infinitely respectable, secretly unscrupulous bookmaker—and he knew that his friends knew it, too. So he was

seeking now to become a man of culture, to cultivate a literary and aesthetic taste, to collect paintings, music, books, and all the rest of it. His little sermon about Rhine wine and Moselle was a part of this thing, this culture that he sought.

"A charming little wine, don't you think?" he said. He was still watching Richard Pratt. I could see him give a rapid furtive glance down the table each time he dropped his head to take a mouthful of whitebait. I could almost *feel* him waiting for the moment when Pratt would take his first sip, and look up from his glass with a smile of pleasure, of astonishment, perhaps even of wonder, and then there would be a discussion and Mike would tell him about the village of Geierslay.

But Richard Pratt did not taste his wine. He was completely engrossed in conversation with Mike's eighteen-year-old daughter, Louise. He was half turned toward her, smiling at her, telling her, so far as I could gather, some story about a chef in a Paris restaurant. As he spoke, he leaned closer and closer to her, seeming in his eagerness almost to impinge upon her, and the poor girl leaned as far as she could away from him, nodding politely, rather desperately, and looking not at his face but at the topmost button of his dinner jacket.

We finished our fish, and the maid came around removing the plates. When she came to Pratt, she saw that he had not yet touched his food, so she hesitated, and Pratt noticed her. He waved her away, broke off his conversation, and quickly began to eat, popping the little crisp brown fish quickly into his mouth with rapid jabbing movements of his fork. Then, when he had finished, he reached for his glass, and in two short swallows he tipped the wine down his throat and turned immediately to resume his conversation with Louise Schofield.

Mike saw it all. I was conscious of him sitting there, very still, containing himself, looking at his guest. His round jovial face seemed to loosen slightly and to sag, but he contained himself and was still and said nothing.

Soon the maid came forward with the second course. This was a large roast of beef. She placed it on the table in front of Mike who stood up and carved it, cutting the slices very thin, laying them gently on the plates for the maid to take around. When he had served everyone, including himself, he put down the carving knife and leaned forward with both hands on the edge of the table.

"Now," he said, speaking to all of us but looking at Richard Pratt. "Now for the claret. I must go and fetch the claret, if you'll excuse me."

"You go and fetch it, Mike?" I said. "Where is it?"

"In my study, with the cork out—breathing."

"Why the study?"

"Acquiring room temperature, of course. It's been there twenty-four hours."

"But why the study?"

"It's the best place in the house. Richard helped me choose it last time he was here."

At the sound of his name, Pratt looked around.

"That's right, isn't it?" Mike said.

"Yes," Pratt answered, nodding gravely. "That's right."

"On top of the green filing cabinet in my study," Mike said. "That's the place we chose. A good draft-free spot in a room with an even temperature. Excuse me now, will you, while I fetch it."

The thought of another wine to play with had restored his humor, and he hurried out the door, to return a minute later more slowly, walking softly, holding in both hands a wine basket in which a dark bottle lay. The label was out of sight, facing downward. "Now!" he cried as he came toward the table. "What about this one, Richard? You'll never name this one!"

Richard Pratt turned slowly and looked up at Mike; then his eyes travelled down to the bottle nestling in its small wicker basket, and he raised his eyebrows, a slight, supercilious arching of the brows, and with it a pushing outward of the wet lower lip, suddenly imperious and ugly.

"You'll never get it," Mike said. "Not in a hundred years."

"A claret?" Richard Pratt asked, condescending.

"Of course."

"I assume, then, that it's from one of the smaller vineyards?"

"Maybe it is, Richard. And then again, maybe it isn't."

"But it's a good year? One of the great years?"

"Yes, I guarantee that."

"Then it shouldn't be too difficult," Richard Pratt said, drawling his words, looking exceedingly bored. Except that, to me, there was something strange about his drawling and his boredom: between the eyes a shadow of something evil, and in his bearing an intentness that gave me a faint sense of uneasiness as I watched him.

"This one is really rather difficult," Mike said, "I won't force you to bet on this one."

"Indeed. And why not?" Again the slow arching of the brows, the cool, intent look.

"Because it's difficult."

"That's not very complimentary to me, you know."

"My dear man," Mike said, "I'll bet you with pleasure, if that's what you wish."

"It shouldn't be too hard to name it."

"You mean you want to bet?"

"I'm perfectly willing to bet," Richard Pratt said.

"All right, then, we'll have the usual. A case of the wine itself."

"You don't think I'll be able to name it, do you?"

"As a matter of fact, and with all due respect, I don't," Mike said. He was making some effort to remain polite, but Pratt was not bothering overmuch to conceal his contempt for the whole proceeding. And yet, curiously, his next question seemed to betray a certain interest.

"You like to increase the bet?"

"No, Richard. A case is plenty."

"Would you like to bet fifty cases?"

"That would be silly."

Mike stood very still behind his chair at the head of the table, carefully holding the bottle in its ridiculous wicker basket. There was a trace of whiteness around his nostrils now, and his mouth was shut very tight.

Pratt was lolling back in his chair, looking up at him, the eyebrows raised, the eyes half closed, a little smile touching the corners of his lips. And again I saw, or thought I saw, something distinctly disturbing about the man's face, that shadow of intentness between the eyes, and in the eyes themselves, right in their centers where it was black, a small slow spark of shrewdness, hiding.

"So you don't want to increase the bet?"

"As far as I'm concerned, old man, I don't give a damn," Mike said. "I'll bet you anything you like."

The three women and I sat quietly, watching the two men. Mike's wife was becoming annoyed; her mouth had gone sour and I felt that at any moment she was going to interrupt. Our roast beef lay before us on our plates, slowly steaming.

"So you'll bet me anything I like?"

"That's what I told you. I'll bet you anything you damn well please, if you want to make an issue out of it."

"Even ten thousand pounds?"

"Certainly I will, if that's the way you want it." Mike was more confident now. He knew quite well that he could call any sum Pratt cared to mention.

"So you say I can name the bet?" Pratt asked again.

"That's what I said."

There was a pause while Pratt looked slowly around the table, first at me, then at the three women, each in turn. He appeared to be reminding us that we were witness to the offer.

"Mike!" Mrs. Schofield said. "Mike, why don't we stop this nonsense and eat our food. It's getting cold."

"But it isn't nonsense," Pratt told her evenly. "We're making a little bet."

I noticed the maid standing in the background holding a dish of vegetables, wondering whether to come forward with them or not.

"All right, then," Pratt said. "I'll tell you what I want you to bet."

"Come on, then," Mike said, rather reckless. "I don't give a damn what it is—you're on."

Pratt nodded, and again the little smile moved the corners of his lips, and then, quite slowly, looking at Mike all the time, he said, "I want you to bet me the hand of your daughter in marriage."

Louise Schofield gave a jump. "Hey!" she cried. "No! That's not funny! Look here, Daddy, that's not funny at all."

"No, dear," her mother said. "They're only joking."

"I'm not joking," Richard Pratt said.

"It's ridiculous," Mike said. He was off balance again now.

"You said you'd bet anything I liked."

"I meant money."

"You didn't *say* money."

"That's what I meant."

"Then it's a pity you didn't say it. But anyway, if you wish to go back on your offer, that's quite all right with me."

"It's not a question of going back on my offer, old man. It's a no-bet anyway, because you can't match the stake. You yourself don't happen to have a daughter to put up against mine in case you lose. And if you had, I wouldn't want to marry her."

"I'm glad of that, dear," his wife said.

"I'll put up anything you like," Pratt announced. "My house, for example. How about my house?"

"Which one?" Mike asked, joking now.

"The country one."

"Why not the other one as well?"

"All right then, if you wish it. Both my houses."

At that point I saw Mike pause. He took a step forward and placed the bottle in its basket gently down on the table. He moved the saltcellar to one side, then the pepper, and then he picked up his knife, studied the blade thoughtfully for a moment, and put it down again. His daughter, too, had seen him pause.

"Now, Daddy!" she cried. "Don't be *absurd!* It's *too* silly for words. I refuse to be betted on like this."

"Quite right, dear," her mother said. "Stop it at once, Mike, and sit down and eat your food."

Mike ignored her. He looked over at his daughter and he smiled, a slow, fatherly, protective smile. But in his eyes, suddenly, there glimmered a little triumph. "You know," he said, smiling as he spoke. "You know, Louise, we ought to think about this a bit."

"Now, stop it, Daddy! I refuse even to listen to you! Why, I've never heard anything so ridiculous in my life!"

"No, seriously, my dear. Just wait a moment and hear what I have to say."

"But I don't *want* to hear it."

"Louise! Please! It's like this. Richard, here, has offered us a serious bet. He is the one who wants to make it, not me. And if he loses, he will have to hand over a considerable amount of property. Now, wait a minute, my dear, don't interrupt. The point is this. *He cannot possibly win.*"

"He seems to think he can."

"Now listen to me, because I know what I'm talking about. The expert, when tasting a claret—so long as it is not one of the famous great wines like Lafite or Latour—can only get a certain way toward naming the vineyard. He can, of course, tell you the Bordeaux district from which the wine comes, whether it is from St. Emilion, Pomerol, Graves, or Médoc. But then each district has several communes, little counties, and each county has many, many small vineyards. It is impossible for a man to differentiate between them all by taste and smell alone. I don't mind telling you that this one I've got here is a wine from a small vineyard that is surrounded by many other small vineyards, and he'll never get it. It's impossible."

"You can't be sure of that," his daughter said.

"I'm telling you I can. Though I say it myself, I understand quite a bit about this wine business, you know. And anyway, heavens alive, girl, I'm your father and you don't think I'd let you in for—for something you didn't want, do you? I'm trying to make you some money."

"Mike!" his wife said sharply. "Stop it now, Mike, please!"

Again he ignored her. "If you will take this bet," he said to his daughter, "in ten minutes you will be the owner of two large houses."

"But I don't want two large houses, Daddy."

"Then sell them. Sell them back to him on the spot. I'll arrange all that for you. And then, just think of it, my dear, you'll be rich! You'll be independent for the rest of your life!"

"Oh, Daddy, I don't like it. I think it's silly."

"So do I," the mother said. She jerked her head briskly up and down as she spoke, like a hen. "You ought to be ashamed of yourself, Michael, ever suggesting such a thing! Your own daughter, too!"

Mike didn't even look at her. "Take it!" he said eagerly, staring hard at the girl. "Take it, quick! I'll guarantee you won't lose."

"But I don't like it, Daddy."

"Come on, girl. Take it!"

Mike was pushing her hard. He was leaning toward her, fixing her with two hard bright eyes, and it was not easy for the daughter to resist him.

"But what if I lose?"

"I keep telling you, you can't lose. I'll guarantee it."

"Oh, Daddy, must I?"

"I'm making you a fortune. So come on now. What do you say, Louise? All right?"

For the last time, she hesitated. Then she gave a helpless little shrug of the shoulders and said, "Oh, all right, then. Just so long as you swear there's no danger of losing."

"Good!" Mike cried. "That's fine! Then it's a bet!"

"Yes," Richard Pratt said, looking at the girl. "It's a bet."

Immediately, Mike picked up the wine, tipped the first thimbleful into his own glass, then skipped excitedly around the table filling up the others. Now everyone was watching Richard Pratt, watching his face as he reached slowly for his glass with his right hand and lifted it to his nose. The man was about fifty years old and he did not have a pleasant face. Somehow, it was all mouth—mouth and lips—the full, wet lips of the professional gourmet, the lower lip hanging downward in the center, a pendulous, permanently open taster's lip, shaped open to receive the rim of a glass or a morsel of food. Like a keyhole, I thought, watching it; his mouth is like a large wet keyhole.

Slowly he lifted the glass to his nose. The point of the nose entered the glass and moved over the surface of the wine, delicately sniffing. He swirled the wine gently around in the glass to receive the bouquet. His concentration was intense. He had closed his eyes, and now the whole top half of his body, the head and neck and chest, seemed to become a kind of huge sensitive smelling-machine, receiving, filtering, analyzing the message from the sniffing nose.

Mike, I noticed, was lounging in his chair, apparently unconcerned, but he was watching every move. Mrs. Schofield, the wife, sat prim and upright at the other end of the table, looking straight ahead, her face tight with disapproval. The daughter, Louise, had shifted her chair away a little, and sidewise, facing the gourmet, and she, like her father, was watching closely.

For at least a minute, the smelling process continued; then, without opening his eyes or moving his head, Pratt lowered the glass to his mouth and tipped in almost half the contents. He paused, his mouth full of wine, getting the first taste; then he permitted some of it to trickle down his throat and I saw his Adam's apple move as it passed by. But most of it he retained in his mouth. And now, without swallowing again, he drew in through his lips a thin breath of air which mingled with the fumes of the wine in the mouth and passed on down into his lungs. He held the breath, blew it out through his nose, and finally began to roll the wine around under the tongue, and chewed it, actually chewed it with his teeth as though it were bread.

It was a solemn, impressive performance, and I must say he did it well.

"Um," he said, putting down the glass, running a pink tongue over his lips. "Um—yes. A very interesting little wine—gentle and gracious, almost feminine in the aftertaste."

There was an excess of saliva in his mouth, and as he spoke he spat an occasional bright speck of it onto the table.

"Now we can start to eliminate," he said. "You will pardon me for doing this carefully, but there is much at stake. Normally I would perhaps take a bit of a chance, leaping forward quickly and landing right in the middle of the vineyard of my choice. But this time— I must move cautiously this time, must I not?" He looked up at Mike and he smiled, a thick-lipped, wet-lipped smile. Mike did not smile back.

"First, then, which district in Bordeaux does this wine come from? That is not too difficult to guess. It is far too light in the body to be from either St. Emilion or Graves. It is obviously a Médoc. There's no doubt about *that.*

"Now—from which commune in Médoc does it come? That also, by elimination, should not be too difficult to decide. Margaux? No. It cannot be Margaux. It has not the violent bouquet of a Margaux. Pauillac? It cannot be Pauillac, either. It is too tender, too gentle and wistful for a Pauillac. The wine of Pauillac has a character that is almost imperious in its taste. And also, to me, a Pauillac contains just a little pith, a curious, dusty, pithy flavor that the grape acquires from the soil of the district. No, no. This— this is a very gentle wine, demure and bashful in the first taste, emerging shyly but quite graciously in the second. A little arch, perhaps, in the second taste, and a little naughty also, teasing the tongue with a trace, just a trace, of tannin. Then, in the aftertaste, delightful—consoling and feminine, with a certain blithely generous quality that one associates only with the wines of the commune of St. Julien. Unmistakably this is a St. Julien."

He leaned back in his chair, held his hands up level with his chest, and placed the fingertips carefully together. He was becoming ridiculously pompous, but I thought that some of it was deliberate, simply to mock his host. I found myself waiting rather tensely for him to go on. The girl Louise was lighting a cigarette. Pratt heard the match strike and he turned on her, flaring suddenly with real anger. "Please!" he said. "Please don't do that! It's a disgusting habit, to smoke at table!"

She looked up at him, still holding the burning match in one hand, the big slow eyes settling on his face, resting there a moment, moving away again, slow and contemptuous. She bent her head and blew out the match, but continued to hold the unlighted cigarette in her fingers.

"I'm sorry, my dear," Pratt said, "but I simply cannot have smoking at table."

She didn't look at him again.

"Now, let me see—where were we?" he said. "Ah, yes. This wine is from Bordeaux, from the commune of St. Julien, in the district of Médoc. So far, so good. But now we come to the more difficult part—the name of the vineyard itself. For in St. Julien there are many vineyards, and as our host so rightly remarked earlier on, there is often not much difference between the wine of one and the wine of another. But we shall see."

He paused again, closing his eyes. "I am trying to establish the 'growth,'" he said. "If I can do that, it will be half the battle. Now, let me see. This wine is obviously not from a first-growth vineyard—nor even a second. It is not a great wine. The quality, the—the—what do you call it?—the radiance, the power, is lacking. But a third growth—that it could be. And yet I doubt it. We know it is a good year—our host has said so—and this is probably flattering it a little bit. I must be careful. I must be very careful here."

He picked up his glass and took another small sip.

"Yes," he said, sucking his lips, "I was right. It is a fourth growth. Now I am sure of it. A fourth growth from a very good year—from a great year, in fact. And that's what made it taste for a moment like a third—or even a second-growth wine. Good! That's better! Now we are closing in! What are the fourth-growth vineyards in the commune of St. Julien?"

Again he paused, took up his glass, and held the rim against that sagging, pendulous lower lip of his. Then I saw the tongue shoot out, pink and narrow, the tip of it dipping into the wine, withdrawing swiftly again—a repulsive sight. When he lowered the glass, his eyes remained closed, the face concentrated, only the lips moving, sliding over each other like two pieces of wet, spongy rubber.

"There it is again!" he cried. "Tannin in the middle taste, and the quick astringent squeeze upon the tongue. Yes, yes, of course! Now I have it! This wine comes from one of those small vineyards around Beychevelle. I remember now. The Beychevelle district, and the river and the little harbor that has silted up so the wine ships can no longer use it. Beychevelle . . . could it actually be a Beychevelle itself? No, I don't think so. Not quite. But it is somewhere very close. Château Talbot? Could it be Talbot? Yes, it could. Wait one moment."

He sipped the wine again, and out of the side of my eye I noticed Mike Schofield and how he was leaning farther and farther forward over the table, his mouth slightly open, his small eyes fixed upon Richard Pratt.

"No. I was wrong. It is not a Talbot. A Talbot comes forward to you just a little quicker than this one; the fruit is nearer to the surface. If it is a '34, which I believe it is, then it couldn't be Talbot. Well, well. Let me think. It is not a Beychevelle and it is not a Talbot, and yet—yet it is so close to both of them, so close, that the vineyard must be almost in between. Now, which could that be?"

He hesitated, and we waited, watching his face. Everyone, even Mike's wife, was watching him now. I heard the maid put down the dish of vegetables on the sideboard behind me, gently, so as not to disturb the silence.

"Ah!" he cried. "I have it! Yes, I think I have it!"

For the last time, he sipped the wine. Then, still holding the glass up near his mouth, he turned to Mike and he smiled, a slow, silky smile, and he said, "You know what this is? This is the little Château Branaire-Ducru."

Mike sat tight, not moving.

"And the year, 1934."

We all looked at Mike, waiting for him to turn the bottle around in its basket and show the label.

"Is that your final answer?" Mike said.

"Yes, I think so."

"Well, is it or isn't it?"

"Yes, it is."

"What was the name again?"

"Château Branaire-Ducru. Pretty little vineyard. Lovely old château. Know it quite well. Can't think why I didn't recognize it at once."

"Come on, Daddy," the girl said. "Turn it round and let's have a peek. I want my two houses."

"Just a minute," Mike said. "Wait just a minute." He was sitting very quiet, bewildered-looking, and his face was becoming puffy and pale, as though all the force was draining slowly out of him.

"Michael!" his wife called sharply from the other end of the table. "What's the matter?"

"Keep out of this, Margaret, will you please."

Richard Pratt was looking at Mike, smiling with his mouth, his eyes small and bright. Mike was not looking at anyone.

"Daddy!" the daughter cried, agonized.

"But, Daddy, you don't mean to say he's guessed it right!"

"Now, stop worrying, my dear," Mike said. "There's nothing to worry about."

I think it was more to get away from his family than anything else that Mike then turned to Richard Pratt and said, "I'll tell you what, Richard. I think you and I better slip off into the next room and have a little chat?"

"I don't want a little chat," Pratt said. "All I want is to see the label on that bottle." He knew he was a winner now; he had the bearing, the quiet arrogance of a winner, and I could see that he was prepared to become thoroughly nasty if there was any trouble. "What are you waiting for?" he said to Mike. "Go on and turn it round."

Then this happened: The maid, the tiny, erect figure of the maid in her white-and-black uniform, was standing beside Richard Pratt, holding something out in her hand. "I believe these are yours, sir," she said.

Pratt glanced around, saw the pair of thin horn-rimmed spectacles that she held out to him, and for a moment he hesitated. "Are they? Perhaps they are. I don't know."

"Yes sir, they're yours." The maid was an elderly woman—nearer seventy than sixty—a faithful family retainer of many years standing. She put the spectacles down on the table beside him.

Without thanking her, Pratt took them up and slipped them into his top pocket, behind the white handkerchief.

But the maid didn't go away. She remained standing beside and slightly behind Richard Pratt, and there was something so unusual in her manner and in the way she stood there, small, motionless, and erect, that I for one found myself watching her with a sudden apprehension. Her old gray face had a frosty, determined look, the lips were compressed, the little chin was out, and the hands were clasped together tight before her. The curious cap on her head and the flash of white down the front of her uniform made her seem like some tiny, ruffled, white-breasted bird.

"You left them in Mr. Schofield's study," she said. Her voice was unnaturally, deliberately polite. "On top of the green filing cabinet in his study, sir, when you happened to go in there by yourself before dinner."

It took a few moments for the full meaning of her words to penetrate, and in the silence that followed I became aware of Mike and how he was slowly drawing himself up in his chair, and the color coming to his face, and the eyes opening wide, and the curl of the mouth, and the dangerous little patch of whiteness beginning to spread around the area of the nostrils.

"Now, Michael!" his wife said. "Keep calm now, Michael, dear! Keep calm!"

KATHARINE BRUSH *Birthday Party*

Katharine Brush (1902-   ) spent most of her childhood in Washington, D. C., and Newbury, Massachusetts. After graduating from Centenary Collegiate Institute, she worked for a Boston newspaper. In 1927 she had her first success with the short story "Night Club." She has written many popular novels and short stories, especially for *The American Magazine* and *Cosmopolitan*. Margaret Culkin Banning has remarked about Katharine Brush that she is "one of the people . . . who proved that popular prose need not be sloppy and sentimental or untrue to life."

"Birthday Party" is one of the shortest of the short short stories, yet character and conflict are set into the enveloping action with such sureness of purpose as to give depth to the story and meaning to the theme.

They were a couple in their late thirties, and they looked unmistakably married. They sat on the banquette opposite us in a little narrow restaurant, having dinner. The man had a round, self-satisfied face, with glasses on it; the woman was fadingly pretty, in a big hat. There was nothing conspicuous about them, nothing particularly noticeable, until the end of their meal, when it suddenly became obvious that this was an Occasion—in fact, the husband's birthday, and the wife had planned a little surprise for him.

It arrived, in the form of a small but glossy birthday cake, with one pink candle burning in the center. The headwaiter brought it in and placed it before the husband, and meanwhile the violin-and-piano orchestra played "Happy Birthday to You" and the wife beamed with shy pride over her little sur-

BIRTHDAY PARTY: Reprinted from *The New Yorker*, March 16, 1946. Copyright 1946 by The New Yorker Magazine, Inc. Reprinted by permission of Harold Ober Associates.

prise, and such few people as there were in the restaurant tried to help out with a pattering of applause. It became clear at once that help was needed, because the husband was not pleased. Instead he was hotly embarrassed, and indignant at his wife for embarrassing him.

You looked at him and you saw this and you thought, "Oh, now, don't *be* like that!" But he was like that, and as soon as the little cake had been deposited on the table, and the orchestra had finished the birthday piece, and the general attention had shifted from the man and the woman, I saw him say something to her under his breath—some punishing thing, quick and curt and unkind. I couldn't bear to look at the woman then, so I stared at my plate and waited for quite a long time. Not long enough, though. She was still crying when I finally glanced over there again. Crying quietly and heartbrokenly and hopelessly, all to herself, under the gay big brim of her best hat.

SAKI (H. H. MUNRO) *The Lumber-Room* *(The Open Window)*

Hector Hugh Munro (1870-1916) is generally known as "Saki," a pseudonym which he took from the name of the cupbearer in *The Rubáiyát of Omar Khayyám*. He was born in Burma, where his father was stationed in the British service. After his schooling in England, he traveled widely in Europe. In 1896 he started to write professionally for London periodicals. From 1902 until 1907 he was in Europe as a correspondent for the London *Morning Post*. When the war broke out in 1914, he enlisted immediately; two years later he was killed in action. His four volumes of stories appeared between 1904 and 1914. A complete collection, *The Short Stories of Saki*, was published in 1930. "Saki" is generally ranked with the most eminent short-story writers. E. V. Lucas has described a perfect hostess as one who puts by the guestroom bed "a volume either of O. Henry or 'Saki' or both."

As with most "Saki" stories, the chief merit and delight of "The Lumber-Room" derive from the ambiguity and irony of the incident on which the story is based.

The children were to be driven, as a special treat, to the sands at Jagborough. Nicholas was not to be of the party; he was in disgrace. Only that morning he had refused to eat his wholesome bread-and-milk on the seemingly frivolous ground that there was a frog in it. Older and wiser and better people had told him that there could not possibly be a frog in his bread-and-milk and that he was not to talk nonsense; he continued, nevertheless, to talk what seemed the veriest nonsense, and described with much detail the colouration and markings of the alleged frog. The dramatic part of the incident was that there really was a frog in Nicholas' basin of bread-and-milk; he had put it there himself, so he felt entitled to know something about it. The sin of taking a frog from the garden and putting it into a bowl of wholesome bread-and-milk was enlarged on at great length, but the fact that stood out clearest in the whole affair, as it presented itself to the mind of Nicholas,

THE LUMBER-ROOM: From *The Short Stories of Saki* by H. H. Munro. Copyright 1930 by The Viking Press, Inc., New York.

was that the older, wiser, and better people had been proved to be profoundly in error in matters about which they had expressed the utmost assurance.

"You said there couldn't possibly be a frog in my bread-and-milk; there *was* a frog in my bread-and-milk," he repeated, with the insistence of a skilled tactician who does not intend to shift from favourable ground.

So his boy-cousin and girl-cousin and his quite uninteresting younger brother were to be taken to Jagborough sands that afternoon and he was to stay home. His cousins' aunt, who insisted, by an unwarranted stretch of imagination, in styling herself his aunt also, had hastily invented the Jagborough expedition in order to impress on Nicholas the delights that he had justly forfeited by his disgraceful conduct at the breakfast-table. It was her habit, whenever one of the children fell from grace, to improvise something of a festival nature from which the offender would be rigorously debarred; if all the children sinned collectively they were suddenly informed of a circus in a neighbouring town, a

circus of unrivalled merit and uncounted elephants, to which, but for their depravity, they
would have been taken that very day.

A few decent tears were looked for on the
part of Nicholas when the moment for the
departure of the expedition arrived. As a
matter of fact, however, all the crying was
done by his girl-cousin, who scraped her knee
rather painfully against the step of the carriage as she was scrambling in.

"How she did howl," said Nicholas cheerfully, as the party drove off without any of
the elation of high spirits that should have
characterized it.

"She'll soon get over that," said the soi-
disant aunt; "it will be a glorious afternoon
for racing about over those beautiful sands.
How they will enjoy themselves!"

"Bobby won't enjoy himself much, and he
won't race much either," said Nicholas with
a grim chuckle; "his boots are hurting him.
They're too tight."

"Why didn't he tell me they were hurting?"
asked the aunt with some asperity.

"He told you twice, but you weren't listening. You often don't listen when we tell you
important things."

"You are not to go into the gooseberry
garden," said the aunt, changing the subject.

"Why not?" demanded Nicholas.

"Because you are in disgrace," said the aunt
loftily.

Nicholas did not admit the flawlessness of
the reasoning; he felt perfectly capable of
being in disgrace and in a gooseberry garden
at the same moment. His face took on an
expression of considerable obstinacy. It was
clear to his aunt that he was determined to
get into the gooseberry garden, "only," as she
remarked to herself, "because I have told him
he is not to."

Now the gooseberry garden had two doors
by which it might be entered, and once a
small person like Nicholas could slip in there
he could effectually disappear from view amid
the masking growth of artichokes, raspberry
canes, and fruit bushes. The aunt had many
other things to do that afternoon, but she
spent an hour or two in trivial gardening
operations among flower beds and shrub-
beries, whence she could keep a watchful eye
on the two doors that led to the forbidden

paradise. She was a woman of few ideas, with
immense powers of concentration.

Nicholas made one or two sorties into the
front garden, wriggling his way with obvious
stealth of purpose towards one or other of
the doors, but never able for a moment to
evade the aunt's watchful eye. As a matter of
fact, he had no intention of trying to get into
the gooseberry garden, but it was extremely
convenient for him that his aunt should believe that he had; it was a belief that would
keep her on self-imposed sentry-duty for the
greater part of the afternoon. Having thoroughly confirmed and fortified her suspicions,
Nicholas slipped back into the house and rapidly put into execution a plan of action that
had long germinated in his brain. By standing on a chair in the library one could reach
a shelf on which reposed a fat, important-
looking key. The key was as important as it
looked; it was the instrument which kept the
mysteries of the lumber-room secure from un-
authorized intrusion, which opened a way
only for aunts and such-like privileged persons. Nicholas had not had much experience
of the art of fitting keys into keyholes and
turning locks, but for some days past he had
practised with the key of the schoolroom
door; he did not believe in trusting too much
to luck and accident. The key turned stiffly
in the lock, but it turned. The door opened,
and Nicholas was in an unknown land, compared with which the gooseberry garden was
a stale delight, a mere material pleasure.

Often and often Nicholas had pictured to
himself what the lumber-room might be like,
that region that was so carefully sealed from
youthful eyes and concerning which no questions were ever answered. It came up to his
expectations. In the first place it was large
and dimly lit, one high window opening on
to the forbidden garden being its only source
of illumination. In the second place it was
a storehouse of unimagined treasures. The
aunt-by-assertion was one of those people
who think that things spoil by use and con-
sign them to dust and damp by way of preserving them. Such parts of the house as
Nicholas knew best were rather bare and
cheerless, but here there were wonderful
things for the eye to feast on. First and foremost there was a piece of framed tapestry that

was evidently meant to be a fire-screen. To Nicholas it was a living, breathing story; he sat down on a roll of Indian hangings, glowing in wonderful colours beneath a layer of dust, and took in all the details of the tapestry picture. A man, dressed in the hunting costume of some remote period, had just transfixed a stag with an arrow; it could not have been a difficult shot because the stag was only one or two paces away from him; in the thickly growing vegetation that the picture suggested it would not have been difficult to creep up to a feeding stag, and the two spotted dogs that were springing forward to join in the chase had evidently been trained to keep to heel till the arrow was discharged. That part of the picture was simple, if interesting, but did the huntsman see, what Nicholas saw, that four galloping wolves were coming in his direction through the wood? There might be more than four of them hidden behind the trees, and in any case would the man and his dogs be able to cope with the four wolves if they made an attack? The man had only two arrows left in his quiver, and he might miss with one or both of them; all one knew about his skill in shooting was that he could hit a large stag at a ridiculously short range. Nicholas sat for many golden minutes revolving the possibilities of the scene; he was inclined to think that there were more than four wolves and that the man and his dogs were in a tight corner.

But there were other objects of delight and interest claiming his instant attention: there were quaint twisted candlesticks in the shape of snakes, and a teapot fashioned like a china duck, out of whose open beak the tea was supposed to come. How dull and shapeless the nursery teapot seemed in comparison! And there was a carved sandal-wood box packed tight with aromatic cotton-wool, and between the layers of cotton-wool were little brass figures, hump-necked bulls, and peacocks and goblins, delightful to see and to handle. Less promising in appearance was a large square book with plain black covers; Nicholas peeped into it, and, behold, it was full of coloured pictures of birds. And such birds! In the garden, and in the lanes when he went for a walk, Nicholas came across a few birds, of which the largest were an occasional magpie

or wood pigeon; here were herons and bustards, kites, toucans, tiger-bitterns, brush turkeys, ibises, golden pheasants, a whole portrait gallery of undreamed-of creatures. And as he was admiring the colouring of the mandarin duck and assigning a life-history to it, the voice of his aunt in shrill vociferation of his name came from the gooseberry garden without. She had grown suspicious at his long disappearance, and had leapt to the conclusion that he had climbed over the wall behind the sheltering screen of the lilac bushes; she was now engaged in energetic and rather hopeless search for him among the artichokes and raspberry canes.

"Nicholas, Nicholas!" she screamed, "you are to come out of this at once. It's no use trying to hide there; I can see you all the time."

It was probably the first time for twenty years that anyone had smiled in that lumber-room.

Presently the angry repetitions of Nicholas' name gave way to a shriek, and a cry for somebody to come quickly. Nicholas shut the book, restored it carefully to its place in a corner, and shook some dust from a neighbouring pile of newspapers over it. Then he crept from the room, locked the door, and replaced the key exactly where he had found it. His aunt was still calling his name when he sauntered into the front garden.

"Who's calling?" he asked.

"Me," came the answer from the other side of the wall; "didn't you hear me? I've been looking for you in the gooseberry garden, and I've slipped into the rain-water tank. Luckily there's no water in it, but the sides are slippery and I can't get out. Fetch the little ladder from under the cherry tree—"

"I was told I wasn't to go into the gooseberry garden," said Nicholas promptly.

"I told you not to, and now I tell you that you may," came the voice from the rain-water tank, rather impatiently.

"Your voice doesn't sound like aunt's," objected Nicholas; "you may be the Evil One tempting me to be disobedient. Aunt often tells me that the Evil One tempts me and that I always yield. This time I'm not going to yield."

"Don't talk nonsense," said the prisoner in the tank; "go and fetch the ladder."

"Will there be strawberry jam for tea?" asked Nicholas innocently.

"Certainly there will be," said the aunt, privately resolving that Nicholas should have none of it.

"Now I know that you are the Evil One and not aunt," shouted Nicholas gleefully; "when we asked aunt for strawberry jam yesterday she said there wasn't any. I know there are four jars of it in the store cupboard, because I looked, and of course you know it's there, but *she* doesn't, because she said there wasn't any. Oh, Devil, you *have* sold yourself!"

There was an unusual sense of luxury in being able to talk to an aunt as though one was talking to the Evil One, but Nicholas knew, with childish discernment, that such luxuries were not to be over-indulged in. He walked noisily away, and it was a kitchen-maid, in search of parsley, who eventually

rescued the aunt from the rain-water tank.

Tea that evening was partaken of in a fearsome silence. The tide had been at its highest when the children had arrived at Jagborough Cove, so there had been no sands to play on— a circumstance that the aunt had overlooked in the haste of organizing her punitive expedition. The tightness of Bobby's boots had had disastrous effect on his temper the whole of the afternoon, and altogether the children could not have been said to have enjoyed themselves. The aunt maintained the frozen muteness of one who has suffered undignified and unmerited detention in a rain-water tank for thirty-five minutes. As for Nicholas, he, too, was silent, in the absorption of one who has much to think about; it was just possible, he considered, that the huntsman would escape with his hounds while the wolves feasted on the stricken stag.

JOHN O'HARA *Where's the Game?*

John O'Hara (1905-   ), the son of a doctor, was born in Pottsville, Pennsylvania. His first success was *Appointment in Samarra*, 1934, a novel dealing with the country-club set. Among his most popular works are his short-story collections; the novels *Butterfield 8*, 1935, and *A Rage to Live*, 1949; and the libretto for the musical comedy *Pal Joey* (based on one of his short stories), which won the Critics Circle and Donaldson awards for the best musical of 1952. Whereas Orville Prescott condemns O'Hara for his "flabby cynicism, moral nihilism and tired misanthropy," Lionel Trilling extols him as "the only American writer to whom America presents itself as a social scene in the way it once presented itself to Howells or Edith Wharton."

"Where's the Game?" reveals O'Hara's mastery of dialogue and his shrewd observations of tribal folkways and social customs. His characters fall into two groups: the victim and the victimizers—both almost equally unattractive.

The moment his wife began to remove the dishes from the table Mr. Garfin got up and went to their bedroom and counted his

WHERE'S THE GAME?: From *Pipe Night* by John O'Hara. Copyright 1945 by John O'Hara. Reprinted by permission of Random House, Inc.

money. Eighty dollars. Actually a little more than eighty dollars, but not enough more to put his bankroll in the ninety-dollar class. There would be enough left over, if he lost the eighty, to bring him home in a taxi and maybe have a rarebit or something.

He put on his hat and coat in the narrow hall and called out to his wife: "I don't know what time I'll be home."

She came out of the kitchen, rubbing her hands on her apron. "Wud you say?"

"I said I don't know what time I'll be home danight."

"You called me out to tell me that? Who *cares, when* you'll be home?" She returned to the kitchen and the dirty dishes.

"Nuts," he said, and went out.

He walked down the short steep street, his cigar sticking up out his mouth. A man spoke to him and he nodded and said, "Moe." Moe, henpecked Moe. For a moment his contempt for Moe gave way to pity. He almost asked Moe to accompany him, but that was out of the question. Tonight might be the night when he would get into a decent game, the game he had been looking for for three, four months. Why run the risk of spoiling it with penny-ante Moe? No, tonight he had a feeling that he would at last get into a decent game, a game where they played for folding money instead of stamp money. The hell with Moe.

A driver in a parked taxi at the corner said, "Taxi?" and Mr. Garfin almost succumbed but he resisted. He would take a taxi home. Now he would take the subway. He bought an early edition of the *News* and read the sports pages until he came to his station. A very shapely blonde girl got off the train when he did; she must have been in another car or surely he would have noticed her on the way down. She was too tall for him but he followed her up the steps anyway. She was a delight to follow up the steps, that figure. And the way her coat fit her over the hips. They got outside and he followed her along 149th Street, taking a kind of proprietary pleasure in the way men looked at her. She looked more like the kind of a broad you might see at the Paradise downtown. She probably was a hostess at one of the dime-a-dance places in this neighborhood, and he was so sure of this guess that he thought of following her into one and having a little fun. Buy a couple bucks' worth of tickets and get something started. Maybe not tonight. Tonight just show her he was a spender. But no, not tonight. Tonight he had other uses for his money.

And then, in front of a cigar store, a young man, dressed flashy, detached himself from a group, and went off with the blonde.

Mr. Garfin continued until he came to a Bar & Grill. He spoke to the cashier, a tired dame with too much lipstick on her. "Hello, dear. The boys here?"

"What boys?"

"The *boys.* Wilkey. Bloom. Harry Smith," said Mr. Garfin.

"Oh, sure. They're sitting in the last booth."

The girl was a dope. Why did she pretend she didn't know him? For three, four months now he had been coming in this joint, two or three nights a week sometimes; and she knew damn well he always sat with Wilkey and Bloom and Harry Smith whenever they were there. A dope girl like that could keep steady customers away.

He went back to the last booth, and when he reached it he stood still. Smith was telling the other two a story and they did not see Garfin coming because their heads were together and they were looking at the salt cellars and Smith was watching the effect of his story on the others. Smith saw Garfin first and nodded, but went on with his story. As the other two saw him they also nodded but continued to listen. At the end of the story the three men burst out laughing, and having laughed the three looked at Garfin. Wilkey and Bloom said nothing. Smith said: "Hello, Big Shot. What's new?"

"Harry. Willie. Abe," said Garfin. "Oh, I don't know. I guess you boys were on that goat yesterday. That Fanciful."

"At Fair Grounds? You mean that one?" said Smith.

"That's the one," said Garfin. "Fanciful."

"No, I wasn't," said Smith. "Were you? You sound like it."

"For a little," said Garfin. "I made a little."

"Like what?" said Bloom.

"Like eighty bucks," said Garfin.

"You don't call that a little," said Bloom. "Don't tell me you can't use eighty dollars. *Any* time."

"He better not tell you," said Willie Wilkey. "Who'd believe him? What I doubt is if he was on her at all." Wilkey was sitting on the aisle. The others were sitting across the table from him. Wilkey made no sign of making room for Garfin, but Garfin took off his coat and hat and pushed in beside Wilkey.

"You got that prosperous look, Big Shot," said Smith. "I bet you were on that Fanciful for plenty. Come on, level with us. How much are you in?"

"Eighty bucks. A little over," said Garfin. "You boys just eat?"

"No, we're just here keeping the seats warm for some fellows from out of town," said Wilkey.

"I ate, but I think I'll have a piece of lemon pie," said Garfin. He called Gus, a waiter, and gave his order. Then he said to Smith: "Where's the game tonight?"

"What game? I didn't hear there was any game. Do you know where one is?"

"Aw, now, Harry," said Garfin.

"No. On the level," said Smith. "What kind of a game? You mean the *hockey* game, down at the Garden? Or, uh, the basketball game. New York U.?"

"Quid it, quid it," said Garfin, smiling. Gus brought the pie and Garfin began to eat, shaking his head and smiling. "You guys."

Wilkey watched him eat and after a bit said: "Garfin, lemme ask you a personal question if you don't mind."

"Not too personal I don't mind."

"Garfin—that's your name, isn't it?" said Wilkey.

"You know it's my name."

"Sure. Well, I often wanted to ask you, what do you do for a living?" said Wilkey.

"I could ask you the same question," said Garfin.

"Everybody knows what I do for a living, Garfin," said Wilkey. "I'm a part-time stool pigeon trying to find out who killed Rothstein. Do you know? I could use that information."

"Everybody knows I killed Rothstein," said Garfin. Smith and Bloom laughed with him.

"Well, then, I guess my work is ended," said Wilkey. "But seriously, when you're not killing Rothstein what do you do? That was a long time ago. You must do something besides that. Come on, level with me."

"You really want to know?"

"Really."

"I'm a salesman."

"Selling what? Papers?" said Wilkey.

"Furniture," said Garfin.

"Furniture. Well, Garfin, I don't want any," said Wilkey.

"That's your privilege," said Garfin.

"That's right. It's my privilege. And you know what else is my privilege? My privilege is I don't like your kisser. You're always coming around here always asking the same question: 'Where's the game tonight?' You always get the same answer, but you keep on asking, 'Where's the game tonight?' I wonder why that is, Garfin. Nobody knows anything about you—"

"Bloom knows me. Bloom went to school with me," said Garfin.

"Bloom told me. He went to school with you for like six months. That was a long time ago, Garfin. Sixth grade, or around there. Twenty years ago at least."

"I used to see him since then, off and on."

"Off and on," said Bloom.

"Right. And Abe was away a few years, remember that," said Wilkey. "Well, this is the way it adds up, Garfin. Bloom is away a few years and then a few months ago you happen to run into him on the street. Happen to. So he can't get rid of you and you come here with him and he introduced you to us and right away you start coming here all the time. A couple times a week. And every night the same question: 'Where's the game tonight?' till I begin to wonder about you, Garfin."

"Why?"

"This is why. I remember about six months ago at an apartment, some fellows I happen to know slightly, they had a game. A poker game. They were playing cards this night in this apartment, and about four o'clock in the morning there was a stick-up. These guys were just friends having a poker game and not letting the whole world know about it, but somebody must have found out because there was a stick-up and the gorills took away about twelve hundred dollars and shot one of the fellows that was playing poker. Do you remember?"

"I read the papers," said Garfin.

"He reads the papers," said Wilkey. "All right. Well, I like to play poker, Garfin. I like all forms of gambling but the best one I like is poker. Now supposing I was sitting here some night and some friends of mine invited me to join them in a game, and you came in and asked your usual question and suppose I said, 'Why, Garfin, old pal. The game is at some address on Tremont Avenya.' Then would you say you hadda make a phone call and when you came back would you say you hadda go home to the little woman, and then I would say too bad and then we would go and play poker without you, and along about four o'clock in the morning some gorills come in and take our money and shoot one of us? Would that ever happen?"

"Certainly not. What do you think I am?"

"I don't know, Garfin. I don't know. But do me a favor, Garfin. Do me a favor and stay out of here. I and the boys talked this over and we decided we don't want you butting in on a private conversation. Do me a favor and get out now. I'll pay for the piece of pie and coffee."

Garfin stared at Wilkey and then quickly looked at Smith and Bloom. They were looking at him coldly, dead-pan. "Okay," he said. He got up and put on his hat and coat. "Okay."

At the desk he told the cashier, "Mr. Wilkey is taking care of my check." He went out into 149th Street and walked a couple of blocks. He caught himself looking at a pretty girl, who stared back at him and sniffed. The hell with her, he thought; he wasn't even thinking about her. Every now and then he would be sick with fear, knowing now what they thought of him. But almost as bad was knowing that he never could go back there again, the only place where he wanted to be. And so he went down into the subway and home.

MARJORIE KINNAN RAWLINGS *Cocks Must Crow*

Marjorie Kinnan Rawlings (1896-1953) was born in Washington, D. C., and began writing and selling stories at the age of eleven. She was a graduate of the University of Wisconsin, where she studied under William Ellery Leonard. In 1928 she bought a seventy-two-acre orange grove at Cross Creek, a small out-of-the-way village in central Florida, and in the next few years became well acquainted with Florida people and their customs. Her attachment to this part of the country was shown by the warmth and fidelity with which she portrayed the Florida scene in her first novel, *South Moon Under*, 1933.

The Yearling, 1938, introduced one of the most appealing boy characters in fiction since Huckleberry Finn. It won for Marjorie Rawlings the Pulitzer Prize for fiction and was a Book of the Month Club choice. In recognition of the understanding with which she had recorded the life of the "Florida cracker," Rollins College in 1939 awarded her the honorary degree of LL.D. Other books by Mrs. Rawlings are Cross Creek, 1942, an autobiographical account of her experiences in her Florida home, and When the Whippoorwill, 1940, a collection of short stories. "Cocks Must Crow" is one of three stories from that volume which center around Quincey Dover, a fat, talkative Florida "cracker."

I got nothing particular against time. Time's a natural thing. Folks is a kind of accident on the face of the earth, but time was here before us. And when we've done finished messing ourselves up, and when the last man turns over to die, saying, "Now how come us to make such a loblolly of living?"— why, time'll rock right on.

It's pure impudence to complain about much of ary thing, excusing human nature, and we all got a just complaint against that. Seems like we could of got borned without so much meanness in us. But just as sure as cooters crawls before a rain, why, we got no right to holler about such things as getting old and dying.

But now what I do hold against time is this: Time be so all-fired slick. It's slick as a otter slide. And how come me to object to

that, don't be on account of you slip down it so fast, but you slip down without noticing what time's a-doing to you. That's what I object to. If time's fixing to change you, why it can't be holpen. But the road's greasy as a darky's cook pot, and what does a feller do? He goes kiyoodling along it, and him changing, like a man getting drunk and not knowing it. And here comes a turn in the road, or a ditch you ain't looking for. And what do you do? You think you got all your senses, and you ain't, and you do the wrong thing and maybe knock your brains out. And if you only had some sign, something to tell you you was drunk instead of sober, something to tell you you was changed, why, you might make it.

Now that happened to me with my Will. I come so clost to losing the only man a woman like me could ever hope to get a-holt of, and a good man to boot, that I can still feel the danger whistling past me like a rattlesnake striking and just missing. And that's it. Time ain't got the decency of a rattlesnake. A rattler most times'll give warning. I almost lost my Will, and me a big fat somebody no man'd look at twicet lessen he was used to me. I almost lost him on account of I had changed and didn't know it, and time never give me the first sign to warn me. Merciful jay bird! No, sir, time's a low-down, sneaking, cottonmouth moccasin, drops its fangs without you knowing it's even in the grass, and was there ary thing I could do about it, I'd do it. Excusing that, I got nothing against time.

My Will married me—some say I married him—when I was a big feather-bolster kind of a gal, pink-cheeked and laughing and easy-going and heavy-eating. I will say, I always did have a tongue in my head, and loved to use it, just like a man with a keen knife loves to keep it sharp. But I used it fair and open. Some said I was lucky to get Will Dover, and some said he was lucky to get me. Will and me was both satisfied. I'd had men was more to look at, come courting me out at Pa's place in the flatwoods, and I'd had men come was nothing but breath and breeches. Will had a gold tooth in the front of his mouth, and I always was a fool for a gold tooth. I takened to the little feller first time I seed him. I was a heap bigger'n him even then.

Third time he come out of a Sunday evening, Pa tipped back in his chair on the porch and said to Will, "Better look out, young feller, Quincey don't take you for a play-dolly."

Will looked him square in the eye.

"You ever tried to hold a hawk in your bare hand?" Will said.

"Why, no," Pa said, "I'd know better."

"Well, a hawk's a heap littler'n you, ain't he? But 'tain't his size or your size makes you leave him be. It's his nature. Now the gal ain't growed so big in these flatwoods, could take me for a play-dolly. I ain't got the size to hold Quincey, here, on my lap. But she shore as hell ain't going to hold me on hers."

Pa laughed and slapped hisself.

"Will Dover," he said, "if you want her and she don't take you, I'll lick her with my own hands."

"Ain't nobody going to lick Quincey but me," Will said, "and I aim just to reason with her."

"Ain't he something?" Pa said to me. "Quincey, I've always told you, you can't judge no man by the length of his suspenders. You got to judge him by the spirit in him."

And I done so. I takened Will first time he offered. The business he was in was just a mite in his favor. He run a livery stable in Oak Bluff, and he come courting in a light trap with a pair of black horses drove tandem. It kind of melted me. I hadn't never see a pair of horses drove tandem.

Me and Will hit it off fine right from the start. He was little and he acted gentle, but couldn't nobody press him no farther than he was o' mind to be pressed. And that was one thing I disremembered as the years went by.

When we was fresh-married I said to him, "You're soft-acting, Will Dover, but you got a will as hard as a gopher shell."

"You ain't fooling me none, neither," he said. "You got a tongue as sharp as a new cane knife, but your heart's as big as your behind, and soft as summer butter." He looked at me with his head on one side, and them blue eyes as bright and quick as a mockingbird's. "And that's why I love you, Quincey Dover," he said.

Ary woman could get along with a man like that. I know now I don't deserve too much credit for us living so nice and friendly. But in them days I takened a mort of credit, on account of I was full of idees about handling men. They was good idees. I still got them. They was mostly this: Man-nature is man-nature, and a woman's a fool to interfere. A man worth his salt can't be helt to heel like a bird dog. Give him his head. Leave him run. If he knows he ain't running under a check-rein, the devil hisself can't get him to run more'n about so far away from his regular rations. Men is the most regular creatures on earth. All they need is to know they can run if they want to. That satisfies them. And that's what I had to go and forget.

Some things about me didn't never change. My tongue didn't never change and, truth to tell, I'd not want it to, for the times I need it I want to know I can count on it. What Will called my big heart, I don't believe didn't never change; for I can't help being tormented when ary living thing, man, woman or dog, be hungry. I can't help feeling all tore up when another grieves. And when a old tabby cat has got no place to birth her kittens, or some poor soul in the woods is fool enough to be bringing another young'un into the world, and not a piece of cloth to wrap it in, and a blessing if it was stillborn, why, I got to light in and fix a bed for that tabby cat or that fool woman.

What did change about me was my size. I had a mighty good start, and seems like a piece of corn bread with a slab of white bacon on top of it has a sweeter taste in my mouth than it do to one of them puny little old scrawny women. And seems like ary piece of rations I've ever ate has just wrapped itself around my middle and stayed there. The last time I weighed myself was a ways back on the scales in the express office, and it balanced two hundred and twenty, and I quit weighing.

"Don't let it fret you," Will said. "You was a big gal when I got you, and I'd purely hate to turn you back to your Maker without I had added something to the good thing was give me."

My Will has been a heap of comfort. Can ary one figure how I could be mean to a man like that? Seems to me, times, like growing into the biggest woman in the county had something to do with it. I growed so big, I reckon I got biggety too. Here was my Will, little and gentle, and here was me, big as Timmons' pond, and used to all Oak Bluff saying, "Go ask Quincey. See what Quincey think."

I can't no-ways recollect when the change in me begun. First time I remember cold-out bearing down on Will was about two years ago. I remember that.

He said to me one evening after supper, "The boys is having a cockfight down to the garage. Reckon I'll ease on down and watch it."

I said, "You'll do no such of a thing. Cockfighting is a low-down nasty business. Men that's got nothing better to do than watch a pair of roosters kill theirselves, isn't fitten company."

Will looked at me slantwise and he said,

"Don't you reckon I can judge my company, Quincey?"

I said, "Judge all you please, but you'll go to no cockfight."

He filled up his pipe and he tamped the tobacco down and he lit it and he said, "Since when you been telling me where I could go?"

I said, "You heered me the first time."

Now I felt mighty righteous about it. That's the trouble with changing, you still feel right about it. I'd never seed a cockfight, but I'd heered tell they was cruel and bloody, and besides, it's agin the law.

Will rocked a while and he smoked a while and he said, "Nothing ain't worth quarreling about. I'll just go on down to the station and wait-see do them automobile parts come in on Number Three."

I said, "All right, but don't you go near no cockfight."

He give me a look I hadn't never seed before, and he said, "No, ma'am," in a funny way, and he went on off.

Now I got to put this together the best way I can. I ain't like them story writers can make a tale come out as even as a first-prize patchwork quilt. Life ain't slick like a story, noways. I got to remember this, and remember that, and when I'm done it'll make sense. The Widow Tippett moving to Oak Bluff don't seem to have a thing to do with me and time mixing it. When she come, I sure as all get-out didn't figure she'd make no marks on my piecrust. But move to Oak Bluff she did, and get messed up in my and Will's business, she done so. And that was about a year and a half ago.

First thing I knowed, I heered a strange widow had bought the old Archer farm at the edge of town. I give her time to get nested down, and one afternoon I went out to welcome her. I takened a basket of my guava preserves and my sour-orange marmalade, and a bundle of cuttings from my porch plants. Minute she come to the door to greet me, I seed she had a chip on her shoulder. She was a quiet kind of a looking woman, right pretty if you like skimmed-milk eyes and sand-colored hair with a permanent wave put to it, and a tippy-tippy way of walking.

"Mis' Tippett?" I said. "I'm Mis' Will

Dover. Quincey Dover. I come to welcome you."

"Pleased to meet you," she said. "I figured that was who 'twas."

I takened a quick look around. I never seed a place kept so careless. The front room looked as if a truck had just backed up to the door and dumped everything out together, and she hadn't never straightened it out and didn't aim to. She hadn't washed her dishes and a big old tomcat was asleep in the dish-pan. There was cats and kittens and dogs and puppies strowed all over the house and yard. A Dominick hen was on the table, peck-ing at the butter.

"Set down," she said. "I hear tell Oak Bluff just couldn't make out without you."

There was something about her voice I mis-trusted right off.

"When I see my duty, I do it," I said.

"That works good when ever'one sees it the same," she said. "You're the lady don't let her husband go to no cockfight, ain't you?"

"You mighty right," I said.

"Ain't it nice to have a man does just like you tell him?" she said.

I looked at her quick to read her mind, for there was pure sandspurs under that easy voice.

"I find it so," I said. "You're a widow, they tell me. Sod?"

"Water. Water and whisky."

"I never heered tell of a water widow."

"He was drunk as ten coots and fell in the water and never did come up. A lake's as good a burying place as any."

"I'm mighty sorry about your loss."

"Don't mention it. I didn't lose much."

I said, "That's a right hard way to speak of the dead."

"So it be," she said, "and the dead was about as hard as they come."

I knowed from then on I didn't like the Widow Tippett and didn't mean to have no truck with her. I got up to go and I gave her the preserves and the cuttings. She didn't offer me my basket back.

I said, "Pleased to of met you. Call on me if a need come," and I walked down the path. I turned at the gate.

"I hope you ain't fixing to farm this land," I said. "It's plumb wore out."

"I thank you," she said. "Just to keep folks from fretting theirselves to death, you can tell Oak Bluff I got steady insurance and aim to raise chickens."

I said to myself, "I'll tell Oak Bluff you're the biggetiest woman I know, to look like a curly-headed mouse."

What she thought of me, she told me when the time come.

Now if I'd of taken to her, I'd of give her settings of my eggs. I have game chickens, on account of they near about feed theirselves, ranging. They lays good, and they grows to fryer size the quickest of ary chicken. The breed is the Roundhead, and the roosters is some kind of handsome bronze and red, and now and again a long white feather mixed in with the shiny green tail. I have to eat them before they get much size to them, for I can't bear to kill them oncet they show up that reddy-bronze and grow them long tail feathers. 'Tain't everybody wants game chickens, on account of the hens'll steal their nests. Could be, I figured, the Widow Tippett'd not crave to raise Roundheads. I felt a mite mean, just the same, not offering. Then I put it out of my mind.

The next thing I can put my finger on was Will asking me for a couple of my frying-size roosters. A year ago past spring I hatched me an early batch of biddies. They growed off big and fine.

"Quincey," Will said, "can I have a couple of them young roosters to give to a friend?"

"I raised them chickens to put in our own bellies," I said. "Anybody you want to invite to set down and eat fried chicken with us, that's another thing."

"I want to give them away," he said.

"Go catch a mess of fish to give away, if you want to feed the county," I said.

A day-two later he said, "Quincey, can I have a setting of them Roundhead eggs to give away?"

I said, "Now who in tarnation are you so fretted about them having chicken to eat?"

"A customer come to the garage."

"No," I said.

"I do pay for the chicken feed, Quincey."

"No."

"Nothing ain't worth quarreling about," he said.

A week later one morning there wasn't an egg in the nests, and two of them frying-size roosters never come up for their feed. I like to had a fit.

"A varmint likely went with them," Will said. "You'd of done better to of give them to me."

"Will," I said, "you reckon that varmint could of had two legs instead of four?" and I looked him in the eye.

He laid a dollar on the table. "Things has come to a pretty pass when a man has to buy eggs and chickens off his own wife," he said.

"Who's this friend you'd steal for?"

"Just a poor soul that don't have much pleasure in life."

"Well, you rob my nests and roosts one more time, and you'll get the living daylights displeasured outen you."

"Yes, ma'am," and he give me that funny look.

A year rocked on. Twice he give me a quarter for a setting of eggs and fifty cents for two more roosters. I knowed there was a preacher he kind of looked out for when times was hard, and I figured it was him he was feeding. Then late this spring, the truth come out. The truth was a red chicken feather in a basket, and ary one thinks a chicken feather in a basket can't boil up hell in a woman, just don't know hell nor women.

I went out to the chicken house on a bright June morning to gather the eggs. I can't see the ground right under my stomach, and my foot catched in something. I backed off so's I could see, and it was a basket. I hadn't left no basket in the chicken house. I looked at it, and I picked it up and I turned it over. It was my basket. It was the basket I'd taken preserves in, and cuttings, to the Widow Tippett. She hadn't never come near me nor returned it. The first thing come to me was, she'd got ashamed of herself for not carrying it back to me, and she'd come and slipped it in my chicken house. But I hadn't seed no woman's tracks in the yard, and me raised in the woods, why, there ain't a polecat, animal or human, can make tracks in the sand of my yard and me not notice it. I looked at the basket again, and there was a bronzy-red chicken feather stuck to the inside of it. It was a tail feather off a Roundhead rooster.

I seed it plain. That slow-speaking, permanent-headed, buttermilk-faced widow with cats in her dishpan had done tolled my Will into her clutches. He'd done stole eggs and chickens from me, his loving and faithful wife, to take and put in her wicked hands. I set right down on the ground of the chicken house, and when I set down on the ground it's serious, for it near about takes a yoke of oxen to get me up again. I didn't even study about getting up again, for it seemed to me life had done gone so black I just as lief lay there and die and be shut of it. It's an awful thing when a woman has done builded her life on a man and she finds his legs is made of sand.

I thought about all the years me and Will had stuck it out together, him losing money on the livery stable, and cars coming in instead of horses, and finally him building the garage on credit, and learning a new trade, and me making a sack of grits last a fortnight. That were the only time in my life I come speaking-close to getting thin. Then things got good, and we prospered, and I fleshened up again, and seemed to me like man and wife couldn't of got along better together lessen they was a pair of angels, and if what they say about heaven be true, married angels couldn't of had near the nice time we had. My Will was always mighty good company.

I set on the ground of the chicken house and I studied. What had I done to deserve such as this? I'd been faithful. 'Course, there'd be them to say a woman as big as me had no choice but being faithful. But I'd been faithful in my mind, and 'tain't every woman goes to the movies can say the same. I'd worked, and I'd saved, and Will Dover hadn't never oncet come in from the garage, no matter how late, and the fruit trucks keeping him busy way into the night, but I had hot rations on the stove. I reckon a woman can put too much store by hot rations. A warm heart'll freshen a man a heap quicker'n hot rations, but all the hot rations in the world can't warm up a cold female tongue.

I set there. I boiled up inside like a sirup kettle filled too full. I boiled up hotter and higher than the fire in a sinner's hell, and I purely boiled over. That cooled the fire a mite, and I panted and fanned myself with my apron and I commenced to study. I laid me a trap for Will. I decided to watch-see when he done ary thing was different from what he generally done, and when I caught him at it I aimed to follow him. I got a-holt of a wall beam for a lever and I finally got myself up off the ground. If Will had of come home then, I like as not wouldn't of held my tongue. When he come in that evening, I was quieted down and I set myself to watching, like an alligator watching for a shote he knows comes to water.

Now the things a suspicioning woman can imagine different about a man would make a new man of him. That evening Will didn't stir from his rocker, just set and smoked. I thought, "Uh-huh, you know I'm watching you." The next evening he put on a clean shirt when he come in from the garage. I thought, "Uh-huh, dressing up for the widow." He didn't have much to say, and it come to me he hadn't been saying much to me for quite some time. I thought, "Uh-huh, saving up them cute things you used to say, for the widow." After supper he eased on out of the house, and I thought, "Uh-huh, I got you now." I followed along a half hour behind him and, bless Katy, there he was setting on the bench in front of the grocery store, visiting with Doc and Uncle Benny.

I said, "I forgot I was out of shortening," and I got me a pound of lard at the store.

Will said, "I'll go on home with you. I come down to hear the fight on the radio, but it's put off."

I thought, "Uh-huh, I just come too soon."

Sunday morning he takened me by surprise. He didn't shave, and he put on the same shirt he'd wore the day before. But he did get out of bed extra early and he acted like he had ants in his pants. I didn't think a thing about it, for he do that, times, of a Sunday. He's a man is restless when he ain't at his work. I never studied on a thing, until I seed him slip off to the fireplace and pull out the loose brick and take out all the money we keep there. Banks is all right, and we got a account in Tray City, but there's nothing feels as safe as a pile of dollar bills under a loose brick in the fireplace. I seed him stuff them in his pocket and look around as sly as a 'possum.

He come to me and he said, "I'm going on down to town. Don't look for me back to dinner."

My heart lept like a mullet jumping. I thought, "Merciful jay bird, now's the time."

I said, "You're missing some mighty good black-eyed peas," and he went on off.

I give him about forty minutes' start and I lit out. I walked the two miles to the Widow Tippett's like a road-runner snake on its way home. I was puffing and blowing when I got to her gate, and I was just as blowed up inside as out.

I thought, "In a minute now I'll see Will Dover setting beside her and holding her hand, and he ain't held mine since spring."

I stopped to figure what I'd do; would I just crack their heads together, or would I say, proud and stiff, "So! This be the end."

While I was panting and studying, the Widow Tippett come out with her hat on.

She said, "Why, Mis' Dover! You look powerful warm."

I said, "I be warm. Tell me the truth, or you'll figure you never knowed what heat was. My Will here?"

"No," she said, "he ain't here."

I looked down in the sand by the gate, and there was his tracks.

"He been here?"

She looked me up and down like a woman trying to make up her mind to step on a cockroach. She throwed back her head.

"Yes," she said. "He's been here."

Now folks talk about seeing red when they're mad. 'Tain't so. Nobody on earth couldn't of been madder'n I was, and what I seed wasn't red. It was white. I seed a white light like looking into the sun, and it was whirling around, and in the middle of it was the Widow Tippett. I closed my eyes against the light.

I said to myself, "O Lord, give my tongue a long reach."

I looked at her. I takened my tongue and I flicked it, like a man flicking a fishing rod. I takened it like a casting line and I laid it down right where I wanted it.

I said, "You figure I aim to leave a man-snatcher like you stay in Oak Bluff? You figure I aim to leave you go from home to home stealing husbands, like a stripety polecat going from nest to nest, stealing eggs? You takened my husband and never returned my preserve basket, and that's how come me to catch up with you, on account of a red chicken feather in that preserve basket. And what I aim to do to Will Dover is my business and not yours, but I ain't aiming to let you clean Oak Bluff out of husbands, for could be they's one or two of them worth keeping."

She tipped back her head and begun to laugh.

I takened my tongue and I drawed it back and I laid it down again. I said, "Devils laughs. Devils with buttermilk faces is the ones laughs. They laughs right on through damnation and brimstone, and that's what'll be your portion."

She said, "You should of been a lady preacher."

I takened my tongue and I purely throwed it.

I said, "I comes to you with a basket of preserves and a bundle of cuttings, and what do you do? You don't even send back a empty basket. Not you. What you sends back is a empty husband. You figure I aim to leave the sun go down on you in Oak Bluff one more time? The sun ain't rose, will set on you in Oak Bluff."

She quit laughing. She licked her lips. I could see her drawing back her tongue like I'd done mine. And when she let it loose, seemed to me like I'd been casting mine full of backlashes, and not coming within ten yards of putting it where I aimed to. For she takened her tongue and she laid it down so accurate I had to stand and admire a expert.

"You was likely a good woman oncet," she said. "You know what you are now? You're nothing but a big old fat hoot-nanny."

I like to of crumpled in the sand. She stepped down off her porch and she walked up to me, and there was nothing between her and me but the gate, and nothing between our souls at all.

She said, "I aim to give you credit for what you was oncet. I come to Oak Bluff, hearing the first day I come that you was a woman wouldn't leave her husband go to no cockfight. I thought, a husband leaves his wife tell him what to do and what not to do, ain't a man no-ways. And then folks begun telling me about you. They told me you was a woman

with a tongue sharp enough to slice soft bacon, and a heart like gold. They told me all the good things you done. And they told me you was always a great one for leaving a man go his man's way, and seemed like you bearing down on yours was something had slipped up on you."

I said, "Go on."

She said, "Who be I, a stranger, to tell you to give a man his freedom? Who be I to tell you a man that has his freedom is the man don't particular want it? And the man drove with a short rein, do he be a man, is the one just ain't going to be drove?"

I said, "Tell me."

She said, "I'll tell you this. I got a man of my own. We're marrying soon as he sells out the stock in his store and crates up his fighting chickens and moves down here. I don't want your man nor no other woman's man. Now you quit your hassling and pull up your petticoat that's showing in the back, and I'll carry you where you can see just what your husband's been a-doing behind your big fat back."

She stalked out the gate and I followed her.

"Where you carrying me?" I said.

"To the cockfight."

Now if ary one had ever of said, "I seed Quincey Dover going to the cockfight on a Sunday morning," I'd of figured what they seed come out of the bottle. And if ary one had ever of told me I'd be walking along humble behind another woman, feeling scairt and as mixed up inside as a Brunswick stew, I'd of figured they was cold-out headed for the insane asylum.

But that's what I was doing. The Widow Tippett was purely stepping it off. It was all I could do to keep up with her.

I said to her back, "I ain't of no mind to follow you, without you tell me what to expect."

She never answered.

I puffed and I blowed and I said, "You could tell me how far we got to go."

She kept right on going. The sun beat down and I begun to sweat. The Widow Tippett was about ten yards ahead of me.

I called out after her, "If you aim to carry me to the cockfight, you got to wait a minute, else I'll be toted in as dead as one of them poor roosters."

She stopped then and we set down under a live-oak tree to rest.

I said, "I be blessed if I see how I can go to no cockfight. I've stood out against them things all my life. I can't go setting up to one of them now."

She said, "Can you climb a tree?"

I said, "Can a elephant fly?"

She said, "Then you'll have to let folks see you there," and she got up and give me a boost to get me up and she set off again.

The place where she takened me was out in Wilson's Woods. We come up on it from the south, and here was a clearing in the woods, and a cockpit in the sand, with a wooden ring around it. On the north side was some men standing, and the trees was between us and them.

The Widow Tippett said to me, "Now how come me to ask you could you climb a tree, is on account of that big camphor tree has a flat bough leans right out over the cockpit, and could you oncet make that first crotch, you could get you a ringside seat and watch the show, and nobody ever know you was near if you set quiet. I aim for you to see the show. Then oncet you've seed it, what you do is your business, for I'm done with you."

I said, "If you was to push me a mite, could be I'd make the crotch."

She said, "You ain't asking much, be you?" but she put her shoulder under me and pushed with a will, and I got myself up into the camphor tree. Like she said, it was easy going oncet I was off the ground, and I pulled up a ways and found me a fine seat partways out the bough, with another bough right over me to hang onto.

"Now keep your big mouth shut," she said, "and with that green dress you got on, nobody won't no more notice you than if you was a owl. A mighty big owl," and she went on over to where the men was standing.

I hadn't no more than made it, for directly men begun coming in from all over. Most of them had gamecocks tucked under their arms. Some was Roundheads, like mine, and some was White Hackles and Irish Grays, and some was Carolina Blues. They had their combs trimmed and their spurs was cut off to a nub

about a half-inch long. Their tail feathers was shaved off till the poor things' butts was naked.

I thought, "Merciful jay bird, them fine roosters throwed to the slaughter."

After I'd looked at the cocks, I begun craning my neck careful to look at the men. Heap of them was strange to me, men had come in from other counties to fight their chickens. And after I'd watched their faces it come to me there was two kinds of men there. One kind had the fighting mark on them. They was men with cold hard eyes and I knowed they'd fight theirselves or their chickens merciless. They had a easy kind of way of moving, a gambler's way. I knowed this kind of man would move slow and talk quiet, and fight until he couldn't get up. And he'd bet his last dollar and his last farm, did the notion take him. He was a kind of man loved to give a licking and could take one, and it was a hard kind of a man, but you had to give him your respect.

Then there was another kind of man there. This kind of man was little, and his eyes was gentle. And I thought to myself, "Now what's that kind of man doing at a cockfight?"

I inched around on my limb so I got a better peephole through the branches. The men milled around, not talking much, just cutting their eyes sideways at t'other feller's chickens. I seed money change hands. The men that was getting their cocks ready was as nervous as brides sewing on their wedding clothes. I could see one man good. He was wrapping little thin strips of leather around the nubs of his rooster's spurs. Then he takened a pair of sharp shiny pointed steel things I knowed must be the gaffs, and he fastened them on, and wrapped them like they was a baby's bandage.

I thought, "Why, them things ain't as cruel as the natural spurs."

I could see they'd go in quick and clean, and if they didn't reach no vital spot they'd not be much more'n a pin prick. It was like a boxer's gloves; they look terrible, but they don't do the harm of a knuckled fist.

A gray-looking feller with his hat on the back of his head stepped into the pit. He drawed three lines acrost the sand with his foot.

He said, "Let's go."

Two men come ambling into the pit with their chickens. They turned their backs one on t'other. Each man on his side of the pit set his cock down on the sand, keeping holt of its wings, and let it run up and down. The cocks lifted their legs high. Their eyes was bright. They was raring to go.

The referee said, "Bill your cocks."

Seemed like electricity goed through all the men. All the easygoing limpness was done gone. They was all stiff and sharp and that high-charged to where you could of lit a match on ary one of them. The two handlers goed up to each other with the cocks cradled in their arms. They poked the cocks' bills together and one cock made him a pass at t'other.

Somebody hollered, "Two to one on the Blue!"

The cocks pecked at each other. Their hackles rose.

The referee said, "Pit your cocks."

The handlers set the birds down, each one on his own line.

The referee said, "Pit!"

The cocks flew at each other. They met in the air. When they come down, one just naturally didn't get up again. The men all relaxed, like a starched napkin had got wet. The handlers picked up the birds and went out. Money passed here and yon.

I thought, "Now nobody much got their money's worth outen that."

The next fight were a dandy. Right off, I picked a big Carolina Blue to win. I never did see such a fight. I'd seed men box and I'd seed men wrestle. I'd seed dogfights and cat-fights. I'd seed a pair of old male 'coons having it. I thought I'd seed fighting. But them game roosters was the fightingest things I ever laid eyes on. They knowed what they was doing. One'd lay quiet for t'other, and he'd flick up his feet, and whip his wings, and pass a lick with them gaffs.

I thought, "Now them fool roosters is following their nature. They're having them some kind of a good time."

I begun to get uneasy about the Blue I'd picked. Seemed to me he was dodging. He lay still oncet when he had him a fine chancet to hit a lick, and I almost hollered, "Get him

now!" Then he kind of shuffled around, and next thing I knowed he laid out the enemy plumb cold. I come near shouting, I was so proud I'd picked the winner. There was three more fights and I picked two of them. I was breathing hard. I leaned back a mite on the camphor bough.

I said to myself, "Quincey Dover, take shame. You're purely enjoying yourself."

'Twas way too late to feel shame. I couldn't scarcely wait for the next fight to begin. I didn't even mind the camphor bough cutting into me. But there was a delay. I could see men look at their watches.

I heered one say, "He knowed he was to fight the Main."

The Widow Tippett called out, "Yonder he comes."

And who come walking in to the cockfight? Who come walking in with a big red Round-head rooster tucked under his arm? My Will come in, that's who come.

Now I can't say I was plumb surprised to see him. I'd figured, the way the Widow Tippett talked, I could look to see him here. I'd a'ready figured that's what she meant about what-all he'd been a-doing behind my back. But I sure didn't look to see him walk in with no fighting cock. I cut my eye at that chicken. And I recognized it. It was one of my prime young roosters, growed up into the biggest, finest, proudest gamecock I ever did see, and the marks of battle was on him. Seemed to me if a rooster had the choice, he'd a heap rather grow up to fight than perish in the cook pot.

Right off I knowed two things. I knowed the Widow Tippett hadn't done a thing but leave Will raise his chickens, and train them, at that sloppy, easygoing place of hers. And I knowed another thing. I knowed my Will was one of them second kind of men come to the cockfight; the little gentle fellers I couldn't make out why they was there. Well, you'd of thought 'twas the Lord of the Jay Birds had come in to the cockfight, 'stead of Will Dover. The men parted a way for him to go into the pit. They closed in after him, talking and joking and asking questions about his rooster.

Will called out, "I got a hundred dollars says this is my day."

I like to shook the camphor tree to pieces.

I near about climbed down to say, "Will Dover, don't you go betting that money from under the fireplace on no cockfight." But I didn't dast give myself away. And truth to tell, I kind of hankered to see could that chicken fight.

Didn't take long to know. The fight was the big fight of the day. Seemed like Will's rooster was a old winner, and the men figured it were his turn to take a licking. Odds was mostly two to one against him. T'other cock was a Carolina Blue, and directly I seed him my heart sank.

"Bill your cocks," said the referee, and Will and t'other feller billed their cocks. They like to of fought right then and there.

"Pit!"

Nobody didn't have to give his rooster no shove. That pair was mixing it time they hit the ground. Will's Roundhead got hung in the Blue.

"Handle!"

The Blue's owner got him a-loose. "Anyways," I thought, "our chicken got in the first lick." Then they was at it again. Now if I hadn't of seed them other fights first, I'd not of appreciated this one. It was a pair of champions, and they both knowed it. They was both shufflers, and it was as neat as a pair of boxers that knowed their footwork. Didn't neither one waste no energy, but when the moment come one seed him a chancet, he was whipping his wings and striking. Now and again they'd both fly up off the ground and pass their licks a foot in the air.

"Handle!"

I wanted to holler so bad I had to put my hand over my mouth. If our Roundhead takened a licking, that Blue was going to wear me out doing it. Both chickens was breathing hard. Will picked his up and run his mouth down along his feathers, from the top of his head on down his back, cooling him and soothing him. He blowed on him and he dipped his bill in a pan of water.

"Pit!"

I mean, anybody that ain't seed a champion cockfight ain't seed a thing.

All of a sudden the Blue begun to take the fight. He got in a lick to the head and while the Roundhead lay hurt and dazed, the Blue followed through with another.

"Time!"

I takened my first breath in about two minutes. I'd of popped directly.

"Pit!"

This time it looked like it was all over. The Blue come in like a whirlwind and he done a heap of damage. He got hung in the Roundhead's back.

"Handle!"

This time when Will turned him a-loose he talked to him. He made queer little sounds, and one of them sounded like a hen a-clucking, like as if he knowed the cock'd fight better if he figured a faithful wife was encouraging him.

"Pit!"

He set him down, and the light of battle was in the Roundhead's eyes. He fought hard and game, but next thing I knowed the Blue had him out cold, with one wing broke. "He's dead," I said, for he lay on his side just scarcely breathing. I could of cried. Seemed like a thing that noble and that fearless had ought to live to be husband to a hundred hens and daddy to a thousand biddies. The referee begun to count. The Blue give the Roundhead an extra lick as he laid there, and everybody figured that finished him. The men that had bet against the Blue reached in their pockets for their money. I begun to sniffle. I didn't someway even mind Will losing the money. I just couldn't bear to see that Roundhead take a licking. Well, I reckon he figured the same. He opened his eyes and he drawed a breath and where he lay he reached up and he put them gaffs in that big Blue standing over him, and the Blue dropped like he'd been shot.

A grunt come outen the men like as if it was them had been hit. And you know that Roundhead wavered up to his feet, dragging that broke wing, and he climbed up on that Blue, and his head wobbled, and he lifted it up, and he flopped his one good wing, and he crowed! He'd won, and he knowed it, and he crowed.

My Will picked him up and stroked him, and wiped the sweat off his own forehead. He kind of lifted up his face and I could see the look on it. And that look made me feel the funniest I've near about ever felt. It was a deep kind of a male satisfaction. And I knowed that without that look a man just ain't a man. And with it, why, he's cock of the walk, no matter how little and runty and put-upon he be. And I knowed why Will loved a cockfight, and I knowed why all them other little gentle-looking fellers loved it. They was men didn't have no other way to be men.

A shame come over me. Times, it's life'll do that to a man. Mostly, it's his woman. And I'd done that to my Will. I'd tried to take his manhood from him, so he didn't have no way to strut but fighting a rooster. Now he'd won, and he was a man again. And I knowed that cocks must crow.

And about that time you know what happened? I reckon I'd been doing a heap of jiggling around in that camphor tree, and a camphor tree's right limber, but there's a limit to what it can stand.

I heered a creak and then I heered a crack, and the limb I was setting on busted off as neat as if you'd put a ax to it, and I slid down it, and I catched holt of the limb below, and I slid down that, and I plunked off down outen the camphor tree right smack in the middle of the cockpit.

I reckon everybody thought it was the end of the world. Nobody couldn't do nothing but gape at me.

"Well, get me up off the ground," I said. "You sure can't fight no chickens with me in the middle of the pit."

Will run to me then, and two-three others, and they hoisted me up. I brushed off my skirt and the Widow Tippett tidied me up. I looked her in the eye.

"I'd be proud to call you my friend," I said to her.

"All you got to do is call it," she said.

I turned to my Will. His face was in knots. The Lord Hisself couldn't of told what he was thinking.

"Well, Will," I said, "we sure got us some kind of a fighting rooster. Now I'd like a mite softer seat for the next fight."

He drawed a long slow breath.

"We ain't staying for the next," he said. "You're like to be hurt. I'm carrying you home."

The men that had lost to him paid him off.

He crammed the bills in his pocket and he tucked up the Roundhead under his arm and he led me off to the car. He cranked up and headed out.

The Roundhead kind of nested down on the seat between us. Directly Will reached in his pocket and he hauled out the money and he dropped it in my lap. I counted out the hundred he'd started with and I put it back in his pocket. Then I divided the rest in two piles, and I put one down inside my blouse and put the other in his pocket. He didn't say the first word.

"Will," I said, "I figured you'd been onfaithful to me with the Widow Tippett."

He shook his head.

"I should of knowed better. You ain't that kind of a man. But something in you had drawed off from me."

He nodded.

"I know why you drawed off," I said. "I'd done drove you to it. And I knowed better than to treat a man the way I'd got to treating you."

He never answered.

"Will," I said, "I hope it's in your heart to forgive me. I didn't use to be thataway. Time changed me, Will, and I didn't never notice it. I'd be proud if you'd blame time for it, and spare me."

He kind of blinked his eyes, like he was fixing to cry.

"Will," I said, "you ain't got to go raising no chickens behind my back. I'll raise them for you."

"No, Quincey," he said, slowlike. "No. I reckon I'll quit cockfighting. It's a foolish business, for a man can lose his shirt at it. And you didn't happen to see one of them long, bloody, ugly fights, makes a man sick to watch it. No, Quincey, I'm done." He looked at me. "Seems like something inside me is satisfied."

Well, I busted out crying. The excitement and the camphor limb cracking, and finding I hadn't plumb lost him, and all, I couldn't stand it. I blubbered like a baby.

"Oh, Will," I said, "I wisht I was young again. An awful thing has done happened to me. You know what I be? I be nothing but a big old fat hoot-nanny."

"Why, Quincey," he said. "Why, Quincey. Don't you dast say such as that. You're my good, sweet Quincey, and I love every hundred pounds of you."

And we busted out laughing.

"Quincey," he said, "you remember when I come courting you and I told you I aimed to fatten you up, for a man couldn't have too much of a good thing?"

I blowed my nose and he put his arm around me.

"Will," I said, "we're on a public highway."

"It's a free road," he said, and he kissed me.

"Will," I said, "home's the place for such as that."

"Ain't I headed for home fast as I can go?" he said, and we laughed like a pair of young'uns.

My Will ain't much to look at, but he's mighty good company.

ANTON CHEKHOV *An Unpleasantness*

Anton Pavlovich Chekhov (1860-1904), the son of a grocer who had been born a serf, took a medical degree at the University of Moscow in 1884 but retired from practice after a single year in order to spend the rest of his life writing. Even while studying medicine, he supported himself by writing comic sketches. In spite of the fact that he suffered from tuberculosis during most of his mature life, he wrote over a thousand stories, novels, and plays and did a great deal to promote public health and education, in which he placed his hope for the future of mankind.

Some critics have interpreted Chekhov's objectivity as cynicism, fatalism, and indifference to good and evil. His writings, when carefully studied, seem to indicate, however, a faith in the progress of society that is also reflected in his public service. He hated sham and could not fail to see and to show in his stories that life poses questions about human experience for which there are no immediate answers.

The impressionistic story as Chekhov wrote it may be described as a completely economical, highly integrated, symbolic revelation of the inner nature of an experience. In "An Unpleasantness" the sensitive Ovchinnikov's agonizing over the slapping incident and the basic tension between the doctor and the assistant illuminate a common problem in human relationships.

Grigory Ivanovich Ovchinnikov, a zemstvo doctor, was a nervous man of about thirty-five, in poor health. He was known to his colleagues by his short papers on medical statistics and for his keen interest in so-called "problems of daily life." One morning he was making the rounds of the wards in the hospital of which he was in charge, followed,

as usual, by his feldscher [medical assistant], Mikhail Zakharych, an elderly man with a fleshy face, greasy hair plastered down over his scalp, and one earring.

No sooner did the doctor start his rounds than one trifling circumstance began to seem very suspicious to him: the feldscher's waistcoat was creased and was continually riding up, in spite of the fact that he kept pulling at it and straightening it. His shirt, too, was mussed and rumpled; there was white fluff on his long, black jacket, on his trousers, and even on his tie. Obviously, the feldscher had slept in his clothes all night, and, to judge by his expression as he pulled at his waist-coat and straightened his tie, he felt uncomfortable in his clothes.

The doctor looked at him closely and grasped the situation. The feldscher was steady on his feet, he answered questions coherently, but the dull and sullen expression of his face, his lustreless eyes, his jerking neck and trembling hands, his disordered clothes, above all, the strenuous efforts he was making to conceal his condition—all pointed to the fact that he had just tumbled out of bed, that he had not had enough sleep, and that he had not got over the effects of the previous night's drinking-bout. . . . He was in the grip of an excruciating hangover and apparently very much displeased with himself.

The doctor, who disliked the feldscher, and had his reasons for it, felt a strong desire to say to him: "I see you're drunk!" All at once he was overcome by a disgust for the waistcoat, the long jacket, the ring in the fleshy ear, but he controlled his irritation and said gently and politely, as usual:

"Did Gerasim get his milk?"

"Yes, sir . . ." Mikhail Zakharych replied, also in a mild tone.

As the doctor talked to Gerasim, he glanced at the temperature chart and was overcome by a new access of loathing. He checked himself, but lost control and asked rudely, choking on the words:

"Why isn't the temperature noted?"

"But it is, sir!" said Mikhail Zakharych quietly; then, glancing at the chart and discovering that the temperature had indeed not been noted, he shrugged his shoulders with an air of confusion and mumbled:

"I don't know, sir, Nadezhda Osipovna must have . . ."

"Last night's temperature wasn't noted, either!" the doctor went on. "All you do is get drunk, damn you! Even now you're as drunk as a cobbler! Where is Nadezhda Osipovna?"

Nadezhda Osipovna, the midwife, was not in the ward, although it was her duty to be present at the dressings every morning. The doctor looked around, and it seemed to him that the ward had not been tidied up, that everything was at sixes and sevens, that nothing had been done that should have been done and that everything was messy, crumpled, covered with fluff, like the feldscher's loathsome waistcoat, and he was filled with a desire to tear off his white apron, to rant, to throw everything up, to send it to the devil and get out. But he mastered himself and continued his rounds.

After Gerasim came a patient who had inflammation of the cellular tissue of the entire right arm. He needed a dressing. The doctor sat down on a stool in front of him and busied himself with the arm.

"Last night they must have had a gay time at a birthday celebration . . ." he thought to himself, slowly removing the bandage. "Wait, I'll show you a birthday! Although, what can I do? I can do nothing."

He felt an abscess on the red, swollen arm, and said:

"A scalpel!"

Mikhail Zakharych, who was at pains to prove that he was steady on his pins and as fit as a fiddle, dashed from where he was standing and quickly handed over a scalpel.

"Not this! A new one," said the doctor.

The assistant walked mincingly across to the stool on which stood the box with supplies and instruments and began hastily rummaging in it. He kept on whispering to the nurses, noisily moving the box about on the stool, and twice he dropped something. Meanwhile, the doctor sat there, waiting, and felt a physical sense of irritation at the whispering and the other noise.

"Well?" he demanded. "You must have left them downstairs. . . ."

The feldscher ran up to him and handed him two scalpels, and in doing so carelessly breathed in the doctor's face.

"Not these," the doctor snapped irritably. "I told you plainly: give me a new one. Never mind, go and get some sleep; you reek like a pothouse. You can't be trusted."

"What other kind of knives do you want?" asked the feldscher, in a tone of irritation and with a lazy shrug of his shoulders.

He was annoyed with himself and ashamed because all the patients and nurses were staring at him, and to hide the fact that he was ashamed, he forced a smirk and repeated:

"What other kind of knives do you want?"

The doctor felt tears rising to his eyes and was conscious of a tremor in his fingers. He made another effort to control himself and brought out in a shaking voice:

"Go and sleep it out! I don't want to talk to a drunk. . . ."

"You can call me to account only for cause," said the assistant, "and if I've had a drop, well, nobody has the right to throw it up to me. I'm on duty, ain't I? What more do you want? I'm on duty, ain't I?"

The doctor leapt to his feet and, without realizing what he was doing, swung his fist and hit the feldscher with all his might. He did not understand why he had done it, but he felt great pleasure because the blow landed smack in the feldscher's face, and that solid citizen, a family man, a churchgoer, substantial, self-respecting, staggered, bounced like a ball and sat down on a stool. The doctor had a passionate urge to hit out again, but when he saw the pale, alarmed faces of the nurses clustered about that hateful countenance, his pleasure died away, he waved his hand in a gesture of desperation and ran out of the ward.

In the courtyard he encountered Nadezhda Osipovna, an unmarried woman about twenty-seven years old, with a sallow complexion and her hair loose over her shoulders, who was on her way to the hospital. The skirt of her pink cotton dress was narrow, and so she walked mincingly. Her dress rustled, she jerked her shoulders in time with her steps and tossed her head as if she were mentally humming a gay tune.

"Aha, the siren!" the doctor said to himself, recalling that in the hospital they called the midwife a siren to tease her. And he took pleasure in the thought that he was about to give a piece of his mind to this mincing, self-infatuated, would-be dressy creature.

"Where on earth have you been?" he exclaimed, as they approached each other. "Why aren't you in the hospital? The temperatures haven't been recorded, everything's at sixes and sevens, the feldscher is drunk, you sleep till noon! . . . You'd better look for another position! You're fired!"

Having reached his apartment, the doctor tore off his white apron and the towel which served him as a belt, angrily tossed both of them into a corner, and began pacing the room.

"God, what people, what people!" he groaned. "They're no help, they just get in the way of the work! I haven't the strength to go on! I can't do it. I'm getting out."

His heart was pounding, he was trembling all over, and he felt like bursting into tears. He tried to quiet himself with the thought that he had been in the right, and that it was a good thing that he had struck the feldscher. In the first place, reflected the doctor, it was abominable that the hospital should have engaged a man not on his own merits but owing to the intercession of his aunt, who was employed as a nursemaid by the chairman of the zemstvo board. It was disgusting to see how this influential nanny, when she drove to the hospital for treatment, behaved as though she were at home and refused to wait her turn. The feldscher was badly trained, knew very little, and did not understand what he had learned. He drank, was insolent, untidy, accepted bribes from the patients, and secretly sold the medicines supplied free by the zemstvo. Moreover, everyone knew that he practiced medicine on the quiet, and treated young men from the town for unmentionable diseases, using remedies of his own concoction. It would not have been so bad if he had simply been a quack, of whom there were plenty, but no—he was a quack who believed in himself, a quack who was furtively in revolt. Behind the doctor's back he cupped and bled dispensary patients, he assisted at operations without having washed his hands, he always examined wounds with a dirty probe. All this was sufficient to show how profoundly and completely he despised the doctors' medicine with its rules and regulations.

When at last his fingers were steady again, the doctor sat down at his desk and wrote a letter to the chairman of the board:

Esteemed Lev Trofimovich!

If on receipt of this note your board does not discharge feldscher Mikhail Zakharych

Smirnovsky, and will not grant me the right to choose my feldscher, I shall regretfully be forced to resign as physician of the N. hospital and request you to secure someone to succeed me. Please remember me to Lubov Fyodorovna and to Yus.

Respectfully,

G. Ovchinnikov.

Having reread this letter, the doctor decided that it was too short and not sufficiently formal. Besides, the mention of Lubov Fyodorovna and of Yus (the nickname of the chairman's younger son) was hardly appropriate in a business letter dealing with an official matter.

"The devil, why bring in Yus?" the doctor said to himself, tore the letter to bits, and started thinking of another. "Dear Sir," he began. Through the open window he could see a flock of ducks with their young. Waddling and stumbling, they were hurrying down the road, apparently on their way to the pond. One duckling picked up a piece of gut that was lying on the ground, tried to swallow it, choked on it and raised an alarmed squeaking. Another duckling ran up, pulled the gut out of its beak and choked on the thing too. . . . At some distance from the fence, in the lacy shadow cast on the grass by the young lindens, the cook Darya was wandering about, picking sorrel for a vegetable soup. . . . Voices were heard. . . . Zot, the coachman, with a bridle in his hand, and Manuilo, the hospital attendant, wearing a dirty apron, were standing by the shed, chatting and laughing.

"They are talking about my having struck the feldscher . . ." thought the doctor. "Before the day is over the whole district will know about this scandal. . . . And so: 'Dear Sir! If your board does not discharge . . .'"

The doctor knew very well that under no circumstance would the board dismiss him rather than the feldscher, that it would let every feldscher in the whole district go, rather than lose such an excellent man as Doctor Ovchinnikov. Certainly, as soon as Lev Trofimovich got the letter he would drive up in his troika and commence: "What's this that you've taken into your head, old man? My dear fellow! What is it? In Christ's name!

Why? What's the matter? Where is he? Fetch the blackguard here! He must be fired! Out with him, by all means! There mustn't be a sign of the fellow here tomorrow!" Then he and the doctor would have dinner, and after dinner he would stretch out on his back on this raspberry-colored couch, cover his face with a newspaper and begin to snore; after a good sleep he would have tea, and then drive the doctor over to his own place for the night. And the upshot of it all would be that the feldscher would remain in the hospital and the doctor would not resign.

But at heart the doctor wanted an altogether different dénouement. His wish was that the feldscher's old aunt should be triumphant, that the board, in spite of his eight years of continuous service, should accept his resignation without a word of protest and, indeed, even with pleasure. He dreamed of how he would leave the hospital, to which he had got accustomed, how he would write a letter to the editor of *The Physician,* how his colleagues would tender him an address of sympathy. . . .

The siren appeared on the road. With a mincing gait and a swish of her dress, she walked over to the window and said:

"Grigory Ivanovich, will you be receiving the patients yourself or do you want us to receive them without you?"

Her eyes were saying: "You lost your temper, but now you have calmed down and you're ashamed of yourself; I am magnanimous, however, and don't notice it."

"I'll come right away," said the doctor.

He put on his apron, belted it with the towel, and went to the hospital.

"It wasn't right that I ran out after I struck him," he thought on the way. "It looked as though I were abashed or frightened. . . . I acted like a schoolboy. . . . It was all wrong!"

It seemed to him that when he entered the ward, the patients would look at him with embarrassment and that he, too, would be discomfited. But when he entered, the patients lay quietly in their beds and scarcely paid any attention to him. The face of the consumptive Gerasim expressed complete indifference and seemed to say: "You were put out with him and you gave him a dressing down. That's as it should be, brother."

The doctor opened two abscesses on the arm and bandaged it. Then he went to the women's ward, where he performed an operation on a peasant woman's eye. The siren was continually at his side and assisted him as though nothing had happened and everything were all right. Then came the turn of the ambulatory patients. In the doctor's small examining room the window was wide open. If you sat down on the window-sill and leaned over slightly, you could see the young grass two or three feet below. There had been a heavy thunderstorm the previous evening, and the grass looked somewhat trampled and glossy. The path which ran just beyond the window and led to the ravine looked washed clean, and the pieces of broken medicine bottles and jars scattered on both sides of it also looked washed, sparkling in the sun and sending out dazzling beams. Farther on, beyond the path, young firs garmented in luxuriant green, pressed close to one another; behind them loomed birches, their trunks white as paper, and through the foliage of the birches that trembled slightly in the breeze, you could see the blue, bottomless sky. When you looked out of the window, there were starlings hopping on the path, turning their foolish beaks in the direction of the window and debating with themselves: to get scared or not? Deciding to get scared, one by one they darted toward the treetops with a gay chirp, as if poking fun at the doctor who didn't know how to fly. . . .

The heavy smell of iodoform could not drown out the freshness and fragrance of the spring day. It was good to breathe!

"Anna Spiridonova!" the doctor called.

A young peasant woman in a red dress entered the examining room and turned to the icon, murmuring a prayer.

"What hurts you?" asked the doctor.

The woman glanced distrustfully at the door through which she had just entered and at the other door which led to the drug dispensary, came closer to the doctor, and whispered:

"No children!"

"Who hasn't registered yet?" the siren shouted from the dispensary. "Report here."

"He is a beast," the doctor thought to

himself as he examined the patient, "just because he made me strike him. I never in my life struck anyone before."

Anna Spiridonova left. Next came an old man who had a venereal disease, then a peasant woman with three children, all suffering from scabies, and things began to hum. There was no sign of the feldscher. Behind the door in the drug dispensary, the siren was making gay little noises, swishing her dress and clinking the bottles. Now and then she came into the examining room, to help with an operation or to fetch a prescription, and all with an air as though everything were as it should be.

"She's glad that I struck him," reflected the doctor, listening to the midwife's voice. "She and the feldscher were like cat and dog, and it will be a red letter day for her if he's discharged. I think the nurses are glad, too. . . . How disgusting!"

When he was at his busiest, he began to feel as though the midwife and the nurses, and the very patients, had purposely assumed an indifferent and even a cheerful expression. It was as though they understood that he was ashamed and pained, but out of delicacy they pretended not to. And he, wishing to show them that he was not ashamed, shouted roughly:

"Hey, you there! Shut the door, it's drafty!"

But he was ashamed, and ill at ease. Having examined forty-five patients, he took his time leaving the hospital.

The midwife had already been to her quarters. A crimson kerchief round her shoulders, a cigarette between her teeth and a flower in her loose hair, she was hurrying off, either on a case or to visit friends. Patients sat on the porch and warmed themselves in the sun. The starlings were still making a racket and chasing beetles. The doctor looked about and reflected that among these untroubled existences of even tenor only two lives, his and the feldscher's, stuck out and were worthless, like two damaged piano keys. The feldscher must surely have gone to bed to sleep it off, but was probably unable to fall asleep because he knew that he was in a bad way, that he had been insulted and had lost his job. His position was excruciating. As for the doctor, who had never struck anyone, he felt as though he had lost his chastity. He no longer blamed the feldscher and exonerated himself, he was only perplexed: how had it happened that he, a decent fellow who had never struck even a dog, could have hit a man? Once in his lodging, he went to his study and lay down on the couch with his face to the back of it, and reflected thus:

"He is a wicked man, he does the patients no good; he's been with me three years now and I'm just fed up; still, what I did was inexcusable. I took advantage of the fact that I was the stronger of the two. He is my subordinate, he was at fault, and, besides, he was drunk; I'm his superior, I was in the right and I was sober. And so I was the stronger. In the second place, I struck him in front of people who look up to me, and so I set them an abominable example."

The doctor was called to dinner. He had scarcely tasted the soup when he left the table and went to lie down again.

"What should I do then?" he continued communing with himself. "As soon as possible he must be given satisfaction. . . . But how? As a hard-headed man, he probably thinks that a duel is stupid, or it doesn't mean anything to him. If I were to apologize to him in that very ward in front of the nurses and the patients, the apology would satisfy me but not him; being a horrid fellow, he would interpret my apology as cowardice, as fear that he would lodge a complaint against me with the authorities. Besides, the apology would just be the end of discipline in the hospital. Shall I offer him money? No, that is immoral and smacks of bribery. Or shall I put the problem up to our immediate superiors, that is, to the board? They could reprimand me or discharge me. But they won't. Besides, it's awkward to get the board mixed up in the intimate affairs of the hospital, and anyway the board has no legal right to deal with these things."

About three hours after dinner the doctor went down to the pond for a swim, and as he walked he was thinking to himself:

"And shouldn't I do what everyone does under such circumstances? Let him sue me. I am unquestionably guilty, I'll put up no defense, and the judge will send me to jail. In this way the injured party will receive satisfaction, and those who look up to me will see that I was in the wrong."

The idea appealed to him. He was pleased, and decided that the problem was settled and that there could be no happier solution.

"Well, that's fine!" he thought, getting into the water and watching the shoals of small golden crucians that were scurrying away from him. "Let him sue me. That will be all the easier for him because he's no longer on the job, and after this scandal one of us obviously must leave the hospital. . . ."

In the evening the doctor ordered his gig, intending to drive over to the captain's to play vint. As he stood in his study, in his coat and hat, putting on his gloves and ready to leave, the outer door opened creakingly and someone noiselessly entered the anteroom.

"Who's there?" the doctor called out.

"It's me, sir . . ." a muffled voice answered.

The doctor felt his heart begin to pound and he was chilled through with shame and a kind of incomprehensible fear. Mikhail Zakharych (it was he) coughed softly, and timidly entered the study. After a pause, he said in a muffled, guilty tone of voice:

"Forgive me, Grigory Ivanovich!"

The doctor was taken aback and didn't know what to say. He realized that the feldscher had come to abase himself and apologize, not out of Christian humility, nor in order to heap coals of fire on the man who had insulted him, but simply for a sordid reason: "I'll force myself to apologize, and perhaps they won't fire me and take the bread out of my mouth. . . ." What could be more degrading?

"Forgive me . . ." repeated the feldscher.

"Listen," began the doctor, without looking at him, and still not knowing what to say. "Listen . . . I insulted you and . . . I must suffer for it, that is, I must give you satisfaction. . . . You're not the man to fight a duel. . . . Nor am I, for that matter. I insulted you and you . . . can lodge a complaint against me with the justice of the peace, and I'll take my punishment. . . . But the two of us can't stay in the same place. . . . One of us, you or I, must go! ('My God! I'm saying just the wrong thing!' the doctor was horrified. 'How stupid, how stupid!') In a word, sue me! But we can't go on working together! . . . It's either you or I! Lodge your complaint to-morrow!"

The feldscher looked at the doctor with a frown, and the frankest contempt flared up in his dark, turbid eyes. He had always thought that the doctor was an impractical, capricious, puerile fellow, and now he despised him for his nervousness, for his incomprehensible, jerky way of speaking.

"I will bring suit," he said, with a look of sullen hatred.

"Well, do!"

"You think I won't sue you? I won't? I will. . . . You've no right to use your fists on me. You ought to be ashamed of yourself! Only drunken peasants fight, and you're an educated man. . . ."

Suddenly the doctor's chest tightened with hatred, and in a voice that did not sound like his own he shouted:

"Get out!"

The feldscher reluctantly took a step or two (he looked as though he wanted to say something further), then walked into the anteroom and stood there, thinking. Having apparently made up his mind, he resolutely went out.

"How stupid, how stupid!" the doctor muttered, when the feldscher was gone. "How stupid and vulgar all this is!"

He felt that his behavior toward the man had been puerile, and he already realized that all his notions about the lawsuit were foolish, that they did not solve the problem but only complicated it.

"How stupid!" he repeated to himself, as he sat in his gig and later while he was playing vint at the captain's. "Is it possible that I am so badly educated and know life so little that I can't solve this simple problem? What shall I do?"

The next morning the doctor saw the feldscher's wife step into a carriage and reflected: "She must be going to his aunt's. Let her!"

The hospital managed to get along without a feldscher. It was necessary to notify the board, but the doctor was still unable to decide what form his letter should take. Now, it seemed to him, the tenor of the letter should be: "I request you to discharge the feldscher, although I am to blame, not he." For a decent person it was almost impossible

to make this statement in a way which would not be stupid and shameful.

Two or three days later the doctor was informed that the feldscher had complained to Lev Trofimovich. The chairman hadn't let him say a word, had stamped his feet and chased him out, shouting: "I know you! Get out! I won't listen to you!" From there the feldscher had gone to the office of the zemstvo and filed a report, in which he did not mention the slap in the face and asked nothing for himself, but informed the board that in his presence the doctor had several times commented unfavorably on the board and its chairman, that he treated patients in a manner contrary to accepted rules, that he was neglectful about making the prescribed rounds of his district, etc., etc. On learning of this, the doctor laughed, and thought: "What a fool!" And he felt shame and pity for the man who was behaving so foolishly; the more stupid things a man does in his defense, the weaker and more helpless he obviously is.

Exactly a week later the doctor received a summons from the justice of the peace.

"This is altogether absurd," he thought as he signed the necessary paper. "You couldn't conceive anything stupider."

As he was on his way to the court on a windless morning under an overcast sky, what he felt was not shame, but annoyance and disgust. He was vexed with himself, with the feldscher, with the situation.

"I'll up and say in court: 'To the devil with the lot of you!'" he raged inwardly. "'You're all asses and you understand nothing!'"

When he reached the building in which court was to be held, he saw in the doorway three of his nurses who had been called as witnesses, and the siren as well. In her impatience she was shifting her weight from one foot to the other, and she even blushed with pleasure when she beheld the principal character in the impending trial. The doctor, furious, was about to swoop down on them like a hawk and stun them by saying: "Who permitted you to leave the hospital? Be good enough to get back to your posts right away!" But he controlled himself and, pretending calmness, made his way through the crowd of peasants to the courtroom. The chamber was empty, and the justice's chain hung on the

back of his armchair. The doctor went into
the clerk's cubbyhole. There he saw a thin-
faced young man wearing a cotton jacket with
bulging pockets—it was the clerk—and the
feldscher. He was sitting at a desk and, having nothing better to do, was paging a law
journal. At the doctor's entrance the clerk
rose, the feldscher looked abashed and rose
also.

"Alexander Arkhipovich isn't here yet?"
asked the doctor, embarrassed.

"Not yet, sir. He's in his own apartments,"
the clerk answered.

The court was located on the justice's estate,
in one of the wings of his large house. The
doctor left the court and walked unhurriedly
toward the justice's apartments. He found
Alexander Arkhipovich in the dining-room,
where a samovar was steaming. The justice,
with his coat off and not even a waistcoat, his
shirt open, so that his chest was bare, was
standing at the table and, holding the tea-
kettle with both hands, was pouring himself
a tumbler of tea black as coffee. When he
saw his visitor, he quietly drew another tumbler toward himself, filled it, and, without
greeting the doctor, asked:

"With or without sugar?"

Long ago the justice of the peace had been
in the cavalry, but now because for many
years he had held elective offices he had the
rank of Actual Councilor of State. Yet he
had not discarded his army uniform or his
military habits. He had long moustaches, the
kind fancied by chiefs of police, wore trousers
with piping, and all his gestures and words
breathed military grace. He spoke with his
head slightly thrown back, and garnishing his
speech with the juicy, dignified "m'yeses" of
a general, he swayed his shoulders and rolled
his eyes. When he greeted you or gave you
a light, he scraped his feet, and when he
walked, he clinked his spurs as gently and
cautiously as if every sound they made caused
him intolerable pain. Having seated the doctor at table and provided him with tea, he
stroked his broad chest and his stomach,
heaved a deep sigh, and said:

"M'yes. . . . Would you perhaps have some
vodka and a bite to eat . . . m'yes?"

"No, thank you, I'm not hungry."

Both felt that they could not avoid the sub-

ject of the scandal at the hospital, and both
felt awkward. The doctor was silent. The justice, with a graceful movement of the hand,
caught an insect which had bit him on his
chest, examined it carefully and let it go.
Then he drew a deep sigh, looked up at the
doctor, and, speaking deliberately, asked:

"Listen, why don't you send him packing?"

The doctor caught a note of sympathy in
his voice; he was suddenly sorry for himself,
and he felt tired and jaded by the disagreeable experiences he had endured in the
course of the preceding week. His face showed
that he had finally reached the end of his
patience. He rose from the table, frowning
irritably and shrugging his shoulders, and
said:

"Send him packing! Good Lord, the logic of
you people! It's astonishing, your logic! Don't
you know that I can't send him packing? You
sit here and think that I'm boss at the hospital and can do what I please! It's astonishing, your logic! Can I send the feldscher packing, if his aunt is employed as a nursemaid by
Lev Trofimovich, and if Lev Trofimovich
wants such gossips and flunkies as this Zakharych? What can I do if the zemstvo people
wipe the floor with us physicians, if they
hinder us at every step? To hell with them,
I don't want to work for them, that's all! I
don't want to!"

"Well, well, well, old man. . . . You're
making a mountain out of a molehill, you
know. . . ."

"The marshal of the nobility goes out of
his way to prove that we're all nihilists, he
spies on us and treats us as his clerks. What
right has he to come to the hospital in my
absence and question the nurses and patients?
Isn't it insulting? And this crazy Semyon
Alexeich of yours, who does his own plowing
and doesn't believe in medicine because he
is as strong as an ox and eats like one, calls
us parasites out loud and to our faces and
begrudges us our salaries. Devil take him! I
work day and night, I get no rest, I'm needed
here more than all these psychopaths, bigots,
reformers, and all the other clowns taken together! I've made myself sick with work, and
what I get instead of gratitude is to have my
salary thrown in my teeth! Many thanks!
And everybody thinks he's entitled to stick his

nose into what's none of his business, to teach me, to discipline me! At one meeting this Kamchatsky, a member of your board, reprimanded the physicians for wasting potassium iodide, and advised us to be careful in using cocaine! What does he know about it, I ask you? How's he concerned? Why doesn't he teach you how to run your court?"

"But he's a cad, my dear fellow, he's a bounder. . . . You mustn't pay any attention to him. . . ."

"A cad, a bounder, and yet you've elected this character to the board and you allow him to stick his nose everywhere! You smile! According to you, these are trifles, bagatelles, but get it into your head that there are so many of these trifles that they make up my whole life, the way grains of sand make a mountain! I can't stand it any longer! I haven't the strength, Alexander Arkhipovich! A little more, and I'll not only use my fists on people, I'll draw a gun on them! Get it into your head, my nerves aren't made of iron. I'm a human being like you. . . ."

Tears came to the doctor's eyes, and his voice quavered; he turned aside and looked out of the window. Silence fell.

"M'yes, my dear fellow . . ." mumbled the justice thoughtfully. "On the other hand, to take a cold-blooded view . . ." (the justice caught a mosquito and, screwing his eyes tight, examined it carefully, crushed it and threw it into the slop-basin). "You see, there's no reason why he should be sent packing. Send him packing, and he'll be replaced by someone just like him or worse. You can try out a hundred men, and you won't find one you want to keep. . . . They're all no good." The justice stroked his armpits and then slowly lit a cigarette. "We must put up with it, bad as it is. Let me tell you that right now honest, sober, reliable workers can be found only among the intellectuals and the peasants, that is at the poles of society and only there. You can find a thoroughly honest physician, let's say, an excellent teacher, an honest plowman or a blacksmith, but the people in between, so to speak, those who no longer belong to the masses and who haven't yet become part of the intelligentsia, are an unreliable element. It's very hard to find an honest and sober feldscher, a clerk, a salesman, and

so forth. Exceedingly hard! I've been in the courts since God knows when, and in all these years I've never had an honest, sober clerk, although I've tried out no end of them in my time. They are people who have no discipline, let alone principles, so to speak. . . ."

"Why is he talking this way?" thought the doctor. "Neither of us is saying what ought to be said."

"Here is a trick my own clerk played on me only last Friday," the justice continued. "In the evening he got together with some drunks, the devil knows who, and all night long they were boozing in my chambers. How do you like that? I've nothing against drinking. Devil take you, drink, but why bring utter strangers into my chambers? Judge for yourself: how long would it take to steal some document, say, a promissory note, from the files? And what do you think? After that orgy I spent two days checking up to see if anything was missing. . . . Well, what are you going to do about this wretch? Send him packing? Very well. . . . And what's the guarantee that the next one won't be worse?"

"Besides, how can you send a man packing?" asked the doctor. "It's easy to say it. How can I fire him and take the bread out of his mouth, when I know that he is a family man and has nothing? Where would he go with his family?"

"Devil take it, I'm saying the wrong thing!" he thought to himself, and it seemed odd to him that he could not fix his mind on some one definite idea or sentiment. "It's because I'm shallow and don't know how to think," he reflected.

"The man in-between, as you called him, is unreliable," he went on. "We send him packing, scold him, slap him in the face, but we also ought to enter into his situation. He is neither a peasant nor a master, neither fish, flesh, nor fowl. His past is bleak, at present he has twenty-five rubles a month, a hungry family and a job in which he's not his own master. The future holds the same twenty-five rubles and the same dependent position, even if he holds on to his job for a hundred years. He has neither education nor property; he has no time to read or to go to church; he doesn't profit by our example, because we don't let him get close enough to us. So he goes on living like that, day in, day out, till he dies, without hoping for anything better, underfed, always afraid that any day he may be evicted from the quarters the Government provides him with, and that his children won't have a roof over their heads. Under such circumstances, how is a man to keep from drinking, from stealing? Under such conditions, how can he have principles?"

"So here we are, solving social problems!" the doctor thought to himself. "And, my God, how awkwardly! And what's all this for?"

The sound of bells was heard. Someone drove into the yard and halted before the wing in which the court chambers were located and then went on and stopped at the porch of the big house.

"Himself is here," said the justice, glancing out of the window. "Well, you'll get it in the neck!"

"Please, let's be done with it, and fast," the doctor pleaded. "If possible, take my case out of turn. I've no time, by Jove!"

"All right, all right. . . . Only, I don't know, old man, if the case is within my jurisdiction. Your relations with the assistant were, so to speak, official, and, besides, you smacked him while he was on duty. But I don't know for certain. Let's ask Lev Trofimovich."

Hurried steps were heard, and heavy breathing, and Lev Trofimovich, chairman of the board, a white-haired, bald-headed old man with a long beard and red eyelids, appeared in the doorway.

"Greetings!" he brought out, panting.

"Ouf! My dears! Tell them to bring me some kvass, judge! I can't stand it. . . ."

He sank into an armchair, but immediately jumped up, trotted over to the doctor and, staring at him angrily, said in a squeaking tenor:

"Many, many thanks to you, Grigory Ivanovich! You've done me a great favor, thank you! I won't forget it to my dying day, amen! Friends don't act like that! Say what you will, it's not decent of you. Why didn't you let me know? What do you think I am? Whom do you take me for? Am I your enemy or an utter stranger to you? Am I your enemy? Have I ever refused you anything? Eh?"

Staring hard and twiddling his fingers, the chairman drank his kvass, wiped his lips hurriedly, and continued:

"Thank you very, very kindly! Why didn't you let me know? If you had had any feeling for me, you would have driven up and talked to me as a friend: 'Lev Trofimovich, my dear fellow, the facts are so-and-so. . . . This is what happened, and so on and so forth . . .' Before you could turn round, I would have arranged everything, and there would have been no scandal. . . . That fool has gone completely crazy, he wanders through the district, concocts stories and gossips with the women, and you, it's really shameful, if you'll excuse my saying so, you've started the devil knows what kind of a row, you've got that fool to sue you! It's shameful! Just shameful! Everybody asks me: What's the matter? What happened? How did it happen? And I, the chairman, know nothing of what's going on. You have no need of me! Many, many thanks, Grigory Ivanovich!"

The chairman made him such a low bow that he turned crimson, then he went over to the window and called:

"Zhigalov, ask Mikhail Zakharych to come up here! Tell him to come up at once! It isn't right, my dear sir!" he said, walking away from the window. "Even my wife has taken offense, and you know how much she likes you. The trouble with you, gentlemen, is that you rely too much on reason! Everything has to be logical with you, you drag in principles, and worry about all the fine points, and as a result all you do is get things balled up!"

"And with you everything has to be illogical, and what is the result?" asked the doctor.

"What's the result? The result is that if I hadn't come here just now, you'd have disgraced yourself, and us, too. . . . It's your luck that I came!"

The feldscher entered and stopped on the threshold. The chairman took up such a position that he was half turned away from the feldscher, put his hands in his pockets, cleared his throat, and said:

"Apologize to the doctor at once!"

The doctor flushed and ran into another room.

"You see, the doctor doesn't want to accept your apology!" the chairman went on. "He wants you to show that you're sorry not in words, but in deeds. Do you give your word of honor that from now on you will follow his orders and lead a sober life?"

"I do," the assistant brought out sullenly, in a deep voice.

"Watch out, then! And Heaven help you, if you don't! I'll fire you before you can say knife. If anything happens, don't come begging for mercy. . . . Now, go on home. . . ."

For the feldscher, who had already accepted his misfortune, such a turn of events was a breath-taking surprise. So much so that he grew pale with joy. He wanted to say something, put out his hand, but could not bring out a word, smiled stupidly and left.

"That's that!" said the chairman. "And there's no need for any trial."

He drew a sigh of relief, and with an air of having just accomplished something difficult and important, he looked closely at the samovar and the glasses, rubbed his hands, and said:

"Blessed are the peacemakers. . . . Pour out a glass for me, Sasha. But wait, have them bring me a bite. . . . And, well, some vodka."

"Gentlemen, this is absurd!" said the doctor, as he entered the dining-room, still flushed, and wringing his hands. "This . . . this is a comedy! It's vile! I can't bear it! It's better to have twenty trials than to settle matters in this farcical fashion. No, I can't stand it!"

"What do you want, then?" the chairman snapped at him. "Shall we fire him? Very well, I'll fire him."

"No, not that. I don't know what I want, but to take such an attitude towards life, gentlemen. . . . Oh, my God! It's torture!"

The doctor started to bustle about nervously, looking for his hat, and failing to find it, sank into an armchair, exhausted.

"It's vile!" he repeated.

"My dear fellow," the justice muttered, "to some extent I fail to understand you, so to speak. . . . You're the one who is at fault in this affair, aren't you? To go about at the end of the nineteenth century, biffing people on the jaw, that is, you will agree, not quite . . . so to speak. . . . He's a scoundrel, bu-u-ut, you will agree, you acted heedlessly, too."

"Of course!" the chairman chimed in.

Vodka and hors d'oeuvres were served.

Before taking his leave the doctor emptied a glass of vodka and ate a radish. As he was returning to the hospital, a mist, such as veils the grass on autumn mornings, was beclouding his thoughts.

"Can it be," he reflected, "that after all that was said and thought and suffered during the past week, the end should be something so absurd and vulgar? How stupid! How stupid!"

He was ashamed of having involved strangers in his personal problem, ashamed of the things he had said to these people, ashamed of having drunk vodka out of a habit of idle drinking and idle living, ashamed of his blunt, shallow mind.

Back in the hospital, he immediately started making the rounds of the wards. The feldscher followed him, stepping softly, like a cat, and answering questions gently. The feldscher, the siren, the nurses, all pretended that nothing had occurred and that everything was as it should be. The doctor himself made every effort to appear indifferent. He issued orders, fumed, cracked jokes with the patients, but in his brain a thought kept stirring:

"Stupid, stupid, stupid . . ."

STEPHEN CRANE *The Open Boat*

Stephen Crane (1871-1900), novelist, poet, journalist, and biographer, started his literary career by writing a startlingly realistic novel, *Maggie: A Girl of the Streets*, 1892. His second novel, *The Red Badge of Courage*, published in 1895, brought him fame. He became a war correspondent and covered the Greco-Turkish War for Hearst's New York *Journal*. After returning from Greece, Crane married and took up residence in England, where he met and became a friend of Joseph Conrad. In 1898 he distinguished himself by his objective reporting from Cuba of the Spanish-American War. He contracted tuberculosis and died when he was only twenty-nine.

Crane did much to revolutionize the technique and style of American fiction by writing in a strongly realistic style. Carl and Mark Van Doren have commented, "Modern American fiction may be said to begin with Stephen Crane." H. G. Wells has called "The Open Boat" the "finest short story in English." While the story is based on an actual experience of Crane's, as the subtitle—"A Fate Intended to be after the Fact: Being the Experience of Four Men from the Sunk Steamer *Commodore*"—indicates, thoughtful readers agree with Conrad, who commented, "The simple humanity of its presentation seems somehow to illustrate the essentials of life itself, like a symbolic tale."

I

None of them knew the color of the sky. Their eyes glanced level, and were fastened upon the waves that swept toward them. These waves were of the hue of slate, save for the tops, which were of foaming white, and all of the men knew the colors of the sea. The horizon narrowed and widened, and dipped and rose, and at all times its edge was jagged with waves that seemed thrust up in points like rocks.

Many a man ought to have a bath-tub larger than the boat which here rode upon the sea. These waves were most wrongfully and barbarously abrupt and tall, and each froth-top was a problem in small-boat navigation.

The cook squatted in the bottom and

THE OPEN BOAT: Reprinted from *Stephen Crane: An Omnibus*, edited by Robert Wooster Stallman, by permission of Alfred A. Knopf, Inc. Copyright 1925 by William H. Crane.

looked with both eyes at the six inches of gunwale which separated him from the ocean. His sleeves were rolled over his fat forearms, and the two flaps of his unbuttoned vest dangled as he bent to bail out the boat. Often he said: "Gawd! That was a narrow clip." As he remarked it he invariably gazed eastward over the broken sea.

The oiler, steering with one of the two oars in the boat, sometimes raised himself suddenly to keep clear of water that swirled in over the stern. It was a thin little oar and it seemed often ready to snap.

The correspondent, pulling at the other oar, watched the waves and wondered why he was there.

The injured captain, lying in the bow, was at this time buried in that profound dejection and indifference which comes, temporarily at least, to even the bravest and most enduring when, willy-nilly, the firm fails, the army loses, the ship goes down. The mind of the master of a vessel is rooted deep in the timbers of her, though he command for a day or a decade, and this captain had on him the stern impression of a scene in the grays of dawn of seven turned faces, and later a stump of a top-mast with a white ball on it that slashed to and fro at the waves, went low and lower, and down. Thereafter there was something strange in his voice. Although steady, it was deep with mourning, and of a quality beyond oration or tears.

"Keep 'er a little more south, Billie," said he.

"A little more south, sir," said the oiler in the stern.

A seat in this boat was not unlike a seat upon a bucking bronco, and, by the same token, a bronco is not much smaller. The craft pranced and reared, and plunged like an animal. As each wave came, and she rose for it, she seemed like a horse making at a fence outrageously high. The manner of her scramble over these walls of water is a mystic thing, and, moreover, at the top of them were ordinarily these problems in white water, the foam racing down from the summit of each wave, requiring a new leap, and a leap from the air. Then, after scornfully bumping a crest, she would slide, and race, and splash down a long incline, and arrive bobbing and nodding in front of the next menace.

A singular disadvantage of the sea lies in the fact that after successfully surmounting one wave you discover that there is another behind it just as important and just as nervously anxious to do something effective in the way of swamping boats. In a ten-foot dinghy one can get an idea of the resources of the sea in the line of waves that is not probable to the average experience which is never at sea in a dinghy. As each slaty wall of water approached, it shut all else from the view of the men in the boat, and it was not difficult to imagine that this particular wave was the final outburst of the ocean, the last effort of the grim water. There was a terrible grace in the move of the waves, and they came in silence, save for the snarling of the crests.

In the wan light, the faces of the men must have been gray. Their eyes must have glinted in strange ways as they gazed steadily astern. Viewed from a balcony, the whole thing would doubtless have been weirdly picturesque. But the men in the boat had no time to see it, and if they had had leisure there were other things to occupy their minds. The sun swung steadily up the sky, and they knew it was broad day because the color of the sea changed from slate to emerald-green, streaked with amber lights, and the foam was like tumbling snow. The process of the breaking day was unknown to them. They were aware only of this effect upon the color of the waves that rolled toward them.

In disjointed sentences the cook and the correspondent argued as to the difference between a life-saving station and a house of refuge. The cook had said: "There's a house of refuge just north of the Mosquito Inlet Light, and as soon as they see us, they'll come off in their boat and pick us up."

"As soon as who see us?" said the correspondent.

"The crew," said the cook.

"Houses of refuge don't have crews," said the correspondent. "As I understand them, they are only places where clothes and grub are stored for the benefit of shipwrecked people. They don't carry crews."

"Oh, yes, they do," said the cook.

"No, they don't," said the correspondent.

"Well, we're not there yet, anyhow," said the oiler, in the stern.

"Well," said the cook, "perhaps it's not a house of refuge that I'm thinking of as being near Mosquito Inlet Light. Perhaps it's a life-saving station."

"We're not there yet," said the oiler, in the stern.

II

As the boat bounced from the top of each wave, the wind tore through the hair of the hatless men, and as the craft plopped her stern down again the spray slashed past them. The crest of each of these waves was a hill, from the top of which the men surveyed, for a moment, a broad tumultuous expanse, shining and wind-driven. It was probably splendid. It was probably glorious, this play of the free sea, wild with lights of emerald and white and amber.

"Bully good thing it's an on-shore wind," said the cook. "If not, where would we be? Wouldn't have a show."

"That's right," said the correspondent.

The busy oiler nodded his assent.

Then the captain, in the bow, chuckled in a way that expressed humor, contempt, tragedy, all in one. "Do you think we've got much of a show now, boys?" said he.

Whereupon the three were silent, save for a trifle of hemming and hawing. To express any particular optimism at this time they felt to be childish and stupid, but they all doubtless possessed this sense of the situation in their mind. A young man thinks doggedly at such times. On the other hand, the ethics of their condition was decidedly against any open suggestion of hopelessness. So they were silent.

"Oh, well," said the captain, soothing his children, "we'll get ashore all right."

But there was that in his tone which made them think, so the oiler quoth: "Yes! If this wind holds!"

The cook was bailing: "Yes! If we don't catch hell in the surf."

Canton flannel gulls flew near and far. Sometimes they sat down on the sea, near patches of brown seaweed that rolled over the waves with a movement like carpets on a line in a gale. The birds sat comfortably in groups, and they were envied by some in the dinghy, for the wrath of the sea was no more to them than it was to a covey of prairie chickens a thousand miles inland. Often they came very close and stared at the men with black bead-like eyes. At these times they were uncanny and sinister in their unblinking scrutiny, and the men hooted angrily at them, telling them to be gone. One came, and evidently decided to alight on the top of the captain's head. The bird flew parallel to the boat and did not circle, but made short sidelong jumps in the air in chicken-fashion. His black eyes were wistfully fixed upon the captain's head. "Ugly brute," said the oiler to the bird. "You look as if you were made with a jackknife." The cook and the correspondent swore darkly at the creature. The captain naturally wished to knock it away with the end of the heavy painter; but he did not dare do it, because anything resembling an emphatic gesture would have capsized this freighted boat, and so with his open hand, the captain gently and carefully waved the gull away. After it had been discouraged from the pursuit the captain breathed easier on account of his hair, and others breathed easier because the bird struck their minds at this time as being somehow gruesome and ominous.

In the meantime the oiler and the correspondent rowed. And also they rowed.

They sat together in the same seat, and each rowed an oar. Then the oiler took both oars; then the correspondent took both oars; then the oiler; then the correspondent. They rowed and they rowed. The very ticklish part of the business was when the time came for the reclining one in the stern to take his turn at the oars. By the very last star of truth, it is easier to steal eggs from under a hen than it was to change seats in the dinghy. First the man in the stern slid his hand along the thwart and moved with care, as if he were of Sèvres. Then the man in the rowing seat slid his hand along the other thwart. It was all done with the most extraordinary care. As the two sidled past each other, the whole party kept watchful eyes on the coming wave, and the captain cried: "Look out now! Steady there!"

The brown mats of seaweed that appeared from time to time were like islands, bits of earth. They were traveling, apparently, neither one way nor the other. They were, to all intents, stationary. They informed the men in the boat that it was making progress slowly toward the land.

The captain, rearing cautiously in the bow, after the dinghy soared on a great swell, said that he had seen the lighthouse at Mosquito Inlet. Presently the cook remarked that he had seen it. The correspondent was at the oars then, and for some reason he too wished to look at the lighthouse, but his back was toward the far shore and the waves were important, and for some time he could not seize an opportunity to turn his head. But at last there came a wave more gentle than the others, and when at the crest of it he swiftly scoured the western horizon.

"See it?" said the captain.

"No," said the correspondent slowly, "I didn't see anything."

"Look again," said the captain. He pointed. "It's exactly in that direction."

At the top of another wave, the correspondent did as he was bid, and this time his eyes chanced on a small still thing on the edge of the swaying horizon. It was precisely like the point of a pin. It took an anxious eye to find a lighthouse so tiny.

"Think we'll make it, captain?"

"If this wind holds and the boat don't swamp, we can't do much else," said the captain.

The little boat, lifted by each towering sea, and splashed viciously by the crests, made progress that in the absence of seaweed was not apparent to those in her. She seemed just a wee thing wallowing, miraculously top up, at the mercy of five oceans. Occasionally, a great spread of water, like white flames, swarmed into her.

"Bail her, cook," said the captain serenely.

"All right, captain," said the cheerful cook.

III

It would be difficult to describe the subtle brotherhood of men that was here established on the seas. No one said that it was so. No one mentioned it. But it dwelt in the boat, and each man felt it warm him. They were a captain, an oiler, a cook, and a correspondent, and they were friends, friends in a more curiously iron-bound degree than may be common. The hurt captain, lying against the water-jar in the bow, spoke always in a low voice and calmly, but he could never command a more ready and swiftly obedient crew than the motley three of the dinghy. It was more than a mere recognition of what was best for the common safety. There was surely in it a quality that was personal and heartfelt. And after this devotion to the commander of the boat there was this comradeship that the correspondent, for instance, who had been taught to be cynical of men, knew even at the time was the best experience of his life. But no one said that it was so. No one mentioned it.

"I wish we had a sail," remarked the captain. "We might try my overcoat on the end of an oar and give you two boys a chance to rest." So the cook and the correspondent held the mast and spread wide the overcoat. The oiler steered, and the little boat made good way with her new rig. Sometimes the oiler had to scull sharply to keep a sea from breaking into the boat, but otherwise sailing was a success.

Meanwhile the lighthouse had been growing slowly larger. It had now almost assumed color, and appeared like a little gray shadow on the sky. The man at the oars could not be prevented from turning his head rather often to try for a glimpse of this little gray shadow.

At last, from the top of each wave the men in the tossing boat could see land. Even as the lighthouse was an upright shadow on the sky, this land seemed but a long black shadow on the sea. It certainly was thinner than paper. "We must be about opposite New Smyrna," said the cook, who had coasted this shore often in schooners. "Captain, by the way, I believe they abandoned that life-saving station there about a year ago."

"Did they?" said the captain.

The wind slowly died away. The cook and the correspondent were not now obliged to slave in order to hold high the oar. But the waves continued their old impetuous swooping at the dinghy, and the little craft, no longer under way, struggled woundily over them. The oiler or the correspondent took the oars again.

Shipwrecks are apropos of nothing. If men could only train for them and have them occur when the men had reached pink condition, there would be less drowning at sea. Of the four in the dinghy none had slept any time worth mentioning for two days and two nights previous to embarking in the dinghy, and in the excitement of clambering about the deck of a foundering ship they had also forgotten to eat heartily.

For these reasons, and for others, neither the oiler nor the correspondent was fond of rowing at this time. The correspondent wondered ingenuously how in the name of all that was sane could there be people who thought it amusing to row a boat. It was not an amusement; it was a diabolical punishment, and even a genius of mental aberrations could never conclude that it was anything but a horror to the muscles and a crime against the back. He mentioned to the boat in general how the amusement of rowing struck him, and the weary-faced oiler smiled in full sympathy. Previously to the foundering, by the way, the oiler had worked double-watch in the engine-room of the ship.

"Take her easy, now, boys," said the captain. "Don't spend yourselves. If we have to run a surf you'll need all your strength, because we'll sure have to swim for it. Take your time."

Slowly the land arose from the sea. From a black line it became a line of black and a line of white, trees and sand. Finally, the captain said that he could make out a house on the shore. "That's the house of refuge, sure," said the cook. "They'll see us before long, and come out after us."

The distant lighthouse reared high. "The keeper ought to be able to make us out now, if he's looking through a glass," said the captain. "He'll notify the life-saving people."

"None of those other boats could have got ashore to give word of the wreck," said the oiler, in a low voice. "Else the lifeboat would be out hunting us."

Slowly and beautifully the land loomed out of the sea. The wind came again. It had veered from the north-east to the south-east. Finally, a new sound struck the ears of the men in the boat. It was the low thunder of the surf on the shore. "We'll never be able to make the lighthouse now," said the captain. "Swing her head a little more north, Billie."

"A little more north, sir," said the oiler.

Whereupon the little boat turned her nose once more down the wind, and all but the oarsman watched the shore grow. Under the influence of this expansion doubt and direful apprehension was leaving the minds of the men. The management of the boat was still most absorbing, but it could not prevent a quiet cheerfulness. In an hour, perhaps, they would be ashore.

Their backbones had become thoroughly used to balancing in the boat, and they now rode this wild colt of a dinghy like circus men. The correspondent thought that he had been drenched to the skin, but happening to feel in the top pocket of his coat, he found therein eight cigars. Four of them were soaked with sea-water; four were perfectly scatheless. After a search, somebody produced three dry matches, and thereupon the four waifs rode impudently in their little boat, and with an assurance of an impending rescue shining in their eyes, puffed at the big cigars and judged well and ill of all men. Everybody took a drink of water.

IV

"Cook," remarked the captain, "there don't seem to be any signs of life about your house of refuge."

"No," replied the cook. "Funny they don't see us!"

A broad stretch of lowly coast lay before the eyes of the men. It was of low dunes topped with dark vegetation. The roar of the surf was plain, and sometimes they could see the white lip of a wave as it spun up the beach. A tiny house was blocked out black upon the sky. Southward, the slim lighthouse lifted its little gray length.

Tide, wind, and waves were swinging the dinghy northward. "Funny they don't see us," said the men.

The surf's roar was here dulled, but its tone was, nevertheless, thunderous and mighty. As the boat swam over the great rollers, the men sat listening to this roar. "We'll swamp sure," said everybody.

It is fair to say here that there was not a life-saving station within twenty miles in either direction, but the men did not know this fact, and in consequence they made dark and opprobrious remarks concerning the eyesight of the nation's life-savers. Four scowling men sat in the dinghy and surpassed records in the invention of epithets.

"Funny they don't see us."

The light-heartedness of a former time had completely faded. To their sharpened minds it was easy to conjure pictures of all kinds of incompetency and blindness and, indeed, cowardice. There was the shore of the populous land, and it was bitter and bitter to them that from it came no sign.

"Well," said the captain, ultimately, "I suppose we'll have to make a try for ourselves. If we stay out here too long, we'll none of us have strength left to swim after the boat swamps."

And so the oiler, who was at the oars, turned the boat straight for the shore. There was a sudden tightening of muscles. There was some thinking.

"If we don't all get ashore—" said the captain. "If we don't all get ashore, I suppose you fellows know where to send news of my finish?"

They then briefly exchanged some addresses and admonitions. As for the reflections of the men, there was a great deal of rage in them. Perchance they might be formulated thus: "If I am going to be drowned—if I am going to be drowned—if I am going to be drowned, why, in the name of the seven mad gods who rule the sea, was I allowed to come thus far and contemplate sand and trees? Was I brought here merely to have my nose dragged away as I was about to nibble the sacred cheese of life? It is preposterous. If this old ninny-woman, Fate, cannot do better than this, she should be deprived of the management of men's fortunes. She is an old hen who knows not her intention. If she has decided to drown me, why did she not do it in the beginning and save me all this trouble? The whole affair is absurd. . . . But no, she cannot mean to drown me. She dare not drown me. She cannot drown me. Not after all this work." Afterward the man might have had an impulse to shake his fist at the clouds: "Just you drown me, now, and then hear what I call you!"

The billows that came at this time were more formidable. They seemed always just about to break and roll over the little boat in a turmoil of foam. There was a preparatory and long growl in the speech of them. No mind unused to the sea would have concluded that the dinghy could ascend these sheer heights in time. The shore was still afar. The oiler was a wily surfman. "Boys," he said swiftly, "she won't live three minutes more, and we're too far out to swim. Shall I take her to sea again, captain?"

"Yes! Go ahead!" said the captain.

This oiler, by a series of quick miracles, and fast and steady oarsmanship, turned the boat in the middle of the surf and took her safely to sea again.

There was a considerable silence as the boat bumped over the furrowed sea to deeper water. Then somebody in gloom spoke. "Well, anyhow, they must have seen us from the shore by now."

The gulls went in slanting flight up the wind toward the gray desolate east. A squall, marked by dingy clouds, and clouds brick-red, like smoke from a burning building, appeared from the south-east.

"What do you think of those life-saving people? Ain't they peaches?"

"Funny they haven't seen us."

"Maybe they think we're out here for sport! Maybe they think we're fishin'. Maybe they think we're damned fools."

It was a long afternoon. A changed tide tried to force them southward, but wind and wave said northward. Far ahead, where coastline, sea, and sky formed their mighty angle, there were little dots which seemed to indicate a city on the shore.

"St. Augustine?"

The captain shook his head. "Too near Mosquito Inlet."

And the oiler rowed, and then the correspondent rowed. Then the oiler rowed. It was a weary business. The human back can become the seat of more aches and pains than are registered in books for the composite anatomy of a regiment. It is a limited area, but it can become the theater of innumerable muscular conflicts, tangles, wrenches, knots, and other comforts.

"Did you ever like to row, Billie?" asked the correspondent.

"No," said the oiler. "Hang it."

When one exchanged the rowing-seat for a place in the bottom of the boat, he suffered a bodily depression that caused him to be careless of everything save an obligation to wiggle one finger. There was cold sea-water swashing to and fro in the boat, and he lay in it. His head, pillowed on a thwart, was within an inch of the swirl of a wave crest, and sometimes a particularly obstreperous sea came in-board and drenched him once more. But these matters did not annoy him. It is almost certain that if the boat had capsized he would have tumbled comfortably out upon the ocean as if he felt sure that it was a great soft mattress.

"Look! There's a man on the shore!"

"Where?"

"There! See 'im? See 'im?"

"Yes, sure! He's walking along."

"Now he's stopped. Look! He's facing us!"

"He's waving at us!"

"So he is! By thunder!"

"Ah, now we're all right! Now we're all right! There'll be a boat out here for us in half an hour."

"He's going on. He's running. He's going up to that house there."

The remote beach seemed lower than the sea, and it required a searching glance to discern the little black figure. The captain saw a floating stick and they rowed to it. A bath-towel was by some weird chance in the boat, and, tying this on the stick, the captain waved it. The oarsman did not dare turn his head, so he was obliged to ask questions.

"What's he doing now?"

"He's standing still again. He's looking, I think. . . . There he goes again. Toward the house. . . . Now he stopped again."

"Is he waving at us?"

"No, not now! He was, though."

"Look! There comes another man!"

"He's running."

"Look at him go, would you!"

"Why, he's on a bicycle. Now he's met the other man. They're both waving at us. Look!"

"There comes something up the beach."

"What the devil is that thing?"

"Why, it looks like a boat."

"Why, certainly it's a boat."

"No, it's on wheels."

"Yes, so it is. Well, that must be the life-boat. They drag them along shore on a wagon."

"That's the life-boat, sure."

"No, by—, it's—it's an omnibus."

"I tell you it's a life-boat."

"It is not! It's an omnibus. I can see it plain. See? One of these big hotel omnibuses."

"By thunder, you're right. It's an omnibus, sure as fate. What do you suppose they are doing with an omnibus? Maybe they are going around collecting the life-crew, hey?"

"That's it, likely. Look! There's a fellow waving a little black flag. He's standing on the steps of the omnibus. There come those other two fellows. Now they're all talking together. Look at the fellow with the flag. Maybe he ain't waving it."

"That ain't a flag, is it? That's his coat. Why, certainly, that's his coat."

"So it is. It's his coat. He's taken it off and

is waving it around his head. But would you look at him swing it."

"Oh, say, there isn't any life-saving station there. That's just a winter resort hotel omnibus that has brought over some of the boarders to see us drown."

"What's that idiot with the coat mean? What's he signaling, anyhow?"

"It looks as if he were trying to tell us to go north. There must be a life-saving station up there."

"No! He thinks we're fishing. Just giving us a merry hand. See? Ah, there, Billie."

"Well, I wish I could make something out of those signals. What do you suppose he means?"

"He don't mean anything. He's just playing."

"Well, if he'd just signal us to try the surf again, or to go to sea and wait, or go north, or go south, or go to hell—there would be some reason in it. But look at him. He just stands there and keeps his coat revolving like a wheel. The ass!"

"There come more people."

"Now there's quite a mob. Look! Isn't that a boat?"

"Where? Oh, I see where you mean. No, that's no boat."

"That fellow is still waving his coat."

"He must think we like to see him do that. Why don't he quit it? It don't mean anything."

"I don't know. I think he is trying to make us go north. It must be that there's a life-saving station there somewhere."

"Say, he ain't tired yet. Look at 'im wave."

"Wonder how long he can keep that up. He's been revolving his coat ever since he caught sight of us. He's an idiot. Why aren't they getting men to bring a boat out? A fishing boat—one of those big yawls—could come out here all right. Why don't he do something?"

"Oh, it's all right, now."

"They'll have a boat out here for us in less than no time, now that they've seen us."

A faint yellow tone came into the sky over the low land. The shadows on the sea slowly deepened. The wind bore coldness with it, and the men began to shiver.

"Holy smoke!" said one, allowing his voice

to express his impious mood, "if we keep on monkeying out here! If we've got to flounder out here all night!"

"Oh, we'll never have to stay here all night! Don't you worry. They've seen us now, and it won't be long before they'll come chasing out after us."

The shore grew dusky. The man waving a coat blended gradually into this gloom, and it swallowed in the same manner the omnibus and the group of people. The spray, when it dashed uproariously over the side, made the voyagers shrink and swear like men who were being branded.

"I'd like to catch the chump who waved that coat. I feel like soaking him one, just for luck."

"Why? What did he do?"

"Oh, nothing, but then he seemed so damned cheerful."

In the meantime the oiler rowed, and then the correspondent rowed, and then the oiler rowed. Gray-faced and bowed forward, they mechanically, turn by turn, plied the leaden oars. The form of the lighthouse had vanished from the southern horizon, but finally a pale star appeared, just lifting from the sea. The streaked saffron in the west passed before the all-merging darkness, and the sea to the east was black. The land had vanished, and was expressed only by the low and drear thunder of the surf.

"If I am going to be drowned—if I am going to be drowned—if I am going to be drowned, why, in the name of the seven mad gods who rule the sea, was I allowed to come thus far and contemplate sand and trees? Was I brought here merely to have my nose dragged away as I was about to nibble the sacred cheese of life?"

The patient captain, drooped over the water-jar, was sometimes obliged to speak to the oarsman.

"Keep her head up! Keep her head up!"

" 'Keep her head up,' sir." The voices were weary and low.

This was surely a quiet evening. All save the oarsman lay heavily and listlessly in the boat's bottom. As for him, his eyes were just capable of noting the tall black waves that swept forward in a most sinister silence, save for an occasional subdued growl of a crest.

The cook's head was on a thwart, and he looked without interest at the water under his nose. He was deep in other scenes. Finally he spoke. "Billie," he murmured, dreamfully, "what kind of pie do you like best?"

V

"Pie," said the oiler and the correspondent, agitatedly. "Don't talk about those things, blast you!"

"Well," said the cook, "I was just thinking about ham sandwiches, and—"

A night on the sea in an open boat is a long night. As darkness settled finally, the shine of the light, lifting from the sea in the south, changed to full gold. On the northern horizon a new light appeared, a small bluish gleam on the edge of the waters. These two lights were the furniture of the world. Otherwise there was nothing but waves.

Two men huddled in the stern, and distances were so magnificent in the dinghy that the rower was enabled to keep his feet partly warmed by thrusting them under his companions. Their legs indeed extended far under the rowing-seat until they touched the feet of the captain forward. Sometimes, despite the efforts of the tired oarsman, a wave came piling into the boat, an icy wave of the night, and the chilling water soaked them anew. They would twist their bodies for a moment and groan, and sleep the dead sleep once more, while the water in the boat gurgled about them as the craft rocked.

The plan of the oiler and the correspondent was for one to row until he lost the ability, and then arouse the other from his sea-water couch in the bottom of the boat.

The oiler plied the oars until his head drooped forward, and the overpowering sleep blinded him. And he rowed yet afterward. Then he touched a man in the bottom of the boat, and called his name. "Will you spell me for a little while?" he said, meekly.

"Sure, Billie," said the correspondent, awakening and dragging himself to a sitting position. They exchanged places carefully, and the oiler, cuddling down in the sea-water at the cook's side, seemed to go to sleep instantly.

The particular violence of the sea had ceased. The waves came without snarling. The obligation of the man at the oars was to keep the boat headed so that the tilt of the rollers would not capsize her, and to preserve her from filling when the crests rushed past. The black waves were silent and hard to be seen in the darkness. Often one was almost upon the boat before the oarsman was aware.

In a low voice the correspondent addressed the captain. He was not sure that the captain was awake, although this iron man seemed to be always awake. "Captain, shall I keep her making for that light north, sir?"

The same steady voice answered him. "Yes. Keep it about two points off the port bow."

The cook had tied a life-belt around himself in order to get even the warmth which this clumsy cork contrivance could donate, and he seemed almost stove-like when a rower, whose teeth invariably chattered wildly as soon as he ceased his labor, dropped down to sleep.

The correspondent, as he rowed, looked down at the two men sleeping underfoot. The cook's arm was around the oiler's shoulders, and, with their fragmentary clothing and haggard faces, they were the babes of the sea, a grotesque rendering of the old babes in the wood.

Later he must have grown stupid at his work, for suddenly there was a growling of water, and a crest came with a roar and a swash into the boat, and it was a wonder that it did not set the cook afloat in his life-belt. The cook continued to sleep, but the oiler sat up, blinking his eyes and shaking with the new cold.

"Oh, I'm awful sorry, Billie," said the correspondent, contritely.

"That's all right, old boy," said the oiler, and lay down again and was asleep.

Presently it seemed that even the captain dozed, and the correspondent thought that he was the one man afloat on all the oceans. The wind had a voice as it came over the waves, and it was sadder than the end.

There was a long, loud swishing astern of the boat, and a gleaming trail of phosphorescence, like blue flame, was furrowed on the black waters. It might have been made by a monstrous knife.

Then there came a stillness, while the correspondent breathed with open mouth and looked at the sea.

Suddenly there was another swish and another long flash of bluish light, and this time it was alongside the boat, and might almost have been reached with an oar. The correspondent saw an enormous fin speed like a shadow through the water, hurling the crystalline spray and leaving the long glowing trail.

The correspondent looked over his shoulder at the captain. His face was hidden, and he seemed to be asleep. He looked at the babes of the sea. They certainly were asleep. So, being bereft of sympathy, he leaned a little way to one side and swore softly into the sea.

But the thing did not then leave the vicinity of the boat. Ahead or astern, on one side or the other, at intervals long or short, fled the long sparkling streak, and there was to be heard the *whiroo* of the dark fin. The speed and power of the thing was greatly to be admired. It cut the water like a gigantic and keen projectile.

The presence of this biding thing did not affect the man with the same horror that it would if he had been a picnicker. He simply looked at the sea dully and swore in an undertone.

Nevertheless, it is true that he did not wish to be alone with the thing. He wished one of his companions to awaken by chance and keep him company with it. But the captain hung motionless over the water-jar, and the oiler and the cook in the bottom of the boat were plunged in slumber.

VI

"If I am going to be drowned—if I am going to be drowned—if I am going to be drowned, why, in the name of the seven mad gods who rule the sea, was I allowed to come thus far and contemplate sand and trees?"

During this dismal night, it may be remarked that a man would conclude that it was really the intention of the seven mad gods to drown him, despite the abominable injustice of it. For it was certainly an abominable injustice to drown a man who had worked so hard, so hard. The man felt it would be a crime most unnatural. Other people had drowned at sea since galleys swarmed with painted sails, but still—

When it occurs to a man that nature does not regard him as important, and that she feels she would not maim the universe by disposing of him, he at first wishes to throw bricks at the temple, and he hates deeply the fact that there are no bricks and no temples. Any visible expression of nature would surely be pelleted with his jeers.

Then, if there be no tangible thing to hoot he feels, perhaps, the desire to confront a personification and indulge in pleas, bowed to one knee, and with hands supplicant, saying: "Yes, but I love myself."

A high cold star on a winter's night is the word he feels that she says to him. Thereafter he knows the pathos of his situation.

The men in the dinghy had not discussed these matters, but each had, no doubt, reflected upon them in silence and according to his mind. There was seldom any expression upon their faces save the general one of complete weariness. Speech was devoted to the business of the boat.

To chime the notes of his emotion, a verse mysteriously entered the correspondent's head. He had even forgotten that he had forgotten this verse, but it suddenly was in his mind.

A soldier of the Legion lay dying in Algiers,
There was lack of woman's nursing, there was
    dearth of woman's tears;
But a comrade stood beside him, and he took
    that comrade's hand,
And he said: "I shall never see my own, my
    native land."

In his childhood, the correspondent had been made acquainted with the fact that a soldier of the Legion lay dying in Algiers, but he had never regarded the fact as important. Myriads of his school-fellows had informed him of the soldier's plight, but the dinning had naturally ended by making him perfectly indifferent. He had never considered it his affair that a soldier of the Legion lay dying in Algiers, nor had it appeared to him as a matter for sorrow. It was less to him than the breaking of a pencil's point.

Now, however, it quaintly came to him as a human, living thing. It was no longer merely a picture of a few throes in the breast of a poet, meanwhile drinking tea and warming

his feet at the grate; it was an actuality—stern, mournful, and fine.

The correspondent plainly saw the soldier. He lay on the sand with his feet out straight and still. While his pale left hand was upon his chest in an attempt to thwart the going of his life, the blood came between his fingers. In the far Algerian distance, a city of low square forms was set against a sky that was faint with the last sunset hues. The correspondent, plying the oars and dreaming of the slow and slower movements of the lips of the soldier, was moved by a profound and perfectly impersonal comprehension. He was sorry for the soldier of the Legion who lay dying in Algiers.

The thing which had followed the boat and waited had evidently grown bored at the delay. There was no longer to be heard the slash of the cutwater, and there was no longer the flame of the long trail. The light in the north still glimmered, but it was apparently no nearer to the boat. Sometimes the boom of the surf rang in the correspondent's ears, and he turned the craft seaward then and rowed harder. Southward, someone had evidently built a watch-fire on the beach. It was too low and too far to be seen, but it made a shimmering, roseate reflection upon the bluff back of it, and this could be discerned from the boat. The wind came stronger, and sometimes a wave suddenly raged out like a mountain-cat, and there was to be seen the sheen and sparkle of a broken crest.

The captain, in the bow, moved on his water-jar and sat erect. "Pretty long night," he observed to the correspondent. He looked at the shore. "Those life-saving people take their time."

"Did you see that shark playing around?"

"Yes, I saw him. He was a big fellow, all right."

"Wish I had known you were awake."

Later the correspondent spoke into the bottom of the boat.

"Billie!" There was a slow and gradual disentanglement. "Billie, will you spell me?"

"Sure," said the oiler.

As soon as the correspondent touched the cold comfortable sea-water in the bottom of the boat and had huddled close to the cook's life-belt he was deep in sleep, despite the fact that his teeth played all the popular airs. This sleep was so good to him that it was but a moment before he heard a voice call his name in a tone that demonstrated the last stages of exhaustion. "Will you spell me?"

"Sure, Billie."

The light in the north had mysteriously vanished, but the correspondent took his course from the wide-awake captain.

Later in the night they took the boat farther out to sea, and the captain directed the cook to take one oar at the stern and keep the boat facing the seas. He was to call out if he should hear the thunder of the surf. This plan enabled the oiler and the correspondent to get respite together. "We'll give those boys a chance to get into shape again," said the captain. They curled down and, after a few preliminary chatterings and trembles, slept once more the dead sleep. Neither knew they had bequeathed to the cook the company of another shark, or perhaps the same shark.

As the boat caroused on the waves, spray occasionally bumped over the side and gave them a fresh soaking, but this had no power to break their repose. The ominous slash of the wind and the water affected them as it would have affected mummies.

"Boys," said the cook, with the notes of every reluctance in his voice, "she's drifted in pretty close. I guess one of you had better take her to sea again." The correspondent, aroused, heard the crash of the toppled crests.

As he was rowing, the captain gave him some whisky-and-water, and this steadied the chills out of him. "If I ever get ashore and anybody shows me even a photograph of an oar—"

At last there was a short conversation.

"Billie . . . Billie, will you spell me?"

"Sure," said the oiler.

VII

When the correspondent again opened his eyes, the sea and the sky were each of the gray hue of the dawning. Later, carmine and gold was painted upon the waters. The morning appeared finally, in its splendor, with a sky of pure blue, and the sunlight flamed on the tips of the waves.

On the distant dunes were set many little black cottages, and a tall white windmill reared above them. No man, nor dog, nor bicycle appeared on the beach. The cottages might have formed a deserted village.

The voyagers scanned the shore. A conference was held in the boat. "Well," said the captain, "if no help is coming, we might better try a run through the surf right away. If we stay out here much longer we will be too weak to do anything for ourselves at all." The others silently acquiesced in this reasoning. The boat was headed for the beach. The correspondent wondered if none ever ascended the tall wind-tower, and if then they never looked seaward. This tower was a giant, standing with its back to the plight of the ants. It represented in a degree, to the correspondent, the serenity of nature amid the struggles of the individual—nature in the wind, and nature in the vision of men. She did not seem cruel to him then, nor beneficent, nor treacherous, nor wise. But she was indifferent, flatly indifferent. It is, perhaps, plausible that a man in this situation, impressed with the unconcern of the universe, should see the innumerable flaws of his life, and have them taste wickedly in his mind and wish for another chance. A distinction between right and wrong seems absurdly clear to him, then, in this new ignorance of the grave-edge, and he understands that if he were given another opportunity he would mend his conduct and his words, and be better and brighter during an introduction or at a tea.

"Now, boys," said the captain, "she is going to swamp sure. All we can do is to work her in as far as possible, and then when she swamps, pile out and scramble for the beach. Keep cool now, and don't jump until she swamps sure."

The oiler took the oars. Over his shoulders he scanned the surf. "Captain," he said, "I think I'd better bring her about, and keep her head-on to the seas and back her in."

"All right, Billie," said the captain. "Back her in." The oiler swung the boat then and, seated in the stern, the cook and the correspondent were obliged to look over their shoulders to contemplate the lonely and indifferent shore.

The monstrous in-shore rollers heaved the boat high until the men were again enabled to see the white sheets of water scudding up the slanted beach. "We won't get in very close," said the captain. Each time a man could wrest his attention from the rollers, he turned his glance toward the shore, and in the expression of the eyes during this contemplation there was a singular quality. The correspondent, observing the others, knew that they were not afraid, but the full meaning of their glances was shrouded.

As for himself, he was too tired to grapple fundamentally with the fact. He tried to coerce his mind into thinking of it, but the mind was dominated at this time by the muscles, and the muscles said they did not care. It merely occurred to him that if he should drown it would be a shame.

There were no hurried words, no pallor, no plain agitation. The men simply looked at the shore. "Now, remember to get well clear of the boat when you jump," said the captain.

Seaward the crest of a roller suddenly fell with a thunderous crash, and the long white comber came roaring down upon the boat. "Steady now," said the captain. The men were silent. They turned their eyes from the shore to the comber and waited. The boat slid up the incline, leaped at the furious top, bounced over it, and swung down the long back of the waves. Some water had been shipped and the cook bailed it out.

But the next crest crashed also. The tumbling boiling flood of white water caught the boat and whirled it almost perpendicular. Water swarmed in from all sides. The correspondent had his hands on the gunwale at this time, and when the water entered at that place he swiftly withdrew his fingers, as if he objected to wetting them.

The little boat, drunken with this weight of water, reeled and snuggled deeper into the sea.

"Bail her out, cook! Bail her out," said the captain.

"All right, captain," said the cook.

"Now, boys, the next one will do for us, sure," said the oiler. "Mind to jump clear of the boat."

The third wave moved forward, huge, furious, implacable. It fairly swallowed the dinghy, and almost simultaneously the men tumbled into the sea. A piece of life-belt had lain in the bottom of the boat, and as the correspondent went overboard he held this to his chest with his left hand.

The January water was icy, and he reflected immediately that it was colder than he had expected to find it off the coast of Florida. This appeared to his dazed mind as a fact important enough to be noted at the time. The coldness of the water was sad; it was tragic. This fact was somehow so mixed and confused with his opinion of his own situation that it seemed almost a proper reason for tears. The water was cold.

When he came to the surface he was conscious of little but the noisy water. Afterward he saw his companions in the sea. The oiler was ahead in the race. He was swimming strongly and rapidly. Off to the correspondent's left, the cook's great white and corked back bulged out of the water, and in the rear the captain was hanging with his one good hand to the keel of the overturned dinghy.

There is a certain immovable quality to a shore, and the correspondent wondered at it amid the confusion of the sea.

It seemed also very attractive, but the correspondent knew that it was a long journey, and he paddled leisurely. The piece of life-preserver lay under him, and sometimes he whirled down the incline of a wave as if he were on a hand-sled.

But finally he arrived at a place in the sea where travel was beset with difficulty. He did not pause swimming to inquire what manner of current had caught him, but there his progress ceased. The shore was set before him like a bit of scenery on a stage, and he looked at it and understood with his eyes each detail of it.

As the cook passed, much farther to the left, the captain was calling to him, "Turn over on your back, cook! Turn over on your back and use the oar."

"All right, sir." The cook turned on his back, and, paddling with an oar, went ahead as if he were a canoe.

Presently the boat also passed to the left of the correspondent with the captain clinging with one hand to the keel. He would have appeared like a man raising himself to look over a board fence, if it were not for the extraordinary gymnastics of the boat. The correspondent marveled that the captain could still hold to it.

They passed on, nearer to shore—the oiler, the cook, the captain—and following them went the water-jar, bouncing gaily over the seas.

The correspondent remained in the grip of this strange new enemy—a current. The shore, with its white slope of sand and its green bluff, topped with little silent cottages, was spread like a picture before him. It was very near to him then, but he was impressed as one who in a gallery looks at a scene from Brittany or Algiers.

He thought: "I am going to drown? Can it be possible? Can it be possible? Can it be possible?" Perhaps an individual must consider his own death to be the final phenomenon of nature.

But later a wave perhaps whirled him out of this small deadly current, for he found suddenly that he could again make progress toward the shore. Later still, he was aware that the captain, clinging with one hand to the keel of the dinghy, had his face turned away from the shore and toward him, and was calling his name. "Come to the boat! Come to the boat!"

In his struggle to reach the captain and the boat, he reflected that when one gets properly wearied, drowning must really be a comfortable arrangement, a cessation of hostilities accompanied by a large degree of relief, and he was glad of it, for the main thing in his mind for some moments had been horror of the temporary agony. He did not wish to be hurt.

Presently he saw a man running along the shore. He was undressing with most remarkable speed. Coat, trousers, shirt, everything flew magically off him.

"Come to the boat," called the captain.

"All right, captain." As the correspondent paddled, he saw the captain let himself down to bottom and leave the boat. Then the correspondent performed his one little marvel of the voyage. A large wave caught him and flung him with ease and supreme speed completely over the boat and far beyond it. It struck him even then as an event in gymnastics, and a true miracle of the sea. An overturned boat in the surf is not a plaything to a swimming man.

The correspondent arrived in water that reached only to his waist, but his condition did not enable him to stand for more than a moment. Each wave knocked him into a heap, and the undertow pulled at him.

Then he saw the man who had been running and undressing, and undressing and running, come bounding into the water. He dragged ashore the cook, and then waded toward the captain, but the captain waved him away, and sent him to the correspondent. He was naked, naked as a tree in winter, but a halo was about his head, and he shone like a saint. He gave a strong pull, and a long drag, and a bully heave at the correspondent's hand. The correspondent, schooled in the minor formulae, said: "Thanks, old man." But suddenly the man cried: "What's that?" He pointed a swift finger. The correspondent said: "Go."

In the shallows, face downward, lay the oiler. His forehead touched sand that was periodically, between each wave, clear of the sea.

The correspondent did not know all that transpired afterward. When he achieved safe ground he fell, striking the sand with each particular part of his body. It was as if he had dropped from a roof, but the thud was grateful to him.

It seems that instantly the beach was populated with men, with blankets, clothes, and flasks, and women with coffee-pots and all the remedies sacred to their minds. The welcome of the land to the men from the sea was warm and generous, but a still and dripping shape was carried slowly up the beach, and the land's welcome for it could only be the different and sinister hospitality of the grave.

When it came night, the white waves paced to and fro in the moonlight, and the wind brought the sound of the great sea's voice to the men on shore, and they felt that they could then be interpreters.

ERNEST HEMINGWAY *A Clean, Well-Lighted Place*

Ernest Hemingway (1898-   ) was born in Oak Park, Illinois. During World War I he volunteered for service in an ambulance corps in France and later transferred to the Italian Army, in which he was seriously wounded. After the war, he became a newspaper correspondent in Paris, where he met Ezra Pound and Gertrude Stein, who profoundly influenced his literary career.

The subject matter of Hemingway's writings is to be found in his personal experience. When he wrote *The Sun Also Rises*, 1926, the novel that made him famous, he was acclaimed as the voice of the "lost generation"—the young men and women who had suffered disillusionment in World War I. His short stories, now collected in *The Short Stories of Ernest Hemingway*, 1954, are further evidence of his variety and versatility. A list of Hemingway's major novels appears in Part I, in the headnote to his essay, "On the Blue Water."

Hemingway's writings reflect his philosophy that man is a a doomed creature, whose only hope is to face the inevitable stoically. Edmund Wilson says that he can "with barometric accuracy" seize "the real moral feeling of the moment" even though "his vision of life is one of perpetual annihilation." In his short stories and in his novels there appears the famous Hemingway dialogue—short, clipped, and bare, the very essence of speech. "A Clean, Well-Lighted Place" is characteristic of both his philosophy and his technique.

It was late and every one had left the café except an old man who sat in the shadow the leaves of the tree made against the electric light. In the day time the street was dusty, but at night the dew settled the dust and the old man liked to sit late because he was deaf and now at night it was quiet and he felt the difference. The two waiters inside the café knew that the old man was a little drunk, and while he was a good client they knew that if he became too drunk he would leave without paying, so they kept watch on him.

"Last week he tried to commit suicide," one waiter said.

"Why?"

"He was in despair."

"What about?"

"Nothing."

"How do you know it was nothing?"

"He has plenty of money."

They sat together at a table that was close against the wall near the door of the café and looked at the terrace where the tables were all empty except where the old man sat in the shadow of the leaves of the tree that moved slightly in the wind. A girl and a soldier went by in the street. The street light shone on the brass number on his collar. The girl wore no head covering and hurried beside him.

"The guard will pick him up," one waiter said.

"What does it matter if he gets what he's after?"

"He had better get off the street now. The guard will get him. They went by five minutes ago."

The old man sitting in the shadow rapped on his saucer with his glass. The younger waiter went over to him.

"What do you want?"

The old man looked at him. "Another brandy," he said.

"You'll be drunk," the waiter said. The old man looked at him. The waiter went away. "He'll stay all night," he said to his colleague. "I'm sleepy now. I never get into bed before three o'clock. He should have killed himself last week."

The waiter took the brandy bottle and another saucer from the counter inside the café and marched out to the old man's table. He put down the saucer and poured the glass full of brandy.

"You should have killed yourself last week," he said to the deaf man. The old man motioned with his finger. "A little more," he said. The waiter poured on into the glass so that the brandy slopped over and ran down the stem into the top saucer of the pile. "Thank you," the old man said. The waiter took the bottle back inside the café. He sat down at the table with his colleague again.

"He's drunk now," he said.

"He's drunk every night."

"What did he want to kill himself for?"

"How should I know."

"How did he do it?"

"He hung himself with a rope."

"Who cut him down?"

"His niece."

"Why did they do it?"

"Fear for his soul."

"How much money has he got?"

"He's got plenty."

"He must be eighty years old."

"Anyway I should say he was eighty."

"I wish he would go home. I never get to bed before three o'clock. What kind of hour is that to go to bed?"

"He stays up because he likes it."

"He's lonely. I'm not lonely. I have a wife waiting in bed for me."

"He had a wife once too."

"A wife would be no good to him now."

"You can't tell. He might be better with a wife."

"His niece looks after him."

"I know. You said she cut him down."

"I wouldn't want to be that old. An old man is a nasty thing."

"Not always. This old man is clean. He drinks without spilling. Even now, drunk. Look at him."

"I don't want to look at him. I wish he would go home. He has no regard for those who must work."

The old man looked from his glass across the square, then over at the waiters.

"Another brandy," he said, pointing to his glass. The waiter who was in a hurry came over.

"Finished," he said, speaking with that omission of syntax stupid people employ when talking to drunken people or foreigners. "No more tonight. Close now."

"Another," said the old man.

"No. Finished." The waiter wiped the edge of the table with a towel and shook his head.

The old man stood up, slowly counted the saucers, took a leather coin purse from his pocket and paid for the drinks, leaving half a peseta tip.

The waiter watched him go down the street, a very old man walking unsteadily but with dignity.

"Why didn't you let him stay and drink?" the unhurried waiter asked. They were putting up the shutters. "It is not half-past two."

"I want to go home to bed."

"What is an hour?"

"More to me than to him."

"An hour is the same."

"You talk like an old man yourself. He can buy a bottle and drink at home."

"It's not the same."

"No, it is not," agreed the waiter with a wife. He did not wish to be unjust. He was only in a hurry.

"And you? You have no fear of going home before your usual hour?"

"Are you trying to insult me?"

"No, hombre, only to make a joke."

"No," the waiter who was in a hurry said, rising from pulling down the metal shutters. "I have confidence. I am all confidence."

"You have youth, confidence, and a job," the older waiter said. "You have everything."

"And what do you lack?"

"Everything but work."

"You have everything I have."

"No. I have never had confidence and I am not young."

"Come on. Stop talking nonsense and lock up."

"I am of those who like to stay late at the café," the older waiter said. "With all those who do not want to go to bed. With all those who need a light for the night."

"I want to go home and into bed."

"We are of two different kinds," the older waiter said. He was now dressed to go home. "It is not only a question of youth and confidence although those things are very beautiful. Each night I am reluctant to close up because there may be someone who needs the café."

"Hombre, there are bodegas open all night long."

"You do not understand. This is a clean and pleasant café. It is well lighted. The light is very good and also, now, there are shadows of the leaves."

"Good night," said the younger waiter.

"Good night," the other said. Turning off the electric light he continued the conversation with himself. It is the light of course but it is necessary that the place be clean and pleasant. You do not want music. Certainly you do not want music. Nor can you stand before a bar with dignity although that is all that is provided for these hours. What did he fear? It was not fear or dread. It was a nothing that he knew too well. It was all a nothing and a man was nothing too. It was

only that and light was all it needed and a certain cleanness and order. Some lived in it and never felt it but he knew it all was nada y pues nada y nada y pues nada. Our nada who are in nada, nada be thy name thy kingdom nada thy will be nada in nada as it is in nada. Give us this nada our daily nada and nada us our nada as we nada our nadas and nada us not into nada but deliver us from nada; pues nada. Hail nothing full of nothing, nothing is with thee. He smiled and stood before a bar with a shining steam pressure coffee machine.

"What's yours?" asked the barman.

"Nada."

"Otro loco mas," said the barman and turned away.

"A little cup," said the waiter.

The barman poured it for him.

"The light is very bright and pleasant but the bar is unpolished," the waiter said.

The barman looked at him but did not answer. It was too late at night for conversation.

"You want another copita?" the barman asked.

"No, thank you," said the waiter and went out. He disliked bars and bodegas. A clean, well-lighted café was a very different thing. Now, without thinking further, he would go home to his room. He would lie in the bed and finally, with daylight, he would go to sleep. After all, he said to himself, it is probably only insomnia. Many must have it.

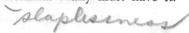

slaplessness

WILLIAM FAULKNER *Spotted Horses*

William Faulkner (1897-   ) has spent most of his life near Oxford, Mississippi, which is the "Jefferson" of his novels and short stories. In World War I he enlisted in the Canadian Air Force. After the war he returned to Oxford, where he took a few courses at the University of Mississippi and supported himself by doing odd jobs.

Faulkner's early novels brought him critical acclaim but little or no popularity or financial remuneration. *Sartoris*, 1929, is the first of his many novels centering loosely around the Sartoris family, suggested by his own wealthy Southern ancestors who had been reduced to genteel poverty by the Civil War. The Snopes family also make their first appearance in this novel and begin accumulating, by various rascalities, the wealth and power once held by the now degenerating aristocracy. In 1931 Faulkner published *Sanctuary*, which he says he deliberately made "horrific" in order to appeal to popular taste and earn enough money to support himself; in this aim he was successful. He has written several other novels and many short stories; the latter were collected in a volume published in 1950. More recently he has published two novels, *Requiem for a Nun*, 1951, and *A Fable*, 1954.

In 1939 Faulkner received the O. Henry Memorial Award, and in 1949, after the publication in 1948 of *Intruder in the Dust*, he received the Nobel Prize for literature "for his forceful and independently artistic contribution to modern American fiction." In all, Faulkner has, with Hemingway, received greater critical acclaim than any other contemporary American novelist.

Few writers achieve so much intense dramatic activity in a story as William Faulkner. In "Spotted Horses," for instance, every detail vibrates with a life of its own and gives added life to other details—the wild, odd-eyed horses, which symbolize the folly of Henry Armstid and his kind; the meek and passive Mrs. Armstid, who objectifies the results of ignorance and rascality; the taciturn and sneaking Flem Snopes; and the calm, sensible Mrs. Littlejohn, who is never deluded by the folly and madness of her neighbors.

Yes sir. Flem Snopes has filled that whole country full of spotted horses. You can hear folks running them all day and all night, whooping and hollering, and the horses running back and forth across them little wooden bridges ever now and then kind of like thunder. Here I was this morning pretty near halfway to town, with the team ambling along and me setting in the buckboard about half asleep, when all of a sudden something come swurging up outen the bushes and jumped the road clean, without touching hoof to it. It flew right over my team big as a billboard and flying through the air like a hawk. It taken me thirty minutes to stop my team and untangle the harness and the buckboard and hitch them up again.

That Flem Snopes. I be dog if he ain't a case, now. One morning about ten years ago the boys was just getting settled down on Varner's porch for a little talk and tobacco, when here come Flem out from behind the counter, with his coat off and his hair all parted, like he might have been clerking for Varner for ten years already. Folks all knowed him; it was a big family of them about five miles down the bottom. That year, at least. Share-cropping. They never stayed on any place over a year. Then they would move on to another place, with the chap or maybe the twins of that year's litter. It was a regular nest of them. But Flem. The rest of them stayed tenant farmers, moving ever year, but here come Flem one day, walking out from behind Jody Varner's counter like he owned it. And he wasn't there but a year or two before folks knowed that if him and Jody was both still in that store in ten years more it would be Jody clerking for Flem Snopes. Why, that fellow could make a nickel where it wasn't but four cents to begin with. He skun me in two trades myself, and the fellow that can do that, I just hope he'll get rich before I do; that's all.

All right. So here Flem was, clerking at Varner's, making a nickel here and there and not telling nobody about it. No, sir. Folks never knowed when Flem got the better of somebody lessen the fellow he beat told it. He'd just set there in the store-chair, chewing his tobacco and keeping his own business to his-self, until about a week later we'd find out it was somebody else's business he was keeping to hisself—provided the fellow he trimmed was mad enough to tell it. That's Flem.

We give him ten years to own ever thing Jody Varner had. But he never waited no ten years. I reckon you-all know that gal of Uncle Billy Varner's, the youngest one, Eula. Jody's sister. Ever Sunday ever yellow-wheeled buggy and curried riding horse in that country would be hitched to Bill Varner's fence, and the young bucks setting on the porch, swarming around Eula like bees around a honey pot. One of these here kind of big, soft-looking gals that could giggle richer than plowed new-ground. Wouldn't none of them leave before the others, and so they would set there on the porch until time to go home, with some of them with nine and ten miles to ride and then get up tomorrow and go back to the

field. So they would all leave together and they would ride in a clump down to the creek ford and hitch them curried horses and yellow-wheeled buggies and get out and fight one another. Then they would get in the buggies again and go on home.

Well, one day about a year ago, one of them yellow-wheeled buggies and one of them curried saddle-horses quit this country. We heard they was heading for Texas. The next day Uncle Billy and Eula and Flem come in to town in Uncle Bill's surrey, and when they come back, Flem and Eula was married. And on the next day we heard that two more of them yellow-wheeled buggies had left the country. They mought have gone to Texas, too. It's a big place.

Anyway, about a month after the wedding, Flem and Eula went to Texas, too. They was gone pretty near a year. Then one day last month, Eula come back, with a baby. We figgered up, and we decided that it was as well-growed a three-months-old baby as we ever see. It can already pull up on a chair. I reckon Texas makes big men quick, being a big place. Anyway, if it keeps on like it started, it'll be chewing tobacco and voting time it's eight years old.

And so last Friday here come Flem himself. He was on a wagon with another fellow. The other fellow had one of these two-gallon hats and a ivory-handled pistol and a box of gingersnaps sticking out of his hind pocket, and tied to the tail-gate of the wagon was about two dozen of them Texas ponies, hitched to one another with barbed wire. They was colored like parrots and they was quiet as doves, and ere a one of them would kill you quick as a rattlesnake. Nere a one of them had two eyes the same color, and nere a one of them had ever see a bridle, I reckon; and when that Texas man got down offen the wagon and walked up to them to show how gentle they was, one of them cut his vest clean offen him, same as with a razor.

Flem had done already disappeared; he had went on to see his wife, I reckon, and to see if that ere baby had done gone on to the field to help Uncle Billy plow, maybe. It was the Texas man that taken the horses on to Mrs. Littlejohn's lot. He had a little trouble at first, when they come to the gate, because they hadn't never see a fence before, and when he finally got them in and taken a pair of wire cutters and unhitched them and got them into the barn and poured some shell corn into the trough, they durn nigh tore down the barn. I reckon they thought that shell corn was bugs, maybe. So he left them in the lot and he announced that the auction would begin at sunup tomorrow.

That night we was setting on Mrs. Little-john's porch. You-all mind the moon was nigh full that night, and we could watch them spotted varmints swirling along the fence and back and forth across the lot same as min-nows in a pond. And then now and then they would all kind of huddle up against the barn and rest themselves by biting and kicking one another. We would hear a squeal, and then a set of hoofs would go Bam! against the barn, like a pistol. It sounded just like a fellow with a pistol, in a nest of cattymounts, taking his time.

It wasn't ere a man knowed yet if Flem owned them things or not. They just knowed one thing: that they wasn't never going to know for sho if Flem did or not, or if maybe he didn't just get on that wagon at the edge of town, for the ride or not. Even Eck Snopes didn't know, Flem's own cousin. But wasn't nobody surprised at that. We knowed that Flem would skin Eck quick as he would ere a one of us.

They was there by sunup next morning, some of them come twelve and sixteen miles, with seed-money tied up in tobacco sacks in their overalls, standing along the fence, when the Texas man come out of Mrs. Littlejohn's after breakfast and clumb onto the gate post with that ere white pistol butt sticking outen his hind pocket. He taken a new box of gin-gersnaps outen his pocket and bit the end offen it like a cigar and spit out the paper, and said the auction was open. And still they was coming up in wagons and a horse- and mule-back and hitching the teams across the road and coming to the fence. Flem wasn't nowhere in sight.

But he couldn't get them started. He begun to work on Eck, because Eck holp him last night to get them into the barn and feed them that shell corn. Eck got out just in time. He come outen that barn like a chip on the crest of a busted dam of water, and clumb into the wagon just in time.

He was working on Eck when Henry Arm-stid come up in his wagon. Eck was saying he was skeered to bid on one of them, because he might get it, and the Texas man says, "Them ponies? Them little horses?" He clumb down offen the gate post and went to-ward the horses. They broke and run, and him following them, kind of chirping to them, with his hand out like he was fixing to catch a fly, until he got three or four of them cor-nered. Then he jumped into them, and then we couldn't see nothing for a while because of the dust. It was a big cloud of it, and them blare-eyed, spotted things swoaring outen it twenty foot to a jump, in forty directions without counting up. Then the dust settled and there they was, that Texas man and the horse. He had its head twisted clean around like a owl's head. Its legs was braced and it was trembling like a new bride and groaning like a sawmill, and him holding its head wrung clean around on its neck so it was snuffing sky. "Look it over," he says, with his heels dug too and that white pistol sticking outen his pocket and his neck swole up like a spreading adder's until you could just tell what he was saying, cussing the horse and talking to us all at once: "Look him over, the fiddle-headed son of fourteen fathers. Try him, buy him; you will get the best—" Then it was all dust again, and we couldn't see nothing but spotted hide and mane, and that ere Texas man's boot-heels like a couple of walnuts on two strings, and after a while that two-gallon hat come sailing out like a fat old hen crossing a fence.

When the dust settled again, he was just getting outen the far fence corner, brushing himself off. He come and got his hat and brushed it off and come and clumb onto the gate post again. He was breathing hard. The hammer-head horse was still running round and round the lot like a merry-go-round at a fair. That was when Henry Armstid come shoving up to the gate in them patched over-alls and one of them dangle-armed shirts of hisn. Hadn't nobody noticed him until then. We was all watching the Texas man and the horses. Even Mrs. Littlejohn; she had done come out and built a fire under the wash-pot in her back yard, and she would stand at the fence a while and then go back into the house and come out again with a arm full of wash and stand at the fence again. Well, here come Henry shoving up, and then we see Mrs. Armstid right behind him, in that ere faded wrapper and sunbonnet and them tennis shoes. "Git on back to that wagon," Henry says.

"Henry," she says.

"Here, boys," the Texas man says; "make room for missus to git up and see. Come on Henry," he says; "here's your chance to buy that saddle-horse missus has been wanting. What about ten dollars, Henry?"

"Henry," Mrs. Armstid says. She put her hand on Henry's arm. Henry knocked her hand down.

"Git on back to that wagon, like I told you," he says.

Mrs. Armstid never moved. She stood behind Henry, with her hands rolled into her dress, not looking at nothing. "He hain't no more despair than to buy one of them things," she says. "And us not five dollars ahead of the pore house, he hain't no more despair." It was the truth, too. They ain't never made more than a bare living offen that place of theirs, and them with four chaps and the very clothes they wears she earns by weaving by the firelight at night while Henry's asleep.

"Shut your mouth and git on back to that wagon," Henry says. "Do you want I taken a wagon stake to you here in the big road?"

Well, that Texas man taken one look at her. Then he begun on Eck again, like Henry wasn't even there. But Eck was skeered. "I can git me a snapping turtle or a water moccasin for nothing. I ain't going to buy none."

So the Texas man said he would give Eck a horse. "To start the auction, and because you holp me last night. If you'll start the bidding on the next horse," he says, "I'll give you that fiddle-head horse."

I wish you could have seen them, standing there with their seed-money in their pockets, watching that Texas man give Eck Snopes a live horse, all fixed to call him a fool if he taken it or not. Finally Eck says he'll take it. "Only I just starts the bidding," he says. "I don't have to buy the next one lessen I ain't overtopped." The Texas man said all right,

and Eck bid a dollar on the next one, with Henry Armstid standing there with his mouth already open, watching Eck and the Texas man like a mad-dog or something. "A dollar," Eck says.

The Texas man looked at Eck. His mouth was already open too, like he had started to say something and what he was going to say had up and died on him. "A dollar? You mean, *one* dollar, Eck?"

"Durn it," Eck says; "two dollars, then."

Well, sir, I wish you could a seen that Texas man. He taken out that gingersnap box and held it up and looked into it, careful, like it might have been a diamond ring in it, or a spider. Then he throwed it away and wiped his face with a bandanna. "Well," he says. "Well. Two dollars. Two dollars. Is your pulse all right, Eck?" he says. "Do you have ager-sweats at night, maybe?" he says. "Well," he says, "I got to take it. But are you boys going to stand there and see Eck get two horses at a dollar a head?"

That done it. I be dog if he wasn't nigh as smart as Flem Snopes. He hadn't no more than got the words outen his mouth before here was Henry Armstid, waving his hand. "Three dollars," Henry says. Mrs. Armstid tried to hold him again. He knocked her hand off, shoving up to the gate post.

"Mister," Mrs. Armstid says, "we got chaps in the house and not corn to feed the stock. We got five dollars I earned my chaps a-weaving after dark, and him snoring in the bed. And he hain't no more despair."

"Henry bid three dollars," the Texas man says. "Raise him a dollar, Eck, and the horse is yours."

"Henry," Mrs. Armstid says.

"Raise him, Eck," the Texas man says.

"Four dollars," Eck says.

"Five dollars," Henry says, shaking his fist. He shoved up right under the gate post. Mrs. Armstid was looking at the Texas man too.

"Mister," she says, "if you take that five dollars I earned my chaps a-weaving for one of them things, it'll be a curse onto you and yourn during all the time of man."

But it wasn't no stopping Henry. He had shoved up, waving his fist at the Texas man. He opened it; the money was in nickels and quarters, and one dollar bill that looked like a cow's cud. "Five dollars," he says. "And the man that raises it'll have to beat my head off, or I'll beat hisn."

"All right," the Texas man says. "Five dollars is bid. But don't you shake your hand at me."

It taken till nigh sundown before the last one was sold. He got them hotted up once and the bidding got up to seven dollars and a quarter, but most of them went around three or four dollars, him setting on the gate post and picking the horses out one at a time by mouth-word, and Mrs. Littlejohn pumping up and down at the tub and stopping and coming to the fence for a while and going back to the tub again. She had done got done too, and the wash was hung on the line in the back yard, and we could smell supper cooking. Finally they was all sold; he swapped the last two and the wagon for a buckboard.

We was all kind of tired, but Henry Armstid looked more like a mad-dog than ever. When he bought, Mrs. Armstid had went back to the wagon, setting in it behind them two rabbit-sized, bone-pore mules, and the wagon itself looking like it would fall all to pieces soon as the mules moved. Henry hadn't even waited to pull it outen the road; it was still in the middle of the road and her setting in it, not looking at nothing, ever since this morning.

Henry was right up against the gate. He went up to the Texas man. "I bought a horse and I paid cash," Henry says. "And yet you expect me to stand around here until they are all sold before I can get my horse. I'm going to take my horse outen that lot."

The Texas man looked at Henry. He talked like he might have been asking for a cup of coffee at the table. "Take your horse," he says.

Then Henry quit looking at the Texas man. He begun to swallow, holding onto the gate. "Ain't you going to help me?" he says.

"It ain't my horse," the Texas man says.

Henry never looked at the Texas man again, he never looked at nobody. "Who'll help me catch my horse?" he says. Never nobody said nothing. "Bring the plowline," Henry says. Mrs. Armstid got outen the wagon and brought the plowline. The Texas man got down offen the post. The woman made to pass him, carrying the rope.

"Don't you go in there, missus," the Texas man says.

Henry opened the gate. He didn't look back. "Come on here," he says.

"Don't you go in there, missus," the Texas man says.

Mrs. Armstid wasn't looking at nobody, neither, with her hands across her middle, holding the rope. "I reckon I better," she says. Her and Henry went into the lot. The horses broke and run. Henry and Mrs. Armstid followed.

"Get him into the corner," Henry says. They got Henry's horse cornered finally, and Henry taken the rope, but Mrs. Armstid let the horse get out. They hemmed it up again, but Mrs. Armstid let it get out again, and Henry turned and hit her with the rope. "Why didn't you head him back?" Henry says. He hit her again. "Why didn't you?" It was about that time I looked around and see Flem Snopes standing there.

It was the Texas man that done something. He moved fast for a big man. He caught the rope before Henry could hit the third time, and Henry whirled and made like he would jump at the Texas man. But he never jumped. The Texas man went and taken Henry's arm and led him outen the lot. Mrs. Armstid come behind them and the Texas man taken some money outen his pocket and he give it into Mrs. Armstid's hand. "Get him into the wagon and take him on home," the Texas man says, like he might have been telling them he enjoyed his supper.

Then here come Flem. "What's that for, Buck?" Flem says.

"Thinks he bought one of them ponies," the Texas man says. "Get him on away, missus."

But Henry wouldn't go. "Give him back that money," he says. "I bought that horse and I aim to have him if I have to shoot him."

And there was Flem, standing there with his hands in his pockets, chewing, like he had just happened to be passing.

"You take your money and I take my horse," Henry says. "Give it back to him," he says to Mrs. Armstid.

"You don't own no horse of mine," the Texas man says. "Get him on home, missus."

Then Henry seen Flem. "You got something to do with these horses," he says. "I bought one. Here's the money for it." He taken the bill outen Mrs. Armstid's hand. He offered it to Flem. "I bought one. Ask him. Here. Here's the money," he says, giving the bill to Flem.

When Flem taken the money, the Texas man dropped the rope he had snatched outen Henry's hand. He had done sent Eck Snopes's boy up to the store for another box of ginger-snaps, and he taken the box outen his pocket and looked into it. It was empty and he dropped it on the ground. "Mr. Snopes will have your money for you tomorrow," he says to Mrs. Armstid. "You can get it from him tomorrow. He don't own no horse. You get him into the wagon and get him on home." Mrs. Armstid went back to the wagon and got in. "Where's that ere buckboard I bought?" the Texas man says. It was after sundown then. And then Mrs. Littlejohn come out on the porch and rung the supper bell.

I come on in and et supper. Mrs. Littlejohn would bring in a pan of bread or something, then she would go out to the porch a minute and come back and tell us. The Texas man had hitched his team to the buckboard he had swapped them last two horses for, and him and Flem had gone, and then she told that the rest of them that never had ropes had went back to the store with I. O. Snopes to get some ropes, and wasn't nobody at the gate but Henry Armstid, and Mrs. Armstid setting in the wagon in the road, and Eck Snopes and that boy of hisn. "I don't care how many of them fool men gets killed by them things," Mrs. Littlejohn says, "but I ain't going to let Eck Snopes take that boy into that lot again." So she went down to the gate, but she come back without the boy or Eck neither.

"It ain't no need to worry about that boy," I says. "He's charmed." He was right behind Eck last night when Eck went to help feed them. The whole drove of them jumped clean over that boy's head and never touched him. It was Eck that touched him. Eck snatched him into the wagon and taken a rope and frailed the tar outen him.

So I had done et and went to my room and was undressing, long as I had a long trip to make next day; I was trying to sell a machine to Mrs. Bundren up past Whiteleaf; when Henry Armstid opened that gate and went in by hisself. They couldn't make him wait for the balance of them to get back with their ropes. Eck Snopes said he tried to make Henry wait, but Henry wouldn't do it. Eck said Henry walked right up to them and that when they broke, they run clean over Henry like a hay-mow breaking down. Eck said he snatched that boy of hisn out of the way just in time and that them things went through that gate like a creek flood and into the wagons and teams hitched side the road, busting wagon tongues and snapping harness like it was fishing-line, with Mrs. Armstid still setting in their wagon in the middle of it like something carved outen wood. Then they scattered, wild horses and tame mules with pieces of harness and singletrees dangling offen them, both ways up and down the road.

"There goes ourn, paw!" Eck said his boy said. "There it goes, into Mrs. Littlejohn's house." Eck says it run right up the steps and into the house like a boarder late for supper. I reckon so. Anyway, I was in my room, in my underclothes, with one sock on and one sock in my hand, leaning out the window when the commotion busted out, when I heard something run into the melodeon in the hall; it sounded like a railroad engine. Then the door to my room come sailing in like when you throw a tin bucket top into the wind and I looked over my shoulder and see something that looked like a fourteen-foot pin-wheel a-blaring its eyes at me. It had to blare them fast, because I was already done jumped out the window.

I reckon it was anxious, too. I reckon it hadn't never seen barbed wire or shell corn before, but I know it hadn't never seen under-clothes before, or maybe it was a sewing-machine agent it hadn't never seen. Anyway, it whirled and turned to run back up the hall and outen the house, when it met Eck Snopes and that boy just coming in, carrying a rope. It swirled again and run down the hall and out the back door just in time to meet Mrs. Littlejohn. She had just gathered up the clothes she had washed, and she was coming onto the back porch with a armful of wash-ing in one hand and a scrubbing-board in the other, when the horse skidded up to her, trying to stop and swirl again. It never taken Mrs. Littlejohn no time a-tall.

"Git outen here, you son," she says. She hit it across the face with the scrubbing-board; that ere scrubbing-board split as neat as ere a axe could have done it, and when the horse swirled to run back up the hall, she hit it again with what was left of the scrubbing-board, not on the head this time. "And stay out," she says.

Eck and that boy was halfway down the hall by this time. I reckon that horse looked like a pinwheel to Eck too. "Git to hell outen here, Ad!" Eck says. Only there wasn't time. Eck dropped flat on his face, but the boy never moved. The boy was about a yard tall maybe, in overalls just like Eck's; that horse swoared over his head without touching a hair. I saw that, because I was just coming back up the front steps, still carrying that ere sock and still in my underclothes, when the horse come onto the porch again. It taken one look at me and swirled again and run to the end of the porch and jumped the banisters and the lot fence like a hen-hawk and lit in the lot running and went out the gate again and jumped eight or ten upside-down wagons and went on down the road. It was a full moon then. Mrs. Armstid was still setting in the wagon like she had done been carved outen wood and left there and forgot.

That horse. It ain't never missed a lick. It was going about forty miles a hour when it come to the bridge over the creek. It would have had a clear road, but it so happened that Vernon Tull was already using the bridge when it got there. He was coming back from town; he hadn't heard about the auction; him and his wife and three daughters and Mrs. Tull's aunt, all setting in chairs in the wagon bed, and all asleep, including the mules. They waked up when the horse hit the bridge one time, but Tull said the first he knew was when the mules tried to turn the wagon around in the middle of the bridge and he seen that spotted varmint run right twixt the mules and run up the wagon tongue like a squirrel. He said he just had time to hit it across the face with his whip-stock, because about that time the mules turned the wagon around on that ere one-way bridge and

that horse clumb across onto the bridge again and went on, with Vernon standing up in the wagon and kicking at it.

Tull said the mules turned in the harness and clumb back into the wagon too, with Tull trying to beat them out again, with the reins wrapped around his wrist. After that he says all he seen was overturned chairs and women-folks' legs and white drawers shining in the moonlight, and his mules and that spotted horse going on up the road like a ghost.

The mules jerked Tull outen the wagon and drug him a spell on the bridge before the reins broke. They thought at first that he was dead, and while they was kneeling around him, picking the bridge splinters outen him, here come Eck and that boy, still carrying the rope. They was running and breathing a little hard. "Where'd he go?" Eck said.

I went back and got my pants and shirt and shoes on just in time to go and help get Henry Armstid outen the trash in the lot. I be dog if he didn't look like he was dead, with his head hanging back and his teeth showing in the moonlight, and a little rim of white under his eye-lids. We could still hear them horses, here and there; hadn't none of them got more than four-five miles away yet, not knowing the country, I reckon. So we could hear them and folks yelling now and then: "Whooey. Head him!"

We toted Henry into Mrs. Littlejohn's. She was in the hall; she hadn't put down the armful of clothes. She taken one look at us, and she laid down the busted scrubbing-board and taken up the lamp and opened a empty door. "Bring him in here," she says.

We toted him in and laid him on the bed. Mrs. Littlejohn set the lamp on the dresser, still carrying the clothes. "I'll declare, you men," she says. Our shadows was way up the wall, tiptoeing too; we could hear ourselves breathing. "Better get his wife," Mrs. Little-john says. She went out, carrying the clothes.

"I reckon we had," Quick says. "Go get her, somebody."

"Whyn't you go?" Winterbottom says.

"Let Ernest git her," Durley says. "He lives neighbors with them."

Ernest went to fetch her. I be dog if Henry didn't look like he was dead. Mrs. Littlejohn come back, with a kettle and some towels.

She went to work on Henry, and then Mrs. Armstid and Ernest come in. Mrs. Armstid come to the foot of the bed and stood there, with her hands rolled into her apron, watching what Mrs. Littlejohn was doing, I reckon.

"You men get outen the way," Mrs. Littlejohn says. "Git outside," she says. "See if you can't find something else to play with that will kill some more of you."

"Is he dead?" Winterbottom says.

"It ain't your fault if he ain't," Mrs. Littlejohn says. "Go tell Will Varner to come up here. I reckon a man ain't so different from a mule, come long come short. Except maybe a mule's got more sense."

We went to get Uncle Billy. It was a full moon. We could hear them, now and then, four miles away: "Whooey. Head him." The country was full of them, one on ever wooden bridge in the land, running across it like thunder: "Whooey. There he goes. Head him."

We hadn't got far before Henry begun to scream. I reckon Mrs. Littlejohn's water had brung him to; anyway, he wasn't dead. We went on to Uncle Billy's. The house was dark. We called to him, and after a while the window opened and Uncle Billy put his head out, peart as a peckerwood, listening. "Are they still trying to catch them durn rabbits?" he says.

He come down, with his britches on over his night-shirt and his suspenders dangling, carrying his horse-doctoring grip. "Yes, sir," he says, cocking his head like a woodpecker; "they're still a-trying."

We could hear Henry before we reached Mrs. Littlejohn's. He was going Ah-Ah-Ah. We stopped in the yard. Uncle Billy went on in. We could hear Henry. We stood in the yard, hearing them on the bridges, this-a-way and that: "Whooey. Whooey."

"Eck Snopes ought to caught hisn," Ernest says.

"Looks like he ought," Winterbottom said.

Henry was going Ah-Ah-Ah steady in the house; then he begun to scream. "Uncle Billy's started," Quick says. We looked into the hall. We could see the light where the door was. Then Mrs. Littlejohn come out.

"Will needs some help," she says. "You, Ernest. You'll do." Ernest went into the house.

"Hear them?" Quick said. "That one was on Four Mile bridge." We could hear them; it sounded like thunder a long way off; it didn't last long:

"Whooey."

We could hear Henry: "Ah-Ah-Ah-Ah-Ah."

"They are both started now," Winterbottom says. "Ernest too."

That was early in the night. Which was a good thing, because it taken a long night for folks to chase them things right and for Henry to lay there and holler, being as Uncle Billy never had none of this here chloryfoam to set Henry's leg with. So it was considerate in Flem to get them started early. And what do you reckon Flem's com-ment was?

That's right. Nothing. Because he wasn't there. Hadn't nobody see him since that Texas man left.

That was Saturday night. I reckon Mrs. Armstid got home about daylight, to see about the chaps. I don't know where they thought her and Henry was. But lucky the oldest one was a gal, about twelve, big enough to take care of the little ones. Which she did for the next two days. Mrs. Armstid would nurse Henry all night and work in the kitchen for hern and Henry's keep, and in the afternoon she would drive home (it was about four miles) to see to the chaps. She would cook up a pot of victuals and leave it on the stove, and the gal would bar the house and keep the little ones quiet. I would hear Mrs. Littlejohn and Mrs. Armstid talking in the kitchen. "How are the chaps making out?" Mrs. Littlejohn says.

"All right," Mrs. Armstid says.

"Don't they git skeered at night?" Mrs. Littlejohn says.

"Ina May bars the door when I leave," Mrs. Armstid says. "She's got the axe in bed with her. I reckon she can make out."

I reckon they did. And I reckon Mrs. Armstid was waiting for Flem to come back to town; hadn't nobody seen him until this morning; to get her money the Texas man said Flem was keeping for her. Sho. I reckon she was.

Anyway, I heard Mrs. Armstid and Mrs. Littlejohn talking in the kitchen this morning while I was eating breakfast. Mrs. Littlejohn had just told Mrs. Armstid that Flem was in town. "You can ask him for that five dollars," Mrs. Littlejohn says.

"You reckon he'll give it to me?" Mrs. Armstid says.

Mrs. Littlejohn was washing dishes, washing them like a man, like they was made out of iron. "No," she says. "But asking him won't do no hurt. It might shame him. I don't reckon it will, but it might."

"If he wouldn't give it back, it ain't no use to ask," Mrs. Armstid says.

"Suit yourself," Mrs. Littlejohn says. "It's your money."

I could hear the dishes.

"Do you reckon he might give it back to me?" Mrs. Armstid says. "That Texas man said he would. He said I could get it from Mr. Snopes later."

"Then go and ask him for it," Mrs. Littlejohn says.

I could hear the dishes.

"He won't give it back to me," Mrs. Armstid says.

"All right," Mrs. Littlejohn says. "Don't ask him for it, then."

I could hear the dishes; Mrs. Armstid was helping. "You don't reckon he would, do you?" she says. Mrs. Littlejohn never said nothing. It sounded like she was throwing the dishes at one another. "Maybe I better go and talk to Henry about it," Mrs. Armstid says.

"I would," Mrs. Littlejohn says. I be dog if it didn't sound like she had two plates in her hands, beating them together. "Then Henry can buy another five-dollar horse with it. Maybe he'll buy one next time that will out and out kill him. If I thought that, I'd give you back the money, myself."

"I reckon I better talk to him first," Mrs. Armstid said. Then it sounded like Mrs. Littlejohn taken up all the dishes and throwed them at the cook-stove, and I come away.

That was this morning. I had been up to Bundren's and back, and I thought that things would have kind of settled down. So after breakfast, I went up to the store. And there was Flem, setting in the store chair and whittling, like he might not have ever moved since he come to clerk for Jody Varner. I. O. was leaning in the door, in his shirt sleeves and with his hair parted too, same as Flem was

before he turned the clerking job over to I. O. It's a funny thing about them Snopes: they all looks alike, yet there ain't ere a two of them that claims brothers. They're always just cousins, like Flem and Eck and Flem and I. O. Eck was there too, squatting against the wall, him and that boy, eating cheese and crackers outen a sack; they told me that Eck hadn't been home a-tall. And that Lon Quick hadn't got back to town, even. He followed his horse clean down to Samson's Bridge, with a wagon and a camp outfit. Eck finally caught one of hisn. It run into a blind lane at Freeman's and Eck and the boy taken and tied their rope across the end of the lane, about three foot high. The horse come to the end of the lane and whirled and run back without ever stopping. Eck says it never seen the rope a-tall. He says it looked just like one of these here Christmas pinwheels. "Didn't it try to run again?" I says.

"No," Eck says, eating a bite of cheese offen his knife blade. "Just kicked some."

"Kicked some?" I says.

"It broke its neck," Eck says.

Well, they was squatting there, about six of them, talking, talking at Flem; never nobody knowed yet if Flem had ere a interest in them horses or not. So finally I come right out and asked him. "Flem's done skun all of us so much," I says, "that we're proud of him. Come on, Flem," I says, "how much did you and that Texas man make offen them horses? You can tell us. Ain't nobody here but Eck that bought one of them; the others ain't got back to town yet, and Eck's your own cousin; he'll be proud to hear, too. How much did you-all make?"

They was all whittling, not looking at Flem, making like they was studying. But you could a heard a pin drop. And I. O. He had been rubbing his back up and down on the door, but he stopped now, watching Flem like a pointing dog. Flem finished cutting the sliver offen his stick. He spit across the porch, into the road. "Twarn't none of my horses," he says.

I. O. cackled, like a hen, slapping his legs with both hands. "You boys might just as well quit trying to get ahead of Flem," he said.

Well, about that time I see Mrs. Armstid

come outen Mrs. Littlejohn's gate, coming up the road. I never said nothing. I says, "Well, if a man can't take care of himself in a trade, he can't blame the man that trims him."

Flem never said nothing, trimming at the stick. He hadn't seen Mrs. Armstid. "Yes, sir," I says. "A fellow like Henry Armstid ain't got nobody but hisself to blame."

"Course he ain't," I. O. says. He ain't seen her, either. "Henry Armstid's a born fool. Always is been. If Flem hadn't a got his money, somebody else would."

We looked at Flem. He never moved. Mrs. Armstid come on up the road.

"That's right," I says. "But come to think of it, Henry never bought no horse." We looked at Flem; you could a heard a match drop. "That Texas man told her to get that five dollars back from Flem next day. I reckon Flem's done already taken that money to Mrs. Littlejohn's and give it to Mrs. Armstid."

We watched Flem. I. O. quit rubbing his back against the door again. After a while Flem raised his head and spit across the porch, into the dust. I. O. cackled, just like a hen. "Ain't he a beating fellow, now?" I. O. says.

Mrs. Armstid was getting closer, so I kept on talking, watching to see if Flem would look up and see her. But he never looked up. I went on talking about Tull, about how he was going to sue Flem, and Flem setting there, whittling his stick, not saying nothing else after he said they wasn't none of his horses.

Then I. O. happened to look around. He seen Mrs. Armstid. "Pssssst!" he says. Flem looked up. "Here she comes!" I. O. says. "Go out the back. I'll tell her you done went in to town today."

But Flem never moved. He just set there, whittling, and we watched Mrs. Armstid come up onto the porch, in that ere faded sunbonnet and wrapper and them tennis shoes that make a kind of hissing noise on the porch. She come onto the porch and stopped, her hands rolled into her dress in front, not looking at nothing.

"He said Saturday," she says, "that he wouldn't sell Henry no horse. He said I could get the money from you."

Flem looked up. The knife never stopped. It went on trimming off a sliver same as if he

was watching it. "He taken that money off with him when he left," Flem says.

Mrs. Armstid never looked at nothing. We never looked at her, neither, except that boy of Eck's. He had a half-et cracker in his hand, watching her, chewing.

"He said Henry hadn't bought no horse," Mrs. Armstid says. "He said for me to get the money from you today."

"I reckon he forgot about it," Flem said. "He taken that money off with him Saturday." He whittled again. I. O. kept on rubbing his back, slow. He licked his lips. After a while the woman looked up the road, where it went on up the hill, toward the graveyard. She looked up that way for a while, with that boy of Eck's watching her and I. O. rubbing his back slow against the door. Then she turned back toward the steps.

"I reckon it's time to get dinner started," she says.

"How's Henry this morning, Mrs. Armstid?" Winterbottom says.

She looked at Winterbottom; she almost stopped. "He's resting, I thank you kindly," she says.

Flem got up, outen the chair, putting his knife away. He spit across the porch. "Wait a minute, Mrs. Armstid," he says. She stopped again. She didn't look at him. Flem went on into the store, with I. O. done quit rubbing his back now, with his head craned after Flem, and Mrs. Armstid standing there with her hands rolled into her dress, not looking at nothing. A wagon come up the road and passed; it was Freeman, on the way to town. Then Flem come out again, with I. O. still watching him. Flem had one of these little striped sacks of Jody Varner's candy; I bet he still owes Jody that nickel, too. He put the sack into Mrs. Armstid's hand, like he would have put it into a hollow stump. He spit again across the porch. "A little sweetening for the chaps," he says.

"You're right kind," Mrs. Armstid says. She held the sack of candy in her hand, not looking at nothing. Eck's boy was watching the sack, the half-et cracker in his hand; he wasn't chewing now. He watched Mrs. Armstid roll the sack into her apron. "I reckon I better get on back and help with dinner," she says. She turned and went back across the porch.

Flem set down in the chair again and opened his knife. He spit across the porch again, past Mrs. Armstid where she hadn't went down the steps yet. Then she went on, in that ere sunbonnet and wrapper all the same color, back down the road toward Mrs. Littlejohn's. You couldn't see her dress move, like a natural woman walking. She looked like a old snag still standing up and moving along on a high water. We watched her turn in at Mrs. Little-

john's and go outen sight. Flem was whittling. I. O. begun to rub his back on the door. Then he begun to cackle, just like a durn hen.

"You boys might just as well quit trying," I. O. says. "You can't git ahead of Flem. You can't touch him. Ain't he a sight, now?"

I be dog if he ain't. If I had brung a herd of wild cattymounts into town and sold them to my neighbors and kinfolks, they would have lynched me. Yes, sir.

FRANK O'CONNOR *Masculine Protest*

Frank O'Connor (1903-   ), whose real name is Michael O'Donovan, was born in Cork and educated by the Christian Brothers. A librarian by profession, he has long been a member of the Irish Academy of Letters. Æ (George Russell, the famous Irish poet and artist) encouraged him to develop his literary talents. He has published about twenty-five books, mainly novels and stories, though several are on travel and literature.

Beginning with his first important book, *Guests of the Nation*, 1931, which is concerned with Michael Collins and the Irish rebellion, he has held close to the Irish scene. He likes to spend his afternoons walking and cycling in the streets of Dublin, where he talks with the people he meets and picks up most of his stories. Only the language and circumstance of his stories, however, are local and national. "All the rest," he says, "is, or should be, a part of human condition. I prefer to write about Ireland and Irish people merely because I know to a syllable how everything in Ireland can be said." William Butler Yeats once remarked: "O'Connor is doing for Ireland what Chekhov did for Russia."

In his theory of the short story, O'Connor stresses its likeness to a pure lyric poem. "It doesn't deal with problems; it doesn't have any solution to offer; it just states a human condition. . . . It is a lyric cry in the face of destiny."

For months things had been getting worse between Mother and me. At the time I was twelve, and we were living in Boharna, a small town twenty miles from the city—Father, Mother, Martha, and I. Father worked in the County Council and we didn't see much of him. I suppose that threw me more on Mother,

MASCULINE PROTEST: Reprinted from *More Stories by Frank O'Connor*, by permission of Alfred A. Knopf, Inc. Copyright 1952, 1954 by Frank O'Connor.

but I could be perfectly happy sitting with her all day if only she let me. She didn't, though. She was always inventing excuses to get rid of me, even giving me money to go to the pictures, which she knew Father didn't like because I wasn't very bright at school and he thought the pictures were bad for me.

I blamed a lot of it on Martha at first. Martha was sly, and she was always trying to get inside me with Mother. She was always saving, whereas I always found money burned a hole in my pocket, and it was only to spite her that I kept a savings bank at all. As well as that, she told Mother about all the scrapes I got into. They weren't what you'd really call scrapes. It was just that we had a gang in our neighbourhood, which was the classy one of the town, and we were always having battles with the slummy kids from the other side of town who wanted to play in our neighbourhood. I was the Chief Gang Leader, and it was my job to keep them from expanding beyond their own frontiers.

Martha let on not to understand why I should be Chief Gang Leader. She let on not to know why we didn't want the slum kids overrunning our locality. Though she knew better than to tell Mother when I made Viking raids on the housekeeping money, she was always at me in a low, blood-curdling voice, following me round like a witch. "You'll be caught yet, Denis Halligan. You'll be caught. The police will be after you. You took three shillings out of Mummy's purse. God sees you!" Sometimes she drove me so wild that I went mad and twisted her arm or pulled her hair, and she went off screeching, and I got a licking.

I had managed to kid myself into the belief that one day Mother would understand; one day she would wake up and see that the affection of Dad and Martha was insincere; that the two of them had long ago ganged up against her, and that I, the black sheep, was the one who really loved her.

This revelation was due to take place in rather unusual circumstances. We were all to be stranded in some dangerous desert, and Mother, with her ankle broken, would tell us to leave her to her fate, the way they did in story-books. Dad and Martha, of course, would leave her, with only a pretence of concern, but I, in my casual way, would simply fold my hands about my knees and ask listlessly: "What use is life to me without you?" Nothing more; I was against any false drama, any raising of the voice. I had never been one for high-flown expressions like Martha: just the lift of the shoulder, the way I pulled a grass-blade to chew (it needn't be a desert), and Mother would realize at last that though I wasn't demonstrative—just a plain, rough,

willing chap—I really had a heart of gold.

The trouble about Mother was that she had a genius for subjecting hearts of gold to intolerable strain. It wasn't that she was actively unkind, for she thought far too much of the impression she wanted to make to be anything like that. It was just that she didn't care a damn. She was always away from home. She visited friends in Galway, Dublin, Birr, and Athlone, and all we ever got to see of her was the flurry between one foray and the next, while she was packing and unpacking.

Things came to a head when she told me she wouldn't be at home for my birthday. At the same time, always conscientious, she had arranged a very nice treat for Martha and me. But the treat wasn't the same thing that I had been planning, when I proposed to bring a couple of fellows along and show Mother off to them, and I began to bawl. The trouble was that the moment I did, I seemed to have no reasons on my side. It was always like that with Mother; she invariably had all the reasons on her side, and made you feel contrary and a pig, but that was worse instead of better. You felt then that she was taking advantage of you. I sobbed and stamped and asked why she hadn't done that to Martha and why she was doing it to me. She looked at me coldly and said I was a pretty picture and that I had no manliness. Of course, I saw she was in the right about that too, and that there was no excuse for a fellow of my age complaining against not being treated like his younger sister, and that only made me madder still.

"Go on!" I screamed. "Who's trying to stop you? All you want is people to admire you."

I knew when I had said it that it was awful, and expected her to give me a clout, but she only drew herself up, looking twice as dignified and beautiful.

"That is a contemptible remark, Denis," she said in a biting tone. "It's one I wouldn't have expected even from you."

The way she said it made me feel like the scum of the earth. And then she went off for the evening in a car with the Clarkes, leaving Martha and me alone. Martha looked at me, half in pity, half in amusement. She was never really disappointed in Mother, because she expected less of her. Martha was born sly.

"What did I tell you?" she said, though she hadn't told me anything.

"Go on!" I said in a thick voice. "You sucker!" Then I went upstairs and bawled and used all the dirty words I knew. I knew now it was all over between Mother and me; that no circumstances would ever occur which would show how much I loved her, because after what had happened I could not live in the same house with her again. For quite a while I thought about suicide, but I put that on one side, because the only way I could contemplate committing suicide was by shooting, and my air pistol was not strong enough for that. I took out my post-office book. I had four pounds fifteen in the bank. As I've said, it was purely out of spite against Martha, but that made no difference now. It was enough to keep me for a month or so till I found some corner where people wanted me; a plain rough-spoken chap who only needed a little affection. I was afraid of nothing in the way of work. I was strong and energetic. At the worst, I could always make for Dublin, where my grandfather and Auntie May lived. I knew they would be glad to help me, because they thought that Dad had married the wrong woman and never pretended to like Mother. When Mother had told me this I was furious, but now I saw that they were probably cleverer than I was. It would give me great satisfaction to reach their door and tell Auntie May in my plain straightforward way: "You were right and I was wrong." For the last time I looked round my bedroom and burst into fresh tears. There is something heart-rending about leaving for the last time a place where you have spent so much of your life. Then, trying to steady myself, I grabbed a little holy picture from the mantelpiece and a favourite story-book from the bookshelf and ran downstairs. Martha heard me taking out my bike and came to see. It had a dynamo lamp and a three-speed gear; a smashing bike!

"Where are you off to?" she asked.

"Never mind!" I said as I cycled off.

I had no particular feelings about seeing Martha for the last time.

Then I had my first shock, because as I cycled into Main Street I saw that all the shops were shuttered for the weekly half-holiday and I knew the post office would be shut

too and I could not draw out my savings. It was the first time I felt what people so often feel in after life, that Fate has made a plaything of you. Why should I have had my final quarrel with Mother on the one day in the week when I could not get away from her? If that wasn't Fate, what was? And I knew my own weakness of character better than anyone. I knew that if I put it off until next day, the sight of Mother would be sufficient to set me servilely seeking for pardon. Even setting off across Ireland without a penny would be better than that.

Then I had what I thought was an inspiration. The city was only twenty miles away, and the General Post Office was bound to be open. I had calculated my time to and from school at twelve miles an hour; even allowing for the distance, it wouldn't take me more than two hours. As well as that, I had been to the city for the Christmas shopping, so I knew the look of it. I could get my money and stay in a hotel or have tea and then set off for Dublin. I liked that idea. Cycling all the way up through Ireland in the dark, through sleeping towns and villages; seeing the dawn break over Dublin as I cycled down the slopes of the Dublin mountains; arriving at Auntie May's door in the Shelbourne Road when she was lighting the fire—that would be smashing. I could imagine how she would greet me—"Child of grace, where did you come from?" "Ah, just cycled." My natural modesty always came out in those day-dreams of mind, for I never, under any circumstances, made a fuss. Absolutely smashing!

All the same, it was no joke, a trip like that. I cycled slowly and undecidedly out the familiar main road where we walked on Sunday, past the little suburban houses. It was queer how hard it was to break away from places and people and things you knew. I thought of letting it go and of doing the best I could to patch it up with Mother. I thought of the gang and at that a real lump rose in my throat. Tomorrow night, when my absence was noticed, there would be a new Chief Gang Leader; somebody like Eddie Humphreys who would be so prim and cautious that he would be afraid to engage the enemy which threatened us on every side. In that moment of weakness I nearly turned back. At the same moment it brought me renewed decision, for I knew that I had not been chosen Chief Gang Leader because I was a little sissy like Eddie Humphreys but because I was afraid of nothing.

At one moment my feet had nearly stopped pedalling; at the next I was pedalling for all I was worth. It was as sudden as that, like the moment when you find yourself out of your depth and two inclinations struggle in you—to swim like hell back to the shallows or strike out boldly for the other side. Up to that I had thought mainly of what was behind me; now I thought only of what was ahead of me, and it was frightening enough. I was aware of great distances, of big cloud masses on the horizon, of the fragility of my tires compared with the rough surface of the road, and I thought only of the two-hour journey ahead of me. The romantic picture of myself cycling across Ireland in the dark disappeared. I should be quite content to get the first stage over me.

For the last ten miles I wasn't even tempted to look at the scenery. I was doubled over the handlebars. Things just happened; the road bent away under me; wide green rivers rose up and slipped away again under me, castles soared from the roadside with great arches blocked out in masses of shadow.

Then at last the little rocky fields closed behind me like a book, and the blessed electric-light poles escorted me up the last hill, and I floated proudly down between comfortable villas with long gardens till I reached the bridge. The city was stretched out on the other side of the river, shining in the evening light, and my heart rose at the thought that I had at least shown Mother whether or not I had manliness. I dismounted from my bicycle and pushed it along the Main Street, looking at the shops. They were far more interesting than the shops at home, and the people looked better too.

I found the post office in a side street and went up to the counter with my savings-bank book.

"I want to draw out my money," I said.

The clerk looked at the clock.

"You can't do that, sonny," he said. "The savings-bank counter is shut."

"When will it open again?" I asked.

"Not till tomorrow. Any time after nine."

"But can't I get it now?"

"No. The clerk is gone home now."

I slouched out of the post office with despair in my heart. I took my bicycle and pushed it wearily back to the Main Street. The crowds were still going by, but now it looked long and wide and lonesome, for I had no money and I didn't know a soul. Without a meal and a rest, I could not even set out for Dublin, if I had the heart, which I knew I hadn't. Nor could I even return home, for it was already late and I was dropping with weariness. One side of the Main Street was in shadow; the shadow seemed to spread with extraordinary rapidity, and you felt that the city was being quenched as with snuffers.

It was only then that I thought of Father. It was funny that I had not thought of him before, even when thinking of Grandfather and Auntie May. I had thought of these as allies against Mother, but I hadn't even considered him as an ally. Now as I thought of him, everything about him seemed different. It wasn't only the hunger and panic. It was something new for me. It was almost love. With fresh energy I pushed my bicycle back to the post office, left it outside the door where I could see it, and went up to the clerk I had already spoken to.

"Could I make a telephone call?" I asked.

"You could to be sure," he said. "Have you the money?"

"No, sir."

"Well, you can't make a call without the money. Where is it to?"

"Boharna," I said.

At once his face took on a severe expression.

"That's one and threepence," he said.

"And I can't ring unless I have the money?"

"Begor, you can't. I couldn't ring myself without that."

I went out and took my bicycle again. This time I could see no way out. I dawdled along the street, leaving my bicycle by the curb and gazing in shop windows. In one I found a mirror in which I could see myself full-length. I looked old and heartbroken. It was just like a picture of a child without a home, and I blinked away my tears.

Then, as I approached a public-house, I saw a barman in shirt sleeves standing by the door. I remembered that I had seen him already on my way down and that he had looked at me. He nodded and smiled and I stopped. I was glad of anyone making a friendly gesture in that strange place.

"Are you waiting for someone?" he asked.

"No," I said. "I wanted to make a phone call."

"You're not from these parts?"

"No," I said. "I'm from Boharna."

"Are you, begor?" he said. "Was it on the bus you came?"

"No," I replied modestly. "I biked it."

"Biked it?"

"Yes."

"That's a hell of a distance," he said.

"It is long," I agreed.

"What did you come all that way for?" he asked in surprise.

"Ah, I was running away from home," I said despondently.

"You were what?" he asked in astonishment. "You're not serious."

"But I am," I said, very close to tears. "I did my best, but then I couldn't stick it any longer and I cleared out." I turned my head away because this time I was really crying.

"Oh, begor, I know what 'tis like," he said in a friendlier tone. "I did it myself."

"Did you?" I asked eagerly, forgetting my grief. This, I felt, was the very man I wanted to meet.

"Ah, indeed I did. I did it three times what's more. By that time they were getting fed up with me. Anyway, they say practice makes perfect. Tell me, is it your old fellow?"

"No," I said with a sigh. "My mother."

"Ah, do you tell me so? That's worse again. 'Tis bad enough to have the old man at you, but 'tis the devil entirely when the mother is against you. What are you going to do now?"

"I don't know," I said. "I wanted to get to Dublin, but the savings bank is shut, and all my money is in it."

"That's tough luck. Sure, you can't get anywhere without money. I'm afraid you'll have to go back and put up with it for another while."

"But I can't," I said. " 'Tis twenty miles."

" 'Tis all of that, begor. You couldn't go on the bus?"

"I can't. I haven't the money. That's what

I asked them in the post office, to let me ring up Daddy, but they wouldn't."

"Where's your daddy?" he asked, and when I told him: "Ah, we'll try and get him for you anyway. Come on in."

There was a phone in the corner, and he rang up and asked for Daddy. Then he gave me a big smile and handed me the receiver. I heard Daddy's voice and I nearly wept with delight.

"Hullo, son," he said in astonishment. "Where on earth are you?"

"In the city, Daddy," I said modestly—even then I couldn't bring myself to make a lot of it, the way another fellow would.

"The city?" he repeated incredulously. "What took you there?"

"I ran away from home, Dad," I said, trying to make it sound as casual as possible.

"Oh!" he exclaimed and there was a moment's pause. I was afraid he was going to get angry, but his tone remained the same. "Had a row?"

"Yes, Dad."

"And how did you get there?"

"On the bike."

"All the way? But you must be dead."

"Just a bit tired," I said modestly.

"Tell me, did you even get a meal?"

"No, Dad. The savings bank was shut."

"Ah, blazes!" he said softly. "Of course, it's the half day. And what are you going to do now?"

"I don't know, Dad. I thought you might tell me."

"Well, what about coming home?" he said, beginning to laugh.

"I don't mind, Dad. Whatever you say."

"Hold on now till I see what the buses are like. . . . Hullo! You can get one in forty minutes' time—seven ten. Tell the conductor I'll be meeting you and I'll pay your fare. Will that be all right?"

"That's grand, Dad," I said, feeling that the world was almost right again.

When I finished, the barman was waiting for me with his coat on. He had got another man to look after the bar for him.

"Now, you'd better come and have a cup of tea with me before your bus goes," he said. "The old bike will be safe outside."

He took me to a café, and I ate cake after

cake and drank tea and he told me about how he'd run away himself. You could see he was a real hard case, worse even than I was. The first time, he'd pinched a bicycle and cycled all the way to Dublin, sleeping in barns and deserted cottages. The police had brought him home and his father had belted hell out of him. They caught him again the second time, but the third time he'd joined the army and not returned home for years.

He put me and my bicycle on the bus and paid my fare. He made me promise to tell Dad that he'd done it and that Dad owed me the money. He said in this world you had to stand up for your rights. He was a rough chap, but you could see he had a good heart. It struck me that maybe only rough chaps had hearts as good as that.

Dad was waiting for me at the bus stop, and he looked at me and laughed.

"Well, the gouger!" he said. "Who ever would think that the son of a good-living, upright man like me would turn into a common tramp."

All the same I could see he was pleased, and as he pushed my bike down the street he made me tell him all about my experiences. He laughed over the barman and promised to give me the fare. Then, seeing him so friendly, I asked the question that had been on my mind the whole way back on the bus.

"Mummy back yet, Dad?"

"No, son," he said. "Not yet. She probably won't be in till late."

What I was really asking him, of course, was "Does she know?" and now I was torn by the desire to ask him not to tell her, but it choked me. It would have seemed too much like trying to gang up against her. But he seemed to know what I was thinking, for he added with a sort of careful casualness that he had sent Martha to the pictures. I guessed that that was to get her out of the way so that she couldn't bring the story to Mother, and when we had supper together and washed up afterwards, I knew I was right.

Mother came in before we went to bed, and Father talked to her just as though nothing had happened. He was a little bit more forthcoming than usual, but that was the only indication he gave, and I was fascinated, watching him create an understanding between us. It was an understanding in more ways than one, because it dawned on me gradually that, like myself and the barman, Dad too had once run away from home, and for some reason—perhaps because the bank was shut or because he was hungry, tired, and lonely—he had come back. People mostly came back, but their protest remained to distinguish them from all the others who had never run away. It was the real sign of their manhood.

I never ran away after that. I never felt I needed to.

THE NOVEL

————— ◆ —————

INTRODUCTION

The novel stems from a rich background, in verse and prose, of tales, romances, and character sketches. It was, however, the Italian *novella*—stories of chivalry and risqué love, of the exploits of corrupt nobility, scandalous women, uncouth country bumpkins, and debased clergy—that gave the novel its narrative form and its name.

Daniel Defoe's *Robinson Crusoe,* a humanized tale of adventure, appeared in England in 1720. This story, told in straightforward manner, reads like a recital of fact. As such, it is generally conceded to be the most immediate forerunner of the novel proper and also to be the first English novel of adventure. To Samuel Richardson, however, is usually given the credit for writing the first novel—defined as a long fictitious prose tale in which characters and action representing those of real life are portrayed in a plot. His *Pamela: or Virtue Rewarded* is a realistic picture of a poor girl who, after resisting the amatory advances of a wild young aristocrat, finally, by a protracted matching of will against will, has her virtuous conduct rewarded by being offered the gallant's hand in marriage. Summarizing the contribution of Richardson to the development of the English novel, Professor Wilbur Cross says: "The first great imaginative success was Richardson's, who made equally real his men and women and the scenes in which he placed them."

Prompted by Defoe's and Richardson's success, Henry Fielding planned a novel which would satirize the bourgeois morality of Richardson's *Pamela;* in 1742 he published *Joseph Andrews,* a story with the reversed situation of a young man exposed to the advances of a young lady. Fielding went beyond his original intention, however, and produced a novel with realistic characters, not caricatures, and with an independently interesting plot. His later and greatest work, *Tom Jones,* is a skillfully woven fabric of diversified incidents, the story of a youth whose inner strength of character eventually corrects many temporary weaknesses in his conduct. At the same time that Fielding was writing, Tobias Smollett and Laurence Sterne were attempting to broaden the scope of the novel—the former with stories of sea adventures and the latter with narratives whose interest centered in character rather than in plot. From their day on through the nineteenth and into the twentieth century, the history of the novel has been one of continuous experimentation resulting in types that vary from the simple narrative incident, with which the novel originated, to perhaps the most complex of all its forms—the stream-of-consciousness novel of modern times.

Huckleberry Finn is a work of refreshing originality, but it would not be so good if Mark Twain had not read and admired many great novels, occasionally copied them, and once in a while made affectionate fun of them. Sometimes, in *Huckleberry Finn,* he refers to these books by name, sometimes he merely suggests their nature, but always his references show how carefully he has studied the masterpieces of the past.

Huckleberry Finn has some of the characteristics of the picaresque type of novel, which in relating the loosely connected adventures of a wandering low-life character, often provides opportunity for satire. Mark Twain knew such picaresque novels as *Histoire de Gil Blas de Santillane* by Le Sage, a Frenchman who wrote his novel in 1715; *Joseph Andrews* and *Tom Jones* by Fielding; *Roderick Random* by Smollett; and *Pickwick Papers* by Charles Dickens, their nineteenth century successor. In these stories the hero encounters all sorts of impostors: magistrates ignorant of the law, worldly priests, doctors who kill their patients, and cowardly soldiers.

Traces of *Don Quixote,* a novel that is sometimes classed as picaresque but is far more than a rogue's story, are plentiful in *Huckleberry Finn.* When Huck was disgusted because Tom Sawyer's attack on "a whole parcel of Spanish merchants and rich A-rabs" turned out to be an attack on a Sunday-school picnic, Tom turned on him and said that "there was A-rabs there, too, and elephants and things. I said, why couldn't we see them, then? He said if I warn't so ignorant, but had read a book called *Don Quixote,* I would know without asking. He said it was all done by enchantment. He said there was hundreds of soldiers there, and elephants and treasure and so on, but we had enemies which he called magicians, and they had turned the whole thing into an infant Sunday-school, just out of spite." Don Quixote, an amiable country gentleman who had read too many romantic books, exactly as Tom had done, attacked windmills thinking they were enchanted castles. His faithful squire, Sancho Panza, knew they were only windmills and sometimes said so, just as Huck did.

When Huck and Jim find an abandoned house and Huck says, "We got an old tin lantern, and a butcher-knife without any handle, and a bran-new Barlow knife worth two bits in any store, and a lot of tallow candles . . . ," we are reminded of a novel where that sort of thing happens all the time. The hero of Daniel Defoe's *Robinson Crusoe* regularly supplies himself in just this happy fashion. Mark Twain may not have been thinking of Defoe when he described Jackson's Island; still, the two authors create the same excitement about being separated from the mainland, and the same horror when a hero who thinks he is safely alone finds there is a stranger about. "I clipped along," says Huck, "and all of a sudden I bounded right on to the ashes of a camp-fire that was still smoking. My heart jumped up amongst my lungs."

In explaining how the magicians turned the "A-rabs" into a Sunday-school picnic, Tom said they had genies to help them. "How do *they* get them?" demanded Huck. "Why, they rub an old tin lamp or an iron ring . . . ," said Tom, for he is living over some adventures from the *Arabian Nights.* And with the *Arabian Nights* we are at the fountainhead of the romantic novel, to which *Huckleberry Finn* also owes some debt.

One of the best of the romantic novelists is Sir Walter Scott, for whom, incidentally, a boat is named in *Huckleberry Finn.* On this boat, appropriately, are a thief tied on the floor and two thieves threatening him with instant death. The Scott who wrote *Waverley* would have thought this a fine situation. Another romantic novelist, Alexandre Dumas, author of *The Count of Monte Cristo,* is responsible for Jim's having to write his sad story on a shirt, cultivate spiders, and be dug out of his cell instead of walking through the front door. "Why," says Tom, "look at one of them prisoners in the bottom dungeon of the Castle Deef, in the harbor of Marseilles, that dug himself out that way; how long was *he* at it, do you reckon? . . . *Thirty-seven year*—and he come out in China."

In his autobiography, H. L. Mencken has written: "My discovery of 'Huckleberry Finn' [was] probably the most stupendous event of my whole life . . . If I undertook to tell you the effect it had upon me my talk would sound frantic, and even delirious. Its impact was genuinely terrific. I had not gone further than the first incomparable chapter before I realized, child though I was, that I had entered a domain of new and gorgeous wonders, and thereafter I pressed on steadily to the last word. . . . I read it over and over. In fact, I read it regularly not less than annually down to my forties, and only a few months ago I hauled it out and read it once more—and found it as magnificent as ever."

These, granted, are the words of an enthusiast. But for all its readers *Huckleberry Finn* can do a few things no other American novel can do. For one thing, it can give a feeling that this world—in spite of ups-and-downs—is a very good place to live in. Who would not like to float down the Mississippi on a raft as Huck and Jim did? "We said there warn't no home like a raft, after all. Other places do seem so cramped up and smothery, but a raft don't. You feel mighty free and easy and comfortable on a raft." And who would not like to be lying in an island cave when it is raining outside? Huckleberry says, "Jim, this is nice. I wouldn't want to be nowhere else but here. Pass me along another hunk of fish and some hot corn-bread."

This novel can give the reader a sense of belonging to the human race and liking nearly all the people in it. Of course there will be exceptions such as the king and the duke, but in general Huck's race is a good one to belong to. The book is filled with fine people like Mary Jane and Buck Grangerford and—standing above them all—Jim, whose common sense, loyalty, and goodness are demonstrated over and over again. *Huckleberry Finn* can give the feeling, too, that this world is worth looking at— "Everything was dead quiet, and it looked late, and *smelt* late. You know what I mean—I don't know the words to put it in."

When Huck says, "I don't know the words to put it in," he is lying a little, for if this novel has one special glory, it is that Mark Twain—and Huck—will always find the right word to describe any situation, and they will always say what they have to say in the words ordinary people use. When Huck says about Colonel Grangerford that "Everybody loved to have him around, too; he was sunshine most always—I mean he made it seem like good weather," he is talking just as Americans talk when they are relaxed. *Huckleberry Finn* sounds as if Mark Twain talked the whole thing before he wrote a word of it. Actually, he wrote it section by section, then read each installment to his family. In that way he managed to cut out anything that bored his little girls, or shocked his wife, or did not sound just right to his own extremely sensitive ear. Anyone can learn to write literary English, but to write English prose with a suggestion of human speech is the gift of only the very best authors.

One of the things we demand of a novel is good construction. In writing a novel that, like *Huckleberry Finn,* resembles the picaresque, the author must achieve unity out of a loose collection of adventures. Even though Mark Twain threatens pain of death to anyone who looks for a plot, in *Huckleberry Finn* he consciously or unconsciously makes the river serve as a unifying force for the episodic narrative; moreover, the uncertain fate of Huck and Jim gives the story a focus throughout. Any weakness of plot structure in the novel is compensated for by the author's clever management of episodic narrative. He closes every chapter with an ending that adds to the excitement of the story. Chapter 12 is typical. Huck has made a mistake by going aboard a boat filled with robbers, as Tom Sawyer might have done—to have "adventures"—and he and Jim prepare to leave by their raft. "Oh, my lordy, lordy!" says Jim. *"Raf'?* Dey ain' no raf' no mo'; she done broke loose en gone!—en here we is!"

There are critics, including Stephen Leacock, who say that the structure of *Huckleberry Finn* is good only to a certain point—ten chapters from the close. In a way, these critics are right. Mark Twain had no idea when he began his story how it would end; he wrote on it for a while, and dropped it, then picked it up again after a trip that he took down the Mississippi in order to get new ideas. Consciously he had no plan for the whole book, and the ending may seem to some a patched-up affair. But in one way it does fit in with the beginning of the book. Huck is, after all, a boy; the novel begins with his boyish adventures with Tom Sawyer—sliding down lightning-rods and robbing a Sunday-school picnic. Then he escapes from his drunken father; he has to take Jim to freedom, and free himself from the duke and the king. Through these serious events, Huck acquires a feeling of responsibility. While Huck is alone, or with Jim, he matures; he learns how to keep inquisitive strangers away from his raft, and how to hide Jim. But by-and-by Tom Sawyer comes along, and whenever Tom appears, Huck retires from leadership. Huck's new adventures are over; it is time for him to be a boy again and let somebody else do his planning. So, in the last ten chapters, he goes back to harum-scarum tricks.

Even though exciting things happen in it, the world in which Huckleberry Finn moves is far from Tom's realm of romantic adventure. The Mississippi that Huck knows, with its brown beauty, its mystery, and its strength also has cruel, deceptive sandbars and snags, dangerous fogs, and swirling eddies. The great river has a personality that Huck Finn instinctively respects; and although Huck would never have put it this way, the river becomes a symbol of a kind of destinal force showing mercy only to those who adjust their lives to its character. Huck is a practical person unwilling to play the role of a romantic hero. His inveterate lying for a worthwhile end, his scorn of respectability, his petty thievery, his aversion to decent grammar, all tend to make him a realistic personage partly bad and partly good. This realistic attitude was characteristic of the period in which this novel was written—the post Civil War years which saw the breakdown of old customs and values associated with the frontier South, for so many decades regarded with romantic idealism. Huck Finn was not the only ragged pioneer who was chafing at being civilized by the new industrialism with its inhibiting influence on freedom of speech and action.

T. S. Eliot has said that *"Huckleberry Finn,* like other great works of imagination, can give to every reader whatever he is capable of taking from it." This is a novel that will continue to reward the person who brings to it an inquiring, receptive mind. Huck grows up and sees the world in truer light as a mixture of good and evil. The reader will find that what begins—and in a sense ends—as a story of childhood becomes, upon increasing and deepened reflection, a mature illumination of the conditions of human life. The reader may also come to find, with the critic Lionel Trilling, that this is "one of the world's great books and one of the central documents of American culture."

SAMUEL L. CLEMENS *The Adventures of Huckleberry Finn*

Samuel Langhorne Clemens (1835-1910) is universally known as Mark Twain, a term used by Mississippi River pilots to designate two fathoms of water. The phrase was first used as a pen name by a pilot named Sellers, who wrote weighty articles for newspapers. Clemens satirized Sellers's pompous style in New Orleans papers under the name "Mark Twain," which he thereafter appropriated.

Mark Twain grew up in the town of Hannibal, Missouri, on the Mississippi River, where he learned first the art of printing at his brother's newspaper and later was apprenticed to a Mississippi River pilot. Then he went West and briefly tried his hand (without any success) at gold mining. Newspaper work, which he attempted next, proved to be a more rewarding profession, and in 1865 he achieved his first fame as a writer with "The Celebrated Jumping Frog of Calaveras County." The success of Twain's later life was dimmed somewhat by financial reverses and by a growing strain of pessimism in his thinking and writing.

Biographers have found in this adventurer an excellent subject. A. B. Paine's *Mark Twain, A Biography* is the most thorough of the biographies; Stephen Leacock's *Mark Twain*, which appears earlier in this text, contains, in briefer form, the essential facts of Clemens's life and writings.

CONTENTS

Explanatory

In this book a number of dialects are used, to wit: the Missouri Negro dialect; the extremist form of the backwoods Southwestern dialect; the ordinary "Pike County" dialect; and four modified varieties of this last. The shadings have not been done in a haphazard fashion, or by guesswork; but painstakingly, and with the trustworthy guidance and support of personal familiarity with these several forms of speech.

I make this explanation for the reason that without it many readers would suppose that all these characters were trying to talk alike and not succeeding.

THE AUTHOR

Notice

Persons attempting to find a motive in this narrative will be prosecuted; persons attempting to find a moral in it will be banished; persons attempting to find a plot in it will be shot.

BY ORDER OF THE AUTHOR,
Per G. G., Chief of Ordnance

THE ADVENTURES OF HUCKLEBERRY FINN

1. I DISCOVER MOSES AND THE BULRUSHERS

You don't know about me without you have read a book by the name of *The Adventures of Tom Sawyer;* but that ain't no matter. That book was made by Mr. Mark Twain, and he told the truth, mainly. There was things which he stretched, but mainly he told the truth. That is nothing. I never seen anybody but lied one time or another, without it was Aunt Polly, or the widow, or maybe Mary. Aunt Polly—Tom's Aunt Polly, she is—and Mary, and the Widow Douglas is all told about in that book, which is mostly a true book, with some stretchers, as I said before.

Now the way that the book winds up is this: Tom and me found the money that the robbers hid in the cave, and it made us rich. We got six thousand dollars apiece—all gold. It was an awful sight of money when it was piled up. Well, Judge Thatcher he took it and put it out at interest, and it fetched us a dollar a day apiece all the year round—more than a body could tell what to do with. The Widow Douglas she took me for her son, and allowed she would civilize me; but it was

rough living in the house all the time, considering how dismal regular and decent the widow was in all her ways; and so when I couldn't stand it no longer I lit out. I got into my old rags and my sugar-hogshead again, and was free and satisfied. But Tom Sawyer he hunted me up and said he was going to start a band of robbers, and I might join if I would go back to the widow and be respectable. So I went back.

The widow she cried over me, and called me a poor lost lamb, and she called me a lot of other names, too, but she never meant no harm by it. She put me in them new clothes again, and I couldn't do nothing but sweat and sweat, and feel all cramped up. Well, then, the old thing commenced again. The widow rung a bell for supper, and you had to come to time. When you got to the table you couldn't go right to eating, but you had to wait for the widow to tuck down her head and grumble a little over the victuals, though there warn't really anything the matter with them—that is, nothing only everything was cooked by itself. In a barrel of odds and ends it is different; things get mixed up, and the juice kind of swaps around, and the things go better.

After supper she got out her book and learned me about Moses and the Bulrushers, and I was in a sweat to find out all about him; but by and by she let it out that Moses had been dead a considerable long time; so then I didn't care no more about him, because I don't take no stock in dead people.

Pretty soon I wanted to smoke, and asked the widow to let me. But she wouldn't. She said it was a mean practice and wasn't clean, and I must try to not do it any more. That is just the way with some people. They get down on a thing when they don't know nothing about it. Here she was a-bothering about Moses, which was no kin to her, and no use to anybody, being gone, you see, yet finding a power of fault with me for doing a thing that had some good in it. And she took snuff, too; of course that was all right, because she done it herself.

Her sister, Miss Watson, a tolerable slim old maid, with goggles on, had just come to live with her, and took a set at me now with a spelling-book. She worked me middling hard for about an hour, and then the widow made her ease up. I couldn't stood it much longer. Then for an hour it was deadly dull, and I was fidgety. Miss Watson would say, "Don't put your feet up there, Huckleberry"; and "Don't scrunch up like that, Huckleberry—set up straight"; and pretty soon she would say, "Don't gap and stretch like that, Huckleberry—why don't you try to behave?" Then she told me all about the bad place, and I said I wished I was there. She got mad then, but I didn't mean no harm. All I wanted was to go somewheres; all I wanted was a change, I warn't particular. She said it was wicked to say what I said; said she wouldn't say it for the whole world; *she* was going to live so as to go to the good place. Well, I couldn't see no advantage in going where she was going, so I made up my mind I wouldn't try for it. But I never said so, because it would only make trouble, and wouldn't do no good.

Now she had got a start, and she went on and told me all about the good place. She said all a body would have to do there was to go around all day long with a harp and sing, forever and ever. So I didn't think much of it.

But I never said so. I asked her if she reckoned Tom Sawyer would go there, and she said not by a considerable sight. I was glad about that, because I wanted him and me to be together.

Miss Watson she kept pecking at me, and it got tiresome and lonesome. By and by they fetched the niggers in and had prayers, and then everybody was off to bed. I went up to my room with a piece of candle, and put it on the table. Then I set down in a chair by the window and tried to think of something cheerful, but it warn't no use. I felt so lonesome I most wished I was dead. The stars were shining, and the leaves rustled in the woods ever so mournful; and I heard an owl, away off, who-whooing about somebody that was dead, and a whippowill and a dog crying about somebody that was going to die; and the wind was trying to whisper something to me, and I couldn't make out what it was, and so it made the cold shivers run over me. Then away out in the woods I heard that kind of a sound that a ghost makes when it wants to tell about something that's on its mind and can't make itself understood, and so can't rest easy in its grave, and has to go about that way every night grieving. I got so downhearted and scared I did wish I had some company. Pretty soon a spider went crawling up my shoulder, and I flipped it off and it lit in the candle; and before I could budge it was all shriveled up. I didn't need anybody to tell me that that was an awful bad sign and would fetch me some bad luck, so I was scared and most shook the clothes off of me. I got up and turned around in my tracks three times and crossed my breast every time; and then I tied up a little lock of my hair with a thread to keep witches away. But I hadn't no confidence. You do that when you've lost a horseshoe that you've found, instead of nailing it up over the door, but I hadn't ever heard anybody say it was any way to keep off bad luck when you'd killed a spider.

I set down again, a-shaking all over, and got out my pipe for a smoke; for the house was all as still as death now, and so the widow wouldn't know. Well, after a long time I heard the clock away off in the town go boom—boom—boom—twelve licks; and all still again—stiller than ever. Pretty soon I heard a twig snap down in the dark amongst the trees—something was a-stirring. I set still and listened. Directly I could just barely hear a *"me-yow! me-yow!"* down there. That was good! Says I, *"me-yow! me-yow!"* as soft as I could, and then I put out the light and scrambled out of the window on to the shed. Then I slipped down to the ground and crawled in among the trees, and, sure enough, there was Tom Sawyer waiting for me.

2. OUR GANG'S DARK OATH

We went tiptoeing along a path amongst the trees back towards the end of the widow's garden, stooping down so as the branches wouldn't scrape our heads. When we was passing by the kitchen I fell over a root and made a noise. We scrouched down and laid still. Miss Watson's big nigger, named Jim, was setting in the kitchen door; we could see him pretty clear, because there was a light behind him. He got up and stretched his neck out about a minute, listening. Then he says:

"Who dah?"

He listened some more; then he came tiptoeing down and stood right between us; we could 'a' touched him, nearly. Well, likely it was minutes and minutes that there warn't a sound, and we all there so close together. There was a place on my ankle that got to itching, but I dasn't scratch it; and then my ear begun to itch; and next my back, right between my shoulders. Seemed like I'd die if I couldn't scratch. Well, I've noticed that thing plenty times since. If you are with the quality, or at a funeral, or trying to go to sleep when you ain't sleepy—if you are anywheres where it don't do for you to scratch, why you will itch all over in upward of a thousand places. Pretty soon Jim says:

"Say, who is you? Whar is you? Dog my cats ef I didn't hear sumf'n. Well, I know what I's gwyne to do: I's gwyne to set down here and listen tell I hears it ag'in."

So he set down on the ground betwixt me and Tom. He leaned his back up against a tree, and stretched his legs out till one of them most touched one of mine. My nose begun to itch. It itched till the tears come into my eyes. But I dasn't scratch. Then it begun to itch on the inside. Next I got to itching underneath. I didn't know how I was going to set still. This miserableness went on as much as six or seven minutes; but it seemed a sight longer than that. I was itching in eleven different places now. I reckoned I couldn't stand it more'n a minute longer, but I set my teeth hard and got ready to try. Just then Jim begun to breathe heavy; next he begun to snore—and then I was pretty soon comfortable again.

Tom he made a sign to me—kind of a little noise with his mouth—and we went creeping away on our hands and knees. When we was ten foot off Tom whispered to me, and wanted to tie Jim to the tree for fun. But I said no; he might wake and make a disturbance, and then they'd find out I warn't in. Then Tom said he hadn't got candles enough, and he would slip in the kitchen and get some more. I didn't want him to try. I said Jim might wake up and come. But Tom wanted to resk it; so we slid in there and got three candles, and Tom laid five cents on the table for pay. Then we got out, and I was in a sweat to get away; but nothing would do Tom but he must crawl to where Jim was, on his hands and knees, and play something on him. I waited, and it seemed a good while, everything was so still and lonesome.

As soon as Tom was back we cut along the path, around the garden fence, and by and by fetched up on the steep top of the hill the other side of the house. Tom said he slipped Jim's hat off of his head and hung it on a limb right over him, and Jim stirred a little, but he didn't wake. Afterward Jim said the witches bewitched him and put him in a trance, and rode him all over the state, and then set him under the trees again, and hung his hat on a limb to show who done it. And next time Jim told it he said they rode him down to New Orleans; and, after that, every time he told it he spread it more and more, till by and by he said they rode him all over the world, and tired him most to death, and his back was all over saddle-boils. Jim was monstrous proud about it, and he got so he wouldn't hardly notice the other niggers. Niggers would come miles to hear Jim tell about it, and he was more looked up to than any nigger in that country. Strange niggers would stand with their mouths open and look him all over, same as if he was a wonder.

Niggers is always talking about witches in the dark by the kitchen fire; but whenever one was talking and letting on to know all about such things, Jim would happen in and say, "Hm! What you know 'bout witches?" and that nigger was corked up and had to take a back seat. Jim always kept that five-center piece round his neck with a string, and said it was a charm the devil give to him with his own hands, and told him he could cure anybody with it and fetch witches whenever he wanted to just by saying something to it; but he never told what it was he said to it. Niggers would come from all around there and give Jim anything they had, just for a sight of that five-center piece; but they wouldn't touch it, because the devil had had his hands on it. Jim was most ruined for a servant, because he got stuck up on account of having seen the devil and been rode by witches.

Well, when Tom and me got to the edge of the hilltop we looked away down into the village and could see three or four lights twinkling, where there was sick folks, maybe; and the stars over us was sparkling ever so fine; and down by the village was the river, a whole mile broad, and awful still and grand. We went down the hill and found Joe Harper and Ben Rogers, and two or three more of the boys, hid in the old tanyard. So we unhitched a skiff and pulled down the river two mile and a half, to the big scar on the hillside, and went ashore.

We went to a clump of bushes, and Tom made everybody swear to keep the secret, and then showed them a hole in the hill, right in the thickest part of the bushes. Then we lit the candles, and crawled in on our hands and knees. We went about two hundred yards, and then the cave opened up. Tom poked about amongst the passages, and pretty soon ducked under a wall where you wouldn't 'a' noticed that there was a hole. We went along a narrow place and got into a kind of room, all damp and sweaty and cold, and there we stopped. Tom says:

"Now, we'll start this band of robbers and call it Tom Sawyer's Gang. Everybody that wants to join has got to take an oath, and write his name in blood."

Everybody was willing. So Tom got out a sheet of paper that he had wrote the oath on, and read it. It swore every boy to stick to the band, and never tell any of the secrets; and if anybody done anything to any boy in the band, whichever boy was ordered to kill that person and his family must do it, and he mustn't eat and he mustn't sleep till he had killed them and hacked a cross in their breasts, which was the sign of the band. And nobody that didn't belong to the band could use that mark, and if he did he must be sued; and if he done it again he must be killed. And if anybody that belonged to the band told the secrets, he must have his throat cut, and then have his carcass burnt up and the ashes scattered all around, and his name blotted off the list with blood and never mentioned again by the gang, but have a curse put on it and be forgot forever.

Everybody said it was a real beautiful oath, and asked Tom if he got it out of his own head. He said some of it, but the rest was out of pirate-books and robber-books, and every gang that was high-toned had it.

Some thought it would be good to kill the *families* of boys that told the secrets. Tom said it was a good idea, so he took a pencil and wrote it in. Then Ben Rogers says:

"Here's Huck Finn, he hain't got no family; what you going to do 'bout him?"

"Well, hain't he got a father?" says Tom Sawyer.

"Yes, he's got a father, but you can't never find him these days. He used to lay drunk with the hogs in the tanyard, but he hain't been seen in these parts for a year or more."

They talked it over, and they was going to rule me out, because they said every boy must have a family or somebody to kill, or else it wouldn't be fair and square for the others. Well, nobody could think of anything to do— everybody was stumped, and set still. I was most ready to cry; but all at once I thought of a way, and so I offered them Miss Watson— they could kill her. Everybody said:

"Oh, she'll do. That's all right. Huck can come in."

Then they all stuck a pin in their fingers to get blood to sign with, and I made my mark on the paper.

"Now," says Ben Rogers, "what's the line of business of this Gang?"

"Nothing only robbery and murder," Tom said.

"But who are we going to rob?—houses, or cattle, or—"

"Stuff! stealing cattle and such things ain't robbery; it's burglary," says Tom Sawyer. "We ain't burglars. That ain't no sort of style. We are highwaymen. We stop stages and carriages on the road, with masks on, and kill the people and take their watches and money."

"Must we always kill the people?"

"Oh, certainly. It's best. Some authorities think different, but mostly it's considered best to kill them—except some that you bring to the cave here, and keep them till they're ransomed."

"Ransomed? What's that?"

"I don't know. But that's what they do. I've seen it in books; and so of course that's what we've got to do."

"But how can we do it if we don't know what it is?"

"Why, blame it all, we've got to do it. Don't I tell you it's in the books? Do you want to go to doing different from what's in the books, and get things all muddled up?"

"Oh, that's all very fine to say, Tom Sawyer, but how in the nation are these fellows going to be ransomed if we don't know how to do it to them?—that's the thing I want to get at. Now, what do you reckon it is?"

"Well, I don't know. But per'aps if we keep them till they're ransomed, it means that we keep them till they're dead."

"Now, that's something like. That'll answer. Why couldn't you said that before? We'll keep them till they're ransomed to death; and a bothersome lot they'll be, too—eating up everything, and always trying to get loose."

"How you talk, Ben Rogers. How can they get loose when there's a guard over them, ready to shoot them down if they move a peg?"

"A guard! Well, that is good. So somebody's got to set up all night and never get any sleep, just so as to watch them. I think that's foolishness. Why can't a body take a club and ransom them as soon as they get here?"

"Because it ain't in the books so—that's why. Now, Ben Rogers, do you want to do things regular, or don't you?—that's the idea. Don't you reckon that the people that made

the books knows what's the correct thing to do? Do you reckon you can learn 'em anything? Not by a good deal. No, sir, we'll just go on and ransom them in the regular way."

"All right. I don't mind; but I say it's a fool way, anyhow. Say, do we kill the women, too?"

"Well, Ben Rogers, if I was as ignorant as you I wouldn't let on. Kill the women? No; nobody ever saw anything in the books like that. You fetch them to the cave, and you're always as polite as pie to them; and by and by they fall in love with you, and never want to go home any more."

"Well, if that's the way I'm agreed, but I don't take no stock in it. Mighty soon we'll have the cave so cluttered up with women, and fellows waiting to be ransomed, that there won't be no place for the robbers. But go ahead, I ain't got nothing to say."

Little Tommy Barnes was asleep now, and when they waked him up he was scared, and cried, and said he wanted to go home to his ma, and didn't want to be a robber any more.

So they all made fun of him, and called him cry-baby, and that made him mad, and he said he would go straight and tell all the secrets. But Tom give him five cents to keep quiet, and said we would all go home and meet next week, and rob somebody and kill some people.

Ben Rogers said he couldn't get out much, only Sundays, and so he wanted to begin next Sunday; but all the boys said it would be wicked to do it on Sunday, and that settled the thing. They agreed to get together and fix a day as soon as they could, and then we elected Tom Sawyer first captain and Joe Harper second captain of the Gang, and so started home.

I clumb up the shed and crept into my window just before day was breaking. My new clothes was all greased up and clayey, and I was dog-tired.

3. WE AMBUSCADE THE A-RABS

Well, I got a good going-over in the morning from old Miss Watson on account of my clothes; but the widow she didn't scold, but only cleaned off the grease and clay, and looked so sorry that I thought I would behave awhile if I could. Then Miss Watson she took me in the closet and prayed, but nothing come of it. She told me to pray every day, and whatever I asked for I would get it. But it warn't so. I tried it. Once I got a fish-line, but no hooks. It warn't any good to me without hooks. I tried for the hooks three or four times, but somehow I couldn't make it work. By and by, one day, I asked Miss Watson to try for me, but she said I was a fool. She never told me why, and I couldn't make it out no way.

I set down one time back in the woods, and had a long think about it. I says to myself, if a body can get anything they pray for, why don't Deacon Winn get back the money he lost on pork? Why can't the widow get back her silver snuff-box that was stole? Why can't Miss Watson fat up? No, says I to myself, there ain't nothing in it. I went and told the widow about it, and she said the thing a body could get by praying for it was "spiritual gifts." This was too many for me, but she told me what she meant—I must help other people, and do everything I could for other people, and look out for them all the time, and never think about myself. This was including Miss Watson, as I took it. I went out in the woods and turned it over in my mind a long time, but I couldn't see no advantage about it— except for the other people; so at last I reckoned I wouldn't worry about it any more, but just let it go. Sometimes the widow would take me one side and talk about Providence in a way to make a body's mouth water; but maybe next day Miss Watson would take hold and knock it all down again. I judged I could see that there was two Providences, and a poor chap would stand considerable show with the widow's Providence, but if Miss Watson's got him there warn't no help for him any more. I thought it all out, and reckoned I would belong to the widow's if he wanted me, though I couldn't make out how he was a-going to be any better off then than what he was before, seeing I was so ignorant, and so kind of low-down and ornery.

Pap he hadn't been seen for more than a year, and that was comfortable for me; I didn't want to see him no more. He used to always whale me when he was sober and could get his hands on me; though I used to take to the woods most of the time when he was around. Well, about this time he was found in the river drownded, about twelve mile above town, so people said. They judged it was him, anyway; said this drownded man was just his size, and was ragged, and had uncommon long hair, which was all like pap; but they couldn't make nothing out of the face, because it had been in the water so long it warn't much like a face at all. They said he was floating on his back in the water. They took him and buried him on the bank. But I warn't comfortable long, because I happened to think of something. I knowed mighty well that a drownded man don't float on his back, but on his face. So I knowed, then, that this warn't pap, but a woman dressed up in a man's clothes. So I was uncomfortable again. I judged the old man would turn up again by and by, though I wished he wouldn't.

We played robber now and then about a month, and then I resigned. All the boys did. We hadn't robbed nobody, hadn't killed any people, but only just pretended. We used to hop out of the woods and go charging down on hog-drivers and women in carts taking garden stuff to market, but we never hived any of them. Tom Sawyer called the hogs "ingots," and he called the turnips and stuff "julery," and we would go to the cave and powwow over what we had done, and how many people we had killed and marked. But I couldn't see no profit in it. One time Tom sent a boy to run about town with a blazing stick, which he called a slogan (which was the sign for the Gang to get together), and then he said he had got secret news by his spies that next day a whole parcel of Spanish merchants and rich A-rabs was going to camp in Cave Hollow with two hundred elephants, and six hundred camels, and over a thousand "sumter" mules, all loaded down with di'monds, and they didn't have only a guard of four hundred soldiers, and so we would lay in ambuscade, as he called it, and kill the lot and scoop the things. He said we must slick up our swords and guns, and get ready. He never could go after even a turnip-cart but he must have the swords and guns all scoured up for it, though they was only lath and broomsticks, and you might scour at them till you rotted, and then they warn't worth a mouthful of ashes more than what they was before. I didn't believe we could lick such a crowd of Spaniards and A-rabs, but I wanted to see the camels and elephants, so I was on hand next day, Saturday, in the ambuscade; and when we got the word we rushed out of the woods and down the hill. But there warn't no Spaniards and A-rabs, and there warn't no camels nor no elephants. It warn't anything but a Sunday-school picnic, and only a primer class at that. We busted it up, and chased the children up the hollow; but we never got anything but some doughnuts and jam, though Ben Rogers got a rag doll, and Joe Harper got a hymn-book and a tract; and then the teacher charged in, and made us drop everything and cut. I didn't see no di'monds, and I told Tom Sawyer so. He said there was loads of them there, anyway; and he said there was A-rabs there, too, and elephants and things. I said, why couldn't we see them, then? He said if I warn't so ignorant, but had read a book called *Don Quixote,* I would know without asking. He said it was all done by enchantment. He said there was hundreds of soldiers there, and elephants and treasure, and so on, but we had enemies which he called magicians, and they had turned the whole thing into an infant Sunday-school, just out of spite. I said, all right; then the thing for us to do was to go for the magicians. Tom Sawyer said I was a numskull.

"Why," said he, "a magician could call up a lot of genies, and they would hash you up like nothing before you could say Jack Robinson. They are as tall as a tree and as big around as a church."

"Well," I says, "s'pose we got some genies to help *us*—can't we lick the other crowd then?"

"How you going to get them?"

"I don't know. How do *they* get them?"

"Why, they rub an old tin lamp or an iron ring, and then the genies come tearing in, with the thunder and lightning a-ripping around and the smoke a-rolling, and everything they're told to do they up and do it. They don't think nothing of pulling a shot-tower up by the roots, and belting a Sunday-school superintendent over the head with it —or any other man."

"Who makes them tear around so?"

"Why, whoever rubs the lamp or the ring. They belong to whoever rubs the lamp or

the ring, and they've got to do whatever he says. If he tells them to build a palace forty miles long out of di'monds, and fill it full of chewing-gum, or whatever you want, and fetch an emperor's daughter from China for you to marry, they've got to do it—and they've got to do it before sun-up next morning, too. And more: they've got to waltz that palace around over the country wherever you want it, you understand."

"Well," says I, "I think they are a pack of flatheads for not keeping the palace themselves 'stead of fooling them away like that. And what's more—if I was one of them I would see a man in Jericho before I would drop my business and come to him for the rubbing of an old tin lamp."

"How you talk, Huck Finn. Why, you'd *have* to come when he rubbed it, whether you wanted to or not."

"What! and I as high as a tree and as big as a church? All right, then; I *would* come; but I lay I'd make that man climb the highest tree there was in the country."

"Shucks, it ain't no use to talk to you, Huck Finn. You don't seem to know anything, some-how—perfect saphead."

I thought all this over for two or three days, and then I reckoned I would see if there was anything in it. I got an old tin lamp and an iron ring, and went out in the woods and rubbed and rubbed till I sweat like an Injun, calculating to build a palace and sell it; but it warn't no use, none of the genies come. So then I judged that all that stuff was only just one of Tom Sawyer's lies. I reckoned he believed in the A-rabs and the elephants, but as for me I think different. It had all the marks of a Sunday-school.

4· THE HAIR-BALL ORACLE

Well, three or four months run along, and it was well into the winter now. I had been to school most all the time and could spell and read and write just a little, and could say the multiplication table up to six times seven is thirty-five, and I don't reckon I could ever get any further than that if I was to live forever. I don't take no stock in mathematics, anyway.

At first I hated the school, but by and by I got so I could stand it. Whenever I got uncommon tired I played hookey, and the hiding I got next day done me good and cheered me up. So the longer I went to school the easier it got to be. I was getting sort of used to the widow's ways, too, and they warn't so raspy on me. Living in a house and sleeping in a bed pulled on me pretty tight mostly, but before the cold weather I used to slide out and sleep in the woods sometimes, and so that was a rest to me. I liked the old ways best, but I was getting so I liked the new ones, too, a little bit. The widow said I was coming along slow but sure, and doing very satisfactory. She said she warn't ashamed of me.

One morning I happened to turn over the salt-cellar at breakfast. I reached for some of it as quick as I could to throw over my left shoulder and keep off the bad luck, but Miss Watson was in ahead of me, and crossed me off. She says, "Take your hands away, Huckleberry; what a mess you are always making!" The widow put in a good word for me, but that warn't going to keep off the bad luck, I knowed that well enough. I started out, after breakfast, feeling worried and shaky, and wondering where it was going to fall on me, and what it was going to be. There is ways to keep off some kinds of bad luck, but this wasn't one of them kind; so I never tried to do anything, but just poked along low-spirited and on the watch-out.

I went down to the front garden and clumb over the stile where you go through the high board fence. There was an inch of new snow on the ground, and I seen somebody's tracks. They had come up from the quarry and stood around the stile awhile, and then went on around the garden fence. It was funny they hadn't come in, after standing around so. I couldn't make it out. It was very curious, somehow. I was going to follow around, but I stooped down to look at the tracks first. I didn't notice anything at first, but next I did. There was a cross in the left boot-heel made with big nails, to keep off the devil.

I was up in a second and shinning down the hill. I looked over my shoulder every now and then, but I didn't see nobody. I was at Judge Thatcher's as quick as I could get there. He said:

"Why, my boy, you are all out of breath. Did you come for your interest?"

"No, sir," I says; "is there some for me?"

"Oh, yes, a half-yearly is in last night—over a hundred and fifty dollars. Quite a fortune for you. You had better let me invest it along with your six thousand, because if you take it you'll spend it."

"No, sir," I says, "I don't want to spend it. I don't want it at all—nor the six thousand, nuther. I want you to take it; I want to give it to you—the six thousand and all."

He looked surprised. He couldn't seem to make it out. He says:

"Why, what can you mean, my boy?"

I says, "Don't you ask me no questions about it, please. You'll take it—won't you?"

He says:

"Well, I'm puzzled. Is something the matter?"

"Please take it," says I, "and don't ask me nothing—then I won't have to tell no lies."

He studied awhile, and then he says:

"Oho-o! I think I see. You want to *sell* all your property to me—not give it. That's the correct idea."

Then he wrote something on a paper and read it over, and says:

"There; you see it says 'for a consideration.' That means I have bought it of you and paid you for it. Here's a dollar for you. Now you sign it."

So I signed it, and left.

Miss Watson's nigger, Jim, had a hair-ball as big as your fist, which had been took out of the fourth stomach of an ox, and he used to do magic with it. He said there was a spirit inside of it, and it knowed everything. So I went to him that night and told him pap was here again, for I found his tracks in the snow. What I wanted to know was, what he was going to do, and was he going to stay? Jim got out his hair-ball and said something over it, and then he held it up and dropped it on the floor. It fell pretty solid, and only rolled about an inch. Jim tried it again, and then another time, and it acted just the same. Jim got down on his knees, and put his ear against it and listened. But it warn't no use; he said it wouldn't talk. He said sometimes it wouldn't talk without money. I told him I had an old slick counterfeit quarter that warn't no good because the brass showed through the silver a little, and it wouldn't pass nohow, even if the brass didn't show, because it was so slick it felt greasy, and so that would tell on it every time. (I reckoned I wouldn't say nothing about the dollar I got from the judge.) I said it was pretty bad money, but maybe the hair-ball would take it, because maybe it wouldn't know the difference. Jim smelt it and bit it and rubbed it, and said he would manage so the hair-ball would think it was good. He said he would split open a raw Irish potato and stick the quarter in between and keep it there all night, and next morning you couldn't see no brass, and it wouldn't feel greasy no more, and so anybody in town would take it in a minute, let alone a hair-ball. Well, I knowed a potato would do that before, but I had forgot it.

Jim put the quarter under the hair-ball, and got down and listened again. This time he said the hair-ball was all right. He said it would tell my whole fortune if I wanted it to. I says, go on. So the hair-ball talked to Jim, and Jim told it to me. He says:

"Yo' ole father doan' know yit what he's a-gwyne to do. Sometimes he spec he'll go 'way, en den ag'in he spec he'll stay. De bes' way is to res' easy en let de ole man take his own way. Dey's two angels hoverin' 'round 'bout him. One uv 'em is white en shiny, en t'other one is black. De white one gits him to go right a little while, den de black one sail in en bust it all up. A body can't tell yit which one gwyne to fetch him at de las'. But you is all right. You gwyne to have considable trouble in yo' life, en considable joy. Sometimes you gwyne to git hurt, en sometimes you gwyne to git sick; but every time you's gwyne to git well ag'in. Dey's two gals flyin' 'bout you in yo' life. One uv 'em's light en t'other one is dark. One is rich en t'other is po'. You's gwyne to marry de po' one fust en de rich one by en by. You wants to keep 'way fum de water as much as you kin, en don't run no resk, 'kase it's down in de bills dat you's gwyne to git hung."

When I lit my candle and went up to my room that night there sat pap—his own self!

5. PAP STARTS IN ON A NEW LIFE

I had shut the door to. Then I turned around, and there he was. I used to be scared of him all the time, he tanned me so much. I reckoned I was scared now, too; but in a minute I see I was mistaken—that is, after the first jolt, as you may say, when my breath sort of hitched, he being so unexpected; but right away after I see I warn't scared of him worth bothring about.

He was most fifty, and he looked it. His hair was long and tangled and greasy, and hung down, and you could see his eyes shining through like he was behind vines. It was all black, no gray; so was his long, mixed-up whiskers. There warn't no color in his face, where his face showed; it was white; not like another man's white, but a white to make a body sick, a white to make a body's flesh crawl —a tree-toad white, a fish-belly white. As for his clothes—just rags, that was all. He had one ankle resting on t'other knee; the boot on that foot was busted, and two of his toes stuck through, and he worked them now and then. His hat was laying on the floor—an old black slouch with the top caved in, like a lid.

I stood a-looking at him; he set there a-looking at me, with his chair tilted back a little. I set the candle down. I noticed the window was up; so he had clumb in by the shed. He kept a-looking me all over. By and by he says:

"Starchy clothes—very. You think you're a good deal of a big-bug, *don't* you?"

"Maybe I am, maybe I ain't," I says.

"Don't you give me none o' your lip," says he. "You've put on considerable many frills since I been away. I'll take you down a peg before I get done with you. You're educated, too, they say—can read and write. You think you're better'n your father, now, don't you, because he can't? *I'll* take it out of you. Who told you you might meddle with such hi-falut'n foolishness, hey?—who told you you could?"

"The widow. She told me."

"The widow, hey?—and who told the widow she could put in her shovel about a thing that ain't none of her business?"

"Nobody never told her."

"Well, I'll learn her how to meddle. And looky here—you drop that school, you hear? I'll learn people to bring up a boy to put on airs over his own father and let on to be better'n what *he* is. You lemme catch you fooling around that school again, you hear? Your mother couldn't read, and she couldn't write, nuther, before she died. None of the family couldn't before *they* died. *I* can't; and here you're a-swelling yourself up like this. I ain't the man to stand it—you hear? Say, lemme hear you read."

I took up a book and begun something about General Washington and the wars. When I'd read about a half a minute, he fetched the book a whack with his hand and knocked it across the house. He says:

"It's so. You can do it. I had my doubts when you told me. Now looky here; you stop that putting on frills. I won't have it. I'll lay for you, my smarty; and if I catch you about that school I'll tan you good. First you know you'll get religion, too. I never see such a son."

He took up a little blue and yaller picture of some cows and a boy, and says:

"What's this?"

"It's something they give me for learning my lessons good."

He tore it up, and says:

"I'll give you something better—I'll give you a cowhide."

He set there a-mumbling and a-growling a minute, and then he says:

"*Ain't* you a sweet-scented dandy, though? A bed; and bed-clothes; and a look'n'-glass; and a piece of carpet on the floor—and your own father got to sleep with the hogs in the tanyard. I never see such a son. I bet I'll take some o' these frills out o' you before I'm done with you. Why, there ain't no end to your airs—they say you're rich. Hey?—how's that?"

"They lie—that's how."

"Looky here—mind how you talk to me; I'm a-standing about all I can stand now—so don't gimme no sass. I've been in town two days, and I hain't heard nothing but about you bein' rich. I heard about it away down the river, too. That's why I come. You git me that money tomorrow—I want it."

"I hain't got no money."

"It's a lie. Judge Thatcher's got it. You git it. I want it."

"I hain't got no money, I tell you. You ask Judge Thatcher; he'll tell you the same."

"All right. I'll ask him; and I'll make him pungle, too, or I'll know the reason why. Say, how much you got in your pocket? I want it."

"I hain't got only a dollar, and I want that to—"

"It don't make no difference what you want it for—you just shell it out."

He took it and bit it to see if it was good, and then he said he was going down-town to get some whisky; said he hadn't had a drink all day. When he had got out on the shed he put his head in again, and cussed me for putting on frills and trying to be better than him; and when I reckoned he was gone he came back and put his head in again, and told me to mind about that school, because he was going to lay for me and lick me if I didn't drop that.

Next day he was drunk, and he went to Judge Thatcher's and bullyragged him, and tried to make him give up the money; but he couldn't, and then he swore he'd make the law force him.

The judge and the widow went to law to get the court to take me away from him and let one of them be my guardian; but it was a new judge that had just come, and he didn't know the old man; so he said courts mustn't interfere and separate families if they could help it; said he'd druther not take a child away from its father. So Judge Thatcher and the widow had to quit on the business.

That pleased the old man till he couldn't rest. He said he'd cowhide me till I was black and blue if I didn't raise some money for him. I borrowed three dollars from Judge Thatcher, and pap took it and got drunk, and went a-blowing around and cussing and whooping and carrying on; and he kept it up all over town, with a tin pan, till most midnight; then they jailed him, and the next day they had him before court, and jailed him again for a week. But he said *he* was satisfied; said he was boss of his son, and he'd make it warm for *him*.

When he got out the new judge said he was a-going to make a man of him. So he took him to his own house, and dressed him up clean and nice, and had him to breakfast and dinner and supper with the family, and was just old pie to him, so to speak. And after supper he talked to him about temperance and such things till the old man cried, and said he'd been a fool, and fooled away his life; but now he was a-going to turn over a new leaf and be a man nobody wouldn't be ashamed of, and he hoped the judge would help him and not look down on him. The judge said he could hug him for them words; so *he* cried, and his wife she cried again; pap said he'd been a man that had always been misunderstood before, and the judge said he believed it. The old man said that what a man wanted that was down was sympathy, and the judge said it was so; so they cried again. And when it was bed-time the old man rose up and held out his hand, and says:

"Look at it, gentlemen and ladies all; take a-hold of it; shake it. There's a hand that was the hand of a hog; but it ain't so no more; it's the hand of a man that's started in on a new life, and'll die before he'll go back. You mark them words—don't forget I said them. It's a clean hand now; shake it—don't be afeard."

So they shook it, one after the other, all around, and cried. The judge's wife she kissed it. Then the old man he signed a pledge—made his mark. The judge said it was the holi-est time on record, or something like that. Then they tucked the old man into a beauti-ful room, which was the spare room, and in the night some time he got powerful thirsty and clumb out on to the porch-roof and slid down a stanchion and traded his new coat for a jug of forty-rod, and clumb back again and had a good old time; and toward daylight he crawled out again, drunk as a fiddler, and rolled off the porch and broke his left arm in two places, and was most froze to death when somebody found him after sun-up. And when they come to look at that spare room they had to take soundings before they could navigate it.

The judge he felt kind of sore. He said he reckoned a body could reform the old man with a shotgun, maybe, but he didn't know no other way.

6. PAP STRUGGLES WITH THE DEATH ANGEL

Well, pretty soon the old man was up and around again, and then he went for Judge Thatcher in the courts to make him give up that money, and he went for me, too, for not stopping school. He catched me a couple of times and thrashed me, but I went to school just the same, and dodged him or outrun him

most of the time. I didn't want to go to school much before, but I reckoned I'd go now to spite pap. That law trial was a slow business—appeared like they warn't ever going to get started on it; so every now and then I'd bor-row two or three dollars off of the judge for him, to keep from getting a cowhiding. Every time he got money he got drunk; and every time he got drunk he raised Cain around town; and every time he raised Cain he got jailed. He was just suited—this kind of thing was right in his line.

He got to hanging around the widow's too much, and so she told him at last that if he didn't quit using around there she would make trouble for him. Well, *wasn't* he mad? He said he would show who was Huck Finn's boss. So he watched out for me one day in the spring, and catched me, and took me up the river about three mile in a skiff, and crossed over to the Illinois shore where it was woody and there warn't no houses but an old log hut in a place where the timber was so thick you couldn't find it if you didn't know where it was.

He kept me with him all the time, and I never got a chance to run off. We lived in that old cabin, and he always locked the door and put the key under his head nights. He had a gun which he had stole, I reckon, and we fished and hunted, and that was what we lived on. Every little while he locked me in and went down to the store, three miles, to the ferry, and traded fish and game for whisky, and fetched it home and got drunk and had a good time, and licked me. The widow she found out where I was by and by, and she sent a man over to try to get hold of me; but pap drove him off with the gun, and it warn't long after that till I was used to being where I was, and liked it—all but the cowhide part.

It was kind of lazy and jolly, laying off comfortable all day, smoking and fishing, and no books nor study. Two months or more run along, and my clothes got to be all rags and dirt, and I didn't see how I'd ever got to like it so well at the widow's, where you had to wash, and eat on a plate, and comb up, and go to bed and get up regular, and be forever bothering over a book, and have old Miss Watson pecking at you all the time. I didn't want to go back no more. I had stopped cussing, because the widow didn't like it; but now I took to it again because pap hadn't no objections. It was pretty good times up in the woods there, take it all around.

But by and by pap got too handy with his hick'ry, and I couldn't stand it. I was all over welts. He got to going away so much, too, and locking me in. Once he locked me in and was gone three days. It was dreadful lonesome. I judged he had got drownded, and I wasn't ever going to get out any more. I was scared. I made up my mind I would fix up some way to leave there. I had tried to get out of that cabin many a time, but I couldn't find no way. There warn't a window to it big enough for a dog to get through. I couldn't get up the chimbly; it was too narrow. The door was thick, solid oak slabs. Pap was pretty careful not to leave a knife or anything in the cabin when he was away; I reckon I had hunted the place over as much as a hundred times; well, I was most all the time at it, because it was about the only way to put in the time. But this time I found something at last; I found an old rusty wood-saw without any handle; it was laid in between a rafter and the clapboards of the roof. I greased it up and went to work. There was an old horse-blanket nailed against the logs at the far end of the cabin behind the table, to keep the wind from blowing through the chinks and putting the candle out. I got under the table and raised the blanket, and went to work to saw a section of the big bottom log out—big enough to let me through. Well, it was a good long job, but I was getting toward the end of it when I heard pap's gun in the woods. I got rid of the signs of my work, and dropped the blanket and hid my saw, and pretty soon pap come in.

Pap warn't in a good humor—so he was his natural self. He said he was down-town, and everything was going wrong. His lawyer said he reckoned he would win his lawsuit and get the money if they ever got started on the trial; but then there was ways to put it off a long time, and Judge Thatcher knowed how to do it. And he said people allowed there'd be another trial to get me away from him and give me to the widow for my guardian, and they guessed it would win this time. This shook me up considerable, because I didn't want to go back to the widow's any more and be so cramped up and civilized, as they called it. Then the old man got to cussing, and cussed everything and everybody he could think of, and then cussed them all over again to make sure he hadn't skipped any, and after that he polished off with a kind of a general cuss all round, including a considerable parcel of people which he didn't know the names of, and so called them what's-his-name when he got to them, and went right along with his cussing.

He said he would like to see the widow get me. He said he would watch out, and if they tried to come any such game on him he knowed of a place six or seven mile off to stow me in, where they might hunt till they dropped and they couldn't find me. That made me pretty uneasy again, but only for a minute; I reckoned I wouldn't stay on hand till he got that chance.

The old man made me go to the skiff and fetch the things he had got. There was a fifty-pound sack of corn meal, and a side of bacon, ammunition, and a four-gallon jug of whisky, and an old book and two newspapers for wadding, besides some tow. I toted up a load, and went back and set down on the bow of the skiff to rest. I thought it all over, and I reckoned I would walk off with the gun and some lines, and take to the woods when I run away. I guessed I wouldn't stay in one place, but just tramp right across the country, mostly night-times, and hunt and fish to keep alive, and so get so far away that the old man nor the widow couldn't ever find me any more. I judged I would saw out and leave that night if pap got drunk enough, and I reckoned he would. I got so full of it I didn't notice how long I was staying till the old man hollered and asked me whether I was asleep or drownded.

I got the things all up to the cabin, and then it was about dark. While I was cooking supper the old man took a swig or two and got sort of warmed up, and went to ripping again. He had been drunk over in town, and laid in the gutter all night, and he was a sight to look at. A body would 'a' thought he was Adam—he was just all mud. Whenever his liquor begun to work he most always went for the govment. This time he says:

"Call this a govment! why, just look at it and see what it's like. Here's the law a-standing ready to take a man's son away from him —a man's own son, which he has had all the trouble and all the anxiety and all the expense of raising. Yes, just as that man has got that son raised at last, and ready to go to work and begin to do suthin' for *him* and give him a rest, the law up and goes for him. And they call *that* govment! That ain't all, nuther. The law backs that old Judge Thatcher up and helps him to keep me out o' my property. Here's what the law does: The law takes a man worth six thousand dollars and up'ards, and jams him into an old trap of a cabin like this, and lets him go round in clothes that ain't fitten for a hog. They call that govment! A man can't get his rights in a govment like this. Sometimes I've a mighty notion to just leave the country for good and all. Yes, and I *told* 'em so; I told old Thatcher so to his face. Lots of 'em heard me, and can tell what I said. Says I, for two cents I'd leave the blamed country and never come a-near it ag'in. Them's the very words. I says, look at my hat—if you call it a hat—but the lid raises up and the rest of it goes down till it's below my chin, and then it ain't rightly a hat at all, but more like my head was shoved up through a jint o' stove-pipe. Look at it, says I—such a hat for me to wear—one of the wealthiest men in this town if I could git my rights.

"Oh, yes, this is a wonderful govment, wonderful. Why, looky here. There was a free nigger there from Ohio—a mulatter, most as white as a white man. He had the whitest shirt on you ever see, too, and the shiniest hat; and there ain't a man in that town that's got as fine clothes as what he had; and he had a gold watch and chain, and a silver-headed cane—the awfulest old gray-headed nabob in the state. And what do you think? They said he was a p'fessor in a college, and could talk all kinds of languages, and knowed everything. And that ain't the wust. They said he could *vote* when he was at home. Well, that let me out. Thinks I, what is the country a-coming to? It was 'lection day, and I was just about to go and vote myself if I warn't too drunk to get there; but when they told me there was a state in this country where they'd let that nigger vote, I drawed out. I says I'll never vote ag'in. Them's the very words I said; they all heard me; and the country may rot for all me —I'll never vote ag'in as long as I live. And to see the cool way of that nigger—why, he wouldn't 'a' give me the road if I hadn't shoved him out o' the way. I says to the people, why ain't this nigger put up at auction and sold?—that's what I want to know. And what do you reckon they said? Why, they said he couldn't be sold till he'd been in the state six months, and he hadn't been there that long yet. There, now—that's a specimen. They call that a govment that can't sell a free nigger till he's been in the state six months. Here's a govment that calls itself a govment, and lets on to be a govment, and thinks it is a govment, and yet's got to set stock-still for six whole months before it can take a-hold of a prowling, thieving, infernal, white-shirted free nigger, and—"

Pap was a-going on so he never noticed where his old limber legs was taking him to, so he went head over heels over the tub of salt pork and barked both shins, and the rest of his speech was all the hottest kind of language —mostly hove at the nigger and the govment, though he give the tub some, too, all along, here and there. He hopped around the cabin considerable, first on one leg and then on the other, holding first one shin and then the other one, and at last he let out with his left foot all of a sudden and fetched the tub a rattling kick. But it warn't good judgment, because that was the boot that had a couple of his toes leaking out of the front end of it; so now he raised a howl that fairly made a body's hair raise, and down he went in the dirt, and rolled there, and held his toes; and the cussing he done then laid over anything he had ever done previous. He said so his own self afterwards. He had heard old Sowberry Hagan in his best days, and he said it laid over him, too; but I reckon that was sort of piling it on, maybe.

After supper pap took the jug, and said he had enough whisky there for two drunks and one delirium tremens. That was always his word. I judged he would be blind drunk in about an hour, and then I would steal the key, or saw myself out, one or t'other. He drank and drank, and tumbled down on his blankets by and by; but luck didn't run my way. He didn't go sound asleep, but was uneasy. He groaned and moaned and thrashed around this way and that for a long time. At last I got so sleepy I couldn't keep my eyes open all I could do, and so before I knowed what I was about I was sound asleep, and the candle burning.

I don't know how long I was asleep, but all of a sudden there was an awful scream and I was up. There was pap looking wild, and skipping around every which way and yelling about snakes. He said they was crawling up his legs; and then he would give a jump and scream, and say one had bit him on the cheek —but I couldn't see no snakes. He started and run round and round the cabin, hollering, "Take him off! take him off! he's biting me on the neck!" I never see a man look so wild in the eyes. Pretty soon he was all fagged out, and fell down panting; then he rolled over and over wonderful fast, kicking things every which way, and striking and grabbing at the air with his hands, and screaming and saying there was devils a-hold of him. He wore out by and by, and laid still awhile, moaning. Then he laid stiller, and didn't make a sound. I could hear the owls and the wolves away off in the woods, and it seemed terrible still. He was laying over by the corner. By and by he raised up part way and listened, with his head to one side. He says, very low:

"Tramp—tramp—tramp; that's the dead; tramp—tramp—tramp; they're coming after me; but I won't go. Oh, they're here! don't touch me—don't! hands off—they're cold; let go. Oh, let a poor devil alone!"

Then he went down on all fours and crawled off, begging them to let him alone, and he rolled himself up in his blanket and wallowed in under the old pine table, still a-begging; and then he went crying. I could hear him through the blanket.

By and by he rolled out and jumped up to his feet looking wild, and he sees me and went for me. He chased me round and round the place with a clasp-knife, calling me the Angel of Death, and saying he would kill me, and then I couldn't come for him no more. I begged, and told him I was only Huck; but he laughed *such* a screechy laugh, and roared and cussed, and kept on chasing me up. Once when I turned short and dodged under his arm he made a grab and got me by the jacket between my shoulders, and I thought I was gone;

but I slid out of the jacket quick as light-ning, and saved myself. Pretty soon he was all tired out, and dropped down with his back against the door, and said he would rest a minute and then kill me. He put his knife under him, and said he would sleep and get strong, and then he would see who was who.

So he dozed off pretty soon. By and by I got the old split-bottom chair and clumb up as easy as I could, not to make any noise, and got down the gun. I slipped the ramrod down it to make sure it was loaded, and then I laid it across the turnip-barrel, pointing towards pap, and set down behind it to wait for him to stir. And how slow and still the time did drag along.

7. I FOOL PAP AND GET AWAY

"Git up! What you 'bout?"

I opened my eyes and looked around trying to make out where I was. It was after sun-up, and I had been sound asleep. Pap was standing over me looking sour—and sick, too. He says:

"What you doin' with this gun?"

I judged he didn't know nothing about what he had been doing, so I says:

"Somebody tried to get in, so I was laying for him."

"Why didn't you roust me out?"

"Well, I tried to, but I couldn't; I couldn't budge you."

"Well, all right. Don't stand there palaver-ing all day, but out with you and see if there's a fish on the lines for breakfast. I'll be along in a minute."

He unlocked the door, and I cleared out up the river-bank. I noticed some pieces of limbs and such things floating down, and a sprin-kling of bark; so I knowed the river had begun to rise. I reckoned I would have great times now if I was over at the town. The June rise used to be always luck for me; because as soon as that rise begins here comes cordwood floating down, and pieces of log rafts—some-times a dozen logs together; so all you have to do is to catch them and sell them to the wood-yards and the sawmill.

I went along up the bank with one eye out for pap and t'other one out for what the rise might fetch along. Well, all at once here comes a canoe; just a beauty, too, about thirteen or fourteen foot long, riding high like a duck. I shot head-first off of the bank like a frog, clothes and all on, and struck out for the canoe. I just expected there'd be somebody laying down in it, because people often done that to fool folks, and when a chap had pulled a skiff out most to it they'd raise up and laugh at him. But it warn't so this time. It was a drift-canoe sure enough, and I clumb in and paddled her ashore. Thinks I, the old man will be glad when he sees this—she's worth ten dollars. But when I got to shore pap wasn't in sight yet, and as I was running her into a little creek like a gully, all hung over with vines and willows, I struck another idea: I judged I'd hide her good, and then, 'stead of taking to the woods when I run off, I'd go down the river about fifty mile and camp in one place for good, and not have such a rough time tramping on foot.

It was pretty close to the shanty, and I thought I heard the old man coming all the time; but I got her hid; and then I out and looked around a bunch of willows, and there was the old man down the path a piece just drawing a bead on a bird with his gun. So he hadn't seen anything.

When he got along I was hard at it taking up a "trot" line. He abused me a little for being so slow; but I told him I fell in the river, and that was what made me so long. I knowed he would see I was wet, and then he would be asking questions. We got five catfish off the lines and went home.

While we laid off after breakfast to sleep up, both of us being about wore out, I got to thinking that if I could fix up some way to keep pap and the widow from trying to follow me, it would be a certainer thing than trusting to luck to get far enough off before they missed me; you see, all kinds of things might happen. Well, I didn't see no way for a while, but by and by pap raised up a minute to drink another barrel of water, and he says:

"Another time a man comes a-prowling round here you roust me out, you hear? That man warn't here for no good. I'd a shot him. Next time you roust me out, you hear?"

Then he dropped down and went to sleep again; what he had been saying give me the very idea I wanted. I says to myself, I can fix it now so nobody won't think of following me.

About twelve o'clock we turned out and went along up the bank. The river was coming up pretty fast, and lots of driftwood going by on the rise. By and by along comes part of a log raft—nine logs fast together. We went out with the skiff and towed it ashore. Then we had dinner. Anybody but pap would 'a' waited and seen the day through, so as to catch more stuff; but that warn't pap's style. Nine logs was enough for one time; he must shove right over to town and sell. So he locked me in and took the skiff, and started off towing the raft about half past three. I judged he wouldn't come back that night. I waited till I reckoned he had got a good start; then I out with my saw, and went to work on that log again. Before he was t'other side of the river I was out of the hole; him and his raft was just a speck on the water away off yonder.

I took the sack of corn meal and took it to where the canoe was hid, and shoved the vines and branches apart and put it in; then I done the same with the side of bacon; then the whisky-jug. I took all the coffee and sugar there was, and all the ammunition; I took the wadding; I took the bucket and gourd; took a dipper and a tin cup, and my old saw and two blankets, and the skillet and the coffee-pot. I took fish-lines and matches and other things—everything that was worth a cent. I cleaned out the place. I wanted an ax, but there wasn't any, only the one out at the woodpile, and I knowed why I was going to leave that. I fetched out the gun, and now I was done.

I had wore the ground a good deal crawling out of the hole and dragging out so many things. So I fixed that as good as I could from the outside by scattering dust on the place, which covered up the smoothness and the sawdust. Then I fixed the piece of log back into its place, and put two rocks under it and one against it to hold it there, for it was bent up at that place and didn't quite touch ground. If you stood four or five foot away and didn't know it was sawed, you wouldn't never notice it; and besides, this was the back of the cabin, and it warn't likely anybody would go fooling around there.

It was all grass clear to the canoe, so I

hadn't left a track. I followed around to see. I stood on the bank and looked out over the river. All safe. So I took the gun and went up a piece into the woods, and was hunting around for some birds when I see a wild pig; hogs soon went wild in them bottoms after they had got away from the prairie-farms. I shot this fellow and took him into camp.

I took the ax and smashed in the door. I beat it and hacked it considerable a-doing it. I fetched the pig in, and took him back nearly to the table and hacked into his throat with the ax, and laid him down on the ground to bleed; I say ground because it *was* ground— hard packed, and no boards. Well, next I took an old sack and put a lot of big rocks in it— all I could drag—and I started it from the pig, and dragged it to the door and through the woods down to the river and dumped it in, and down it sunk, out of sight. You could easy see that something had been dragged over the ground. I did wish Tom Sawyer was there; I knowed he would take an interest in this kind of business, and throw in the fancy touches. Nobody could spread himself like Tom Sawyer in such a thing as that.

Well, last I pulled out some of my hair, and blooded the ax good, and stuck it on the back side, and slung the ax in the corner. Then I took up the pig and held him to my breast with my jacket (so he couldn't drip) till I got a good piece below the house and then dumped him into the river. Now I thought of something else. So I went and got the bag of meal and my old saw out of the canoe, and fetched them to the house. I took the bag to where it used to stand, and ripped a hole in the bottom of it with the saw, for there warn't no knives and forks on the place —pap done everything with his clasp-knife about the cooking. Then I carried the sack about a hundred yards across the grass and through the willows east of the house, to a shallow lake that was five mile wide and full of rushes—and ducks too, you might say, in the season. There was a slough or a creek leading out of it on the other side that went miles away, I don't know where, but it didn't go to the river. The meal sifted out and made a little track all the way to the lake. I dropped pap's whetstone there too, so as to look like it had been done by accident. Then I tied up the rip in the meal-sack with a string, so it wouldn't leak no more, and took it and my saw to the canoe again.

It was about dark now; so I dropped the canoe down the river under some willows that hung over the bank, and waited for the moon to rise. I made fast to a willow; then I took a bite to eat, and by and by laid down in the canoe to smoke a pipe and lay out a plan. I says to myself, they'll follow the track of that sackful of rocks to the shore and then drag the river for me. And they'll follow that meal track to the lake and go browsing down the creek that leads out of it to find the robbers that killed me and took the things. They won't ever hunt the river for anything but my dead carcass. They'll soon get tired of that, and won't bother no more about me. All right; I can stop anywhere I want to. Jackson's Island is good enough for me; I know that island pretty well, and nobody ever comes there. And then I can paddle over to town nights, and slink around and pick up things I want. Jackson's Island's the place.

I was pretty tired, and the first thing I knowed I was asleep. When I woke up I didn't know where I was for a minute. I set up and looked around, a little scared. Then I remembered. The river looked miles and miles across. The moon was so bright I could 'a' counted the drift-logs that went a-slipping along, black and still, hundreds of yards out from shore. Everything was dead quiet, and it looked late, and *smelt* late. You know what I mean—I don't know the words to put it in.

I took a good gap and a stretch, and was just going to unhitch and start when I heard a sound away over the water. I listened. Pretty soon I made it out. It was that dull kind of a regular sound that comes from oars working in rowlocks when it's a still night. I peeped out through the willow branches, and there it was—a skiff, away across the water. I couldn't tell how many was in it. It kept a-coming, and when it was abreast of me I see there warn't but one man in it. Thinks I, maybe it's pap, though I warn't expecting him. He dropped below me with the current, and by and by he came a-swinging up shore in the easy water, and he went by so close I could 'a' reached out the gun and touched him. Well, it *was* pap, sure enough—and sober, too, by the way he laid his oars.

I didn't lose no time. The next minute I was a-spinning down-stream soft, but quick, in the shade of the bank. I made two mile and a half, and then struck out a quarter of a mile or more toward the middle of the river, because pretty soon I would be passing the ferry-landing, and people might see me and hail me. I got out amongst the driftwood, and then laid down in the bottom of the canoe and let her float. I laid there, and had a good rest and a smoke out of my pipe, looking away into the sky; not a cloud in it. The sky looks ever so deep when you lay down on your back in the moonshine; I never knowed it before. And how far a body can hear on the water such nights! I heard people talking at the ferry-landing. I heard what they said, too—every word of it. One man said it was getting towards the long days and the short nights now. T'other one said *this* warn't one of the short ones, he reckoned—and then they laughed, and he said it over again, and they laughed again; then they waked up another fellow and told him, and laughed, but he didn't laugh; he ripped out something brisk, and said let him alone. The first fellow said he 'lowed to tell it to his old woman—she would think it was pretty good; but he said that warn't nothing to some things he had said in his time. I heard one man say it was nearly three o'clock, and he hoped daylight wouldn't wait more than about a week longer. After that the talk got further and further away, and I couldn't make out the words any more; but I could hear the mumble, and now and then a laugh, too, but it seemed a long ways off.

I was away below the ferry now. I rose up, and there was Jackson's Island, about two mile and a half down-stream, heavy-timbered and standing up out of the middle of the river, big and dark and solid, like a steamboat without any lights. There warn't any signs of the bar at the head—it was all under water now.

It didn't take me long to get there. I shot past the head at a ripping rate, the current was so swift, and then I got into the dead water and landed on the side towards the Illinois shore. I run the canoe into a deep dent in the bank that I knowed about; I had

to part the willow branches to get in; and when I made fast nobody could 'a' seen the canoe from the outside.

I went up and set down on a log at the head of the island, and looked out on the big river and the black driftwood and away over to the town, three mile away, where there was three or four lights twinkling. A monstrous big lumber-raft was about a mile upstream, coming along down, with a lantern in the middle of it. I watched it come creeping down, and when it was most abreast of where I stood I heard a man say, "Stern oars, there! heave her head to stabboard!" I heard that just as plain as if the man was by my side.

There was a little gray in the sky now; so I stepped into the woods, and laid down for a nap before breakfast.

8. I SPARE MISS WATSON'S JIM

The sun was up so high when I waked that I judged it was after eight o'clock. I laid there in the grass and the cool shade thinking about things, and feeling rested and ruther comfortable and satisfied. I could see the sun out at one or two holes, but mostly it was big trees all about, and gloomy in there amongst them. There was freckled places on the ground where the light sifted down through the leaves, and the freckled places swapped about a little, showing there was a little breeze up there. A couple of squirrels set on a limb and jabbered at me very friendly.

I was powerful lazy and comfortable—didn't want to get up and cook breakfast. Well, I was dozing off again when I thinks I hears a deep sound of "boom!" away up the river. I rouses up, and rests on my elbow and listens; pretty soon I hears it again. I hopped up, and went and looked out at a hole in the leaves, and I see a bunch of smoke laying on the water a long ways up—about abreast the ferry. And there was the ferryboat full of people floating along down. I knowed what was the matter now. "Boom!" I see the white smoke squirt out of the ferryboat's side. You see, they was firing cannon over the water, trying to make my carcass come to the top.

I was pretty hungry, but it warn't going to do for me to start a fire, because they might see the smoke. So I set there and watched the cannon-smoke and listened to the boom. The river was a mile wide there, and it always looks pretty on a summer morning—so I was having a good enough time seeing them hunt for my remainders if I only had a bite to eat. Well, then I happened to think how they always put quicksilver in loaves of bread and float them off, because they always go right to the drownded carcass and stop there. So, says I, I'll keep a lookout, and if any of them's floating around after me I'll give them a show. I changed to the Illinois edge of the island to see what luck I could have, and I warn't disappointed. A big double loaf come along, and I most got it with a long stick, but my foot slipped and she floated out further. Of course I was where the current set in the closest to the shore—I knowed enough for that. But by and by along comes another one, and this time I won. I took out the plug and shook out the little dab of quicksilver, and set my teeth in. It was "baker's bread"—what the quality eat; none of your low-down corn-pone.

I got a good place amongst the leaves, and set there on a log, munching the bread and watching the ferryboat, and very well satisfied. And then something struck me. I says, now I reckon the widow or the parson or somebody prayed that this bread would find me, and here it has gone and done it. So there ain't no doubt but there is something in that thing—that is, there's something in it when a body like the widow or the parson prays, but it don't work for me, and I reckon it don't work for only just the right kind.

I lit a pipe and had a good long smoke, and went on watching. The ferryboat was floating with the current, and I allowed I'd have a chance to see who was aboard when she come along, because she would come in close, where the bread did. When she'd got pretty well along down towards me, I put out my pipe and went to where I fished out the bread, and laid down behind a log on the bank in a little open place. Where the log forked I could peep through.

By and by she come along, and she drifted in so close that they could 'a' run out a plank and walked ashore. Most everybody was on the boat. Pap, and Judge Thatcher, and Bessie Thatcher, and Joe Harper, and Tom Sawyer, and his old Aunt Polly, and Sid and Mary, and plenty more. Everybody was talking about the murder, but the captain broke in and says:

"Look sharp, now; the current sets in the closest here, and maybe he's washed ashore and got tangled amongst the brush at the water's edge. I hope so, anyway."

I didn't hope so. They all crowded up and leaned over the rails, nearly in my face, and kept still, watching with all their might. I could see them first-rate, but they couldn't see me. Then the captain sung out: "Stand away!" and the cannon let off such a blast right before me that it made me deef with the noise and pretty near blind with the smoke, and I judged I was gone. If they'd 'a' had some bullets in, I reckon they'd 'a' got the corpse they was after. Well, I see I warn't hurt, thanks to goodness. The boat floated on and went out of sight around the shoulder of the island. I could hear the booming now and then, further and further off, and by and by, after an hour, I didn't hear it no more. The island was three mile long. I judged they had got to the foot, and was giving it up. But they didn't yet awhile. They turned around the foot of the island and started up the channel on the Missouri side, under steam, and booming once in a while as they went. I crossed over to that side and watched them. When they got abreast the head of the island they quit shooting and dropped over to the Missouri shore and went home to the town.

I knowed I was all right now. Nobody else would come a-hunting after me. I got my traps out of the canoe and made me a nice camp in the thick woods. I made a kind of a tent out of my blankets to put my things under so the rain couldn't get at them. I catched a catfish and haggled him open with my saw, and towards sundown I started my camp-fire and had supper. Then I set out a line to catch some fish for breakfast.

When it was dark I set by my camp-fire smoking, and feeling pretty well satisfied; but by and by it got sort of lonesome, and so I went and set on the bank and listened to the current swashing along, and counted the stars and drift-logs and rafts that come down, and then went to bed; there ain't no better way to put in time when you are lonesome; you can't stay so, you soon get over it.

And so for three days and nights. No difference—just the same thing. But the next day I went exploring around down through the island. I was boss of it; it all belonged to me, so to say, and I wanted to know all about it; but mainly I wanted to put in the time. I found plenty strawberries, ripe and prime; and green summer grapes, and green razberries; and the green blackberries was just beginning to show. They would all come handy by and by, I judged.

Well, I went fooling along in the deep woods till I judged I warn't far from the foot of the island. I had my gun along, but I hadn't shot nothing; it was for protection; thought I would kill some game nigh home. About this time I mighty near stepped on a good-sized snake, and it went sliding off through the grass and flowers, and I after it, trying to get a shot at it. I clipped along, and all of a sudden I bounded right on to the ashes of a camp-fire that was still smoking.

My heart jumped up amongst my lungs. I never waited for to look further, but uncocked my gun and went sneaking back on my tiptoes as fast as ever I could. Every now and then I stopped a second amongst the thick leaves and listened, but my breath come so hard I couldn't hear nothing else. I slunk along another piece further, then listened again; and so on, and so on. If I see a stump, I took it for a man; if I trod on a stick and broke it, it made me feel like a person had cut one of my breaths in two and I only got half, and the short half, too.

When I got to camp I warn't feeling very brash, there warn't much sand in my craw; but I says, this ain't no time to be fooling around. So I got all my traps into my canoe again so as to have them out of sight, and I put out the fire and scattered the ashes around to look like an old last-year's camp, and then clumb a tree.

I reckon I was up in the tree two hours; but I didn't see nothing, I didn't hear nothing—I only *thought* I heard and seen as much as a thousand things. Well, I couldn't stay up there forever; so at last I got down, but I kept in the thick woods and on the lookout all the time. All I could get to eat was berries and what was left over from breakfast.

By the time it was night I was pretty hungry. So when it was good and dark I slid out from shore before moonrise and paddled over to the Illinois bank—about a quarter of a mile. I went out in the woods and cooked a supper, and I had about made up my mind I would stay there all night when I hear a *plunkety-plunk, plunkety-plunk,* and says to myself, horses coming; and next I hear people's voices. I got everything into the canoe as quick as I could, and then went creeping through the woods to see what I could find out. I hadn't got far when I hear a man say: "We better camp here if we can find a good place; the horses is about beat out. Let's look around."

I didn't wait, but shoved out and paddled away easy. I tied up in the old place, and reckoned I would sleep in the canoe.

I didn't sleep much. I couldn't, somehow, for thinking. And every time I waked up I thought somebody had me by the neck. So the sleep didn't do me no good. By and by I says to myself, I can't live this way; I'm a-going to find out who it is that's here on the island with me; I'll find it out or bust. Well, I felt better right off.

So I took my paddle and slid out from shore just a step or two, and then let the canoe drop along down amongst the shadows. The moon was shining, and outside of the shadows it made it most as light as day. I poked along well on to an hour, everything still as rocks and sound asleep. Well, by this time I was most down to the foot of the island. A little ripply, cool breeze begun to blow, and that was as good as saying the night was about done. I give her a turn with the paddle and brung her nose to shore; then I got my gun and slipped out and into the edge of the woods. I sat down there on a log, and looked out through the leaves. I see the moon go off watch, and the darkness begin to blanket the river. But in a little while I see a pale streak over the treetops, and knowed the day was coming. So I took my gun and slipped off towards where I had run across that camp-fire, stopping every minute or two to listen. But I hadn't no luck somehow; I couldn't seem to find the place. But by and by, sure enough, I catched a glimpse of fire away through the trees. I went for it, cautious and slow. By and by I was close enough to have a look, and there laid a man on the ground. It most give me the fantods. He had a blanket around his head, and his head was nearly in the fire. I set there behind a clump of bushes in about six foot of him, and kept my eyes on him steady. It was getting gray daylight now. Pretty soon he gapped and stretched himself and hove off the blanket, and it was Miss Watson's Jim! I bet I was glad to see him. I says:

"Hello, Jim!" and skipped out.

He bounced up and stared at me wild. Then he drops down on his knees, and puts his hands together and says:

"Doan' hurt me—don't! I hain't ever done no harm to a ghos'. I alwuz liked dead people, en done all I could for 'em. You go en git in de river ag'in, whah you b'longs, en doan' do nuffn to Ole Jim, 'at 'uz alwuz yo' fren'."

Well, I warn't long making him understand I warn't dead. I was ever so glad to see Jim. I warn't lonesome now. I told him I warn't afraid of *him* telling the people where I was. I talked along, but he only set there and looked at me; never said nothing. Then I says:

"It's good daylight. Le's get breakfast. Make up your camp-fire good."

"What's de use er makin' up de camp-fire to cook strawbries en sich truck? But you got a gun, hain't you? Den we kin git sumfn better den strawbries."

"Strawberries and such truck," I says. "Is that what you live on?"

"I couldn't git nuffn else," he says.

"Why, how long you been on the island, Jim?"

"I come heah de night arter you's killed."

"What, all that time?"

"Yes-indeedy."

"And ain't you had nothing but that kind of rubbage to eat?"

"No, sah—nuffn else."

"Well, you must be most starved, ain't you?"

"I reck'n I could eat a hoss. I think I could. How long you ben on de islan'?"

"Since the night I got killed."

"No! W'y, what has you lived on? But you got a gun. Oh, yes, you got a gun. Dat's good. Now you kill sumfn en I'll make up de fire."

So we went over to where the canoe was, and while he built a fire in a grassy open place amongst the trees, I fetched meal and bacon and coffee, and coffee-pot and frying-pan, and sugar and tin cups, and the nigger was set back considerable, because he reckoned it was all done with witchcraft. I catched a good big catfish, too, and Jim cleaned him with his knife, and fried him.

When breakfast was ready we lolled on the grass and eat it smoking hot. Jim laid it in with all his might, for he was most about starved. Then when we had got pretty well stuffed, we laid off and lazied.

By and by Jim says:

"But looky here, Huck, who wuz it dat 'uz killed in dat shanty ef it warn't you?"

Then I told him the whole thing, and he said it was smart. He said Tom Sawyer couldn't get up no better plan than what I had. Then I says:

"How do you come to be here, Jim, and how'd you get here?"

He looked pretty uneasy, and didn't say nothing for a minute. Then he says:

"Maybe I better not tell."

"Why, Jim?"

"Well, dey's reasons. But you wouldn't tell on me ef I 'uz to tell you, would you, Huck?"

"Blamed if I would, Jim."

"Well, I b'lieve you, Huck I—I *run off.*"

"Jim!"

"But mind, you said you wouldn' tell—you know you said you wouldn' tell, Huck."

"Well, I did. I said I wouldn't, and I'll stick to it. Honest *injun,* I will. People would call me a low-down Abolitionist and despise me for keeping mum—but that don't make no difference. I ain't a-going to tell, and I ain't a-going back there, anyways. So, now, le's know all about it."

"Well, you see, it 'uz dis way. Ole missus—dat's Miss Watson—she pecks on me all de time, en treats me pooty rough, but she awluz said she wouldn' sell me down to Orleans. But I noticed dey wuz a nigger trader roun' de place considable lately, en I begin to git oneasy. Well, one night I creeps to de do' pooty late, en de do' warn't quite shet, en I hear old missus tell de widder she gwyne to sell me down to Orleans, but she didn' want to, but she could git eight hund'd dollars for me, en it 'uz sich a big stack o' money she couldn' resis'. De widder she try to git her to say she wouldn't do it, but I never waited to hear de res'. I lit out mighty quick, I tell you.

"I tuck out en shin down de hill, en 'spec to steal a skift 'long de sho' som'ers 'bove de town, but dey wuz people a-stirring yit, so I hid in de ole tumbledown cooper shop on de bank to wait for everybody to go 'way. Well, I wuz dah all night. Dey wuz somebody roun' all de time. 'Long 'bout six in de mawnin' skifts begin to go by, en 'bout eight er nine every skift dat went 'long wuz talkin' 'bout how yo' pap come over to de town en say you's killed. Dese las' skifts wuz full o' ladies en genlmen a-goin' over for to see de place. Sometimes dey'd pull up at de sho' en take a res' b'fo' dey started acrost, so by de talk I got to know all 'bout de killin'. I 'uz powerful sorry you's killed, Huck, but I ain't no mo' now.

"I laid dah under de shavin's all day. I 'uz hungry, but I warn't afeard; bekase I knowed ole missus en de widder wuz goin' to start to de camp-meet'n' right arter breakfas' en be gone all day, en dey knows I goes off wid de cattle 'bout daylight, so dey wouldn' 'spec to see me roun' de place, en so dey wouldn' miss me tell arter dark in de evenin'. De yuther servants wouldn' miss me, kase dey'd shin out en take holiday soon as de ole folks 'uz out'n de way.

"Well, when it come dark I tuck out up de river road, en went 'bout two mile er more to whah dey warn't no houses. I'd made up my mine 'bout what I's a-gwyne to do. You see, ef I kep' on tryin' to git away afoot, de dogs 'ud track me; ef I stole a skift to cross over, dey'd miss dat skift, you see, en dey'd know 'bout whah I'd lan' on de yuther side, en whah to pick up my track. So I says, a raff is what I's arter; it doan' *make* no track.

"I see a light a-comin' roun' de p'int by-meby, so I wade' in en shove' a log ahead o' me en swum more'n half-way acrost de river, en got in 'mongst de driftwood, en kep' my head down low, en kinder swum agin de current tell de raff come along. Den I swum to de stern uv it en tuck a-holt. It clouded up en 'uz pooty dark for a little while. So I clumb up en laid down on de planks. De men 'uz all 'way yonder in de middle, whah de lantern wuz. De river wuz a-risin', en dey wuz a good current; so I reck'n'd 'at by fo' in de mawnin' I'd be twenty-five mile down de river, en den

I'd slip in jis b'fo' daylight en swim asho', en take to de woods on de Illinois side.

"But I didn' have no luck. When we 'uz mos' down to de head er de islan' a man begin to come aft wid de lantern. I see it warn't no use fer to wait, so I slid overboard en struck out fer de islan'. Well, I had a notion I could lan' mos' anywhers, but I couldn't—bank too bluff. I 'uz mos' to de foot er de islan' b'fo' I foun' a good place. I went into de woods en jedged I wouldn' fool wid raffs no mo', long as dey move de lantern roun' so. I had my pipe en a plug er dog-leg en some matches in my cap, en dey warn't wet, so I 'uz all right."

"And so you ain't had no meat nor bread to eat all this time? Why didn't you get mud-turkles?"

"How you gwyne to git 'm? You can't slip up on um en grab um; en how's a body gwyne to hit um wid a rock? How could a body do it in de night? En I warn't gwyne to show mysef on de bank in de daytime."

"Well, that's so. You've had to keep in the woods all the time, of course. Did you hear 'em shooting the cannon?"

"Oh, yes. I knowed dey was arter you. I see um go by heah—watched um thoo de bushes."

Some young birds come along, flying a yard or two at a time and lighting. Jim said it was a sign it was going to rain. He said it was a sign when young chickens flew that way, and so he reckoned it was the same way when young birds done it. I was going to catch some of them, but Jim wouldn't let me. He said it was death. He said his father laid mighty sick once, and some of them catched a bird, and his old granny said his father would die, and he did.

And Jim said you mustn't count the things you are going to cook for dinner, because that would bring bad luck. The same if you shook the tablecloth after sundown. And he said if a man owned a beehive and that man died, the bees must be told about it before sun-up next morning, or else the bees would all weaken down and quit work and die. Jim said bees wouldn't sting idiots; but I didn't believe that, because I had tried them lots of times myself, and they wouldn't sting me.

I had heard about some of these things before, but not all of them. Jim knowed all kinds of signs. He said he knowed most everything. I said it looked to me like all the signs was about bad luck, and so I asked him if there warn't any good-luck signs. He says:

"Mighty few—an' *dey* ain't no use to a body. What you want to know when good luck's a-comin' for? Want to keep it off?" And he said: "Ef you's got hairy arms en a hairy breas', it's a sign dat you's a-gwyne to be rich. Well, dey's some use in a sign like dat, 'kase it's so fur ahead. You see, maybe you's got to be po' a long time fust, en so you might git discourage' en kill yo'sef 'f you didn' know by de sign dat you gwyne to be rich bymeby."

"Have you got hairy arms and a hairy breast, Jim?"

"What's de use to ax dat question? Don't you see I has?"

"Well, are you rich?"

"No, but I ben rich wunst, and gwyne to be rich ag'in. Wunst I had foteen dollars, but I tuck to specalat'n', en got busted out."

"What did you speculate in, Jim?"

"Well, fust I tackled stock."

"What kind of stock?"

"Why, live stock—cattle, you know. I put ten dollars in a cow. But I ain't gwyne to resk no mo' money in stock. De cow up 'n' died on my han's."

"So you lost the ten dollars."

"No, I didn't lose it all. I on'y los' 'bout nine of it. I sole de hide en taller for a dollar en ten cents."

"You had five dollars and ten cents left. Did you speculate any more?"

"Yes. You know that one-laigged nigger dat b'longs to old Misto Bradish? Well, he sot up a bank, en say anybody dat put in a dollar would git fo' dollars mo' at de en' er de year. Well, all de niggers went in, but dey didn't have much. I wuz de on'y one dat had much. So I stuck out for mo' dan fo' dollars, en I said 'f I didn't git it I'd start a bank mysef. Well, o' course dat nigger want' to keep me out er de business, bekase he says dey warn't business 'nough for two banks, so he say I could put in my five dollars en he pay me thirty-five at de 'en er de year.

"So I done it. Den I reck'n'd I'd inves' de thirty-five dollars right off en keep things a-movin'. Dey wuz a nigger name' Bob, dat had ketched a wood-flat, en his marster didn' know it; en I bought it off'n him en told him to take de thirty-five dollars when de en' er de year come; but somebody stole de wood-flat dat night, en nex' day de one-laigged nigger say de bank's busted. So dey didn' none uv us git no money."

"What did you do with the ten cents, Jim?"

"Well, I 'uz gwyne to spen' it, but I had a dream, en de dream tole me to give it to a nigger name' Balum—Balum's Ass dey call him for short; he's one er dem chuckleheads, you know. But he's lucky, dey say, en I see I warn't lucky. De dream say let Balum inves' de ten cents en he'd make a raise for me. Well, Balum he tuck de money, en when he wuz in church he hear de preacher say dat whoever give to de po' len' to de Lord, en boun' to git his money back a hund'd times. So Balum he tuck en give de ten cents to de po', en laid low to see what wuz gwyne to come of it."

"Well, what did come of it, Jim?"

"Nuffn never come of it. I couldn' manage to k'leck dat money no way; en Balum he couldn'. I ain' gwyne to len' no mo' money 'dout I see de security. Boun' to git yo' money back a hund'd times, de preacher says! Ef I could git de ten *cents* back, I'd call it squah, en be glad er de chanst."

"Well, it's all right anyway, Jim, long as you're going to be rich again some time or other."

"Yes; en I's rich now, come to look at it. I owns mysef, en I's wuth eight hund'd dollars. I wisht I had de money, I wouldn' want no mo'."

9. THE HOUSE OF DEATH FLOATS BY

I wanted to go and look at a place right about the middle of the island that I'd found when I was exploring; so we started and soon got to it, because the island was only three miles long and a quarter of a mile wide.

This place was a tolerable long, steep hill or ridge about forty foot high. We had a rough time getting to the top, the sides was so steep and the bushes so thick. We tramped and clumb around all over it, and by and by found a good big cavern in the rock, most up to the top on the side towards Illinois. The cavern was as big as two or three rooms bunched together, and Jim could stand up straight in it. It was cool in there. Jim was for putting our traps in there right away, but I said we didn't want to be climbing up and down there all the time.

Jim said if we had the canoe hid in a good place, and had all the traps in the cavern, we could rush there if anybody was to come to the island, and they would never find us without dogs. And, besides, he said them little birds had said it was going to rain, and did I want the things to get wet?

So we went back and got the canoe, and paddled up abreast the cavern, and lugged all the traps up there. Then we hunted up a place close by to hide the canoe in, amongst the thick willows. We took some fish off of the lines and set them again, and begun to get ready for dinner.

The door of the cavern was big enough to roll a hogshead in, and on one side of the door the floor stuck out a little bit, and was flat and a good place to build a fire on. So we built it there and cooked dinner.

We spread the blankets inside for a carpet, and eat our dinner in there. We put all the other things handy at the back of the cavern. Pretty soon it darkened up, and begun to thunder and lighten; so the birds was right about it. Directly it begun to rain, and it rained like all fury, too, and I never see the wind blow so. It was one of these regular summer storms. It would get so dark that it looked all blue-black outside, and lovely; and the rain would thrash along by so thick that the trees off a little ways looked dim and spider-webby; and here would come a blast of wind that would bend the trees down and turn up the pale underside of the leaves; and then a perfect ripper of a gust would follow along and set the branches to tossing their arms as if they was just wild; and next, when it was just about the bluest and blackest—*fst!* it was as bright as glory, and you'd have a little glimpse of treetops a-plunging about away off yonder in the storm, hundreds of yards further than you could see before; dark as sin again in a second, and now you'd hear the thunder let go with an awful crash, and then go rumbling, grumbling, tumbling, down the sky towards the under side of the world, like rolling empty barrels down-stairs—where it's long

stairs and they bounce a good deal, you know.

"Jim, this is nice," I says. "I wouldn't want to be nowhere else but here. Pass me along another hunk of fish and some hot cornbread."

"Well, you wouldn't 'a' ben here 'f it hadn't 'a' ben for Jim. You'd 'a' ben down dah in de woods widout any dinner, en gittin' mos' drownded, too; dat you would, honey. Chickens knows when it's gwyne to rain, en so do de birds, chile."

The river went on raising and raising for ten or twelve days, till at last it was over the banks. The water was three or four foot deep on the island in the low places and on the Illinois bottom. On that side it was a good many miles wide, but on the Missouri side it was the same old distance across—a half a mile—because the Missouri shore was just a wall of high bluffs.

Daytimes we paddled all over the island in the canoe. It was mighty cool and shady in the deep woods, even if the sun was blazing outside. We went winding in and out amongst the trees, and sometimes the vines hung so thick we had to back away and go some other way. Well, on every old broken-down tree you could see rabbits and snakes and such things; and when the island had been overflowed a day or two they got so tame, on account of being hungry, that you could paddle right up and put your hand on them if you wanted to; but not the snakes and turtles—they would slide off in the water. The ridge our cavern was in was full of them. We could 'a' had pets enough if we'd wanted them.

One night we catched a little section of a lumber-raft—nice pine planks. It was twelve foot wide and about fifteen or sixteen foot long, and the top stood above water six or seven inches—a solid, level floor. We could see saw-logs go by in the daylight sometimes, but we let them go; we didn't show ourselves in daylight.

Another night when we was up at the head of the island, just before daylight, here comes a frame-house down, on the west side. She was a two-story, and tilted over considerable. We paddled out and got aboard—clumb in at an up-stairs window. But it was too dark to see yet, so we made the canoe fast and set in her to wait for daylight.

The light begun to come before we got to the foot of the island. Then we looked in at the window. We could make out a bed, and a table, and two old chairs, and lots of things around about on the floor, and there was clothes hanging against the wall. There was something laying on the floor in the far corner that looked like a man. So Jim says:

"Hello, you!"

But it didn't budge. So I hollered again, and then Jim says:

"De man ain't asleep—he's dead. You hold still—I'll go en see."

He went, and bent down and looked, and says:

"It's a dead man. Yes, indeedy; naked, too. He's ben shot in de back. I reck'n he's ben dead two er three days. Come in, Huck, but doan' look at his face—it's too gashly."

I didn't look at him at all. Jim throwed some old rags over him, but he needn't done it; I didn't want to see him. There was heaps of old greasy cards scattered around over the floor, and old whisky-bottles, and a couple of masks made out of black cloth; and all over the walls was the ignorantest kind of words and pictures made with charcoal. There was two old dirty calico dresses, and a sun-bonnet, and some women's underclothes hanging against the wall, and some men's clothing, too. We put the lot into the canoe—it might come good. There was a boy's old speckled straw hat on the floor; I took that, too. And there was a bottle that had had milk in it, and it had a rag stopper for a baby to suck. We would 'a' took the bottle, but it was broke. There was a seedy old chest, and an old hair trunk with the hinges broke. They stood open, but there warn't nothing left in them that was any account. The ways things was scattered about we reckoned the people left in a hurry, and warn't fixed so as to carry off most of their stuff.

We got an old tin lantern, and a butcher-knife without any handle, and a bran-new Barlow knife worth two bits in any store, and a lot of tallow candles, and a tin candlestick, and a gourd, and a tin cup, and a ratty old bedquilt off the bed, and a reticule with needles and pins and beeswax and buttons and thread and all such truck in it, and a hatchet and some nails, and a fish-line as thick as my little finger with some monstrous hooks on it, and a roll of buckskin, and a leather dog-collar, and a horseshoe, and some vials of medicine that didn't have no label on them; and just as we was leaving I found a tolerable good currycomb, and Jim he found a ratty old fiddle-bow, and a wooden leg. The straps was broke off of it, but, barring that, it was a good enough leg, though it was too long for me and not long enough for Jim, and we couldn't find the other one, though we hunted all around.

And so, take it all around, we made a good haul. When we was ready to shove off we was a quarter of a mile below the island, and it was pretty broad day; so I made Jim lay down in the canoe and cover up with a quilt, because if he set up people could tell he was a nigger a good ways off. I paddled over to the Illinois shore, and drifted down most a half a mile doing it. I crept up the dead water under the bank, and hadn't no accidents and didn't see nobody. We got home all safe.

10. WHAT COMES OF HANDLIN' SNAKE-SKIN

After breakfast I wanted to talk about the dead man and guess out how he come to be killed, but Jim didn't want to. He said it would fetch bad luck; and besides, he said, he might come and ha'nt us; he said a man that warn't buried was more likely to go a-ha'nting around than one that was planted and comfortable. That sounded pretty reasonable, so I didn't say no more; but I couldn't keep from studying over it and wishing I knowed who shot the man, and what they done it for.

We rummaged the clothes we'd got, and found eight dollars in silver sewed up in the lining of an old blanket overcoat. Jim said he reckoned the people in that house stole the coat, because if they'd 'a' knowed the money was there they wouldn't 'a' left it. I said I reckoned they killed him, too; but Jim didn't want to talk about that. I says:

"Now you think it's bad luck; but what did you say when I fetched in the snake-skin that I found on the top of the ridge day before yesterday? You said it was the worst bad luck in the world to touch a snake-skin with my hands. Well, here's your bad luck! We've raked in all this truck and eight dollars besides. I wish we could have some bad luck like this every day, Jim."

"Never you mind, honey, never you mind. Don't you git too peart. It's a-comin'. Mind I tell you, it's a-comin'."

It did come, too. It was a Tuesday that we had that talk. Well, after dinner Friday we was laying around in the grass at the upper end of the ridge, and got out of tobacco. I went to the cavern to get some, and found a rattlesnake in there. I killed him, and curled him up on the foot of Jim's blanket, ever so natural, thinking there'd be some fun when Jim found him there. Well, by night I forgot all about the snake, and when Jim flung himself down on the blanket while I struck a light the snake's mate was there, and bit him.

He jumped up yelling, and the first thing the light showed was the varmint curled up and ready for another spring. I laid him out in a second with a stick, and Jim grabbed pap's whisky-jug and begun to pour it down.

He was barefooted, and the snake bit him right on the heel. That all comes of my being such a fool as to not remember that wherever you leave a dead snake its mate always comes there and curls around it. Jim told me to chop off the snake's head and throw it away, and then skin the body and roast a piece of it. I done it, and he eat it and said it would help cure him. He made me take off the rattles and tie them around his wrist, too. He said that that would help. Then I slid out quiet and throwed the snakes clear away amongst the bushes; for I warn't going to let Jim find out it was all my fault, not if I could help it.

Jim sucked and sucked at the jug, and now and then he got out of his head and pitched around and yelled; but every time he come to himself he went to sucking at the jug again. His foot swelled up pretty big, and so did his leg; but by and by the drunk begun to come, and so I judged he was all right; but I'd druther been bit with a snake than pap's whisky.

Jim was laid up for four days and nights. Then the swelling was all gone and he was around again. I made up my mind I wouldn't ever take a-holt of a snake-skin again with my hands, now that I see what had come of it. Jim said he reckoned I would believe him next time. And he said that handling a snake-skin was such awful bad luck that maybe we hadn't got to the end of it yet. He said he druther see the new moon over his left shoulder as much as a thousand times than take up a snake-skin in his hand. Well, I was getting to feel that way myself, though I've always reckoned that looking at the new moon over your left shoulder is one of the carelessest and foolishest things a body can do. Old Hank Bunker done it once, and bragged about it; and in less than two years he got drunk and fell off of the shot-tower, and spread himself out so that he was just a kind of a layer, as you may say; and they slid him edgeways between two barn doors for a coffin, and buried him so, so they say, but I didn't see it. Pap told me. But anyway it all come of looking at the moon that way, like a fool.

Well, the days went along, and the river went down between its banks again; and about the first thing we done was to bait one of the big hooks with a skinned rabbit and set it and catch a catfish that was as big as a man, being six foot two inches long, and weighed over two hundred pounds. We couldn't handle him, of course; he would 'a' flung us into Illinois. We just set there and watched him rip and tear around till he drownded. We found a brass button in his stomach and a round ball, and lots of rubbage. We split the ball open with a hatchet, and there was a spool in it. Jim said he'd had it there a long time, to coat it over so and make a ball of it. It was as big a fish as was ever catched in the Mississippi, I reckon. Jim said he hadn't ever seen a bigger one. He would 'a' been worth a good deal over at the village. They peddle out such a fish as that by the pound in the market-house there; everybody buys some of him; his meat's as white as snow and makes a good fry.

Next morning I said it was getting slow and dull, and I wanted to get a stirring-up some way. I said I reckoned I would slip over the river and find out what was going on. Jim liked that notion; but he said I must go in the dark and look sharp. Then he studied it over and said, couldn't I put on some of them old things and dress up like a girl? That was a good notion, too. So we shortened up one of the calico gowns, and I turned up my trouser-legs to my knees and got into it. Jim hitched it behind with the hooks, and it was a fair fit. I put on the sun-bonnet and tied it under my chin, and then for a body to look in and see my face was like looking down a joint of stove-pipe. Jim said nobody would know me, even in the daytime, hardly. I practised around all day to get the hang of the things, and by and by I could do pretty well in them, only Jim said I didn't walk like a girl; and he said I must quit pulling up my gown to get at my britches-pocket. I took notice, and done better.

I started up the Illinois shore in the canoe just after dark.

I started across to the town from a little below the ferry-landing, and the drift of the current fetched me in at the bottom of the town. I tied up and started along the bank. There was a light burning in a little shanty that hadn't been lived in for a long time, and I wondered who had took up quarters there. I slipped up and peeped in at the window. There was a woman about forty year old in there knitting by a candle that was on a pine table. I didn't know her face; she was a stranger, for you couldn't start a face in that town that I didn't know. Now this was lucky, because I was weakening; I was getting afraid I had come; people might know my voice and find me out. But if this woman had been in such a little town two days she could tell me all I wanted to know; so I knocked at the door, and made up my mind I wouldn't forget I was a girl.

11. THEY'RE AFTER US!

"Come in," says the woman, and I did. She says: "Take a cheer."

I done it. She looked me all over with her little shiny eyes, and says:

"What might your name be?"

"Sarah Williams."

"Where'bouts do you live? In this neighborhood?"

"No'm. In Hookerville, seven mile below. I've walked all the way and I'm all tired out."

"Hungry, too, I reckon. I'll find you something."

"No'm, I ain't hungry. I was so hungry I had to stop two miles below here at a farm; so I ain't hungry no more. It's what makes me so late. My mother's down sick, and out of

money and everything, and I come to tell my uncle Abner Moore. He lives at the upper end of the town, she says. I hain't ever been here before. Do you know him?"

"No; but I don't know everybody yet. I haven't lived here quite two weeks. It's a considerable ways to the upper end of the town. You better stay here all night. Take off your bonnet."

"No," I says; "I'll rest awhile, I reckon, and go on. I ain't afeard of the dark."

She said she wouldn't let me go by myself, but her husband would be in by and by, maybe in an hour and a half, and she'd send him along with me. Then she got to talking about her husband, and about her relations up the river, and her relations down the river, and about how much better off they used to was, and how they didn't know but they'd made a mistake coming to our town, instead of letting well alone—and so on and so on, till I was afeard I had made a mistake coming to her to find out what was going on in the town; but by and by she dropped on to pap and the murder, and then I was pretty willing to let her clatter right along. She told about me and Tom Sawyer finding the twelve thousand dollars (only she got it twenty) and all about pap and what a hard lot he was, and what a hard lot I was, and at last she got down to where I was murdered. I says:

"Who done it? We've heard considerable about these goings-on down in Hookerville, but we don't know who 'twas that killed Huck Finn."

"Well, I reckon there's a right smart chance of people *here* that 'd like to know who killed him. Some think old Finn done it himself."

"No—is that so?"

"Most everybody thought it at first. He'll never know how nigh he come to getting lynched. But before night they changed around and judged it was done by a runaway nigger named Jim."

"Why *he*—"

I stopped. I reckoned I better keep still. She run on, and never noticed I had put in at all:

"The nigger run off the very night Huck Finn was killed. So there's a reward out for him—three hundred dollars. And there's a reward out for old Finn, too—two hundred dollars. You see, he come to town the morning after the murder, and told about it, and was out with 'em on the ferryboat hunt, and right away after he up and left. Before night they wanted to lynch him, but he was gone, you see. Well, next day they found out the nigger was gone; they found out he hadn't ben seen sence ten o'clock the night the murder was done. So then they put it on him, you see; and while they was full of it, next day, back comes old Finn, and went boo-hooing to Judge Thatcher to get money to hunt for the nigger all over Illinois with. The judge gave him some, and that evening he got drunk, and was around till after midnight with a couple of mighty hard-looking strangers, and then went off with them. Well, he hain't come back sence, and they ain't looking for him back till this thing blows over a little, for people thinks now that he killed his boy and fixed things so folks would think robbers done it, and then he'd get Huck's money without having to bother a long time with a lawsuit. People do say he warn't any too good to do it. Oh, he's sly, I reckon. If he don't come back for a year he'll be all right. You can't prove anything on him, you know; everything will be quieted down then, and he'll walk in Huck's money as easy as nothing."

"Yes, I reckon so, 'm. I don't see nothing in the way of it. Has everybody quit thinking the nigger done it?"

"Oh, no, not everybody. A good many thinks he done it. But they'll get the nigger pretty soon now, and maybe they can scare it out of him."

"Why, are they after him yet?"

"Well, you're innocent, ain't you! Does three hundred dollars lay around every day for people to pick up? Some folks think the nigger ain't far from here. I'm one of them— but I hain't talked it around. A few days ago I was talking with an old couple that lives next door in the log shanty, and they happened to say hardly anybody ever goes to that island over yonder that they call Jackson's Island. Don't anybody live there? says I. No, nobody, says they. I didn't say any more, but I done some thinking. I was pretty near certain I'd seen smoke over there, about the head of the island, a day or two before that, so I says to myself, like as not that nigger's hiding over there; anyway, says I, it's worth the trouble to give the place a hunt. I hain't seen any smoke sence, so I reckon maybe he's gone, if it was him; but husband's going over to see—him and another man. He was gone up the river; but he got back today, and I told him as soon as he got here two hours ago."

I had got so uneasy I couldn't set still. I had to do something with my hands; so I took up a needle off of the table and went to threading it. My hands shook, and I was making a bad job of it. When the woman stopped talking I looked up, and she was looking at me pretty curious and smiling a little. I put down the needle and thread, and let on to be interested—and I was, too—and says:

"Three hundred dollars is a power of money. I wish my mother could get it. Is your husband going over there tonight?"

"Oh, yes. He went up-town with the man I was telling you of, to get a boat and see if they could borrow another gun. They'll go over after midnight."

"Couldn't they see better if they was to wait till daytime?"

"Yes. And couldn't the nigger see better, too? After midnight he'll likely be asleep, and they can slip around through the woods and hunt up his camp-fire all the better for the dark, if he's got one."

"I didn't think of that."

The woman kept looking at me pretty curious, and I didn't feel a bit comfortable. Pretty soon she says:

"What did you say your name was, honey?"

"M—Mary Williams."

Somehow it didn't seem to me that I said it was Mary before, so I didn't look up—seemed to me I said it was Sarah; so I felt sort of cornered, and was afeard maybe I was looking it, too. I wished the woman would say something more; the longer she set still the uneasier I was. But now she says:

"Honey, I thought you said it was Sarah when you first come in?"

"Oh, yes'm, I did. Sarah Mary Williams. Sarah's my first name. Some calls me Sarah, some calls me Mary."

"Oh, that's the way of it?"

"Yes'm."

I was feeling better then, but I wished I was out of there, anyway. I couldn't look up yet.

Well, the woman fell to talking about how hard times was, and how poor they had to live, and how the rats was as free as if they owned the place, and so forth and so on, and then I got easy again. She was right about the rats. You'd see one stick his nose out of a hole in the corner every little while. She said she had to have things handy to throw at them when she was alone, or they wouldn't give her no peace. She showed me a bar of lead twisted up into a knot, and said she was a good shot with it generly, but she'd wrenched her arm a day or two ago, and didn't know whether she could throw true now. But she watched for a chance, and directly banged away at a rat; but she missed him wide, and said, "Ouch!" it hurt her arm so. Then she told me to try for the next one. I wanted to be getting away before the old man got back, but of course I didn't let on. I got the thing, and the first rat that showed his nose I let drive, and if he'd 'a' stayed where he was he'd 'a' been a tolerable sick rat. She said that was first-rate, and she reckoned I would hive the next one. She went and got the lump of lead and fetched it back, and brought along a hank of yarn which she wanted me to help her with. I held up my two hands and she put the hank over them, and went on talking about her and her husband's matters. But she broke off to say:

"Keep your eye on the rats. You better have the lead in your lap, handy."

So she dropped the lump into my lap just at that moment, and I clapped my legs together on it and she went on talking. But only about a minute. Then she took off the hank and looked me straight in the face, and very pleasant, and says:

"Come, now, what's your real name?"

"Wh-hat, mum?"

"What's your real name? Is it Bill, or Tom, or Bob?—or what is it?"

I reckon I shook like a leaf, and I didn't know hardly what to do. But I says:

"Please to don't poke fun at a poor girl like me, mum. If I'm in the way here, I'll—"

"No, you won't. Set down and stay where you are. I ain't going to hurt you, and I ain't going to tell on you, nuther. You just tell me your secret, and trust me. I'll keep it; and, what's more, I'll help you. So'll my old man

if you want him to. You see, you're a runaway 'prentice, that's all. It ain't anything. There ain't no harm in it. You've been treated bad, and you made up your mind to cut. Bless you, child, I wouldn't tell on you. Tell me all about it now, that's a good boy."

So I said it wouldn't be no use to try to play it any longer, and I would just make a clean breast and tell her everything, but she mustn't go back on her promise. Then I told her my father and mother was dead, and the law had bound me out to a mean old farmer in the country thirty mile back from the river, and he treated me so bad I couldn't stand it no longer; he went away to be gone a couple of days, and so I took my chance and stole some of his daughter's old clothes and cleared out, and I had been three nights coming the thirty miles. I traveled nights, and hid daytimes and slept, and the bag of bread and meat I carried from home lasted me all the way, and I had a-plenty. I said I believed my uncle Abner Moore would take care of me, and so that was why I struck out for this town of Goshen.

"Goshen, child? This ain't Goshen. This is St. Petersburg. Goshen's ten mile further up the river. Who told you this was Goshen?"

"Why, a man I met at daybreak this morning, just as I was going to turn into the woods for my regular sleep. He told me when the roads forked I must take the right hand, and five mile would fetch me to Goshen."

"He was drunk, I reckon. He told you just exactly wrong."

"Well, he did act like he was drunk, but it ain't no matter now. I got to be moving along. I'll fetch Goshen before daylight."

"Hold on a minute. I'll put you up a snack to eat. You might want it."

So she put me up a snack, and says:

"Say, when a cow's laying down, which end of her gets up first? Answer up prompt now—don't stop to study over it. Which end gets up first?"

"The hind end, mum."

"Well, then, a horse?"

"The for'rard end, mum."

"Which side of a tree does the moss grow on?"

"North side."

"If fifteen cows is browsing on a hillside,

how many of them eats with their heads pointed the same direction?"

"The whole fifteen, mum."

"Well, I reckon you *have* lived in the country. I thought maybe you was trying to hocus me again. What's your real name, now?"

"George Peters, mum."

"Well, try to remember it, George. Don't forget and tell me it's Elexander before you go, and then get out by saying it's George Elexander when I catch you. And don't go about women in that old calico. You do a girl tolerable poor, but you might fool men, maybe. Bless you, child, when you set out to thread a needle don't hold the thread still and fetch the needle up to it; hold the needle still and poke the thread at it; that's the way a woman most always does, but a man always does t'other way. And when you throw at a rat or anything, hitch yourself up a-tiptoe and fetch your hand up over your head as awkward as you can, and miss your rat about six or seven foot. Throw stiff-armed from the shoulder, like there was a pivot there for it to turn on, like a girl; not from the wrist and elbow, with your arm out to one side, like a boy. And, mind you, when a girl tries to catch anything in her lap she throws her knees apart; she don't clap them together, the way you did when you catched the lump of lead. Why, I spotted you for a boy when you was threading the needle; and I contrived the other things just to make certain. Now trot along to your uncle, Sarah Mary Williams George Elexander Peters, and if you get into trouble you send word to Mrs. Judith Loftus, which is me, and I'll do what I can to get you out of it. Keep the river road all the way, and next time you tramp take shoes and socks with you. The river road's a rocky one, and your feet'll be in condition when you get to Goshen, I reckon."

I went up the bank about fifty yards, and then I doubled on my tracks and slipped back to where my canoe was, a good piece below the house. I jumped in, and was off in a hurry. I went up-stream far enough to make the head of the island, and then started across. I took off the sun-bonnet, for I didn't want no blinders on then. When I was about the middle I heard the clock begin to strike, so I stops and listens; the sound come faint over the water but clear—eleven. When I struck the head of the island I never waited to blow, though I was most winded, but I shoved right into the timber where my old camp used to be, and started a good fire there on a high and dry spot.

Then I jumped in the canoe and dug out for our place, a mile and a half below, as hard as I could go. I landed, and slopped through the timber and up the ridge, and into the cavern. There Jim laid, sound asleep on the ground. I roused him out and says:

"Git up and hump yourself, Jim! There ain't a minute to lose. They're after us!"

Jim never asked no questions, he never said a word; but the way he worked for the next half an hour showed about how he was scared. By that time everything we had in the world was on our raft, and she was ready to be shoved out from the willow cove where she was hid. We put out the camp-fire at the cavern the first thing, and didn't show a candle outside after that.

I took the canoe out from the shore a little piece, and took a look; but if there was a boat around I couldn't see it, for stars and shadows ain't good to see by. Then we got out the raft and slipped along down in the shade, past the foot of the island dead still—never saying a word.

12. "BETTER LET BLAME WELL ALONE"

It must 'a' been close on to one o'clock when we got below the island at last, and the raft did seem to go mighty slow. If a boat was to come along we was going to take to the canoe and break for the Illinois shore; and it was well a boat didn't come, for we hadn't ever thought to put the gun in the canoe, or a fishing-line, or anything to eat. We was in ruther too much of a sweat to think of so many things. It warn't good judgment to put *everything* on the raft.

If the men went to the island I just expect they found the camp-fire I built, and watched it all night for Jim to come. Anyways, they stayed away from us, and if my building the fire never fooled them it warn't no fault of mine. I played it as low down on them as I could.

When the first streak of day began to show

we tied up to a towhead in a big bend on the Illinois side, and hacked off cottonwood branches with the hatchet, and covered up the raft with them so she looked like there had been a cave-in in the bank there. A towhead is a sand-bar that has cottonwoods on it as thick as harrow-teeth.

We had mountains on the Missouri shore and heavy timber on the Illinois side, and the channel was down the Missouri shore at that place, so we warn't afraid of anybody running across us. We laid there all day, and watched the rafts and steamboats spin down the Missouri shore, and up-bound steamboats fight the big river in the middle. I told Jim all about the time I had jabbering with that woman; and Jim said she was a smart one, and if she was to start after us herself *she* wouldn't set down and watch a camp-fire—no, sir, she'd fetch a dog. Well, then, I said, why couldn't she tell her husband to fetch a dog? Jim said he bet she did think of it by the time the men was ready to start, and he believed they must 'a' gone up-town to get a dog and so they lost all that time, or else we wouldn't be here on a towhead sixteen or seventeen mile below the village—no, indeedy, we would be in that same old town again. So I said I didn't care what was the reason they didn't get us as long as they didn't.

When it was beginning to come on dark we poked our heads out of the cottonwood thicket, and looked up and down and across; nothing in sight; so Jim took up some of the top planks of the raft and built a snug wigwam to get under in blazing weather and rainy, and to keep the things dry. Jim made a floor for the wigwam, and raised it a foot or more above the level of the raft, so now the blankets and all the traps was out of reach of steamboat waves. Right in the middle of the wigwam we made a layer of dirt about five or six inches deep with a frame around it for to hold it to its place; this was to build a fire on in sloppy weather or chilly; the wigwam would keep it from being seen. We made an extra steering-oar, too, because one of the others might get broke on a snag or something. We fixed up a short forked stick to hang the old lantern on, because we must always light the lantern whenever we see a steamboat coming down-stream, to keep from getting run over; but we wouldn't have to light it for up-stream boats unless we see we was in what they call a "crossing"; for the river was pretty high yet, very low banks being still a little under water; so up-bound boats didn't always run the channel, but hunted easy water.

This second night we run between seven and eight hours, with a current that was making over four mile an hour. We catched fish and talked, and we took a swim now and then to keep off sleepiness. It was kind of solemn, drifting down the big, still river, laying on our backs looking up at the stars, and we didn't ever feel like talking loud, and it warn't often that we laughed—only a little kind of a low chuckle. We had mighty good weather as a general thing, and nothing ever happened to us at all—that night, nor the next, nor the next.

Every night we passed towns, some of them away up on black hillsides, nothing but just a shiny bed of lights; not a house could you see. The fifth night we passed St. Louis, and it was like the whole world lit up. In St. Petersburg they used to say there was twenty or thirty thousand people in St. Louis, but I never believed it till I see that wonderful spread of lights at two o'clock that still night. There warn't a sound there; everybody was asleep.

Every night now I used to slip ashore toward ten o'clock at some little village, and buy ten or fifteen cents' worth of meal or bacon or other stuff to eat; and sometimes I lifted a chicken that warn't roosting comfortable, and took him along. Pap always said, take a chicken when you get a chance, because if you don't want him yourself you can easy find somebody that does, and a good deed ain't ever forgot. I never see pap when he didn't want the chicken himself, but that is what he used to say, anyway.

Mornings before daylight I slipped into corn-fields and borrowed a watermelon, or a mushmelon, or a punkin, or some new corn, or things of that kind. Pap always said it warn't no harm to borrow things if you was meaning to pay them back some time; but the widow said it warn't anything but a soft name for stealing, and no decent body would do it. Jim said he reckoned the widow was partly right and pap was partly right; so the best way would be for us to pick out two or three things from the list and say we wouldn't borrow them any more—then he reckoned it wouldn't be no harm to borrow the others. So we talked it over all one night, drifting along down the river, trying to make up our minds whether to drop the watermelons, or the cantelopes, or the mushmelons, or what. But toward daylight we got all settled satisfactory, and concluded to drop crabapples and p'simmons. We warn't feeling just right before that, but it was all comfortable now. I was glad the way it come out, too, because crabapples ain't ever good, and the p'simmons wouldn't be ripe for two or three months yet.

We shot a water-fowl now and then that got up too early in the morning or didn't go to bed early enough in the evening. Take it all round, we lived pretty high.

The fifth night below St. Louis we had a big storm after midnight, with a power of thunder and lightning, and the rain poured down in a solid sheet. We stayed in the wigwam and let the raft take care of itself. When the lightning glared out we could see a big straight river ahead, and high, rocky bluffs on both sides. By and by says I, "Hel-*lo*, Jim, looky yonder!" It was a steamboat that had killed herself on a rock. We was drifting straight down for her. The lightning showed her very distinct. She was leaning over, with part of her upper deck above water, and you could see every little chimbly-guy clean and clear, and a chair by the big bell, with an old slouch hat hanging on the back of it, when the flashes come.

Well, it being away in the night and stormy, and all so mysterious-like, I felt just the way any other boy would 'a' felt when I seen that wreck laying there so mournful and lonesome in the middle of the river. I wanted to get aboard of her and slink around a little, and see what there was there. So I says:

"Le's land on her, Jim."

But Jim was dead against it at first. He says:

"I doan' want to go fool'n' 'long er no wrack. We's doin' blame' well, en we better let blame' well alone, as de good book says. Like as not dey's a watchman on dat wrack."

"Watchman your grandmother," I says; "there ain't nothing to watch but the texas

and the pilot-house; and do you reckon anybody's going to resk his life for a texas and a pilot-house such a night as this, when it's likely to break up and wash off down the river any minute?" Jim couldn't say nothing to that, so he didn't try. "And besides," I says, "we might borrow something worth having out of the captain's stateroom. Seegars, *I* bet you —and cost five cents apiece, solid cash. Steamboat captains is always rich, and get sixty dollars a month, and *they* don't care a cent what a thing costs, you know, long as they want it. Stick a candle in your pocket; I can't rest, Jim, till we give her a rummaging. Do you reckon Tom Sawyer would ever go by this thing? Not for pie, he wouldn't. He'd call it an adventure—that's what he'd call it; and he'd land on that wreck if it was his last act. And wouldn't he throw style into it?—wouldn't he spread himself, nor nothing? Why, you'd think it was Christopher C'lumbus discovering Kingdom Come. I wish Tom Sawyer *was* here."

Jim he grumbled a little, but give in. He said we mustn't talk any more than we could help, and then talk mighty low. The lightning showed us the wreck again just in time, and we fetched the stabboard derrick, and made fast there.

The deck was high out here. We went sneaking down the slope of it to labboard, in the dark, towards the texas, feeling our way slow with our feet, and spreading our hands out to fend off the guys, for it was so dark we couldn't see no sign of them. Pretty soon we struck the forward end of the skylight, and clumb on it; and the next step fetched us in front of the captain's door, which was open, and by Jiminy, away down through the texas-hall we see a light! and all in the same second we seem to hear low voices in yonder!

Jim whispered and said he was feeling powerful sick, and told me to come along. I says, all right, and was going to start for the raft; but just then I heard a voice wail out and say:

"Oh, please don't, boys; I swear I won't ever tell!"

Another voice said, pretty loud:

"It's a lie, Jim Turner. You've acted this way before. You always want more'n your share of the truck, and you've always got it, too, because you've swore 't if you didn't you'd tell. But this time you've said it jest one time too many. You're the meanest, treacherousest hound in this country."

By this time Jim was gone for the raft. I was just a-biling with curiosity; and I says to myself, Tom Sawyer wouldn't back out now, and so I won't either; I'm a-going to see what's going on here. So I dropped on my hands and knees in the little passage, and crept aft in the dark till there warn't but one stateroom betwixt me and the cross-hall of the texas. Then in there I see a man stretched on the floor and tied hand and foot, and two men standing over him, and one of them had a dim lantern in his hand, and the other one had a pistol. This one kept pointing the pistol at the man's head on the floor, and saying:

"I'd *like* to! And I orter, too—a mean skunk!"

The man on the floor would shrivel up and say, "Oh, please don't, Bill; I hain't ever goin' to tell."

And every time he said that the man with the lantern would laugh and say:

" 'Deed you ain't! You never said no truer thing 'n that, you bet you." And once he said: "Hear him beg! and yit if we hadn't got the best of him and tied him he'd 'a' killed us both. And what *for?* Jist for noth'n'. Jist because we stood on our *rights*—that's what for. But I lay you ain't a-goin' to threaten nobody any more, Jim Turner. Put *up* that pistol, Bill."

Bill says:

"I don't want to, Jake Packard. I'm for killin' him—and didn't he kill old Hatfield jist the same way—and don't he deserve it?"

"But I don't *want* him killed, and I've got my reasons for it."

"Bless yo' heart for them words, Jake Packard! I'll never forgit you long's I live!" says the man on the floor, sort of blubbering.

Packard didn't take no notice of that, but hung up his lantern on a nail and started toward where I was, there in the dark, and motioned Bill to come. I crawfished as fast as I could about two yards, but the boat slanted so that I couldn't make very good time; so to keep from getting run over and catched I crawled into a stateroom on the upper side. The man came a-pawing along in the dark,

and when Packard got to my stateroom, he says:

"Here—come in here."

And in he come, and Bill after him. But before they got in I was up in the upper berth, cornered, and sorry I come. Then they stood there, with their hands on the ledge of the berth, and talked. I couldn't see them, but I could tell where they was by the whisky they'd been having. I was glad I didn't drink whisky; but it wouldn't made much difference anyway, because most of the time they couldn't 'a' treed me because I didn't breathe. I was too scared. And, besides, a body *couldn't* breathe and hear such talk. They talked low and earnest. Bill wanted to kill Turner. He says:

"He's said he'll tell, and he will. If we was to give both our shares to him *now* it wouldn't make no difference after the row and the way we've served him. Shore's you're born, he'll turn state's evidence; now you hear *me.* I'm for putting him out of his troubles."

"So'm I," says Packard, very quiet.

"Blame it, I'd sorter begun to think you wasn't. Well, then, that's all right. Le's go and do it."

"Hold on a minute; I hain't had my say yit. You listen to me. Shooting's good, but there's quieter ways if the thing's *got* to be done. But what *I* say is this: it ain't good sense to go court'n' around after a halter if you can git at what you're up to in some way that's jist as good and at the same time don't bring you into no resks. Ain't that so?"

"You bet it is. But how you goin' to manage it this time?"

"Well, my idea is this: we'll rustle around and gather up whatever pickin's we've overlooked in the staterooms, and shove for shore and hide the truck. Then we'll wait. Now I say it ain't a-goin' to be more'n two hours befo' this wrack breaks up and washes off down the river. See? He'll be drownded, and won't have nobody to blame for it but his own self. I reckon that's a considerable sight better 'n killin' of him. I'm unfavorable to killin' a man as long as you can git aroun' it; it ain't good sense, it ain't good morals. Ain't I right?"

"Yes, I reck'n you are. But s'pose she *don't* break up and wash off?"

"Well, we can wait the two hours anyway and see, can't we?"

"All right, then; come along."

So they started, and I lit out, all in a cold sweat, and scrambled forward. It was dark as pitch there; but I said, in a kind of a coarse whisper, "Jim!" and he answered up, right at my elbow, with a sort of a moan, and I says:

"Quick, Jim, it ain't no time for fooling around and moaning; there's a gang of murderers in yonder, and if we don't hunt up their boat and set her drifting down the river so these fellows can't get away from the wreck there's one of 'em going to be in a bad fix. But if we find their boat we can put *all* of 'em in a bad fix—for the sheriff 'll get 'em. Quick —hurry! I'll hunt the labboard side, you hunt the stabboard. You start at the raft, and—"

"Oh, my lordy, lordy! *Raf'?* Dey ain' no raf' no mo'; she done broke loose en gone!—en here we is!"

13. HONEST LOOT FROM THE "WALTER SCOTT"

Well, I catched my breath and most fainted. Shut up on a wreck with such a gang as that! But it warn't no time to be sentimentering. We'd *got* to find that boat now—had to have it for ourselves. So we went a-quaking and shaking down the stabboard side, and slow work it was, too—seemed a week before we got to the stern. No sign of a boat. Jim said he didn't believe he could go any farther—so scared he hadn't hardly any strength left, he said. But I said, come on, if we get left on this wreck we are in a fix, sure. So on we prowled again. We struck for the stern of the texas, and found it, and then scrabbled along forwards on the skylight, hanging on from shutter to shutter, for the edge of the skylight was in the water. When we got pretty close to the cross-hall door there was the skiff, sure enough! I could just barely see her. I felt ever so thankful. In another second I would 'a' been aboard of her, but just then the door opened. One of the men stuck his head out only about a couple of foot from me, and I thought I was gone; but he jerked it in again, and says:

"Heave that blame lantern out o' sight, Bill!"

He flung a bag of something into the boat, and then got in himself and set down. It was Packard. Then Bill *he* come out and got in. Packard says, in a low voice:

"All ready—shove off!"

I couldn't hardly hang on to the shutters, I was so weak. But Bill says:

"Hold on—'d you go through him?"

"No. Didn't you?"

"No. So he's got his share o' the cash yet."

"Well, then, come along; no use to take truck and leave money."

"Say, won't he suspicion what we're up to?"

"Maybe he won't. But we got to have it anyway. Come along."

So they got out and went in.

The door slammed to because it was on the careened side; and in a half second I was in the boat, and Jim come tumbling after me. I out with my knife and cut the rope, and away we went!

We didn't touch an oar, and we didn't speak nor whisper, nor hardly even breathe. We went gliding swift along, dead silent, past the tip of the paddlebox, and past the stern; then in a second or two more we was a hundred yards below the wreck, and the darkness soaked her up, every last sign of her, and we was safe, and knowed it.

When we was three or four hundred yards down-stream we see the lantern show like a little spark at the texas door for a second, and we knowed by that that the rascals had missed their boat, and was beginning to understand that they was in just as much trouble now as Jim Turner was.

Then Jim manned the oars, and we took out after our raft. Now was the first time that I begun to worry about the men—I reckon I hadn't had time to before. I begun to think how dreadful it was, even for murderers, to be in such a fix. I says to myself, there ain't no telling but I might come to be a murderer myself yet, and then how would I like it? So says I to Jim:

"The first light we see we'll land a hundred yards below it or above it, in a place where it's a good hiding-place for you and the skiff, and then I'll go and fix up some kind of a yarn, and get somebody to go for that gang and get them out of their scrape, so they can be hung when their time comes."

But that idea was a failure; for pretty soon

it begun to storm again, and this time worse than ever. The rain poured down, and never a light showed; everybody in bed, I reckon. We boomed along down the river, watching for lights and watching for our raft. After a long time the rain let up, but the clouds stayed, and the lightning kept whimpering, and by and by a flash showed us a black thing ahead, floating, and we made for it.

It was the raft, and mighty glad was we to get aboard of it again. We seen a light now away down to the right, on shore. So I said I would go for it. The skiff was half full of plunder which that gang had stole there on the wreck. We hustled it on to the raft in a pile, and I told Jim to float along down, and show a light when he judged he had gone about two mile, and keep it burning till I come; then I manned my oars and shoved for the light. As I got down towards it three or four more showed—up on a hillside. It was a village. I closed in above the shore light, and laid on my oars and floated. As I went by I see it was a lantern hanging on the jackstaff of a double-hull ferryboat. I skimmed around for the watchman, a-wondering whereabouts he slept; and by and by I found him roosting on the bitts forward, with his head down between his knees. I gave his shoulder two or three little shoves, and begun to cry.

He stirred up in a kind of a startlish way; but when he see it was only me he took a good gap and stretch, and then he says:

"Hello, what's up? Don't cry, bub. What's the trouble?"

I says:

"Pap, and mam, and sis, and—"

Then I broke down. He says:

"Oh, dang it now, *don't* take on so; we all has to have our troubles, with this 'n 'll come out all right. What's the matter with 'em?"

"They're—they're—are you the watchman of the boat?"

"Yes," he says, kind of pretty-well-satisfied like. "I'm the captain and the owner and the mate and the pilot and watchman and head deck-hand; and sometimes I'm the freight and passengers. I ain't as rich as old Jim Hornback, and I can't be so blame' generous and good to Tom, Dick, and Harry as what he is, and slam around money the way he does; but I've told him a many a time 't I wouldn't

trade places with him; for, says I, a sailor's life's the life for me, and I'm derned if *I'd* live two mile out o' town, where there ain't nothing ever goin' on, not for all his spondulicks and as much more on top of it. Says I—"

I broke in and says:

"They're in an awful peck of trouble, and—"

"*Who* is?"

"Why, pap and mam and sis and Miss Hooker; and if you'd take your ferryboat and go up there—"

"Up where? Where are they?"

"On the wreck."

"What wreck?"

"Why, there ain't but one."

"What, you don't mean the *Walter Scott?*"

"Yes."

"Good land! what are they doin' *there,* for gracious sakes?"

"Well, they didn't go there a-purpose."

"I bet they didn't! Why, great goodness, there ain't no chance for 'em if they don't git off mighty quick! Why, how in the nation did they ever git into such a scrape?"

"Easy enough. Miss Hooker was a-visiting up there to the town—"

"Yes. Booth's Landing—go on."

"She was a-visiting there at Booth's Landing, and just in the edge of the evening she started over with her nigger woman in the horse-ferry to stay all night at her friend's house, Miss What-you-may-call-her—I disremember her name—and they lost their steering-oar, and swung around and went a-floating down, stern first, about two mile, and saddle-baggsed on the wreck, and the ferryman and the nigger woman and the horses was all lost, but Miss Hooker she made a grab and got aboard the wreck. Well, about an hour after dark we come along down in our trading-scow, and it was so dark we didn't notice the wreck till we was right on it; and so *we* saddle-baggsed; but all of us was saved but Bill Whipple—and oh, he *was* the best cretur!—I most wish 't it had been me, I do."

"My George! It's the beatenest thing I ever struck. And *then* what did you all do?"

"Well, we hollered and took on, but it's so wide there we couldn't make nobody hear. So pap said somebody got to get ashore and get help somehow. I was the only one that could swim, so I made a dash for it, and Miss Hooker she said if I didn't strike help sooner, come here and hunt up her uncle, and he'd fix the thing. I made the land about a mile below, and been fooling along ever since, trying to get people to do something, but they said, 'What, in such a night and such a current? There ain't no sense in it; go for the steam-ferry.' Now if you'll go and—"

"By Jackson, I'd *like* to, and, blame it, I don't know but I will; but who in the ding-nation's a-going to *pay* for it? Do you reckon your pap—"

"Why *that's* all right. Miss Hooker she tole me, *particular*, that her uncle Hornback—"

"Great guns! is *he* her uncle? Looky here, you break for that light over yonder-way, and turn out west when you git there, and about a quarter of a mile out you'll come to the tavern; tell 'em to dart you out to Jim Hornback's, and he'll foot the bill. And don't you fool around any, because he'll want to know the news. Tell him I'll have his niece all safe before he can get to town. Hump yourself, now; I'm a-going up around the corner here to roust out my engineer."

I struck for the light, but as soon as he turned the corner I went back and got into my skiff and bailed her out, and then pulled up shore in the easy water about six hundred yards, and tucked myself in among some wood-boats; for I couldn't rest easy till I could see the ferryboat start. But take it all around, I was feeling ruther comfortable on accounts of taking all this trouble for that gang, for not many would 'a' done it. I wished the widow knowed about it. I judged she would be proud of me for helping these rapscallions, because rapscallions and dead-beats is the kind the widow and good people takes the most interest in.

Well, before long here comes the wreck, dim and dusky, sliding along down! A kind of cold shiver went through me, and then I struck out for her. She was very deep, and I see in a minute there warn't much chance for anybody being alive in her. I pulled all around her and hollered a little, but there wasn't any answer; all dead still. I felt a little bit heavy-hearted about the gang, but not much, for I reckoned if they could stand it I could.

Then here comes the ferryboat; so I shoved for the middle of the river on a long downstream slant; and when I judged I was out of eye-reach I laid on my oars, and looked back and see her go and smell around the wreck of Miss Hooker's remainders, because the captain would know her uncle Hornback would want them; and then pretty soon the ferryboat give it up and went for the shore, and I laid into my work and went a-booming down the river.

It did seem a powerful long time before Jim's light showed up; and when it did show it looked like it was a thousand mile off. By the time I got there the sky was beginning to get a little gray in the east; so we struck for an island, and hid the raft, and sunk the skiff, and turned in and slept like dead people.

14. WAS SOLOMON WISE?

By and by, when we got up, we turned over the truck the gang had stole off of the wreck, and found boots, blankets, and clothes, and all sorts of other things, and a lot of books, and a spy-glass, and three boxes of seegars. We hadn't ever been this rich before in neither of our lives. The seegars was prime. We laid off all the afternoon in the woods talking, and me reading the books, and having a general good time. I told Jim all about what happened inside the wreck and at the ferryboat, and I said these kinds of things was adventures; but he said he didn't want no more adventures. He said that when I went in the texas and he crawled back to get on the raft and found her gone he nearly died, because he judged it was all up with *him* anyway it could be fixed; for if he didn't get saved he would get drownded; and if he did get saved, whoever saved him would send him back home so as to get the reward, and then Miss Watson would sell him South, sure. Well, he was right; he was most always right; he had an uncommon level head for a nigger.

I read considerable to Jim about kings and dukes and earls and such, and how gaudy they dressed, and how much style they put on, and called each other your majesty, and your grace, and your lordship, and so on, 'stead of mister; and Jim's eyes bugged out, and he was interested. He says:

"I didn't know dey was so many un um. I hain't hearn 'bout none un um, skasely, but ole King Sollermun, onless you counts dem kings dat's in a pack er k'yards. How much do a king git?"

"Get?" I says; "why, they get a thousand dollars a month if they want it; they can have just as much as they want; everything belongs to them."

"*Ain'* dat gay? En what dey got to do, Huck?"

"*They* don't do nothing! Why, how you talk! They just set around."

"No; is dat so?"

"Of course it is. They just set around—except, maybe, when there's a war; then they go to the war. But other times they just lazy around; or go hawking—just hawking and sp— Sh!—d'you hear a noise?"

We skipped out and looked; but it warn't nothing but the flutter of a steamboat's wheel away down, coming around the point; so we come back.

"Yes," says I, "and other times, when things is dull, they fuss with the parlyment; and if everybody don't go just so he whacks their heads off. But mostly they hang round the harem."

"Roun' de which?"

"Harem."

"What's de harem?"

"The place where he keeps his wives. Don't you know about the harem? Solomon had one; he had about a million wives."

"Why, yes, dat's so; I—I'd done forgot it. A harem's a bo'd'n-house, I reck'n. Mos' likely dey has rackety times in de nussery. En I reck'n de wives quarrels considable; en dat 'crease de racket. Yit dey say Sollermun de wises' man dat ever liv'. I doan' take no stock in dat. Bekase why: would a wise man want to live in de mids' er sich a blim-blammin' all de time? No—'deed he wouldn't. A wise man 'ud take en buil' a biler-factry; en den he could shet *down* de biler-factry when he want to res'."

"Well, but he *was* the wisest man, anyway; because the widow she told me so, her own self."

"I doan' k'yer what de widder say, he *warn't* no wise man nuther. He had some er de dad-fetchedes' ways I ever see. Does you know

'bout dat chile dat he 'uz gwyne to chop in two?"

"Yes, the widow told me all about it."

"*Well,* den! Warn' dat de beatenes' notion in de worl'? You jes' take en look at it a minute. Dah's de stump, dah—dat's one er de women; heah's you—dat's de yuther one; I's Sollermun; en dish yer dollar bill's de chile. Bofe un you claims it. What does I do? Does I shin aroun' mongs' de neighbors en fine out which un you de bill *do* b'long to, en han' it over to de right one, all safe en soun', de way dat anybody dat had any gumption would? No; I taken en whack de bill in *two,* en give half un it to you, en de yuther half to de yuther woman. Dat's de way Sollermun was gwyne to do wid de chile. Now I want to ast you: what's de use er dat half a bill?—can't buy noth'n wid it. En what use is a half a chile? I wouldn' give a dern for a million un um."

"But hang it, Jim, you've clean missed the point—blame it, you've missed it a thousand mile."

"Who? Me? Go 'long. Doan' talk to *me* 'bout yo' pints. I reck'n I knows sense when I sees it; en dey ain' no sense in sich doin's as dat. De 'spute warn't 'bout a half a chile, de 'spute was 'bout a whole chile; en de man dat think he kin settle a 'spute 'bout a whole chile wid a half a chile doan' know enough to come in out'n de rain. Doan' talk to me 'bout Sollermun, Huck, I knows him by de back."

"But I tell you you don't get the point."

"Blame de point! I reck'n I knows what I knows. En mine you, de *real* pint is down furder—it's down deeper. It lays in de way Sollermun was raised. You take a man dat's got on'y one or two chillen; is dat man gwyne to be wasteful o' chillen? No, he ain't; he can't 'ford it. *He* knows how to value 'em. But you take a man dat's got 'bout five million chillen runnin' roun' de house, en it's diffunt. *He* as soon chop a chile in two as a cat. Dey's plenty mo'. A chile er two, mo' er less, warn't no consekens to Sollermun, dad fetch him!"

I never see such a nigger. If he got a notion in his head once, there warn't no getting it out again. He was the most down on Solomon of any nigger I ever see. So I went to talking about other kings, and let Solomon slide. I told about Louis Sixteenth that got his head cut off in France long time ago; and about his little boy the dolphin, that would 'a' been a king, but they took and shut him up in jail, and some say he died there.

"Po' little chap."

"But some says he got out and got away, and come to America."

"Dat's good! But he'll be pooty lonesome—dey ain' no kings here, is dey, Huck?"

"No."

"Den he cain't git no situation. What he gwyne to do?"

"Well, I don't know. Some of them gets on the police, and some of them learns people how to talk French."

"Why, Huck, doan' de French people talk de same way we does?"

"*No,* Jim; you couldn't understand a word they said—not a single word."

"Well, now, I be ding-busted! How do dat come?"

"*I* don't know; but it's so. I got some of their jabber out of a book. S'pose a man was to come to you and say Polly-voo-franzy—what would you think?"

"I wouldn't think nuffn; I'd take en bust him over de head—dat is, if he warn't white. I wouldn't 'low no nigger to call me dat."

"Shucks, it ain't calling you anything. It's only saying, do you know how to talk French?"

"Well, den, why couldn't he say it?"

"Why, he *is* a-saying it. That's a Frenchman's *way* of saying it."

"Well, it's a blame ridicklous way, en I doan' want to hear no mo' 'bout it. Dey ain' no sense in it."

"Looky here, Jim; does a cat talk like we do?"

"No, a cat don't."

"Well, does a cow?"

"No, a cow don't, nuther."

"Does a cat talk like a cow, or a cow talk like a cat?"

"No, dey don't."

"It's natural and right for 'em to talk different from each other, ain't it?"

"Course."

"And ain't it natural and right for a cat and a cow to talk different from *us?*"

"Why, mos' sholy it is."

"Well, then, why ain't it natural and right for a *Frenchman* to talk different from us? You answer me that."

"Is a cat a man, Huck?"

"No."

"Well, den, dey ain't no sense in a cat talkin' like a man. Is a cow a man?—er is a cow a cat?"

"No, she ain't either of them."

"Well, den, she ain't got no business to talk like either one er the yuther of 'em. Is a Frenchman a man?"

"Yes."

"*Well,* den! Dad blame it, why doan' he *talk* like a man? You answer me *dat!*"

I see it warn't no use wasting words—you can't learn a nigger to argue. So I quit.

15. FOOLING POOR OLD JIM

We judged that three nights more would fetch us to Cairo, at the bottom of Illinois, where the Ohio River comes in, and that was what we was after. We would sell the raft and get on a steamboat and go way up the Ohio amongst the free states, and then be out of trouble.

Well, the second night a fog begun to come on, and we made for a towhead to tie to, for it wouldn't do to try to run in a fog; but when I paddled ahead in the canoe, with the line to make fast, there warn't anything but little saplings to tie to. I passed the line around one of them right on the edge of the cut bank, but there was a stiff current, and the raft come booming down so lively she tore it out by the roots and away she went. I see the fog closing down, and it made me so sick and scared I couldn't budge for most a half a minute it seemed to me—and then there warn't no raft in sight; you couldn't see twenty yards. I jumped into the canoe and run back to the stern, and grabbed the paddle and set her back a stroke. But she didn't come. I was in such a hurry I hadn't untied her. I got up and tried to untie her, but I was so excited my hands shook so I couldn't hardly do anything with them.

As soon as I got started I took out after the raft, hot and heavy, right down the towhead. That was all right as far as it went, but the towhead warn't sixty yards long, and the minute I flew by the foot of it I shot out into the solid white fog, and hadn't no more idea which way I was going than a dead man. Thinks I, it won't do to paddle; first I know

I'll run into the bank or a towhead or something; I got to set still and float, and yet it's mighty fidgety business to have to hold your hands still at such a time. I whooped and listened. Away down there somewheres I hears a small whoop, and up comes my spirits. I went tearing after it, listening sharp to hear it again. The next time it come I see I warn't heading for it, but heading away to the right of it. And the next time I was heading away to the left of it—and not gaining on it much either, for I was flying around, this way and that and t'other, but it was going straight ahead all the time.

I did wish the fool would think to beat a tin pan, and beat it all the time, but he never did, and it was the still places between the whoops that was making the trouble for me. Well, I fought along, and directly I hears the whoop *behind* me. I was tangled good now. That was somebody else's whoop, or else I was turned around.

I throwed the paddle down. I heard the whoop again; it was behind me yet, but in a different place; it kept coming, and kept changing its place, and I kept answering, till by and by it was in front of me again, and I knowed the current had swung the canoe's head down-stream, and I was all right if that was Jim and not some other raftsman hollering. I couldn't tell nothing about voices in a fog, for nothing don't look natural nor sound natural in a fog.

The whooping went on, and in about a minute I come a-booming down on a cut bank with smoky ghosts of big trees on it, and the current throwed me off to the left and shot by, amongst a lot of snags that fairly roared, the current was tearing by them so swift.

In another second or two it was solid white and still again. I set perfectly still then, listening to my heart thump, and I reckon I didn't draw a breath while it thumped a hundred.

I just give up then. I knowed what the matter was. That cut bank was an island, and Jim had gone down t'other side of it. It warn't no towhead that you could float by in ten minutes. It had the big timber of a regular island; it might be five or six miles long and more than half a mile wide.

I kept quiet, with my ears cocked, about fifteen minutes, I reckon. I was floating along, of course, four or five miles an hour; but you don't ever think of that. No, you *feel* like you are laying dead still on the water; and if a little glimpse of a snag slips by you don't think to yourself how fast *you're* going, but you catch your breath and think, my! how that snag's tearing along. If you think it ain't dismal and lonesome out in a fog that way by yourself in the night, you try it once—you'll see.

Next, for about a half an hour, I whoops now and then; at last I hears the answer a long ways off, and tries to follow it, but I couldn't do it, and directly I judged I'd got into a nest of towheads, for I had little dim glimpses of them on both sides of me—sometimes just a narrow channel between, and some that I couldn't see I knowed was there because I'd hear the wash of the current against the old dead brush and trash that hung over the banks. Well, I warn't long losing the whoops down amongst the towheads; and I only tried to chase them a little while, anyway, because it was worse than chasing a Jack-o'-lantern. You never knowed a sound dodge around so, and swap places so quick and so much.

I had to claw away from the bank pretty lively four or five times, to keep from knocking the islands out of the river; and so I judged the raft must be butting into the bank every now and then, or else it would get further ahead and clear out of hearing—it was floating a little faster than what I was.

Well, I seemed to be in the open river again by and by, but I couldn't hear no sign of a whoop nowheres. I reckoned Jim had fetched up on a snag, maybe, and it was all up with him. I was good and tired, so I laid down in the canoe and said I wouldn't bother no more. I didn't want to go to sleep, of course; but I was so sleepy I couldn't help it; so I thought I would take jest one little cat-nap.

But I reckon it was more than a cat-nap, for when I waked up the stars was shining bright, the fog was all gone, and I was spinning down a big bend stern first. First I didn't know where I was; I thought I was dreaming; and when things began to come back to me they seemed to come up dim out of last week.

It was a monstrous big river here, with the tallest and the thickest kind of timber on both banks; just a solid wall, as well as I could see by the stars. I looked away down-stream, and seen a black speck on the water. I took after it; but when I got to it it warn't nothing but a couple of saw-logs made fast together. Then I see another speck, and chased that; then another, and this time I was right. It was the raft.

When I got to it Jim was setting there with his head down between his knees, asleep, with his right arm hanging over the steering-oar. The other oar was smashed off, and the raft was littered up with leaves and branches and dirt. So she'd had a rough time.

I made fast and laid down under Jim's nose on the raft, and began to gap, and stretch my fists out against Jim, and says: "Hello, Jim, have I been asleep? Why didn't you stir me up?"

"Goodness gracious, is dat you, Huck? En you ain' dead—you ain' drownded—you's back ag'in? It's too good for true, honey, it's too good for true. Lemme look at you, chile, lemme feel o' you. No, you ain' dead! you's back ag'in, 'live en soun', jis de same ole Huck —de same ole Huck, thanks to goodness!"

"What's the matter with you, Jim? You been a-drinking?"

"Drinkin'? Has I ben a-drinkin'? Has I had a chance to be a-drinkin'?"

"Well, then, what makes you talk so wild?"

"How does I talk wild?"

"*How?* Why, hain't you been talking about my coming back, and all that stuff, as if I'd been gone away?"

"Huck—Huck Finn, you look me in de eye; look me in de eye. *Hain't* you ben gone away?"

"Gone away? Why, what in the nation do you mean? *I* hain't been gone anywheres. Where would I go to?"

"Well, looky here, boss, dey's sumfn wrong, dey is. Is I *me*, or who *is* I? Is I heah, or whah *is* I? Now dat's what I wants to know."

"Well, I think you're here, plain enough, but I think you're a tangle-headed old fool, Jim."

"I is, is I? Well, you answer me dis: Didn't you tote out de line in de canoe fer to make fas' to de towhead?"

"No, I didn't. What towhead? I hain't seen no towhead."

"You hain't seen no towhead? Looky here, didn't de line pull loose en de raf' go a-hummin' down de river, en leave you en de canoe behine in de fog?"

"What fog?"

"Why, *de* fog!—de fog dat's been aroun' all night. En didn't you whoop, en didn't I whoop, tell we got mix' up in de islands en one un us got los' en t'other one was jis' as good as los', 'kase he didn' know whah he wuz? En didn't I bust up again a lot er dem islands en have a turrible time en mos' git drownded? Now ain't dat so, boss—ain't it so? You answer me dat."

"Well, this is too many for me, Jim. I hain't seen no fog, nor no islands, nor no troubles, nor nothing. I been setting here talking with you all night till you went to sleep about ten minutes ago, and I reckon I done the same. You couldn't 'a' got drunk in that time, so of course you've been dreaming."

"Dad fetch it, how is I gwyne to dream all dat in ten minutes?"

"Well, hang it all, you did dream it, because there didn't any of it happen."

"But, Huck, it's all jis' as plain to me as—"

"It don't make no difference how plain it is; there ain't nothing in it. I know, because I've been here all the time."

Jim didn't say nothing for about five minutes, but set there studying over it. Then he says:

"Well, den, I reck'n I did dream it, Huck; but dog my cats ef it ain't de powerfulest dream I ever see. En I hain't ever had no dream b'fo' dat's tired me like dis one."

"Oh, well, that's all right, because a dream does tire a body like everything sometimes. But this one was a staving dream; tell me all about it, Jim."

So Jim went to work and told me the whole thing right through, just as it happened, only he painted it up considerable. Then he said he must start in and " 'terpret" it, because it was sent for a warning. He said the first towhead stood for a man that would try to do us some good, but the current was another man that would get us away from him. The whoops was warnings that would come to us every now and then, and if we didn't try hard to make out to understand them they'd just take us into bad luck, 'stead of keeping us out of it. The lot of towheads was troubles we was going to get into with quarrelsome people and all kinds of mean folks, but if we minded our business and didn't talk back and aggravate them, we would pull through and get out of the fog and into the big clear river, which was the free states, and wouldn't have no more trouble.

It had clouded up pretty dark just after I got on to the raft, but it was clearing up again now.

"Oh, well, that's all interpreted well enough as far as it goes, Jim," I says; "but what does *these* things stand for?"

It was the leaves and rubbish on the raft and the smashed oar. You could see them first-rate now.

Jim looked at the trash, and then looked at me, and back at the trash again. He had got the dream fixed so strong in his head that he couldn't seem to shake it loose and get the facts back into its place again right away. But when he did get the thing straightened around he looked at me steady without ever smiling, and says:

"What do dey stan' for? I's gwyne to tell you. When I got all wore out wid work, en wid de callin' for you, en went to sleep, my heart wuz mos' broke bekase you wuz los', en I didn' k'yer no' mo' what become er me en de raf'. En when I wake up en find you back ag'in, all safe en soun', de tears come, en I could 'a' got down on my knees en kiss yo' foot, I's so thankful. En all you wuz thinkin' 'bout wuz how you could make a fool uv ole Jim wid a lie. Dat truck dah is *trash*; en trash is what people is dat puts dirt on de head er dey fren's en makes 'em ashamed."

Then he got up slow and walked to the wigwam, and went in there without saying anything but that. But that was enough. It made me feel so mean I could almost kissed *his* foot to get him to take it back.

It was fifteen minutes before I could work myself up to go and humble myself to a nigger; but I done it, and I warn't ever sorry for it afterward, neither. I didn't do him no more mean tricks, and I wouldn't done that one if I'd 'a' knowed it would make him feel that way.

16. THE RATTLESNAKE-SKIN DOES ITS WORK

We slept most all day, and started out at night, a little ways behind a monstrous long raft that was as long going by as a procession. She had four long sweeps at each end, so we judged she carried as many as thirty men, likely. She had five big wigwams aboard, wide apart, and an open camp-fire in the middle, and a tall flag-pole at each end. There was a power of style about her. It *amounted* to something being a raftsman on such a craft as that.

We went drifting down into a big bend, and the night clouded up and got hot. The river was very wide, and was walled with solid timber on both sides; you couldn't see a break in it hardly ever, or a light. We talked about Cairo, and wondered whether we would know it when we got to it. I said likely we wouldn't, because I had heard say there warn't but about a dozen houses there, and if they didn't happen to have them lit up, how was we going to know we was passing a town? Jim said if the two big rivers joined together there, that would show. But I said maybe we might think we was passing the foot of an island and coming into the same old river again. That disturbed Jim—and me too. So the question was, what to do? I said, paddle ashore the first time a light showed, and tell them pap was behind, coming along with a trading-scow, and was a green hand at the business, and wanted to know how far it was to Cairo. Jim thought it was a good idea, so we took a smoke on it and waited.

There warn't nothing to do now but to look out sharp for the town, and not pass it without seeing it. He said he'd be mighty sure to see it, because he'd be a free man the minute he seen it, but if he missed it he'd be in a slave country again and no more show for freedom. Every little while he jumps up and says:

"Dah she is?"

But it warn't. It was Jack-o'-lanterns, or lightning-bugs; so he set down again, and went to watching, same as before. Jim said it made him all over trembly and feverish to be so close to freedom. Well, I can tell you it made me all over trembly and feverish, too, to hear him, because I begun to get it through my head that he *was* most free—and who was to blame for it? Why, *me*. I couldn't get that out of my conscience, no how nor no way. It got to troubling me so I couldn't rest; I couldn't stay still in one place. It hadn't ever come home to me before, what this thing was that I was doing. But now it did; and it stayed with me, and scorched me more and more. I tried to make out to myself that *I* warn't to blame, because *I* didn't run Jim off from his rightful owner; but it warn't no use, conscience up and says, every time, "But you knowed he was running for his freedom, and you could 'a' paddled ashore and told somebody." That was so—I couldn't get around that no way. That was where it pinched. Conscience says to me, "What had poor Miss Watson done to you that you could see her nigger go off right under your eyes and never say one single word? What did that poor old woman do to you that you could treat her so mean? Why, she tried to learn you your book, she tried to learn you your manners, she tried to be good to you every way she knowed how. *That's* what she done."

I got to feeling so mean and so miserable I most wished I was dead. I fidgeted up and down the raft, abusing myself to myself, and Jim was fidgeting up and down past me. We neither of us could keep still. Every time he danced around and says, "Dah's Cairo!" it went through me like a shot, and I thought if it *was* Cairo I reckoned I would die of miserableness.

Jim talked out loud all the time while I was talking to myself. He was saying how the first thing he would do when he got to a free state he would go to saving up money and never spend a single cent, and when he got enough he would buy his wife, which was owned on a farm close to where Miss Watson lived; and then they would both work to buy the two children, and if their master wouldn't sell them, they'd get an Ab'litionist to go and steal them.

It most froze me to hear such talk. He wouldn't ever dared to talk such talk in his life before. Just see what a difference it made in him the minute he judged he was about free. It was according to the old saying, "Give a nigger an inch and he'll take an ell." Thinks I, this is what comes of my not thinking. Here

was this nigger, which I had as good as helped to run away, coming right out flat-footed and saying he would steal his children—children that belonged to a man I didn't even know; a man that hadn't ever done me no harm.

I was sorry to hear Jim say that, it was such a lowering of him. My conscience got to stirring me up hotter than ever, until at last I says to it, "Let up on me—it ain't too late yet—I'll paddle ashore at the first light and tell." I felt easy and happy and light as a feather right off. All my troubles was gone. I went to looking out sharp for a light, and sort of singing to myself. By and by one showed. Jim sings out:

"We's safe, Huck, we's safe! Jump up and crack yo' heels! Dat's de good ole Cairo at las', I jis knows it!"

I says:

"I'll take the canoe and go and see, Jim. It mightn't be, you know."

He jumped and got the canoe ready, and put his old coat in the bottom for me to set on, and give me the paddle; and as I shoved off, he says:

"Pooty soon I'll be a-shout'n' for joy, en I'll say, it's all on accounts o' Huck; I's a free man, en I couldn't ever ben free ef it hadn't ben for Huck; Huck done it. Jim won't ever forgit you, Huck; you's de bes' fren' Jim's ever had; en you's de *only* fren' ole Jim's got now."

I was paddling off, all in a sweat to tell on him; but when he says this, it seemed to kind of take the tuck all out of me. I went along slow then, and I warn't right down certain whether I was glad I started or whether I warn't. When I was fifty yards off, Jim says:

"Dah you goes, de ole true Huck; de on'y white genlman dat ever kep' his promise to ole Jim."

Well, I just felt sick. But I says, I *got* to do it—I can't get *out* of it. Right then along comes a skiff with two men in it with guns, and they stopped and I stopped. One of them says:

"What's that yonder?"

"A piece of raft," I says.

"Do you belong on it?"

"Yes, sir."

"Any men on it?"

"Only one, sir."

"Well, there's five niggers run off tonight

up yonder, above the head of the bend. Is your man white or black?"

I didn't answer up promptly. I tried to, but the words wouldn't come. I tried for a second or two to brace up and out with it, but I warn't man enough—hadn't the spunk of a rabbit. I see I was weakening; so I just give up trying, and up and says:

"He's white."

"I reckon we'll go and see for ourselves."

"I wish you would," says I, "because it's pap that's there, and maybe you'd help me tow the raft ashore where the light is. He's sick —and so is mam and Mary Ann."

"Oh, the devil! we're in a hurry, boy. But I s'pose we've got to. Come, buckle to your paddle, and let's get along."

I buckled to my paddle and they laid to their oars. When we had made a stroke or two, I says:

"Pap'll be mighty much obleeged to you, I can tell you. Everybody goes away when I want them to help me tow the raft ashore, and I can't do it by myself."

"Well, that's infernal mean. Odd, too. Say, boy, what's the matter with your father?"

"It's the—a—the—well, it ain't anything much."

They stopped pulling. It warn't but a mighty little ways to the raft now. One says:

"Boy, that's a lie. What *is* the matter with your pap? Answer up square now, and it'll be the better for you."

"I will, sir, I will, honest—but don't leave us, please. It's the—the— Gentlemen, if you'll only pull ahead, and let me heave you the headline, you won't have to come a-near the raft—please do."

"Set her back, John, set her back!" says one. They backed water. "Keep away, boy—keep to looard. Confound it, I just expect the wind has blowed it to us. Your pap's got the small-pox, and you know it precious well. Why didn't you come out and say so? Do you want to spread it all over?"

"Well," says I, a-blubbering, "I've told everybody before, and they just went away and left us."

"Poor devil, there's something in that. We are right down sorry for you, but we—well, hang it, we don't want the smallpox, you see. Look here, I'll tell you what to do. Don't you

try to land by yourself, or you'll smash everything to pieces. You float along down about twenty miles, and you'll come to a town on the left-hand side of the river. It will be long after sun-up then, and when you ask for help you tell them your folks are all down with chills and fever. Don't be a fool again, and let people guess what is the matter. Now we're trying to do you a kindness; so you just put twenty miles between us, that's a good boy. It wouldn't do any good to land yonder where the light is—it's only a wood-yard. Say, I reckon your father's poor, and I'm bound to say he's in pretty hard luck. Here, I'll put a twenty-dollar gold piece on this board, and you get it when it floats by. I feel mighty mean to leave you; but my kingdom! it won't do to fool with smallpox, don't you see?"

"Hold on, Parker," says the man, "here's a twenty to put on the board for me. Good-by, boy; you do as Mr. Parker told you, and you'll be all right."

"That's so, my boy—good-by, good-by. If you see any runaway niggers you get help and nab them, and you can make some money by it."

"Good-by, sir," says I; "I won't let no runaway niggers get by me if I can help it."

They went off and I got aboard the raft, feeling bad and low, because I knowed very well I had done wrong, and I see it warn't no use for me to try to learn to do right; a body that don't get *started* right when he's little ain't got no show—when the pinch comes there ain't nothing to back him up and keep him to his work, and so he gets beat. Then I thought a minute, and says to myself, hold on; s'pose you'd 'a' done right and give Jim up, would you felt better than what you do now? No, says I, I'd feel bad—I'd feel just the same way I do now. Well, then, says I, what's the use you learning to do right when it's troublesome to do right and ain't no trouble to do wrong, and the wages is just the same? I was stuck. I couldn't answer that. So I reckoned I wouldn't bother no more about it, but after this always do whichever come handiest at the time.

I went into the wigwam; Jim warn't there. I looked all around; he warn't anywhere. I says:

"Jim!"

"Here I is, Huck. Is dey out o' sight yit? Don't talk loud."

He was in the river under the stern oar, with just his nose out. I told him they were out of sight, so he come aboard. He says:

"I was a-listenin' to all de talk, en I slips into de river en was gwyne to shove for sho' if dey come aboard. Den I was gwyne to swim to de raf' agin when dey was gone. But lawsy, how you did fool 'em, Huck! Dat *wuz* de smartes' dodge! I tell you, chile, I 'spec it save' ole Jim—ole Jim ain't going to forgit you for dat, honey."

Then we talked about the money. It was a pretty good raise—twenty dollars apiece. Jim said we could take deck passage on a steamboat now, and the money would last us as far as we wanted to go in the free states. He said twenty mile more warn't far for the raft to go, but he wished we was already there.

Towards daybreak we tied up, and Jim was mighty particular about hiding the raft good. Then he worked all day fixing things in bundles, and getting all ready to quit rafting.

That night about ten we hove in sight of the lights of a town away down in a left-hand bend.

I went off in the canoe to ask about it. Pretty soon I found a man out in the river with a skiff, setting a trot-line. I ranged up and says:

"Mister, is that town Cairo?"

"Cairo? No. You must be a blame' fool."

"What town is it, mister?"

"If you want to know, go and find out. If you stay here botherin' around me for about a half a minute longer you'll get something you won't want."

I paddled to the raft. Jim was awful disappointed, but I said never mind, Cairo would be the next place, I reckoned.

We passed another town before daylight, and I was going out again; but it was high ground, so I didn't go. No high ground about Cairo, Jim said. I had forgot it. We laid up for the day on a towhead tolerable close to the left-hand bank. I begun to suspicion something. So did Jim. I says:

"Maybe we went by Cairo in the fog that night."

He says:

"Doan' le's talk about it, Huck. Po' niggers can't have no luck. I alwuz 'spected dat rattle-snake-skin warn't done wid its work."

"I wish I'd never seen that snake-skin, Jim—I do wish I'd never laid eyes on it."

"It ain't yo' fault, Huck; you didn't know. Don't you blame yo'self 'bout it."

When it was daylight, here was the clear Ohio water inshore, sure enough, and outside was the old regular Muddy! So it was all up with Cairo.

We talked it all over. It wouldn't do to take to the shore; we couldn't take the raft up the stream, of course. There warn't no way but to wait for dark, and start back in the canoe and take the chances. So we slept all day amongst the cottonwood thicket, so as to be fresh for the work, and when we went back to the raft about dark the canoe was gone!

We didn't say a word for a good while. There warn't anything to say. We both knowed well enough it was some more work of the rattlesnake-skin; so what was the use to talk about it? It would only look like we was finding fault, and that would be bound to fetch more bad luck—and keep on fetching it, too, till we knowed enough to keep still.

By and by we talked about what we better do, and found there warn't no way but just to go along down with the raft till we got a chance to buy a canoe to go back in. We warn't going to borrow it when there warn't anybody around, the way pap would do, for that might set people after us.

So we shoved out after dark on the raft.

Anybody that don't believe yet that it's foolishness to handle a snake-skin, after all that that snake-skin done for us, will believe it now if they read on and see what more it done for us.

The place to buy canoes is off of rafts laying up at shore. But we didn't see no rafts laying up; so we went along during three hours and more. Well, the night got gray and ruther thick, which is the next meanest thing to fog. You can't tell the shape of the river, and you can't see no distance. It got to be very late and still, and then along comes a steamboat up the river. We lit the lantern, and judged she would see it. Up-stream boats didn't generly come close to us; they go out and follow the bars and hunt for easy water under the reefs; but nights like this they bull right up the channel against the whole river.

We could hear her pounding along, but we didn't see her good till she was close. She aimed right for us. Often they do that and try to see how close they can come without touching; sometimes the wheel bites off a sweep, and then the pilot sticks his head out and laughs, and thinks he's mighty smart. Well, here she comes, and we said she was going to try and shave us; but she didn't seem to be sheering off a bit. She was a big one, and she was coming in a hurry, too, looking like a black cloud with rows of glow-worms around it; but all of a sudden she bulged out, big and scary, with a long row of wide-open furnace doors shining like red-hot teeth, and her monstrous bows and guards hanging right over us. There was a yell at us, and a jingling of bells to stop the engines, a powwow of cussing, and whistling of steam—and as Jim went overboard on one side and I on the other, she come smashing straight through the raft.

I dived—and I aimed to find the bottom, too, for a thirty-foot wheel had got to go over me, and I wanted it to have plenty of room. I could always stay under water a minute; this time I reckoned I stayed under a minute and a half. Then I bounced for the top in a hurry, for I was nearly busting. I popped out to my armpits and blowed the water out of my nose, and puffed a bit. Of course there was a booming current; and of course that boat started her engines again ten seconds after she stopped them, for they never cared much for raftsmen; so now she was churning along up the river, out of sight in the thick weather, though I could hear her.

I sung out for Jim about a dozen times, but I didn't get any answer; so I grabbed a plank that touched me while I was "treading water," and struck out for shore, shoving it ahead of me. But I made out to see that the drift of the current was towards the left-hand shore, which meant that I was in a crossing; so I changed off and went that way.

It was one of these long, slanting, two-mile crossings; so I was a good long time in getting over. I made a safe landing, and clumb up the bank. I couldn't see but a little ways, but I went poking along over rough ground for a

quarter of a mile or more, and then I run across a big old-fashioned double log house before I noticed it. I was going to rush by and get away, but a lot of dogs jumped out and went to howling and barking at me, and I knowed better than to move another peg.

17. THE GRANGERFORDS TAKE ME IN

In about a minute somebody spoke out of a window without putting his head out, and says:

"Be done, boys! Who's there?"

I says:

"It's me."

"Who's me?"

"George Jackson, sir."

"What do you want?"

"I don't want nothing, sir. I only want to go along by, but the dogs won't let me."

"What are you prowling around here this time of night for—hey?"

"I warn't prowling around, sir; I fell overboard off of the steamboat."

"Oh, you did, did you? Strike a light there, somebody. What did you say your name was?"

"George Jackson, sir. I'm only a boy."

"Look here, if you're telling the truth you needn't be afraid—nobody'll hurt you. But don't try to budge; stand right where you are. Rouse out Bob and Tom, some of you, and fetch the guns. George Jackson, is there anybody with you?"

"No, sir, nobody."

I heard the people stirring around in the house now, and see a light. The man sung out:

"Snatch that light away, Betsy, you old fool—ain't you got any sense? Put it on the floor behind the front door. Bob, if you and Tom are ready, take your places."

"All ready."

"Now, George Jackson, do you know the Shepherdsons?"

"No, sir; I never heard of them."

"Well, that may be so, and it mayn't. Now, all ready. Step forward, George Jackson. And mind, don't you hurry—come mighty slow. If there's anybody with you, let him keep back—if he shows himself he'll be shot. Come along now. Come slow; push the door open yourself—just enough to squeeze in, d'you hear?"

I didn't hurry; I couldn't if I'd a-wanted to.

I took one slow step at a time and there warn't a sound, only I thought I could hear my heart. The dogs were as still as the humans, but they followed a little behind me. When I got to the three log doorsteps I heard them unlocking and unbarring and unbolting. I put my hand on the door and pushed it a little and a little more till somebody said, "There, that's enough—put your head in." I done it, but I judged they would take it off.

The candle was on the floor, and there they all was, looking at me, and me at them, for about a quarter of a minute: Three big men with guns pointed at me, which made me wince, I tell you; the oldest, gray and about sixty, the other two thirty or more—all of them fine and handsome—and the sweetest old gray-headed lady, and back of her two young women which I couldn't see right well. The old gentleman says:

"There; I reckon it's all right. Come in."

As soon as I was in the old gentleman he locked the door and barred it and bolted it, and told the young men to come in with their guns, and they all went in a big parlor that had a new rag carpet on the floor, and got together in a corner that was out of the range of the front windows—there warn't none on the side. They held the candle, and took a good look at me, and all said, "Why, *he* ain't a Shepherdson—no, there ain't any Shepherdson about him." Then the old man said he hoped I wouldn't mind being searched for arms, because he didn't mean no harm by it —it was only to make sure. So he didn't pry into my pockets, but only felt outside with his hands, and said it was all right. He told me to make myself easy and at home, and tell all about myself; but the old lady says:

"Why, bless you, Saul, the poor thing's as wet as he can be; and don't you reckon it may be he's hungry?"

"True for you, Rachel—I forgot."

So the old lady says:

"Betsy" (this was a nigger woman), "you fly around and get him something to eat as quick as you can, poor thing; and one of you girls go and wake up Buck and tell him—oh, here he is himself. Buck, take this little stranger and get the wet clothes off from him and dress him up in some of yours that's dry."

Buck looked about as old as me—thirteen or fourteen or along there, though he was a little bigger than me. He hadn't on anything but a shirt, and he was very frowzy-headed. He came in gaping and digging one fist in his eyes, and he was dragging a gun along with the other one. He says:

"Ain't they no Shepherdsons around?"

They said, no, 'twas a false alarm.

"Well," he says, "if they'd 'a' ben some, I reckon I'd 'a' got one."

They all laughed, and Bob says:

"Why, Buck, they might have scalped us all, you've been so slow in coming."

"Well, nobody come after me, and it ain't right. I'm always kept down; I don't get no show."

"Never mind, Buck, my boy," says the old man, "you'll have show enough, all in good time, don't you fret about that. Go 'long with you now, and do as your mother told you."

When we got up-stairs to his room he got me a coarse shirt and a roundabout and pants of his, and I put them on. While I was at it he asked me what my name was, but before I could tell him he started to tell me about a bluejay and a young rabbit he had catched in the woods day before yesterday, and he asked me where Moses was when the candle went out. I said I didn't know; I hadn't heard about it before, no way.

"Well, guess," he says.

"How'm I going to guess," says I, "when I never heard tell of it before?"

"But you can guess, can't you? It's just as easy."

"*Which* candle?" I says.

"Why, any candle," he says.

"I don't know where he was," says I; "where was he?"

"Why, he was in the *dark!* That's where he was!"

"Well, if you knowed where he was, what did you ask me for?"

"Why, blame it, it's a riddle, don't you see? Say, how long are you going to stay here? You got to stay always. We can just have booming times—they don't have no school now. Do you own a dog? I've got a dog—and he'll go in the river and bring out chips that you throw in. Do you like to comb up Sundays, and all that kind of foolishness? You bet I don't, but ma she makes me. Confound these ole britches!

I reckon I'd better put 'em on, but I'd ruther not, it's so warm. Are you all ready? All right. Come along, old hoss."

Cold corn-pone, cold corn-beef, butter and butter-milk—that is what they had for me down there, and there ain't nothing better that ever I've come across yet. Buck and his ma and all of them smoked cob pipes, except the nigger woman, which was gone, and the two young women. They all smoked and talked, and I eat and talked. The young women had quilts around them, and their hair down their backs. They all asked me questions, and I told them how pap and me and all the family was living on a little farm down at the bottom of Arkansaw, and my sister Mary Ann run off and got married and never was heard of no more, and Bill went to hunt them and he warn't heard of no more, and Tom and Mort died, and then there warn't nobody but just me and pap left, and he was just trimmed down to nothing, on account of his troubles; so when he died I took what there was left, because the farm didn't belong to us, and started up the river, deck passage, and fell overboard; and that was how I come to be here. So they said I could have a home there as long as I wanted it. Then it was most daylight and everybody went to bed, and I went to bed with Buck, and when I waked up in the morning, drat it all, I had forgot what my name was. So I laid there about an hour trying to think, and when Buck waked up I says:

"Can you spell, Buck?"

"Yes," he says.

"I bet you can't spell my name," says I.

"I bet you what you dare I can," says he.

"All right," says I, "go ahead."

"G-e-o-r-g-e J-a-x-o-n—there now," he says.

"Well," says I, "you done it, but I didn't think you could. It ain't no slouch of a name to spell—right off without studying."

I set it down, private, because somebody might want *me* to spell it next, and so I wanted to be handy with it and rattle it off like I was used to it.

It was a mighty nice family, and a mighty nice house, too. I hadn't seen no house out in the country before that was so nice and had so much style. It didn't have an iron latch on the front door, nor a wooden one with a buckskin string, but a brass knob to turn, the same as houses in town. There warn't no bed in the parlor, nor a sign of a bed; but heaps of parlors in towns has beds in them. There was a big fireplace that was bricked on the bottom, and the bricks was kept clean and red by pouring water on them and scrubbing them with another brick; sometimes they wash them over with red water-paint that they call Spanish-brown, same as they do in town. They had big brass dog-irons that could hold up a saw-log. There was a clock on the middle of the mantelpiece, with a picture of a town painted on the bottom half of the glass front, and a round place in the middle of it for the sun, and you could see the pendulum swinging behind it. It was beautiful to hear that clock tick; and sometimes when one of these peddlers had been along and scoured her up and got her in good shape, she would start in and strike a hundred and fifty before she got tuckered out. They wouldn't took any money for her.

Well, there was a big outlandish parrot on each side of the clock, made out of something like chalk, and painted up gaudy. By one of the parrots was a cat made of crockery, and a crockery dog by the other; and when you pressed down on them they squeaked, but didn't open their mouths nor look different nor interested. They squeaked through underneath. There was a couple of big wild-turkey-wing fans spread out behind those things. On the table in the middle of the room was a kind of a lovely crockery basket that had apples and oranges and peaches and grapes piled up in it, which was much redder and yellower and prettier than real ones is, but they warn't real because you could see where pieces had got chipped off and showed the white chalk, or whatever it was, underneath.

This table had a cover made out of beautiful oil-cloth, with a red and blue spread-eagle painted on it, and a painted border all around. It come all the way from Philadelphia, they said. There was some books, too, piled up perfectly exact, on each corner of the table. One was a big family Bible full of pictures. One was *Pilgrim's Progress,* about a man that left his family, it didn't say why. I read considerable in it now and then. The statements was interesting, but tough. Another was *Friendship's Offering,* full of beautiful stuff and poetry; but I didn't read the poetry. Another was Henry Clay's Speeches, and another was Dr. Gunn's *Family Medicine,* which told you all about what to do if a body was sick or dead. There was a hymn-book, and a lot of other books. And there was nice split-bottom chairs, and perfectly sound, too—not bagged down in the middle and busted, like an old basket.

They had pictures hung on the walls— mainly Washingtons and Lafayettes, and battles, and Highland Marys, and one called "Signing the Declaration." There was some that they called crayons, which one of the daughters which was dead made her own self when she was only fifteen years old. They was different from any pictures I ever see before —blacker, mostly, than is common. One was a woman in a slim black dress, belted small under the armpits, with bulges like a cabbage in the middle of the sleeves, and a large black scoop-shovel bonnet with a black veil, and white slim ankles crossed about with black tape, and very wee black slippers, like a chisel, and she was leaning pensive on a tombstone on her right elbow, under a weeping willow, and her other hand hanging down her side holding a white handkerchief and a reticule, and underneath the picture it said "Shall I Never See Thee More Alas." Another one was a young lady with her hair all combed up straight to the top of her head, and knotted there in front of a comb like a chair-back, and she was crying into a handkerchief and had a dead bird laying on its back in her other hand with its heels up, and underneath the picture it said "I Shall Never Hear Thy Sweet Chirrup More Alas." There was one where a young lady was at a window looking up at the moon, and tears running down her cheeks; and she had an open letter in one hand with black sealing-wax showing on one edge of it, and she was mashing a locket with a chain to it against her mouth, and underneath the picture it said "And Art Thou Gone Yes Thou Art Gone Alas." These was all nice pictures, I reckon, but I didn't somehow seem to take to them, because if ever I was down a little they always give me the fantods. Everybody was sorry she died, because she had laid out a lot more of these pictures to do, and a body could see by what she had

done what they had lost. But I reckoned that with her disposition she was having a better time in the graveyard. She was at work on what they said was her greatest picture when she took sick, and every day and every night it was her prayer to be allowed to live till she got it done, but she never got the chance. It was a picture of a young woman in a long white gown, standing on the rail of a bridge all ready to jump off, with her hair all down her back, and looking up to the moon, with the tears running down her face, and she had two arms folded across her breast, and two arms stretched out in front, and two more reaching up toward the moon—and the idea was to see which pair would look best, and then scratch out all the other arms; but, as I was saying, she died before she got her mind made up, and now they kept this picture over the head of the bed in her room, and every time her birthday come they hung flowers on it. Other times it was hid with a little curtain. The young woman in the picture had a kind of a nice sweet face, but there was so many arms it made her look too spidery, seemed to me.

This young girl kept a scrap-book when she was alive, and used to paste obituaries and accidents and cases of patient suffering in it out of the *Presbyterian Observer,* and write poetry after them out of her own head. It was very good poetry. This is what she wrote about a boy by the name of Stephen Dowling Bots that fell down a well and was drownded:

ODE TO STEPHEN DOWLING BOTS, DEC'D

And did young Stephen sicken,
  And did young Stephen die?
And did the sad hearts thicken,
  And did the mourners cry?

No; such was not the fate of
  Young Stephen Dowling Bots;
Though sad hearts round him thickened,
  'Twas not from sickness' shots.

No whooping-cough did rack his frame,
  Nor measles drear with spots;
Not these impaired the sacred name
  Of Stephen Dowling Bots.

Despised love struck not with woe
  That head of curly knots,
Nor stomach troubles laid him low,
  Young Stephen Dowling Bots.

O no. Then list with tearful eye,
    Whilst I his fate do tell.
His soul did from this cold world fly
    By falling down a well.

They got him out and emptied him;
    Alas it was too late;
His spirit was gone for to sport aloft
    In the realms of the good and great.

If Emmeline Grangerford could make poetry like that before she was fourteen, there ain't no telling what she could 'a' done by and by. Buck said she could rattle off poetry like nothing. She didn't ever have to stop to think. He said she would slap down a line, and if she couldn't find anything to rhyme with it would just scratch it out and slap down another one, and go ahead. She warn't particular; she could write about anything you choose to give her to write about just so it was sadful. Every time a man died, or a woman died, or a child died, she would be on hand with her "tribute" before he was cold. She called them tributes. The neighbors said it was the doctor first, then Emmeline, then the undertaker—the undertaker never got in ahead of Emmeline but once, and then she hung fire on a rhyme for the dead person's name, which was Whistler. She warn't ever the same after that; she never complained, but she kinder pined away and did not live long. Poor thing, many's the time I made myself go up to the little room that used to be hers and get out her poor old scrapbook and read in it when her pictures had been aggravating me and I had soured on her a little. I liked all that family, dead ones and all, and warn't going to let anything come between us. Poor Emmeline made poetry about all the dead people when she was alive, and it didn't seem right that there warn't nobody to make some about her now she was gone; so I tried to sweat out a verse or two myself, but I couldn't seem to make it go somehow. They kept Emmeline's room trim and nice, and all the things fixed in it just the way she liked to have them when she was alive, and nobody ever slept there. The old lady took care of the room herself, though there was plenty of niggers, and she sewed there a good deal and read her Bible there mostly.

Well, as I was saying about the parlor, there was beautiful curtains on the windows: white, with pictures painted on them of castles with vines all down the walls, and cattle coming down to drink. There was a little old piano, too, that had tin pans in it, I reckon, and nothing was ever so lovely as to hear the young ladies sing "The Last Link is Broken" and play "The Battle of Prague" on it. The walls of all the rooms was plastered, and most had carpets on the floors, and the whole house was whitewashed on the outside.

It was a double house, and the big open place betwixt them was roofed and floored, and sometimes the table was set there in the middle of the day, and it was a cool, comfortable place. Nothing couldn't be better. And warn't the cooking good, and just bushels of it too!

18. WHY HARNEY RODE AWAY FOR HIS HAT

Col. Grangerford was a gentleman, you see. He was a gentleman all over; and so was his family. He was well born, as the saying is, and that's worth as much in a man as it is in a horse, so the Widow Douglas said, and nobody ever denied that she was of the first aristocracy in our town; and pap he always said it, too, though he warn't no more quality than a mudcat himself. Col. Grangerford was very tall and very slim, and had a darkish-paly complexion, not a sign of red in it anywheres; he was clean-shaved every morning all over his thin face, and he had the thinnest kind of lips, and the thinnest kind of nostrils, and a high nose, and heavy eyebrows, and the blackest kind of eyes, sunk so deep back that they seemed like they was looking out of caverns at you, as you may say. His forehead was high, and his hair was gray and straight and hung to his shoulders. His hands was long and thin, and every day of his life he put on a clean shirt and a full suit from head to foot made out of linen so white it hurt your eyes to look at it; and on Sundays he wore a blue tailcoat with brass buttons on it. He carried a mahogany cane with a silver head to it. There warn't no frivolishness about him, not a bit, and he warn't ever loud. He was as kind as he could be—you could feel that, you know, and so you had confidence. Sometimes he smiled,

and it was good to see; but when he straightened himself up like a liberty-pole, and the
lightning begun to flicker out from under his
eyebrows, you wanted to climb a tree first,
and find out what the matter was afterwards.
He didn't ever have to tell anybody to mind
their manners—everybody was always good-
mannered where he was. Everybody loved to
have him around, too; he was sunshine most
always—I mean he made it seem like good
weather. When he turned into a cloud-bank
it was awful dark for half a minute, and that
was enough; there wouldn't nothing go wrong
again for a week.

When him and the old lady come down in
the morning all the family got up out of their
chairs and give them good day, and didn't set
down again till they had set down. Then Tom
and Bob went to the sideboard where the de-
canter was, and mixed a glass of bitters and
handed it to him, and he held it in his hand
and waited till Tom's and Bob's was mixed,
and then they bowed and said, "Our duty to
you, sir, and madam"; and *they* bowed the
least bit in the world and said thank you, and
so they drank, all three, and Bob and Tom
poured a spoonful of water on the sugar and
the mite of whisky or apple-brandy in the
bottom of their tumblers, and give it to me
and Buck, and we drank to the old people too.

Bob was the oldest and Tom next—tall,
beautiful men with very broad shoulders and
brown faces, and long black hair and black
eyes. They dressed in white linen from head to
foot, like the old gentleman, and wore broad
Panama hats.

Then there was Miss Charlotte; she was
twenty-five, and tall and proud and grand,
but as good as she could be when she warn't
stirred up; but when she was she had a look
that would make you wilt in your tracks, like
her father. She was beautiful.

So was her sister, Miss Sophia, but it was a
different kind. She was gentle and sweet like
a dove, and she was only twenty.

Each person had their own nigger to wait
on them—Buck too. My nigger had a monstrous easy time, because I warn't used to having anybody do anything for me, but Buck's
was on the jump most of the time.

This was all there was of the family now,
but there used to be more—three sons; they
got killed; and Emmeline that died.

The old gentleman owned a lot of farms
and over a hundred niggers. Sometimes a stack
of people would come there, horseback, from
ten or fifteen miles around, and stay five or
six days, and have such junketings round
about and on the river, and dances and pic-
nics in the woods daytimes, and balls at the
house nights. These people was mostly kinfolks of the family. The men brought their
guns with them. It was a handsome lot of
quality, I tell you.

There was another clan of aristocracy
around there—five or six families—mostly of
the name of Shepherdson. They was as high-
toned and well born and rich and grand as
the tribe of Grangerfords. The Shepherdsons
and Grangerfords used the same steamboat-
landing, which was about two mile above our
house; so sometimes when I went up there
with a lot of our folks I used to see a lot of
the Shepherdsons there on their fine horses.

One day Buck and me was away out in the
woods hunting, and heard a horse coming.
We was crossing the road. Buck says:

"Quick! Jump for the woods!"

We done it, and then peeped down the
woods through the leaves. Pretty soon a splendid young man came galloping down the road,
setting his horse easy and looking like a soldier. He had his gun across his pommel. I had
seen him before. It was young Harney Shepherdson. I heard Buck's gun go off at my ear,
and Harney's hat tumbled off from his head.
He grabbed his gun and rode straight to the
place where we was hid. But we didn't wait.
We started through the woods on a run. The
woods warn't thick, so I looked over my
shoulder to dodge the bullet, and twice I seen
Harney cover Buck with his gun; and then he
rode away the way he come—to get his hat,
I reckon, but I couldn't see. We never stopped
running till we got home. The old gentleman's eyes blazed a minute—'twas pleasure,
mainly, I judged—then his face sort of
smoothed down, and he says, kind of gentle:

"I don't like that shooting from behind a
bush. Why didn't you step into the road, my
boy?"

"The Shepherdsons don't, father. They always take advantage."

Miss Charlotte she held her head up like a queen while Buck was telling his tale, and her nostrils spread and her eyes snapped. The two young men looked dark, but never said nothing. Miss Sophia she turned pale, but the color come back when she found the man warn't hurt.

Soon as I could get Buck down by the corn-cribs under the trees by ourselves, I says:

"Did you want to kill him, Buck?"

"Well, I bet I did."

"What did he do to you?"

"Him? He never done nothing to me."

"Well, then, what did you want to kill him for?"

"Why, nothing—only it's on account of the feud."

"What's a feud?"

"Why, where was you raised? Don't you know what a feud is?"

"Never heard of it before—tell me about it."

"Well," says Buck, "a feud is this way: A man has a quarrel with another man, and kills him; then that other man's brother kills *him;* then the other brothers, on both sides, goes for one another; then the *cousins* chip in—and by and by everybody's killed off, and there ain't no more feud. But it's kind of slow, and takes a long time."

"Has this one been going on long, Buck?"

"Well, I should *reckon!* It started thirty year ago, or som'ers along there. There was trouble 'bout something, and then a lawsuit to settle it; and the suit went agin one of the men, and so he up and shot the man that won the suit—which he would naturally do, of course. Anybody would."

"What was the trouble about, Buck?—land?"

"I reckon maybe—I don't know."

"Well, who done the shooting? Was it a Grangerford or a Shepherdson?"

"Laws, how do *I* know? It was so long ago."

"Don't anybody know?"

"Oh, yes, pa knows, I reckon, and some of the other old people; but they don't know now what the row was about in the first place."

"Has there been many killed, Buck?"

"Yes; right smart chance of funerals. But they don't always kill. Pa's got a few buckshot in him; but he don't mind it 'cuz he don't weigh much, anyway. Bob's been carved up some with a bowie, and Tom's been hurt once or twice."

"Has anybody been killed this year, Buck?"

"Yes; we got one and they got one. 'Bout three months ago my cousin Bud, fourteen year old, was riding through the woods on t'other side of the river, and didn't have no weapon with him, which was blame' foolishness, and in a lonesome place he hears a horse a-coming behind him, and sees old Baldy Shepherdson a-linkin' after him with his gun in his hand and his white hair a-flying in the wind; and 'stead of jumping off and taking to the brush, Bud 'lowed he could outrun him; so they had it, nip and tuck, for five mile or more, the old man a-gaining all the time; so at last Bud seen it warn't any use, so he stopped and faced around so as to have the bullet-holes in front, you know, and the old man he rode up and shot him down. But he didn't git much chance to enjoy his luck, for inside of a week our folks laid *him* out."

"I reckon that old man was a coward, Buck."

"I reckon he *warn't* a coward. Not by a blame' sight. There ain't a coward amongst them Shepherdsons—not a one. And there ain't no cowards amongst the Grangerfords either. Why, that old man kep' up his end in a fight one day for half an hour against three Grangerfords, and come out winner. They was all a-horseback; he lit off of his horse and got behind a little woodpile, and kep' his horse before him to stop the bullets; but the Grangerfords stayed on their horses and ca-pered around the old man, and peppered away at him, and he peppered away at them. Him and his horse both went home pretty leaky and crippled, but the Grangerfords had to be *fetched* home—and one of 'em was dead, and another died the next day. No, sir; if a body's out hunting for cowards he don't want to fool away any time amongst them Shepherd-sons, becuz they don't breed any of that *kind.*"

Next Sunday we all went to church, about three mile, everybody a-horseback. The men took their guns along, so did Buck, and kept them between their knees or stood them handy against the wall. The Shepherdsons done the same. It was pretty ornery preaching—all about brotherly love, and such-like tiresomeness; but everybody said it was a good sermon, and they all talked it over going home, and had such a powerful lot to say about faith and good works and free grace and preforeordestination, and I don't know what all, that it did seem to me to be one of the roughest Sundays I had run across yet.

About an hour after dinner everybody was dozing around, some in their chairs and some in their rooms, and it got to be pretty dull. Buck and a dog was stretched out on the grass in the sun sound asleep. I went up to our room, and judged I would take a nap myself. I found that sweet Miss Sophia standing in her door, which was next to ours, and she took me in her room and shut the door very soft, and asked me if I liked her, and I said I did; and she asked me if I would do something for her and not tell anybody, and I said I would. Then she said she'd forgot her Testament, and left it in the seat at church between two other books, and would I slip out quiet and go there and fetch it to her, and not say nothing to nobody. I said I would. So I slid out and slipped off up the road, and there warn't anybody at the church, except maybe a hog or two, for there warn't any lock on the door, and hogs likes a puncheon floor in summer-time because it's cool. If you notice, most folks don't go to church only when they've got to; but a hog is different.

Says I to myself, something's up; it ain't natural for a girl to be in such a sweat about a Testament. So I give it a shake, and out drops a little piece of paper with *"Half past two"* wrote on it with a pencil. I ransacked it, but couldn't find anything else. I couldn't make anything out of that, so I put the paper in the book again, and when I got home and upstairs there was Miss Sophia in her door waiting for me. She pulled me in and shut the door; then she looked in the Testament till she found the paper, and as soon as she read it she looked glad; and before a body could think she grabbed me and give me a squeeze, and said I was the best boy in the world, and not to tell anybody. She was mighty red in the face for a minute, and her eyes lighted up, and it made her powerful pretty. I was a good deal astonished, but when I got my breath I asked her what the paper was about, and she asked me if I had read it, and I said no, and she asked me if I could

read writing, and I told her "no, only coarse-hand," and then she said the paper warn't anything but a book-mark to keep her place, and I might go and play now.

I went off down to the river, studying over this thing, and pretty soon I noticed that my nigger was following along behind. When we was out of sight of the house he looked back and around a second, and then comes a-running, and says:

"Mars Jawge, if you'll come down into de swamp I'll show you a whole stack o' water-moccasins."

Thinks I, that's mighty curious; he said that yesterday. He oughter know a body don't love water-moccasins enough to go around hunting for them. What is he up to, anyway? So I says:

"All right; trot ahead."

I followed a half a mile; then he struck out over the swamp, and waded ankle-deep as much as another half-mile. We come to a little flat piece of land which was dry and very thick with trees and bushes and vines, and he says:

"You shove right in dah jist a few steps, Mars Jawge; dah's whah dey is. I's seed 'm befo'; I don't k'yer to see 'em no mo'."

Then he slopped right along and went away, and pretty soon the trees hid him. I poked into the place a ways and come to a little open patch as big as a bedroom all hung around with vines, and found a man laying there asleep—and, by jings, it was my old Jim!

I waked him up, and I reckoned it was going to be a grand surprise to him to see me again, but it warn't. He nearly cried he was so glad, but he warn't surprised. Said he swum along behind me that night, and heard me yell every time, but dasn't answer, because he didn't want nobody to pick *him* up and take him into slavery again. Says he:

"I got hurt a little, en couldn't swim fas', so I wuz a considerable ways behine you towards de las'; when you landed I reck'ned I could ketch up wid you on de lan' 'dout havin' to shout at you, but when I see dat house I begin to go slow. I 'uz off too fur to hear what dey say to you—I wuz 'fraid o' de dogs; but when it 'uz all quiet ag'in I knowed you's in de house, so I struck out for de woods to wait for day. Early in de mawnin' some er de niggers come along, gwyne to de fields, en dey tuk me en showed me dis place, whah de dogs can't track me on accounts o' de water, en dey brings me truck to eat every night, en tells me how you's a-gittin' along."

"Why didn't you tell my Jack to fetch me here sooner, Jim?"

"Well, 'twarn't no use to 'sturb you, Huck, tell we could do sumfn—but we're all right now. I ben a-buyin' pots en pans en vittles, as I got a chanst, en a-patchin' up de raf' nights when—"

"*What* raft, Jim?"

"Our ole raf'."

"You mean to say our old raft warn't smashed all to flinders?"

"No, she warn't. She was tore up a good deal—one en' of her was; but dey warn't no great harm done, on'y our traps was mos' all los'. Ef we hadn' dive' so deep en swum so fur under water, en de night hadn't ben so dark, en we warn't so sk'yerd, en ben sich punkin-heads, as de sayin' is, we'd a seed de raf'. But it's jis' as well we didn't, 'kase now she's all fixed up ag'in mos' as good as new, en we's got a new lot o' stuff, in de place o' what 'uz los'."

"Why, how did you get hold of the raft again, Jim—did you catch her?"

"How I gwyne to ketch her en I out in de woods? No; some er de niggers foun' her ketched on a snag along heah in de ben', en dey hid her in a crick 'mongst de willows, en dey wuz so much jawin' 'bout which un 'um she b'long to de mos' dat I come to heah 'bout it pooty soon, so I ups en settles de trouble by tellin' 'um she don't b'long to none uv 'um, but to you en me; en I ast 'm if dey gwyne to grab a young white genlman's propaty, en git a hid'n for it? Den I gin 'm ten cents apiece, en dey 'uz mighty well satisfied, en wisht some mo' raf's 'ud come along en make 'm rich ag'in. Dey's mighty good to me, dese niggers is, en whatever I wants 'm to do fur me I doan' have to ast 'm twice, honey. Dat Jack's a good nigger, en pooty smart."

"Yes, he is. He ain't ever told me you was here; told me to come, and he'd show me a lot of water-moccasins. If anything happens *he* ain't mixed up in it. He can say he never seen us together, and it'll be the truth."

I don't want to talk much about the next day. I reckon I'll cut it pretty short. I waked up about dawn, and was a-going to turn over and go to sleep again when I noticed how still it was—didn't seem to be anybody stirring. That warn't usual. Next I noticed that Buck was up and gone. Well, I gets up, a-wondering, and goes down-stairs—nobody around; everything as still as a mouse. Just the same outside. Thinks I, what does it mean? Down by the woodpile I comes across my Jack, and says:

"What's it all about?"

Says he:

"Don't you know, Mars Jawge?"

"No," says I, "I don't."

"Well, den, Miss Sophia's run off! 'deed she has. She run off in de night some time—nobody don't know jis' when; run off to get married to dat young Harney Shepherdson, you know—leastways, so dey 'spec. De fambly foun' it out 'bout half an hour ago—maybe a little mo'—en' I *tell* you dey warn't no time los'. Sich another hurryin' up guns en hosses *you* never see! De women folks has gone for to stir up de relations, en ole Mars Saul en de boys tuck dey guns en rode up de river road for to try to ketch dat young man en kill him 'fo' he kin git acrost de river wid Miss Sophia. I reck'n dey's gwyne to be mighty rough times."

"Buck went off 'thout waking me up."

"Well, I reck'n he *did!* Dey warn't gwyne to mix you up in it. Mars Buck he loaded up his gun en 'lowed he's gwyne to fetch home a Shepherdson or bust. Well, dey'll be plenty un 'm dah, I reck'n, en you bet you he'll fetch one ef he gits a chanst."

I took up the river road as hard as I could put. By and by I begin to hear guns a good ways off. When I came in sight of the log store and the woodpile where the steamboats lands I worked along under the trees and brush till I got to a good place, and then I clumb up into the forks of a cottonwood that was out of reach, and watched. There was a wood-rank four foot high a little ways in front of the tree, and first I was going to hide behind that; but maybe it was luckier I didn't.

There was four or five men cavorting around on their horses in the open place before the log store, cussing and yelling, and trying to get at a couple of young chaps that was behind the wood-rank alongside of the steam-boat-landing; but they couldn't come it. Every time one of them showed himself on the river side of the woodpile he got shot at. The two boys was squatting back to back behind the pile, so they could watch both ways.

By and by the men stopped cavorting around and yelling. They started riding towards the store; then up gets one of the boys, draws a steady bead over the wood-rank, and drops one of them out of his saddle. All the men jumped off of their horses and grabbed the hurt one and started to carry him to the store; and that minute the two boys started on the run. They got half-way to the tree I was in before the men noticed. Then the men see them, and jumped on their horses and took out after them. They gained on the boys, but it didn't do no good, the boys had too good a start; they got to the woodpile that was in front of my tree, and slipped in behind it, and so they had the bulge on the men again. One of the boys was Buck, and the other was a slim young chap about nineteen years old.

The men ripped around awhile, and then rode away. As soon as they was out of sight I sung out to Buck and told him. He didn't know what to make of my voice coming out of the tree at first. He was awful surprised. He told me to watch out sharp and let him know when the men come in sight again; said they was up to some devilment or other—wouldn't be gone long. I wished I was out of that tree, but I dasn't come down. Buck begun to cry and rip, and 'lowed that him and his cousin Joe (that was the other young chap) would make up for this day yet. He said his father and his two brothers was killed, and two or three of the enemy. Said the Shepherdsons laid for them in ambush. Buck said his father and brothers ought to waited for their rela-tions—the Shepherdsons was too strong for them. I asked him what was become of young Harney and Miss Sophia. He said they'd got across the river and was safe. I was glad of that; but the way Buck did take on because he didn't manage to kill Harney that day he shot at him—I hain't ever heard anything like it.

All of a sudden, bang! bang! bang! goes three or four guns—the men had slipped around through the woods and come in from behind without their horses! The boys jumped for the river—both of them hurt—and as they swum down the current the men run along the bank shooting at them and singing out, "Kill them, kill them!" It made me so sick I most fell out of the tree. I ain't a-going to tell *all* that happened—it would make me sick again if I was to do that. I wished I hadn't ever come ashore that night to see such things. I ain't ever going to get shut of them—lots of times I dream about them.

I stayed in the tree till it begun to get dark, afraid to come down. Sometimes I heard guns away off in the woods; and twice I seen little gangs of men gallop past the log store with guns; so I reckoned the trouble was still a-going on. I was mighty downhearted; so I made up my mind I wouldn't ever go anear that house again, because I reckoned I was to blame, somehow. I judged that that piece of paper meant that Miss Sophia was to meet Harney somewheres at half past two and run off; and I judged I ought to told her father about that paper and the curious way she acted, and then maybe he would 'a' locked her up, and this awful mess wouldn't ever hap-pened.

When I got down out of the tree I crept along down the river-bank a piece, and found the two bodies laying in the edge of the water, and tugged at them till I got them ashore; then I covered up their faces, and got away as quick as I could. I cried a little when I was covering up Buck's face, for he was mighty good to me.

It was just dark now. I never went near the house, but struck through the woods and made for the swamp. Jim warn't on his island, so I tramped off in a hurry for the crick, and crowded through the willows, red-hot to jump aboard and get out of that awful country. The raft was gone! My souls, but I was scared! I couldn't get my breath for most a minute. Then I raised a yell. A voice not twenty-five foot from me says:

"Good lan'! is dat you, honey? Doan' make no noise."

It was Jim's voice—nothing ever sounded so good before. I run along the bank a piece and got aboard, and Jim he grabbed me and hugged me, he was so glad to see me. He says:

"Laws bless you, chile, I 'uz right down sho' you's dead ag'in. Jack's been heah; he say he reck'n you's ben shot, kase you didn' come home no mo'; so I's jes' dis minute a-startin' de raf' down towards de mouf er de crick, so's to be all ready for to shove out en leave soon as Jack comes ag'in en tells me for certain you *is* dead. Lawsy, I's mighty glad to git you back ag'in, honey."

I says:

"All right—that's mighty good; they won't find me, and they'll think I've been killed, and floated down the river—there's something up there that'll help them think so—so don't you lose no time, Jim, but just shove off for the big water as fast as ever you can."

I never felt easy till the raft was two mile below there and out in the middle of the Mississippi. Then we hung up our signal lantern, and judged that we was free and safe once more. I hadn't had a bite to eat since yesterday, so Jim he got out some corn-dodgers and buttermilk, and pork and cabbage and greens—there ain't nothing in the world so good when it's cooked right—and whilst I eat my supper we talked and had a good time. I was powerful glad to get away from the feuds, and so was Jim to get away from the swamp. We said there warn't no home like a raft, after all. Other places do seem so cramped up and smothery, but a raft don't. You feel mighty free and easy and comfortable on a raft.

19. THE DUKE AND THE DAUPHIN COME ABOARD

Two or three days and nights went by; I reckon I might say they swum by, they slid along so quiet and smooth and lovely. Here is the way we put in the time. It was a monstrous big river down there—sometimes a mile and a half wide; we run nights, and laid up and hid daytimes; soon as night was most gone we stopped navigating and tied up—nearly always in the dead water under a tow-head; and then cut young cottonwoods and willows, and hid the raft with them. Then we set out the lines. Next we slid into the river and had a swim, so as to freshen up and cool off; then we set down on the sandy bottom where the water was about knee-deep, and watched the daylight come. Not a sound any-wheres—perfectly still—just like the whole world was asleep, only sometimes the bull-frogs a-cluttering, maybe. The first thing to see, looking away over the water, was a kind of dull line—that was the woods on t'other side; you couldn't make nothing else out; then a pale place in the sky; then more paleness spreading around; then the river softened up away off, and warn't black any more, but gray; you could see little dark spots drifting along ever so far away—trading-scows, and such things; and long black streaks—rafts; sometimes you could hear a sweep screaking; or jumbled-up voices, it was so still, and sounds come so far; and by and by you could see a streak on the water which you know by the look of the streak that there's a snag there in a swift current which breaks on it and makes that streak look that way; and you see the mist curl up off of the water, and the east reddens up, and the river, and you make out a log cabin in the edge of the woods, away on the bank on t'other side of the river, being a wood-yard, likely, and piled by them cheats so you can throw a dog through it any-wheres; then the nice breeze springs up, and comes fanning you from over there, so cool and fresh and sweet to smell on account of the woods and the flowers; but sometimes not that way, because they've left dead fish laying around, gars and such, and they do get pretty rank; and next you've got the full day, and everything smiling in the sun, and the song-birds just going it!

A little smoke couldn't be noticed now, so we would take some fish off of the lines and cook up a hot breakfast. And afterwards we would watch the lonesomeness of the river, and kind of lazy along, and by and by lazy off to sleep. Wake up by and by, and look to see what done it, and maybe see a steamboat coughing along up-stream, so far off towards the other side you couldn't tell nothing about her only whether she was a stern-wheel or side-wheel; then for about an hour there wouldn't be nothing to hear nor nothing to see—just solid lonesomeness. Next you'd see a raft sliding by, away off yonder, and maybe a galoot on it chopping, because they're most always doing it on a raft; you'd see the ax flash and come down—you don't hear nothing; you see that ax go up again, and by the time it's above the man's head then you hear the *k'chunk!*—it had took all that time to come over the water. So we would put in the day, lazying around, listening to the stillness. Once there was a thick fog, and the rafts and things that went by was beating tin pans so the steamboats wouldn't run over them. A scow or a raft went by so close we could hear them talking and cussing and laughing—heard them plain; but we couldn't see no sign of them; it made you feel crawly; it was like spirits carrying on that way in the air. Jim said he believed it was spirits; but I says:

"No; spirits wouldn't say, 'Dern the dern fog.'"

Soon as it was night out we shoved; when we got her out to about the middle we let her alone, and let her float wherever the current wanted her to; then we lit the pipes, and dangled our legs in the water, and talked about all kinds of things—we was always naked, day and night, whenever the mosquitoes would let us—the new clothes Buck's folks made for me was too good to be comfortable, and besides I didn't go much on clothes, nohow.

Sometimes we'd have that whole river all to ourselves for the longest time. Yonder was the banks and the islands, across the water; and maybe a spark—which was a candle in a cabin window; and sometimes on the water you could see a spark or two—on a raft or a scow, you know; and maybe you could hear a fiddle or a song coming over from one of them crafts. It's lovely to live on a raft. We had the sky up there, all speckled with stars, and we used to lay on our backs and look up at them, and discuss about whether they was made or only just happened. Jim he allowed they was made, but I allowed they happened; I judged it would have took too long to *make* so many. Jim said the moon could 'a' *laid* them; well, that looked kind of reasonable, so I didn't say nothing against it, because I've seen a frog lay most as many, so of course it could be done. We used to watch the stars that fell, too, and see them streak down. Jim allowed they'd got spoiled and was hove out of the nest.

Once or twice of a night we would see a steamboat slipping along in the dark, and now and then she would belch a whole world of sparks up out of her chimbleys, and they would rain down in the river and look awful pretty; then she would turn a corner and her lights would wink out and her powwow shut off and leave the river still again; and by and by her waves would get to us, a long time after she was gone, and joggle the raft a bit, and after that you wouldn't hear nothing for you couldn't tell how long, except maybe frogs or something.

After midnight the people on shore went to bed, and then for two or three hours the shores was black—no more sparks in the cabin windows. These sparks was our clock—the first one that showed again meant morning was coming, so we hunted a place to hide and tie up right away.

One morning about daybreak I found a canoe and crossed over a chute to the main shore—it was only two hundred yards—and paddled about a mile up a crick amongst the cypress woods, to see if I couldn't get some berries. Just as I was passing a place where a kind of a cowpath crossed the crick, here comes a couple of men tearing up the path as tight as they could foot it. I thought I was a goner, for whenever anybody was after anybody I judged it was *me*—or maybe Jim. I was about to dig out from there in a hurry, but they was pretty close to me then, and sung out and begged me to save their lives—said they hadn't been doing nothing, and was being chased for it—said there was men and dogs a-coming. They wanted to jump right in, but I says:

"Don't you do it. I don't hear the dogs and horses yet; you've got time to crowd through the brush and get up the crick a little ways; then you take to the water and wade down to me and get in—that'll throw the dogs off the scent."

They done it, and soon as they was aboard I lit out for our towhead, and in about five or ten minutes we heard the dogs and the men away off, shouting. We heard them come along towards the crick, but couldn't see them; they seemed to stop and fool around awhile; then, as we got further and further away all the time, we couldn't hardly hear them at all; by the time we had left a mile of woods behind us and struck the river, everything was quiet, and we paddled over to the towhead and hid in the cottonwoods and was safe.

One of these fellows was about seventy or

upwards, and had a bald head and very gray whiskers. He had an old battered-up slouch hat on, and a greasy blue woolen shirt, and ragged old blue jeans britches stuffed into his boot-tops, and home-knit galluses—no, he only had one. He had an old long-tailed blue jeans coat with slick brass buttons flung over his arm, and both of them had big, fat, ratty-looking carpet-bags.

The other fellow was about thirty, and dressed about as ornery. After breakfast we all laid off and talked, and the first thing that come out was that these chaps didn't know one another.

"What got you into trouble?" says the bald-head to t'other chap.

"Well, I'd been selling an article to take the tartar off the teeth—and it does take it off, too, and generly the enamel along with it—but I stayed about one night longer than I ought to, and was just in the act of sliding out when I ran across you on the trail this side of town, and you told me they were coming, and begged me to help you to get off. So I told you I was expecting trouble myself, and would scatter out *with* you. That's the whole yarn—what's yourn?"

"Well, I'd ben a-runnin' a little temperance revival thar 'bout a week, and was the pet of the women folks, big and little, for I was makin' it mighty warm for the rummies, I *tell* you, and takin' as much as five or six dollars a night—ten cents a head, children and niggers free—and business a-growin' all the time, when somehow or another a little report got around last night that I had a way of puttin' in my time with a private jug on the sly. A nigger rousted me out this mornin', and told me the people was getherin' on the quiet with their dogs and horses, and they'd be along pretty soon and give me 'bout half an hour's start, and then run me down if they could; and if they got me they'd tar and feather me and ride me on a rail, sure. I didn't wait for no breakfast—I warn't hungry."

"Old man," said the young one, "I reckon we might double-team it together; what do you think?"

"I ain't undisposed. What's your line—mainly?"

"Jour printer by trade; do a little in patent medicines; theater-actor—tragedy, you know;

take a turn to mesmerism and phrenology when there's a chance; teach singing-geography school for a change; sling a lecture sometimes —oh, I do lots of things—most anything that comes handy, so it ain't work. What's your lay?"

"I've done considerble in the doctoring way in my time. Layin' on o' hands is my best holt—for cancer and paralysis, and sich things; and I k'n tell a fortune pretty good when I've got somebody along to find out the facts for me. Preachin's my line, too, and workin' camp-meetin's, and missionaryin' around."

Nobody never said anything for a while; then the young man hove a sigh and says:

"Alas!"

"What 're you alassin' about?" says the bald-head.

"To think I should have lived to be leading such a life, and be degraded down into such company." And he begun to wipe the corner of his eye with a rag.

"Dern your skin, ain't the company good enough for you?" says the baldhead, pretty pert and uppish.

"Yes, it *is* good enough for me; it's as good as I deserve; for who fetched me so low when I was so high? *I* did myself. I don't blame *you,* gentlemen—far from it; I don't blame anybody. I deserve it all. Let the cold world do its worst; one thing I know—there's a grave somewhere for me. The world may go on just as it's always done, and take everything from me—loved ones, property, everything; but it can't take that. Some day I'll lie down in it and forget it all, and my poor broken heart will be at rest." He went on a-wiping.

"Drot your pore broken heart," says the baldhead; "what are you heaving your pore broken heart at *us* f'r? *We* hain't done nothing."

"No, I know you haven't. I ain't blaming you, gentlemen. I brought myself down—yes, I did it myself. It's right I should suffer—perfectly right—I don't make any moan."

"Brought you down from whar? Whar was you brought down from?"

"Ah, you would not believe me; the world never believes—let it pass—'tis no matter. The secret of my birth—"

"The secret of your birth! Do you mean to say—"

"Gentlemen," says the young man, very solemn, "I will reveal it to you, for I feel I may have confidence in you. By rights I am a duke!"

Jim's eyes bugged out when he heard that; and I reckon mine did, too. Then the baldhead says: "No! you can't mean it?"

"Yes. My great-grandfather, eldest son of the Duke of Bridgewater, fled to this country about the end of the last century, to breathe the pure air of freedom; married here, and died, leaving a son, his own father dying about the same time. The second son of the late duke seized the titles and estates—the infant real duke was ignored. I am the lineal descendant of that infant—I am the rightful Duke of Bridgewater; and here am I, forlorn, torn from my high estate, hunted of men, despised by the cold world, ragged, worn, heartbroken, and degraded to the companionship of felons on a raft!"

Jim pitied him ever so much, and so did I. We tried to comfort him, but he said it warn't much use, he couldn't be much comforted; said if we was a mind to acknowledge him, that would do him more good than most anything else; so we said we would, if he would tell us how. He said we ought to bow when we spoke to him, and say "Your Grace," or "My Lord," or "Your Lordship"—and he wouldn't mind it if we called him plain "Bridgewater," which, he said, was a title anyway, and not a name; and one of us ought to wait on him at dinner, and do any little thing for him he wanted done.

Well, that was all easy, so we done it. All through dinner Jim stood around and waited on him, and says, "Will yo' Grace have some o' dis or some o' dat?" and so on, and a body could see it was mighty pleasing to him.

But the old man got pretty silent by and by —didn't have much to say, and didn't look pretty comfortable over all that petting that was going on around that duke. He seemed to have something on his mind. So, along in the afternoon, he says:

"Looky here, Bilgewater," he says, "I'm nation sorry for you, but you ain't the only person that's had troubles like that."

"No?"

"No, you ain't. You ain't the only person that's ben snaked down wrongfully out'n a high place."

"Alas!"

"No, you ain't the only person that's had a secret of his birth." And, by jings, *he* begins to cry.

"Hold! What do you mean?"

"Bilgewater, kin I trust you?" says the old man, still sort of sobbing.

"To the bitter death!" He took the old man by the hand and squeezed it, and says, "That secret of your being: speak!"

"Bilgewater, I am the late Dauphin!"

You bet you, Jim and me stared this time. Then the duke says:

"You are what?"

"Yes, my friend, it is too true—your eyes is lookin' at this very moment on the pore disappeared Dauphin, Looy the Seventeen, son of Looy the Sixteen and Marry Antonette."

"You! At your age! No! You mean you're the late Charlemagne; you must be six or seven hundred years old, at the very least."

"Trouble has done it, Bilgewater, trouble has done it; trouble has brung these gray hairs and this premature balditude. Yes, gentlemen, you see before you, in blue jeans and misery, the wanderin', exiled, trampled-on, and sufferin' rightful King of France."

Well, he cried and took on so that me and Jim didn't know hardly what to do, we was so sorry—and so glad and proud we'd got him with us, too. So we set in, like we done before with the duke, and tried to comfort *him*. But he said it warn't no use, nothing but to be dead and done with it all could do him any good; though he said it often made him feel easier and better for a while if people treated him according to his rights, and got down on one knee to speak to him, and always called him "Your Majesty," and waited on him first at meals, and didn't set down in his presence till he asked them. So Jim and me set to majestying him, and doing this and that and t'other for him, and standing up till he told us we might set down. This done him heaps of good, and so he got cheerful and comfortable. But the duke kind of soured on him, and didn't look a bit satisfied with the way things was going; still, the king acted real friendly towards him, and said the duke's great-grandfather and all the other Dukes of

Bilgewater was a good deal thought of by *his* father, and was allowed to come to the palace considerable; but the duke stayed huffy a good while, till by and by the king says:

"Like as not we got to be together a blamed long time on this h-yer raft, Bilgewater, and so what's the use o' your bein' sour? It'll only make things oncomfortable. It ain't my fault I warn't born a duke, it ain't your fault you warn't born a king—so what's the use to worry? Make the best o' things the way you find 'em, says I—that's my motto. This ain't no bad thing that we've struck here—plenty grub and an easy life—come, give us your hand, duke, and le's all be friends."

The duke done it, and Jim and me was pretty glad to see it. It took away all the uncomfortableness and we felt mighty good over it, because it would 'a' been a miserable business to have any unfriendliness on the raft; for what you want, above all things, on a raft, is for everybody to be satisfied, and feel right and kind towards the others.

It didn't take me long to make up my mind that these liars warn't no kings nor dukes at all, but just low-down humbugs and frauds. But I never said nothing, never let on; kept it to myself; it's the best way; then you don't have no quarrels, and don't get into no trouble. If they wanted us to call them kings and dukes, I hadn't no objections, 'long as it would keep peace in the family; and it warn't no use to tell Jim, so I didn't tell him. If I never learnt nothing else out of pap, I learnt that the best way to get along with his kind of people is to let them have their own way.

20. WHAT ROYALTY DID TO PARKVILLE

They asked us considerable many questions; wanted to know what we covered up the raft that way for, and laid by in the daytime instead of running—was Jim a runaway nigger? Says I:

"Goodness sakes! would a runaway nigger run *south?*"

No, they allowed he wouldn't. I had to account for things some way, so I says:

"My folks was living in Pike County, in Missouri, where I was born, and they all died off but me and pa and my brother Ike. Pa, he 'lowed he'd break up and go down and live with Uncle Ben, who's got a little one-horse place on the river forty-four mile below Orleans. Pa was pretty poor, and had some debts; so when he'd squared up there warn't nothing left but sixteen dollars and our nigger, Jim. That warn't enough to take us fourteen hundred mile, deck passage nor no other way. Well, when the river rose pa had a streak of luck one day; he ketched this piece of a raft; so we reckoned we'd go down to Orleans on it. Pa's luck didn't hold out; a steamboat run over the forrard corner of the raft one night, and we all went overboard and dove under the wheel; Jim and me come up all right, but pa was drunk, and Ike was only four years old, so they never come up no more. Well, for the next day or two we had considerable trouble, because people was always coming out in skiffs and trying to take Jim away from me, saying they believed he was a runaway nigger. We don't run daytimes no more now; nights they don't bother us."

The duke says:

"Leave me alone to cipher out a way so we can run in the daytime if we want to. I'll think the thing over—I'll invent a plan that 'll fix it. We'll let it alone for today, because of course we don't want to go by that town yonder in daylight—it mightn't be healthy."

Towards night it begun to darken up and look like rain; the heat-lightning was squirting around low down in the sky, and the leaves was beginning to shiver—it was going to be pretty ugly, it was easy to see that. So the duke and the king went to overhauling our wigwam, to see what the beds was like. My bed was a straw tick—better than Jim's, which was a corn-shuck tick; there's always cobs around about in a shuck tick, and they poke into you and hurt; and when you roll over the dry shucks sound like you was rolling over in a pile of dead leaves; it makes such a rustling that you wake up. Well, the duke allowed he would take my bed; but the king allowed he wouldn't. He says:

"I should 'a' reckoned the difference in rank would 'a' sejested to you that a corn-shuck bed warn't just fitten for me to sleep on. Your Grace 'll take the shuck bed yourself."

Jim and me was in a sweat again for a minute, being afraid there was going to be some more trouble amongst them; so we was pretty glad when the duke says:

"'Tis my fate to be always ground into the mire under the iron heel of oppression. Misfortune has broken my once haughty spirit; I yield, I submit; 'tis my fate. I am alone in the world—let me suffer; I can bear it."

We got away as soon as it was good and dark. The king told us to stand well out towards the middle of the river, and not show a light till we got a long ways below the town. We come in sight of the little bunch of lights by and by—that was the town, you know—and slid by, about a half a mile out, all right. When we was three-quarters of a mile below we hoisted up our signal lantern; and about ten o'clock it come on to rain and blow and thunder and lighten like everything; so the king told us to both stay on watch till the weather got better; then him and the duke crawled into the wigwam and turned in for the night. It was my watch below till twelve, but I wouldn't 'a' turned in anyway if I'd had a bed, because a body don't see such a storm as that every day in the week, not by a long sight. My souls, how the wind did scream along! And every second or two there'd come a glare that lit up the white-caps for a half a mile around, and you'd see the islands looking dusty through the rain, and the trees thrashing around in the wind; then comes a *h-whack!*—bum! bum! bumble-umble-um-bum-bum-bum-bum—and the thunder would go rumbling and grumbling away, and quit—and then *rip* comes another flash and another sockdolager. The waves most washed me off the raft sometimes, but I hadn't any clothes on, and didn't mind. We didn't have no trouble about snags; the lightning was glaring and flittering around so constant that we could see them plenty soon enough to throw her head this way or that and miss them.

I had the middle watch, you know, but I was pretty sleepy by that time, so Jim he said he would stand the first half of it for me; he was always mighty good that way, Jim was. I crawled into the wigwam, but the king and the duke had their legs sprawled around so there warn't no show for me; so I laid outside —I didn't mind the rain, because it was warm, and the waves warn't running so high now. About two they come up again, though, and

Jim was going to call me; but he changed his mind, because he reckoned they warn't high enough yet to do any harm; but he was mistaken about that, for pretty soon all of a sudden along comes a regular ripper and washed me overboard. It most killed Jim a-laughing. He was the easiest nigger to laugh that ever was, anyway.

I took the watch, and Jim he laid down and snored away; and by and by the storm let up for good and all; and the first cabin-light that showed I rousted him out, and we slid the raft into hiding-quarters for the day.

The king got out an old ratty deck of cards after breakfast, and him and the duke played seven-up awhile, five cents a game. Then they got tired of it, and allowed they would "lay out a campaign," as they called it. The duke went down into his carpet-bag, and fetched up a lot of little printed bills and read them out loud. One bill said, "The celebrated Dr. Armand de Montalban, of Paris," would "lecture on the Science of Phrenology" at such and such a place, on the blank day of blank, at ten cents admission, and "furnish charts of character at twenty-five cents apiece." The duke said that was *him*. In another bill he was the "world-renowned Shakespearian tragedian, Garrick the Younger, of Drury Lane, London." In other bills he had a lot of other names and done other wonderful things, like finding water and gold with a "diving-rod," "dissipating witch spells," and so on. By and by he says:

"But the histrionic muse is the darling. Have you ever trod the boards, Royalty?"

"No," says the king.

"You shall, then, before you're three days older, Fallen Grandeur," says the duke. "The first good town we come to we'll hire a hall and do the swordfight in 'Richard III.' and the balcony scene in 'Romeo and Juliet.' How does that strike you?"

"I'm in, up to the hub, for anything that will pay, Bilgewater; but, you see, I don't know nothing about play-actin', and hain't ever seen much of it. I was too small when pap used to have 'em at the palace. Do you reckon you can learn me?"

"Easy!"

"All right. I'm jist a-freezin' for something fresh, anyway. Le's commence right away."

So the duke told him all about who Romeo was and who Juliet was, and said he was used to being Romeo, so the king could be Juliet.

"But if Juliet's such a young gal, duke, my peeled head and my white whiskers is goin' to look oncommon odd on her, maybe."

"No, don't you worry; these country jakes won't ever think of that. Besides, you know, you'll be in costume, and that makes all the difference in the world; Juliet's in a balcony, enjoying the moonlight before she goes to bed, and she's got on her nightgown and her ruffled nightcap. Here are the costumes for the parts."

He got out two or three curtain-calico suits, which he said was meedyevil armor for Richard III. and t'other chap, and a long white cotton nightshirt and a ruffled nightcap to match. The king was satisfied; so the duke got out his book and read the parts over in the most splendid spread-eagle way, prancing around and acting at the same time, to show how it had got to be done; then he give the book to the king and told him to get his part by heart.

There was a little one-horse town about three mile down the bend, and after dinner the duke said he had ciphered out his idea about how to run in daylight without it being dangersome for Jim; so he allowed he would go down to the town and fix that thing. The king allowed he would go, too, and see if he couldn't strike something. We was out of coffee, so Jim said I better go along with them in the canoe and get some.

When we got there there warn't nobody stirring; streets empty, and perfectly dead and still, like Sunday. We found a sick nigger sunning himself in a back yard, and he said everybody that warn't too young or too sick or too old was gone to camp-meeting, about two mile back in the woods. The king got the directions, and allowed he'd go and work that camp-meeting for all it was worth, and I might go, too.

The duke said what he was after was a printing-office. We found it; a little bit of a concern, up over a carpenter-shop—carpenters and printers all gone to the meeting, and no doors locked. It was a dirty, littered-up place, and had ink-marks, and handbills with pictures of horses and runaway niggers on them, all over the walls. The duke shed his coat and

said he was all right now. So me and the king lit out for the camp-meeting.

We got there in about a half an hour fairly dripping, for it was a most awful hot day. There was as much as a thousand people there from twenty mile around. The woods was full of teams and wagons, hitched everywheres, feeding out of the wagon-troughs and stomping to keep off the flies. There was sheds made out of poles and roofed over with branches, where they had lemonade and gingerbread to sell, and piles of watermelons and green corn and such-like truck.

The preaching was going on under the same kinds of sheds, only they was bigger and held crowds of people. The benches was made out of outside slabs of logs, with holes bored in the round side to drive sticks into for legs. They didn't have no backs. The preachers had high platforms to stand on at one end of the sheds. The women had on sun-bonnets; and some had linsey-woolsey frocks, some gingham ones, and a few of the young ones had on calico. Some of the young men was barefooted, and some of the children didn't have on any clothes but just a tow-linen shirt. Some of the old women was knitting, and some of the young folks was courting on the sly.

The first shed we come to the preacher was lining out a hymn. He lined out two lines, everybody sung it, and it was kind of grand to hear it, there was so many of them and they done it in such a rousing way; then he lined out two more for them to sing—and so on. The people woke up more and more, and sung louder and louder; and towards the end some begun to groan, and some begun to shout. Then the preacher begun to preach, and begun in earnest, too; and went weaving first to one side of the platform and then the other, and then a-leaning down over the front of it, and his arms and his body going all the time, and shouting his words out with all his might; and every now and then he would hold up his Bible and spread it open, and kind of pass it around this way and that, shouting, "It's the brazen serpent in the wilderness! Look upon it and live!" And people would shout out, "Glory!—A-a-*men!*" And so he went on, and the people groaning and crying and saying amen:

"Oh, come to the mourners' bench! come,

black with sin! (*amen!*) come, sick and sore! (*amen!*) come, lame and halt and blind! (*amen!*) come, pore and needy, sunk in shame! (*a-a-men!*) come, all that's worn and soiled and suffering!—come with a broken spirit! come with a contrite heart! come in your rags and sin and dirt! the waters that cleanse is free, the door of heaven stands open—oh, enter in and be at rest!" (*a-a-men! glory, glory hallelujah!*)

And so on. You couldn't make out what the preacher said any more, on account of the shouting and crying. Folks got up everywheres in the crowd, and worked their way just by main strength to the mourners' bench, with the tears running down their faces; and when all the mourners had got up there to the front benches in a crowd, they sung and shouted and flung themselves down on the straw, just crazy and wild.

Well, the first I knowed the king got a-going, and you could hear him over everybody; and next he went a-charging up onto the platform, and the preacher he begged him to speak to the people, and he done it. He told them he was a pirate—been a pirate for thirty years out in the Indian Ocean—and his crew was thinned out considerable last spring in a fight, and he was home now to take out some fresh men, and thanks to goodness he'd been robbed last night and put ashore off of a steamboat without a cent, and he was glad of it; it was the blessedest thing that ever happened to him, because he was a changed man now, and happy for the first time in his life; and, poor as he was, he was going to start right off and work his way back to the Indian Ocean, and put in the rest of his life trying to turn the pirates into the true path; for he could do it better than anybody else, being acquainted with all pirate crews in that ocean; and though it would take him a long time to get there without money, he would get there anyway, and every time he convinced a pirate he would say to him, "Don't you thank me, don't you give me no credit; it all belongs to them dear people in Pokeville camp-meeting, natural brothers and benefactors of the race, and that dear preacher there, the truest friend a pirate ever had!"

And then he busted into tears, and so did everybody. Then somebody sings out, "Take up a collection for him, take up a collection!" Well, a half a dozen made a jump to do it, but somebody sings out, "Let *him* pass the hat around!" Then everybody said it, the preacher too.

So the king went all through the crowd with his hat, swabbing his eyes, and blessing the people and praising them and thanking them for being so good to the poor pirates away off there; and every little while the prettiest kind of girls, with the tears running down their cheeks, would up and ask him would he let them kiss him for to remember him by; and he always done it; and some of them he hugged and kissed as many as five or six times—and he was invited to stay a week; and everybody wanted him to live in their houses, and said they'd think it was an honor; but he said as this was the last day of the camp-meeting he couldn't do no good, and besides he was in a sweat to get to the Indian Ocean right off and go to work on the pirates.

When we got back to the raft and he come to count up he found he had collected eighty-seven dollars and seventy-five cents. And then he had fetched away a three-gallon jug of whisky, too, that he found under a wagon when he was starting home through the woods. The king said, take it all around, it laid over any day he'd ever put in in the missionarying line. He said it warn't no use talking, heathens don't amount to shucks alongside of pirates to work a camp-meeting with.

The duke was thinking *he'd* been doing pretty well till the king come to show up, but after that he didn't think so so much. He had set up and printed off two little jobs for farmers in that printing-office—horse bills—and took the money, four dollars. And he had got in ten dollars' worth of advertisements for the paper, which he said he would put in for four dollars if they would pay in advance—so they done it. The price of the paper was two dollars a year, but he took in three subscriptions for half a dollar apiece on condition of them paying him in advance; they were going to pay in cordwood and onions as usual, but he said he had just bought the concern and knocked down the price as low as he could afford it, and was going to run it for cash. He set up a little piece of poetry, which he made, himself, out of his own head—three verses—kind of sweet and saddish—the name of it was, "Yes, crush, cold world, this breaking heart"—and he left that all set up and ready to print in the paper, and didn't charge nothing for it. Well, he took in nine dollars and a half, and said he'd done a pretty square day's work for it.

Then he showed us another little job he'd printed and hadn't charged for, because it was for us. It had a picture of a runaway nigger with a bundle on a stick over his shoulder, and "$200 reward" under it. The reading was all about Jim and just described him to a dot. It said he run away from St. Jacques's plantation, forty mile below New Orleans, last winter, and likely went north, and whoever would catch him and send him back he could have the reward and expenses.

"Now," says the duke, "after tonight we can run in the daytime if we want to. Whenever we see anybody coming we can tie Jim hand and foot with a rope, and lay him in the wigwam and show this handbill and say we captured him up the river, and were too poor to travel on a steamboat, so we got this little raft on credit from our friends and are going down to get the reward. Handcuffs and chains would look still better on Jim, but it wouldn't go well with the story of us being so poor. Too much like jewelry. Ropes are the correct thing—we must preserve the unities, as we say on the boards."

We all said the duke was pretty smart, and there couldn't be no trouble about running daytimes. We judged we could make miles enough that night to get out of the reach of the powwow we reckoned the duke's work in the printing-office was going to make in that little town; then we could boom right along if we wanted to.

We laid low and kept still, and never shoved out till nearly ten o'clock; then we slid by, pretty wide away from the town, and didn't hoist our lantern till we was clear out of sight of it.

When Jim called me to take the watch at four in the morning, he says:

"Huck, does you reck'n we gwyne to run acrost any mo' kings on dis trip?"

"No," I says, "I reckon not."

"Well," says he, "dat's all right, den. I doan'

mine one er two kings, but dat's enough. Dis one's powerful drunk, en de duke ain' much better."

I found Jim had been trying to get him to talk French, so he could hear what it was like; but he said he had been in this country so long, and had so much trouble, he'd forgot it.

21. AN ARKANSAW DIFFICULTY

It was after sun-up now, but we went right on and didn't tie up. The king and the duke turned out by and by looking pretty rusty; but after they'd jumped overboard and took a swim it chippered them up a good deal. After breakfast the king he took a seat on the corner of the raft, and pulled off his boots and rolled up his britches, and let his legs dangle in the water, so as to be comfortable, and lit his pipe, and went to getting his "Romeo and Juliet" by heart. When he had got it pretty good him and the duke begun to practise it together. The duke had to learn him over and over again how to say every speech; and he made him sigh, and put his hand on his heart, and after a while he said he done it pretty well; "only," he says, "you mustn't bellow out *Romeo!* that way, like a bull—you must say it soft and sick and languishy, so—R-o-o-meo! that is the idea; for Juliet's a dear sweet mere child of a girl, you know, and she doesn't bray like a jackass."

Well, next they got out a couple of long swords that the duke made out of oak laths, and begun to practise the sword-fight—the duke called himself Richard III.; and the way they laid on and pranced around the raft was grand to see. But by and by the king tripped and fell overboard, and after that they took a rest, and had a talk about all kinds of adventures they'd had in other times along the river.

After dinner the duke says:

"Well, Capet, we'll want to make this a first-class show, you know, so I guess we'll add a little more to it. We want a little something to answer encores with, anyway."

"What's onkores, Bilgewater?"

The duke told him, and then says:

"I'll answer by doing the Highland fling or the sailor's hornpipe; and you—well, let me see—oh, I've got it—you can do Hamlet's soliloquy."

"Hamlet's which?"

"Hamlet's soliloquy, you know; the most celebrated thing in Shakespeare. Ah, it's sublime, sublime! Always fetches the house. I haven't got it in the book—I've only got one volume—but I reckon I can piece it out from memory. I'll just walk up and down a minute, and see if I can call it back from recollection's vaults."

So he went to marching up and down, thinking, and frowning horrible every now and then; then he would hoist up his eyebrows; next he would squeeze his hand on his forehead and stagger back and kind of moan; next he would sigh, and next he'd let on to drop a tear. It was beautiful to see him. By and by he got it. He told us to give attention. Then he strikes a most noble attitude, with one leg shoved forwards, and his arms stretched away up, and his head tilted back, looking up at the sky; and then he begins to rip and rave and grit his teeth; and after that, all through his speech, he howled, and spread around, and swelled up his chest, and just knocked the spots out of any acting ever *I* see before. This is the speech—I learned it, easy enough, while he was learning it to the king:

To be, or not to be; that is the bare bodkin
That makes calamity of so long life;
For who would fardels bear, till Birnam Wood do
    come to Dunsinane,
But that the fear of something after death
Murders the innocent sleep,
Great nature's second course,
And makes us rather sling the arrows of outrageous
    fortune
Than fly to others that we know not of.
There's the respect must give us pause:
Wake Duncan with thy knocking! I would thou
    couldst;
For who would bear the whips and scorns of time,
The oppressor's wrong, the proud man's con-
    tumely,
The law's delay, and the quietus which his pangs
    might take,
In the dead waste and middle of the night, when
    churchyards yawn
In customary suits of solemn black,
But that the undiscovered country from whose
    bourne no traveler returns,
Breathes forth contagion on the world,

And thus the native hue of resolution, like the
    poor cat i' the adage,
Is sicklied o'er with care,
And all the clouds that lowered o'er our housetops,
With this regard their currents turn awry,
And lose the name of action.
'Tis a consummation devoutly to be wished. But
    soft you, the fair Ophelia:
Ope not thy ponderous and marble jaws,
But get thee to a nunnery—go!

Well, the old man he liked that speech, and he mighty soon got it so he could do it first rate. It seemed like he was just born for it; and when he had his hand in and was excited, it was perfectly lovely the way he would rip and tear and rair up behind when he was getting it off.

The first chance we got the duke he had some show-bills printed; and after that, for two or three days as we floated along, the raft was a most uncommon lively place, for there warn't nothing but sword-fighting and rehearsing—as the duke called it—going on all the time. One morning, when we was pretty well down the state of Arkansaw, we come in sight of a little one-horse town in a big bend; so we tied up about three-quarters of a mile above it, in the mouth of a crick which was shut in like a tunnel by the cypress trees, and all of us but Jim took the canoe and went down there to see if there was any chance in that place for our show.

We struck it mighty lucky; there was going to be a circus there that afternoon, and the country-people was already beginning to come in, all kinds of old shackly wagons, and on horses. The circus would leave before night, so our show would have a pretty good chance. The duke he hired the court-house, and we went around and stuck up our bills. They read like this:

Shaksperean Revival ! ! !
Wonderful Attraction!
For One Night Only!
The world renowned tragedians,
David Garrick the younger,
of Drury Lane Theatre, London,
and
Edmund Kean the elder, of the Royal Haymarket
Theatre, Whitechapel, Pudding Lane, Picca-
dilly, London, and the Royal Continental
Theatres, in their sublime Shak-
sperean Spectacle entitled

The Balcony Scene
in
Romeo and Juliet ! ! !

Romeo ....Mr. Garrick
Juliet ....Mr. Kean
Assisted by the whole strength of the company!
New costumes, new scenery, new appointments!
Also:
The thrilling, masterly, and blood-curdling
Broad-sword conflict
In Richard III. ! ! !

Richard III ....Mr. Garrick
Richmond ....Mr. Kean
Also:
(by special request)
Hamlet's Immortal Soliloquy ! !
By the Illustrious Kean!
Done by him 300 consecutive nights in Paris!
For One Night Only,
On account of imperative European engagements!
Admission 25 cents; children and servants, 10 cents.

Then we went loafing around town. The stores and houses was most all old, shackly, dried-up frame concerns that hadn't ever been painted; they was set up three or four foot above ground on stilts, so as to be out of reach of the water when the river was overflowed. The houses had little gardens around them, but they didn't seem to raise hardly anything in them but jimpson-weeds, and sunflowers, and ash-piles, and old curled-up boots and shoes, and pieces of bottles, and rags, and played-out tinware. The fences was made of different kinds of boards, nailed on at different times; and they leaned every which way, and had gates that didn't generly have but one hinge—a leather one. Some of the fences had been white-washed some time or another, but the duke said it was in Columbus's time, like enough. There was generly hogs in the garden, and people driving them out.

All the stores was along one street. They had white domestic awnings in front, and the country-people hitched their horses to the awning-posts. There was empty dry-goods boxes under the awnings, and loafers roosting on them all day long, whittling them with their Barlow knives; and chawing tobacco, and gaping and yawning and stretching—a mighty ornery lot. They generly had on yellow straw hats most as wide as an umbrella, but didn't wear no coats nor waistcoats; they called one another Bill, and Buck, and Hank, and Joe, and Andy, and talked lazy and drawly, and used considerable many cusswords. There was as many as one loafer leaning up against every awning-post, and he most always had his hands in his britches pockets, except when he fetched them out to lend a chaw of tobacco or scratch. What a body was hearing amongst them all the time was:

"Gimme a chaw 'v tobacker, Hank."

"Cain't; I hain't got but one chaw left. Ask Bill."

Maybe Bill he gives him a chaw; maybe he lies and says he ain't got none. Some of them kinds of loafers never has a cent in the world, nor a chaw of tobacco of their own. They get all their chawing by borrowing; they say to a fellow, "I wisht you'd len' me a chaw, Jack, I jist this minute give Ben Thompson the last chaw I had"—which is a lie pretty much every time; it don't fool nobody but a stranger; but Jack ain't no stranger, so he says:

"*You* give him a chaw, did you? So did your sister's cat's grandmother. You pay me back the chaws you've awready borry'd off'n me, Lafe Buckner, then I'll loan you one or two ton of it, and won't charge you no back intrust, nuther."

"Well, I *did* pay you back some of it wunst."

"Yes, you did—'bout six chaws. You borry'd store tobacker and paid back nigger-head."

Store tobacco is flat black plug, but these fellows mostly chaws the natural leaf twisted. When they borrow a chaw they don't generly cut it off with a knife, but set the plug in between their teeth, and gnaw with their teeth and tug at the plug with their hands till they get it in two; then sometimes the one that owns the tobacco looks mournful at it when it's handed back, and says, sarcastic:

"Here, gimme the *chaw*, and you take the *plug*."

All the streets and lanes was just mud; they warn't nothing else *but* mud—mud as black as tar and nigh about a foot deep in some places, and two or three inches deep in *all* the places. The hogs loafed and grunted around everywheres. You'd see a muddy sow and a litter of pigs come lazying along the street and whollop herself right down in the way, where folks had to walk around her, and she'd stretch out and shut her eyes and wave her ears whilst the pigs was milking her, and look as happy as if she was on salary. And pretty soon you'd hear a loafer sing out, "Hi! *so* boy! sick him, Tige!" and away the sow would go, squealing most horrible, with a dog or two swinging to each ear, and three or four dozen more a-coming; and then you would see all the loafers get up and watch the thing out of sight, and laugh at the fun and look grateful for the noise. Then they'd settle back again till there was a dog-fight. There couldn't anything wake them up all over, and make them happy all over, like a dog-fight—unless it might be putting turpentine on a stray dog and setting fire to him, or tying a tin pan to his tail and see him run himself to death.

On the river-front some of the houses was sticking out over the bank, and they was bowed and bent, and about ready to tumble in. The people had moved out of them. The bank was caved away under one corner of some others, and that corner was hanging over. People lived in them yet, but it was dangersome, because sometimes a strip of land as wide as a house caves in at a time. Sometimes a belt of land a quarter of a mile deep will start in and cave along and cave along till it all caves into the river in one summer. Such a town as that has to be always moving back, and back, and back, because the river's always gnawing at it.

The nearer it got to noon that day the thicker and thicker was the wagons and horses in the streets, and more coming all the time. Families fetched their dinners with them from the country, and eat them in the wagons. There was considerable whisky-drinking going on, and I seen three fights. By and by somebody sings out:

"Here comes old Boggs!—in from the country for his little old monthly drunk; here he comes, boys!"

All the loafers looked glad; I reckoned they was used to having fun out of Boggs. One of them says:

"Wonder who he's a-gwyne to chaw up this time. If he'd a-chawed up all the men he's ben a-gwyne to chaw up in the last twenty year he'd have considerable reputation now."

Another one says, "I wisht old Boggs 'd threaten me, 'cuz then I'd know I warn't gwyne to die for a thousan' year."

Boggs comes a-tearing along on his horse, whooping and yelling like an Injun, and singing out:

"Cler the track, thar. I'm on the waw-path, and the price uv coffins is a-gwyne to raise."

He was drunk, and weaving about in his saddle; he was over fifty year old, and had a very red face. Everybody yelled at him and laughed at him and sassed him, and he sassed back, and said he'd attend to them and lay them out in their regular turns, but he couldn't wait now because he'd come to town to kill old Colonel Sherburn, and his motto was, "Meat first, and spoon vittles to top off on."

He see me, and rode up and says:

"Whar'd you come f'm, boy? You prepared to die?"

Then he rode on. I was scared, but a man says:

"He don't mean nothing; he's always a-carryin' on like that when he's drunk. He's the best-naturedest old fool in Arkansaw—never hurt nobody, drunk nor sober."

Boggs rode up before the biggest store in town, and bent his head down so he could see under the curtain of the awning and yells:

"Come out here, Sherburn! Come out and meet the man you've swindled. You're the houn' I'm after, and I'm a-gwyne to have you, too!"

And so he went on, calling Sherburn everything he could lay his tongue to, and the whole street packed with people listening and laughing and going on. By and by a proud-looking man about fifty-five—and he was a heap the best-dressed man in that town, too—steps out of the store, and the crowd drops back on each side to let him come. He says to Boggs, mighty ca'm and slow—he says:

"I'm tired of this, but I'll endure it till one o'clock. Till one o'clock, mind—no longer. If you open your mouth against me only once after that time you can't travel so far but I will find you."

Then he turns and goes in. The crowd looked mighty sober; nobody stirred, and there warn't no more laughing. Boggs rode off blackguarding Sherburn as loud as he could yell, all down the street; and pretty soon back he comes and stops before the store, still keeping it up. Some men crowded around him and tried to get him to shut up, but he wouldn't; they told him it would be one o'clock in about fifteen minutes, and so he *must* go home—he must go right away. But it didn't do no good. He cussed away with all his might, and throwed his hat down in the mud and rode over it, and pretty soon away he went a-raging down the street again, with his gray hair a-flying. Everybody that could get a chance at him tried their best to coax him off of his horse so they could lock him up and get him sober; but it warn't no use—up the street he would tear again, and give Sherburn another cussing. By and by somebody says:

"Go for his daughter!—quick, go for his daughter; sometimes he'll listen to her. If anybody can persuade him, she can."

So somebody started on a run. I walked down street a ways and stopped. In about five or ten minutes here comes Boggs again, but not on his horse. He was a-reeling across the street towards me, bareheaded, with a friend on both sides of him a-holt of his arms and hurrying him along. He was quiet, and looked uneasy; and he warn't hanging back any, but was doing some of the hurrying himself. Somebody sings out:

"Boggs!"

I looked over there to see who said it, and it was that Colonel Sherburn. He was standing perfectly still in the street, and had a pistol raised in his right hand—not aiming it, but holding it out with the barrel tilted up towards the sky. The same second I see a young girl coming on the run, and two men with her. Boggs and the men turned round to see who called him, and when they see the pistol the men jumped to one side, and the pistol-barrel come down slow and steady to a level—both barrels cocked. Boggs throws up both of his hands and says, "O Lord, don't shoot!" Bang! goes the first shot, and he staggers back, clawing at the air—bang! goes the second one, and he tumbles backward onto the ground, heavy and solid, with his arms spread out. That young girl screamed out and comes rushing, and down she throws herself on her father, crying, and saying, "Oh, he's killed him, he's killed him!" The crowd closed up around them, and shouldered and jammed one another, with their necks stretched, trying to see,

and people on the inside trying to shove them back and shouting,

"Back, back! give him air, give him air!"

Colonel Sherburn he tossed his pistol onto the ground, and turned around on his heels and walked off.

They took Boggs to a little drug store, the crowd pressing around just the same, and the whole town following, and I rushed and got a good place at the window, where I was close to him and could see in. They laid him on the floor and put one large Bible under his head, and opened another one and spread it on his breast; but they tore open his shirt first, and I seen where one of the bullets went in. He made about a dozen long gasps, his breast lifting the Bible up when he drawed in his breath, and letting it down again when he breathed it out—and after that he laid still; he was dead. Then they pulled his daughter away from him, screaming and crying, and took her off. She was about sixteen, and very sweet and gentle looking, but awful pale and scared.

Well, pretty soon the whole town was there, squirming and scrouging and pushing and shoving to get at the window and have a look, but people that had the places wouldn't give them up, and folks behind them was saying all the time, "Say, now, you've looked enough, you fellows; 'tain't right and 'tain't fair for you to stay thar all the time, and never give nobody a chance; other folks has their rights as well as you."

There was considerable jawing back, so I slid out, thinking maybe there was going to be trouble. The streets was full, and everybody was excited. Everybody that seen the shooting was telling how it happened, and there was a big crowd packed around each one of these fellows, stretching their necks and listening. One long, lanky man, with long hair and a big white fur stovepipe hat on the back of his head, and a crooked-handled cane, marked out the places on the ground where Boggs stood and where Sherburn stood, and the people following him around from one place to t'other and watching everything he done, and bobbing their heads to show they understood, and stooping a little and resting their hands on their thighs to watch him mark the places on the ground with his cane; and then he stood up straight and stiff where Sherburn had stood, frowning and having his hat-brim down over his eyes, and sung out, "Boggs!" and then fetched his cane down slow to a level, and says "Bang!" staggered backward, says "Bang!" again, and fell down flat on his back. The people that had seen the thing said he done it perfect; said it was just exactly the way it all happened. Then as much as a dozen people got out their bottles and treated him.

Well, by and by somebody said Sherburn ought to be lynched. In about a minute everybody was saying it; so away they went, mad and yelling, and snatching down every clothesline they come to to do the hanging with.

22. WHY THE LYNCHING BEE FAILED

They swarmed up towards Sherburn's house, a-whooping and raging like Injuns, and everything had to clear the way or get run over and tromped to mush, and it was awful to see. Children was heeling it ahead of the mob, screaming and trying to get out of the way; and every window along the road was full of women's heads, and there was nigger boys in every tree, and bucks and wenches looking over every fence; and as soon as the mob would get nearly to them they would break and skaddle back out of reach. Lots of the women and girls was crying and taking on, scared most to death.

They swarmed up in front of Sherburn's palings as thick as they could jam together, and you couldn't hear yourself think for the noise. It was a little twenty-foot yard. Some sung out "Tear down the fence! tear down the fence!" Then there was a racket of ripping and tearing and smashing, and down she goes, and the front wall of the crowd begins to roll in like a wave.

Just then Sherburn steps out onto the roof of his little front porch, with a double-barrel gun in his hand, and takes his stand, perfectly ca'm and deliberate, not saying a word. The racket stopped, and the wave sucked back.

Sherburn never said a word—just stood there, looking down. The stillness was awful creepy and uncomfortable. Sherburn run his eyes slow along the crowd; and wherever it struck the people tried a little to outgaze him, but they couldn't; they dropped their eyes and looked sneaky. Then pretty soon Sherburn sort of laughed; not the pleasant kind, but the kind that makes you feel like when you are eating bread that's got sand in it.

Then he says, slow and scornful:

"The idea of *you* lynching anybody! It's amusing. The idea of you thinking you had pluck enough to lynch a *man!* Because you're brave enough to tar and feather poor friendless cast-out women that come along here, did that make you think you had grit enough to lay your hands on a *man?* Why, a *man's* safe in the hands of ten thousand of your kind— as long as it's daytime and you're not behind him.

"Do I know you? I know you clear through. I was born and raised in the South, and I've lived in the North; so I know the average all around. The average man's a coward. In the North he lets anybody walk over him that wants to, and goes home and prays for a humble spirit to bear it. In the South one man, all by himself, has stopped a stage full of men in the daytime, and robbed the lot. Your newspapers call you a brave people so much that you think you *are* braver than any other people—whereas you're just *as* brave, and no braver. Why don't your juries hang murderers? Because they're afraid the man's friends will shoot them in the back, in the dark—and it's just what they *would* do.

"So they always acquit; and then a *man* goes in the night, with a hundred masked cowards at his back, and lynches the rascal. Your mistake is, that you didn't bring a man with you; that's one mistake, and the other is that you didn't come in the dark and fetch your masks. You brought *part* of a man—Buck Harkness, there—and if you hadn't had him to start you, you'd 'a' taken it out in blowing.

"You didn't want to come. The average man don't like trouble and danger. *You* don't like trouble and danger. But if only *half* a man—like Buck Harkness, there—shouts 'Lynch him! lynch him!' you're afraid to back down—afraid you'll be found out to be what you are—*cowards*—and so you raise a yell, and hang yourselves onto that half-a-man's coattail, and come raging up here, swearing what big things you're going to do. The pitifulest thing out is a mob; that's what an army is—

a mob; they don't fight with courage that's born in them, but with courage that's borrowed from their mass, and from their officers. But a mob without any *man* at the head of it is *beneath* pitifulness. Now the thing for *you* to do is to droop your tails and go home and crawl in a hole. If any real lynching's going to be done it will be done in the dark, Southern fashion; and when they come they'll bring their masks, and fetch a *man* along. Now *leave*—and take your half-a-man with you"—tossing his gun up across his left arm and cocking it when he says this.

The crowd washed back sudden, and then broke all apart, and went tearing off every which way, and Buck Harkness he heeled it after them, looking tolerable cheap. I could 'a' stayed if I wanted to, but I didn't want to.

I went to the circus and loafed around the back side till the watchman went by, and then dived in under the tent. I had my twenty-dollar gold piece and some other money, but I reckoned I better save it, because there ain't no telling how soon you are going to need it, away from home and amongst strangers that way. You can't be too careful. I ain't opposed to spending money on circuses when there ain't no other way, but there ain't no use in *wasting* it on them.

It was a real bully circus. It was the splendidest sight that ever was when they all come riding in, two and two, and gentleman and lady, side by side, the men just in their drawers and undershirts, and no shoes nor stirrups, and resting their hands on their thighs easy and comfortable—there must 'a' been twenty of them—and every lady with a lovely complexion, and perfectly beautiful, and looking just like a gang of real sure-enough queens, and dressed in clothes that cost millions of dollars, and just littered with diamonds. It was a powerful fine sight; I never see anything so lovely. And then one by one they got up and stood, and went a-weaving around the ring so gentle and wavy and graceful, the men looking ever so tall and airy and straight, with their heads bobbing and skimming along, away up there under the tent-roof, and every lady's rose-leafy dress flapping soft and silky around her hips, and she looking like the most loveliest parasol.

And then faster and faster they went, all of them dancing, first one foot out in the air and then the other, the horses leaning more and more, and the ringmaster going round and round the center pole, cracking his whip and shouting "Hi!—hi!" and the clown cracking jokes behind him; and by and by all hands dropped the reins, and every lady put her knuckles on her hips and every gentleman folded his arms, and then how the horses did lean over and hump themselves. And so one after the other they all skipped off into the ring, and made the sweetest bow I ever see, and then scampered out, and everybody clapped their hands and went just about wild.

Well, all through the circus they done the most astonishing things; and all the time that clown carried on so it most killed the people. The ringmaster couldn't ever say a word to him but he was back at him quick as a wink with the funniest things a body ever said; and how he ever *could* think of so many of them, and so sudden and so pat, was what I couldn't no way understand. Why, I couldn't 'a' thought of them in a year. And by and by a drunken man tried to get into the ring—said he wanted to ride; said he could ride as well as anybody that ever was. They argued and tried to keep him out, but he wouldn't listen, and the whole show come to a standstill. Then the people begun to holler at him and make fun of him, and that made him mad, and he begun to rip and tear; so that stirred up the people, and a lot of men begun to pile down off of the benches and swarm toward the ring, saying, "Knock him down! throw him out!" and one or two women begun to scream. So, then, the ringmaster he made a little speech, and said he hoped there wouldn't be no disturbance, and if the man would promise he wouldn't make no more trouble he would let him ride if he thought he could stay on the horse. So everybody laughed and said all right, and the man got on. The minute he was on, the horse begun to rip and tear and jump and cavort around, with two circus men hanging on to his bridle trying to hold him, and the drunken man hanging on to his neck, and his heels flying in the air every jump, and the whole crowd of people standing up shouting and laughing till tears rolled down. And at last, sure enough, all the circus men could do, the horse broke loose, and away he went like the very nation, round and round the ring, with that sot laying down on him and hanging to his neck, with first one leg hanging most to the ground on one side, and then t'other one on t'other side, and the people just crazy. It warn't funny to me, though; I was all of a tremble to see his danger. But pretty soon he struggled up astraddle and grabbed the bridle, a-reeling this way and that; and the next minute he sprung up and dropped the bridle and stood! and the horse a-going like a house afire, too. He just stood up there, a-sailing around as easy and comfortable as if he warn't ever drunk in his life—and then he began to pull off his clothes and sling them. He shed them so thick they kind of clogged up the air, and altogether he shed seventeen suits. And, then, there he was, slim and handsome, and dressed the gaudiest and prettiest you ever saw, and he lit into that horse with his whip and made him fairly hum—and finally skipped off, and made his bow and danced off to the dressing-room, and everybody just a-howling with pleasure and astonishment.

Then the ringmaster he see how he had been fooled, and he *was* the sickest ringmaster you ever see, I reckon. Why, it was one of his own men! He had got up that joke all out of his own head, and never let on to nobody. Well, I felt sheepish enough to be took in so, but I wouldn't 'a' been in that ringmaster's place, not for a thousand dollars. I don't know; there may be bullier circuses than what that one was, but I never struck them yet. Anyways, it was plenty good enough for *me;* and wherever I run across it, it can have all of *my* custom every time.

Well, that night we had *our* show; but there warn't only about twelve people there —just enough to pay expenses. And they laughed all the time, and that made the duke mad; and everybody left, anyway, before the show was over, but one boy which was asleep. So the duke said these Arkansaw lunkheads couldn't come up to Shakespeare; what they wanted was low comedy—and maybe something ruther worse than low comedy, he reckoned. He said he could size their style. So next morning he got some big sheets of wrapping-paper and some black paint, and drawed off

some handbills, and stuck them up all over the village. The bills said:

AT THE COURT HOUSE!
FOR 3 NIGHTS ONLY!
The World-Renowned Tragedians
DAVID GARRICK THE YOUNGER!
AND
EDMUND KEAN THE ELDER!
Of the London and Continental Theatres,
In their Thrilling Tragedy of
THE KING'S CAMELEOPARD,
OR
THE ROYAL NONESUCH! ! !
Admission 50 cents.

Then at the bottom was the biggest line of all, which said:

LADIES AND CHILDREN NOT ADMITTED

"There," says he, "if that line don't fetch them, I don't know Arkansaw!"

23. THE ORNERINESS OF KINGS

Well, all day him and the king was hard at it, rigging up a stage and a curtain and a row of candles for footlights; and that night the house was jam full of men in no time. When the place couldn't hold no more, the duke he quit tending door and went around the back way and come onto the stage and stood up before the curtain and made a little speech, and praised up this tragedy, and said it was the most thrillingest one that ever was; and so he went on a-bragging about the tragedy, and about Edmund Kean the Elder, which was to play the main principal part in it; and at last when he'd got everybody's expectations up high enough, he rolled up the curtain, and the next minute the king come a-prancing out on all fours, naked; and he was painted all over, ring-streaked-and-striped, all sorts of colors, as splendid as a rainbow. And —but never mind the rest of his outfit; it was just wild, but it was awful funny. The people most killed themselves laughing; and when the king got done capering and capered off behind the scenes, they roared and clapped and stormed and haw-hawed till he come back and done it over again, and after that they made him do it another time. Well, it would make a cow laugh to see the shines that old idiot cut.

Then the duke he lets the curtain down, and bows to the people, and says the great tragedy will be performed only two nights more, on accounts of pressing London engagements, where the seats is all sold already for it in Drury Lane; and then he makes them another bow, and says if he has succeeded in pleasing them and instructing them, he will be deeply obleeged if they will mention it to their friends and get them to come and see it.

Twenty people sings out:

"What, is it over? Is that *all?*"

The duke says yes. Then there was a fine time. Everybody sings out, "Sold!" and rose up mad, and was a-going for that stage and them tragedians. But a big, fine-looking man jumps up on a bench and shouts:

"Hold on! Just a word, gentlemen." They stopped to listen. "We are sold—mighty badly sold. But we don't want to be the laughing-stock of this whole town, I reckon, and never hear the last of this thing as long as we live. *No.* What we want is to go out of here quiet, and talk this show up, and sell the *rest* of the town! Then we'll all be in the same boat. Ain't that sensible?" ("You bet it is!—the jedge is right!" everybody sings out.) "All right, then—not a word about any sell. Go along home, and advise everybody to come and see the tragedy."

Next day you couldn't hear nothing around that town but how splendid that show was. House was jammed again that night, and we sold this crowd the same way. When me and the king and the duke got home to the raft we all had a supper; and by and by, about midnight, they made Jim and me back her out and float her down the middle of the river, and fetch her in and hide her about two mile below town.

The third night the house was crammed again—and they warn't new-comers this time, but people that was at the show the other two nights. I stood by the duke at the door, and I see that every man that went in had his pockets bulging, or something muffled up under his coat—and I see it warn't no perfumery, neither, not by a long sight. I smelt sickly eggs by the barrel, and rotten cabbages, and such things; and if I know the signs of a dead cat being around, and I bet I do, there was sixty-four of them went in. I shoved in there for

a minute, but it was too various for me; I couldn't stand it. Well, when the place couldn't hold no more people the duke he give a fellow a quarter and told him to tend door for him a minute, and then he started around for the stage door, I after him; but the minute we turned the corner and was in the dark he says:

"Walk fast now till you get away from the houses, and then shin for the raft like the dickens was after you!"

I done it, and he done the same. We struck the raft at the same time, and in less than two seconds we was gliding down-stream, all dark and still, and edging towards the middle of the river, nobody saying a word. I reckoned the poor king was in for a gaudy time of it with the audience, but nothing of the sort; pretty soon he crawls out from under the wigwam, and says:

"Well, how'd the old thing pan out this time, duke?" He hadn't been up-town at all.

We never showed a light till we was about ten mile below the village. Then we lit up and had a supper, and the king and the duke fairly laughed their bones loose over the way they'd served them people. The duke says:

"Greenhorns, flatheads! *I* knew the first house would keep mum and let the rest of the town get roped in; and I knew they'd lay for us the third night, and consider it was *their* turn now. Well, it *is* their turn, and I'd give something to know how much they'd take for it. I *would* just like to know how they're putting in their opportunity. They can turn it into a picnic if they want to—they brought plenty provisions."

Them rapscallions took in four hundred and sixty-five dollars in that three nights. I never see money hauled in by the wagon-load like that before.

By and by, when they was asleep and snoring, Jim says:

"Don't it s'prise you de way dem kings carries on, Huck?"

"No," I says, "it don't."

"Why don't it, Huck?"

"Well, it don't, because it's in the breed. I reckon they're all alike."

"But, Huck, dese kings o' ourn is reglar rapscallions; dat's jist what dey is; dey's reglar rapscallions."

"Well, that's what I'm a-saying; all kings is mostly rapscallions, as fur as I can make out."

"Is dat so?"

"You read about them once—you'll see. Look at Henry the Eight; this 'n' 's a Sunday-school Superintendent to *him*. And look at Charles Second, and Louis Fourteen, and Louis Fifteen, and James Second, and Edward Second, and Richard Third, and forty more; besides all them Saxon heptarchies that used to rip around so in old times and raise Cain. My, you ought to seen old Henry the Eight when he was in bloom. He *was* a blossom. He used to marry a new wife every day, and chop off her head next morning. And he would do it just as indifferent as if he was ordering up eggs. 'Fetch up Nell Gwynn,' he says. They fetch her up. Next morning, 'Chop off her head!' And they chop it off. 'Fetch up Jane Shore,' he says; and up she comes. Next morning, 'Chop off her head'—and they chop it off. 'Ring up Fair Rosamun.' Fair Rosamun answers the bell. Next morning, 'Chop off her head.' And he made every one of them tell him a tale every night; and he kept that up till he had hogged a thousand and one tales that way, and then he put them all in a book, and called it Domesday Book—which was a good name and stated the case. You don't know kings, Jim, but I know them; and this old rip of ourn is one of the cleanest I've struck in history. Well, Henry he takes a notion he wants to get up some trouble with this country. How does he go at it—give notice?— give the country a show? No. All of a sudden he heaves all the tea in Boston Harbor overboard, and whacks out a declaration of independence, and dares them to come on. That was *his* style—he never give anybody a chance. He had suspicions of his father, the Duke of Wellington. Well, what did he do? Ask him to show up? No—drownded him in a butt of mamsey, like a cat. S'pose people left money laying around where he was—what did he do? He collared it. S'pose he contracted to do a thing, and you paid him, and didn't set down there and see that he done it—what did he do? He always done the other thing. S'pose he opened his mouth—what then? If he didn't shut it up powerful quick he'd lose a lie every time. That's the kind of a bug Henry was; and if we'd 'a' had him along 'stead of our kings he'd 'a' fooled that town a heap worse than ourn done. I don't say that ourn is lambs, because they ain't, when you come right down to the cold facts; but they ain't nothing to *that* old ram, anyway. All I say is, kings is kings, and you got to make allowances. Take them all around, they're a mighty ornery lot. It's the way they're raised."

"But dis one do *smell* so like de nation, Huck."

"Well, they all do, Jim. *We* can't help the way a king smells; history don't tell no way."

"Now de duke, he's a tolerble likely man in some ways."

"Yes, a duke's different. But not very different. This one's a middling hard lot for a duke. When he's drunk there ain't no near-sighted man could tell him from a king."

"Well, anyways, I doan' hanker for no mo' un um, Huck. Dese is all I kin stan'."

"It's the way I feel, too, Jim. But we've got them on our hands, and we got to remember what they are, and make allowances. Sometimes I wish we could hear of a country that's out of kings."

What was the use to tell Jim these warn't real kings and dukes? It wouldn't 'a' done no good; and, besides, it was just as I said: you couldn't tell them from the real kind.

I went to sleep, and Jim didn't call me when it was my turn. He often done that. When I waked up just at daybreak he was sitting there with his head down betwixt his knees, moaning and mourning to himself. I didn't take notice nor let on. I knowed what it was about. He was thinking about his wife and his children, away up yonder, and he was low and homesick; because he hadn't ever been away from home before in his life; and I do believe he cared just as much for his people as white folks does for their'n. It don't seem natural, but I reckon it's so. He was often moaning and mourning that way nights, when he judged I was asleep, and saying, "Po' little 'Lizabeth! po' little Johnny! it's mighty hard; I spec' I ain't ever gwyne to see you no mo', no mo'!" He was a mighty good nigger, Jim was.

But this time I somehow got to talking to him about his wife and young ones; and by and by he says:

"What makes me feel so bad dis time 'uz

bekase I hear sumpn over yonder on de bank like a whack, er a slam, while ago, en it mine me er de time I treat my little 'Lizabeth so ornery. She warn't on'y 'bout fo' year ole en she tuck de sk'yarlet fever, en had a powful rough spell; but she got well, en one day she was a-stannin' aroun', en I says to her, I says:

" 'Shet de do'.'

"She never done it; jis' stood dah, kiner smilin' up at me. It make me mad; en I says ag'in, mighty loud, I says:

" 'Doan you hear me? Shet de do'!'

"She jis' stood de same way, kiner smilin' up. I was a-bilin'! I says:

" 'I lay I *make* you mine!'

"En wid dat I fetch' her a slap side de head dat sont her a-sprawlin'. Den I went into de yuther room, en 'uz gone 'bout ten minutes; en when I come back dah was dat do' a-stannin' open *yit*, en dat chile stannin' mos' right in it, a-lookin' down and mournin', en de tears runnin' down. My, but I *wuz* mad! I was a-gwyne for de chile, but jis' den—it was a do' dat open innerds—jis' den, 'long come de wind en slam it to, behine de chile, ker-*blam*!—en my lan', de chile never move'! My breff mos' hop outer me; en I feel so—so—I doan' know *how* I feel. I crope out, all a-tremblin', en crope aroun' en open de do' easy en slow, en poke my head in behine de chile, sof' en still, en all uv a sudden I says *pow!* jis' as loud as I could yell. *She never budge!* Oh, Huck, I bust out a-cryin' en grab her up in my arms, en say, 'Oh, de po' little thing! De Lord God Amighty fogive po' ole Jim, kaze he never gwyne to fogive hisself as long's he live!' Oh, she was plumb deef en dumb, Huck, plumb deef en dumb—en I'd ben a-treat'n her so!"

24. THE KING TURNS PARSON

Next day, towards night, we laid up under a little willow towhead out in the middle, where there was a village on each side of the river, and the duke and the king begun to lay out a plan for working them towns. Jim he spoke to the duke, and said he hoped it wouldn't take but a few hours, because it got mighty heavy and tiresome to him when he had to lay all day in the wigwam tied with the rope. You see, when we left him all alone we had to tie him, because if anybody happened on to him all by himself and not tied it wouldn't look much like he was a runaway nigger, you know. So the duke said it *was* kind of hard to have to lay roped all day, and he'd cipher out some way to get around it.

He was uncommon bright, the duke was, and he soon struck it. He dressed Jim up in King Lear's outfit—it was a long curtain-calico gown, and a white horse-hair wig and whiskers; and then he took his theater paint and painted Jim's face and hands and ears and neck all over a dead, dull solid blue, like a man that's been drownded nine days. Blamed if he warn't the horriblest-looking outrage I ever see. Then the duke took and wrote out a sign on a shingle so:

Sick Arab—but harmless when not out of his head.

And he nailed that shingle to a lath, and stood the lath up four or five foot in front of the wigwam. Jim was satisfied. He said it was a sight better than lying tied a couple of years every day, and trembling all over every time there was a sound. The duke told him to make himself free and easy, and if anybody ever come meddling around, he must hop out of the wigwam, and carry on a little, and fetch a howl or two like a wild beast, and he reckoned they would light out and leave him alone. Which was sound enough judgment; but you take the average man, and he wouldn't wait for him to howl. Why, he didn't only look like he was dead, he looked considerable more than that.

These rapscallions wanted to try the Nonesuch again, because there was so much money in it, but they judged it wouldn't be safe, because maybe the news might 'a' worked along down by this time. They couldn't hit no project that suited exactly; so at last the duke said he reckoned he'd lay off and work his brains an hour or two and see if he couldn't put up something on the Arkansaw village; and the king he allowed he would drop over to t'other village without any plan, but just trust in Providence to lead him the profitable way—meaning the devil, I reckon. We had all bought store clothes where we stopped last; and now the king put his'n on, and he told me to put mine on. I done it, of course. The king's duds was all black, and he did look real swell and starchy. I never knowed how clothes could change a body before. Why, before, he looked like the orneriest old rip that ever was; but now, when he'd take off his new white beaver and make a bow and do a smile, he looked that grand and good and pious that you'd say he had walked right out of the ark, and maybe was old Leviticus himself. Jim cleaned up the canoe, and I got my paddle ready. There was a big steamboat laying at the shore away up under the point, about three mile above the town—been there a couple of hours, taking on freight. Says the king:

"Seein' how I'm dressed, I reckon maybe I better arrive down from St. Louis or Cincinnati, or some other big place. Go for the steamboat, Huckleberry; we'll come down to the village on her."

I didn't have to be ordered twice to go and take a steamboat ride. I fetched the shore a half a mile above the village, and then went scooting along the bluff bank in the easy water. Pretty soon we come to a nice innocent-looking young country jake setting on a log swabbing the sweat off of his face, for it was powerful warm weather; and he had a couple of big carpet-bags by him.

"Run her nose inshore," says the king. I done it. "Wher' you bound for, young man?"

"For the steamboat; going to Orleans."

"Git aboard," says the king. "Hold on a minute, my servant 'll he'p you with them bags. Jump out and he'p the gentleman, Adolphus"—meaning me, I see.

I done so, and then we all three started on again. The young chap was mighty thankful; said it was tough work toting his baggage such weather. He asked the king where he was going, and the king told him he'd come down the river and landed at the other village this morning, and now he was going up a few mile to see an old friend on a farm up there. The young fellow says:

"When I first see you I says to myself, 'It's Mr. Wilks, sure, and he come mighty near getting here in time.' But then I says again, 'No, I reckon it ain't him, or else he wouldn't be paddling up the river.' You *ain't* him, are you?"

"No, my name's Blodgett—Elexander Blodgett—*Reverend* Elexander Blodgett, I s'pose I must say, as I'm one o' the Lord's poor servants. But still I'm jist as able to be sorry for Mr. Wilks for not arriving in time, all the same, if he's missed anything by it—which I hope he hasn't."

"Well, he don't miss any property by it, because he'll get that all right; but he's missed seeing his brother Peter die—which he mayn't mind, nobody can tell as to that—but his brother would 'a' give anything in this world to see *him* before he died; never talked about nothing else all these three weeks; hadn't seen him since they was boys together—and hadn't ever seen his brother William at all—that's the deef and dumb one—William ain't more than thirty or thirty-five. Peter and George were the only ones that come out here; George was the married brother; him and his wife both died last year. Harvey and William's the only ones that's left now; and, as I was saying, they haven't got here in time."

"Did anybody send 'em word?"

"Oh, yes; a month or two ago, when Peter was first took; because Peter said then that he sorter felt like he warn't going to get well this time. You see, he was pretty old, and George's g'yirls was too young to be much company for him, except Mary Jane, the red-headed one; and so he was kinder lonesome after George and his wife died, and didn't seem to care much to live. He most desperately wanted to see Harvey—and William, too, for that matter—because he was one of them kind that can't bear to make a will. He left a letter behind for Harvey, and said he'd told in it where his money was hid, and how he wanted the rest of the property divided up so George's g'yirls would be all right—for George didn't leave nothing. And that letter was all they could get him to put a pen to."

"Why do you reckon Harvey don't come? Wher' does he live?"

"Oh, he lives in England—Sheffield—preaches there—hasn't ever been in this country. He hasn't had any too much time—and besides he mightn't 'a' got the letter at all, you know."

"Too bad, too bad he couldn't 'a' lived to see his brothers, poor soul. You going to Orleans, you say?"

"Yes, but that ain't only a part of it. I'm going in a ship, next Wednesday, for Ryo Janeero, where my uncle lives."

"It's a pretty long journey. But it 'll be

lovely; I wisht I was a-going. Is Mary Jane the oldest? How old is the others?"

"Mary Jane's nineteen, Susan's fifteen, and Joanna's about fourteen—that's the one that gives herself to good works and has a hare-lip."

"Poor things! to be left alone in the cold world so."

"Well, they could be worse off. Old Peter had friends, and they ain't going to let them come to no harm. There's Hobson, the Baptis' preacher; and Deacon Lot Hovey, and Ben Rucker, and Abner Shackleford, and Levi Bell, the lawyer; and Dr. Robinson, and their wives, and the widow Bartley, and—well, there's a lot of them; but these are the ones that Peter was thickest with, and used to write about sometimes, when he wrote home; so Harvey 'll know where to look for friends when he gets here."

Well, the old man went on asking questions till he just fairly emptied that young fellow. Blamed if he didn't inquire about everybody and everything in that blessed town, and all about the Wilkses; and about Peter's business—which was a tanner; and about George's—which was a carpenter; and about Harvey's—which was a dissentering minister; and so on, and so on. Then he says:

"What did you want to walk all the way up to the steamboat for?"

"Because she's a big Orleans boat, and I was afeared she mightn't stop there. When they're deep they won't stop for a hail. A Cincinnati boat will, but this is a St. Louis one."

"Was Peter Wilks well off?"

"Oh, yes, pretty well off. He had houses and land, and it's reckoned he left three or four thousand in cash hid up som'ers."

"When did you say he died?"

"I didn't say, but it was last night."

"Funeral tomorrow, likely?"

"Yes, 'bout the middle of the day."

"Well, it's all terrible sad; but we've all got to go, one time or another. So what we want to do is to be prepared; then we're all right."

"Yes, sir, it's the best way. Ma used to always say that."

When we struck the boat she was about done loading, and pretty soon she got off. The king never said nothing about going aboard, so I lost my ride, after all. When the boat was gone the king made me paddle up another mile to a lonesome place, and then he got ashore and says:

"Now hustle back, right off, and fetch the duke up here, and the new carpet-bags. And if he's gone over to t'other side, go over there and git him. And tell him to git himself up regardless. Shove along, now."

I see what he was up to; but I never said nothing, of course. When I got back with the duke we hid the canoe, and then they set down on a log, and the king told him everything, just like the young fellow had said it—every last word of it. And all the time he was a-doing it he tried to talk like an Englishman; and he done it pretty well, too, for a slouch. I can't imitate him, and so I ain't a-going to try to; but he really done it pretty good. Then he says:

"How are you on the deef and dumb, Bilgewater?"

The duke said, leave him alone for that; said he had played a deef and dumb person on the histrionic boards. So then they waited for a steamboat.

About the middle of the afternoon a couple of little boats come along, but they didn't come from high enough up the river; but at last there was a big one, and they hailed her. She sent out her yawl, and we went aboard, and she was from Cincinnati; and when they found we only wanted to go four or five mile they were booming mad, and gave us a cussing, and said they wouldn't land us. But the king was ca'm. He says:

"If gentlemen kin afford to pay a dollar a mile apiece to be took on and put off in a yawl, a steamboat kin afford to carry 'em, can't it?"

So they softened down and said it was all right; and when we got to the village they yawled us ashore. About two dozen men flocked down when they see the yawl a-coming, and when the king says:

"Kin any of you gentlemen tell me wher' Mr. Peter Wilks lives?" they give a glance at one another, and nodded their heads, as much as to say, "What 'd I tell you?" Then one of them says, kind of soft and gentle:

"I'm sorry, sir, but the best we can do is to tell you where he *did* live yesterday evening."

Sudden as winking the ornery old cretur

went all to smash, and fell up against the man, and put his chin on his shoulder, and cried down his back, and says:

"Alas, alas, our poor brother—gone, and we never got to see him; oh, it's too, *too* hard!"

Then he turns around, blubbering, and makes a lot of idiotic signs to the duke on his hands, and blamed if *he* didn't drop a carpet-bag and bust out a-crying. If they warn't the beatenest lot, them two frauds, that ever I struck.

Well, the men gathered around and sympathized with them, and said all sorts of kind things to them, and carried their carpet-bags up the hill for them, and let them lean on them and cry, and told the king all about his brother's last moments, and the king he told it all over again on his hands to the duke, and both of them took on about that dead tanner like they'd lost the twelve disciples. Well, if ever I struck anything like it, I'm a nigger. It was enough to make a body ashamed of the human race.

25. ALL FULL OF TEARS AND FLAPDOODLE

The news was all over town in two minutes, and you could see the people tearing down on the run from every which way, some of them putting on their coats as they come. Pretty soon we was in the middle of a crowd, and the noise of the tramping was like a soldier march. The windows and dooryards was full; and every minute somebody would say, over a fence:

"Is it *them*?"

And somebody trotting along with the gang would answer back and say:

"You bet it is."

When we got to the house the street in front of it was packed, and the three girls was standing in the door. Mary Jane *was* red-headed, but that don't make no difference, she was most awful beautiful, and her face and her eyes was all lit up like glory, she was so glad her uncles was come. The king he spread his arms, and Mary Jane she jumped for them, and the hare-lip jumped for the duke, and there they *had* it! Everybody most, leastways women, cried for joy to see them meet again at last and have such good times.

Then the king he hunched the duke private

—I see him do it—and then he looked around and see the coffin, over in the corner on two chairs; so then him and the duke, with a hand across each other's shoulder, and t'other hand to their eyes, walked slow and solemn over there, everybody dropping back to give them room, and all the talk and noise stopping, people saying " 'Sh!" and all the men taking their hats off and drooping their heads, so you could 'a' heard a pin fall. And when they got there they bent over and looked in the coffin, and took one sight, and then they bust out a-crying so you could 'a' heard them to Orleans, most; and then they put their arms around each other's necks, and hung their chins over each other's shoulders; and then for three minutes, or maybe four, I never seen two men leak the way they done. And, mind you, everybody was doing the same; and the place was that damp I never see anything like it. Then one of them got on one side of the coffin, and t'other on t'other side, and they kneeled down and rested their foreheads on the coffin, and let on to pray all to themselves. Well, when it come to that it worked the crowd like you never see anything like it, and everybody broke down and went to sobbing right out loud—the poor girls, too; and every woman, nearly, went up to the girls, without saying a word, and kissed them, solemn, on the forehead, and then put their hand on their head, and looked up towards the sky, with the tears running down, and then busted out and went off sobbing and swabbing, and give the next woman a show. I never see anything so disgusting.

Well, by and by the king he gets up and comes forward a little, and works himself up and slobbers out a speech, all full of tears and flapdoodle, about its being a sore trial for him and his poor brother to lose the diseased, and to miss seeing diseased alive after the long journey of four thousand mile, but it's a trial that's sweetened and sanctified to us by this dear sympathy and these holy tears, and so he thanks them out of his heart and out of his brother's heart, because out of their mouths they can't, words being too weak and cold, and all that kind of rot and slush, till it was just sickening; and then he blubbers out a pious goody-goody Amen, and turns himself loose and goes to crying fit to bust.

And the minute the words were out of his mouth somebody over in the crowd struck up the doxolojer and everybody joined in with all their might, and it just warmed you up and made you feel as good as church letting out. Music *is* a good thing; and after all that soul-butter and hogwash I never see it freshen up things so, and sound so honest and bully.

Then the king begins to work his jaw again, and says how him and his nieces would be glad if a few of the main principal friends of the family would take supper here with them this evening, and help set up with the ashes of the diseased; and says if his poor brother laying yonder could speak he knows who he would name, for they was names that was very dear to him, and mentioned often in his letters, and so he will name the same, to wit, as follows, viz.:—Rev. Mr. Hobson, and Deacon Lot Hovey, and Mr. Ben Rucker, and Abner Shackleford, and Levi Bell, and Dr. Robinson, and their wives, and the widow Bartley.

Rev. Hobson and Dr. Robinson was down to the end of the town a-hunting together—that is, I mean the doctor was shipping a sick man to t'other world, and the preacher was pinting him right. Lawyer Bell was away up to Louisville on business. But the rest was on hand, and so they all come and shook hands with the king and thanked him and talked to him; and then they shook hands with the duke and didn't say nothing, but just kept a-smiling and bobbing their heads like a passel of sapheads whilst he made all sorts of signs with his hands and said "Goo-goo—goo-goo-goo" all the time, like a baby that can't talk.

So the king he blattered along, and managed to inquire about pretty much everybody and dog in town, by his name, and mentioned all sorts of little things that happened one time or another in the town, or to George's family, or to Peter. And he always let on that Peter wrote him the things; but that was a lie: he got every blessed one of them out of that young flathead that we canoed up to the steamboat.

Then Mary Jane she fetched the letter her father left behind, and the king he read it out loud and cried over it. It give the dwelling-house and three thousand dollars, gold, to the girls; and it give the tanyard (which was do-ing a good business), along with some other houses and land (worth about seven thousand), and three thousand dollars in gold to Harvey and William, and told where the six thousand cash was hid down cellar. So these two frauds said they'd go and fetch it up, and have everything square and above-board; and told me to come with a candle. We shut the cellar door behind us, and when they found the bag they spilt it out on the floor, and it was a lovely sight, all them yaller-boys. My, the way the king's eyes did shine! He slaps the duke on the shoulder and says:

"Oh, *this* ain't bully nor noth'n'! Oh, no, I reckon not! Why, Biljy, it beats the Nonesuch, *don't* it?"

The duke allowed it did. They pawed the yaller-boys, and sifted them through their fingers and let them jingle down on the floor; and the king says:

"It ain't no use talkin'; bein' brothers to a rich dead man and representatives of furrin heirs that's got left is the line for you and me, Bilge. Thish yer comes of trust'n to Providence. It's the best way, in the long run. I've tried 'em all, and ther' ain't no better way."

Most everybody would 'a' been satisfied with the pile, and took it on trust; but no, they must count it. So they counts it, and it comes out four hundred and fifteen dollars short. Says the king:

"Dern him, I wonder what he done with that four hundred and fifteen dollars?"

They worried over that awhile, and ransacked all around for it. Then the duke says:

"Well, he was a pretty sick man, and likely he made a mistake—I reckon that's the way of it. The best way's to let it go, and keep still about it. We can spare it."

"Oh, shucks, yes, we can *spare* it. I don't k'yer noth'n 'bout that—it's the *count* I'm thinkin' about. We want to be awful square and open and above-board here, you know. We want to lug this h'yer money up-stairs and count it before everybody—then ther' ain't noth'n suspicious. But when the dead man says ther's six thous'n dollars, you know, we don't want to—"

"Hold on," says the duke. "Le's make up the deffisit," and he begun to haul out yaller-boys out of his pocket.

"It's a most amaz'n' good idea, duke—you

have got a rattlin' clever head on you," says the king. "Blest if the old Nonesuch ain't a-heppin' us out ag'in," and *he* begun to haul out yaller-jackets and stack them up.

It most busted them, but they made up the six thousand clean and clear.

"Say," says the duke, "I got another idea. Le's go up-stairs and count this money, and then take and *give it to the girls.*"

"Good land, duke, lemme hug you! It's the most dazzling idea 'at ever a man struck. You have cert'nly got the most astonishin' head I ever see. Oh, this is the boss dodge, ther' ain't no mistake 'bout it. Let 'em fetch along their suspicions now if they want to—this 'll lay 'em out."

When we got up-stairs everybody gethered around the table, and the king he counted it and stacked it up, three hundred dollars in a pile—twenty elegant little piles. Everybody looked hungry at it, and licked their chops. Then they raked it into the bag again, and I see the king begin to swell himself up for another speech. He says:

"Friends all, my poor brother that lays yonder has done generous by them that's left behind in the vale of sorrers. He has done generous by these yer poor little lambs that he loved and sheltered, and that's left fatherless and motherless. Yes, and we that knowed him knows that he would 'a' done *more* generous by 'em if he hadn't ben afeard o' woundin' his dear William and me. Now, *wouldn't* he? Ther' ain't no question 'bout it in *my* mind. Well, then, what kind o' brothers would it be that 'd stand in his way at sech a time? And what kind o' uncles would it be that 'd rob—yes, *rob*—sech poor sweet lambs as these 'at he loved so at sech a time? If I know William—and I *think* I do—he—well, I'll jest ask him." He turned around and began to make a lot of signs to the duke with his hands, and the duke he looks at him stupid and leather-headed awhile; then all of a sudden he seems to catch his meaning, and jumps for the king, goo-gooing with all his might for joy, and hugs him about fifteen times before he lets up. Then the king says, "I knowed it; I reckon *that* 'll convince anybody the way *he* feels about it. Here, Mary Jane, Susan, Joanner, take the money—take it *all.* It's the gift of him that lays yonder, cold but joyful."

Mary Jane she went for him, Susan and the hare-lip went for the duke, and then such another hugging and kissing I never see yet. And everybody crowded up with the tears in their eyes, and most shook the hands off of them frauds, saying all the time:

"You *dear* good souls!—how *lovely!*—how *could* you!"

Well, then, pretty soon all hands got to talking about the diseased again, and how good he was, and what a loss he was, and all that; and before long a big iron-jawed man worked himself in there from outside, and stood a-listening and looking, and not saying anything; and nobody saying anything to him either, because the king was talking and they was all busy listening. The king was saying—in the middle of something he'd started in on—

"—they bein' partickler friends o' the diseased. That's why they're invited here this evenin'; but tomorrow we want *all* to come—everybody; for he respected everybody, he liked everybody, and so it's fitten that his funeral orgies sh'd be public."

And so he went a-mooning on and on, liking to hear himself talk, and every little while he fetched in his funeral orgies again, till the duke he couldn't stand it no more; so he writes on a little scrap of paper, "*Obsequies,* you old fool," and folds it up, and goes to goo-gooing and reaching it over people's heads to him. The king he reads it and puts it in his pocket, and says:

"Poor William, afflicted as he is, his *heart's* aluz right. Asks me to invite everybody to come to the funeral—wants me to make 'em all welcome. But he needn't 'a' worried—it was jest what I was at."

Then he weaves along again, perfectly ca'm, and goes to dropping in his funeral orgies again every now and then, just like he done before. And when he done it the third time he says:

"I say orgies, not because it's the common term, because it ain't—obsequies bein' the common term—but because orgies is the right term. Obsequies ain't used in England no more now—it's gone out. We say orgies now in England. Orgies is better, because it means the thing you're after more exact. It's a word that's made up out'n the Greek *orgo,* outside, open, abroad; and the Hebrew *jeesum,* to plant, cover up; hence in*ter.* So, you see, funeral orgies is an open er public funeral."

He was the *worst* I ever struck. Well, the iron-jawed man he laughed right in his face. Everybody was shocked. Everybody says, "Why, *doctor!*" and Abner Shackleford says:

"Why, Robinson, hain't you heard the news? This is Harvey Wilks."

The king he smiled eager, and shoved out his flapper, and says:

"*Is* it my poor brother's dear good friend and physician? I—"

"Keep your hands off me!" says the doctor. "*You* talk like an Englishman, *don't* you? It's the worst imitation I ever heard. *You* Peter Wilks's brother! You're a fraud, that's what you are!"

Well, how they all took on! They crowded around the doctor and tried to quiet him down, and tried to explain to him and tell him how Harvey's showed in forty ways that he *was* Harvey, and knowed everybody by name, and the names of the very dogs, and begged and *begged* him not to hurt Harvey's feelings and the poor girls' feelings, and all that. But it warn't no use; he stormed right along, and said any man that pretended to be an Englishman and couldn't imitate the lingo no better than what he did was a fraud and a liar. The poor girls was hanging to the king and crying; and all of a sudden the doctor ups and turns on *them.* He says:

"I was your father's friend, and I'm your friend; and I warn you *as* a friend, and an honest one that wants to protect you and keep you out of harm and trouble, to turn your backs on that scoundrel and have nothing to do with him, the ignorant tramp, with his idiotic Greek and Hebrew, as he calls it. He is the thinnest kind of an impostor—has come here with a lot of empty names and facts which he picked up somewheres; and you take them for *proofs,* and are helped to fool yourselves by these foolish friends here, who ought to know better. Mary Jane Wilks, you know me for your friend, and for your unselfish friend, too. Now listen to me; turn this pitiful rascal out—I *beg* you to do it. Will you?"

Mary Jane straightened herself up, and my, but she was handsome! She says:

"*Here* is my answer." She hove up the bag

of money and put it in the king's hands, and says, "Take this six thousand dollars, and invest for me and my sisters any way you want to, and don't give us no receipt for it."

Then she put her arm around the king on one side, and Susan and the hare-lip done the same on the other. Everybody clapped their hands and stomped on the floor like a perfect storm, whilst the king held up his head and smiled proud. The doctor says:

"All right; I wash *my* hands of the matter. But I warn you all that a time's coming when you're going to feel sick whenever you think of this day." And away he went.

"All right, doctor," says the king, kinder mocking him; "we'll try and get 'em to send for you"; which made them all laugh, and they said it was a prime good hit.

26. I STEAL THE KING'S PLUNDER

Well, when they was all gone the king he asks Mary Jane how they was off for spare rooms, and she said she had one spare room, which would do for Uncle William, and she'd give her own room to Uncle Harvey, which was a little bigger, and she would turn into the room with her sisters and sleep on a cot; and up garret was a little cubby, with a pallet in it. The king said the cubby would do for his valley—meaning me.

So Mary Jane took us up, and she showed them their rooms, which was plain but nice. She said she'd have her frocks and a lot of other traps took out of her room if they was in Uncle Harvey's way, but he said they warn't. The frocks was hung along the wall, and before them was a curtain made out of calico that hung down to the floor. There was an old hair trunk in one corner, and a guitar-box in another, and all sorts of little knick-knacks and jimcracks around, like girls brisken up a room with. The king said it was all the more homely and more pleasanter for these fixings, and so don't disturb them. The duke's room was pretty small, but plenty good enough, and so was my cubby.

That night they had a big supper, and all them men and women was there, and I stood behind the king and the duke's chairs and waited on them, and the niggers waited on the rest. Mary Jane she set at the head of the table, with Susan alongside of her, and said how bad the biscuits was, and how mean the preserves was, and how ornery and tough the fried chickens was—and all that kind of rot, the way women always do for to force out compliments; and the people all knowed everything was tiptop, and said so—said "How *do* you get biscuits to brown so nice?" and "Where, for the land's sake, *did* you get these amaz'n pickles?" and all that kind of humbug talky-talk, just the way people always does at a supper, you know.

And when it was all done me and the hare-lip had supper in the kitchen off of the leav-ings, whilst the others was helping the niggers clean up the things. The hare-lip she got to pumping me about England, and blest if I didn't think the ice was getting mighty thin sometimes. She says:

"Did you ever see the king?"

"Who? William Fourth? Well, I bet I have —he goes to our church." I knowed he was dead years ago, but I never let on. So when I says he goes to our church, she says:

"What—regular?"

"Yes—regular. His pew's right over opposite ourn—on t'other side the pulpit."

"I thought he lived in London?"

"Well, he does. Where *would* he live?"

"But I thought *you* lived in Sheffield?"

I see I was up a stump. I had to let on to get choked with a chicken-bone, so as to get time to think how to get down again. Then I says:

"I mean he goes to our church regular when he's in Sheffield. That's only in the summer-time, when he comes there to take the sea baths."

"Why, how you talk—Sheffield ain't on the sea."

"Well, who said it was?"

"Why, you did."

"I *didn't*, nuther."

"You did!"

"I didn't."

"You did."

"I never said nothing of the kind."

"Well, what *did* you say, then?"

"Said he come to take the sea *baths*—that's what I said."

"Well, then, how's he going to take the sea baths if it ain't on the sea?"

"Looky here," I says; "did you ever see any Congress-water?"

"Yes."

"Well, did you have to go to Congress to get it?"

"Why, no."

"Well, neither does William Fourth have to go to the sea to get a sea bath."

"How does he get it, then?"

"Gets it the way people down here gets Congress-water—in barrels. There in the pal-ace at Sheffield they've got furnaces, and he wants his water hot. They can't bile that amount of water away off there at the sea. They haven't got no conveniences for it."

"Oh, I see, now. You might 'a' said that in the first place and saved time."

When she said that I see I was out of the woods again, and so I was comfortable and glad. Next, she says:

"Do you go to church, too?"

"Yes—regular."

"Where do you set?"

"Why, in our pew."

"*Whose* pew?"

"Why, *ourn*—your Uncle Harvey's."

"His'n? What does *he* want with a pew?"

"Wants it to set in. What did you *reckon* he wanted with it?"

"Why, I thought he'd be in the pulpit."

Rot him, I forgot he was a preacher. I see I was up a stump again, so I played another chicken-bone and got another think. Then I says:

"Blame it, do you suppose there ain't but one preacher to a church?"

"Why, what do they want with more?"

"What!—to preach before a king? I never did see such a girl as you. They don't have no less than seventeen."

"Seventeen! My land! Why, I wouldn't set out such a string as that, not if I *never* got to glory. It must take 'em a week."

"Shucks, they don't *all* of 'em preach the same day—only *one* of 'em."

"Well, then, what does the rest of 'em do?"

"Oh, nothing much. Loll around, pass the plate—and one thing or another. But mainly they don't do nothing."

"Well, then, what are they *for*?"

"Why, they're for *style*. Don't you know nothing?"

"Well, I don't *want* to know no such fool-ishness as that. How is servants treated in England? Do they treat 'em better 'n we treat our niggers?"

"*No!* A servant ain't nobody there. They treat them worse than dogs."

"Don't they give 'em holidays, the way we do, Christmas and New Year's week, and Fourth of July?"

"Oh, just listen! A body could tell *you* hain't ever been to England by that. Why, Hare-l—why, Joanna, they never see a holiday from year's end to year's end; never go to the circus, nor theater, nor nigger shows, nor nowheres."

"Nor church?"

"Nor church."

"But *you* always went to church."

Well, I was gone up again. I forgot I was the old man's servant. But next minute I whirled in on a kind of an explanation how a valley was different from a common servant, and *had* to go to church whether he wanted to or not, and set with the family, on account of its being the law. But I didn't do it pretty good, and when I got done I see she warn't satisfied. She says:

"Honest injun, now, hain't you been telling me a lot of lies?"

"Honest injun," says I.

"None of it at all?"

"None of it at all. Not a lie in it," says I.

"Lay your hand on this book and say it."

I see it warn't nothing but a dictionary, so I laid my hand on it and said it. So then she looked a little better satisfied, and says:

"Well, then, I'll believe some of it; but I hope to gracious if I'll believe the rest."

"What is it you won't believe, Jo?" says Mary Jane, stepping in with Susan behind her. "It ain't right nor kind for you to talk so to him, and him a stranger and so far from his people. How would you like to be treated so?"

"That's always your way, Maim—always sailing in to help somebody before they're hurt. I hain't done nothing to him. He's told some stretchers, I reckon, and I said I wouldn't swallow it all; and that's every bit and grain I *did* say. I reckon he can stand a little thing like that, can't he?"

"I don't care whether 'twas little or whether 'twas big; he's here in our house and a stranger, and it wasn't good of you to say it. If you was in his place it would make you feel ashamed; and so you oughtn't to say a thing to another person that will make *them* feel ashamed."

"Why, Maim, he said—"

"It don't make no difference what he *said*—that ain't the thing. The thing is for you to treat him *kind,* and not be saying things to make him remember he ain't in his own coun-try and amongst his own folks."

I says to myself, *this* is a girl that I'm letting that old reptile rob her of her money!

Then Susan *she* waltzed in; and if you'll believe me, she did give Hare-lip hark from the tomb!

Says I to myself, and this is *another* one that I'm letting him rob her of her money!

Then Mary Jane she took another inning, and went in sweet and lovely again—which was her way; but when she got done there warn't hardly anything left o' poor Hare-lip. So she hollered.

"All right, then," says the other girls; "you just ask his pardon."

She done it, too; and she done it beautiful. She done it so beautiful it was good to hear; and I wished I could tell her a thousand lies, so she could do it again.

I says to myself, this is *another* one that I'm letting him rob her of her money. And when she got through they all jest laid theirselves out to make me feel at home and know I was amongst friends. I felt so ornery and low down and mean that I says to myself, my mind's made up; I'll hive that money for them or bust.

So then I lit out—for bed, I said, meaning some time or another. When I got by myself I went to thinking the thing over. I says to myself, shall I go to that doctor, private, and blow on these frauds? No—that won't do. He might tell who told him; then the king and the duke would make it warm for me. Shall I go, private, and tell Mary Jane? No—I dasn't do it. Her face would give them a hint, sure; they've got the money, and they'd slide right out and get away with it. If she was to fetch in help I'd get mixed up in the business before it was done with, I judge. No; there ain't no good way but one. I got to steal that money, somehow; and I got to steal it some way that they won't suspicion that I done it. They've got a good thing here, and they ain't a-going to leave till they've played this family and this town for all they're worth, so I'll find a chance time enough. I'll steal it and hide it; and by and by, when I'm away down the river, I'll write a letter and tell Mary Jane where it's hid. But I better hive it tonight if I can, because the doctor maybe hasn't let up as much as he lets on he has; he might scare them out of here yet.

So, thinks I, I'll go and search them rooms. Up-stairs the hall was dark, but I found the duke's room, and started to paw around it with my hands; but I recollected it wouldn't be much like the king to let anybody else take care of that money but his own self; so then I went to his room and begun to paw around there. But I see I couldn't do nothing without a candle, and I dasn't light one, of course. So I judged I'd got to do the other thing—lay for them and eavesdrop. About that time I hears their footsteps coming, and was going to skip under the bed; I reached for it, but it wasn't where I thought it would be; but I touched the curtain that hid Mary Jane's frocks, so I jumped in behind that and snuggled in amongst the gowns, and stood there perfectly still.

They come in and shut the door; and the first thing the duke done was to get down and look under the bed. Then I was glad I hadn't found the bed when I wanted it. And yet, you know, it's kind of natural to hide under the bed when you are up to anything private. They sets down then, and the king says:

"Well, what is it? And cut it middlin' short, because it's better for us to be down there a-whooping up the mournin' than up here givin' 'em a chance to talk us over."

"Well, this is it, Capet. I ain't easy; I ain't comfortable. That doctor lays on my mind. I wanted to know your plans. I've got a notion, and I think it's a sound one."

"What is it, duke?"

"That we better glide out of this before three in the morning, and clip it down the river with what we've got. Specially, seeing we got it so easy—*given* back to us, flung at our heads, as you may say, when of course we allowed to have to steal it back. I'm for knocking off and lighting out."

That made me feel pretty bad. About an hour or two ago it would 'a' been a little different, but now it made me feel bad and disappointed. The king rips out and says:

"What! And not sell out the rest o' the property? March off like a passel of fools and leave eight or nine thous'n' dollars' worth o' property layin' around jest sufferin' to be scooped in?—and all good, salable stuff, too."

The duke he grumbled; said the bag of gold was enough, and he didn't want to go no deeper—didn't want to rob a lot of orphans of *everything* they had.

"Why, how you talk!" says the king. "We sha'n't rob 'em of nothing at all but jest this money. The people that *buys* the property is the suff'rers; because as soon 's it's found out 'at we didn't own it—which won't be long after we've slid—the sale won't be valid, and it 'll all go back to the estate. These yer orphans 'll git their house back ag'in, and that's enough for *them;* they're young and spry, and k'n easy earn a livin'. *They* ain't a-goin' to suffer. Why, jest think—there's thous'n's and thous'n's that ain't nigh so well off. Bless you, *they* ain't got noth'n' to complain of."

Well, the king he talked him blind; so at last he give in, and said all right, but said he believed it was blamed foolishness to stay, and that doctor hanging over them. But the king says:

"Cuss the doctor! What do we k'yer for *him?* Hain't we got all the fools in town on our side? And ain't that a big enough majority in any town?"

So they got ready to go down-stairs again. The duke says:

"I don't think we put that money in a good place."

That cheered me up. I'd begun to think I warn't going to get a hint of no kind to help me. The king says:

"Why?"

"Because Mary Jane 'll be in mourning from this out; and first you know the nigger that does up the rooms will get an order to box these duds up and put 'em away; and do you reckon a nigger can run across money and not borrow some of it?"

"Your head's level ag'in, duke," says the king; and he comes a-fumbling under the curtain two or three foot from where I was. I stuck tight to the wall and kept mighty still, though quivery; and I wondered what them fellows would say to me if they catched me; and I tried to think what I'd better do if they did catch me. But the king he got the bag before I could think more than about a half a thought, and he never suspicioned I was around. They took and shoved the bag through a rip in the straw tick that was under the feather-bed, and crammed it in a foot or two amongst the straw and said it was all right now, because a nigger only makes up the feather-bed, and don't turn over the straw tick only about twice a year, and so it warn't in no danger of getting stole now.

But I knowed better. I had it out of there before they was half-way down-stairs. I groped along up to my cubby, and hid it there till I could get a chance to do better. I judged I better hide it outside of the house some-wheres, because if they missed it they would give the house a good ransacking: I knowed that very well. Then I turned in, with my clothes all on; but I couldn't 'a' gone to sleep if I'd 'a' wanted to, I was in such a sweat to get through with the business. By and by I heard the king and the duke come up; so I rolled off my pallet and laid with my chin at the top of my ladder, and waited to see if anything was going to happen. But nothing did.

So I held on till all the late sounds had quit and the early ones hadn't begun yet; and then I slipped down the ladder.

27. DEAD PETER HAS HIS GOLD

I crept to their doors and listened; they was snoring. So I tiptoed along, and got down-stairs all right. There warn't a sound any-wheres. I peeped through a crack of the din-ing-room door, and see the men that was watching the corpse all sound asleep on their chairs. The door was open into the parlor, where the corpse was laying, and there was a candle in both rooms. I passed along, and the parlor door was open; but I see there warn't nobody in there but the remainders of Peter; so I shoved on by; but the front door was locked, and the key wasn't there. Just then I heard somebody coming down the stairs, back behind me. I run in the parlor and took a

swift look around, and the only place I see to hide the bag was in the coffin. The lid was shoved along about a foot, showing the dead man's face down in there, with a wet cloth over it, and his shroud on. I tucked the money-bag in under the lid, just down beyond where his hands was crossed, which made me creep, they was so cold, and then I run back across the room and in behind the door.

The person coming was Mary Jane. She went to the coffin, very soft, and kneeled down and looked in; then she put up her handker-chief, and I see she begun to cry, though I couldn't hear her, and her back was to me. I slid out, and as I passed the dining-room I thought I'd make sure them watchers hadn't seen me; so I looked through the crack, and everything was all right. They hadn't stirred.

I slipped up to bed, feeling ruther blue, on accounts of the thing playing out that way after I had took so much trouble and run so much resk about it. Says I, if it could stay where it is, all right; because when we get down the river a hundred mile or two I could write back to Mary Jane, and she could dig him up again and get it; but that ain't the thing that's going to happen; the thing that's going to happen is, the money'll be found when they come to screw on the lid. Then the king 'll get it again, and it 'll be a long day before he gives anybody another chance to smouch it from him. Of course I *wanted* to slide down and get it out of there, but I dasn't try it. Every minute it was getting earlier now, and pretty soon some of them watchers would begin to stir, and I might get catched—catched with six thousand dollars in my hands that nobody hadn't hired me to take care of. I don't wish to be mixed up in no such business as that, I says to myself.

When I got down-stairs in the morning the parlor was shut up, and the watchers was gone. There warn't nobody around but the family and the widow Bartley and our tribe. I watched their faces to see if anything had been happening, but I couldn't tell.

Towards the middle of the day the under-taker come with his man, and they set the coffin in the middle of the room on a couple of chairs, and then set all our chairs in rows, and borrowed more from the neighbors till the hall and the parlor and the dining-room was full. I see the coffin lid was the way it was before, but I dasn't go to look in under it, with folks around.

Then the people begun to flock in, and the beats and the girls took seats in the front row at the head of the coffin, and for a half an hour the people filed around slow, in single rank, and looked down at the dead man's face a minute, and some dropped in a tear, and it was all very still and solemn, only the girls and the beats holding handkerchiefs to their eyes and keeping their heads bent, and sobbing a little. There warn't no other sound but the scraping of the feet on the floor and blowing noses—because people always blows them more at a funeral than they do at other places except church.

When the place was packed full the undertaker he slid around in his black gloves with his softy soothering ways, putting on the last touches, and getting people and things all ship-shape and comfortable, and making no more sound than a cat. He never spoke; he moved people around, he squeezed in late ones, he opened up passageways, and done it with nods, and signs with his hands. Then he took his place over against the wall. He was the softest, glidingest, stealthiest man I ever see; and there warn't no more smile to him than there is to a ham.

They had borrowed a melodeum—a sick one; and when everything was ready a young woman set down and worked it, and it was pretty skreeky and colicky, and everybody joined in and sung, and Peter was the only one that had a good thing, according to my notion. Then the Reverend Hobson opened up, slow and solemn, and begun to talk; and straight off the most outrageous row busted out in the cellar a body ever heard; it was only one dog, but he made a most powerful racket, and he kept it up right along; the parson he had to stand there, over the coffin, and wait—you couldn't hear yourself think. It was right down awkward, and nobody didn't seem to know what to do. But pretty soon they see that long-legged undertaker make a sign to the preacher as much as to say, "Don't you worry—just depend on me." Then he stooped down and begun to glide along the wall, just his shoulders showing over the people's heads. So he glided along, and the powwow and

racket getting more and more outrageous all the time; and at last, when he had gone around two sides of the room, he disappears down cellar. Then in about two seconds we heard a whack, and the dog he finished up with a most amazing howl or two, and then everything was dead still, and the parson begun his solemn talk where he left off. In a minute or two here comes this undertaker's back and shoulders gliding along the wall again; and so he glided and glided around three sides of the room, and then rose up, and shaded his mouth with his hands, and stretched his neck out towards the preacher, over the people's heads, and says, in a kind of a coarse whisper, *"He had a rat!"* Then he drooped down and glided along the wall again to his place. You could see it was a great satisfaction to the people, because naturally they wanted to know. A little thing like that don't cost nothing, and it's just the little things that makes a man to be looked up to and liked. There warn't no more popular man in town than what that undertaker was.

Well, the funeral sermon was very good, but pison long and tiresome; and then the king he shoved in and got off some of his usual rubbage, and at last the job was through, and the undertaker begun to sneak up on the coffin with his screw-driver. I was in a sweat then, and watched him pretty keen. But he never meddled at all; just slid the lid along as soft as mush, and screwed it down tight and fast. So there I was! I didn't know whether the money was in there or not. So, says I, s'pose somebody has hogged that bag on the sly?—now how do *I* know whether to write to Mary Jane or not? S'pose she dug him up and didn't find nothing, what would she think of me? Blame it, I says, I might get hunted up and jailed; I'd better lay low and keep dark, and not write at all; the thing's awful mixed now; trying to better it, I've worsened it a hundred times, and I wish to goodness I'd just let it alone, dad fetch the whole business!

They buried him, and we come back home, and I went to watching faces again—I couldn't help it, and I couldn't rest easy. But nothing come of it; the faces didn't tell me nothing.

The king he visited around in the evening, and sweetened everybody up, and made himself ever so friendly; and he give out the idea that his congregation over in England would be in a sweat about him, so he must hurry and settle up the estate right away and leave for home. He was very sorry he was so pushed, and so was everybody; they wished he could stay longer, but they said they could see it couldn't be done. And he said of course him and William would take the girls home with them; and that pleased everybody too, because then the girls would be well fixed and amongst their own relations; and it pleased the girls, too—tickled them so they clean forgot they ever had a trouble in the world; and told him to sell out as quick as he wanted to, they would be ready. Them poor things was that glad and happy it made my heart ache to see them getting fooled and lied to so, but I didn't see no safe way for me to chip in and change the general tune.

Well, blamed if the king didn't bill the house and the niggers and all the property for auction straight off—sale two days after the funeral; but anybody could buy private beforehand if they wanted to.

So the next day after the funeral, along about noontime, the girls' joy got the first jolt. A couple of nigger-traders come along, and the king sold them the niggers reasonable, for three-day drafts as they called it, and away they went, the two sons up the river to Memphis, and their mother down the river to Orleans. I thought them poor girls and them niggers would break their hearts for grief; they cried around each other, and took on so it most made me down sick to see it. The girls said they hadn't ever dreamed of seeing the family separated or sold away from the town. I can't ever get it out of my memory, the sight of them poor miserable girls and niggers hanging around each other's necks and crying; and I reckoned I couldn't 'a' stood it all, but would 'a' had to bust out and tell on our gang if I hadn't knowed the sale warn't no account and the niggers would be back home in a week or two.

The thing made a big stir in the town, too, and a good many come out flatfooted and said it was scandalous to separate the mother and the children that way. It injured the frauds some; but the old fool he bulled right along, spite of all the duke could say or do, and I tell you the duke was powerful uneasy.

Next day was auction day. About broad day in the morning the king and the duke come up in the garret and woke me up, and I see by their look that there was trouble. The king says:

"Was you in my room night before last?"

"No, your majesty"—which was the way I always called him when nobody but our gang warn't around.

"Was you in there yisterday er last night?"

"No, your majesty."

"Honor bright, now—no lies."

"Honor bright, your majesty, I'm telling you the truth. I hain't been a-near your room since Miss Mary Jane took you and the duke and showed it to you."

The duke says:

"Have you seen anybody else go in there?"

"No, your grace, not as I remember, I believe."

"Stop and think."

I studied awhile and see my chance; then I says:

"Well, I see the niggers go in there several times."

Both of them gave a little jump, and looked like they hadn't ever expected it, and then like they *had*. Then the duke says:

"What, *all* of them?"

"No—leastways, not all at once—that is, I don't think I ever see them all come *out* at once but just one time."

"Hello! When was that?"

"It was the day we had the funeral. In the morning. It warn't early, because I overslept. I was just staring down the ladder, and I see them."

"Well, go on, *go* on! What did they do? How'd they act?"

"They didn't do nothing. And they didn't act anyway much, as fur as I see. They tiptoed away; so I seen, easy enough, that they'd shoved in there to do up your majesty's room, or something, s'posing you was up; and found you *warn't* up, and so they was hoping to slide out of the way of trouble without waking you up, if they hadn't already waked you up."

"Great guns, *this* is a go!" says the king; and both of them looked pretty sick and tolerable silly. They stood there a-thinking and scratching their heads a minute, and the duke he bust into a kind of a little raspy chuckle, and says:

"It does beat all how neat the niggers played their hand. They let on to be *sorry* they was going out of this region! And I believed they *was* sorry, and so did you, and so did everybody. Don't ever tell *me* any more that a nigger ain't got any histrionic talent. Why, the way they played that thing it would fool *anybody*. In my opinion, there's a fortune in 'em. If I had capital and a theater, I wouldn't want a better lay-out than that—and here we've gone and sold 'em for a song. Yes, and ain't privileged to sing the song yet. Say, where *is* that song—that draft?"

"In the bank for to be collected. Where *would* it be?"

"Well, *that's* all right then, thank goodness."

Says I, kind of timid-like:

"Is something gone wrong?"

The king whirls on me and rips out:

"None o' your business! You keep your head shet, and mind y'r own affairs—if you got any. Long as you're in this town don't you forget *that*—you hear?" Then he says to the duke, "We got to jest swaller it and say noth'n': mum's the word for *us*."

As they was starting down the ladder the duke he chuckles again, and says:

"Quick sales *and* small profits! It's a good business—yes."

The king snarls around on him and says:

"I was trying to do for the best in sellin' 'em out so quick. If the profits has turned out to be none, lackin' considable, and none to carry, is it my fault any more'n it's yourn?"

"Well, *they'd* be in this house yet and we *wouldn't* if I could 'a' got my advice listened to."

The king sassed back as much as was safe for him, and then swapped around and lit into *me* again. He give me down the banks for not coming and *telling* him I see the niggers come out of his room acting that way—said any fool would 'a' *knowed* something was up. And then waltzed in and cussed *himself* awhile, and said it all come of him not laying late and taking his natural rest that morning, and he'd be blamed if he'd ever do it again. So they went off a-jawing; and I felt dreadful glad I'd worked it all off onto the niggers, and yet hadn't done the niggers no harm by it.

28. OVERREACHING DON'T PAY

By and by it was getting-up time. So I come down the ladder and started for down-stairs; but as I come to the girls' room the door was open, and I see Mary Jane setting by her old hair trunk, which was open and she'd been packing things in it—getting ready to go to England. But she had stopped now with a folded gown in her lap, and had her face in her hands, crying. I felt awful bad to see it; of course anybody would. I went in there and says:

"Miss Mary Jane, you can't a-bear to see people in trouble, and *I* can't—most always. Tell me about it."

So she done it. And it was the niggers—I just expected it. She said the beautiful trip to England was most about spoiled for her; she didn't know *how* she was ever going to be happy there, knowing the mother and the children warn't ever going to see each other no more—and then busted out bitterer than ever, and flung up her hands, and says:

"Oh, dear, dear, to think they ain't *ever* going to see each other any more!"

"But they *will*—and inside of two weeks—and I *know* it!" says I.

Laws, it was out before I could think! And before I could budge she throws her arms around my neck and told me to say it *again*, say it *again*, say it *again*!

I see I had spoke too sudden and said too much, and was in a close place. I asked her to let me think a minute; and she set there, very impatient and excited and handsome, but looking kind of happy and eased-up, like a person that's had a tooth pulled out. So I went to studying it out. I says to myself, I reckon a body that ups and tells the truth when he is in a tight place is taking considerable many resks, though I ain't had no experience, and can't say for certain; but it looks so to me, anyway; and yet here's a case where I'm blest if it don't look to me like the truth is better and actuly *safer* than a lie. I must lay it by in my mind, and think it over some time or other, it's so kind of strange and unregular. I never see nothing like it. Well, I says to myself at last, I'm a-going to chance it; I'll up and tell the truth this time, though it does seem most like setting down on a kag of powder and touching it off just to see where you'll go to. Then I says:

"Miss Mary Jane, is there any place out of town a little ways where you could go and stay three or four days?"

"Yes; Mr. Lothrop's. Why?"

"Never mind why yet. If I'll tell you how I know the niggers will see each other again—inside of two weeks—here in this house—and *prove* how I know it—will you go to Mr. Lothrop's and stay four days?"

"Four days!" she says; "I'll stay a year!"

"All right," I says, "I don't want nothing more out of *you* than just your word—I druther have it than another man's kiss-the-Bible." She smiled and reddened up very sweet, and I says, "If you don't mind it, I'll shut the door—and bolt it."

Then I come back and set down again, and says:

"Don't you holler. Just set still and take it like a man. I got to tell the truth, and you want to brace up, Miss Mary, because it's a bad kind, and going to be hard to take, but there ain't no help for it. These uncles of yourn ain't no uncles at all; they're a couple of frauds—regular dead-beats. There, now we're over the worst of it, you can stand the rest middling easy."

It jolted her up like everything, of course; but I was over the shoal water now, so I went right along, her eyes a-blazing higher and higher all the time, and told her every blame thing, from where we first struck that young fool going up to the steamboat, clear through to where she flung herself onto the king's breast at the front door and he kissed her sixteen or seventeen times—and then up she jumps, with her face afire like sunset, and says:

"The brute! Come, don't waste a minute—not a *second*—we'll have them tarred and feathered, and flung in the river!"

Says I:

"Cert'nly. But do you mean *before* you go to Mr. Lothrop's, or—"

"Oh," she says, "what am I *thinking* about!" she says, and set right down again. "Don't mind what I said—please don't—you *won't*, now, *will* you?" Laying her silky hand on

mine in that kind of a way that I said I would die first. "I never thought, I was so stirred up," she says; "now go on, and I won't do so any more. You tell me what to do, and whatever you say I'll do it."

"Well," I says, "it's a rough gang, them two frauds, and I'm fixed so I got to travel with them a while longer, whether I want to or not—I druther not tell you why; and if you was to blow on them this town would get me out of their claws, and *I'd* be all right; but there'd be another person that you don't know about who'd be in big trouble. Well, we got to save *him*, hain't we? Of course. Well, then, we won't blow on them."

Saying them words put a good idea in my head. I see how maybe I could get me and Jim rid of the frauds; get them jailed here, and then leave. But I didn't want to run the raft in the daytime without anybody aboard to answer questions but me; so I didn't want the plan to begin working till pretty late tonight. I says:

"Miss Mary Jane, I'll tell you what we'll do, and you won't have to stay at Mr. Lothrop's so long, nuther. How fur is it?"

"A little short of four miles—right out in the country, back here."

"Well, that'll answer. Now you go along out there, and lay low till nine or half past tonight, and then get them to fetch you home again—tell them you've thought of something. If you get here before eleven put a candle in this window, and if I don't turn up wait *till* eleven, and *then* if I don't turn up it means I'm gone, and out of the way, and safe. Then you come out and spread the news around, and get these beats jailed."

"Good," she says, "I'll do it."

"And if it just happens so that I don't get away, but get took up along with them, you must up and say I told you the whole thing beforehand, and you must stand by me all you can."

"Stand by you! indeed I will. They sha'n't touch a hair of your head!" she says, and I see her nostrils spread and her eyes snap when she said it, too.

"If I get away I sha'n't be here," I says, "to prove these rapscallions ain't your uncles, and I couldn't do it if I *was* here. I could swear they was beats and bummers, that's all, though that's worth something. Well, there's others can do that better than what I can, and they're people that ain't going to be doubted as quick as I'd be. I'll tell you how to find them. Gimme a pencil and a piece of paper. There—'Royal Nonesuch, Bricksville.' Put it away, and don't lose it. When the court wants to find out something about these two, let them send up to Bricksville and say they've got the man that played the 'Royal Nonesuch,' and ask for some witnesses—why, you'll have that entire town down here before you can hardly wink, Miss Mary. And they'll come a-biling, too."

I judged we had got everything fixed about right now. So I says:

"Just let the auction go right along, and don't worry. Nobody don't have to pay for the things they buy till a whole day after the auction on accounts of the short notice, and they ain't going out of this till they get that money; and the way we've fixed it the sale ain't going to count, and they ain't going to get no money. It's just like the way it was with the niggers —it warn't no sale, and the niggers will be back before long. Why, they can't collect the money for the niggers yet—they're in the worst kind of a fix, Miss Mary."

"Well," she says, "I'll run down to breakfast now, and then I'll start straight for Mr. Lothrop's."

"'Deed, that ain't the ticket, Miss Mary Jane," I says, "by no manner of means; go before breakfast."

"Why?"

"What did you reckon I wanted you to go at all for, Miss Mary?"

"Well, I never thought—and come to think, I don't know. What was it?"

"Why, it's because you ain't one of these leather-face people. I don't want no better book than what your face is. A body can set down and read it off like coarse print. Do you reckon you can go and face your uncles when they come to kiss you good-morning, and never—"

"There, there, don't! Yes, I'll go before breakfast—I'll be glad to. And leave my sisters with them?"

"Yes; never mind about them. They've got to stand it yet awhile. They might suspicion something if all of you was to go. I don't want you to see them, nor your sisters, nor nobody

in this town; if a neighbor was to ask how is your uncles this morning your face would tell something. No, you go right along, Miss Mary Jane, and I'll fix it with all of them. I'll tell Miss Susan to give your love to your uncles and say you've went away for a few hours for to get a little rest and change, or to see a friend, and you'll be back tonight or early in the morning."

"Gone to see a friend is all right, but I won't have my love given to them."

"Well, then, it sha'n't be." It was well enough to tell her so—no harm in it. It was only a little thing to do, and no trouble; and it's the little things that smooths people's roads the most, down here below; it would make Mary Jane comfortable, and it wouldn't cost nothing. Then I says: "There's one more thing—that bag of money."

"Well, they've got that; and it makes me feel pretty silly to think how they got it."

"No, you're out, there. They hain't got it."

"Why, who's got it?"

"I wish I knowed, but I don't. I had it, because I stole it from them; and I stole it to give to you; and I know where I hid it, but I'm afraid it ain't there no more. I'm awful sorry, Miss Mary Jane, I'm just as sorry as I can be; but I done the best I could; I did honest. I come nigh getting caught, and I had to shove it into the first place I come to, and run—and it warn't a good place."

"Oh, stop blaming yourself—it's too bad to do it, and I won't allow it—you couldn't help it; it wasn't your fault. Where did you hide it?"

I didn't want to set her to thinking about her troubles again; and I couldn't seem to get my mouth to tell her what would make her see that corpse laying in the coffin with that bag of money on his stomach. So for a minute I didn't say nothing; then I says:

"I'd ruther not tell you where I put it, Miss Mary Jane, if you don't mind letting me off; but I'll write it for you on a piece of paper, and you can read it along the road to Mr. Lothrop's, if you want to. Do you reckon that 'll do?"

"Oh, yes."

So I wrote: "I put it in the coffin. It was in there when you was crying there, away in the night. I was behind the door, and I was mighty sorry for you, Miss Mary Jane."

It made my eyes water a little to remember her crying there all by herself in the night, and them devils laying there right under her own roof, shaming her and robbing her; and when I folded it up and give it to her I see the water come into her eyes, too; and she shook me by the hand, hard, and says:

"*Good*-by. I'm going to do everything just as you've told me; and if I don't ever see you again, I sha'n't ever forget you, and I'll think of you a many and a many a time, and I'll *pray* for you, too!"—and she was gone.

Pray for me! I reckoned if she knowed me she'd take a job that was more nearer her size. But I bet she done it, just the same—she was just that kind. She had the grit to pray for Judas if she took the notion—there warn't no backdown to her, I judge. You may say what you want to, but in my opinion she had more sand in her than any girl I ever see; in my opinion she was just full of sand. It sounds like flattery, but it ain't no flattery. And when it comes to beauty—and goodness, too—she lays over them all. I hain't ever seen her since that time that I see her go out of that door; no, I hain't ever seen her since, but I reckon I've thought of her a many and a many a million times, and of her saying she would pray for me; and if ever I'd 'a' thought it would do any good for me to pray for *her*, blamed if I wouldn't 'a' done it or bust.

Well, Mary Jane she lit out the back way, I reckon; because nobody see her go. When I struck Susan and the hare-lip, I says:

"What's the name of them people over on t'other side of the river that you all goes to see sometimes?"

They says:

"There's several; but it's the Proctors, mainly."

"That's the name," I says; "I most forgot it. Well, Miss Mary Jane she told me to tell you she's gone over there in a dreadful hurry—one of them's sick."

"Which one?"

"I don't know; leastways, I kinder forgot; but I thinks it's—"

"Sakes alive, I hope it ain't *Hanner*?"

"I'm sorry to say it," I says, "but Hanner's the very one."

"My goodness, and she so well only last week! Is she took bad?"

"It ain't no name for it. They set up with her all night, Miss Mary Jane said, and they don't think she'll last many hours."

"Only think of that, now! What's the matter with her?"

I couldn't think of anything reasonable, right off that way, so I says:

"Mumps."

"Mumps your granny! They don't set up with people that's got the mumps."

"They don't, don't they? You better bet they do with *these* mumps. These mumps is different. It's a new kind, Miss Mary Jane said."

"How's it a new kind?"

"Because it's mixed up with other things."

"What other things?"

"Well, measles, and whooping-cough, and erysiplas, and consumption, and yaller janders, and brain fever, and I don't know what all."

"My land! And they call it the *mumps*?"

"That's what Miss Mary Jane said."

"Well, what in the nation do they call it the *mumps* for?"

"Why, because it *is* the mumps. That's what it starts with."

"Well, ther' ain't no sense in it. A body might stump his toe, and take pison, and fall down the well, and break his neck, and bust his brains out, and somebody come along and ask what killed him, and some numskull up and say, 'Why, he stumped his *toe*.' Would ther' be any sense in that? *No.* And ther' ain't no sense in *this*, nuther. Is it ketching?"

"Is it *ketching*? Why, how you talk. Is a *harrow* catching—in the dark? If you don't hitch on to one tooth, you're bound to on another, ain't you? And you can't get away with that tooth without fetching the whole harrow along, can you? Well, these kind of mumps is a kind of a harrow, as you may say—and it ain't no slouch of a harrow, nuther, you come to get it hitched on good."

"Well, it's awful, *I* think," says the hare-lip. "I'll go to Uncle Harvey and—"

"Oh, yes," I says, "I *would*. Of *course* I would. I wouldn't lose no time."

"Well, why wouldn't you?"

"Just look at it a minute, and maybe you can see. Hain't your uncles obleeged to get along home to England as fast as they can? And do you reckon they'd be mean enough to go off and leave you to go all that journey by yourselves? *You* know they'll wait for you. So fur, so good. Your Uncle Harvey's a preacher, ain't he? Very well, then; is a *preacher* going to deceive a steamboat clerk? is he going to deceive a *ship clerk?*—so as to get them to let Miss Mary Jane go aboard? Now *you* know he ain't. What *will* he do, then? Why, he'll say, 'It's a great pity, but my church matters has got to get along the best way they can; for my niece has been exposed to the dreadful pluribus-unum mumps, and so it's my bounden duty to set down here and wait the three months it takes to show on her if she's got it.' But never mind, if you think it's best to tell your Uncle Harvey—"

"Shucks, and stay fooling around here when we could all be having good times in England whilst we was waiting to find out whether Mary Jane's got it or not? Why, you talk like a muggins."

"Well, anyway, maybe you'd better tell some of the neighbors."

"Listen at that, now. You do beat all for natural stupidity. Can't you *see* that *they'd* go and tell? Ther' ain't no way but just to not tell anybody at *all*."

"Well, maybe you're right—yes, I judge you *are* right."

"But I reckon we ought to tell Uncle Harvey she's gone out awhile, anyway, so he won't be uneasy about her?"

"Yes, Miss Mary Jane she wanted you to do that. She says, 'Tell them to give Uncle Harvey and William my love and a kiss, and say I've run over the river to see Mr.'—Mr.—what *is* the name of that rich family your uncle Peter used to think so much of?—I mean the one that—"

"Why, you must mean the Apthorps, ain't it?"

"Of course; bother them kind of names, a body can't ever seem to remember them, half the time, somehow. Yes, she said, say she has run over for to ask the Apthorps to be sure and come to the auction and buy this house, because she allowed her uncle Peter would ruther they had it than anybody else; and she's going to stick to them till they say they'll come, and then, if she ain't too tired, she's

coming home; and if she is, she'll be home in the morning anyway. She said, don't say nothing about the Proctors, but only about the Apthorps—which 'll be perfectly true, because she *is* going there to speak about their buying the house; I know it, because she told me so herself."

"All right," they said, and cleared out to lay for their uncles, and give them the love and the kisses, and tell them the message.

Everything was all right now. The girls wouldn't say nothing because they wanted to go to England; and the king and the duke would ruther Mary Jane was off working for the auction than around in reach of Doctor Robinson. I felt very good; I judged I had done it pretty neat—I reckoned Tom Sawyer couldn't 'a' done it no neater himself. Of course he would 'a' throwed more style into it, but I can't do that very handy, not being brung up to it.

Well, they held the auction in the public square, along towards the end of the afternoon, and it strung along, and strung along, and the old man he was on hand and looking his level pisonest, up there longside of the auctioneer, and chipping in a little Scripture now and then, or a little goody-goody saying of some kind, and the duke he was around goo-gooing for sympathy all he knowed how, and just spreading himself generly.

But by and by the thing dragged through, and everything was sold—everything but a little old trifling lot in the graveyard. So they'd got to work *that* off—I never see such a girafft as the king was for wanting to swallow *every thing*. Well, whilst they was at it a steamboat landed, and in about two minutes up comes a crowd a-whooping and yelling and laughing and carrying on, and singing out:

"*Here's* your opposition line! here's your two sets o' heirs to old Peter Wilks—and you pays your money and you takes your choice!"

29. I LIGHT OUT IN THE STORM

They was fetching a very nice-looking old gentleman along, and a nice-looking younger one, with his right arm in a sling. And, my souls, how the people yelled and laughed, and kept it up. But I didn't see no joke about it, and I judged it would strain the duke and the king some to see any. I reckoned they'd turn pale. But no, nary a pale did *they* turn. The duke he never let on he suspicioned what was up, but just went a goo-gooing around, happy and satisfied, like a jug that's googling out buttermilk; and as for the king, he just gazed and gazed down sorrowful on them new-comers like it give him the stomache-ache in his very heart to think there could be such frauds and rascals in the world. Oh, he done it admirable. Lots of the principal people gethered around the king, to let him see they was on his side. That old gentleman that had just come looked all puzzled to death. Pretty soon he begun to speak, and I see straight off he pronounced *like* an Englishman—not the king's way, though the king's *was* pretty good for an imitation. I can't give the old gent's words, nor I can't imitate him; but he turned around to the crowd, and says, about like this:

"This is a surprise to me which I wasn't looking for; and I'll acknowledge, candid and frank, I ain't very well fixed to meet it and answer it; for my brother and me has had mis-fortunes; he's broke his arm, and our baggage got put off at a town above here last night in the night by a mistake. I am Peter Wilks's brother Harvey, and this is his brother Wil-liam, which can't hear nor speak—and can't even make signs to amount to much, now't he's only got one hand to work them with. We are who we say we are; and in a day or two, when I get the baggage, I can prove it. But up till then I won't say nothing more, but go to the hotel and wait."

So him and the new dummy started off; and the king he laughs, and blethers out:

"Broke his arm—*very* likely, *ain't* it?—and very convenient, too, for a fraud that's got to make signs, and ain't learnt how. Lost their baggage! That's *mighty* good!—and mighty ingenious—under the *circumstances!*"

So he laughed again; and so did everybody else, except three or four, or maybe half a dozen. One of these was that doctor; another one was a sharp-looking gentleman, with a carpet-bag of the old-fashioned kind made out of carpet-stuff, that had just come off of the steamboat and was talking to him in a low voice, and glancing towards the king now and then and nodding their heads—it was Levi Bell, the lawyer that was gone up to Louis-

ville; and another one was a big rough husky that come along and listened to all the old gentlemen said, and was listening to the king now. And when the king got done this husky up and says:

"Say, looky here; if you are Harvey Wilks, when'd you come to this town?"

"The day before the funeral, friend," says the king.

"But what time o' day?"

"In the evenin'—'bout an hour er two before sundown."

"How'd you come?"

"I come down on the *Susan Powell* from Cincinnati."

"Well, then, how'd you come to be up at the Pint in the *mornin'*—in a canoe?"

"I warn't up at the Pint in the mornin'."

"It's a lie."

Several of them jumped for him and begged him not to talk that way to an old man and a preacher.

"Preacher be hanged, he's a fraud and a liar. He was up at the Pint that mornin'. I live up there, don't I? Well, I was up there, and he was up there. I *see* him there. He come in a canoe, along with Tim Collins and a boy."

The doctor he up and says:

"Would you know the boy again if you was to see him, Hines?"

"I reckon I would, but I don't know. Why, yonder he is, now. I know him perfectly easy."

It was me he pointed at. The doctor says:

"Neighbors, I don't know whether the new couple is frauds or not; but if *these* two ain't frauds, I am an idiot, that's all. I think it's our duty to see that they don't get away from here till we've looked into this thing. Come along, Hines; come along, the rest of you. We'll take these fellows to the tavern and affront them with t'other couple, and I reckon we'll find out *something* before we get through."

It was nuts for the crowd, though maybe not for the king's friends; so we all started. It was about sundown. The doctor he led me along by the hand, and was plenty kind enough, but he never let *go* my hand.

We all got in a big room in the hotel, and lit up some candles, and fetched in the new couple. First, the doctor says:

"I don't wish to be too hard on these two

men, but *I* think they're frauds, and they may have complices that we don't know nothing about. If they have, won't the complices get away with that bag of gold Peter Wilks left? It ain't unlikely. If these men ain't frauds, they won't object to sending for that money and letting us keep it till they prove they're all right—ain't that so?"

Everybody agreed to that. So I judged they had our gang in a pretty tight place right at the outstart. But the king he only looked sorrowful, and says:

"Gentlemen, I wish the money was there, for I ain't got no disposition to throw anything in the way of a fair, open, out-and-out investigation o' this misable business; but, alas, the money ain't there; you k'n send and see, if you want to."

"Where is it, then?"

"Well, when my niece give it to me to keep for her I took and hid it inside o' the straw tick o' my bed, not wishin' to bank it for the few days we'd be here, and considerin' the bed a safe place, we not bein' used to niggers, and suppos'n' 'em honest, like servants in England. The niggers stole it the very next mornin' after I had went down-stairs; and when I sold 'em I hadn't missed the money yit, so they got clean away with it. My servant here k'n tell you 'bout it, gentlemen."

The doctor and several said "Shucks!" and I see nobody didn't altogether believe him. One man asked me if I see the niggers steal it. I said no, but I see them sneaking out of the room and hustling away, and I never thought nothing, only I reckoned they was afraid they had waked up my master and was trying to get away before he made trouble with them. That was all they asked me. Then the doctor whirls on me and says:

"Are *you* English, too?"

I says yes; and him and some others laughed, and said, "Stuff!"

Well, then they sailed in on the general investigation, and there we had it, up and down, hour in, hour out, and nobody never said a word about supper, nor ever seemed to think about it—and so they kept it up, and kept it up; and it *was* the worst mixed-up thing you ever see. They made the king tell his yarn, and they made the old gentleman tell his'n; and anybody but a lot of prejudiced chuckle-heads would 'a' *seen* that the old gentleman was spinning truth and t'other one lies. And by and by they had me up to tell what I knowed. The king he give me a left-handed look out of the corner of his eye, and so I knowed enough to talk on the right side. I begun to tell about Sheffield, and how we lived there, and all about the English Wilkses, and so on; but I didn't get pretty fur till the doctor begun to laugh; and Levi Bell, the lawyer, says:

"Set down, my boy; I wouldn't strain myself if I was you. I reckon you ain't used to lying, it don't seem to come handy; what you want is practice. You do it pretty awkward."

I didn't care nothing for the compliment, but I was glad to be let off, anyway.

The doctor he started to say something, and turns and says:

"If you'd been in town at first, Levi Bell—"

The king broke in and reached out his hand, and says:

"Why, is this my poor dead brother's old friend that he's wrote so often about?"

The lawyer and him shook hands, and the lawyer smiled and looked pleased, and they talked right along awhile, and then got to one side and talked low; and at last the lawyer speaks up and says:

"That 'll fix it. I'll take the order and send it, along with your brother's, and then they'll know it's all right."

So they got some paper and a pen, and the king he set down and twisted his head to one side, and chawed his tongue, and scrawled off something; and then they give the pen to the duke—and then for the first time the duke looked sick. But he took the pen and wrote. So then the lawyer turns to the new old gentleman and says:

"You and your brother please write a line or two and sign your names."

The old gentleman wrote, but nobody couldn't read it. The lawyer looked powerful astonished, and says:

"Well, it beats *me*—" and snaked a lot of old letters out of his pocket, and examined them, and then examined the old man's writing, and then *them* again; and then says: "These old letters is from Harvey Wilks; and here's *these* two handwritings, and anybody can see *they* didn't write them" (the king and the duke looked sold and foolish, I tell you, to see how the lawyer had took them in), "and here's *this* old gentleman's handwriting, and anybody can tell, easy enough, *he* didn't write them—fact is, the scratches he makes ain't properly *writing* at all. Now, here's some letters from—"

The new old gentleman says:

"If you please, let me explain. Nobody can read my hand but my brother there—so he copies for me. It's *his* hand you've got there, not mine."

"*Well!*" says the lawyer, "this *is* a state of things. I've got some of William's letters, too; so if you'll get him to write a line or so we can com—"

"He *can't* write with his left hand," says the old gentleman. "If he could use his right hand, you would see that he wrote his own letters and mine too. Look at both, please—they're by the same hand."

The lawyer done it, and says:

"I believe it's so—and if it ain't so, there's a heap stronger resemblance than I'd noticed before, anyway. Well, well, well! I thought we was right on the track of a solution, but it's gone to grass, partly. But anyway, *one* thing is proved—*these* two ain't either of 'em Wilkses"—and he wagged his head towards the king and the duke.

Well, what do you think? That mule-headed old fool wouldn't give in *then!* Indeed he wouldn't. Said it warn't no fair test. Said his brother William was the cussedest joker in the world, and hadn't *tried* to write—he see William was going to play one of his jokes the minute he put the pen to paper. And so he warmed up and went warbling right along till he was actuly beginning to believe what he was saying *himself;* but pretty soon the new gentleman broke in, and says:

"I've thought of something. Is there anybody here that helped to lay out my br—helped to lay out the late Peter Wilks for burying?"

"Yes," says somebody, "me and Ab Turner done it. We're both here."

Then the old man turns toward the king, and says:

"Peraps this gentleman can tell me what was tattooed on his breast?"

Blamed if the king didn't have to brace up mighty quick, or he'd 'a' squshed down like a bluff bank that the river has cut under, it took him so sudden; and, mind you, it was a thing that was calculated to make most *anybody* sqush to get fetched such a solid one as that without any notice, because how was *he* going to know what was tattooed on the man? He whitened a little; he couldn't help it; and it was mighty still in there, and everybody bending a little forwards and gazing at him. Says I to myself, *Now* he'll throw up the sponge—there ain't no more use. Well, did he? A body can't hardly believe it, but he didn't. I reckon he thought he'd keep the thing up till he tired them people out, so they'd thin out, and him and the duke could break loose and get away. Anyway, he set there, and pretty soon he begun to smile, and says:

"Mf! It's a *very* tough question, *ain't it!* Yes, sir, I k'n tell you what's tattooed on his breast. It's jest a small, thin, blue arrow—that's what it is; and if you don't look close, you can't see it. *Now* what do you say—hey?"

Well, *I* never see anything like that old blister for clean out-and-out cheek.

The new old gentleman turns brisk towards Ab Turner and his pard, and his eye lights up like he judged he'd got the king *this* time, and says:

"There—you've heard what he said! Was there any such mark on Peter Wilks's breast?"

Both of them spoke up and says:

"We didn't see no such mark."

"Good!" says the old gentleman. "Now, what you *did* see on his breast was a small dim P, and a B (which is an initial he dropped when he was young), and a W, and dashes between them, so: P—B—W"—and he marked them that way on a piece of paper. "Come, ain't that what you saw?"

Both of them spoke up again, and says:

"No, we *didn't*. We never seen any marks at all."

Well, everybody *was* in a state of mind now, and they sings out:

"The whole *bilin'* of 'm 's frauds! Le's duck 'em! le's drown 'em! le's ride 'em on a rail!" and everybody was whooping at once, and there was a rattling powwow. But the lawyer he jumps on the table and yells, and says:

"Gentlemen—gentle*men!* Hear me just a

word—just a *single* word—if you PLEASE! There's one way yet—let's go and dig up the corpse and look."

That took them.

"Hooray!" they all shouted, and was starting right off; but the lawyer and the doctor sung out:

"Hold on, hold on! Collar all these four men and the boy, and fetch *them* along, too!"

"We'll do it!" they all shouted; "and if we don't find them marks we'll lynch the whole gang!"

I *was* scared, now, I tell you. But there warn't no getting away, you know. They gripped us all, and marched us right along, straight for the graveyard, which was a mile and a half down the river, and the whole town at our heels, for we made noise enough, and it was only nine in the evening.

As we went by our house I wished I hadn't sent Mary Jane out of town; because now if I could tip her the wink she'd light out and save me, and blow on our dead-beats.

Well, we swarmed along down the river road, just carrying on like wildcats; and to make it more scary the sky was darking up, and the lightning beginning to wink and flitter, and the wind to shiver amongst the leaves. This was the most awful trouble and most dangersome I ever was in; and I was kinder stunned; everything was going so different from what I had allowed for; stead of being fixed so I could take my own time if I wanted to, and see all the fun, and have Mary Jane at my back to save me and set me free when the close-fit come, here was nothing in the world betwixt me and sudden death but just them tattoo-marks. If they didn't find them—

I couldn't bear to think about it; and yet, somehow, I couldn't think about nothing else. It got darker and darker, and it was a beautiful time to give the crowd the slip; but that big husky had me by the wrist—Hines—and a body might as well try to give Goliar the slip. He dragged me right along, he was so excited, and I had to run to keep up.

When they got there they swarmed into the graveyard and washed over it like an overflow. And when they got to the grave they found they had about a hundred times as many shovels as they wanted, but nobody hadn't thought to fetch a lantern. But they sailed into digging anyway by the flicker of the lightning, and sent a man to the nearest house, a half a mile off, to borrow one.

So they dug and dug like everything; and it got awful dark, and the rain started, and the wind swished and swushed along, and the lightning come brisker and brisker, and the thunder boomed; but them people never took no notice of it, they was so full of this business; and one minute you could see everything and every face in that big crowd, and the shovelfuls of dirt sailing up out of the grave, and the next second the dark wiped it all out, and you couldn't see nothing at all.

At last they got out the coffin and begun to unscrew the lid, and then such another crowding and shouldering and shoving as there was, to scrouge in and get a sight, you never see; and in the dark, that way, it was awful. Hines he hurt my wrist dreadful pulling and tugging so, and I reckon he clean forgot I was in the world, he was so excited and panting.

All of a sudden the lightning let go a perfect sluice of white glare, and somebody sings out:

"By the living jingo, here's the bag of gold on his breast!"

Hines let out a whoop, like everybody else, and dropped my wrist and give a big surge to bust his way in and get a look, and the way I lit out and shinned for the road in the dark there ain't nobody can tell.

I had the road all to myself, and I fairly flew—leastways, I had it all to myself except the solid dark, and the now-and-then glares, and the buzzing of the rain, and the thrashing of the wind, and the splitting of the thunder; and sure as you are born I did clip it along!

When I struck the town I see there warn't nobody out in the storm, so I never hunted for no back streets, but humped it straight through the main one; and when I begun to get towards our house I aimed my eye and set it. No light there; the house all dark—which made me feel sorry and disappointed, I didn't know why. But at last, just as I was sailing by, *flash* comes the light in Mary Jane's window! and my heart swelled up sudden, like to bust; and the same second the house and all was behind me in the dark, and wasn't ever going to be before me no more in this world. She *was* the best girl I ever see, and had the most sand.

The minute I was far enough above the town to see I could make the towhead, I begun to look sharp for a boat to borrow, and the first time the lightning showed me one that wasn't chained I snatched it and shoved. It was a canoe, and warn't fastened with nothing but a rope. The towhead was a rattling big distance off, away out there in the middle of the river, but I didn't lose no time; and when I struck the raft at last I was so fagged I would 'a' just laid down to blow and gasp if I could afforded it. But I didn't. As I sprung aboard I sung out:

"Out with you, Jim, and set her loose! Glory be to goodness, we're shut of them!"

Jim lit out, and was a-coming for me with both arms spread, he was so full of joy; but when I glimpsed him in the lightning my heart shot up in my mouth and I went overboard backwards; for I forgot he was old King Lear and a drownded A-rab all in one, and it most scared the livers and lights out of me. But Jim fished me out, and was going to hug me and bless me, and so on, he was so glad I was back and we was shut of the king and the duke, but I says:

"Not now; have it for breakfast, have it for breakfast! Cut loose and let her slide!"

So in two seconds away we went a-sliding down the river, and it *did* seem so good to be free again and all by ourselves on the big river, and nobody to bother us. I had to skip around a bit, and jump up and crack my heels a few times—I couldn't help it; but about the third crack I noticed a sound that I knowed mighty well, and held my breath and listened and waited; and sure enough, when the next flash busted out over the water, here they come!—and just a-laying to their oars and making their skiff hum! It was the king and duke.

So I wilted right down onto the planks then, and give up; and it was all I could do to keep from crying.

30. THE GOLD SAVES THE THIEVES

When they got aboard the king went for me, and shook me by the collar, and says:

"Tryin' to give us the slip, was ye, you pup! Tired of our company, hey?"

I says:

"No, your majesty, we warn't—*please* don't, your majesty!"

"Quick, then, and tell us what *was* your idea, or I'll shake the insides out o' you!"

"Honest, I'll tell you everything just as it happened, your majesty. The man that had a-holt of me was very good to me, and kept saying he had a boy about as big as me that died last year, and he was sorry to see a boy in such a dangerous fix; and when they was all took by surprise by finding the gold, and made a rush for the coffin, he lets go of me and whispers, 'Heel it now, or they'll hang ye, sure!' and I lit out. It didn't seem no good for *me* to stay—I couldn't do nothing, and I didn't want to be hung if I could get away. So I never stopped running till I found the canoe; and when I got here I told Jim to hurry, or they'd catch me and hang me yet, and said I was afeared you and the duke wasn't alive now, and I was awful sorry, and so was Jim, and was awful glad when we see you coming; you may ask Jim if I didn't."

Jim said it was so; and the king told him to shut up, and said, "Oh, yes, it's *mighty* likely!" and shook me up again, and said he reckoned he'd drownd me. But the duke says:

"Leggo the boy, you old idiot! Would *you* 'a' done any different? Did you inquire around for *him* when you got loose? *I* don't remember it."

So the king let go of me, and begun to cuss that town and everybody in it. But the duke says:

"You better a blame' sight give *yourself* a good cussing, for you're the one that's entitled to it most. You hain't done a thing from the start that had any sense in it, except coming out so cool and cheeky with that imaginary blue-arrow mark. That *was* bright—it was right down bully; and it was the thing that saved us. For if it hadn't been for that they'd 'a' jailed us till them Englishmen's baggage come—and then—the penitentiary, you bet! But that trick took 'em to the graveyard, and the gold done us a still bigger kindness; for if the excited fools hadn't let go all holts and made that rush to get a look we'd 'a' slept in our cravats tonight—cravats warranted to *wear*, too—longer than *we'd* need 'em."

They was still a minute—thinking; then the king says, kind of absent-minded like:

"Mf! And we reckoned the *niggers* stole it!"

That made me squirm!

"Yes," says the duke, kinder slow and deliberate and sarcastic, "*we* did."

After about a half a minute the king drawls out:

"Leastways, *I* did."

The duke says, the same way:

"On the contrary, *I* did."

The king kind of ruffles up, and says:

"Looky here, Bilgewater, what'r you referrin' to?" The duke says, pretty brisk:

"When it comes to that, maybe you'll let me ask what was *you* referring to?"

"Shucks!" says the king, very sarcastic; "but *I* don't know—maybe you was asleep, and didn't know what you was about."

The duke bristles up now, and says:

"Oh, let *up* on this cussed nonsense; do you take me for a blame' fool? Don't you reckon *I* know who hid that money in that coffin?"

"*Yes,* sir! I know you *do* know, because you done it yourself!"

"It's a lie!"—and the duke went for him. The king sings out:

"Take y'r hands off!—leggo my throat!—I take it all back!"

The duke says:

"Well, you just own up, first, that you *did* hide that money there, intending to give me the slip one of these days, and come back and dig it up, and have it all to yourself."

"Wait jest a minute, duke—answer me this one question, honest and fair; if you didn't put the money there, say it, and I'll b'lieve you, and take back everything I said."

"You old scoundrel, I didn't, and you know I didn't. There, now!"

"Well, then, I b'lieve you. But answer me only jest this one more—now *don't* git mad; didn't you have it in your *mind* to hook the money and hide it?"

The duke never said nothing for a little bit; then he says:

"Well, I don't care if I *did*, I didn't *do* it, anyway. But you not only had it in mind to do it, but you *done* it."

"I wisht I never die if I done it, duke, and that's honest. I won't say I warn't *goin'* to do it, because I *was;* but you—I mean somebody—got in ahead o' me."

"It's a lie! You done it, and you got to *say* you done it, or—"

The king began to gurgle, and then he gasps out:

"'Nough!—I *own* up!"

I was very glad to hear him say that; it made me feel much more easier than what I was feeling before. So the duke took his hands off and says:

"If you ever deny it again I'll drown you. It's *well* for you to set there and blubber like a baby—it's fitten for you, after the way you've acted. I never see such an old ostrich for wanting to gobble everything—and I a-trusting you all the time, like you was my own father. You ought to been ashamed of yourself to stand by and hear it saddled on to a lot of poor niggers, and you never say a word for 'em. It makes me feel ridiculous to think I was soft enough to *believe* that rubbage. Cuss you, I can see now why you was so anxious to make up the deffisit—you wanted to get what money I'd got out of the 'Nonesuch' and one thing or another, and scoop it *all!*"

The king says, timid, and still a-snuffling:

"Why, duke, it was you that said make up the deffersit; it warn't me."

"Dry up! I don't want to hear no more *out* of you!" says the duke. "And *now* you see what you *got* by it. They've got all their own money back, and all of *ourn* but a shekel or two *besides*. G'long to bed, and don't you deffersit *me* no more deffersits, long's *you* live!"

So the king sneaked into the wigwam and took to his bottle for comfort; and before long the duke tackled *his* bottle; and so in about a half an hour they was as thick as thieves again, and the tighter they got the lovinger they got, and went off a-snoring in each other's arms. They both got powerful mellow, but I noticed the king didn't get mellow enough to forget to remember to not deny about hiding the money-bag again. That made me feel easy and satisfied. Of course when they got to snoring we had a long gabble, and I told Jim everything.

31. YOU CAN'T PRAY A LIE

We dasn't stop again at any town for days and days; kept right along down the river. We was down south in the warm weather now, and a mighty long ways from home. We begun to come to trees with Spanish moss on them, hanging down from the limbs like long, gray beards. It was the first I ever see it growing, and it made the woods look solemn and dismal. So now the frauds reckoned they was out of danger, and they begun to work the villages again.

First they done a lecture on temperance; but they didn't make enough for them both to get drunk on. Then in another village they started a dancing-school; but they didn't know no more how to dance than a kangaroo does; so the first prance they made the general public jumped in and pranced them out of town. Another time they tried to go at yellocution; but they didn't yellocute long till the audience got up and give them a solid good cussing, and made them skip out. They tackled missionarying, and mesmerizing, and doctoring, and telling fortunes, and a little of everything; but they couldn't seem to have no luck. So at last they got just about dead broke, and laid around the raft as she floated along, thinking and thinking, and never saying nothing, by the half a day at a time, and dreadful blue and desperate.

And at last they took a change and begun to lay their heads together in the wigwam and talk low and confidential two or three hours at a time. Jim and me got uneasy. We didn't like the look of it. We judged they was studying up some kind of worse deviltry than ever. We turned it over and over, and at last we made up our minds they was going to break into somebody's house or store, or was going into the counterfeit-money business, or something. So then we was pretty scared, and made up an agreement that we wouldn't have nothing in the world to do with such actions, and if we ever got the least show we would give them the cold shake and clear out and leave them behind. Well, early one morning we hid the raft in a good, safe place about two mile below a little bit of a shabby village named Pikesville, and the king he went ashore and told us all to stay hid whilst he went up to town and smelt around to see if anybody

had got any wind of the "Royal Nonesuch" there yet. ("House to rob, you *mean*," says I to myself; "and when you get through robbing it you'll come back here and wonder what has become of me and Jim and the raft—and you'll have to take it out in wondering.") And he said if he warn't back by midday the duke and me would know it was all right, and we was to come along.

So we stayed where we was. The duke he fretted and sweated around, and was in a mighty sour way. He scolded us for everything, and we couldn't seem to do nothing right; he found fault with every little thing. Something was a-brewing, sure. I was good and glad when midday come and no king; we could have a change, anyway—and maybe a chance for *the* chance on top of it. So me and the duke went up to the village, and hunted around there for the king, and by and by we found him in the back room of a little low doggery, very tight, and a lot of loafers bullyragging him for sport, and he a-cussing and a-threatening with all his might, and so tight he couldn't walk, and couldn't do nothing to them. The duke he begun to abuse him for an old fool, and the king begun to sass back, and the minute they was fairly at it I lit out and shook the reefs out of my hind legs, and spun down the river road like a deer, for I see our chance; and I made up my mind that it would be a long day before they ever see me and Jim again. I got down there all out of breath but loaded up with joy, and sung out:

"Set her loose, Jim; we're all right now!"

But there warn't no answer, and nobody come out of the wigwam. Jim was gone! I set up a shout—and then another—and then another one; and run this way and that in the woods, whooping and screeching; but it warn't no use—old Jim was gone. Then I set down and cried; I couldn't help it. But I couldn't set still long. Pretty soon I went out on the road, trying to think what I better do, and I run across a boy walking, and asked him if he'd seen a strange nigger dressed so and so, and he says:

"Yes."

"Whereabouts?" says I.

"Down to Silas Phelps's place, two mile below here. He's a runaway nigger, and they've got him. Was you looking for him?"

"You bet I ain't! I run across him in the woods about an hour or two ago, and he said if I hollered he'd cut my livers out—and told me to lay down and stay where I was; and I done it. Been there ever since; afeared to come out."

"Well," he says, "you needn't be afeared no more, becuz they've got him. He run off f'm down South, som'ers."

"It's a good job they got him."

"Well, I *reckon!* There's two hundred dollars' reward on him. It's like picking up money out'n the road."

"Yes, it is—and *I* could 'a' had it if I'd been big enough; I see him *first.* Who nailed him?"

"It was an old fellow—a stranger—and he sold out his chance in him for forty dollars, becuz he's got to go up the river and can't wait. Think o' that, now! You bet *I'd* wait, if it was seven year."

"That's me, every time," says I. "But maybe his chance ain't worth no more than that, if he'll sell it so cheap. Maybe there's something ain't straight about it."

"But it *is,* though—straight as a string. I see the handbill myself. It tells all about him, to a dot—paints him like a picture, and tells the plantation he's frum, below New*r*leans. No-sirree-*bob,* they ain't no trouble 'bout *that* speculation, you bet you. Say, gimme a chaw tobacker, won't ye?"

I didn't have none, so he left. I went to the raft, and set down in the wigwam to think. But I couldn't come to nothing. I thought till I wore my head sore, but I couldn't see no way out of the trouble. After all this long journey, and after all we'd done for them scoundrels, here it was all come to nothing, everything all busted up and ruined, because they could have the heart to serve Jim such a trick as that, and make him a slave again all his life, and amongst strangers, too, for forty dirty dollars.

Once I said to myself it would be a thousand times better for Jim to be a slave at home where his family was, as long as he'd *got* to be a slave, and so I'd better write a letter to Tom Sawyer and tell him to tell Miss Watson where he was. But I soon give up that notion for two things: she'd be mad and disgusted at his rascality and ungratefulness for leaving her, and so she'd sell him straight down the river again; and if she didn't, everybody naturally despises an ungrateful nigger, and they'd make Jim feel it all the time, and so he'd feel ornery and disgraced. And then think of *me!* It would get all around that Huck Finn helped a nigger to get his freedom; and if I was ever to see anybody from that town again I'd be ready to get down and lick his boots for shame. That's just the way: a person does a low-down thing, and then he don't want to take no consequences of it. Thinks as long as he can hide, it ain't no disgrace. That was my fix exactly. The more I studied about this the more my conscience went to grinding me, and the more wicked and low-down and ornery I got to feeling. And at last, when it hit me all of a sudden that here was the plain hand of Providence slapping me in the face and letting me know my wickedness was being watched all the time from up there in heaven, whilst I was stealing a poor old woman's nigger that hadn't ever done me no harm, and now was showing me there's One that's always on the lookout, and ain't a-going to allow no such miserable doings to go only just so fur and no further, I most dropped in my tracks I was so scared. Well, I tried the best I could to kinder soften it up somehow for myself by saying I was brung up wicked, and so I warn't so much to blame; but something inside of me kept saying, "There was the Sunday-school, you could 'a' gone to it; and if you'd 'a' done it they'd 'a' learnt you there that people that acts as I'd been acting about that nigger goes to everlasting fire."

It made me shiver. And I about made up my mind to pray, and see if I couldn't try to quit being the kind of a boy I was and be better. So I kneeled down. But the words wouldn't come. Why wouldn't they? It warn't no use to try and hide it from Him. Nor from *me,* neither. I knowed very well why they wouldn't come. It was because my heart warn't right; it was because I warn't square; it was because I was playing double. I was letting *on* to give up sin, but away inside of me I was holding on to the biggest one of all. I was trying to make my mouth *say* I would do the right thing and the clean thing, and go and write to that nigger's owner and tell where he was; but deep down in me I knowed it was a lie, and He knowed it. You can't pray a lie —I found that out.

So I was full of trouble, full as I could be; and didn't know what to do. At last I had an idea; and I says, I'll go and write the letter— and *then* see if I can pray. Why, it was astonishing, the way I felt as light as a feather right straight off, and my troubles all gone. So I got a piece of paper and a pencil, all glad and excited, and set down and wrote:

Miss Watson, your runaway nigger Jim is down here two mile below Pikesville, and Mr. Phelps has got him and he will give him up for the reward if you send.   HUCK FINN.

I felt good and all washed clean of sin for the first time I had ever felt so in my life, and I knowed I could pray now. But I didn't do it straight off, but laid the paper down and set there thinking—thinking how good it was all this happened so, and how near I come to being lost and going to hell. And went on thinking. And got to thinking over our trip down the river; and I see Jim before me all the time: in the day and in the night-time, sometimes moonlight, sometimes storms, and we a-floating along, talking and singing and laughing. But somehow I couldn't seem to strike no places to harden me against him, but only the other kind. I'd see him standing my watch on top of his'n, 'stead of calling me, so I could go on sleeping; and see him how glad he was when I come back out of the fog; and when I come to him again in the swamp, up there where the feud was; and such-like times; and would always call me honey, and pet me, and do everything he could think of for me, and how good he always was; and at last I struck the time I saved him by telling the men we had small-pox aboard, and he was so grateful, and said I was the best friend old Jim ever had in the world, and the *only* one he's got now; and then I happened to look around and see that paper.

It was a close place. I took it up, and held it in my hand. I was a-trembling, because I'd got to decide, forever, betwixt two things, and I knowed it. I studied a minute, sort of holding my breath, and then says to myself:

"All right, then, I'll *go* to hell"—and tore it up.

It was awful thoughts and awful words, but they was said. And I let them stay said; and never thought no more about reforming. I shoved the whole thing out of my head, and said I would take up wickedness again, which was in my line, being brung up to it, and the other warn't. And for a starter I would go to work and steal Jim out of slavery again; and if I could think up anything worse, I would do that, too; because as long as I was in, and in for good, I might as well go the whole hog.

Then I set to thinking over how to get at it, and turned over some considerable many ways in my mind; and at last fixed up a plan that suited me. So then I took the bearings of a woody island that was down the river a piece, and as soon as it was fairly dark I crept out with my raft and went for it, and hid it there, and then turned in. I slept the night through, and got up before it was light, and had my breakfast, and put on my store clothes, and tied up some others and one thing or another in a bundle, and took the canoe and cleared for shore. I landed below where I judged was Phelps's place, and hid my bundle in the woods, and then filled up the canoe with water, and loaded rocks into her and sunk her where I could find her again when I wanted her, about a quarter of a mile below a little steam-sawmill that was on the bank.

Then I struck up the road, and when I passed the mill I see a sign on it, "Phelps's Sawmill," and when I come to the farm-houses, two or three hundred yards further along, I kept my eyes peeled, but didn't see nobody around, though it was good day-light now. But I didn't mind, because I didn't want to see nobody just yet—I only wanted to get the lay of the land. According to my plan, I was going to turn up there from the village, not from below. So I just took a look, and shoved along, straight for town. Well, the very first man I see when I got there was the duke. He was sticking up a bill for the "Royal Nonesuch" —three-night performance, like that other time. *They* had the cheek, them frauds! I was right on him before I could shirk. He looked astonished, and says:

"Hel-*lo!* where'd *you* come from?" Then he says, kind of glad and eager, "Where's the raft?—got her in a good place?"

I says:

"Why, that's just what I was going to ask your grace."

Then he didn't look so joyful, and says:

"What was your idea for asking *me?*" he says.

"Well," I says, "when I see the king in that doggery yesterday I says to myself, we can't get him home for hours, till he's soberer; so I went a-loafing around town to put in the time and wait. A man up and offered me ten cents to help him pull a skiff over the river and back to fetch a sheep, and so I went along; but when we was dragging him to the boat, and the man left me a-holt of the rope and went behind him to shove him along, he was too strong for me and jerked loose and run, and we after him. We didn't have no dog, and so we had to chase him all over the country till we tired him out. We never got him till dark; then we fetched him over, and I started down for the raft. When I got there and see it was gone, I says to myself, 'They've got into trouble and had to leave; and they've took my nigger, which is the only nigger I've got in the world, and now I'm in a strange country, and ain't got no property no more, nor nothing, and no way to make my living'; so I set down and cried. I slept in the woods all night. But what *did* become of the raft, then?—and Jim—poor Jim!"

"Blamed if *I* know—that is, what's become of the raft. That old fool had made a trade and got forty dollars, and when we found him in the doggery the loafers had matched half-dollars with him and got every cent but what he'd spent for whisky; and when I got him home late last night and found the raft gone, we said, 'That little rascal has stole our raft and shook us, and run off down the river.'"

"I wouldn't shake my *nigger,* would I?—the only nigger I had in the world, and the only property."

"We never thought of that. Fact is, I reckon we'd come to consider him *our* nigger; yes, we did consider him so—goodness knows we had trouble enough for him. So when we see the raft was gone and we flat broke, there warn't anything for it but to try the 'Royal Nonesuch' another shake. And I've pegged along ever since, dry as a powder-horn. Where's that ten cents? Give it here."

I had considerable money, so I give him ten cents, but begged him to spend it for something to eat, and give me some, because it was all the money I had, and I hadn't had nothing to eat since yesterday. He never said nothing. The next minute he whirls on me and says:

"Do you reckon that nigger would blow on us? We'd skin him if he done that!"

"How can he blow? Hain't he run off?"

"No! That old fool sold him, and never divided with me, and the money's gone."

"*Sold* him?" I says, and begun to cry; "why, he was *my* nigger, and that was my money. Where is he?—I want my nigger."

"Well, you can't *get* your nigger, that's all —so dry up your blubbering. Looky here— do you think *you'd* venture to blow on us? Blamed if I think I trust you. Why, if you *was* to blow on us—"

He stopped, but I never seen the duke look so ugly out of his eyes before. I went on a-whimpering, and says:

"I don't want to blow on nobody; and I ain't got no time to blow, nohow; I got to turn out and find my nigger."

He looked kinder bothered, and stood there with his bills fluttering on his arm, thinking, and wrinkling up his forehead. At last he says:

"I'll tell you something. We got to be here three days. If you'll promise you won't blow, and won't let the nigger blow, I'll tell you where to find him."

So I promised, and he says:

"A farmer by the name of Silas Ph—" and then he stopped. You see, he started to tell me the truth; but when he stopped that way, and begun to study and think again, I reckoned he was changing his mind. And so he was. He wouldn't trust me; he wanted to make sure of having me out of the way the whole three days. So pretty soon he says:

"The man that brought him is named Abram Foster—Abram G. Foster—and he lives forty mile back here in the country, on the road to Lafayette."

"All right," I says, "I can walk it in three days. And I'll start this very afternoon."

"No, you won't, you'll start *now;* and don't you lose any time about it, neither, nor do any gabbling by the way. Just keep a tight tongue in your head and move right along, and then you won't get into trouble with *us*, d'ye hear?"

That was the order I wanted, and that was the one I played for. I wanted to be left free to work my plans.

"So clear out," he says; "and you can tell Mr. Foster whatever you want to. Maybe you can get him to believe that Jim *is* your nigger—some idiots don't require documents—leastways I've heard there's such down South here. And when you tell him the handbill and the reward's bogus, maybe he'll believe you when you explain to him what the idea was for getting 'em out. Go 'long now, and tell him anything you want to; but mind you don't work your jaw any *between* here and there."

So I left, and struck for the back country. I didn't look around, but I kinder felt like he was watching me. But I knowed I could tire him out at that. I went straight out in the country as much as a mile before I stopped; then I doubled back through the woods towards Phelps's. I reckoned I better start in on my plan straight off without fooling around, because I wanted to stop Jim's mouth till these fellows could get away. I didn't want no trouble with their kind. I'd seen all I wanted to of them, and wanted to get entirely shut of them.

32. I HAVE A NEW NAME

When I got there it was all still and Sunday-like, and hot and sunshiny; the hands was gone to the fields; and there was them kind of faint dronings of bugs and flies in the air that makes it seem so lonesome and like everybody's dead and gone; and if a breeze fans along and quivers the leaves it makes you feel mournful, because you feel like it's spirits whispering—spirits that's been dead ever so many years—and you always think they're talking about *you*. As a general thing it makes a body wish *he* was dead, too, and done with it all.

Phelps's was one of these little one-horse cotton plantations, and they all look alike. A rail fence round a two-acre yard; a stile made out of logs sawed off and up-ended in steps, like barrels of a different length, to climb over the fence with, and for the women to stand on when they are going to jump onto a horse; some sickly grass-patches in the big yard, but

mostly it was bare and smooth, like an old hat with the nap rubbed off; big double log house for the white folks—hewed logs, with the chinks stopped up with mud or mortar, and these mud-stripes been whitewashed some time or another; round-log kitchen, with a big broad, open but roofed passage joining it to the house; log smokehouse back of the kitchen; three little log nigger cabins in a row t'other side of the smokehouse; one little hut all by itself away down against the back fence, and some outbuildings down a piece the other side; ash-hopper and big kettle to bile soap in by the little hut; bench by the kitchen door, with bucket of water and a gourd; hound asleep there in the sun; more hounds asleep round about; about three shade trees away off in a corner; some currant bushes and gooseberry bushes in one place by the fence; outside of the fence a garden and a watermelon patch; then the cottonfields begins, and after the fields the woods.

I went around and clumb over the back stile by the ash-hopper, and started for the kitchen. When I got a little ways I heard the dim hum of a spinning-wheel wailing along up and sinking along down again; and then I knowed for certain I wished I was dead—for that *is* the lonesomest sound in the whole world.

I went right along, not fixing up any particular plan, but just trusting to Providence to put the right words in my mouth when the time come; for I'd noticed that Providence always did put the right words in my mouth if I left it alone.

When I got half-way, first one hound and then another got up and went for me, and of course I stopped and faced them, and kept still. And such another powwow as they made! In a quarter of a minute I was a kind of a hub of a wheel, as you may say—spokes made out of dogs—circle of fifteen of them packed together around me, with their necks and noses stretched up towards me, a-barking and howling; and more a-coming; you could see them sailing over fences and around corners from everywheres.

A nigger woman come tearing out of the kitchen with a rolling-pin in her hand, singing out, "Begone! *you* Tige! you Spot! begone sah!" and she fetched first one and then another of them a clip and sent them howling, and then the rest followed; and the next second half of them come back, wagging their tails around me, and making friends with me. There ain't no harm in a hound, nohow.

And behind the woman comes a little nigger girl and two little nigger boys without anything on but tow-linen shirts, and they hung on to their mother's gown, and peeped out from behind her at me, bashful, the way they always do. And here comes the white woman running from the house, about forty-five or fifty year old, bareheaded, and her spinning-stick in her hand; and behind her comes her little white children, acting the same way the little niggers was going. She was smiling all over so she could hardly stand— and says:

"It's *you*, at last!—*ain't* it?"

I out with a "Yes'm" before I thought.

She grabbed me and hugged me tight; and then gripped me by both hands and shook and shook; and the tears come in her eyes, and run down over; and she couldn't seem to hug and shake enough, and kept saying, "You don't look as much like your mother as I reckoned you would; but law sakes, I don't care for that, I'm *so* glad to see you! Dear, dear, it does seem like I could eat you up! Children, it's your cousin Tom!—tell him howdy."

But they ducked their heads, and put their fingers in their mouths, and hid behind her. So she run on:

"Lize, hurry up and get him a hot breakfast right away—or did you get your breakfast on the boat?"

I said I had got it on the boat. So then she started for the house, leading me by the hand, and the children tagging after. When we got there she set me down in a split-bottomed chair, and set herself down on a little low stool in front of me, holding both of my hands, and says:

"Now I can have a *good* look at you; and, laws-a-me, I've been hungry for it a many and a many a time, all these long years, and it's come at last! We been expecting you a couple of days and more. What kep' you?— boat get aground?"

"Yes'm—she—"

"Don't say yes'm—say Aunt Sally. Where'd she get aground?"

I didn't rightly know what to say, because I didn't know whether the boat would be coming up the river or down. But I go a good deal on instinct; and my instinct said she would be coming up—from down towards Orleans. That didn't help me much, though; for I didn't know the names of bars down that way. I see I'd got to invent a bar, or forget the name of the one we got aground on—or—Now I struck an idea, and fetched it out:

"It warn't the grounding—that didn't keep us back but a little. We blowed out a cylinder-head."

"Good gracious! anybody hurt?"

"No'm. Killed a nigger."

"Well, it's lucky; because sometimes people do get hurt. Two years ago last Christmas your uncle Silas was coming up from Newrleans on the old *Lally Rook,* and she blowed out a cylinder-head and crippled a man. And I think he died afterwards. He was a Baptist. Your uncle Silas knowed a family in Baton Rouge that knowed his people very well. Yes, I remember now, he *did* die. Mortification set in, and they had to amputate him. But it didn't save him. Yes, it was mortification— that was it. He turned blue all over, and died in the hope of a glorious resurrection. They say he was a sight to look at. Your uncle's been up to the town every day to fetch you. And he's gone again, not more'n an hour ago; he'll be back any minute now. You must 'a' met him on the road, didn't you?—oldish man, with a—"

"No, I didn't see nobody, Aunt Sally. The boat landed just at daylight, and I left my baggage on the wharf-boat and went looking around the town and out a piece in the country, to put in the time and not get here too soon; and so I come down the back way."

"Who'd you give the baggage to?"

"Nobody."

"Why, child, it'll be stole!"

"Not where *I* hid it I reckon it won't," I says.

"How'd you get your breakfast so early on the boat?"

It was kinder thin ice, but I says:

"The captain see me standing around, and told me I better have something to eat before I went ashore; so he took me in the texas to the officers' lunch, and give me all I wanted."

I was getting so uneasy I couldn't listen good. I had my mind on the children all the time; I wanted to get them out to one side and pump them a little, and find out who I was. But I couldn't get no show, Mrs. Phelps kept it up and run on so. Pretty soon she made the cold chills streak all down my back, because she says:

"But here we're a-running on this way, and you hain't told me a word about Sis, nor any of them. Now I'll rest my works a little, and you start up yourn; just tell me *everything*— tell me all about 'm all—every one of 'em; and how they are, and what they're doing, and what they told you to tell me; and every last thing you can think of."

Well, I see I was up a stump—and up it good. Providence had stood by me this fur all right, but I was hard and tight aground now. I see it warn't a bit of use to try to go ahead —I'd *got* to throw up my hand. So I says to myself, here's another place where I got to resk the truth. I opened my mouth to begin; but she grabbed me and hustled me in behind the bed, and says:

"Here he comes! Stick your head down lower—there, that 'll do; you can't be seen now. Don't you let on you're here. I'll play a joke on him. Children, don't you say a word."

I see I was in a fix now. But it warn't no use to worry; there warn't nothing to do but just hold still, and try and be ready to stand from under when the lightning struck.

I had just one little glimpse of the old gentleman when he come in; then the bed hid him. Mrs. Phelps she jumps for him, and says:

"Has he come?"

"No," says her husband.

"Good-*ness* gracious!" she says, "what in the world *can* have become of him?"

"I can't imagine," says the old gentleman; "and I must say it makes me dreadful uneasy."

"Uneasy!" she says; "I'm ready to go distracted! He *must* 'a' come; and you've missed him along the road. I *know* it's so—something *tells* me so."

"Why, Sally, I *couldn't* miss him along the road—*you* know that."

"But oh, dear, dear, what *will* Sis say! He must 'a' come! You must 'a' missed him. He—"

"Oh, don't distress me any more'n I'm already distressed. I don't know what in the world to make of it. I'm at my wit's end, and I don't mind acknowledging 't I'm right down scared. But there's no hope that he's come; for he *couldn't* come and me miss him. Sally, it's terrible—just terrible—something's happened to the boat, sure!"

"Why, Silas! Look yonder!—up the road!— ain't that somebody coming?"

He sprung to the window at the head of the bed, and that give Mrs. Phelps the chance she wanted. She stooped down quick at the foot of the bed and give me a pull, and out I come; and when he turned back from the window there she stood, a-beaming and a-smiling like a house afire, and I standing pretty meek and sweaty alongside. The old gentleman stared, and says:

"Why, who's that?"

"Who do you reckon 'tis?"

"I hain't no idea. Who *is* it?"

"It's *Tom Sawyer!*"

By jings, I most slumped through the floor! But there warn't no time to swap knives; the old man grabbed me by the hand and shook, and kept on shaking; and all the time how the woman did dance around and laugh and cry; and then how they both did fire off questions about Sid, and Mary, and the rest of the tribe.

But if they was joyful, it warn't nothing to what I was; for it was like being born again, I was so glad to find out who I was. Well, they froze to me for two hours; and at last, when my chin was so tired it couldn't hardly go any more, I had told them more about my family—I mean the Sawyer family—than ever happened to any six Sawyer families. And I explained all about how we blowed out a cylinder-head at the mouth of White River and it took us three days to fix it. Which was all right, and worked first-rate; because *they* didn't know but what it would take three days to fix it. If I'd 'a' called it a bolt-head it would 'a' done just as well.

Now I was feeling pretty comfortable all down one side, and pretty uncomfortable all up the other. Being Tom Sawyer was easy and comfortable, and it stayed easy and comfortable till by and by I hear a **steamboat**

coughing along down the river. Then I says
to myself, s'pose Tom Sawyer comes down on
that boat? And s'pose he steps in here any
minute, and sings out my name before I can
throw him a wink to keep quiet?

Well, I couldn't *have* it that way; it
wouldn't do at all. I must go up the road
and waylay him. So I told the folks I reckoned
I would go up to the town and fetch down
my baggage. The old gentleman was for going along with me, but I said no, I could drive
the horse myself, and I druther he wouldn't
take no trouble about me.

33. THE PITIFUL ENDING OF ROYALTY

So I started for town in the wagon, and
when I was half-way I see a wagon coming,
and sure enough it was Tom Sawyer, and I
stopped and waited till he come along. I says
"Hold on!" and it stopped alongside, and his
mouth opened up like a trunk, and stayed so;
and he swallowed two or three times like a
person that's got a dry throat, and then says:

"I hain't ever done you no harm. You
know that. So, then, what you want to come
back and ha'nt *me* for?"

I says:

"I hain't come back—I hain't been *gone.*"

When he heard my voice it righted him up
some, but he warn't quite satisfied yet. He
says:

"Don't you play nothing on me, because I
wouldn't on you. Honest injun, you ain't a
ghost?"

"Honest injun, I ain't," I says.

"Well—I—I—well, that ought to settle it, of
course; but I can't somehow seem to understand it no way. Looky here, warn't you ever
murdered *at all?*"

"No. I warn't ever murdered at all—I played
it on them. You come in here and feel of me
if you don't believe me."

So he done it; and it satisfied him; and he
was that glad to see me again he didn't know
what to do. And he wanted to know all about
it right off, because it was a grand adventure,
and mysterious, and so it hit him where he
lived. But I said, leave it alone till by and by;
and told his driver to wait, and we drove off
a little piece, and I told him the kind of a
fix I was in, and what did he reckon we better

do? He said, let him alone a minute, and don't
disturb him. So he thought and thought, and
pretty soon he says:

"It's all right; I've got it. Take my trunk
in your wagon, and let on it's yourn; and you
turn back and fool along slow, so as to get
to the house about the time you ought to;
and I'll go towards town a piece, and take a
fresh start, and get there a quarter or a half
an hour after you; and you needn't let on to
know me at first."

I says:

"All right; but wait a minute. There's one
more thing—a thing that *nobody* don't know
but me. And that is, there's a nigger here that
I'm a-trying to steal out of slavery, and his
name is *Jim*—old Miss Watson's Jim."

He says:

"What! Why, Jim is—"

He stopped and went to studying. I says:

"*I* know what you'll say. You'll say it's dirty,
low-down business; but what if it is? *I'm* low
down; and I'm a-going to steal him, and I
want you to keep mum and not let on. Will
you?"

His eye lit up, and he says:

"I'll *help* you steal him!"

Well, I let go all holts then, like I was shot.
It was the most astonishing speech I ever
heard—and I'm bound to say Tom Sawyer
fell considerable in my estimation. Only I
couldn't believe it. Tom Sawyer a *nigger-
stealer!*

"Oh, shucks!" I says; "you're joking."

"I ain't joking, either."

"Well, then," I says, "joking or no joking,
if you hear anything said about a runaway
nigger, don't forget to remember that *you*
don't know nothing about him, and *I* don't
know nothing about him."

Then he took the trunk and put it in my
wagon, and he drove off his way and I drove
mine. But of course I forgot all about driving
slow on accounts of being glad and full of
thinking; so I got home a heap too quick for
that length of a trip. The old gentleman was
at the door, and he says:

"Why, this is wonderful! Whoever would
'a' thought it was in that mare to do it? I wish
we'd 'a' timed her. And she hain't sweated
a hair—not a hair. It's wonderful. Why, I
wouldn't take a hundred dollars for that horse

now—I wouldn't, honest; and yet I'd 'a' sold her for fifteen before, and thought 'twas all she was worth."

That's all he said. He was the innocentest, best old soul I ever see. But it warn't surprising; because he warn't only just a farmer, he was a preacher, too, and had a little one-horse log church down back of the plantation, which he built it himself at his own expense, for a church and schoolhouse, and never charged nothing for his preaching, and it was worth it, too. There was plenty other farmer-preachers like that, and done the same way, down South.

In about half an hour Tom's wagon drove up to the front stile, and Aunt Sally she see it through the window, because it was only about fifty yards, and says:

"Why, there's somebody come! I wonder who 'tis? Why, I do believe it's a stranger. Jimmy" (that's one of the children), "run and tell Lize to put on another plate for dinner."

Everybody made a rush for the front door, because, of course, a stranger don't come *every* year, and so he lays over the yaller-fever, for interest, when he does come. Tom was over the stile and starting for the house, the wagon was spinning up the road for the village, and we was all bunched in the front door. Tom had his store clothes on, and an audience— and that was always nuts for Tom Sawyer. In them circumstances it warn't no trouble to him to throw in an amount of style that was suitable. He warn't a boy to meeky along up that yard like a sheep; no, he come ca'm and important, like the ram. When he got a-front of us he lifts his hat ever so gracious and dainty, like it was the lid of a box that had butterflies asleep in it and he didn't want to disturb them, and says:

"Mr. Archibald Nichols, I presume?"

"No, my boy," says the old gentleman, "I'm sorry to say 't your driver has deceived you; Nichols's place is down a matter of three mile more. Come in, come in."

Tom he took a look back over his shoulder, and says, "Too late—he's out of sight."

"Yes, he's gone, my son, and you must come in and eat your dinner with us; and then we'll hitch up and take you down to Nichols's."

"Oh, I *can't* make you so much trouble; I

couldn't think of it. I'll walk—I don't mind the distance."

"But we won't *let* you walk—it wouldn't be Southern hospitality to do it. Come right in."

"Oh, *do*," says Aunt Sally; "it ain't a bit of trouble to us, not a bit in the world. You *must* stay. It's a long, dusty three mile, and we *can't* let you walk. And, besides, I've already told 'em to put on another plate when I see you coming; so you mustn't disappoint us. Come right in and make yourself at home."

So Tom he thanked them very hearty and handsome, and let himself be persuaded, and come in; and when he was in he said he was a stranger from Hicksville, Ohio, and his name was William Thompson—and he made another bow.

Well, he run on, and on, and on, making up stuff about Hicksville and everybody in it he could invent, and I getting a little nervous, and wondering how this was going to help me out of my scrape; and at last, still talking along, he reached over and kissed Aunt Sally right on the mouth, and then settled back again in his chair comfortable, and was going on talking; but she jumped up and wiped it off with the back of her hand, and says:

"You owdacious puppy!"

He looked kind of hurt, and says:

"I'm surprised at you, m'am."

"You're s'rp— Why, what do you reckon *I* am? I've a good notion to take and— Say, what do you mean by kissing me?"

He looked kind of humble, and says:

"I didn't mean nothing, m'am. I didn't mean no harm. I—I—thought you'd like it."

"Why, you born fool!" She took up the spinning-stick, and it looked like it was all she could do to keep from giving him a crack with it. "What made you think I'd like it?"

"Well, I don't know. Only, they—they—told me you would."

"*They* told you I would. Whoever told you's *another* lunatic. I never heard the beat of it. Who's *they?*"

"Why, everybody. They all said so, m'am."

It was all she could do to hold in; and her eyes snapped, and her fingers worked like she wanted to scratch him; and she says:

"Who's 'everybody'? Out with their names, or ther'll be an idiot short."

He got up and looked distressed, and fumbled his hat, and says:

"I'm sorry, and I warn't expecting it. They told me to. They all told me to. They all said, kiss her; and said she'd like it. They all said it—every one of them. But I'm sorry, m'am, and I won't do it no more—I won't, honest."

"You won't, won't you? Well, I sh'd *reckon* you won't!"

"No'm, I'm honest about it; I won't ever do it again—till you ask me."

"Till I *ask* you! Well, I never see the beat of it in my born days! I lay you'll be the Methusalem-numskull of creation before ever *I* ask you—or the likes of you."

"Well," he says, "it does surprise me so. I can't make it out, somehow. They said you would, and I thought you would. But—" He stopped and looked around slow, like he wished he could run across a friendly eye somewheres, and fetched up on the old gentleman's, and says, "Didn't *you* think she'd like me to kiss her, sir?"

"Why, no; I—I—well, no, I b'lieve I didn't."

Then he looks on around the same way to me, and says:

"Tom, didn't *you* think Aunt Sally 'd open out her arms and say, 'Sid Sawyer—'"

"My land!" she says, breaking in and jumping for him, "you impudent young rascal, to fool a body so—" and was going to hug him, but he fended her off, and says:

"No, not till you've asked me first."

So she didn't lose no time, but asked him; and hugged him and kissed him over and over again, and then turned him over to the old man, and he took what was left. And after they got a little quiet again she says:

"Why, dear me, I never see such a surprise. We warn't looking for *you* at all, but only Tom. Sis never wrote to me about anybody coming but him."

"It's because it warn't *intended* for any of us to come but Tom," he says; "but I begged and begged, and at the last minute she let me come, too; so, coming down the river, me and Tom thought it would be a first-rate surprise for him to come here to the house first, and for me to by and by tag along and drop in, and let on to be a stranger. But it was a mistake, Aunt Sally. This ain't no healthy place for a stranger to come."

"No—not impudent whelps, Sid. You ought to had your jaws boxed; I hain't been so put out since I don't know when. But I don't care, I don't mind the terms—I'd be willing to stand a thousand such jokes to have you here. Well, to think of that performance! I don't deny it, I was most putrified with astonishment when you give me that smack."

We had dinner out in that broad open passage betwixt the house and the kitchen; and there was things enough on that table for seven families—and all hot, too; none of your flabby, tough meat that's laid in a cupboard in a damp cellar all night and tastes like a hunk of old cold cannibal in the morning. Uncle Silas he asked a pretty long blessing over it, but it was worth it; and it didn't cool it a bit, neither, the way I've seen them kind of interruptions do lots of times.

There was a considerable good deal of talk all the afternoon, and me and Tom was on the lookout all the time; but it warn't no use, they didn't happen to say nothing about any runaway nigger, and we was afraid to try to work up to it. But at supper, at night, one of the little boys says:

"Pa, mayn't Tom and Sid and me go to the show?"

"No," says the old man, "I reckon there ain't going to be any; and you couldn't go if there was; because the runaway nigger told Burton and me all about that scandalous show, and Burton said he would tell the people; so I reckon they've drove the owdacious loafers out of town before this time."

So there it was!—but I couldn't help it. Tom and me was to sleep in the same room and bed; so, being tired, we bid good night and went up to bed right after supper, and clumb out of the window and down the lightning-rod, and shoved for the town; for I didn't believe anybody was going to give the king and the duke a hint, and so if I didn't hurry up and give them one they'd get into trouble sure.

On the road Tom told me all about how it was reckoned I was murdered, and how pap disappeared pretty soon, and didn't come back no more, and what a stir there was when Jim run away; and I told Tom all about our "Royal Nonesuch" rapscallions, and as much of the raft voyage as I had time to; and as we struck into the town and up through the middle of it—it was as much as half after eight then—here comes a raging rush of people with torches, and an awful whooping and yelling, and banging tin pans and blowing horns; and we jumped to one side to let them go by; and as they went by I see they had the king and the duke astraddle of a rail—that is, I knowed it *was* the king and the duke, though they was all over tar and feathers, and didn't look like nothing in the world that was human—just looked like a couple of monstrous big soldier-plumes. Well, it made me sick to see it; and I was sorry for them poor pitiful rascals, it seemed like I couldn't ever feel any hardness against them any more in the world. It was a dreadful thing to see. Human beings *can* be awful cruel to one another.

We see we was too late—couldn't do no good. We asked some stragglers about it, and they said everybody went to the show looking very innocent; and laid low and kept dark till the poor old king was in the middle of his cavortings on the stage; then somebody give a signal, and the house rose up and went for them.

So we poked along back home, and I warn't feeling so brash as I was before, but kind of ornery, and humble, and to blame, somehow—though *I* hadn't done nothing. But that's always the way; it don't make no difference whether you do right or wrong, a person's conscience ain't got no sense, and just goes for him *anyway*. If I had a yaller dog that didn't know no more than a person's conscience does I would pison him. It takes up more room than all the rest of a person's insides, and yet ain't no good, nohow. Tom Sawyer he says the same.

34. WE CHEER UP JIM

We stopped talking, and got to thinking. By and by Tom says:

"Looky here, Huck, what fools we are to not think of it before! I bet I know where Jim is."

"No! Where?"

"In that hut down by the ash-hopper. Why, looky here. When we was at dinner, didn't you see a nigger man go in there with some vittles?"

"Yes."

"What did you think the vittles was for?"

"For a dog."

"So 'd I. Well, it wasn't for a dog."

"Why?"

"Because part of it was watermelon."

"So it was—I noticed it. Well, it does beat all that I never thought about a dog not eating watermelon. It shows how a body can see and don't see at the same time."

"Well, the nigger unlocked the padlock when he went in, and he locked it again when he came out. He fetched uncle a key about the time we got up from table—same key, I bet. Watermelon shows man, lock shows prisoner; and it ain't likely there's two prisoners on such a little plantation, and where the people's all so kind and good. Jim's the prisoner. All right—I'm glad we found it out detective fashion; I wouldn't give shucks for any other way. Now you work your mind, and study out a plan to steal Jim, and I will study out one, too; and we'll take the one we like the best."

What a head for just a boy to have! If I had Tom Sawyer's head I wouldn't trade it off to be a duke, nor mate of a steamboat, nor clown in a circus, nor nothing I can think of. I went to thinking out a plan, but only just to be doing something; I knowed very well where the right plan was going to come from. Pretty soon Tom says:

"Ready?"

"Yes," I says.

"All right—bring it out."

"My plan is this," I says. "We can easy find out if it's Jim in there. Then get up my canoe tomorrow night, and fetch my raft over from the island. Then the first dark night that comes steal the key out of the old man's britches after he goes to bed, and shove off down the river on the raft with Jim, hiding daytimes and running nights, the way me and Jim used to do before. Wouldn't that plan work?"

"*Work?* Why, cert'nly it would work, like rats a-fighting. But it's too blame' simple; there ain't nothing *to* it. What's the good of a plan that ain't no more trouble than that? It's as mild as goosemilk. Why, Huck, it wouldn't make no more talk than breaking into a soap factory."

I never said nothing, because I warn't expecting nothing different; but I knowed mighty well that whenever he got *his* plan ready it wouldn't have none of them objections to it.

And it didn't. He told me what it was, and I see in a minute it was worth fifteen of mine for style, and would make Jim just as free a man as mine would, and maybe get us all killed besides. So I was satisfied, and said we would waltz in on it. I needn't tell what it was here, because I knowed it wouldn't stay the way it was. I knowed he would be changing it around every which way as we went along, and heaving in new bullinesses wherever he got a chance. And that is what he done.

Well, one thing was dead sure, and that was that Tom Sawyer was in earnest, and was actuly going to help steal that nigger out of slavery. That was the thing that was too many for me. Here was a boy that was respectable and well brung up; and had a character to lose; and folks at home that had characters; and he was bright and not leatherheaded; and knowing and not ignorant; and not mean, but kind; and yet here he was, without any more pride, or rightness, or feeling, than to stoop to this business, and make himself a shame, and his family a shame, before everybody. I *couldn't* understand it no way at all. It was outrageous, and I knowed I ought to just up and tell him so; and so be his true friend, and let him quit the thing right where he was and save himself. And I *did* start to tell him; but he shut me up and says:

"Don't you reckon I know what I'm about? Don't I generly know what I'm about?"

"Yes."

"Didn't I *say* I was going to help steal the nigger?"

"Yes."

"*Well,* then."

That's all he said, and that's all I said. It warn't no use to say any more; because when he said he'd do a thing, he always done it. But *I* couldn't make out how he was willing to go into this thing; so I just let it go, and never bothered no more about it. If he was bound to have it so, *I* couldn't help it.

When we got home the house was all dark and still; so we went on down to the hut by the ash-hopper for to examine it. We went through the yard so as to see what the hounds would do. They knowed us, and didn't make no more noise than country dogs is always doing when anything comes by in the night. When we got to the cabin we took a look at the front and the two sides; and on the side I warn't acquainted with—which was the north side—we found a square window-hole, up tolerable high, with just one stout board nailed across it. I says:

"Here's the ticket. This hole's big enough for Jim to get through if we wrench off the board."

Tom says:

"It's as simple as tit-tat-toe, three-in-a-row, and as easy as playing hooky. I should *hope* we can find a way that's a little more complicated than *that,* Huck Finn."

"Well, then," I says, "how'll it do to saw him out, the way I done before I was murdered that time?"

"That's more *like,*" he says. "It's real mysterious, and troublesome, and good," he says; "but I bet we can find a way that's twice as long. There ain't no hurry; le's keep on looking around."

Betwixt the hut and the fence, on the back side, was a lean-to that joined the hut at the eaves, and was made out of plank. It was as long as the hut, but narrow—only about six foot wide. The door to it was at the south end, and was padlocked. Tom he went to the soap-kettle and searched around, and fetched back the iron thing they lift the lid with; so he took it and prized out one of the staples. The chain fell down, and we opened the door and went in, and shut it, and struck a match, and see the shed was only built against a cabin and hadn't no connection with it; and there warn't no floor to the shed, nor nothing in it but some old rusty played-out hoes and spades and picks and a crippled plow. The match went out, and so did we, and shoved in the staple again, and the door was locked as good as ever. Tom was joyful. He says:

"Now we're all right. We'll *dig* him out. It 'll take about a week!"

Then we started for the house, and I went in the back door—you only have to pull a buckskin latchstring, they don't fasten the doors—but that warn't romantical enough for

Tom Sawyer; no way would do him but he must climb up the lightning-rod. But after he got up half-way about three times, and missed fire and fell every time, and the last time most busted his brains out, he thought he'd got to give it up; but after he was rested he allowed he would give her one more turn for luck, and this time he made the trip.

In the morning we was up at break of day, and down to the nigger cabins to pet the dogs and make friends with the nigger that fed Jim—if it *was* Jim that was being fed. The niggers was just getting through breakfast and starting for the fields; and Jim's nigger was piling up a tin pan with bread and meat and things; and whilst the others was leaving, the key come from the house.

This nigger had a good-natured, chuckle-headed face, and his wool was all tied up in little bunches with thread. That was to keep witches off. He said the witches was pestering him awful these nights, and making him see all kinds of strange things, and hear all kinds of strange words and noises, and he didn't believe he was ever witched so long before in his life. He got so worked up, and got to running on so about his troubles, he forgot all about what he'd been a-going to do. So Tom says:

"What's the vittles for? Going to feed the dogs?"

The nigger kind of smiled around gradually over his face, like when you heave a brickbat in a mud-puddle, and he says:

"Yes, Mars Sid, *a* dog. Cur'us dog, too. Does you want to go en look at 'im?"

"Yes."

I hunched Tom, and whispers:

"You going, right here in the daybreak? *That* warn't the plan."

"No, it warn't; but it's the plan *now*."

So, drat him, we went along, but I didn't like it much. When we got in we couldn't hardly see anything, it was so dark; but Jim was there, sure enough, and could see us; and he sings out:

"Why, *Huck!* En good *lan'!* ain' dat Misto Tom?"

I just knowed how it would be; I just expected it. *I* didn't know nothing to do; and if I had I couldn't 'a' done it, because that nigger busted in and says:

"Why, de gracious sakes! do he know you genlmen?"

We could see pretty well now. Tom he looked at the nigger, steady and kind of wondering, and says:

"Does *who* know us?"

"Why, dis-yer runaway nigger."

"I don't reckon he does; but what put that into your head?"

"What *put* it dar? Didn't he jis' dis minute sing out like he knowed you?"

Tom says, in a puzzled-up kind of way:

"Well, that's mighty curious. *Who* sung out? *When* did he sing out? *What* did he sing out?" And turns to me, perfectly ca'm, and says, "Did *you* hear anybody sing out?"

Of course there warn't nothing to be said but the one thing, so I says:

"No; *I* ain't heard nobody say nothing."

Then he turns to Jim, and looks him over like he never see him before, and says:

"Did you sing out?"

"No, sah," says Jim; "*I* hain't said nothing, sah."

"Not a word?"

"No, sah, I hain't said a word."

"Did you ever see us before?"

"No, sah; not as *I* knows on."

So Tom turns to the nigger, which was looking wild and distressed, and says, kind of severe:

"What do you reckon's the matter with you, anyway? What made you think somebody sung out?"

"Oh, it's de dad-blame' witches, sah, en I wisht I was dead, I do. Dey's awluz at it, sah, en dey do mos' kill me, dey sk'yers me so. Please to don't tell nobody 'bout it, sah, er ole Mars Silas he'll scole me; 'kase he say dey *ain't* no witches. I jis' wish to goodness he was heah now—*den* what would he say! I jis' bet he couldn' fine no way to git aroun' it *dis* time. But it's awluz jis' so; people dat's *sot*, stays sot; dey won't look into noth'n' en fine it out f'r deyselves, en when *you* fine it out en tell um 'bout it, dey doan' b'lieve you."

Tom give him a dime, and said we wouldn't tell nobody; and told him to buy some more thread to tie up his wool with; and then looks at Jim, and says:

"I wonder if Uncle Silas is going to hang this nigger. If I was to catch a nigger that was ungrateful enough to run away, *I* wouldn't give him up, I'd hang him." And whilst the nigger stepped to the door to look at the dime and bite it to see if it was good, he whispers to Jim and says:

"Don't ever let on to know us. And if you hear any digging going on nights, it's us; we're going to set you free."

Jim only had time to grab us by the hand and squeeze it; then the nigger come back, and we said we'd come again some time if the nigger wanted us to; and he said he would, more particular if it was dark, because the witches went for him mostly in the dark, and it was good to have folks around then.

35. DARK, DEEP-LAID PLANS

It would be most an hour yet till breakfast, so we left and struck down into the woods; because Tom said we got to have *some* light to see how to dig by, and a lantern makes too much, and might get us into trouble; what we must have was a lot of them rotten chunks that's called fox-fire, and just makes a soft kind of a glow when you lay them in a dark place. We fetched an armful and hid it in the weeds, and set down to rest, and Tom says, kind of dissatisfied:

"Blame it, this whole thing is just as easy and awkward as it can be. And so it makes it so rotten difficult to get up a difficult plan. There ain't no watchman to be drugged— now there *ought* to be a watchman. There ain't even a dog to give a sleeping-mixture to. And there's Jim chained by one leg, with a ten-foot chain, to the leg of his bed; why, all you got to do is to lift up the bedstead and slip off the chain. And Uncle Silas he trusts everybody; sends the key to the punkin-headed nigger, and don't send nobody to watch the nigger. Jim could 'a' got out of that window-hole before this, only there wouldn't be no use trying to travel with a ten-foot chain on his leg. Why, drat it, Huck, it's the stupidest arrangement I ever see. You got to invent *all* the difficulties. Well, we can't help it; we got to do the best we can with the materials we've got. Anyhow, there's one thing—there's more honor in getting him out through a lot of difficulties and dangers, where there warn't one of them furnished to you by the people who it was their duty to furnish them, and you had to contrive them all out of your own head. Now look at just that one thing of the lantern. When you come down to the cold facts, we simply got to *let on* that a lantern's resky. Why, we could work with a torchlight procession if we wanted to, *I* believe. Now, whilst I think of it, we got to hunt up something to make a saw out of the first chance we get."

"What do we want of a saw?"

"What do we *want* of a saw? Hain't we got to saw the leg of Jim's bed off, so as to get the chain loose?"

"Why, you just said a body could lift up the bedstead and slip the chain off."

"Well, if that ain't just like you, Huck Finn. You *can* get up the infant-schooliest ways of going at a thing. Why, hain't you ever read any books at all?—Baron Trenck, nor Casanova, nor Benvenuto Chelleeny, nor Henri IV., nor none of them heroes? Who ever heard of getting a prisoner loose in such an old-maidy way as that? No; the way all the best authorities does is to saw the bed-leg in two, and leave it just so, and swallow the sawdust, so it can't be found, and put some dirt and grease around the sawed place so the very keenest seneskal can't see no sign of its being sawed, and thinks the bed-leg is perfectly sound. Then, the night you're ready, fetch the leg a kick, down she goes; slip off your chain, and there you are. Nothing to do but hitch your rope ladder to the battlements, shin down it, break your leg in the moat—because a rope ladder is nineteen foot too short, you know—and there's your horses and your trusty vassles, and they scoop you up and fling you across a saddle, and away you go to your native Langudoc, or Navarre, or wherever it is. It's gaudy, Huck. I wish there was a moat to this cabin. If we get time, the night of the escape, we'll dig one."

I says:

"What do we want of a moat when we're going to snake him out from under the cabin?"

But he never heard me. He had forgot me and everything else. He had his chin in his hand, thinking. Pretty soon he sighs and shakes his head; then sighs again, and says:

"No, it wouldn't do—there ain't necessity enough for it."

"For what?" I says.

"Why, to saw Jim's leg off," he says.

"Good land!" I says; "why, there ain't *no* necessity for it. And what would you want to saw his leg off for, anyway?"

"Well, some of the best authorities has done it. They couldn't get the chain off, so they just cut their hand off and shoved. And a leg would be better still. But we got to let that go. There ain't necessity enough in this case; and, besides, Jim's a nigger, and wouldn't understand the reasons for it, and how it's the custom in Europe; so we'll let it go. But there's one thing—he can have a rope ladder; we can tear up our sheets and make him a rope ladder easy enough. And we can send it to him in a pie; it's mostly done that way. And I've et worse pies."

"Why, Tom Sawyer, how you talk," I says; "Jim ain't got no use for a rope ladder."

"He *has* got use for it. How *you* talk, you better say; you don't know nothing about it. He's *got* to have a rope ladder; they all do."

"What in the nation can he *do* with it?"

"*Do* with it? He can hide it in his bed, can't he? That's what they all do; and *he's* got to, too. Huck, you don't ever seem to want to do anything that's regular; you want to be starting something fresh all the time. S'pose he *don't* do nothing with it? ain't it there in his bed, for a clue, after he's gone? and don't you reckon they'll want clues? Of course they will. And you wouldn't leave them any? That would be a *pretty* howdy-do, *wouldn't* it! I never heard of such a thing."

"Well," I says, "if it's in the regulations, and he's got to have it, all right, let him have it; because I don't wish to go back on no regulations; but there's one thing, Tom Sawyer— if we go to tearing up our sheets to make Jim a rope ladder, we're going to get into trouble with Aunt Sally, just as sure as you're born. Now, the way I look at it, a hickry-bark ladder don't cost nothing, and don't waste nothing, and is just as good to load up a pie with, and hide in a straw tick, as any rag ladder you can start; and as for Jim, he ain't had no experience, and so he don't care what kind of a—"

"Oh, shucks, Huck Finn, if I was as ignorant as you I'd keep still—that's what *I'd* do. Who ever heard of a state prisoner escaping by a hickry-bark ladder? Why, it's perfectly ridiculous."

"Well, all right, Tom, fix it your own way; but if you'll take my advice, you'll let me borrow a sheet off of the clothes-line."

He said that would do. And that gave him another idea, and he says:

"Borrow a shirt, too."

"What do we want of a shirt, Tom?"

"Want it for Jim to keep a journal on."

"Journal your granny—*Jim* can't write."

"S'pose he *can't* write—he can make marks on the shirt, can't he, if we make him a pen out of an old pewter spoon or a piece of an old iron barrel-hoop?"

"Why, Tom, we can pull a feather out of a goose and make him a better one; and quicker, too."

"*Prisoners* don't have geese running around the donjon-keep to pull pens out of, you muggins. They *always* make their pens out of the hardest, toughest, troublesomest piece of old brass candlestick or something like that they can get their hands on; and it takes them weeks and weeks and months and months to file it out, too, because they've got to do it by rubbing it on the wall. *They* wouldn't use a goose-quill if they had it. It ain't regular."

"Well, then, what'll we make him the ink out of?"

"Many makes it out of iron-rust and tears; but that's the common sort and women; the best authorities uses their own blood. Jim can do that; and when he wants to send any little common ordinary mysterious message to let the world know where he's captivated, he can write it on the bottom of a tin plate with a fork and throw it out of the window. The Iron Mask always done that, and it's a blame' good way, too."

"Jim ain't got no tin plate. They feed him in a pan."

"That ain't nothing; we can get him some."

"Can't nobody *read* his plates."

"That ain't got anything to *do* with it, Huck Finn. All *he's* got to do is to write on the plate and throw it out. You don't *have* to be able to read it. Why, half the time you can't read anything a prisoner writes on a tin plate, or anywhere else."

"Well, then, what's the sense in wasting the plates?"

"Why, blame it all, it ain't the *prisoner's* plates."

"But it's *somebody's* plates, ain't it?"

"Well, spos'n it is? What does the *prisoner* care whose—"

He broke off there, because we heard the breakfast-horn blowing. So we cleared out for the house.

Along during the morning I borrowed a sheet and a white shirt off of the clothes-line; and I found an old sack and put them in it, and we went down and got the fox-fire, and put that in too. I called it borrowing, because that was what pap always called it; but Tom said it warn't borrowing, it was stealing. He said we was representing prisoners; and prisoners don't care how they get a thing so they get it, and nobody don't blame them for it, either. It ain't no crime in a prisoner to steal the thing he needs to get away with, Tom said; it's his right; and so, as long as we was representing a prisoner, we had a perfect right to steal anything on this place we had the least use for to get ourselves out of prison with. He said if we warn't prisoners it would be a very different thing, and nobody but a mean, ornery person would steal when he warn't a prisoner. So we allowed we would steal everything there was that come handy. And yet he made a mighty fuss, one day, after that, when I stole a watermelon out of the nigger patch and eat it; and he made me go and give the niggers a dime without telling them what it was for. Tom said that what he meant was, we could steal anything we *needed*. Well, I says, I needed the watermelon. But he said I didn't need it to get out of prison with; there's where the difference was. He said if I'd 'a' wanted it to hide a knife in, and smuggle it to Jim to kill the seneskal with, it would 'a' been all right. So I let it go at that, though I couldn't see no advantage in my representing a prisoner if I got to set down and chaw over a lot of gold-leaf distinctions like that everytime I see a chance to hog a watermelon.

Well, as I was saying, we waited that morning till everybody was settled down to business, and nobody in sight around the yard; then Tom he carried the sack into the lean-to whilst I stood off a piece to keep watch. By and by he come out, and we went and set down on the woodpile to talk. He says:

"Everything's all right now except tools; and that's easy fixed."

"Tools?" I says.

"Yes."

"Tools for what?"

"Why, to dig with. We ain't a-going to *gnaw* him out, are we?"

"Ain't them old crippled picks and things in there good enough to dig a nigger out with?" I says.

He turns on me, looking pitying enough to make a body cry, and says:

"Huck Finn, did you *ever* hear of a prisoner having picks and shovels, and all the modern conveniences in his wardrobe to dig himself out with? Now I want to ask you—if you got any reasonableness in you at all—what kind of a show would *that* give him to be a hero? Why, they might as well lend him the key and done with it. Picks and shovels—why, they wouldn't furnish 'em to a king."

"Well, then," I says, "if we don't want the picks and shovels, what do we want?"

"A couple of case-knives."

"To dig the foundations out from under that cabin with?"

"Yes."

"Confound it, it's foolish, Tom."

"It don't make no difference how foolish it is, it's the *right* way—and it's the regular way. And there ain't no *other* way, that ever *I* heard of, and I've read all the books that gives any information about these things. They always dig out with a case-knife—and not through dirt, mind you; generly it's through solid rock. And it takes them weeks and weeks and weeks, and for ever and ever. Why, look at one of them prisoners in the bottom dungeon of the Castle Deef, in the harbor of Marseilles, that dug himself out that way; how long was *he* at it, you reckon?"

"I don't know."

"Well, guess."

"I don't know. A month and a half."

"*Thirty-seven year*—and he come out in China. *That's* the kind. I wish the bottom of *this* fortress was solid rock."

"*Jim* don't know nobody in China."

"What's *that* got to do with it? Neither did that other fellow. But you're always a-wandering off on a side issue. Why can't you stick to the main point?"

"All right—*I* don't care where he comes out, so he *comes* out; and Jim don't, either, I reckon. But there's one thing, anyway—Jim's too old to be dug out with a case-knife. He won't last."

"Yes he will *last,* too. You don't reckon it's going to take thirty-seven years to dig out through a *dirt* foundation, do you?"

"How long will it take, Tom?"

"Well, we can't resk being as long as we ought to, because it mayn't take very long for Uncle Silas to hear from down there by New Orleans. He'll hear Jim ain't from there. Then his next move will be to advertise Jim, or something like that. So we can't resk being as long digging him out as we ought to. By rights I reckon we ought to be a couple of years; but we can't. Things being so uncertain, what I recommend is this: that we really dig right in, as quick as we can; and after that, we can *let on,* to ourselves, that we was at it thirty-seven years. Then we can snatch him out and rush him away the first time there's an alarm. Yes, I reckon that 'll be the best way."

"Now, there's *sense* in that," I says. "Letting on don't cost nothing; letting on ain't no trouble; and if it's any object, I don't mind letting on we was at it a hundred and fifty year. It wouldn't strain me none, after I got my hand in. So I'll mosey along now, and smouch a couple of case-knives."

"Smouch three," he says; "we want one to make a saw out of."

"Tom, if it ain't unregular and irreligious to sejest it," I says, "there's an old rusty saw-blade around yonder sticking under the weather-boarding behind the smokehouse."

He looked kind of weary and discouraged-like, and says:

"It ain't no use to try to learn you nothing, Huck. Run along and smouch the knives—three of them." So I done it.

36. TRYING TO HELP JIM

As soon as we reckoned everybody was asleep that night we went down the lightning-rod, and shut ourselves up in the lean-to, and got out our pile of fox-fire, and went to work. We cleared everything out of the way, about

four or five foot along the middle of the bottom log. Tom said we was right behind Jim's bed now, and we'd dig in under it, and when we got through there couldn't nobody in the cabin ever know there was any hole there, because Jim's counterpin hung down most to the ground, and you'd have to raise it up and look under to see the hole. So we dug and dug with the case-knives till most midnight: and then we was dog-tired, and our hands was blistered, and yet you couldn't see we'd done anything hardly. At last I says:

"This ain't no thirty-seven-year job; this is a thirty-eight-year job, Tom Sawyer."

He never said nothing. But he sighed, and pretty soon he stopped digging, and then for a good little while I knowed that he was thinking. Then he says:

"It ain't no use, Huck, it ain't a-going to work. If we was prisoners it would, because then we'd have as many years as we wanted, and no hurry; and we wouldn't get but a few minutes to dig, every day, while they was changing watches, and so our hands wouldn't get blistered, and we could keep it up right along, year in and year out, and do it right, and the way it ought to be done. But *we* can't fool along; we got to rush; we ain't got no time to spare. If we was to put in another night this way we'd have to knock off for a week to let our hands get well—couldn't touch a case-knife with them sooner."

"Well, then, what we going to do, Tom?"

"I'll tell you. It ain't right, and it ain't moral, and I wouldn't like it to get out; but there ain't only just the one way: we got to dig him out with the picks, and *let on* it's case-knives."

"*Now* you're *talking!*" I says; "your head gets leveler and leveler all the time, Tom Sawyer," I says. "Picks is the thing, moral or no moral; and as for me, I don't care shucks for the morality of it, nohow. When I start in to steal a nigger, or a watermelon, or a Sunday-school book, I ain't no ways particular how it's done so it's done. What I want is my nigger; or what I want is my watermelon; or what I want is my Sunday-school book; and if a pick's the handiest thing, that's the thing I'm a-going to dig that nigger or that watermelon or that Sunday-school book out with;

and I don't give a dead rat what the authorities thinks about it nuther."

"Well," he says, "there's excuse for picks and letting on in a case like this; if it warn't so, I wouldn't approve of it, nor I wouldn't stand by and see the rules broke—because right is right, and wrong is wrong, and a body ain't got no business doing wrong when he ain't ignorant and knows better. It might answer for *you* to dig Jim out with a pick, *without* any letting on, because you don't know no better; but it wouldn't for me, because I do know better. Gimme a case-knife."

He had his own by him, but I handed him mine. He flung it down, and says:

"Gimme a *case-knife*."

I didn't know just what to do—but then I thought. I scratched around amongst the old tools, and got a pickax and give it to him, and he took it and went to work, and never said a word.

He was always just that particular. Full of principle.

So then I got a shovel, and then we picked and shoveled, turn about, and made the fur fly. We stuck to it about a half an hour, which was as long as we could stand up; but we had a good deal of a hole to show for it. When I got up-stairs I looked out at the window and see Tom doing his level best with the lightning-rod, but he couldn't come it, his hands was so sore. At last he says:

"It ain't no use, it can't be done. What you reckon I better do? Can't you think of no way?"

"Yes," I says, "but I reckon it ain't regular. Come up the stairs, and let on it's a lightning-rod."

So he done it.

Next day Tom stole a pewter spoon and a brass candle-stick in the house, for to make some pens for Jim out of, and six tallow candles; and I hung around the nigger cabins and laid for a chance, and stole three tin plates. Tom says it wasn't enough; but I said nobody wouldn't ever see the plates that Jim throwed out, because they'd fall in the dog-fennel and jimpson weeds under the window-hole—then we could tote them back and he could use them over again. So Tom was satisfied. Then he says:

"Now, the thing to study out is, how to get the things to Jim."

"Take them in through the hole," I says, "when we get it done."

He only just looked scornful, and said something about nobody ever heard of such an idiotic idea, and then he went to studying. By and by he said he had ciphered out two or three ways, but there warn't no need to decide on any of them yet. Said we'd got to post Jim first.

That night we went down the lightning-rod a little after ten, and took one of the candles along, and listened under the window-hole and heard Jim snoring; so we pitched it in, and it didn't wake him. Then we whirled in with the pick and shovel, and in about two hours and a half the job was done. We crept in under Jim's bed and into the cabin, and pawed around and found the candle and lit it, and stood over Jim awhile, and found him looking hearty and healthy, and then we woke him up gentle and gradual. He was so glad to see us he most cried; and called us honey, and all the pet names he could think of; and was for having us hunt up a cold-chisel to cut the chain off of his leg with right away, and clearing out without losing any time. But Tom he showed him how unregular it would be, and set down and told him all about our plans, and how we could alter them in a minute any time there was an alarm; and not to be the least afraid, because we would see he got away, *sure*. So Jim he said it was all right, and we set there and talked over old times awhile, and then Tom asked a lot of questions, and when Jim told him Uncle Silas come in every day or two to pray with him, and Aunt Sally come in to see if he was comfortable and had plenty to eat, and both of them was kind as they could be, Tom says:

"*Now* I know how to fix it. We'll send you some things by them."

I said, "Don't do nothing of the kind; it's one of the most jackass ideas I ever struck"; but he never paid no attention to me; went right on. It was his way when he'd got his plans set.

So he told Jim how we'd have to smuggle in the rope-ladder pie and other large things by Nat, the nigger that fed him, and he must be on the lookout, and not be surprised, and not let Nat see him open them; and we would put small things in uncle's coat pockets and he must steal them out; and we would tie things to aunt's apron-strings or put them in her apron pocket, if we got a chance; and told him what they would be and what they was for. And told him how to keep a journal on the shirt with his blood, and all that. He told him everything. Jim he couldn't see no sense in the most of it, but he allowed we was white folks and knowed better than him; so he was satisfied, and said he would do it all just as Tom said.

Jim had plenty of corn-cob pipes and to-bacco; so we had a right down good sociable time; then we crawled out through the hole, and so home to bed, with hands that looked like they'd been chawed. Tom was in high spirits. He said it was the best fun he ever had in his life, and the most intellectural; and said if he only could see his way to it we would keep it up all the rest of our lives and leave Jim to our children to get out; for he believed Jim would come to like it better and better the more he got used to it. He said that in that way it could be strung out to as much as eighty year, and would be the best time on record. And he said it would make us all cele-brated that had a hand in it.

In the morning we went out to the wood-pile and chopped up the brass candlesticks into handy sizes, and Tom put them and the pewter spoon in his pocket. Then we went to the nigger cabins, and while I got Nat's notice off, Tom shoved a piece of candlestick into the middle of a corn-pone that was in Jim's pan, and we went along with Nat to see how it would work, and it just worked noble; when Jim bit into it it most mashed all his teeth out; and there warn't ever anything could 'a' worked better. Tom said so himself. Jim he never let on but what it was only just a piece of rock or something like that that's always getting into bread, you know; but after that he never bit into nothing but what he jabbed his fork into it in three or four places first.

And whilst we was a-standing there in the dimmish light, here comes a couple of the hounds bulging in from under Jim's bed; and they kept on piling in till there was eleven of them, and there warn't hardly room in there to get your breath. By jings, we forgot to fasten that lean-to door! The nigger Nat he only just hollered "Witches" once, and keeled over onto the floor amongst the dogs, and begun to groan like he was dying. Tom jerked the door open and flung out a slab of Jim's meat, and the dogs went for it, and in two seconds he was out himself and back again and shut the door, and I knowed he'd fixed the other door too. Then he went to work on the nigger, coaxing him and petting him, and asking him if he'd been imagining he saw something again. He raised up, and blinked his eyes around, and says:

"Mars Sid, you'll say I's a fool, but if I didn't b'lieve I see most a million dogs, er devils, er some'n, I wisht I may die right heah in dese tracks. I did, mos' sholy. Mars Sid, I *felt* um—I *felt* um, sah; dey was all over me. Dad fetch it, I jis' wisht I could git my han's on one er dem witches jis' wunst—on'y jis' wunst—it's all *I'd* ast. But mos'ly I wisht dey'd lemme 'lone, I does."

Tom says:

"Well, I tell you what *I* think. What makes them come here just at this runaway nigger's breakfast-time? It's because they're hungry; that's the reason. You make them a witch pie; that's the thing for *you* to do."

"But my lan', Mars Sid, how's I gwyne to make 'm a witch pie? I doan' know how to make it. I hain't ever hearn er sich a thing b'fo'."

"Well, then, I'll have to make it myself."

"Will you do it, honey?—will you? I'll wus-shup de groun' und' yo' foot, I will!"

"All right, I'll do it, seeing it's you, and you've been good to us and showed us the runaway nigger. But you got to be mighty careful. When we come around, you turn your back; and then whatever we've put in the pan, don't you let on you see it at all. And don't you look when Jim unloads the pan—something might happen, I don't know what. And above all, don't you *handle* the witch things."

"*Hannel* 'm, Mars Sid? What *is* you a-talkin' 'bout? I wouldn' lay de weight er my finger on um, not f'r ten hund'd thous'n billion dol-lars, I wouldn't."

37. JIM GETS HIS WITCH-PIE

That was all fixed. So then we went away and went to the rubbage-pile in the back yard, where they keep the old boots, and rags, and pieces of bottles, and wore-out tin things, and all such truck, and scratched around and found an old tin washpan, and stopped up the holes as well as we could, to bake the pie in, and took it down cellar and stole it full of flour and started for breakfast, and found a couple of shingle-nails that Tom said would be handy for a prisoner to scrabble his name and sorrows on the dungeon walls with, and dropped one of them in Aunt Sally's apron pocket which was hanging on a chair, and t'other we stuck in the band of Uncle Silas's hat, which was on the bureau, because we heard the children say their pa and ma was going to the runaway nigger's house this morning, and then went to breakfast, and Tom dropped the pewter spoon in Uncle Silas's coat pocket, and Aunt Sally wasn't come yet, so we had to wait a little while.

And when she come she was hot and red and cross, and couldn't hardly wait for the blessing; and then she went to sluicing out coffee with one hand and cracking the handiest child's head with her thimble with the other, and says:

"I've hunted high and I've hunted low, and it does beat all what *has* become of your other shirt."

My heart fell down amongst my lungs and livers and things, and a hard piece of corn-crust started down my throat after it and got met on the road with a cough, and was shot across the table, and took one of the children in the eye and curled him up like a fishing-worm, and let a cry out of him the size of a war-whoop, and Tom he turned kinder blue around the gills, and it all amounted to a considerable state of things for about a quarter of a minute or as much as that, and I would 'a' sold out for half price if there was a bidder. But after that we was all right again —it was the sudden surprise of it that knocked us so kind of cold. Uncle Silas he says:

"It's most uncommon curious, I can't understand it. I know perfectly well I took it *off*, because—"

"Because you ain't got but one *on*. Just *listen* at the man! I know you took it off, and know it by a better way than your wool-gethering memory, too, because it was on the clo's-line yesterday—I see it there myself. But it's gone, that's the long and the short of it, and you'll just have to change to a red flann'l one till I can get time to make a new one. And it 'll be the third I've made in two years. It just keeps a body on the jump to keep you in shirts; and whatever you do manage to *do* with 'm all is more'n *I* can make out. A body'd think you *would* learn to take some sort of care of 'em at your time of life."

"I know it, Sally, and I do try all I can. But it oughtn't to be altogether my fault, because, you know, I don't see them nor have nothing to do with them except when they're on me; and I don't believe I've ever lost one of them *off* of me."

"Well, it ain't *your* fault if you haven't, Silas; you'd 'a' done it if you could, I reckon. And the shirt ain't all that's gone, nuther. Ther's a spoon gone; and *that* ain't all. There was ten, and now ther's only nine. The calf got the shirt, I reckon, but the calf never took the spoon, *that's* certain."

"Why, what else is gone, Sally?"

"Ther's six *candles* gone—that's what. The rats could 'a' got the candles, and I reckon they did; I wonder they don't walk off with the whole place, the way you're always going to stop their holes and don't do it; and if they warn't fools they'd sleep in your hair, Silas—*you'd* never find it out; but you can't lay the *spoon* on the rats, and that I *know*."

"Well, Sally, I'm in fault, and I acknowledge it; I've been remiss; but I won't let to-morrow go by without stopping up them holes."

"Oh, I wouldn't hurry; next year 'll do. Matilda Angelina Araminta *Phelps!*"

Whack comes the thimble, and the child snatches her claws out of the sugar-bowl without fooling around any. Just then the nigger woman steps onto the passage, and says:

"Missus, dey's a sheet gone."

"A *sheet* gone! Well, for the land's sake!"

"I'll stop up them holes today," says Uncle Silas, looking sorrowful.

"Oh, *do* shet up!—s'pose the rats took the *sheet? Where's* it gone, Lize?"

"Clah to goodness I hain't no notion, Miss'

Sally. She wuz on de clo's-line yistiddy, but she done gone: she ain' dah no mo' now."

"I reckon the world *is* coming to an end. I *never* see the beat of it in all my born days. A shirt, and a sheet, and a spoon, and six can—"

"Missus," comes a young yaller wench, "dey's a brass cannelstick mis'n."

"Cler out from here, you hussy, er I'll take a skillet to ye!"

Well, she was just a-biling. I begun to lay for a chance; I reckoned I would sneak out and go for the woods till the weather moderated. She kept a-raging right along, running her insurrection all by herself, and everybody else mighty meek and quiet; and at last Uncle Silas, looking kind of foolish, fishes up that spoon out of his pocket. She stopped, with her mouth open and her hands up; and as for me, I wished I was in Jerusalem or somewheres. But not long, because she says:

"It's *just* as I expected. So you had it in your pocket all the time; and like as not you've got the other things there, too. How'd it get there?"

"I reely don't know, Sally," he says, kind of apologizing, "or you know I would tell. I was a-studying over my text in Acts Seventeen before breakfast, and I reckon I put it in there, not noticing, meaning to put my Testament in, and it must be so, because my Testament ain't in; but I'll go and see; and if the Testament is where I had it, I'll know I didn't put it in, and that will show that I laid the Testament down and took up the spoon, and—"

"Oh, for the land's sake! Give a body a rest! Go 'long now, the whole kit and biling of ye; and don't come nigh me again till I've got back my peace of mind."

I'd 'a' heard her if she'd 'a' said it to herself, let alone speaking it out; and I'd 'a' got up and obeyed her if I'd 'a' been dead. As we was passing through the setting-room the old man he took up his hat, and the shingle-nail fell out on the floor, and he just merely picked it up and laid it on the mantel-shelf, and never said nothing, and went out. Tom see him do it, and remembered about spoon, and says:

"Well, it ain't no use to send things by *him* no more, he ain't reliable." Then he says: "But he done us a good turn with the spoon, anyway, without knowing it, and so we'll go

and do him one without *him* knowing it—stop up his rat-holes."

There was a noble good lot of them down cellar, and it took us a whole hour, but we done the job tight and good and shipshape. Then we heard steps on the stairs, and blowed out our light and hid; and here comes the old man, with a candle in one hand and a bundle of stuff in t'other, looking as absent-minded as year before last. He went a-mooning around, first to one rat-hole and then another, till he'd been to them all. Then he stood about five minutes, picking tallow-drip off of his candle and thinking. Then he turns off slow and dreamy towards the stairs, saying:

"Well, for the life of me I can't remember when I done it. I could show her now that I warn't to blame on account of the rats. But never mind—let it go. I reckon it wouldn't do no good."

And so he went on a-mumbling up-stairs, and then we left. He was a mighty nice old man. And always is.

Tom was a good deal bothered about what to do for a spoon, but he said we'd got to have it; so he took a think. When he had ciphered it out he told me how we was to do; then we went and waited around the spoon-basket till we see Aunt Sally coming, and then Tom went to counting the spoons and laying them out to one side, and I slid one of them up my sleeve, and Tom says:

"Why, Aunt Sally, there ain't but nine spoons *yet*."

She says:

"Go 'long to your play, and don't bother me. I know better, I counted 'm myself."

"Well, I've counted them twice, Aunty, and I can't make but nine."

She looked out of all patience, but of course she come to count—anybody would.

"I declare to gracious ther' *ain't* but nine!" she says. "Why, what in the world—plague *take* the things, I'll count 'm again."

So I slipped back the one I had, and when she got done counting, she says:

"Hang the troublesome rubbage, ther's *ten* now!" and she looked huffy and bothered both. But Tom says:

"Why, Aunty, *I* don't think there's ten."

"You numskull, didn't you see me *count* 'm?"

"I know, but—"

"Well, I'll count 'm again."

So I smouched one, and they come out nine, same as the other time. Well, she *was* in a tearing way—just a-trembling all over, she was so mad. But she counted and counted till she got that addled she'd start to count in the *basket* for a spoon sometimes; and so, three times they come out right, and three times they come out wrong. Then she grabbed up the basket and slammed it across the house and knocked the cat galley-west; and she said cler out and let her have some peace, and if we come bothering around her again betwixt that and dinner she'd skin us. So we had the odd spoon, and dropped it in her apron pocket whilst she was a-giving us our sailing orders, and Jim got it all right, along with her shingle-nail, before noon. We was very well satisfied with this business, and Tom allowed it was worth twice the trouble it took, because he said *now* she couldn't ever count them spoons twice alike again to save her life; and wouldn't believe she'd counted them right if she *did;* and said that after she'd about counted her head off for the next three days he judged she'd give it up and offer to kill anybody that wanted her to ever count them any more.

So we put the sheet back on the line that night, and stole one out of her closet; and kept on putting it back and stealing it again for a couple of days till she didn't know how many sheets she had any more, and she didn't *care,* and warn't a-going to bullyrag the rest of her soul out about it, and wouldn't count them again not to save her life; she druther die first.

So we was all right now, as to the shirt and the sheet and the spoon and the candles, by the help of the calf and the rats and the mixed-up counting; and as to the candlestick, it warn't no consequence, it would blow over by and by.

But that pie was a job; we had no end of trouble with that pie. We fixed it up away down in the woods, and cooked it there; and we got it done at last, and very satisfactory, too; but not all in one day; and we had to use up three washpans full of flour before we got through, and we got burnt pretty much all over, in places, and eyes put out with the smoke; because, you see, we didn't want

nothing but a crust, and we couldn't prop it up right, and she would always cave in. But of course we thought of the right way at last—which was to cook the ladder, too, in the pie. So then we laid in with Jim the second night, and tore up the sheet all in little strings and twisted them together, and long before daylight we had a lovely rope that you could 'a' hung a person with. We let on it took nine months to make it.

And in the forenoon we took it down to the woods, but it wouldn't go into the pie. Being made of a whole sheet, that way, there was rope enough for forty pies if we'd 'a' wanted them, and plenty left over for soup, or sausages, or anything you choose. We could 'a' had a whole dinner.

But we didn't need it. All we needed was just enough for the pie, and so we throwed the rest away. We didn't cook none of the pies in the washpan—afraid the solder would melt; but Uncle Silas he had a noble brass warming-pan which he thought considerable of, because it belonged to one of his ancestors with a long wooden handle that come over from England with William the Conqueror in the *Mayflower* or one of them early ships and was hid away up garret with a lot of other old pots and things that was valuable, not on account of being any account, because they warn't, but on account of them being relicts, you know, and we snaked her out, private, and took her down there, but she failed on the first pies, because we didn't know how, but she come up smiling on the last one. We took and lined her with dough, and set her in the coals, and loaded her up with rag rope, and put on a dough roof, and shut down the lid, and put hot embers on top, and stood off five foot, with the long handle, cool and comfortable, and in fifteen minutes she turned out a pie that was a satisfaction to look at. But the person that et it would want to fetch a couple of kags of toothpicks along, for if that rope ladder wouldn't cramp him down to business I don't know nothing what I'm talking about, and lay him in enough stomach-ache to last him till next time, too.

Nat didn't look when we put the witch pie in Jim's pan; and we put the three tin plates in the bottom of the pan under the vittles; and so Jim got everything all right, and as soon as he was by himself he busted into the pie and hid the rope ladder inside of his straw tick, and scratched some marks on a tin plate and throwed it out of the window-hole.

38. "HERE A CAPTIVE HEART BUSTED"

Making them pens was a distressid tough job, and so was the saw; and Jim allowed the inscription was going to be the toughest of all. That's the one which the prisoner has to scribble on the wall. But he had to have it; Tom said he'd *got* to; there warn't no case of a state prisoner not scrabbling his inscription to leave behind, and his coat of arms.

"Look at Lady Jane Grey," he says; "look at Gilford Dudley; look at old Northumberland! Why, Huck, s'pose it *is* considerble trouble?—what you going to do?—how you going to get around it? Jim's *got* to do his inscription and coat of arms. They all do."

Jim says:

"Why, Mars Tom, I hain't got no coat o' arm; I hain't got nuffn but dish yer ole shirt, en you knows I got to keep de journal on dat."

"Oh, you don't understand, Jim; a coat of arms is very different."

"Well," I says, "Jim's right, anyway, when he says he ain't got no coat of arms, because he hain't."

"I reckon *I* knowed that," Tom says, "but you bet he'll have one before he goes out of this—because he's going out *right,* and there ain't going to be no flaws in his record."

So whilst me and Jim filed away at the pens on a brickbat apiece, Jim a-making his'n out of the brass and I making mine out of the spoon, Tom set to work to think out the coat of arms. By and by he said he'd struck so many good ones he didn't hardly know which to take, but there was one which he reckoned he'd decide on. He says:

"On the scutcheon we'll have a bend *or* in the dexter base, a saltire *murrey* in the fess, with a dog, couchant, for common charge, and under his foot a chain embattled, for slavery, with a chevron *vert* in a chief engrailed, and three invected lines on a field *azure,* with the nombril points rampant on a dancette indented; crest, a runaway nigger, *sable,* with his bundle over his shoulder on a bar sinister; and a couple of gules for supporters, which is

you and me; motto, *Maggiore fretta, minore atto.* Got it out of a book—means the more haste the less speed."

"Geewhillikins," I says, "but what does the rest of it mean?"

"We ain't got no time to bother over that," he says; "we got to dig in like all git-out."

"Well, anyway," I says, "what's *some* of it? What's a fess?"

"A fess—a fess is—*you* don't need to know what a fess is. I'll show him how to make it when he gets to it."

"Shucks, Tom," I says, "I think you might tell a person. What's a bar sinister?"

"Oh, *I* don't know. But he's got to have it. All the nobility does."

That was just his way. If it didn't suit him to explain a thing to you, he wouldn't do it. You might pump at him a week, it wouldn't make no difference.

He'd got all that coat-of-arms business fixed, so now he started in to finish up the rest of that part of the work, which was to plan out a mournful inscription—said Jim got to have one, like they all done. He made up a lot, and wrote them out on a paper, and read them off, so:

1. Here a captive heart busted.
2. Here a poor prisoner, forsook by the world and friends, fretted his sorrowful life.
3. Here a lonely heart broke, and a worn spirit went to its rest, after thirty-seven years of solitary captivity.
4. Here, homeless and friendless, after thirty-seven years of bitter captivity, perished a noble stranger, natural son of Louis XIV.

Tom's voice trembled whilst he was reading them, and he most broke down. When he got done he couldn't no way make up his mind which one for Jim to scrabble onto the wall, they was all so good; but at last he allowed he would let him scrabble them all on. Jim said it would take him a year to scrabble such a lot of truck onto the logs with a nail, and he didn't know how to make letters, besides; but Tom said he would block them out for him, and then he wouldn't have nothing to do but just follow the lines. Then pretty soon he says:

"Come to think, the logs ain't a-going to do; they don't have log walls in a dungeon: we got to dig the inscriptions into a rock. We'll fetch a rock."

Jim said the rock was worse than the logs; he said it would take him such a pison long time to dig them into a rock he wouldn't ever get out. But Tom said he would let me help him do it. Then he took a look to see how me and Jim was getting along with the pens. It was most pesky tedious hard work and slow, and didn't give my hands no show to get well of the sores, and we didn't seem to make no headway, hardly; so Tom says:

"I know how to fix it. We got to have a rock for the coat of arms and mournful inscriptions, and we can kill two birds with that same rock. There's a gaudy big grindstone down at the mill, and we'll smouch it, and carve the things on it, and file out the pens and the saw on it, too."

It warn't no slouch of an idea; and it warn't no slouch of a grindstone nuther; but we allowed we'd tackle it. It warn't quite midnight yet, so we cleared out for the mill, leaving Jim at work. We smouched the grindstone, and set out to roll her home, but it was a most nation tough job. Sometimes, do what we could, we couldn't keep her from falling over, and she come mighty near mashing us every time. Tom said she was going to get one of us, sure, before we got through. We got her halfway; and then we was plumb played out, and most drownded with sweat. We see it warn't no use; we got to go and fetch Jim. So he raised up his bed and slid the chain off of the bed-leg, and wrapt it round and round his neck, and we crawled out through our hole and down there, and Jim and me laid into that grindstone and walked her along like nothing; and Tom superintended. He could out-superintend any boy I ever see. He knowed how to do everything.

Our hole was pretty big, but it warn't big enough to get the grindstone through; but Jim he took the pick and soon made it big enough. Then Tom marked out them things on it with the nail, and set Jim to work on them, with the nail for a chisel and an iron bolt from the rubbage in the lean-to for a hammer, and told him to work till the rest of his candle quit on him, and then he could go to bed, and hide the grindstone under his straw tick and sleep on it. Then we helped

him fix his chain back on the bed-leg, and was ready for bed ourselves. But Tom thought of something, and says:

"You got any spiders in here, Jim?"

"No, sah, thanks to goodness I hain't, Mars Tom."

"All right, we'll get you some."

"But bless you, honey, I doan' *want* none. I's afeard un um. I jis' 's soon have rattlesnakes aroun'."

Tom thought a minute or two, and says:

"It's a good idea. And I reckon it's been done. It *must* 'a' been done; it stands to reason. Yes, it's a prime good idea. Where could you keep it?"

"Keep what, Mars Tom?"

"Why, a rattlesnake."

"De goodness gracious alive, Mars Tom! Why, if dey was a rattlesnake to come in heah I'd take en bust right out thoo dat log wall, I woud, wid my head."

"Why, Jim, you wouldn't be afraid of it after a little. You could tame it."

"*Tame* it!"

"Yes—easy enough. Every animal is grateful for kindness and petting, and they wouldn't *think* of hurting a person that pets them. Any book will tell you that. You try— that's all I ask; just try for two or three days. Why, you can get him so in a little while that he'll love you; and sleep with you; and won't stay away from you a minute; and will let you wrap him round your neck and put his head in your mouth."

"*Please*, Mars Tom—*doan'* talk so! I can't *stan'* it! He'd *let* me shove his head in my mouf—fer a favor, hain't it? I lay he'd wait a pow'ful long time 'fo' I *ast* him. En mo' en dat, I doan' *want* him to sleep with me."

"Jim, don't act so foolish. A prisoner's *got* to have some kind of a dumb pet, and if a rattlesnake hain't ever been tried, why, there's more glory to be gained in your being the first to ever try it than any other way you could ever think of to save your life."

"Why, Mars Tom, I doan' *want* no sich glory. Snake take 'n bite Jim's chin off, den *whah* is de glory? No, sah, I doan' want no sich doin's."

"Blame it, can't you *try*? I only *want* you to try—you needn't keep it up if it don't work."

"But de trouble all *done* ef de snake bite me while I's a-tryin' him. Mars Tom, I's willin' to tackle mos' anything 'at ain't onreasonable, but ef you en Huck fetches a rattlesnake in heah for me to tame, I's gwyne to *leave*, dat's *shore*."

"Well, then, let it go, let it go, if you're so bullheaded about it. We can get you some gartersnakes, and you can tie some buttons on their tails, and let on they're rattlesnakes, and I reckon that 'll have to do."

"I k'n stan' *dem*, Mars Tom, but blame' 'f I couldn' get along widout um, I tell you dat. I never knowed b'fo' 'twas so much bother and trouble to be a prisoner."

"Well, it *always* is when it's done right. You got any rats around here?"

"No, sah, I hain't seed none."

"Well, we'll get you some rats."

"Why, Mars Tom, I doan' *want* no rats. Dey's de dad-blamedest creturs to 'sturb a body, en rustle roun' over 'im, en bite his feet, when he's tryin' to sleep, I ever see. No, sah, gimme g'yarter-snakes, 'f I's got to have 'm, but doan' gimme no rats; I hain't got no use f'r um, skasely."

"But, Jim, you *got* to have 'em—they all do. So don't make no more fuss about it. Prisoners ain't ever without rats. There ain't no instance of it. And they train them, and pet them, and learn them tricks, and they get to be as sociable as flies. But you got to play music to them. You got anything to play music on?"

"I ain' got nuffin but a coase comb en a piece o' paper, en a juice-harp; but I reck'n dey wouldn' take no stock in a juice-harp."

"Yes they would. *They* don't care what kind of music 'tis. A jew's-harp's plenty good enough for a rat. All animals like music—in a prison they dote on it. Specially, painful music; and you can't get no other kind out of a jew's-harp. It always interests them; they come out to see what's the matter with you. Yes, you're all right; you're fixed very well. You want to set on your bed nights before you go to sleep, and early in the mornings, and play your jew's-harp; play 'The Last Link is Broken'—that's the thing that 'll scoop a rat quicker 'n anything else; and when you've played about two minutes you'll see all the rats, and the snakes, and spiders and things begin to feel worried about you, and come. And they'll just fairly swarm over you, and have a noble good time."

"Yes, *dey* will, I reck'n, Mars Tom, but what kine er time is *Jim* havin'? Blest if I kin see de pint. But I'll do it ef I got to. I reck'n I better keep de animals satisfied, en not have no trouble in de house."

Tom waited to think it over, and see if there wasn't nothing else; and pretty soon he says:

"Oh, there's one thing I forgot. Could you raise a flower here, do you reckon?"

"I doan' know but maybe I could, Mars Tom; but it's tolable dark in heah, en I ain' got no use f'r no flower, nohow, en she'd be a pow'ful sight o' trouble."

"Well, you try it, anyway. Some other prisoners has done it."

"One er dem big cat-tail-lookin' mullen-stalks would grow in heah, Mars Tom, I reck'n, but she wouldn't be wuth half de trouble she'd coss."

"Don't you believe it. We'll fetch you a little one, and you plant it in the corner over there, and raise it. And don't call it mullen, call it Pitchiola—that's its right name when it's in a prison. And you want to water it with your tears."

"Why, I got plenty spring water, Mars Tom."

"You don't *want* spring water; you want to water it with your tears. It's the way they always do."

"Why, Mars Tom, I lay I kin raise one er dem mullen-stalks twyste wid spring water whiles another man's a *start'n* one wid tears."

"That ain't the idea. You *got* to do it with tears."

"She'll die on my han's, Mars Tom, she sholy will; kase I doan' skasely ever cry."

So Tom was stumped. But he studied it over, and then said Jim would have to worry along the best he could with an onion. He promised he would go to the nigger cabins and drop one, private, in Jim's coffee-pot, in the morning. Jim said he would "jis' 's soon have tobacker in his coffee"; and found so much fault with it, and with the work and bother of raising the mullen, and jew's-harping the rats, and petting and flattering up the snakes and spiders and things, on top of all the other work he had to do on pens, and inscriptions, and journals, and things, which made it more trouble and worry and responsibility to be a prisoner than anything he ever undertook, that Tom most lost all patience with him; and said he was just loadened down with more gaudier chances than a prisoner ever had in the world to make a name for himself, and yet he didn't know enough to appreciate them, and they was just about wasted on him. So Jim he was sorry, and said he wouldn't behave so no more, and then me and Tom shoved for bed.

39. TOM WRITES NONNAMOUS LETTERS

In the morning we went up to the village and bought a wire rat-trap and fetched it down, and unstopped the best rat-hole, and in about an hour we had fifteen of the bulliest kind of ones; and then we took it and put it in a safe place under Aunt Sally's bed. But while we was gone for spiders little Thomas Franklin Benjamin Jefferson Elexander Phelps found it there, and opened the door of it to see if the rats would come out, and they did; and Aunt Sally she come in, and when we got back she was a-standing on top of the bed raising Cain, and the rats was doing what they could to keep off the dull times for her. So she took and dusted us both with the hickry, and we was as much as two hours catching another fifteen or sixteen, drat that meddlesome cub, and they warn't the likeliest, nuther, because the first haul was the pick of the flock. I never see a likelier lot of rats than what that first haul was.

We got a splendid stock of sorted spiders, and bugs, and frogs, and caterpillars, and one thing or another; and we like to got a hornet's nest, but we didn't. The family was at home. We didn't give it right up, but stayed with them as long as we could; because we allowed we'd tire them out or they'd got to tire us out, and they done it. Then we got allycumpain and rubbed on the places, and was pretty near all right again, but couldn't set down convenient. And so we went for the snakes, and grabbed a couple of dozen garters and housesnakes, and put them in a bag, and put it in our room, and by that time it was suppertime, and a rattling good honest day's work:

and hungry?—oh, no, I reckon not! And there warn't a blessed snake up there when we went back—we didn't half tie the sack, and they worked out somehow, and left. But it didn't matter much, because they was still on the premises somewheres. So we judged we could get some of them again. No, there warn't no real scarcity of snakes about the house for a considerable spell. You'd see them dripping from the rafters and places every now and then; and they generly landed in your plate, or down the back of your neck, and most of the time where you didn't want them. Well, they was handsome and striped, and there warn't no harm in a million of them; but that never made no difference to Aunt Sally; she despised snakes, be the breed what they might, and she couldn't stand them no way you could fix it; and every time one of them flopped down on her, it didn't make no difference what she was doing, she would just lay that work down and light out. I never see such a woman. And you could hear her whoop to Jericho. You couldn't get her to take a-holt of one of them with the tongs. And if she turned over and found one in bed she would scramble out and lift a howl that you would think the house was afire. She disturbed the old man so that he said he could most wish there hadn't ever been no snakes created. Why, after every last snake had been gone clear out of the house for as much as a week Aunt Sally warn't over it yet; she warn't near over it; when she was setting thinking about something you could touch her on the back of her neck with a feather and she would jump right out of her stockings. It was very curious. But Tom said all women was just so. He said they was made that way for some reason or other.

We got a licking every time one of our snakes come in her way, and she allowed these lickings warn't nothing to what she would do if we ever loaded up the place again with them. I didn't mind the lickings, because they didn't amount to nothing; but I minded the trouble we had to lay in another lot. But we got them laid in, and all the other things; and you never see a cabin as blithesome as Jim's was when they'd all swarm out for music and go for him. Jim didn't like the spiders, and the spiders didn't like Jim; and so they'd lay for him, and make it mighty warm for him. And he said that between the rats and the snakes and the grindstone there warn't no room in bed for him, skasely; and when there was, a body couldn't sleep, it was so lively, and it was always lively, he said, because *they* never all slept at one time, but took turn about, so when the snakes was asleep the rats was on deck, and when the rats turned in the snakes come on watch, so he always had one gang under him, in his way, and t'other gang having a circus over him, and if he got up to hunt a new place the spiders would take a chance at him as he crossed over. He said if he ever got out this time he wouldn't ever be a prisoner again, not for a salary.

Well, by the end of three weeks everything was in pretty good shape. The shirt was sent in early, in a pie, and every time a rat bit Jim he would get up and write a line in his journal whilst the ink was fresh; the pens was made, the inscriptions and so on was all carved on the grindstone; the bed-leg was sawed in two, and we had et up the sawdust, and it give us a most amazing stomach-ache. We reckoned we was all going to die, but didn't. It was the most undigestible sawdust I ever see; and Tom said the same. But as I was saying, we'd got all the work done now, at last; and we was all pretty much fagged out, too, but mainly Jim. The old man had wrote a couple of times to the plantation below Orleans to come and get their runaway nigger, but hadn't got no answer, because there warn't no such plantation; so he allowed he would advertise Jim in the St. Louis and New Orleans papers; and when he mentioned the St. Louis ones it give me the cold shivers, and I see we hadn't no time to lose. So Tom said, now for the nonnamous letters.

"What's them?" I says.

"Warnings to the people that something is up. Sometimes it's done one way, sometimes another. But there's always somebody spying around that gives notice to the governor of the castle. When Louis XVI. was going to light out of the Tooleries a servant-girl done it. It's a very good way, and so is the nonnamous letters. We'll use them both. And it's usual for the prisoner's mother to change clothes with him, and she stays in, and he slides out in her clothes. We'll do that, too."

"But looky here, Tom, what do we want to *warn* anybody for that something's up? Let them find it out for themselves—it's their lookout."

"Yes, I know; but you can't depend on them. It's the way they've acted from the very start —left us to do *everything*. They're so confiding and mullet-headed they don't take notice of nothing at all. So if we don't *give* them notice there won't be nobody nor nothing to interfere with us, and so after all our hard work and trouble this escape'll go off perfectly flat; won't amount to nothing—won't be nothing *to* it."

"Well, as for me, Tom, that's the way I'd like."

"Shucks!" he says, and looked disgusted. So I says:

"But I ain't going to make no complaint. Any way that suits you suits me. What you going to do about the servant-girl?"

"You'll be her. You slide in, in the middle of the night, and hook that yaller girl's frock."

"Why, Tom, that 'll make trouble next morning; because, of course, she prob'ly hain't got any but that one."

"I know; but you don't want it but fifteen minutes, to carry the nonnamous letter and shove it under the front door."

"All right, then, I'll do it; but I could carry it just as handy in my own togs."

"You wouldn' look like a servant-girl *then,* would you?"

"No, but there won't be nobody to see what I look like, *anyway*."

"That ain't got nothing to do with it. The thing for us to do is just to do our *duty*, and not worry about whether anybody *sees* us do it or not. Hain't you got no principle at all?"

"All right, I ain't saying nothing; I'm the servant-girl. Who's Jim's mother?"

"I'm his mother. I'll hook a gown from Aunt Sally."

"Well, then, you'll have to stay in the cabin when me and Jim leaves."

"Not much. I'll stuff Jim's clothes full of straw and lay it on his bed to represent his mother in disguise, and Jim 'll take the nigger woman's gown off of me and wear it, and we'll all evade together. When a prisoner of style escapes it's called an evasion. It's always called so when a king escapes, f'r instance.

And the same with a king's son; it don't make no difference whether he's a natural one or an unnatural one."

So Tom he wrote the nonnamous letter, and I smouched the yaller wench's frock that night, and put it on, and shoved it under the front door, the way Tom told me to. It said:

Beware. Trouble is brewing. Keep a sharp look-out.   UNKNOWN FRIEND.

Next night we struck a picture, which Tom drawed in blood, of a skull and crossbones on the front door; and next night another one of a coffin on the back door. I never see a family in such a sweat. They couldn't 'a' been worse scared if the place had 'a' been full of ghosts laying for them behind everything and under the beds and shivering through the air. If a door banged, Aunt Sally she jumped and said "ouch!" if anything fell, she jumped and said "ouch!" if you happened to touch her, when she warn't noticing, she done the same; she couldn't face no way and be satisfied, because she allowed there was something behind her every time—so she was always a-whirling around sudden, and saying "ouch," and before she'd got two-thirds around she'd whirl back again, and say it again; and she was afraid to go to bed, but she dasn't set up. So the thing was working very well, Tom said; he said he never see a thing work more satisfactory. He said it showed it was done right.

So he said, now for the grand bulge! So the very next morning at the streak of dawn we got another letter ready, and was wondering what we better do with it, because we heard them say at supper they was going to have a nigger on watch at both doors all night. Tom he went down the lightning-rod to spy around; and the nigger at the back door was asleep, and he stuck it in the back of his neck and come back. This letter said:

Don't betray me, I wish to be your friend. There is a desperate gang of cutthroats from over in the Indian Territory going to steal your runaway nigger tonight, and they have been trying to scare you so as you will stay in the house and not bother them. I am one of the gang, but have got religgion and wish to quit it and lead an honest life again, and will betray the helish design. They will sneak down from northards, along the fence, at midnight exact, with a false key, and go in the nigger's cabin to get him. I am to be off a piece and blow a tin horn if I see any danger; but stead of that I will BA like a sheep soon as they get in and not blow at all; then whilst they are getting his chains loose, you slip there and lock them in, and can kill them at your leasure. Don't do anything but just the way I am telling you; if you do they will suspicion something and raise whoop-jamboreehoo. I do not wish any reward but to know I have done the right thing.   UNKNOWN FRIEND.

40. A MIXED-UP AND SPLENDID RESCUE

We was feeling pretty good after breakfast, and took my canoe and went over the river a-fishing, with a lunch, and had a good time, and took a look at the raft and found her all right, and got home late to supper, and found them in such a sweat and worry they didn't know which end they was standing on, and made us go right off to bed the minute we was done supper, and wouldn't tell us what the trouble was, and never let on a word about the new letter, but didn't need to, because we knowed as much about it as anybody did, and as soon as we was half up-stairs and her back was turned we slid for the cellar cupboard and loaded up a good lunch and took it up to our room and went to bed, and got up about half past eleven, and Tom put on Aunt Sally's dress that he stole and was going to start with the lunch, but says:

"Where's the butter?"

"I laid out a hunk of it," I says, "on a piece of a corn-pone."

"Well, you *left* it laid out, then—it ain't here."

"We can get along without it," I says.

"We can get along *with* it, too," he says; "just you slide down cellar and fetch it. And then mosey right down the lightning-rod and come along. I'll go and stuff the straw into Jim's clothes to represent his mother in disguise, and be ready to *ba* like a sheep and shove soon as you get there."

So out he went, and down cellar went I. The hunk of butter, big as a person's fist, was where I had left it, so I took up the slab of corn-pone with it on, and blowed out my light, and started up-stairs very stealthy, and got up to the main floor all right, but here comes Aunt Sally with a candle, and I clapped the truck in my hat, and clapped my hat on my head, and the next second she see me; and she says:

"You been down cellar?"

"Yes'm."

"What you been doing down there?"

"Noth'n."

"*Noth'n!*"

"No'm."

"Well, then, what possessed you to go down there this time of night?"

"I don't know 'm."

"You don't *know?* Don't answer me that way. Tom, I want to know what you been *doing* down there."

"I hain't been doing a single thing, Aunt Sally, I hope to gracious if I have."

I reckoned she'd let me go now, and as a generl thing she would; but I s'pose there was so many strange things going on she was just in a sweat about every little thing that warn't yard-stick straight; so she says, very decided:

"You just march into that sitting-room and stay there till I come. You been up to something you no business to, and I lay I'll find out what it is before *I'm* done with you."

So she went away as I opened the door and walked into the setting-room. My, but there was a crowd there! Fifteen farmers, and every one of them had a gun. I was most powerful sick, and slunk to a chair and set down. They was setting around, some of them talking a little, in a low voice, and all of them fidgety and uneasy, but trying to look like they warn't; but I knowed they was, because they was always taking off their hats, and putting them on, and scratching their heads, and changing their seats, and fumbling with their buttons. I warn't easy myself, but I didn't take my hat off, all the same.

I did wish Aunt Sally would come, and get done with me, and lick me, if she wanted to, and let me get away and tell Tom how we'd overdone this thing, and what a thundering hornet's nest we'd got ourselves into, so we could stop fooling around straight off, and clear out with Jim before these rips got out of patience and come for us.

At last she come and begun to ask me questions, but I *couldn't* answer them straight, I didn't know which end of me was up; because these men was in such a fidget now that some

was wanting to start right *now* and lay for them desperadoes, and saying it warn't but a few minutes to midnight; and others was trying to get them to hold on and wait for the sheep-signal; and here was Aunty pegging away at the questions, and me a-shaking all over and ready to sink down in my tracks I was that scared; and the place getting hotter and hotter, and the butter beginning to melt and run down my neck and behind my ears; and pretty soon, when one of them says, *"I'm* for going and getting in the cabin *first* and right *now,* and catching them when they come," I most dropped; and a streak of butter comes a-trickling down my forehead, and Aunt Sally she see it, and turns white as a sheet, and says:

"For the land's sake, what *is* the matter with the child? He's got the brain-fever as shore as you're born, and they're oozing out!"

And everybody runs to see, and she snatches off my hat, and out comes the bread and what was left of the butter, and she grabbed me, and hugged me, and says:

"Oh, what a turn you did give me! and how glad and grateful I am it ain't no worse; for luck's against us, and it never rains but it pours, and when I see that truck I thought we'd lost you, for I knowed by the color and all it was just like your brains would be if— Dear, dear, whyd'n't you *tell* me that was what you'd been down there for, *I* wouldn't 'a' cared. Now cler out to bed, and don't lemme see no more of you till morning!"

I was up-stairs in a second, and down the lightning-rod in another one, and shinning through the dark for the lean-to. I couldn't hardly get my words out, I was so anxious; but I told Tom as quick as I could we must jump for it now, and not a minute to lose— the house full of men, yonder, with guns!

His eyes just blazed; and he says:

"No!—is that so? *Ain't* it bully! Why, Huck, if it was to do over again, I bet I could fetch two hundred! If we could put it off till—"

"Hurry! *hurry!"* I says. "Where's Jim?"

"Right at your elbow; if you reach out your arm you can touch him. He's dressed, and everything's ready. Now we'll slide out and give the sheep-signal."

But when we heard the tramp of men coming to the door, and heard them begin to fumble with the padlock, and heard a man say:

"I *told* you we'd be too soon; they haven't come—the door is locked. Here, I'll lock some of you into the cabin, and you lay for 'em in the dark and kill 'em when they come; and the rest scatter around a piece, and listen if you can hear 'em coming."

So in they come, but couldn't see us in the dark, and most trod on us whilst we was hustling to get under the bed. But we got under all right, and out through the hole, swift but soft—Jim first, me next, and Tom last, which was according to Tom's orders. Now we was in the lean-to, and heard trampings close by outside. So we crept to the door, and Tom stopped us there and put his eye to the crack, but couldn't make out nothing, it was so dark; and whispered and said he would listen for the steps to get further, and when he nudged us Jim must glide out first, and him last. So he set his ear to the crack and listened, and listened, and listened, and the steps a-scraping around out there all the time; and at last he nudged us, and we slid out, and stooped down, not breathing, and not making the least noise, and slipped stealthy towards the fence in Injun file, and got to it all right, and me and Jim over it; but Tom's britches catched fast on a splinter on the top rail, and then he hear the steps coming, so he had to pull loose, which snapped the splinter and made a noise; and as he dropped on our tracks and started somebody sings out:

"Who's that? Answer, or I'll shoot!"

But we didn't answer; we just unfurled our heels and shoved. Then there was a rush, and a *bang, bang, bang!* and the bullets fairly whizzed around us! We heard them sing out:

"Here they are! They've broke for the river! After 'em, boys, and turn loose the dogs!"

So here they come, full tilt. We could hear them because they wore boots and yelled, but we didn't wear no boots and didn't yell. We was in the path to the mill; and when they got pretty close onto us we dodged into the bush and let them go by, and then dropped in behind them. They'd had all the dogs shut up, so they wouldn't scare off the robbers; but by this time somebody had let them loose, and here they come, making powwow enough for a million; but they was our dogs; so we

stopped in our tracks till they catched up; and when they see it warn't nobody but us, and no excitement to offer them, they only just said howdy, and tore right ahead towards the shouting and clattering; and then we upsteam again, and whizzed along after them till we was nearly to the mill, and then struck up through the bush to where my canoe was tied, and hopped in and pulled for dear life towards the middle of the river, but didn't make no more noise than we was obleeged to. Then we struck out, easy and comfortable for the island where my raft was; and we could hear them yelling and barking at each other all up and down the bank, till we was so far away the sounds got dim and died out. And when we stepped onto the raft I says:

"*Now,* old Jim, you're a free man *again,* and I bet you won't ever be a slave no more."

"En a mighty good job it wuz, too, Huck. It 'uz planned beautiful, en it 'uz *done* beautiful; en dey ain't *nobody* kin git up a plan dat's mo' mixed up en splendid den what dat one wuz."

We was all glad as we could be, but Tom was the gladdest of all because he had a bullet in the calf of his leg.

When me and Jim heard that we didn't feel as brash as what we did before. It was hurting him considerable, and bleeding; so we laid him in the wigwam and tore up one of the duke's shirts for to bandage him, but he says:

"Gimme the rags; I can do it myself. Don't stop now; don't fool around here, and the evasion booming along so handsome; man the sweeps, and set her loose! Boys, we done it elegant!—'deed we did. I wish *we'd* 'a' had the handling of Louis XVI., there wouldn't 'a' been no 'Son of Saint Louis, ascend to heaven!' wrote down in *his* biography; no, sir, we'd 'a' whooped him over the *border*—that's what we'd 'a' done with *him*—and done it just as slick as nothing at all, too. Man the sweeps—man the sweeps!"

But me and Jim was consulting—and thinking. And after we'd thought a minute, I says:

"Say it, Jim."

So he says:

"Well, den, dis is de way it look to me, Huck. Ef it wuz *him* dat 'uz bein' sot free, en one er de boys wuz to git shot, would he say, 'Go on en save me, nemmine 'bout a doctor f'r to save dis one'? Is dat like Mars Tom Sawyer? Would he say dat? You *bet* he wouldn't! *Well,* den, is *Jim* gwyne to say it? No, sah—I doan' budge a step out'n dis place 'dout a *doctor;* not if it's forty year!"

I knowed he was white inside, and I reckoned he'd say what he did say—so it was all right now, and I told Tom I was a-going for a doctor. He raised considerable row about it, but me and Jim stuck to it and wouldn't budge; so he was for crawling out and setting the raft loose himself; but we wouldn't let him. Then he give us a piece of his mind, but it didn't do no good.

So when he sees me getting the canoe ready, he says:

"Well, then, if you're bound to go, I'll tell you the way to do when you get to the village. Shut the door and blindfold the doctor tight and fast, and make him swear to be silent as the grave, and put a purse full of gold in his hand, and then take and lead him all around the back alleys and everywheres in the dark, and then fetch him here in the canoe, in a roundabout way amongst the islands, and search him and take his chalk away from him, and don't give it back to him till you get him back to the village, or else he will chalk this raft so he can find it again. It's the way they all do."

So I said I would, and left, and Jim was to hide in the woods when he see the doctor coming till he was gone again.

41. "MUST 'A' BEEN SPERITS"

The doctor was an old man; a very nice, kind-looking old man when I got him up. I told him me and my brother was over on Spanish Island hunting yesterday afternoon, and camped on a piece of a raft we found, and about midnight he must 'a' kicked his gun in his dreams, for it went off and shot him in the leg, and we wanted him to go over there and fix it and not say nothing about it, nor let anybody know, because we wanted to come home this evening and surprise the folks.

"Who is your folks?" he says.

"The Phelpses, down yonder."

"Oh," he says. And after a minute, he says:

"How'd you say he got shot?"

"He had a dream," I says, "and it shot him."

"Singular dream," he says.

So he lit up his lantern, and got his saddlebags, and we started. But when he see the canoe he didn't like the look of her—said she was big enough for one, but didn't look pretty safe for two. I says:

"Oh, you needn't be afeard, sir, she carried the three of us easy enough."

"What three?"

"Why, me and Sid, and—and—and *the guns;* that's what I mean."

"Oh," he says.

But he put his foot on the gunnel and rocked her, and shook his head, and said he reckoned he'd look around for a bigger one. But they was all locked and chained; so he took my canoe, and said for me to wait till he come back, or I could hunt around further, or maybe I better go down home and get them ready for the surprise if I wanted to. But I said I didn't; so I told him just how to find the raft, and then he started.

I struck an idea pretty soon. I says to myself, spos'n he can't fix that leg just in three shakes of a sheep's tail, as the saying is? spos'n it takes him three or four days? What are we going to do?—lay around there till he lets the cat out of the bag? No, sir; I know what *I'll* do. I'll wait, and when he comes back if he says he's got to go any more I'll get down there, too, if I swim; and we'll take and tie him, and keep him, and shove out down the river; and when Tom's done with him we'll give him what it's worth, or all we got, and then let him get ashore.

So then I crept into a lumber-pile to get some sleep; and next time I waked up the sun was away up over my head! I shot out and went for the doctor's house, but they told me he'd gone away in the night some time or other, and warn't back yet. Well, thinks I, that looks powerful bad for Tom, and I'll dig out for the island right off. So away I shoved, and turned the corner, and nearly rammed my head into Uncle Silas's stomach! He says:

"Why, *Tom!* Where you been all this time, you rascal?"

"*I* hain't been nowheres," I said, "only just hunting for the runaway nigger—me and Sid."

"Why, where ever did you go?" he says. "Your aunt's been mighty uneasy."

"She needn't," I says, "because we was all right. We followed the men and the dogs, but they outrun us, and we lost them; but we thought we heard them on the water, so we got a canoe and took out after them and crossed over, but couldn't find nothing of them; so we cruised along up-shore till we got kind of tired and beat out; and tied up the canoe and went to sleep, and never waked up till about an hour ago; then we paddled over here to hear the news, and Sid's at the post-office to see what he can hear, and I'm a-branching out to get something to eat for us, and then we're going home."

So then we went to the post-office to get "Sid"; but just as I suspicioned, he warn't there; so the old man he got a letter out of the office, and we waited awhile longer, but Sid didn't come; so the old man said, come along, let Sid foot it home, or canoe it, when he got done fooling around—but we would ride. I couldn't get him to let me stay and wait for Sid; and he said there warn't no use in it, and I must come along, and let Aunt Sally see we was all right.

When we got home Aunt Sally was that glad to see me she laughed and cried both, and hugged me, and give me one of them lickings of hern that don't amount to shucks, and said she'd serve Sid the same when he come.

And the place was plumb full of farmers and farmers' wives, to dinner; and such another clack a body never heard. Old Mrs. Hotchkiss was the worst; her tongue was a-going all the time. She says:

"Well, Sister Phelps, I've ransacked that-air cabin over, an' I b'lieve the nigger was crazy. I says to Sister Damrell—didn't I, Sister Damrell?—s'I, he's crazy, s'I—them's the very words, I said. You all hearn me: he's crazy, s'I; everything shows it, s'I. Look at that-air grindstone, s'I; want to tell me't any cretur 't's in his right mind 's a-goin' to scrabble all them crazy things onto a grindstone? s'I. Here sich 'n' such a person busted his heart; 'n' here so 'n' so pegged along for thirty-seven year, 'n' all that—natcherl son o' Louis somebody, 'n' sich everlast'n rubbage. He's plumb crazy, s'I; it's what I says in the fust place, it's what I says in the middle, 'n' it's what I says last 'n' all the time—the nigger's crazy—crazy 's Nebokoodnezzer, s'I."

"An' look at that-air ladder made out'n rags, Sister Hotchkiss," says old Mrs. Damrell; "what in the name o' goodness *could* he ever want of—"

"The very words I was a-sayin' no longer ago th'n this minute to Sister Utterback, 'n' she'll tell you so herself. Sh-she, look at that-air rag ladder, sh-she; 'n' s'I, yes, *look* at it, s'I —what *could* he 'a' wanted of it? s'I. Sh-she, Sister Hotchkiss, sh-she—"

"But how in the nation'd they ever *git* that grindstone *in* there, *anyway*? 'n' who dug that-air *hole*? 'n' who—"

"My very *words*, Brer Penrod! I was a-sayin' —pass that-air sasser o' m'lasses, won't ye?—I was a-sayin' to Sister Dunlap, jist this minute, how *did* they git that grindstone in there? s'I. Without *help*, mind you—'thout *help*! Thar's where 'tis. Don't tell *me*, s'I; there *wuz* help, s'I; 'n' ther' wuz a *plenty* help, too, s'I; ther's ben a *dozen* a-helpin' that nigger, 'n' I lay I'd skin every last nigger on this place but *I'd* find out who done it, s'I; 'n' moreover, s'I—"

"A *dozen* says you!—*forty* couldn't 'a' done everything that's been done. Look at them case-knife saws and things, how tedious they've been made; look at that bed-leg sawed off with 'm, a week's work for six men: look at that nigger made out'n straw on the bed; and look at—"

"You may *well* say it, Brer Hightower! It's jist as I was a-sayin' to Brer Phelps, his own self. S'e, what do *you* think of it, Sister Hotchkiss? s'e. Think o' what, Brer Phelps? s'I. Think o' that bed-leg sawed off that a way? s'e. *Think* of it? s'I. I lay it never sawed *itself* off, s'I—somebody *sawed* it, s'I; that's my opinion, take it or leave it, it mayn't be no 'count, s'I, but sich as 't is, it's my opinion, s'I, 'n' if anybody k'n start a better one, s'I, let him *do* it, s'I, that's all. I says to Sister Dunlap, s'I—"

"Why, dog my cats, they must 'a' ben a house-full o' niggers in there every night for four weeks to 'a' done all that work, Sister Phelps. Look at that shirt—every last inch of it kivered over with secret African writ'n done with blood! Must 'a' ben a raft uv 'm at it right along, all the time, amost. Why, I'd give two dollars to have it read to me; 'n' as for the niggers that wrote it, I 'low I'd take 'n' lash 'm t'll—"

"People to *help* him, Brother Marples! Well, I reckon you'd *think* so if you'd 'a' been in this house for a while back. Why, they've stole everything they could lay their hands on —and we a-watching all the time, mind you. They stole that shirt right off o' the line! and as for that sheet they made the rag ladder out of, ther' ain't no telling how many times they *didn't* steal that; and flour, and candles, and candlesticks, and spoons, and the old warming-pan, and most a thousand things that I disremember now, and my new calico dress; and me and Silas and my Sid and Tom on the constant watch day *and* night, as I was a-telling you, and not a one of us could catch hide nor hair nor sight nor sound of them; and here at the last minute, lo and behold you, they slides right in under our noses and fools us, and not only fools *us* but the Injun Territory robbers too, and actuly gets *away* with that nigger safe and sound, and that with sixteen men and twenty-two dogs right on their very heels at that very time! I tell you, it just bangs anything I ever *heard* of. Why, *sperits* couldn't 'a' done better and been no smarter. And I reckon they must 'a' *been* sperits—because, *you* know our dogs, and ther' ain't no better; well, them dogs never even got on the *track* of 'm once! You explain *that* to me if you can!—*any* of you!"

"Well, it does beat—"

"Laws alive, I never—"

"So help me, I wouldn't 'a' be—"

"*House*-thieves as well as—"

"Goodnessgracioussakes, I'd 'a' ben afeard to *live* in sich a—"

" 'Fraid to *live!*—why, I was that scared I dasn't hardly go to bed, or get up, or lay down, or *set* down, Sister Ridgeway. Why, they'd steal the very—why, goodness sakes, you can guess what kind of a fluster *I* was in by the time midnight come last night. I hope to gracious if I warn't afraid they'd steal some o' the family! I was just to that pass I didn't have no reasoning faculties no more. It looks foolish enough *now,* in the daytime; but I says to myself, there's my two poor boys asleep, 'way up-stairs in that lonesome room, and I declare to goodness I was that uneasy 't I crep' up there and locked 'em in! I *did.* And anybody would. Because, you know, when you get scared that way, and it keeps running on, and getting worse and worse all the time, and your wits gets to addling, and you get to doing all

sorts o' wild things, and by and by you think to yourself, spos'n *I* was a boy, and was away up there, and the door ain't locked, and you—" She stopped, looking kind of wondering, and then she turned her head around slow, and when her eye lit on me—I got up and took a walk.

Says I to myself, I can explain better how we come to not be in that room this morning if I go out to one side and study over it a little. So I done it. But I dasn't go fur, or she'd 'a' sent for me. And when it was late in the day the people all went, and then I come in and told her the noise and shooting waked up me and "Sid," and the door was locked, and we wanted to see the fun, so we went down the lightning-rod, and both of us got hurt a little, and we didn't never want to try *that* no more. And then I went on and told her all what I told Uncle Silas before; and then she said she'd forgive us, and maybe it was all right enough anyway, and about what a body might expect of boys, for all boys was a pretty harum-scarum lot as fur as she could see; and so, as long as no harm hadn't come of it, she judged she better put in her time being grateful we was alive and well and she had us still, stead of fretting over what was past and done. So then she kissed me, and patted me on the head, and dropped into a kind of a brown-study; and pretty soon jumps up, and says:

"Why, lawsamercy, it's most night, and Sid not come yet! What *has* become of that boy?"

I see my chance; so I skips up and says:

"I'll run right up to town and get him," I says.

"No, you won't," she says. "You'll stay right wher' you are; one's enough to be lost at a time. If he ain't here to supper, your uncle 'll go."

Well, he warn't there to supper; so right after supper uncle went.

He come back about ten a little bit uneasy; hadn't run across Tom's track. Aunt Sally was a good *deal* uneasy; but Uncle Silas he said there warn't no occasion to be—boys will be boys, he said, and you'll see this one turn up in the morning all sound and right. So she had to be satisfied. But she said she'd set up for him awhile anyway, and keep a light burning so he could see it.

And then when I went up to bed she come up with me and fetched her candle, and tucked me in, and mothered me so good I felt mean, and like I couldn't look her in the face; and she set down on the bed and talked with me a long time, and said what a splendid boy Sid was, and didn't seem to want to ever stop talking about him; and kept asking me every now and then if I reckoned he could 'a' got lost, or hurt, or maybe drownded, and might be laying at this minute somewheres suffering or dead, and she not by him to help him, and so the tears would drip down silent, and I would tell her that Sid was all right, and would be home in the morning, sure; and she would squeeze my hand, or maybe kiss me, and tell me to say it again, and keep on saying it, because it done her good, and she was in so much trouble. And when she was going away she looked down in my eyes so steady and gentle, and says:

"The door ain't going to be locked, Tom, and there's the window and the rod; but you'll be good, *won't* you? And you won't go? For *my* sake."

Laws knows I *wanted* to go bad enough to see about Tom, and was all intending to go; but after that I wouldn't 'a' went, not for kingdoms.

But she was on my mind and Tom was on my mind, so I slept very restless. And twice I went down the rod away in the night, and slipped around front, and see her setting there by her candle in the window with her eyes towards the road and the tears in them; and I wished I could do something for her, but I couldn't, only to swear that I wouldn't never do nothing to grieve her any more. And the third time I waked up at dawn, and slid down, and she was there yet, and her candle was most out, and her old gray head was resting on her hands, and she was asleep.

42. WHY THEY DIDN'T HANG JIM

The old man was up-town again before breakfast, but couldn't get no track of Tom; and both of them set at the table thinking, and not saying nothing, and looking mournful, and their coffee getting cold, and not eating anything. And by and by the old man says:

"Did I give you the letter?"

"What letter?"

"The one I got yesterday out of the post office."

"No, you didn't give me no letter."

"Well, I must 'a' forgot it."

So he rummaged his pockets, and then went off somewheres where he had laid it down, and fetched it, and give it to her. She says:

"Why, it's from St. Petersburg—it's from Sis."

I allowed another walk would do me good; but I couldn't stir. But before she could break it open she dropped it and run—for she see something. And so did I. It was Tom Sawyer on a mattress; and that old doctor; and Jim, in *her* calico dress, with his hands tied behind him; and a lot of people. I hid the letter behind the first thing that come handy, and rushed. She flung herself at Tom, crying, and says:

"Oh, he's dead, he's dead, I know he's dead!"

And Tom he turned his head a little, and muttered something or other, which showed he warn't in his right mind; then she flung up her hands, and says:

"He's alive, thank God! And that's enough!" and she snatched a kiss of him, and flew for the house to get the bed ready, and scattering orders right and left at the niggers and everybody else, as fast as her tongue could go, every jump of the way.

I followed the men to see what they was going to do with Jim; and the old doctor and Uncle Silas followed after Tom into the house. The men was very huffy, and some of them wanted to hang Jim for an example to all the other niggers around there, so they wouldn't be trying to run away like Jim done, and making such a raft of trouble, and keeping a whole family scared most to death for days and nights. But the others said, don't do it, it wouldn't answer at all; he ain't our nigger, and his owner would turn up and make us pay for him, sure. So that cooled them down a little, because the people that's always the most anxious for to hang a nigger that hain't done just right is always the very ones that ain't the most anxious to pay for him when they've got their satisfaction out of him.

They cussed Jim considerable, though, and

give him a cuff or two side the head once in a while, but Jim never said nothing, and he never let on to know me, and they took him to the same cabin, and put his own clothes on him, and chained him again, and not to no bed-leg this time, but to a big staple drove into the bottom log, and chained his hands, too, and both legs, and said he warn't to have nothing but bread and water to eat after this till his owner come, or he was sold at auction because he didn't come in a certain length of time, and filled up our hole, and said a couple of farmers with guns must stand watch around about the cabin every night, and a bulldog tied to the door in the daytime; and about this time they was through with the job and was tapering off with a kind of generl good-by cussing, and then the old doctor comes and takes a look, and says:

"Don't be no rougher on him than you're obleeged to, because he ain't a bad nigger. When I got to where I found the boy I see I couldn't cut the bullet out without some help, and he warn't in no condition for me to leave to go and get help; and he got a little worse and a little worse, and after a long time he went out of his head, and wouldn't let me come a-nigh him any more, and said if I chalked his raft he'd kill me, and no end of wild foolishness like that, and I see I couldn't do anything at all with him; so I says, I got to have *help* somehow; and the minute I says it out crawls this nigger from somewheres and says he'll help, and he done it, too, and done it very well. Of course I judged he must be a runaway nigger, and there I *was!* and there I had to stick right straight along all the rest of the day and all night. It was a fix, I tell you! I had a couple of patients with the chills, and of course I'd of liked to run up to town and see them, but I dasn't, because the nigger might get away, and then I'd be to blame; and yet never a skiff come close enough for me to hail. So there I had to stick plumb until daylight this morning; and I never see a nigger that was a better nuss or faithfuler, and yet he was risking his freedom to do it, and was all tired out, too, and I see plain enough he'd been worked main hard lately. I liked the nigger for that; I tell you, gentlemen, a nigger like that is worth a thousand dollars—and kind treatment, too. I

had everything I needed, and the boy was doing as well there as he would 'a' done at home—better, maybe, because it was so quiet; but there I *was,* with both of 'm on my hands, and there I had to stick till about dawn this morning; then some men in a skiff come by, and as good luck would have it the nigger was setting by the pallet with his head propped on his knees sound asleep; so I motioned them in quiet, and they slipped up on him and grabbed him and tied him before he knowed what he was about, and we never had no trouble. And the boy being in a kind of a flighty sleep, too, we muffled the oars and hitched the raft on, and towed her over very nice and quiet, and the nigger never made the least row nor said a word from the start. He ain't no bad nigger, gentlemen; that's what I think about him."

Somebody says:

"Well, it sounds very good, doctor, I'm obleeged to say."

Then the others softened up a little, too, and I was mighty thankful to that old doctor for doing Jim that good turn; and I was glad it was according to my judgment of him, too; because I thought he had a good heart in him and was a good man the first time I see him. Then they all agreed that Jim had acted very well, and was deserving to have some notice took of it, and reward. So every one of them promised, right out and hearty, that they wouldn't cuss him no more.

Then they come out and locked him up. I hoped they was going to say he could have one or two of the chains took off, because they was rotten heavy, or could have meat and greens with his bread and water; but they didn't think of it, and I reckoned it warn't best for me to mix in, but I judged I'd get the doctor's yarn to Aunt Sally somehow or other as soon as I'd got through the breakers that was laying just ahead of me—explanations, I mean, of how I forgot to mention about Sid being shot when I was telling how him and me put in that dratted night paddling around hunting the runaway nigger.

But I had plenty time. Aunt Sally she stuck to the sick-room all day and all night, and every time I see Uncle Silas mooning around I dodged him.

Next morning I heard Tom was a good

deal better, and they said Aunt Sally was gone to get a nap. So I slips to the sick-room, and if I found him awake I reckoned we could put up a yarn for the family that would wash. But he was sleeping, and sleeping very peaceful, too; and pale, not fire-faced the way he was when he come. So I set down and laid for him to wake. In about half an hour Aunt Sally comes gliding in, and there I was, up a stump again! She motioned me to be still, and set down by me, and begun to whisper, and said we could all be joyful now, because all the symptoms was first-rate, and he'd been sleeping like that for ever so long, and looking better and peacefuler all the time, and ten to one he'd wake up in his right mind.

So we set there watching, and by and by he stirs a bit, and opens his eyes very natural, and takes a look, and says:

"Hello!—why, I'm at *home!* How's that? Where's the raft?"

"It's all right," I says.

"And *Jim?*"

"The same," I says, but couldn't say it pretty brash. But he never noticed, but says:

"Good! Splendid! *Now* we're all right and safe! Did you tell Aunty?"

I was going to say yes; but she chipped in and says:

"About what, Sid?"

"Why, about the way the whole thing was done."

"What whole thing?"

"Why, *the* whole thing. There ain't but one; how we set the runaway nigger free—me and Tom."

"Good land! Set the run— What *is* the child talking about! Dear, dear, out of his head again!"

"*No,* I ain't out of my HEAD; I know all what I'm talking about. We *did* set him free—me and Tom. We laid out to do it, and we *done* it. And we done it elegant, too." He'd got a start, and she never checked him up, just set and stared and stared, and let him clip along, and I see it warn't no use for *me* to put in. "Why, Aunty, it cost us a power of work— weeks of it—hours and hours, every night, whilst you was all asleep. And we had to steal candles, and the sheet, and the shirt, and your dress, and spoons, and tin plates, and case-knives, and the warming-pan, and the grind-

stone, and flour, and just no end of things, and you can't think what work it was to make the saws, and pens, and inscriptions, and one thing or another, and you can't think *half* the fun it was. And we had to make up the pictures of coffins and things, and nonnamous letters from the robbers, and get up and down the lightning-rod, and dig the hole into the cabin, and make the rope ladder and send it in cooked up in a pie, and send in spoons and things to work with in your apron pocket—"

"Mercy sakes!"

"—and load up the cabin with rats and snakes and so on, for company for Jim; and then you kept Tom here so long with the butter in his hat that you come near spiling the whole business, because the men come before we was out of the cabin, and we had to rush, and they heard us and let drive at us, and I got my share, and we dodged out of the path and let them go by, and when the dogs come they warn't interested in us, but went for the most noise, and we got our canoe, and made for the raft, and was all safe, and Jim was a free man, and we done it all by ourselves, and *wasn't* it bully, Aunty!"

"Well, I never heard the likes of it in all my born days! So it was *you,* you little rapscallions, that's been making all this trouble, and turned everybody's wits clean inside out and scared us all most to death. I've as good a notion as ever I had in my life to take it out o' you this very minute. To think, here I've been, night after night, a—*you* just get well once, you young scamp, and I lay I'll tan the Old Harry out o' both o' ye!"

But Tom, he *was* so proud and joyful, he just *couldn't* hold in, and his tongue just *went* it—she a-chipping in, and spitting fire all along, and both of them going it at once, like a cat convention; and she says:

"*Well,* you get all the enjoyment you can out of it *now,* for mind I tell you if I catch you meddling with him again—"

"Meddling with *who?*" Tom says, dropping his smile and looking surprised.

"With *who?* Why, the runaway nigger, of course. Who'd you reckon?"

Tom looks at me very grave, and says:

"Tom, didn't you just tell me he was all right? Hasn't he got away?"

"*Him?*" says Aunt Sally; "the runaway nigger? 'Deed he hasn't. They've got him back, safe and sound, and he's in that cabin again, on bread and water, and loaded down with chains, till he's claimed or sold!"

Tom rose square up in bed, with his eye hot, and his nostrils opening and shutting like gills, and sings out to me:

"They hain't no *right* to shut him up! *Shove!*—and don't you lose a minute. Turn him loose! he ain't no slave; he's as free as any cretur that walks this earth!"

"What *does* the child mean?"

"I mean every word I *say*, Aunt Sally, and if somebody don't go, *I'll* go. I've knowed him all his life, and so has Tom, there. Old Miss Watson died two months ago, and she was ashamed she ever was going to sell him down the river, and *said* so; and she set him free in her will."

"Then what on earth did *you* want to set him free for, seeing he was already free?"

"Well, that *is* a question, I must say; and *just* like women! Why, I wanted the *adventure* of it; and I'd 'a' waded neck-deep in blood to—goodness alive, AUNT POLLY!"

If she warn't standing right there, just inside the door, looking as sweet and contented as an angel half full of pie, I wish I may never!

Aunt Sally jumped for her, and most hugged the head off of her, and cried over her, and I found a good enough place for me under the bed, for it was getting pretty sultry for *us*, seemed to me. And I peeped out, and in a little while Tom's Aunt Polly shook herself loose and stood there looking across at Tom over her spectacles—kind of grinding him into the earth, you know. And then she says:

"Yes, you *better* turn y'r head away—I would if I was you, Tom."

"Oh, deary me!" says Aunt Sally; "*is* he changed so? Why, that ain't *Tom*, it's Sid; Tom's—Tom's—why, where is Tom? He was here a minute ago."

"You mean where's Huck *Finn*—that's what you mean! I reckon I hain't raised such a scamp as my Tom all these years not to know him when I *see* him. That *would* be a pretty howdy-do. Come out from under that bed, Huck Finn."

So I done it. But not feeling brash.

Aunt Sally she was one of the mixed-upest-

looking persons I ever see—except one, and that was Uncle Silas, when he come in and they told it all to him. It kind of made him drunk, as you may say, and he didn't know nothing at all the rest of the day, and preached a prayer-meeting sermon that night that give him a rattling ruputation, because the oldest man in the world couldn't 'a' understood it. So Tom's Aunt Polly, she told all about who I was, and what; and I had to up and tell how I was in such a tight place that when Mrs. Phelps took me for Tom Sawyer—she chipped in and says, "Oh, go on and call me Aunt Sally, I'm used to it now, and 'taint no need to change"—that when Aunt Sally took me for Tom Sawyer I had to stand it—there warn't no other way, and I knowed he wouldn't mind, because it would be nuts for him, being a mystery, and he'd make an adventure out of it, and be perfectly satisfied. And so it turned out, and he let on to be Sid, and made things as soft as he could for me.

And his Aunt Polly she said Tom was right about old Miss Watson setting Jim free in her will; and so, sure enough, Tom Sawyer had gone and took all that trouble and bother to set a free nigger free! and I couldn't ever understand before, until that minute and that talk, how he *could* help a body set a nigger free with his bringing-up.

Well, Aunt Polly she said that when Aunt Sally wrote to her that Tom and *Sid* had come all right and safe, she says to herself:

"Look at that, now! I might have expected it, letting him go off that way without anybody to watch him. So now I got to go and trapse all the way down the river, eleven hundred mile, and find out what that creetur's up to *this* time, as long as I couldn't seem to get any answer out of you about it."

"Why, I never heard nothing from you," says Aunt Sally.

"Well, I wonder! Why, I wrote you twice to ask you what you could mean by Sid being here."

"Well, I never got 'em, Sis."

Aunt Polly she turns around slow and severe, and says:

"You, Tom!"

"Well—*what?*" he says, kind of pettish.

"Don't you what *me,* you impudent thing —hand out them letters."

"What letters?"

"*Them* letters. I be bound, if I have to take a-holt of you I'll—"

"They're in the trunk. There, now. And they're just the same as they was when I got them out of the office. I hain't looked into them, I hain't touched them. But I knowed they'd make trouble, and I thought if you warn't in no hurry, I'd—"

"Well, you *do* need skinning, there ain't no mistake about it. And I wrote another one to tell you I was coming; and I s'pose he—"

"No, it come yesterday; I hain't read it yet, but *it's* all right, I've got that one."

I wanted to offer to bet two dollars she hadn't, but I reckoned maybe it was just as safe to not to. So I never said nothing.

Chapter the Last

NOTHING MORE TO WRITE

The first time I catched Tom private I asked him what was his idea, time of the evasion?—what it was he'd planned to do if the evasion worked all right and he managed to set a nigger free that was already free before? And he said, what he had planned in his head from the start, if we got Jim out all safe, was for us to run him down the river on the raft, and have adventures plumb to the mouth of the river, and then tell him about his being free, and take him back up home on a steamboat, in style, and pay him for his lost time, and write word ahead and get out all the niggers around, and have them waltz him into town with a torch-light procession and a brass-band, and then he would be a hero, and so would we. But I reckoned it was about as well the way it was.

We had Jim out of the chains in no time, and when Aunt Polly and Uncle Silas and Aunt Sally found out how good he helped the doctor nurse Tom, they made a heap of fuss over him, and fixed him up prime, and give him all he wanted to eat, and a good time, and nothing to do. And we had him up to the sick-room, and had a high talk; and Tom give Jim forty dollars for being prisoner for us so patient, and doing it up so good, and

Jim was pleased most to death, and busted out, and says:

"*Dah,* now, Huck, what I tell you?—what I tell you up dah on Jackson Islan'? I *tole* you I got a hairy breas', en what's de sign un it; en I *tole* you I ben rich wunst, en gwineter be rich *ag'in; en it's come true; en heah she *is!* Dah,* now! doan' talk to *me*—signs is *signs,* mine I tell you; en I knowed jis' 's well 'at I 'uz gwineter be rich ag'in as I's a-stannin' heah dis minute!"

And then Tom he talked along and talked along, and says, le's all three slide out of here one of these nights and get an outfit, and go for howling adventures amongst the Injuns, over in the territory, for a couple of weeks or two; and I says, all right, that suits me, but I ain't got no money for to buy the outfit, and I reckon I couldn't get none from home, because it's likely pap's been back before now, and got it all away from Judge Thatcher and drunk it up.

"No, he hain't," Tom says; "it's all there yet—six thousand dollars and more; and your pap hain't ever been back since. Hadn't when I come away, anyhow."

Jim says, kind of solemn:

"He ain't a-comin' back no mo', Huck."

I says:

"Why, Jim?"

"Nemmine why, Huck—but he ain't comin' back no mo'."

But I kept at him; so at last he says:

"Doan' you 'member de house dat was float'n down de river, en dey wuz a man in dah, kivered up, en I went in en unkivered him and didn' let you come in? Well, den, you kin git yo' money when you wants it, kase dat wuz him."

Tom's most well now, and got his bullet around his neck on a watch-guard for a watch, and is always seeing what time it is, and so there ain't nothing more to write about, and I am rotten glad of it, because if I'd 'a' knowed what a trouble it was to make a book I wouldn't 'a' tackled it, and ain't a-going to no more. But I reckon I got to light out for the territory ahead of the rest, because Aunt Sally she's going to adopt me and civilize me, and I can't stand it. I been there before.

First act, Death of a Salesman

INTRODUCTION

Drama has its genesis in several closely related human characteristics, most important of which perhaps are the urge to imitate and the love of make-believe. Such tendencies are everywhere apparent, in the games small children play—cowboys and Indians, or cops and robbers—and in the entertainments older people often enjoy—masquerades and costume parties. To lose oneself, for a short time, within the identity of some imagined creature—a Lone Ranger or a Queen of the Pirates—seems to answer a deeply felt need in the human heart. And both this tendency to imitate and this love of make-believe culminate in drama—the impulse to make a story live again through action.

The ancient Greeks, an agricultural people, met on semiannual feast days to honor the god Dionysus, who ruled over the harvest and wine press. At first, their worship of Dionysus seems to have been expressed in choral songs and dances performed by elaborately trained and costumed choruses; but with time, more and more of a dramatic element crept in. During an intermission, perhaps, the leader of the chorus would tell of some exploit in the life of Dionysus; and at a later date he came to *represent* the god himself and tell his story in the first person. Finally, some minor member of the chorus answered the rhetorical utterances of Dionysus, and thus dramatic dialogue and impersonation came into being. To describe this activity, the word *drama,* derived from a Greek verb *dran,* meaning *to act* or *to do,* was used. By its own etymology, drama implies action, the essence of every dramatic composition.

Greek comedy and tragedy both originated in such seasonal festivals. From the broad jesting and burlesque natural to a rustic carnival developed comedy. From the serious side of worship developed tragedy, which reached its culmination in three great writers—Aeschylus, Sophocles, and Euripides—all of whose works emphasize the Greek ideal of artistic restraint and balance.

During the Dark Ages, when Greek drama was temporarily forgotten, another form of drama emerged in western Europe in the morality plays of the medieval Christian Church. Everywhere confronted by ignorance and lack of schooling, the priests realized that the easiest way to tell the Christian story to the people was through the dramatic representation of the Easter and Christmas stories in the cathedrals. What started out as devices for religious instruction became so popular as entertainment that it was necessary to find a larger place for their presentation. Once outside the church, these plays soon fell into secular hands, as when the trade guilds in certain cities produced an elaborate series of pageants telling the Biblical story from the Creation to the Crucifixion and Resurrection.

Out of these religious plays of the late Middle Ages and out of the school and university revivals of long-neglected Greek and Roman dramas during the Renaissance grew the new drama of western Europe. In the English tradition this means pre-eminently the dramas of William Shakespeare; but there were many other playwrights in the sixteenth and seventeenth centuries who contributed their share toward making English drama worthy of comparison with drama anywhere in the world. After Goldsmith and Sheridan in the late eighteenth century, British drama went into a decline that lasted until Henrik Ibsen revolutionized the drama of all Europe. Profiting in part from this foreign influence, writers like Shaw and Pinero re-established British drama in the world's esteem, and so it has continued to our own day. In the United States a powerful and original drama scarcely emerged until after World War I, when Eugene O'Neill began producing the plays that were to win for him the Nobel Prize for literature in 1936. By this latter date such writers as Maxwell Anderson, Sidney Howard, Robert Sherwood, and Thornton Wilder had clearly demonstrated that American drama was not inferior to the best contemporary drama found anywhere in the world. More recently, Tennessee Williams and Arthur Miller have affirmed the psychological power and lyricism of the American theater.

Both comedy and tragedy are likely to be built around a central figure involved in some kind of conflict of wills—the wills of two persons who oppose each other, the will of a person to win out over unfavorable circumstances, or the internally conflicting emotions of a person torn between two irreconcilable desires. Generally speaking, if the central character is in the end defeated, the play is tragic; if he is triumphant, the play is comic. Aristotle, the ancient Greek philosopher, believed that tragedy must excite the emotions of pity and fear. To accomplish this end, it must be single and complete in action, must present a reversal of fortune involving persons renowned and of superior attainments, and finally must be written in poetry of the highest sort.

Later tragedy has changed some of these requirements. The interest that can be aroused in tragic conflict is usually in direct proportion to the impressiveness of character displayed by the central figure in the drama. Comedies can be written about trivial people, but a tragedy usually centers around a great personality going down in defeat before forces too great even for him to match. It is doubtless this need for a certain magnitude in the central character that long compelled dramatists to center their tragedies around people of exalted rank, such as kings and princesses. Shakespeare to some extent demonstrated that people of humbler station can be fit subjects for tragedy, and subsequently Ibsen set the example for modern dramatists not only by choosing tragic characters from common life but also by utilizing prose instead of poetry as the language of tragedy.

In contrast with tragedy, comedy, by conventional definition at least, is light and amusing. Where amusement is all, it becomes farce or burlesque. But at its best comedy is scarcely less serious in purpose than tragedy and is equally exacting in plot, dialogue, and characterization. Since the comic effect derives primarily from the exposure of some kind of incongruity, it reveals to us absurd, illogical, or pretentious speech, action, or character. The function of comedy, as George Meredith observed, is to provoke thoughtful laughter, the sort that arises out of our realization of human foibles and inconsistencies. Consequently, comedy lends itself well to satire and becomes a means whereby the dramatist chastises the world for its vices and shortcomings.

The categories of tragedy and comedy, however, cannot be rigidly applied to all plays. *Cyrano de Bergerac*, compounded of wit and spectacle, was written as a heroic comedy for the French comedian Coquelin, but recent productions on stage, screen, and television have tended to emphasize its romantic and tragic aspects. No doubt both points of view are valid; and the play could fairly be assigned the compromise label of "tragicomedy." In *Pygmalion* George Bernard Shaw ironically paraphrases Greek myth to create comedy which blends the ingredients of romance (Shaw so designates the play), drawing-room comedy, and the comedy of ideas, the last being the special domain of George Bernard Shaw. *Death of a Salesman* certainly does not satisfy Aristotles' conception of the tragic hero and the tragic flaw, but no one can see a performance of *Death of a Salesman* without feeling that he has shared a tragic vision of life.

Since plays are written to be acted, the technique of play reading is somewhat different from that of reading a short story or a novel; and enjoyment of plays can therefore be increased greatly if one stops to consider some special problems that the reading of plays presents.

If plays are to be read successfully—that is, with the fullest degree of understanding and enjoyment—the reader is compelled, with his own creative imagination, to visualize characters speaking, gesticulating, and moving about in a setting which playwrights, especially the modern ones, frequently describe in detail. From the cast of characters and from the stage directions, the reader can determine many things about the people of the play, particularly the main characters—what they look like, how old they are, what relation exists between one and the other, and what their special mannerisms and peculiarities imply. Another help to intelligent reading of plays is to observe the play's structure. In the conventional play much of the first scene is devoted to getting the play under way. This portion of the play—the "exposition" as it is technically called—should be carefully read in order to get one's bearings early. As soon as the exposition is finished, most playwrights get their main plot started. In many modern dramas new scenes indicate the introduction of a new character or a new element in the story. The reader should watch for these developments as they unfold.

If the reader follows these suggestions, the experience of reading a play may equal, if not surpass, the experience of seeing all but the very best performance.

EDMOND ROSTAND *Cyrano de Bergerac*

Translation by Brian Hooker

Edmond Rostand (1868-1918), French dramatist and poet, was born in Marseilles. His father, a well-known economist and journalist, wanted his son to enter government service and educated him in law. While still a student, however, young Rostand showed literary inclinations. He was awarded a prize for an essay and collaborated on a drama. Although he finished his legal training and was admitted to the bar, he never practiced but concentrated entirely on writing. His literary career may be said to have begun with a volume of verse, *Les Musardises*, 1890. During the following decade, he wrote five dramas: *Les Romanesques*, 1894 (his first success); *La Princesse Lointaine*, 1895; *La Samaritaine*, 1897; *Cyrano de Bergerac*, 1897; *L'Aiglon*, 1900. *Cyrano de Bergerac*, produced when Rostand was only twenty-nine, established his position among the foremost European playwrights. At the age of thirty-three he was elected to the French Academy, the youngest writer ever to be accorded this honor.

Cyrano was an immediate success on its first appearance not only because of its merit but also because it marked a complete reaction against the realism of the problem plays then in vogue. In the midst of a period of naturalism, Rostand had revived and given new vitality to poetic drama and heroic comedy. In *Cyrano de Bergerac*, the playgoers of 1897 found a fresh, romantic drama with a spectacular hero masterfully impersonated by the able French actor Coquelin.

Although the play was based on fact, Rostand freely romanticized his sources. The scenes are laid in Paris and Arras, and the time is the middle of the seventeenth century. Cyrano, the central figure, was a poet, a contemporary of Molière, born in 1619 of Gascon origin. These and other details of the play are matters of record. But while of interest to the reader, or viewer, of *Cyrano*, these facts are by no means essential to his understanding and enjoyment of the play. Whenever presented—through the medium of the stage, motion picture, or television—*Cyrano de Bergerac* has been enthusiastically received for more than fifty years. Its variety of action and rapid changes of mood partly account for this appeal. Elements of comedy, tragedy, character delineation, and poetry are skillfully combined for dramatic enjoyment. Indeed, it may not be too extravagant to claim that Rostand's formula for *Cyrano* has much in common with the dramaturgy that has perpetually made Shakespeare's plays "good theater."

THE PERSONS

CYRANO DE BERGERAC	CUIGY	*A Capuchin*
CHRISTIAN DE NEUVILLETTE	BRISSAILLE	*Two Musicians*
COMTE DE GUICHE	*A Meddler*	*The Poets*
RAGUENEAU	*A Musketeer*	*The Pastrycooks*
LE BRET	*Another Musketeer*	*The Pages*
CARBON DE CASTEL-JALOUX	*A Spanish Officer*	ROXANE
The Cadets	*A Cavalier*	HER DUENNA
LIGNIÈRE	*The Porter*	LISE
VICOMTE DE VALVERT	*A Citizen*	THE ORANGE GIRL
A MARQUIS	*His Son*	MOTHER MARGUÉRITE DE JÉSUS
Second Marquis	*A Cut-Purse*	SISTER MARTHE
Third Marquis	*A Spectator*	SISTER CLAIRE
Montfleury	*A Sentry*	*An Actress*
Bellerose	*Bertrandou the Fifer*	*A Soubrette*
Jodelet		*The Flower Girl*

The Crowd, Citizens, Marquis, Musketeers, Thieves, Pastrycooks, Poets, Cadets of Gascoyne, Actors, Violins, Pages, Children, Spanish Soldiers, Spectators, Intellectuals, Academicians, Nuns, etc.

(The first four Acts in 1640; the fifth in 1655.)

FIRST ACT: A Performance at the Hôtel de Bourgogne.   THIRD ACT: Roxane's Kiss.
SECOND ACT: The Bakery of the Poets.   FOURTH ACT: The Cadets of Gascoyne.
FIFTH ACT: Cyrano's Gazette.

THE FIRST ACT

A Performance at the Hôtel de Bourgogne

THE HALL OF THE HÔTEL DE BOURGOGNE *in* 1640. *A sort of Tennis Court, arranged and decorated for Theatrical productions.*

The Hall is a long rectangle; we see it diagonally, in such a way that one side of it forms the back scene, which begins at the First Entrance on the Right and runs up to the Last Entrance on the Left, where it makes a right angle with the Stage which is seen obliquely.

This Stage is provided on either hand with benches placed along the wings. The curtain is formed by two lengths of Tapestry which can be drawn apart. Above a Harlequin cloak, the Royal Arms. Broad steps lead from the Stage down to the floor of the Hall. On either side of these steps, a place for the Musicians. A row of candles serves as footlights. Two tiers of Galleries along the side of the Hall; the upper one divided into boxes. There are no seats upon the Floor, which is

the actual stage of our theatre; but toward the back of the Hall, on the right, a few benches are arranged; and underneath a stairway on the extreme right, which leads up to the galleries, and of which only the lower portion is visible, there is a sort of Sideboard, decorated with little tapers, vases of flowers, bottles and glasses, plates of cake, et cetera.

Farther along, toward the centre of our stage, is the Entrance to the Hall: a great double door which opens only slightly to admit the Audience. On one of the panels of this door, as also in other places about the Hall, and in particular just over the Sideboard, are Playbills in red, upon which we may read the title LA CLORISE.

As the CURTAIN RISES, the Hall is dimly lighted and still empty. The Chandeliers are lowered to the floor, in the middle of the Hall, ready for lighting.

(*Sounds of voices outside the door. Then a* CAVA-
LIER *enters abruptly.*)

PORTER. (*Follows him*) Hallo there!—Fifteen sols!
CAV.   I enter free.
PORT. Why?

CAV.   Soldier of the Household of the King!

PORT. (*Turns to* ANOTHER CAVALIER *who has just entered*) You?

2ND CAV.   I pay nothing.

PORT.   Why not?

2ND CAV.   Musketeer!

1ST CAV. (*To the Second*)
The play begins at two. Plenty of time—
And here's the whole floor empty. Shall we try
Our exercise?   (*They fence with the foils
which they have brought*)

LACKEY. (*Enters*) —Pst! . . . Flanquin! . . .

ANOTHER. (*Already on stage*) What, Champagne?

1ST LACK. (*Showing games which he takes out of his doublet*) Cards. Dice. Come on.
(*Sits on the floor*)

2ND LACK. (*Same action*) Come on, old cock!

1ST LACK. (*Takes from his pocket a bit of candle, lights it, sets it on the floor*) I have stolen
A little of my master's fire.

A GUARDSMAN. (*To a* FLOWER GIRL *who comes forward*)   How sweet
Of you, to come before they light the hall!
(*Puts his arm around her*)

1ST CAV. (*Receives a thrust of the foil*)
A hit!

2ND LACK. A club!

GUARD (*Pursuing the* GIRL) A kiss!

GIRL. (*Pushing away from him*) They'll see us!—

GUARD. (*Draws her into a dark corner*) No danger!

A MAN. (*Sits on the floor, together with several others who have brought packages of food*)
When we come early, we have time to eat.

A CITIZEN. (*Escorting his son, a* BOY *of sixteen*)
Sit here, my son.

1ST LACK.   Mark the Ace!

ANOTHER MAN. (*Draws a bottle from under his cloak and sits down with the others*) Here's the spot
For a jolly old sot to suck his Burgundy— (*Drinks*)
Here—in the house of the Burgundians!

CIT. (*To his son*)
Would you not think you were in some den of vice?
(*Points with his cane at the drunkard*)
Drunkards—   (*In stepping back, one of the
CAVALIERS trips him up*)
Bullies!— (*He falls between the* LACKEYS)
Gamblers!—

GUARD. (*Behind him as he rises, still struggling
with the* FLOWER GIRL)   One kiss—

CIT. (*Draws his son quickly away*) Good God!—
Here!—And to think, my son, that in this hall
They play Rotrou!

BOY.   Yes, father—and Corneille!

PAGES. (*Dance in, holding hands and singing*)
Tra-la-la-la-la-la-la-la-la-lère . . .

PORT. You pages there—no nonsense!

1ST PAGE. (*With wounded dignity*) Oh, Monsieur!
Really! How could you? (*To the* SECOND, *the moment the* PORTER *turns his back*) Pst!—a bit of string?

2ND PAGE. (*Shows fishline with hook*)
Yes—and a hook.

1ST PAGE.   Up in the gallery,
And fish for wigs!

A CUT-PURSE. (*Gathers around him several evil-looking young fellows*) Now then, you picaroons,
Perk up, and hear me mutter. Here's your bout—
Bustle around some cull, and bite his bung . . .

2ND PAGE. (*Calls to other* PAGES *already in the gallery*) Hey! Brought your pea-shooters?

3RD PAGE. (*From above*)   And our peas, too!
(*Blows, and showers them with peas*)

BOY. What is the play this afternoon?

CIT.   *Clorise*.

BOY. Who wrote that?

CIT.   Balthasar Baro. What a play! . . .
(*He takes the* BOY's *arm and leads him upstage*)

CUT-PURSE. (*To his pupils*)
Lace now, on those long sleeves, you cut it off—
(*Gesture with thumb and finger,
as if using scissors*)

SPECTATOR. (*To another, pointing upward toward the gallery*)
Ah, *Le Cid*!—Yes, the first night, I sat there—

CUT-PURSE. Watches—
(*Gesture as of picking a pocket*)

CIT. (*Coming down with his son*)
Great actors we shall see today—

CUT-PURSE. Handkerchiefs— (*Gesture of holding
the pocket with left hand, and drawing
out handkerchief with right*)

CIT.   Montfleury—

A VOICE. (*In the gallery*) Lights! Light the lights!

CIT. Bellerose, l'Epy, Beaupré, Jodelet—

PAGE. (*On the floor*) Here cômes the orange-girl.

ORANGE-GIRL.   Oranges, milk,
Raspberry syrup, lemonade— (*Noise at the door*)

A FALSETTO VOICE. (*Outside*) Make way,
Brutes!

1ST LACK. What, the Marquis—on the floor?
(*The* MARQUIS *enters in a little group*)

2ND LACK.   Not long—
Only a few moments; they'll go and sit
On the stage presently.

1ST MARQ. (*Seeing the hall half empty*)
How now! We enter
Like tradespeople—no crowding, no disturbance!—
No treading on the toes of citizens?
Oh fie! Oh fie!   (*He encounters two gentlemen
who have already arrived*)
          Cuigy! Brissaille!   (*Great embracings*)
CUIGY.   The faithful! (*Looks around him*)
We are here before the candles.
1ST MARQ.   Ah, be still!
You put me in a temper.
2ND MARQ.   Console yourself,
Marquis— The lamplighter!
THE CROWD. (*Applauding the appearance of the
lamplighter*)   Ah! . . .
(*A group gathers around the chandelier while he
lights it. A few people have already taken their
place in the gallery.* LIGNIÈRE *enters the hall, arm
in arm with* CHRISTIAN DE NEUVILLETTE. LIGNIÈRE *is
a slightly disheveled figure, dissipated and yet distinguished looking.* CHRISTIAN, *elegantly but rather
unfashionably dressed, appears pre-occupied and
keeps looking up at the boxes.*)
CUIGY.   Lignière!—
BRISSAILLE. (*Laughing*) Still sober—at this hour?
LIG. (*To* CHRISTIAN)   May I present you?
                    (CHRISTIAN *assents*)
Baron Christian de Neuvillette.   (*They salute*)
THE CROWD. (*Applauding as the lighted chande-
lier is hoisted into place*)   Ah!—
CUIGY. (*Aside to* BRISSAILLE, *looking at* CHRISTIAN)
                              Rather
A fine head, is it not? The profile . . .
1ST MARQ. (*Who has overheard*)   Peuh!
LIG. (*Presenting them to* CHRISTIAN)
Messieurs de Cuigy . . . de Brissaille . . .
CHRIS. (*Bows*)   Enchanted!
1ST MARQ. (*To the second*)
He is not ill-looking; possibly a shade
Behind the fashion.
LIG. (*To* CUIGY)   Monsieur is recently
From the Touraine.
CHRIS.   Yes, I have been in Paris
Two or three weeks only. I join the Guards
Tomorrow.
1ST MARQ. (*Watching the people who come into
the boxes*) Look—Madame la Présidente
Aubry!
OR. GIRL. Oranges, milk—
THE VIOLINS. (*Tuning up*) La . . . la . . .

CUIGY. (*To* CHRISTIAN, *calling his attention to
the increasing crowd*)   We have
An audience today!
CHRIS.   A brilliant one.
1ST MARQ. Oh, yes, all our own people—the gay
   world!
(*They name the ladies who enter the boxes elab-
orately dressed. Bows and smiles are exchanged.*)
2ND MARQ. Madame de Guéméné . . .
CUIGY.   De Bois-Dauphin . . .
1ST MARQ. Whom we adore—
BRIS.   Madame de Chavigny . . .
2ND MARQ. Who plays with all our hearts—
LIG.   Why, there's Corneille
Returned from Rouen!
BOY. (*To his father*)   Are the Academy
All here?
CIT. I see some of them . . . there's Boudu—
Boissat—Cureau—Porchères—Colomby—
Bourzeys—Bourdon—Arbaut—
                    Ah, those great names,
Never to be forgotten!
1ST MARQ.   Look—at last!
Our Intellectuals! Barthénoide,
Urimédonte, Félixérie . . .
2ND MARQ. (*Languishing*) Sweet heaven!
How exquisite their surnames are! Marquis,
You know them all?
1ST MARQ.   I know them all, Marquis!
LIG. (*Draws* CHRISTIAN *aside*)
My dear boy, I came here to serve you— Well,
But where's the lady? I'll be going.
CHRIS.   Not yet—
A little longer! She is always here.
Please! I must find some way of meeting her.
I am dying of love! And you—you know
Everyone, the whole court and the whole town,
And put them all into your songs—at least
You can tell me her name!
FIRST VIOLIN. (*Raps on his desk with his bow*)
                    Pst— Gentlemen! (*Raises his bow*)
OR. GIRL. Macaroons, lemonade—
CHRIS.   Then she may be
One of those aesthetes . . . Intellectuals,
You call them— How can I talk to a woman
In that style? I have no wit. This fine manner
Of speaking and of writing nowadays—
Not for me! I am a soldier—and afraid.
That's her box, on the right—the empty one.
LIG. (*Starts for the door*) I am going.
CHRIS. (*Restrains him*)   No—wait!

LIG.   Not I. There's a tavern
Not far away—and I am dying of thirst.

OR.-GIRL. (*Passes with her tray*)
Orange juice?

LIG.   No!

OR. GIRL.   Milk?

LIG.   Pouah!

OR. GIRL.   Muscatel?

LIG. Here! Stop! (*To* CHRISTIAN) I'll stay a little.
              (*To the* GIRL) Let me see
Your Muscatel. (*He sits down by the sideboard.*
        The GIRL *pours out wine for him.*)

VOICES. (*In the crowd about the door, upon the
entrance of a spruce little man, rather fat, with a
beaming smile*) Ragueneau!

LIG. (*To* CHRISTIAN)   Ragueneau,
Poet and pastrycook—a character!

RAGUENEAU. (*Dressed like a confectioner in his
Sunday clothes, advances quickly to* LIGNIÈRE)
Sir, have you seen Monsieur de Cyrano?

LIG. (*Presents him to* CHRISTIAN)
Permit me . . . Ragueneau, confectioner,
The chief support of modern poetry.

RAG. (*Bridling*) Oh—too much honor!

LIG.   Patron of the Arts—
Maecenas! Yes, you are—

RAG.   Undoubtedly,
The poets gather round my hearth.

LIG.   On credit—
Himself a poet—

RAG.   So they say—

LIG.   Maintains
The Muses.

RAG.   It is true that for an ode—

LIG. You give a tart—

RAG.   A tartlet—

LIG.   Modesty!
And for a triolet you give—

RAG.   Plain bread!

LIG. (*Severely*)
Bread and milk! And you love the theatre?

RAG. I adore it!

LIG.   Well, pastry pays for all.
Your place today now— Come, between ourselves,
What did it cost you?

RAG. (*Looking about*) Four pies; fourteen cakes
But— Cyrano not here? Astonishing!

LIG. Why so?

RAG.   Why— Montfleury plays!

LIG.   Yes, I hear
That hippopotamus assumes the rôle
Of Phédon. What is that to Cyrano?

RAG. Have you not heard? Monsieur de Bergerac
So hates Montfleury, he has forbidden him
For three weeks to appear upon the stage.

LIG. (*Who is, by this time, at his fourth glass*)
Well?

RAG. Montfleury plays!—

CUIGY. (*Strolls over to them*) Yes—what then?

RAG.   Ah! That
Is what I came to see.

1ST MARQ.   This Cyrano—
Who is he?

CUIGY.   Oh, he is the lad with the long sword.

2ND MARQ. Noble?

CUIGY.   Sufficiently; he is in the Guards.
     (*Points to a gentleman who comes and goes
about the hall as though seeking for someone*)
His friend Le Bret can tell you more.
                (*Calls to him*) Le Bret!
        (LE BRET *comes down to them*)
Looking for Bergerac?

LE BRET.   Yes. And for trouble.

CUIGY. Is he not an extraordinary man?

LE B. The best friend and the bravest soul alive!

RAG. Poet—

CUIGY.   Swordsman—

LE B.   Musician—

BRIS.   Philosopher—

LIG. Such a remarkable appearance, too!

RAG. Truly, I should not look to find his portrait
By the grave hand of Philippe de Champagne.
He might have been a model for Callot—
One of those wild swashbucklers in a masque—
Hat with three plumes, and doublet with six
     points—
His cloak behind him over his long sword
Cocked, like the tail of strutting Chanticleer—
Prouder than all the swaggering Tamburlaines
Hatched out of Gascony. And to complete
This Punchinello figure—such a nose!—
My lords, there is no such nose as that nose—
You cannot look upon it without crying: "Oh, no,
Impossible! Exaggerated!" Then
You smile, and say: "Of course— I might have
     known;
Presently he will take it off." But that
Monsieur de Bergerac will never do.

LIG. (*Grimly*)
He keeps it—and God help the man who smiles!

RAG. His sword is one half of the shears of Fate!

1ST MARQ. (*Shrugs*) He will not come.

RAG.   Will he not? Sir, I'll lay you
A pullet à la Ragueneau!

1ST MARQ. (*Laughing*) Done!

(*Murmurs of admiration;* ROXANE *has just appeared in her box. She sits at the front of the box, and her Duenna takes a seat toward the rear.* CHRISTIAN, *busy paying the* ORANGE-GIRL, *does not see her at first.*)

2ND MARQ. (*With little excited cries*) Ah! Oh! Oh! Sweet sirs, look yonder! Is she not Frightfully ravishing?

1ST MARQ.   Bloom of the peach—
Blush of the strawberry—

2ND MARQ.   So fresh—so cool,
That our hearts, grown all warm with loving her,
May catch their death of cold!

CHRIS (*Looks up, sees* ROXANE, *and seizes* LIGNIÈRE *by the arm*)   There! Quick—up there—
In the box! Look!—

LIG. (*Coolly*)   Herself?

CHRIS.   Quickly— Her name?

LIG. (*Sipping his wine, and speaking between sips*) Madeleine Robin, called Roxane . . . refined . . .
Intellectual . . .

CHRIS.   Ah!—

LIG.   Unmarried . . .

CHRIS.   Oh!—

LIG. No title . . . rich enough . . . an orphan
. . . cousin
To Cyrano . . . of whom we spoke just now . . .

(*At this point, a very distinguished looking gentleman, the Cordon Bleu around his neck, enters the box, and stands a moment talking with* ROXANE)

CHRIS. (*Starts*) And the man? . . .

LIG. (*Beginning to feel his wine a little; cocks his eye at them*)
        Oho! That man? . . . Comte de Guiche . . .
In love with her . . . married himself, however,
To the niece of the Cardinal—Richelieu . . .
Wishes Roxane, therefore, to marry one
Monsieur de Valvert . . . Vicomte . . . friend of
his . . .
A somewhat melancholy gentleman . . .
But . . . well, accommodating! . . . She says No . . .
Nevertheless, de Guiche is powerful . . .
Not above persecuting . . .

(*He rises, swaying a little, and very happy*)
                I have written
A little song about his little game . . .
Good little song, too . . . Here, I'll sing it for
you . . .
Make de Guiche furious . . . naughty little
song . . .

Not so bad, either— Listen! . . . (*He stands with
his glass held aloft, ready to sing*)

CHRIS.   No. Adieu.

LIG. Whither away?

CHRIS.   To Monsieur de Valvert!

LIG. Careful! The man's a swordsman . . .

(*Nods toward* ROXANE, *who is
watching* CHRISTIAN)
                Wait! Someone
Looking at you—

CHRIS.   Roxane! . . .

(*He forgets everything, and stands spellbound, gazing toward* ROXANE. *The* CUT-PURSE *and his crew, observing him transfixed, his eyes raised and his mouth half open, begin edging in his direction.*)

LIG.   Oh! Very well,
Then I'll be leaving you . . . Good day . . . Good
day! . . .   (CHRISTIAN *remains motionless*)
Everywhere else, they like to hear me sing!—
Also, I am thirsty.

(*He goes out, navigating carefully.* LE BRET, *having made the circuit of the hall, returns to* RAGUENEAU, *somewhat reassured.*)

LE B.   No sign anywhere
Of Cyrano!

RAG. (*Incredulous*) Wait and see!

LE B.   Humph! I hope
He has not seen the bill.

THE CROWD.   The play!—The play!—

1ST MARQ. (*Observing* DE GUICHE, *as he descends from* ROXANE'S *box and crosses the floor, followed by a knot of obsequious gentlemen, the* VICOMTE DE VALVERT *among them*)
This man de Guiche—what ostentation!

2ND MARQ.   Bah!—
Another Gascon!

1ST MARQ.   Gascon, yes—but cold
And calculating—certain to succeed—
My word for it. Come, shall we make our bow?
We shall be none the worse, I promise you . . .

(*They go toward* DE GUICHE)

2ND MARQ. Beautiful ribbons, Count! That color,
now,
What is it—*Kiss-me-Dear* or *Startled-Fawn?*

DE GUICHE. I call that shade *The Dying Spaniard.*

1ST MARQ.   Ha!
And no false colors either—thanks to you
And your brave troops, in Flanders before long
The Spaniard will die daily.

DE G.   Shall we go
And sit upon the stage? Come, Valvert.

CHRIS. (*Starts at the name*)   Valvert!—
The Vicomte— Ah, that scoundrel! Quick—my
    glove—
I'll throw it in his face— (*Reaching into his pocket
for his glove, he catches the hand of the* CUT-PURSE)
CUT-PURSE.   Oh!—
CHRIS. (*Holding fast to the man's wrist*)
                              Who are you?
I was looking for a glove—
    CUT-PURSE. (*Cringing*)   You found a hand.
(*Hurriedly*) Let me go—I can tell you something—
    CHRIS. (*Still holding him*)   Well?
    CUT-PURSE. Lignière—that friend of yours—
    CHRIS. (*Same business*)   Well?
    CUT-PURSE.   Good as dead—
Understand? Ambuscaded. Wrote a song
About—no matter. There's a hundred men
Waiting for him tonight—I'm one of them.
    CHRIS. A hundred! Who arranged this?
    CUT-PURSE.   Secret.
    CHRIS.   Oh!
    CUT-PURSE. (*With dignity*) Professional secret.
    CHRIS.   Where are they to be?
    CUT-PURSE. Porte de Nesle. On his way home.
    Tell him so.
Save his life.
    CHRIS. (*Releases the man*)
              Yes, but where am I to find him?
    CUT-PURSE. Go round the taverns. There's the
    Golden Grape,
The Pineapple, The Bursting Belt, The Two
Torches, The Three Funnels—in every one
You leave a line of writing—understand?
To warn him.
    CHRIS (*Starts for the door*)
              I'll go! God, what swine—a hundred
Against one man! . . .
          (*Stops and looks longingly at* ROXANE)
              Leave *her* here!—
          (*Savagely, turning toward* VALVERT)
                    And leave *him*!—
(*Decidedly*) I must save Lignière!   (*Exit*)
(DE GUICHE, VALVERT, *and all the* MARQUIS *have
disappeared through the curtains, to take their
seats upon the stage. The floor is entirely filled;
not a vacant seat remains in the gallery or in the
boxes.*)
    CROWD.   The play! The play!
Begin the play!
    CIT. (*As his wig is hoisted into the air on the*

end of a fishline, in the hands of a page in the
gallery)   My wig!!
    CRIES OF JOY.   He's bald! Bravo,
You pages! Ha ha ha!
    CIT. (*Furious, shakes his fist at the boy*)
                    Here, you young villain!
    CRIES AND LAUGHTER. (*Beginning very loud, then
suddenly repressed*)
HA HA! Ha Ha! ha ha. . . .   (*Complete silence*)
    LE B. (*Surprised*)   That sudden hush! . . .
          (*A* SPECTATOR *whispers in his ear*)
Yes?
    SPECTATOR. I was told on good authority . . .
    MURMURS. (*Here and there*)
What? . . . Here? . . . No . . . Yes . . . Look—
    in the latticed box—
The Cardinal! . . . The Cardinal! . . .
    PAGE.   The Devil!—
Now we shall all have to behave ourselves!
          (*Three raps on the stage. The audience
                    becomes motionless. Silence.*)
    VOICE OF A MARQUIS. (*From the stage, behind the
curtains*) Snuff that candle!
    ANOTHER MARQUIS. (*Puts his head out through the
curtains*)   A chair! . . .
(*A chair is passed from hand to hand over the
heads of the crowd. He takes it, and disappears
behind the curtains, not without having blown a
few kisses to the occupants of the boxes.*)
    SPECTATOR.   Silence!
    VOICES.   Hssh! . . . Hssh! . . .
(*Again the three raps on the stage. The curtains
part. TABLEAU. The* MARQUIS *seated on their chairs
to right and left of the stage, insolently posed.
Back drop representing a pastoral scene, bluish in
tone. Four little crystal chandeliers light up the
stage. The violins play softly.*)
    LE B. (*In a low tone to* RAGUENEAU)
Montfleury enters now?
    RAG. (*Nods*)   Opens the play.
    LE B. (*Much relieved*)
Then Cyrano is not here!
    RAG.   I lose . . .
    LE B.   Humph!
So much the better!
(*The melody of a Musette is heard.* MONTFLEURY
*appears upon the scene, a ponderous figure in the
costume of a rustic shepherd, a hat garlanded with
roses tilted over one ear, playing upon a berib-
boned pastoral pipe.*)
    CROWD. (*Applauds*) Montfleury! . . . Bravo! . . .

MONTFLEURY. (*After bowing to the applause, begins the rôle of Phédon*)
"Thrice happy he who hides from pomp and power
In sylvan shade or solitary bower;
Where balmy zephyrs fan his burning cheeks—"
VOICE. (*From the midst of the hall*)
Wretch! Have I not forbade you these three weeks?
    (*Sensation. Every one turns to look. Murmurs.*)
SEVERAL VOICES. What? . . . Where? . . . Who is it? . . .
CUIGY. Cyrano!
LE B. (*In alarm*) Himself!
VOICE. King of clowns! Leave the stage—*at once!*
CROWD.   Oh!
MONT.   Now,
Now, now—
VOICE.   You disobey me?
SEVERAL VOICES. (*From the floor, from the boxes*)
              Hsh! Go on—
Quiet!—Go on, Montfleury!—Who's afraid?—
MONT. (*In a voice of no great assurance*)
"Thrice happy he who hides from . . ."
VOICE. (*More menacingly*) Well? Well? Well? . . .
Monarch of mountebanks! Must I come and plant
A forest on your shoulders? (*A cane at the end of a long arm shakes above the heads of the crowd*)
MONT. (*In a voice increasingly feeble*)
"Thrice hap—"   (*The cane is violently agitated*)
VOICE.   GO!!!
CROWD. Ah! . . .
CYRANO. (*Arises in the centre of the floor, erect upon a chair, his arms folded, his hat cocked ferociously, his moustache bristling, his nose terrible*)
    Presently I shall grow angry!
        (*Sensation at his appearance*)
MONT. (*To the* MARQUIS)   Messieurs,
If you protect me—
MARQ. (*Nonchalantly*) Well—proceed!
CYR.   Fat swine!
If you dare breathe one balmy zephyr more,
I'll fan your cheeks for you!
MARQ.   Quiet down there!
CYR. Unless these gentlemen retain their seats,
My cane may bite their ribbons!
ALL THE MARQUIS. (*On their feet*) That will do!—
Montfleury—
CYR. Fly, goose! Shoo! Take to your wings,
Before I pluck your plumes, and draw your gorge!
VOICE. See here!—
CYR.   Off stage!
ANOTHER VOICE.   One moment—

CYR.   What—still there?
    (*Turns back his cuffs deliberately*)
Very good—then I enter—*Left—with knife—*
To carve this large Italian sausage.
MONT. (*Desperately attempting dignity*) Sir,
When you insult me, you insult the Muse!
CYR. (*With great politeness*)
Sir, if the Muse, who never knew your name,
Had the honor to meet you—then be sure
That after one glance at that face of yours,
That figure of a mortuary urn—
She would apply her buskin—toward the rear!
CROWD. Montfleury! . . . Montfleury! . . . The play! The play!
CYR. (*To those who are shouting and crowding about him*)
Pray you, be gentle with my scabbard here—
She'll put her tongue out at you presently!—
        (*The circle enlarges*)
CROWD. (*Recoiling*) Keep back—
CYR. (*To* MONTFLEURY) Begone!
CROWD. (*Pushing in closer, and growling*)
        Ahr! . . . ahr! . . .
CYR. (*Turns upon them*) Did some one speak?
        (*They recoil again*)
VOICE. (*In the back of the hall, sings*)
    Monsieur de Cyrano
      Must be another Caesar—
    Let Brutus lay him low,
      And play us La Clorise!
ALL THE CROWD. (*Singing*)
    La Clorise! La Clorise!
CYR. Let me hear one more word of that same song,
And I destroy you all!
CIT.   Who might you be?
Samson?—
CYR.   Precisely. Would you kindly lend me
Your jawbone?
LADY. (*In one of the boxes*) What an outrage!
NOBLE.   Scandalous!
CIT. Annoying!
PAGE.   What a game!
CROWD.   Kss! Montfleury!
Cyrano!
CYR.   Silence!
CROWD. (*Delirious*) Woof! Woof! Baaa! Cockadoo!
CYR. I—
PAGE.   Meow!

CYR.   I say be silent!—
(*His voice dominates the uproar. Momentary hush.*)
                                        And I offer
One universal challenge to you all!
Approach, young heroes—I will take your names.
Each in his turn—no crowding! One, two, three—
Come, get your numbers—who will head the list—
You, sir? No— You? Ah, no. To the first man
Who falls I'll build a monument! . . . Not one?
Will all who wish to die, please raise their
        hands? . . .
I see. You are so modest, you might blush
Before a sword naked. Sweet innocence! . . .
Not one name? Not one finger? . . . Very well,
Then I go on: (*Turning back toward the stage,
        where* MONTFLEURY *waits in despair*)
                    I'd have our theatre cured
Of this carbuncle. Or if not, why then—
                    (*His hand on his sword hilt*)
The lancet!
    MONT.   I—
    CYR. (*Descends from his chair, seats himself comfortably in the centre of the circle which has formed around him, and makes himself quite at home*)   Attend to me—full moon!
I clap my hands, three times—thus. At the third
You will eclipse yourself.
    CROWD. (*Amused*)   Ah!
    CYR.   Ready? *One.*
    MONT. I—
    VOICE. (*From the boxes*) No!
    CROWD.   He'll go— He'll stay—
    MONT.   I really think,
Gentlemen—
    CYR.   *Two.*
    MONT.   Perhaps I had better—
    CYR.   *Three!*
(MONTFLEURY *disappears, as if through a trap-door.
    Tempest of laughter, hoots and hisses.*)
    CROWD. Yah!—Coward— Come back—
    CYR. (*Beaming, drops back in his chair and crosses his legs*)   Let him—if he dare!
    CIT. The Manager! Speech! Speech!
                    (BELLEROSE *advances and bows*)
    BOXES.   Ah! Bellerose!
    BELLEROSE (*With elegance*)
Most noble—most fair—
    CROWD.   No! The Comedian—
Jodelet!—
    JODELET. (*Advances, and speaks through his nose*)
            Lewd fellows of the baser sort—
    CROWD. Ha! Ha! Not bad! Bravo!

    JOD.   No Bravos here!
Our heavy tragedian with the voluptuous bust
Was taken suddenly—
    CROWD.   Yah! Coward!
    JOD.   I mean . . .
He had to be excused—
    CROWD.   Call him back— No!—
Yes!—
    BOY. (*To* CYRANO)
        After all, Monsieur, what reason have you
To hate this Montfleury?
    CYR. (*Graciously, still seated*)
                    My dear young man,
I have two reasons, either one alone
Conclusive. *Primo:* A lamentable actor,
Who mouths his verse and moans his tragedy,
And heaves up— Ugh!—like a hod-carrier, lines
That ought to soar on their own wings. *Secundo:*—
Well—that's my secret.
    OLD CITIZEN (*Behind him*)
                    But you close the play—
La Clorise—by Baro! Are we to miss
Our entertainment, merely—
    CYR. (*Respectfully, turns his chair toward the old man*)   My dear old boy,
The poetry of Baro being worth
Zero, or less, I feel that I have done
Poetic justice!
    INTELLECTUALS. (*In the boxes*)
                    Really!—our Baro!—
My dear!—Who ever?—Ah, dieu! The idea!—
    CYR. (*Gallantly, turns his chair toward the boxes*)
Fair ladies—shine upon us like the sun,
Blossom like flowers around us—be our songs,
Heard in a a dream— Make sweet the hour of
        death,
Smiling upon us as you close our eyes—
Inspired, but do not try to criticize!
    BEL. Quite so!—and the mere money—possibly
You would like that returned— Yes?
    CYR.   Bellerose,
You speak the first word of intelligence!
I will not wound the mantle of the Muse—
Here, catch!—   (*Throws him a purse*)
            And hold your tongue.
    CROWD. (*Astonished*)   Ah! Ah!
    JOD. (*Deftly catches the purse, weighs it in his hand*)   Monsieur
You are hereby authorized to close our play
Every night, on the same terms.
    CROWD.   Boo!

JOD.   And welcome!
Let us be booed together, you and I!
BEL. Kindly pass out quietly . . .
JOD. (*Burlesquing* BELLEROSE)   Quietly . . .
(*They begin to go out, while* CYRANO *looks about
him with satisfaction. But the exodus ceases pres-
ently during the ensuing scene. The ladies in the
boxes who have already risen and put on their
wraps, stop to listen, and finally sit down again.*)
LE B. (*To* CYRANO) Idiot!
MEDDLER. (*Hurries up to* CYRANO)
                  But what a scandal! Montfleury—
The great Montfleury! Did you know the Duc
De Candale was his patron? Who is yours?
  CYR. No one.
  MED.   No one—no patron?
  CYR.   I said no.
  MED. What, no great lord, to cover with his
    name—
  CYR. (*With visible annoyance*)
No, I have told you twice. Must I repeat?
No sir, no patron—   (*His hand on his sword*)
            But a patroness!
  MED. And when do you leave Paris?
  CYR.   That's as may be.
  MED. The Duc de Candale has a long arm.
  CYR.   Mine
Is longer (*Drawing his sword*), by three feet of steel.
  MED.   Yes, yes,
But do you dream of daring—
  CYR.   I do dream
Of daring . . .
  MED.   But—
  CYR.   You may go now.
  MED.   But—
  CYR.   You may go—
Or tell me why are you staring at my nose!
  MED. (*In confusion*) No—I—
  CYR. (*Stepping up to him*) Does it astonish you?
  MED. (*Drawing back*)   Your grace
Misunderstands my—
  CYR.   Is it long and soft
And dangling, like a trunk?
  MED. (*Same business*)   I never said—
  CYR. Or crooked, like an owl's beak?
  MED.   I—
  CYR.   Perhaps
A pimple ornaments the end of it?
  MED. No—
  CYR.   Or a fly parading up and down?
What is this portent?
  MED.   Oh!—

  CYR.   This phenomenon?
  MED. But I have been careful not to look—
  CYR.   And why
Not, if you please?
  MED.   Why—
  CYR.   It disgusts you, then?
  MED. My dear sir—
  CYR.   Does its color appear to you
Unwholesome?
  MED.   Oh, by no means!
  CYR.   Or its form
Obscene?
  MED. Not in the least—
  CYR.   Then why assume
This deprecating manner? Possibly
You find it just a trifle large?
  MED. (*Babbling*)   Oh, no!—
Small, very small, infinitesimal—
  CYR. (*Roars*)   What!
How? You accuse me of absurdity?
Small—*my nose?* Why—
  MED. (*Breathless*)   My God!—
  CYR.   Magnificent,
My nose! . . . You pug, you knob, you button-
    head,
Know that I glory in this nose of mine,
For a great nose indicates a great man—
Genial, courteous, intellectual,
Virile, courageous—as I am—and such
As you—poor wretch—will never dare to be
Even in imagination. For that face—
That blank, inglorious concavity
Which my right hand finds—   (*He strikes him*)
  MED.   Ow!
  CYR.   —on top of you,
Is as devoid of pride, of poetry,
Of soul, of picturesqueness, of contour,
Of character, of NOSE in short—as that
      (*Takes him by the shoulders and turns him
        around suiting the action to the word*)
Which at the end of that limp spine of yours
My left foot—
  MED. (*Escaping*) Help! The Guard!
  CYR.   Take notice, all
Who find this feature of my countenance
A theme for comedy! When the humorist
Is noble, then my custom is to show
Appreciation proper to his rank—
More heartfelt . . . and more pointed. . . .
  DE GUICHE. (*Who has come down from the stage,
surrounded by the* MARQUIS)   Presently
This fellow will grow tiresome.

VALVERT. (*Shrugs*)   Oh, he blows
His trumpet!

DE G.   Well—will no one interfere?

VAL. No one?   (*Looks round*)
                   Observe. I myself will proceed
To put him in his place. (*He walks up to* CYRANO,
*who has been watching him, and stands there,
        looking him over with an affected air*)
                   Ah . . . your nose . . . hem! . . .
Your nose is . . . rather large!

CYR. (*Gravely*)   Rather.

VAL. (*Simpering*)   Oh, well—

CYR. (*Coolly*) Is that all?

VAL. (*Turns away, with a shrug*)
                        Well, of course—

CYR.   Ah, no, young sir!
You are too simple. Why, you might have said—
Oh, a great many things! Mon dieu, why waste
Your opportunity? For example, thus:—
AGGRESSIVE: I, sir, if that nose were mine,
I'd have it amputated—on the spot!
FRIENDLY: How do you drink with such a nose?
You ought to have a cup made specially.
DESCRIPTIVE: 'Tis a rock—a crag—a cape—
A cape? say rather, a peninsula!
INQUISITIVE: What is that receptacle—
A razor-case or a portfolio?
KINDLY: Ah, do you love the little birds
So much that when they come and sing to you,
You give them this to perch on? INSOLENT:
Sir, when you smoke, the neighbors must suppose
Your chimney is on fire. CAUTIOUS: Take care—
A weight like that might make you topheavy.
THOUGHTFUL: Somebody fetch my parasol—
Those delicate colors fade so in the sun!
PEDANTIC: Does not Aristophanes
Mention a mythologic monster called
Hippocampelephantocamelos?
Surely we have here the original!
FAMILIAR: Well, old torchlight! Hang your hat
Over that chandelier—it hurts my eyes.
ELOQUENT: When it blows, the typhoon howls,
And the clouds darken. DRAMATIC: When it bleeds—
The Red Sea! ENTERPRISING: What a sign
For some perfumer! LYRIC: Hark—the horn
Of Roland calls to summon Charlemagne!—
SIMPLE: When do they unveil the monument?
RESPECTFUL: Sir, I recognize in you
A man of parts, a man of prominence—
RUSTIC: Hey? What? Call that a nose? Na, na—
I be no fool like what you think I be—
That there's a blue cucumber! MILITARY:

Point against cavalry! PRACTICAL: Why not
A lottery with this for the grand prize?
Or—parodying Faustus in the play—
"Was this the nose that launched a thousand ships
And burned the topless towers of Ilium?"
These, my dear sir, are things you might have said
Had you some tinge of letters, or of wit
To color your discourse. But wit,—not so,
You never had an atom—and of letters,
You need but three to write you down—an Ass.
Moreover,—if you had the invention, here
Before these folk to make a jest of me—
Be sure you would not then articulate
The twentieth part of half a syllable
Of the beginning! For I say these things
Lightly enough myself, about myself,
But I allow none else to utter them.

DE G. (*Tries to lead away the amazed* VALVERT)
Vicomte—come.

VAL. (*Choking*) Oh— These arrogant grand airs!—
A clown who—look at him—not even gloves!
No ribbons—no lace—no buckles on his shoes—

CYR. I carry my adornments on my soul.
I do not dress up like a popinjay;
But inwardly, I keep my daintiness.
I do not bear with me, by any chance,
An insult not yet washed away—a conscience
Yellow with unpurged bile—an honor frayed
To rags, a set of scruples badly worn.
I go caparisoned in gems unseen,
Trailing white plumes of freedom, garlanded
With my good name—no figure of a man,
But a soul clothed in shining armor, hung
With deeds for decorations, twirling—thus—
A bristling wit, and swinging at my side
Courage, and on the stones of this old town
Making the sharp truth ring, like golden spurs!

VAL. But—

CYR.   But I have no gloves! A pity too!
I had one—the last one of an old pair—
And lost that. Very careless of me. Some
Gentleman offered me an impertinence.
I left it—in his face.

VAL.   Dolt, bumpkin, fool.
Insolent puppy, jobbernowl!

CYR. (*Removes his hat and bows*) Ah, yes?
And I—Cyrano-Savinien-Hercule
De Bergerac!

VAL. (*Turns away*) Buffoon!

CYR. (*Cries out as if suddenly taken with a cramp*)
                        Oh!

VAL. (*Turns back*)   Well, what now?
CYR. (*With grimaces of anguish*)
I must do something to relieve these cramps—
This is what comes of lack of exercise—
Ah!—
VAL. What is all this?
CYR.   My sword has gone to sleep!
VAL. (*Draws*) So be it!
CYR.   You shall die exquisitely.
VAL. (*Contemptuously*) Poet!
CYR.   Why, yes, a poet, if you will;
So while we fence, I'll make you a Ballade
Extempore.
VAL.   A Ballade?
CYR.   Yes. You know
What that is?
VAL.   I—
CYR.   The Ballade, sir, is formed
Of three stanzas of eight lines each—
VAL.   Oh, come!
CYR. And a refrain of four.
VAL.   You—
CYR.   I'll compose
One, while I fight with you; and at the end
Of the last line—thrust home!
VAL.   Will you?
CYR.   I will. (*Declaims*)
"Ballade of the duel at the Hôtel de Bourgogne
Between de Bergerac and a Boeotian.
VAL. (*Sneering*) What do you mean by that?
CYR.   Oh, that? The title.
CROWD. (*Excited*) Come on—
                    A circle—
                        Quiet—
                            Down in front!
(TABLEAU. *A ring of interested spectators in the
centre of the floor, the* MARQUIS *and the Officers
mingling with the citizens and common folk. Pages
swarming up on men's shoulders to see better;
the Ladies in the boxes standing and leaning over.
To the right,* DE GUICHE *and his following; to the
left,* LE BRET, CUIGY, RAGUENEAU, *and others of*
CYRANO's *friends.*)
CYR. (*Closes his eyes for an instant*) Stop . . .
    Let me choose my rimes. . . . Now! Here we
go—   (*He suits the action to the word,
                        throughout the following*)

Lightly I toss my hat away,
    Languidly over my arm let fall
The cloak that covers my bright array—
    Then out swords, and to work withal!

A Launcelot, in his Lady's hall . . .
A Spartacus, at the Hippodrome! . . .
    I dally awhile with you, dear jackal,
Then, as I end the refrain, thrust home.
                (*The swords cross—the fight is on*)

Where shall I skewer my peacock? . . . Nay,
    Better for you to have shunned this brawl!—
Here, in the heart, thro' your ribbons gay?
    —In the belly, under your silken shawl?
Hark, how the steel rings musical!
Mark how my point floats, light as the foam,
    Ready to drive you back to the wall,
Then, as I end the refrain, thrust home!

Ho, for a rime! . . . You are white as whey—
    You break, you cower, you cringe, you . . .
        crawl!
Tac!—and I parry your last essay:
    So may the turn of a hand forestall
Life with its honey, death with its gall;
So may the turn of my fancy roam
    Free, for a time, till the rimes recall,
Then, as I end the refrain, thrust home!
                (*He announces solemnly*)

REFRAIN

Prince! Pray God, that is Lord of all,
Pardon your soul, for your time has come!
    Beat—pass—fling you aslant, asprawl—
Then, as I end the refrain . . .
(*He lunges;* VALVERT *staggers back and falls into
the arms of his friends.* CYRANO *recovers, and sa-
lutes.*)
                            —Thrust home!
(*Shouts. Applause from the boxes. Flowers and
handkerchiefs come fluttering down. The Officers
surround* CYRANO *and congratulate him.* RAGUE-
NEAU *dances for joy.* LE BRET *is unable to conceal
his enthusiasm. The friends of* VALVERT *hold him
up and help him away.*)
CROWD. (*In one long cry*) Ah-h!
CAV.   Superb!
WOMAN.   Simply sweet!
RAG.   Magnelephant!
MARQ. A novelty!
LE B.   Bah!
CROWD. (*Thronging around* CYRANO)
                    Compliments—regards—
Bravo!—
WOMAN'S VOICE. Why, he's a hero!
MUSKETEER. (*Advances quickly to* CYRANO, *with
outstretched hands*)   Monsieur, will you

Permit me?—It was altogether fine!
I think I may appreciate these things—
Moreover, I have been stamping for pure joy!
            (*He retires quickly*)
CYR. (*To* CUIGY)
What was that gentleman's name?
        CUIGY.   Oh . . . D'Artagnan.
LE B. (*Takes* CYRANO'S *arm*)
Come here and tell me—
        CYR.   Let this crowd go first—
(*To* BELLEROSE) May we stay?
        BEL. (*With great respect*)   Certainly!
                (*Cries and catcalls off stage*)
JOD. (*Comes down from the door where he has
been looking out*)   Hark!— Montfleury—
They are hooting him.
        BEL. (*Solemnly*)   Sic transit gloria!
                (*Changes his tone and shouts
                to the* PORTER *and the* LAMPLIGHTER)
—Strike! . . . Close the house! . . . Leave the
lights— We rehearse
The new farce after dinner. (JODELET *and* BELLEROSE
        go out after elaborately saluting CYRANO)
PORTER. (*To* CYRANO)   You do not dine?
CYR. I?—No!   (*The* PORTER *turns away*)
LE B.   Why not?
CYR. (*Haughtily*)   Because—
                (*Changing his tone when he sees
                the* PORTER *has gone*)
                        Because I have
No money.
        LE B. (*Gesture of tossing*) But—the purse of gold?
CYR.   Farewell,
Paternal pension!
        LE B.   So you have, until
The first of next month—?
        CYR.   Nothing.
        LE B.   What a fool!—
CYR. But—what a gesture!
        OR. GIRL. (*Behind her little counter; coughs*)
                        Hem!
        (CYRANO *and* LE BRET *look around;
                she advances timidly*)
                Pardon, Monsieur . . .
A man ought never to go hungry . . .
                (*Indicating the sideboard*)
                        See,
I have everything here . . .   (*Eagerly*)
                Please!—
        CYR. (*Uncovers*)   My dear child,
I cannot bend this Gascon pride of mine
To accept such a kindness— Yet, for fear

That I may give you pain if I refuse,
I will take . . .
(*He goes to the sideboard and makes his selection*)
                Oh, not very much! A grape . . .
                (*She gives him the bunch;
                he removes a single grape*)
One only! And a glass of water . . .
        (*She starts to pour wine into it; he stops her*)
                                Clear!
And . . . half a macaroon!
                (*He gravely returns the other half*)
        LE B.   Old idiot!
        OR. GIRL. Please!—Nothing more?
        CYR.   Why, yes— Your hand to kiss.
        (*He kisses the hand which she holds out,
                as he would the hand of a princess*)
        OR. GIRL. Thank you, sir.   (*She curtseys*)
                Good-night. (*She goes out*)
        CYR.   Now, I am listening.
                (*Plants himself before the sideboard
                and arranges thereon—*)
Dinner!— (—*the macaroon*)
        Drink!— (—*the glass of water*)
                Dessert!— (—*the grape*)
                There—now I'll sit down.
                        (*Seats himself*)
Lord, I was hungry! Abominably!   (*Eating*)
                                Well!
        LE B. These fatheads with the bellicose grand airs
Will have you ruined if you listen to them;
Talk to a man of sense and hear how all
Your swagger impresses him.
        CYR. (*Finishes his macaroon*) Enormously.
        LE B. The Cardinal—
        CYR. (*Beaming*) Was he there?
        LE B.   He must have thought you—
        CYR. Original.
        LE B.   Well, but—
        CYR.   He is himself
A playwright. He will not be too displeased
That I have closed another author's play.
        LE B. But look at all the enemies you have made!
        CYR. (*Begins on the grape*)
How many—do you think?
        LE B.   Just forty-eight
Without the women.
        CYR.   Count them.
        LE B.   Montfleury,
Baro, de Guiche, the Vicomte, the Old Man,
All the Academy—
        CYR.   Enough! You make me
Happy!

LE B. But where is all this leading you?
What is your plan?

CYR.   I have been wandering—
Wasting my force upon too many plans.
Now I have chosen one.

LE B   What one?

CYR.   The simplest—
To make myself in all things admirable!

LE B. Hmph!—Well, then, the real reason why
    you hate
Montfleury— Come, the truth, now!

CYR. (Rises)   That Silenus,
Who cannot hold his belly in his arms,
Still dreams of being sweetly dangerous
Among the women—sighs and languishes
Making sheeps' eyes out of his great frog's face—
I hate him ever since one day he dared
Smile upon—
                        Oh, my friend, I seemed to see
Over some flower a great snail crawling!

LE B. (Amazed)   How?
What? Is it possible?—

CYR. (With a bitter smile)
                        For me to love? . . .
                        (Changing his tone; seriously)
I love.

LE B. May I know? You have never said—

CYR. Whom I love? Think a moment. Think of
    me—
Me, whom the plainest woman would despise—
Me, with this nose of mine that marches on
Before me by a quarter of an hour!
Whom should I love? Why—of course—it must be
The woman in the world most beautiful.

LE B. Most beautiful?

CYR.   In all this world—most sweet
Also; most wise; most witty, and most fair!

LE B. Who and what is this woman?

CYR.   Dangerous
Mortally, without meaning; exquisite
Without imagining. Nature's own snare
To allure manhood. A white rose wherein
Love lies in ambush for his natural prey.
Who knows her smile has known a perfect thing.
She creates grace in her own image, brings
Heaven to earth in one movement of her hand—
Nor thou, O Venus! balancing thy shell
Over the Mediterranean blue, nor thou,
Diana! marching through broad, blossoming woods,
Art so divine as when she mounts her chair,
And goes abroad through Paris!

LE B.   Oh, well—of course,
That makes everything clear!

CYR.   Transparently.

LE B. Madeleine Robin—your cousin?

CYR.   Yes; Roxane.

LE B. And why not? If you love her, tell her so!
You have covered yourself with glory in her eyes
This very day.

CYR.   My old friend—look at me,
And tell me how much hope remains for me
With its protuberance! Oh, I have no more
Illusions! Now and then—bah! I may grow
Tender, walking alone in the blue cool
Of evening, through some garden fresh with flowers
After the benediction of the rain;
My poor big devil of a nose inhales
April . . . and so I follow with my eyes
Where some boy, with a girl upon his arm,
Passes a patch of silver . . . and I feel
Somehow, I wish I had a woman too,
Walking with little steps under the moon,
And holding my arm so, and smiling. Then
I dream—and I forget. . . .
                        And then I see
The shadow of my profile on the wall!

LE B. My friend! . . .

CYR.   My friend, I have my bitter days,
Knowing myself so ugly, so alone.
Sometimes—

LE B.   You weep?

CYR. (Quickly)   Oh, not that ever! No,
That would be too grotesque—tears trickling down
All the long way along this nose of mine?
I will not so profane the dignity
Of sorrow. Never any tears for me!
Why, there is nothing more sublime than tears,
Nothing!—Shall I make them ridiculous
In my poor person?

LE B.   Love's no more than chance!

CYR. (Shakes his head)
No. I love Cleopatra; do I appear
Caesar? I adore Beatrice; have I
The look of Dante?

LE B.   But your wit—your courage—
Why, that poor child who offered you just now
Your dinner!—She—you saw with your own eyes,
Her eyes did not avoid you.

CYR. (Thoughtful)   That is true . . .

LE B. Well then! Roxane herself, watching your
    duel,
Paler than—

CYR.   Pale?—

LE B.   Her lips parted, her hand
Thus at her breast— I saw it! Speak to her
Speak, man!

CYR.   Through my nose? She might laugh at me.
That is the one thing in this world I fear!

PORTER. (*Followed by the* DUENNA, *approaches*
CYRANO *respectfully*) A lady asking for Monsieur.

CYR.   Mon dieu . . .
Her Duenna!—

DUENNA (*A sweeping curtsey*) Monsieur . . .
                          A message for you:
From our good cousin we desire to know
When and where we may see him privately.

CYR. (*Amazed*) To see me?

DUEN. (*An elaborate reverence*)
            To see you. We have certain things
To tell you.

CYR.   Certain—

DUEN.   Things.

CYR. (*Trembling*)   Mon dieu! . . .

DUEN.   We go
Tomorrow, at the first flush of the dawn,
To hear Mass at St. Roch. Then afterwards,
Where can we meet and talk a little?

CYR. (*Catching* LE BRET's *arm*)   Where?
I— Ah, mon dieu! . . . mon dieu! . . .

DUEN.   Well?

CYR.   I am thinking . . .

DUEN. And you think?

CYR.   I . . . The shop of Ragueneau . . .
Ragueneau—pastrycook . . .

DUEN.   Who dwells?—

CYR.   Mon dieu! . . .
Oh, yes . . . Ah, mon dieu! . . . Rue St.-Honoré.

DUEN. We are agreed. Remember—seven o'clock.
(*Reverence*) Until then—

CYR.   I'll be there. (*The* DUENNA *goes out.*
CYRANO *falls into the arms of* LE BRET.)
            Me . . . to see me! . . .

LE B. You are not quite so gloomy.

CYR.   After all,
She knows that I exist—no matter why!

LE B. So now, you are going to be happy.

CYR.   Now! . . . (*Beside himself*)
I—I am going to be a storm—a flame—
I need to fight whole armies all alone;
I have ten hearts; I have a hundred arms; I feel
Too strong to war with mortals—
            (*He shouts at the top of his voice*)
                BRING ME GIANTS!

(*A moment since, the shadows of the comedians
have been visible moving and posturing upon the
stage. The violins have taken their places.*)

VOICE. (*From the stage*)
Hey—pst—less noise! We are rehearsing here!

CYR. (*Laughs*) We are going.

(*He turns up stage. Through the street door enter*
CUIGY, BRISSAILLE, *and a number of officers, supporting* LIGNIÈRE, *who is now thoroughly drunk.*)

CUIGY. Cyrano!

CYR.   What is it?

CUIGY.   Here—
Here's your stray lamb!

CYR. (*Recognizes* LIGNIÈRE)
                Lignière—What's wrong with him?

CUIGY. He wants you.

BRIS.   He's afraid to go home.

CYR.   Why?

LIG. (*Showing a crumpled scrap of paper and
speaking with the elaborate logic of profound in-
toxication*)
This letter—hundred against one—that's me—
I'm the one—all because of little song—
Good song— Hundred men, waiting, understand?
Porte de Nesle—way home— Might be dangerous—
Would you permit me spend the night with you?

CYR. A hundred—is that all? You are going home!

LIG. (*Astonished*) Why—

CYR. (*In a voice of thunder, indicating the
lighted lantern which the* PORTER *holds up curiously as he regards the scene*)
            Take that lantern!
            (LIGNIÈRE *precipitately seizes the lantern*)
                    Forward march! I say
I'll be the man tonight that sees you home.
                    (*To the officers*)
You others follow—I want an audience!

CUIGY. A hundred against one—

CYR.   Those are the odds
Tonight! (*The Comedians in their costumes are
descending from the stage and joining the group*)

LE B.   But why help this—

CYR.   There goes Le Bret
Growling!

LE B.   —This drunkard here?

CYR. (*His hand on* LE BRET's *shoulder*)
                    Because this drunkard—
This tun of sack, this butt of Burgundy—
Once in his life has done one lovely thing:
After the Mass, according to the form,
He saw, one day, the lady of his heart
Take holy water for a blessing. So

This one, who shudders at a drop of rain,
This fellow here—runs headlong to the font
Bends down and drinks it dry!

SOUBRETTE.   I say that was
A pretty thought!

CYR.   Ah, was it not?

SOUBRETTE. (*To the others*)   But why
Against one poor poet, a hundred men?

CYR. March!   (*To the officers*)
          And you gentlemen, remember now,
No rescue— Let me fight alone.

COMEDIENNE (*Jumps down from the stage*)
                        Come on!
I'm going to watch—

CYR.   Come along!

ANOTHER COMEDIENNE. (*Jumps down, speaks to a
          Comedian costumed as an old man*)
                        You, Cassandre?

CYR. Come all of you—the Doctor, Isabelle,
Léandre—the whole company—a swarm
Of murmuring, golden bees—we'll parody
Italian farce and Tragedy-of-Blood;
Ribbons for banners, masks for blazonry,
And tambourines to be our rolling drums!

ALL THE WOMEN. (*Jumping for joy*)
Bravo!—My hood— My cloak— Hurry!

JOD. (*Mock heroic*)   Lead on!—

CYR. (*To the violins*)
You violins—play us an overture—
(*The violins join the procession which is forming.
The lighted candles are snatched from the stage
and distributed; it becomes a torchlight procession.*)
Bravo!—Officers— Ladies in costume—
And twenty paces in advance. . . .

                (*He takes his station as he speaks*)
                        Myself,
Alone, with glory fluttering over me,
Alone as Lucifer at war with heaven!
Remember—no one lifts a hand to help—
Ready there? One . . . two . . . three! Porter, the
     doors! . . .
(*The* PORTER *flings wide the great doors. We see
in the dim moonlight a corner of old Paris, purple
                and picturesque.*)
Look—Paris dreams—nocturnal, nebulous,
Under blue moonbeams hung from wall to wall—
Nature's own setting for the scene we play!—
Yonder, behind her veil of mist, the Seine,
Like a mysterious and magic mirror
Trembles—
                And you shall see what you shall see!

ALL. To the Porte de Nesle!

CYR. (*Erect upon the threshold*)
                        To the Porte de Nesle!
(*He turns back for a moment to the* SOUBRETTE)
Did you not ask, my dear, why against one
Singer they send a hundred swords?

                (*Quietly, drawing his own sword*)
                        Because
They know this one man for a friend of mine!
(*He goes out. The procession follows:* LIGNIÈRE
zigzagging at its head, then, the COMEDIENNES *on
the arms of the* OFFICERS, *then the* COMEDIANS, *leaping and dancing as they go. It vanishes into the
night to the music of the violins, illuminated by
the flickering glimmer of the candles.*)

[CURTAIN]

THE SECOND ACT

The Bakery of the Poets

THE SHOP OF RAGUENEAU, *Baker and Pastrycook:
a spacious affair at the corner of the Rue St.-
Honoré and the Rue de l'Arbre Sec. The street,
seen vaguely through the glass panes in the door
at the back, is grey in the first light of dawn.*

*In the foreground, at the Left, a Counter is sur-
mounted by a Canopy of wrought iron from which
are hanging ducks, geese, and white peacocks.
Great crockery jars hold bouquets of common
flowers, yellow sunflowers in particular. On the
same side farther back, a huge fireplace; in front
of it, between great andirons, of which each one
supports a little saucepan, roast fowls revolve and
weep into their dripping-pans. To the Right at the
First Entrance, a door. Beyond it, Second Entrance, a staircase leads up to a little dining-room
under the eaves, its interior visible through open
shutters. A table is set there and a tiny Flemish
candlestick is lighted; there one may retire to eat
and drink in private. A wooden gallery, extending
from the head of the stairway, seems to lead to
other little dining-rooms.*

*In the centre of the shop, an iron ring hangs
by a rope over a pulley so that it can be raised or
lowered; adorned with game of various kinds hung
from it by hooks, it has the appearance of a sort of
gastronomic chandelier.*

*In the shadow under the staircase, ovens are
glowing. The spits revolve; the copper pots and
pans gleam ruddily. Pastries in pyramids. Hams
hanging from the rafters. The morning baking is*

in progress: a bustle of tall cooks and timid scullions and scurrying apprentices; a blossoming of white caps adorned with cock's feathers or the wings of guinea fowl. On wicker trays or on great metal platters they bring in rows of pastries and fancy dishes of various kinds.

Tables are covered with trays of cakes and rolls; others with chairs placed about them are set for guests.

One little table in a corner disappears under a heap of papers. At the CURTAIN RISE RAGUENEAU *is seated there. He is writing poetry.*

PASTRYCOOK. (*Brings in a dish*)
Fruits *en gelée!*

2ND PASTRYCOOK. (*Brings dish*) Custard!

3RD PASTRYCOOK. (*Brings roast peacock ornamented with feathers*)   Peacock *roti!*

4TH PASTRYCOOK. (*Brings tray of cakes*)
Cakes and confections!

5TH PASTRYCOOK. (*Brings earthen dish*)
                    Beef *en casserole!*

RAG. (*Raises his head; returns to mere earth*)
Over the coppers of my kitchen flows
The frost-silver dawn. Silence awhile
The god who sings within thee, Ragueneau!
Lay down the lute—the oven calls for thee!
            (*Rises; goes to one of the cooks*)
Here's a hiatus in your sauce; fill up
The measure.

COOK.   How much?

RAG. (*Measures on his finger*) One more dactyl.

COOK.   Huh? . . .

1ST PASTRYCOOK. Rolls!

2ND PASTRYCOOK.   Roulades!

RAG. (*Before the fireplace*)
                    Veil, O Muse, thy virgin eyes
From the lewd gleam of these terrestrial fires!
                    (*To* 1ST PASTRYCOOK)
Your rolls lack balance. Here's the proper form—
An equal hemistich on either side,
And the caesura in between.
        (*To another, pointing out an unfinished pie*)
                              Your house
Of crust should have a roof upon it.
            (*To another, who is seated on the hearth, placing poultry on a spit*)
                              And you—
Along the interminable spit, arrange
The modest pullet and the lordly Turk
Alternately, my son—as great Malherbe
Alternates male and female rimes. Remember,

A couplet, or a roast, should be well turned.

APPRENTICE. (*Advances with a dish covered by a napkin*) Master, I thought of you when I designed
This, hoping it might please you.

RAG.   Ah! A Lyre—

APPRENTICE. In puff-paste—

RAG.   And the jewels—candied fruit!

APPRENTICE. And the strings, barley-sugar!

RAG. (*Gives him money*)   Go and drink
My health.   (LISE *enters*)
              St!—My wife— Circulate, and hide
That money!
        (*Shows the Lyre to* LISE, *with a languid air*)
                    Graceful—yes?

LISE.   Ridiculous!
(*She places on the counter a pile of paper bags*)

RAG. Paper bags? Thank you . . .
                    (*He looks at them*)
                    Ciel! My manuscripts!
The sacred verses of my poets—rent
Asunder, limb from limb—butchered to make
Base packages of pastry! Ah, you are one
Of those insane Bacchantes who destroyed
Orpheus!

LISE.   Your dirty poets left them here
To pay for eating half our stock-in-trade:
We ought to make some profit out of them!

RAG. Ant! Would you blame the locust for his
    song?

LISE. I blame the locust for his appetite!
There used to be a time—before you had
Your hungry friends—you never called me Ants—
No, nor Bacchantes!

RAG.   What a way to use
Poetry!

LISE. Well, what is the use of it?

RAG. But, my dear girl, what would you do with
    prose?   (*Two* CHILDREN *enter*)
Well, dears?

CHILD.   Three little patties.

RAG. (*Serves them*)   There we are!
All hot and brown.

CHILD.   Would you mind wrapping them?

RAG. One of my paper bags! . . .
                    Oh, certainly.
            (*Reads from the bag, as he is about to wrap the patties in it*)
"Ulysses, when he left Penelope"—
Not that one!   (*Takes another bag; reads*)
        "Phoebus, golden-crowned"—
                    Not that one.

LISE. Well? They are waiting!

RAG.   Very well, very well!—
The Sonnet to Phyllis . . .
                        Yet—it does seem hard . . .
LISE. Made up your mind—at last! Mph! Jack-o'-
Dreams!
RAG. (*As her back is turned, calls back the* CHIL-
DREN, *who are already at the door*)
Pst!—Children— Give me back the bag. Instead
Of three patties, you shall have six of them!
(*Makes the exchange. The* CHILDREN *go out. He
reads from the bag, as he smoothes it out tenderly.*)
"Phyllis"—
            A spot of butter on her name!—
"Phyllis"—
CYR. (*Enters hurriedly*) What is the time?
RAG.   Six o'clock.
CYR.   One
Hour more . . .
RAG.   Felicitations!
CYR.   And for what?
RAG. Your victory! I saw it all—
CYR.   Which one?
RAG. At the Hôtel de Bourgogne.
CYR.   Oh—the duel!
RAG. The duel in Rime!
LISE.   He talks of nothing else.
CYR. Nonsense!
RAG. (*Fencing and foining with a spit, which he
snatches up from the hearth*)
       "Then, as I end the refrain, thrust home!"
"Then, as I end the refrain"—
                        Gods! What a line!
"Then, as I end"—
CYR.   What time now, Ragueneau?
RAG. (*Petrified at the full extent of a lunge,
while he looks at the clock*)
Five after six—   (*Recovers*)
            "—thrust home!"
                        A Ballade, too!
LISE. (*To* CYRANO, *who in passing has mechan-
ically shaken hands with her*)
Your hand—what have you done?
CYR.   Oh, my hand?—Nothing.
RAG. What danger now—
CYR.   No danger.
LISE   I believe
He is lying.
CYR.   Why? Was I looking down my nose!
That must have been a devil of a lie!
            (*Changing his tone; to* RAGUENEAU)
I expect someone. Leave us here alone,
When the time comes.

RAG.   How can I? In a moment,
My poets will be here.
LISE.   To break their . . . fast!
CYR. Take them away, then, when I give the sign.
—What time?
RAG.   Ten minutes after.
CYR.   Have you a pen?
RAG. (*Offers him a pen*)
An eagle's feather!
MUSKETEER. (*Enters, and speaks to* LISE *in a sten-
torian voice*)   Greeting!
CYR. (*To* RAGUENEAU)   Who is this?
RAG. My wife's friend. A terrific warrior,
So he says.
CYR.   Ah— I see. (*Takes up the pen; waves
            RAGUENEAU away*)
                Only to write—
To fold— To give it to her—and to go . . .
                (*Throws down the pen*)
Coward! And yet—the Devil take my soul
If I dare speak one word to her . . .
                (*To* RAGUENEAU) What time now?
RAG. A quarter after six.
CYR. (*Striking his breast*)—One little word
Of all the many thousand I have here!
Whereas in writing . . . (*Takes up the pen*)
                Come, I'll write to her
That letter I have written on my heart,
Torn up, and written over many times—
So many times . . . that all I have to do
Is to remember, and to write it down.
(*He writes. Through the glass of the door appear
vague and hesitating shadows. The* POETS *enter
clothed in rusty black and spotted with mud.*)
LISE. (*To* RAGUENEAU)
Here come your scarecrows!
1ST POET.   Comrade!
2ND POET. (*Takes both* RAGUENEAU'S *hands*)
                My dear brother!
3RD POET. (*Sniffing*)
O Lord of Roasts, how sweet thy dwellings are!
4TH POET. Phoebus Apollo of the Silver Spoon!
5TH POET. Cupid of Cookery!
RAG. (*Surrounded, embraced, beaten on the back*)
                These geniuses,
They put one at one's ease!
1ST POET.   We were delayed
By the crowd at the Porte de Nesle.
2ND POET.   Dead men
All scarred and gory, scattered on the stones,
Villainous-looking scoundrels—eight of them.

CYR. (*Looks up an instant*)
Eight? I thought only seven—

RAG.   Do you know
The hero of this hecatomb?

CYR.   I? . . . No.

LISE. (*To the* MUSKETEER) Do you?

MUSK.   Hmm—perhaps!

1ST POET.   They say one man alone
Put to flight all this crowd.

2ND POET   Everywhere lay
Swords, daggers, pikes, bludgeons—

CYR. (*Writing*)   "Your eyes . . ."

3RD POET.   As far
As the Quai des Orfevres, hats and cloaks—

1ST POET. Why, that man must have been the
devil!

CYR.   "Your lips . . ."

1ST POET. Some savage monster might have done
this thing!

CYR. "Looking upon you, I grow faint with
fear . . ."

2ND POET. What have you written lately, Ragueneau?

CYR.   "Your Friend—Who loves you . . ."
                    So. No signature;
I'll give it to her myself.

RAG.   A Recipe
In Rime.

3RD POET. Read us your rimes!

4TH POET.   Here's a brioche
Cocking its hat at me.   (*He bites off the top of it*)

1ST POET.   Look how those buns
Follow the hungry poet with their eyes—
Those almond eyes!

2ND POET.   We are listening—

3RD POET.   See this cream-puff—
Fat little baby, drooling while it smiles!

2ND POET. (*Nibbling at the pastry Lyre*)
For the first time, the Lyre is my support.

RAG. (*Coughs, adjusts his cap, strikes an attitude*)
A Recipe in Rime—

2ND POET. (*Gives* FIRST POET *a dig with his elbow*)
                    Your breakfast?

1ST POET.   Dinner!

RAG. (*Declaims*)

A Recipe for Making Almond Tarts.

Beat your eggs, the yolk and white,
        Very light;
Mingle with their creamy fluff
Drops of lime-juice, cool and green;

Then pour in
Milk of Almonds, just enough.

Dainty patty-pans, embraced
        In puff-paste—
Have these ready within reach;
    With your thumb and finger, pinch
        Half an inch
Up around the edge of each—

Into these, a score or more,
        Slowly pour
All your store of custard; so
    Take them, bake them golden-brown—
        Now sit down! . . .
Almond tartlets, Ragueneau!

POET. Delicious! Melting!

POET (*Chokes*)   Humph!

CYR. (*To* RAGUENEAU)   Do you not see
Those fellows fattening themselves?—

RAG.   I know.
I would not look—it might embarrass them—
You see, I love a friendly audience.
Besides—another vanity—I am pleased
When they enjoy my cooking.

CYR. (*Slaps him on the back*) Be off with you!—
                    (RAGUENEAU *goes up stage*)
Good little soul!   (*Calls to* LISE)
                    Madame!—
(*She leaves the* MUSKETEER *and comes down to him*)
                    This musketeer—
He is making love to you?

LISE. (*Haughtily*)   If any man
Offends my virtue—all I have to do
Is look at him—once!

CYR. (*Looks at her gravely; she drops her eyes*)
                    I do not find
Those eyes of yours unconquerable.

LISE. (*Panting*)   —Ah!

CYR. (*Raising his voice a little*)
Now listen— I am fond of Ragueneau;
I allow no one—do you understand?—
To . . . take his name in vain!

LISE.   You think—

CYR. (*Ironic emphasis*)   I think
I interrupt you.
(*He salutes the* MUSKETEER, *who has heard without
daring to resent the warning.* LISE *goes to the* MUS-
KETEER *as he returns* CYRANO'S *salute*)

LISE.   You—you swallow that?—
You ought to have pulled his nose!

MUSK.   His nose? His nose! . . .

(He goes out hurriedly. ROXANE *and the* DUENNA *appear outside the door.)*

CYR. *(Nods to* RAGUENEAU) Pst!—

RAG. *(To the* POETS)   Come inside—

CYR. *(Impatient)*   Pst! . . . Pst! . . .

RAG.   We shall be more Comfortable . . .

(He leads the POETS *into inner room)*

1ST POET. The cakes!

2ND POET.   Bring them along! *(They go out)*

CYR. If I can see the faintest spark of hope,

Then—   *(Throws door open—bows)*

Welcome!   (ROXANE *enters, followed by the* DUENNA, *whom* CYRANO *detains)*

Pardon me—one word—

DUEN.   Take two.

CYR. Have you a good digestion?

DUEN.   Wonderful!

CYR. Good. Here are two sonnets, by Benserade—

DUEN. Euh?

CYR.   Which I fill for you with éclairs.

DUEN.   Ooo!

CYR. Do you like cream-puffs?

DUEN.   Only with whipped cream.

CYR. Here are three . . . six—embosomed in a poem

By Saint-Amant. This ode of Chapelin

Looks deep enough to hold—a jelly roll.

—Do you love Nature?

DUEN.   Mad about it.

CYR.   Then

Go out and eat these in the street. Do not

Return—

DUEN. Oh, but—

CYR.   Until you finish them.

        (Down to ROXANE)

Blessed above all others be the hour

When you remembered to remember me,

And came to tell me . . . what?

ROX. *(Takes off her mask)* First let me thank you

Because . . . That man . . . that creature, whom your sword

Made sport of yesterday— His patron, one—

CYR. De Guiche?—

ROX.   —who thinks himself in love with me

Would have forced that man upon me for—

a husband—

CYR.   I understand—so much the better then!

I fought, not for my nose, but your bright eyes.

ROX. And then, to tell you—but before I can

Tell you— Are you, I wonder, still the same

Big brother—almost—that you used to be

When we were children, playing by the pond

In the old garden down there—

CYR.   I remember—

Every summer you came to Bergerac! . . .

ROX. You used to make swords out of bulrushes—

CYR. You dandelion-dolls with golden hair—

ROX. And those green plums—

CYR.   And those black mulberries—

ROX. In those days, you did everything I wished!

CYR. Roxane, in short skirts, was called Madeleine.

ROX. Was I pretty?

CYR.   Oh—not too plain!

ROX.   Sometimes

When you had hurt your hand you used to come

Running to me—and I would be your mother,

And say— Oh, in a very grown-up voice:

        (She takes his hand)

"Now, what have you been doing to yourself?

Let me see—"   *(She sees the hand—starts)*

        Oh!—

            Wait—I said *Let me see!*

Still—at your age! How did you do that?

CYR.   Playing

With the big boys, down by the Porte de Nesle.

ROX. *(Sits at a table and wets her handkerchief in a glass of water)* Come here to me.

CYR.   —Such a wise little mother!

ROX. And tell me, while I wash this blood away,

How many you—played with?

CYR.   Oh, about a hundred.

ROX. Tell me.

CYR.   No. Let me go. Tell me what *you*

Were going to tell *me*—if you dared?

ROX. *(Still holding his hand)*   I think

I do dare—now. It seems like long ago

When I could tell you things. Yes—I dare . . .

    Listen:

I . . . love someone.

CYR.   Ah! . . .

ROX.   Someone who does not know.

CYR. Ah! . . .

ROX.   At least—not yet.

CYR.   Ah! . . .

ROX.   But he will know

Some day.

CYR. Ah! . . .

ROX.   A big boy who loves me too,

And is afraid of me, and keeps away,

And never says one word.

CYR.   Ah! . . .

ROX.   Let me have
Your hand a moment—why, how hot it is!—
I know. I see him trying . . .

CYR.   Ah! . . .

ROX.   There now!
Is that better?—   (*She finishes bandaging the
                    hand with her handkerchief*)
                    Besides—only to think—
(This is a secret.) He is a soldier too,
In your own regiment—

CYR.   Ah! . . .

ROX.   Yes, in the Guards.
Your company too.

CYR.   Ah! . . .

ROX.   And such a man!—
He is proud—noble—young—brave—beautiful—

CYR. (*Turns pale; rises*) Beautiful!—

ROX.   What's the matter?

CYR. (*Smiling*)   Nothing—this—
My sore hand!

ROX.   Well, I love him. That is all.
Oh—and I never saw him anywhere
Except the *Comédie*.

CYR.   You have never spoken?—

ROX. Only our eyes . . .

CYR.   Why, then— How do you know?—

ROX. People talk about people; and I hear
Things . . . and I know.

CYR.   You say he is in the Guards:
His name?

ROX. Baron Christian de Neuvillette.

CYR. He is not in the Guards.

ROX.   Yes. Since this morning.
Captain Carbon de Castel-Jaloux.

CYR.   So soon! . . .
So soon we lose our hearts!—
                          But, my dear child.—

DUEN. (*Opens the door*)
I have eaten the cakes, Monsieur de Bergerac!

CYR. Good! Now go out and read the poetry!
                    (*The* DUENNA *disappears*)
—But, my dear child! You, who love only words,
Wit, the grand manner— Why, for all you know,
The man may be a savage, or a fool.

ROX. His curls are like a hero from D'Urfé.

CYR. His mind may be as curly as his hair.

ROX. Not with such eyes. I read his soul in them.

CYR. Yes, all our souls are written in our eyes!
But—if he be a bungler?

ROX.   Then I shall die—
There!

CYR. (*After a pause*)
          And you brought me here to tell me this?
I do not yet quite understand, Madame,
The reason for your confidence.

ROX.   They say
That in your company— It frightens me—
You are all Gascons . . .

CYR.   And we pick a quarrel
With any flat-foot who intrudes himself,
Whose blood is not pure Gascon like our own?
Is this what you have heard?

ROX.   I am so afraid
For him!

CYR. (*Between his teeth*) Not without reason!—

ROX.   And I thought
You . . . You were so brave, so invincible
Yesterday, against all those brutes!—If you,
Whom they all fear—

CYR.   Oh, well—I will defend
Your little Baron.

ROX.   Will you? Just for me?
Because I have always been—your friend!

CYR.   Of course . . .

ROX. Will you be *his* friend?

CYR.   I will be his friend.

ROX. And never let him fight a duel?

CYR.   No—never.

ROX. Oh, but you are a darling!—I must go—
You never told me about last night— Why,
You must have been a hero! Have him write
And tell me all about it—will you?

CYR.   Of course . . .

ROX. (*Kisses her hand*)
I always did love you!—A hundred men
Against one— Well. . . . Adieu. We are great
     friends,
Are we not?

CYR.   Of course . . .

ROX.   He *must* write to me—
A hundred— You shall tell me the whole story
Some day, when I have time. A hundred men—
What courage!

CYR. (*Salutes as she goes out*)
                          Oh . . . I have done better since!
(*The door closes after her.* CYRANO *remains motionless, his eyes on the ground. Pause. The other
     door opens;* RAGUENEAU *puts in his head.*)

RAG. May I come in?

CYR. (*Without moving*) Yes . . .
(RAGUENEAU *and his friends re-enter. At the same
time,* CARBON DE CASTEL-JALOUX *appears at the*

street door in uniform as Captain of the Guards; recognizes CYRANO with a sweeping gesture.)

CARB. Here he is!—Our hero!

CYR. (Raises his head and salutes) Our Captain!

CARB.   We know! All our company Are here—

CYR. (Recoils) No—

CARB.   Come! They are waiting for you.

CYR.   No!

CARB. (Tries to lead him out) Only across the street— Come!

CYR.   Please—

CARB. (Goes to the door and shouts in a voice of thunder)   Our champion Refuses! He is not feeling well today!

VOICE OUTSIDE. Ah! Sandious! (Noise outside of swords and trampling feet approaching)

CARB.   Here they come now!

CADETS. (Entering the shop)   Mille dious!— Mordious!—Capdedious!—Pocapdedious!

RAG. (In astonishment)   Gentlemen— You are all Gascons?

CADETS.   All!

1ST CADET. (To CYRANO) Bravo!

CYR.   Baron!

ANOTHER CADET. (Takes both his hands) Vivat!

CYR. Baron!

3RD CADET. Come to my arms!

CYR.   Baron!

OTHERS. To mine!— To mine!—

CYR. Baron . . . Baron . . . Have mercy—

RAG. You are all Barons too?

CADETS.   Are we?

RAG.   Are they? . . .

1ST CADET. Our coronets would star the midnight sky!

LE B. (Enters; hurries to CYRANO) The whole Town's looking for you! Raving mad— A triumph! Those who saw the fight—

CYR.   I hope You have not told them where I—

LE B. (Rubbing his hand)   Certainly I told them!

CITIZEN. (Enters, followed by a group) Listen! Shut the door!—Here comes All Paris!

(The street outside fills with a shouting crowd. Chairs and carriages stop at the door.)

LE B. (Aside to CYRANO, smiling) And Roxane?

CYR. (Quickly)   Hush!

CROWD OUTSIDE.   Cyrano!

(A mob bursts into the shop. Shouts, acclamations, general disturbance.)

RAG. (Standing on a table) My shop invaded— They'll break everything— Glorious!

SEVERAL MEN. (Crowding about CYRANO) My friend! . . . My friend! . . .

CYR.   Why, yesterday I did not have so many friends!

LE B.   Success At last!

MARQUIS (Runs to CYRANO, with outstretched hands) My dear—really!—

CYR. (Coldly)   So? And how long Have I been dear to you?

ANOTHER MARQUIS.   One moment—pray! I have two ladies in my carriage here; Let me present you—

CYR.   Certainly! And first, Who will present you, sir,—to me?

LE B. (Astounded)   Why, what The devil?—

CYR.   Hush!

MAN OF LETTERS (With a portfolio)   May I have the details? . . .

CYR. You may not.

LE B. (Plucking CYRANO's sleeve)   Theophraste Renaudot!—Editor Of the Gazette—your reputation! . . .

CYR.   No!

POET. (Advances) Monsieur—

CYR.   Well?

POET.   Your full name? I will compose A pentacrostic—

ANOTHER.   Monsieur—

CYR.   That will do!

(Movement. The crowd arranges itself. DE GUICHE appears, escorted by CUIGY, BRISSAILLE, and the other officers who were with CYRANO at the close of the First Act.)

CUIGY. (Goes to CYRANO) Monsieur de Guiche!— (Murmur. Everyone moves.)   A message from the Marshal De Gassion—

DE G. (Saluting CYRANO) Who wishes to express Through me his admiration. He has heard Of your affair—

CROWD.   Bravo!

CYR. (Bowing)   The Marshal speaks As an authority.

DE G.   He said just now
The story would have been incredible
Were it not for the witness—

CUIGY.   Of our eyes!

LE B. (*Aside to* CYRANO) What is it?

CYR.   Hush!—

LE B.   Something is wrong with you;
Are you in pain?

CYR. (*Recovering himself*)
                In pain? Before this crowd?
(*His moustache bristles. He throws out his chest.*)
I? In pain? You shall see!

DE G. (*To whom* CUIGY *has been whispering*)
                Your name is known
Already as a soldier. You are one
Of those wild Gascons, are you not?

CYR.   The Guards,
Yes. A Cadet.

CADET. (*In a voice of thunder*) One of ourselves!

DE G.   Ah! So
Then all these gentlemen with the haughty air,
These are the famous—

CARB.   Cyrano!

CYR.   Captain?

CARB. Our troop being all present, be so kind
As to present them to the Comte de Guiche!

CYR. (*With a gesture presenting the Cadets to* DE
GUICHE, *declaims*)

The Cadets of Gascoyne—the defenders
    Of Carbon de Castel-Jaloux:
Free fighters, free lovers, free spenders—
The Cadets of Gascoyne—the defenders
Of old homes, old names, and old splendors—
    A proud and a pestilent crew!
The Cadets of Gascoyne, the defenders
    Of Carbon de Castel-Jaloux.

Hawk-eyed, they stare down all contenders—
    The wolf bares his fangs as they do—
Make way there, you fat money-lenders!
(Hawk-eyed, they stare down all contenders)
Old boots that have been to the menders,
    Old cloaks that are worn through and through—
Hawk-eyed, they stare down all contenders—
    The wolf bares his fangs as they do!

Skull-breakers they are, and sword-benders;
    Red blood is their favorite brew;
Hot haters and loyal befrienders,
Skull-breakers they are, and sword-benders

Wherever a quarrel engenders,
    They're ready and waiting for you!
Skull-breakers they are, and sword-benders;
    Red blood in their favorite brew!

Behold them, our Gascon defenders
    Who win every woman they woo!
There's never a dame but surrenders—
Behold them, our Gascon defenders!
Young wives who are clever pretenders—
    Old husbands who house the cuckoo—
Behold them—our Gascon defenders
    Who win every woman they woo!

DE G. (*Languidly, sitting in a chair*)
Poets are fashionable nowadays
To have about one. Would you care to join
My following?

CYR.   No, sir. I do not follow.

DE G. Your duel yesterday amused my uncle
The Cardinal. I might help you there.

LE B.   Grand Dieu!

DE G. I suppose you have written a tragedy—
They all have.

LE B. (*Aside to* CYRANO)
                Now at last you'll have it played—
Your *Agrippine!*

DE G.   Why not? Take it to him.

CYR. (*Tempted*) Really—

DE G.   He is himself a dramatist;
Let him rewrite a few lines here and there,
And he'll approve the rest.

CYR. (*His face falls again*) Impossible.
My blood curdles to think of altering
One comma.

DE G.   Ah, but when he likes a thing
He pays well.

CYR.   Yes—but not so well as I—
When I have made a line that sings itself
So that I love the sound of it—I pay
Myself a hundred times.

DE G.   You are proud, my friend.

CYR. You have observed that?

CADET. (*Enters with a drawn sword, along the
whole blade of which is transfixed a collection of
disreputable hats, their plumes draggled, their
crowns cut and torn*)   Cyrano! See here—
Look what we found this morning in the street—
The plumes dropped in their flight by those fine
    birds
Who showed the white feather!

CARB.   Spoils of the hunt—
Well mounted!

CROWD.   Ha-ha-ha!

CUIGY.   Whoever hired
Those rascals, he must be an angry man
Today!

BRIS. Who was it? Do you know?

DE G.   Myself!— (*The laughter ceases*)
I hired them to do the sort of work
We do not soil our hands with—punishing
A drunken poet. . . .   (*Uncomfortable silence*)

CADET. (*To* CYRANO) What shall we do with them?
They ought to be preserved before they spoil—

CYR. (*Takes the sword, and in the gesture of
saluting* DE GUICHE *with it, makes all the hats slide
off at his feet*)
Sir, will you not return these to your friends?

DE G. My chair—my porters here—immediately!
(*To* CYRANO *violently*)—As for you, sir!—

VOICE. (*In the street*) The chair of Monseigneur
Le Comte de Guiche!—

DE G. (*Who has recovered his self-control; smiling*)
                Have you read *Don Quixote?*

CYR. I have—and found myself the hero.

PORTER. (*Appears at the door*)   Chair
Ready!

DE G. Be so good as to read once more
The chapter of the windmills.

CYR. (*Gravely*)   Chapter Thirteen.

DE G. Windmills, remember, if you fight with
    them—

CYR. My enemies change, then, with every wind?

DE G.—May swing round their huge arms and
    cast you down
Into the mire.

CYR.   Or up—among the stars!
(DE GUICHE *goes out. We see him get into the chair.
The Officers follow murmuring among themselves.*
LE BRET *goes up with them. The crowd goes out.*)

CYR. (*Saluting with burlesque politeness, those
who go out without daring to take leave of him*)
Gentlemen. . . . Gentlemen. . . .

LE B. (*As the door closes, comes down, shaking
his clenched hands to heaven*)
                    You have done it now—
You have made your fortune!

CYR.   There you go again,
Growling!—

LE B.   At least this latest pose of yours—
Ruining every chance that comes your way—
Becomes exaggerated—

CYR.   Very well,
Then I exaggerate!

LE B. (*Triumphantly*) Oh, you do!

CYR.   Yes;
On principle. There are things in this world
A man does well to carry to extremes.

LE B. Stop trying to be Three Musketeers in
    one!
Fortune and glory—

CYR.   What would you have me do?
Seek for the patronage of some great man,
And like a creeping vine on a tall tree
Crawl upward, where I cannot stand alone?
No, thank you! Dedicate, as others do,
Poems to pawnbrokers? Be a buffoon
In the vile hope of teasing out a smile
On some cold face? No, thank you! Eat a toad
For breakfast every morning? Make my knees
Callous, and cultivate a supple spine,—
Wear out my belly grovelling in the dust?
No, thank you! Scratch the back of any swine
That roots up gold for me? Tickle the horns
Of Mammon with my left hand, while my right
Too proud to know his partner's business,
Takes in the fee? No, thank you! Use the fire
God gave me to burn incense all day long
Under the nose of wood and stone? No, thank you!
Shall I go leaping into ladies' laps
And licking fingers?—or—to change the form—
Navigating with madrigals for oars,
My sails full of the sighs of dowagers?
No, thank you! Publish verses at my own
Expense? No, thank you! Be the patron saint
Of a small group of literary souls
Who dine together every Tuesday? No,
I thank you! Shall I labor night and day
To build a reputation on one song,
And never write another? Shall I find
True genius only among Geniuses,
Palpitate over little paragraphs,
And struggle to insinuate my name
Into the columns of the *Mercury?*
No, thank you! Calculate, scheme, be afraid,
Love more to make a visit than a poem,
Seek introductions, favors, influences?—
No, thank you! No, I thank you! And again
I thank you!—But . . .
                    To sing, to laugh, to dream,
To walk in my own way and be alone,
Free, with an eye to see things as they are,
A voice that means manhood—to cock my hat
Where I choose—At a word, a *Yes*, a *No*,

To fight—or write. To travel any road
Under the sun, under the stars, nor doubt
If fame or fortune lie beyond the bourne—
Never to make a line I have not heard
In my own heart; yet, with all modesty
To say: "My soul, be satisfied with flowers,
With fruit, with weeds even; but gather them
In the one garden you may call your own."
So, when I win some triumph, by some chance,
Render no share to Caesar—in a word,
I am too proud to be a parasite,
And if my nature wants the germ that grows
Towering to heaven like the mountain pine,
Or like the oak, sheltering multitudes—
I stand, not high it may be—but alone!

LE B. Alone, yes!—but why stand against the
    world?
What devil has possessed you now, to go
Everywhere making yourself enemies?

CYR. Watching you other people making friends
Everywhere—as a dog makes friends! I mark
The manner of these canine courtesies
And think: "My friends are of a cleaner breed;
Here comes—thank God!—another enemy!"

LE B. But this is madness!

CYR.   Method, let us say.
It is my pleasure to displease. I love
Hatred. Imagine how it feels to face
The volley of a thousand angry eyes—
The bile of envy and the froth of fear
Spattering little drops about me— You—
Good nature all around you, soft and warm—
You are like those Italians, in great cowls
Comfortable and loose— Your chin sinks down
Into the folds, your shoulders droop. But I—
The Spanish ruff I wear around my throat
Is like a ring of enemies; hard, proud,
Each point another pride, another thorn—
So that I hold myself erect perforce,
Wearing the hatred of the common herd
Haughtily, the harsh collar of Old Spain,
At once a fetter and—a halo!

LE B.   Yes . . .
    (After a silence, draws CYRANO's
                arm through his own)
Tell this to all the world— And then to me
Say very softly that . . . She loves you not.

CYR. (Quickly) Hush!

(A moment since, CHRISTIAN has entered and mingled with the CADETS, who do not offer to speak
to him. Finally, he sits down alone at a small table,
where he is served by LISE.)

CADET. (Rises from a table up stage, his glass in
his hand)   Cyrano!—Your story!

CYR.   Presently . . .
    (He goes up, on the arm of LE BRET, talking
        to him. The CADETS come down stage.)

CADET. The story of the combat! An example
For—
(He stops by the table where CHRISTIAN is sitting)
    —this young tadpole here.

CHRIS. (Looks up)   Tadpole?

ANOTHER CADET.   Yes, you!—
You narrow-gutted Northerner!

CHRIS.   Sir?

1ST CADET.   Hark ye,
Monsieur de Neuvillette: You are to know
There is a certain subject—I would say,
A certain object—never to be named
Among us: utterly unmentionable!

CHRIS. And that is?

3RD CADET. (In an awful voice)
                    Look at me! . . .
            (He strikes his nose three times
                with his finger, mysteriously)
                        You understand?

CHRIS. Why, yes; the—

4TH CADET. Sh! . . . We never speak that word—
            (Indicating CYRANO by a gesture)
To breathe it is to have to do with HIM!

5TH CADET. (Speaks through his nose)
He has exterminated several
Whose tone of voice suggested . . .

6TH CADET. (In a hollow tone; rising from under
the table on all fours)   Would you die
Before your time? Just mention anything
Convex . . . or cartilaginous . . .

7TH CADET. (His hand on CHRISTIAN's shoulder)
                                One word—
One syllable—one gesture—nay, one sneeze—
Your handkerchief becomes your winding-sheet!
    (Silence. In a circle around CHRISTIAN, arms
        crossed, they regard him expectantly.)

CHRIS. (Rises and goes to CARBON, who is conversing with an officer, and pretending not to see
what is taking place) Captain!

CARB. (Turns, and looks him over) Sir?

CHRIS.   What is the proper thing to do
When Gascons grow too boastful?

CARB.   Prove to them
That one may be a Norman, and have courage.
                            (Turns his back)

CHRIS. I thank you.

1ST CADET. (To CYRANO) Come—the story!

ALL. The story!

CYR. (*Comes down*) Oh,
My story? Well . . .
(*They all draw up their stools and group them-
selves around him, eagerly.* CHRISTIAN *places him-
self astride of a chair, his arms on the back of it.*)
I marched on, all alone
To meet those devils. Overhead, the moon
Hung like a gold watch at the fob of heaven,
Till suddenly some Angel rubbed a cloud,
As it might be his handkerchief, across
The shining crystal, and—the night came down.
No lamps in those back streets— It was so dark—
Mordious! You could not see beyond—

CHRIS. Your nose.
(*Silence. Every man slowly rises to his feet. They
look at* CYRANO *almost with terror. He has stopped
short, utterly astonished. Pause.*)

CYR. Who is that man there?

CADET (*In a low voice*) A recruit—arrived
This morning.

CYR. (*Takes a step toward* CHRISTIAN) A recruit—

CARB. (*In a low voice*) His name is Christian
De Neuvil—

CYR. (*Suddenly motionless*) Oh . . .
(*He turns pale, flushes, makes a movement
as if to throw himself upon* CHRISTIAN)
I
(*Controls himself, and goes on in a choking voice*)
I see. Very well,
As I was saying— (*With a sudden burst of rage*)
Mordious! . . .
(*He goes on in a natural tone*)
It grew dark,
You could not see your hand before your eyes.
I marched on, thinking how, all for the sake
Of one old souse
(*They slowly sit down, watching him*)
who wrote a bawdy song
Whenever he took—

CHRIS. A noseful—
(*Everyone rises.* CHRISTIAN *balances
himself on two legs of his chair.*)

CYR. (*Half strangled*) —Took a notion . . .
Whenever he took a notion— For his sake,
I might antagonize some dangerous man,
One powerful enough to make me pay—

CHRIS. Through the nose—

CYR. (*Wipes the sweat from his forehead*)
—Pay the Piper. After all,
I thought, why am I putting in my—

CHRIS. Nose—

CYR.—My oar . . . Why am I putting in my oar?
The quarrel's none of mine. However—now
I am here, I may as well go through with it.
Come, Gascon—do your duty!—Suddenly
A sword flashed in the dark. I caught it fair—

CHRIS. On the nose—

CYR. On my blade. Before I knew it,
There I was—

CHRIS. Rubbing noses—

CYR. (*Pale and smiling*) Crossing swords
With half a score at once. I handed one—

CHRIS. A nosegay—

CYR. (*Leaping at him*) Ventre-Saint-Gris! . . .
(*The Gascons tumble over each other to get a good
view. Arrived in front of* CHRISTIAN, *who has not
moved an inch,* CYRANO *masters himself again, and
continues.*)
He went down;
The rest gave way; I charged—

CHRIS. Nose in the air—

CYR. I skewered two of them—disarmed a third—
Another lunged— Paf! And I countered—

CHRIS. Pif!

CYR. (*Bellowing*)
TONNERRE! Out of here—All of you!
(*All the* CADETS *rush for the door*)

1ST CADET. At last—
The old lion wakes!

CYR. All of you! Leave me here
Alone with that man!
(*The lines following are heard brokenly, in
the confusion of getting through the door*)

2ND CADET. Bigre! He'll have the fellow
Chopped into sausage—

RAG. Sausage?—

3RD CADET. Mince-meat, then—
One of your pies!—

RAG. Am I pale? You look white
As a fresh napkin—

CARB. (*At the door*) Come!

4TH CADET. He'll never leave
Enough of him to—

5TH CADET. Why, it frightens ME
To think of what will—

6TH CADET. (*Closing the door*)
Something horrible
Beyond imagination . . .
(*They are all gone: some through the street door,
some by the inner doors to right and left. A few
disappear up the staircase.* CYRANO *and* CHRISTIAN
*stand face to face a moment, and look at each
other.*)

CYR.   To my arms!

CHRIS. Sir? . . .

CYR.   You have courage!

CHRIS.   Oh, that! . . .

CYR.   You are brave—
That pleases me.

CHRIS.   You mean? . . .

CYR.   Do you not know
I am her brother? Come!

CHRIS.   Whose?—

CYR.   Hers—Roxane!

CHRIS. Her . . . brother? You? (Hurries to him)

CYR.   Her cousin. Much the same.

CHRIS. And she has told you? . . .

CYR.   Everything.

CHRIS.   She loves me?

CYR. Perhaps.

CHRIS. (Takes both his hands)
              My dear sir—more than I can say,
I am honored—

CYR.   This is rather sudden.

CHRIS.   Please
Forgive me—

CYR. (Holds him at arm's length, looking at him)
         Why, he is a handsome devil,
This fellow!

CHRIS.   On my honor—if you knew
How much I have admired—

CYR.   Yes, yes—and all
Those Noses which—

CHRIS.   Please! I apologize.

CYR. (Change of tone) Roxane expects a letter—

CHRIS.   Not from me?—

CYR. Yes. Why not?

CHRIS.   Once I write, that ruins all!

CYR. And why?

CHRIS.   Because . . . because I am a fool!
Stupid enough to hang myself!

CYR.   But no—
You are no fool; you call yourself a fool,
There's proof enough in that. Besides, you did not
Attack me like a fool.

CHRIS.   Bah! Anyone
Can pick a quarrel. Yes, I have a sort
Of rough and ready soldier's tongue. I know
That. But with any woman—paralyzed,
Speechless, dumb. I can only look at them.
Yet sometimes, when I go away, their eyes . . .

CYR. Why not their hearts, if you should wait
    and see?

CHRIS. No. I am one of those— I know—those
    men
Who never can make love.

CYR.   Strange. . . . Now it seems
I, if I gave my mind to it, I might
Perhaps make love well.

CHRIS.   Oh, if I had words
To say what I have here!

CYR.   If I could be
A handsome little Musketeer with eyes!—

CHRIS. Besides—you know Roxane—how sensi-
    tive—
One rough word, and the sweet illusion—gone!

CYR. I wish you might be my interpreter.

CHRIS. I wish I had your wit—

CYR.   Borrow it, then!—
Your beautiful young manhood—lend me that,
And we two make one hero of romance!

CHRIS. What?

CYR.   Would you dare repeat to her the words
I gave you, day by day?

CHRIS.   You mean?

CYR.   I mean
Roxane shall have no disillusionment!
Come, shall we win her both together? Take
The soul within this leathern jack of mine,
And breathe it into you?
                    (Touches him on the breast)
                    So—there's my heart
Under your velvet, now!

CHRIS.   But— Cyrano!—

CYR. But— Christian, why not?

CHRIS.   I am afraid—

CYR.   I know—
Afraid that when you have her all alone,
You lose all. Have no fear. It is yourself
She loves—give her yourself put into words—
My words, upon your lips!

CHRIS.   But . . . but your eyes! . . .
They burn like—

CYR.   Will you? . . . Will you?

CHRIS.   Does it mean
So much to you?

CYR. (Besides himself) It means—
                    (Recovers, changes tone)
                    A Comedy,
A situation for a poet! Come,
Shall we collaborate? I'll be your cloak
Of darkness, your enchanted sword, your ring
To charm the fairy Princess!

CHRIS.   But the letter—
I cannot write—
CYR.   Oh, yes, the letter.
                        (*He takes from his pocket*
                        the letter which he has written)
                                            Here.

CHRIS. What is this?
CYR.   All there; all but the address.
CHRIS. I—
CYR.   Oh, you may send it. It will serve.
CHRIS.   But why
Have you done this?
    CYR.   I have amused myself
As we all do, we poets—writing vows
To Chloris, Phyllis—any pretty name—
You might have had a pocketful of them!
Take it, and turn to facts my fantasies—
I loosed these loves like doves into the air;
Give them a habitation and a home.
Here, take it— You will find me all the more
Eloquent, being insincere! Come!
    CHRIS.   First,
There must be a few changes here and there—
Written at random, can it fit Roxane?
    CYR. Like her own glove.
    CHRIS.   No, but—
    CYR.   My son, have faith—
Faith in the love of women for themselves—
Roxane will know this letter for her own!
        CHRIS. (*Throws himself into the arms of* CYRANO.
They stand embraced.) My friend!
(*The door up stage opens a little. A* CADET *steals in.*)
    CADET.   Nothing. A silence like the tomb . . .
I hardly dare look—   (*He sees the two*)
                Wha-at?
(*The other* CADETS *crowd in behind him and see*)
CADETS.   No!—No!
2ND CADET.   Mon dieu!
MUSK. (*Slaps his knee*) Well, well, well!
    CARB.   Here's our devil . . . Christianized!
Offend one nostril, and he turns the other.
    MUSK. Now we are allowed to talk about his
        nose!
(*Calls*) Hey, Lise! Come here—
            (*Affectedly*) Snf! What a horrid smell!
What is it? . . .
            (*Plants himself in front of* CYRANO, *and*
            looks at his nose in an impolite manner)
            You ought to know about such things;
What seems to have died around here?

CYR. (*Knocks him backward over a bench*)
                            Cabbage-heads!
(*Joy. The* CADETS *have found their old*
CYRANO again. General disturbance.)

[CURTAIN]

THE THIRD ACT

Roxane's Kiss

A little square in the old Marais: old houses,
and a glimpse of narrow streets. On the Right,
THE HOUSE OF ROXANE *and her garden wall, over-*
hung with tall shrubbery. Over the door of the
house a balcony and a tall window; to one side of
the door, a bench.
Ivy clings to the wall; jasmine embraces the
balcony, trembles, and falls away.
By the bench and the jutting stonework of the
wall one might easily climb up to the balcony.
Opposite, an ancient house of the like char-
acter, brick and stone, whose front door forms an
Entrance. The knocker on this door is tied up in
linen like an injured thumb.

At the CURTAIN RISE *the* DUENNA *is seated on the*
bench beside the door. The window is wide open
on ROXANE'S *balcony; a light within suggests that*
it is early evening. By the DUENNA *stands* RAGUE-
NEAU *dressed in what might be the livery of one*
attached to the household. He is by way of telling
her something, and wiping his eyes meanwhile.

RAG.—And so she ran off with a Musketeer!
I was ruined— I was alone— Remained
Nothing for me to do but hang myself,
So I did that. Presently along comes
Monsieur de Bergerac, and cuts me down,
And makes me steward to his cousin.
    DUEN.   Ruined?—
I thought your pastry was a great success!
RAG. (*Shakes his head*)
Lise loved the soldiers, and I loved the poets—
Mars ate up all the cakes Apollo left;
It did not take long. . . .
    DUEN. (*Calls up to window*)
                    Roxane! Are you ready?
We are late!
    VOICE OF ROXANE. (*Within*) Putting on my cape—
    DUEN. (*To* RAGUENEAU, *indicating the house op-*
posite)
                                    Clomire
Across the way receives on Thursday nights—

We are to have a psycho-colloquy
Upon the Tender Passion.

RAG.   Ah—the Tender . . .

DUEN. (*Sighs*)—Passion! . . . (*Calls up to window*)
            Roxane!—Hurry, dear—we shall miss
The Tender Passion!

ROX.   Coming!— (*Music of stringed
            instruments off stage approaching*)

VOICE OF CYRANO. (*Singing*)   La, la, la!—

DUEN. A serenade?—How pleasant—

CYR.   No, no, no!—
F natural, you natural-born fool!
(*Enters, followed by two* PAGES, *carrying theorbos*)

1ST PAGE. (*Ironically*)
No doubt your honor knows F natural
When he hears—

CYR.   I am a musician, infant!—
A pupil of Gassendi.

PAGE. (*Plays and sings*) La, la,—

CYR.   Here—
Give me that—   (*He snatches the instrument
            from the* PAGE *and continues the tune*)
            La, la, la, la—

ROX. (*Appears on the Balcony*) Is that you,
Cyrano?

CYR. (*Singing*) I, who praise your lilies fair,
But long to love your ro . . . ses!

ROX.   I'll be down—
Wait—   (*Goes in through window*)

DUEN. Did you train these virtuosi?

CYR.   No—
I won them on a bet from D'Assoucy.
We were debating a fine point of grammar
When, pointing out these two young nightingales
Dressed up like peacocks, with their instruments,
He cries: "No, but I KNOW! I'll wager you
A day of music." Well, of course he lost;
And so until tomorrow they are mine,
My private orchestra. Pleasant at first,
But they become a trifle—   (*To the* PAGES)
                    Here! Go play
A minuet to Montfleury—and tell him
I sent you!   (*The* PAGES *go up to the exit.*
            CYRANO *turns to the* DUENNA.)
            I came here as usual
To inquire after our friend—   (*To* PAGES)
                    Play out of tune.
And keep on playing!
            (*The* PAGES *go out. He turns to the* DUENNA.)
            —Our friend with the great soul.

ROX. (*Enters in time to hear the last words*)
He is beautiful and brilliant—and I love him!

CYR. Do you find Christian . . . intellectual?

ROX. More so than you, even.

CYR.   I am glad.

ROX.   No man
Ever so beautifully said those things—
Those pretty nothings that are everything.
Sometimes he falls into a reverie;
His inspiration fails—then all at once,
He will say something absolutely . . . Oh! . . .

CYR. Really!

ROX.   How like a man! You think a man
Who has a handsome face must be a fool.

CYR. He talks well about . . . matters of the
    heart?

ROX. He does not *talk*; he rhapsodizes . . .
    dreams . . .

CYR. (*Twisting his moustache*)
He . . . writes well?

ROX.   Wonderfully: Listen now:
            (*Reciting as from memory*)
"Take my heart; I shall have it all the more;
Plucking the flowers, we keep the plant in bloom—"
Well?

CYR. Pooh!

ROX.   And this:
                "Knowing you have in store
More heart to give than I to find heart-room—"

CYR. First he has too much, then too little; just
How much heart does he need?

ROX. (*Tapping her foot*)   You are teasing me!
You are jealous!

CYR. (*Startled*) Jealous?

ROX.   Of his poetry—
You poets are like that . . .
                    And these last lines
Are they not the last word in tenderness?—
"There is no more to say: only believe
That unto you my whole heart gives one cry,
And writing, writes down more than you receive;
Sending you kisses through my finger-tips—
Lady, O read my letter with your lips!"

CYR. H'm, yes—those last lines . . . but he over-
    writes!

ROX. Listen to this—

CYR.   You know them all by heart?

ROX. Every one!

CYR. (*Twisting his moustache*)
                I may call that flattering . . .

ROX. He is a master!

CYR.   Oh—come!

ROX.   Yes—a master!

CYR. (*Bowing*) A master—if you will!

DUEN. (*Comes down stage quickly*)

        Monsieur de Guiche!—

 (*To* CYRANO, *pushing him toward the house*)
Go inside— If he does not find you here,
It may be just as well. He may suspect—

ROX.—My secret! Yes; he is in love with me
And he is powerful. Let him not know—
One look would frost my roses before bloom.

 CYR. (*Going into house*) Very well, very well!

 ROX. (*To* DE GUICHE, *as he enters*)

         We were just going—

 DE G. I came only to say farewell.

 ROX.   You leave
Paris?

 DE G. Yes—for the front.

 ROX.   Ah!

 DE G.   And tonight!

 ROX. Ah!

 DE G. We have orders to besiege Arras.

 ROX. Arras?

 DE G. Yes. My departure leaves you . . . cold?

 ROX (*Politely*) Oh! Not that.

 DE G.   It has left me desolate—
When shall I see you? Ever? Did you know
I was made Colonel?

 ROX. (*Indifferent*) Bravo!

 DE G.   Regiment
Of the Guards.

 ROX. (*Catching her breath*) Of the Guards?—

 DE G.   *His* regiment,
Your cousin, the mighty man of words!— (*Grimly*)

         Down there
We may have an accounting!

 ROX. (*Suffocating*)   Are you sure
The Guards are ordered?

 DE G.   Under my command!

 ROX. (*Sinks down, breathless, on the bench; aside*)
Christian!—

 DE G. What is it?

 ROX. (*Losing control of herself*)

      To the war—perhaps
Never again to— When a woman cares,
Is that nothing?

 DE G. (*Surprised and delighted*)

     You say this now—to me—
Now, at the very moment?—

 ROX. (*Recovers—changes her tone*)

      Tell me something:
My cousin— You say you mean to be revenged
On him. Do you mean that?

 DE G. (*Smiles*) Why? Would you care?

 ROX. Not for him.

 DE G. Do you see him?

 ROX.   Now and then.

 DE G. He goes about everywhere nowadays
With one of the Cadets—de Neuve—Neuville—
Neuvillers—

 ROX. (*Coolly*) A tall man?—

 DE G.   Blond—

 ROX.   Rosy cheeks?

 DE G. Handsome!—

 ROX.   Pooh!—

 DE G.   And a fool.

 ROX. (*Languidly*) So he appears . . .
(*Animated*) But Cyrano? What will you do to him?
Order him into danger? He loves that!
I know what *I* should do. . . .

 DE G.   What?

 ROX.   Leave him here
With his Cadets, while all the regiment
Goes on to glory! That would torture him—
To sit all through the war with folded arms—
I know his nature. If you hate that man,
Strike at his self-esteem.

 DE G.   Oh, woman—woman!
Who but a woman would have thought of this?

 ROX. He'll eat his heart out, while his Gascon
  friends
Bite their nails all day long in Paris here.
And you will be avenged!

 DE G.   You love me then,
A little? . . . (*She smiles*)
    Making my enemies your own,
Hating them—I should like to see in that
A sign of love, Roxane.

 ROX.   Perhaps it is one . . .

 DE G. (*Shows a number of folded despatches*)
Here are the orders—for each company—
Ready to send . . .   (*Selects one*)
    So— This is for the Guards—
I'll keep that. Aha, Cyrano! (*To* ROXANE)
      You too,
You play your little games, do you?

 ROX. (*Watching him*) Sometimes . . .

 DE G. (*Close to her, speaking hurriedly*)
And you!—Oh, I am mad over you!—

         Listen—
I leave tonight—but—let you through my hands
Now, when I feel you trembling?—Listen— Close
 by,
In the Rue d'Orleans, the Capuchins
Have their new convent. By their law, no layman
May pass inside those walls. I'll see to that—
Their sleeves are wide enough to cover me—

The servants of my Uncle-Cardinal
Will fear his nephew. So—I'll come to you
Masked, after everyone knows I have gone—
Oh, let me wait one day!—

ROX.   If this be known,
Your honor—

DE G.   Bah!

ROX.   The war—your duty—

DE G. (*Blows away an imaginary feather*) Phoo!—
Only say yes!

ROX.   No!

DE G.   Whisper . . .

ROX. (*Tenderly*)   I ought not
To let you . . .

DE G.   Ah! . . .

ROX. (*Pretends to break down*) Ah, go! (*Aside*)
—Christian remains—
                (*Aloud—heroically*)
I must have you a hero—Antoine . . .

DE G.   Heaven! . . .
So you can love—

ROX.   One for whose sake I fear.

DE G. (*Triumphant*) I go!
        Will that content you? (*Kisses her hand*)

ROX.   Yes—my friend! (*He goes out*)

DUEN. (*As* DE GUICHE *disappears, making a deep
curtsey behind his back, and imitating* ROXANE'S
intense tone) Yes—my friend!

ROX. (*Quickly, close to her*)
                        Not a word to Cyrano—
He would never forgive me if he knew
I stole his war!   (*She calls toward the house*)
                Cousin!

    (CYRANO *comes out of the house; she turns
        to him, indicating the house opposite*)
                We are going over—
Alcandre speaks tonight—and Lysimon.

DUEN. (*Puts finger in her ear*)
My little finger says we shall not hear
Everything.

CYR.   Never mind me—

DUEN. (*Across the street*)   Look— Oh, look!
The knocker tied up in a napkin— Yes,
They muzzled you because you bark too loud
And interrupt the lecture—little beast!

ROX. (*As the door opens*) Enter . . .
(*To* CYRANO) If Christian comes, tell him to wait.

CYR. Oh—   (ROXANE *returns*)
    When he comes, what will you talk about?
You always know beforehand.

ROX.   About . . .

CYR.   Well?

ROX. You will not tell him, will you?

CYR.   I am dumb.

ROX. About nothing! Or about everything—
I shall say: "Speak of love in your own words—
Improvise! Rhapsodize! Be eloquent!"

CYR. (*Smiling*) Good!

ROX.   Sh!—

CYR.   Sh!—

ROX.   Not a word!
                (*She goes in; the door closes*)

CYR. (*Bowing*)   Thank you so much—

ROX. (*Opens door and puts out her head*)
He must be unprepared—

CYR.   Of course!

ROX.   Sh!— (*Goes in again*)

CYR. (*Calls*)   Christian!
                (CHRISTIAN *enters*)
I have your theme—bring on your memory!—
Here is your chance now to surpass yourself,
No time to lose— Come! Look intelligent—
Come home and learn your lines.

CHRIS.   No.

CYR.   What?

CHRIS.   I'll wait
Here for Roxane.

CYR.   What lunacy is this?
Come quickly!

CHRIS.   No, I say! I have had enough—
Taking my words, my letters, all from you—
Making our love a little comedy!
It was a game at first; but now—she cares . . .
Thanks to you. I am not afraid. I'll speak
For myself now.

CYR.   Undoubtedly!

CHRIS.   I will!
Why not? I am no such fool—you shall see!
Besides—my dear friend—you have taught me much;
I ought to know something . . . By God, I know
Enough to take a woman in my arms!
        (ROXANE *appears in the doorway, opposite*)
There she is now . . . Cyrano, wait! Stay here!

CYR. (*Bows*) Speak for yourself, my friend!
                        (*He goes out*)

ROX. (*Taking leave of the company*)
                        —Barthénoide!
Alcandre! . . . Grémione! . . .

DUEN.   I told you so—
We missed the Tender Passion!
                (*She goes into* ROXANE'S *house*)

ROX.   Urimédonte!—
Adieu!   (As the guests disappear down
            the street, she turns to CHRISTIAN)
      Is that you, Christian? Let us stay
Here, in the twilight. They are gone. The air
Is fragrant. We shall be alone. Sit down
There—so . . .   (They sit on the bench)
            Now tell me things.
    CHRIS. (After a silence)   I love you.
    ROX. (Closes her eyes)   Yes,
Speak to me about love . . .
    CHRIS.   I love you.
    ROX.   Now
Be eloquent! . . .
    CHRIS.   I love—
    ROX. (Opens her eyes)   You have your theme—
Improvise! Rhapsodize!
    CHRIS.   I love you so!
    ROX. Of course. And then? . . .
    CHRIS.   And then . . . Oh, I should be
So happy if you loved me too! Roxane,
Say that you love me too!
    ROX. (Making a face)   I ask for cream—
You give me milk and water. Tell me first
A little, how you love me.
    CHRIS.   Very much.
    ROX. Oh—tell me how you feel!
    CHRIS. (Coming nearer and devouring her with
his eyes)   Your throat . . . If only
I might . . . kiss it—
    ROX.   Christian!
    CHRIS.   I love you so!
    ROX. (Makes as if to rise) Again?
    CHRIS. (Desperately, restraining her)
            No, not again— I do not love you—
    ROX. (Settles back) That is better . . .
    CHRIS.   I adore you!
    ROX.   Oh!—
            (Rises and moves away)
    CHRIS.   I know;
I grow absurd.
    ROX. (Coldly) And that displeases me
As much as if you had grown ugly.
    CHRIS.   I—
    ROX. Gather your dreams together into words!
    CHRIS. I love—
    ROX.   I know; you love me. Adieu.
                (She goes to the house)
    CHRIS.   No,
But wait—please—let me— I was going to say—
    ROX. (Pushes the door open)
That you adore me. Yes; I know that too.

No! . . . Go away! . . .
        (She goes in and shuts the door in his face)
    CHRIS.   I . . . I . . .
    CYR. (Enters)   A great success!
    CHRIS. Help me!
    CYR.   Not I.
    CHRIS.   I cannot live unless
She loves me—now, this moment!
    CYR.   How the devil
Am I to teach you now—this moment?
    CHRIS. (Catches him by the arm)   —Wait!—
Look! Up there!—Quick—
            (The light shows in ROXANE's window)
    CYR.   Her window—
    CHRIS. (Wailing)   I shall die!—
    CYR. Less noise!
    CHRIS.   Oh, I—
    CYR.   It does seem fairly dark—
    CHRIS. (Excitedly) Well?—Well?—Well?—
    CYR.   Let us try what can be done;
It is more than you deserve—stand over there,
Idiot—there!—before the balcony—
Let me stand underneath. I'll whisper you
What to say.
    CHRIS.   She may hear—she may—
    CYR.   Less noise!
            (The PAGES appear up stage)
    1ST PAGE. Hep!—
    CYR. (Finger to lips) Sh!—
    1ST PAGE. (Low voice)
                We serenaded Montfleury!—
What next?
    CYR.   Down to the corner of the street—
One this way—and the other over there—
If anybody passes, play a tune!
    PAGE. What tune, O musical Philosopher?
    CYR. Sad for a man, or merry for a woman—
Now go!
(The PAGES disappear, one toward each corner of
            the street)
    CYR. (To CHRISTIAN) Call her!
    CHRIS.   Roxane!
    CYR.   Wait . . .
(Gathers up a handful of pebbles) Gravel . . .
            (Throws it at the window) There!—
    ROX. (Opens the window) Who is calling?
    CHRIS.   I—
    ROX.   Who?
    CHRIS.   Christian.
    ROX.   You again?
    CHRIS. I had to tell you—

CYR. (*Under the balcony*)
                    Good— Keep your voice down.
ROX. No. Go away. You tell me nothing.
CHRIS.   Please!—
ROX. You do not love me any more—
CHRIS. (*To whom* CYRANO *whispers his words*)
                                No—no—
Not any more— I love you . . . evermore . . .
And ever . . . more and more!
    ROX. (*About to close the window—pauses*)
                            A little better . . .
CHRIS. (*Same business*)
Love grows and struggles like . . . an angry child
Breaking my heart . . . his cradle . . .
    ROX. (*Coming out on the balcony*) Better still—
But . . . such a babe is dangerous; why not
Have smothered it new-born?
    CHRIS. (*Same business*)   And so I do . . .
And yet he lives . . . I found . . . as you shall
find . . .
This new-born babe . . . an infant . . . Hercules!
    ROX. (*Further forward*) Good!—
CHRIS. (*Same business*)
Strong enough . . . at birth . . . to strangle those
Two serpents—Doubt and . . . Pride.
    ROX. (*Leans over balcony*)   Why, very well!
Tell me now why you speak so haltingly—
Has your imagination gone lame?
    CYR. (*Thrusts* CHRISTIAN *under the balcony, and
stands in his place*)   Here—
This grows too difficult!
    ROX.   Your words tonight
Hesitate. Why?
    CYR. (*In a low tone, imitating* CHRISTIAN)
                    Through the warm summer gloom
They grope in darkness toward the light of you.
    ROX. My words, well aimed, find you more
        readily.
    CYR. My heart is open wide and waits for them—
Too large a mark to miss! My words fly home,
Heavy with honey like returning bees,
To your small secret ear. Moreover—yours
Fall to me swiftly. Mine more slowly rise.
    ROX. Yet not so slowly as they did at first.
    CYR. They have learned the way, and you have
        welcomed them.
    ROX. (*Softly*) Am I so far above you now?
    CYR.   So far—
If you let fall upon me one hard word,
Out of that height—you crush me!
    ROX. (*Turns*)   I'll come down—
    CYR. (*Quickly*) No!

ROX. (*Points out the bench under the balcony*)
            Stand you on the bench. Come nearer!
    CYR. (*Recoils into the shadow*)   No!—
    ROX. And why—so great a *No?*
    CYR. (*More and more overcome by emotion*)
                            Let me enjoy
The one moment I ever—my one chance
To speak to you . . . unseen!
    ROX.   Unseen?—
    CYR.   Yes!—yes . . .
Night, making all things dimly beautiful,
One veil over us both— You only see
The darkness of a long cloak in the gloom,
And I the whiteness of a summer gown—
You are all light— I am all shadow! . . . How
Can you know what this moment means to me?
If I was ever eloquent—
    ROX.   You were
Eloquent—
    CYR.   —You have never heard till now
My own heart speaking!
    ROX.   Why not?
    CYR.   Until now,
I spoke through . . .
    ROX.   Yes?—
    CYR.   —through that sweet drunkenness
You pour into the world out of your eyes!
But tonight . . . But tonight, I indeed speak
For the first time!
    ROX.   For the first time— Your voice,
Even, is not the same.
    CYR. (*Passionately; moves nearer*)
                        How should it be?
I have another voice tonight—my own,
Myself, daring—
(*He stops, confused; then tries to recover himself*)
                        Where was I? . . . I forget!
Forgive me. This is all sweet like a dream . . .
Strange—like a dream . . .
    ROX.   How, strange?
    CYR.   Is it not so
To be myself to you, and have no fear
Of moving you to laughter?
    ROX.   Laughter— why?
    CYR. (*Struggling for an explanation*)
Because . . . What am I . . . What is any man,
That he dare ask for you? Therefore my heart
Hides behind phrases. There's a modesty
In these things too— I come here to pluck down
Out of the sky the evening star—then smile.
And stoop to gather little flowers.

ROX.   Are they
Not sweet, those little flowers?

CYR.   Not enough sweet
For you and me, tonight!

ROX. (*Breathless*)   You never spoke
To me like this . . .

CYR.   Little things, pretty things—
Arrows and hearts and torches—roses red,
And violets blue—are these all? Come away,
And breathe fresh air! Must we keep on and on
Sipping stale honey out of tiny cups
Decorated with golden tracery,
Drop by drop, all day long? We are alive;
We thirst— Come away, plunge, and drink, and
     drown
In the great river flowing to the sea!

ROX. But . . . Poetry?

CYR.   I have made rimes for you—
Not now— Shall we insult Nature, this night,
These flowers, this moment—shall we set all these
To phrases from a letter by Voiture?
Look once at the high stars that shine in heaven,
And put off artificiality!
Have you not seen great gaudy hothouse flowers,
Barren, without fragrance?—Souls are like that:
Forced to show all, they soon become all show—
The means to Nature's end ends meaningless!

ROX. But . . . Poetry?

CYR.   Love hates that game of words!
It is a crime to fence with life— I tell you,
There comes one moment, once—and God help
     those
Who pass that moment by!—when Beauty stands
Looking into the soul with grave, sweet eyes
That sicken at pretty words!

ROX.   If that be true—
And when that moment comes to you and me—
What words will you? . . .

CYR.   All those, all those, all those
That blossom in my heart, I'll fling to you—
Armfuls of loose bloom! Love, I love beyond
Breath, beyond reason, beyond love's own power
Of loving! Your name is like a golden bell
Hung in my heart; and when I think of you,
I tremble, and the bell swings and rings—
                              Roxane! . . .
Roxane! . . . along my veins, *Roxane!* . . .
                              I know
All small forgotten things that once meant You—
I remember last year, the First of May,
A little before noon, you had your hair
Drawn low, that one time only. Is that strange?

You know how, after looking at the sun,
One sees red suns everywhere—so, for hours
After the flood of sunshine that you are,
My eyes are blinded by your burning hair!

ROX. (*Very low*) Yes . . . that is . . . Love—

CYR.   Yes, that is Love—that wind
Of terrible and jealous beauty, blowing
Over me—that dark fire, that music . . .
                              Yet
Love seeketh not his own! Dear, you may take
My happiness to make you happier,
Even though you never know I gave it you—
Only let me hear sometimes, all alone,
The distant laughter of your joy! . . .
                              I never
Look at you, but there's some new virtue born
In me, some new courage. Do you begin
To understand, a little? Can you feel
My soul, there in the darkness, breathe on you?
—Oh, but tonight, now, I dare say these things—
I . . . to you . . . and you hear them! . . . It is
     too much!
In my most sweet unreasonable dreams,
I have not hoped for this! Now let me die,
Having lived. It is my voice, mine, my own,
That makes you tremble there in the green gloom
Above me—for you do tremble, as a blossom
Among the leaves— You tremble, and I can feel,
All the way down along these jasmine branches,
Whether you will or no, the passion of you
Trembling . . .   (*He kisses wildly the end
                    of a drooping spray of jasmine*)

ROX.   Yes, I do tremble . . . and I weep . . .
And I love you . . . and I am yours . . . and you
Have made me thus!

CYR. (*After a pause; quietly*)
                    What is death like, I wonder?
I know everything else now . . .
                              I have done
This, to you—I, myself . . .
                              Only let me
Ask one thing more—

CHRIS. (*Under the balcony*)
                    One kiss!

ROX. (*Startled*)   One?—

CYR. (*To* CHRISTIAN)   You! . . .

ROX.   You ask me
For—

CYR. I . . . Yes, but—I mean— (*To* CHRISTIAN)
                    You go too far!

CHRIS. She is willing!—Why not make the most
of it?

CYR. (*To* ROXANE)

I did ask . . . but I know I ask too much . . .

ROX. Only one— Is that all?

CYR.   All!—How much more
Than all!—I know—I frighten you—I ask . . .
I ask you to refuse—

CHRIS (*To* CYRANO) But why? Why? Why?

CYR. Christian, be quiet!

ROX. (*Leaning over*)   What is that you say
To yourself?

CYR.   I am angry with myself
Because I go too far, and so I say
To myself: "Christian, be quiet!"

                            (*The theorbos begin to play*)
                                        Hark—someone
Is coming—

(ROXANE *closes her window.* CYRANO *listens to the
theorbos, one of which plays a gay melody, the
other a mournful one.*)

                    A sad tune, a merry tune—
Man, woman—what do they mean?—

(*A Capuchin enters; he carries a lantern, and goes
from house to house, looking at the doors*)

                                        Aha!—a priest!
                              (*To the* CAPUCHIN)
What is this new game of Diogenes?

CAPUCHIN. I am looking for the house of
Madame—

CHRIS. (*Impatient*) Bah!—

CAP. Madeleine Robin—

CHRIS.   What does he want?

CYR. (*To the* CAPUCHIN; *points out a street*)
                                        This way—
To the right—keep to the right—

CAP.   I thank you, sir!—
I'll say my beads for you to the last grain.

CYR. Good fortune, father, and my service to you!
                        (*The* CAPUCHIN *goes out*)

CHRIS. Win me that kiss!

CYR.   No.

CHRIS.   Sooner or later—

CYR.   True . . .
That is true . . . Soon or late, it will be so
Because you are young and she is beautiful—
                              (*To himself*)
Since it must be, I had rather be myself
                  (*The window re-opens.* CHRISTIAN
                        hides under the balcony.)
The cause of . . . what must be.

ROX. (*Out on the balcony*)   Are you still there?
We were speaking of—

CYR.   A kiss. The word is sweet--
What will the deed be? Are your lips afraid
Even of its burning name? Not much afraid—
Not too much! Have you not unwittingly
Laid aside laughter, slipping beyond speech
Insensibly, already, without fear,
From words to smiles . . . from smiles to sighs
        . . . from sighing,
Even to tears? One step more—only one—
From a tear to a kiss—one step, one thrill!

ROX. Hush!—

CYR.   And what is a kiss, when all is done?
A promise given under seal—a vow
Taken before the shrine of memory—
A signature acknowledged—a rosy dot
Over the i of Loving—a secret whispered
To listening lips apart—a moment made
Immortal, with a rush of wings unseen—
A sacrament of blossoms, a new song
Sung by two hearts to an old simple tune—
The ring of one horizon around two souls
Together, all alone!

ROX.   Hush! . . .

CYR.   Why, what shame?—
There was a Queen of France, not long ago,
And a great lord of England—a queen's gift,
A crown jewel!—

ROX.   Indeed!

CYR.   Indeed, like him,
I have my sorrows and my silences;
Like her, you are the queen I dare adore;
Like him I am faithful and forlorn—

ROX.   Like him,
Beautiful—

CYR. (*Aside*) So I am—I forgot that!

ROX. Then— Come! . . . Gather your sacred
    blossom . . .

CYR. (*To* CHRISTIAN) Go!—

ROX. Your crown jewel . . .

CYR.   Go on!—

ROX.   Your old new song . . .

CYR. Climb!—

CHRIS. (*Hesitates*) No— Would you?—not yet—

ROX.   Your moment made
Immortal . . .

CYR. (*Pushing him*)
              Climb up, animal!

(CHRISTIAN *springs on the bench, and climbs by
the pillars, the branches, the vines, until he be
strides the balcony railing*)

CHRIS.   Roxane! . . .
(*He takes her in his arms and bends over her*)

CYR. (*Very low*) Ah! . . . *Roxane!* . . .
> I have won what I have won—

The feast of love—and I am Lazarus!
Yet . . . I have something here that is mine now
And was not mine before I spoke the words
That won her—not for me! . . . Kissing my words,
My words, upon your lips!
> (*The theorbos begin to play*)
> A merry tune—

A sad tune— So! The Capuchin!
(*He pretends to be running, as if he had arrived
    from a distance; then calls up to the balcony*)
> Holo!

ROX. Who is it?
CYR.   I. Is Christian there with you?
CHRIS. (*Astonished*) Cyrano!
ROX.   Good morrow, Cousin!
CYR.   Cousin, . . . good morrow!
ROX. I am coming down. (*She disappears into the
    house. The* CAPUCHIN *enters up stage.*)
CHRIS. (*Sees him*)   Oh—again!
CAP. (*To* CYRANO)   She lives *here*,
Madeleine Robin!
CYR.   You said RO-LIN.
CAP.   No—
R-O-B-I-N
ROX. (*Appears on the threshold of the house, fol-
lowed by* RAGUENEAU *with a lantern, and by* CHRIS-
TIAN)   What is it?
CAP.   A letter.
CHRIS.   Oh! . . .
CAP. (*To* ROXANE)
Some matter profitable to the soul—
A very noble lord gave it to me!
ROX. (*To* CHRISTIAN) De Guiche!
CHRIS.   He dares?—
ROX.   It will not be for long;
When he learns that I love you . . .
(*By the light of the lantern which* RAGUENEAU *holds,
she reads the letter in a low tone, as if to herself*)
> "Mademoiselle,

The drums are beating, and the regiment
Arms for the march. Secretly I remain
Here, in the Convent. I have disobeyed;
I shall be with you soon. I send this first
By an old monk, as simple as a sheep,
Who understands nothing of this. Your smile
Is more than I can bear, and seek no more.
Be alone tonight, waiting for one who dares
To hope you will forgive . . . —" etcetera—
> (*To the* CAPUCHIN)

Father, this letter concerns you . . .

> (*To* CHRISTIAN)—and you

Listen: (*The others gather around her.
> She pretends to read from the letter, aloud.*)
> "Mademoiselle:
> The Cardinal

Will have his way, although against your will;
That is why I am sending this to you
By a most holy man, intelligent,
Discreet. You will communicate to him
Our order to perform, here and at once
The rite of . . .   (*Turns the page*)
> —Holy Matrimony. You

And Christian will be married privately
In your house. I have sent him to you. I know
You hesitate. Be resigned, nevertheless,
To the Cardinal's command, who sends herewith
His blessing. Be assured also of my own
Respect and high consideration—*signed,*
Your very humble and—etcetera—"
CAP. A noble lord! I said so—never fear—
A worthy lord!—a very worthy lord!—
ROX. (*To* CHRISTIAN) Am I a good reader of let-
ters?
CHRIS. (*Motions toward the* CAPUCHIN)
> Careful!—

ROX. (*In a tragic tone*) Oh, this is terrible!
CAP. (*Turns the light of his lantern on* CYRANO)
> You are to be—

CHRIS. *I* am the bridegroom!
CAP. (*Turns his lantern upon* CHRISTIAN; *then, as
if some suspicion crossed his mind, upon seeing
the young man so handsome*) Oh—why, you . . .
ROX. (*Quickly*)   Look here—
"*Postscript:* Give to the Convent in my name
One hundred and twenty pistoles"—
CAP.   Think of it!
A worthy lord—a very worthy lord! . . .
> (*To* ROXANE, *solemnly*)

Daughter, resign yourself!
ROX. (*With an air of martyrdom*)
> I am resigned . . .

(*While* RAGUENEAU *opens the door for the* CAPU-
CHIN *and* CHRISTIAN *invites him to enter, she turns
to* CYRANO)
De Guiche may come. Keep him out here with you.
Do not let him—
CYR.   I understand! (*To the* CAPUCHIN)
> How long

Will you be?—
CAP.   Oh, a quarter of an hour.
CYR. (*Hurrying them into the house*)
Hurry—I'll wait here—

ROX. (*To* CHRISTIAN) Come!

(*They go into the house*)

CYR.   Now then, to make
His Grace delay that quarter of an hour . . .
I have it!—up here— (*He steps on the bench, and
climbs up the wall toward the balcony. The theorbos begin to play a mournful melody.*)

Sad music— Ah, a man! . . .

(*The music pauses on a sinister tremolo*)
Oh—very much a man! (*He sits astride of the railing, and, drawing toward him a long branch of one
of the trees which border the garden wall, he grasps
it with both hands, ready to swing himself down*)

So—not too high—

(*He peers down at the ground*)
I must float gently through the atmosphere—

DE G. (*Enters, masked, groping in the dark
toward the house*)
Where is that cursed, bleating Capuchin?

CYR. What if he knows my voice?—the devil!—
Tic-tac,
Bergerac—we unlock our Gascon tongue;
A good strong accent—

DE G.   Here is the house—all dark—
Damn this mask!—
(*As he is about to enter the house,* CYRANO *leaps
from the balcony, still holding fast to the branch,
which bends and swings him between* DE GUICHE
*and the door; then he releases the branch and pre-
tends to fall heavily as though from a height. He
lands flatlong on the ground, where he lies motionless, as if stunned.* DE GUICHE *leaps back.*)

What is that?
(*When he lifts his eyes, the branch has sprung back
into place. He can see nothing but the sky; he does
not understand.*)

Why . . . where did this man
Fall from?

CYR. (*Sits up, and speaks with a strong accent*)
—The moon!

DE G.   You—

CYR.   From the moon, the moon!
I fell out of the moon!

DE G.   The fellow is mad—

CYR. (*Dreamily*) Where am I?

DE G.   Why—

CYR.   What time is it? What place
Is this? What day? What season?

DE G.   You—

CYR.   I am stunned!

DE G. My dear sir—

CYR. . . .   Like a bomb—a bomb—I fell
From the moon!

DE G.   Now, see here—

CYR. (*Rising to his feet, and speaking in a terrible voice*)   I say, the moon!

DE G. (*Recoils*) Very well—if you say so—

(*Aside*) Raving mad!—

CYR. (*Advancing upon him*)
I am not speaking metaphorically!

DE G. Pardon.

CYR.   A hundred years—an hour ago—
I really cannot say how long I fell—
I was in yonder shining sphere—

DE G. (*Shrugs*)   Quite so.
Please let me pass.

CYR. (*Interposes himself*)
                    Where am I? Tell the truth—
I can bear it. In what quarter of the globe
Have I descended like a meteorite?

DE G. Morbleu!

CYR.   I could not choose my place to fall—
The earth spun round so fast— Was it the Earth,
I wonder?—Or is this another world?
Another moon? Whither have I been drawn
By the dead weight of my posterior?

DE G. Sir, I repeat—

CYR. (*With a sudden cry, which causes* DE GUICHE
to recoil again)   His face! My God—black!

DE G. (*Carries his hand to his mask*)   Oh—

CYR. (*Terrified*) Are you a native? Is this Africa?

DE G.—This mask!

CYR. (*Somewhat reassured*)
                    Are we in Venice? Genoa?

DE G. (*Tries to pass him*)
A lady is waiting for me.

CYR. (*Quite happy again*) So this is Paris!

DE G. (*Smiling in spite of himself*)
This fool becomes amusing.

CYR.   Ah! You smile?

DE G. I do. Kindly permit me—

CYR. (*Delighted*)   Dear old Paris—
Well, well!—
(*Wholly at his ease, smiles, bows, arranges his dress*)
                    Excuse my appearance. I arrive
By the last thunderbolt—a trifle singed
As I came through the ether. These long jour-
neys—
You know! There are so few conveniences!
My eyes are full of star-dust. On my spurs,
Some sort of fur . . . Planet's apparently . . .

(*Plucks something from his sleeve*)
Look—on my doublet— That's a Comet's hair!

(He blows something from the back of his hand)
Phoo!

DE G. *(Grows angry)* Monsieur—

CYR. *(As* DE GUICHE *is about to push past, thrusts his leg in the way)* Here's a tooth, stuck in my boot,
From the Great Bear. Trying to get away,
I tripped over the Scorpion and came down
Slap, into one scale of the Balances—
The pointer marks my weight this moment . . .
                    (Pointing upward) See?
          *(*DE GUICHE *makes a sudden movement.* CYRANO *catches his arm.)*
Be careful! If you struck me on the nose,
It would drip milk!

DE G.   Milk?

CYR.   From the Milky Way!

DE G. Hell!

CYR.   No, no—Heaven. *(Crossing his arms)*
                    Curious place up there—
Did you know Sirius wore a nightcap? True!
                    (Confidentially)
The Little Bear is still too young to bite.
                    (Laughing)
My foot caught in the Lyre, and broke a string.
                    (Proudly)
Well—when I write my book, and tell the tale
Of my adventures—all these little stars
That shake out of my cloak—I must save those
To use for asterisks!

DE G.   That will do now—
I wish—

CYR.   Yes, yes—I know—

DE G.   Sir—

CYR.   You desire
To learn from my own lips the character
Of the moon's surface—its inhabitants
If any—

DE G. *(Loses patience and shouts)*
          I desire no such thing! I—

CYR. *(Rapidly)*
You wish to know by what mysterious means
I reached the moon?—well—confidentially—
It was a new invention of my own.

DE G. *(Discouraged)*
Drunk too—as well as mad!

CYR.   I scorned the eagle
Of Regiomontanus, and the dove
Of Archytas!

DE G.   A learned lunatic!—

CYR. I imitated no one. I myself
Discovered not one scheme merely, but six—
Six ways to violate the virgin sky!

*(*DE GUICHE *has succeeding in passing him, and moves toward the door of* ROXANE'S *house.* CYRANO *follows, ready to use violence if necessary.)*

DE G. *(Looks around)* Six?

CYR. *(With increasing volubility)*
          As for instance— Having stripped myself
Bare as a wax candle, adorn my form
With crystal vials filled with morning dew,
And so be drawn aloft, as the sun rises
Drinking the mist of dawn!

DE G. *(Takes a step toward* CYRANO*)*
                    Yes—that makes one.

CYR. *(Draws back to lead him away from the door; speaks faster and faster)*
Or, sealing up the air in a cedar chest,
Rarefy it by means of mirrors, placed
In an icosahedron.

DE G. *(Takes another step)* Two.

CYR. *(Still retreating)*   Again,
I might construct a rocket, in the form
Of a huge locust, driven by impulses
Of villainous saltpetre from the rear,
Upward, by leaps and bounds.

DE G. *(Interested in spite of himself, and counting on his fingers)*   Three.

CYR. *(Same business)*   Or again,
Smoke having a natural tendency to rise,
Blow in a globe enough to raise me.

DE G. *(Same business, more and more astonished)*
                    Four!

CYR. Or since Diana, as old fables tell,
Draws forth to fill her crescent horn, the marrow
Of bulls and goats—to anoint myself therewith.

DE G. *(Hypnotized)* Five!—

CYR. *(Has by this time led him all the way across the street, close to a bench)*
                    Finally—seated on an iron plate,
To hurl a magnet in the air—the iron
Follows—I catch the magnet—throw again—
And so proceed indefinitely.

DE G.   Six!—
All excellent,—and which did you adopt?

CYR. *(Coolly)*
Why, none of them. . . . A seventh.

DE G.   Which was?—

CYR.   Guess!—

DE G. An interesting idiot, this!

CYR. *(Imitates the sound of waves with his voice, and their movement by large, vague gestures)*
                    Hoo! . . . Hoo! . . .

DE G. Well?

CYR.   Have you guessed it yet?

DE G.   Why, no.
CYR. *(Grandiloquent)*   The ocean! . . .
What hour its rising tide seeks the full moon,
I laid me on the strand, fresh from the spray,
My head fronting the moonbeams, since the hair
Retains moisture—and so I slowly rose
As upon angels' wings, effortlessly,
Upward—then suddenly I felt a shock!—
And then . . .
    DE G. *(Overcome by curiosity, sits down on the bench)*   And then?
    CYR.   And then—
        (Changes abruptly to his natural voice)
                            The time is up!—
Fifteen minutes, your Grace!—You are now free;
And—they are bound—in wedlock.
    DE G. *(Leaping up)*   Am *I* drunk?
That voice . . .
(The door of ROXANE'S *house opens; lackeys appear, bearing lighted candles.* LIGHTS UP. CYRANO *removes his hat.)*
            And that nose!—Cyrano!
    CYR. *(Saluting)*   Cyrano! . . .
This very moment, they have exchanged rings.
    DE G. Who?
(He turns up stage. TABLEAU: *between the lackeys.* ROXANE *and* CHRISTIAN *appear, hand in hand. The* CAPUCHIN *follows them, smiling.* RAGUENEAU *holds aloft a torch. The* DUENNA *brings up the rear, in a negligée, and a pleasant flutter of emotion.)*
            Zounds!   *(To* ROXANE)
        You?—   *(Recognizes* CHRISTIAN)
        He?—   *(Saluting* ROXANE)
                    My sincere compliments!
(To CYRANO) You also, my inventor of machines!
Your rigmarole would have detained a saint
Entering Paradise—decidedly
You must not fail to write that book some day!
    CYR. *(Bowing)* Sir, I engage myself to do so.
    CAP. *(Leads the bridal pair down to* DE GUICHE *and strokes with great satisfaction his long white beard)*   My lord,
The handsome couple you—and God—have joined
Together!
    DE G. *(Regarding him with a frosty eye)*
        Quite so.   *(Turns to* ROXANE)
            Madame, kindly bid
Your . . . husband farewell.
    ROX.   Oh!—
    DE G. *(To* CHRISTIAN)   Your regiment
Leaves tonight, sir. Report at once!

                        ROX.   You mean
For the front? The war?
    DE G.   Certainly!
    ROX.   I thought
The Cadets were not going—
    DE G.   Oh, yes, they are!
        (Taking out the despatch from his pocket)
Here is the order—   *(To* CHRISTIAN)
            Baron! Deliver this.
    ROX. *(Throws herself into* CHRISTIAN'S *arms)*
Christian!
    DE G. *(To* CYRANO, *sneering)*
            The bridal night is not so near!
    CYR. *(Aside)*
Somehow that news fails to disquiet me.
    CHRIS. *(To* ROXANE) Your lips again . . .
    CYR.   There . . . That will do now— Come!
    CHRIS. *(Still holding* ROXANE)
You do not know how hard it is—
    CYR. *(Tries to drag him away)* I know!
    (The beating of drums is heard in the distance)
    DE G. *(Up stage)* The regiment—on the march!
    ROX. *(As* CYRANO *tries to lead* CHRISTIAN *away, follows, and detains them)*   Take care of him
For me— *(Appealingly)*
            Promise me never to let him do
Anything dangerous!
    CYR.   I'll do my best—
I cannot promise—
    ROX. *(Same business)* Make him be careful!
    CYR.   Yes—
I'll try—
    ROX. *(Same business)*
            Be sure you keep him dry and warm!
    CYR. Yes, yes—if possible—
    ROX. *(Same business; confidentially, in his ear)*
                    See that he remains
Faithful—
    CYR.   Of course! If—
    ROX. *(Same business)* And have him write to me
Every single day.
    CYR. *(Stops)*   That, I promise you!

                    [CURTAIN]

THE FOURTH ACT

The Cadets of Gascoyne

THE POST *occupied by the Company of* CARBON
DE CASTEL-JALOUX *at* THE SIEGE OF ARRAS.
In the background, a Rampart traversing the en-

tire scene; beyond this, and apparently below, a Plain stretches away to the horizon. The country is cut up with earthworks and other suggestions of the siege. In the distance against the sky-line, the houses and the walls of Arras.

Tents; scattered Weapons; Drums, et cetera. It is near daybreak, and the East is yellow with approaching dawn. Sentries at intervals. Camp-fires.

CURTAIN RISE *discovers the* CADETS *asleep, rolled in their cloaks.* CARBON DE CASTEL-JALOUX *and* LE BRET *keep watch. They are both very thin and pale.* CHRISTIAN *is asleep among the others, wrapped in his cloak, in the foreground, his face lighted by the flickering fire. Silence.*

LE B. Horrible!

CARB.   Why, yes. All of that.

LE B.   Mordious!

CARB. (*Gesture toward the sleeping* CADETS) Swear gently— You might wake them. (*To* CADETS)
                                    Go to sleep—
Hush!   (*To* LE BRET)
      Who sleeps dines.

LE B.   I have insomnia.
God! What a famine.   (*Firing off stage*)

CARB.   Curse that musketry!
They'll wake my babies.   (*To the men*)
                      Go to sleep!—

CADET. (*Rouses*)   Diantre!
Again?

CARB. No—only Cyrano coming home.
(*The heads which have been raised sink back again*)

SENTRY. (*Off stage*) Halt! Who goes there?

VOICE OF CYRANO.   Bergerac!

SENTRY ON THE PARAPET.   Halt! Who goes?—

CYR. (*Appears on the parapet*) Bergerac, idiot!

LE B. (*Goes to meet him*)   Thank God again!

CYR. (*Signs to him not to wake anyone*)
Hush!

LE B. Wounded?—

CYR   No— They always miss me—quite
A habit by this time!

LE B.   Yes— Go right on—
Risk your life every morning before breakfast
To send a letter!

CYR. (*Stops near* CHRISTIAN)
             I promised he should write
Every single day . . .   (*Looks down at him*)
             Hm— The boy looks pale
When he is asleep—thin too—starving to death—
If that poor child knew! Handsome, none the
   less . . .

LE B. Go and get some sleep!

CYR. (*Affectionately*)   Now, now—you old bear,
No growling!—I am careful—you know I am—
Every night, when I cross the Spanish lines
I wait till they are all drunk.

LE B.   You might bring
Something with you.

CYR.   I have to travel light
To pass through— By the way, there will be news
For you today; the French will eat or die,
If what I saw means anything.

LE B.   Tell us!

CYR.   No—
I am not sure—we shall see!

CARB.   What a war,
When the besiegers starve to death!

LE B.   Fine war—
Fine situation! We besiege Arras—
The Cardinal Prince of Spain besieges us—
And—here we are!

CYR.   Someone might besiege *him.*

CARB. A hungry joke!

CYR.   Ho, ho!

LE B.   Yes, you can laugh—
Risking a life like yours to carry letters—
Where are you going now?

CYR. (*At the tent door*)
             To write another. (*Goes into tent*)
(*A little more daylight. The clouds redden. The town of Arras shows on the horizon. A cannon shot is heard, followed immediately by a roll of drums, far away to the left. Other drums beat a little nearer. The drums go on answering each other here and there, approach, beat loudly almost on the stage, and die away toward the right, across the camp. The camp awakes. Voices of officers in the distance.*)

CARB. (*Sighs*)
Those drums!—another good nourishing sleep
Gone to the devil. (*The* CADETS *rouse themselves*)
             Now then!—

1ST CADET. (*Sits up, yawns*)   God! I'm hungry!

2ND CADET. Starving!

ALL. (*Groan*)   Aoh!

CARB.   Up with you!

3RD CADET.   Not another step!

4TH CADET. Not another movement!

1ST CADET.   Look at my tongue—
I said this air was indigestible!

5TH CADET. My coronet for half a pound of cheese!

6TH CADET. I have no stomach for this war—
I'll stay
In my tent—like Achilles.

ANOTHER.   Yes—no bread,
No fighting—

CARB.   Cyrano!

OTHERS.   May as well die—

CARB. Come out here!—You know how to talk to
them.
Get them laughing—

2ND CADET. (Rushes up to FIRST CADET who is
eating something)   What are you gnawing there?

1ST CADET. Gun wads and axle-grease. Fat country this
Around Arras.

ANOTHER. (Enters) I have been out hunting!

ANOTHER. (Enters)   I
Went fishing, in the Scarpe!

ALL. (Leaping up and surrounding the newcom-
ers)   Find anything?
Any fish? Any game? Perch? Partridges?
Let me look!

FISHERMAN. Yes—one gudgeon.   (Shows it)

HUNTER.   One fat . . . sparrow. (Shows it)

ALL. Ah!—See here, this—mutiny!—

CARB.   Cyrano!
Come and help!

CYR. (Enters from tent) Well?
    (Silence. To the FIRST CADET who is walking
        away, with his chin on his chest.)
                    You there, with the long face?

1ST CADET. I have something on my mind that
    troubles me.

CYR. What is that?

1ST CADET.   My stomach,

CYR.   So have I.

1ST CADET.   No doubt
You enjoy this!

CYR. (Tightens his belt)
            It keeps me looking young.

2ND CADET. My teeth are growing rusty.

CYR.   Sharpen them!

3RD CADET. My belly sounds as hollow as a drum.

CYR. Beat the long roll on it!

4TH CADET.   My ears are ringing.

CYR. Liar! A hungry belly has no ears.

5TH CADET. Oh for a barrel of good wine!

CYR. (Offers him his own helmet)   Your casque!

6TH CADET. I'll swallow anything!

CYR. (Throws him the book which he has in his
hand)   Try the Iliad.

7TH CADET. The Cardinal, he has four meals a
    day—
What does he care!

CYR.   Ask him; he really ought
To send you . . . a spring lamb out of his flock,
Roasted whole—

CADET.   Yes, and a bottle—

CYR. (Exaggerates the manner of one speaking
to a servant)   If you please,
Richelieu—a little more of the Red Seal . . .
Ah, thank you!

CADET.   And the salad—

CYR.   Of course—Romaine!

ANOTHER CADET (Shivering)
I am as hungry as a wolf.

CYR. (Tosses him a cloak) Put on
Your sheep's clothing.

1ST CADET. (With a shrug)
                Always the clever answer!

CYR. Always the answer—yes! Let me die so—
Under some rosy-golden sunset, saying
A good thing, for a good cause! By the sword,
The point of honor—by the hand of one
Worthy to be my foeman, let me fall—
Steel in my heart, and laughter on my lips!

VOICES HERE AND THERE. All very well— We are
hungry!

CYR.   Bah! You think
Of nothing but yourselves.
(His eye singles out the old fifer in the background)
                    Here, Bertrandou,
You were a shepherd once— Your pipe now! Come,
Breathe, blow.—Play to these belly-worshippers
The old airs of the South—
                "Airs with a smile in them,
Airs with a sigh in them, airs with the breeze
And the blue of the sky in them—"
                    Small, demure tunes
Whose every note is like a little sister—
Songs heard only in some long silent voice
Not quite forgotten— Mountain melodies
Like thin smoke rising from brown cottages
In the still noon, slowly— Quaint lullabies,
Whose very music has a Southern tongue—
    (The old man sits down and prepares his fife)
Now let the fife, that dry old warrior,
Dream, while over the stops your fingers dance
A minuet of little birds—let him
Dream beyond ebony and ivory;
Let him remember he was once a reed
Out of the river, and recall the spirit
Of innocent, untroubled country days . . .

(The fifer begins to play a Provençal melody)
Listen, you Gascons! Now it is no more
The shrill fife— It is the flute, through woodlands
    far
Away, calling—no longer the hot battle-cry,
But the cool, quiet pipe our goatherds play!
Listen—the forest glens . . . the hills . . . the
    downs . . .
The green sweetness of night on the Dordogne . . .
Listen, you Gascons! It is all Gascoyne! . . .
*(Every head is bowed; every eye cast down. Here
    and there a tear is furtively brushed away with
    the back of a hand, the corner of a cloak.)*
    CARB. *(Softly to* CYRANO*)* You make them weep—
    CYR.   For homesickness—a hunger
More noble than that hunger of the flesh;
It is their hearts now that are starving.
    CARB.   Yes,
But you melt down their manhood.
    CYR. *(Motions the drummer to approach)*
                                    You think so?
Let them be. There is iron in their blood
Not easily dissolved in tears. You need
Only—   *(He makes a gesture; the drum beats)*
    ALL. *(Spring up and rush toward their weapons)*
            What's that? Where is it?—What?—
    CYR. *(Smiles)*   You see—
Let Mars snore in his sleep once—and farewell
Venus—sweet dreams—regrets—dear thoughts of
    home—
All the fife lulls to rest wakes at the drums!
    CADET. *(Looks up stage)*
Aha— Monsieur de Guiche!
    CADETS. *(Mutter among themselves)* Ugh! . . .
    CYR. *(Smiles)*   Flattering
Murmur!
    CADET. He makes me weary!
    ANOTHER.   With his collar
Of lace over his corselet—
    ANOTHER.   Like a ribbon
Tied round a sword!
    ANOTHER.   Bandages for a boil
On the back of his neck—
    2ND CADET.   A courtier always!
    ANOTHER. The Cardinal's nephew!
    CARB.   None the less—a Gascon.
    1ST CADET. A counterfeit! Never you trust that
    man—
Because we Gascons, look you, are all mad—
This fellow is reasonable—nothing more
Dangerous than a reasonable Gascon!
    LE B. He looks pale.

    ANOTHER.   Oh, he can be hungry too,
Like any other poor devil—but he wears
So many jewels on that belt of his
That his cramps glitter in the sun!
    CYR. *(Quickly)*   Is he
To see us looking miserable? Quick—
Pipes!—Cards!—Dice!—
*(They all hurriedly begin to play, on their stools,
on the drums, or on their cloaks spread on the
    ground, lighting their long pipes meanwhile)*
                      As for me, I read Descartes.
*(He walks up and down, reading a small book
which he takes from his pocket.* TABLEAU: DE
GUICHE *enters, looking pale and haggard. All are
absorbed in their games. General air of content-
ment.* DE GUICHE *goes to* CARBON. *They look at each
other askance, each observing with satisfaction the
                condition of the other.)*
    DE G. Good morning!   *(Aside)*
                        He looks yellow.
    CARB. *(Same business)*   He is all eyes.
    DE G. *(Looks at the* CADETS*)*
What have we here? Black looks? Yes, gentlemen—
I am informed I am not popular;
The hill-nobility, barons of Béarn,
The pomp and pride of Périgord—I learn
They disapprove their colonel; call him courtier,
Politician—they take it ill that I
Cover my steel with lace of Genoa.
It is a great offense to be a Gascon
And not to be a beggar!
                    (Silence. They smoke. They play.)
                        Well— Shall I have
Your captain punish you? . . . No.
    CARB.   As to that,
It would be impossible.
    DE G.   Oh?
    CARB.   I am free;
I pay my company; it is my own;
I obey military orders.
    DE G.   Oh!
That will be quite enough.   *(To the* CADETS*)*
                        I can afford
Your little hates. My conduct under fire
Is well known. It was only yesterday
I drove the Count de Bucquoi from Bapaume,
Pouring my men down like an avalanche,
I myself led the charge—
    CYR. *(Without looking up from his book)*
                        And your white scarf?
    DE G. *(Surprised and gratified)*
You heard that episode? Yes—rallying

My men for the third time, I found myself
Carried among a crowd of fugitives
Into the enemy's lines. I was in danger
Of being shot or captured; but I thought
Quickly—took off and flung away the scarf
That marked my military rank—and so
Being inconspicuous, escaped among
My own force, rallied them, returned again
And won the day! . . .

(*The* CADETS *do not appear to be listening, but
here and there the cards and the dice boxes remain motionless, the smoke is retained in their
cheeks*)

                    What do you say to that?
Presence of mind—yes?

CYR.   Henry of Navarre
Being outnumbered, never flung away
His white plume.   (*Silent enjoyment. The cards
        flutter, the dice roll, the smoke puffs out.*)

DE G.   My device was a success,
However!   (*Same attentive pause, interrupting
                the games and the smoking*)

CYR.   Possibly . . . An officer
Does not lightly resign the privilege
Of being a target. (*Cards, dice, and smoke fall, roll,
        and float away with increasing satisfaction*)
                Now, if I had been there—
Your courage and my own differ in this—
When your scarf fell, I should have put it on.

DE G. Boasting again!

CYR.   Boasting? Lend it to me
Tonight; I'll lead the first charge, with your scarf
Over my shoulder!

DE G.   Gasconnade once more!
You are safe making that offer, and you know it—
My scarf lies on the river bank between
The lines, a spot swept by artillery
Impossible to reach alive!

CYR. (*Produces the scarf from his pocket*)
                    Yes. Here . . .

(*Silence. The* CADETS *stifle their laughter behind
their cards and their dice boxes.* DE GUICHE *turns to
look at them. Immediately they resume their gravity and their game. One of them whistles carelessly
the mountain air which the fifer was playing.*)

DE G. (*Takes the scarf*)
Thank you! That bit of white is what I need
To make a signal. I was hesitating—
You have decided me.

(*He goes up to the parapet, climbs upon it, and
waves the scarf at arm's length several times*)

ALL.   What is he doing?—
What?—

SENTRY ON THE PARAPET. There's a man down
    there running away!

DE G. (*Descending*)
A Spaniard. Very useful as a spy
To both sides. He informs the enemy
As I instruct him. By his influence
I can arrange their dispositions.

CYR.   Traitor!

DE G. (*Folding the scarf*)
A traitor, yes; but useful . . .
                    We were saying? . . .
Oh, yes— Here is a bit of news for you:
Last night we had hopes of reprovisioning
The army. Under cover of the dark,
The Marshal moved to Dourlens. Our supplies
Are there. He may reach them. But to return
Safely, he needs a large force—at least half
Our entire strength. At present, we have here
Merely a skeleton.

CARB.   Fortunately,
The Spaniards do not know that.

DE G.   Oh, yes; they know.
They will attack.

CARB.   Ah!

DE G.   From that spy of mine
I learned of their intention. His report
Will determine the point of their advance.
The fellow asked me what to say! I told him:
"Go out between the lines; watch for my signal;
Where you see that, let them attack there."

CARB. (*To the* CADETS)   Well,
Gentlemen!   (*All rise. Noise of sword
            belts and breast-plates being buckled on.*)

DE G.   You may have perhaps an hour.

1ST CADET. Oh— An hour!   (*They all sit down
                and resume their games once more*)

DE G. (*To* CARBON) The great thing is to gain
    time.
Any moment the Marshal may return.

CARB. And to gain time?

DE G.   You will all be so kind
As to lay down your lives!

CYR.   Ah! Your revenge?

DE G. I make no great pretense of loving you!
But—since you gentlemen esteem yourselves
Invincible, the bravest of the brave,
And all that—why need we be personal?
I serve the king in choosing . . . as I choose!

CYR. (*Salutes*) Sir, permit me to offer—all our
    thanks.

DE G. (*Returns the salute*)
You love to fight a hundred against one;
Here is your opportunity!
>   (*He goes up stage with* CARBON)

CYR. (*To the* CADETS)   My friends,
We shall add now to our old Gascon arms
With their six chevrons, blue and gold, a seventh—
Blood-red!
(DE GUICHE *talks in a low tone to* CARBON *up stage.
Orders are given. The defense is arranged.* CYRANO
goes to CHRISTIAN, *who has remained motionless
with folded arms.*)
>   Christian? (*Lays a hand on his shoulder*)

CHRIS. (*Shakes his head*) Roxane . . .

CYR.   Yes.

CHRIS.   I should like
To say farewell to her, with my whole heart
Written for her to keep.

CYR.   I thought of that—
>   (*Takes a letter from his doublet*)
I have written your farewell.

CHRIS.   Show me!

CYR.   You wish
To read it?

CHRIS.   Of course!   (*He takes the letter;
>   begins to read, looks up suddenly*)
>   What?—

CYR.   What is it?

CHRIS.   Look—
This little circle—

CYR. (*Takes back the letter quickly; and looks
innocent*)   Circle?—

CHRIS.   Yes—a tear!

CYR. So it is! . . . Well—a poet while he writes
Is like a lover in his lady's arms,
Believing his imagination—all
Seems true—you understand? There's half the
    charm
Of writing— Now, this letter as you see
I have made so pathetic that I wept
While I was writing it!

CHRIS.   You—wept?

CYR.   Why, yes—
Because . . . it is a little thing to die,
But—not to see her . . . that is terrible!
And I shall never—   (CHRISTIAN *looks at him*)
>   We shall never—   (*Quickly*)
>   You
Will never—

CHRIS. (*Snatches the letter*) Give me that!
(*Noise in the distance on the outskirts of the camp*)

VOICE OF A SENTRY.   Halt—who goes there?
>   (*Shots, shouting, jingle of harness*)

CARB. What is it?—

SENTRY ON THE PARAPET. Why, a coach.
>   (*They rush to look*)

CONFUSED VOICES.   What? In the Camp?
A coach? Coming this way— It must have driven
Through the Spanish lines—what the devil— Fire!—
No— Hark! The driver shouting—what does he say?
Wait— He said: "On the service of the King!"
>   (*They are all on the parapet looking over.
>   The jingling comes nearer.*)

DE G. Of the King?
>   (*They come down and fall into line*)

CARB.   Hats off, all!

DE G. (*Speaks off stage*)   The King! Fall in,
Rascals!—
(*The coach enters at full trot. It is covered with
mud and dust. The curtains are drawn. Two footmen are seated behind. It stops suddenly.*)

CARB. (*Shouts*) Beat the assembly—
>   (*Roll of drums. All the* CADETS *uncover.*)

DE G. Lower the steps—open the door—
>   (*Two men rush to the coach. The door opens.*)

ROX. (*Comes out of the coach*)   Good morning!
>   (*At the sound of a woman's voice, every
>   head is raised. Sensation.*)

DE G. On the King's service— You?

ROX.   Yes—my own king—
Love!

CYR. (*Aside*) God is merciful . . .

CHRIS. (*Hastens to her*)   You! Why have you—

ROX. Your war lasted so long!

CHRIS.   But why?—

ROX.   Not now—

CYR. (*Aside*) I wonder if I dare to look at her . . .

DE G. You cannot remain here!

ROX.   Why, certainly!
Roll that drum here, somebody . . .
>   (*She sits on the drum, which is brought to her*)
>   Thank you— There! (*She laughs*)
Would you believe—they fired upon us?
>   —My coach
Looks like the pumpkin in the fairy tale,
Does it not? And my footmen—
>   (*She throws a kiss to* CHRISTIAN)
>   How do you do? (*She looks about*)
How serious you all are! Do you know,
It is a long drive here—from Arras? (*Sees* CYRANO)
>   Cousin,
I am glad to see you!

CYR. (*Advances*)   Oh— How did you come?

ROX. How did I find you? Very easily—
I followed where the country was laid waste
—Oh, but I saw such things! I had to see
To believe. Gentlemen, is that the service
Of your King? I prefer my own!

CYR.   But how
Did you come through?

ROX.   Why, through the Spanish lines,
Of course!

1ST CADET. They let you pass?—

DE G.   What did you say?
How did you manage?

LE B.   Yes, that must have been
Difficult!

ROX.   No— I simply drove along.
Now and then some hidalgo scowled at me
And I smiled back—my best smile; whereupon,
The Spaniards being (without prejudice
To the French) the most polished gentlemen
In the world—I passed!

CARB.   Certainly that smile
Should be a passport! Did they never ask
Your errand or your destination?

ROX.   Oh,
Frequently! Then I drooped my eyes and said:
"I have a lover . . ." Whereupon, the Spaniard
With an air of ferocious dignity
Would close the carriage door—with such a gesture
As any king might envy, wave aside
The muskets that were levelled at my breast,
Fall back three paces, equally superb
In grace and gloom, draw himself up, thrust forth
A spur under his cloak, sweeping the air
With his long plumes, bow very low, and say:
"Pass, Señorita!"

CHRIS.   But, Roxane—

ROX.   I know—
I said "a lover"—but you understand—
Forgive me!—If I said "I am going to meet
My husband," no one would believe me!

CHRIS.   Yes,
But—

ROX. What then?

DE G.   You must leave this place.

CYR.   At once.

ROX. I?

LE B.   Yes—immediately.

ROX.   And why?

CHRIS. (Embarrassed)   Because . . .

CYR. (Same) In half an hour . . .

DE G. (Same)   Or three quarters . . .

CARB. (Same)   Perhaps
It might be better . . .

LE B.   If you . . .

ROX.   Oh— I see!
You are going to fight. I remain here.

ALL.   No—no!

ROX. He is my husband—
        (Throws herself in CHRISTIAN's arms)
                        I will die with you!

CHRIS. Your eyes! . . . Why do you?—

ROX.   You know why . . .

DE G. (Desperate)   This post
Is dangerous—

ROX. (Turns) How—dangerous?

CYR.   The proof
Is, we are ordered—

ROX. (To DE GUICHE) Oh—you wish to make
A widow of me?

DE G.   On my word of honor—

ROX. No matter. I am just a little mad—
I will stay. It may be amusing.

CYR.   What.
A heroine—our intellectual?

ROX. Monsieur de Bergerac, I am your cousin!

CADET. We'll fight now! Hurrah!

ROX. (More and more excited)
                I am safe with you—my friends!

ANOTHER. (Carried away)
The whole camp breathes of lilies!—

ROX.   And I think,
This hat would look well on the battlefield! . . .
But perhaps—   (Looks at DE GUICHE)
        The Count ought to leave us. Any moment
Now, there may be danger.

DE G.   This is too much!
I must inspect my guns. I shall return—
You may change your mind— There will yet be
    time—

ROX. Never!   (DE GUICHE goes out)

CHRIS. (Imploring) Roxane! . . .

ROX.   No!

1ST CADET. (To the rest)   She stays here!

ALL. (Rushing about, elbowing each other, brush-
ing off their clothes)   A comb!—
Soap!—Here's a hole in my— A needle!—Who
Has a ribbon?—Your mirror, quick!—My cuffs—
A razor—

ROX. (To CYRANO, who is still urging her)
        No! I shall not stir one step!

CARB. (Having, like the others, tightened his belt,
dusted himself, brushed off his hat, smoothed out

his plume and put on his lace cuffs, advances to
ROXANE *ceremoniously*)
In that case, may I not present to you
Some of these gentlemen who are to have
The honor of dying in your presence?

ROX. (*Bows*) Please!—
(*She waits, standing, on the
arm of* CHRISTIAN, *while*

CARB. (—*presents*) Baron de Peyrescous de Co-
lignac!

CADET. (*Salutes*) Madame . . .

ROX. Monsieur . . .

CARB. (*Continues*) Baron de Casterac
De Cahuzac— Vidame de Malgouyre
Estressac Lésbas d'Escarabiot—

VIDAME. Madame . . .

CARB. Chevalier d'Antignac-Juzet—
Baron Hillot de Blagnac-Saléchan
De Castel-Crabioules—

BARON. Madame . . .

ROX. How many
Names you all have!

BARON. Hundreds!

CARB. (*To* ROXANE) Open the hand
That holds your handkerchief.

ROX. (*Opens her hand; the handkerchief falls*)
Why?
(*The whole company makes a movement toward it*)

CARB. (*Picks it up quickly*) My company
Was in want of a banner. We have now
The fairest in the army!

ROX. (*Smiling*) Rather small—

CARB. (*Fastens the handkerchief to his lance*)
Lace—and embroidered!

CADET. (*To the others*) With her smiling on me,
I could die happy, if I only had
Something in my—

CARB. (*Turns upon him*)
Shame on you! Feast your eyes
And forget your—

ROX. (*Quickly*) It must be this fresh air—
I am starving! Let me see . . .
Cold partridges,
Pastry, a little white wine—that would do.
Will someone bring that to me?

CADET. (*Aside*) Will someone!—

ANOTHER. Where the devil are we to find—

ROX. (*Overhears; sweetly*) Why, there—
In my carriage.

ALL. Wha-at?

ROX. All you have to do
Is to unpack, and carve, and serve things.
Oh,
Notice my coachman; you may recognize
An old friend.

CADETS. (*Rush to the coach*) Ragueneau!

ROX. (*Follows them with her eyes*)
Poor fellows . . .

CADETS. (*Acclamations*) Ah!
Ah!

CYR. (*Kisses her hand*) Our good fairy!

RAG. (*Standing on his box, like a mountebank
before a crowd*) Gentlemen!— (*Enthusiasm*)

CADETS. Bravo!
Bravo!

RAG. The Spaniards, basking in our smiles,
Smiled on our baskets! (*Applause*)

CYR. (*Aside to* CHRISTIAN) Christian!—

RAG. They adored
The Fair, and missed— (*He takes from under the
seat a dish, which he holds aloft*)
the Fowl!
(*Applause. The dish is passed from hand to hand.*)

CYR. (*As before, to* CHRISTIAN) One moment—

RAG. Venus
Charmed their eyes while Adonis quietly
(*Brandishing a ham*)
Brought home the Boar! (*Applause; the ham is
seized by a score of hands outstretched*)

CYR. (*As before*) Pst— Let me speak to you—

ROX. (*As the* CADETS *return, their arms full of
provisions*) Spread them out on the ground. (*Calls*)
Christian! Come here;
Make yourself useful.

(CHRISTIAN *turns to her, at the moment when*
CYRANO *was leading him aside. She arranges the
food, with his aid and that of the two imper-
turbable footmen.*)

RAG. Peacock, *aux truffes!*

1ST CADET. (*Comes down, cutting a huge slice of
the ham*) Tonnerre!
We are not going to die without a gorge—
(*Sees* ROXANE; *corrects himself hastily*)
Pardon—a banquet!

RAG. (*Tossing out the cushions of the carriage*)
Open these—they are full
Of ortolans!
(*Tumult; laughter; the cushions are eviscerated*)

3RD CADET. Lucullus!

RAG. (*Throws out bottles of red wine*)
Flasks of ruby— (*And of white*)
Flasks of topaz—

ROX. (*Throws a tablecloth at the head of* CYRANO)
                    Come back out of your dreams!
Unfold this cloth—
    RAG. (*Takes off one of the lanterns of the carriage, and flourishes it*)
                    Our lamps are bonbonnières!
    CYR. (*To* CHRISTIAN)
I must see you before you speak with her—
    RAG. (*More and more lyrical*)
My whip-handle is one long sausage!
    ROX. (*Pouring wine; passing the food*) We
Being about to die, first let us dine!
Never mind the others—all for Gascoyne!
And if de Guiche comes, he is not invited!
                    (*Going from one to another*)
Plenty of time—you need not eat so fast—
Hold your cup—   (*To another*)
            What's the matter?
    CADET. (*Sobbing*)   You are so good
To us . . .
    ROX.   There, there! Red or white wine?
                    —Some bread
For Monsieur de Carbon!—Napkins— A knife—
Pass your plate— Some of the crust? A little more—
Light or dark?—Burgundy?—
    CYR. (*Follows her with an armful of dishes, helping to serve*)   Adorable!
    ROX. (*Goes to* CHRISTIAN)
What would you like?
    CHRIS.   Nothing.
    ROX.   Oh, but you must!—
A little wine? A biscuit?
    CHRIS.   Tell me first
Why you came—
    ROX.   By and by. I must take care
Of these poor boys—
    LE B. (*Who has gone up stage to pass up food to the sentry on the parapet, on the end of a lance*)
                    De Guiche!
    CYR.   Hide everything
Quick!—Dishes, bottles, tablecloth—
                    Now look
Hungry again—   (*To* RAGUENEAU)
            You there! Up on your box—
—Everything out of sight?—
(*In a twinkling, everything has been pushed inside the tents, hidden in their hats or under their cloaks.* DE GUICHE *enters quickly, then stops, sniffing the air. Silence.*)
    DE G.   It smells good here.
    CADET. (*Humming with an air of great unconcern*)
Sing ha-ha-ha and ho-ho-ho—

DE G. (*Stares at him; he grows embarrassed*)
                    You there—
What are you blushing for?
    CADET.   Nothing—my blood
Stirs at the thought of battle.
    ANOTHER.   Pom . . . pom . . . pom! . . .
DE G. (*Turns upon him*) What is that?
    CADET. (*Slightly stimulated*)
                    Only song—only little song—
    DE G. You appear happy!
    CADET.   Oh, yes—always happy
Before a fight—
    DE G. (*Calls to* CARBON, *for the purpose of giving him an order*) Captain! I— (*Stops and looks at him*)
                    What the devil—
You are looking happy too!—
    CARB. (*Pulls a long face and hides a bottle behind his back*)   No!
    DE G.   Here—I had
One gun remaining. I have had it placed
                    (*He points off stage*)
There—in that corner—for your men.
    CADET. (*Simpering*)   So kind!—
Charming attention!
    ANOTHER. (*Same business; burlesque*)
                    Sweet solicitude!—
    DE G. (*Contemptuous*)
I believe you are both drunk—   (*Coldly*)
                    Being unaccustomed
To guns—take care of the recoil!
    1ST CADET. (*Gesture*)   Ah-h . . . Pfft!
    DE G. (*Goes up to him, furious*) How dare you?
    1ST CADET.   A Gascon's gun never recoils!
    DE G. (*Shakes him by the arm*) You are drunk—
    1ST CADET. (*Superbly*) With the smell of powder!
    DE G. (*Turns away with a shrug*)   Bah!
(*To* ROXANE) Madame, have you decided?
    ROX.   I stay here.
    DE G. You have time to escape—
    ROX.   No!
    DE G.   Very well—
Someone give me a musket!
    CARB.   What!
    DE G.   I stay
Here also.
    CYR. (*Formally*) Sir, you show courage!
    1ST CADET.   A Gascon
In spite of all that lace!
    ROX.   Why—
    DE G.   Must I run
Away, and leave a woman?

2ND CADET. (*To* FIRST CADET) We might give him
Something to eat—what do you say?
      (*All the food reappears, as if by magic*)
DE G. (*His face lights up*)   A feast!
3RD CADET. Here a little, there a little—
DE G. (*Recovers his self-control; haughtily*)
          Do you think
I want your leavings?
CYR. (*Saluting*)   Colonel—you improve!
DE G. I can fight as I am!
1ST CADET. (*Delighted*)   Listen to him—
He has an accent!
DE G. (*Laughs*) Have I so?
1ST CADET.   A Gascon!—
A Gascon, after all!   (*They all begin to dance*)
CARB. (*Who has disappeared for a moment be-
hind the parapet, reappears on top of it*)
       I have placed my pikemen
Here.   (*Indicates a row of pikes show-
         ing above the parapet*)
DE G. (*Bows to* ROXANE)
   We'll review them; will you take my arm?
(*She takes his arm; they go up on the parapet.
The rest uncover, and follow them up stage.*)
CHRIS. (*Goes hurriedly to* CYRANO)
Speak quickly!
(*At the moment when* ROXANE *appears on the para-
pet the pikes are lowered in salute, and a cheer is
heard. She bows.*)
PIKEMEN. (*Off stage*) Hurrah!
CHRIS.   What is it?
CYR.   If Roxane . . .
CHRIS. Well?
CYR.   Speaks about your letters . . .
CHRIS.   Yes—I know!
CYR. Do not make the mistake of showing . . .
CHRIS.   What?
CYR. Showing surprise.
CHRIS.   Surprise—why?
CYR.   I must tell you! . . .
It is quite simple—I had forgotten it
Until just now. You have . . .
CHRIS.   Speak quickly!
CYR.   You
Have written oftener than you think.
CHRIS.   Oh—have I!
CYR. I took upon me to interpret you;
And wrote—sometimes . . . without . . .
CHRIS.   My knowing. Well?
CYR. Perfectly simple!

CHRIS.   Oh, yes, perfectly!—
For a month, we have been blockaded here!—
How did you send all these letters?
CYR.   Before
Daylight, I managed—
CHRIS.   I see. That was also
Perfectly simple!
    —So I wrote to her,
How many times a week? Twice? Three times?
   Four?
CYR. Oftener.
CHRIS.   Every day?
CYR.   Yes—every day . . .
Every single day . . .
CHRIS. (*Violently*)   And that wrought you up
Into such a flame that you faced death—
CYR. (*Sees* ROXANE *returning*)   Hush—
Not before her!   (*He goes quickly into the
     tent.* ROXANE *comes up to* CHRISTIAN.)
ROX.   Now—Christian!
CHRIS. (*Takes her hands*)   Tell me now
Why you came here—over these ruined roads—
Why you made your way among mosstroopers
And ruffians—you—to join me here?
ROX.   Because—
Your letters . . .
CHRIS.   Meaning?
ROX.   It was your own fault
If I ran into danger! I went mad—
Mad with you! Think what you have written me,
How many times, each one more wonderful
Than the last!
CHRIS.   All this for a few absurd
Love-letters—
ROX.   Hush—absurd! How can you know?
I thought I loved you, ever since one night
When a voice that I never would have known
Under my window breathed your soul to me . . .
But—all this time, your letters—every one
Was like hearing your voice there in the dark,
All around me, like your arms around me . . .
     (*More lightly*) At last
I came. Anyone would! Do you suppose
The prim Penelope had stayed at home
Embroidering,—if Ulysses wrote like you?
She would have fallen like another Helen—
Tucked up those linen petticoats of hers
And followed him to Troy!
CHRIS.   But you—
ROX.   I read them
Over and over. I grew faint reading them.
I belonged to you. Every page of them

Was like a petal fallen from your soul—
Like the light and the fire of a great love,
Sweet and strong and true—
    CHRIS. Sweet . . . and strong . . . and true . . .
You felt that, Roxane?—
    ROX.   You know how I feel! . . .
    CHRIS. So—you came . . .
    ROX.   Oh, my Christian, oh my king,—
Lift me up if I fall upon my knees—
It is the heart of me that kneels to you,
And will remain forever at your feet—
You cannot lift that!—
               I came here to say
"Forgive me"—(It is time to be forgiven
Now, when we may die presently)—forgive me
For being light and vain and loving you
Only because you were beautiful.
    CHRIS. (*Astonished*)   Roxane! . . .
    ROX. Afterwards I knew better. Afterwards
(I had to learn to use my wings) I loved you
For yourself too—knowing you more, and loving
More of you. And now—
    CHRIS.   Now? . . .
    ROX.   It is yourself
I love now: your own self.
    CHRIS. (*Taken aback*)   Roxane!
    ROX. (*Gravely*)   Be happy!—
You must have suffered; for you must have seen
How frivolous I was; and to be loved
For the mere costume, the poor casual body
You went about in—to a soul like yours,
That must have been torture! Therefore with
     words
You revealed your heart. Now that image of you
Which filled my eyes first—I see better now,
And I see it no more!
    CHRIS.   Oh!—
    ROX.   You still doubt
Your victory?
    CHRIS. (*Miserably*) Roxane!—
    ROX.   I understand:
You cannot perfectly believe in me—
A love like this—
    CHRIS.   I want no love like this!
I want love only for—
    ROX.   Only for what
Every woman sees in you? I can do
Better than that!
    CHRIS.   No—it was best before!
    ROX. You do not altogether know me . . . Dear,
There is more of me than there was—with this,
I can love more of you—more of what makes

You your own self—Truly! . . . If you were less
Lovable—
    CHRIS. No!
    ROX.   —Less charming—ugly even—
I should love you still.
    CHRIS.   You mean that?
    ROX.   I do
Mean that!
    CHRIS.   Ugly? . . .
    ROX.   Yes. Even then!
    CHRIS. (*Agonized*)   Oh . . . God! . . .
    ROX. Now are you happy?
    CHRIS. (*Choking*)   Yes . . .
    ROX.   What is it?
    CHRIS. (*Pushes her away gently*)   Only . . .
Nothing . . . one moment . . .
    ROX.   But—
    CHRIS. (*Gesture toward the* CADETS)
                  I am keeping you
From those poor fellows— Go and smile at them;
They are going to die!
    ROX. (*Softly*)   Dear Christian!
    CHRIS.   Go—
          (*She goes up among the Gascons,
          who gather round her respectfully*)
Cyrano!
    CYR. (*Comes out of the tent, armed for the battle*)
       What is wrong? You look—
    CHRIS.   She does not
Love me any more.
    CYR. (*Smiles*)   You think not?
    CHRIS.   She loves
You.
    CYR. No!—
    CHRIS. (*Bitterly*) She loves only my soul.
    CYR.   No!
    CHRIS.   Yes—
That means you. And you love her.
    CYR.   I?
    CHRIS.   I see—
I know!
    CYR.   That is true . . .
    CHRIS.   More than—
    CYR. (*Quietly*)   More than that.
    CHRIS. Tell her so!
    CYR.   No.
    CHRIS.   Why not?
    CYR.   Why—look at me!
    CHRIS. She would love me if I were ugly.
    CYR. (*Startled*)   She—
Said that?
    CHRIS.   Yes. Now then!

CYR. (*Half to himself*)   It was good of her
To tell you that . . .   (*Change of tone*)
                        Nonsense! Do not believe
Any such madness—
                It was good of her
To tell you . . .
                Do not take her at her word!
Go on—you never will be ugly— Go!
She would never forgive me.
        CHRIS.   That is what
We shall see.
        CYR.   No, no—
        CHRIS.   Let her choose between us!
Tell her everything!
        CYR.   No—you torture me—
        CHRIS. Shall I ruin your happiness, because
I have a cursed pretty face? That seems
Too unfair!
        CYR.   And am I to ruin yours
Because I happen to be born with power
To say what you—perhaps—feel?
        CHRIS.   Tell her!
        CYR.   Man—
Do not try me too far!
        CHRIS.   I am tired of being
My own rival!
        CYR.   Christian!—
        CHRIS.   Our secret marriage—
No witnesses—fraudulent—that can be
Annulled—
        CYR.   Do not try me—
        CHRIS.   I want her love
For the poor fool I am—or not at all!
Oh, I am going through with this! I'll know,
One way or the other. Now I shall walk down
To the end of the post. Go tell her. Let her choose
One of us.
        CYR.   It will be you.
        CHRIS.   God—I hope so! (*He turns and calls*)
Roxane!
        CYR.   No—no—
        ROX. (*Hurries down to him*) Yes, Christian?
        CHRIS.   Cyrano
Has news for you—important.
        (*She turns to* CYRANO. CHRISTIAN *goes out.*)
        ROX. (*Lightly*)   Oh—important?
        CYR. He is gone . . .   (*To* ROXANE)
                Nothing—only Christian thinks
You ought to know—
        ROX.   I do know. He still doubts
What I told him just now. I saw that.

CYR. (*Takes her hand*)   Was it
True—what you told him just now?
        ROX.   It was true!
I said that I should love him even . . .
        CYR. (*Smiling sadly*)   The word
Comes hard—before me?
        ROX.   Even if he were . . .
        CYR.   Say it—
I shall not be hurt!—Ugly?
        ROX.   Even then
I should love him.
                (*A few shots, off stage, in the direction
                in which* CHRISTIAN *disappeared*)
                Hark! The guns—
        CYR.   Hideous?
        ROX. Hideous.
        CYR.   Disfigured?
        ROX.   Or disfigured.
        CYR.   Even
Grotesque?
        ROX.   How could he ever be grotesque—
Ever—to me!
        CYR.   But you could love him so,
As much as?—
        ROX.   Yes—and more!
        CYR. (*Aside, excitedly*)   It is true!—true!—
Perhaps—God! This is too much happiness . . .
(*To* ROXANE) I—Roxane—listen—
        LE B. (*Enters quickly; calls to* CYRANO *in a low
tone*)   Cyrano—
        CYR. (*Turns*)   Yes?
        LE B.   Hush! . . .
                (*Whispers a few words to him*)
        CYR. (*Lets fall* ROXANE's *hand*) Ah!
        ROX.   What is it?
        CYR. (*Half stunned, and aside*) All gone . . .
        ROX. (*More shots*)   What is it? Oh,
They are fighting!— (*She goes up to look off stage*)
        CYR.   All gone. I cannot ever
Tell her, now . . . ever . . .
        ROX. (*Starts to rush away*)
                What has happened?
        CYR. (*Restrains her*)   Nothing.
(*Several* CADETS *enter. They conceal something
which they are carrying, and form a group so as
to prevent* ROXANE *from seeing their burden.*)
        ROX. These men—
        CYR.   Come away . . .
                (*He leads her away from the group*)
        ROX.   You were telling me
Something—

CYR.   Oh, that? Nothing . . .   (*Gravely*)
I swear to you
That the spirit of Christian—that his soul
Was—   (*Corrects himself quickly*)
That his soul is no less great—
ROX. (*Catches at the word*)   Was?
(*Crying out*) Oh!—
(*She rushes among the men, and scatters them*)
CYR. All gone . . .
ROX (*Sees* CHRISTIAN *lying upon his cloak*)
Christian!
LE B. (*To* CYRANO)   At the first volley.
(ROXANE *throws herself upon the body of* CHRISTIAN.
*Shots; at first scattered, then increasing. Drums.
Voices shouting.*)
CARB. (*Sword in hand*)   Here
They come!—Ready!—   (*Followed by the* CADETS,
he climbs over the parapet and disappears)
ROX.   Christian!
CARB. (*Off stage*)   Come on, there, You!
ROX. Christian!
CARB.   Fall in!
ROX.   Christian!
CARB.   Measure your fuse!
(RAGUENEAU *hurries up, carrying
a helmet full of water*)
CHRIS. (*Faintly*) Roxane! . . .
CYR. (*Low and quick, in* CHRISTIAN's *ear, while*
ROXANE *is dipping into the water a strip of linen
torn from her dress*)
I have told her; she loves you.
(CHRISTIAN *closes his eyes*)
ROX. (*Turns to* CHRISTIAN)   Yes,
My darling?
CARB.   Draw your ramrods!
ROX. (*To* CYRANO)   He is not dead? . . .
CARB. Open your charges!
ROX.   I can feel his cheek
Growing cold against mine—
CARB.   Take aim!
ROX.   A letter—
Over his heart—   (*She opens it*)
For me.
CYR. (*Aside*)   My letter . . .
CARB.   Fire!
(*Musketry, cries and groans. Din of battle*)
CYR. (*Trying to withdraw his hand, which* ROX-
ANE, *still upon her knees, is holding*)
But, Roxane—they are fighting—
ROX.   Wait a little . . .
He is dead. No one else knew him but you . . .
(*She weeps quietly*)

Was he not a great lover, a great man,
A hero?
CYR. (*Standing, bareheaded*) Yes, Roxane.
ROX.   A poet, unknown,
Adorable?
CYR.   Yes, Roxane.
ROX.   A fine mind?
CYR. Yes, Roxane.
ROX.   A heart deeper than we knew—
A soul magnificently tender?
CYR. (*Firmly*)   Yes,
Roxane!
ROX. (*Sinks down upon the breast of* CHRISTIAN)
He is dead now . . .
CYR. (*Aside; draws his sword*) Why, so am I—
For I am dead, and my love mourns for me
And does not know . . . (*Trumpets in distance*)
DE G. (*Appears on the parapet, disheveled,
wounded on the forehead, shouting*)
The signal—hark—the trumpets!
The army has returned— Hold them now!— Hold
them!
The army!—
ROX.   On his letter—blood . . . and tears
VOICE. (*Off stage*) Surrender!
CADETS.   No!
RAG.   This place is dangerous!
CYR. (*To* DE GUICHE)
Take her away—I am going—
ROX. (*Kisses the letter; faintly*)
His blood . . . his tears . . .
RAG. (*Leaps down from the coach and runs to
her*) She has fainted—
DE G. (*On the parapet; savagely, to the* CADETS)
Hold them!
VOICE OFF STAGE.   Lay down your arms!
VOICES.   No! No!
CYR. (*To* DE GUICHE)
Sir, you have proved yourself— Take care of her.
DE G. (*Hurries to* ROXANE *and takes her up in his
arms*) As you will—we can win, if you hold on
A little longer—
CYR.   Good!
(*Calls out to* ROXANE, *as she is carried away,
fainting, by* DE GUICHE *and* RAGUENEAU)
Adieu, Roxane!
(*Tumult, outcries. Several* CADETS *come back
wounded and fall on the stage.* CYRANO, *rushing
to the fight, is stopped on the crest of the parapet
by* CARBON, *covered with blood.*)
CARB. We are breaking—I am twice wounded—

CYR. (*Shouts to the Gascons*)   Hardi!
Reculez pas, Drollos! (*To* CARBON, *holding him up*)
So—never fear!
I have two deaths to avenge now—Christian's
And my own!
(*They come down.* CYRANO *takes from him the
lance with* ROXANE's *handkerchief still fastened
to it.*)
Float, little banner, with her name!
(*He plants it on the parapet;
then shouts to the* CADETS)
Toumbé dessus! Escrasas lous!
(*To the fifer*) Your fife!
Music!
(*Fife plays. The wounded drag themselves to their
feet. Other* CADETS *scramble over the parapet and
group themselves around* CYRANO *and his tiny flag.
The coach is filled and covered with men, bristling
with muskets, transformed into a redoubt.*)
CADET. (*Reels backward over the wall, still fight-
ing, shouts*) They are climbing over!—
(*And falls dead*)
CYR.   Very good—
Let them come!— A salute now—
(*The parapet is crowned for an instant with a rank
of enemies. The imperial banner of Spain is raised
aloft.*)
Fire! (*General volley*)
VOICE (*Among the ranks of the enemy*) Fire!
(*Murderous counter-fire; the
CADETS fall on every side*)
SPANISH OFFICER. (*Uncovers*)
Who are these men who are so fond of death?
CYR. (*Erect amid the hail of bullets, declaims*)
The Cadets of Gascoyne, the defenders
Of Carbon de Castel-Jaloux—
Free fighters, free lovers, free spenders—
(*He rushes forward, followed by a few survivors*)
The Cadets of Gascoyne . . .
(*The rest is lost in the din of battle*)

[CURTAIN]

THE FIFTH ACT

Cyrano's Gazette

Fifteen years later, in 1655. THE PARK OF THE CON-
VENT *occupied by the Ladies of the Cross, at Paris.
Magnificent foliage. To the Left, the House
upon a broad Terrace at the head of a flight of
steps, with several Doors opening upon the Terrace. In the centre of the scene an enormous Tree
alone in the centre of a little open space. Toward
the Right, in the foreground, among Boxwood
Bushes, a semicircular Bench of stone.
All the way across the Background of the scene,
an Avenue overarched by the chestnut trees, leading to the door of a Chapel on the Right, just
visible among the branches of the trees. Beyond
the double curtain of the trees, we catch a glimpse
of bright lawns and shaded walks, masses of shrubbery; the perspective of the Park; the sky.
A little side door of the Chapel opens upon a
Colonnade, garlanded with Autumnal vines, and
disappearing on the Right behind the box-trees.
It is late October. Above the still living green of
the turf all the foliage is red and yellow and brown.
The evergreen masses of Box and Yew stand out
darkly against this Autumnal coloring. A heap of
dead leaves under every tree. The leaves are falling everywhere. They rustle underfoot along the
walks; the Terrace and the Bench are half covered with them.
Before the Bench on the Right, on the side
toward the Tree, is placed a tall embroidery frame
and beside it a little Chair. Baskets filled with
skeins of many-colored silks and balls of wool. Tapestry unfinished on the Frame.
At the* CURTAIN RISE *the nuns are coming and
going across the Park; several of them are seated
on the Bench around* MOTHER MARGUÉRITE DE JÉSUS.
The leaves are falling.

SISTER MARTHE. (*To* MOTHER MARGUÉRITE)
Sister Claire has been looking in the glass
At her new cap; twice!
M. MARG. (*To* SISTER CLAIRE)
It is very plain;
Very.
SISTER CLAIRE. And Sister Marthe stole a plum
Out of the tart this morning!
M. MARG. (*To* SISTER MARTHE) That was wrong;
Very wrong.
S. C.   Oh, but such a little look!
S. MAR. Such a little plum!
M. MARG. (*Severely*)   I shall tell Monsieur
De Cyrano, this evening.
S. C.   No! Oh no!—
He will make fun of us.
S. MAR.   He will say nuns
Are so gay!
S. C.   And so greedy!
M. MARG. (*Smiling*)   And so good . . .

S. C. It must be ten years, Mother Marguérite,
That he has come here every Saturday,
Is it not?

M. MARG. More than ten years; ever since
His cousin came to live among us here—
Her worldly weeds among our linen veils,
Her widowhood and our virginity—
Like a black dove among white doves.

S. MAR.   No one
Else ever turns that happy sorrow of hers
Into a smile.

ALL THE NUNS. He is such fun!—He makes us
Almost laugh!—And he teases everyone—
And pleases everyone— And we all love him—
And he likes our cake, too—

S. MAR.   I am afraid
He is not a good Catholic.

S. C.   Some day
We shall convert him.

NUNS.   Yes—yes!

M. MARG.   Let him be;
I forbid you to worry him. Perhaps
He might stop coming here.

S. MAR.   But . . . God?

M. MARG.   You need not
Be afraid. God knows all about him.

S. MAR.   Yes . . .
But every Saturday he says to me,
Just as if he were proud of it: "Well, Sister,
I ate meat yesterday!"

M. MARG.   He tells you so?
The last time he said that, he had not eaten
Anything for two days.

S. MAR.   Mother!—

M. MARG.   He is poor;
Very poor.

S. MAR.   Who said so?

M. MARG.   Monsieur Le Bret.

S. MAR. Why does not someone help him?

M. MARG.   He would be
Angry; very angry . . .
(Between the trees up stage, ROXANE appears, all in
black, with a widow's cap and long veils. DE GUICHE,
magnificently grown old, walks beside her. They
move slowly. MOTHER MARGUÉRITE rises.)
                    Let us go in—
Madame Madeleine has a visitor.

S. MAR. (To SISTER CLAIRE)
The Duc de Grammont, is it not? The Marshal?

S. C. (Looks toward DE GUICHE) I think so—yes.

S. MAR.   He has not been to see her
For months—

NUNS.   He is busy—the Court!—The Camp!—

S. C.   The world . . .
(They go out. DE GUICHE and ROXANE come down in
silence, and stop near the embroidery frame. Pause.)

DE G. And you remain here, wasting all that
gold—
For ever in mourning?

ROX.   For ever.

DE G.   And still faithful?

ROX. And still faithful . . .

DE G. (After a pause)   Have you forgiven me?

ROX. (Simply, looking up at the cross of the Convent) I am here.   (Another pause)

DE G.   Was Christian . . . all that?

ROX.   If you knew him.

DE G. Ah? We were not precisely . . . intimate . . .
And his last letter—always at your heart?

ROX. It hangs here, like a holy reliquary.

DE G. Dead—and you love him still!

ROX.   Sometimes I think
He has not altogether died; our hearts
Meet, and his love flows all around me, living.

DE G. (After another pause)
You see Cyrano often?

ROX.   Every week.
My old friend takes the place of my Gazette,
Brings me all the news. Every Saturday,
Under that tree where you are now, his chair
Stands, if the day be fine. I wait for him,
Embroidering; the hour strikes; then I hear,
(I need not turn to look!) at the last stroke,
His cane tapping the steps. He laughs at me
For my eternal needlework. He tells
The story of the past week—
          (LE BRET appears on the steps)
                    There's Le Bret!—
          (LE BRET approaches)
How is it with our friend?

LE B.   Badly.

DE G.   Indeed?

ROX. (To DE GUICHE) Oh, he exaggerates!

LE B.   Just as I said—
Loneliness, misery—I told him so!—
His satires make a host of enemies—
He attacks the false nobles, the false saints,
The false heroes, the false artists—in short,
Everyone!

ROX.   But they fear that sword of his—
No one dare touch him!

DE G. (With a shrug) H'm—that may be so.

LE B. It is not violence I fear for him,
But solitude—poverty—old gray December,
Stealing on wolf's feet, with a wolf's green eyes,
Into his darkening room. Those bravoes yet
May strike our Swordsman down! Every day now,
He draws his belt up one hole; his poor nose
Looks like old ivory; he has one coat
Left—his old black serge.

DE G.   That is nothing strange
In this world! No, you need not pity him
Overmuch.

LE B. (*With a bitter smile*)
         My lord Marshal! . . .

DE G.   I say, do not
Pity him overmuch. He lives his life,
His own life, his own way—thought, word, and
    deed
Free!

LE B. (*As before*) My lord Duke! . . .

DE G. (*Haughtily*)   Yes, I know—I have all;
He has nothing. Nevertheless, today
I should be proud to shake his hand . . .
         (*Saluting* ROXANE) Adieu.

ROX. I will go with you.
         (DE GUICHE *salutes* LE BRET, *and turns*
         with ROXANE *toward the steps*)

DE G. (*Pauses on the steps, as she climbs*)
         Yes—I envy him
Now and then . . .
         Do you know, when a man wins
Everything in this world, when he succeeds
Too much—he feels, having done nothing wrong
Especially, Heaven knows!—he feels somehow
A thousand small displeasures with himself,
Whose whole sum is not quite Remorse, but rather
A sort of vague disgust . . . The ducal robes
Mounting up, step by step, to pride and power,
Somewhere among their folds draw after them
A rustle of dry illusions, vain regrets
As your veil, up the stairs here, draws along
The whisper of dead leaves.

ROX. (*Ironical*)   The sentiment
Does you honor.

DE G.   Oh, yes . . . (*Pausing suddenly*)
         Monsieur Le Bret!—
         (*To* ROXANE)
You pardon us?—
    (*He goes to* LE BRET, *and speaks in a low tone*)
         One moment— It is true
That no one dares attack your friend. Some people
Dislike him, none the less. The other day

At Court, such a one said to me: "This man
Cyrano may die—accidentally."

LE B. (*Coldly*)   Thank you.

DE G.   You may thank me. Keep him at home
All you can. Tell him to be careful.

LE B. (*Shaking his hands to heaven*) Careful!—
He is coming here. I'll warn him—yes, but! . . .

ROX. (*Still on the steps, to a* NUN *who approaches
her*)   Here
I am—what is it?

NUN.   Madame, Ragueneau
Wishes to see you.

ROX.   Bring him here.
         (*To* LE BRET *and* DE GUICHE)
         He comes
For sympathy—having been first of all
A Poet, he became since then, in turn,
A Singer—

LE B.   Bath-house keeper—

ROX.   Sacristan—

LE B. Actor—

ROX.   Hairdresser—

LE B.   Music-master—

ROX.   Now,
Today—

RAG. (*Enters hurriedly*)
         Madame!—   (*He sees* LE BRET)
         Monsieur!—

ROX. (*Smiling*)   First tell your troubles
To Le Bret for a moment.

RAG.   But, Madame—
    (*She goes out, with* DE GUICHE, *not hearing
him.* RAGUENEAU *comes to* LE BRET.)
After all, I had rather— You are here—
She need not know so soon— I went to see him
Just now— Our friend— As I came near his door,
I saw him coming out. I hurried on
To join him. At the corner of the street,
As he passed— Could it be an accident?—
I wonder!—At the window overhead,
A lackey with a heavy log of wood
Let it fall—

LE B.   Cyrano!

RAG.   I ran to him—

LE B. God! The cowards!

RAG.   I found him lying there—
A great hole in his head—

LE B.   Is he alive?

RAG. Alive—yes. But . . . I had to carry him
Up to his room—Dieu! Have you seen his room?—

LE B. Is he suffering?

RAG.   No; unconscious.

LE B.   Did you
Call a doctor?

RAG.   One came—for charity.

LE B. Poor Cyrano!—We must not tell Roxane
All at once . . . Did the doctor say?—

RAG.   He said
Fever, and lesions of the— I forget
Those long names— Ah, if you had seen him there,
His head all white bandages!—Let us go
Quickly—there is no one to care for him—
All alone— If he tries to raise his head,
He may die!

LE B. (*Draws him away to the Right*)
                        This way— It is shorter—through
The Chapel—

ROX. (*Appears on the stairway, and calls to* LE
BRET *as he is going out by the colonnade which
leads to the small door of the Chapel*)
                        Monsieur Le Bret!—
(LE BRET *and* RAGUENEAU *rush off without hearing*)
                        Running away
When I call to him? Poor dear Ragueneau
Must have been very tragic!
(*She comes slowly down the stair, toward the tree*)
                        What a day! . . .
Something in these bright Autumn afternoons
Happy and yet regretful—an old sorrow
Smiling . . . as though poor little April dried
Her tears long ago—and remembered . . .
(*She sits down at her work. Two* NUNS *come out
of the house carrying a great chair and set it under
the tree.*)
                        Ah—
The old chair, for my old friend!—

S. MAR.   The best one
In our best parlor!—

ROX.   Thank you, Sister—
                        (*The* NUNS *withdraw*)
                        There—
(*She begins embroidering. The clock strikes.*)
The hour!—He will be coming now—my silks—
All done striking? He never was so late
Before! The sister at the door—my thimble . . .
Here it is—she must be exhorting him
To repent all his sins . . .   (*A pause*)
                        He ought to be
Converted, by this time— Another leaf—
(*A dead leaf falls on her work; she brushes it away*)
Certainly nothing could—my scissors—ever
Keep him away—

NUN. (*Appears on the steps*)
                        Monsieur de Bergerac.

ROX. (*Without turning*)
What was I saying? . . . Hard, sometimes, to
   match
These faded colors! . . .
(*While she goes on working,* CYRANO *appears at
the top of the steps, very pale, his hat drawn over
his eyes. The* NUN *who has brought him in goes
away. He begins to descend the steps leaning on
his cane, and holding himself on his feet only by
an evident effort.* ROXANE *turns to him, with a
tone of friendly banter.*)
                        After fourteen years,
Late—for the first time!

CYR. (*Reaches the chair, and sinks into it, his
gay tone contrasting with his tortured face*)
                        Yes, yes—maddening!
I was detained by—

ROX.   Well?

CYR.   A visitor,
Most unexpected.

ROX. (*Carelessly, still sewing*)   Was your visitor
Tiresome?

CYR.   Why, hardly that—inopportune,
Let us say—an old friend of mine—at least
A very old acquaintance.

ROX.   Did you tell him
To go away?

CYR.   For the time being, yes.
I said: "Excuse me—this is Saturday—
I have a previous engagement, one
I cannot miss, even for you— Come back
An hour from now."

ROX.   Your friend will have to wait;
I shall not let you go till dark.

CYR. (*Very gently*)   Perhaps
A little before dark, I must go . . .
(*He leans back in the chair, and closes his eyes.*
SISTER MARTHE *crosses above the stairway.* ROXANE
sees her, motions her to wait, then turns to CYRANO.)

ROX.   Look—
Somebody waiting to be teased.

CYR. (*Quickly, opens his eyes*) Of course!
                        (*In a big, comic voice*)
Sister, approach!
                        (SISTER MARTHE *glides toward him*)
                        Beautiful downcast eyes!—
So shy—

S. MAR. (*Looks up, smiling*)
            You—   (*She sees his face*)
                        Oh!—

CYR. (*Indicates* ROXANE) Sh!—Careful!
(*Resumes his burlesque tone*)
                                        Yesterday,
I ate meat again!
    S. MAR.   Yes, I know. (*Aside*)
                                        That is why
He looks so pale . . . (*To him: low and quickly*)
                                        In the refectory,
Before you go—come to me there—
                                        I'll make you
A great bowl of hot soup—will you come?
    CYR. (*Boisterously*)   Ah—
Will I come!
    S. MAR.   You are quite reasonable
Today!
    ROX. Has she converted you?
    S. MAR.   Oh, no—
Not for the world!—
    CYR.   Why, now I think of it,
That is so— You, bursting with holiness,
And yet you never preach! Astonishing
I call it . . .   (*With burlesque ferocity*)
                Ah—now I'll astonish you—
I am going to—   (*With the air of seeking
                    for a good joke and finding it*)
                —let you pray for me
Tonight, at vespers!
    ROX.   Aha!
    CYR.   Look at her—
Absolutely struck dumb!
    S. MAR. (*Gently*)   I did not wait
For you to say I might.   (*She goes out*)
    CYR. (*Returns to* ROXANE, *who is bending over
her work*)   Now, may the devil
Admire me, if I ever hope to see
The end of that embroidery!
    ROX. (*Smiling*)   I thought
It was time you said that.
        (*A breath of wind causes a few leaves to fall*)
    CYR.   The leaves—
    ROX. (*Raises her head and looks away through
the trees*)   What color—
Perfect Venetian red! Look at them fall.
    CYR. Yes—they know how to die. A little way
From the branch to the earth, a little fear
Of mingling with the common dust—and yet
They go down gracefully—a fall that seems
Like flying!
    ROX.   Melancholy—you?
    CYR.   Why, no,
Roxane!

    ROX.   Then let the leaves fall. Tell me now
The Court news—my Gazette!
    CYR.   Let me see—
    ROX.   Ah!
    CYR. (*More and more pale, struggling against
pain*) Saturday, the nineteenth: The King fell ill,
After eight helpings of grape marmalade.
His malady was brought before the court,
Found guilty of high treason; whereupon
His Majesty revived. The royal pulse
Is now normal. *Sunday, the twentieth:*
The Queen gave a grand ball, at which they burned
Seven hundred and sixty-three wax candles. *Note:*
They say our troops have been victorious
In Austria. *Later:* Three sorcerers
Have been hung. *Special post:* The little dog
Of Madame d'Athis was obliged to take
Four pills before—
    ROX.   Monsieur de Bergerac,
Will you kindly be quiet!
    CYR.   Monday . . . nothing.
Lygdamire has a new lover.
    ROX.   Oh,
    CYR. (*His face more and more altered*)
                            Tuesday,
The twenty-second: All the court has gone
To Fontainebleau. *Wednesday:* The Comte de
    Fiesque
Spoke to Madame de Montglat; she said No.
Thursday: Mancini was the Queen of France
Or—very nearly! *Friday:* La Montglat
Said Yes. *Saturday, twenty-sixth.* . . .
        (*His eyes close; his head sinks back; silence*)
    ROX. (*Surprised at not hearing any more, turns,
looks at him, and rises, frightened*) He has fainted—
                    (*She runs to him, crying out*)
Cyrano!
    CYR. (*Opens his eyes*) What . . . What is it? . . .
(*He sees* ROXANE *leaning over him, and quickly
pulls his hat down over his head and leans back
            away from her in the chair*)
                            No—oh no—
It is nothing—truly!
    ROX.   But—
    CYR.   My old wound—
At Arras—sometimes—you know. . . .
    ROX.   My poor friend!
    CYR. Oh it is nothing; it will soon be gone. . . .
                            (*Forcing a smile*)
There! It is gone!
    ROX. (*Standing close to him*)
                    We all have our old wounds—

I have mine—here . . . *(Her hand at her breast)*
  under this faded scrap
Of writing. . . . It is hard to read now—all
But the blood—and the tears. . . .
  (Twilight begins to fall)
CYR.   His letter! . . . Did you
Not promise me that some day . . . that some day
You would let me read it?
ROX.   His letter?—You . . .
You wish—
CYR.   I do wish it—today.
ROX. *(Gives him the little silken bag from around
her neck)*   Here. . . .
CYR. May I . . . open it?
ROX.   Open it, and read.
  *(She goes back to her work, folds
  it again, rearranges her silks)*
CYR. *(Unfolds the letter; reads)*
"Farewell, Roxane, because today I die—"
ROX. *(Looks up, surprised)* Aloud?
CYR. *(Reads)*   "I know that it will be today,
My own dearly beloved—and my heart
Still so heavy with love I have not told,
And I die without telling you! No more
Shall my eyes drink the sight of you like wine,
Never more, with a look that is a kiss,
Follow the sweet grace of you—"
ROX.   How you read it—
His letter!
CYR. *(Continues)* "I remember now the way
You have, of pushing back a lock of hair
With one hand, from your forehead—and my heart
Cries out—"
ROX.   His letter . . . and you read it so . . .
  (The darkness increases imperceptibly)
CYR. "Cries out and keeps crying: 'Farewell, my
  dear,
My dearest—'"
ROX.   In a voice . . .
CYR.   "—My own heart's own.
My own treasure—"
ROX. *(Dreamily)* In such a voice. . . .
CYR.   —"My love—"
ROX.—As I remember hearing . . .
  (She trembles) —long ago. . . .
*(She comes near him, softly, without his seeing
  her; passes the chair, leans over silently, look-
  ing at the letter. The darkness increases.)*
CYR. "—I am never away from you. Even now,
I shall not leave you. In another world,
I shall be still that one who loves you, loves you
Beyond measure, beyond—"

ROX. *(Lays her hand on his shoulder)*
  How can you read
Now? It is dark. . . .
  *(He starts, turns, and sees her there close to
  him. A little movement of surprise, almost of
  fear; then he bows his head.
A long pause; then in the twilight now completely
  fallen, she says very softly, clasping her hands)*
  And all these fourteen years,
He has been the old friend, who came to me
To be amusing.
CYR.   Roxane!—
ROX.   It was you.
CYR. No, no, Roxane, no!
ROX.   And I might have known,
Every time that I heard you speak my name! . . .
CYR. No— It was not I—
ROX.   It was . . . you!
CYR.   I swear—
ROX. I understand everything now: The letters—
That was you . . .
CYR.   No!
ROX.   And the dear, foolish words—
That was you. . . .
CYR.   No!
ROX.   And the voice . . . in the dark . . .
That was . . . you!
CYR.   On my honor—
ROX.   And . . . the Soul!—
That was all you.
CYR.   I never loved you—
ROX.   Yes,
You loved me.
CYR. *(Desperately)* No— He loved you—
ROX.   Even now,
You love me!
CYR. *(His voice weakens)* No!
ROX. *(Smiling)*   And why . . . so great a *No?*
CYR. No, no, my own dear love, I love you
  not! . . .   *(Pause)*
ROX. How many things have died . . . and are
  new-born! . . .
Why were you silent for so many years,
All the while, every night and every day,
He gave me nothing—you knew that— You knew
Here, in this letter lying on my breast,
Your tears— You knew they were your tears—
CYR. *(Holds the letter out to her)*   The blood
Was his.
ROX.   Why do you break that silence now,
Today?

CYR. Why? Oh, because—
(LE BRET *and* RAGUENEAU *enter, running*)
LE B.   What recklessness—
I knew it! He is here!
CYR. (*Smiling, and trying to rise*)
                          Well? Here I am!
RAG. He has killed himself, Madame, coming
here!
ROX. He— Oh, God. . . . And that faintness
. . . was that?—
CYR.   No,
Nothing! I did not finish my Gazette—
Saturday, twenty-sixth: An hour or so
Before dinner, Monsieur de Bergerac
Died, foully murdered. (*He uncovers his head, and
                          shows it swathed in bandages*)
ROX.   Oh, what does he mean?—
Cyrano!—What have they done to you?—
CYR.   "Struck down
By the sword of a hero, let me fall—
Steel in my heart, and laughter on my lips!"
Yes, I said that once. How Fate loves a jest!—
Behold me ambushed—taken in the rear—
My battlefield a gutter—my noble foe
A lackey, with a log of wood! . . .
                          It seems
Too logical— I have missed everything,
Even my death!
RAG. (*Breaks down*) Ah, Monsieur!—
CYR.   Ragueneau,
Stop blubbering!   (*Takes his hand*)
                    What are you writing nowadays,
Old poet?
RAG. (*Through his tears*) I am not a poet now;
I snuff the—light the candles—for Molière!
CYR. Oh—Molière!
RAG.   Yes, but I am leaving him
Tomorrow. Yesterday they played *Scapin*—
He has stolen your scene—
LE B.   The whole scene—word for word!
RAG. Yes: "What the devil was he doing there"—
That one!
LE B. (*Furious*)
          And Molière stole it all from you—
Bodily!—
CYR.   Bah— He showed good taste. . . .
               (*To* RAGUENEAU) The Scene
Went well? . . .
RAG. Ah, Monsieur, they laughed—and laughed—
How they did laugh!
CYR.   Yes—that has been my life.
Do you remember that night Christian spoke

Under your window? It was always so!
While I stood in the darkness underneath,
Others climbed up to win the applause—the kiss!—
Well—that seems only justice— I still say,
Even now, on the threshold of my tomb—
"Molière has genius—Christian had good looks—"
(*The chapel bell is ringing. Along the avenue of
trees above the stairway, the* NUNS *pass in proces-
sion to their prayers.*)
They are going to pray now; there is the bell.
ROX (*Raises herself and calls to them*)
Sister!—Sister!—
CYR. (*Holding on to her hand*)
               No,—do not go away—
I may not still be here when you return. . . .
               (*The* NUNS *have gone into the
               chapel. The organ begins to play.*)
A little harmony is all I need—
Listen. . . .
ROX.   You shall not die! I love you!—
CYR.   No—
That is not in the story! You remember
When Beauty said "I love you" to the Beast
That was a fairy prince, his ugliness
Changed and dissolved, like magic. . . . But you
               see
I am still the same.
ROX.   And I—I have done
This to you! All my fault—mine!
CYR.   You? Why, no,
On the contrary! I had never known
Womanhood and its sweetness but for you.
My mother did not love to look at me—
I never had a sister— Later on,
I feared the mistress with a mockery
Behind her smile. But you—because of you
I have had one friend not quite all a friend—
Across my life, one whispering silken gown! . . .
LE B. (*Points to the rising moon which begins to
shine down between the trees*)
Your other friend is looking at you.
CYR. (*Smiling at the moon*)   I see. . . .
ROX. I never loved but one man in my life,
And I have lost him—twice. . . .
CYR. Le Bret—I shall be up there presently
In the moon—without having to invent
Any flying-machines!
ROX.   What are you saying? . . .
CYR. The moon—yes, that would be the place for
     me—
My kind of paradise! I shall find there

Those other souls who should be friends of mine—
Socrates—Galileo—
LE B. (*Revolting*) No! No! No!
It is too idiotic—too unfair—
Such a friend—such a poet—such a man
To die so—to die so!—
CYR. (*Affectionately*) There goes Le Bret,
Growling!
LE B. (*Breaks down*) My friend!—
CYR. (*Half raises himself, his eye wanders*)
                    The Cadets of Gascoyne,
The Defenders. . . . The elementary mass—
Ah—there's the point! Now, then . . .
    LE B.   Delirious—
And all that learning—
    CYR.   On the other hand,
We have Copernicus—
    ROX.   Oh!
CYR. (*More and more delirious*) "Very well,
But what the devil was he doing there?—
What the devil was he doing there, up there?" . . .
                    (*He declaims*)

Philosopher and scientist,
Poet, musician, duellist—
    He flew high, and fell back again!
A pretty wit—whose like we lack—
A lover . . . not like other men. . . .
    Here likes Hercule-Savinien
De Cyrano de Bergerac—
Who was all things—and all in vain!

Well, I must go—pardon— I cannot stay!
My moonbeam comes to carry me away. . . .
    (*He falls back into the chair, half fainting. The
    sobbing of* ROXANE *recalls him to reality. Gradu-
    ally his mind comes back to him. He looks at her,
        stroking the veil that hides her hair.*)
I would not have you mourn any the less
That good, brave, noble Christian; but perhaps—
I ask you only this—when the great cold
Gathers around my bones, that you may give
A double meaning to your widow's weeds
And the tears you let fall for him may be
For a little—my tears. . . .
    ROX. (*Sobbing*)   Oh, my love! . . .
CYR. (*Suddenly shaken as with a fever fit, he
raises himself erect and pushes her away*)
                    —Not here!—

Not lying down! . . .   (*They spring forward
        to help him; he motions them back*)
                    Let no one help me—no one!—
Only the tree. . . .
    (*He sets his back against the trunk. Pause.*)
                    It is coming . . . I feel
Already shod with marble . . . gloved with
    lead . . .
                    (*Joyously*)
Let the old fellow come now! He shall find me
On my feet—sword in hand—   (*Draws his sword*)
    LE B.   Cyrano!—
ROX. (*Half fainting*)   Oh,
Cyrano!
    CYR. I can see him there—he grins—
He is looking at my nose—that skeleton
—What's that you say? Hopeless?—Why, very well!—
But a man does not fight merely to win!
No—no—better to know one fights in vain! . . .
You there— Who are you? A hundred against one—
I know them now, my ancient enemies—
                    (*He lunges at the empty air*)
Falsehood! . . . There! There! Prejudice— Com-
    promise—
Cowardice—   (*Thrusting*)
        What's that? No! Surrender? No!
Never—never! . . .
                    Ah, you too, Vanity!
I knew you would overthrow me in the end—
No! I fight on! I fight on! I fight on!
(*He swings the blade in great circles, then pauses,
gasping. When he speaks again, it is another tone.*)
Yes, all my laurels you have riven away
And all my roses; yet in spite of you,
There is one crown I bear away with me,
And tonight, when I enter before God,
My salute shall sweep all the stars away
From the blue threshold! One thing without stain,
Unspotted from the world, in spite of doom
Mine own!—
                    (*He springs forward, his sword aloft*)
                    And that is . . .
(*The sword escapes from his hand; he totters, and
    falls into the arms of* LE BRET *and* RAGUENEAU)
    ROX. (*Bends over him and kisses him on the
forehead*)   —That is . . .
    CYR. (*Opens his eyes and smiles up at her*)
                    My white plume. . . .

                    [CURTAIN]

GEORGE BERNARD SHAW *Pygmalion*

George Bernard Shaw (1856-1950), the greatest English playwright of the twentieth century, is also one of the myths of our time. His patriarchal beard, vegetarian habits, socialist views, scathing pronouncements on a variety of subjects—all these have contributed to form a legendary picture which, according to Shaw, must most resolutely be banished from the mind before we can understand Shaw the literary artist. Yet his plays are the extension of his personality, a personality that was part clown, part "intellectual cheesemite," in the words of Ezra Pound, and part genuine prophet.

After several experiments with the novel, Shaw distinguished himself in the writing of music and drama criticism. In his reviews and in the brilliantly argued prefaces to his plays, he developed a prose more lucid and sinuous than anything since Swift. Five years of playwriting finally brought success with *Candida* in 1898, and by 1912 Shaw had reached the apex of his career with *Androcles and the Lion* and *Pygmalion*. In 1925 he received the Nobel Prize for literature, and he continued to write for the theater until the very day of his death at the age of ninety-four.

Though not so great as *St. Joan*, 1923, nor so perfectly contrived as *Candida*, *Pygmalion* has over the years probably been Shaw's most popular play. It was a huge box-office success at His Majesty's Theatre, London, in 1914, after earlier successes in Berlin and Vienna. It has had three noteworthy runs on Broadway, the last time in 1945 with Gertrude Lawrence as Eliza Doolittle and Raymond Massey as Higgins. It was, in 1938, Shaw's first play to be made into a movie, with Wendy Hiller and Leslie Howard, and plans are now afoot to turn it into a musical comedy.

One of Shaw's crotchets was a passion for language reforms, among them the phonetic spelling of English. Fortunately, in spite of the play's avowedly didactic intent, *Pygmalion* is not a treatise on phonetics, nor is it excessively burdened with weighty discourse. Much has been made of Shaw the thinker—and there is no denying his intellectual genius—but the distinction of *Pygmalion* lies in the subtle co-operation of intellect and emotion, mind and heart, in a thoroughly engaging comedy.

PREFACE TO PYGMALION—
A PROFESSOR OF PHONETICS

As will be seen later on, Pygmalion needs, not a preface, but a sequel, which I have supplied in its due place. The English have no respect for their language, and will not teach their children to speak it. They spell it so abominably that no man can teach himself what it sounds like. It is impossible for an Englishman to open his mouth with-

out making some other Englishman hate or despise him. German and Spanish are accessible to foreigners: English is not accessible even to Englishmen. The reformer England needs today is an energetic phonetic enthusiast: that is why I have made such a one the hero of a popular play. There have been heroes of that kind crying in the wilderness for many years past. When I became interested in the subject towards the end of the eighteen-seventies, the illustrious Alexander Melville Bell, the inventor of Visible Speech, had emigrated to Canada, where his son invented the telephone; but Alexander J. Ellis was still a London patriarch, with an impressive head always covered by a velvet skull cap, for which he would apologize to public meetings in a very courtly manner. He and Tito Pagliardini, another phonetic veteran, were men whom it was impossible to dislike. Henry Sweet, then a young man, lacked their sweetness of character: he was about as conciliatory to conventional mortals as Ibsen or Samuel Butler. His great ability as a phonetician (he was, I think, the best of them all at his job) would have entitled him to high official recognition, and perhaps enabled him to popularize his subject, but for his Satanic contempt for all academic dignitaries and persons in general who thought more of Greek than of phonetics. Once, in the days when the Imperial Institute rose in South Kensington, and Joseph Chamberlain was booming the Empire, I induced the editor of a leading monthly review to commission an article from Sweet on the imperial importance of his subject. When it arrived, it contained nothing but a savagely derisive attack on a professor of language and literature whose chair Sweet regarded as proper to a phonetic expert only. The article, being libellous, had to be returned as impossible; and I had to renounce my dream of dragging its author into the limelight. When I met him afterwards, for the first time for many years, I found to my astonishment that he, who had been a quite tolerably presentable young man, had actually managed by sheer scorn to alter his personal appearance until he had become a sort of walking repudiation of Oxford and all its traditions. It must have been largely in his own despite that he was squeezed into something called a Readership of phonetics there. The future of phonetics rests probably with his pupils, who all swore by him; but nothing could bring the man himself into any sort of compliance with the university to which he nevertheless clung by divine right in an intensely Oxonian way. I daresay his papers, if he has left any, include some satires that may be published without too destructive results fifty years hence. He was, I believe, not in the least an illnatured man: very much the opposite, I should say; but he would not suffer fools gladly.

Those who knew him will recognize in my third act the allusion to the patent shorthand in which he used to write postcards, and which may be acquired from a four and sixpenny manual published by the Clarendon Press. The postcards which Mrs Higgins describes are such as I have received from Sweet. I would decipher a sound which a cockney would represent by *zerr*, and a Frenchman by *seu*, and then write demanding with some heat what on earth it meant. Sweet, with boundless contempt for my stupidity, would reply that it not only meant but obviously was the word Result, as no other word containing that sound, and capable of making sense with the context, existed in any language spoken on earth. That less expert mortals should require fuller indications was beyond Sweet's patience. Therefore, though the whole point of his Current Shorthand is that it can express every sound in the language perfectly, vowels as well as consonants, and that your hand has to make no stroke except the easy and current ones with which you write m, n, and u, l, p, and q, scribbling them at whatever angle comes easiest to you, his unfortunate determination to make this remarkable and quite legible script serve also as a shorthand reduced it in his own practice to the most inscrutable of cryptograms. His true objective was the provision of a full, accurate, legible script for our noble but ill-dressed language; but he was led past that by his contempt for the popular Pitman system of shorthand, which he called the Pitfall system. The triumph of Pitman was a triumph of business organization: there was a weekly paper to persuade you to learn Pitman: there were cheap textbooks and exercise books and transcripts of speeches for you to copy, and schools where experienced teachers coached you up to the necessary proficiency. Sweet could not organize his market in that fashion. He might as well have been the Sybil who tore up the leaves of prophecy that nobody would attend to. The four and sixpenny manual, mostly in his lithographed handwriting, that was never vulgarly advertized, may perhaps some day be taken up by a syndicate and pushed upon the public as The Times pushed the Encyclopædia Britannica; but until then it will certainly not prevail against Pitman. I have bought three copies of it during my lifetime; and I am informed by the publishers that its cloistered existence is still a steady and healthy one. I actually learned the system two several times; and yet the shorthand in which I am writing these lines is Pitman's. And the reason is, that my secretary cannot transcribe Sweet, having been perforce taught in the schools of Pitman. Therefore, Sweet railed at Pitman as vainly as Thersites railed at Ajax: his raillery, however it may have eased his soul, gave no popular vogue to Current Shorthand.

Pygmalion Higgins is not a portrait of Sweet, to whom the adventure of Eliza Doolittle would have been impossible; still, as will be seen, there are touches of Sweet in the play. With Higgins's physique and temperament Sweet might have set the Thames on fire. As it was, he impressed himself professionally on Europe to an extent that made his comparative personal obscurity, and the failure of Oxford to do justice to his eminence, a puzzle to foreign specialists in his subject. I do not blame Oxford, because I think Oxford is quite right in demanding a certain social amenity from its nurslings (heaven knows it is not exorbitant in its requirements!); for although I well know how hard it is for a man of genius with a seriously underrated subject to maintain serene and kindly relations with the men who underrate it, and who keep all the best places for less important subjects which they profess without originality and sometimes without much capacity for them, still, if he overwhelms them with wrath and disdain, he cannot expect them to heap honors on him.

Of the later generations of phoneticians I know little. Among them towers the Poet Laureate, to whom perhaps Higgins may owe his Miltonic sympathies, though here again I must disclaim all portraiture. But if the play makes the public aware that there are such people as phoneticians, and that they are among the most important people in England at present, it will serve its turn.

I wish to boast that Pygmalion has been an extremely successful play all over Europe and North America as well as at home. It is so intensely and deliberately didactic, and its subject is esteemed so dry, that I delight in throwing it at the heads of the wiseacres who repeat the parrot cry that art should never be didactic. It goes to prove my contention that art should never be anything else.

Finally, and for the encouragement of people troubled with accents that cut them off from all high employment, I may add that the change wrought by Professor Higgins in the flower girl is neither impossible nor uncommon. The modern concierge's daughter who fulfils her ambition by playing the Queen of Spain in Ruy Blas at the Théâtre Français is only one of many thousands of men and women who have sloughed off their native dialects and acquired a new tongue. But the thing has to be done scientifically, or the last state of the aspirant may be worse than the first. An honest and natural slum dialect is more tolerable than the attempt of a phonetically untaught person to imitate the vulgar dialect of the golf club; and I am sorry to say that in spite of the efforts of our Royal Academy of Dramatic Art, there is still too much sham golfing English on our stage, and too little of the noble English of Forbes Robertson.

ACT I

Covent Garden at 11.15 *p.m. Torrents of heavy summer rain. Cab whistles blowing frantically in all directions. Pedestrians running for shelter into the market and under the portico of St Paul's Church, where there are already several people, among them a lady and her daughter in evening dress. They are all peering out gloomily at the rain, except one man with his back turned to the rest, who seems wholly preoccupied with a notebook in which he is writing busily.*

The church clock strikes the first quarter.

THE DAUGHTER (*in the space between the central pillars, close to the one on her left*). I'm getting chilled to the bone. What can Freddy be doing all this time? He's been gone twenty minutes.

THE MOTHER (*on her daughter's right*). Not so long. But he ought to have got us a cab by this.

A BYSTANDER (*on the lady's right*). He wont get no cab not until half-past eleven, missus, when they come back after dropping their theatre fares.

THE MOTHER. But we must have a cab. We cant stand here until half-past eleven. It's too bad.

THE BYSTANDER. Well, it aint my fault, missus.

THE DAUGHTER. If Freddy had a bit of gumption, he would have got one at the theatre door.

THE MOTHER. What could he have done, poor boy?

THE DAUGHTER. Other people got cabs. Why couldnt he?

FREDDY *rushes in out of the rain from the Southampton Street side, and comes between them closing a dripping umbrella. He is a young man of twenty, in evening dress, very wet round the ankles.*

THE DAUGHTER. Well, havnt you got a cab?

FREDDY. Theres not one to be had for love or money.

THE MOTHER. Oh, Freddy, there must be one. You cant have tried.

THE DAUGHTER. It's too tiresome. Do you expect us to go and get one ourselves?

FREDDY. I tell you theyre all engaged. The rain was so sudden: nobody was prepared; and everybody had to take a cab. Ive been to Charing Cross one way and nearly to Ludgate Circus the other; and they were all engaged.

THE MOTHER. Did you try Trafalgar Square?

FREDDY. There wasnt one at Trafalgar Square.

THE DAUGHTER. Did you try?

FREDDY. I tried as far as Charing Cross Station. Did you expect me to walk to Hammersmith?

THE DAUGHTER. You havnt tried at all.

THE MOTHER. You really are very helpless, Freddy. Go again; and dont come back until you have found a cab.

FREDDY. I shall simply get soaked for nothing.

THE DAUGHTER. And what about us? Are we to stay here all night in this draught, with next to nothing on? You selfish pig—

FREDDY. Oh, very well: I'll go, I'll go. (*He opens his umbrella and dashes off Strandwards, but comes into collision with a flower girl, who is hurrying in for shelter, knocking her basket out of her hands. A blinding flash of lightning, followed instantly by a rattling peal of thunder, orchestrates the incident.*)

THE FLOWER GIRL. Nah then, Freddy: look wh' y' gowin, deah.

FREDDY. Sorry (*he rushes off*).

THE FLOWER GIRL (*picking up her scattered flowers and replacing them in the basket*). Theres menners f' yer! Te-oo banches o voylets trod into the mad. (*She sits down on the plinth of the column, sorting her flowers, on the lady's right. She is not at all an attractive person. She is perhaps eighteen, perhaps twenty, hardly older. She wears a little sailor hat of black straw that has long been exposed to the dust and soot of London and has seldom if ever been brushed. Her hair needs washing rather badly: its mousy color can hardly be natural. She wears a shoddy black coat that reaches nearly to her knees and is shaped to her waist. She has a brown skirt with a coarse apron. Her boots are much the worse for wear. She is no doubt as clean as she can afford to be; but compared to the ladies she is very dirty. Her features are no worse than theirs; but their condition leaves something to be desired; and she needs the services of a dentist.*)

THE MOTHER. How do you know that my son's name is Freddy, pray?

THE FLOWER GIRL. Ow, eez ye-ooa san, is e?

Wal, fewd dan y' de-ooty bawmz a mather should, eed now bettern to spawl a pore gel's flahrzn than ran awy athaht pyin. Will ye-oo py me f' them? (*Here, with apologies, this desperate attempt to represent her dialect without a phonetic alphabet must be abandoned as unintelligible outside London.*)

THE DAUGHTER. Do nothing of the sort, mother. The idea!

THE MOTHER. Please allow me, Clara. Have you any pennies?

THE DAUGHTER. No. Ive nothing smaller than sixpence.

THE FLOWER GIRL (*hopefully*). I can give you change for a tanner, kind lady.

THE MOTHER (*to* CLARA). Give it to me. (CLARA *parts reluctantly.*) Now (*to* THE GIRL) this is for your flowers.

THE FLOWER GIRL. Thank you kindly, lady.

THE DAUGHTER. Make her give you the change. These things are only a penny a bunch.

THE MOTHER. Do hold your tongue, Clara. (*To* THE GIRL) You can keep the change.

THE FLOWER GIRL. Oh, thank you, lady.

THE MOTHER. Now tell me how you know that young gentleman's name.

THE FLOWER GIRL. I didnt.

THE MOTHER. I heard you call him by it. Dont try to deceive me.

THE FLOWER GIRL (*protesting*). Who's trying to deceive you? I called him Freddy or Charlie same as you might yourself if you was talking to a stranger and wished to be pleasant. (*She sits down beside her basket.*)

THE DAUGHTER. Sixpence thrown away! Really, mamma, you might have spared Freddy *that*. (*She retreats in disgust behind the pillar.*)

An elderly gentleman of the amiable military type rushes into the shelter, and closes a dripping umbrella. He is in the same plight as Freddy, very wet about the ankles. He is in evening dress, with a light overcoat. He takes the place left vacant by the daughter's retirement.

THE GENTLEMAN. Phew!

THE MOTHER (*to* THE GENTLEMAN). Oh, sir, is there any sign of its stopping?

THE GENTLEMAN. I'm afraid not. It started worse than ever about two minutes ago. (*He goes to the plinth beside the flower girl; puts* up his foot on it; and stoops to turn down his trouser ends.)

THE MOTHER. Oh dear! (*She retires sadly and joins her daughter.*)

THE FLOWER GIRL (*taking advantage of the military gentleman's proximity to establish friendly relations with him*). If it's worse, it's a sign it's nearly over. So cheer up, Captain; and buy a flower off a poor girl.

THE GENTLEMAN. I'm sorry. I havnt any change.

THE FLOWER GIRL. I can give you change, Captain.

THE GENTLEMAN. For a sovereign! Ive nothing less.

THE FLOWER GIRL. Garn! Oh do buy a flower off me, Captain. I can change half-a-crown. Take this for tuppence.

THE GENTLEMAN. Now dont be troublesome: theres a good girl. (*Trying his pockets*) I really havnt any change—Stop: heres three hapence, if thats any use to you (*he retreats to the other pillar*).

THE FLOWER GIRL (*disappointed, but thinking three halfpence better than nothing*). Thank you, sir.

THE BYSTANDER (*to THE GIRL*). You be careful: give him a flower for it. Theres a bloke here behind taking down every blessed word youre saying. (*All turn to the man who is taking notes.*)

THE FLOWER GIRL (*springing up terrified*). I aint done nothing wrong by speaking to the gentleman. Ive a right to sell flowers if I keep off the kerb. (*Hysterically*) I'm a respectable girl: so help me, I never spoke to him except to ask him to buy a flower off me. (*General hubbub, mostly sympathetic to the flower girl, but deprecating her excessive sensibility. Cries of* Dont start hollerin. Who's hurting you? Nobody's going to touch you. Whats the good of fussing? Steady on. Easy easy, etc., *come from the elderly staid spectators, who pat her comfortingly. Less patient ones bid her shut her head, or ask her roughly what is wrong with her. A remoter group, not knowing what the matter is, crowd in and increase the noise with question and answer:* Whats the row? Whatshe do? Where is he? A tec taking her down. What! him? Yes: him over there: Took money off the gentleman, etc. THE FLOWER GIRL, *distraught and mobbed, breaks through*

them to THE GENTLEMAN, *crying wildly*) Oh, sir, dont let him charge me. You dunno what it means to me. Theyll take away my character and drive me on the streets for speaking to gentlemen. They—

THE NOTE TAKER (*coming forward on her right, the rest crowding after him*). There, there, there, there! who's hurting you, you silly girl? What do you take me for?

THE BYSTANDER. It's all right: he's a gentleman: look at his boots. (*Explaining to THE NOTE TAKER*) She thought you was a copper's nark, sir.

THE NOTE TAKER (*with quick interest*). Whats a copper's nark?

THE BYSTANDER (*inapt at definition*). It's a— well, it's a copper's nark, as you might say. What else would you call it? A sort of informer.

THE FLOWER GIRL (*still hysterical*). I take my Bible oath I never said a word—

THE NOTE TAKER (*overbearing but good-humored*). Oh, shut up, shut up. Do I look like a policeman?

THE FLOWER GIRL (*far from reassured*). Then what did you take down my words for? How do I know whether you took me down right? You just shew me what youve wrote about me. (THE NOTE TAKER *opens his book and holds it steadily under her nose, though the pressure of the mob trying to read it over his shoulders would upset a weaker man.*) Whats that? *That* aint proper writing. I cant read that.

THE NOTE TAKER. I can. (*Reads, reproducing her pronunciation exactly*) "Cheer ap, Keptin; n' baw ya flahr orf a pore gel."

THE FLOWER GIRL (*much distressed*). It's because I called him Captain. I meant no harm. (*To THE GENTLEMAN*) Oh, sir, dont let him lay a charge agen me for a word like that. You—

THE GENTLEMAN. Charge! I make no charge. (*To THE NOTE TAKER*) Really, sir, if you are a detective, you need not begin protecting me against molestation by young women until I ask you. Anybody could see that the girl meant no harm.

THE BYSTANDERS GENERALLY (*demonstrating against police espionage*). Course they could. What business is it of yours? You mind your own affairs. He wants promotion, he does.

Taking down people's words! Girl never said a word to him. What harm if she did? Nice thing a girl cant shelter from the rain without being insulted, etc., etc., etc. (*She is conducted by the more sympathetic demonstrators back to her plinth, where she resumes her seat and struggles with her emotion.*)

THE BYSTANDER. He aint a tec. He's a blooming busybody: thats what he is. I tell you, look at his boots.

THE NOTE TAKER (*turning on him genially*). And how are all your people down at Selsey?

THE BYSTANDER (*suspiciously*). Who told you my people come from Selsey?

THE NOTE TAKER. Never you mind. They did. (*To* THE GIRL) How do you come to be up so far east? You were born in Lisson Grove.

THE FLOWER GIRL (*appalled*). Oh, what harm is there in my leaving Lisson Grove? It wasnt fit for a pig to live in; and I had to pay four-and-six a week. (*In tears*) Oh, boo—hoo—oo—

THE NOTE TAKER. Live where you like; but stop that noise.

THE GENTLEMAN (*to* THE GIRL). Come, come! he cant touch you: you have a right to live where you please.

A SARCASTIC BYSTANDER (*thrusting himself between* THE NOTE TAKER *and* THE GENTLEMAN). Park Lane, for instance. I'd like to go into the Housing Question with you, I would.

THE FLOWER GIRL (*subsiding into a brooding melancholy over her basket, and talking very low-spiritedly to herself*). I'm a good girl, I am.

THE SARCASTIC BYSTANDER (*not attending to her*). Do you know where *I* come from?

THE NOTE TAKER (*promptly*). Hoxton.

Titterings. Popular interest in THE NOTE TAKER's *performance increases.*

THE SARCASTIC ONE (*amazed*). Well, who said I didnt? Bly me! You know everything, you do.

THE FLOWER GIRL (*still nursing her sense of injury*). Aint no call to meddle with me, he aint.

THE BYSTANDER (*to her*). Of course he aint. Dont you stand it from him. (*To* THE NOTE TAKER) See here: what call have you to know about people what never offered to meddle with you? Wheres your warrant?

SEVERAL BYSTANDERS (*encouraged by this seeming point of law*). Yes: wheres your warrant?

THE FLOWER GIRL. Let him say what he likes. I dont want to have no truck with him.

THE BYSTANDER. You take us for dirt under your feet, dont you? Catch you taking liberties with a gentleman!

THE SARCASTIC BYSTANDER. Yes: tell *him* where he come from if you want to go fortune-telling.

THE NOTE TAKER. Cheltenham, Harrow, Cambridge, and India.

THE GENTLEMAN. Quite right. (*Great laughter. Reaction in* THE NOTE TAKER's *favor. Exclamations of* He knows all about it. Told him proper. Hear him tell the toff where he come from? etc.) May I ask, sir, do you do this for your living at a music hall?

THE NOTE TAKER. Ive thought of that. Perhaps I shall some day.

The rain has stopped; and the persons on the outside of the crowd begin to drop off.

THE FLOWER GIRL (*resenting the reaction*). He's no gentleman, he aint, to interfere with a poor girl.

THE DAUGHTER (*out of patience, pushing her way rudely to the front and displacing* THE GENTLEMAN, *who politely retires to the other side of the pillar*). What on earth is Freddy doing? I shall get pneumonia if I stay in this draught any longer.

THE NOTE TAKER (*to himself, hastily making a note of her pronunciation of "monia"*). Earlscourt.

THE DAUGHTER (*violently*). Will you please keep your impertinent remarks to yourself.

THE NOTE TAKER. Did I say that out loud? I didnt mean to. I beg your pardon. Your mother's Epsom, unmistakably.

THE MOTHER (*advancing between her daughter and* THE NOTE TAKER). How very curious! I was brought up in Largelady Park, near Epsom.

THE NOTE TAKER (*uproariously amused*). Ha! ha! What a devil of a name! Excuse me. (*To* THE DAUGHTER) You want a cab, do you?

THE DAUGHTER. Dont dare speak to me.

THE MOTHER. Oh please, please, Clara. (*Her daughter repudiates her with an angry shrug and retires haughtily.*) We should be so grateful to you, sir, if you found us a cab.

(THE NOTE TAKER *produces a whistle.*) Oh, thank you. (*She joins her daughter.*)

THE NOTE TAKER *blows a piercing blast.*

THE SARCASTIC BYSTANDER. There! I knowed he was a plain-clothes copper.

THE BYSTANDER. That aint a police whistle: thats a sporting whistle.

THE FLOWER GIRL (*still preoccupied with her wounded feelings*). He's no right to take away my character. My character is the same to me as any lady's.

THE NOTE TAKER. I dont know whether youve noticed it; but the rain stopped about two minutes ago.

THE BYSTANDER. So it has. Why didnt you say so before? and us losing our time listening to your silliness! (*He walks off towards the Strand.*)

THE SARCASTIC BYSTANDER. I can tell where *you* come from. You come from Anwell. Go back there.

THE NOTE TAKER (*helpfully*). Hanwell.

THE SARCASTIC BYSTANDER (*affecting great distinction of speech*). Thenk you, teacher. Haw haw! So long (*he touches his hat with mock respect and strolls off*).

THE FLOWER GIRL. Frightening people like that! How would he like it himself?

THE MOTHER. It's quite fine now, Clara. We can walk to a motor bus. Come. (*She gathers her skirts above her ankles and hurries off towards the Strand.*)

THE DAUGHTER. But the cab—(*her mother is out of hearing*). Oh, how tiresome! (*She follows angrily.*)

All the rest have gone except THE NOTE TAKER, THE GENTLEMAN, *and* THE FLOWER GIRL, *who sits arranging her basket and still pitying herself in murmurs.*

THE FLOWER GIRL. Poor girl! Hard enough for her to live without being worried and chivied.

THE GENTLEMAN (*returning to his former place on* THE NOTE TAKER's *left*). How do you do it, if I may ask?

THE NOTE TAKER. Simply phonetics. The science of speech. Thats my profession: also my hobby. Happy is the man who can make a living by his hobby! You can spot an Irishman or a Yorkshireman by his brogue. *I* can place any man within six miles. I can place

him within two miles in London. Sometimes within two streets.

THE FLOWER GIRL. Ought to be ashamed of himself, unmanly coward!

THE GENTLEMAN. But is there a living in that?

THE NOTE TAKER. Oh yes. Quite a fat one. This is an age of upstarts. Men begin in Kentish Town with £80 a year, and end in Park Lane with a hundred thousand. They want to drop Kentish Town; but they give themselves away every time they open their mouths. Now I can teach them—

THE FLOWER GIRL. Let him mind his own business and leave a poor girl—

THE NOTE TAKER (*explosively*). Woman: cease this detestable boohooing instantly; or else seek the shelter of some other place of worship.

THE FLOWER GIRL (*with feeble defiance*). Ive a right to be here if I like, same as you.

THE NOTE TAKER. A woman who utters such depressing and disgusting sounds has no right to be anywhere—no right to live. Remember that you are a human being with a soul and the divine gift of articulate speech: that your native language is the language of Shakespear and Milton and The Bible: and dont sit there crooning like a bilious pigeon.

THE FLOWER GIRL (*quite overwhelmed, looking up at him in mingled wonder and deprecation without daring to raise her head*). Ah-ah-ah-ow-ow-ow-oo!

THE NOTE TAKER (*whipping out his book*). Heavens! what a sound! (*He writes; then holds out the book and reads, reproducing her vowels exactly.*) Ah-ah-ah-ow-ow-ow-oo!

THE FLOWER GIRL (*tickled by the performance, and laughing in spite of herself*). Garn!

THE NOTE TAKER. You see this creature with her kerbstone English: the English that will keep her in the gutter to the end of her days. Well, sir, in three months I could pass that girl off as a duchess at an ambassador's garden party. I could even get her a place as lady's maid or shop assistant, which requires better English. Thats the sort of thing I do for commercial millionaires. And on the profits of it I do genuine scientific work in phonetics, and a little as a poet on Miltonic lines.

THE GENTLEMAN. I am myself a student of Indian dialects; and—

THE NOTE TAKER (*eagerly*). Are you? Do you know Colonel Pickering, the author of Spoken Sanscrit?

THE GENTLEMAN. I *am* Colonel Pickering. Who are you?

THE NOTE TAKER. Henry Higgins, author of Higgins's Universal Alphabet.

PICKERING (*with enthusiasm*). I came from India to meet you.

HIGGINS. I was going to India to meet you.

PICKERING. Where do you live?

HIGGINS. 27A Wimpole Street. Come and see me tomorrow.

PICKERING. I'm at the Carlton. Come with me now and lets have a jaw over some supper.

HIGGINS. Right you are.

THE FLOWER GIRL (*to* PICKERING, *as he passes her*). Buy a flower, kind gentleman. I'm short for my lodging.

PICKERING. I really havnt any change. I'm sorry (*he goes away*).

HIGGINS (*shocked at the girl's mendacity*). Liar. You said you could change half-a-crown.

THE FLOWER GIRL (*rising in desperation*). You ought to be stuffed with nails, you ought. (*Flinging the basket at his feet*) Take the whole blooming basket for sixpence.

The church clock strikes the second quarter.

HIGGINS (*hearing in it the voice of God, rebuking him for his Pharisaic want of charity to the poor girl*). A reminder. (*He raises his hat solemnly; then throws a handful of money into the basket and follows* PICKERING.)

THE FLOWER GIRL (*picking up a half-crown*). Ah-ow-ooh! (*Picking up a couple of florins*) Aaah-ow-ooh! (*Picking up several coins*) Aaaaaah-ow-ooh! (*Picking up a half-sovereign*) Aaaaaaaaaaaa-ow-ooh!!!

FREDDY (*springing out of a taxicab*). Got one at last. Hallo! (*To* THE GIRL) Where are the two ladies that were here?

THE FLOWER GIRL. They walked to the bus when the rain stopped.

FREDDY. And left me with a cab on my hands! Damnation!

THE FLOWER GIRL (*with grandeur*). Never mind, young man. I'm going home in a taxi. (*She sails off to the cab. The driver puts his hand behind him and holds the door firmly shut against her. Quite understanding his mistrust, she shews him her handful of money.*) Eightpence aint no object to me, Charlie. (*He grins and opens the door.*) Angel Court, Drury Lane, round the corner of Micklejohn's oil shop. Lets see how fast you can make her hop it. (*She gets in and pulls the door to with a slam as the taxicab starts.*)

FREDDY. Well, I'm dashed!

ACT II

Next day at 11 a.m. Higgins's laboratory in Wimpole Street. It is a room on the first floor, looking on the street, and was meant for the drawing room. The double doors are in the middle of the back wall; and persons entering find in the corner to their right two tall file cabinets at right angles to one another against the walls. In this corner stands a flat writing-table, on which are a phonograph, a laryngoscope, a row of tiny organ pipes with bellows, a set of lamp chimneys for singing flames with burners attached to a gas plug in the wall by an indiarubber tube, several tuning-forks of different sizes, a life-size image of half a human head, shewing in section the vocal organs, and a box containing a supply of wax cylinders for the phonograph.

Further down the room, on the same side, is a fireplace, with a comfortable leather-covered easy-chair at the side of the hearth nearest the door, and a coal-scuttle. There is a clock on the mantelpiece. Between the fireplace and the phonograph table is a stand for newspapers.

On the other side of the central door, to the left of the visitor, is a cabinet of shallow drawers. On it is a telephone and the telephone directory. The corner beyond, and most of the side wall, is occupied by a grand piano, with the keyboard at the end furthest from the door, and a bench for the player extending the full length of the keyboard. On the piano is a dessert dish heaped with fruit and sweets, mostly chocolates.

The middle of the room is clear. Besides the easy-chair, the piano bench, and two chairs at the phonograph table, there is one stray chair. It stands near the fireplace. On the walls, engravings: mostly Piranesis and mezzotint portraits. No paintings.

PICKERING *is seated at the table, putting down some cards and a tuning-fork which he has been using.* HIGGINS *is standing up near him, closing two or three file drawers which are hanging out. He appears in the morning light as a robust, vital, appetizing sort of man of forty or thereabouts, dressed in a professional-looking black frock-coat with a white linen collar and black silk tie. He is of the energetic, scientific type, heartily, even violently interested in everything that can be studied as a scientific subject, and careless about himself and other people, including their feelings. He is, in fact, but for his years and size, rather like a very impetuous baby "taking notice" eagerly and loudly, and requiring almost as much watching to keep him out of unintended mischief. His manner varies from genial bullying when he is in a good humor to stormy petulance when anything goes wrong; but he is so entirely frank and void of malice that he remains likeable even in his least reasonable moments.*

HIGGINS (*as he shuts the last drawer*). Well, I think thats the whole show.

PICKERING. It's really amazing. I havnt taken half of it in, you know.

HIGGINS. Would you like to go over any of it again?

PICKERING (*rising and coming to the fireplace, where he plants himself with his back to the fire*). No, thank you; not now. I'm quite done up for this morning.

HIGGINS (*following him, and standing beside him on his left*). Tired of listening to sounds?

PICKERING. Yes. It's a fearful strain. I rather fancied myself because I can pronounce twenty-four distinct vowel sounds; but your hundred and thirty beat me. I cant hear a bit of difference between most of them.

HIGGINS (*chuckling, and going over to the piano to eat sweets*). Oh, that comes with practice. You hear no difference at first; but you keep on listening, and presently you find theyre all as different as A from B. (MRS PEARCE *looks in: she is Higgins's housekeeper.*) Whats the matter?

MRS PEARCE (*hesitating, evidently perplexed*). A young woman wants to see you, sir.

HIGGINS. A young woman! What does she want?

MRS PEARCE. Well, sir, she says youll be glad to see her when you know what she's

come about. She's quite a common girl, sir. Very common indeed. I should have sent her away, only I thought perhaps you wanted her to talk into your machines. I hope Ive not done wrong; but really you see such queer people sometimes—youll excuse me, I'm sure, sir—

HIGGINS. Oh, thats all right, Mrs Pearce. Has she an interesting accent?

MRS PEARCE. Oh, something dreadful, sir, really. I dont know how you can take an interest in it.

HIGGINS (*to* PICKERING). Lets have her up. Shew her up, Mrs Pearce (*he rushes across to his working table and picks out a cylinder to use on the phonograph*).

MRS PEARCE (*only half resigned to it*). Very well, sir. It's for you to say. (*She goes downstairs.*)

HIGGINS. This is rather a bit of luck. I'll shew you how I make records. We'll set her talking; and I'll take it down first in Bell's Visible Speech; then in broad Romic; and then we'll get her on the phonograph so that you can turn her on as often as you like with the written transcript before you.

MRS PEARCE (*returning*). This is the young woman, sir.

THE FLOWER GIRL *enters in state. She has a hat with three ostrich feathers, orange, sky-blue, and red. She has a nearly clean apron, and the shoddy coat has been tidied a little. The pathos of this deplorable figure, with its innocent vanity and consequential air, touches* PICKERING, *who has already straightened himself in the presence of Mrs Pearce. But as to* HIGGINS, *the only distinction he makes between men and women is that when he is neither bullying nor exclaiming to the heavens against some feather-weight cross, he coaxes women as a child coaxes its nurse when it wants to get anything out of her.*

HIGGINS (*brusquely, recognizing her with unconcealed disappointment, and at once, baby-like, making an intolerable grievance of it*). Why, this is the girl I jotted down last night. She's no use: Ive got all the records I want of the Lisson Grove lingo; and I'm not going to waste another cylinder on it. (*To* THE GIRL) Be off with you: I dont want you.

THE FLOWER GIRL. Dont you be so saucy. You

aint heard what I come for yet. (*To* MRS PEARCE, *who is waiting at the door for further instructions*) Did you tell him I come in a taxi?

MRS PEARCE. Nonsense, girl! what do you think a gentleman like Mr Higgins cares what you came in?

THE FLOWER GIRL. Oh, we are proud! He aint above giving lessons, not him: I heard him say so. Well, I aint come here to ask for any compliment; and if my money's not good enough I can go elsewhere.

HIGGINS. Good enough for what?

THE FLOWER GIRL. Good enough for ye-oo. Now you know, dont you? I'm come to have lessons, I am. And to pay for em too: make no mistake.

HIGGINS (*stupent*). Well!!! (*Recovering his breath with a gasp*) What do you expect me to say to you?

THE FLOWER GIRL. Well, if you was a gentleman, you might ask me to sit down, I think. Dont I tell you I'm bringing you business?

HIGGINS. Pickering: shall we ask this baggage to sit down, or shall we throw her out of the window?

THE FLOWER GIRL (*running away in terror to the piano, where she turns at bay*). Ah-ah-oh-ow-ow-ow-oo! (*Wounded and whimpering*) I wont be called a baggage when Ive offered to pay like any lady.

Motionless, the two men stare at her from the other side of the room, amazed.

PICKERING (*gently*). What is it you want, my girl?

THE FLOWER GIRL. I want to be a lady in a flower shop stead of selling at the corner of Tottenham Court Road. But they wont take me unless I can talk more genteel. He said he could teach me. Well, here I am ready to pay him—not asking any favor—and he treats me as if I was dirt.

MRS PEARCE. How can you be such a foolish ignorant girl as to think you could afford to pay Mr Higgins?

THE FLOWER GIRL. Why shouldnt I? I know what lessons cost as well as you do; and I'm ready to pay.

HIGGINS. How much?

THE FLOWER GIRL (*coming back to him, triumphant*). Now youre talking! I thought youd come off it when you saw a chance of getting back a bit of what you chucked at me last night. (*Confidentially*) Youd had a drop in, hadnt you?

HIGGINS (*peremptorily*). Sit down.

THE FLOWER GIRL. Oh, if youre going to make a compliment of it—

HIGGINS (*thundering at her*). Sit down.

MRS PEARCE (*severely*). Sit down, girl. Do as youre told. (*She places the stray chair near the hearthrug between* HIGGINS *and* PICKERING, *and stands behind it waiting for the girl to sit down.*)

THE FLOWER GIRL. Ah-ah-ah-ow-ow-oo! (*She stands, half rebellious, half bewildered.*)

PICKERING (*very courteous*). Wont you sit down?

THE FLOWER GIRL (*coyly*). Dont mind if I do. (*She sits down.* PICKERING *returns to the hearthrug.*)

HIGGINS. Whats your name?

THE FLOWER GIRL. Liza Doolittle.

HIGGINS (*declaiming gravely*).

Eliza, Elizabeth, Betsy and Bess,
They went to the woods to get a bird's nes':

PICKERING. They found a nest with four eggs in it:

HIGGINS. They took one apiece, and left three in it.

They laugh heartily at their own wit.

LIZA. Oh, dont be silly.

MRS PEARCE. You mustnt speak to the gentleman like that.

LIZA. Well, why wont he speak sensible to me?

HIGGINS. Come back to business. How much do you propose to pay me for the lessons?

LIZA. Oh. I know whats right. A lady friend of mine gets French lessons for eighteenpence an hour from a real French gentleman. Well, you wouldnt have the face to ask me the same for teaching me my own language as you would for French; so I wont give more than a shilling. Take it or leave it.

HIGGINS (*walking up and down the room, rattling his keys and his cash in his pockets*). You know, Pickering, if you consider a shilling, not as a simple shilling, but as a percentage of this girl's income, it works out as fully equivalent to sixty or seventy guineas from a millionaire.

PICKERING. How so?

HIGGINS. Figure it out. A millionaire has

about £150 a day. She earns about half-a-crown.

LIZA (*haughtily*). Who told you I only—

HIGGINS (*continuing*). She offers me two-fifths of her day's income for a lesson. Two-fifths of a millionaire's income for a day would be somewhere about £60. It's handsome. By George, it's enormous! it's the biggest offer I ever had.

LIZA (*rising, terrified*). Sixty pounds! What are you talking about? I never offered you sixty pounds. Where would I get—

HIGGINS. Hold your tongue.

LIZA (*weeping*). But I aint got sixty pounds. Oh—

MRS PEARCE. Dont cry, you silly girl. Sit down. Nobody is going to touch your money.

HIGGINS. Somebody is going to touch you, with a broomstick, if you dont stop snivelling. Sit down.

LIZA (*obeying slowly*). Ah-ah-ah-ow-oo-o! One would think you was my father.

HIGGINS. If I decide to teach you, I'll be worse than two fathers to you. Here (*he offers her his silk handkerchief*)!

LIZA. Whats this for?

HIGGINS. To wipe your eyes. To wipe any part of your face that feels moist. Remember: thats your handkerchief; and thats your sleeve. Dont mistake the one for the other if you wish to become a lady in a shop.

LIZA, *utterly bewildered, stares helplessly at him.*

MRS PEARCE. It's no use talking to her like that, Mr Higgins: she doesnt understand you. Besides, youre quite wrong: she doesnt do it that way at all (*she takes the handkerchief*).

LIZA (*snatching it*). Here! You give me that handkerchief. He give it to me, not to you.

PICKERING (*laughing*). He did. I think it must be regarded as her property, Mrs Pearce.

MRS PEARCE (*resigning herself*). Serve you right, Mr Higgins.

PICKERING. Higgins: I'm interested. What about the ambassador's garden party? I'll say youre the greatest teacher alive if you make that good. I'll bet you all the expenses of the experiment you cant do it. And I'll pay for the lessons.

LIZA. Oh, you are real good. Thank you, Captain.

HIGGINS (*tempted, looking at her*). It's al-most irresistible. She's so deliciously low—so horribly dirty—

LIZA (*protesting extremely*). Ah-ah-ah-ah-ow-ow-oo-oo!!! I aint dirty: I washed my face and hands afore I come, I did.

PICKERING. Youre certainly not going to turn her head with flattery, Higgins.

MRS PEARCE (*uneasy*). Oh, dont say that, sir: theres more ways than one of turning a girl's head; and nobody can do it better than Mr Higgins, though he may not always mean it. I do hope, sir, you wont encourage him to do anything foolish.

HIGGINS (*becoming excited as the idea grows on him*). What is life but a series of inspired follies? The difficulty is to find them to do. Never lose a chance: it doesnt come every day. I shall make a duchess of this draggletailed guttersnipe.

LIZA (*strongly deprecating this view of her*). Ah-ah-ah-ow-ow-oo!

HIGGINS (*carried away*). Yes: in six months—in three if she has a good ear and a quick tongue—I'll take her anywhere and pass her off as anything. We'll start today: now! this moment! Take her away and clean her, Mrs Pearce. Monkey Brand, if it wont come off any other way. Is there a good fire in the kitchen?

MRS PEARCE (*protesting*). Yes; but—

HIGGINS (*storming on*). Take all her clothes off and burn them. Ring up Whiteley or somebody for new ones. Wrap her up in brown paper til they come.

LIZA. Youre no gentleman, youre not, to talk of such things. I'm a good girl, I am; and I know what the like of you are, I do.

HIGGINS. We want none of your Lisson Grove prudery here, young woman. Youve got to learn to behave like a duchess. Take her away, Mrs Pearce. If she gives you any trouble, wallop her.

LIZA (*springing up and running between PICKERING and MRS PEARCE for protection*). No! I'll call the police, I will.

MRS PEARCE. But Ive no place to put her.

HIGGINS. Put her in the dustbin.

LIZA. Ah-ah-ah-ow-ow-oo!

PICKERING. Oh come, Higgins! be reasonable.

MRS PEARCE (*resolutely*). You *must* be reasonable, Mr Higgins: really you must. You cant walk over everybody like this.

HIGGINS, *thus scolded, subsides. The hurricane is succeeded by a zephyr of amiable surprise.*

HIGGINS (*with professional exquisiteness of modulation*). *I* walk over everybody! My dear Mrs Pearce, my dear Pickering, I never had the slightest intention of walking over anyone. All I propose is that we should be kind to this poor girl. We must help her to prepare and fit herself for her new station in life. If I did not express myself clearly it was because I did not wish to hurt her delicacy, or yours.

LIZA, *reassured, steals back to her chair.*

MRS PEARCE (*to* PICKERING). Well, did you ever hear anything like that, sir?

PICKERING (*laughing heartily*). Never, Mrs Pearce: never.

HIGGINS (*patiently*). Whats the matter?

MRS PEARCE. Well, the matter is, sir, that you cant take a girl up like that as if you were picking up a pebble on the beach.

HIGGINS. Why not?

MRS PEARCE. Why not! But you dont know anything about her. What about her parents? She may be married.

LIZA. Garn!

HIGGINS. There! As the girl very properly says, Garn! Married indeed! Dont you know that a woman of that class looks a worn out drudge of fifty a year after she's married?

LIZA. Whood marry me?

HIGGINS (*suddenly resorting to the most thrillingly beautiful low tones in his best elocutionary style*). By George, Eliza, the streets will be strewn with the bodies of men shooting themselves for your sake before Ive done with you.

MRS PEARCE. Nonsense, sir. You mustnt talk like that to her.

LIZA (*rising and squaring herself determinedly*). I'm going away. He's off his chump, he is. I dont want no balmies teaching me.

HIGGINS (*wounded in his tenderest point by her insensibility to his elocution*). Oh, indeed! I'm mad, am I? Very well, Mrs Pearce: you neednt order the new clothes for her. Throw her out.

LIZA (*whimpering*). Nah-ow. You got no right to touch me.

MRS PEARCE. You see now what comes of being saucy. (*Indicating the door*) This way, please.

LIZA (*almost in tears*). I didnt want no clothes. I wouldnt have taken them (*she throws away the handkerchief*). I can buy my own clothes.

HIGGINS (*deftly retrieving the handkerchief and intercepting her on her reluctant way to the door*). Youre an ungrateful wicked girl. This is my return for offering to take you out of the gutter and dress you beautifully and make a lady of you.

MRS PEARCE. Stop, Mr Higgins. I wont allow it. It's you that are wicked. Go home to your parents, girl; and tell them to take better care of you.

LIZA. I ain't got no parents. They told me I was big enough to earn my own living and turned me out.

MRS PEARCE. Wheres your mother?

LIZA. I aint got no mother. Her that turned me out was my sixth stepmother. But I done without them. And I'm a good girl, I am.

HIGGINS. Very well, then, what on earth is all this fuss about? The girl doesnt belong to anybody—is no use to anybody but me. (*He goes to* MRS PEARCE *and begins coaxing.*) You can adopt her, Mrs Pearce: I'm sure a daughter would be a great amusement to you. Now dont make any more fuss. Take her downstairs; and—

MRS PEARCE. But whats to become of her? Is she to be paid anything? Do be sensible, sir.

HIGGINS. Oh, pay her whatever is necessary: put it down in the housekeeping book. (*Impatiently*) What on earth will she want with money? She'll have her food and her clothes. She'll only drink if you give her money.

LIZA (*turning on him*). Oh you *are* a brute. It's a lie: nobody ever saw the sign of liquor on me. (*She goes back to her chair and plants herself there defiantly.*)

PICKERING (*in good-humored remonstrance*). Does it occur to you, Higgins, that the girl has some feelings?

HIGGINS (*looking critically at her*). Oh no, I dont think so. Not any feelings that we need bother about. (*Cheerily*) Have you, Eliza?

LIZA. I got my feelings same as anyone else.

HIGGINS (*to* PICKERING, *reflectively*). You see the difficulty?

PICKERING. Eh? What difficulty?

HIGGINS. To get her to talk grammar. The mere pronunciation is easy enough.

LIZA. I dont want to talk grammar. I want to talk like a lady.

MRS PEARCE. Will you please keep to the point, Mr Higgins? I want to know on what terms the girl is to be here. Is she to have any wages? And what is to become of her when youve finished your teaching? You must look ahead a little.

HIGGINS (impatiently). Whats to become of her if I leave her in the gutter? Tell me that, Mrs Pearce.

MRS PEARCE. Thats her own business, not yours, Mr Higgins.

HIGGINS. Well, when Ive done with her, we can throw her back into the gutter; and then it will be her own business again; so thats all right.

LIZA. Oh, youve no feeling heart in you: you dont care for nothing but yourself (she rises and takes the floor resolutely). Here! Ive had enough of this. I'm going (making for the door). You ought to be ashamed of yourself, you ought.

HIGGINS (snatching a chocolate cream from the piano, his eyes suddenly beginning to twinkle with mischief). Have some chocolates, Eliza.

LIZA (halting, tempted). How do I know what might be in them? Ive heard of girls being drugged by the like of you.

HIGGINS whips out his penknife; cuts a chocolate in two; puts one half into his mouth and bolts it; and offers her the other half.

HIGGINS. Pledge of good faith, Eliza. I eat one half: you eat the other. (LIZA opens her mouth to retort: he pops the half chocolate into it.) You shall have boxes of them, barrels of them, every day. You shall live on them. Eh?

LIZA (who has disposed of the chocolate after being nearly choked by it). I wouldnt have ate it, only I'm too ladylike to take it out of my mouth.

HIGGINS. Listen, Eliza. I think you said you came in a taxi.

LIZA. Well, what if I did? Ive as good a right to take a taxi as anyone else.

HIGGINS. You have, Eliza; and in future you shall have as many taxis as you want. You shall go up and down and round the town in a taxi every day. Think of that, Eliza.

MRS PEARCE. Mr Higgins: youre tempting the girl. It's not right. She should think of the future.

HIGGINS. At her age! Nonsense! Time enough to think of the future when you havnt any future to think of. No, Eliza: do as this lady does: think of other people's futures; but never think of your own. Think of chocolates, and taxis, and gold, and diamonds.

LIZA. No: I dont want no gold and no diamonds. I'm a good girl, I am. (She sits down again, with an attempt at dignity.)

HIGGINS. You shall remain so, Eliza, under the care of Mrs Pearce. And you shall marry an officer in the Guards, with a beautiful moustache: the son of a marquis, who will disinherit him for marrying you, but will relent when he sees your beauty and goodness—

PICKERING. Excuse me, Higgins; but I really must interfere. Mrs Pearce is quite right. If this girl is to put herself in your hands for six months for an experiment in teaching, she must understand thoroughly what she's doing.

HIGGINS. How can she? She's incapable of understanding anything. Besides, do any of us understand what we are doing? If we did, would we ever do it?

PICKERING. Very clever, Higgins; but not sound sense. (To ELIZA) Miss Doolittle—

LIZA (overwhelmed). Ah-ah-ow-oo!

HIGGINS. There! Thats all youll get out of Eliza. Ah-ah-ow-oo! No use explaining. As a military man you ought to know that. Give her her orders: thats what she wants. Eliza: you are to live here for the next six months, learning how to speak beautifully, like a lady in a florist's shop. If youre good and do whatever youre told, you shall sleep in a proper bedroom, and have lots to eat, and money to buy chocolates and take rides in taxis. If youre naughty and idle you will sleep in the back kitchen among the black beetles, and be walloped by Mrs Pearce with a broomstick. At the end of six months you shall go to Buckingham Palace in a carriage, beautifully dressed. If the King finds out youre not a lady, you will be taken by the police to the Tower of London, where your head will be cut off as a warning to other presumptuous flower girls. If you are not found out, you shall have a present of seven-and-sixpence to start life with as a lady in a shop. If you refuse this offer you will be a most ungrateful and wicked girl; and the angels will weep for you. (*To* PICKERING) Now are you satisfied, Pickering? (*To* MRS PEARCE) Can I put it more plainly and fairly, Mrs Pearce?

MRS PEARCE (*patiently*). I think youd better let me speak to the girl properly in private. I dont know that I can take charge of her or consent to the arrangement at all. Of course I know you dont mean her any harm; but when you get what you call interested in people's accents, you never think or care what may happen to them or you. Come with me, Eliza.

HIGGINS. Thats all right. Thank you, Mrs Pearce. Bundle her off to the bathroom.

LIZA (*rising reluctantly and suspiciously*). Youre a great bully, you are. I wont stay here if I dont like. I wont let nobody wallop me. I never asked to go to Bucknam Palace, I didnt. I was never in trouble with the police, not me. I'm a good girl—

MRS PEARCE. Dont answer back, girl. You dont understand the gentleman. Come with me. (*She leads the way to the door, and holds it open for* ELIZA.)

LIZA (*as she goes out*). Well, what I say is right. I wont go near the King, not if I'm going to have my head cut off. If I'd known what I was letting myself in for, I wouldnt have come here. I always been a good girl; and I never offered to say a word to him; and I dont owe him nothing; and I dont care; and I wont be put upon; and I have my feelings the same as anyone else—

MRS PEARCE *shuts the door; and* ELIZA's *plaints are no longer audible.* PICKERING *comes from the hearth to the chair and sits astride it with his arms on the back.*

PICKERING. Excuse the straight question, Higgins. Are you a man of good character where women are concerned?

HIGGINS (*moodily*). Have you ever met a man of good character where women are concerned?

PICKERING. Yes: very frequently.

HIGGINS (*dogmatically, lifting himself on his hands to the level of the piano, and sitting on it with a bounce*). Well, I havnt. I find that the moment I let a woman make friends with me, she becomes jealous, exacting, suspicious, and a damned nuisance. I find that the moment I let myself make friends with a woman, I become selfish and tyrannical. Women upset everything. When you let them into your life, you find that the woman is driving at one thing and youre driving at another.

PICKERING. At what, for example?

HIGGINS (*coming off the piano restlessly*). Oh, Lord knows! I suppose the woman wants to live her own life; and the man wants to live his; and each tries to drag the other on to the wrong track. One wants to go north and the other south; and the result is that both have to go east, though they both hate the east wind. (*He sits down on the bench at the keyboard.*) So here I am, a confirmed old bachelor, and likely to remain so.

PICKERING (*rising and standing over him gravely*). Come, Higgins! You know what I mean. If I'm to be in this business I shall feel responsible for that girl. I hope it's understood that no advantage is to be taken of her position.

HIGGINS. What! That thing! Sacred, I assure you. (*Rising to explain*) You see, she'll be a pupil; and teaching would be impossible unless pupils were sacred. Ive taught scores of American millionairesses how to speak English: the best looking women in the world. I'm seasoned. They might as well be blocks of wood. *I* might as well be a block of wood. It's—

MRS PEARCE *opens the door. She has Eliza's hat in her hand.* PICKERING *retires to the easy-chair at the hearth and sits down.*

HIGGINS (*eagerly*). Well, Mrs Pearce: is it all right?

MRS PEARCE (*at the door*). I just wish to trouble you with a word, if I may, Mr Higgins.

HIGGINS. Yes, certainly. Come in. (*She comes forward.*) Dont burn that, Mrs Pearce. I'll keep it as a curiosity. (*He takes the hat.*)

MRS PEARCE. Handle it carefully, sir, *please*. I had to promise her not to burn it; but I had better put it in the oven for a while.

HIGGINS (*putting it down hastily on the piano*). Oh! thank you. Well, what have you to say to me?

PICKERING. Am I in the way?

MRS PEARCE. Not at all, sir. Mr Higgins: will

you please be very particular what you say before the girl?

HIGGINS (*sternly*). Of course. I'm always particular about what I say. Why do you say this to me?

MRS PEARCE (*unmoved*). No, sir: youre not at all particular when youve mislaid anything or when you get a little impatient. Now it doesnt matter before me: I'm used to it. But you really must not swear before the girl.

HIGGINS (*indignantly*). *I* swear! (*Most emphatically*) I never swear. I detest the habit. What the devil do you mean?

MRS PEARCE (*stolidly*). Thats what I mean, sir. You swear a great deal too much. I dont mind your damning and blasting, and *what* the devil and *where* the devil and *who* the devil—

HIGGINS. Mrs Pearce: this language from your lips! Really!

MRS PEARCE (*not to be put off*)—but there is a certain word I must ask you not to use. The girl has just used it herself because the bath was too hot. It begins with the same letter as bath. She knows no better: she learnt it at her mother's knee. But she must not hear it from *your* lips.

HIGGINS (*loftily*). I cannot charge myself with having ever uttered it, Mrs Pearce. (*She looks at him steadfastly. He adds, hiding an uneasy conscience with a judicial air*) Except perhaps in a moment of extreme and justifiable excitement.

MRS PEARCE. Only this morning, sir, you applied it to your boots, to the butter, and to the brown bread.

HIGGINS. Oh, that! Mere alliteration, Mrs Pearce, natural to a poet.

MRS PEARCE. Well, sir, whatever you choose to call it, I beg you not to let the girl hear you repeat it.

HIGGINS. Oh, very well, very well. Is that all?

MRS PEARCE. No, sir. We shall have to be very particular with this girl as to personal cleanliness.

HIGGINS. Certainly. Quite right. Most important.

MRS PEARCE. I mean not to be slovenly about her dress or untidy in leaving things about.

HIGGINS (*going to her solemnly*). Just so. I intended to call your attention to that. (*He passes on to* PICKERING, *who is enjoying the*

conversation *immensely*.) It is these little things that matter, Pickering. Take care of the pence and the pounds will take care of themselves is as true of personal habits as of money. (*He comes to anchor on the hearthrug, with the air of a man in an unassailable position.*)

MRS PEARCE. Yes, sir. Then might I ask you not to come down to breakfast in your dressing-gown, or at any rate not to use it as a napkin to the extent you do, sir. And if you would be so good as not to eat everything off the same plate, and to remember not to put the porridge saucepan out of your hand on the clean tablecloth, it would be a better example to the girl. You know you nearly choked yourself with a fishbone in the jam only last week.

HIGGINS (*routed from the hearthrug and drifting back to the piano*). I may do these things sometimes in absence of mind; but surely I dont do them habitually. (*Angrily*) By the way: my dressing-gown smells most damnably of benzine.

MRS PEARCE. No doubt it does, Mr Higgins. But if you *will* wipe your fingers—

HIGGINS (*yelling*). Oh very well, very well: I'll wipe them in my hair in future.

MRS PEARCE. I hope youre not offended, Mr Higgins.

HIGGINS (*shocked at finding himself thought capable of an unamiable sentiment*). Not at all, not at all. Youre quite right, Mrs Pearce: I shall be particularly careful before the girl. Is that all?

MRS PEARCE. No, sir. Might she use some of those Japanese dresses you brought from abroad? I really cant put her back into her old things.

HIGGINS. Certainly. Anything you like. Is *that* all?

MRS PEARCE. Thank you, sir. Thats all. (*She goes out.*)

HIGGINS. You know, Pickering, that woman has the most extraordinary ideas about me. Here I am, a shy, diffident sort of man. Ive never been able to feel really grown-up and tremendous, like other chaps. And yet she's firmly persuaded that I'm an arbitrary overbearing bossing kind of person. I cant account for it.

MRS PEARCE *returns*.

MRS PEARCE. If you please, sir, the trouble's beginning already. Theres a dustman downstairs, Alfred Doolittle, wants to see you. He says you have his daughter here.

PICKERING (*rising*). Phew! I say! (*He retreats to the hearthrug.*)

HIGGINS (*promptly*). Send the blackguard up.

MRS PEARCE. Oh, very well, sir. (*She goes out.*)

PICKERING. He may not be a blackguard, Higgins.

HIGGINS. Nonsense. Of course he's a blackguard.

PICKERING. Whether he is or not, I'm afraid we shall have some trouble with him.

HIGGINS (*confidently*). Oh no: I think not. If theres any trouble he shall have it with me, not I with him. And we are sure to get something interesting out of him.

PICKERING. About the girl?

HIGGINS. No. I mean his dialect.

PICKERING. Oh!

MRS PEARCE (*at the door*). Doolittle, sir. (*She admits* DOOLITTLE *and retires.*)

ALFRED DOOLITTLE *is an elderly but vigorous dustman, clad in the costume of his profession, including a hat with a black brim covering his neck and shoulders. He has well marked and rather interesting features, and seems equally free from fear and conscience. He has a remarkably expressive voice, the result of a habit of giving vent to his feelings without reserve. His present pose is that of wounded honor and stern resolution.*

DOOLITTLE (*at the door, uncertain which of the two gentlemen is his man*). Professor Higgins?

HIGGINS. Here. Good morning. Sit down.

DOOLITTLE. Morning, Governor. (*He sits down magisterially.*) I come about a very serious matter, Governor.

HIGGINS (*to* PICKERING). Brought up in Hounslow. Mother Welsh, I should think. (DOOLITTLE *opens his mouth, amazed.* HIGGINS *continues*) What do you want, Doolittle?

DOOLITTLE (*menacingly*). I want my daughter: thats what I want. See?

HIGGINS. Of course you do. Youre her father, arnt you? You dont suppose anyone else wants her, do you? I'm glad to see you have some spark of family feeling left. She's upstairs. Take her away at once.

DOOLITTLE (*rising, fearfully taken aback*). What!

HIGGINS. Take her away. Do you suppose I'm going to keep your daughter for you?

DOOLITTLE (*remonstrating*). Now, now, look here, Governor. Is this reasonable? Is it fairity to take advantage of a man like this? The girl belongs to me. You got her. Where do I come in? (*He sits down again.*)

HIGGINS. Your daughter had the audacity to come to my house and ask me to teach her how to speak properly so that she could get a place in a flower shop. This gentleman and my housekeeper have been here all the time. (*Bullying him*) How dare you come here and attempt to blackmail me? You sent her here on purpose.

DOOLITTLE (*protesting*). No, Governor.

HIGGINS. You must have. How else could you possibly know that she is here?

DOOLITTLE. Dont take a man up like that, Governor.

HIGGINS. The police shall take you up. This is a plant—a plot to extort money by threats. I shall telephone for the police. (*He goes resolutely to the telephone and opens the directory.*)

DOOLITTLE. Have I asked you for a brass farthing? I leave it to the gentleman here: have I said a word about money?

HIGGINS (*throwing the book aside and marching down on* DOOLITTLE *with a poser*). What else did you come for?

DOOLITTLE (*sweetly*). Well, what *would* a man come for? Be human, Governor.

HIGGINS (*disarmed*). Alfred: did you put her up to it?

DOOLITTLE. So help me, Governor, I never did. I take my Bible oath I aint seen the girl these two months past.

HIGGINS. Then how did you know she was here?

DOOLITTLE (*"most musical, most melancholy"*). I'll tell you, Governor, if youll only let me get a word in. I'm willing to tell you. I'm wanting to tell you. I'm waiting to tell you.

HIGGINS. Pickering: this chap has a certain natural gift of rhetoric. Observe the rhythm of his native woodnotes wild. "I'm willing to tell you: I'm wanting to tell you: I'm waiting to tell you." Sentimental rhetoric! thats the

Welsh strain in him. It also accounts for his mendacity and dishonesty.

PICKERING. Oh, *please*, Higgins: I'm west country myself. (*To* DOOLITTLE) How did you know the girl was here if you didnt send her?

DOOLITTLE. It was like this, Governor. The girl took a boy in the taxi to give him a jaunt. Son of her landlady, he is. He hung about on the chance of her giving him another ride home. Well, she sent him back for her luggage when she heard you was willing for her to stop here. I met the boy at the corner of Long Acre and Endell Street.

HIGGINS. Public house. Yes?

DOOLITTLE. The poor man's club, Governor: why shouldnt I?

PICKERING. Do let him tell his story, Higgins.

DOOLITTLE. He told me what was up. And I ask you, what was my feelings and my duty as a father? I says to the boy, "You bring me the luggage," I says--

PICKERING. Why didnt you go for it yourself?

DOOLITTLE. Landlady wouldnt have trusted me with it, Governor. She's that kind of woman: you know. I had to give the boy a penny afore he trusted me with it, the little swine. I brought it to her just to oblige you like, and make myself agreeable. Thats all.

HIGGINS. How much luggage?

DOOLITTLE. Musical instrument, Governor. A few pictures, a trifle of jewelry, and a bird-cage. She said she didnt want no clothes. What was I to think from that, Governor? I ask you as a parent what was I to think?

HIGGINS. So you came to rescue her from worse than death, eh?

DOOLITTLE (*appreciatively: relieved at being so well understood*). Just so, Governor. Thats right.

PICKERING. But why did you bring her luggage if you intended to take her away?

DOOLITTLE. Have I said a word about taking her away? Have I now?

HIGGINS (*determinedly*). Youre going to take her away, double quick. (*He crosses to the hearth and rings the bell.*)

DOOLITTLE (*rising*). No, Governor. Dont say that. I'm not the man to stand in my girl's light. Heres a career opening for her, as you might say; and--

MRS PEARCE *opens the door and awaits orders.*

HIGGINS. Mrs Pearce: this is Eliza's father. He has come to take her away. Give her to him. (*He goes back to the piano, with an air of washing his hands of the whole affair.*)

DOOLITTLE. No. This is a misunderstanding. Listen here--

MRS PEARCE. He cant take her away, Mr Higgins: how can he? You told me to burn her clothes.

DOOLITTLE. Thats right. I cant carry the girl through the streets like a blooming monkey, can I? I put it to you.

HIGGINS. You have put it to me that you want your daughter. Take your daughter. If she has no clothes go out and buy her some.

DOOLITTLE (*desperate*). Wheres the clothes she come in? Did I burn them or did your missus here?

MRS PEARCE. I am the housekeeper, if you please. I have sent for some clothes for your girl. When they come you can take her away. You can wait in the kitchen. This way, please.

DOOLITTLE, *much troubled, accompanies her to the door; then hesitates; finally turns confidently to* HIGGINS.

DOOLITTLE. Listen here, Governor. You and me is men of the world, aint we?

HIGGINS. Oh! Men of the world, are we? Youd better go, Mrs Pearce.

MRS PEARCE. I think so, indeed, sir. (*She goes, with dignity.*)

PICKERING. The floor is yours, Mr Doolittle.

DOOLITTLE (*to* PICKERING). I thank you, Governor. (*To* HIGGINS, *who takes refuge on the piano bench, a little overwhelmed by the proximity of his visitor; for* DOOLITTLE *has a professional flavor of dust about him*) Well, the truth is, Ive taken a sort of fancy to you, Governor; and if you want the girl, I'm not so set on having her back home again but what I might be open to an arrangement. Regarded in the light of a young woman, she's a fine handsome girl. As a daughter she's not worth her keep; and so I tell you straight. All I ask is my rights as a father; and youre the last man alive to expect me to let her go for nothing; for I can see youre one of the straight sort, Governor. Well, whats a five-pound note to you? And whats Eliza to me? (*He returns to his chair and sits down judicially.*)

PICKERING. I think you ought to know, Doolittle, that Mr Higgins's intentions are entirely honorable.

DOOLITTLE. Course they are, Governor. If I thought they wasnt, I'd ask fifty.

HIGGINS (*revolted*). Do you mean to say, you callous rascal, that you would sell your daughter for £50?

DOOLITTLE. Not in a general way I wouldnt; but to oblige a gentleman like you I'd do a good deal, I do assure you.

PICKERING. Have you no morals, man?

DOOLITTLE (*unabashed*). Cant afford them, Governor. Neither could you if you was as poor as me. Not that I mean any harm, you know. But if Liza is going to have a bit out of this, why not me too?

HIGGINS (*troubled*). I dont know what to do, Pickering. There can be no question that as a matter of morals it's a positive crime to give this chap a farthing. And yet I feel a sort of rough justice in his claim.

DOOLITTLE. Thats it, Governor. Thats all I say. A father's heart, as it were.

PICKERING. Well, I know the feeling; but really it seems hardly right—

DOOLITTLE. Dont say that, Governor. Dont look at it that way. What am I, Governors both? I ask you, what am I? I'm one of the undeserving poor: thats what I am. Think of what that means to a man. It means that he's up agen middle class morality all the time. If theres anything going, and I put in for a bit of it, it's always the same story: "Youre undeserving; so you cant have it." But my needs is as great as the most deserving widow's that ever got money out of six different charities in one week for the death of the same husband. I dont need less than a deserving man: I need more. I dont eat less hearty than him; and I drink a lot more. I want a bit of amusement, cause I'm a thinking man. I want cheerfulness and a song and a band when I feel low. Well, they charge me just the same for everything as they charge the deserving. What is middle class morality? Just an excuse for never giving me anything. Therefore, I ask you, as two gentlemen, not to play that game on me. I'm playing straight with you. I aint pretending to be deserving. I'm undeserving; and I mean to go on being undeserving. I like it; and thats the truth. Will you

take advantage of a man's nature to do him out of the price of his own daughter what he's brought up and fed and clothed by the sweat of his brow until she's growed big enough to be interesting to you two gentlemen? Is five pounds unreasonable? I put it to you; and I leave it to you.

HIGGINS (*rising, and going over to* PICKERING). Pickering: if we were to take this man in hand for three months, he could choose between a seat in the Cabinet and a popular pulpit in Wales.

PICKERING. What do you say to that, Doolittle?

DOOLITTLE. Not me, Governor, thank you kindly. Ive heard all the preachers and all the prime ministers—for I'm a thinking man and game for politics or religion or social reform same as all the other amusements—and I tell you it's a dog's life any way you look at it. Undeserving poverty is my line. Taking one station in society with another, it's—it's—well, it's the only one that has any ginger in it, to my taste.

HIGGINS. I suppose we must give him a fiver.

PICKERING. He'll make a bad use of it, I'm afraid.

DOOLITTLE. Not me, Governor, so help me I wont. Dont you be afraid that I'll save it and spare it and live idle on it. There wont be a penny of it left by Monday: I'll have to go to work same as if I'd never had it. It wont pauperize me, you bet. Just one good spree for myself and the missus, giving pleasure to ourselves and employment to others, and satisfaction to you to think it's not been throwed away. You couldnt spend it better.

HIGGINS (*taking out his pocket book and coming between* DOOLITTLE *and the piano*). This is irresistible. Lets give him ten. (*He offers two notes to the dustman.*)

DOOLITTLE. No, Governor. She wouldnt have the heart to spend ten; and perhaps I shouldnt neither. Ten pounds is a lot of money: it makes a man feel prudent like; and then goodbye to happiness. You give me what I ask you, Governor: not a penny more, and not a penny less.

PICKERING. Why dont you marry that missus of yours? I rather draw the line at encouraging that sort of immorality.

DOOLITTLE. Tell her so, Governor: tell her so. I'm willing. It's me that suffers by it. Ive no hold on her. I got to be agreeable to her. I got to give her presents. I got to buy her clothes something sinful. I'm a slave to that woman, Governor, just because I'm not her lawful husband. And she knows it too. Catch her marrying me! Take my advice, Governor: marry Eliza while she's young and dont know no better. If you dont youll be sorry for it after. If you do, *she'll* be sorry for it after; but better her than you, because youre a man, and she's only a woman and dont know how to be happy anyhow.

HIGGINS. Pickering: if we listen to this man another minute, we shall have no convictions left. (*To* DOOLITTLE) Five pounds I think you said.

DOOLITTLE. Thank you kindly, Governor.

HIGGINS. Youre sure you wont take ten?

DOOLITTLE. Not now. Another time, Governor.

HIGGINS (*handing him a five-pound note*). Here you are.

DOOLITTLE. Thank you, Governor. Good morning. (*He hurries to the door, anxious to get away with his booty. When he opens it he is confronted with a dainty and exquisitely clean young Japanese lady in a simple blue cotton kimono printed cunningly with small white jasmine blossoms.* MRS PEARCE *is with her. He gets out of her way deferentially and apologizes.*) Beg pardon, miss.

THE JAPANESE LADY. Garn! Dont you know your own daughter?

DOOLITTLE. ⎤ (*exclaiming* ⎡ Bly me! it's Eliza!
HIGGINS. ⎬ *simul-* ⎨ Whats that! This!
PICKERING. ⎦ *taneously*) ⎣ By Jove!

LIZA. Dont I look silly?

HIGGINS. Silly?

MRS PEARCE (*at the door*). Now, Mr Higgins, please dont say anything to make the girl conceited about herself.

HIGGINS (*conscientiously*). Oh! Quite right, Mrs Pearce. (*To* ELIZA) Yes: damned silly.

MRS PEARCE. Please, sir.

HIGGINS (*correcting himself*). I mean extremely silly.

LIZA. I should look all right with my hat on. (*She takes up her hat; puts it on; and walks across the room to the fireplace with a fashionable air.*)

HIGGINS. A new fashion, by George! And it ought to look horrible!

DOOLITTLE (*with fatherly pride*). Well, I never thought she'd clean up as good looking as that, Governor. She's a credit to me, aint she?

LIZA. I tell you, it's easy to clean up here. Hot and cold water on tap, just as much as you like, there is. Woolly towels, there is; and a towel horse so hot, it burns your fingers. Soft brushes to scrub yourself, and a wooden bowl of soap smelling like primroses. Now I know why ladies is so clean. Washing's a treat for them. Wish they saw what it is for the like of me!

HIGGINS. I'm glad the bathroom met with your approval.

LIZA. It didnt: not all of it; and I dont care who hears me say it. Mrs Pearce knows.

HIGGINS. What was wrong, Mrs Pearce?

MRS PEARCE (*blandly*). Oh, nothing, sir. It doesnt matter.

LIZA. I had a good mind to break it. I didnt know which way to look. But I hung a towel over it, I did.

HIGGINS. Over what?

MRS PEARCE. Over the looking glass, sir.

HIGGINS. Doolittle: you have brought your daughter up too strictly.

DOOLITTLE. Me! I never brought her up at all, except to give her a lick of a strap now and again. Dont put it on me, Governor. She aint accustomed to it, you see: thats all. But she'll soon pick up your free-and-easy ways.

LIZA. I'm a good girl, I am; and I wont pick up no free-and-easy ways.

HIGGINS. Eliza: if you say again that youre a good girl, your father shall take you home.

LIZA. Not him. You dont know my father. All he come here for was to touch you for some money to get drunk on.

DOOLITTLE. Well, what else would I want money for? To put into the plate in church, I suppose. (*She puts out her tongue at him. He is so incensed by this that* PICKERING *presently finds it necessary to step between them.*) Dont you give me none of your lip; and dont let me hear you giving this gentleman any of it neither, or youll hear from me about it. See?

HIGGINS. Have you any further advice to

give her before you go, Doolittle? Your blessing, for instance.

DOOLITTLE. No, Governor: I aint such a
mug as to put up my children to all I know
myself. Hard enough to hold them in without that. If you want Eliza's mind improved,
Governor, you do it yourself with a strap. So
long, gentlemen. (*He turns to go.*)

HIGGINS (*impressively*). Stop. Youll come
regularly to see your daughter. It's your duty,
you know. My brother is a clergyman; and he
could help you in your talks with her.

DOOLITTLE (*evasively*). Certainly. I'll come,
Governor. Not just this week, because I have
a job at a distance. But later on you may
depend on me. Afternoon, gentlemen. Afternoon, maam. (*He takes off his hat to* MRS
PEARCE, *who disdains the salutation and goes
out. He winks at* HIGGINS, *thinking him probably a fellow-sufferer from* MRS PEARCE'S *difficult disposition, and follows her.*)

LIZA. Dont you believe the old liar. He'd
as soon you set a bull-dog on him as a clergyman. You wont see him again in a hurry.

HIGGINS. I dont want to, Eliza. Do you?

LIZA. Not me. I dont want never to see him
again, I dont. He's a disgrace to me, he is, collecting dust, instead of working at his trade.

PICKERING. What is his trade, Eliza?

LIZA. Taking money out of other people's
pockets into his own. His proper trade's a
navvy; and he works at it sometimes too—for
exercise—and earns good money at it. Aint
you going to call me Miss Doolittle any
more?

PICKERING. I beg your pardon, Miss Doolittle. It was a slip of the tongue.

LIZA. Oh, I dont mind; only it sounded so
genteel. I *should* just like to take a taxi to
the corner of Tottenham Court Road and
get out there and tell it to wait for me, just
to put the girls in their place a bit. I wouldnt
speak to them, you know.

PICKERING. Better wait til we get you something really fashionable.

HIGGINS. Besides, you shouldnt cut your old
friends now that you have risen in the world.
Thats what we call snobbery.

LIZA. You dont call the like of them my
friends now, I should hope. Theyve took it
out of me often enough with their ridicule
when they had the chance; and now I mean

to get a bit of my own back. But if I'm to
have fashionable clothes, I'll wait. I should
like to have some. Mrs Pearce says youre
going to give me some to wear in bed at night
different to what I wear in the daytime; but
it do seem a waste of money when you could
get something to shew. Besides, I never could
fancy changing into cold things on a winter
night.

MRS PEARCE (*coming back*). Now, Eliza. The
new things have come for you to try on.

LIZA. Ah-ow-oo-ooh! (*She rushes out.*)

MRS PEARCE (*following her*). Oh, dont rush
about like that, girl. (*She shuts the door behind her.*)

HIGGINS. Pickering: we have taken on a stiff
job.

PICKERING (*with conviction*). Higgins: we
have.

ACT III

It is MRS HIGGINS'S *at-home day. Nobody
has yet arrived. Her drawing room, in a flat
on Chelsea Embankment, has three windows
looking on the river; and the ceiling is not so
lofty as it would be in an older house of the
same pretension. The windows are open, giving access to a balcony with flowers in pots.
If you stand with your face to the windows,
you have the fireplace on your left and the
door in the right-hand wall close to the corner
nearest the windows.*

MRS HIGGINS *was brought up on Morris and
Burne Jones; and her room, which is very unlike her son's room in Wimpole Street, is not
crowded with furniture and little tables and
nicknacks. In the middle of the room there
is a big ottoman; and this, with the carpet,
the Morris wall-papers, and the Morris chintz
window curtains and brocade covers of the
ottoman and its cushions, supply all the ornament, and are much too handsome to be
hidden by odds and ends of useless things. A
few good oil-paintings from the exhibitions
in the Grosvenor Gallery thirty years ago (the
Burne Jones, not the Whistler side of them)
are on the walls. The only landscape is a
Cecil Lawson on the scale of a Rubens. There
is a portrait of* MRS HIGGINS *as she was when
she defied fashion in her youth in one of
the beautiful Rosettian costumes which, when*

*caricatured by people who did not understand,
led to the absurdities of popular estheticism
in the eighteen-seventies.*

In the corner diagonally opposite the door
MRS HIGGINS, *now over sixty and long past
taking the trouble to dress out of the fashion,
sits writing at an elegantly simple writing-
table with a bell button within reach of her
hand. There is a Chippendale chair further
back in the room between her and the window nearest her side. At the other side of the
room, further forward, is an Elizabethan chair
roughly carved in the taste of Inigo Jones. On
the same side a piano in a decorated case.
The corner between the fireplace and the window is occupied by a divan cushioned in
Morris chintz.*

*It is between four and five in the afternoon.
The door is opened violently; and* HIGGINS
enters with his hat on.

MRS HIGGINS (*dismayed*). Henry (*scolding
him*)! What are you doing here today? It is
my at-home day: you promised not to come.
(*As he bends to kiss her, she takes his hat off,
and presents it to him.*)

HIGGINS. Oh bother! (*He throws the hat
down on the table.*)

MRS HIGGINS. Go home at once.

HIGGINS (*kissing her*). I know, mother. I
came on purpose.

MRS HIGGINS. But you mustnt. I'm serious,
Henry. You offend all my friends: they stop
coming whenever they meet you.

HIGGINS. Nonsense! I know I have no small
talk; but people dont mind. (*He sits on the
settee.*)

MRS HIGGINS. Oh! dont they? Small talk indeed! What about your large talk? Really,
dear, you mustnt stay.

HIGGINS. I must. Ive a job for you. A phonetic job.

MRS HIGGINS. No use, dear. I'm sorry; but
I cant get round your vowels; and though I
like to get pretty postcards in your patent
shorthand, I always have to read the copies
in ordinary writing you so thoughtfully send
me.

HIGGINS. Well, this isnt a phonetic job.

MRS HIGGINS. You said it was.

HIGGINS. Not your part of it. Ive picked up
a girl.

MRS HIGGINS. Does that mean that some girl
has picked you up?

HIGGINS. Not at all. I dont mean a love
affair.

MRS HIGGINS. What a pity!

HIGGINS. Why?

MRS HIGGINS. Well, you never fall in love
with anyone under forty-five. When will you
discover that there are some rather nice-looking young women about?

HIGGINS. Oh, I cant be bothered with young
women. My idea of a lovable woman is something as like you as possible. I shall never get
into the way of seriously liking young women:
some habits lie too deep to be changed. (*Rising abruptly and walking about, jingling his
money and his keys in his trouser pockets*)
Besides, theyre all idiots.

MRS HIGGINS. Do you know what you would
do if you really loved me, Henry?

HIGGINS. Oh bother! What? Marry, I suppose?

MRS HIGGINS. No. Stop fidgeting and take
your hands out of your pockets. (*With a gesture of despair, he obeys and sits down again.*)
Thats a good boy. Now tell me about the girl.

HIGGINS. She's coming to see you.

MRS HIGGINS. I dont remember asking her.

HIGGINS. You didnt. *I* asked her. If youd
known her you wouldnt have asked her.

MRS HIGGINS. Indeed! Why?

HIGGINS. Well, it's like this. She's a common
flower girl. I picked her off the kerbstone.

MRS HIGGINS. And invited her to my at-
home!

HIGGINS (*rising and coming to her to coax
her*). Oh, thatll be all right. Ive taught her to
speak properly; and she has strict orders as to
her behavior. She's to keep to two subjects:
the weather and everybody's health—Fine day
and How do you do, you know—and not to
let herself go on things in general. That will
be safe.

MRS HIGGINS. Safe! To talk about our health!
about our insides! perhaps about our out-
sides! How could you be so silly, Henry?

HIGGINS (*impatiently*). Well, she must talk
about something. (*He controls himself and
sits down again.*) Oh, she'll be all right: dont
you fuss. Pickering is in it with me. Ive a sort
of bet on that I'll pass her off as a duchess in
six months. I started on her some months

ago; and she's getting on like a house on fire. I shall win my bet. She has a quick ear; and she's been easier to teach than my middle class pupils because she's had to learn a complete new language. She talks English almost as you talk French.

MRS HIGGINS. Thats satisfactory, at all events.

HIGGINS. Well, it is and it isnt.

MRS HIGGINS. What does that mean?

HIGGINS. You see, Ive got her pronunciation all right; but you have to consider not only *how* a girl pronounces, but *what* she pronounces; and thats where—

They are interrupted by THE PARLOR-MAID, *announcing guests.*

THE PARLOR-MAID. Mrs and Miss Eynsford Hill. (*She withdraws.*)

HIGGINS. Oh Lord! (*He rises; snatches his hat from the table; and makes for the door; but before he reaches it his mother introduces him.*)

MRS *and* MISS EYNSFORD HILL *are the mother and daughter who sheltered from the rain in Covent Garden. The mother is well bred, quiet, and has the habitual anxiety of strait-ened means. The daughter has acquired a gay air of being very much at home in society: the bravado of genteel poverty.*

MRS EYNSFORD HILL (*to* MRS HIGGINS). How do you do? (*They shake hands.*)

MISS EYNSFORD HILL. How d'you do? (*She shakes.*)

MRS HIGGINS (*introducing*). My son Henry.

MRS EYNSFORD HILL. Your celebrated son! I have so longed to meet you, Professor Higgins.

HIGGINS (*glumly, making no movement in her direction*). Delighted. (*He backs against the piano and bows brusquely.*)

MISS EYNSFORD HILL (*going to him with confident familiarity*). How do you do?

HIGGINS (*staring at her*). Ive seen you before somewhere. I havnt the ghost of a notion where; but Ive heard your voice. (*Drearily*) It doesnt matter. Youd better sit down.

MRS HIGGINS. I'm sorry to say that my celebrated son has no manners. You mustnt mind him.

MISS EYNSFORD HILL (*gaily*). I dont. (*She sits in the Elizabethan chair.*)

MRS EYNSFORD HILL (*a little bewildered*). Not at all. (*She sits on the ottoman between her

daughter and* MRS HIGGINS, *who has turned her chair away from the writing-table.*)

HIGGINS. Oh, have I been rude? I didnt mean to be.

He goes to the central window, through which, with his back to the company, he contemplates the river and the flowers in Battersea Park on the opposite bank as if they were a frozen desert.

THE PARLOR-MAID *returns, ushering in* PICKERING.

THE PARLOR-MAID. Colonel Pickering. (*She withdraws.*)

PICKERING. How do you do, Mrs Higgins?

MRS HIGGINS. So glad youve come. Do you know Mrs Eynsford Hill—Miss Eynsford Hill? (*Exchange of bows.* THE COLONEL *brings the Chippendale chair a little forward between* MRS HILL *and* MRS HIGGINS, *and sits down.*)

PICKERING. Has Henry told you what weve come for?

HIGGINS (*over his shoulder*). We were interrupted: damn it!

MRS HIGGINS. Oh Henry, Henry, really!

MRS EYNSFORD HILL (*half rising*). Are we in the way?

MRS HIGGINS (*rising and making her sit down again*). No, no. You couldnt have come more fortunately: we want you to meet a friend of ours.

HIGGINS (*turning hopefully*). Yes, by George! We want two or three people. Youll do as well as anybody else.

THE PARLOR-MAID *returns, ushering* FREDDY.

THE PARLOR-MAID. Mr Eynsford Hill.

HIGGINS (*almost audibly, past endurance*). God of Heaven! another of them.

FREDDY (*shaking hands with* MRS HIGGINS). Ahdedo?

MRS HIGGINS. Very good of you to come. (*Introducing*) Colonel Pickering.

FREDDY (*bowing*). Ahdedo?

MRS HIGGINS. I dont think you know my son, Professor Higgins.

FREDDY (*going to* HIGGINS). Ahdedo?

HIGGINS (*looking at him much as if he were a pickpocket*). I'll take my oath Ive met *you* before somewhere. Where was it?

FREDDY. I dont think so.

HIGGINS (*resignedly*). It dont matter, anyhow. Sit down.

He shakes FREDDY's *hand, and almost slings him on to the ottoman with his face to the windows; then comes round to the other side of it.*

HIGGINS. Well, here we are, anyhow! (*He sits down on the ottoman next* MRS EYNSFORD HILL, *on her left.*) And now, what the devil are we going to talk about until Eliza comes?

MRS HIGGINS. Henry: you are the life and soul of the Royal Society's soirées; but really youre rather trying on more commonplace occasions.

HIGGINS. Am I? Very sorry. (*Beaming suddenly*) I suppose I am, you know. (*Uproariously*) Ha, ha!

MISS EYNSFORD HILL (*who considers* HIGGINS *quite eligible matrimonially*). I sympathize. I havnt any small talk. If people would only be frank and say what they really think!

HIGGINS (*relapsing into gloom*). Lord forbid!

MRS EYNSFORD HILL (*taking up her daughter's cue*). But why?

HIGGINS. What they think they ought to think is bad enough, Lord knows; but what they really think would break up the whole show. Do you suppose it would be really agreeable if I were to come out now with what *I* really think?

MISS EYNSFORD HILL (*gaily*). Is it so very cynical?

HIGGINS. Cynical! Who the dickens said it was cynical? I mean it wouldnt be decent.

MRS EYNSFORD HILL (*seriously*). Oh! I'm sure you dont mean that, Mr Higgins.

HIGGINS. You see, we're all savages, more or less. We're supposed to be civilized and cultured—to know all about poetry and philosophy and art and science, and so on; but how many of us know even the meanings of these names? (*To* MISS HILL) What do *you* know of poetry? (*To* MRS HILL) What do *you* know of science? (*Indicating* FREDDY) What does *he* know of art or science or anything else? What the devil do you imagine I know of philosophy?

MRS HIGGINS (*warningly*). Or of manners, Henry?

THE PARLOR-MAID (*opening the door*). Miss Doolittle. (*She withdraws.*)

HIGGINS (*rising hastily and running to* MRS HIGGINS). Here she is, mother. (*He stands on tiptoe and makes signs over his mother's head*

to ELIZA *to indicate to her which lady is* **her** *hostess.*)

ELIZA, *who is exquisitely dressed, produces an impression of such remarkable distinction and beauty as she enters that they all rise, quite fluttered. Guided by* HIGGINS's *signals, she comes to* MRS HIGGINS *with studied grace.*

LIZA (*speaking with pedantic correctness of pronunciation and great beauty of tone*). How do you do, Mrs Higgins? (*She gasps slightly in making sure of the H in Higgins, but is quite successful.*) Mr Higgins told me I might come.

MRS HIGGINS (*cordially*). Quite right: I'm very glad indeed to see you.

PICKERING. How do you do, Miss Doolittle?

LIZA (*shaking hands with him*). Colonel Pickering, is it not?

MRS EYNSFORD HILL. I feel sure we have met before, Miss Doolittle. I remember your eyes.

LIZA. How do you do? (*She sits down on the ottoman gracefully in the place just left vacant by* HIGGINS.)

MRS EYNSFORD HILL (*introducing*). My daughter Clara.

LIZA. How do you do?

CLARA (*impulsively*). How do you do? (*She sits down on the ottoman beside* ELIZA, *devouring her with her eyes.*)

FREDDY (*coming to their side of the ottoman*). Ive certainly had the pleasure.

MRS EYNSFORD HILL (*introducing*). My son Freddy.

LIZA. How do you do?

FREDDY *bows and sits down in the Elizabethan chair, infatuated.*

HIGGINS (*suddenly*). By George, yes: it all comes back to me! (*They stare at him.*) Covent Garden! (*Lamentably*) What a damned thing!

MRS HIGGINS. Henry, please! (*He is about to sit on the edge of the table.*) Dont sit on my writing-table: youll break it.

HIGGINS (*sulkily*). Sorry.

He goes *to the divan, stumbling into the fender and over the fire-irons on his way; extricating himself with muttered imprecations; and finishing his disastrous journey by throwing himself so impatiently on the divan that he almost breaks it.* MRS HIGGINS *looks at him, but controls herself and says nothing.*

A long and painful pause ensues.

MRS HIGGINS (*at last, conversationally*). Will it rain, do you think?

LIZA. The shallow depression in the west of these islands is likely to move slowly in an easterly direction. There are no indications of any great change in the barometrical situation.

FREDDY. Ha! ha! how awfully funny!

LIZA. What is wrong with that, young man? I bet I got it right.

FREDDY. Killing!

MRS EYNSFORD HILL. I'm sure I hope it wont turn cold. Theres so much influenza about. It runs right through our whole family regularly every spring.

LIZA (*darkly*). My aunt died of influenza: so they said.

MRS EYNSFORD HILL (*clicks her tongue sympathetically*)!!!

LIZA (*in the same tragic tone*). But it's my belief they done the old woman in.

MRS HIGGINS (*puzzled*). Done her in?

LIZA. Y-e-e-e-es, Lord love you! Why should *she* die of influenza? She come through diphtheria right enough the year before. I saw her with my own eyes. Fairly blue with it, she was. They all thought she was dead; but my father he kept ladling gin down her throat til she came to so sudden that she bit the bowl off the spoon.

MRS EYNSFORD HILL (*startled*). Dear me!

LIZA (*piling up the indictment*). What call would a woman with that strength in her have to die of influenza? What become of her new straw hat that should have come to me? Somebody pinched it; and what I say is, them as pinched it done her in.

MRS EYNSFORD HILL. What does doing her in mean?

HIGGINS (*hastily*). Oh, thats the new small talk. To do a person in means to kill them.

MRS EYNSFORD HILL (*to* ELIZA, *horrified*). You surely dont believe that your aunt was killed?

LIZA. Do I not! Them she lived with would have killed her for a hat-pin, let alone a hat.

MRS EYNSFORD HILL. But it cant have been right for your father to pour spirits down her throat like that. It might have killed her.

LIZA. Not her. Gin was mother's milk to her. Besides, he'd poured so much down his own throat that he knew the good of it.

MRS EYNSFORD HILL. Do you mean that he drank?

LIZA. Drank! My word! Something chronic.

MRS EYNSFORD HILL. How dreadful for you!

LIZA. Not a bit. It never did him no harm what I could see. But then he did not keep it up regular. (*Cheerfully*) On the burst, as you might say, from time to time. And always more agreeable when he had a drop in. When he was out of work, my mother used to give him fourpence and tell him to go out and not come back until he'd drunk himself cheerful and loving-like. Theres lots of women has to make their husbands drunk to make them fit to live with. (*Now quite at her ease*) You see, it's like this. If a man has a bit of a conscience, it always takes him when he's sober; and then it makes him low-spirited. A drop of booze just takes that off and makes him happy. (*To* FREDDY, *who is in convulsions of suppressed laughter*) Here! what are you sniggering at?

FREDDY. The new small talk. You do it so awfully well.

LIZA. If I was doing it proper, what was you laughing at? (*To* HIGGINS) Have I said anything I oughtnt?

MRS HIGGINS (*interposing*). Not at all, Miss Doolittle.

LIZA. Well, thats a mercy, anyhow. (*Expansively*) What I always say is—

HIGGINS (*rising and looking at his watch*). Ahem!

LIZA (*looking round at him; taking the hint; and rising*). Well: I must go. (*They all rise.* FREDDY *goes to the door.*) So pleased to have met you. Goodbye. (*She shakes hands with* MRS HIGGINS.)

MRS HIGGINS. Goodbye.

LIZA. Goodbye, Colonel Pickering.

PICKERING. Goodbye, Miss Doolittle. (*They shake hands.*)

LIZA (*nodding to the others*). Goodbye, all.

FREDDY (*opening the door for her*). Are you walking across the Park, Miss Doolittle? If so—

LIZA. Walk! Not bloody likely. (*Sensation.*) I am going in a taxi. (*She goes out.*)

PICKERING *gasps and sits down.* FREDDY *goes out on the balcony to catch another glimpse of* ELIZA.

MRS EYNSFORD HILL (*suffering from shock*). Well, I really cant get used to the new ways.

CLARA (*throwing herself discontentedly into the Elizabethan chair*). Oh, it's all right, mamma, quite right. People will think we never go anywhere or see anybody if you are so old-fashioned.

MRS EYNSFORD HILL. I daresay I am very old-fashioned; but I do hope you wont begin using that expression, Clara. I have got accustomed to hear you talking about men as rotters, and calling everything filthy and beastly; though I do think it horrible and unladylike. But this last is really too much. Dont you think so, Colonel Pickering?

PICKERING. Dont ask me. Ive been away in India for several years; and manners have changed so much that I sometimes dont know whether I'm at a respectable dinner-table or in a ship's forecastle.

CLARA. It's all a matter of habit. Theres no right or wrong in it. Nobody means anything by it. And it's so quaint, and gives such a smart emphasis to things that are not in themselves very witty. I find the new small talk delightful and quite innocent.

MRS EYNSFORD HILL (*rising*). Well, after that, I think it's time for us to go.

PICKERING *and* HIGGINS *rise*.

CLARA (*rising*). Oh yes: we have three at-homes to go to still. Goodbye, Mrs Higgins. Goodbye, Colonel Pickering. Goodbye, Professor Higgins.

HIGGINS (*coming grimly at her from the divan, and accompanying her to the door*). Goodbye. Be sure you try on that small talk at the three at-homes. Dont be nervous about it. Pitch it in strong.

CLARA (*all smiles*). I will. Goodbye. Such nonsense, all this early Victorian prudery!

HIGGINS (*tempting her*). Such damned nonsense!

CLARA. Such bloody nonsense!

MRS EYNSFORD HILL (*convulsively*). Clara!

CLARA. Ha! ha! (*She goes out radiant, conscious of being thoroughly up to date, and is heard descending the stairs in a stream of silvery laughter.*)

FREDDY (*to the heavens at large*). Well, I ask you— (*He gives it up, and comes to* MRS HIGGINS.) Goodbye.

MRS HIGGINS (*shaking hands*). Goodbye. Would you like to meet Miss Doolittle again?

FREDDY (*eagerly*). Yes, I should, most awfully.

MRS HIGGINS. Well, you know my days.

FREDDY. Yes. Thanks awfully. Goodbye. (*He goes out.*)

MRS EYNSFORD HILL. Goodbye, Mr Higgins.

HIGGINS. Goodbye. Goodbye.

MRS EYNSFORD HILL (*to* PICKERING). It's no use. I shall never be able to bring myself to use that word.

PICKERING. Dont. It's not compulsory, you know. Youll get on quite well without it.

MRS EYNSFORD HILL. Only, Clara is so down on me if I am not positively reeking with the latest slang. Goodbye.

PICKERING. Goodbye. (*They shake hands.*)

MRS EYNSFORD HILL (*to* MRS HIGGINS). You mustnt mind Clara. (PICKERING, *catching from her lowered tone that this is not meant for him to hear, discreetly joins* HIGGINS *at the window.*) We're so poor! and she gets so few parties, poor child! She doesnt quite know. (MRS HIGGINS, *seeing that her eyes are moist, takes her hand sympathetically and goes with her to the door.*) But the boy is nice. Dont you think so?

MRS HIGGINS. Oh, quite nice. I shall always be delighted to see him.

MRS EYNSFORD HILL. Thank you, dear. Goodbye. (*She goes out.*)

HIGGINS (*eagerly*). Well? Is Eliza presentable? (*He swoops on his mother and drags her to the ottoman, where she sits down in* ELIZA's *place with her son on her left.*)

PICKERING *returns to his chair on her right.*

MRS HIGGINS. You silly boy, of course she's not presentable. She's a triumph of your art and of her dressmaker's; but if you suppose for a moment that she doesnt give herself away in every sentence she utters, you must be perfectly cracked about her.

PICKERING. But dont you think something might be done? I mean something to eliminate the sanguinary element from her conversation.

MRS HIGGINS. Not as long as she is in Henry's hands.

HIGGINS (*aggrieved*). Do you mean that *my* language is improper?

MRS HIGGINS. No, dearest: it would be quite proper—say on a canal barge; but it would not be proper for her at a garden party.

HIGGINS (*deeply injured*). Well I must say—

PICKERING (*interrupting him*). Come, Higgins: you must learn to know yourself. I havnt heard such language as yours since we used to review the volunteers in Hyde Park twenty years ago.

HIGGINS (*sulkily*). Oh, well, if *you* say so, I suppose I dont always talk like a bishop.

MRS HIGGINS (*quieting* HENRY *with a touch*). Colonel Pickering: will you tell me what is the exact state of things in Wimpole Street?

PICKERING (*cheerfully: as if this completely changed the subject*). Well, I have come to live there with Henry. We work together at my Indian Dialects; and we think it more convenient—

MRS HIGGINS. Quite so. I know all about that: it's an excellent arrangement. But where does this girl live?

HIGGINS. With us, of course. Where *should* she live?

MRS HIGGINS. But on what terms? Is she a servant? If not, what is she?

PICKERING (*slowly*). I think I know what you mean, Mrs Higgins.

HIGGINS. Well, dash me if *I* do! Ive had to work at the girl every day for months to get her to her present pitch. Besides, she's useful. She knows where my things are, and remembers my appointments and so forth.

MRS HIGGINS. How does your housekeeper get on with her?

HIGGINS. Mrs Pearce? Oh, she's jolly glad to get so much taken off her hands; for before Eliza came, *she* used to have to find things and remind me of my appointments. But she's got some silly bee in her bonnet about Eliza. She keeps saying "You dont *think,* sir": doesnt she, Pick?

PICKERING. Yes: thats the formula. "You dont *think,* sir." Thats the end of every conversation about Eliza.

HIGGINS. As if I ever stop thinking about the girl and her confounded vowels and consonants. I'm worn out, thinking about her, and watching her lips and her teeth and her tongue, not to mention her soul, which is the quaintest of the lot.

MRS HIGGINS. You certainly are a pretty pair of babies, playing with your live doll.

HIGGINS. Playing! The hardest job I ever tackled: make no mistake about that, mother. But you have no idea how frightfully interesting it is to take a human being and change her into a quite different human being by creating a new speech for her. It's filling up the deepest gulf that separates class from class and soul from soul.

PICKERING (*drawing his chair closer to* MRS HIGGINS *and bending over to her eagerly*). Yes: it's enormously interesting. I assure you, Mrs Higgins, we take Eliza very seriously. Every week—every day almost—there is some new change. (*Closer again*) We keep records of every stage—dozens of gramophone disks and photographs—

HIGGINS (*assailing her at the other ear*). Yes, by George: it's the most absorbing experiment I ever tackled. She regularly fills our lives up: doesnt she, Pick?

PICKERING. We're always talking Eliza.

HIGGINS. Teaching Eliza.

PICKERING. Dressing Eliza.

MRS HIGGINS. What!

HIGGINS. Inventing new Elizas.

	(*speaking together*)	
HIGGINS.		You know, she has the most extraordinary quickness of ear:
PICKERING.		I assure you, my dear Mrs Higgins, that girl
HIGGINS.		just like a parrot. Ive tried her with every
PICKERING.		is a genius. She can play the piano quite beautifully.
HIGGINS.		possible sort of sound that a human being can make—
PICKERING.		We have taken her to classical concerts and to music
HIGGINS.		Continental dialects, African dialects, Hottentot
PICKERING.		halls; and it's all the same to her: she plays everything
HIGGINS.		clicks, things it took me years to get hold of; and
PICKERING.		she hears right off when she comes home, whether

HIGGINS. | she picks them up like a shot, right away, as if she had

PICKERING. | it's Beethoven and Brahms or Lehar and Lionel Monckton;

HIGGINS. | been at it all her life.

PICKERING. | though six months ago, she'd never as much as touched a piano—

MRS HIGGINS (*putting her fingers in her ears, as they are by this time shouting one another down with an intolerable noise*). Sh-sh-sh—sh! (*They stop.*)

PICKERING. I beg your pardon. (*He draws his chair back apologetically.*)

HIGGINS. Sorry. When Pickering starts shouting nobody can get a word in edgeways.

MRS HIGGINS. Be quiet, Henry. Colonel Pickering: dont you realize that when Eliza walked into Wimpole Street, something walked in with her?

PICKERING. Her father did. But Henry soon got rid of him.

MRS HIGGINS. It would have been more to the point if her mother had. But as her mother didnt something else did.

PICKERING. But what?

MRS HIGGINS (*unconsciously dating herself by the word*). A problem.

PICKERING. Oh, I see. The problem of how to pass her off as a lady.

HIGGINS. I'll solve that problem. Ive half solved it already.

MRS HIGGINS. No, you two infinitely stupid male creatures: the problem of what is to be done with her afterwards.

HIGGINS. I dont see anything in that. She can go her own way, with all the advantages I have given her.

MRS HIGGINS. The advantages of that poor woman who was here just now! The manners and habits that disqualify a fine lady from earning her own living without giving her a fine lady's income! Is that what you mean?

PICKERING (*indulgently, being rather bored*). Oh, that will be all right, Mrs Higgins. (*He rises to go.*)

HIGGINS (*rising also*). We'll find her some light employment.

PICKERING. She's happy enough. Dont you worry about her. Goodbye. (*He shakes hands as if he were consoling a frightened child, and makes for the door.*)

HIGGINS. Anyhow, theres no good bothering now. The thing's done. Goodbye, mother. (*He kisses her, and follows* PICKERING.)

PICKERING (*turning for a final consolation*). There are plenty of openings. We'll do whats right. Goodbye.

HIGGINS (*to* PICKERING *as they go out together*). Let's take her to the Shakespear exhibition at Earlscourt.

PICKERING. Yes: lets. Her remarks will be delicious.

HIGGINS. She'll mimic all the people for us when we get home.

PICKERING. Ripping. (*Both are heard laughing as they go downstairs.*)

MRS HIGGINS (*rises with an impatient bounce, and returns to her work at the writing-table. She sweeps a litter of disarranged papers out of her way; snatches a sheet of paper from her stationery case; and tries resolutely to write. At the third line she gives it up; flings down her pen; grips the table angrily and exclaims*) Oh, men! men!! men!!!

ACT IV

The Wimpole Street laboratory. Midnight. Nobody in the room. The clock on the mantelpiece strikes twelve. The fire is not alight: it is a summer night.

Presently HIGGINS *and* PICKERING *are heard on the stairs.*

HIGGINS (*calling down to* PICKERING). I say, Pick: lock up, will you? I shant be going out again.

PICKERING. Right. Can Mrs Pearce go to bed? We dont want anything more, do we?

HIGGINS. Lord, no!

ELIZA *opens the door and is seen on the lighted landing in opera cloak, brilliant evening dress, and diamonds, with fan, flowers, and all accessories. She comes to the hearth, and switches on the electric lights there. She is tired: her pallor contrasts strongly with her dark eyes and hair; and her expression is almost tragic. She takes off her cloak; puts her fan and flowers on the piano; and sits down on the bench, brooding and silent.* HIGGINS, *in evening dress, with overcoat and hat, comes in, carrying a smoking jacket which he has picked up downstairs. He takes off the hat and overcoat; throws them carelessly on the newspaper stand; disposes of his coat in the same way; puts on the smoking jacket; and throws himself wearily into the easy-chair at the hearth.* PICKERING, *similarly attired, comes in. He also takes off his hat and overcoat, and is about to throw them on* HIGGINS's *when he hesitates.*

PICKERING. I say: Mrs Pearce will row if we leave these things lying about in the drawing room.

HIGGINS. Oh, chuck them over the bannisters into the hall. She'll find them there in the morning and put them away all right. She'll think we were drunk.

PICKERING. We are, slightly. Are there any letters?

HIGGINS. I didnt look. (PICKERING *takes the overcoats and hats and goes downstairs.* HIGGINS *begins half singing half yawning an air from La Fanciulla del Golden West. Suddenly he stops and exclaims.*) I wonder where the devil my slippers are!

ELIZA *looks at him darkly; then rises suddenly and leaves the room.*

HIGGINS *yawns again, and resumes his song.*

PICKERING *returns, with the contents of the letter-box in his hand.*

PICKERING. Only circulars, and this coroneted billet-doux for you. (*He throws the circulars into the fender, and posts himself on the hearthrug, with his back to the grate.*)

HIGGINS (*glancing at the billet-doux*). Money-lender. (*He throws the letter after the circulars.*)

ELIZA *returns with a pair of large down-at-heel slippers. She places them on the carpet before* HIGGINS, *and sits as before without a word.*

HIGGINS (*yawning again*). Oh Lord! What an evening! What a crew! What a silly tom-foolery! (*He raises his shoe to unlace it, and catches sight of the slippers. He stops unlacing and looks at them as if they had appeared there of their own accord.*) Oh! theyre there, are they?

PICKERING (*stretching himself*). Well, I feel a bit tired. It's been a long day. The garden party, a dinner party, and the opera! Rather too much of a good thing. But youve won your bet, Higgins. Eliza did the trick, and something to spare, eh?

HIGGINS (*fervently*). Thank God it's over!

ELIZA *flinches violently; but they take no notice of her; and she recovers herself and sits stonily as before.*

PICKERING. Were you nervous at the garden party? *I* was. Eliza didnt seem a bit nervous.

HIGGINS. Oh, *she* wasnt nervous. I knew she'd be all right. No: it's the strain of putting the job through all these months that has told on me. It was interesting enough at first, while we were at the phonetics; but after that I got deadly sick of it. If I hadnt backed myself to do it I should have chucked the whole thing up two months ago. It was a silly notion: the whole thing has been a bore.

PICKERING. Oh come! the garden party was frightfully exciting. My heart began beating like anything.

HIGGINS. Yes, for the first three minutes. But when I saw we were going to win hands down, I felt like a bear in a cage, hanging about doing nothing. The dinner was worse: sitting gorging there for over an hour, with nobody but a damned fool of a fashionable woman to talk to! I tell you, Pickering, never again for me. No more artificial duchesses. The whole thing has been simple purgatory.

PICKERING. Youve never been broken in properly to the social routine. (*Strolling over to the piano*) I rather enjoy dipping into it occasionally myself: it makes me feel young again. Anyhow, it was a great success: an immense success. I was quite frightened once or twice because Eliza was doing it so well. You see, lots of the real people cant do it at all: theyre such fools that they think style comes by nature to people in their position; and so they never learn. Theres always something professional about doing a thing superlatively well.

HIGGINS. Yes: thats what drives me mad: the silly people dont know their own silly business. (*Rising*) However, it's over and done with; and now I can go to bed at last without dreading tomorrow.

ELIZA's *beauty becomes murderous.*

PICKERING. I think I shall turn in too. Still, it's been a great occasion: a triumph for you. Goodnight. (*He goes.*)

HIGGINS (*following him*). Goodnight. (*Over his shoulder, at the door*) Put out the lights, Eliza; and tell Mrs Pearce not to make coffee for me in the morning: I'll take tea. (*He goes out.*)

ELIZA *tries to control herself and feel indifferent as she rises and walks across to the hearth to switch off the lights. By the time she gets there she is on the point of screaming. She sits down in Higgins's chair and holds on hard to the arms. Finally she gives way and flings herself furiously on the floor, raging.*

HIGGINS (*in despairing wrath outside*). What the devil have I done with my slippers? (*He appears at the door.*)

LIZA (*snatching up the slippers, and hurling them at him one after the other with all her force*). There are your slippers. And there. Take your slippers; and may you never have a day's luck with them!

HIGGINS (*astounded*). What on earth—! (*He comes to her.*) Whats the matter? Get up. (*He pulls her up.*) Anything wrong?

LIZA (*breathless*). Nothing wrong—with you. Ive won your bet for you, havnt I? Thats enough for you. *I* dont matter, I suppose.

HIGGINS. *You* won my bet! You! Presumptuous insect! *I* won it. What did you throw those slippers at me for?

LIZA. Because I wanted to smash your face. I'd like to kill you, you selfish brute. Why didnt you leave me where you picked me out of—in the gutter? You thank God it's all over, and that now you can throw me back again there, do you? (*She crisps her fingers frantically.*)

HIGGINS (*looking at her in cool wonder*). The creature is nervous, after all.

LIZA (*gives a suffocated scream of fury, and instinctively darts her nails at his face*)!!

HIGGINS (*catching her wrists*). Ah! would you? Claws in, you cat. How dare you shew your temper to me? Sit down and be quiet. (*He throws her roughly into the easy-chair.*)

LIZA (*crushed by superior strength and weight*). Whats to become of me? Whats to become of me?

HIGGINS. How the devil do I know whats to become of you? What does it matter what becomes of you?

LIZA. You dont care. I know you dont care.

You wouldnt care if I was dead. I'm nothing to you—not so much as them slippers.

HIGGINS (*thundering*). *Those* slippers.

LIZA (*with bitter submission*). Those slippers. I didnt think it made any difference now.

A pause. ELIZA *hopeless and crushed.* HIGGINS *a little uneasy.*

HIGGINS (*in his loftiest manner*). Why have you begun going on like this? May I ask whether you complain of your treatment here?

LIZA. No.

HIGGINS. Has anybody behaved badly to you? Colonel Pickering? Mrs Pearce? Any of the servants?

LIZA. No.

HIGGINS. I presume you dont pretend that *I* have treated you badly?

LIZA. No.

HIGGINS. I am glad to hear it. (*He moderates his tone.*) Perhaps youre tired after the strain of the day. Will you have a glass of champagne? (*He moves towards the door.*)

LIZA. No. (*Recollecting her manners*) Thank you.

HIGGINS (*good-humored again*). This has been coming on you for some days. I suppose it was natural for you to be anxious about the garden party. But thats all over now. (*He pats her kindly on the shoulder. She writhes.*) Theres nothing more to worry about.

LIZA. No. Nothing more for *you* to worry about. (*She suddenly rises and gets away from him by going to the piano bench, where she sits and hides her face.*) Oh God! I wish I was dead.

HIGGINS (*staring after her in sincere surprise*). Why? In heaven's name, why? (*Reasonably, going to her*) Listen to me, Eliza. All this irritation is purely subjective.

LIZA. I dont understand. I'm too ignorant.

HIGGINS. It's only imagination. Low spirits and nothing else. Nobody's hurting you. Nothing's wrong. You go to bed like a good girl and sleep it off. Have a little cry and say your prayers: that will make you comfortable.

LIZA. I heard your prayers. "Thank God it's all over!"

HIGGINS (*impatiently*). Well, *dont* you thank God it's all over? Now you are free and can do what you like.

LIZA (*pulling herself together in desperation*). What am I fit for? What have you left me fit for? Where am I to go? What am I to do? Whats to become of me?

HIGGINS (*enlightened, but not at all impressed*). Oh thats whats worrying you, is it? (*He thrusts his hands into his pockets, and walks about in his usual manner, rattling the contents of his pockets, as if condescending to a trivial subject out of pure kindness.*) I shouldnt bother about it if I were you. I should imagine you wont have much difficulty in settling yourself somewhere or other, though I hadnt quite realized that you were going away. (*She looks quickly at him: he does not look at her, but examines the dessert stand on the piano and decides that he will eat an apple.*) You might marry, you know. (*He bites a large piece out of the apple and munches it noisily.*) You see, Eliza, all men are not confirmed old bachelors like me and the Colonel. Most men are the marrying sort (poor devils!); and youre not bad-looking: it's quite a pleasure to look at you sometimes—not now, of course, because youre crying and looking as ugly as the very devil; but when youre all right and quite yourself, youre what I should call attractive. That is, to the people in the marrying line, you understand. You go to bed and have a good nice rest; and then get up and look at yourself in the glass; and you wont feel so cheap.

ELIZA *again looks at him, speechless, and does not stir.*

The look is quite lost on him: he eats his apple with a dreamy expression of happiness, as it is quite a good one.

HIGGINS (*a genial afterthought occurring to him*). I daresay my mother could find some chap or other who would do very well.

LIZA. We were above that at the corner of Tottenham Court Road.

HIGGINS (*waking up*). What do you mean?

LIZA. I sold flowers. I didnt sell myself. Now youve made a lady of me I'm not fit to sell anything else. I wish youd left me where you found me.

HIGGINS (*slinging the core of the apple decisively into the grate*). Tosh, Eliza. Dont you insult human relations by dragging all this cant about buying and selling into it. You neednt marry the fellow if you dont like him.

LIZA. What else am I to do?

HIGGINS. Oh, lots of things. What about your old idea of a florist's shop? Pickering could set you up in one: he's lots of money. (*Chuckling*) He'll have to pay for all those togs you have been wearing to-day; and that, with the hire of the jewellery, will make a big hole in two hundred pounds. Why, six months ago you would have thought it the millennium to have a flower shop of your own. Come! youll be all right. I must clear off to bed: I'm devilish sleepy. By the way, I came down for something: I forget what it was.

LIZA. Your slippers.

HIGGINS. Oh yes, of course. You shied them at me. (*He picks them up, and is going out when she rises and speaks to him.*)

LIZA. Before you go, sir—

HIGGINS (*dropping the slippers in his surprise at her calling him Sir*). Eh?

LIZA. Do my clothes belong to me or to Colonel Pickering?

HIGGINS (*coming back into the room as if her question were the very climax of unreason*). What the devil use would they be to Pickering?

LIZA. He might want them for the next girl you pick up to experiment on.

HIGGINS (*shocked and hurt*). Is *that* the way you feel towards us?

LIZA. I dont want to hear anything more about that. All I want to know is whether anything belongs to me. My own clothes were burnt.

HIGGINS. But what does it matter? Why need you start bothering about that in the middle of the night?

LIZA. I want to know what I may take away with me. I dont want to be accused of stealing.

HIGGINS (*now deeply wounded*). Stealing! You shouldnt have said that, Eliza. That shews a want of feeling.

LIZA. I'm sorry. I'm only a common ignorant girl; and in *my* station I have to be careful. There cant be any feelings between the like of you and the like of me. Please will you tell me what belongs to me and what doesnt?

HIGGINS (*very sulky*). You may take the whole damned houseful if you like. Except the jewels. Theyre hired. Will that satisfy you? (*He turns on his heel and is about to go in extreme dudgeon.*)

LIZA (*drinking in his emotion like nectar, and nagging him to provoke a further supply*). Stop, please. (*She takes off her jewels.*) Will you take these to your room and keep them safe? I dont want to run the risk of their being missing.

HIGGINS (*furious*). Hand them over. (*She puts them into his hands.*) If these belonged to me instead of to the jeweller, I'd ram them down your ungrateful throat. (*He perfunctorily thrusts them into his pockets, unconsciously decorating himself with the protruding ends of the chains.*)

LIZA (*taking a ring off*). This ring isnt the jeweller's: it's the one you bought me in Brighton. I dont want it now. (HIGGINS *dashes the ring violently into the fireplace, and turns on her so threateningly that she crouches over the piano with her hands over her face, and exclaims*) Dont you hit me.

HIGGINS. Hit you! You infamous creature, how dare you accuse me of such a thing? It is you who have hit me. You have wounded me to the heart.

LIZA (*thrilling with hidden joy*). I'm glad. Ive got a little of my own back, anyhow.

HIGGINS (*with dignity, in his finest professional style*). You have caused me to lose my temper: a thing that has hardly ever happened to me before. I prefer to say nothing more tonight. I am going to bed.

LIZA (*pertly*). Youd better leave a note for Mrs Pearce about the coffee; for she wont be told by me.

HIGGINS (*formally*). Damn Mrs Pearce; and damn the coffee; and damn you; and damn my own folly in having lavished hard-earned knowledge and the treasure of my regard and intimacy on a heartless guttersnipe. (*He goes out with impressive decorum, and spoils it by slamming the door savagely.*)

ELIZA *smiles for the first time; expresses her feelings by a wild pantomime in which an imitation of* HIGGINS's *exit is confused with her own triumph; and finally goes down on her knees on the hearthrug to look for the ring.*

ACT V

MRS HIGGINS's *drawing room. She is at her writing-table as before.* THE PARLOR-MAID *comes in.*

THE PARLOR-MAID (*at the door*). Mr Henry, maam, is downstairs with Colonel Pickering.

MRS HIGGINS. Well, shew them up.

THE PARLOR-MAID. Theyre using the telephone, maam. Telephoning to the police, I think.

MRS HIGGINS. What!

THE PARLOR-MAID (*coming further in and lowering her voice*). Mr Henry is in a state, maam. I thought I'd better tell you.

MRS HIGGINS. If you had told me that Mr Henry was not in a state it would have been more surprising. Tell them to come up when theyve finished with the police. I suppose he's lost something.

THE PARLOR-MAID. Yes, maam (*going*).

MRS HIGGINS. Go upstairs and tell Miss Doolittle that Mr Henry and the Colonel are here. Ask her not to come down til I send for her.

THE PARLOR-MAID. Yes, maam.

HIGGINS *bursts in. He is, as* THE PARLOR-MAID *has said, in a state.*

HIGGINS. Look here, mother: heres a confounded thing!

MRS HIGGINS. Yes, dear. Good morning. (*He checks his impatience and kisses her, whilst* THE PARLOR-MAID *goes out.*) What is it?

HIGGINS. Eliza's bolted.

MRS HIGGINS (*calmly continuing her writing*). You must have frightened her.

HIGGINS. Frightened her! nonsense! She was left last night, as usual, to turn out the lights and all that; and instead of going to bed she changed her clothes and went right off: her bed wasnt slept in. She came in a cab for her things before seven this morning; and that fool Mrs Pearce let her have them without telling me a word about it. What am I to do?

MRS HIGGINS. Do without, I'm afraid, Henry. The girl has a perfect right to leave if she chooses.

HIGGINS (*wandering distractedly across the room*). But I cant find anything. I dont know what appointments Ive got. I'm— (PICKERING *comes in.* MRS HIGGINS *puts down her pen and turns away from the writing-table.*)

PICKERING (*shaking hands*). Good morning, Mrs Higgins. Has Henry told you? (*He sits down on the ottoman.*)

HIGGINS. What does that ass of an inspector say? Have you offered a reward?

MRS HIGGINS (*rising in indignant amazement*). You dont mean to say you have set the police after Eliza.

HIGGINS. Of course. What are the police for? What else could we do? (*He sits in the Elizabethan chair.*)

PICKERING. The inspector made a lot of difficulties. I really think he suspected us of some improper purpose.

MRS HIGGINS. Well, of course he did. What right have you to go to the police and give the girl's name as if she were a thief, or a lost umbrella, or something? Really! (*She sits down again, deeply vexed.*)

HIGGINS. But we want to find her.

PICKERING. We cant let her go like this, you know, Mrs Higgins. What were we to do?

MRS HIGGINS. You have no more sense, either of you, than two children. Why—

THE PARLOR-MAID *comes in and breaks off the conversation.*

THE PARLOR-MAID. Mr Henry: a gentleman wants to see you very particular. He's been sent on from Wimpole Street.

HIGGINS. Oh, bother! I cant see anyone now. Who is it?

THE PARLOR-MAID. A Mr Doolittle, sir.

PICKERING. Doolittle! Do you mean the dustman?

THE PARLOR-MAID. Dustman! Oh no, sir: a gentleman.

HIGGINS (*springing up excitedly*). By George, Pick, it's some relative of hers that she's gone to. Somebody we know nothing about. (*To* THE PARLOR-MAID) Send him up, quick.

THE PARLOR-MAID. Yes, sir. (*She goes.*)

HIGGINS (*eagerly, going to his mother*). Genteel relatives! now we shall hear something. (*He sits down in the Chippendale chair.*)

MRS HIGGINS. Do you know any of her people?

PICKERING. Only her father: the fellow we told you about.

THE PARLOR-MAID (*announcing*). Mr Doolittle. (*She withdraws.*)

DOOLITTLE *enters. He is brilliantly dressed in a new fashionable frock-coat, with white waistcoat and grey trousers. A flower in his buttonhole, a dazzling silk hat, and patent leather shoes complete the effect. He is too concerned with the business he has come on to notice* MRS HIGGINS. *He walks straight to* HIGGINS, *and accosts him with vehement reproach.*

DOOLITTLE (*indicating his own person*). See here! Do you see this? You done this.

HIGGINS. Done what, man?

DOOLITTLE. This, I tell you. Look at it. Look at this hat. Look at this coat.

PICKERING. Has Eliza been buying you clothes?

DOOLITTLE. Eliza! not she. Not half. Why would she buy me clothes?

MRS HIGGINS. Good morning, Mr. Doolittle. Wont you sit down?

DOOLITTLE (*taken aback as he becomes conscious that he has forgotten his hostess*). Asking your pardon, maam. (*He approaches her and shakes her proffered hand.*) Thank you. (*He sits down on the ottoman, on* PICKERING's *right.*) I am that full of what has happened to me that I cant think of anything else.

HIGGINS. What the dickens *has* happened to you?

DOOLITTLE. I shouldnt mind if it had only happened to me: anything might happen to anybody and nobody to blame but Providence, as you might say. But this is something that you done to me: yes, you, Henry Higgins.

HIGGINS. Have you found Eliza? Thats the point.

DOOLITTLE. Have you lost her?

HIGGINS. Yes.

DOOLITTLE. You have all the luck, you have. I aint found her; but she'll find me quick enough now after what you done to me.

MRS HIGGINS. But what has my son done to you, Mr Doolittle?

DOOLITTLE. Done to me! Ruined me. Destroyed my happiness. Tied me up and delivered me into the hands of middle class morality.

HIGGINS (*rising intolerantly and standing over* DOOLITTLE). Youre raving. Youre drunk. Youre mad. I gave you five pounds. After that I had two conversations with you, at half-a-crown an hour. Ive never seen you since.

DOOLITTLE. Oh! Drunk! am I? Mad? am I? Tell me this. Did you or did you not write a letter to an old blighter in America that was giving five millions to found Moral Reform Societies all over the world, and that wanted you to invent a universal language for him?

HIGGINS. What! Ezra D. Wannafeller! He's dead. (*He sits down again carelessly.*)

DOOLITTLE. Yes: he's dead; and I'm done for. Now did you or did you not write a letter to him to say that the most original moralist at present in England, to the best of your knowledge, was Alfred Doolittle, a common dustman.

HIGGINS. Oh, after your last visit I remember making some silly joke of the kind.

DOOLITTLE. Ah! you may well call it a silly joke. It put the lid on me right enough. Just give him the chance he wanted to shew that Americans is not like us: that they recognize and respect merit in every class of life, however humble. Them words is in his blooming will, in which, Henry Higgins, thanks to your silly joking, he leaves me a share in his Predigested Cheese Trust worth three thousand a year on condition that I lecture for his Wannafeller Moral Reform World League as often as they ask me up to six times a year.

HIGGINS. The devil he does! Whew! (*Brightening suddenly*) What a lark!

PICKERING. A safe thing for you, Doolittle. They wont ask you twice.

DOOLITTLE. It aint the lecturing I mind. I'll lecture them blue in the face, I will, and not turn a hair. It's making a gentleman of me that I object to. Who asked him to make a gentleman of me? I was happy. I was free. I touched pretty nigh everybody for money when I wanted it, same as I touched you, Henry Higgins. Now I am worrited; tied neck and heels; and everybody touches me for money. It's a fine thing for you, says my solicitor. Is it? says I. You mean it's a good thing for you, I says. When I was a poor man and had a solicitor once when they found a pram in the dust cart, he got me off, and got shut of me and got me shut of him as quick as he could. Same with the doctors: used to shove me out of the hospital before I could hardly stand on my legs, and nothing to pay. Now they finds out that I'm not a healthy man and cant live unless they looks after me twice a day. In the house I'm not let do a hand's turn for myself: somebody else must do it and touch me for it. A year ago I hadnt a relative in the world except two or three that wouldnt speak to me. Now Ive fifty, and not a decent week's wages among the lot of them. I have to live for others and not for myself: thats middle class morality. You talk of losing Eliza. Dont you be anxious: I bet she's on my doorstep by this: she that could support herself easy by selling flowers if I wasnt respectable. And the next one to touch me will be you, Henry Higgins. I'll have to learn to speak middle class language from you, instead of speaking proper English. Thats where youll come in; and I daresay thats what you done it for.

MRS HIGGINS. But, my dear Mr Doolittle, you need not suffer all this if you are really in earnest. Nobody can force you to accept this bequest. You can repudiate it. Isnt that so, Colonel Pickering?

PICKERING. I believe so.

DOOLITTLE (*softening his manner in deference to her sex*). Thats the tragedy of it, maam. It's easy to say chuck it; but I havnt the nerve. Which of us has? We're all intimidated. Intimidated, maam: thats what we are. What is there for me if I chuck it but the workhouse in my old age? I have to dye my hair already to keep my job as a dustman. If I was one of the deserving poor, and had put by a bit, I could chuck it; but then why should I, acause the deserving poor might as well be millionaires for all the happiness they ever has. They dont know what happiness is. But I, as one of the undeserving poor, have nothing between me and the pauper's uniform but this here blasted three thousand a year that shoves me into the middle class. (Excuse the expression, maam: youd use it yourself if you had my provocation.) Theyve got you every way you turn: it's a choice between the Skilly of the workhouse and the Char Bydis of the middle class; and I havnt the nerve for the workhouse. Intimidated: thats what I am. Broke. Brought up. Happier men than me will call for my dust, and touch me for their tip; and I'll look on helpless, and envy them. And thats what your son has brought me to. (*He is overcome by emotion.*)

MRS HIGGINS. Well, I'm very glad youre not going to do anything foolish, Mr Doolittle. For this solves the problem of Eliza's future. You can provide for her now.

DOOLITTLE (*with melancholy resignation*). Yes, maam: I'm expected to provide for everyone now, out of three thousand a year.

HIGGINS (*jumping up*). Nonsense! he cant provide for her. He shant provide for her. She doesnt belong to him. I paid him five pounds for her. Doolittle: either youre an honest man or a rogue.

DOOLITTLE (*tolerantly*). A little of both, Henry, like the rest of us: a little of both.

HIGGINS. Well, you took that money for the girl; and you have no right to take her as well.

MRS HIGGINS. Henry: dont be absurd. If you want to know where Eliza is, she is upstairs.

HIGGINS (*amazed*). Upstairs!!! Then I shall jolly soon fetch her downstairs. (*He makes resolutely for the door.*)

MRS HIGGINS (*rising and following him*). Be quiet, Henry. Sit down.

HIGGINS. I—

MRS HIGGINS. Sit down, dear; and listen to me.

HIGGINS. Oh very well, very well, very well. (*He throws himself ungraciously on the ottoman, with his face towards the windows.*) But I think you might have told us this half an hour ago.

MRS HIGGINS. Eliza came to me this morning. She passed the night partly walking about in a rage, partly trying to throw herself into the river and being afraid to, and partly in the Carlton Hotel. She told me of the brutal way you two treated her.

HIGGINS (*bounding up again*). What!

PICKERING (*rising also*). My dear Mrs Higgins, she's been telling you stories. We didnt treat her brutally. We hardly said a word to her; and we parted on particularly good terms. (*Turning on* HIGGINS) Higgins: did you bully her after I went to bed?

HIGGINS. Just the other way about. She threw my slippers in my face. She behaved in the most outrageous way. I never gave her the slightest provocation. The slippers came bang into my face the moment I entered the room—before I had uttered a word. And used perfectly awful language.

PICKERING (*astonished*). But why? What did we do to her?

MRS HIGGINS. I think I know pretty well what you did. The girl is naturally rather affectionate, I think. Isnt she, Mr Doolittle?

DOOLITTLE. Very tender-hearted, maam. Takes after me.

MRS HIGGINS. Just so. She had become attached to you both. She worked very hard for you, Henry! I dont think you quite realize what anything in the nature of brain work means to a girl like that. Well, it seems that when the great day of trial came, and she did this wonderful thing for you without making a single mistake, you two sat there and never said a word to her, but talked together of how glad you were that it was all over and how you had been bored with the whole thing. And then you were surprised because she threw your slippers at you! *I* should have thrown the fire-irons at you.

HIGGINS. We said nothing except that we were tired and wanted to go to bed. Did we, Pick?

PICKERING (*shrugging his shoulders*). That was all.

MRS HIGGINS (*ironically*). Quite sure?

PICKERING. Absolutely. Really, that was all.

MRS HIGGINS. You didnt thank her, or pet her, or admire her, or tell her how splendid she'd·been.

HIGGINS (*impatiently*). But she knew all about that. We didnt make speeches to her, if thats what you mean.

PICKERING (*conscience stricken*). Perhaps we were a little inconsiderate. Is she very angry?

MRS HIGGINS (*returning to her place at the writing-table*). Well, I'm afraid she wont go back to Wimpole Street, especially now that Mr Doolittle is able to keep up the position you have thrust on her; but she says she is quite willing to meet you on friendly terms and to let bygones be bygones.

HIGGINS (*furious*). Is she, by George? Ho!

MRS HIGGINS. If you promise to behave yourself, Henry, I'll ask her to come down. If not, go home; for you have taken up quite enough of my time.

HIGGINS. Oh, all right. Very well. Pick: you behave yourself. Let us put on our best Sunday manners for this creature that we picked out of the mud. (*He flings himself sulkily into the Elizabethan chair.*)

DOOLITTLE (*remonstrating*). Now, now, Henry Higgins! have some consideration for my feelings as a middle class man.

MRS HIGGINS. Remember your promise, Henry. (*She presses the bell-button on the writing-table.*) Mr Doolittle: will you be so good as to step out on the balcony for a moment. I dont want Eliza to have the shock of your news until she has made it up with these two gentlemen. Would you mind?

DOOLITTLE. As you wish, lady. Anything to help Henry to keep her off my hands. (*He disappears through the window.*)

THE PARLOR-MAID *answers the bell.* PICKERING *sits down in* DOOLITTLE's *place.*

MRS HIGGINS. Ask Miss Doolittle to come down, please.

THE PARLOR-MAID. Yes, maam. (*She goes out.*)

MRS HIGGINS. Now, Henry: be good.

HIGGINS. I am behaving myself perfectly.

PICKERING. He is doing his best, Mrs Higgins.

A pause. HIGGINS *throws back his head; stretches out his legs; and begins to whistle.*

MRS HIGGINS. Henry, dearest, you dont look at all nice in that attitude.

HIGGINS (*pulling himself together*). I was not trying to look nice, mother.

MRS HIGGINS. It doesnt matter, dear. I only wanted to make you speak.

HIGGINS. Why?

MRS HIGGINS. Because you cant speak and whistle at the same time.

HIGGINS *groans. Another very trying pause.*

HIGGINS (*springing up, out of patience*). Where the devil is that girl? Are we to wait here all day?

ELIZA *enters, sunny, self-possessed, and giving a staggeringly convincing exhibition of ease of manner. She carries a little workbasket, and is very much at home.* PICKERING *is too much taken aback to rise.*

LIZA. How do you do, Professor Higgins? Are you quite well?

HIGGINS (*choking*). Am I— (*He can say no more.*)

LIZA. But of course you are: you are never ill. So glad to see you again, Colonel Pickering. (*He rises hastily; and they shake hands.*) Quite chilly this morning, isnt it? (*She sits down on his left. He sits beside her.*)

HIGGINS. Dont you dare try this game on me. I taught it to you; and it doesnt take me

in. Get up and come home; and dont be a fool.

ELIZA *takes a piece of needlework from her basket, and begins to stitch at it, without taking the least notice of this outburst.*

MRS HIGGINS. Very nicely put, indeed, Henry. No woman could resist such an invitation.

HIGGINS. You let her alone, mother. Let her speak for herself. You will jolly soon see whether she has an idea that I havnt put into her head or a word that I havnt put into her mouth. I tell you I have created this thing out of the squashed cabbage leaves of Covent Garden; and now she pretends to play the fine lady with me.

MRS HIGGINS (*placidly*). Yes, dear; but youll sit down, wont you?

HIGGINS *sits down again, savagely.*

LIZA (*to* PICKERING, *taking no apparent notice of* HIGGINS, *and working away deftly*). Will *you* drop me altogether now that the experiment is over, Colonel Pickering?

PICKERING. Oh dont. You mustnt think of it as an experiment. It shocks me, somehow.

LIZA. Oh, I'm only a squashed cabbage leaf—

PICKERING (*impulsively*). No.

LIZA (*continuing quietly*).—but I owe so much to you that I should be very unhappy if you forgot me.

PICKERING. It's very kind of you to say so, Miss Doolittle.

LIZA. It's not because you paid for my dresses. I know you are generous to everybody with money. But it was from you that I learnt really nice manners; and that is what makes one a lady, isnt it? You see it was so very difficult for me with the example of Professor Higgins always before me. I was brought up to be just like him, unable to control myself, and using bad language on the slightest provocation. And I should never have known that ladies and gentlemen didnt behave like that if you hadnt been there.

HIGGINS. Well!!

PICKERING. Oh, thats only his way, you know. He doesnt mean it.

LIZA. Oh, *I* didnt mean it either, when I was a flower girl. It was only my way. But you see I did it; and thats what makes the difference after all.

PICKERING. No doubt. Still, he taught you

to speak; and I couldnt have done that, you know.

LIZA (*trivially*). Of course: that is his profession.

HIGGINS. Damnation!

LIZA (*continuing*). It was just like learning to dance in the fashionable way: there was nothing more than that in it. But do you know what began my real education?

PICKERING. What?

LIZA (*stopping her work for a moment*). Your calling me Miss Doolittle that day when I first came to Wimpole Street. That was the beginning of self-respect for me. (*She resumes her stitching.*) And there were a hundred little things you never noticed, because they came naturally to you. Things about standing up and taking off your hat and opening doors—

PICKERING. Oh, that was nothing.

LIZA. Yes: things that shewed you thought and felt about me as if I were something better than a scullery-maid; though of course I know you would have been just the same to a scullery-maid if she had been let into the drawing room. You never took off your boots in the dining room when I was there.

PICKERING. You mustnt mind that. Higgins takes off his boots all over the place.

LIZA. I know. I am not blaming him. It is his way, isnt it? But it made *such* a difference to me that you didnt do it. You see, really and truly, apart from the things anyone can pick up (the dressing and the proper way of speaking, and so on), the difference between a lady and a flower girl is not how she behaves, but how she's treated. I shall always be a flower girl to Professor Higgins, because he always treats me as a flower girl, and always will; but I know I can be a lady to you, because you always treat me as a lady, and always will.

MRS HIGGINS. Please dont grind your teeth, Henry.

PICKERING. Well, this is really very nice of you, Miss Doolittle.

LIZA. I should like you to call me Eliza, now, if you would.

PICKERING. Thank you. Eliza, of course.

LIZA. And I should like Professor Higgins to call me Miss Doolittle.

HIGGINS. I'll see you damned first.

MRS HIGGINS. Henry! Henry!

PICKERING (*laughing*). Why dont you slang back at him? Dont stand it. It would do him a lot of good.

LIZA. I cant. I could have done it once; but now I cant go back to it. Last night, when I was wandering about, a girl spoke to me; and I tried to get back into the old way with her; but it was no use. You told me, you know, that when a child is brought to a foreign country, it picks up the language in a few weeks, and forgets its own. Well, I am a child in your country. I have forgotten my own language, and can speak nothing but yours. Thats the real break-off with the corner of Tottenham Court Road. Leaving Wimpole Street finishes it.

PICKERING (*much alarmed*). Oh! but youre coming back to Wimpole Street, arnt you? Youll forgive Higgins?

HIGGINS (*rising*). Forgive! Will she, by George! Let her go. Let her find out how she can get on without us. She will relapse into the gutter in three weeks without me at her elbow.

DOOLITTLE *appears at the centre window. With a look of dignified reproach at* HIGGINS, *he comes slowly and silently to his daughter, who, with her back to the window, is unconscious of his approach.*

PICKERING. He's incorrigible, Eliza. You wont relapse, will you?

LIZA. No: not now. Never again. I have learnt my lesson. I dont believe I could utter one of the old sounds if I tried. (DOOLITTLE *touches her on her left shoulder. She drops her work, losing her self-possession utterly at the spectacle of her father's splendor.*) A-a-a-a-ah-ow-ooh!

HIGGINS (*with a crow of triumph*). Aha! Just so. A-a-a-a-ahowooh! A-a-a-a-ahowooh! A-a-a-ahowooh! Victory! Victory! (*He throws himself on the divan, folding his arms, and spraddling arrogantly.*)

DOOLITTLE. Can you blame the girl? Dont look at me like that, Eliza. It aint my fault. Ive come into some money.

LIZA. You must have touched a millionaire this time, dad.

DOOLITTLE. I have. But I'm dressed something special today. I'm going to St George's,

Hanover Square. Your stepmother is going to marry me.

LIZA (*angrily*). Youre going to let yourself down to marry that low common woman!

PICKERING (*quietly*). He ought to, Eliza. (*To* DOOLITTLE) Why has she changed her mind?

DOOLITTLE (*sadly*). Intimidated, Governor. Intimidated. Middle class morality claims its victim. Wont you put on your hat, Liza, and come and see me turned off?

LIZA. If the Colonel says I must, I—I'll (*almost sobbing*) I'll demean myself. And get insulted for my pains, like enough.

DOOLITTLE. Dont be afraid: she never comes to words with anyone now, poor woman! respectability has broke all the spirit out of her.

PICKERING (*squeezing* ELIZA's *elbow gently*). Be kind to them, Eliza. Make the best of it.

LIZA (*forcing a little smile for him through her vexation*). Oh well, just to shew theres no ill feeling. I'll be back in a moment. (*She goes out.*)

DOOLITTLE (*sitting down beside* PICKERING). I feel uncommon nervous about the ceremony, Colonel. I wish youd come and see me through it.

PICKERING. But youve been through it before, man. You were married to Eliza's mother.

DOOLITTLE. Who told you that, Colonel?

PICKERING. Well, nobody told me. But I concluded—naturally—

DOOLITTLE. No: that aint the natural way, Colonel: it's only the middle class way. My way was always the undeserving way. But dont say nothing to Eliza. She dont know: I always had a delicacy about telling her.

PICKERING. Quite right. We'll leave it so, if you dont mind.

DOOLITTLE. And youll come to the church, Colonel, and put me through straight?

PICKERING. With pleasure. As far as a bachelor can.

MRS HIGGINS. May I come, Mr Doolittle? I should be very sorry to miss your wedding.

DOOLITTLE. I should indeed be honored by your condescension, maam; and my poor old woman would take it as a tremenjous compliment. She's been very low, thinking of the happy days that are no more.

MRS HIGGINS (*rising*). I'll order the carriage and get ready. (*The men rise, except* HIGGINS.) I shant be more than fifteen minutes. (*As she goes to the door* ELIZA *comes in, hatted and buttoning her gloves.*) I'm going to the church to see your father married, Eliza. You had better come in the brougham with me. Colonel Pickering can go on with the bridegroom.

MRS HIGGINS *goes out.* ELIZA *comes to the middle of the room between the centre window and the ottoman.* PICKERING *joins her.*

DOOLITTLE. Bridegroom! What a word! It makes a man realize his position, somehow. (*He takes up his hat and goes towards the door.*)

PICKERING. Before I go, Eliza, do forgive him and come back to us.

LIZA. I dont think papa would allow me. Would you, dad?

DOOLITTLE (*sad but magnanimous*). They played you off very cunning, Eliza, them two sportsmen. If it had been only one of them, you could have nailed him. But you see, there was two; and one of them chaperoned the other, as you might say. (*To* PICKERING) It was artful of you, Colonel; but I bear no malice: I should have done the same myself. I been the victim of one woman after another all my life; and I dont grudge you two getting the better of Eliza. I shant interfere. It's time for us to go, Colonel. So long, Henry. See you in St George's, Eliza. (*He goes out.*)

PICKERING (*coaxing*). Do stay with us, Eliza. (*He follows* DOOLITTLE.)

ELIZA *goes out on the balcony to avoid being alone with* HIGGINS. *He rises and joins her there. She immediately comes back into the room and makes for the door; but he goes along the balcony quickly and gets his back to the door before she reaches it.*

HIGGINS. Well, Eliza, youve had a bit of your own back, as you call it. Have you had enough? and are you going to be reasonable? Or do you want any more?

LIZA. You want me back only to pick up your slippers and put up with your tempers and fetch and carry for you.

HIGGINS. I havnt said I wanted you back at all.

LIZA. Oh, indeed. Then what are we talking about?

HIGGINS. About you, not about me. If you come back I shall treat you just as I have always treated you. I cant change my nature; and I dont intend to change my manners. My manners are exactly the same as Colonel Pickering's.

LIZA. Thats not true. He treats a flower girl as if she was a duchess.

HIGGINS. And I treat a duchess as if she was a flower girl.

LIZA. I see. (*She turns away composedly, and sits on the ottoman, facing the window.*) The same to everybody.

HIGGINS. Just so.

LIZA. Like father.

HIGGINS (*grinning, a little taken down*). Without accepting the comparison at all points, Eliza, it's quite true that your father is not a snob, and that he will be quite at home in any station of life to which his eccentric destiny may call him. (*Seriously*) The great secret, Eliza, is not having bad manners or good manners or any other particular sort of manners, but having the same manner for all human souls: in short, behaving as if you were in Heaven, where there are no third-class carriages, and one soul is as good as another.

LIZA. Amen. You are a born preacher.

HIGGINS (*irritated*). The question is not whether I treat you rudely, but whether you ever heard me treat anyone else better.

LIZA (*with sudden sincerity*). I dont care how you treat me. I dont mind your swearing at me. I dont mind a black eye: Ive had one before this. But (*standing up and facing him*) I wont be passed over.

HIGGINS. Then get out of my way; for I wont stop for you. You talk about me as if I were a motor bus.

LIZA. So you are a motor bus: all bounce and go, and no consideration for anyone. But I can do without you: dont think I cant.

HIGGINS. I know you can. I told you you could.

LIZA (*wounded, getting away from him to the other side of the ottoman with her face to the hearth*). I know you did, you brute. You wanted to get rid of me.

HIGGINS. Liar.

LIZA. Thank you. (*She sits down with dignity.*)

HIGGINS. You never asked yourself, I suppose, whether *I* could do without you.

LIZA (*earnestly*). Dont you try to get round me. Youll *have* to do without me.

HIGGINS (*arrogant*). I can do without anybody. I have my own soul: my own spark of divine fire. But (*with sudden humility*) I shall miss you, Eliza. (*He sits down near her on the ottoman.*) I have learnt something from your idiotic notions: I confess that humbly and gratefully. And I have grown accustomed to your voice and appearance. I like them, rather.

LIZA. Well, you have both of them on your gramophone and in your book of photographs. When you feel lonely without me, you can turn the machine on. It's got no feelings to hurt.

HIGGINS. I cant turn your soul on. Leave me those feelings; and you can take away the voice and the face. They are not you.

LIZA. Oh, you *are* a devil. You can twist the heart in a girl as easy as some could twist her arms to hurt her. Mrs Pearce warned me. Time and again she has wanted to leave you; and you always got round her at the last minute. And you dont care a bit for her. And you dont care a bit for me.

HIGGINS. I care for life, for humanity; and you are a part of it that has come my way and been built into my house. What more can you or anyone ask?

LIZA. I wont care for anybody that doesnt care for me.

HIGGINS. Commercial principles, Eliza. Like (*reproducing her Covent Garden pronunciation with professional exactness*) s'yollin voylets (*selling violets*), isnt it?

LIZA. Dont sneer at me. It's mean to sneer at me.

HIGGINS. I have never sneered in my life. Sneering doesnt become either the human face or the human soul. I am expressing my righteous contempt for Commercialism. I dont and wont trade in affection. You call me a brute because you couldnt buy a claim on me by fetching my slippers and finding my spectacles. You were a fool: I think a woman fetching a man's slippers is a disgusting sight: did I ever fetch *your* slippers? I think a good deal more of you for throwing them in my face. No use slaving for me and then saying you want to be cared for: who cares for a slave? If you come back, come back for the sake of good fellowship; for youll get nothing else. Youve had a thousand times as much out of me as I have out of you; and if you dare to set up your little dog's tricks of fetching and carrying slippers against my creation of a Duchess Eliza, I'll slam the door in your silly face.

LIZA. What did you do it for if you didnt care for me?

HIGGINS (heartily). Why, because it was my job.

LIZA. You never thought of the trouble it would make for me.

HIGGINS. Would the world ever have been made if its maker had been afraid of making trouble? Making life means making trouble. Theres only one way of escaping trouble; and thats killing things. Cowards, you notice, are always shrieking to have troublesome people killed.

LIZA. I'm no preacher: I dont notice things like that. I notice that you dont notice me.

HIGGINS (jumping up and walking about intolerantly). Eliza: youre an idiot. I waste the treasures of my Miltonic mind by spreading them before you. Once for all, understand that I go my way and do my work without caring twopence what happens to either of us. I am not intimidated, like your father and your stepmother. So you can come back or go to the devil: which you please.

LIZA. What am I to come back for?

HIGGINS (bouncing up on his knees on the ottoman and leaning over it to her). For the fun of it. Thats why I took you on.

LIZA (with averted face). And you may throw me out to-morrow if I dont do everything you want me to?

HIGGINS. Yes; and you may walk out to-morrow if I dont do everything you want me to.

LIZA. And live with my stepmother?

HIGGINS. Yes, or sell flowers.

LIZA. Oh! if I only could go back to my flower basket! I should be independent of both you and father and all the world! Why did you take my independence from me? Why did I give it up? I'm a slave now, for all my fine clothes.

HIGGINS. Not a bit. I'll adopt you as my daughter and settle money on you if you like. Or would you rather marry Pickering?

LIZA (looking fiercely round at him). I wouldnt marry you if you asked me; and youre nearer my age than what he is.

HIGGINS (gently). Than he is: not "than what he is."

LIZA (losing her temper and rising). I'll talk as I like. Youre not my teacher now.

HIGGINS (reflectively). I dont suppose Pickering would, though. He's as confirmed an old bachelor as I am.

LIZA. Thats not what I want; and dont you think it. Ive always had chaps enough wanting me that way. Freddy Hill writes to me twice and three times a day, sheets and sheets.

HIGGINS (disagreeably surprised). Damn his impudence! (He recoils and finds himself sitting on his heels.)

LIZA. He has a right to if he likes, poor lad. And he does love me.

HIGGINS (getting off the ottoman). You have no right to encourage him.

LIZA. Every girl has a right to be loved.

HIGGINS. What! By fools like that?

LIZA. Freddy's not a fool. And if he's weak and poor and wants me, may be he'd make me happier than my betters that bully me and dont want me.

HIGGINS. Can he make anything of you? Thats the point.

LIZA. Perhaps I could make something of him. But I never thought of us making anything of one another; and you never think of anything else. I only want to be natural.

HIGGINS. In short, you want me to be as infatuated about you as Freddy? Is that it?

LIZA. No I dont. Thats not the sort of feeling I want from you. And dont you be too sure of yourself or of me. I could have been a bad girl if I'd liked. Ive seen more of some things than you, for all your learning. Girls like me can drag gentlemen down to make love to them easy enough. And they wish each other dead the next minute.

HIGGINS. Of course they do. Then what in thunder are we quarrelling about?

LIZA (much troubled). I want a little kindness. I know I'm a common ignorant girl, and you a book-learned gentleman; but I'm not dirt under your feet. What I done (correcting herself) what I did was not for the dresses and the taxis: I did it because we were pleasant together and I come—came—to care for you; not to want you to make love to me, and not forgetting the difference between us, but more friendly like.

HIGGINS. Well, of course. Thats just how I feel. And how Pickering feels. Eliza: youre a fool.

LIZA. Thats not a proper answer to give me. (*She sinks on the chair at the writing-table in tears.*)

HIGGINS. It's all youll get until you stop being a common idiot. If youre going to be a lady, youll have to give up feeling neglected if the men you know dont spend half their time snivelling over you and the other half giving you black eyes. If you cant stand the coldness of my sort of life, and the strain of it, go back to the gutter. Work til you are more a brute than a human being; and then cuddle and squabble and drink til you fall asleep. Oh, it's a fine life, the life of the gutter. It's real: it's warm: it's violent: you can feel it through the thickest skin: you can taste it and smell it without any training or any work. Not like Science and Literature and Classical Music and Philosophy and Art. You find me cold, unfeeling, selfish, dont you? Very well: be off with you to the sort of people you like. Marry some sentimental hog or other with lots of money, and a thick pair of lips to kiss you with and a thick pair of boots to kick you with. If you cant appreciate what youve got, youd better get what you can appreciate.

LIZA (*desperate*). Oh, you *are* a cruel tyrant. I cant talk to you: you turn everything against me: I'm always in the wrong. But you know very well all the time that youre nothing but a bully. You know I cant go back to the gutter, as you call it, and that I have no real friends in the world but you and the Colonel. You know well I couldnt bear to live with a low common man after you two; and it's wicked and cruel of you to insult me by pretending I could. You think I must go back to Wimpole Street because I have nowhere else to go but father's. But dont you be too sure that you have me under your feet to be trampled on and talked down. I'll marry Freddy, I will, as soon as he's able to support me.

HIGGINS (*sitting down beside her*). Rubbish! You shall marry an ambassador. You shall marry the Governor-General of India or the Lord-Lieutenant of Ireland, or somebody who wants a deputy-queen. I'm not going to have my masterpiece thrown away on Freddy.

LIZA. You think I like you to say that. But I havnt forgot what you said a minute ago; and I wont be coaxed round as if I was a baby or a puppy. If I cant have kindness, I'll have independence.

HIGGINS. Independence? Thats middle class blasphemy. We are all dependent on one another, every soul of us on earth.

LIZA (*rising determinedly*). I'll let you see whether I'm dependent on you. If you can preach, I can teach. I'll go and be a teacher.

HIGGINS. Whatll you teach, in heaven's name?

LIZA. What you taught me. I'll teach phonetics.

HIGGINS. Ha! ha! ha!

LIZA. I'll offer myself as an assistant to Professor Nepean.

HIGGINS (*rising in a fury*). What! That impostor! that humbug! that toadying ignoramus! Teach him *my* methods! *my* discoveries! You take one step in his direction and I'll wring your neck. (*He lays hands on her.*) Do you hear?

LIZA (*defiantly non-resistant*). Wring away. What do I care? I knew youd strike me some day. (*He lets her go, stamping with rage at having forgotten himself, and recoils so hastily that he stumbles back into his seat on the ottoman.*) Aha! Now I know how to deal with you. What a fool I was not to think of it before! You cant take away the knowledge you gave me. You said I had a finer ear than you. And I can be civil and kind to people, which is more than you can. Aha! Thats done you, Henry Higgins, it has. Now I dont care *that* (*snapping her fingers*) for your bullying and your big talk. I'll advertize it in the papers that your duchess is only a flower girl that you taught, and that she'll teach anybody to be a duchess just the same in six months for a thousand guineas. Oh, when I think of myself crawling under your feet and being trampled on and called names, when all the time I had only to lift up my finger to be as good as you, I could just kick myself.

HIGGINS (*wondering at her*). You damned impudent slut, you! But it's better than snivelling; better than fetching slippers and finding spectacles, isnt it? (*Rising*) By George, Eliza, I said I'd make a woman of you; and I have. I like you like this.

LIZA. Yes: you turn round and make up to

me now that I'm not afraid of you, and can do without you.

HIGGINS. Of course I do, you little fool. Five minutes ago you were like a millstone round my neck. Now youre a tower of strength: a consort battleship. You and I and Pickering will be three old bachelors together instead of only two men and a silly girl.

MRS HIGGINS *returns, dressed for the wedding.* ELIZA *instantly becomes cool and elegant.*

MRS HIGGINS. The carriage is waiting, Eliza. Are you ready?

LIZA. Quite. Is the Professor coming?

MRS HIGGINS. Certainly not. He cant behave himself in church. He makes remarks out loud all the time on the clergyman's pronunciation.

LIZA. Then I shall not see you again, Professor. Goodbye. (*She goes to the door.*)

MRS HIGGINS (*coming to* HIGGINS). Goodbye, dear.

HIGGINS. Goodbye, mother. (*He is about to kiss her, when he recollects something.*) Oh, by the way, Eliza, order a ham and a Stilton cheese, will you? And buy me a pair of reindeer gloves, number eights, and a tie to match that new suit of mine, at Eale & Binman's. You can choose the color. (*His cheerful, careless, vigorous voice shows that he is incorrigible.*)

LIZA (*disdainfully*). Buy them yourself. (*She sweeps out.*)

MRS HIGGINS. I'm afraid youve spoiled that girl, Henry. But never mind, dear: I'll buy you the tie and gloves.

HIGGINS (*sunnily*). Oh, dont bother. She'll buy em all right enough. Goodbye.

They kiss. MRS HIGGINS *runs out.* HIGGINS, *left alone, rattles his cash in his pocket; chuckles; and disports himself in a highly self-satisfied manner.*

The rest of the story need not be shewn in action, and indeed, would hardly need telling if our imaginations were not so enfeebled by their lazy dependence on the ready-mades and reach-medowns of the ragshop in which Romance keeps its stock of "happy endings" to misfit all stories. Now, the history of Eliza Doolittle, though called a romance because the transfiguration it records seems exceedingly improbable, is common enough. Such transfigurations have been achieved by hundreds of resolutely ambitious young women since Nell Gwynne set them the example by playing queens

and fascinating kings in the theatre in which she began by selling oranges. Nevertheless, people in all directions have assumed, for no other reason than that she became the heroine of a romance, that she must have married the hero of it. This is unbearable, not only because her little drama, if acted on such a thoughtless assumption, must be spoiled, but because the true sequel is patent to anyone with a sense of human nature in general, and of feminine instinct in particular.

Eliza, in telling Higgins she would not marry him if he asked her, was not coquetting: she was announcing a well-considered decision. When a bachelor interests, and dominates, and teaches, and becomes important to a spinster, as Higgins with Eliza, she always, if she has character enough to be capable of it, considers very seriously indeed whether she will play for becoming that bachelor's wife, especially if he is so little interested in marriage that a determined and devoted woman might capture him if she set herself resolutely to do it. Her decision will depend a good deal on whether she is really free to choose; and that, again, will depend on her age and income. If she is at the end of her youth, and has no security for her livelihood, she will marry him because she must marry anybody who will provide for her. But at Eliza's age a good-looking girl does not feel that pressure: she feels free to pick and choose. She is therefore guided by her instinct in the matter. Eliza's instinct tells her not to marry Higgins. It does not tell her to give him up. It is not in the slightest doubt as to his remaining one of the strongest personal interests in her life. It would be very sorely strained if there was another woman likely to supplant her with him. But as she feels sure of him on that last point, she has no doubt at all as to her course, and would not have any, even if the difference of twenty years in age, which seems so great to youth, did not exist between them.

As our own instincts are not appealed to by her conclusion, let us see whether we cannot discover some reason in it. When Higgins excused his indifference to young women on the ground that they had an irresistible rival in his mother, he gave the clue to his inveterate old-bachelordom. The case is uncommon only to the extent that remarkable mothers are uncommon. If an imaginative boy has a sufficiently rich mother who has intelligence, personal grace, dignity of character without harshness, and a cultivated sense of the best art of her time to enable her to make her house beautiful, she sets a standard for him against which very few women can struggle, besides effecting for him a disengagement of his affections, his sense of beauty, and his idealism from his specifically sexual impulses. This makes him a standing puzzle to the huge number of uncultivated people who have been brought up in tasteless homes by commonplace or disagreeable parents, and to whom, consequently, literature, painting, sculpture, music, and affectionate personal relations come as modes of sex if they come at all. The word passion means nothing else to them; and that Higgins could have a passion for phonetics and idealize his mother instead of Eliza, would seem to them absurd and unnatural. Nevertheless, when we look round and see that hardly anyone is too ugly or disagreeable to find a wife or a husband if he or she wants one, whilst many old maids and bachelors are above the average in quality and culture, we cannot help suspecting that the disentanglement of sex from the associations with which it is so commonly confused, a disentanglement which persons of genius achieve by sheer intellectual analysis, is sometimes produced or aided by parental fascination.

Now, though Eliza was incapable of thus explaining to herself Higgins's formidable powers of resistance to the charm that prostrated Freddy at the first glance, she was instinctively aware that she could never obtain a complete grip of him, or come between him and his mother (the first necessity of the married woman). To put it shortly, she knew that for some mysterious reason he had not the makings of a married man in him, according to her conception of a husband as one to whom she would be his nearest and fondest and warmest interest. Even had there been no mother-rival, she would still have refused to accept an interest in herself that was secondary to philosophic interests. Had Mrs Higgins died, there would still have been Milton and the Universal Alphabet. Landor's remark that to those who have the greatest power of loving, love is a secondary affair, would not have recommended Landor to Eliza. Put that along with her resentment of Higgins's domineering superiority, and her mistrust of his coaxing cleverness in getting round her and evading her wrath when he had gone too far with his impetuous bullying, and you will see that Eliza's instinct had good grounds for warning her not to marry her Pygmalion.

And now, whom did Eliza marry? For if Higgins was a predestinate old bachelor, she was most certainly not a predestinate old maid. Well, that can be told very shortly to those who have not guessed it from the indications she has herself given them. Almost immediately after Eliza is stung into proclaiming her considered determination not to marry Higgins, she mentions the fact that young Mr Frederick Eynsford Hill is pouring out his love for her daily through the post. Now Freddy is young, practically twenty years younger than Higgins: he is a gentleman (or, as Eliza would

qualify him, a toff), and speaks like one; he is nicely dressed, is treated by the Colonel as an equal, loves her unaffectedly, and is not her master, nor ever likely to dominate her in spite of his advantage of social standing. Eliza has no use for the foolish romantic tradition that all women love to be mastered, if not actually bullied and beaten. "When you go to women," says Nietzsche, "take your whip with you." Sensible despots have never confined that precaution to women: they have taken their whips with them when they have dealt with men, and been slavishly idealized by the men over whom they have flourished the whip much more than by women. No doubt there are slavish women as well as slavish men: and women, like men, admire those that are stronger than themselves. But to admire a strong person and to live under that strong person's thumb are two different things. The weak may not be admired and hero-worshipped; but they are by no means disliked or shunned; and they never seem to have the least difficulty in marrying people who are too good for them. They may fail in emergencies; but life is not one long emergency: it is mostly a string of situations for which no exceptional strength is needed, and with which even rather weak people can cope if they have a stronger partner to help them out. Accordingly, it is a truth everywhere in evidence that strong people, masculine or feminine, not only do not marry stronger people, but do not shew any preference for them in selecting their friends. When a lion meets another with a louder roar "the first lion thinks the last a bore." The man or woman who feels strong enough for two, seeks for every other quality in a partner than strength.

The converse is also true. Weak people want to marry strong people who do not frighten them too much; and this often leads them to make the mistake we describe metaphorically as "biting off more than they can chew." They want too much for too little; and when the bargain is unreasonable beyond all bearing, the union becomes impossible: it ends in the weaker party being either discarded or borne as a cross, which is worse. People who are not only weak, but silly or obtuse as well, are often in these difficulties.

This being the state of human affairs, what is Eliza fairly sure to do when she is placed between Freddy and Higgins? Will she look forward to a lifetime of fetching Higgins's slippers or to a lifetime of Freddy fetching hers? There can be no doubt about the answer. Unless Freddy is biologically repulsive to her, and Higgins biologically attractive to a degree that overwhelms all her other instincts, she will, if she marries either of them, marry Freddy.

And that is just what Eliza did.

Complications ensued; but they were economic, not romantic. Freddy had no money and no occupation. His mother's jointure, a last relic of the opulence of Largelady Park, had enabled her to struggle along in Earlscourt with an air of gentility, but not to procure any serious secondary education for her children, much less give the boy a profession. A clerkship at thirty shillings a week was beneath Freddy's dignity, and extremely distasteful to him besides. His prospects consisted of a hope that if he kept up appearances somebody would do something for him. The something appeared vaguely to his imagination as a private secretaryship or a sinecure of some sort. To his mother it perhaps appeared as a marriage to some lady of means who could not resist her boy's niceness. Fancy her feelings when he married a flower girl who had become déclassée under extraordinary circumstances which were now notorious!

It is true that Eliza's situation did not seem wholly ineligible. Her father, though formerly a dustman, and now fantastically disclassed, had become extremely popular in the smartest society by a social talent which triumphed over every prejudice and every disadvantage. Rejected by the middle class, which he loathed, he had shot up at once into the highest circles by his wit, his dustmanship (which he carried like a banner), and his Nietzschean transcendence of good and evil. At intimate ducal dinners he sat on the right hand of the Duchess; and in country houses he smoked in the pantry and was made much of by the butler when he was not feeding in the dining room and being consulted by cabinet ministers. But he found it almost as hard to do all this on four thousand a year as Mrs Eynsford Hill to live in Earlscourt on an income so pitiably smaller that I have not the heart to disclose its exact figure. He absolutely refused to add the last straw to his burden by contributing to Eliza's support.

Thus Freddy and Eliza, now Mr and Mrs Eynsford Hill, would have spent a penniless honeymoon but for a wedding present of £500 from the Colonel to Eliza. It lasted a long time because Freddy did not know how to spend money, never having had any to spend, and Eliza, socially trained by a pair of old bachelors, wore her clothes as long as they held together and looked pretty, without the least regard to their being many months out of fashion. Still, £500 will not last two young people for ever; and they both knew, and Eliza felt as well, that they must shift for themselves in the end. She could quarter herself on Wimpole Street because it had come to be her home; but she was quite aware that she ought not

to quarter Freddy there, and that it would not be good for his character if she did.

Not that the Wimpole Street bachelors objected. When she consulted them, Higgins declined to be bothered about her housing problem when that solution was so simple. Eliza's desire to have Freddy in the house with her seemed of no more importance than if she had wanted an extra piece of bedroom furniture. Pleas as to Freddy's character, and the moral obligation on him to earn his own living, were lost on Higgins. He denied that Freddy had any character, and declared that if he tried to do any useful work some competent person would have the trouble of undoing it: a procedure involving a net loss to the community, and great unhappiness to Freddy himself, who was obviously intended by Nature for such light work as amusing Eliza, which, Higgins declared, was a much more useful and honorable occupation than working in the city. When Eliza referred again to her project of teaching phonetics, Higgins abated not a jot of his violent opposition to it. He said she was not within ten years of being qualified to meddle with his pet subject; and as it was evident that the Colonel agreed with him, she felt she could not go against them in this grave matter, and that she had no right, without Higgins's consent, to exploit the knowledge he had given her; for his knowledge seemed to her as much his private property as his watch: Eliza was no communist. Besides, she was superstitiously devoted to them both, more entirely and frankly after her marriage than before it.

It was the Colonel who finally solved the problem, which had cost him much perplexed cogitation. He one day asked Eliza, rather shyly, whether she had quite given up her notion of keeping a flower shop. She replied that she had thought of it, but had put it out of her head, because the Colonel had said, that day at Mrs Higgins's, that it would never do. The Colonel confessed that when he said that, he had not quite recovered from the dazzling impression of the day before. They broke the matter to Higgins that evening. The sole comment vouchsafed by him very nearly led to a serious quarrel with Eliza. It was to the effect that she would have in Freddy an ideal errand boy.

Freddy himself was next sounded on the subject. He said he had been thinking of a shop himself; though it had presented itself to his pennilessness as a small place in which Eliza should sell tobacco at one counter whilst he sold newspapers at the opposite one. But he agreed that it would be extraordinarily jolly to go early every morning with Eliza to Covent Garden and buy flowers on the scene of their first meeting: a sentiment which earned him many kisses from his wife. He added that he had always been afraid to propose anything of the sort, because Clara would make an awful row about a step that must damage her matrimonial chances, and his mother could not be expected to like it after clinging for so many years to that step of the social ladder on which retail trade is impossible.

This difficulty was removed by an event highly unexpected by Freddy's mother. Clara, in the course of her incursions into those artistic circles which were the highest within her reach, discovered that her conversational qualifications were expected to include a grounding on the novels of Mr H. G. Wells. She borrowed them in various directions so energetically that she swallowed them all within two months. The result was a conversion of a kind quite common today. A modern Acts of the Apostles would fill fifty whole Bibles if anyone were capable of writing it.

Poor Clara, who appeared to Higgins and his mother as a disagreeable and ridiculous person, and to her own mother as in some inexplicable way a social failure, had never seen herself in either light; for, though to some extent ridiculed and mimicked in West Kensington like everybody else there, she was accepted as a rational and normal—or shall we say inevitable?—sort of human being. At worst they called her The Pusher; but to them no more than to herself had it ever occurred that she was pushing the air, and pushing it in a wrong direction. Still, she was not happy. She was growing desperate. Her one asset, the fact that her mother was what the Epsom greengrocer called a carriage lady, had no exchange value, apparently. It had prevented her from getting educated, because the only education she could have afforded was education with the Earlscourt greengrocer's daughter. It had led her to seek the society of her mother's class; and that class simply would not have her, because she was much poorer than the greengrocer, and, far from being able to afford a maid, could not afford even a housemaid, and had to scrape along at home with an illiberally treated general servant. Under such circumstances nothing could give her an air of being a genuine product of Largelady Park. And yet its tradition made her regard a marriage with anyone within her reach as an unbearable humiliation. Commercial people and professional people in a small way were odious to her. She ran after painters and novelists; but she did not charm them; and her bold attempts to pick up and practice artistic and literary talk irritated them. She was, in short, an utter failure, an ignorant, incompetent, pretentious, unwelcome, penniless, useless little snob; and though she did not admit these disqualifications (for nobody ever faces unpleasant truths of this

kind until the possibility of a way out dawns on them) she felt their effects too keenly to be satisfied with her position.

Clara had a startling eyeopener when, on being suddenly wakened to enthusiasm by a girl of her own age who dazzled her and produced in her a gushing desire to take her for a model, and gain her friendship, she discovered that this exquisite apparition had graduated from the gutter in a few months time. It shook her so violently, that when Mr H. G. Wells lifted her on the point of his puissant pen, and placed her at the angle of view from which the life she was leading and the society to which she clung appeared in its true relation to real human needs and worthy social structure, he effected a conversion and a conviction of sin comparable to the most sensational feats of General Booth or Gypsy Smith. Clara's snobbery went bang. Life suddenly began to move with her. Without knowing how or why, she began to make friends and enemies. Some of the acquaintances to whom she had been a tedious or indifferent or ridiculous affliction, dropped her: others became cordial. To her amazement she found that some "quite nice" people were saturated with Wells, and that this accessibility to ideas was the secret of their niceness. People she had thought deeply religious, and had tried to conciliate on that tack with disastrous results, suddenly took an interest in her, and revealed a hostility to conventional religion which she had never conceived possible except among the most desperate characters. They made her read Galsworthy; and Galsworthy exposed the vanity of Largelady Park and finished her. It exasperated her to think that the dungeon in which she had languished for so many unhappy years had been unlocked all the time, and that the impulses she had so carefully struggled with and stifled for the sake of keeping well with society, were precisely those by which alone she could have come into any sort of sincere human contact. In the radiance of these discoveries, and the tumult of their reaction, she made a fool of herself as freely and conspicuously as when she so rashly adopted Eliza's expletive in Mrs Higgins's drawing room; for the newborn Wellsian had to find her bearings almost as ridiculously as a baby; but nobody hates a baby for its ineptitudes, or thinks the worse of it for trying to eat the matches; and Clara lost no friends by her follies. They laughed at her to her face this time; and she had to defend herself and fight it out as best she could.

When Freddy paid a visit to Earlscourt (which he never did when he could possibly help it) to make the desolating announcement that he and his Eliza were thinking of blackening the Largelady scutcheon by opening a shop, he found the little household already convulsed by a prior announcement from Clara that she also was going to work in an old furniture shop in Dover Street, which had been started by a fellow Wellsian. This appointment Clara owed, after all, to her old social accomplishment of Push. She had made up her mind that, cost what it might, she would see Mr Wells in the flesh; and she had achieved her end at a garden party. She had better luck than so rash an enterprise deserved. Mr Wells came up to her expectations. Age had not withered him, nor could custom stale his infinite variety in half an hour. His pleasant neatness and compactness, his small hands and feet, his teeming ready brain, his unaffected accessibility, and a certain fine apprehensiveness which stamped him as susceptible from his topmost hair to his tipmost toe, proved irresistible. Clara talked of nothing else for weeks and weeks afterwards. And as she happened to talk to the lady of the furniture shop, and that lady also desired above all things to know Mr Wells and sell pretty things to him, she offered Clara a job on the chance of achieving that end through her.

And so it came about that Eliza's luck held, and the expected opposition to the flower shop melted away. The shop is in the arcade of a railway station not very far from the Victoria and Albert Museum; and if you live in that neighborhood you may go there any day and buy a buttonhole from Eliza.

Now here is a last opportunity for romance. Would you not like to be assured that the shop was an immense success, thanks to Eliza's charms and her early business experience in Covent Garden? Alas! the truth is the truth: the shop did not pay for a long time, simply because Eliza and her Freddy did not know how to keep it. True, Eliza had not to begin at the very beginning: she knew the names and prices of the cheaper flowers; and her elation was unbounded when she found that Freddy, like all youths educated at cheap, pretentious, and thoroughly inefficient schools, knew a little Latin. It was very little, but enough to make him appear to her a Porson or Bentley, and to put him at his ease with botanical nomenclature. Unfortunately he knew nothing else; and Eliza, though she could count money up to eighteen shillings or so, and had acquired a certain familiarity with the language of Milton from her struggles to qualify herself for winning Higgins's bet, could not write out a bill without utterly disgracing the establishment. Freddy's power of stating in Latin that Balbus built a wall and that Gaul was divided into three parts did not carry with it the slightest knowledge of accounts or business: Colonel Pickering had to explain to him what a cheque book and a bank account meant. And the

pair were by no means easily teachable. Freddy backed up Eliza in her obstinate refusal to believe that they could save money by engaging a bookkeeper with some knowledge of the business. How, they argued, could you possibly save money by going to extra expense when you already could not make both ends meet? But the Colonel, after making the ends meet over and over again, at last gently insisted; and Eliza, humbled to the dust by having to beg from him so often, and stung by the uproarious derision of Higgins, to whom the notion of Freddy succeeding at anything was a joke that never palled, grasped the fact that business, like phonetics, has to be learned.

On the piteous spectacle of the pair spending their evenings in shorthand schools and polytechnic classes, learning bookkeeping and typewriting with incipient junior clerks, male and female, from the elementary schools, let me not dwell. There were even classes at the London School of Economics, and a humble personal appeal to the director of that institution to recommend a course bearing on the flower business. He, being a humorist, explained to them the method of the celebrated Dickensian essay on Chinese Metaphysics by the gentleman who read an article on China and an article on Metaphysics and combined the information. He suggested that they should combine the London School with Kew Gardens. Eliza, to whom the procedure of the Dickensian gentleman seemed perfectly correct (as in fact it was) and not in the least funny (which was only her ignorance), took his advice with entire gravity. But the effort that cost her the deepest humiliation was a request to Higgins, whose pet artistic fancy, next to Milton's verse, was calligraphy, and who himself wrote a most beautiful Italian hand, that he would teach her to write. He declared that she was congenitally incapable of forming a single letter worthy of the least of Milton's words; but she persisted; and again he suddenly threw himself into the task of teaching her with a combination of stormy intensity, concentrated patience, and occasional bursts of interesting disquisition on the beauty and nobility, the august mission and destiny, of human handwriting. Eliza ended by acquiring an extremely uncommercial script which was a positive extension of her personal beauty, and spending three times as much on stationery as anyone else because certain qualities and shapes of paper became indispensable to her. She could not even address an envelope in the usual way because it made the margins all wrong.

Their commercial schooldays were a period of disgrace and despair for the young couple. They seemed to be learning nothing about flower shops.

At last they gave it up as hopeless, and shook the dust of the shorthand schools, and the polytechnics, and the London School of Economics from their feet for ever. Besides, the business was in some mysterious way beginning to take care of itself. They had somehow forgotten their objections to employing other people. They came to the conclusion that their own way was the best, and that they had really a remarkable talent for business. The Colonel, who had been compelled for some years to keep a sufficient sum on current account at his bankers to make up their deficits, found that the provision was unnecessary: the young people were prospering. It is true that there was not quite fair play between them and their competitors in trade. Their week-ends in the country cost them nothing, and saved them the price of their Sunday dinners; for the motor car was the Colonel's; and he and Higgins paid the hotel bills. Mr F. Hill, florist and greengrocer (they soon discovered that there was money in asparagus; and asparagus led to other vegetables), had an air which stamped the business as classy; and in private life he was still Frederick Eynsford Hill, Esquire. Not that there was any swank about him: nobody but Eliza knew that he had been christened Frederick Challoner. Eliza herself swanked like anything.

That is all. That is how it has turned out. It is astonishing how much Eliza still manages to meddle in the housekeeping at Wimpole Street in spite of the shop and her own family. And it is notable that though she never nags her husband, and frankly loves the Colonel as if she were his favorite daughter, she has never got out of the habit of nagging Higgins that was established on the fatal night when she won his bet for him. She snaps his head off on the faintest provocation, or on none. He no longer dares to tease her by assuming an abysmal inferiority of Freddy's mind to his own. He storms and bullies and derides: but she stands up to him so ruthlessly that the Colonel has to ask her from time to time to be kinder to Higgins; and it is the only request of his that brings a mulish expression into her face. Nothing but some emergency or calamity great enough to break down all likes and dislikes, and throw them both back on their common humanity—and may they be spared any such trial!—will ever alter this. She knows that Higgins does not need her, just as her father did not need her. The very scrupulousness with which he told her that day that he had become used to having her there, and dependent on her for all sorts of little services, and that he should miss her if she went away (it would never have occurred to Freddy or the Colonel to say anything of the sort) deepens her inner certainty that she is "no more to him than them slippers"; yet she has a sense, too, that his indifference is deeper than the infatuation of commoner souls. She is immensely interested in him. She has even secret mischievous moments in which she wishes she could get him alone, on a desert island, away from all ties and with nobody else in the world to consider, and just drag him off his pedestal and see him making love like any common man. We all have private imaginations of that sort. But when it comes to business, to the life that she really leads as distinguished from the life of dreams and fancies, she likes Freddy and she likes the Colonel; and she does not like Higgins and Mr Doolittle. Galatea never does quite like Pygmalion: his relation to her is too godlike to be altogether agreeable.

ARTHUR MILLER *Death of a Salesman*

Arthur Miller (1916-   ) was born to a lower-middle-class family in New York's Harlem district. He was educated in the public schools of Brooklyn and at the University of Michigan, where his talent for play writing won him the Hopwood Award for two successive years and the Theatre Guild National Award.

After his graduation in 1938 he worked with the Federal Theater Project and wrote scripts for the Columbia Broadcasting System. He also had an unsuccessful try at Hollywood, which he described as "swimming in a sea of gumdrops." During the war he was assigned to collect material for the scenario of Ernie Pyle's *The Story of G.I. Joe*. Some of this material provided the subject for his volume of reportage, *Situation Normal*, 1944. *Focus*, 1945, is an exciting novel dealing with anti-Semitism.

His first professional production on Broadway, *The Man Who Had All the Luck*, 1944, lasted "just long enough for the actors to put on their make-up." His next play, *All My Sons*, 1947, however, ran for three hundred performances and received the Drama Critics Circle Award. *Death of a Salesman*, 1949, was a triumph. It won five awards including the Drama Critics Circle Award and the Pulitzer Prize. Brooks Atkinson pronounced it "one of the finest dramas in the whole range of the American theatre." In 1955 two one-act plays—*A Memory of Two Mondays* and *A View from the Bridge*—were produced under the collective title *A View from the Bridge*.

Mr. Miller takes his fame modestly and is content to live the life of a suburbanite in Brooklyn. In his writing he is concerned primarily with the life and problems of the middle class. In fact his plays are written with the professed intention of making theater going a vivid and enriching experience for the ordinary middle-class American citizen.

The great success of *Death of a Salesman* has raised a critical controversy about the nature of its power. Can it be called tragedy? Is Willy Loman a tragic hero? Does the stature of the tragic hero depend upon his inner dignity alone, or does it depend upon the worth and universality of the things for which he sacrifices himself? Can the audience find value in Willy's devotion to his dream of success, worthless though it be? Mr. Miller himself feels that Willy is a tragic hero and defends his conception by saying that Willy's "tragic flaw" is his "inherent unwillingness to remain passive in the face of what he conceives to be a challenge to his dignity, his image of his rightful status."

Death of a Salesman is a landmark in the history of the American stage, for it carries forward the endeavor of American dramatists such as Eugene O'Neill, Clifford Odets, and Tennessee Williams to create a realistically critical expression of American life. The common man—you might say, the man next door—is the hero; and the speech and manners, though the drama is poetic, are rooted in American life.

CHARACTERS

Salesman
wife
sons

WILLY LOMAN   HOWARD WAGNER
LINDA   JENNY
BIFF   STANLEY
HAPPY   MISS FORSYTHE
BERNARD   LETTA
THE WOMAN   CHARLEY
UNCLE BEN

THE PLACE

Willy Loman's house and yard and various places he visits in the New York and Boston of today.

Throughout the play, in the stage directions, left and right mean stage left and stage right.

ACT I

A melody is heard, played upon a flute. It is small and fine, telling of grass and trees and the horizon. The curtain rises.

Before us is the Salesman's house. We are aware of towering, angular shapes behind it, surrounding it on all sides. Only the blue light of the sky falls upon the house and forestage; the surrounding area shows an angry glow of orange. As more light appears, we see a solid vault of apartment houses around the small, fragile-seeming home. An air of the dream clings to the place, a dream rising out of reality. The kitchen at center seems actual enough, for there is a kitchen table with three chairs, and a refrigerator. But no other fixtures are seen. At the back of the kitchen there is a draped entrance, which leads to the living-room. To the right of the kitchen, on a level raised two feet, is a bedroom furnished only with a brass bedstead and a straight chair. On a shelf over the bed a silver athletic trophy stands. A window opens onto the apartment house at the side.

Behind the kitchen, on a level raised six and a half feet, is the boys' bedroom, at present barely visible. Two beds are dimly seen, and at the back of the room a dormer window. (This bedroom is above the unseen living-room.) At the left a stairway curves up to it from the kitchen.

The entire setting is wholly or, in some places, partially transparent. The roof-line of the house is one-dimensional; under and over it we see the apartment buildings. Before the house lies an apron, curving beyond the fore-stage into the orchestra. This forward area serves as the back yard as well as the locale of all WILLY's imaginings and of his city scenes. Whenever the action is in the present the actors observe the imaginary wall-lines, entering the house only through its door at the left. But in the scenes of the past these boundaries are broken, and characters enter or leave a room by stepping "through" a wall onto the forestage.

From the right, WILLY LOMAN, the Salesman, enters, carrying two large sample cases. The flute plays on. He hears but is not aware of it. He is past sixty years of age, dressed quietly. Even as he crosses the stage to the doorway of the house, his exhaustion is apparent. He unlocks the door, comes into the kitchen, and thankfully lets his burden down, feeling the soreness of his palms. A word-sigh escapes his lips—it might be "Oh, boy, oh, boy." He closes the door, then carries his cases out into the living-room, through the draped kitchen doorway.

LINDA, his wife, has stirred in her bed at the right. She gets out and puts on a robe, listening. Most often jovial, she has developed an iron repression of her exceptions to WILLY's behavior—she more than loves him, she admires him, as though his mercurial nature, his temper, his massive dreams and little cruelties, served her only as sharp reminders of the turbulent longings within him, longings which she shares but lacks the temperament to utter and follow to their end.

LINDA (*hearing* WILLY *outside the bedroom, calls with some trepidation*). Willy!

WILLY. It's all right. I came back.

LINDA. Why? What happened? (*Slight pause*) Did something happen, Willy?

WILLY. No, nothing happened.

LINDA. You didn't smash the car, did you?

WILLY (*with casual irritation*). I said nothing happened. Didn't you hear me?

LINDA. Don't you feel well?

WILLY. I'm tired to the death. (*The flute has faded away. He sits on the bed beside her, a little numb.*) I couldn't make it. I just couldn't make it, Linda.

LINDA (*very carefully, delicately*). Where were you all day? You look terrible.

WILLY. I got as far as a little above Yonkers. I stopped for a cup of coffee. Maybe it was the coffee.

LINDA. What?

WILLY (*after a pause*). I suddenly couldn't drive any more. The car kept going off onto the shoulder, y'know?

LINDA (*helpfully*). Oh. Maybe it was the steering again. I don't think Angelo knows the Studebaker.

WILLY. No, it's me, it's me. Suddenly I realize I'm goin' sixty miles an hour and I don't remember the last five minutes. I'm—I can't seem to—keep my mind to it.

LINDA. Maybe it's your glasses. You never went for your new glasses.

WILLY. No, I see everything. I came back ten miles an hour. It took me nearly four hours from Yonkers.

LINDA (*resigned*). Well, you'll just have to take a rest, Willy, you can't continue this way.

WILLY. I just got back from Florida.

LINDA. But you didn't rest your mind. Your mind is overactive, and the mind is what counts, dear.

WILLY. I'll start out in the morning. Maybe I'll feel better in the morning. (*She is taking off his shoes.*) These goddam arch supports are killing me.

LINDA. Take an aspirin. Should I get you an aspirin? It'll soothe you.

WILLY (*with wonder*). I was driving along, you understand? And I was fine. I was even observing the scenery. You can imagine, me looking at scenery, on the road every week

of my life. But it's so beautiful up there, Linda, the trees are so thick, and the sun is warm. I opened the windshield and just let the warm air bathe over me. And then all of a sudden I'm goin' off the road! I'm tellin' ya, I absolutely forgot I was driving. If I'd've gone the other way over the white line I might've killed somebody. So I went on again—and five minutes later I'm dreamin' again, and I nearly— (*He presses two fingers against his eyes.*) I have such thoughts, I have such strange thoughts.

LINDA. Willy, dear. Talk to them again. There's no reason why you can't work in New York.

WILLY. They don't need me in New York. I'm the New England man. I'm vital in New England.

LINDA. But you're sixty years old. They can't expect you to keep traveling every week.

WILLY. I'll have to send a wire to Portland. I'm supposed to see Brown and Morrison tomorrow morning at ten o'clock to show the line. Goddammit, I could sell them! (*He starts putting on his jacket.*)

LINDA (*taking the jacket from him*). Why don't you go down to the place tomorrow and tell Howard you've simply got to work in New York? You're too accommodating, dear.

WILLY. If old man Wagner was alive I'd a been in charge of New York now! That man was a prince, he was a masterful man. But that boy of his, that Howard, he don't appreciate. When I went north the first time, the Wagner Company didn't know where New England was!

LINDA. Why don't you tell those things to Howard, dear?

WILLY (*encouraged*). I will, I definitely will. Is there any cheese?

LINDA. I'll make you a sandwich.

WILLY. No, go to sleep. I'll take some milk. I'll be up right away. The boys in?

LINDA. They're sleeping. Happy took Biff on a date tonight.

WILLY (*interested*). That so?

LINDA. It was so nice to see them shaving together, one behind the other, in the bathroom. And going out together. You notice? The whole house smells of shaving lotion.

WILLY. Figure it out. Work a lifetime to

pay off a house. You finally own it, and there's nobody to live in it.

LINDA. Well, dear, life is a casting off. It's always that way.

WILLY. No, no, some people—some people accomplish something. Did Biff say anything after I went this morning?

LINDA. You shouldn't have criticized him, Willy, especially after he just got off the train. You mustn't lose your temper with him.

WILLY. When the hell did I lose my temper? I simply asked him if he was making any money. Is that a criticism?

LINDA. But, dear, how could he make any money?

WILLY (worried and angered). There's such an undercurrent in him. He became a moody man. Did he apologize when I left this morning?

LINDA. He was crestfallen, Willy. You know how he admires you. I think if he finds himself, then you'll both be happier and not fight any more.

WILLY. How can he find himself on a farm? Is that a life? A farmhand? In the beginning, when he was young, I thought, well, a young man, it's good for him to tramp around, take a lot of different jobs. But it's more than ten years now and he has yet to make thirty-five dollars a week!

LINDA. He's finding himself, Willy.

WILLY. Not finding yourself at the age of thirty-four is a disgrace!

LINDA. Shh!

WILLY. The trouble is he's lazy, goddammit!

LINDA. Willy, please!

WILLY. Biff is a lazy bum!

LINDA. They're sleeping. Get something to eat. Go on down.

WILLY. Why did he come home? I would like to know what brought him home.

LINDA. I don't know. I think he's still lost, Willy. I think he's very lost.

WILLY. Biff Loman is lost. In the greatest country in the world a young man with such—personal attractiveness, gets lost. And such a hard worker. There's one thing about Biff—he's not lazy.

LINDA. Never.

WILLY (with pity and resolve). I'll see him in the morning; I'll have a nice talk with him. I'll get him a job selling. He could be big in no time. My God! Remember how they used to follow him around in high school? When he smiled at one of them their faces lit up. When he walked down the street. . . . (He loses himself in reminiscences.)

LINDA (trying to bring him out of it). Willy, dear, I got a new kind of American-type cheese today. It's whipped.

WILLY. Why do you get American when I like Swiss?

LINDA. I just thought you'd like a change—

WILLY. I don't want a change! I want Swiss cheese. Why am I always being contradicted?

LINDA (with a covering laugh). I thought it would be a surprise.

WILLY. Why don't you open a window in here, for God's sake?

LINDA (with infinite patience). They're all open, dear.

WILLY. The way they boxed us in here. Bricks and windows, windows and bricks.

LINDA. We should've bought the land next door.

WILLY. The street is lined with cars. There's not a breath of fresh air in the neighborhood. The grass don't grow any more, you can't raise a carrot in the back yard. They should've had a law against apartment houses. Remember those two beautiful elm trees out there? When I and Biff hung the swing between them?

LINDA. Yeah, like being a million miles from the city.

WILLY. They should've arrested the builder for cutting those down. They massacred the neighborhood. (Lost) More and more I think of those days, Linda. This time of year it was lilac and wisteria. And then the peonies would come out, and the daffodils. What fragrance in this room!

LINDA. Well, after all, people had to move somewhere.

WILLY. No, there's more people now.

LINDA. I don't think there's more people. I think—

WILLY. There's more people! That's what's ruining this country! Population is getting out of control. The competition is maddening! Smell the stink from that apartment house! And another one on the other side . . . How can they whip cheese?

(On WILLY's last line, BIFF and HAPPY raise themselves up in their beds, listening.)

LINDA. Go down, try it. And be quiet.

WILLY (turning to LINDA, guiltily). You're not worried about me, are you, sweetheart?

BIFF. What's the matter?

HAPPY. Listen!

LINDA. You've got too much on the ball to worry about.

WILLY. You're my foundation and my support, Linda.

LINDA. Just try to relax, dear. You make mountains out of molehills.

WILLY. I won't fight with him any more. If he wants to go back to Texas, let him go.

LINDA. He'll find his way.

WILLY. Sure. Certain men just don't get started till later in life. Like Thomas Edison, I think. Or B. F. Goodrich. One of them was deaf. (He starts for the bedroom doorway.) I'll put my money on Biff.

LINDA. And Willy—if it's warm Sunday we'll drive in the country. And we'll open the windshield, and take lunch.

WILLY. No, the windshields don't open on the new cars.

LINDA. But you opened it today.

WILLY. Me? I didn't. (He stops.) Now isn't that peculiar! Isn't that a remarkable— (He breaks off in amazement and fright as the flute is heard distantly.)

LINDA. What, darling?

WILLY. That is the most remarkable thing.

LINDA. What, dear?

WILLY. I was thinking of the Chevvy. (Slight pause) Nineteen twenty-eight . . . when I had that red Chevvy— (Breaks off) That's funny? I coulda sworn I was driving that Chevvy today.

LINDA. Well, that's nothing. Something must've reminded you.

WILLY. Remarkable. Ts. Remember those days? The way Biff used to simonize that car? The dealer refused to believe there was eighty thousand miles on it. (He shakes his head.) Heh! (To LINDA) Close your eyes, I'll be right up. (He walks out of the bedroom.)

HAPPY (to BIFF). Jesus, maybe he smashed up the car again!

LINDA (calling after WILLY). Be careful on the stairs, dear! The cheese is on the middle shelf! (She turns, goes over to the bed, takes his jacket, and goes out of the bedroom.)

(Light has risen on the boys' room. Unseen, WILLY is heard talking to himself, "Eighty thousand miles," and a little laugh. BIFF gets out of bed, comes downstage a bit, and stands attentively. BIFF is two years older than his brother HAPPY, well built, but in these days bears a worn air and seems less self-assured. He has succeeded less, and his dreams are stronger and less acceptable than HAPPY's. HAPPY is tall, powerfully made. Sexuality is like a visible color on him, or a scent that many women have discovered. He, like his brother, is lost, but in a different way, for he has never allowed himself to turn his face toward defeat and is thus more confused and hard-skinned, although seemingly more content.)

HAPPY (getting out of bed). He's going to get his license taken away if he keeps that up. I'm getting nervous about him, y'know, Biff?

BIFF. His eyes are going.

HAPPY. No, I've driven with him. He sees all right. He just doesn't keep his mind on it. I drove into the city with him last week. He stops at a green light and then it turns red and he goes. (He laughs.)

BIFF. Maybe he's color-blind.

HAPPY. Pop? Why he's got the finest eye for color in the business. You know that.

BIFF (sitting down on his bed). I'm going to sleep.

HAPPY. You're not still sour on Dad, are you, Biff?

BIFF. He's all right, I guess.

WILLY (underneath them, in the living-room). Yes, sir, eighty thousand miles—eighty-two thousand!

BIFF. You smoking?

HAPPY (holding out a pack of cigarettes). Want one?

BIFF (taking a cigarette). I can never sleep when I smell it.

WILLY. What a simonizing job, heh!

HAPPY (with deep sentiment). Funny, Biff, y'know? Us sleeping in here again? The old beds. (He pats his bed affectionately.) All the talk that went across those two beds, huh? Our whole lives.

BIFF. Yeah. Lotta dreams and plans.

HAPPY (with a deep and masculine laugh).

About five hundred women would like to know what was said in this room.

(*They share a soft laugh.*)

BIFF. Remember that big Betsy something—what the hell was her name—over on Bushwick Avenue?

HAPPY (*combing his hair*). With the collie dog!

BIFF. That's the one. I got you in there, remember?

HAPPY. Yeah, that was my first time—I think. Boy, there was a pig! (*They laugh, almost crudely.*) You taught me everything I know about women. Don't forget that.

BIFF. I bet you forgot how bashful you used to be. Especially with girls.

HAPPY. Oh, I still am, Biff.

BIFF. Oh, go on.

HAPPY. I just control it, that's all. I think I got less bashful and you got more so. What happened, Biff? Where's the old humor, the old confidence? (*He shakes* BIFF's *knee.* BIFF *gets up and moves restlessly about the room.*) What's the matter?

BIFF. Why does Dad mock me all the time?

HAPPY. He's not mocking you, he—

BIFF. Everything I say there's a twist of mockery on his face. I can't get near him.

HAPPY. He just wants you to make good, that's all. I wanted to talk to you about Dad for a long time, Biff. Something's—happening to him. He—talks to himself.

BIFF. I noticed that this morning. But he always mumbled.

HAPPY. But not so noticeable. It got so embarrassing I sent him to Florida. And you know something? Most of the time he's talking to you.

BIFF. What's he say about me?

HAPPY. I can't make it out.

BIFF. What's he say about me?

HAPPY. I think the fact that you're not settled, that you're still kind of up in the air . . .

BIFF. There's one or two other things depressing him, Happy.

HAPPY. What do you mean?

BIFF. Never mind. Just don't lay it all to me.

HAPPY. But I think if you just got started—I mean—is there any future for you out there?

BIFF. I tell ya, Hap, I don't know what the future is. I don't know—what I'm supposed to want.

HAPPY. What do you mean?

BIFF. Well, I spent six or seven years after high school trying to work myself up. Shipping clerk, salesman, business of one kind or another. And it's a measly manner of existence. To get on that subway on the hot mornings in summer. To devote your whole life to keeping stock, or making phone calls, or selling or buying. To suffer fifty weeks of the year for the sake of a two-week vacation, when all you really desire is to be outdoors, with your shirt off. And always to have to get ahead of the next fella. And still—that's how you build a future.

HAPPY. Well, you really enjoy it on a farm? Are you content out there?

BIFF (*with rising agitation*). Hap, I've had twenty or thirty different kinds of jobs since I left home before the war, and it always turns out the same. I just realized it lately. In Nebraska when I herded cattle, and the Dakotas, and Arizona, and now in Texas. It's why I came home now, I guess, because I realized it. This farm I work on, it's spring there now, see? And they've got about fifteen new colts. There's nothing more inspiring or —beautiful than the sight of a mare and a new colt. And it's cool there now, see? Texas is cool now, and it's spring. And whenever spring comes to where I am, I suddenly get the feeling, my God, I'm not gettin' anywhere! What the hell am I doing, playing around with horses, twenty-eight dollars a week! I'm thirty-four years old, I oughta be makin' my future. That's when I come running home. And now, I get here, and I don't know what to do with myself. (*After a pause*) I've always made a point of not wasting my life, and everytime I come back here I know that all I've done is to waste my life.

HAPPY. You're a poet, you know that, Biff? You're a—you're an idealist!

BIFF. No, I'm mixed up very bad. Maybe I oughta get married. Maybe I oughta get stuck into something. Maybe that's my trouble. I'm like a boy. I'm not married, I'm not in business, I just—I'm like a boy. Are you content, Hap? You're a success, aren't you? Are you content?

HAPPY. Hell, no!

BIFF. Why? You're making money, aren't you?

HAPPY (*moving about with energy, expressiveness*). All I can do now is wait for the merchandise manager to die. And suppose I get to be merchandise manager? He's a good friend of mine, and he just built a terrific estate on Long Island. And he lived there about two months and sold it, and now he's building another one. He can't enjoy it once it's finished. And I know that's just what I would do. I don't know what the hell I'm workin' for. Sometimes I sit in my apartment—all alone. And I think of the rent I'm paying. And it's crazy. But then, it's what I always wanted. My own apartment, a car, and plenty of women. And still, goddammit, I'm lonely.

BIFF (*with enthusiasm*). Listen, why don't you come out West with me?

HAPPY. You and I, heh?

BIFF. Sure, maybe we could buy a ranch. Raise cattle, use our muscles. Men built like we are should be working out in the open.

HAPPY (*avidly*). The Loman Brothers, heh?

BIFF (*with vast affection*). Sure, we'd be known all over the counties!

HAPPY (*enthralled*). That's what I dream about, Biff. Sometimes I want to just rip my clothes off in the middle of the store and outbox that goddam merchandise manager. I mean I can outbox, outrun, and outlift anybody in that store, and I have to take orders from those common, petty sons-of-bitches till I can't stand it any more.

BIFF. I'm tellin' you, kid, if you were with me I'd be happy out there.

HAPPY (*enthused*). See, Biff, everybody around me is so false that I'm constantly lowering my ideals. . . .

BIFF. Baby, together we'd stand up for one another, we'd have someone to trust.

HAPPY. If I were around you—

BIFF. Hap, the trouble is we weren't brought up to grub for money. I don't know how to do it.

HAPPY. Neither can I!

BIFF. Then let's go!

HAPPY. The only thing is—what can you make out there?

BIFF. But look at your friend. Builds an es-

tate and then hasn't the peace of mind to live in it.

HAPPY. Yeah, but when he walks into the store the waves part in front of him. That's fifty-two thousand dollars a year coming through the revolving door, and I got more in my pinky finger than he's got in his head.

BIFF. Yeah, but you just said—

HAPPY. I gotta show some of those pompous, self-important executives over there that Hap Loman can make the grade. I want to walk into the store the way he walks in. Then I'll go with you, Biff. We'll be together yet, I swear. But take those two we had tonight. Now weren't they gorgeous creatures?

BIFF. Yeah, yeah, most gorgeous I've had in years.

HAPPY. I get that any time I want, Biff. Whenever I feel disgusted. The only trouble is, it gets like bowling or something. I just keep knockin' them over and it doesn't mean anything. You still run around a lot?

BIFF. Naa. I'd like to find a girl—steady, somebody with substance.

HAPPY. That's what I long for.

BIFF. Go on! You'd never come home.

HAPPY. I would! Somebody with character, with resistance! Like Mom, y'know? You're gonna call me a bastard when I tell you this. That girl Charlotte I was with tonight is engaged to be married in five weeks. (*He tries on his new hat.*)

BIFF. No kiddin'!

HAPPY. Sure, the guy's in line for the vice-presidency of the store. I don't know what gets into me, maybe I just have an over-developed sense of competition or something, but I went and ruined her, and furthermore I can't get rid of her. And he's the third executive I've done that to. Isn't that a crummy characteristic? And to top it all, I go to their weddings! (*Indignantly, but laughing*) Like I'm not supposed to take bribes. Manufacturers offer me a hundred-dollar bill now and then to throw an order their way. You know how honest I am, but it's like this girl, see. I hate myself for it. Because I don't want the girl, and, still, I take it and—I love it!

BIFF. Let's go to sleep.

HAPPY. I guess we didn't settle anything, heh?

BIFF. I just got one idea that I think I'm going to try.

HAPPY. What's that?

BIFF. Remember Bill Oliver?

HAPPY. Sure, Oliver is very big now. You want to work for him again?

BIFF. No, but when I quit he said something to me. He put his arm on my shoulder, and he said, "Biff, if you ever need anything, come to me."

HAPPY. I remember that. That sounds good.

BIFF. I think I'll go to see him. If I could get ten thousand or even seven or eight thousand dollars I could buy a beautiful ranch.

HAPPY. I bet he'd back you. 'Cause he thought highly of you, Biff. I mean, they all do. You're well liked, Biff. That's why I say to come back here, and we both have the apartment. And I'm tellin' you, Biff, any babe you want. . . .

BIFF. No, with a ranch I could do the work I like and still be something. I just wonder though. I wonder if Oliver still thinks I stole that carton of basketballs.

HAPPY. Oh, he probably forgot that long ago. It's almost ten years. You're too sensitive. Anyway, he didn't really fire you.

BIFF. Well, I think he was going to. I think that's why I quit. I was never sure whether he knew or not. I know he thought the world of me, though. I was the only one he'd let lock up the place.

WILLY (below). You gonna wash the engine, Biff?

HAPPY. Shh!

(BIFF looks at HAPPY, who is gazing down, listening. WILLY is mumbling in the parlor.)

HAPPY. You hear that?

(They listen. WILLY laughs warmly.)

BIFF (growing angry). Doesn't he know Mom can hear that?

WILLY. Don't get your sweater dirty, Biff!

(A look of pain crosses BIFF's face.)

HAPPY. Isn't that terrible? Don't leave again, will you? You'll find a job here. You gotta stick around. I don't know what to do about him, it's getting embarrassing.

WILLY. What a simonizing job!

BIFF. Mom's hearing that!

WILLY. No kiddin', Biff, you got a date? Wonderful!

HAPPY. Go on to sleep. But talk to him in the morning, will you?

BIFF (reluctantly getting into bed). With her in the house. Brother!

HAPPY (getting into bed). I wish you'd have a good talk with him.

(The light on their room begins to fade.)

BIFF (to himself in bed). That selfish, stupid . . .

HAPPY. Sh . . . Sleep, Biff.

(Their light is out. Well before they have finished speaking, WILLY's form is dimly seen below in the darkened kitchen. He opens the refrigerator, searches in there, and takes out a bottle of milk. The apartment houses are fading out, and the entire house and surroundings become covered with leaves. Music insinuates itself as the leaves appear.)

WILLY. Just wanna be careful with those girls, Biff, that's all. Don't make any promises. No promises of any kind. Because a girl, y'know, they always believe what you tell 'em, and you're very young, Biff, you're too young to be talking seriously to girls.

(Light rises on the kitchen. WILLY, talking, shuts the refrigerator door and comes downstage to the kitchen table. He pours milk into a glass. He is totally immersed in himself, smiling faintly.)

WILLY. Too young entirely, Biff. You want to watch your schooling first. Then when you're all set, there'll be plenty of girls for a boy like you. (He smiles broadly at a kitchen chair.) That so? The girls pay for you? (He laughs.) Boy, you must really be makin' a hit.

(WILLY is gradually addressing—physically— a point offstage, speaking through the wall of the kitchen, and his voice has been rising in volume to that of a normal conversation.)

WILLY. I been wondering why you polish the car so careful. Ha! Don't leave the hubcaps, boys. Get the chamois to the hubcaps. Happy, use newspaper on the windows, it's the easiest thing. Show him how to do it, Biff! You see, Happy? Pad it up, use it like a pad. That's it, that's it, good work. You're doin' all right, Hap. (He pauses, then nods in approbation for a few seconds, then looks upward.) Biff, first thing we gotta do when we get time is clip that big branch over the house. Afraid it's gonna fall in a storm and hit the roof. Tell you what. We get a rope and sling her around, and then we climb up there with a couple of saws and take her down. Soon as you finish the car, boys, I wanna see ya. I got a surprise for you, boys.

BIFF (*offstage*). Whatta ya got, Dad?

WILLY. No, you finish first. Never leave a job till you're finished—remember that. (*Looking toward the "big trees"*) Biff, up in Albany I saw a beautiful hammock. I think I'll buy it next trip, and we'll hang it right between those two elms. Wouldn't that be something? Just swingin' there under those branches. Boy, that would be. . . .

(YOUNG BIFF *and* YOUNG HAPPY *appear from the direction* WILLY *was addressing.* HAPPY *carries rags and a pail of water.* BIFF, *wearing a sweater with a block "S," carries a football.*)

BIFF (*pointing in the direction of the car offstage*). How's that, Pop, professional?

WILLY. Terrific. Terrific job, boys. Good work, Biff.

HAPPY. Where's the surprise, Pop?

WILLY. In the back seat of the car.

HAPPY. Boy! (*He runs off.*)

BIFF. What is it, Dad? Tell me, what'd you buy?

WILLY (*laughing, cuffs him*). Never mind, something I want you to have.

BIFF (*turns and starts off*). What is it, Hap?

HAPPY (*offstage*). It's a punching bag!

BIFF. Oh, Pop!

WILLY. It's got Gene Tunney's signature on it!

(HAPPY *runs onstage with a punching bag.*)

BIFF. Gee, how'd you know we wanted a punching bag?

WILLY. Well, it's the finest thing for the timing.

HAPPY (*lies down on his back and pedals with his feet*). I'm losing weight, you notice, Pop?

WILLY (*to* HAPPY). Jumping rope is good too.

BIFF. Did you see the new football I got?

WILLY (*examining the ball*). Where'd you get a new ball?

BIFF. The coach told me to practice my passing.

WILLY. That so? And he gave you the ball, heh?

BIFF. Well, I borrowed it from the locker room. (*He laughs confidentially.*)

WILLY (*laughing with him at the theft*). I want you to return that.

HAPPY. I told you he wouldn't like it!

BIFF (*angrily*). Well, I'm bringing it back!

WILLY (*stopping the incipient argument, to* HAPPY). Sure, he's gotta practice with a regulation ball, doesn't he? (*To* BIFF) Coach'll probably congratulate you on your initiative!

BIFF. Oh, he keeps congratulating my initiative all the time, Pop.

WILLY. That's because he likes you. If somebody else took that ball there'd be an uproar. So what's the report, boys, what's the report?

BIFF. Where'd you go this time, Dad? Gee, we were lonesome for you.

WILLY (*pleased, puts an arm around each boy and they come down to the apron*). Lonesome, heh?

BIFF. Missed you every minute.

WILLY. Don't say? Tell you a secret, boys. Don't breathe it to a soul. Someday I'll have my own business, and I'll never have to leave home any more.

HAPPY. Like Uncle Charley, heh?

WILLY. Bigger than Uncle Charley! Because Charley is not—liked. He's liked, but he's not —well liked.

BIFF. Where'd you go this time, Dad?

WILLY. Well, I got on the road, and I went north to Providence. Met the Mayor.

BIFF. The Mayor of Providence!

WILLY. He was sitting in the hotel lobby.

BIFF. What'd he say?

WILLY. He said, "Morning!" And I said, "You got a fine city here, Mayor." And then he had coffee with me. And then I went to Waterbury. Waterbury is a fine city. Big clock city, the famous Waterbury clock. Sold a nice bill there. And then Boston—Boston is the cradle of the Revolution. A fine city. And a couple of other towns in Mass., and on to Portland and Bangor and straight home!

BIFF. Gee, I'd love to go with you sometime, Dad.

WILLY. Soon as summer comes.

HAPPY. Promise?

WILLY. You and Hap and I, and I'll show you all the towns. America is full of beautiful towns and fine, upstanding people. And they know me, boys, they know me up and down New England. The finest people. And when I bring you fellas up, there'll be open sesame for all of us, 'cause one thing, boys: I have friends. I can park my car in any street in New England, and the cops protect it like their own. This summer, heh?

BIFF AND HAPPY (*together*). Yeah! You bet!

WILLY. We'll take our bathing suits.

HAPPY. We'll carry your bags, Pop!

WILLY. Oh, won't that be something! Me comin' into the Boston stores with you boys carryin' my bags. What a sensation!

(BIFF *is prancing around, practicing passing the ball.*)

WILLY. You nervous, Biff, about the game?

BIFF. Not if you're gonna be there.

WILLY. What do they say about you in school, now that they made you captain?

HAPPY. There's a crowd of girls behind him everytime the classes change.

BIFF (*taking* WILLY's *hand*). This Saturday, Pop, this Saturday—just for you, I'm going to break through for a touchdown.

HAPPY. You're supposed to pass.

BIFF. I'm takin' one play for Pop. You watch me, Pop, and when I take off my helmet, that means I'm breakin' out. Then you watch me crash through that line!

WILLY (*kisses* BIFF). Oh, wait'll I tell this in Boston!

(BERNARD *enters in knickers. He is younger than* BIFF, *earnest and loyal, a worried boy.*)

BERNARD. Biff, where are you? You're supposed to study with me today.

WILLY. Hey, looka Bernard. What're you lookin' so anemic about, Bernard?

BERNARD. He's gotta study, Uncle Willy. He's got Regents next week.

HAPPY (*tauntingly, spinning* BERNARD *around*). Let's box, Bernard!

BERNARD. Biff! (*He gets away from* HAPPY.) Listen, Biff, I heard Mr. Birnbaum say that if you don't start studyin' math he's gonna flunk you, and you won't graduate. I heard him!

WILLY. You better study with him, Biff. Go ahead now.

BERNARD. I heard him!

BIFF. Oh, Pop, you didn't see my sneakers! (*He holds up a foot for* WILLY *to look at.*)

WILLY. Hey, that's a beautiful job of printing!

BERNARD (*wiping his glasses*). Just because he printed University of Virginia on his sneak-

ers doesn't mean they've got to graduate him, Uncle Willy!

WILLY (*angrily*). What're you talking about? With scholarships to three universities they're gonna flunk him?

BERNARD. But I heard Mr. Birnbaum say—

WILLY. Don't be a pest, Bernard! (*To his boys*) What an anemic!

BERNARD. Okay, I'm waiting for you in my house, Biff.

(BERNARD *goes off.* THE LOMANS *laugh.*)

WILLY. Bernard is not well liked, is he?

BIFF. He's liked, but he's not well liked.

HAPPY. That's right, Pop.

WILLY. That's just what I mean. Bernard can get the best marks in school, y'understand, but when he gets out in the business world, y'understand, you are going to be five times ahead of him. That's why I thank Almighty God you're both built like Adonises. Because the man who makes an appearance in the business world, the man who creates personal interest, is the man who gets ahead. Be liked and you will never want. You take me, for instance. I never have to wait in line to see a buyer. "Willy Loman is here!" That's all they have to know, and I go right through.

BIFF. Did you knock them dead, Pop?

WILLY. Knocked 'em cold in Providence, slaughtered 'em in Boston.

HAPPY (*on his back, pedaling again*). I'm losing weight, you notice, Pop?

(LINDA *enters, as of old, a ribbon in her hair, carrying a basket of washing.*)

LINDA (*with youthful energy*). Hello, dear!

WILLY. Sweetheart!

LINDA. How'd the Chevvy run?

WILLY. Chevrolet, Linda, is the greatest car ever built. (*To the boys*) Since when do you let your mother carry wash up the stairs?

BIFF. Grab hold there, boy!

HAPPY. Where to, Mom?

LINDA. Hang them up on the line. And you better go down to your friends, Biff. The cellar is full of boys. They don't know what to do with themselves.

BIFF. Ah, when Pop comes home they can wait!

WILLY (*laughs appreciatively*). You better go down and tell them what to do, Biff.

BIFF. I think I'll have them sweep out the furnace room.

WILLY. Good work, Biff.

BIFF (*goes through wall-line of kitchen to doorway at back and calls down*). Fellas! Everybody sweep out the furnace room! I'll be right down!

VOICES. All right! Okay, Biff.

BIFF. George and Sam and Frank, come out back! We're hangin' up the wash! Come on, Hap, on the double! (*He and* HAPPY *carry out the basket.*)

LINDA. The way they obey him!

WILLY. Well, that's training, the training. I'm tellin' you, I was sellin' thousands and thousands, but I had to come home.

LINDA. Oh, the whole block'll be at that game. Did you sell anything?

WILLY. I did five hundred gross in Providence and seven hundred gross in Boston.

LINDA. No! Wait a minute, I've got a pencil. (*She pulls pencil and paper out of her apron pocket.*) That makes your commission. . . . Two hundred—my God! Two hundred and twelve dollars!

WILLY. Well, I didn't figure it yet, but. . . .

LINDA. How much did you do?

WILLY. Well, I—I did—about a hundred and eighty gross in Providence. Well, no—it came to—roughly two hundred gross on the whole trip.

LINDA (*without hesitation*). Two hundred gross. That's. . . . (*She figures.*)

WILLY. The trouble was that three of the stores were half closed for inventory in Boston. Otherwise I woulda broke records.

LINDA. Well, it makes seventy dollars and some pennies. That's very good.

WILLY. What do we owe?

LINDA. Well, on the first there's sixteen dollars on the refrigerator—

WILLY. Why sixteen?

LINDA. Well, the fan belt broke, so it was a dollar eighty.

WILLY. But it's brand new.

LINDA. Well, the man said that's the way it is. Till they work themselves in, y'know.

(*They move through the wall-line into the kitchen.*)

WILLY. I hope we didn't get stuck on that machine.

LINDA. They got the biggest ads of any of them!

WILLY. I know, it's a fine machine. What else?

LINDA. Well, there's nine-sixty for the washing machine. And for the vacuum cleaner there's three and a half due on the fifteenth. Then the roof, you got twenty-one dollars remaining.

WILLY. It don't leak, does it?

LINDA. No, they did a wonderful job. Then you owe Frank for the carburetor.

WILLY. I'm not going to pay that man! That goddam Chevrolet, they ought to prohibit the manufacture of that car!

LINDA. Well, you owe him three and a half. And odds and ends, comes to around a hundred and twenty dollars by the fifteenth.

WILLY. A hundred and twenty dollars! My God, if business don't pick up I don't know what I'm gonna do!

LINDA. Well, next week you'll do better.

WILLY. Oh, I'll knock 'em dead next week. I'll go to Hartford. I'm very well liked in Hartford. You know, the trouble is, Linda, people don't seem to take to me.

(*They move onto the forestage.*)

LINDA. Oh, don't be foolish.

WILLY. I know it when I walk in. They seem to laugh at me.

LINDA. Why? Why would they laugh at you? Don't talk that way, Willy.

(WILLY *moves to the edge of the stage.* LINDA *goes into the kitchen and starts to darn stockings.*)

WILLY. I don't know the reason for it, but they just pass me by. I'm not noticed.

LINDA. But you're doing wonderful, dear. You're making seventy to a hundred dollars a week.

WILLY. But I gotta be at it ten, twelve hours a day. Other men—I don't know—they do it easier. I don't know why—I can't stop myself —I talk too much. A man oughta come in with a few words. One thing about Charley. He's a man of few words, and they respect him.

LINDA. You don't talk too much, you're just lively.

WILLY (*smiling*). Well, I figure, what the hell, life is short, a couple of jokes. (*To himself*) I joke too much! (*The smile goes.*)

LINDA. Why? You're—

WILLY. I'm fat. I'm very—foolish to look at,

LINDA. I didn't tell you, but Christmas time I happened to be calling on F. H. Stewarts, and a salesman I know, as I was going in to see the buyer I heard him say something about —walrus. And I—I cracked him right across the face. I won't take that. I simply will not take that. But they do laugh at me. I know that.

LINDA. Darling. . . .

WILLY. I gotta overcome it. I know I gotta overcome it. I'm not dressing to advantage, maybe.

LINDA. Willy, darling, you're the handsomest man in the world—

WILLY. Oh, no, Linda.

LINDA. To me you are. (*Slight pause*) The handsomest.

(*From the darkness is heard the laughter of a woman.* WILLY *doesn't turn to it, but it continues through* LINDA's *lines.*)

LINDA. And the boys, Willy. Few men are idolized by their children the way you are.

(*Music is heard as behind a scrim, to the left of the house,* THE WOMAN, *dimly seen, is dressing.*)

WILLY (*with great feeling*). You're the best there is, Linda, you're a pal, you know that? On the road—on the road I want to grab you sometimes and just kiss the life outa you.

(*The laughter is loud now, and he moves into a brightening area at the left, where* THE WOMAN *has come from behind the scrim and is standing, putting on her hat, looking into a "mirror" and laughing.*)

WILLY. 'Cause I get so lonely—especially when business is bad and there's nobody to talk to. I get the feeling that I'll never sell anything again, that I won't make a living for you, or a business, a business for the boys. (*He talks through* THE WOMAN's *subsiding laughter;* THE WOMAN *primps at the "mirror."*) There's so much I want to make for—

THE WOMAN. Me? You didn't make me, Willy. I picked you.

WILLY (*pleased*). You picked me?

THE WOMAN (*who is quite proper-looking,* WILLY's *age*). I did. I've been sitting at that desk watching all the salesmen go by, day in, day out. But you've got such a sense of humor, and we do have such a good time together, don't we?

WILLY. Sure, sure. (*He takes her in his arms.*) Why do you have to go now?

THE WOMAN. It's two o'clock. . . .

WILLY. No, come on in! (*He pulls her.*)

THE WOMAN. . . . my sisters'll be scandalized. When'll you be back?

WILLY. Oh, two weeks about. Will you come up again?

THE WOMAN. Sure thing. You do make me laugh. It's good for me. (*She squeezes his arm, kisses him.*) And I think you're a wonderful man.

WILLY. You picked me, heh?

THE WOMAN. Sure. Because you're so sweet. And such a kidder.

WILLY. Well, I'll see you next time I'm in Boston.

THE WOMAN. I'll put you right through to the buyers.

WILLY (*slapping her bottom*). Right. Well, bottoms up!

THE WOMAN (*slaps him gently and laughs*). You just kill me, Willy. (*He suddenly grabs her and kisses her roughly.*) You kill me. And thanks for the stockings. I love a lot of stockings. Well, good night.

WILLY. Good night. And keep your pores open!

THE WOMAN. Oh, Willy!

(THE WOMAN *bursts out laughing, and* LINDA's *laughter blends in.* THE WOMAN *disappears into the dark. Now the area at the kitchen table brightens.* LINDA *is sitting where she was at the kitchen table, but now is mending a pair of her silk stockings.*)

LINDA. You are, Willy. The handsomest man. You've got no reason to feel that—

WILLY (*coming out of* THE WOMAN's *dimming area and going over to* LINDA). I'll make it all up to you, Linda, I'll—

LINDA. There's nothing to make up, dear. You're doing fine, better than—

WILLY (*noticing her mending*). What's that?

LINDA. Just mending my stockings. They're so expensive—

WILLY (*angrily, taking them from her*). I won't have you mending stockings in this house! Now throw them out!

(LINDA *puts the stockings in her pocket.*)

BERNARD (*entering on the run*). Where is he? If he doesn't study!

WILLY (*moving to the forestage, with great agitation*). You'll give him the answers!

BERNARD. I do, but I can't on a Regents! That's a state exam! They're liable to arrest me!

WILLY. Where is he? I'll whip him, I'll whip him!

LINDA. And he'd better give back that football, Willy, it's not nice.

WILLY. Biff! Where is he? Why is he taking everything?

LINDA. He's too rough with the girls, Willy. All the mothers are afraid of him!

WILLY. I'll whip him!

BERNARD. He's driving the car without a license!

(THE WOMAN's *laugh is heard.*)

WILLY. Shut up!

LINDA. All the mothers—

WILLY. Shut up!

BERNARD (*backing quietly away and out*). Mr. Birnbaum says he's stuck up.

WILLY. Get outa here!

BERNARD. If he doesn't buckle down he'll flunk math! (*He goes off.*)

LINDA. He's right, Willy, you've gotta—

WILLY (*exploding at her*). There's nothing the matter with him! You want him to be a worm like Bernard? He's got spirit, personality. . . .

(*As he speaks,* LINDA, *almost in tears, exits into the living-room.* WILLY *is alone in the kitchen, wilting and staring. The leaves are gone. It is night again, and the apartment houses look down from behind.*)

WILLY. Loaded with it. Loaded! What is he stealing? He's giving it back, isn't he? Why is he stealing? What did I tell him? I never in my life told him anything but decent things.

(HAPPY *in pajamas has come down the stairs;* WILLY *suddenly becomes aware of* HAPPY's *presence.*)

HAPPY. Let's go now, come on.

WILLY (*sitting down at the kitchen table*). Huh! Why did she have to wax the floors herself? Everytime she waxes the floors she keels over. She knows that!

HAPPY. Shh! Take it easy. What brought you back tonight?

WILLY. I got an awful scare. Nearly hit a kid in Yonkers. God! Why didn't I go to Alaska with my brother Ben that time! Ben! That man was a genius, that man was success incarnate! What a mistake! He begged me to go.

HAPPY. Well, there's no use in—

WILLY. You guys! There was a man started with the clothes on his back and ended up with diamond mines!

HAPPY. Boy, someday I'd like to know how he did it.

WILLY. What's the mystery? The man knew what he wanted and went out and got it! Walked into a jungle, and comes out, the age of twenty-one, and he's rich! The world is an oyster, but you don't crack it open on a mattress!

HAPPY. Pop, I told you I'm gonna retire you for life.

WILLY. You'll retire me for life on seventy goddam dollars a week? And your women and your car and your apartment, and you'll retire me for life! Christ's sake, I couldn't get past Yonkers today! Where are you guys, where are you? The woods are burning! I can't drive a car!

(CHARLEY *has appeared in the doorway. He is a large man, slow of speech, laconic, immovable. In all he says, despite what he says, there is pity, and, now, trepidation. He has a robe over pajamas, slippers on his feet. He enters the kitchen.*)

CHARLEY. Everything all right?

HAPPY. Yeah, Charley, everything's . . .

WILLY. What's the matter?

CHARLEY. I heard some noise. I thought something happened. Can't we do something about the walls? You sneeze in here, and in my house hats blow off.

HAPPY. Let's go to bed, Dad. Come on.

(CHARLEY *signals to* HAPPY *to go.*)

WILLY. You go ahead, I'm not tired at the moment.

HAPPY (*to* WILLY). Take it easy, huh? (*He exits.*)

WILLY. What're you doin' up?

CHARLEY (*sitting down at the kitchen table opposite* WILLY). Couldn't sleep good. I had a heartburn.

WILLY. Well, you don't know how to eat.

CHARLEY. I eat with my mouth.

WILLY. No, you're ignorant. You gotta know about vitamins and things like that.

CHARLEY. Come on, let's shoot. Tire you out a little.

WILLY (*hesitantly*). All right. You got cards?

CHARLEY (*taking a deck from his pocket*). Yeah, I got them. Someplace. What is it with those vitamins?

WILLY (*dealing*). They build up your bones. Chemistry.

CHARLEY. Yeah, but there's no bones in a heartburn.

WILLY. What are you talkin' about? Do you know the first thing about it?

CHARLEY. Don't get insulted.

WILLY. Don't talk about something you don't know anything about.

(*They are playing. Pause*)

CHARLEY. What're you doin' home?

WILLY. A little trouble with the car.

CHARLEY. Oh. (*Pause*) I'd like to take a trip to California.

WILLY. Don't say.

CHARLEY. You want a job?

WILLY. I got a job, I told you that. (*After a slight pause*) What the hell are you offering me a job for?

CHARLEY. Don't get insulted.

WILLY. Don't insult me.

CHARLEY. I don't see no sense in it. You don't have to go on this way.

WILLY. I got a good job. (*Slight pause*) What do you keep comin' in here for?

CHARLEY. You want me to go?

WILLY (*after a pause, withering*). I can't understand it. He's going back to Texas again. What the hell is that?

CHARLEY. Let him go.

WILLY. I got nothin' to give him, Charley, I'm clean, I'm clean.

CHARLEY. He won't starve. None a them starve. Forget about him.

WILLY. Then what have I got to remember?

CHARLEY. You take it too hard. To hell with it. When a deposit bottle is broken you don't get your nickel back.

WILLY. That's easy enough for you to say.

CHARLEY. That ain't easy for me to say.

WILLY. Did you see the ceiling I put up in the living-room?

CHARLEY. Yeah, that's a piece of work. To put up a ceiling is a mystery to me. How do you do it?

WILLY. What's the difference?

CHARLEY. Well, talk about it.

WILLY. You gonna put up a ceiling?

CHARLEY. How could I put up a ceiling?

WILLY. Then what the hell are you bothering me for?

CHARLEY. You're insulted again.

WILLY. A man who can't handle tools is not a man. You're disgusting.

CHARLEY. Don't call me disgusting, Willy.

(UNCLE BEN, *carrying a valise and an umbrella, enters the forestage from around the right corner of the house. He is a stolid man, in his sixties, with a mustache and an authoritative air. He is utterly certain of his destiny, and there is an aura of far places about him. He enters exactly as* WILLY *speaks.*)

WILLY. I'm getting awfully tired, Ben.

(BEN's *music is heard.* BEN *looks around at everything.*)

CHARLEY. Good, keep playing; you'll sleep better. Did you call me Ben?

(BEN *looks at his watch.*)

WILLY. That's funny. For a second there you reminded me of my brother Ben.

BEN. I only have a few minutes. (*He strolls, inspecting the place.* WILLY *and* CHARLEY *continue playing.*)

CHARLEY. You never heard from him again, heh? Since that time?

WILLY. Didn't Linda tell you? Couple of weeks ago we got a letter from his wife in Africa. He died.

CHARLEY. That so.

BEN (*chuckling.*) So this is Brooklyn, eh?

CHARLEY. Maybe you're in for some of his money.

WILLY. Naa, he had seven sons. There's just one opportunity I had with that man. . . .

BEN. I must make a train, William. There are several properties I'm looking at in Alaska.

WILLY. Sure, sure! If I'd gone with him to Alaska that time, everything would've been totally different.

CHARLEY. Go on, you'd froze to death up there.

WILLY. What're you talking about?

BEN. Opportunity is tremendous in Alaska, William. Surprised you're not up there.

WILLY. Sure, tremendous.

CHARLEY. Heh?

WILLY. There was the only man I ever met who knew the answers.

CHARLEY. Who?

BEN. How are you all?

WILLY (*taking a pot, smiling*). Fine, fine.

CHARLEY. Pretty sharp tonight.

BEN. Is Mother living with you?

WILLY. No, she died a long time ago.

CHARLEY. Who?

BEN. That's too bad. Fine specimen of a lady, Mother.

WILLY (*to* CHARLEY). Heh?

BEN. I'd hoped to see the old girl.

CHARLEY. Who died?

BEN. Heard anything from Father, have you?

WILLY (*unnerved*). What do you mean, who died?

CHARLEY (*taking a pot*). What're you talkin' about?

BEN (*looking at his watch*). William, it's half-past eight!

WILLY (*as though to dispel his confusion he angrily stops* CHARLEY's *hand*). That's my build!

CHARLEY. I put the ace—

WILLY. If you don't know how to play the game I'm not gonna throw my money away on you!

CHARLEY (*rising*). It was my ace, for God's sake!

WILLY. I'm through, I'm through!

BEN. When did Mother die?

WILLY. Long ago. Since the beginning you never knew how to play cards.

CHARLEY (*picks up the cards and goes to the door*). All right! Next time I'll bring a deck with five aces.

WILLY. I don't play that kind of game!

CHARLEY (*turning to him*). You ought to be ashamed of yourself!

WILLY. Yeah?

CHARLEY. Yeah! (*He goes out.*)

WILLY (*slamming the door after him*). Ignoramus!

BEN (*as* WILLY *comes toward him through the wall-line of the kitchen*). So you're William.

WILLY (*shaking* BEN's *hand*). Ben! I've been waiting for you so long! What's the answer? How did you do it?

BEN. Oh, there's a story in that.

(LINDA *enters the forestage, as of old, carrying the wash basket.*)

LINDA. Is this Ben?

BEN (*gallantly*). How do you do, my dear.

LINDA. Where've you been all these years? Willy's always wondered why you—

WILLY (*pulling* BEN *away from her impatiently*). Where is Dad? Didn't you follow him? How did you get started?

BEN. Well, I don't know how much you remember.

WILLY. Well, I was just a baby, of course, only three or four years old—

BEN. Three years and eleven months.

WILLY. What a memory, Ben!

BEN. I have many enterprises, William, and I have never kept books.

WILLY. I remember I was sitting under the wagon in—was it Nebraska?

BEN. It was South Dakota, and I gave you a bunch of wild flowers.

WILLY. I remember you walking away down some open road.

BEN (*laughing*). I was going to find Father in Alaska.

WILLY. Where is he?

BEN. At that age I had a very faulty view of geography, William. I discovered after a few days that I was heading due south, so instead of Alaska, I ended up in Africa.

LINDA. Africa!

WILLY. The Gold Coast!

BEN. Principally diamond mines.

LINDA. Diamond mines!

BEN. Yes, my dear. But I've only a few minutes—

WILLY. No! Boys! Boys! (YOUNG BIFF *and* HAPPY *appear.*) Listen to this. This is your Uncle Ben, a great man! Tell my boys, Ben!

BEN. Why, boys, when I was seventeen I walked into the jungle, and when I was twenty-one I walked out. (*He laughs.*) And by God I was rich.

WILLY (*to the boys*). You see what I been talking about? The greatest things can happen!

BEN (*glancing at his watch*). I have an appointment in Ketchikan Tuesday week.

WILLY. No, Ben! Please tell about Dad. I want my boys to hear. I want them to know the kind of stock they spring from. All I remember is a man with a big beard, and I was in Mamma's lap, sitting around a fire, and some kind of high music.

BEN. His flute. He played the flute.

WILLY. Sure, the flute, that's right!

(*New music is heard, a high, rollicking tune.*)

BEN. Father was a very great and a very wild-hearted man. We would start in Boston, and he'd toss the whole family into the wagon, and then he'd drive the team right across the country; through Ohio, and Indiana, Michigan, Illinois, and all the Western states. And we'd stop in the towns and sell the flutes that he'd made on the way. Great inventor, Father. With one gadget he made more in a week than a man like you could make in a lifetime.

WILLY. That's just the way I'm bringing them up, Ben—rugged, well liked, all-around.

BEN. Yeah? (*To* BIFF) Hit that, boy—hard as you can. (*He pounds his stomach.*)

BIFF. Oh, no, sir!

BEN (*taking boxing stance*). Come on, get to me! (*He laughs.*)

WILLY. Go to it, Biff! Go ahead, show him!

BIFF. Okay! (*He cocks his fists and starts in.*)

LINDA (*to* WILLY). Why must he fight, dear?

BEN (*sparring with* BIFF). Good boy! Good boy!

WILLY. How's that, Ben, heh?

HAPPY. Give him the left, Biff!

LINDA. Why are you fighting?

BEN. Good boy! (*Suddenly comes in, trips* BIFF, *and stands over him, the point of his umbrella poised over* BIFF's *eye*)

LINDA. Look out, Biff!

BIFF. Gee!

BEN (*patting* BIFF's *knee*). Never fight fair with a stranger, boy. You'll never get out of the jungle that way. (*Taking* LINDA's *hand and bowing*) It was an honor and a pleasure to meet you, Linda.

LINDA (*withdrawing her hand coldly, frightened*). Have a nice—trip.

BEN (*to* WILLY). And good luck with your— what do you do?

WILLY. Selling.

BEN. Yes. Well . . . (*He raises his hand in farewell to all.*)

WILLY. No, Ben, I don't want you to think . . . (*He takes* BEN's *arm to show him.*) It's Brooklyn, I know, but we hunt too.

BEN. Really, now.

WILLY. Oh, sure, there's snakes and rabbits and—that's why I moved out here. Why, Biff can fell any one of these trees in no time!

Boys! Go right over to where they're building the apartment house and get some sand. We're gonna rebuild the entire front stoop right now! Watch this, Ben!

BIFF. Yes, sir! On the double, Hap!

HAPPY (*as he and* BIFF *run off*). I lost weight, Pop, you notice?

(CHARLEY *enters in knickers, even before the boys are gone.*)

CHARLEY. Listen, if they steal any more from that building the watchman'll put the cops on them!

LINDA (*to* WILLY). Don't let Biff . . .

(BEN *laughs lustily.*)

WILLY. You shoulda seen the lumber they brought home last week. At least a dozen six-by-tens worth all kinds a money.

CHARLEY. Listen, if that watchman—

WILLY. I gave them hell, understand. But I got a couple of fearless characters there.

CHARLEY. Willy, the jails are full of fearless characters.

BEN (*clapping* WILLY *on the back, with a laugh at* CHARLEY). And the stock exchange, friend!

WILLY (*joining in* BEN's *laughter*). Where are the rest of your pants?

CHARLEY. My wife bought them.

WILLY. Now all you need is a golf club and you can go upstairs and go to sleep. (*To* BEN) Great athlete! Between him and his son Bernard they can't hammer a nail!

BERNARD (*rushing in*). The watchman's chasing Biff!

WILLY (*angrily*). Shut up! He's not stealing anything!

LINDA (*alarmed, hurrying off left*). Where is he? Biff, dear! (*She exits.*)

WILLY (*moving toward the left, away from* BEN). There's nothing wrong. What's the matter with you?

BEN. Nervy boy. Good!

WILLY (*laughing*). Oh, nerves of iron, that Biff!

CHARLEY. Don't know what it is. My New England man comes back and he's bleedin', they murdered him up there.

WILLY. It's contacts, Charley, I got important contacts!

CHARLEY (*sarcastically*). Glad to hear it, Willy. Come in later, we'll shoot a little casino. I'll take some of your Portland money. (*He laughs at* WILLY *and exits.*)

WILLY (*turning to* BEN). Business is bad, it's murderous. But not for me, of course.

BEN. I'll stop by on my way back to Africa.

WILLY (*longingly*). Can't you stay a few days? You're just what I need, Ben, because I—I have a fine position here, but I—well, Dad left when I was such a baby and I never had a chance to talk to him and I still feel—kind of temporary about myself.

BEN. I'll be late for my train.

(*They are at opposite ends of the stage.*)

WILLY. Ben, my boys—can't we talk? They'd go into the jaws of hell for me, see, but I—

BEN. William, you're being first-rate with your boys. Outstanding, manly chaps!

WILLY (*hanging on to his words*). Oh, Ben, that's good to hear! Because sometimes I'm afraid that I'm not teaching them the right kind of— Ben, how should I teach them?

BEN (*giving great weight to each word, and with a certain vicious audacity*). William, when I walked into the jungle, I was seventeen. When I walked out I was twenty-one. And, by God, I was rich! (*He goes off into darkness around the right corner of the house.*)

WILLY. . . . was rich! That's just the spirit I want to imbue them with! To walk into a jungle! I was right! I was right! I was right!

(BEN *is gone, but* WILLY *is still speaking to him as* LINDA, *in nightgown and robe, enters the kitchen, glances around for* WILLY, *then goes to the door of the house, looks out and sees him. Comes down to his left. He looks at her.*)

LINDA. Willy, dear? Willy?

WILLY. I was right!

LINDA. Did you have some cheese? (*He can't answer.*) It's very late, darling. Come to bed, heh?

WILLY (*looking straight up*). Gotta break your neck to see a star in this yard.

LINDA. You coming in?

WILLY. Whatever happened to that diamond watch fob? Remember? When Ben came from Africa that time? Didn't he give me a watch fob with a diamond in it?

LINDA. You pawned it, dear. Twelve, thirteen years ago. For Biff's radio correspondence course.

WILLY. Gee, that was a beautiful thing. I'll take a walk.

LINDA. But you're in your slippers.

WILLY (*starting to go around the house at the left*). I was right! I was! (*Half to* LINDA, *as he goes, shaking his head*) What a man! There was a man worth talking to. I was right!

LINDA (*calling after* WILLY). But in your slippers, Willy!

(WILLY *is almost gone when* BIFF, *in his pajamas, comes down the stairs and enters the kitchen.*)

BIFF. What is he doing out there?

LINDA. Sh!

BIFF. God Almighty, Mom, how long has he been doing this?

LINDA. Don't, he'll hear you.

BIFF. What the hell is the matter with him?

LINDA. It'll pass by morning.

BIFF. Shouldn't we do anything?

LINDA. Oh, my dear, you should do a lot of things, but there's nothing to do, so go to sleep.

(HAPPY *comes down the stairs and sits on the steps.*)

HAPPY. I never heard him so loud, Mom.

LINDA. Well, come around more often; you'll hear him. (*She sits down at the table and mends the lining of* WILLY's *jacket.*)

BIFF. Why didn't you ever write me about this, Mom?

LINDA. How would I write to you? For over three months you had no address.

BIFF. I was on the move. But you know I thought of you all the time. You know that, don't you, pal?

LINDA. I know, dear, I know. But he likes to have a letter. Just to know that there's still a possibility for better things.

BIFF. He's not like this all the time, is he?

LINDA. It's when you come home he's always the worst.

BIFF. When I come home?

LINDA. When you write you're coming, he's all smiles, and talks about the future, and—he's just wonderful. And then the closer you seem to come, the more shaky he gets, and then, by the time you get here, he's arguing, and he seems angry at you. I think it's just that maybe he can't bring himself to—to open up to you. Why are you so hateful to each other? Why is that?

BIFF (*evasively*). I'm not hateful, Mom.

LINDA. But you no sooner come in the door than you're fighting!

BIFF. I don't know why. I mean to change. I'm tryin', Mom, you understand?

LINDA. Are you home to stay now?

BIFF. I don't know. I want to look around, see what's doin'.

LINDA. Biff, you can't look around all your life, can you?

BIFF. I just can't take hold, Mom. I can't take hold of some kind of a life.

LINDA. Biff, a man is not a bird, to come and go with the springtime.

BIFF. Your hair. . . . (*He touches her hair.*) Your hair got so gray.

LINDA. Oh, it's been gray since you were in high school. I just stopped dyeing it, that's all.

BIFF. Dye it again, will ya? I don't want my pal looking old. (*He smiles.*)

LINDA. You're such a boy! You think you can go away for a year and . . . You've got to get it into your head now that one day you'll knock on this door and there'll be strange people here—

BIFF. What are you talking about? You're not even sixty, Mom.

LINDA. But what about your father?

BIFF (*lamely*). Well, I meant him too.

HAPPY. He admires Pop.

LINDA. Biff, dear, if you don't have any feeling for him, then you can't have any feeling for me.

BIFF. Sure I can, Mom.

LINDA. No. You can't just come to see me, because I love him. (*With a threat, but only a threat, of tears*) He's the dearest man in the world to me, and I won't have anyone making him feel unwanted and low and blue. You've got to make up your mind now, darling, there's no leeway any more. Either he's your father and you pay him that respect, or else you're not to come here. I know he's not easy to get along with—nobody knows that better than me—but . . .

WILLY (*from the left, with a laugh*). Hey, hey, Biffo!

BIFF (*starting to go out after* WILLY). What the hell is the matter with him?

(HAPPY *stops him.*)

LINDA. Don't—don't go near him!

BIFF. Stop making excuses for him! He always, always wiped the floor with you. Never had an ounce of respect for you.

HAPPY. He's always had respect for—

BIFF. What the hell do you know about it?

HAPPY (*surlily*). Just don't call him crazy!

BIFF. He's got no character— Charley wouldn't do this. Not in his own house—spewing out that vomit from his mind.

HAPPY. Charley never had to cope with what he's got to.

BIFF. People are worse off than Willy Loman. Believe me, I've seen them.

LINDA. Then make Charley your father, Biff. You can't do that, can you? I don't say he's a great man. Willy Loman never made a lot of money. His name was never in the paper. He's not the finest character that ever lived. But he's a human being, and a terrible thing is happening to him. So attention must be paid. He's not to be allowed to fall into his grave like an old dog. Attention, attention must be finally paid to such a person. You called him crazy—

BIFF. I didn't mean—

LINDA. No, a lot of people think he's lost his—balance. But you don't have to be very smart to know what his trouble is. The man is exhausted.

HAPPY. Sure!

LINDA. A small man can be just as exhausted as a great man. He works for a company thirty-six years this March, opens up unheard-of territories to their trademark, and now in his old age they take his salary away.

HAPPY (*indignantly*). I didn't know that, Mom.

LINDA. You never asked, my dear! Now that you get your spending money someplace else you don't trouble your mind with him.

HAPPY. But I gave you money last—

LINDA. Christmas time, fifty dollars! To fix the hot water it cost ninety-seven fifty! For five weeks he's been on straight commission, like a beginner, an unknown!

BIFF. Those ungrateful bastards!

LINDA. Are they any worse than his sons? When he brought them business, when he was young, they were glad to see him. But now his old friends, the old buyers that loved him so and always found some order to hand him in a pinch—they're all dead, retired. He used to be able to make six, seven calls a day in Boston. Now he takes his valises out of the car and puts them back and takes them out again and he's exhausted. Instead of walking he talks now. He drives seven hundred miles, and when he gets there no one knows him any more, no one welcomes him. And what goes through a man's mind, driving seven hundred miles home without having earned a cent? Why shouldn't he talk to himself? Why? When he has to go to Charley and borrow fifty dollars a week and pretend to me that it's his pay? How long can that go on? How long? You see what I'm sitting here and waiting for? And you tell me he has no character? The man who never worked a day but for your benefit? When does he get the medal for that? Is this his reward—to turn around at the age of sixty-three and find his sons, who he loved better than his life, one a philandering bum—

HAPPY. Mom!

LINDA. That's all you are, my baby! (*To* BIFF) And you! What happened to the love you had for him? You were such pals! How you used to talk to him on the phone every night! How lonely he was till he could come home to you!

BIFF. All right, Mom. I'll live here in my room, and I'll get a job. I'll keep away from him, that's all.

LINDA. No, Biff. You can't stay here and fight all the time.

BIFF. He threw me out of this house, remember that.

LINDA. Why did he do that? I never knew why.

BIFF. Because I know he's a fake and he doesn't like anybody around who knows!

LINDA. Why a fake? In what way? What do you mean?

BIFF. Just don't lay it all at my feet. It's between me and him—that's all I have to say. I'll chip in from now on. He'll settle for half my pay check. He'll be all right. I'm going to bed. (*He starts for the stairs.*)

LINDA. He won't be all right.

BIFF (*turning on the stairs, furiously*). I hate this city and I'll stay here. Now what do you want?

LINDA. He's dying, Biff.

(HAPPY *turns quickly to her, shocked.*)

BIFF (*after a pause*). Why is he dying?

LINDA. He's been trying to kill himself.

BIFF (*with great horror*). How?

LINDA. I live from day to day.

BIFF. What're you talking about?

LINDA. Remember I wrote you that he smashed up the car again? In February?

BIFF. Well?

LINDA. The insurance inspector came. He said that they have evidence. That all these accidents in the last year—weren't—weren't—accidents.

HAPPY. How can they tell that? That's a lie.

LINDA. It seems there's a woman. . . . (*She takes a breath as*)

BIFF (*sharply but contained*). What woman?

LINDA (*simultaneously*). . . . and this woman . . .

LINDA. What?

BIFF. Nothing. Go ahead.

LINDA. What did you say?

BIFF. Nothing. I just said what woman?

HAPPY. What about her?

LINDA. Well, it seems she was walking down the road and saw his car. She says that he wasn't driving fast at all, and that he didn't skid. She says he came to that little bridge, and then deliberately smashed into the railing, and it was only the shallowness of the water that saved him.

BIFF. Oh, no, he probably just fell asleep again.

LINDA. I don't think he fell asleep.

BIFF. Why not?

LINDA. Last month . . . (*With great difficulty*) Oh, boys, it's so hard to say a thing like this! He's just a big stupid man to you, but I tell you there's more good in him than in many other people. (*She chokes, wipes her eyes.*) I was looking for a fuse. The lights blew out, and I went down the cellar. And behind the fuse box—it happened to fall out—was a length of rubber pipe—just short.

HAPPY. No kidding?

LINDA. There's a little attachment on the end of it. I knew right away. And sure enough, on the bottom of the water heater there's a new little nipple on the gas pipe.

HAPPY (*angrily*). That—jerk.

BIFF. Did you have it taken off?

LINDA. I'm—I'm ashamed to. How can I mention it to him? Every day I go down and take away that little rubber pipe. But, when he comes home, I put it back where it was. How can I insult him that way? I don't know what to do. I live from day to day, boys. I tell you, I know every thought in his mind. It sounds so old-fashioned and silly, but I tell you he put his whole life into you and you've turned your backs on him. (*She is bent over in the chair, weeping, her face in her hands.*) Biff, I swear to God! Biff, his life is in your hands!

HAPPY (*to* BIFF). How do you like that damned fool!

BIFF (*kissing her*). All right, pal, all right. It's all settled now. I've been remiss. I know that, Mom. But now I'll stay, and I swear to you, I'll apply myself. (*Kneeling in front of her, in a fever of self-reproach*) It's just—you see, Mom, I don't fit in business. Not that I won't try. I'll try, and I'll make good.

HAPPY. Sure you will. The trouble with you in business was you never tried to please people.

BIFF. I know, I—

HAPPY. Like when you worked for Harrison's. Bob Harrison said you were tops, and then you go and do some damn fool thing like whistling whole songs in the elevator like a comedian.

BIFF (*against* HAPPY). So what? I like to whistle sometimes.

HAPPY. You don't raise a guy to a responsible job who whistles in the elevator!

LINDA. Well, don't argue about it now.

HAPPY. Like when you'd go off and swim in the middle of the day instead of taking the line around.

BIFF (*his resentment rising*). Well, don't you run off? You take off sometimes, don't you? On a nice summer day?

HAPPY. Yeah, but I cover myself!

LINDA. Boys!

HAPPY. If I'm going to take a fade the boss can call any number where I'm supposed to be and they'll swear to him that I just left. I'll tell you something that I hate to say, Biff, but in the business world some of them think you're crazy.

BIFF (*angered*). Screw the business world!

HAPPY. All right, screw it! Great, but cover yourself!

LINDA. Hap, Hap!

BIFF. I don't care what they think! They've laughed at Dad for years, and you know why? Because we don't belong in this nuthouse of a city! We should be mixing cement on some open plain, or—or carpenters. A carpenter is allowed to whistle!

(WILLY *walks in from the entrance of the house, at left.*)

WILLY. Even your grandfather was better than a carpenter. (*Pause. They watch him.*) You never grew up. Bernard does not whistle in the elevator, I assure you.

BIFF (*as though to laugh* WILLY *out of it*). Yeah, but you do, Pop.

WILLY. I never in my life whistled in an elevator! And who in the business world thinks I'm crazy?

BIFF. I didn't mean it like that, Pop. Now don't make a whole thing out of it, will ya?

WILLY. Go back to the West! Be a carpenter, a cowboy, enjoy yourself!

LINDA. Willy, he was just saying—

WILLY. I heard what he said!

HAPPY (*trying to quiet* WILLY). Hey, Pop, come on now. . . .

WILLY (*continuing over* HAPPY's *line*). They laugh at me, heh? Go to Filene's, go to the Hub, go to Slattery's, Boston. Call out the name Willy Loman and see what happens! Big shot!

BIFF. All right, Pop.

WILLY. Big!

BIFF. All right!

WILLY. Why do you always insult me?

BIFF. I didn't say a word. (*To* LINDA) Did I say a word?

LINDA. He didn't say anything, Willy.

WILLY (*going to the doorway of the living-room*). All right, good night, good night.

LINDA. Willy, dear, he just decided. . . .

WILLY (*to* BIFF). If you get tired hanging around tomorrow, paint the ceiling I put up in the living-room.

BIFF. I'm leaving early tomorrow.

HAPPY. He's going to see Bill Oliver, Pop.

WILLY (*interestedly*). Oliver? For what?

BIFF (*with reserve, but trying, trying*). He always said he'd stake me. I'd like to go into business, so maybe I can take him up on it.

LINDA. Isn't that wonderful?

WILLY. Don't interrupt. What's wonderful about it? There's fifty men in the City of New

York who'd stake him. (*To* BIFF) Sporting goods?

BIFF. I guess so. I know something about it and—

WILLY. He knows something about it! You know sporting goods better than Spalding, for God's sake! How much is he giving you?

BIFF. I don't know, I didn't even see him yet, but—

WILLY. Then what're you talkin' about?

BIFF (*getting angry*). Well, all I said was I'm gonna see him, that's all!

WILLY (*turning away*). Ah, you're counting your chickens again.

BIFF (*starting left for the stairs*). Oh, Jesus, I'm going to sleep!

WILLY (*calling after him*). Don't curse in this house!

BIFF (*turning*). Since when did you get so clean?

HAPPY (*trying to stop them*). Wait a . . . .

WILLY. Don't use that language to me! I won't have it!

HAPPY (*grabbing* BIFF, *shouts*). Wait a minute! I got an idea. I got a feasible idea. Come here, Biff, let's talk this over now, let's talk some sense here. When I was down in Florida last time, I thought of a great idea to sell sporting goods. It just came back to me. You and I, Biff—we have a line, the Loman Line. We train a couple of weeks, and put on a couple of exhibitions, see?

WILLY. That's an idea!

HAPPY. Wait! We form two basketball teams, see? Two water-polo teams. We play each other. It's a million dollars' worth of publicity. Two brothers, see? The Loman Brothers. Displays in the Royal Palms—all the hotels. And banners over the ring and the basketball court: "Loman Brothers." Baby, we could sell sporting goods!

WILLY. That is a one-million-dollar idea!

LINDA. Marvelous!

BIFF. I'm in great shape as far as that's concerned.

HAPPY. And the beauty of it is, Biff, it wouldn't be like a business. We'd be out playin' ball again. . . .

BIFF (*enthused*). Yeah, that's. . . .

WILLY. Million-dollar. . . .

HAPPY. And you wouldn't get fed up with it, Biff. It'd be the family again. There'd be

the old honor, and comradeship, and if you wanted to go off for a swim or somethin'—well, you'd do it! Without some smart cooky gettin' up ahead of you!

WILLY. Lick the world! You guys together could absolutely lick the civilized world.

BIFF. I'll see Oliver tomorrow. Hap, if we could work that out. . . .

LINDA. Maybe things are beginning to—

WILLY (*wildly enthused, to* LINDA). Stop interrupting! (*To* BIFF) But don't wear sport jacket and slacks when you see Oliver.

BIFF. No, I'll—

WILLY. A business suit, and talk as little as possible, and don't crack any jokes.

BIFF. He did like me. Always liked me.

LINDA. He loved you!

WILLY (*to* LINDA). Will you stop! (*To* BIFF) Walk in very serious. You are not applying for a boy's job. Money is to pass. Be quiet, fine, and serious. Everybody likes a kidder, but nobody lends him money.

HAPPY. I'll try to get some myself, Biff. I'm sure I can.

WILLY. I see great things for you kids, I think your troubles are over. But remember, start big and you'll end big. Ask for fifteen. How much you gonna ask for?

BIFF. Gee, I don't know—

WILLY. And don't say "Gee." "Gee" is a boy's word. A man walking in for fifteen thousand dollars does not say "Gee!"

BIFF. Ten, I think, would be top though.

WILLY. Don't be so modest. You always started too low. Walk in with a big laugh. Don't look worried. Start off with a couple of your good stories to lighten things up. It's not what you say, it's how you say it—because personality always wins the day.

LINDA. Oliver always thought the highest of him—

WILLY. Will you let me talk?

BIFF. Don't yell at her, Pop, will ya?

WILLY (*angrily*). I was talking, wasn't I?

BIFF. I don't like you yelling at her all the time, and I'm tellin' you, that's all.

WILLY. What're you, takin' over this house?

LINDA. Willy—

WILLY (*turning on her*). Don't take his side all the time, goddammit!

BIFF (*furiously*). Stop yelling at her!

WILLY (*suddenly pulling on his cheek, beaten*

down, guilt ridden). Give my best to Bill Oliver—he may remember me. (*He exits through the living-room doorway.*)

LINDA (*her voice subdued*). What'd you have to start that for? (BIFF *turns away.*) You see how sweet he was as soon as you talked hopefully? (*She goes over to* BIFF.) Come up and say good night to him. Don't let him go to bed that way.

HAPPY. Come on, Biff, let's buck him up.

LINDA. Please, dear. Just say good night. It takes so little to make him happy. Come. (*She goes through the living-room doorway, calling upstairs from within the living-room.*) Your pajamas are hanging in the bathroom, Willy!

HAPPY (*looking toward where* LINDA *went out*). What a woman! They broke the mold when they made her. You know that, Biff?

BIFF. He's off salary. My God, working on commission!

HAPPY. Well, let's face it: he's no hot-shot selling man. Except that sometimes, you have to admit, he's a sweet personality.

BIFF (*deciding*). Lend me ten bucks, will ya? I want to buy some new ties.

HAPPY. I'll take you to a place I know. Beautiful stuff. Wear one of my striped shirts tomorrow.

BIFF. She got gray. Mom got awful old. Gee, I'm gonna go in to Oliver tomorrow and knock him for a—

HAPPY. Come on up. Tell that to Dad. Let's give him a whirl. Come on.

BIFF (*steamed up*). You know, with ten thousand bucks, boy!

HAPPY (*as they go into the living-room*). That's the talk, Biff, that's the first time I've heard the old confidence out of you! (*From within the living-room, fading off*) You're gonna live with me, kid, and any babe you want just say the word. . . . (*The last lines are hardly heard. They are mounting the stairs to their parents' bedroom.*)

LINDA (*entering her bedroom and addressing* WILLY, *who is in the bathroom. She is straightening the bed for him*). Can you do anything about the shower? It drips.

WILLY (*from the bathroom*). All of a sudden everything falls to pieces! Goddam plumbing, oughta be sued, those people. I hardly finished putting it in and the thing. . . . (*His words rumble off.*)

LINDA. I'm just wondering if Oliver will remember him. You think he might?

WILLY (*coming out of the bathroom in his pajamas*). Remember him? What's the matter with you, you crazy? If he'd've stayed with Oliver he'd be on top by now! Wait'll Oliver gets a look at him. You don't know the average caliber any more. The average young man today—(*he is getting into bed*)—is got a caliber of zero. Greatest thing in the world for him was to bum around.

(BIFF *and* HAPPY *enter the bedroom. Slight pause*)

WILLY (*stops short, looking at* BIFF). Glad to hear it, boy.

HAPPY. He wanted to say good night to you, sport.

WILLY (*to* BIFF). Yeah. Knock him dead, boy. What'd you want to tell me?

BIFF. Just take it easy, Pop. Good night. (*He turns to go.*)

WILLY (*unable to resist*). And if anything falls off the desk while you're talking to him —like a package or something—don't you pick it up. They have office boys for that.

LINDA. I'll make a big breakfast—

WILLY. Will you let me finish? (*To* BIFF) Tell him you were in the business in the West. Not farm work.

BIFF. All right, Dad.

LINDA. I think everything—

WILLY (*going right through her speech*). And don't undersell yourself. No less than fifteen thousand dollars.

BIFF (*unable to bear him*). Okay. Good night, Mom. (*He starts moving.*)

WILLY. Because you got a greatness in you, Biff, remember that. You got all kinds a greatness. . . . (*He lies back, exhausted.* BIFF *walks out.*)

LINDA (*calling after* BIFF). Sleep well, darling!

HAPPY. I'm gonna get married, Mom. I wanted to tell you.

LINDA. Go to sleep, dear.

HAPPY (*going*). I just wanted to tell you.

WILLY. Keep up the good work. (HAPPY *exits.*) God. . . . remember that Ebbets Field game? The championship of the city?

LINDA. Just rest. Should I sing to you?

WILLY. Yeah. Sing to me. (LINDA *hums a soft*

lullaby.) When that team came out—he was the tallest, remember?

LINDA. Oh, yes. And in gold.

(BIFF *enters the darkened kitchen, takes a cigarette, and leaves the house. He comes downstage into a golden pool of light. He smokes, staring at the night.*)

WILLY. Like a young god. Hercules—something like that. And the sun, the sun all around him. Remember how he waved to me? Right up from the field, with the representatives of three colleges standing by? And the buyers I brought, and the cheers when he came out—Loman, Loman, Loman! God Almighty, he'll be great yet. A star like that, magnificent, can never really fade away!

(*The light on* WILLY *is fading. The gas heater begins to glow through the kitchen wall, near the stairs, a blue flame beneath red coils.*)

LINDA (*timidly*). Willy dear, what has he got against you?

WILLY. I'm so tired. Don't talk any more.

(BIFF *slowly returns to the kitchen. He stops, stares toward the heater.*)

LINDA. Will you ask Howard to let you work in New York?

WILLY. First thing in the morning. Everything'll be all right.

(BIFF *reaches behind the heater and draws out a length of rubber tubing. He is horrified and turns his head toward* WILLY's *room, still dimly lit, from which the strains of* LINDA's *desperate but monotonous humming rise.*)

WILLY (*staring through the window into the moonlight*). Gee, look at the moon moving between the buildings!

(BIFF *wraps the tubing around his hand and quickly goes up the stairs.*)

CURTAIN

ACT II

Music is heard, gay and bright. The curtain rises as the music fades away. WILLY, *in shirt sleeves, is sitting at the kitchen table, sipping coffee, his hat in his lap.* LINDA *is filling his cup when she can.*

WILLY. Wonderful coffee. Meal in itself.

LINDA. Can I make you some eggs?

WILLY. No. Take a breath.

LINDA. You look so rested, dear.

WILLY. I slept like a dead one. First time in months. Imagine, sleeping till ten on a Tuesday morning. Boys left nice and early, heh?

LINDA. They were out of here by eight o'clock.

WILLY. Good work!

LINDA. It was so thrilling to see them leaving together. I can't get over the shaving lotion in this house!

WILLY (*smiling*). Mmm—

LINDA. Biff was very changed this morning. His whole attitude seemed to be hopeful. He couldn't wait to get downtown to see Oliver.

WILLY. He's heading for a change. There's no question, there simply are certain men that take longer to get—solidified. How did he dress?

LINDA. His blue suit. He's so handsome in that suit. He could be a—anything in that suit!

(WILLY *gets up from the table.* LINDA *holds his jacket for him.*)

WILLY. There's no question, no question at all. Gee, on the way home tonight I'd like to buy some seeds.

LINDA (*laughing*). That'd be wonderful. But not enough sun gets back there. Nothing'll grow any more.

WILLY. You wait, kid, before it's all over we're gonna get a little place out in the country, and I'll raise some vegetables, a couple of chickens. . . .

LINDA. You'll do it yet, dear.

(WILLY *walks out of his jacket.* LINDA *follows him.*)

WILLY. And they'll get married, and come for a weekend. I'd build a little guest house. 'Cause I got so many fine tools, all I'd need would be a little lumber and some peace of mind.

LINDA (*joyfully*). I sewed the lining. . . .

WILLY. I could build two guest houses, so they'd both come. Did he decide how much he's going to ask Oliver for?

LINDA (*getting him into the jacket*). He didn't mention it, but I imagine ten or fifteen thousand. You going to talk to Howard today?

WILLY. Yeah. I'll put it to him straight and simple. He'll just have to take me off the road.

LINDA. And, Willy, don't forget to ask for a little advance, because we've got the insurance premium. It's the grace period now.

WILLY. That's a hundred . . . ?

LINDA. A hundred and eight, sixty-eight. Because we're a little short again.

WILLY. Why are we short?

LINDA. Well, you had the motor job on the car . . .

WILLY. That goddam Studebaker!

LINDA. And you got one more payment on the refrigerator . . .

WILLY. But it just broke again!

LINDA. Well, it's old, dear.

WILLY. I told you we should've bought a well-advertised machine. Charley bought a General Electric and it's twenty years old and it's still good, that son-of-a-bitch.

LINDA. But, Willy—

WILLY. Whoever heard of a Hastings refrigerator? Once in my life I would like to own something outright before it's broken! I'm always in a race with the junkyard! I just finished paying for the car and it's on its last legs. The refrigerator consumes belts like a goddam maniac. They time those things. They time them so when you finally paid for them, they're used up.

LINDA (buttoning up his jacket as he unbuttons it). All told, about two hundred dollars would carry us, dear. But that includes the last payment on the mortgage. After this payment, Willy, the house belongs to us.

WILLY. It's twenty-five years!

LINDA. Biff was nine years old when we bought it.

WILLY. Well, that's a great thing. To weather a twenty-five year mortgage is—

LINDA. It's an accomplishment.

WILLY. All the cement, the lumber, the reconstruction I put in this house! There ain't a crack to be found in it any more.

LINDA. Well, it served its purpose.

WILLY. What purpose? Some stranger'll come along, move in, and that's that. If only Biff would take this house, and raise a family. . . . (He starts to go.) Good-by, I'm late.

LINDA (suddenly remembering). Oh, I forgot! You're supposed to meet them for dinner.

WILLY. Me?

LINDA. At Frank's Chop House on Forty-eighth near Sixth Avenue.

WILLY. Is that so! How about you?

LINDA. No, just the three of you. They're gonna blow you to a big meal!

WILLY. Don't say! Who thought of that?

LINDA. Biff came to me this morning, Willy, and he said, "Tell Dad, we want to blow him to a big meal." Be there six o'clock. You and your two boys are going to have dinner.

WILLY. Gee whiz! That's really somethin'. I'm gonna knock Howard for a loop, kid. I'll get an advance, and I'll come home with a New York job. Goddammit, now I'm gonna do it!

LINDA. Oh, that's the spirit, Willy!

WILLY. I will never get behind a wheel the rest of my life!

LINDA. It's changing, Willy, I can feel it changing!

WILLY. Beyond a question. G'by, I'm late. (He starts to go again.)

LINDA (calling after him as she runs to the kitchen table for a handkerchief). You got your glasses?

WILLY (feels for them, then comes back in). Yeah, yeah, got my glasses.

LINDA (giving him the handkerchief). And a handkerchief.

WILLY. Yeah, handkerchief.

LINDA. And your saccharine?

WILLY. Yeah, my saccharine.

LINDA. Be careful on the subway stairs.

(She kisses him, and a silk stocking is seen hanging from her hand. WILLY notices it.)

WILLY. Will you stop mending stockings? At least while I'm in the house. It gets me nervous. I can't tell you. Please.

(LINDA hides the stocking in her hand as she follows WILLY across the forestage in front of the house.)

LINDA. Remember, Frank's Chop House.

WILLY (passing the apron). Maybe beets would grow out there.

LINDA (laughing). But you tried so many times.

WILLY. Yeah. Well, don't work hard today. (He disappears around the right corner of the house.)

LINDA. Be careful!

(As WILLY vanishes, LINDA waves to him. Suddenly the phone rings. She runs across the stage and into the kitchen and lifts it.)

LINDA. Hello? Oh, Biff! I'm so glad you called, I just. . . . Yes, sure, I just told him. Yes, he'll be there for dinner at six o'clock, I didn't forget. Listen, I was just dying to tell you. You know that little rubber pipe I told you about? That he connected to the gas heater? I finally decided to go down the cellar this morning and take it away and destroy it. But it's gone! Imagine? He took it away himself, it isn't there! (*She listens.*) When? Oh, then you took it. Oh—nothing, it's just that I'd hoped he'd taken it away himself. Oh, I'm not worried, darling, because this morning he left in such high spirits, it was like the old days! I'm not afraid any more. Did Mr. Oliver see you? . . . Well, you wait there then. And make a nice impression on him, darling. Just don't perspire too much before you see him. And have a nice time with Dad. He may have big news too! . . . That's right, a New York job. And be sweet to him tonight, dear. Be loving to him. Because he's only a little boat looking for a harbor. (*She is trembling with sorrow and joy.*) Oh, that's wonderful, Biff, you'll save his life. Thanks, darling. Just put your arm around him when he comes into the restaurant. Give him a smile. That's the boy. . . . Good-by, dear. . . . You got your comb? . . . That's fine. Good-by, Biff dear.

(*In the middle of her speech,* HOWARD WAGNER, *thirty-six, wheels on a small typewriter table on which is a wire-recording machine and proceeds to plug it in. This is on the left forestage. Light slowly fades on* LINDA *as it rises on* HOWARD. HOWARD *is intent on threading the machine and only glances over his shoulder as* WILLY *appears.*)

WILLY. Pst! Pst!

HOWARD. Hello, Willy, come in.

WILLY. Like to have a little talk with you, Howard.

HOWARD. Sorry to keep you waiting. I'll be with you in a minute.

WILLY. What's that, Howard?

HOWARD. Didn't you ever see one of these? Wire recorder.

WILLY. Oh. Can we talk a minute?

HOWARD. Records things. Just got delivery yesterday. Been driving me crazy, the most terrific machine I ever saw in my life. I was up all night with it.

WILLY. What do you do with it?

HOWARD. I bought it for dictation, but you can do anything with it. Listen to this. I had it home last night. Listen to what I picked

up. The first one is my daughter. Get this. (*He flicks the switch and "Roll out the Barrel" is heard being whistled.*) Listen to that kid whistle.

WILLY. That is lifelike, isn't it?

HOWARD. Seven years old. Get that tone.

WILLY. Ts, ts. Like to ask a little favor if you . . .

(*The whistling breaks off, and the voice of* HOWARD's *daughter is heard.*)

HIS DAUGHTER. "Now you, Daddy."

HOWARD. She's crazy for me! (*Again the same song is whistled.*) That's me! Ha! (*He winks.*)

WILLY. You're very good!

(*The whistling breaks off again. The machine runs silent for a moment.*)

HOWARD. Sh! Get this now, this is my son.

HIS SON. "The capital of Alabama is Montgomery; the capital of Arizona is Phoenix; the capital of Arkansas is Little Rock; the capital of California is Sacramento . . ." (*and on, and on.*)

HOWARD (*holding up five fingers.*) Five years old, Willy!

WILLY. He'll make an announcer some day!

HIS SON (*continuing*). "The capital . . ."

HOWARD. Get that—alphabetical order! (*The machine breaks off suddenly.*) Wait a minute. The maid kicked the plug out.

WILLY. It certainly is a—

HOWARD. Sh, for God's sake!

HIS SON. "It's nine o'clock, Bulova watch time. So I have to go to sleep."

WILLY. That really is—

HOWARD. Wait a minute! The next is my wife.

(*They wait.*)

HOWARD'S VOICE. "Go on, say something." (*Pause*) "Well, you gonna talk?"

HIS WIFE. "I can't think of anything."

HOWARD'S VOICE. "Well, talk—it's turning."

HIS WIFE (*shyly, beaten*). "Hello." (*Silence*) "Oh, Howard, I can't talk into this . . ."

HOWARD (*snapping the machine off*). That was my wife.

WILLY. That is a wonderful machine. Can we—

HOWARD. I tell you, Willy, I'm gonna take my camera, and my bandsaw, and all my hobbies, and out they go. This is the most fascinating relaxation I ever found.

WILLY. I think I'll get one myself.

HOWARD. Sure, they're only a hundred and a half. You can't do without it. Supposing you wanna hear Jack Benny, see? But you can't be at home at that hour. So you tell the maid to turn the radio on when Jack Benny comes on, and this automatically goes on with the radio. . . .

WILLY. And when you come home you. . . .

HOWARD. You can come home twelve o'clock, one o'clock, any time you like, and you get yourself a Coke and sit yourself down, throw the switch, and there's Jack Benny's program in the middle of the night!

WILLY. I'm definitely going to get one. Because lots of time I'm on the road, and I think to myself, what I must be missing on the radio!

HOWARD. Don't you have a radio in the car?

WILLY. Well, yeah, but who ever thinks of turning it on?

HOWARD. Say, aren't you supposed to be in Boston?

WILLY. That's what I want to talk to you about, Howard. You got a minute? (*He draws a chair in from the wing.*)

HOWARD. What happened? What're you doing here?

WILLY. Well. . . .

HOWARD. You didn't crack up again, did you?

WILLY. Oh, no. No. . . .

HOWARD. Geez, you had me worried there for a minute. What's the trouble?

WILLY. Well, tell you the truth, Howard. I've come to the decision that I'd rather not travel any more.

HOWARD. Not travel! Well, what'll you do?

WILLY. Remember, Christmas time, when you had the party here? You said you'd try to think of some spot for me here in town.

HOWARD. With us?

WILLY. Well, sure.

HOWARD. Oh, yeah, yeah. I remember. Well, I couldn't think of anything for you, Willy.

WILLY. I tell ya, Howard. The kids are all grown up, y'know. I don't need much any more. If I could take home—well, sixty-five dollars a week, I could swing it.

HOWARD. Yeah, but Willy, see I—

WILLY. I tell ya why, Howard. Speaking frankly and between the two of us, y'know— I'm just a little tired.

HOWARD. Oh, I could understand that, Willy. But you're a road man, Willy, and we do a road business. We've only got a half-dozen salesmen on the floor here.

WILLY. God knows, Howard, I never asked a favor of any man. But I was with the firm when your father used to carry you in here in his arms.

HOWARD. I know that, Willy, but—

WILLY. Your father came to me the day you were born and asked me what I thought of the name of Howard, may he rest in peace.

HOWARD. I appreciate that, Willy, but there just is no spot here for you. If I had a spot I'd slam you right in, but I just don't have a single solitary spot.

(*He looks for his lighter.* WILLY *has picked it up and gives it to him. Pause.*)

WILLY (*with increasing anger*). Howard, all I need to set my table is fifty dollars a week.

HOWARD. But where am I going to put you, kid?

WILLY. Look, it isn't a question of whether I can sell merchandise, is it?

HOWARD. No, but it's a business, kid, and everybody's gotta pull his own weight.

WILLY (*desperately*). Just let me tell you a story, Howard—

HOWARD. 'Cause you gotta admit, business is business.

WILLY (*angrily*). Business is definitely business, but just listen for a minute. You don't understand this. When I was a boy—eighteen, nineteen—I was already on the road. And there was a question in my mind as to whether selling had a future for me. Because in those days I had a yearning to go to Alaska. See, there were three gold strikes in one month in Alaska, and I felt like going out. Just for the ride, you might say.

HOWARD (*barely interested*). Don't say.

WILLY. Oh, yeah, my father lived many years in Alaska. He was an adventurous man. We've got quite a little streak of self-reliance in our family. I thought I'd go out with my older brother and try to locate him, and maybe settle in the North with the old man. And I was almost decided to go, when I met a salesman in the Parker House. His name was Dave Singleman. And he was eighty-four years old, and he'd drummed merchandise in thirty-one states. And old Dave, he'd go up to his room, y'understand, put on his green velvet slippers—I'll never forget—and pick up his phone and call the buyers, and without ever leaving his room, at the age of eighty-four, he made his living. And when I saw that, I realized that selling was the greatest career a man could want. 'Cause what could be more satisfying than to be able to go, at the age of eighty-four, into twenty or thirty different cities, and pick up a phone, and be remembered and loved and helped by so many different people? Do you know? when he died—and by the way he died the death of a salesman, in his green velvet slippers in the smoker of the New York, New Haven and Hartford, going into Boston—when he died, hundreds of salesmen and buyers were at his funeral. Things were sad on a lotta trains for months after that. (*He stands up.* HOWARD *has not looked at him.*) In those days there was personality in it, Howard. There was respect, and comradeship, and gratitude in it. Today, it's all cut and dried, and there's no chance for bringing friendship to bear—or personality. You see what I mean? They don't know me any more.

HOWARD (*moving away, to the right*). That's just the thing, Willy.

WILLY. If I had forty dollars a week—that's all I'd need. Forty dollars, Howard.

HOWARD. Kid, I can't take blood from a stone, I—

WILLY (*desperation is on him now*). Howard, the year Al Smith was nominated, your father came to me and—

HOWARD (*starting to go off*). I've got to see some people, kid.

WILLY (*stopping him*). I'm talking about your father! There were promises made across this desk! You mustn't tell me you've got people to see—I put thirty-four years into this firm, Howard, and now I can't pay my insurance! You can't eat the orange and throw the peel away—a man is not a piece of fruit! (*After a pause*) Now pay attention. Your father—in 1928 I had a big year. I averaged a hundred and seventy dollars a week in commissions.

HOWARD (*impatiently*). Now, Willy, you never averaged—

WILLY (*banging his hand on the desk*). I averaged a hundred and seventy dollars a week in the year of 1928! And your father came to me—or rather, I was in the office here—it was right over this desk—and he put his hand on my shoulder—

HOWARD (*getting up*). You'll have to excuse me, Willy, I gotta see some people. Pull yourself together. (*Going out*) I'll be back in a little while.

(*On* HOWARD's *exit, the light on his chair grows very bright and strange.*)

WILLY. Pull myself together! What the hell did I say to him? My God, I was yelling at him! How could I! (WILLY *breaks off, staring at the light, which occupies the chair, animating it. He approaches this chair, standing across the desk from it.*) Frank, Frank, don't you remember what you told me that time? How you put your hand on my shoulder, and Frank . . . (*He leans on the desk and as he speaks the dead man's name he accidentally switches on the recorder, and instantly*)

HOWARD's SON. ". . . of New York is Albany. The capital of Ohio is Cincinnati, the capital of Rhode Island is . . ." (*The recitation continues.*)

WILLY (*leaping away with fright, shouting*). Ha! Howard! Howard! Howard!

HOWARD (*rushing in*). What happened?

WILLY (*pointing at the machine, which continues nasally, childishly, with the capital cities*). Shut it off! Shut it off!

HOWARD (*pulling the plug out*). Look, Willy . . .

WILLY (*pressing his hands to his eyes*). I gotta get myself some coffee. I'll get some coffee . . .

(WILLY *starts to walk out.* HOWARD *stops him.*)

HOWARD (*rolling up the cord*). Willy, look . . .

WILLY. I'll go to Boston.

HOWARD. Willy, you can't go to Boston for us.

WILLY. Why can't I go?

HOWARD. I don't want you to represent us. I've been meaning to tell you for a long time now.

WILLY. Howard, are you firing me?

HOWARD. I think you need a good long rest, Willy.

WILLY. Howard—

HOWARD. And when you feel better, come

back, and we'll see if we can work something out.

WILLY. But I gotta earn money, Howard. I'm in no position to—

HOWARD. Where are your sons? Why don't your sons give you a hand?

WILLY. They're working on a very big deal.

HOWARD. This is no time for false pride, Willy. You go to your sons and you tell them that you're tired. You've got two great boys, haven't you?

WILLY. Oh, no question, no question, but in the meantime . . .

HOWARD. Then that's that, heh?

WILLY. All right, I'll go to Boston tomorrow.

HOWARD. No, no.

WILLY. I can't throw myself on my sons. I'm not a cripple!

HOWARD. Look, kid, I'm busy this morning.

WILLY (grasping HOWARD's arm). Howard, you've got to let me go to Boston!

HOWARD (hard, keeping himself under control). I've got a line of people to see this morning. Sit down, take five minutes, and pull yourself together, and then go home, will ya? I need the office, Willy. (He starts to go, turns, remembering the recorder, starts to push off the table holding the recorder.) Oh, yeah. Whenever you can this week, stop by and drop off the samples. You'll feel better, Willy, and then come back and we'll talk. Pull yourself together, kid, there's people outside.

(HOWARD exits, pushing the table off left. WILLY stares into space, exhausted. Now the music is heard—BEN's music—first distantly, then closer, closer. As WILLY speaks, BEN enters from the right. He carries valise and umbrella.)

WILLY. Oh, Ben, how did you do it? What is the answer? Did you wind up the Alaska deal already?

BEN. Doesn't take much time if you know what you're doing. Just a short business trip. Boarding ship in an hour. Wanted to say good-by.

WILLY. Ben, I've got to talk to you.

BEN (glancing at his watch). Haven't the time, William.

WILLY (crossing the apron to BEN). Ben, nothing's working out. I don't know what to do.

BEN. Now, look here, William. I've bought

timberland in Alaska and I need a man to look after things for me.

WILLY. God, timberland! Me and my boys in those grand outdoors!

BEN. You've a new continent at your doorstep, William. Get out of these cities, they're full of talk and time payments and courts of law. Screw on your fists and you can fight for a fortune up there.

WILLY. Yes, yes! Linda, Linda!

(LINDA enters as of old, with the wash.)

LINDA. Oh, you're back?

BEN. I haven't much time.

WILLY. No, wait! Linda, he's got a proposition for me in Alaska.

LINDA. But you've got— (To BEN) He's got a beautiful job here.

WILLY. But in Alaska, kid, I could—

LINDA. You're doing well enough, Willy!

BEN (to LINDA). Enough for what, my dear?

LINDA (frightened of BEN and angry at him). Don't say those things to him! Enough to be happy right here, right now. (To WILLY, while BEN laughs) Why must everybody conquer the world? You're well liked, and the boys love you, and someday—(to BEN)—why, old man Wagner told him just the other day that if he keeps it up he'll be a member of the firm, didn't he, Willy?

WILLY. Sure, sure. I am building something with this firm, Ben, and if a man is building something he must be on the right track, mustn't he?

BEN. What are you building? Lay your hand on it. Where is it?

WILLY (hesitantly). That's true, Linda, there's nothing.

LINDA. Why? (To BEN) There's a man eighty-four years old—

WILLY. That's right, Ben, that's right. When I look at that man I say, what is there to worry about?

BEN. Bah!

WILLY. It's true, Ben. All he has to do is go into any city, pick up the phone, and he's making his living and you know why?

BEN (picking up his valise). I've got to go.

WILLY (holding BEN back). Look at this boy!

(BIFF, in his high school sweater, enters carrying suitcase. HAPPY carries BIFF's shoulder guards, gold helmet, and football pants.)

WILLY. Without a penny to his name, three

great universities are begging for him, and from there the sky's the limit, because it's not what you do, Ben. It's who you know and the smile on your face! It's contacts, Ben, contacts! The whole wealth of Alaska passes over the lunch table at the Commodore Hotel, and that's the wonder, the wonder of this country, that a man can end with diamonds here on the basis of being liked! (*He turns to* BIFF.) And that's why when you get out on that field today it's important. Because thousands of people will be rooting for you and loving you. (*To* BEN, *who has again begun to leave*) And Ben! when he walks into a business office his name will sound out like a bell and all the doors will open to him! I've seen it, Ben, I've seen it a thousand times! You can't feel it with your hand like timber, but it's there!

BEN. Good-by, William.

WILLY. Ben, am I right? Don't you think I'm right? I value your advice.

BEN. There's a new continent at your doorstep, William. You could walk out rich. Rich! (*He is gone.*)

WILLY. We'll do it here, Ben! You hear me? We're gonna do it here!

(YOUNG BERNARD *rushes in. The gay music of* THE BOYS *is heard.*)

BERNARD. Oh, gee, I was afraid you left already!

WILLY. Why? What time is it?

BERNARD. It's half-past one!

WILLY. Well, come on, everybody! Ebbets Field next stop! Where's the pennants? (*He rushes through the wall-line of the kitchen and out into the living-room.*)

LINDA (*to* BIFF). Did you pack fresh underwear?

BIFF (*who has been limbering up*). I want to go!

BERNARD. Biff, I'm carrying your helmet, ain't I?

HAPPY. No, I'm carrying the helmet.

BERNARD. Oh, Biff, you promised me.

HAPPY. I'm carrying the helmet.

BERNARD. How am I going to get in the locker room?

LINDA. Let him carry the shoulder guards. (*She puts her coat and hat on in the kitchen.*)

BERNARD. Can I, Biff? 'Cause I told everybody I'm going to be in the locker room.

HAPPY. In Ebbets Field it's the clubhouse.

BERNARD. I meant the clubhouse, Biff!

HAPPY. Biff!

BIFF (*grandly, after a slight pause*). Let him carry the shoulder guards.

HAPPY (*as he gives* BERNARD *the shoulder guards*). Stay close to us now.

(WILLY *rushes in with the pennants.*)

WILLY (*handing them out*). Everybody wave when Biff comes out on the field. (HAPPY *and* BERNARD *run off.*) You set now, boy?

(*The music has died away.*)

BIFF. Ready to go, Pop. Every muscle is ready.

WILLY (*at the edge of the apron*). You realize what this means?

BIFF. That's right, Pop.

WILLY (*feeling* BIFF's *muscles*). You're comin' home this afternoon captain of the All-Scholastic Championship Team of the City of New York.

BIFF. I got it, Pop. And remember, pal, when I take off my helmet, that touchdown is for you.

WILLY. Let's go! (*He is starting out, with his arm around* BIFF, *when* CHARLEY *enters, as of old, in knickers.*) I got no room for you, Charley.

CHARLEY. Room? For what?

WILLY. In the car.

CHARLEY. You goin' for a ride? I wanted to shoot some casino.

WILLY (*furiously*). Casino! (*Incredulously*) Don't you realize what today is?

LINDA. Oh, he knows, Willy. He's just kidding you.

WILLY. That's nothing to kid about!

CHARLEY. No, Linda, what's goin' on?

LINDA. He's playing in Ebbets Field.

CHARLEY. Baseball in this weather?

WILLY. Don't talk to him. Come on, come on! (*He is pushing them out.*)

CHARLEY. Wait a minute, didn't you hear the news?

WILLY. What?

CHARLEY. Don't you listen to the radio? Ebbets Field just blew up.

WILLY. You go to hell! (CHARLEY *laughs. Pushing them out*) Come on, come on! We're late.

CHARLEY (*as they go*). Knock a homer, Biff, knock a homer!

WILLY (*the last to leave, turning to* CHARLEY).

I don't think that was funny, Charley. This is the greatest day of his life.

CHARLEY. Willy, when are you going to grow up?

WILLY. Yeah, heh? When this game is over, Charley, you'll be laughing out of the other side of your face. They'll be calling him another Red Grange. Twenty-five thousand a year.

CHARLEY (kidding). Is that so?

WILLY. Yeah, that's so.

CHARLEY. Well, then, I'm sorry, Willy. But tell me something.

WILLY. What?

CHARLEY. Who is Red Grange?

WILLY. Put up your hands. Goddam you, put up your hands!

(CHARLEY, chuckling, shakes his head and walks away, around the left corner of the stage. WILLY follows him. The music rises to a mocking frenzy.)

WILLY. Who the hell do you think you are, better than everybody else? You don't know everything, you big, ignorant, stupid . . . Put up your hands!

(Light rises, on the right side of the forestage, on a small table in the reception room of CHARLEY's office. Traffic sounds are heard. BERNARD, now mature, sits whistling to himself. A pair of tennis rackets and an overnight bag are on the floor beside him.)

WILLY (offstage). What are you walking away for? Don't walk away! If you're going to say something say it to my face! I know you laugh at me behind my back. You'll laugh out of the other side of your goddam face after this game. Touchdown! Touchdown! Eighty thousand people! Touchdown! Right between the goal posts.

(BERNARD is a quiet, earnest, but self-assured young man. WILLY's voice is coming from right upstage now. BERNARD lowers his feet off the table and listens. JENNY, his father's secretary, enters.)

JENNY (distressed). Say, Bernard, will you go out in the hall?

BERNARD. What is that noise? Who is it?

JENNY. Mr. Loman. He just got off the elevator.

BERNARD (getting up). Who's he arguing with?

JENNY. Nobody. There's nobody with him.

I can't deal with him any more, and your father gets all upset everytime he comes. I've got a lot of typing to do, and your father's waiting to sign it. Will you see him?

WILLY (entering). Touchdown! Touch— (He sees JENNY.) Jenny, Jenny, good to see you. How're ya? Workin'? Or still honest?

JENNY. Fine. How've you been feeling?

WILLY. Not much any more, Jenny. Ha, Ha! (He is surprised to see the rackets.)

BERNARD. Hello, Uncle Willy.

WILLY (almost shocked). Bernard! Well, look who's here! (He comes quickly, guiltily, to BERNARD and warmly shakes his hand.)

BERNARD. How are you? Good to see you.

WILLY. What are you doing here?

BERNARD. Oh, just stopped by to see Pop. Get off my feet till my train leaves. I'm going to Washington in a few minutes.

WILLY. Is he in?

BERNARD. Yes, he's in his office with the accountant. Sit down.

WILLY (sitting down). What're you going to do in Washington?

BERNARD. Oh, just a case I've got there, Willy.

WILLY. That so? (Indicating the rackets) You going to play tennis there?

BERNARD. I'm staying with a friend who's got a court.

WILLY. Don't say. His own tennis court. Must be fine people, I bet.

BERNARD. They are, very nice. Dad tells me Biff's in town.

WILLY (with a big smile). Yeah, Biff's in. Working on a very big deal, Bernard.

BERNARD. What's Biff doing?

WILLY. Well, he's been doing very big things in the West. But he decided to establish himself here. Very big. We're having dinner. Did I hear your wife had a boy?

BERNARD. That's right. Our second.

WILLY. Two boys! What do you know!

BERNARD. What kind of a deal has Biff got?

WILLY. Well, Bill Oliver—very big sporting goods man—he wants Biff very badly. Called him in from the West. Long distance, carte blanche, special deliveries. Your friends have their own private tennis court?

BERNARD. You still with the old firm, Willy?

WILLY (after a pause). I'm—I'm overjoyed to see how you made the grade, Bernard, overjoyed. It's an encouraging thing to see a young man really—really— Looks very good for Biff—very— (*He breaks off, then*) Bernard— (*He is so full of emotion, he breaks off again.*)

BERNARD. What is it, Willy?

WILLY (*small and alone*). What—what's the secret?

BERNARD. What secret?

WILLY. How—how did you? Why didn't he ever catch on?

BERNARD. I wouldn't know that, Willy.

WILLY (*confidentially, desperately*). You were his friend, his boyhood friend. There's something I don't understand about it. His life ended after that Ebbets Field game. From the age of seventeen nothing good ever happened to him.

BERNARD. He never trained himself for anything.

WILLY. But he did, he did. After high school he took so many correspondence courses. Radio mechanics; television; God knows what, and never made the slightest mark.

BERNARD (*taking off his glasses*). Willy, do you want to talk candidly?

WILLY (*rising, faces* BERNARD). I regard you as a very brilliant man, Bernard. I value your advice.

BERNARD. Oh, the hell with the advice, Willy. I couldn't advise you. There's just one thing I've always wanted to ask you. When he was supposed to graduate, and the math teacher flunked him—

WILLY. Oh, that son-of-a-bitch ruined his life.

BERNARD. Yeah, but, Willy, all he had to do was go to summer school and make up that subject.

WILLY. That's right, that's right.

BERNARD. Did you tell him not to go to summer school?

WILLY. Me? I begged him to go. I ordered him to go!

BERNARD. Then why wouldn't he go?

WILLY. Why? Why! Bernard, that question has been trailing me like a ghost for the last fifteen years. He flunked the subject, and laid down and died like a hammer hit him!

BERNARD. Take it easy, kid.

WILLY. Let me talk to you—I got nobody to talk to. Bernard, Bernard, was it my fault? Y'see? It keeps going around in my mind, maybe I did something to him. I got nothing to give him.

BERNARD. Don't take it so hard.

WILLY. Why did he lay down? What is the story there? You were his friend!

BERNARD. Willy, I remember, it was June, and our grades came out. And he'd flunked math.

WILLY. That son-of-a-bitch!

BERNARD. No, it wasn't right then. Biff just got very angry, I remember, and he was ready to enroll in summer school.

WILLY (*surprised*). He was?

BERNARD. He wasn't beaten by it at all. But then, Willy, he disappeared from the block for almost a month. And I got the idea that he'd gone up to New England to see you. Did he have a talk with you then?

(WILLY *stares in silence.*)

BERNARD. Willy?

WILLY (*with a strong edge of resentment in his voice*). Yeah, he came to Boston. What about it?

BERNARD. Well, just that when he came back—I'll never forget this, it always mystifies me. Because I thought so well of Biff, even though he'd always taken advantage of me. I loved him, Willy, y'know? And he came back after that month and took his sneakers—remember those sneakers with "University of Virginia" printed on them? He was so proud of those, wore them every day. And he took them down in the cellar, and burned them up in the furnace. We had a fist fight. It lasted at least half an hour. Just the two of us, punching each other down the cellar, and crying right through it. I've often thought of how strange it was that I knew he'd given up his life. What happened in Boston, Willy?

(WILLY *looks at him as at an intruder.*)

BERNARD. I just bring it up because you asked me.

WILLY (*angrily*). Nothing. What do you mean, "What happened?" What's that got to do with anything?

BERNARD. Well, don't get sore.

WILLY. What are you trying to do, blame it on me? If a boy lays down is that my fault?

BERNARD. Now, Willy, don't get—

WILLY. Well, don't—don't talk to me that way! What does that mean, "What happened?"

(CHARLEY *enters. He is in his vest, and he carries a bottle of bourbon.*)

CHARLEY. Hey, you're going to miss that train. (*He waves the bottle.*)

BERNARD. Yeah, I'm going. (*He takes the bottle.*) Thanks, Pop. (*He picks up his rackets and bag.*) Good-by, Willy, and don't worry about it. You know, "If at first you don't succeed . . ."

WILLY. Yes, I believe in that.

BERNARD. But sometimes, Willy, it's better for a man just to walk away.

WILLY. Walk away?

BERNARD. That's right.

WILLY. But if you can't walk away?

BERNARD (*after a slight pause*). I guess that's when it's tough. (*Extending his hand*) Good-by, Willy.

WILLY (*shaking* BERNARD'S *hand*). Good-by, boy.

CHARLEY (*an arm on* BERNARD'S *shoulder*). How do you like this kid? Gonna argue a case in front of the Supreme Court.

BERNARD (*protesting*). Pop!

WILLY (*genuinely shocked, pained, and happy*). No! The Supreme Court!

BERNARD. I gotta run. 'By, Dad!

CHARLEY. Knock 'em dead, Bernard!

(BERNARD *goes off.*)

WILLY (*as* CHARLEY *takes out his wallet*). The Supreme Court! And he didn't even mention it!

CHARLEY (*counting out money on the desk*). He don't have to—he's gonna do it.

WILLY. And you never told him what to do, did you? You never took any interest in him.

CHARLEY. My salvation is that I never took any interest in anything. There's some money —fifty dollars. I got an accountant inside.

WILLY. Charley, look . . . (*With difficulty*) I got my insurance to pay. If you can manage it—I need a hundred and ten dollars.

(CHARLEY *doesn't reply for a moment; merely stops moving.*)

WILLY. I'd draw it from my bank but Linda would know, and I. . . .

CHARLEY. Sit down, Willy.

WILLY (*moving toward the chair*). I'm keeping an account of everything, remember. I'll pay every penny back. (*He sits.*)

CHARLEY. Now listen to me, Willy.

WILLY. I want you to know I appreciate . . .

CHARLEY (*sitting down on the table*). Willy, what're you doin'? What the hell is goin' on in your head?

WILLY. Why? I'm simply. . . .

CHARLEY. I offered you a job. You can make fifty dollars a week. And I won't send you on the road.

WILLY. I've got a job.

CHARLEY. Without pay? What kind of a job is a job without pay? (*He rises.*) Now, look, kid, enough is enough. I'm no genius but I know when I'm being insulted.

WILLY. Insulted!

CHARLEY. Why don't you want to work for me?

WILLY. What's the matter with you? I've got a job.

CHARLEY. Then what're you walkin' in here every week for?

WILLY (*getting up*). Well, if you don't want me to walk in here—

CHARLEY. I am offering you a job.

WILLY. I don't want your goddam job!

CHARLEY. When the hell are you going to grow up?

WILLY (*furiously*). You big ignoramus, if you say that to me again I'll rap you one! I don't care how big you are! (*He's ready to fight.*)

(*Pause*)

CHARLEY (*kindly, going to him*). How much do you need, Willy?

WILLY. Charley, I'm strapped. I'm strapped. I don't know what to do. I was just fired.

CHARLEY. Howard fired you?

WILLY. That snotnose. Imagine that? I named him. I named him Howard.

CHARLEY. Willy, when're you gonna realize that them things don't mean anything? You named him Howard, but you can't sell that. The only thing you got in this world is what you can sell. And the funny thing is that you're a salesman, and you don't know that.

WILLY. I've always tried to think otherwise, I guess. I always felt that if a man was impressive, and well liked, that nothing—

CHARLEY. Why must everybody like you? Who liked J. P. Morgan? Was he impressive? In a Turkish bath he'd look like a butcher. But with his pockets on he was very well liked. Now listen, Willy, I know you don't like me, and nobody can say I'm in love with you, but I'll give you a job because—just for the hell of it, put it that way. Now what do you say?

WILLY. I—I just can't work for you, Charley.

CHARLEY. What're you, jealous of me?

WILLY. I can't work for you, that's all, don't ask me why.

CHARLEY (angered, takes out more bills). You been jealous of me all your life, you damned fool! Here, pay your insurance. (He puts the money in WILLY's hand.)

WILLY. I'm keeping strict accounts.

CHARLEY. I've got some work to do. Take care of yourself. And pay your insurance.

WILLY (moving to the right). Funny, y'know? After all the highways, and the trains, and the appointments, and the years, you end up worth more dead than alive.

CHARLEY. Willy, nobody's worth nothin' dead. (After a slight pause) Did you hear what I said?

(WILLY stands still, dreaming.)

CHARLEY. Willy!

WILLY. Apologize to Bernard for me when you see him. I didn't mean to argue with him. He's a fine boy. They're all fine boys, and they'll end up big—all of them. Someday they'll all play tennis together. Wish me luck, Charley. He saw Bill Oliver today.

CHARLEY. Good luck.

WILLY (on the verge of tears). Charley, you're the only friend I got. Isn't that a remarkable thing? (He goes out.)

CHARLEY. Jesus!

(CHARLEY stares after him a moment and follows. All light blacks out. Suddenly raucous music is heard, and a red glow rises behind the screen at right. STANLEY, a young waiter, appears, carrying a table, followed by HAPPY, who is carrying two chairs.)

STANLEY (putting the table down). That's all right, Mr. Loman, I can handle it myself. (He turns and takes the chairs from HAPPY and places them at the table.)

HAPPY (glancing around). Oh, this is better.

STANLEY. Sure, in the front there you're in the middle of all kinds a noise. Whenever you got a party, Mr. Loman, you just tell me and I'll put you back here. Y'know, there's a lotta people they don't like it private, because when they go out they like to see a lotta action around them because they're sick and tired to stay in the house by theirself. But I know you, you ain't from Hackensack. You know what I mean?

HAPPY (sitting down). So how's it coming, Stanley?

STANLEY. Ah, it's a dog's life. I only wish during the war they'd a took me in the Army. I coulda been dead by now.

HAPPY. My brother's back, Stanley.

STANLEY. Oh, he come back, heh? From the Far West.

HAPPY. Yeah, big cattle man, my brother, so treat him right. And my father's coming too.

STANLEY. Oh, your father too!

HAPPY. You got a couple of nice lobsters?

STANLEY. Hundred per cent, big.

HAPPY. I want them with the claws.

STANLEY. Don't worry, I don't give you no mice. (HAPPY laughs.) How about some wine? It'll put a head on the meal.

HAPPY. No. You remember, Stanley, that recipe I brought you from overseas? With the champagne in it?

STANLEY. Oh, yeah, sure. I still got it tacked up yet in the kitchen. But that'll have to cost a buck apiece anyways.

HAPPY. That's all right.

STANLEY. What'd you, hit a number or somethin'?

HAPPY. No, it's a little celebration. My brother is—I think he pulled off a big deal today. I think we're going into business together.

STANLEY. Great! That's the best for you. Because a family business, you know what I mean?—that's the best.

HAPPY. That's what I think.

STANLEY. 'Cause what's the difference? Somebody steals? It's in the family. Know what I mean? (Sotto voce) Like this bartender here. The boss is goin' crazy what kinda leak he's got in the cash register. You put it in but it don't come out.

HAPPY (raising his head). Sh!

STANLEY. What?

HAPPY. You notice I wasn't lookin' right or left, was I?

STANLEY. No.

HAPPY. And my eyes are closed.

STANLEY. So what's the—?

HAPPY. Strudel's comin'.

STANLEY (*catching on, looks around*). Ah, no, there's no—

(*He breaks off as a furred, lavishly dressed girl enters and sits at the next table. Both follow her with their eyes.*)

STANLEY. Geez, how'd ya know?

HAPPY. I got radar or something. (*Staring directly at her profile*) Oooooooo . . . Stanley.

STANLEY. I think that's for you, Mr. Loman.

HAPPY. Look at that mouth. Oh, God. And the binoculars.

STANLEY. Geez, you got a life, Mr. Loman.

HAPPY. Wait on her.

STANLEY (*going to the* GIRL's *table*). Would you like a menu, ma'am?

GIRL. I'm expecting someone, but I'd like a—

HAPPY. Why don't you bring her—excuse me, miss, do you mind? I sell champagne, and I'd like you to try my brand. Bring her a champagne, Stanley.

GIRL. That's awfully nice of you.

HAPPY. Don't mention it. It's all company money. (*He laughs.*)

GIRL. That's a charming product to be selling, isn't it?

HAPPY. Oh, gets to be like everything else. Selling is selling, y'know.

GIRL. I suppose.

HAPPY. You don't happen to sell, do you?

GIRL. No, I don't sell.

HAPPY. Would you object to a compliment from a stranger? You ought to be on a magazine cover.

GIRL (*looking at him a little archly*). I have been.

(STANLEY *comes in with a glass of champagne.*)

HAPPY. What'd I say before, Stanley? You see? She's a cover girl.

STANLEY. Oh, I could see, I could see.

HAPPY (*to the* GIRL). What magazine?

GIRL. Oh, a lot of them. (*She takes the drink.*) Thank you.

HAPPY. You know what they say in France, don't you? "Champagne is the drink of the complexion"—Hya, Biff!

(BIFF *has entered and sits with* HAPPY.)

BIFF. Hello, kid. Sorry I'm late.

HAPPY. I just got here. Uh, Miss—?

GIRL. Forsythe.

HAPPY. Miss Forsythe, this is my brother.

BIFF. Is Dad here?

HAPPY. His name is Biff. You might've heard of him. Great football player.

GIRL. Really? What team?

HAPPY. Are you familiar with football?

GIRL. No, I'm afraid I'm not.

HAPPY. Biff is quarterback with the New York Giants.

GIRL. Well, that is nice, isn't it? (*She drinks.*)

HAPPY. Good health.

GIRL. I'm happy to meet you.

HAPPY. That's my name. Hap. It's really Harold, but at West Point they called me Happy.

GIRL (*now really impressed*). Oh, I see. How do you do? (*She turns her profile.*)

BIFF. Isn't Dad coming?

HAPPY. You want her?

BIFF. Oh, I could never make that.

HAPPY. I remember the time that idea would never come into your head. Where's the old confidence, Biff?

BIFF. I just saw Oliver—

HAPPY. Wait a minute. I've got to see that old confidence again. Do you want her? She's on call.

BIFF. Oh, no. (*He turns to look at the* GIRL.)

HAPPY. I'm telling you. Watch this. (*Turning to the* GIRL) Honey? (*She turns to him.*) Are you busy?

GIRL. Well, I am . . . but I could make a phone call.

HAPPY. Do that, will you, honey? And see if you can get a friend. We'll be here for a while. Biff is one of the greatest football players in the country.

GIRL (*standing up*). Well, I'm certainly happy to meet you.

HAPPY. Come back soon.

GIRL. I'll try.

HAPPY. Don't try, honey, try hard.

(*The* GIRL *exits*. STANLEY *follows, shaking his head in bewildered admiration.*)

HAPPY. Isn't that a shame now? A beautiful girl like that? That's why I can't get married. There's not a good woman in a thousand. New York is loaded with them, kid!

BIFF. Hap, look—

HAPPY. I told you she was on call!

BIFF (*strangely unnerved*). Cut it out, will ya? I want to say something to you.

HAPPY. Did you see Oliver?

BIFF. I saw him all right. Now look, I want to tell Dad a couple of things and I want you to help me.

HAPPY. What? Is he going to back you?

BIFF. Are you crazy? You're out of your goddam head, you know that?

HAPPY. Why? What happened?

BIFF (breathlessly). I did a terrible thing today, Hap. It's been the strangest day I ever went through. I'm all numb, I swear.

HAPPY. You mean he wouldn't see you?

BIFF. Well, I waited six hours for him, see? All day. Kept sending my name in. Even tried to date his secretary so she'd get me to him, but no soap.

HAPPY. Because you're not showin' the old confidence, Biff. He remembered you, didn't he?

BIFF (stopping HAPPY with a gesture). Finally, about five o'clock, he comes out. Didn't remember who I was or anything. I felt like such an idiot, Hap.

HAPPY. Did you tell him my Florida idea?

BIFF. He walked away. I saw him for one minute. I got so mad I could've torn the walls down! How the hell did I ever get the idea I was a salesman there? I even believed myself that I'd been a salesman for him! And then he gave me one look and—I realized what a ridiculous lie my whole life has been! We've been talking in a dream for fifteen years. I was a shipping clerk.

HAPPY. What'd you do?

BIFF (with great tension and wonder). Well, he left, see. And the secretary went out. I was all alone in the waiting-room. I don't know what came over me, Hap. The next thing I know I'm in his office—paneled walls, everything. I can't explain it. I— Hap, I took his fountain pen.

HAPPY. Geez, did he catch you?

BIFF. I ran out. I ran down all eleven flights. I ran and ran and ran.

HAPPY. That was an awful dumb—what'd you do that for?

BIFF (agonized). I don't know, I just— wanted to take something, I don't know. You gotta help me, Hap, I'm gonna tell Pop.

HAPPY. You crazy? What for?

BIFF. Hap, he's got to understand that I'm not the man somebody lends that kind of money to. He thinks I've been spiting him all these years and it's eating him up.

HAPPY. That's just it. You tell him something nice.

BIFF. I can't.

HAPPY. Say you got a lunch date with Oliver tomorrow.

BIFF. So what do I do tomorrow?

HAPPY. You leave the house tomorrow and come back at night and say Oliver is thinking it over. And he thinks it over for a couple of weeks, and gradually it fades away and nobody's the worse.

BIFF. But it'll go on forever!

HAPPY. Dad is never so happy as when he's looking forward to something!

(WILLY enters.)

HAPPY. Hello, scout!

WILLY. Gee, I haven't been here in years!

(STANLEY has followed WILLY in and sets a chair for him. STANLEY starts off but HAPPY stops him.)

HAPPY. Stanley!

(STANLEY stands by, waiting for an order.)

BIFF (going to WILLY with guilt, as to an invalid). Sit down, Pop. You want a drink?

WILLY. Sure, I don't mind.

BIFF. Let's get a load on.

WILLY. You look worried.

BIFF. N-no. (To STANLEY) Scotch all around. Make it doubles.

STANLEY. Doubles, right. (He goes.)

WILLY. You had a couple already, didn't you?

BIFF. Just a couple, yeah.

WILLY. Well, what happened, boy? (Nodding affirmatively, with a smile) Everything go all right?

BIFF (takes a breath, then reaches out and grasps WILLY's hand). Pal . . . (He is smiling bravely, and WILLY is smiling too.) I had an experience today.

HAPPY. Terrific, Pop.

WILLY. That so? What happened?

BIFF (high, slightly alcoholic, above the earth). I'm going to tell you everything from first to last. It's been a strange day. (Silence. He looks around, composes himself as best he can, but his breath keeps breaking the rhythm of his voice.) I had to wait quite a while for him, and—

WILLY. Oliver?

BIFF. Yeah, Oliver. All day, as a matter of cold fact. And a lot of—instances—facts, Pop, facts about my life came back to me. Who was it, Pop? Who ever said I was a salesman with Oliver?

WILLY. Well, you were.

BIFF. No, Dad, I was a shipping clerk.

WILLY. But you were practically—

BIFF (with determination). Dad, I don't know who said it first, but I was never a salesman for Bill Oliver.

WILLY. What're you talking about?

BIFF. Let's hold on to the facts tonight, Pop. We're not going to get anywhere bullin' around. I was a shipping clerk.

WILLY (angrily). All right, now listen to me—

BIFF. Why don't you let me finish?

WILLY. I'm not interested in stories about the past or any crap of that kind because the woods are burning, boys, you understand? There's a big blaze going on all around. I was fired today.

BIFF (shocked). How could you be?

WILLY. I was fired, and I'm looking for a little good news to tell your mother, because the woman has waited and the woman has suffered. The gist of it is that I haven't got a story left in my head, Biff. So don't give me a lecture about facts and aspects. I am not interested. Now what've you got to say to me?

(STANLEY enters with three drinks. They wait until he leaves.)

WILLY. Did you see Oliver?

BIFF. Jesus, Dad!

WILLY. You mean you didn't go up there?

HAPPY. Sure he went up there.

BIFF. I did. I—saw him. How could they fire you?

WILLY (on the edge of his chair). What kind of a welcome did he give you?

BIFF. He won't even let you work on commission?

WILLY. I'm out! (Driving) So tell me, he gave you a warm welcome?

HAPPY. Sure, Pop, sure!

BIFF (driven). Well, it was kind of—

WILLY. I was wondering if he'd remember you. (To HAPPY) Imagine, man doesn't see him for ten, twelve years and gives him that kind of a welcome!

HAPPY. Damn right!

BIFF (trying to return to the offensive). Pop look—

WILLY. You know why he remembered you, don't you? Because you impressed him in those days.

BIFF. Let's talk quietly and get this down to the facts, huh?

WILLY (as though BIFF had been interrupting). Well, what happened? It's great news, Biff. Did he take you into his office or'd you talk in the waiting-room?

BIFF. Well, he came in, see, and—

WILLY (with a big smile). What'd he say? Betcha he threw his arm around you.

BIFF. Well, he kinda—

WILLY. He's a fine man. (To HAPPY) Very hard man to see, y'know.

HAPPY (agreeing). Oh, I know.

WILLY (to BIFF). Is that where you had the drinks?

BIFF. Yeah, he gave me a couple of—no, no!

HAPPY (cutting in). He told him my Florida idea.

WILLY. Don't interrupt. (To BIFF) How'd he react to the Florida idea?

BIFF. Dad, will you give me a minute to explain?

WILLY. I've been waiting for you to explain since I sat down here! What happened? He took you into his office and what?

BIFF. Well—I talked. And—and he listened, see.

WILLY. Famous for the way he listens, y'know. What was his answer?

BIFF. His answer was— (He breaks off, suddenly angry.) Dad, you're not letting me tell you what I want to tell you!

WILLY (accusing, angered). You didn't see him, did you?

BIFF. I did see him!

WILLY. What'd you insult him or something? You insulted him, didn't you?

BIFF. Listen, will you let me out of it, will you just let me out of it!

HAPPY. What the hell!

WILLY. Tell me what happened!

BIFF (to HAPPY). I can't talk to him!

(A single trumpet note jars the ear. The light of green leaves stains the house, which holds the air of night and a dream. YOUNG BERNARD enters and knocks on the door of the house.)

YOUNG BERNARD (*frantically*). Mrs. Loman, Mrs. Loman!

HAPPY. Tell him what happened!

BIFF (*to* HAPPY). Shut up and leave me alone!

WILLY. No, no! You had to go and flunk math!

BIFF. What math? What're you talking about?

YOUNG BERNARD. Mrs. Loman, Mrs. Loman!
   (LINDA *appears in the house, as of old.*)

WILLY (*wildly*). Math, math, math!

BIFF. Take it easy, Pop!

YOUNG BERNARD. Mrs. Loman!

WILLY (*furiously*). If you hadn't flunked you'd've been set by now!

BIFF. Now, look, I'm gonna tell you what happened, and you're going to listen to me.

YOUNG BERNARD. Mrs. Loman!

BIFF. I waited six hours—

HAPPY. What the hell are you saying?

BIFF. I kept sending in my name but he wouldn't see me. So finally he . . . (*He continues unheard as light fades low on the restaurant.*)

YOUNG BERNARD. Biff flunked math!

LINDA. No!

YOUNG BERNARD. Birnbaum flunked him! They won't graduate him!

LINDA. But they have to. He's gotta go to the university. Where is he? Biff! Biff!

YOUNG BERNARD. No, he left. He went to Grand Central.

LINDA. Grand— You mean he went to Boston!

YOUNG BERNARD. Is Uncle Willy in Boston?

LINDA. Oh, maybe Willy can talk to the teacher. Oh, the poor, poor boy!

   (*Light on house area snaps out.*)

BIFF (*at the table, now audible, holding up a gold fountain pen*). . . . so I'm washed up with Oliver, you understand? Are you listening to me?

WILLY (*at a loss*). Yeah, sure. If you hadn't flunked—

BIFF. Flunked what? What're you talking about?

WILLY. Don't blame everything on me! I didn't flunk math—you did! What pen?

HAPPY. That was awful dumb, Biff, a pen like that is worth—

WILLY (*seeing the pen for the first time*). You took Oliver's pen?

BIFF (*weakening*). Dad, I just explained it to you.

WILLY. You stole Bill Oliver's fountain pen!

BIFF. I didn't exactly steal it! That's just what I've been explaining to you!

HAPPY. He had it in his hand and just then Oliver walked in, so he got nervous and stuck it in his pocket!

WILLY. My God, Biff!

BIFF. I never intended to do it, Dad!

OPERATOR'S VOICE. Standish Arms, good evening!

WILLY (*shouting*). I'm not in my room!

BIFF (*frightened*). Dad, what's the matter? (*He and* HAPPY *stand up.*)

OPERATOR. Ringing Mr. Loman for you!

WILLY. I'm not there, stop it!

BIFF (*horrified, gets down on one knee before* WILLY). Dad, I'll make good, I'll make good. (WILLY *tries to get to his feet.* BIFF *holds him down.*) Sit down now.

WILLY. No, you're no good, you're no good for anything.

BIFF. I am, Dad, I'll find something else, you understand? Now don't worry about anything. (*He holds up* WILLY's *face.*) Talk to me, Dad.

OPERATOR. Mr. Loman does not answer. Shall I page him?

WILLY (*attempting to stand, as though to rush and silence the* OPERATOR). No, no, no!

HAPPY. He'll strike something, Pop.

WILLY. No, no . . .

BIFF (*desperately, standing over* WILLY). Pop, listen! Listen to me! I'm telling you something good. Oliver talked to his partner about the Florida idea. You listening? He—he talked to his partner, and he came to me . . . I'm going to be all right, you hear? Dad, listen to me, he said it was just a question of the amount!

WILLY. Then you . . . got it?

HAPPY. He's gonna be terrific, Pop!

WILLY (*trying to stand*). Then you got it, haven't you? You got it! You got it!

BIFF (*agonized, holds* WILLY *down*). No, no. Look, Pop. I'm supposed to have lunch with them tomorrow. I'm just telling you this so you'll know that I can still make an impression, Pop. And I'll make good somewhere, but I can't go tomorrow, see?

WILLY. Why not? You simply—

BIFF. But the pen, Pop!

WILLY. You give it to him and tell him it was an oversight!

HAPPY. Sure, have lunch tomorrow!

BIFF. I can't say that—

WILLY. You were doing a crossword puzzle and accidentally used his pen!

BIFF. Listen, kid, I took those balls years ago, now I walk in with his fountain pen? That clinches it, don't you see? I can't face him like that! I'll try elsewhere.

PAGE'S VOICE. Paging Mr. Loman!

WILLY. Don't you want to be anything?

BIFF. Pop, how can I go back?

WILLY. You don't want to be anything, is that what's behind it?

BIFF (*now angry at* WILLY *for not crediting his sympathy*). Don't take it that way! You think it was easy walking into that office after what I'd done to him? A team of horses couldn't have dragged me back to Bill Oliver!

WILLY. Then why'd you go?

BIFF. Why did I go? Why did I go! Look at you! Look at what's become of you!

(*Off left,* THE WOMAN *laughs.*)

WILLY. Biff, you're going to go to that lunch tomorrow, or—

BIFF. I can't go. I've got no appointment!

HAPPY. Biff, for . . . !

WILLY. Are you spiting me?

BIFF. Don't take it that way! Goddammit!

WILLY (*strikes* BIFF *and falters away from the table*). You rotten little louse! Are you spiting me?

THE WOMAN. Someone's at the door, Willy!

BIFF. I'm no good, can't you see what I am?

HAPPY (*separating them*). Hey, you're in a restaurant! Now cut it out, both of you! (*The* GIRLS *enter.*) Hello, girls, sit down.

(THE WOMAN *laughs, off left.*)

MISS FORSYTHE. I guess we might as well. This is Letta.

THE WOMAN. Willy, are you going to wake up?

BIFF (*ignoring* WILLY). How're ya, miss, sit down. What do you drink?

MISS FORSYTHE. Letta might not be able to stay long.

LETTA. I gotta get up very early tomorrow.

I got jury duty. I'm so excited! Were you fellows ever on a jury?

BIFF. No, but I been in front of them! (*The* GIRLS *laugh.*) This is my father.

LETTA. Isn't he cute? Sit down with us, Pop.

HAPPY. Sit him down, Biff!

BIFF (*going to him*). Come on, slugger, drink us under the table. To hell with it! Come on, sit down, pal.

(*On* BIFF's *last insistence,* WILLY *is about to sit.*)

THE WOMAN (*now urgently*). Willy, are you going to answer the door!

(THE WOMAN's *call pulls* WILLY *back. He starts right, befuddled.*)

BIFF. Hey, where are you going?

WILLY. Open the door.

BIFF. The door?

WILLY. The washroom . . . the door . . . where's the door?

BIFF (*leading* WILLY *to the left*). Just go straight down.

(WILLY *moves left.*)

THE WOMAN. Willy, Willy, are you going to get up. get up, get up, get up?

(WILLY *exits left.*)

LETTA. I think it's sweet you bring your daddy along.

MISS FORSYTHE. Oh, he isn't really your father!

BIFF (*at left, turning to her resentfully*). Miss Forsythe, you've just seen a prince walk by. A fine, troubled prince. A hard-working, unappreciated prince. A pal, you understand? A good companion. Always for his boys.

LETTA. That's so sweet.

HAPPY. Well, girls, what's the program? We're wasting time. Come on, Biff. Gather round. Where would you like to go?

BIFF. Why don't you do something for him?

HAPPY. Me!

BIFF. Don't you give a damn for him, Hap?

HAPPY. What're you talking about? I'm the one who—

BIFF. I sense it, you don't give a good goddam about him. (*He takes the rolled-up hose from his pocket and puts it on the table in front of* HAPPY.) Look what I found in the cellar, for Christ's sake. How can you bear to let it go on?

HAPPY. Me? Who goes away? Who runs off and—

BIFF. Yeah, but he doesn't mean anything to you. You could help him—I can't! Don't you understand what I'm talking about? He's going to kill himself, don't you know that?

HAPPY. Don't I know it! Me!

BIFF. Hap, help him! Jesus . . . help him . . . Help me, help me, I can't bear to look at his face! (*Ready to weep, he hurries out, up right.*)

HAPPY (*starting after him*). Where are you going?

MISS FORSYTHE. What's he so mad about?

HAPPY. Come on, girls, we'll catch up with him.

MISS FORSYTHE (*as* HAPPY *pushes her out*). Say, I don't like that temper of his!

HAPPY. He's just a little overstrung, he'll be all right!

WILLY (*off left, as* THE WOMAN *laughs*). Don't answer! Don't answer!

LETTA. Don't you want to tell your father—

HAPPY. No, that's not my father. He's just a guy. Come on, we'll catch Biff, and, honey, we're going to paint this town! Stanley, where's the check! Hey, Stanley!

(*They exit.* STANLEY *looks toward left.*)

STANLEY (*calling to* HAPPY *indignantly*). Mr. Loman! Mr. Loman!

(STANLEY *picks up a chair and follows them off. Knocking is heard off left.* THE WOMAN *enters, laughing.* WILLY *follows her. She is in a black slip; he is buttoning his shirt. Raw, sensuous music accompanies their speech.*)

WILLY. Will you stop laughing? Will you stop?

THE WOMAN. Aren't you going to answer the door? He'll wake the whole hotel.

WILLY. I'm not expecting anybody.

THE WOMAN. Whyn't you have another drink, honey, and stop being so damn self-centered?

WILLY. I'm so lonely.

THE WOMAN. You know you ruined me, Willy? From now on, whenever you come to the office, I'll see that you go right through to the buyers. No waiting at my desk any more, Willy. You ruined me.

WILLY. That's nice of you to say that.

THE WOMAN. Gee, you are self-centered! Why so sad? You are the saddest, self-centeredest soul I ever did see-saw. (*She laughs. He kisses her.*) Come on inside, drum-mer boy. It's silly to be dressing in the middle of the night. (*As knocking is heard*) Aren't you going to answer the door?

WILLY. They're knocking on the wrong door.

THE WOMAN. But I felt the knocking. And he heard us talking in here. Maybe the hotel's on fire!

WILLY (*his terror rising*). It's a mistake.

THE WOMAN. Then tell him to go away!

WILLY. There's nobody there.

THE WOMAN. It's getting on my nerves, Willy. There's somebody standing out there and it's getting on my nerves!

WILLY (*pushing her away from him*). All right, stay in the bathroom here, and don't come out. I think there's a law in Massachusetts about it, so don't come out. It may be that new room clerk. He looked very mean. So don't come out. It's a mistake, there's no fire.

(*The knocking is heard again. He takes a few steps away from her, and she vanishes into the wing. The light follows him, and now he is facing* YOUNG BIFF, *who carries a suitcase.* BIFF *steps toward him. The music is gone.*)

BIFF. Why didn't you answer?

WILLY. Biff! What are you doing in Boston?

BIFF. Why didn't you answer? I've been knocking for five minutes, I called you on the phone—

WILLY. I just heard you. I was in the bathroom and had the door shut. Did anything happen home?

BIFF. Dad—I let you down.

WILLY. What do you mean?

BIFF. Dad . . .

WILLY. Biffo, what's this about? (*Putting his arm around* BIFF) Come on, let's go downstairs and get you a malted.

BIFF. Dad, I flunked math.

WILLY. Not for the term?

BIFF. The term. I haven't got enough credits to graduate.

WILLY. You mean to say Bernard wouldn't give you the answers?

BIFF. He did, he tried, but I only got a sixty-one.

WILLY. And they wouldn't give you four points.

BIFF. Birnbaum refused absolutely. I begged him, Pop, but he won't give me those points.

You gotta talk to him before they close the school. Because if he saw the kind of man you are, and you just talked to him in your way, I'm sure he'd come through for me. The class came right before practice, see, and I didn't go enough. Would you talk to him? He'd like you, Pop. You know the way you could talk.

WILLY. You're on. We'll drive right back.

BIFF. Oh, Dad, good work! I'm sure he'll change it for you!

WILLY. Go downstairs and tell the clerk I'm checkin' out. Go right down.

BIFF. Yes, sir! See, the reason he hates me, Pop—one day he was late for class so I got up at the blackboard and imitated him. I crossed my eyes and talked with a lithp.

WILLY (laughing). You did? The kids like it?

BIFF. They nearly died laughing!

WILLY. Yeah? What'd you do?

BIFF. The thquare root of thixthy twee is . . . (WILLY bursts out laughing; BIFF joins him.) And in the middle of it he walked in!

(WILLY laughs and THE WOMAN joins in offstage.)

WILLY (without hesitation). Hurry downstairs and—

BIFF. Somebody in there?

WILLY. No, that was next door.

(THE WOMAN laughs offstage.)

BIFF. Somebody got in your bathroom!

WILLY. No, it's the next room, there's a party—

THE WOMAN (enters, laughing. She lisps this). Can I come in? There's something in the bathtub, Willy, and it's moving!

(WILLY looks at BIFF, who is staring openmouthed and horrified at THE WOMAN.)

WILLY. Ah—you better go back to your room. They must be finished painting by now. They're painting her room so I let her take a shower here. Go back, go back . . . (He pushes her.)

THE WOMAN (resisting). But I've got to get dressed, Willy, I can't—

WILLY. Get out of here! Go back, go back . . . (Suddenly striving for the ordinary) This is Miss Francis, Biff, she's a buyer. They're painting her room. Go back, Miss Francis, go back . . .

THE WOMAN. But my clothes, I can't go out naked in the hall!

WILLY (pushing her offstage). Get outa here! Go back, go back!

(BIFF slowly sits down on his suitcase as the argument continues offstage.)

THE WOMAN. Where's my stockings? You promised me stockings, Willy!

WILLY. I have no stockings here!

THE WOMAN. You had two boxes of size nine sheers for me, and I want them!

WILLY. Here, for God's sake, will you get outa here!

THE WOMAN (enters holding a box of stockings). I just hope there's nobody in the hall. That's all I hope. (To BIFF) Are you football or baseball?

BIFF. Football.

THE WOMAN (angry, humiliated). That's me too. G'night. (She snatches her clothes from WILLY and walks out.)

WILLY (after a pause). Well, better get going. I want to get to the school first thing in the morning. Get my suits out of the closet. I'll get my valise. (BIFF doesn't move.) What's the matter? (BIFF remains motionless, tears falling.) She's a buyer. Buys for J. H. Simmons. She lives down the hall—they're painting. You don't imagine— (He breaks off. After a pause) Now listen, pal, she's just a buyer. She sees merchandise in her room and they have to keep it looking just so . . . (Pause. Assuming command) All right, get my suits. (BIFF doesn't move.) Now stop crying and do as I say. I gave you an order. Biff, I gave you an order! Is that what you do when I give you an order? How dare you cry! (Putting his arm around BIFF) Now look, Biff, when you grow up you'll understand about these things. You mustn't—you mustn't overemphasize a thing like this. I'll see Birnbaum first thing in the morning.

BIFF. Never mind.

WILLY (getting down beside BIFF). Never mind! He's going to give you those points. I'll see to it.

BIFF. He wouldn't listen to you.

WILLY. He certainly will listen to me. You need those points for the U. of Virginia.

BIFF. I'm not going there.

WILLY. Heh? If I can't get him to change that mark you'll make it up in summer school. You've got all summer to—

BIFF (his weeping breaking from him). Dad . . .

WILLY (*infected by it*). Oh, my boy . . .

BIFF. Dad . . .

WILLY. She's nothing to me, Biff. I was lonely, I was terribly lonely.

BIFF. You—you gave her Mama's stockings! (*His tears break through and he rises to go.*)

WILLY (*grabbing for* BIFF). I gave you an order!

BIFF. Don't touch me, you—liar!

WILLY. Apologize for that!

BIFF. You fake! You phony little fake! You fake! (*Overcome, he turns quickly and weeping fully goes out with his suitcase.* WILLY *is left on the floor on his knees.*)

WILLY. I gave you an order! Biff, come back here or I'll beat you! Come back here! I'll whip you!

(STANLEY *comes quickly in from the right and stands in front of* WILLY.)

WILLY (*shouts at* STANLEY). I gave you an order . . .

STANLEY. Hey, let's pick it up, pick it up, Mr. Loman. (*He helps* WILLY *to his feet.*) Your boys left with the chippies. They said they'll see you home.

(*A second waiter watches some distance away.*)

WILLY. But we were supposed to have dinner together.

(*Music is heard,* WILLY'S *theme.*)

STANLEY. Can you make it?

WILLY. I'll—sure, I can make it. (*Suddenly concerned about his clothes*) Do I—I look all right?

STANLEY. Sure, you look all right. (*He flicks a speck off* WILLY'S *lapel.*)

WILLY. Here—here's a dollar.

STANLEY. Oh, your son paid me. It's all right.

WILLY (*putting it in* STANLEY'S *hand*). No, take it. You're a good boy.

STANLEY. Oh, no, you don't have to . . .

WILLY. Here—here's some more, I don't need it any more. (*After a slight pause*) Tell me—is there a seed store in the neighborhood?

STANLEY. Seeds? You mean like to plant?

(*As* WILLY *turns,* STANLEY *slips the money back into his jacket pocket.*)

WILLY. Yes. Carrots, peas . . .

STANLEY. Well, there's hardware stores on Sixth Avenue, but it may be too late now.

WILLY (*anxiously*). Oh, I'd better hurry. I've got to get some seeds. (*He starts off to the right.*) I've got to get some seeds, right away. Nothing's planted. I don't have a thing in the ground.

(WILLY *hurries out as the light goes down.* STANLEY *moves over to the right after him, watches him off. The other waiter has been staring at* WILLY.)

STANLEY (*to the waiter*). Well, whatta you looking at?

(*The waiter picks up the chairs and moves off right.* STANLEY *takes the table and follows him. The light fades on this area. There is a long pause, the sound of the flute coming over. The light gradually rises on the kitchen, which is empty.* HAPPY *appears at the door of the house, followed by* BIFF. HAPPY *is carrying a large bunch of long-stemmed roses. He enters the kitchen, looks around for* LINDA. *Not seeing her, he turns to* BIFF, *who is just outside the house door, and makes a gesture with his hands, indicating "Not here, I guess." He looks into the living-room and freezes. Inside,* LINDA, *unseen, is seated,* WILLY'S *coat on her lap. She rises ominously and quietly and moves toward* HAPPY, *who backs up into the kitchen, afraid.*)

HAPPY. Hey, what're you doing up? (LINDA *says nothing but moves toward him implacably.*) Where's Pop? (*He keeps backing to the right, and now* LINDA *is in full view in the doorway to the living-room.*) Is he sleeping?

LINDA. Where were you?

HAPPY (*trying to laugh it off*). We met two girls, Mom, very fine types. Here, we brought you some flowers. (*Offering them to her*) Put them in your room, Ma.

(*She knocks them to the floor at* BIFF'S *feet. He has now come inside and closed the door behind him. She stares at* BIFF, *silent.*)

HAPPY. Now what'd you do that for? Mom, I want you to have some flowers—

LINDA (*cutting* HAPPY *off, violently to* BIFF). Don't you care whether he lives or dies?

HAPPY (*going to the stairs*). Come upstairs, Biff.

BIFF (*with a flare of disgust, to* HAPPY). Go away from me! (*To* LINDA) What do you mean, lives or dies? Nobody's dying around here, pal.

LINDA. Get out of my sight! Get out of here!

BIFF. I wanna see the boss.

LINDA. You're not going near him!

BIFF. Where is he? (*He moves into the living-room and* LINDA *follows.*)

LINDA (*shouting after* BIFF). You invite him for dinner. He looks forward to it all day— (BIFF *appears in his parents' bedroom, looks around, and exits*)—and then you desert him there. There's no stranger you'd do that to!

HAPPY. Why? He had a swell time with us. Listen, when I—(LINDA *comes back into the kitchen*)—desert him I hope I don't outlive the day!

LINDA. Get out of here!

HAPPY. Now look, Mom . . .

LINDA. Did you have to go to women tonight? You and your lousy rotten whores!

(BIFF *re-enters the kitchen.*)

HAPPY. Mom, all we did was follow Biff around trying to cheer him up! (*To* BIFF) Boy, what a night you gave me!

LINDA. Get out of here, both of you, and don't come back! I don't want you tormenting him any more. Go on now, get your things together! (*To* BIFF) You can sleep in his apartment. (*She starts to pick up the flowers and stops herself.*) Pick up this stuff, I'm not your maid any more. Pick it up, you bum, you!

(HAPPY *turns his back to her in refusal.* BIFF *slowly moves over and gets down on his knees, picking up the flowers.*)

LINDA. You're a pair of animals! Not one, not another living soul would have had the cruelty to walk out on that man in a restaurant!

BIFF (*not looking at her*). Is that what he said?

LINDA. He didn't have to say anything. He was so humiliated he nearly limped when he came in.

HAPPY. But, Mom, he had a great time with us—

BIFF (*cutting him off violently*). Shut up! (*Without another word,* HAPPY *goes upstairs.*)

LINDA. You! You didn't even go in to see if he was all right!

BIFF (*still on the floor in front of* LINDA, *the flowers in his hand; with self-loathing*). No. Didn't. Didn't do a damned thing. How do you like that, heh? Left him babbling in a toilet.

LINDA. You louse. You . . .

BIFF. Now you hit it on the nose! (*He gets up, throws the flowers in the wastebasket.*)

The scum of the earth, and you're looking at him!

LINDA. Get out of here!

BIFF. I gotta talk to the boss, Mom. Where is he?

LINDA. You're not going near him. Get out of this house!

BIFF (*with absolute assurance, determination*). No. We're gonna have an abrupt conversation, him and me.

LINDA. You're not talking to him!

(*Hammering is heard from outside the house, off right.* BIFF *turns toward the noise.*)

LINDA (*suddenly pleading*). Will you please leave him alone?

BIFF. What's he doing out there?

LINDA. He's planting the garden!

BIFF (*quietly*). Now? Oh, my God!

(BIFF *moves outside,* LINDA *following. The light dies down on them and comes up on the center of the apron as* WILLY *walks into it. He is carrying a flashlight, a hoe, and a handful of seed packets. He raps the top of the hoe sharply to fix it firmly, and then moves to the left, measuring off the distance with his foot. He holds the flashlight to look at the seed packets, reading off the instructions. He is in the blue of night.*)

WILLY. Carrots . . . quarter-inch apart. Rows . . . one-foot rows. (*He measures it off.*) One foot. (*He puts down a package and measures off.*) Beets. (*He puts down another package and measures again.*) Lettuce. (*He reads the package, puts it down.*) One foot— (*He breaks off as* BEN *appears at the right and moves slowly down to him.*) What a proposition, ts, ts. Terrific, terrific. 'Cause she's suffered, Ben, the woman has suffered. You understand me? A man can't go out the way he came in, Ben, a man has got to add up to something. You can't, you can't— (BEN *moves toward him as though to interrupt.*) You gotta consider, now. Don't answer so quick. Remember, it's a guaranteed twenty-thousand-dollar proposition. Now look, Ben, I want you to go through the ins and outs of this thing with me. I've got nobody to talk to, Ben, and the woman has suffered, you hear me?

BEN (*standing still, considering*). What's the proposition?

WILLY. It's twenty thousand dollars on the

barrelhead. Guaranteed, gilt-edged, you understand?

BEN. You don't want to make a fool of yourself. They might not honor the policy.

WILLY. How can they dare refuse? Didn't I work like a coolie to meet every premium on the nose? And now they don't pay off? Impossible!

BEN. It's called a cowardly thing, William.

WILLY. Why? Does it take more guts to stand here the rest of my life ringing up a zero?

BEN (*yielding*). That's a point, William. (*He moves, thinking, turns.*) And twenty thousand—that *is* something one can feel with the hand, it is there.

WILLY (*now assured, with rising power*). Oh, Ben, that's the whole beauty of it! I see it like a diamond, shining in the dark, hard and rough, that I can pick up and touch in my hand. Not like—like an appointment! This would not be another damned-fool appointment, Ben, and it changes all the aspects. Because he thinks I'm nothing, see, and so he spites me. But the funeral— (*Straightening up*) Ben, that funeral will be massive! They'll come from Maine, Massachusetts, Vermont, New Hampshire! All the old-timers with the strange license plates—that boy will be thunder-struck, Ben, because he never realized—I am known! Rhode Island, New York, New Jersey—I am known, Ben, and he'll see it with his eyes once and for all. He'll see what I am, Ben! He's in for a shock, that boy!

BEN (*coming down to the edge of the garden*). He'll call you a coward.

WILLY (*suddenly fearful*). No, that would be terrible.

BEN. Yes. And a damned fool.

WILLY. No, no, he mustn't, I won't have that! (*He is broken and desperate.*)

BEN. He'll hate you, William.

(*The gay music of* THE BOYS *is heard.*)

WILLY. Oh, Ben, how do we get back to all the great times? Used to be so full of light, and comradeship, the sleigh-riding in winter and the ruddiness on his cheeks. And always some kind of good news coming up, always something nice coming up ahead. And never even let me carry the valises in the house, and simonizing, simonizing that little red car!

Why, why can't I give him something and not have him hate me?

BEN. Let me think about it. (*He glances at his watch.*) I still have a little time. Remarkable proposition, but you've got to be sure you're not making a fool of yourself.

(BEN *drifts off upstage and goes out of sight.* BIFF *comes down from the left.*)

WILLY (*suddenly conscious of* BIFF, *turns and looks up at him, then begins picking up the packages of seeds in confusion*). Where the hell is that seed? (*Indignantly*) You can't see nothing out here! They boxed in the whole goddam neighborhood!

BIFF. There are people all around here. Don't you realize that?

WILLY. I'm busy. Don't bother me.

BIFF (*taking the hoe from* WILLY). I'm saying good-by to you, Pop. (WILLY *looks at him, silent, unable to move.*) I'm not coming back any more.

WILLY. You're not going to see Oliver tomorrow?

BIFF. I've got no appointment, Dad.

WILLY. He put his arm around you, and you've got no appointment?

BIFF. Pop, get this now, will you? Everytime I've left it's been a fight that sent me out of here. Today I realized something about myself and I tried to explain it to you and I— I think I'm just not smart enough to make any sense out of it for you. To hell with whose fault it is or anything like that. (*He takes* WILLY's *arm.*) Let's just wrap it up, heh? Come on in, we'll tell Mom. (*He gently tries to pull* WILLY *to left.*)

WILLY (*frozen, immobile, with guilt in his voice*). No, I don't want to see her.

BIFF. Come on! (*He pulls again, and* WILLY *tries to pull away.*)

WILLY (*highly nervous*). No, no, I don't want to see her.

BIFF (*tries to look into* WILLY's *face, as if to find the answer there*). Why don't you want to see her?

WILLY (*more harshly now*). Don't bother me, will you?

BIFF. What do you mean, you don't want to see her? You don't want them calling you yellow, do you? This isn't your fault; it's me, I'm a bum. Now come inside! (WILLY *strains to get away.*) Did you hear what I said to you?

(WILLY *pulls away and quickly goes by him- self into the house.* BIFF *follows.*)

LINDA (*to* WILLY). Did you plant, dear?

BIFF (*at the door, to* LINDA). All right, we had it out. I'm going and I'm not writing any more.

LINDA (*going to* WILLY *in the kitchen*). I think that's the best way, dear. 'Cause there's no use drawing it out, you'll just never get along.

(WILLY *doesn't respond.*)

BIFF. People ask where I am and what I'm doing, you don't know, and you don't care. That way it'll be off your mind and you can start brightening up again. All right? That clears it, doesn't it? (WILLY *is silent, and* BIFF *goes to him.*) You gonna wish me luck, scout? (*He extends his hand.*) What do you say?

LINDA. Shake his hand, Willy.

WILLY (*turning to her, seething with hurt*). There's no necessity to mention the pen at all, y'know.

BIFF (*gently*). I've got no appointment, Dad.

WILLY (*erupting fiercely*). He put his arm around . . . ?

BIFF. Dad, you're never going to see what I am, so what's the use of arguing? If I strike oil I'll send you a check. Meantime forget I'm alive.

WILLY (*to* LINDA). Spite, see?

BIFF. Shake hands, Dad.

WILLY. Not my hand.

BIFF. I was hoping not to go this way.

WILLY. Well, this is the way you're going. Good-by.

(BIFF *looks at him a moment, then turns sharply and goes to the stairs.*)

WILLY (*stops him with*). May you rot in hell if you leave this house!

BIFF (*turning*). Exactly what is it that you want from me?

WILLY. I want you to know, on the train, in the mountains, in the valleys, wherever you go, that you cut down your life for spite!

BIFF. No, no.

WILLY. Spite, spite, is the word of your un- doing! And when you're down and out, re- member what did it. When you're rotting somewhere beside the railroad tracks, remem- ber, and don't you dare blame it on me!

BIFF. I'm not blaming it on you!

WILLY. I won't take the rap for this, you hear?

(HAPPY *comes down the stairs and stands on the bottom step, watching.*)

BIFF. That's just what I'm telling you!

WILLY (*sinking into a chair at the table, with full accusation*). You're trying to put a knife in me—don't think I don't know what you're doing!

BIFF. All right, phony! Then let's lay it on the line. (*He whips the rubber tube out of his pocket and puts it on the table.*)

HAPPY. You crazy—

LINDA. Biff! (*She moves to grab the hose, but* BIFF *holds it down with his hand.*)

BIFF. Leave it there! Don't move it!

WILLY (*not looking at it*). What is that?

BIFF. You know goddam well what that is.

WILLY (*caged, wanting to escape*). I never saw that.

BIFF. You saw it. The mice didn't bring it into the cellar! What is this supposed to do, make a hero out of you? This supposed to make me sorry for you?

WILLY. Never heard of it.

BIFF. There'll be no pity for you, you hear it? No pity!

WILLY (*to* LINDA). You hear the spite!

BIFF. No, you're going to hear the truth— what you are and what I am!

LINDA. Stop it!

WILLY. Spite!

HAPPY (*coming down toward* BIFF). You cut it now!

BIFF (*to* HAPPY). The man don't know who we are! The man is gonna know! (*To* WILLY) We never told the truth for ten minutes in this house!

HAPPY. We always told the truth!

BIFF (*turning on him*). You big blow, are you the assistant buyer? You're one of the two assistants to the assistant, aren't you?

HAPPY. Well, I'm practically—

BIFF. You're practically full of it! We all are! And I'm through with it (*To* WILLY) Now hear this, Willy, this is me.

WILLY. I know you!

BIFF. You know why I had no address for three months? I stole a suit in Kansas City and I was in jail. (*To* LINDA, *who is sobbing*) Stop crying. I'm through with it.

(LINDA *turns away from them, her hands covering her face.*)

WILLY. I suppose that's my fault!

BIFF. I stole myself out of every good job since high school!

WILLY. And whose fault is that?

BIFF. And I never got anywhere because you blew me so full of hot air I could never stand taking orders from anybody! That's whose fault it is!

WILLY. I hear that!

LINDA. Don't, Biff!

BIFF. It's goddam time you heard that! I had to be boss big shot in two weeks, and I'm through with it!

WILLY. Then hang yourself! For spite, hang yourself!

BIFF. No! Nobody's hanging himself, Willy! I ran down eleven flights with a pen in my hand today. And suddenly I stopped, you hear me? And in the middle of that office building, do you hear this? I stopped in the middle of that building and I saw—the sky. I saw the things that I love in this world. The work and the food and time to sit and smoke. And I looked at the pen and said to myself, what the hell am I grabbing this for? Why am I trying to become what I don't want to be? What am I doing in an office, making a contemptuous, begging fool of myself, when all I want is out there, waiting for me the minute I say I know who I am! Why can't I say that, Willy? (*He tries to make* WILLY *face him, but* WILLY *pulls away and moves to the left.*)

WILLY (*with hatred, threateningly*). The door of your life is wide open!

BIFF. Pop! I'm a dime a dozen, and so are you!

WILLY (*turning on him now in an uncontrolled outburst*). I am not a dime a dozen! I am Willy Loman, and you are Biff Loman!

(BIFF *starts for* WILLY, *but is blocked by* HAPPY. *In his fury,* BIFF *seems on the verge of attacking his father.*)

BIFF. I am not a leader of men, Willy, and neither are you. You were never anything but a hard-working drummer who landed in the ash can like all the rest of them! I'm one dollar an hour, Willy! I tried seven states and couldn't raise it. A buck an hour! Do you gather my meaning? I'm not bringing home

any prizes any more, and you're going to stop waiting for me to bring them home!

WILLY (*directly to* BIFF). You vengeful, spiteful mutt!

(BIFF *breaks from* HAPPY. WILLY, *in fright, starts up the stairs.* BIFF *grabs him.*)

BIFF (*at the peak of his fury*). Pop, I'm nothing! I'm nothing, Pop. Can't you understand that? There's no spite in it any more. I'm just what I am, that's all.

(BIFF's *fury has spent itself, and he breaks down, sobbing, holding on to* WILLY, *who dumbly fumbles for* BIFF's *face.*)

WILLY (*astonished*). What're you doing? What're you doing? (*To* LINDA) Why is he crying?

BIFF (*crying, broken*). Will you let me go, for Christ's sake? Will you take that phony dream and burn it before something happens? (*Struggling to contain himself, he pulls away and moves to the stairs.*) I'll go in the morning. Put him—put him to bed. (*Exhausted,* BIFF *moves up the stairs to his room.*)

WILLY (*after a long pause, astonished, elevated*). Isn't that—isn't that remarkable? Biff—he likes me!

LINDA. He loves you, Willy!

HAPPY (*deeply moved*). Always did, Pop.

WILLY. Oh, Biff! (*Staring wildly*) He cried! Cried to me. (*He is choking with his love, and now cries out his promise.*) That boy—that boy is going to be magnificent!

(BEN *appears in the light just outside the kitchen.*)

BEN. Yes, outstanding, with twenty thousand behind him.

LINDA (*sensing the racing of his mind, fearfully, carefully*). Now come to bed, Willy. It's all settled now.

WILLY (*finding it difficult not to rush out of the house*). Yes, we'll sleep. Come on. Go to sleep, Hap.

BEN. And it does take a great kind of a man to crack the jungle.

(*In accents of dread,* BEN's *idyllic music starts up.*)

HAPPY (*his arm around* LINDA). I'm getting married, Pop, don't forget it. I'm changing everything. I'm gonna run that department before the year is up. You'll see, Mom. (*He kisses her.*)

BEN. The jungle is dark but full of diamonds, Willy.

(WILLY *turns, moves, listening to* BEN.)

LINDA. Be good. You're both good boys, just act that way, that's all.

HAPPY. 'Night, Pop. (*He goes upstairs.*)

LINDA (*to* WILLY). Come, dear.

BEN (*with greater force*). One must go in to fetch a diamond out.

WILLY (*to* LINDA, *as he moves slowly along the edge of the kitchen, toward the door*). I just want to get settled down, Linda. Let me sit alone for a little.

LINDA (*almost uttering her fear*). I want you upstairs.

WILLY (*taking her in his arms*). In a few minutes, Linda. I couldn't sleep right now. Go on, you look awful tired. (*He kisses her.*)

BEN. Not like an appointment at all. A diamond is rough and hard to the touch.

WILLY. Go on now. I'll be right up.

LINDA. I think this is the only way, Willy.

WILLY. Sure, it's the best thing.

BEN. Best thing!

WILLY. The only way. Everything is gonna be—go on, kid, get to bed. You look so tired.

LINDA. Come right up.

WILLY. Two minutes.

(LINDA *goes into the living-room, then reappears in her bedroom.* WILLY *moves just outside the kitchen door.*)

WILLY. Loves me. (*Wonderingly*) Always loved me. Isn't that a remarkable thing? Ben, he'll worship me for it!

BEN (*with promise*). It's dark there, but full of diamonds.

WILLY. Can you imagine that magnificence with twenty thousand dollars in his pocket?

LINDA (*calling from her room*). Willy! Come up!

WILLY (*calling into the kitchen*). Yes! Yes. Coming! It's very smart, you realize that, don't you, sweetheart? Even Ben sees it. I gotta go, baby. 'By! 'By! (*Going over to* BEN, *almost dancing*) Imagine? When the mail comes he'll be ahead of Bernard again!

BEN. A perfect proposition all around.

WILLY. Did you see how he cried to me? Oh, if I could kiss him, Ben!

BEN. Time, William, time!

WILLY. Oh, Ben, I always knew one way or another we were gonna make it, Biff and I!

BEN (*looking at his watch*). The boat. We'll be late. (*He moves slowly off into the darkness.*)

WILLY (*elegiacally, turning to the house*). Now when you kick off, boy, I want a seventy-yard boot, and get right down the field under the ball, and when you hit, hit low and hit hard, because it's important, boy. (*He swings around and faces the audience.*) There's all kinds of important people in the stands, and the first thing you know . . . (*Suddenly realizing he is alone*) Ben! Ben, where do I . . . ? (*He makes a sudden movement of search.*) Ben, how do I . . . ?

LINDA (*calling*). Willy, you coming up?

WILLY (*uttering a gasp of fear, whirling about as if to quiet her*). Sh! (*He turns around as if to find his way; sounds, faces, voices, seem to be swarming in upon him and he flicks at them, crying*) Sh! Sh! (*Suddenly music, faint and high, stops him. It rises in intensity, almost to an unbearable scream. He goes up and down on his toes, and rushes off around the house.*) Shhh!

LINDA. Willy?

(*There is no answer.* LINDA *waits.* BIFF *gets up off his bed. He is still in his clothes.* HAPPY *sits up.* BIFF *stands listening.*)

LINDA (*with real fear*). Willy, answer me! Willy!

(*There is the sound of a car starting and moving away at full speed.*)

LINDA. No!

BIFF (*rushing down the stairs*). Pop!

(*As the car speeds off, the music crashes down in a frenzy of sound, which becomes the soft pulsation of a single cello string.* BIFF *slowly returns to his bedroom. He and* HAPPY *gravely don their jackets.* LINDA *slowly walks out of her room. The music has developed into a dead march. The leaves of day are appearing over everything.* CHARLEY *and* BERNARD, *somberly dressed, appear and knock on the kitchen door.* BIFF *and* HAPPY *slowly descend the stairs to the kitchen as* CHARLEY *and* BERNARD *enter. All stop a moment when* LINDA, *in clothes of mourning, bearing a little bunch of roses, comes through the draped doorway into the kitchen. She goes to* CHARLEY *and takes his arm. Now all move toward the audience, through the wall-line of the kitchen. At the limit of the apron,* LINDA *lays down the flowers, kneels, and sits back on her heels. All stare down at the grave.*)

REQUIEM

CHARLEY. It's getting dark, Linda.

(LINDA *doesn't react. She stares at the grave.*)

BIFF. How about it, Mom? Better get some rest, heh? They'll be closing the gate soon.

(LINDA *makes no move. Pause*)

HAPPY (*deeply angered*). He had no right to do that. There was no necessity for it. We would've helped him.

CHARLEY (*grunting*). Hmmm.

BIFF. Come along, Mom.

LINDA. Why didn't anybody come?

CHARLEY. It was a very nice funeral.

LINDA. But where are all the people he knew? Maybe they blame him.

CHARLEY. Naa. It's a rough world, Linda. They wouldn't blame him.

LINDA. I can't understand it. At this time especially. First time in thirty-five years we were just about free and clear. He only needed a little salary. He was even finished with the dentist.

CHARLEY. No man only needs a little salary.

LINDA. I can't understand it.

BIFF. There were a lot of nice days. When he'd come home from a trip; or on Sundays, making the stoop; finishing the cellar; putting on the new porch; when he built the extra bathroom; and put up the garage. You know something, Charley, there's more of him in that front stoop than in all the sales he ever made.

CHARLEY. Yeah. He was a happy man with a batch of cement.

LINDA. He was so wonderful with his hands.

BIFF. He had the wrong dreams. All, all, wrong.

HAPPY (*almost ready to fight* BIFF). Don't say that!

BIFF. He never knew who he was.

CHARLEY (*stopping* HAPPY's *movement and reply. To* BIFF). Nobody dast blame this man. You don't understand: Willy was a salesman. And for a salesman, there is no rock bottom to the life. He don't put a bolt to a nut, he don't tell you the law or give you medicine. He's a man way out there in the blue, riding on a smile and a shoeshine. And when they start not smiling back—that's an earthquake. And then you get yourself a couple of spots on your hat, and you're finished. Nobody dast blame this man. A salesman is got to dream, boy. It comes with the territory.

BIFF. Charley, the man didn't know who he was.

HAPPY (*infuriated*). Don't say that!

BIFF. Why don't you come with me, Happy?

HAPPY. I'm not licked that easily. I'm staying right in this city, and I'm gonna beat this racket! (*He looks at* BIFF, *his chin set.*) The Loman Brothers!

BIFF. I know who I am, kid.

HAPPY. All right, boy. I'm gonna show you and everybody else that Willy Loman did not die in vain. He had a good dream. It's the only dream you can have—to come out number-one man. He fought it out here, and this is where I'm gonna win it for him.

BIFF (*with a hopeless glance at* HAPPY, *bends toward his mother*). Let's go, Mom.

LINDA. I'll be with you in a minute. Go on, Charley. (*He hesitates.*) I want to, just for a minute. I never had a chance to say good-by.

(CHARLEY *moves away, followed by* HAPPY. BIFF *remains a slight distance up and left of* LINDA. *She sits there, summoning herself. The flute begins, not far away, playing behind her speech.*)

LINDA. Forgive me, dear. I can't cry. I don't know what it is, but I can't cry. I don't understand it. Why did you ever do that? Help me, Willy, I can't cry. It seems to me that you're just on another trip. I keep expecting you. Willy, dear, I can't cry. Why did you do it? I search and search and I search, and I can't understand it, Willy. I made the last payment on the house today. Today, dear. And there'll be nobody home. (*A sob rises in her throat.*) We're free and clear. (*Sobbing more fully, released*) We're free. (BIFF *comes slowly toward her.*) We're free . . . We're free . . .

(BIFF *lifts her to her feet and moves out up right with her in his arms.* LINDA *sobs quietly.* BERNARD *and* CHARLEY *come together and follow them, followed by* HAPPY. *Only the music of the flute is left on the darkening stage as over the house the hard towers of the apartment buildings rise into sharp focus, and*)

THE CURTAIN FALLS

POETRY

INTRODUCTION

Poetry is a form of literature that many readers hold in a special kind of affectionate admiration. From the earliest times, probably even before language was written, poets have been the oracles and prophets of their peoples. Poets have always reflected the temper of the ages in which they live: Homer epitomizes a glorious epoch in Greek history, as Hardy epitomizes the perplexity and despair of late Victorian England.

THE NATURE OF POETRY. Poetry cannot be precisely defined, but some of its distinguishing characteristics can be described. Poetry deals in matters beyond direct statement—in meanings conditioned by emotional attitudes—and its intention is to evoke the full flavor and impact of experience. Poetry often achieves its effects by selecting words that are suggestive not only of sensory experience but also of emotional attitudes, by using figurative comparisons and by rime and rhythm. Finally, the most distinctive feature of poetry is the organic quality achieved by the close organization of its component parts. The poet in a sense is a maker of experiences. (The Old English word for poet is *scop,* "the maker.") Life is so cluttered with detail that to most of us it often seems chaotic. Like other artists, the poet discards the confusing detail, selects and arranges the remainder to communicate his impression, and thereby creates a meaningful experience which he passes on to his reader.

What one receives from a poem, then, is an experience. I. A. Richards, perhaps the most stimulating of the contemporary critics of poetry, has pointed out that a poem has a "Total Meaning" which is a blend of the poet's *sense* (what the poem is apparently about), his *feeling* (the poet's attitude toward his subject matter), his *tone* (attitude toward his reader), and his *intention* (aim, or effect). A poet is more or less aware of this fact and, as he writes, expresses all the meanings as fully as his ability and his medium will permit. The reader, in turn, will profit by considering all of them when trying to arrive at a full realization of a poem.

Consider, for example, the following occasional poem by Thomas Hardy, "On an Invitation to the United States." [1]

I

My ardours for emprize nigh lost   Where the new regions claim them free
Since life has bared its bones to me,   From that long drip of human tears
I shrink to seek a modern coast   Which peoples old in tragedy
Whose riper times have yet to be;   Have left upon the centuried years.

[1] From *Collected Poems* by Thomas Hardy. Copyright 1925 by The Macmillan Company and used with their permission.

II

For, wonning in these ancient lands,	Though my own Being bear no bloom
Enchased and lettered as a tomb,	I trace the lives such scenes enshrine,
And scored with prints of perished hands,	Give past exemplars present room,
And chronicled with dates of doom,	And their experience count as mine.

Obviously, the poem is about Hardy's declining an invitation to visit the United States—his reaction to an invitation to come to a land of more promising future but a less historic past. But statement of the *sense* of the poem is not the equivalent of the poem. In fact, even the following full paraphrase of the sense of the poem falls far short of the poem itself: "I have almost lost my taste for adventure since I discovered how grim life is; I hesitate to seek a new country that has not yet reached full fruition, and has not had a tragic-storied past. Living in this old land, which is much like a tombstone with its inscriptions, I—even though I do not prosper personally—study the lives of the great people of England's history and consider their experience as mine."

For full comprehension we need to absorb the poet's *feeling* about the material. Hardy presents that feeling by implying a contrast between the pasts of the United States and England and by suggesting a relationship between his own past and that of his country. He hints some mild doubt of the United States—a country raw and un-tried by a long history of adversities and tribulations, though perhaps of a promising future. Just as indirectly he communicates, without sentimentality, his love of England by imagery that pictures her long and tragic history, full of adversities, trials, and strug-gles; and he makes clear his desire to share what he feels is England's unhappy lot.

We need also to grasp his *tone,* or his attitude toward his reader. His tone, like his feeling, is complex, for, though he is addressing himself particularly to the people of the United States, the people who extended to him the invitation that occasioned the poem, in the background he includes among his audience English compatriots. With neither condescension to the inviters nor depreciation of the worth of their regard, he courteously declines. Though he reminds his background audience, the English, of their mournful history, and indirectly rededicates them as well as himself to his resolve to endure and to be proud of enduring, he steers as widely clear of national conceit and chauvinism as he does of a defensive attitude that would be un-comfortable to English and American alike.

Hardy's full poetic *intention* is to comment feelingly on the individual's rela-tion to his country's history and on his goal in life. Furthermore, he intends to imply the judgment that to assume a share of the unhappy human lot may be a greater act than to achieve purely personal well-being—the attitude of a true pessimist.

The total meaning of "On an Invitation to the United States," therefore, depends on its *sense, feeling, tone,* and *intention.* Briefly, Hardy says that he cannot accept the invitation, acknowledges the favorable prospects of America and expresses his love of England, shows to those who invited him a courteous but not deferential apprecia-tion, and takes the opportunity to comment on the value of tradition. In other words, the communication of this complex meaning provides an experience for the reader, an experience which *is* the poem.

THE METHOD OF POETRY. As "On an Invitation to the United States" reveals, there is more to a poem than the *sense* which can be translated into direct prose statement or paraphrase. Poets characteristically communicate by suggestion or implication; that is, they say more than their words and word combinations literally mean. Perhaps *indirection* is the best term to summarize the way by which poets say so much in so few words.

Diction. The words of poetry are for the most part the same words that people use to carry on the plain business of living. Individually those words stand for about the same things and have approximately the same sounds in poems as they have in everyday speech. But in poetry words are used more precisely and are ordered more carefully than in conversation. Moreover, a poem does not depend solely upon meanings of words; what the words suggest—their connotative rather than their denotative values —may be even more important to its effect. Consider the implications of some of the words in "On an Invitation to the United States": *modern, riper, emprize, wonning.* In context *modern* has just a slightly unfavorable overtone; it suggests, though faintly, that Hardy had in mind an overmodernity, an excessive degree of modernity. Much the same is true of the word *riper* in its context here: Hardy seems to imply that the United States is presently lacking the maturity he cherishes in England. *Emprize* and *wonning* are also highly implicative words. Their effect here is to promote, by supplying atmosphere, Hardy's intention of getting the reader to understand and approve his cherishing of the past. Both are archaic—*emprize* having been supplanted by the modern form *enterprise* or *adventure;* and *wonning,* by *dwelling, residing, living.* By using these archaisms along with such other words as *old, centuried, ancient, chronicled, dates of doom,* Hardy reminds the reader of Norse and Norman invaders, the Anglo-Saxon Chronicle, Alfred and Harold, the Domesday Book, and Runnymede and Magna Charta.

Imagery. The selection of language in poetry is governed primarily by the poet's desire to give his reader sensory experience—as Coleridge says, "to instill that energy into the mind, which compels the imagination to produce the picture." By appealing to some one or more of the physical senses, the poet arouses both the mind and the emotion of the reader so that he in a measure experiences physical sensation. These things imaginatively sensed are collectively known as *imagery.*

The Concrete Word. Doubtless the simplest device to evoke imagery is the single concrete word, a word such as *scored* or *chronicled* in Hardy's poem. Hardy might have written *marked* "with prints of perished hands" instead of "*scored* with prints of perished hands." But he chose *scored* because it supplies to the reader's imagination the image Hardy desired, that of signs much deeper and more permanent than mere surface "marks." So with *chronicled.* Hardy chose a word to suggest a whole complex of meaning, the Anglo-Saxon Chronicle and even England's whole history.

Figurative Language. Another device poets use to create imagery is figurative language. Basically, most figures are comparisons, expressed or implied, of things not ordinarily thought of as being alike—comparisons that do not on the surface seem logical but that on closer inspection prove illuminating. For instance, Hardy says "life has bared its bones to me." He is using a *metaphor* here, an implied comparison that not only suggests his interpretation of the true character of life, but also vividly reveals Hardy's state of mind. Again, Hardy in a *simile* directly compares England to a tomb—"ancient lands,/Enchased and lettered as a tomb." Thus he suggests to the reader the richness of England's past—the multitude of deeds and personages that make up England's history. As the inscriptions on tombs record the deeds and exploits (as well as the vital statistics) of the persons buried in the tombs, so England is filled with places and covered with monuments and shrines that recall the richness of her past.

Rhythm and Rime. Another kind of indirection prominent in the method of poetry is the use of sound effects to intensify meaning. Along with the attempt to communicate his total meaning by choosing words and images which convey his sense, feeling, and tone, the poet attempts to organize his words into a pattern of sound that is a part of that total meaning. The sound of poetry, then, like the diction and the imagery, is to be considered only in relation to the total design of the poem.

Sound effects are the products of organized repetitions. *Rhythm* is the result of systematically *stressing* or *accenting* words and syllables, whereas *rime* repeats similar sounds in some apparent scheme. Both rhythm and rime arouse interest in the reader, for as soon as he grasps their patterns he unconsciously expects them to continue. Expecting their continuation, he is more attentive not only to the sound itself but also to the sense, feeling, and tone of the poet.

Different rhythms tend to arouse different emotions.

> Scots, wha hae wi' Wallace bled,　　　　Now's the day, and now's the hour:
> Scots, wham Bruce has aften led,　　　　See the front o' battle lour;
> Welcome to your gory bed,　　　　　　　See approach proud Edward's power—
> 　　Or to victory!　　　　　　　　　　　　Chains and slavery! [2]

The rhythmic beat here, along with the sense of the words, sounds a grim, determined battle cry and stirs the reader to a quicker beating of the blood.

> God of our fathers, known of old—　　　Dominion over palm and pine—
> 　Lord of our far-flung battle-line—　　Lord God of Hosts, be with us yet
> Beneath whose awful Hand we hold　　　Lest we forget—lest we forget! [3]

Here the rhythm helps to induce in the reader the solemnity and even reverence that accompany pomp and ceremony.

Rhythms exist for the full gamut of emotions, since the only limitation upon the variety of rhythms is that which word-meaning imposes. Thus rhythms can easily be found for those quieter emotions accompanying meditation and reflection:

> "A cold coming we had of it,
> Just the worst time of the year
> For a journey, and such a long journey:
> The ways deep and the weather sharp,
> The very dead of winter."
> And the camels galled, sore-footed, refractory,
> Lying down in the melting snow.[4]

[2] From "Scots Wha Hae" by Robert Burns.
[3] From "Recessional" by Rudyard Kipling. See page 711 of this text.
[4] From "Journey of the Magi" by T. S. Eliot. See page 706 of this text.

This rhythm is less patterned than the preceding two. The poet here has departed from a strict rhythmic movement much more frequently and prominently than have either of the two preceding poets. These departures, while preserving a reflective mood, make for informality and a conversational tone. Variation from a rigid metrical pattern is often found in poetry, especially in modern poetry.

Rime—a patterned recurrence of like or similar sounds—also functions indirectly to intensify meaning. It is a further impressing of design upon material in order to achieve an intention in sense, feeling, and tone. It serves as a binding and unifying element and lends continuity. It may also be used for emphasis, especially when, as often occurs, the rime word at the end of a line concludes a phrase or clause. And rime, like rhythm, affords pleasure at the fulfillment of a pattern the reader has unconsciously recognized. Since most poetry is rimed, when Kipling writes

> God of our fathers, known of old

the reader has, at least unconsciously, recognized the likelihood that Kipling will somewhere, perhaps in the very next line, come back to a sound similar to the one on which he stopped the first. The reader is pleased when he finds that expectation fulfilled:

> God of our fathers, known of old—
> Lord of our far-flung battle-line—
> Beneath whose awful Hand we hold . . .

Closely allied to metrical and rime pattern, are a number of textural devices—devices that are similar to rime in that they involve correspondence of sounds. These devices tend to occur within the line unit of poetry but affect the total sound pattern. Alliteration, assonance, consonance give ease and speed to pronunciation, stepping up melody and tempo. Such pleasantness of sound is called euphony. Not always, however, is euphony desirable. In fact, cacophony, its opposite, may better achieve the poet's intention. For instance, in Eliot's line

> And the camels galled, sore-footed, refractory

the last three words, galled, sore-footed, refractory, cause a sense of strain and slowing of tempo appropriate to the experience he is describing.

The nature of poetry and the method of poetry are so dependent upon each other that one cannot be conceived without the other. Their relationship is organic; it is not a mere mechanical association. In other words, the way of saying a thing is a large degree of what is said. A poem does much more than say or state. It transmutes sense, feeling, tone, and intention into experience, into being itself.

ALFRED NOYES *The Highwayman*

PART ONE

The wind was a torrent of darkness among the gusty trees,
The moon was a ghostly galleon tossed upon cloudy seas,
The road was a ribbon of moonlight over the purple moor,
And the highwayman came riding—
        Riding—riding—
The highwayman came riding, up to the old inn-door.

He'd a French cocked-hat on his forehead, a bunch of lace at his chin,
A coat of the claret velvet, and breeches of brown doe-skin;
They fitted with never a wrinkle: his boots were up to the thigh!
And he rode with a jewelled twinkle,   10
        His pistol butts a-twinkle,
His rapier hilt a-twinkle, under the jewelled sky.

Over the cobbles he clattered and clashed in the dark inn-yard,
And he tapped with his whip on the shutters, but all was locked and barred;
He whistled a tune to the window, and who should be waiting there
But the landlord's black-eyed daughter,
        Bess, the landlord's daughter,
Plaiting a dark red love-knot into her long black hair.

And dark in the dark old inn-yard a stable-wicket creaked
Where Tim, the ostler, listened; his face was white and peaked;   20
His eyes were hollows of madness, his hair like mouldy hay,
But he loved the landlord's daughter,
        The landlord's red-lipped daughter.
Dumb as a dog he listened, and he heard the robber say—

"One kiss, my bonny sweetheart, I'm after a prize tonight,
But I shall be back with the yellow gold before the morning light;
Yet if they press me sharply, and harry me through the day,
Then look for me by moonlight,
        Watch for me by moonlight,
I'll come to thee by moonlight, though hell should bar the way."   30

He rose upright in the stirrups; he scarce could reach her hand,
But she loosened her hair i' the casement! His face burnt like a brand
As the black cascade of perfume came tumbling over his breast;
And he kissed its waves in the moonlight,
        (Oh, sweet black waves in the moonlight,)
Then he tugged at his reins in the moonlight, and galloped away to the west.

PART TWO

He did not come in the dawning; he did not come at noon;
And out of the tawny sunset, before the rise o' the moon,
When the road was a gypsy's ribbon, looping the purple moor,
A red-coat troop came marching—   40
        Marching—marching—
King George's men came marching, up to the old inn-door.

They said no word to the landlord, they drank his ale instead,
But they gagged his daughter and bound her to the foot of her narrow bed;
Two of them knelt at her casement, with muskets at the side!
There was death at every window;
        And Hell at one dark window;
For Bess could see, through her casement, the road that *he* would ride.

They had tied her up to attention, with many a sniggering jest;
They had bound a musket beside her, with the barrel beneath her breast!   50
"Now keep good watch!" and they kissed her.
        She heard the dead man say—
Look for me by moonlight;
        Watch for me by moonlight;
I'll come to thee by moonlight, though hell should bar the way!

She twisted her hands behind her; but all the knots held good!
She writhed her hands till her fingers were wet with sweat or blood!
They stretched and strained in the darkness, and the hours crawled by like years,
Till, now, on the stroke of midnight,
        Cold, on the stroke of midnight,   60
The tip of one finger touched it! The trigger at least was hers!

The tip of one finger touched it; she strove no more for the rest!
Up, she stood to attention, with the barrel beneath her breast,
She would not risk their hearing: she would not strive again;
For the road lay bare in the moonlight;
        Blank and bare in the moonlight;
And the blood of her veins in the moonlight throbbed to her love's refrain.

Tlot-tlot; tlot-tlot! Had they heard it? The horse-hoofs ringing clear—
Tlot-tlot, tlot-tlot in the distance? Were they deaf that they did not hear?
Down the ribbon of moonlight, over the brow of the hill,   70
The highwayman came riding,
        Riding, riding!
The red-coats looked to their priming! She stood up straight and still!

Tlot-tlot, in the frosty silence! *Tlot-tlot* in the echoing night!
Nearer he came and nearer! Her face was like a light!
Her eyes grew wide for a moment; she drew one last deep breath,
Then her finger moved in the moonlight,
        Her musket shattered the moonlight,
Shattered her breast in the moonlight and warned him—with her death.

He turned; he spurred him westward; he did not know who stood   80
Bowed with her head o'er the musket, drenched with her own red blood!
Not till the dawn he heard it, and slowly blanched to hear

How Bess, the landlord's daughter,
      The landlord's black-eyed daughter,
Had watched for her love in the moonlight, and died in the darkness there.

Back, he spurred like a madman, shrieking a curse to the sky,
With the white road smoking behind him, and his rapier brandished high!
Blood-red were his spurs i' the golden moon; wine-red was his velvet coat;
When they shot him down on the highway,
      Down like a dog on the highway,   90
And he lay in his blood on the highway, with the bunch of lace at his throat.

And still of a winter's night, they say, when the wind is in the trees,
When the moon is a ghostly galleon tossed upon cloudy seas,
When the road is a ribbon of moonlight over the purple moor,
A highwayman comes riding—
      Riding—riding—
A highwayman comes riding, up to the old inn-door.

Over the cobbles he clatters and clangs in the dark inn-yard;
And he taps with his whip on the shutters, but all is locked and barred;
He whistles a tune to the window, and who should be waiting there   100
But the landlord's black-eyed daughter,
      Bess, the landlord's daughter,
Plaiting a dark red love-knot into her long black hair.

JAMES WELDON JOHNSON

The Creation

And God stepped out on space,
And He looked around and said,
"I'm lonely—
I'll make me a world."

And far as the eye of God could see
Darkness covered everything,
Blacker than a hundred midnights
Down in a cypress swamp.

Then God smiled,
And the light broke,   10
And the darkness rolled up on one side,
And the light stood shining on the other,
And God said, *"That's good!"*

Then God reached out and took the light in His
   hands,
And God rolled the light around in His hands
Until He made the sun;
And He set that sun a-blazing in the heavens.
And the light that was left from making the sun
God gathered up in a shining ball

THE CREATION: From *God's Trombones* by James Weldon Johnson. Copyright 1927 by The Viking Press, Inc., 1955 by Grace Nail Johnson. Reprinted by permission of The Viking Press, Inc., New York.

And flung it against the darkness,   20
Spangling the night with the moon and stars.
Then down between
The darkness and the light
He hurled the world;
And God said, *"That's good!"*

Then God Himself stepped down—
And the sun was on His right hand,
And the moon was on His left;
The stars were clustered about His head,
And the earth was under His feet.   30
And God walked, and where He trod
His footsteps hollowed the valleys out
And bulged the mountains up.

Then He stopped and looked and saw
That the earth was hot and barren.
So God stepped over to the edge of the world
And He spat out the seven seas;
He batted His eyes, and the lightnings flashed;
He clapped His hands, and the thunders rolled;
And the waters above the earth came down,   40
The cooling waters came down.

Then the green grass sprouted,
And the little red flowers blossomed,
The pine-tree pointed his finger to the sky,
And the oak spread out his arms;
The lakes cuddled down in the hollows of the
   ground,

And the rivers ran down to the sea;
And God smiled again,
And the rainbow appeared,
And curled itself around His shoulder.   50

Then God raised His arm and He waved His hand
Over the sea and over the land,
And He said, *"Bring forth! Bring forth!"*
And quicker than God could drop His hand,
Fishes and fowls
And beasts and birds
Swam the rivers and the seas,
Roamed the forests and the woods,
And split the air with their wings.
And God said, *"That's good!"*   60

Then God walked around
And God looked around
On all that He had made.
He looked at His sun,
And He looked at His moon,
And He looked at His little stars;
He looked on His world
With all its living things,
And God said, *"I'm lonely still."*

Then God sat down—   70
On the side of a hill where He could think;
By a deep, wide river He sat down;
With His head in His hands,
God thought and thought,
Till He thought, *"I'll make me a man!"*

Up from the bed of the river
God scooped the clay;
And by the bank of the river
He kneeled Him down;
And there the great God Almighty,   80
Who lit the sun and fixed it in the sky,
Who flung the stars to the most far corner of the
    night,
Who rounded the earth in the middle of His
    hand—
This Great God,
Like a mammy bending over her baby,
Kneeled down in the dust
Toiling over a lump of clay
Till He shaped it in His own image;

Then into it He blew the breath of life,
And man became a living soul.   90
Amen. Amen.

WILLIAM BUTLER YEATS

The Ballad of Father Gilligan

The old priest Peter Gilligan
Was weary night and day;
For half his flock were in their beds,
Or under green sods lay.

Once, while he nodded on a chair,
At the moth-hour of eve,
Another poor man sent for him,
And he began to grieve.

"I have no rest, nor joy, nor peace,
For people die and die";   10
And after cried he, "God forgive!
My body spake, not I!"

He knelt, and leaning on the chair
He prayed and fell asleep;
And the moth-hour went from the fields,
And stars began to peep.

They slowly into millions grew,
And leaves shook in the wind;
And God covered the world with shade,
And whispered to mankind.   20

Upon the time of sparrow-chirp
When the moths came once more,
The old priest Peter Gilligan
Stood upright on the floor.

"Mavrone, mavrone! the man has died
While I slept on the chair";
He roused his horse out of its sleep,
And rode with little care.

He rode now as he never rode,
By rocky lane and fen;   30
The sick man's wife opened the door:
"Father! You come again!"

"And is the poor man dead?" he cried.
"He died an hour ago."
The old priest Peter Gilligan
In grief swayed to and fro.

"When you were gone, he turned and died
As merry as a bird."
The old priest Peter Gilligan
He knelt him at that word.   40

"He who hath made the night of stars
For souls who tire and bleed,
Sent one of His great angels down
To help me in my need.

"He who is wrapped in purple robes,
With planets in His care,
Had pity on the least of things
Asleep upon a chair."

ANONYMOUS *Ballad*

Sir Patrick Spens

The king sits in Dumferling toune,
  Drinking the blude-reid wine:
"O whar will I get guid sailor,
  To sail this schip of mine?"

Up and spak an eldern knicht,
  Sat at the kings richt kne:
"Sir Patrick Spens is the best sailor,
  That sails upon the se."

The king has written a braid letter,
  And signd it wi his hand,   10
And sent it to Sir Patrick Spens,
  Was walking on the sand.

The first line that Sir Patrick red,
  A loud lauch laughèd he;
The next line that Sir Patrick red,
  The teir blinded his ee.

"O wha is this has don this deid,
  This ill deid don to me,
To send me out this time o' the yeir,
  To sail upon the se!   20

"Mak hast, mak hast, my mirry men all,
  Our guid schip sails the morne:"
"O say na sae, my master deir,
  For I feir a deadlie storme.

"Late, late yestreen I saw the new moone,
  Wi the auld moone in hir arme,
And I feir, I feir, my deir master,
  That we will cum to harme."

O our Scots nobles were richt laith
  To weet their cork-heild schoone;   30
Bot lang owre a' the play wer playd,
  Thair hats they swam aboone.

O lang, lang may thair ladies sit,
  Wi thair fans into thair hand,

Or eir they se Sir Patrick Spens
  Cum sailing to the land.

O lang, lang may the ladies stand,
  Wi thair gold kems in thair hair,
Waiting for thair ain deir lords,
  For they'll se thame na mair.   40

Haf owre, haf owre to Aberdour,
  It's fiftie fadom deip,
And thair lies guid Sir Patrick Spens,
  Wi the Scots lords at his feit.

ANONYMOUS

The Three Ravens

There were three ravens sat on a tree,
  Downe a downe, hay downe, hay downe
There were three ravens sat on a tree,
  With a downe

There were three ravens sat on a tree,
They were as blacke as they might be.
  With a downe derrie, derrie, derrie, downe,
  downe.

The one of them said to his mate,
"Where shall we our breakfast take?"

"Downe in yonder greene field,   10
There lies a knight slain under his shield.

"His hounds they lie downe at his feete,
So well they can their master keepe.

"His haukes they flie so eagerly,
There's no fowle dare him come nie."

Downe there comes a fallow doe,
As great with yong as she might goe.

She lift up his bloudy hed,
And kist his wounds that were so red.

She got him up upon her backe,   20
And carried him to earthen lake.[1]

She buried him before the prime,
She was dead herselfe ere euen-song time.

God send every gentleman,
Such haukes, such hounds, and such a leman.[2]

¹ pit. ² lover.

ANONYMOUS

fabulation murder disloyalty (handwritten)

The Twa Corbies

(cynical version/best known version) (handwritten, left margin)

As I was walking all alane,
I heard twa corbies making a mane;[1]
The tane[2] unto the t'other say,
"Where sall we gang[3] and dine today?"

"In behint yon auld fail dyke,[4]
I wot[5] there lies a new slain knight;
And naebody kens[6] that he lies there
But his hawk, his hound, and lady fair.

"His hound is to the hunting gane,
His hawk to fetch the wild-fowl hame,   10

His lady's ta'en another mate,
So we may mak our dinner sweet.

"Ye'll sit on his white hause-bane,[7]
And I'll pike out his bonny blue een;
Wi ae lock o his gowden hair
We'll theek[8] our nest when it grows bare.

"Mony a one for him makes mane,
But nane sall ken where he is gane;
Oer his white banes, when they are bare,
The wind sall blaw for evermair."   20

[1] moan. [2] one. [3] go. [4] turf wall. [5] know. [6] knows.
[7] neckbone. [8] thatch.

ALFRED, LORD TENNYSON   *The Revenge*

1

At Flores in the Azores, Sir Richard Grenville lay,
And a pinnace, like a fluttered bird, came flying from far away;
"Spanish ships of war at sea! we have sighted fifty-three!"
Then sware Lord Thomas Howard: " 'Fore God I am no coward;
But I cannot meet them here, for my ships are out of gear,
And the half my men are sick. I must fly, but follow quick.
We are six ships of the line; can we fight with fifty-three?"

2

Then spake Sir Richard Grenville: "I know you are no coward;
You fly them for a moment to fight with them again.
But I've ninety men and more that are lying sick ashore.   10
I should count myself the coward if I left them, my Lord Howard,
To these Inquisition dogs and the devildoms of Spain."

3

So Lord Howard past away with five ships of war that day,
Till he melted like a cloud in the silent summer heaven;
But Sir Richard bore in hand all his sick men from the land
Very carefully and slow,
Men of Bideford in Devon,
And we laid them on the ballast down below;
For we brought them all aboard,
And they blest him in their pain, that they were not left to Spain,   20
To the thumbscrew and the stake, for the glory of the Lord.

4

He had only a hundred seamen to work the ship and to fight,
And he sailed away from Flores till the Spaniards came in sight,
With his huge sea-castles heaving upon the weather bow.
"Shall we fight or shall we fly?
Good Sir Richard, tell us now,
For to fight is but to die!

There'll be little of us left by the time this sun be set."
And Sir Richard said again: "We be all good Englishmen.
Let us bang these dogs of Seville, the children of the devil,   30
For I never turned my back upon Don or devil yet."

5

Sir Richard spoke and he laughed, and we roared a hurrah, and so
The little *Revenge* ran on sheer into the heart of the foe,
With her hundred fighters on deck, and her ninety sick below;
For half of their fleet to the right and half to the left were seen,
And the little *Revenge* ran on through the long sea-lane between.

6

Thousands of their soldiers looked down from their decks and laughed,
Thousands of their seamen made mock at the mad little craft
Running on and on, till delayed
By their mountain-like *San Philip* that, of fifteen hundred tons,   40
And up-shadowing high above us with her yawning tiers of guns,
Took the breath from our sails, and we stayed.

7

And while now the great *San Philip* hung above us like a cloud
Whence the thunderbolt will fall
Long and loud,
Four galleons drew away
From the Spanish fleet that day,
And two upon the larboard and two upon the starboard lay,
And the battle thunder broke from them all.

8

But anon the great *San Philip,* she bethought herself and went,   50
Having that within her womb that had left her ill content;
And the rest they came aboard us, and they fought us hand to hand,
For a dozen times they came with their pikes and musketeers,
And a dozen times we shook 'em off as a dog that shakes his ears
When he leaps from the water to the land.

9

And the sun went down, and the stars came out far over the summer sea,
But never a moment ceased the fight of the one and the fifty-three.
Ship after ship, the whole night long, their high-built galleons came,
Ship after ship, the whole night long, with her battle-thunder and flame;
Ship after ship, the whole night long, drew back with her dead and her shame.   60
For some were sunk and many were shattered, and so could fight us no more—
God of battles, was ever a battle like this in the world before?

10

For he said, "Fight on! fight on!"
Though his vessel was all but a wreck;
And it chanced that, when half of the summer night was gone,
With a grisly wound to be drest he had left the deck,
But a bullet struck him that was dressing it suddenly dead,
And himself he was wounded again in the side and the head,
And he said, "Fight on! Fight on!"

11

And the night went down, and the sun smiled out far over the summer sea,   70
And the Spanish fleet with broken sides lay round us all in a ring;
But they dared not touch us again, for they feared that we still could sting,
So they watched what the end would be.
And we had not fought them in vain,
But in perilous plight were we,
Seeing forty of our poor hundred were slain,
And half of the rest of us maimed for life
In the crash of the cannonades and the desperate strife;
And the sick men down in the hold were most of them stark and cold,
And the pikes were all broken or bent, and the powder was all of it spent;   80
And the masts and the rigging were lying over the side;
But Sir Richard cried in his English pride,
"We have fought such a fight, for a day and a night
As may never be fought again!
We have won great glory, my men!
And a day less or more
At sea or ashore,
We die—does it matter when?
Sink me the ship, Master Gunner—sink her, split her in twain!
Fall into the hands of God, not into the hands of Spain!"   90

12

And the gunner said, "Ay, ay," but the seamen made reply:
"We have children, we have wives,
And the Lord hath spared our lives.
We will make the Spaniard promise, if we yield, to let us go;
We shall live to fight again and to strike another blow."
And the lion there lay dying, and they yielded to the foe.

13

And the stately Spanish men to their flagship bore him then,
Where they laid him by the mast, old Sir Richard caught at last,
And they praised him to his face with their courtly foreign grace;
But he rose upon their decks, and he cried:
"I have fought for Queen and Faith like a valiant man and true;   100
I have only done my duty as a man is bound to do:
With a joyful spirit I Sir Richard Grenville die!"
And he fell upon their decks, and he died.

14

And they stared at the dead that had been so valiant and true,
And had holden the power and glory of Spain so cheap
That he dared her with one little ship and his English few;
Was he devil or man? He was devil for aught they knew,
But they sank his body with honour down into the deep,
And they manned the *Revenge* with a swarthier alien crew,   110
And away she sailed with her loss and longed for her own;
When a wind from the lands they had ruined awoke from sleep,
And the water began to heave and the weather to moan,
And or ever that evening ended a great gale blew,
And a wave like the wave that is raised by an earthquake grew,
Till it smote on their hulls and their sails and their masts and their flags,
And the whole sea plunged and fell on the shot-shattered navy of Spain,
And the little *Revenge* herself went down by the island crags
To be lost evermore in the main.

A. E. HOUSMAN

Hell Gate

Onward led the road again
Through the sad uncoloured plain
Under twilight brooding dim,
And along the utmost rim
Wall and rampart risen to sight
Cast a shadow not of night,
And beyond them seemed to glow
Bonfires lighted long ago.
And my dark conductor broke
Silence at my side and spoke,   10
Saying, "You conjecture well:
Yonder is the gate of hell."

Ill as yet the eye could see
The eternal masonry,
But beneath it on the dark
To and fro there stirred a spark.
And again the sombre guide
Knew my question, and replied:
"At hell gate the damned in turn
Pace for sentinel and burn."   20

Dully at the leaden sky
Staring, and with idle eye
Measuring the listless plain,
I began to think again.
Many things I thought of then,
Battle, and the loves of men,
Cities entered, oceans crossed,
Knowledge gained and virtue lost,
Cureless folly done and said,
And the lovely way that led   30
To the slimepit and the mire
And the everlasting fire.
And against a smoulder dun
And a dawn without a sun
Did the nearing bastion loom,
And across the gate of gloom
Still one saw the sentry go,
Trim and burning, to and fro,
One for women to admire
In his finery of fire.   40
Something, as I watched him pace,
Minded me of time and place,
Soldiers of another corps
And a sentry known before.

Ever darker hell on high
Reared its strength upon the sky,

And our footfall on the track
Fetched the daunting echo back.
But the soldier pacing still
The insuperable sill,   50
Nursing his tormented pride,
Turned his head to neither side,
Sunk into himself apart
And the hell-fire of his heart.
But against our entering in
From the drawbridge Death and Sin
Rose to render key and sword
To their father and their lord.
And the portress foul to see
Lifted up her eyes on me   60
Smiling, and I made reply:
"Met again, my lass," said I.
Then the sentry turned his head,
Looked, and knew me, and was Ned.

Once he looked, and halted straight,
Set his back against the gate,
Caught his musket to his chin,
While the hive of hell within
Sent abroad a seething hum
As of towns whose king is come   70
Leading conquest home from far
And the captives of his war,
And the car of triumph waits,
And they open wide the gates.
But across the entry barred
Straddled the revolted guard,
Weaponed and accoutred well
From the arsenals of hell;
And beside him, sick and white,
Sin to left and Death to right   80
Turned a countenance of fear
On the flaming mutineer.
Over us the darkness bowed,
And the anger in the cloud
Clenched the lightning for the stroke;
But the traitor musket spoke.

And the hollowness of hell
Sounded as its master fell,
And the mourning echo rolled
Ruin through his kingdom old.   90
Tyranny and terror flown
Left a pair of friends alone,
And beneath the nether sky
All that stirred was he and I.

Silent, nothing found to say,
We began the backward way;
And the ebbing lustre died
From the soldier at my side,

As in all his spruce attire
Failed the everlasting fire.   **100**
Midmost of the homeward track
Once we listened and looked back;
But the city, dusk and mute,
Slept, and there was no pursuit.

T. S. ELIOT

Journey of the Magi

"A cold coming we had of it,
Just the worst time of the year
For a journey, and such a long journey:
The ways deep and the weather sharp,
The very dead of winter."
And the camels galled, sore-footed, refractory,
Lying down in the melting snow.
There were times we regretted
The summer palaces on slopes, the terraces,
And the silken girls bringing sherbet.   **10**
Then the camel men cursing and grumbling
And running away, and wanting their liquor and
    women,
And the night-fires going out, and the lack of
    shelters,
And the cities hostile and the towns unfriendly
And the villages dirty and charging high prices:
A hard time we had of it.
At the end we preferred to travel all night,
Sleeping in snatches,

JOURNEY OF THE MAGI: From *Collected Poems, 1909-1935* by T. S. Eliot, copyright, 1936, by Harcourt, Brace and Company, Inc.

With the voices singing in our ears, saying
That this was all folly.   **20**

Then at dawn we came down to a temperate
    valley,
Wet, below the snow line, smelling of vegetation;
With a running stream and a water-mill beating
    the darkness,
And three trees on the low sky,
And an old white horse galloped away in the
    meadow.
Then we came to a tavern with vine-leaves over
    the lintel,
Six hands at an open door dicing for pieces of
    silver,
And feet kicking the empty wine-skins.
But there was no information, and so we
    continued   **29**
And arrived at evening, not a moment too soon
Finding the place; it was (you may say) satisfactory.

All this was a long time ago, I remember,
And I would do it again, but set down
This set down
This: were we led all that way for
Birth or Death? There was a Birth, certainly,
We had evidence and no doubt. I had seen birth
    and death,
But had thought they were different; this Birth was
Hard and bitter agony for us, like Death, our
    death.
We returned to our places, these Kingdoms,   **40**
But no longer at ease here, in the old dispensation,
With an alien people clutching their gods.
I should be glad of another death.

PERCY BYSSHE SHELLEY

Love's Philosophy

The fountains mingle with the river
  And the rivers with the Ocean,
The winds of Heaven mix for ever
  With a sweet emotion;
Nothing in the world is single;
  All things by a law divine
In one spirit meet and mingle.
  Why not I with thine?—

See the mountains kiss high Heaven
  And the waves clasp one another;   10
No sister-flower would be forgiven
  If it disdained its brother;
And the sunlight clasps the earth
  And the moonbeams kiss the sea:
What is all this sweet work worth
  If thou kiss not me?

ROBERT HERRICK

To the Virgins, to Make Much of Time

Gather ye rose-buds while ye may,
  Old Time is still a-flying,
And this same flower that smiles to-day,
  To-morrow will be dying.

The glorious lamp of Heaven, the sun,
  The higher he's a-getting,
The sooner will his race be run,
  And nearer he's to setting.

That age is best which is the first,
  When youth and blood are warmer;   10
But being spent, the worse, and worst
  Times still succeed the former.

Then be not coy, but use your time,
  And while ye may, go marry;
For having lost but once your prime,
  You may for ever tarry.

EDMUND WALLER

Go, Lovely Rose

Go, lovely Rose!
Tell her that wastes her time and me
  That now she knows,
When I resemble her to thee,
How sweet and fair she seems to be.

Tell her that's young,
And shuns to have her graces spied,
  That hadst thou sprung
In deserts, where no men abide,
Thou must have uncommended died.   10

Small is the worth
Of beauty from the light retired;
  Bid her come forth,
Suffer herself to be desired,
And not blush so to be admired.

Then die! that she
The common fate of all things rare
  May read in thee;
How small a part of time they share,
That are so wondrous sweet and fair!   20

GEORGE NOEL GORDON, LORD BYRON

So, We'll Go No More a Roving

So, we'll go no more a roving
  So late into the night,
Though the heart be still as loving,
  And the moon be still as bright.

For the sword outwears its sheath,
  And the soul wears out the breast,
And the heart must pause to breathe,
  And love itself have rest.

Though the night was made for loving,
  And the day return too soon,   10
Yet we'll go no more a roving
  By the light of the moon.

JOHN DONNE

Song

Sweetest love, I do not go,
   For weariness of thee,
Nor in hope the world can show
   A fitter love for me;
     But since that I
Must die at last, 'tis best,
To use myself in jest
     Thus by feign'd deaths to die;

Yesternight the sun went hence,
   And yet is here today,   10
He hath no desire nor sense,
   Nor half so short a way:
     Then fear not me,
But believe that I shall make
Speedier journeys, since I take
     More wings and spurs than he.

O how feeble is man's power,
   That if good fortune fall,
Cannot add another hour,
   Nor a lost hour recall!   20
     But come bad chance,
And we join to'it our strength,
And we teach it art and length,
     Itself o'er us t'advance.

When thou sigh'st, thou sigh'st not wind,
   But sigh'st my soul away,
When thou weep'st, unkindly kind,
   My life's blood doth decay.
     It cannot be
That thou lov'st me, as thou say'st,   30
If in thine my life thou waste,
     That art the best of me.

Let not thy divining heart
   Forethink me any ill,
Destiny may take thy part,
   And may thy fears fulfill;
     But think that we
Are but turn'd aside to sleep;
They who one another keep
     Alive, ne'er parted be.   40

SIR PHILIP SIDNEY

With How Sad Steps, O Moon

With how sad steps, O moon, thou climb'st the
   skies!
How silently, and with how wan a face!
What! may it be that even in heavenly place

That busy archer his sharp arrows tries?
Sure, if that long-with-love-acquainted eyes
   Can judge of love, thou feel'st a lover's case;
   I read it in thy looks; thy languished grace
   To me, that feel the like, thy state descries.
Then, even of fellowship, O moon, tell me,
   Is constant love deemed there but want of wit?
   Are beauties there as proud as here they be?   11
Do they above love to be loved, and yet
   Those lovers scorn whom that love doth possess?
   Do they call virtue there ungratefulness?

WILLIAM SHAKESPEARE

*Let Me Not to the Marriage
of True Minds*

Let me not to the marriage of true minds
Admit impediments. Love is not love
Which alters when it alteration finds,
Or bends with the remover to remove:
O, no! it is an ever-fixèd mark,
That looks on tempests and is never shaken;
It is the star to every wand'ring bark,
Whose worth's unknown, although his height be
   taken.
Love's not Time's fool, though rosy lips and
   cheeks
Within his bending sickle's compass come;   10
Love alters not with his brief hours and weeks,
But bears it out even to the edge of doom:—
   If this be error and upon me proved,
   I never writ, nor no man ever loved.

EDNA ST. VINCENT MILLAY

I Know I Am But Summer

I know I am but summer to your heart,
And not the full four seasons of the year;
And you must welcome from another part
Such noble moods as are not mine, my dear.
No gracious weight of golden fruits to sell
Have I, nor any wise and wintry thing;
And I have loved you all too long and well
To carry still the high sweet breast of Spring.
Wherefore I say: O love, as summer goes,
I must be gone, steal forth with silent drums,   10
That you may hail anew the bird and rose
When I come back to you, as summer comes.
Else will you seek, at some not distant time,
Even your summer in another clime.

WILLIAM BUTLER YEATS *Down by the Salley Gardens*

Down by the salley gardens my love and I did meet;
She passed the salley gardens with little snow-white feet.
She bid me take love easy, as the leaves grow on the tree;
But I, being young and foolish, with her would not agree.

In a field by a river my love and I did stand,
And on my leaning shoulder she laid her snow-white hand.
She bid me take life easy, as the grass grows on the weirs;
But I was young and foolish, and now am full of tears.

ARCHIBALD MAC LEISH *"Not Marble nor the Gilded Monuments"*

The praisers of women in their proud and beautiful poems
Naming the grave mouth and the hair and the eyes
Boasted those they loved should be forever remembered
These were lies

The words sound but the face in the Istrian sun is forgotten
The poet speaks but to her dead ears no more
The sleek throat is gone—and the breast that was troubled to listen
Shadow from door

Therefore I will not praise your knees nor your fine walking
Telling you men shall remember your name as long   10
As lips move or breath is spent or the iron of English
Rings from a tongue

I shall say you were young and your arms straight and your mouth scarlet
I shall say you will die and none will remember you
Your arms change and none remember the swish of your garments
Nor the click of your shoe

Not with my hand's strength not with difficult labor
Springing the obstinate words to the bones of your breast
And the stubborn line to your young stride and the breath to your breathing
And the beat to your haste   20
Shall I prevail on the hearts of unborn men to remember

(What is a dead girl but a shadowy ghost
Or a dead man's voice but a distant and vain affirmation
Like dream words most)
Therefore I will not speak of the undying glory of women
I will say you were young and straight and your skin fair
And you stood in the door and the sun was a shadow of leaves on your shoulders
And a leaf on your hair

I will not speak of the famous beauty of dead women
I will say the shape of a leaf lay once on your hair   30
Till the world ends and the eyes are out and the mouths broken
Look! It is there.

DOWN BY THE SALLEY GARDENS: From *Collected Poems* by William Butler Yeats. Copyright 1934 by The Macmillan Company and used with their permission.
"NOT MARBLE NOR THE GILDED MONUMENTS": From *Poems, 1924-1933*, by Archibald MacLeish. Reprinted by permission of Houghton Mifflin Company, publishers.

CARL SANDBURG *Jazz Fantasia*

Drum on your drums, batter on your banjoes,
sob on the long cool winding saxophones.
Go to it, O jazzmen.

Sling your knuckles on the bottoms of the happy
tin pans, let your trombones ooze, and go husha-
husha-hush with the slippery sand-paper.

Moan like an autumn wind high in the lonesome treetops, moan soft like you wanted
somebody terrible, cry like a racing car slipping away from a motorcycle cop, bang-bang!
you jazzmen, bang altogether drums, traps, banjoes, horns, tin cans—make two people
fight on the top of a stairway and scratch each other's eyes in a clinch tumbling down the
stairs.

Can the rough stuff . . . Now a Mississippi steamboat pushes up the night river with
a hoo-hoo-hoo-oo . . . and the green lanterns calling to the high soft stars . . . a red
moon rides on the humps of the low river hills . . . Go to it, O jazzmen.

WALT WHITMAN *I Hear America Singing*

I hear America singing, the varied carols I hear,
Those of mechanics, each one singing his as it should be blithe and strong,
The carpenter singing his as he measures his plank or beam,
The mason singing his as he makes ready for work, or leaves off work,
The boatman singing what belongs to him in his boat, the deckhand singing on the
    steamboat deck,
The shoemaker singing as he sits on his bench, the hatter singing as he stands,
The woodcutter's song, the plowboy's on his way in the morning, or at noon intermission
    or at sundown,
The delicious singing of the mother, or of the young wife at work, or of the girl sewing
    or washing,
Each singing what belongs to him or her and to none else,
The day what belongs to the day—at night the party of young fellows, robust, friendly, 10
Singing with open mouths their strong melodious songs.

ROBERT FROST

A Soldier

He is that fallen lance that lies as hurled,
That lies unlifted now, come dew, come rust,
But still lies pointed as it plowed the dust.
If we who sight along it round the world,
See nothing worthy to have been its mark,
It is because like men we look too near,
Forgetting that as fitted to the sphere,

Our missiles always make too short an arc.
They fall, they rip the grass, they intersect
The curve of earth, and striking, break their own;
They make us cringe for metal-point on stone.   11
But this we know, the obstacle that checked
And tripped the body, shot the spirit on
Further than target ever showed or shone.

RUDYARD KIPLING
Lymn written to celebrate Diamond Jubilee of Queen Victoria June 22, 1897

Recessional

God of our fathers, known of old—
  Lord of our far-flung battle-line—
Beneath whose awful Hand we hold
  Dominion over palm and pine—
Lord God of Hosts, be with us yet,
Lest we forget—lest we forget!

The tumult and the shouting dies—
  The Captains and the Kings depart—
Still stands Thine ancient Sacrifice,
  An humble and a contrite heart.   10
Lord God of Hosts, be with us yet,
Lest we forget—lest we forget!

Far-called our navies melt away—
  On dune and headland sinks the fire—
Lo, all our pomp of yesterday
  Is one with Nineveh and Tyre!

Judge of the Nations, spare us yet,
Lest we forget—lest we forget!

If, drunk with sight of power, we loose
  Wild tongues that have not Thee in awe— 20
Such boasting as the Gentiles use
  Or lesser breeds without the Law—
Lord God of Hosts, be with us yet,
Lest we forget—lest we forget!

For heathen heart that puts her trust
  In reeking tube and iron shard—
All valiant dust that builds on dust,
  And guarding calls not Thee to guard—
For frantic boast and foolish word,
Thy mercy on Thy people, Lord!   30
    Amen.

JOHN MASEFIELD *Sea-Fever*

I must go down to the seas again, to the lonely sea and the sky,
And all I ask is a tall ship and a star to steer her by,
And the wheel's kick and the wind's song and the white sail's shaking,
And a grey mist on the sea's face and a grey dawn breaking.

I must go down to the seas again, for the call of the running tide
Is a wild call and a clear call that may not be denied;
And all I ask is a windy day with the white clouds flying,
And the flung spray and the blown spume, and the sea-gulls crying.

I must go down to the seas again to the vagrant gypsy life,
To the gull's way and the whale's way where the wind's like a whetted knife; 10
And all I ask is a merry yarn from a laughing fellow-rover,
And quiet sleep and a sweet dream when the long trick's over.

WALTER DE LA MARE *you can't go home again pigeon house*

Silver

Slowly, silently, now the moon
Walks the night in her silver shoon;
This way, and that, she peers, and sees
Silver fruit upon silver trees;
One by one the casements catch
Her beams beneath the silvery thatch;
Couched in his kennel, like a log,

With paws of silver sleeps the dog;
From their shadowy cote the white breasts peep
Of doves in a silver-feathered sleep; 10
A harvest mouse goes scampering by,
With silver claws, and silver eye;
And moveless fish in the water gleam,
By silver reeds in a silver stream.

ROBERT P. TRISTRAM COFFIN

Strange Holiness

There is strange holiness around
Our common days on common ground.
I have heard it in the birds
Whose voices reach above all words,
Going upward, bars on bars,
Until they sound as high as stars.
I have seen it in the snake,
A flowing jewel in the brake.
It has sparkled in my eyes
In luminous breath of fireflies.   10
I have come upon its track
Where trilliums curled their petals back.
I have seen it flash in under
The towers of the midnight thunder.
Once, I met it face to face
In a fox pressed by the chase.
He came down the road on feet,
Quiet and fragile, light as heat.
He had a fish still wet and bright
In his slender jaws held tight.   20
His ears were conscious whetted darts,
His eyes had small flames in their hearts.
The preciousness of life and breath
Glowed through him as he outran death.
Strangeness and secrecy and pride
Ran rippling down his golden hide.
His beauty was not meant for me,
With my dull eyes, so close to see.
Unconscious of me, rapt, alone,
He came, and then stopped still as stone.   30
His eyes went out as in a gust,
His beauty crumbled into dust.
There was but a ruin there,
A hunted creature, stripped and bare.
Then he faded at one stroke,
Like a dingy, melting smoke.
But there his fish lay like a key
To the bright lost mystery.

EMILY DICKINSON

I'll Tell You How the Sun Rose

I'll tell you how the sun rose,—
A ribbon at a time.
The steeples swam in amethyst,
The news like squirrels ran.

The hills untied their bonnets,
The bobolinks begun.
Then I said softly to myself,
"That must have been the sun!"

But how he set, I know not.
There seemed a purple stile   10
Which little boys and girls
Were climbing all the while

Till when they reached the other side,
A dominie in gray
Put gently up the evening bars,
And led the flock away.

EMILY DICKINSON

A Narrow Fellow in the Grass

A narrow fellow in the grass
Occasionally rides;
You may have met him,—did you not?
His notice sudden is.

The grass divides as with a comb,
A spotted shaft is seen;
And then it closes at your feet
And opens further on.

He likes a boggy acre,
A floor too cool for corn.   10
Yet when a child, and barefoot,
I more than once, at morn,

Have passed, I thought, a whip-lash
Unbraiding in the sun,—
When, stopping to secure it,
It wrinkled, and was gone.

Several of nature's people
I know, and they know me;
I feel for them a transport
Of cordiality;   20

But never met this fellow,
Attended or alone,
Without a tighter breathing,
And zero at the bone.

STRANGE HOLINESS: From *Collected Poems* by Robert
P. Tristram Coffin. Copyright 1935 by The Macmillan
Company and used with their permission.

I'LL TELL YOU HOW THE SUN ROSE and A NARROW
FELLOW IN THE GRASS: From *Poems by Emily Dickinson*
edited by Martha Dickinson Bianchi and Alfred Leete
Hampson, Little, Brown and Company.

WILLIAM WORDSWORTH

The Solitary Reaper

Behold her, single in the field,
Yon solitary Highland Lass!
Reaping and singing by herself;
Stop here, or gently pass!
Alone she cuts and binds the grain,
And sings a melancholy strain;
O listen! for the Vale profound
Is overflowing with the sound.

No Nightingale did ever chaunt
More welcome notes to weary bands   10
Of travelers in some shady haunt,
Among Arabian sands:
A voice so thrilling ne'er was heard
In spring time from the Cuckoo-bird,
Breaking the silence of the seas
Among the farthest Hebrides.

Will not one tell me what she sings?—
Perhaps the plaintive numbers flow
For old, unhappy, far-off things,
And battles long ago: 20
Or is it some more humble lay,
Familiar matter of to-day?
Some natural sorrow, loss, or pain,
That has been, and may be again?

Whate'er the theme, the Maiden sang
As if her song could have no ending;
I saw her singing at her work,
And o'er the sickle bending;
I listened, motionless and still;
And, as I mounted up the hill,   30
The music in my heart I bore,
Long after it was heard no more.

W. H. AUDEN

Look, Stranger, on This Island Now

Look, stranger, on this island now
The leaping light for your delight discovers,
Stand stable here
And silent be,
That through the channels of the ear
May wander like a river
The swaying sound of the sea.
Here at the small field's ending pause

When the chalk wall falls to the foam and its tall
     ledges
Oppose the pluck   10
And knock of the tide,
And the shingle scrambles after the sucking surf,
And the gull lodges
A moment on its sheer side.

Far off like floating seeds the ships
Diverge on urgent voluntary errands,
And the full view
Indeed may enter
And move in memory as now these clouds do,
That pass the harbour mirror   20
And all the summer through the water saunter.

THOMAS HARDY

The Darkling Thrush

I leant upon a coppice gate
     When Frost was spectre-gray,
And Winter's dregs made desolate
     The weakening eye of day.
The tangled bine-stems scored the sky
     Like strings of broken lyres,
And all mankind that haunted nigh
     Had sought their household fires.

The land's sharp features seemed to be
     The Century's corpse outleant;   10
His crypt the cloudy canopy,
     The wind his death-lament.
The ancient pulse of germ and birth
     Was shrunken hard and dry,
And every spirit upon earth
     Seemed fervourless as I.

At once a voice arose among
     The bleak twigs overhead
In a full-hearted evensong
     Of joy illimited;   20
An aged thrush, frail, gaunt and small,
     In blast-beruffled plume,
Had chosen thus to fling his soul
     Upon the growing gloom.

So little cause for carolings
     Of such ecstatic sound
Was written on terrestrial things
     Afar or nigh around,
That I could think there trembled through
     His happy good-night air   30
Some blessed Hope, whereof he knew
     And I was unaware.

ROBERT FROST

Stopping by Woods
on a Snowy Evening

Whose woods these are I think I know.
His house is in the village though;
He will not see me stopping here
To watch his woods fill up with snow.

My little horse must think it queer
To stop without a farmhouse near
Between the woods and frozen lake
The darkest evening of the year.

He gives his harness bells a shake
To ask if there is some mistake.   10
The only other sound's the sweep
Of easy wind and downy flake.

The woods are lovely, dark and deep.
But I have promises to keep,
And miles to go before I sleep,
And miles to go before I sleep.

ORLANDO GIBBONS

The Silver Swan

The silver swan, who living had no note,
When death approached, unlocked her silent
    throat;
Leaning her breast against the reedy shore,
Thus sung her first and last, and sung no more.
Farewell, all joys; O death, come close mine eyes;
More geese than swans now live, more fools than
    wise.

THE BIBLE

Psalm XIX

1. The heavens declare the glory of God; and
the firmament sheweth his handywork.
2. Day unto day uttereth speech, and night unto
night sheweth knowledge.
3. There is no speech nor language, where their
voice is not heard.
4. Their line is gone out through all the earth,
and their words to the end of the world. In them
hath he set a tabernacle for the sun,

STOPPING BY WOODS ON A SNOWY EVENING: From *Complete Poems of Robert Frost*. Copyright, 1930, 1949, by Henry Holt and Company, Inc. Copyright, 1936, 1948, by Robert Frost. Reprinted by permission of the publishers.

5. Which is as a bridegroom coming out of his
chamber, and rejoiceth as a strong man to run a
race.
6. His going forth is from the end of the heaven,
and his circuit unto the ends of it: and there is
nothing hid from the heat thereof.
7. The law of the Lord is perfect, converting
the soul: the testimony of the Lord is sure, making
wise the simple.
8. The statutes of the Lord are right, rejoicing
the heart: the commandment of the Lord is pure,
enlightening the eyes.
9. The fear of the Lord is clean, enduring for
ever: the judgments of the Lord are true and
righteous altogether.
10. More to be desired are they than gold, yea,
than much fine gold: sweeter also than honey and
the honeycomb.
11. Moreover by them is thy servant warned:
and in keeping of them there is great reward.
12. Who can understand his errors? cleanse thou
me from secret faults.
13. Keep back thy servant also from presumptuous sins; let them not have dominion over me:
then shall I be upright, and I shall be innocent
from the great transgression.
14. Let the words of my mouth, and the meditation of my heart, be acceptable in thy sight,
O Lord, my strength, and my redeemer.

JOSEPH ADDISON

The Spacious Firmament

The Spacious Firmament on high,
With all the blue Ethereal Sky,
And spangled Heav'ns, a Shining Frame,
Their great Original proclaim:
Th' unwearied Sun, from Day to Day,
Does his Creator's Power display,
And publishes to every Land
The Work of an Almighty Hand.

Soon as the Evening Shades prevail,
The Moon takes up the wondrous Tale,   10
And nightly to the list'ning Earth
Repeats the Story of her Birth:
Whilst all the Stars that round her burn,
And all the Planets, in their turn,
Confirm the Tidings as they roll,
And spread the Truth from Pole to Pole.

What though, in solemn Silence, all
Move round the dark terrestrial Ball?

What tho' nor real Voice nor Sound
Amid their radiant Orbs be found?   20
In Reason's Ear they all rejoice,
And utter forth a glorious Voice,
For ever singing, as they shine,
"The Hand that made us is Divine."

EMILY DICKINSON

I Never Saw a Moor

I never saw a moor,
I never saw the sea;
Yet know I how the heather looks,
And what a wave must be.

I never spoke with God,
Nor visited in heaven;
Yet certain am I of the spot
As if the chart were given.

G. K. CHESTERTON

The Donkey

When fishes flew and forests walked
    And figs grew upon thorn,
Some moment when the moon was blood,
    Then surely I was born;

With monstrous head and sickening cry
    And ears like errant wings,
The devil's walking parody
    On all four-footed things.

The tattered outlaw of the earth,
    Of ancient crooked will;   10
Starve, scourge, deride me: I am dumb;
    I keep my secret still.

Fools! For I also had my hour;
    One far, fierce hour and sweet.
There was a shout about my ears,
    And palms before my feet.

GEORGE HERBERT   The Pulley

When God at first made man,
Having a glass of blessings standing by,
"Let us," said he, "pour on him all we can;
Let the world's riches, which dispersèd lie,
    Contract into a span."

So strength first made a way,
Then beauty flowed, then wisdom, honor, pleasure.
When almost all was out, God made a stay,
Perceiving that, alone of all his treasure,
    Rest in the bottom lay.   10

"For if I should," said he,
"Bestow this jewel also on my creature,
He would adore my gifts instead of me,
And rest in Nature, not the God of Nature;
    So both should losers be.

"Yet let him keep the rest,
But keep them with repining restlessness;
Let him be rich and weary, that at least,
If goodness lead him not, yet weariness
    May toss him to my breast."   20

I NEVER SAW A MOOR: From *Poems by Emily Dickinson* edited by Martha Dickinson Bianchi and Alfred Leete Hampson, Little, Brown and Company.

THE DONKEY: From the book *The Wild Knight and Other Poems* by Gilbert K. Chesterton, published by E. P. Dutton and Company, Inc.

RICHARD ARMOUR

Bee Lines

Russian experts claim to have trained bees to seek nectar and pollen from specific plants and to ignore others.—News item.

How doth the regimented bee
  Improve each shining hour?
He flies to each selected tree
  And designated flower.

The State directs his every course,
  The State defines the sector.
The State prescribes his pollen's source
  And allocates his nectar.

No longer flying fancy-free,
  No longer ranging bold. . . .   10
How doth the regimented bee?
  He doth as he is told.

RICHARD ARMOUR

Hiding Place

A speaker at a meeting of the New York State Frozen Food Locker Association declared that the best hiding place in event of an atomic explosion is a frozen-food locker, where "radiation will not penetrate."—News item.

Move over, ham
  And quartered cow,
My Geiger says
  The time is now.

Yes, now I lay me
  Down to sleep,
And if I die,
  At least I'll keep.

BEE LINES and HIDING PLACE: Reprinted from *Light Armour,* published by the McGraw-Hill Book Company, Inc., N.Y.C. Copyright, 1954, by Richard Armour.

ETHEL JACOBSON

Atomic Courtesy

To smash the simple atom
All mankind was intent.
  Now any day
  The atom may
Return the compliment.

ANONYMOUS

Flight

A fly and a flea in a flue
Were imprisoned, so what could they do?
  Said the fly, "Let us flee!"
  "Let us fly!" said the flea.
So they flew through the flaw in the flue.

ANONYMOUS

The Archdeacon

There was a young man of Kilpeacon
Whose nose was as red as a beacon.
  But by saying, "It's white!"
  Thirty times, day and night,
He cured it and died an archdeacon.

PHYLLIS MC GINLEY

A Garland of Precepts

Though a seeker since my birth,
Here is all I've learned on earth,
This the gist of what I know:
Give advice and buy a foe.
Random truths are all I find

ATOMIC COURTESY: Reprinted from *Collier's,* February 25, 1950, by permission of the author and the publishers.
A GARLAND OF PRECEPTS: From *The Love Letters of Phyllis McGinley;* originally appeared in *The New Yorker.* Copyright 1954 by Phyllis McGinley. Reprinted by permission of The Viking Press, Inc., New York.

Stuck like burs about my mind.
Salve a blister. Burn a letter.
Do not wash a cashmere sweater.
Tell a tale but seldom twice.
Give a stone before advice.   10

Pressed for rules and verities,
All I recollect are these:
Feed a cold to starve a fever.
Argue with no true believer.
Think-too-long is never-act.
Scratch a myth and find a fact.
Stitch in time saves twenty stitches.
Give the rich, to please them, riches.
Give to love your health and hall.
But do not give advice at all.   20

ARTHUR GUITERMAN

On the Vanity of Earthly Greatness

The tusks that clashed in mighty brawls
Of mastodons, are billiard balls.

The sword of Charlemagne the Just
Is ferric oxide, known as rust.

The grizzly bear whose potent hug
Was feared by all, is now a rug.

Great Caesar's bust is on the shelf,
And I don't feel so well myself!

ARTHUR GUITERMAN   *Sea-Chill*

When Mrs. John Masefield and her husband, the author of "I Must Go Down to the Seas Again," arrived here on a liner, she said to a reporter, "It was too uppy-downy, and Mr. Masefield was ill."—News item.

I must go down to the seas again, where the billows romp and reel,
So all I ask is a large ship that rides on an even keel,
And a mild breeze and a broad deck with a slight list to leeward,
And a clean chair in a snug nook and a nice, kind steward.

I must go down to the seas again, the sport of wind and tide,
As the gray wave and the green wave play leapfrog over the side.
And all I want is a glassy calm with a bone-dry scupper,
A good book and a warm rug and a light, plain supper.

I must go down to the seas again, though there I'm a total loss,
And can't say which is worst, the pitch, the plunge, the roll, the toss.   10
But all I ask is a safe retreat in a bar well tended,
And a soft berth and a smooth course till the long trip's ended.

A. E. HOUSMAN

Oh, When I Was in Love with You

Oh, when I was in love with you,
  Then I was clean and brave,
And miles around the wonder grew
  How well did I behave.

And now the fancy passes by,
  And nothing will remain,
And miles around they'll say that I
  Am quite myself again.

MORRIS BISHOP

The Naughty Preposition

I lately lost a preposition;
  It hid, I thought, beneath my chair.
And angrily I cried: "Perdition!
  Up from out of in under there!"

Correctness is my vade mecum,
  And straggling phrases I abhor;
And yet I wondered: "What should he come
  Up from out of in under for?"

ON THE VANITY OF EARTHLY GREATNESS and SEA-CHILL: From the book *Gaily the Troubadour* by Arthur Guiterman. Copyright, 1936, by E. P. Dutton & Co., Inc., Publishers.
OH, WHEN I WAS IN LOVE WITH YOU: From *The Collected Poems of A. E. Housman*. Copyright, 1940, by Henry Holt and Company, Inc. Reprinted by permission of the publishers.
THE NAUGHTY PREPOSITION: Reprinted from *A Bowl of Bishop* by Morris Bishop. Copyright 1954 by Morris Bishop; used with his permission. This poem first appeared in *The New Yorker*.

OGDEN NASH   *Lines in Dispraise of Dispraise*

I hereby bequeath to the Bide-a-Wee Home all people who have statistics to prove that
    a human
Is nothing but a combination of iron and water and potash and albumen.
That may very well be the truth
But it's just like saying that a cocktail is nothing but ice and gin and vermouth.
People who go around analyzing
Are indeed very tanalizing.
They always want to get at the bottom
Of everything from spring to ottom.
They can't just look at a Rembrandt or a Bartolozzi
And say, Boy! that's pretty hozzi-tozzi!   10
No, they have to break it up into its component parts
And reconstruct it with blueprints and charts.
My idea is that while after looking around me and even at me I may not be proud of
    being a human
I object to having attention called to my iron and water and potash and albumen.
In the first place, it's undignified,
And in the second place, nothing by it is signified.
Because it isn't potash et cetera that makes people Republicans or Democrats or Ghibel-
    lines or Guelphs,
It's the natural perversity of the people themselves.
No, no, you old analysts, away with the whole kit and kaboodle of you.
I wouldn't even make mincemeat to give to a poodle of you.   20

MORRIS BISHOP

With Every Regret

For many years the undersigned
Has struggled to improve his mind;
He now is mortified and moved
To find it is not much improved.

His unremitting efforts were
To build a sterling character;
The best that he can really claim
Is that it is about the same.

He went through many a tedious drill
Developing the power of will,   10
The muscles, and the memory.
They're roughly what they used to be.

Alas! The inference is plain
That Education is in vain,
And all the end of our endeavor
Is to be just as dumb as ever.

OGDEN NASH

The Purist

I give you now Professor Twist,
A conscientious scientist.
Trustees exclaimed, "He never bungles!"
And sent him off to distant jungles.
Camped on a tropic riverside,
One day he missed his loving bride.
She had, the guide informed him later,
Been eaten by an alligator.
Professor Twist could not but smile.
"You mean," he said, "a crocodile."   10

ROBERT FROST

Departmental

An ant on the tablecloth
Ran into a dormant moth
Of many times his size.
He showed not the least surprise.
His business wasn't with such.
He gave it scarcely a touch,
And was off on his duty run.
Yet if he encountered one
Of the hive's enquiry squad
Whose work is to find out God   10
And the nature of time and space,
He would put him onto the case.
Ants are a curious race;
One crossing with hurried tread
The body of one of their dead
Isn't given a moment's arrest—
Seems not even impressed.
But he no doubt reports to any
With whom he crosses antennae,
And they no doubt report   20
To the higher up at court.
Then word goes forth in Formic:
"Death's come to Jerry McCormic,
Our selfless forager Jerry.
Will the special Janizary
Whose office it is to bury
The dead of the commissary
Go bring him home to his people.
Lay him in state on a sepal.
Wrap him for shroud in a petal.   30
Embalm him with ichor of nettle.
This is the word of your Queen."
And presently on the scene
Appears a solemn mortician;
And taking formal position
With feelers calmly atwiddle,
Seizes the dead by the middle,
And heaving him high in air,
Carries him out of there.
No one stands round to stare.   40
It is nobody else's affair.

It couldn't be called ungentle.
But how thoroughly departmental.

ROBERT FROST

The Hardship of Accounting

Never ask of money spent
Where the spender thinks it went.
Nobody was ever meant
To remember or invent
What he did with every cent.

RUPERT BROOKE

Heaven

Fish (fly-replete, in depth of June,
Dawdling away their wat'ry noon)
Ponder deep wisdom, dark or clear,
Each secret fishy hope or fear.
Fish say, they have their Stream and Pond;
But is there anything Beyond?
This life cannot be All, they swear,
For how unpleasant, if it were!
One may not doubt that, somehow, Good
Shall come of Water and of Mud;   10
And, sure, the reverent eye must see
A Purpose in Liquidity.
We darkly know, by Faith we cry,
The future is not Wholly Dry.
Mud unto mud!—Death eddies near—
Not here the appointed End, not here!
But somewhere, beyond Space and Time,
Is wetter water, slimier slime!
And there (they trust) there swimmeth One
Who swam ere rivers were begun,   20
Immense, of fishy form and mind,
Squamous, omnipotent, and kind;
And under that Almighty Fin,
The littlest fish may enter in.
Oh! never fly conceals a hook,
Fish say, in the Eternal Brook,
But more than mundane weeds are there,
And mud, celestially fair;
Fat caterpillars drift around,
And Paradisal grubs are found;   30
Unfading moths, immortal flies,
And the worm that never dies.
And in that Heaven of all their wish,
There shall be no more land, say fish.

GEORGE NOEL GORDON, LORD BYRON

She Walks in Beauty

She walks in beauty, like the night
  Of cloudless climes and starry skies;
And all that's best of dark and bright
  Meet in her aspect and her eyes:
Thus mellowed to that tender light
  Which heaven to gaudy day denies.

One shade the more, one ray the less,
  Had half impaired the nameless grace
Which waves in every raven tress,
  Or softly lightens o'er her face;   10
Where thoughts serenely sweet express
  How pure, how dear their dwelling-place.

And on that cheek, and o'er that brow,
  So soft, so calm, yet eloquent,
The smiles that win, the tints that glow,
  But tell of days in goodness spent,
A mind at peace with all below,
  A heart whose love is innocent!

EDWIN ARLINGTON ROBINSON

Uncle Ananias

His words were magic and his heart was true,
  And everywhere he wandered he was blessed.
Out of all ancient men my childhood knew
  I choose him and I mark him for the best.
Of all authoritative liars, too,
  I crown him loveliest.

How fondly I remember the delight
  That always glorified him in the spring;
The joyous courage and the benedight
  Profusion of his faith in everything!
He was a good old man, and it was right   10
  That he should have his fling.

And often, underneath the apple-trees,
  When we surprised him in the summer time,
With what superb magnificence and ease

UNCLE ANANIAS: From *The Town Down the River* by Edwin Arlington Robinson; copyright 1910 by Charles Scribner's Sons, 1938 by Ruth Nivison. Reprinted by permission of the publishers.

MR. FLOOD'S PARTY: From *Collected Poems* by Edwin Arlington Robinson. Copyright 1925 and 1949 by The Macmillan Company and used with their permission.

He sinned enough to make the day sublime!
And if he liked us there about his knees,
  Truly it was no crime.

All summer long we loved him for the same
  Perennial inspiration of his lies;   20
And when the russet wealth of autumn came,
  There flew but fairer visions to our eyes—
Multiple, tropical, winged with a feathery flame,
  Like birds of paradise.

So to the sheltered end of many a year
  He charmed the seasons out with pageantry
Wearing upon his forehead, with no fear,
  The laurel of approved iniquity.
And every child who knew him, far or near,
  Did love him faithfully.   30

EDWIN ARLINGTON ROBINSON

Mr. Flood's Party

Old Eben Flood, climbing alone one night
Over the hill between the town below
And the forsaken upland hermitage.
That held as much as he should ever know
On earth again of home, paused warily.
The road was his with not a native near;
And Eben, having leisure, said aloud,
For no man else in Tilbury Town to hear:

"Well, Mr. Flood, we have the harvest moon
Again, and we may not have many more;   10
The bird is on the wing, the poet says,
And you and I have said it here before.
Drink to the bird." He raised up to the light
The jug that he had gone so far to fill,
And answered huskily: "Well, Mr. Flood,
Since you propose it, I believe I will."

Alone, as if enduring to the end
A valiant armor of scarred hopes outworn,
He stood there in the middle of the road
Like Roland's ghost winding a silent horn.   20
Below him, in the town among the trees,
Where friends of other days had honored him,
A phantom salutation of the dead
Rang thinly till old Eben's eyes were dim.

Then, as a mother lays her sleeping child
Down tenderly, fearing it may awake,
He set the jug down slowly at his feet
With trembling care, knowing that most things
    break;
And only when assured that on firm earth
It stood, as the uncertain lives of men   30
Assuredly did not, he paced away,
And with his hand extended paused again:

"Well, Mr. Flood, we have not met like this
In a long time; and many a change has come
To both of us, I fear, since last it was
We had a drop together. Welcome home!"
Convivially returning with himself,
Again he raised the jug up to the light;
And with an acquiescent quaver said:
"Well, Mr. Flood, if you insist, I might.   40

"Only a very little, Mr. Flood—
For auld lang syne. No more, sir; that will do."
So, for the time, apparently it did,
And Eben evidently thought so too;
For soon amid the silver loneliness
Of night he lifted up his voice and sang,
Secure, with only two moons listening,
Until the whole harmonious landscape rang—

"For auld lang syne." The weary throat gave out,
The last word wavered; and the song being done,
He raised again the jug regretfully   51
And shook his head, and was again alone.
There was not much that was ahead of him,
And there was nothing in the town below—
Where strangers would have shut the many doors
That many friends had opened long ago.

EMILY DICKINSON

He Preached upon "Breadth"

He preached upon "breadth" till it argued him
    narrow,—
The broad are too broad to define;
And of "truth" until it proclaimed him a liar,—
The truth never flaunted a sign.

Simplicity fled from his counterfeit presence
As gold the pyrites would shun.
What confusion would cover the innocent Jesus
To meet so enabled a man!

HE PREACHED UPON "BREADTH": From *Poems by Emily Dickinson* edited by Martha Dickinson Bianchi and Alfred Leete Hampson, Little, Brown and Company.

PHYLLIS MC GINLEY

Simeon Stylites

On top of a pillar Simeon sat.
He wore no mantle,
He had no hat,
But bare as a bird
Sat night and day.
And hardly a word
Did Simeon say.

Under the sun of the desert sky
He sat on a pillar
Nine feet high   10
When Fool and his brother
Came round to admire,
He raised it another
Nine feet high'r.

The seasons circled about his head.
He lived on water
And crusts of bread
(Or so one hears)
From pilgrims' store,
For thirty years   20
And a little more.

And why did Simeon sit like that,
Without a garment,
Without a hat,
In a holy rage
For the world to see?
It puzzles the age,
It puzzles me.
It puzzled many
A Desert Father.   30
And I think it puzzled the Good Lord, rather.

ALFRED, LORD TENNYSON

Ulysses

It little profits that an idle king,
By this still hearth, among these barren crags,
Matched with an agèd wife, I mete and dole
Unequal laws unto a savage race,
That hoard, and sleep, and feed, and know not me.
I cannot rest from travel; I will drink
Life to the lees. All times I have enjoyed
Greatly, have suffered greatly, both with those

SIMEON STYLITES: From *The Love Letters of Phyllis McGinley*. Copyright 1954 by Phyllis McGinley. Reprinted by permission of The Viking Press, Inc., New York.

That loved me, and alone; on shore, and when
Through scudding drifts the rainy Hyades   10
Vexed the dim sea. I am become a name;
For always roaming with a hungry heart
Much have I seen and known—cities of men,
And manners, climates, councils, governments,
Myself not least, but honored of them all—
And drunk delight of battle with my peers,
Far on the ringing plains of windy Troy.
I am a part of all that I have met;
Yet all experience is an arch wherethrough
Gleams that untraveled world, whose margin fades
Forever and forever when I move.   21
How dull it is to pause, to make an end,
To rust unburnished, not to shine in use!
As though to breathe were life! Life piled on life
Were all too little, and of one to me
Little remains: but every hour is saved
From that eternal silence, something more,
A bringer of new things; and vile it were
For some three suns to store and hoard myself,
And this gray spirit yearning in desire   30
To follow knowledge like a sinking star,
Beyond the utmost bound of human thought.

This is my son, mine own Telemachus,
To whom I leave the scepter and the isle—
Well-loved of me, discerning to fulfill
This labor, by slow prudence to make mild
A rugged people, and through soft degrees
Subdue them to the useful and the good.
Most blameless is he, centered in the sphere
Of common duties, decent not to fail   40
In offices of tenderness, and pay
Meet adoration to my household gods,
When I am gone. He works his work, I mine.

There lies the port; the vessel puffs her sail;
There gloom the dark broad seas. My mariners,
Souls that have toiled, and wrought, and thought
    with me,—
That ever with a frolic welcome took
The thunder and the sunshine, and opposed
Free hearts, free foreheads,—you and I are old;
Old age hath yet his honor and his toil.   50
Death closes all; but something ere the end,
Some work of noble note, may yet be done,
Not unbecoming men that strove with Gods.
The lights begin to twinkle from the rocks;
The long day wanes; the slow moon climbs; the
    deep
Moans round with many voices. Come, my friends,
'Tis not too late to seek a newer world.
Push off, and sitting well in order smite
The sounding furrows; for my purpose holds
To sail beyond the sunset, and the baths   60
Of all the western stars, until I die.
It may be that the gulfs will wash us down;
It may be we shall touch the Happy Isles,

And see the great Achilles, whom we knew.
Though much is taken, much abides; and though
We are not now that strength which in old days
Moved earth and heaven; that which we are, we
    are;
One equal temper of heroic hearts,
Made weak by time and fate, but strong in will
To strive, to seek, to find, and not to yield.   70

ROBERT BROWNING

Soliloquy of the Spanish Cloister

Gr-r-r—there go, my heart's abhorrence!
    Water your damned flower-pots, do!
If hate killed men, Brother Lawrence,
    God's blood, would not mine kill you!
What? your myrtle-bush wants trimming?
    Oh, that rose has prior claims—
Needs its leaden vase filled brimming?
    Hell dry you up with its flames!

At the meal we sit together:
    Salve tibi! I must hear   10
Wise talk of the kind of weather,
    Sort of season, time of year:
*Not a plenteous cork-crop: scarcely
    Dare we hope oak-galls, I doubt:
What's the Latin name for "parsley"?*
    What's the Greek name for Swine's Snout?

Whew! We'll have our platter burnished,
    Laid with care on our own shelf!
With a fire-new spoon we're furnished,
    And a goblet for ourself,   20
Rinsed like something sacrificial
    Ere 'tis fit to touch our chaps—
Marked with L for our initial!
    (He-he! There his lily snaps!)

Saint, forsooth! While brown Dolores
    Squats outside the Convent bank
With Sanchicha, telling stories,
    Steeping tresses in the tank,
Blue-black, lustrous, thick like horse-hairs,
    —Can't I see his dead eye glow,   30
Bright as 'twere a Barbary corsair's?
    (That is, if he'd let it show!)

When he finishes refection,
    Knife and fork he never lays
Cross-wise, to my recollection,
    As do I, in Jesu's praise.
I the Trinity illustrate,
    Drinking watered orange-pulp—

In three sips the Arian frustrate;
    While he drains his at one gulp.   40

Oh, those melons! If he's able
    We're to have a feast! so nice!
One goes to the Abbot's table,
    All of us get each a slice.
How go on your flowers? None double?
    Not one fruit-sort can you spy?
Strange!—And I, too, at such trouble
    Keep them close-nipped on the sly!

There's a great text in Galatians,
    Once you trip on it, entails   50
Twenty-nine distinct damnations,
    One sure, if another fails:
If I trip him just a-dying,
    Sure of heaven as sure can be,
Spin him round and send him flying
    Off to hell, a Manichee!

Or, my scrofulous French novel
    On gray paper with blunt type!
Simply glance at it, you grovel
    Hand and foot in Belial's gripe: 60
If I double down its pages
    At the woeful sixteenth print,
When he gathers his greengages,
    Ope a sieve and slip it in't?

Or, there's Satan! one might venture
    Pledge one's soul to him, yet leave
Such a flaw in the indenture
    As he'd miss till, past retrieve,
Blasted lay that rose-acacia
    We're so proud of! *Hy, Zy, Hine* . . .   70
'St, there's Vespers! *Plena gratia,*
    Ave, Virgo! Gr-r-r—you swine!

STEPHEN SPENDER

Judas Iscariot

The eyes of twenty centuries
Pursue me along corridors to where
I am painted at their ends on many walls.
    Ever-revolving future recognize

JUDAS ISCARIOT: From *The Edge of Being*. Copyright 1949 by Stephen Spender. Reprinted by permission of Random House, Inc.

This red hair and red beard, where I am seated
Within the dark cave of the feast of light.
    Out of my heart-shaped shadow I stretch my hand
Across the white table into the dish
But not to dip the bread. It is as though
The cloth on each side of one dove-bright face   10
Spread dazzling wings on which the apostles ride
Uplifting them into the vision
Where their eyes watch themselves enthroned.
    My russet hand across the dish
Plucks enviously against one feather
    —But still the rushing wings spurn me below!

    Saint Sebastian of wickedness
I stand: all eyes legitimate arrows piercing through
The darkness of my wickedness. They recognize
My halo hammered from thirty silver pieces   20
And the hemp rope around my neck
Soft as that Spirit's hanging arms
When on my cheek he answered with the kiss
Which cuts for ever—
                My strange stigmata,
All love and hate, all fire and ice!

    But who betrayed whom? O you,
Whose light gaze forms the azure corridor
Through which those other pouring eyes
Arrow into me—answer! Who
Betrayed whom? Who read   30
In his mind's light from the first day
That the kingdom of heaven on earth must always
Reiterate the garden of Eden,
And each day's revolution be betrayed
Within man's heart, each day?
                Who wrapped
The whispering serpent round the tree
And hung between the leaves the glittering purse
And trapped the fangs with God-appointed poison?
Who knew
I must betray the truth, and made the lie   40
Betray its truth in me?

    Those hypocrite eyes which aimed at you
Now aim at me. And yet, beyond their world
Each turning on his pole of truth, your pole
Invisible light, and mine
Becoming what man is. We stare
Across two thousand years, and heaven, and hell,
Into each other's gaze.

WALTER SAVAGE LANDOR

Rose Aylmer

Ah, what avails the sceptred race,
　Ah, what the form divine!
What every virtue, every grace!
　Rose Aylmer, all were thine.

Rose Aylmer, whom these wakeful eyes
　May weep, but never see,
A night of memories and of sighs
　I consecrate to thee.

ROBERT BURNS

Highland Mary

Ye banks and braes and streams around
　The castle o' Montgomery,
Green be your woods, and fair your flowers,
　Your waters never drumlie!
There simmer first unfauld her robes,
　And there the langest tarry;
For there I took the last fareweel
　O' my sweet Highland Mary.

How sweetly bloomed the gay green birk,
　How rich the hawthorn's blossom,   10
As underneath their fragrant shade
　I clasped her to my bosom!
The golden hours on angel wings
　Flew o'er me and my dearie;
For dear to me as light and life
　Was my sweet Highland Mary.

Wi' monie a vow and locked embrace
　Our parting was fu' tender;
And, pledging aft to meet again,
　We tore ourselves asunder;   20
But oh! fell Death's untimely frost,
　That nipped my flower sae early!
Now green's the sod, and cauld's the clay,
　That wraps my Highland Mary!

O pale, pale now, those rosy lips
　I aft hae kissed sae fondly!
And closed for aye the sparkling glance

That dwelt on me sae kindly!
And mould'ring now in silent dust,
　That heart that lo'ed me dearly!   30
But still within my bosom's core
　Shall live my Highland Mary.

A. E. HOUSMAN

To an Athlete Dying Young

The time you won your town the race
We chaired you through the market-place;
Man and boy stood cheering by,
And home we brought you shoulder-high.

Today, the road all runners come,
Shoulder-high we bring you home,
And set you at your threshold down,
Townsman of a stiller town.

Smart lad, to slip betimes away
From fields where glory does not stay,   10
And early though the laurel grows
It withers quicker than the rose.

Eyes the shady night has shut
Cannot see the record cut,
And silence sounds no worse than cheers
After earth has stopped the ears:

Now you will not swell the rout
Of lads that wore their honours out,
Runners whom renown outran
And the name died before the man.   20

So set, before its echoes fade,
The fleet foot on the sill of shade,
And hold to the low lintel up
The still-defended challenge-cup.

And round that early-laureled head
Will flock to gaze the strengthless dead,
And find unwithered on its curls
The garland briefer than a girl's.

TO AN ATHLETE DYING YOUNG: From *The Collected Poems of A. E. Housman.* Copyright, 1940, by Henry Holt and Company, Inc. Reprinted by permission of the publishers.

JOHN CROWE RANSOM

Bells for John Whiteside's Daughter

There was such speed in her little body,
And such lightness in her footfall,
It is no wonder her brown study
Astonishes us all.

Her wars were bruited in our high window.
We looked among orchard trees and beyond,
Where she took arms against her shadow,
Or harried unto the pond

The lazy geese, like a snow cloud
Dripping their snow on the green grass,   10
Tricking and stopping, sleepy and proud,
Who cried in goose, Alas,

For the tireless heart within the little
Lady with rod that made them rise
From their noon apple-dreams and scuttle
Goose-fashion under the skies!

But now go the bells, and we are ready,
In one house we are sternly stopped
To say we are vexed at her brown study,
Lying so primly propped.   20

E E CUMMINGS   Buffalo Bill's

Buffalo Bill's
defunct
           who used to
           ride a watersmooth-silver
                                          stallion
and break onetwothreefourfive pigeonsjustlikethat
                                          Jesus
he was a handsome man
                         and what i want to know is
how do you like your blueeyed boy
Mister Death

ROBERT BRIDGES   Elegy

The wood is bare: a river-mist is steeping
     The trees that winter's chill of life bereaves:
Only their stiffened boughs break silence, weeping
     Over their fallen leaves;

That lie upon the dank earth brown and rotten,
     Miry and matted in the soaking wet:
Forgotten with the spring, that is forgotten
     By them that can forget.

Yet it was here we walked when ferns were springing,
     And through the mossy bank shot bud and blade:—   10
Here found in summer, when the birds were singing,
     A green and pleasant shade.

'Twas here we loved in sunnier days and greener;
     And now, in this disconsolate decay,
I come to see her where I most have seen her,
     And touch the happier day.

BELLS FOR JOHN WHITESIDE'S DAUGHTER: Reprinted from *Selected Poems* by John Crowe Ransom, by permission of Alfred A. Knopf, Inc. Copyright 1924, 1945 by Alfred A. Knopf, Inc.
BUFFALO BILL'S: From *Poems: 1923-1954*. Harcourt, Brace and Company. Copyright, 1923, by E. E. Cummings. Reprinted by permission of Brandt and Brandt.
ELEGY: From *The Shorter Poems of Robert Bridges*, by permission of The Clarendon Press, Oxford.

For on this path, at every turn and corner,
The fancy of her figure on me falls:
Yet walks she with the slow step of a mourner,
Nor hears my voice that calls.   20

So through my heart there winds a track of feeling,
A path of memory, that is all her own:
Whereto her phantom beauty ever stealing
Haunts the sad spot alone.

About her steps the trunks are bare, the branches
Drip heavy tears upon her downcast head;
And bleed from unseen wounds that no sun stanches,
For the year's sun is dead.

And dead leaves wrap the fruits that summer planted:
And birds that love the South have taken wing.   30
The wanderer, loitering o'er the scene enchanted,
Weeps, and despairs of spring.

KARL SHAPIRO

Elegy for a Dead Soldier

I

A white sheet on the tail-gate of a truck
Becomes an altar; two small candlesticks
Sputter at each side of the crucifix
Laid round with flowers brighter than the blood,
Red as the red of our apocalypse,
Hibiscus that a marching man will pluck
To stick into his rifle or his hat,
And great blue morning-glories pale as lips
That shall no longer taste or kiss or swear.
The wind begins a low magnificat,   10
The chaplain chats, the palmtrees swirl their hair,
The columns come together through the mud.

II

We too are ashes as we watch and hear
The psalm, the sorrow, and the simple praise
Of one whose promised thoughts of other days
Were such as ours, but now wholly destroyed,
The service record of his youth wiped out,
His dream dispersed by shot, must disappear.
What can we feel but wonder at a loss
That seems to point at nothing but the doubt   20
Which flirts our sense of luck into the ditch?
Reader of Paul who prays beside this fosse,
Shall we believe our eyes or legends rich
With glory and rebirth beyond the void?

ELEGY FOR A DEAD SOLDIER: From *V-Letter and Other Poems* by Karl Shapiro, copyright 1944 by Karl Shapiro. Reprinted by permission of Random House, Inc.

III

For the comrade is dead, dead in the war,
A young man out of millions yet to live,
One cut away from all that war can give,
Freedom of self and peace to wander free.
Who mourns in all this sober multitude
Who did not feel the bite of it before   30
The bullet found its aim? This worthy flesh,
This boy laid in a coffin and reviewed—
Who has not wrapped himself in this same flag,
Heard the light fall of dirt, his wound still fresh,
Felt his eyes closed, and heard the distant brag
Of the last volley of humanity?

IV

By chance I saw him die, stretched on the ground,
A tattooed arm lifted to take the blood
Of someone else sealed in a tin. I stood
During the last delirium that stays   40
The intelligence a tiny moment more,
And then the strangulation, the last sound.
The end was sudden, like a foolish play,
A stupid fool slamming a foolish door,
The absurd catastrophe, half-prearranged,
And all the decisive things still left to say.
So we disbanded, angrier and unchanged,
Sick with the utter silence of dispraise.

V

We ask for no statistics of the killed,
For nothing political impinges on   50
This single casualty, or all those gone,
Missing or healing, sinking or dispersed,

Hundreds of thousands counted, millions lost.
More than an accident and less than willed
Is every fall, and this one like the rest.
However others calculate the cost,
To us the final aggregate is *one*,
One with a name, one transferred to the blest;
And though another stoops and takes the gun,
We cannot add the second to the first.   60

VI

I would not speak for him who could not speak
Unless my fear were true: he was not wronged,
He knew to which decision he belonged
But let it choose itself. Ripe in instinct,
Neither the victim nor the volunteer,
He followed, and the leaders could not seek
Beyond the followers. Much of this he knew;
The journey was a detour that would steer
Into the Lincoln Highway of a land
Remorselessly improved, excited, new,   70
And that was what he wanted. He had planned
To earn and drive. He and the world had winked.

VII

No history deceived him, for he knew
Little of times and armies not his own;
He never felt that peace was but a loan,
Had never questioned the idea of gain.
Beyond the headlines once or twice he saw
The gathering of a power by the few
But could not tell their names; he cast his vote,
Distrusting all the elected but not the law.   80
He laughed at socialism; *on mourrait*
Pour les industriels? He shed his coat
And not for brotherhood, but for his pay.
To him the red flag marked the sewer main.

VIII

Above all else he loathed the homily,
The slogan and the ad. He paid his bill
But not for Congressmen at Bunker Hill.
Ideals were few and those were not made
For conversation. He belonged to church
But never spoke of God. The Christmas tree,   90
The Easter egg, baptism, he observed,
Never denied the preacher on his perch,
And would not sign Resolved That or Whereas.
Softness he had and hours and nights reserved
For thinking, dressing, dancing to the jazz.
His laugh was real, his manners were home made.

IX

Of all men poverty pursued him least;
He was ashamed of all the down and out,
Spurned the panhandler like an uneasy doubt,
And saw the unemployed as a vague mass   100
Incapable of hunger or revolt.
He hated other races, south or east,
And shoved them to the margin of his mind.
He could recall the justice of the Colt,
Take interest in a gang-war like a game.
His ancestry was somewhere far behind
And left him only his peculiar name.
Doors opened, and he recognized no class.

X

His children would have known a heritage,
Just or unjust, the richest in the world,   110
The quantum of all art and science curled
In the horn of plenty, bursting from the horn,
A people bathed in honey, Paris come,
Vienna transferred with the highest wage,
A World's Fair spread to Phoenix, Jacksonville,
Earth's capitol, the new Byzantium,
Kingdom of man—who knows? Hollow or firm,
No man can ever prophesy until
Out of our death some undiscovered germ,
Whole toleration or pure peace is born.   120

XI

The time to mourn is short that best becomes
The military dead. We lift and fold the flag,
Lay bare the coffin with its written tag,
And march away. Behind, four others wait
To lift the box, the heaviest of loads.
The anesthetic afternoon benumbs,
Sickens our senses, forces back our talk.
We know that others on tomorrow's roads
Will fall, ourselves perhaps, the man beside,
Over the world the threatened, all who walk: 130
And could we mark the grave of him who died
We would write this beneath his name and date:

EPITAPH

Underneath this wooden cross there lies
A Christian killed in battle. You who read,
Remember that this stranger died in pain;
And passing here, if you can lift your eyes
Upon a peace kept by a human creed,
Know that one soldier has not died in vain.

W. H. AUDEN

In Memory of W. B. Yeats

1

He disappeared in the dead of winter:
The brooks were frozen, the airports almost
    deserted,
And snow disfigured the public statues;
The mercury sank in the mouth of the dying day.
O all the instruments agree
The day of his death was a dark cold day.

Far from his illness
The wolves ran on through the evergreen forests,
The peasant river was untempted by the fashion-
    able quays;
By mourning tongues   10
The death of the poet was kept from his poems.

But for him it was his last afternoon as himself,
An afternoon of nurses and rumors;
The provinces of his body revolted,
The squares of his mind were empty,
Silence invaded the suburbs,
The current of his feeling failed: he became his
    admirers.

Now he is scattered among a hundred cities
And wholly given over to unfamiliar affections;
To find his happiness in another kind of wood   20
And be punished under a foreign code of
    conscience.
The words of a dead man
Are modified in the guts of the living.

But in the importance and noise of tomorrow
When the brokers are roaring like beasts on the
    floor of the Bourse,
And the poor have the sufferings to which they
    are fairly accustomed,
And each in the cell of himself is almost convinced
    of his freedom;
A few thousand will think of this day
As one thinks of a day when one did something
    slightly unusual.

O all the instruments agree   30
The day of his death was a dark cold day.

2

You were silly like us: your gift survived it all;
The parish of rich women, physical decay,

IN MEMORY OF W. B. YEATS: From *Another Time* by
W. H. Auden, copyright 1940 by W. H. Auden. Reprinted by permission of Random House, Inc.

Yourself; mad Ireland hurt you into poetry.
Now Ireland has her madness and her weather still,
For poetry makes nothing happen: it survives
In the valley of its saying where executives
Would never want to tamper; it flows south
From ranches of isolation and the busy griefs,
Raw towns that we believe and die in; it survives,
A way of happening, a mouth.   41

3

Earth, receive an honored guest;
William Yeats is laid to rest:
Let the Irish vessel lie
Emptied of its poetry.

Time that is intolerant
Of the brave and innocent,
And indifferent in a week
To a beautiful physique,

Worships language and forgives   50
Everyone by whom it lives;
Pardons cowardice, conceit,
Lays its honors at their feet.

Time that with this strange excuse
Pardoned Kipling and his views,
And will pardon Paul Claudel,
Pardons him for writing well.

In the nightmare of the dark
All the dogs of Europe bark,
And the living nations wait,   60
Each sequestered in its hate;

Intellectual disgrace
Stares from every human face,
And the seas of pity lie
Locked and frozen in each eye.

Follow, poet, follow right
To the bottom of the night,
With your unconstraining voice
Still persuade us to rejoice;

With the farming of a verse   70
Make a vineyard of the curse,
Sing of human unsuccess
In a rapture of distress;

In the deserts of the heart
Let the healing fountain start,
In the prison of his days
Teach the free man how to praise.

PERCY BYSSHE SHELLEY

Ozymandias

I met a traveler from an antique land
Who said: Two vast and trunkless legs of stone
Stand in the desert. Near them, on the sand,
Half sunk, a shattered visage lies, whose frown,
And wrinkled lip, and sneer of cold command,
Tell that its sculptor well those passions read
Which yet survive, stamped on these lifeless things,
The hand that mocked them, and the heart that
    fed.
And on the pedestal these words appear:
"My name is Ozymandias, king of kings;   10
Look on my works, ye Mighty, and despair!"
Nothing beside remains. Round the decay
Of that colossal wreck, boundless and bare,
The lone and level sands stretch far away.

WILLIAM WORDSWORTH

London, 1802

Milton! thou shouldst be living at this hour:
England hath need of thee: she is a fen
Of stagnant waters: altar, sword, and pen,
Fireside, the heroic wealth of hall and bower,
Have forfeited their ancient English dower
Of inward happiness. We are selfish men;
Oh! raise us up, return to us again;
And give us manners, virtue, freedom, power.
Thy soul was like a Star, and dwelt apart;
Thou hadst a voice whose sound was like the sea:
Pure as the naked heavens, majestic, free,   11
So didst thou travel on life's common way,
In cheerful godliness; and yet thy heart
The lowliest duties on herself did lay.

CARL SANDBURG   Chicago

Hog Butcher for the World,
Tool Maker, Stacker of Wheat,
Player with Railroads and the Nation's Freight Handler;
Stormy, husky, brawling,
City of the Big Shoulders:

They tell me you are wicked and I believe them, for I have seen your painted women
    under the gas lamps luring the farm boys.
And they tell me you are crooked and I answer:
Yes, it is true I have seen the gunman kill and go free to kill again.
And they tell me you are brutal and my reply is: On the faces of women and children
    I have seen the marks of wanton hunger.
And having answered so I turn once more to those who sneer at this my city, and I
    give them back the sneer and say to them: 10
Come and show me another city with lifted head singing so proud to be alive and coarse
    and strong and cunning.
Flinging magnetic curses amid the toil of piling job on job, here is a tall bold slugger
    set vivid against the little soft cities;
Fierce as a dog with tongue lapping for action, cunning as a savage pitted against the
    wilderness,
        Bareheaded,
        Shoveling,
        Wrecking,
        Planning,
        Building, breaking, rebuilding.

Under the smoke, dust all over his mouth, laughing with white teeth,
Under the terrible burden of destiny laughing as a young man laughs,   20
Laughing even as an ignorant fighter laughs who has never lost a battle,
Bragging and laughing that under his wrist is the pulse, and under his ribs the heart
    of the people,
               Laughing!
Laughing the stormy, husky, brawling laughter of Youth, half-naked, sweating, proud to
    be Hog Butcher, Tool Maker, Stacker of Wheat, Player with Railroads and Freight
    Handler to the Nation.

WILLIAM ROSE BENÉT

Third Row, Centre

The stage is lighted, the first act half over.
These, the too ample ones, subside and fret,
Fussing with furs, with program and lorgnette,
And finally the dialogue, discover
Where the bright leading-lady with her lover
Moves in the scenic brilliance of the set.
Expressionless they stare at the duet
And gradually their sighing breath recover.

Their escorts, redolent of excellent wine,
Liqueurs, and quite superior cigars,   10
Slump in their seats and estimate the star's
Height, weight, and substance, and relax the spine
Musing upon the question of her charms
Were she transferred to their own broadcloth arms.

Fish-eyed, they drowse for two hours and a half
Save for the intermissions when they push
Into the aisle and join the lobby's crush
And stare about, and vacuously laugh,
Innerly woeful with no more to quaff,
Putting the barnyard waddlers to the blush   20
For solid flesh, and sure in any hush
To give the play a brazen epitaph.

So the plot thickens, and the second act,
That even pricks the critics with its pace,
Brings something near to pathos on each face,
As the eyes goggle and the brows contract
And yearningly those vasty bosoms heave,
And, like the mute stalled ox, those others grieve.

Uncomfortably they stir and cough and stir
And wonder dimly what it's all about,   30
Sniffing at truffles with a quivering snout
When any questionable lines occur,
But otherwise in trance, as they prefer.

And so, at last, their evening is worn out;
And the house-lights come on; and with the rout
They exit in their usual hauteur.

High above Broadway blaze the great sky-signs.
Blare, in the street, a thousand taxi klaxons.
All over town Semites and Anglo-Saxons
Strengthen their old commercial battle-lines . . .
And now in chariots of a newer Rome   41
The furs and opera-hats are bowling home.

WILFRED OWEN

Dulce et Decorum Est

Bent double, like old beggars under sacks,
Knock-kneed, coughing like hags, we cursed
    through sludge,
Till on the haunting flares we turned our backs,
And towards our distant rest began to trudge.
Men marched asleep. Many had lost their boots,
But limped on, blood-shod. All went lame, all
    blind;
Drunk with fatigue; deaf even to the hoots
Of gas-shells dropping softly behind.

Gas! Gas! Quick, boys!—An ecstasy of fumbling,
Fitting the clumsy helmets just in time,   10
But some one still was yelling out and stumbling
And flound'ring like a man in fire or lime.
Dim through the misty panes and thick green
    light,
As under a green sea, I saw him drowning.

In all my dreams before my helpless sight
He plunges at me, guttering, choking, drowning.

If in some smothering dreams, you too could pace
Behind the wagon that we flung him in,
And watch the white eyes wilting in his face,
His hanging face, like a devil's sick of sin,   20
If you could hear, at every jolt, the blood
Come gargling from the froth-corrupted lungs

Bitten as the cud
Of vile, incurable sores on innocent tongues,—
My friend, you would not tell with such high zest
To children ardent for some desperate glory,
The old lie: Dulce et decorum est
Pro patria mori.

ROBINSON JEFFERS

The Bloody Sire

It is not bad. Let them play.
Let the guns bark and the bombing-plane
Speak his prodigious blasphemies.
It is not bad, it is high time,
Stark violence is still the sire of all the world's
    values.

What but the wolf's tooth whittled so fine
The fleet limbs of the antelope?
What but fear winged the birds, and hunger
Jeweled with such eyes the great goshawk's head?
Violence has been the sire of all the world's
    values.   10

Who would remember Helen's face
Lacking the terrible halo of spears?
Who formed Christ but Herod and Caesar,
The cruel and bloody victories of Caesar?
Violence, the bloody sire of all the world's values.

Never weep, let them play,
Old violence is not too old to beget new values.

A. E. HOUSMAN

"Terence, This Is Stupid Stuff—"

"Terence, this is stupid stuff:
You eat your victuals fast enough;
There can't be much amiss, 'tis clear,
To see the rate you drink your beer.
But oh, good Lord, the verse you make,
It gives a chap the belly-ache.
The cow, the old cow, she is dead;
It sleeps well, the horned head:
We poor lads, 'tis our turn now

THE BLOODY SIRE: From *Be Angry at the Sun* by Robinson Jeffers, copyright 1941 by Robinson Jeffers. Reprinted by permission of Random House, Inc.
"TERENCE, THIS IS STUPID STUFF—": From *The Collected Poems of A. E. Housman.* Copyright, 1940, by Henry Holt and Company, Inc. Reprinted by permission of the publishers.

To hear such tunes as killed the cow.   10
Pretty friendship 'tis to rhyme
Your friends to death before their time
Moping melancholy mad:
Come, pipe a tune to dance to, lad."

Why, if 'tis dancing you would be,
There's brisker pipes than poetry.
Say, for what were hop-yards meant,
Or why was Burton built on Trent?
Oh many a peer of England brews
Livelier liquor than the Muse,   20
And malt does more than Milton can
To justify God's ways to man.
Ale, man, ale's the stuff to drink
For fellows whom it hurts to think:
Look into the pewter pot
To see the world as the world's not.
And faith, 'tis pleasant till 'tis past:
The mischief is that 'twill not last.
Oh I have been to Ludlow fair
And left my necktie God knows where,   30
And carried half-way home, or near,
Pints and quarts of Ludlow beer:
Then the world seemed none so bad,
And I myself a sterling lad;
And down in lovely muck I've lain,
Happy till I woke again.
Then I saw the morning sky:
Heigho, the tale was all a lie;
The world, it was the old world yet,
I was I, my things were wet,   40
And nothing now remained to do
But begin the game anew.

Therefore, since the world has still
Much good, but much less good than ill,
And while the sun and moon endure
Luck's a chance, but trouble's sure,
I'd face it as a wise man would,
And train for ill and not for good.
'Tis true, the stuff I bring for sale
Is not so brisk a brew as ale: 50
Out of a stem that scored the hand
I wrung it in a weary land.
But take it: if the smack is sour,
The better for the embittered hour;
It should do good to heart and head
When your soul is in my soul's stead;
And I will friend you, if I may,
In the dark and cloudy day.

There was a king reigned in the East:
There, when kings will sit to feast,   60
They get their fill before they think
With poisoned meat and poisoned drink.
He gathered all that springs to birth

From the many-venomed earth;
First a little, thence to more,
He sampled all her killing store;
And easy, smiling, seasoned sound
Sate the king when healths went round.
They put arsenic in his meat
And stared aghast to watch him eat;   70
They poured strychnine in his cup
And shook to see him drink it up:
They shook, they stared as white's their shirt:
Them it was their poison hurt.
—I tell the tale that I heard told.
Mithridates, he died old.

DYLAN THOMAS

In My Craft or Sullen Art

In my craft or sullen art
Exercised in the still night
When only the moon rages
And the lovers lie abed
With all their griefs in their arms,
I labour by singing light
Not for ambition or bread
Or the strut and trade of charms
On the ivory stages
But for the common wages   10
Of their most secret heart.
Not for the proud man apart
From the raging moon I write
On these spindrift pages
Not for the towering dead
With their nightingales and psalms
But for the lovers, their arms
Round the griefs of the ages,
Who pay no praise or wages
Nor heed my craft or art.   20

JOHN KEATS

Ode to a Nightingale

My heart aches, and a drowsy numbness pains
  My sense, as though of hemlock I had drunk,
Or emptied some dull opiate to the drains
  One minute past, and Lethe-wards had sunk:
'Tis not through envy of thy happy lot,
  But being too happy in thine happiness,—
    That thou, light-wingèd Dryad of the trees,
      In some melodious plot
Of beechen green, and shadows numberless,
  Singest of summer in full-throated ease.   10

O for a draught of vintage! that hath been
  Cooled a long age in the deep-delvèd earth,
Tasting of Flora and the country green,
  Dance, and Provençal song, and sunburnt mirth!
O for a beaker full of the warm South,
  Full of the true, the blushful Hippocrene,
    With beaded bubbles winking at the brim,
      And purple-stainèd mouth;
That I might drink, and leave the world unseen,
  And with thee fade away into the forest dim:

Fade far away, dissolve, and quite forget   21
  What thou among the leaves hast never known,
The weariness, the fever, and the fret
  Here, where men sit and hear each other groan;
Where palsy shakes a few, sad, last gray hairs,
  Where youth grows pale, and specter-thin, and
      dies;
    Where but to think is to be full of sorrow
      And leaden-eyed despairs,
  Where Beauty cannot keep her lustrous eyes,
    Or new Love pine at them beyond tomorrow.

Away! away! for I will fly to thee,   31
  Not charioted by Bacchus and his pards,
But on the viewless wings of Poesy,
  Though the dull brain perplexes and retards:
Already with thee! tender is the night,
  And haply the Queen-Moon is on her throne,
    Clustered around by all her starry Fays;
      But here there is no light,
Save what from heaven is with the breezes blown
    Through verdurous glooms and winding mossy
      ways.   40

I cannot see what flowers are at my feet,
  Nor what soft incense hangs upon the boughs,
But, in embalmèd darkness, guess each sweet
  Wherewith the seasonable month endows
The grass, the thicket, and the fruit-tree wild;
  White hawthorn, and the pastoral eglantine;
    Fast fading violets covered up in leaves;
      And mid-May's eldest child,
The coming musk-rose, full of dewy wine,
    The murmurous haunt of flies on summer
      eves.   50

Darkling I listen; and, for many a time
  I have been half in love with easeful Death,
Called him soft names in many a musèd rhyme,
  To take into the air my quiet breath;
Now more than ever seems it rich to die,
  To cease upon the midnight with no pain,
    While thou art pouring forth thy soul abroad
      In such an ecstasy!
Still wouldst thou sing, and I have ears in vain—
    To thy high requiem become a sod.   60

Thou wast not born for death, immortal Bird!
  No hungry generations tread thee down;
The voice I hear this passing night was heard
  In ancient days by emperor and clown:
Perhaps the self-same song that found a path
  Through the sad heart of Ruth, when, sick for
      home,
    She stood in tears amid the alien corn;
      The same that oft-times hath
Charmed magic casements, opening on the foam
  Of perilous seas, in faery lands forlorn. 70

Forlorn! the very word is like a bell
  To toll me back from thee to my sole self!
Adieu! the fancy cannot cheat so well
  As she is famed to do, deceiving elf.
Adieu! adieu! thy plaintive anthem fades
  Past the near meadows, over the still stream,
  Up the hill-side; and now 'tis buried deep
    In the next valley-glades:
Was it a vision, or a waking dream?
  Fled is that music:—Do I wake or sleep? 80

MATTHEW ARNOLD

Dover Beach

The sea is calm tonight,
The tide is full, the moon lies fair
Upon the straits;—on the French coast the light
Gleams and is gone; the cliffs of England stand,
Glimmering and vast, out in the tranquil bay.
Come to the window, sweet is the night-air!
Only, from the long line of spray
Where the sea meets the moon-blanched land,
Listen! you hear the grating roar
Of pebbles which the waves draw back, and fling,
At their return, up the high strand, 11
Begin, and cease, and then again begin,
With tremulous cadence slow, and bring
The eternal note of sadness in.

Sophocles long ago
Heard it on the Aegean, and it brought
Into his mind the turbid ebb and flow
Of human misery; we
Find also in the sound a thought,
Hearing it by this distant northern sea. 20

The Sea of Faith
Was once, too, at the full, and round earth's shore
Lay like the folds of a bright girdle furled.
But now I only hear
Its melancholy, long, withdrawing roar,
Retreating, to the breath

Of the night-wind, down the vast edges drear
And naked shingles of the world.

Ah, love, let us be true
To one another! for the world, which seems 30
To lie before us like a land of dreams,
So various, so beautiful, so new,
Hath really neither joy, nor love, nor light,
Nor certitude, nor peace, nor help for pain;
And we are here as on a darkling plain
Swept with confused alarms of struggle and flight,
Where ignorant armies clash by night.

ARTHUR HUGH CLOUGH

Say Not the Struggle Nought Availeth

Say not the struggle nought availeth,
  The labor and the wounds are vain,
The enemy faints not, nor faileth,
  And as things have been they remain.

If hopes were dupes, fears may be liars;
  It may be, in yon smoke concealed,
Your comrades chase e'en now the fliers,
  And, but for you, possess the field.

For while the tired waves, vainly breaking,
  Seem here no painful inch to gain, 10
Far back, through creeks and inlets making,
  Comes silent, flooding in, the main.

And not by eastern windows only,
  When daylight comes, comes in the light,
In front, the sun climbs slow, how slowly,
  But westward, look, the land is bright.

THOMAS HARDY

Hap

If but some vengeful god would call to me
From up the sky, and laugh: "Thou suffering thing,
Know that thy sorrow is my ecstasy,
That thy love's loss is my hate's profiting!"

Then would I bear it, clench myself, and die,
Steeled by the sense of ire unmerited;
Half-eased in that a Powerfuller than I
Had willed and meted me the tears I shed.

HAP: From Collected Poems by Thomas Hardy. Copyright 1925 by The Macmillan Company and used with their permission.

But not so. How arrives it joy lies slain,
And why unblooms the best hope ever sown?   10
—Crass Casualty obstructs the sun and rain,
And dicing Time for gladness casts a moan. . . .
These purblind Doomsters had as readily strown
Blisses about my pilgrimage as pain.

COUNTEE CULLEN

Ultimatum

I hold not with the fatalist creed
Of what must be must be;
There is enough to meet my need
In this most meagre me.

These two slim arms were made to rein
My steed, to ward and fend;
There is more gold in this small brain
Than I can ever spend.

The seed I plant is chosen well;
Ambushed by no sly sweven,   10
I plant it if it droops to hell,
Or if it blooms to heaven.

EDWIN ARLINGTON ROBINSON

Karma

Christmas was in the air and all was well
With him, but for a few confusing flaws
In divers of God's images. Because
A friend of his would neither buy nor sell,
Was he to answer for the axe that fell?
He pondered; and the reason for it was,
Partly, a slowly freezing Santa Claus
Upon the corner, with his beard and bell.

Acknowledging an improvident surprise,
He magnified a fancy that he wished   10
The friend whom he had wrecked were here again.
Not sure of that, he found a compromise;
And from the fullness of his heart he fished
A dime for Jesus who had died for men.

EMILY DICKINSON

He Ate and Drank the Precious Words

He ate and drank the precious words,
His spirit grew robust;
He knew no more that he was poor,
Nor that his frame was dust.
He danced along the dingy days,
And this bequest of wings
Was but a book. What liberty
A loosened spirit brings!

EMILY DICKINSON

The Bustle in a House

The bustle in a house
The morning after death
Is solemnest of industries
Enacted upon earth,—

The sweeping up the heart,
And putting love away
We shall not want to use again
Until eternity.

JOHN MILTON

On His Blindness

When I consider how my light is spent
Ere half my days in this dark world and wide,
And that one talent, which is death to hide,
Lodged with me useless, though my soul more bent
To serve therewith my Maker, and present
My true account, lest He returning chide;
"Doth God exact day-labor, light denied?"
I fondly ask. But Patience, to prevent
That murmur, soon replies, "God doth not need
Either man's work or his own gifts. Who best   10
Bear His mild yoke, they serve Him best. His state
Is kingly. Thousands at His bidding speed
And post o'er land and ocean without rest.
They also serve who only stand and wait.

ROBERT FROST

Provide, Provide

The witch that came (the withered hag)
To wash the steps with pail and rag,
Was once the beauty Abishag,

The picture pride of Hollywood.
Too many fall from great and good
For you to doubt the likelihood.

Die early and avoid the fate.
Or if predestined to die late,
Make up your mind to die in state.

Make the whole stock exchange your own!   10
If need be occupy a throne,
Where nobody can call *you* crone.

Some have relied on what they knew;
Others on being simply true.
What worked for them might work for you.

No memory of having starred
Atones for later disregard,
Or keeps the end from being hard.

Better to go down dignified
With boughten friendship at your side   20
Than none at all. Provide, provide!

THOMAS HARDY

The Oxen

Christmas Eve, and twelve of the clock.
  "Now they are all on their knees,"
An elder said as we sat in a flock
  By the embers in hearthside ease.

We pictured the meek mild creatures where
  They dwelt in their strawy pen,
Nor did it occur to one of us there
  To doubt they were kneeling then.

So fair a fancy few would weave
  In these years! Yet, I feel,   10

If someone said on Christmas Eve,
  "Come; see the oxen kneel,

"In the lonely barton by yonder coomb
  Our childhood used to know,"
I should go with him in the gloom,
  Hoping it might be so.

MARIANNE MOORE

Silence

My father used to say,
"Superior people never make long visits,
have to be shown Longfellow's grave
or the glass flowers at Harvard.
Self-reliant like the cat—
that takes its prey to privacy,
the mouse's limp tail hanging like a shoelace from
  its mouth—
they sometimes enjoy solitude,
and can be robbed of speech
by speech which has delighted them.   10
The deepest feeling always shows itself in silence;
not in silence, but restraint."
Nor was he insincere in saying, "Make my house
  your inn."
Inns are not residences.

ELINOR WYLIE

The Eagle and the Mole

Avoid the reeking herd,
Shun the polluted flock,
Live like that stoic bird,
The eagle of the rock.

The huddled warmth of crowds
Begets and fosters hate;
He keeps, above the clouds,
His cliff inviolate.

When flocks are folded warm,
And herds to shelter run,   10
He sails above the storm,
He stares into the sun.

If in the eagle's track
Your sinews cannot leap,
Avoid the lathered pack,
Turn from the steaming sheep.

If you would keep your soul
From spotted sight or sound,
Live like the velvet mole;
Go burrow underground.   20

And there hold intercourse
With roots of trees and stones,
With rivers at their source,
And disembodied bones.

WILLIAM BLAKE

The Tiger

Tiger! Tiger! burning bright
In the forests of the night,
What immortal hand or eye
Could frame thy fearful symmetry?

In what distant deeps or skies
Burnt the fire of thine eyes?
On what wings dare he aspire?
What the hand dare seize the fire?

And what shoulder, and what art,
Could twist the sinews of thy heart?   10
And when thy heart began to beat,
What dread hand? and what dread feet?

What the hammer? what the chain?
In what furnace was thy brain?
What the anvil? what dread grasp
Dare its deadly terrors clasp?

When the stars threw down their spears,
And watered heaven with their tears,
Did he smile his work to see?
Did he who made the Lamb make thee?   20

Tiger! Tiger! burning bright
In the forests of the night,
What immortal hand or eye
Could frame thy fearful symmetry?

GEORGE MEREDITH

Lucifer in Starlight

On a starred night Prince Lucifer uprose.
  Tired of his dark dominion swung the fiend
  Above the rolling ball in cloud part screened,

Where sinners hugged their specter of repose.
Poor prey to his hot fit of pride were those.
  And now upon his western wing he leaned,
  Now his huge bulk o'er Afric's sands careened.
Now the black planet shadowed Arctic snows.
Soaring through wider zones that pricked his scars
  With memory of the old revolt from Awe,   10
He reached a middle height, and at the stars,
  Which are the brain of heaven, he looked, and
    sank.
  Around the ancient track marched, rank on rank,
The army of unalterable law.

GERARD MANLEY HOPKINS

Spring and Fall: To a Young Child

Margaret, are you grieving
Over Goldengrove unleaving?
Leaves, like the things of man, you
With your fresh thoughts care for, can you?
Ah! as the heart grows older
It will come to such sights colder
By and by, nor spare a sigh
Though worlds of wanwood leafmeal lie;
And yet you will weep and know why.
Now no matter, child, the name: 10
Sorrow's springs are the same.
Nor mouth had, no nor mind, expressed
What heart heard of, ghost guessed:
It is the blight man was born for,
It is Margaret you mourn for.

T. S. ELIOT

Animula

"Issues from the hand of God, the simple soul"
To a flat world of changing lights and noise,
To light, dark, dry or damp, chilly or warm;
Moving between the legs of tables and of chairs,
Rising or falling, grasping at kisses and toys,
Advancing boldly, sudden to take alarm,
Retreating to the corner of arm and knee,
Eager to be reassured, taking pleasure
In the fragrant brilliance of the Christmas tree,
Pleasure in the wind, the sunlight and the sea;   10
Studies the sunlit pattern on the floor
And running stags around a silver tray;
Confounds the actual and the fanciful,
Content with playing-cards and kings and queens,
What the fairies do and what the servants say.

ANIMULA: From *Collected Poems, 1909-1935* by T. S.
Eliot, copyright, 1936, by Harcourt, Brace and Company, Inc.

The heavy burden of the growing soul
Perplexes and offends more, day by day;
Week by week, offends and perplexes more
With the imperatives of "is and seems"
And may and may not, desire and control.   20
The pain of living and the drug of dreams
Curl up the small soul in the window seat
Behind the *Encyclopædia Britannica*.
Issues from the hand of time the simple soul
Irresolute and selfish, misshapen, lame,
Unable to fare forward or retreat,
Fearing the warm reality, the offered good,
Denying the importunity of the blood,
Shadow of its own shadows, spectre in its own
    gloom,
Leaving disordered papers in a dusty room;   30
Living first in the silence after the viaticum.

Pray for Guiterriez, avid of speed and power,
For Boudin, blown to pieces,
For this one who made a great fortune,
And that one who went his own way.
Pray for Floret, by the boarhound slain between
    the yew trees,
Pray for us now and at the hour of our birth.

WILLIAM BUTLER YEATS

Sailing to Byzantium

I

That is no country for old men. The young
In one another's arms, birds in the trees,
—Those dying generations—at their song,
The salmon-falls, the mackerel-crowded seas,
Fish, flesh, or fowl, commend all summer long

Whatever is begotten, born, and dies.
Caught in that sensual music all neglect
Monuments of unaging intellect.

II

An aged man is but a paltry thing,
A tattered coat upon a stick, unless   10
Soul clap its hands and sing, and louder sing
For every tatter in its mortal dress,
Nor is there singing school but studying
Monuments of its own magnificence;
And therefore I have sailed the seas and come
To the holy city of Byzantium.

III

O sages standing in God's holy fire
As in the gold mosaic of a wall,
Come from the holy fire, perne in a gyre,
And be the singing-masters of my soul.   20
Consume my heart away; sick with desire
And fastened to a dying animal
It knows not what it is; and gather me
Into the artifice of eternity.

IV

Once out of nature I shall never take
My bodily form from any natural thing,
But such a form as Grecian goldsmiths make
Of hammered gold and gold enameling
To keep a drowsy Emperor awake;
Or set upon a golden bough to sing   30
To lords and ladies of Byzantium
Of what is past, or passing, or to come.

DYLAN THOMAS *Fern Hill*

Now as I was young and easy under the apple boughs
About the lilting house and happy as the grass was green,
    The night above the dingle starry,
        Time let me hail and climb
    Golden in the heydays of his eyes,
And honoured among wagons I was prince of the apple towns
And once below a time I lordly had the trees and leaves
        Trail with daisies and barley
    Down the rivers of the windfall light.

And as I was green and carefree, famous among the barns   10
About the happy yard and singing as the farm was home,

In the sun that is young once only,
    Time let me play and be
Golden in the mercy of his means,
And green and golden I was huntsman and herdsman, the calves
Sang to my horn, the foxes on the hills barked clear and cold,
    And the sabbath rang slowly
    In the pebbles of the holy streams.

All the sun long it was running, it was lovely, the hay-
Fields high as the house, the tunes from the chimneys, it was air   20
    And playing, lovely and watery
        And fire green as grass.
    And nightly under the simple stars
As I rode to sleep the owls were bearing the farm away,
All the moon long I heard, blessed among stables, the night-jars
    Flying with the ricks, and the horses
        Flashing into the dark.

And then to awake, and the farm, like a wanderer white
With the dew, come back, the cock on his shoulder: it was all
    Shining, it was Adam and maiden,   30
        The sky gathered again
    And the sun grew round that very day.
So it must have been after the birth of the simple light
In the first, spinning place, the spellbound horses walking warm
    Out of the whinnying green stable
        On to the fields of praise.

And honoured among foxes and pheasants by the gay house
Under the new made clouds and happy as the heart was long,
    In the sun born over and over,
        I ran my heedless ways,   40
        My wishes raced through the house-high hay
And nothing I cared, at my sky blue trades, that time allows
In all his tuneful turnings so few and such morning songs
    Before the children green and golden
        Follow him out of grace.

Nothing I cared, in the lamb white days, that time would take me
Up to the swallow thronged loft by the shadow of my hand,
    In the moon that is always rising,
        Nor that riding to sleep
    I should hear him fly with the high fields   50
And wake to the farm forever fled from the childless land.
Oh as I was young and easy in the mercy of his means,
        Time held me green and dying
    Though I sang in my chains like the sea.

FRANCIS THOMPSON

The Hound of Heaven

I fled Him, down the nights and down the days;   I hid from Him, and under running laughter.
    I fled Him, down the arches of the years;   Up vistaed hopes I sped;
I fled Him, down the labyrinthine ways   And shot, precipitated,
    Of my own mind; and in the midst of tears   Adown Titanic glooms of chasmèd fears,

From those strong Feet that followed, followed after.
        But with unhurrying chase,   10
        And unperturbèd pace,
    Deliberate speed, majestic instancy,
        They beat—and a Voice beat
        More instant than the Feet—
    "All things betray thee, who betrayest Me."

        I pleaded, outlaw-wise,
By many a hearted casement, curtained red,
    Trellised with intertwining charities
(For, though I knew His love Who followèd,
        Yet was I sore adread   20
Lest, having Him, I must have naught beside);
But, if one little casement parted wide,
    The gust of His approach would clash it to:
Fear wist not to evade, as Love wist to pursue.
Across the margent of the world I fled,
    And troubled the gold gateways of the stars,
    Smiting for shelter on their clangèd bars
        Fretted to dulcet jars
And silvern chatter the pale ports o' the moon.
I said to Dawn: Be sudden—to Eve: Be soon;   30
    With thy young skiey blossoms heap me over
        From this tremendous Lover—
Float thy vague veil about me, lest He see!
    I tempted all His servitors, but to find
My own betrayal in their constancy,
In faith to Him their fickleness to me,
    Their traitorous trueness, and their loyal deceit.
To all swift things for swiftness did I sue;
    Clung to the whistling mane of every wind.
        But whether they swept, smoothly fleet,   40
    The long savannahs of the blue;
        Or whether, Thunder-driven,
        They clanged his chariot 'thwart a heaven,
Plashy with flying lightnings round the spurn o'
    their feet:—
    Fear wist not to evade as Love wist to pursue.
        Still with unhurrying chase,
        And unperturbèd pace,
    Deliberate speed, majestic instancy,
        Came on the following Feet,
        And a Voice above their beat—   50
    "Naught shelters thee, who wilt not shelter
    Me."

I sought no more that after which I strayed
    In face of man or maid;
But still within the little children's eyes
    Seems something, something that replies,
They at least are for me, surely for me!
I turned me to them very wistfully;
But just as their young eyes grew sudden fair
    With dawning answers there,
Their angel plucked them from me by the hair.   60
"Come then, ye other children, Nature's—share

With me" (said I) "your delicate fellowship;
    Let me greet you lip to lip,
    Let me twine with you caresses,
        Wantoning
    With our Lady-Mother's vagrant tresses,
        Banqueting
    With her in her wind-walled palace,
    Underneath her azured daïs,
    Quaffing, as your taintless way is,   70
        From a chalice
Lucent-weeping out of the dayspring."
    So it was done:
I in their delicate fellowship was one—
Drew the bolt of Nature's secrecies.
I knew all the swift importings
    On the willful face of skies;
    I knew how the clouds arise
    Spumèd of the wild sea-snortings;
    All that's born or dies   80
    Rose and drooped with; made them
    shapers
Of mine own moods, or wailful or divine;
    With them joyed and was bereaven.
    I was heavy with the even,
    When she lit her glimmering tapers
    Round the day's dead sanctities.
    I laughed in the morning's eyes.
I triumphed and I saddened with all weather,
    Heaven and I wept together,
And its sweet tears were salt with mortal mine;   90
Against the red throb of its sunset-heart
    I laid my own to beat,
    And share commingling heat;
But not by that, by that, was eased my human
    smart.
In vain my tears were wet on Heaven's gray cheek.
For ah! we know not what each other says,
    These things and I; in sound *I* speak—
Their sound is but their stir, they speak by silences.
Nature, poor stepdame, cannot slake my drouth;
    Let her, if she would owe me,   100
Drop yon blue bosom-veil of sky, and show me
    The breasts o' her tenderness:
Never did any milk of hers once bless
    My thirsting mouth.
    Nigh and nigh draws the chase,
    With unperturbèd pace,
    Deliberate speed, majestic instancy;
    And past those noisèd Feet
    A Voice comes yet more fleet—
    "Lo! naught contents thee, who content'st
    not Me."   110

Naked I wait Thy love's uplifted stroke!
My harness piece by piece Thou hast hewn from
    me,

And smitten me to my knee;
I am defenseless utterly.
I slept, methinks, and woke,
And, slowly gazing, find me stripped in sleep.
In the rash lustihead of my young powers,
I shook the pillaring hours,
And pulled my life upon me; grimed with smears,
I stand amid the dust o' the mounded years—   120
My mangled youth lies dead beneath the heap.
My days have crackled and gone up in smoke,
Have puffed and burst as sun-starts on a stream.
Yea, faileth now even dream
The dreamer, and the lute the lutanist;
Even the linked fantasies, in whose blossomy twist
I swung the earth a trinket at my wrist,
Are yielding; cords of all too weak account
For earth with heavy griefs so overplused.
Ah! is Thy love indeed   130
A weed, albeit an amaranthine weed,
Suffering no flowers except its own to mount?
Ah! must—
Designer infinite!—
Ah! must Thou char the wood ere Thou canst
limn with it?
My freshness spent its wavering shower i' the dust;
And now my heart is as a broken fount,
Wherein tear-dripping stagnate, spilt down ever
From the dank thoughts that shiver
Upon the sighful branches of my mind.   140
Such is; what is to be?
The pulp so bitter, how shall taste the rind?
I dimly guess what Time in mists confounds;
Yet ever and anon a trumpet sounds
From the hid battlements of Eternity;
Those shaken mists a space unsettle, then
Round the half-glimpsèd turrets slowly wash again.
But not ere him who summoneth

I first have seen, enwound
With glooming robes purpureal, cypress-crowned;
His name I know, and what his trumpet saith.   151
Whether man's heart or life it be which yields
Thee harvest, must Thy harvest-fields
Be dunged with rotten death?

Now of that long pursuit
Comes on at hand the bruit;
That Voice is round me like a bursting sea:
"And is thy earth so marred,
Shattered in shard on shard?
Lo, all things fly thee, for thou fliest Me!
Strange, piteous, futile thing!   161
Wherefore should any set thee love apart?
See none but I makes much of naught" (He said),
"And human love needs human meriting:
How hast thou merited—
Of all man's clotted clay the dingiest clot?
Alack, thou knowest not
How little worthy of any love thou art!
Whom wilt thou find to love ignoble thee
Save Me, save only Me?   170
All which I took from thee I did but take,
Not for thy harms,
But just that thou might'st seek it in My arms.
All which thy child's mistake
Fancies as lost, I have stored for thee at home:
Rise, clasp My hand, and come!"

Halts by me that footfall:
Is my gloom, after all,
Shade of His hand, outstretched caress-
ingly?
"Ah, fondest, blindest, weakest,   180
I am He Whom thou seekest!
Thou dravest love from thee, who dravest Me."

ACCENT. Stress or emphasis given to a poetic syllable. *See* Prosody.

ALLEGORY. A narrative in which objects and persons stand for meanings outside the narrative itself; an elaborated metaphor. *See* Figurative Language.

ALLITERATION. The repetition of initial consonant sounds or of accented consonant sounds. *See* Rime, Texture.

ALLUSION. A reference to something outside the primary content of the poem, often figurative in effect.

ANALOGY. A comparison, bordering on metaphor, of particular points of resemblance between two obviously different things.

ANAPEST. *See* Meter, Prosody.

APOSTROPHE. Direct address to a person, object or abstract idea, often treating the dead as living, the nonhuman as human, and the absent as present. *See* Figurative Language.

ASSONANCE. Repetition of vowel sounds that are not followed, as in rime, by similar consonants. *See* Rime, Texture.

BALLAD. In its original form a simple, highly concentrated verse-story, often sung. The more recent literary ballad is a consciously artistic imitation. *See* Narrative, Types of Poetry.

BLANK VERSE. Unrimed iambic pentameter. *See* Prosody, Stanza, Verse Paragraphs.

CACOPHONY. Harsh, unpleasant sound. *See* Euphony, Texture.

CADENCE. Rhythmic, though not regularly metrical, flow of language. Cadence is influenced by much the same factors as those determining rhythm. *See* Rhythm.

CAESURA. The main sense pause within a line of poetry. *See* Prosody.

CONSONANCE. Identity of the pattern of consonants (*deer, door*); unlike rime in that the vowels involved differ. *See* Rime, Texture.

COUPLET. The form of verse with two successive lines riming. *See* Stanza.

DACTYL. *See* Meter, Prosody.

DIMETER. *See* Line, Meter, Prosody.

DRAMATIC. That one of the three major types of poetry which uses methods that resemble the methods of drama. *See* Types of Poetry.

DRAMATIC MONOLOGUE. Poem which is the speech of a single character.

ELEGY. A subjective, meditative poem, usually expressing emotions associated with grief or death. *See* Lyric, Types of Poetry.

END-STOPPED LINE. Line whose end coincides with a pause in sense. *See* Prosody.

ENVOY. A short stanza in the nature of a postscript at the end of a poem.

EPIC. A long narrative poem dealing in elevated style with heroic personalities and great actions. *See* Narrative, Types of Poetry.

EUPHONY. Sound combinations, consonant or vowel, that are pleasing to the ear. *See* Cacophony, Texture.

EYE-RIME. A terminal pairing of words or syllables that appear from the spelling to rime but in pronunciation do not (*yea, tea*).

FIGURATIVE LANGUAGE. Words used out of their literal sense to convey a special effect and meaning. Many figures of speech are based upon comparison or intensification. The more common figures are simile and metaphor, which are based on comparison. Other figurative comparisons are symbol and allegory. Some figures based on intensification are personification, apostrophe, hyperbole, litotes or understatement, and irony.

FOOT. A metrical unit composed of one accented syllable and one or more unaccented syllables. *See* Meter, Prosody.

FREE VERSE. Verse with loose or irregular rhythm. *See* Stanza.

HEPTAMETER. *See* Line, Meter, Prosody.

HEXAMETER. *See* Line, Meter, Prosody.

HYPERBOLE. The figure of speech using an exaggerated statement not intended to be taken literally; overstatement. *See* Understatement, Figurative Language.

IAMB. *See* Meter, Prosody.

IMAGERY. The representation of sensory experience by use of allusions and figurative language in general. *See* Allusion, Figurative Language.

INTERNAL RIME. Rime occurring within a single line of poetry. *See* Rime.

IRONY. An implication opposite to the literal meaning of the words used; a situation or effect opposite to the expected and the normally appropriate one. *See* Figurative Language.

ITALIAN SONNET. *See* Sonnet.

LINE. A typographical unit of one or more metrical feet in verse. The poetic line is described by the predominant kind of foot and the number of feet it contains. *See* Foot, Meter, Prosody.

LYRIC. A poem meant to be sung, or an especially musical or highly subjective poem; one of the three main types of poetry. *See* Types of Poetry.

METAPHOR. Narrowly, the figure of speech expressing indirectly (by implication, not using *as* or *like*) a resemblance, in one or more points, of an object in one class to an object of another class. Broadly, figurative language in general. *See* Figurative Language, Simile.

METER. The relationship of accented and unaccented syllables. Used both to designate the kind of metrical foot and the number of feet in a line of verse. The common kinds of meter in English are anapest, dactyl, trochee, iamb. The spondee, a metrical foot of two accented syllables, is only approximated in English prosody. Common line lengths (reckoned in number of metrical feet) are monometer, dimeter, trimeter, tetrameter, pentameter, hexameter, heptameter. *See* Line, Rhythm, Prosody.

MONOMETER. *See* Line, Meter, Prosody.

NARRATIVE. A story; the one of the three major types of poetry that tells a connected series of events. *See* Types of Poetry.

OCTAVE. Stanza of eight lines, or the first eight lines of a sonnet. *See* Sonnet.

ODE. Usually a serious, formal poem that follows a set, complicated metrical pattern and is written for a special purpose and occasion. *See* Lyric, Types of Poetry.

ONOMATOPOEIA. Words formed in imitation of the natural sounds they name. *See* Texture.

PARODY. An imitation of the language, style, and ideas of another work for comic or critical effect.

PASTORAL. Narrowly, a type of classical poetry, or, broadly, any favorable treatment of rural life. *See* Lyric, Types of Poetry.

PENTAMETER. *See* Line, Meter, Prosody.

PERSONIFICATION. Figure of speech in which human qualities are given to nonhuman objects or abstract qualities. *See* Figurative Language.

PETRARCHAN SONNET. *See* Sonnet.

PROSODY. Art of metrical composition, or a special theory or practice in metrics. *See* fuller discussion of prosody, pp. 743-44.

QUATRAIN. Four-line stanza in any of a number of end-rime schemes. *See* Prosody, Stanza.

RHYTHM. Literally, the measured motion of language. Rhythm is primarily a product of the relationship of accented and unaccented syllables or sounds, though pitch, tempo, syllabic length, and sentence structure are other influential factors. Often rhythm refers to regular metrical pattern. *See* Meter.

RIME. Usually refers to end rime, the similarity or correspondence of the terminal sounds of words; but, in general, rime is any degree of correspondence of sound combinations whether terminal or internal (within a line). Slant or partial rime is an approximate correspondence of sounds. Textural effects—assonance, consonance, alliteration—are themselves forms of rime. *See* End Rime, Internal Rime, Texture.

RIME SCHEME. The patterns of end rime in a stanza. Small letters are ordinarily used to indicate this pattern, thus: couplet, *aa;* ballad quatrain, *abcb;* envelope quatrain, *abba;* Rubáiyát quatrain, *aaba;* Spenserian stanza, *ababbcbcc. See* Stanza.

RUN-ON LINE. A line in which the sense is not concluded but continues into the next line without pause. *See* Prosody, End-stopped Line.

SCANSION. The determining of the relationship between accented and unaccented syllables in verse. *See* Prosody.

SESTET. Stanza of six lines, or the first six lines of a sonnet. *See* Sonnet.

SHAKESPEAREAN SONNET. *See* Sonnet.

SIMILE. The figure of speech expressing directly (with *as* or *like*) a resemblance in one or more points of an object of one class to an object of another class. *See* Figurative Language, Metaphor.

SLANT RIME. Loose or approximate rime (*run, tone*). *See* Rime.

SONNET. A poem of fourteen lines in iambic pentameter. The Petrarchan or Italian sonnet commonly divides itself into an octave riming *abbaabba,* in which the theme is presented, and a sestet riming *cdecde,* or sometimes more freely, in which the conclusion to the theme is presented. The Shakespearean sonnet, riming *ababcdcdefefgg,* commonly develops the theme in three quatrains and concludes it in a couplet.

SPONDEE. *See* Meter, Prosody.

STANZA. A pattern of lines and rimes in verse.

Stanzas are identified on the basis of the type of meter, number of metrical feet in each line, number of lines, and the pattern of rime when rime is employed. Many stanzaic patterns have been long established and have conventional names—couplet, ballad quatrain, Spenserian, etc. Blank verse (unrimed iambic pentameter) and other non-stanzaic verse forms (like free verse) may be broken into verse paragraphs which are determined more by content than by form. See Prosody.

SYMBOL. In the broadest sense, something that suggests or stands for an idea, quality, or conception larger than itself, as the lion is the symbol of courage, the cross the symbol of Christianity. In poetic usage, a symbol is a more central and pervasive comparison than either simile or metaphor, often providing the basic imagery of an entire poem. It represents a step beyond metaphor in that the first term of the comparison is not supplied. See Figurative Language.

TEMPO. Rate of articulation or delivery of words and syllables. See Rhythm.

TETRAMETER. See Line, Meter, Prosody.

TEXTURE. As applied to poetry, texture is the general relationship of sounds, not generally including the more exact forms of rime. Important textural devices are cacophony and euphony, onomatopoeia, alliteration, assonance, consonance. See Rime.

TRIMETER. See Line, Meter, Prosody.

TROCHEE. See Meter, Prosody.

TYPES OF POETRY. Generally, poetry is divided into three main types: the narrative, which is the story poem; the dramatic, which uses many of the direct concrete methods of the drama itself; and the lyric, which is highly musical, emotional, subjective. Some common types of dramatic poetry are the dramatic monologue and the verse-drama. Some common types of lyric are the descriptive lyric, the didactic lyric, the elegy, the hymn, the sonnet, the ode, the pastoral, the reflective or philosophical lyric, and the satiric lyric. See Dramatic, Lyric, Narrative.

UNDERSTATEMENT. Popular designation of the figure of speech classically known as litotes. Understatement is the saying less about an occasion than might normally be expected. See Figurative Language.

VERSE. A single line of a poem. A literary composition with a systematic metrical pattern as opposed to prose. Sometimes verse is used disparagingly in reference to such compositions as attain only the outward and mechanical features and not the high quality of poetry.

VERSE PARAGRAPHS. Thought divisions in non-stanzaic verse forms such as blank verse and free verse. See Stanza.

PROSODY

Prosody, generally defined as the "science of versification," rises above mere attention to the mechanical considerations of metrical structure to become an art of communication in which the sound furthers the sense and in which the sense intensifies the sound. Since English verse is primarily accentual and not quantitative (that is, primarily dependent upon emphasis given a syllable rather than on length of syllable), English prosody is much a matter of studying the occurrence of accents.

The prosodic structure of a stanza is analyzed by a process known as scansion. In scanning, one examines (1) the prevailing metrical foot: (2) the line length; (3) the placement of pauses; and (4) the number of lines and, if the verse is rimed, the pattern of end rime.

1. METRICAL FEET

Iamb: Unaccented syllable, accented syllable (a-go).

Trochee: Accented syllable, unaccented syllable (dwel-ling).

Anapest: Two unaccented syllables, accented syllable (of the sun).

Dactyl: Accented syllable, two unaccented syllables (mer-ri-ly).

Spondee: A fifth kind of metrical foot, in which two consecutive accented syllables from different metrical feet occur or in which a primary and secondary accent occur consecutively (play-house).

2. LINE

The line length in metrical feet is monometer if the line has one foot, dimeter if two feet, trimeter if three, tetrameter if four, pentameter if five, hexameter (Alexandrine) if six, heptameter if seven, octameter if eight. In theory there may be more than eight feet in a line, but in practice a line longer than heptameter tends to break up into two or more lines.

3. PAUSES

Also important, especially in blank verse, alliterative verse, and the heroic couplet, is the location of pauses ending sense units—phrases, clauses, sentences—within the line. A main pause, known as the *caesura*, and secondary pauses are common. (In scansion they are indicated by the symbols // and /.) A line is termed *end-stopped* when it ends with a sense pause, *run-on* when the sense extends into the next line.

Little verse is metrically perfect, for metrical perfection does not permit the flexibility necessary to combine sense and sound most fittingly. Nearly all English verse is iambic, but substitution of another type of foot is common and substantial passages of trochee, dactyl, and anapest can be found.

4. PATTERN OF LINES AND RIMES

The number of lines and the rime pattern are described as *couplet* (aa); *tercet* or *triplet* (terza rima, aba-bcb-cdc, etc.); *quatrain* (ballad, abcb; Rubáiyát, aaba; In Memoriam, abba); *octave*; etc.

Following are metrical descriptions of some common verse patterns.

Blank verse: Iambic pentameter unrimed.

The world | was all | before | them, // where | to
    choose
Their place | of rest, | // and Prov | idence | their
    guide.
They, / hand | in hand, | // with wan | dering steps |
    and slow,
Through E | den took | their sol | itar | y way.

Heroic couplet: Iambic pentameter rimed (aa); first couplet below is run-on, second couplet end-stopped.

Of all | the caus | es which | conspire | to blind
Man's er | ring judge | ment, and | misguide | the
    mind.

What the | weak head | with strong | est bi | as rules,
Is Pride, // the nev | er fail | ing vice | of fools.

Ballad measure: Iambic, first and third lines tetrameter, second and fourth lines trimeter, and second and fourth lines riming (i.e., iambic, 4-3-4-3, abcb).

And soon | I heard | a roar | ing wind;
    It did | not come | anear;
But with | its sound | it shook | the sails
    That were | so thin | and sear.

Rubáiyát quatrain: Iambic pentameter rimed aaba.

Come, fill | the cup, | // and in | the fire | of Spring
Your Win | ter-gar | ment of | Repen | tance fling.
    The Bird | of Time | has but | a lit | tle way
To flut | ter // —and | the Bird | is on | the Wing.

Spenserian stanza: Iambic pentameter rimed ababbcbcc, the last line being hexameter (Alexandrine).

And still | she slept | an az | ure-lid | ded sleep,
In blan | chèd lin | en, / smooth, | and lav | en-
    dered,
While he | from forth | the clos | et brought | a
    heap
Of can | died ap | ple, quince, | and plum, | and
    gourd,
With jel | lies sooth | er than | the cream | y curd,
And lu | cent syr | ops, // tinct | with cin | namon;
Manna | and dates, | in ar | gosy | transferred
From Fez; | and spic | èd dain | ties, ev | ery one,
From sil | ken Sam | arcand | to ce | dared Leb |
    anon.

JOSEPH ADDISON (1672-1719), English essayist, poet, dramatist, and statesman, helped to establish the essay as a literary form by his urbane and polished writing for the *Tatler* and the *Spectator*.

RICHARD ARMOUR (1906-   ), professor, editor, and biographer, is popular as a writer of light verse.

MATTHEW ARNOLD (1822-1888), an English poet and critic greatly interested in social and religious topics, was strongly affected by the science of his day. In both his poetry and his prose he revealed wide learning and a deep respect for culture, which he defined as "the best that has been thought and said in the world."

W. H. AUDEN (1907-   ), a British-born, Oxford-educated poet now a naturalized American citizen, was, in the 1930's, a leader of a group of young English poets who wrote about the political and social problems of our times. More recently, Auden's verse has shown a religious and philosophical outlook.

WILLIAM ROSE BENÉT (1886-1950) was one of the founders of the *Saturday Review*. He was equally distinguished as an editor, a poet, and a critic.

MORRIS GILBERT BISHOP (1893-   ) was educated at Cornell University. After serving in the United States Infantry during World War I, engaging in business, and holding various government positions, he returned to Cornell, where he is now Professor of Romance Literature. *A Bowl of Bishop* is his twelfth book.

WILLIAM BLAKE (1757-1827), the self-educated son of a London tradesman, was a rare combination of poet and painter. In his lyrics and in his highly original paintings, notably those for *The Book of Job*, he expressed a mystical awareness of the Divine.

ROBERT BRIDGES (1844-1930), British surgeon, essayist, poet, and playwright, became poet laureate in 1913. He is admired particularly for his skill in using varied verse forms.

RUPERT BROOKE (1887-1915), after a short but brilliant poetic career, enlisted in the British Army in World War I, and died of sunstroke. His best poems are probably his sonnets.

ROBERT BROWNING (1812-1889), English poet of the Victorian period, wrote for many years without attracting public attention or critical approval, but he lived to become a hero in the literary world with cults founded solely to study his works. He is especially known for his employment of the dramatic verse monologue to reveal character and personality.

ROBERT BURNS (1759-1796), Scotland's greatest poet and national hero, was born a peasant. His love poems, his character studies, his celebration of the common man—most of all, his command of melody —make him a universal favorite.

GEORGE NOEL GORDON, LORD BYRON (1788-1824), versatile poet of early nineteenth-century England, was an adventurer. His poetic heroes are romantic; his manner of expression is fluent and lyrically intense; his ideas are liberal, sometimes extreme; but he often wrote biting satire that is closer in spirit to the Age of Pope than to the Age of Romanticism in which he lived.

G. K. CHESTERTON (1874-1936), often called the master of paradox, began his literary career as a critic of art books. A versatile writer, his literary output included fiction (he is best remembered in this field as the creator of Father Brown, a whimsical priest-detective), biography, criticism, poetry, essays, and plays.

ARTHUR HUGH CLOUGH (1819-1861), poet and teacher, received his early education at Rugby, where he fell under the influence of Thomas Arnold, Rugby's great headmaster and Matthew Arnold's father. At Oxford he acquired religious doubts that influenced his later thinking and writing. Like Matthew Arnold, he was troubled by the effect of scientific discovery on traditional religious doctrines.

ROBERT P. TRISTRAM COFFIN (1892-1954), a scholar whose special field of interest was English and classical literature, was a prolific nature poet and historian of Maine, his native state. He spent much time lecturing and giving poetry recitations, and conducted a number of writers' conferences.

COUNTEE CULLEN (1903-1946), a Negro poet who was popular during the 'twenties and 'thirties, wrote seven volumes of verse (*Color* was the first; *On These I Stand*, the last) largely about the feelings and aspirations of Negroes.

E. E. CUMMINGS (1894-   ) was born in Cambridge, Massachusetts, and was educated at Harvard University. He has published several books of verse, most recently the definitive *Poems 1923-1954.* The unconventional punctuation and form of his poetry are technical devices which indicate the way the poem should be read.

WALTER DE LA MARE (1873-   ), English novelist and poet, writes verse marked by music and mystery, for children and adults.

EMILY DICKINSON (1830-1886), now accounted one of America's greatest poets, spent most of her life in self-imposed seclusion. She published only four poems in her lifetime and won no wide audience until the 1920's. Though uniformly brief, her poems show close observation, intensity, and illuminating, often whimsical, metaphor.

JOHN DONNE (1572-1631), who, after an intense spiritual struggle, became the most famous Anglican preacher of his day, won his lasting reputation not so much on his *Sermons* as on two groups of poems, the love lyrics of his youth and the religious lyrics of his maturity.

T. S. ELIOT (1888-   ), an American-born critic and poet, now a British citizen, has influenced a whole generation of writers, particularly through his long, controversial poem *The Waste Land.* His major theme is the frustration, and the consequent spiritual inadequacy, of our times.

ROBERT FROST (1875-   ), though born in San Francisco, is identified with the New England of his forebears. As a young man, he taught, farmed, and wrote poetry there—all with little initial success. Not until he went to England for the years 1912-15 did he come to the attention of critics and public. After his return to New England, his reputation grew steadily—he has won the Pulitzer Prize four times and is now considered America's foremost living poet.

ORLANDO GIBBONS (1583-1625), an illustrious Elizabethan musician, is especially famed for his anthems and hymns and for his collection of madrigals.

ARTHUR GUITERMAN (1871-1943), an American lecturer and magazine editor, wrote light verse with wry humor and unexpected twists.

THOMAS HARDY (1840-1928), one of the two or three English writers who have produced both great poetry and great novels, was trained as an architect. His earliest writings were poems; about 1870 he turned to the novel and wrote all his novels in the succeeding twenty-six years; in 1896,

discouraged by harsh criticism of *Jude the Obscure,* he returned to poetry. In this final period of his work he wrote *The Dynasts,* a great epic drama in verse and the most ambitious of his poems.

GEORGE HERBERT (1593-1633) was born into one of the great families of England. Under the influence of his mother, a woman of exceptional brilliance, he entered the church, but only after passing through a period of worldly ambition. The last years of his short life were spent quietly in the service of St. Andrew's Church at Bemerton—one of the smallest churches in England. In his verse Herbert celebrates, with intense simplicity, his religious experience.

ROBERT HERRICK (1591-1674), the most popular of the Cavalier poets, was, like Donne and Herbert, a churchman as well as a poet. Like Donne, too, he is best known for his love lyrics and religious lyrics. His graceful, light secular poems usually treat of the simple pleasures of life and of love.

GERARD MANLEY HOPKINS (1844-1898), a brilliant Oxford graduate, became converted to Catholicism and entered the priesthood. His poetry, which was experimental in its imagery and rhythm, was not known until 1918, when Robert Bridges published a volume of his verse.

A. E. HOUSMAN (1859-1936), English scholar and poet, was not a prolific writer; he produced only three small volumes of lyrics. But the simplicity, irony, and flawlessness of these lyrics place him among the chief English poets.

ETHEL JACOBSON grew up in New York City but now lives in California with her family (a husband and two daughters), "a houseful of Siamese cats and a dog Rover." She has contributed light verse to the *Saturday Evening Post,* the *Atlantic,* and other national magazines.

ROBINSON JEFFERS (1877-   ) has been called American poetry's apostle of negation. Jeffers' poetic line resembles Whitman's in length, vigor, and rhythm, but the philosophies of the two poets are at opposite poles. Jeffers' creed is the renunciation of humanity and the glorification of unspoiled nature.

JAMES WELDON JOHNSON (1871-1938), Negro lawyer, diplomat, and writer, served as United States Consul in Venezuela and Nicaragua and as professor of creative literature at Fisk University. He wrote light opera, novels, autobiography, spirituals, and other poetry reflecting the religious life of the Negro.

JOHN KEATS (1795-1821), English poet of the Romantic movement, produced a remarkable number of richly sensuous, melodic verses before he died of tuberculosis at the age of twenty-six.

RUDYARD KIPLING (1865-1936) wrote poems with swinging rhythms and vigorous themes that won him great popular favor. For his poetry, stories, and novels, most of them about life in India under British rule, he was awarded the Nobel Prize in 1907.

WALTER SAVAGE LANDOR (1775-1864), English classical scholar and poet, is best known for his *Imaginary Conversations,* in which historical figures discuss classical, medieval, and modern themes. His carefully chiseled short poems are often modeled after Greek and Latin originals.

PHYLLIS MC GINLEY (1905-   ), a suburban housewife, is a writer of light verse. She has published several volumes and contributed widely to national magazines.

ARCHIBALD MAC LEISH (1892-   ), an important public figure as well as a literary man, has been Librarian of Congress and an Undersecretary of State. In 1949, he was awarded the Boylston Professorship of Oratory and Rhetoric at Harvard University.

JOHN MASEFIELD (1878-   ), poet laureate of England since 1930, achieved fame with long, realistic narrative poems—*The Everlasting Mercy, Dauber, Reynard the Fox*—but he is probably better known today for his short poems of the sea. He has been a prolific writer of poetry, prose, and drama.

GEORGE MEREDITH (1828-1909), Victorian novelist and poet, tried his hand at various aspects of the publishing business and finally settled down as a publisher's reader—a job he held for thirty-five years. His novels (*The Ordeal of Richard Feverel, Diana of the Crossways,* and others) are brilliantly witty and reveal a keen perception of human motivations. Meredith's best-known group of poems is the pseudo-sonnet sequence *Modern Love.*

EDNA ST. VINCENT MILLAY (1892-1950), Pulitzer Prize winner for poetry in 1922, was born in Rockland, Maine; attended school at Vassar; and after a varied career as journalist, actress, dramatist, and libretto writer, devoted the remainder of her life to writing poetry. Her verse is distinguished by its passionate zest for life, its revolt against Victorian prudery, and its intense emotions. *Renascence and Other Poems,* published in 1917,

established her reputation among the brilliant young poets of her generation.

JOHN MILTON (1608-1674), one of the greatest poets of the late Renaissance, was educated at Christ's College, Cambridge. He served as Latin Secretary to the Council of State under Oliver Cromwell, during which time he became blind. The Restoration of Charles II brought both political and financial reverses to Milton, who was an ardent Puritan and a champion of political freedom. Though he is best known as the author of the epic, *Paradise Lost,* he was also an important sonnet writer.

MARIANNE MOORE (1887-   ) is noted for the effective imagery and keen wit of her poems. Her first book of verse, *Poems,* 1921, was published by her friends without her assistance. Since then she has published several collections of poetry and recently a highly praised translation of La Fontaine's *Fables.*

OGDEN NASH (1902-   ), master of light verse, uses an irregular rhythm and an intriguingly clever rime in his poetic commentaries on the modern scene.

ALFRED NOYES (1880-   ), English critic, novelist, and poet, has produced a large amount of readable rhythmic verse. Perhaps his most ambitious works are the epic, *Drake,* 1908, and *Tales of the Mermaid Tavern,* 1913.

WILFRED OWEN (1893-1918), British poet of World War I, returned to the Western Front after having been wounded and invalided home, was decorated for gallantry, and was killed in action one week before the Armistice.

JOHN CROWE RANSOM (1888-   ), a native Tennesseean, was educated at Vanderbilt and Oxford. He is now Carnegie Professor of Poetry at Kenyon College. As editor of the *Kenyon Review,* he is one of the leading contemporary literary critics in America. Among his books are *Chills and Fever,* 1924, *Two Gentlemen in Bonds,* 1927, and *Selected Poems of John Crowe Ransom,* 1945.

EDWIN ARLINGTON ROBINSON (1869-1935), three-time Pulitzer Prize winner, is in the first rank of American poets. He wrote character studies in verse, revealing the inner triumphs and outward failures of man.

CARL SANDBURG (1878-   ), poet, Lincoln biographer, and authority on American folk songs, worked as a barber, a dish washer, and a harvest hand, among other jobs, before his thoughts turned to literature during his college days. This background equipped him well to write about the vitality and variety of American life. In line, language, and subject matter he extends the Whitman tradition.

WILLIAM SHAKESPEARE (1564-1616), England's, and perhaps the world's, greatest dramatic poet, produced some thirty plays, many of which contain memorable short songs. Apart from his plays, his chief work was a sonnet sequence.

KARL SHAPIRO (1913-   ) published two books of poetry while stationed in the Pacific during World War II (*Person, Place and Thing* and *V-Letter and Other Poems*). Like many other contemporary poets, Shapiro is a teacher.

PERCY BYSSHE SHELLEY (1792-1822), English Romantic poet, was an idealist who revolted against tyranny in all forms—political, social, and moral—and who led an unconventional life in accordance with his ideals. His major theme is the possibility of human perfection.

SIR PHILIP SIDNEY (1554-1586), who more than any other Elizabethan represents the ideal Renaissance man, was a courtier, diplomat, soldier, novelist, critic, and poet. His sonnet sequence *Astrophel and Stella* was his chief poetic work.

STEPHEN SPENDER (1909-   ) was a fellow student of Auden at Oxford and was much influenced by him. Like Auden he has been chiefly concerned in his writing with social and political problems.

ALFRED, LORD TENNYSON (1809-1892) is, in many ways, the poet who best represents the spirit of Victoria's England. After an early period of neglect and adverse criticism, he perfected his poetic craftsmanship and won public favor, which he held to his death. He became poet laureate in 1850.

DYLAN THOMAS (1914-1953), considered by many the greatest lyric poet of the younger generation, was born in the Welsh seaport of Swansea. He was early steeped in Welsh lore and poetry and in the Bible, all of which left their mark on his rich, startling imagery and driving rhythm. He made his living by radio broadcasting, scenario writing, storytelling, and readings of his poetry. His first book, *Eighteen Poems,* was published when he was twenty. His *Collected Poems, 1934-1952* contains, in the poet's own words, "all, up to the present year, that I wish to preserve."

FRANCIS THOMPSON (1859-1907), an English poet whose life was marked by failure and spiritual conflict, wrote one of the greatest religious poems of modern times, "The Hound of Heaven."

EDMUND WALLER (1606-1687), English Royalist poet, is best known for his witty love lyrics. A contemporary of Dryden, he helped to perfect the closed couplet verse form.

WALT WHITMAN (1819-1892) created the free verse form. His *Leaves of Grass,* published in 1855, was a revolutionary book. In it Whitman spoke as the prophet of democracy and a worshiper of the common man. His technique has influenced two generations of later poets, including Sandburg, MacLeish, and Jeffers.

WILLIAM WORDSWORTH (1770-1850), English Romantic poet, found most of his subjects in nature and the life of simple people. He had the genius to see and record the beauty and wonder of the familiar.

ELINOR WYLIE (1885-1928), whose poems are always controlled, exact, and brilliant, was in her personal life a rebel against social convention. Her peak of popularity came in the early 1920's when, as the wife of William Rose Benét, she took an active part in the literary life of New York City.

WILLIAM BUTLER YEATS (1865-1939), foremost figure of the Irish Renaissance and one of the great poets of our century, was also an editor, folklorist, and playwright, and took an active interest in politics. His best poetry is sinewy, conversational, and musical.

part three

Speaking and Listening

HENRY PHILIP CONSTANS *Fundamentals of Speech*

The Importance of Speaking Well

Early man communicated through speech, however rudimentary, long before he had worked out a set of symbols with which he could write or read. Modern man relies entirely on oral communication for his first five or six years, and throughout the remainder of his life transacts most of his affairs—in his home and in society and business—by means of speech. Indeed, that part of the world's work which relies upon communication is carried on largely by people speaking to one another or to groups. Learning to speak clearly and effectively is a prime consideration for anyone who wishes to meet fully his social responsibilities.

Speaking is closely linked with thinking. We frequently hear someone say, "I am just thinking out loud." What does he mean? Putting it in simplest terms, he means he is speaking. Let us then ask, What would he be doing if he were thinking *not* out loud? The answer is he would be speaking to himself, that is, he would be using word symbols, though not audibly expressed. In either case he is speaking, using words which are symbols of ideas. When we think, most of us do so in terms of words. While it is said to be possible to think without resorting to language, few people claim to have achieved so abstract a degree of thinking.

This close relationship between speaking and thinking leads us to some important con-

siderations. If we are not to be misunderstood, it is important that we say what we mean and mean what we say. To put it another way, straight thinking is expressed in accurate speaking. When a student impulsively says, "There are eight traffic lights between the campus and Main Street and all of them are unnecessary," he is probably exaggerating. But more important than that, he is probably neither saying what he means nor meaning what he says. If he actually means what he says, he must be able to support his statements with evidence; he must be not merely giving unrestrained expression to his emotions because he has been delayed—apparently unnecessarily—by a traffic light.

Speaking is likely to lead to clearer thinking because the ideas expressed are subject to examination by the listeners. When we know that others are going to pass judgment on what we say, we are more likely to examine our reasoning and test its soundness. Moreover, we know that the listener will not only evaluate our ideas but will also judge us as a person. Most of us prefer to have that judgment reflect credit upon us.

Often in reply to a question we may hear a fellow student say, "I know what it is but I can't say it." To what extent is this correct? Does not the student deceive himself or his hearers? If he knows the answer, he knows it in terms of words; if he cannot express it in words, he does not know it. He may lack the words to express it accurately, adequately, clearly, or completely; *but what he knows he can say*. The broader one's command of language, the better his thinking; the better one's thinking, the better his speaking; conversely, the better one's speaking, the better his thinking.

Of all classroom activities, speaking produces the greatest degree of interaction. The speaker reacts to his fellow students; they react to him. When a student writes a composition, too often it is directed to one person, the instructor. The instructor reads the composition and returns it to the writer with comments, suggestions, and a grade. Rarely will the instructor read the paper aloud to the class; even less frequently will the writer be asked to read aloud his own paper to the class. That is, his written ideas, feelings, and reasoning are seldom subjected to public examination. How different when the student speaks! The group looks at him, listens to him, evaluates what he says and does, and judges him for what he is or appears to be. This is true whether the speaker is explaining the solution of a problem in algebra, giving a demonstration of a chemical reaction, answering a question in history, or making a talk before a class in forestry, music, or education.

Every speaker is judged by the audience even before he begins to speak. As he sits in the classroom, at the front of the class, or on a platform, he is the object of attention. His observers decide whether they like his appearance, the clothes he wears, the way he deports himself—all this before he has spoken a word. Men in the public eye know this and endeavor to capitalize upon it. Consider, for instance, the personality expressed in the mere appearance of Winston Churchill. But every speaker, professional or amateur, knows that as soon as he begins speaking, the previous judgment of the audience may be shifted; it may swing from positive to neutral to negative, or vice versa. The speaker may begin his talk with these words: "I know most of you are ignorant of conditions in Hawaii, so I am going to enlighten you." Or he may start as follows: "I believe you are familiar with this passage from Shakespeare's *Hamlet*." Another speaker's opening words may be: "I am going to talk about hunting." When you hear any of these introductory statements, your response to the speaker is immediate. You say to yourself, "I like him; he's all right." Or, "He's got the big head; he's a blowhard; look at the conceited fool." Or, "Here we go again with the same old stuff." Every speaker is judged by every member of his audience on the basis of what he looks like, what he does, and what he says. Since this is true, it is important for the speaker to be judged at his best.

The quality of one's speech is considered a measure of one's education. An educated person is expected to be able to present his ideas in a logical, grammatical, and effective manner. As a college-trained man, you may be invited to speak to the high school assembly, the community club, the women's club, the church or Sunday school, or some other group. You will be expected to do a creditable job of speaking; in fact, your degree of educational attainment may be judged in no small part by how you "measure up."

Whatever profession or occupation you plan to enter, you should realize that, almost of necessity, you will probably be called upon to do a considerable amount of speaking. If you expect to be a lawyer, preacher, teacher, salesman, county demonstration agent, athletic coach, recreation director, or candidate for political office, you will no doubt concede the necessity for your being able to speak effectively in public. In brief, speaking is a part of the "stock in trade" of people in those professions or occupations. You may, however, say that you are going to be an engineer or a doctor and will not need to be an effective public speaker. But as an engineer you will almost certainly find that you will be presenting plans, drawings, sketches, or specifications to a board of public works, a city commission, county trustees, or the manager of a plant. And approval of those plans is dependent, to a considerable extent, on your ability to make an effective oral presentation. The engineer's success, then, may actually be dependent upon his speaking ability. Likewise, a brief examination of the storm of controversy occasioned by proposals for socialized or state medical service suggests that the members of the medical profession need to be effective spokesmen. Indeed, it is almost impossible to choose a career of any kind today in which effective speaking is not an invaluable asset.

Furthermore, and regardless of your occupational plans for the future, as a citizen in a democracy it is important for you to be able to speak well. It is a truism to say that if our representative form of government is to function effectively, the citizenry must be enlightened. And this does not mean merely that the individual will himself be informed on the crucial issues. The citizen owes an obligation to society to see that others are informed, and the greater his ability, the greater his obligation. He shirks his responsibility when he remains silent. The passive citizen may say, "I'll let someone else speak for me." But someone else may not say what the passive citizen would say (if he were not passive), what he wants said, what should be said. Good citizenship demands that each one speak for himself.

In times of stress, when the decision to be made, the action to be taken, the course to be pursued vitally affect the group, the spoken word is resorted to. Mediation between management and employees, annual meetings of boards of directors, sales meetings, all call for conferences—face-to-face speaking.

It will be remembered how John Paul Jones aroused the fighting spirit of a nation with his words "I have not yet begun to fight"; how Colonel C. E. Stanton, during a speech at Lafayette's grave in 1917, symbolized the spirit of the Allies when he said, "Lafayette, we are here." No one can accurately measure the impact of Winston Churchill when with the phrase "blood, toil, tears, and sweat" he rallied a nation. No one knows how many fearful spirits were calmed and reassured by Franklin D. Roosevelt's saying, "The only thing we have to fear is fear itself." Churchill and Roosevelt could have resorted to the press and had their words printed; instead, they *spoke* to millions. The printed symbol seldom has the power of the spoken word.

Some Criteria of Good Speaking

A speaker should always be impelled by a desire to communicate. But communication is always a two-way process—there must be a listener who responds. This brings us to the point that every talk can and must be tested in terms of audience response. A speaker must decide early in his preparation what response he hopes to secure. The first criterion of good speaking, then, is that every speech must have a definite purpose. Here are some of the major purposes for speaking:

To inform. The informative speech presents a body of fact, explains a process, or describes an event or scene. The test of the effectiveness of this type of speech is whether the material can easily be understood by every listener.

To entertain. The after-dinner talk, the telling of a story, the relating of an amusing incident have as their primary purpose the entertainment of the audience. The test of their effectiveness is whether the audience listens with delight and enjoyment.

To stimulate. The sermon, the community "booster" speech, the college "pep talk," and the talk at a political rally are types of speeches whose main purpose is to stimulate. The test of their effectiveness is whether the listeners feel inspired, whether they experience an emotional lift.

To convince. The businessman in conference, the lawyer pleading a case, and the speaker addressing a legislative assembly are chiefly interested in convincing their listeners. The test of their effectiveness is whether the hearers agree with what the speaker has said, whether they accept the argument he has presented.

To actuate. Talks designed to sell, to raise funds, or to secure votes are intended to stir up action. The test of their effectiveness is whether the audience takes the definite action, frequently physical, advocated by the speaker.

These purposes are not mutually exclusive; they may and do overlap. It may be desirable to entertain, inform, and convince before you can get your hearers to take the step which is the real goal, the purpose of your talk. The important thing to remember is that if your speaking is to be effective, you must have a definite purpose expressed in terms of audience reaction. Without a purpose, you are almost certain to fail; with it, you have satisfied one of the criteria of effective speaking.

Many years ago the famous orator Wendell Phillips was described as a "gentleman conversing." In his day the idea that good speaking is conversation at its best was revolutionary. Now it is generally accepted and is commonly called the conversational mode of speaking. Conversation at its best carries with it certain implications of which, upon reflection, we are all aware. What are the marks of good conversation? Many might be cited, but three should be borne in mind by a student learning to speak in public. They are *directness, genuineness,* and *liveliness.*

When conversation is direct, we feel the speaker is personally concerned with us and with our reaction. This is true even though others may be present. He probably looks at us, inclines his head in our direction, possibly emphasizes a point with a gesture. No barrier, real or imaginary, is between us.

The second characteristic of conversation at its best is genuineness. The participants are being themselves. The false front and the artificial social manner crumble in real conversation. We feel that the man is speaking not for effect, to show off, or to impress others. Rather, he is the real man speaking sincerely.

Conversation at its best is also lively. It moves along with an undercurrent of eagerness to participate. It may take on the aspects of a game of tennis when a volley is in progress: the conversational ball goes back and forth from one to the other with a rapidity of exchange that may make it difficult to follow. But liveliness should not be confused with speed of utterance; many times it is not the rate of speaking but rather the inherent interest the conversationalist shows that makes for liveliness. This interest frequently reveals itself in the bodily set and the radiant glow of enjoyment that suffuses the speaker.

Conversation at its best is not limited by the number of participants. The size of the group should not change the conversational aspect of the speaking situation. True, the person speaking before a large audience may speak louder, may speak from a platform, may use more care in diction, may be clothed in academic regalia; but if he is to be very effective, he must exemplify the gentleman conversing—he must be direct, genuine, and lively.

All of us have heard, or been subjected to, speakers who, forgetting the qualities of effective conversation, fail because they think speaking before an audience calls for a certain manner of delivery different from that of good conversation. Three of these types may be designated as *Miss Pedantic, Senator Stump,* and *Dr. Dry Dust.*

Miss Pedantic talks to her class of high school students with the patronizing air of superiority, the overpreciseness which she confuses with correctness, or the stiffness of the person who feels she must guard her dignity. Having once mounted the pedagogical pedestal, she dares not communicate as a genuine human being. Fortunately, her kind is becoming scarce.

Senator Stump, seizing every occasion to speak, launches forth in stentorian tones accompanied with a vocal vibrato that would be the envy of a coloratura soprano. "To you good pee-pul of Mon-u-ah-men-tah County, my fel-low cit-i-zens of this guh-rate and guh-lory-us state, I want to state that I ah-pear before you as a guh-rate-ful ser-vunt of the pee-pul," he begins—and continues. He lacks genuineness and directness. He talks *at,* not *with,* his hearers. Fortunately the number of his kind is decreasing, too.

Dr. Dry Dust appears before his audience or his university class armed with a series of lecture cards or copious notes and proceeds to read or speak from them with little apparent regard for his listeners. His eyes, when not fixed on his notes, search the ceiling or gaze vaguely out the window. If he is interested in what he is doing, he is careful to conceal it. In a desire to be objective, he frequently becomes detached; his audience ceases to impinge on his consciousness. He fails as a speaker in large part because he is indirect and dull. Unfortunately, too many of this type are still with us, even though they are also in a decreasing minority.

Perhaps because these types of speaker—Senator Stump's style has been greatly altered by modern public-address and broadcasting systems—are not so numerous as they once were, and because they represent professional and political groups, you may think that the problems of avoiding nonconversational styles of speaking do not concern you greatly. Let us leave public life and enter your classroom for a brief survey of the speaking habits of your classmates. There you may find the mumbler, who exerts no effort to make anyone hear him. His enunciation is so indistinct and his voice so low and monotonous that his hearers are under constant strain to understand his in-articulate mutterings. Or you may find the fidgeter, who takes seriously the statement that for every action there is a reaction. Consequently, he acts and reacts until his hearers are totally unaware of what he is attempting to say. They watch him as visitors at a zoo watch the antics of a caged monkey. Look further. You may discover another fellow student who blocks his own communication—the "and-uh" vocalist. Instead of making a clean pause at the end of a thought, he fills the pause with meaningless sounds, making it difficult for his hearers to get the interrelationship of his thought units.

Survey your own speaking habits and those of your classmates for these ineffective modes of speaking. You may detect other faulty mannerisms. Be alert to avoid any style or mode of speaking which interferes with clear-cut communication.

Given a purpose for speaking and a style resembling conversation at its best, the speaker still has at least two considerations to take into account. You may have said of a speaker, "I enjoyed him, but he never said a thing." Or, you may have remarked, "What he was talking about is very important, but he failed to hold the attention of his audience." Both statements describe unfortunate extremes. We should strive for the happy solution expressed in the Duke of Wellington's famous theory of style, "Have something to say, and say it."

One point is never so obvious but that it will bear repeating: Whatever the purpose of the speaker may be—to inform, to entertain, to stimulate, to convince, to actuate—the hearers should feel fully repaid for their time. The speaker should avail himself of every possible source—his own experience, the opinions of others, what has been written or said about the topic—to the end that he may be well informed and prepared for the occasion. And, being well prepared will not only make for effective speaking but will also be found a good cure for stage fright and fear of the speaking situation in general. Another criterion of good speaking is adequate coverage of a timely topic.

Appropriate level of language and proper diction (assuming clear enunciation and correct pronunciation) are as requisite for an effective speech as for any other form of verbal composition. Even as skilled an orator as Patrick Henry, invited on one occasion to speak in a remote mountain locality of Virginia, made the error of speaking to his unlettered but not unlearned hearers in their own language pattern. Knowing he did not usually talk as he did that day, they thought he was belittling them and resented his effort to meet them on their level. There is a level of language usage for the occasion just as there is an appropriate attire. The use of ornate language when simple language is more in keeping may make the speaker, though he is in dead earnest, seem merely ludicrous. In any situation, the use of abstract or general words instead of concrete or specific ones may not only reflect the speaker's laziness but also prevent the hearers from getting any explicit meaning or direct information. Couch your speech in appropriate, concrete, and simple language that says exactly what you mean. (For a more detailed treatment of the various levels of language usage see the *Harbrace Handbook,* Section 19a[5].)

Overcoming Common Hindrances to Effective Speaking

Most beginning speakers get along with little or no difficulty. Those who have hindrances often find they arise from two sources, one psychological and the other physical. The psychological ones result from fear—usually unfounded; the physical ones from the speaker's realization for the first time that certain parts of his body seem to get in the way when he attempts to make a speech. An examination of these hindrances—their source, manifestation, and cure—may be helpful.

The feeling of inadequacy, rooted in fear, or "being afraid," has several possible sources. The student has been used to reciting in class, talking before classmates, and possibly appearing before high school assemblies or civic groups in his home town. On these occasions he doubtless spoke with comparative ease and confidence; he knew many of his listeners, possibly all of them. Now he is called upon to prepare and deliver a talk before a college class. He does not know many of his audience—maybe a few, possibly none well. In his mind's eye he sees himself standing before a group of strangers where there is no friendly eye, no familiar face, to turn to. Even the room looks different, possibly somewhat forbidding. Mentally he dwells on the strange, the new, and the unfamiliar aspects of the speaking situation which is to confront him; possibly he exaggerates the circumstances until the prospect is drear indeed. If you find yourself with this mental and emotional attitude toward speaking, what can you do about it? First, the most helpful suggestion is for you to practice. Practice before your roommate or a small group of friends. Practice will build your confidence. Each time you speak before the class it will be easier than the preceding time; soon the unfamiliar situation has become familiar.

To the beginner, the thought of failure frequently looms large. He thinks that if he fails to live up to his hopes and desires, the result will be fatal. In actuality, such fears are not reasonable. Seldom does a student altogether fail as a speaker if he actually tries to do his best. But suppose he does not come up to the expectations of himself or others? The answer is that the consequences are slight. After all, nothing particularly serious is at stake; he, like others, is learning; and the classroom is the place in which to learn. He who has an opportunity to study speaking in college has a double advantage in that he will have several chances to speak and will do his speaking under the direction of an instructor who is trained as a critic. The important thing is to make the best of every speaking opportunity.

Unfortunately, many persons associate speaking with speaking from memory. They believe that it is not only desirable but necessary for the beginning speaker to write out and "learn by heart" his entire speech. Actually, he may be afraid not to commit the talk to memory; and then having memorized it he is afraid he may forget it. All of us have been present at speaking contests or commencement exercises where the contestant or graduate who has memorized the talk until he is "letter perfect" forgets. We have all held our breath during that painful pause that ensued, physically and emotionally tried to help him over the barrier of forgetfulness, and agonized if he could not recall, or sighed with relief if after the pause he continued. How can we

ensure the speaker against this type of painful experience? How can we be certain that he will not forget? The answer is a simple one. *You can't forget if you don't memorize.* Do not attempt to memorize the talk! Make an outline of the talk, put it on a small card, put the card face down on the table or lectern. Refer to the outline only in case of absolute necessity. The only thing you have to learn, or memorize, is the relatively few main points in the outline. Even if you forget these you can turn over the card, glance at the outline, and then again place the card face down. Learn to speak by doing it the easier, the better way—*don't memorize the talk.*

Occasionally, the thought occurs to the student that his listeners may be hostile and that potential cheers may turn to jeers. Actually, this almost never happens in the classroom. When it does, the fault has been not with the listeners, but with the speaker who, with an air of arrogance, conceit, or cocksureness, has turned the listeners against him. Your classmates believe in giving a man a chance, a chance to be heard; in short, in fair play. In this connection let us look a little more closely at the speaking situation in a college class. Upon examination we see that the listener cannot afford to be hostile. He may be called on to speak next; as surely as his name is on the class roll his turn to speak will come. This is another way of saying that the members of the class, or your audience, are all in the same position—they cannot afford to be hostile. But on the positive side, since we all like a winner, the chances are that they hope you will speak well, and the better you speak, the better they will like it. As a matter of fact, they will, in all likelihood, fervently hope for your success. You can approach your classroom speaking situations confident in the thought that your listeners will accord you courtesy and kindness. They, like you, are beginners desirous of learning.

It is common experience for nervous tensions to manifest themselves in physical behavior; sometimes they are so severe that the muscles become rigid and no action is possible. But this is unusual; most of us when under nervous tension are given to too much action, or action that we cannot control. The result is that we shake, mainly in the arms and legs.

What are we to do about it? The first and best suggestion is to relax. Try to relax mentally and physically before you get up to speak. If, after you start speaking, you find that your leg muscles are shaking, move around. Do not stand still. Take several steps. You will find that often you can literally "walk it off"; you can dissipate muscular tensions by moving. This does not mean that you are to pace regularly back and forth like a caged animal; however, it is better to move too much than not at all.

In most conversations, we look at our listener because we can judge in part his reaction to what we are saying by watching his facial expression. In speaking, you are equally concerned with the listeners' reaction; consequently, you watch for the audience's response. It is obvious that you cannot know what is going on in the audience if you are looking at the ceiling, the floor, or out the window. Even if nervousness impels you to avoid looking at the listeners, force yourself to do so. Fix your gaze at about their eye level; avoid looking merely at the hearers as a group or at any individual for too long a time.

You may find that the first time or two you speak you have difficulty with your breathing. You cannot get enough air, or your chest seems tight. Again it is excessive nervous tension. If you will pause before you begin to speak and, while you pause, look at your audience, you will gain considerable control over your breathing. And while you are pausing, if you will take a deep breath and slowly exhale, then another and exhale, you will start the breathing process going regularly and evenly. This will help you get "over the hump." Do not hurry; do not worry; take it easy.

The question of what the speaker should do with his hands is a pertinent one. Many a beginning speaker takes a deathlike grip on the lectern, buttons and unbuttons his coat, thrusts a hand in his coat pocket or both hands in his trouser pockets, and finally, in near desperation, puts his hands behind his back and locks them together in a viselike grip. The young woman frequently resorts to fumbling needlessly with her handkerchief, toying with a necklace, or assuming the clasped-hands-at-waist position usually characteristic of women singers.

What should the speaker do with his hands? Do nothing! Leave them alone and they will take care of themselves. The natural position for the hands is at the sides; they look well there; they are readily available for use. If, perchance, you may be impelled to make some gesture, the hands will be ready. Remember, for as many years as you are old your hands have been a part of you and have never been a problem. Do not let them become one now. If you let your hands hang easily at your sides, you will find that gaining control over this part of the body will help relieve the excessive nervous tension of the entire body.

The preceding paragraphs have discussed some means of controlling excessive nervous tension. In this connection, let us remember that it is natural to have some nervous tension before and during a talk. Effective, experienced speakers feel it. But we must conceal and control this natural nervousness. If we let it control us, it becomes an enemy that defeats us. If we control it, it becomes an ally that aids us. For we should be under just enough nervous tension to have a feeling of anticipation, of buoyancy, of alertness.

Finally, one of the best ways to overcome excessive nervous tension is to have a definite purpose, an appropriate topic, a satisfactory outline, and effective illustrative materials. Nothing will defeat you as quickly as lack of preparation; nothing will give you the same degree of calm assurance as thorough preparation. Resolve to give yourself that added confidence that comes only from having something to say.

Selecting and Organizing Materials for a Speech

Neither as a student who is learning to speak nor as a college graduate who is invited to address some group should you permit the problem "What shall I speak about?" to become bothersome. Always, regardless of the speaking situation that may confront you, choose a subject—or some phase of an assigned subject—that interests you and about which you have some knowledge. Then decide what your purpose is to be in terms of the response you seek to obtain from your audience.

Once a subject in which you are genuinely interested is selected, consider the sources of material available. Turn first to yourself and explore your own resources. What do you know about this subject, especially as a result of firsthand experience or observation? Let us assume that you have decided to talk on the general subject "Causes of Automobile Accidents." You are genuinely interested in this general subject; you know something about it; and you believe you can gather sufficient material on the topic for an effective talk. You realize, of course, that the subject is too general, too broad, too extensive to be covered in a brief talk, perhaps even in a long one. But, even before you attempt to narrow the subject, you might well explore the general sources of material that are available.

Begin, then, with an examination of your own knowledge of the subject. What do you yourself know about it? Presumably you may know that automobile accidents are increasing in the nation, you may remember seeing some predictions about the number of automobile accidents that would occur over the Labor Day week end, you may recall that the predictions proved reasonably accurate. But all of this is general and rather vague. What firsthand experience or observation do you have to present? More than likely you have witnessed an accident, or come upon the scene soon after an accident has occurred. Possibly you have been the unfortunate victim of an accident. You got out to inspect the damage done, you sensed the acrid odor of the friction-burned tires, you looked at the skid tracks. You decided this accident occurred because the driver of the other car was going too fast, had waited too long before applying his brakes, was operating a mechanically defective car, or had ignored the caution sign. Possibly the fault lay with you. At any rate, right now you have some impressions, some recollections of automobile accidents; in short, you have some firsthand knowledge of the general subject "Causes of Automobile Accidents."

Feeling the need to supplement your knowledge, you may write letters to persons who are informed on the subject—for instance, the director of your state highway patrol, the traffic officer of some city, or the chairman of the highway safety commission—for facts and figures on the number and causes of automobile accidents and for other available pertinent material. On the national level your Congressman will be glad to answer your letter seeking information, or he will refer it to the appropriate government agency, which will send you the material you want. The American Automobile Association and the National Highway Safety Conference will be glad to supply available information. A little thinking on your part and a few intelligent inquiries will reveal the names of additional persons or agencies to whom a letter seeking specific information may be written. In your letter remember to request *specific* information.

In most instances the college student has an unusual opportunity to secure information from members of the faculty who can qualify, at least to some extent, as experts. Though not necessarily exhaustively informed on that aspect of the subject about which the student is seeking additional information, some faculty member probably has a grasp of the underlying principles involved. In the case of "Causes of Automobile Accidents" an interview with a psychologist, a sociologist, or an engineer is likely to be rewarding. A member of the law faculty may be able to supply graphic data from his legal experience. There are other sources in your community. Talk to the chief of police or the officer in charge of the traffic department, call on the judge in whose court traffic violations are tried, pay a visit to the city or county attorney. These people can be a great help to you as sources of material for your talk.

Although many radio and television programs do not add to the listener's knowledge, except in a most incidental and indirect way, nevertheless, every radio or television station has some programs that can be a source of material for a talk. This is particularly true of forums, interviews, round tables, and educational farm or home programs. For many years five-minute talks on highway safety, interviews with state highway patrol officers, and fifteen-minute shows dramatizing highway accidents have been broadcast by radio stations in many states. Not infrequently the talk by a government official or even the speech of a political campaigner may supply you with material for a talk. For example, a candidate for the governorship who has a better-highway plank in his platform will present a plan for the reduction of accidents in partial support of this particular plank. An examination of the radio and television schedule printed in the local newspaper will apprise you of the opportunities for using radio and television as a source of material for talks.

You may well wonder why books, magazines, and newspapers—the most obvious source of material for a talk—were not mentioned first. This is the only reason: it is almost axiomatic that in searching for such material you would immediately think of going to the library,[1] looking in the *Readers' Guide to Periodical Literature* under the heading of "Highways" or "Accidents," finding in the designated magazine an article on highway accidents, reading it, jotting down some notes or possibly a quotation or so—and then return to your room satisfied that you had the necessary material for a talk. Because you would think of such printed matter first, you might also think of it as the only source, overlooking the other sources that not infrequently will be of greater aid to you. Newspapers, magazines, and books are always available to the student who has the initiative to go to the library and do some reading. He should use this source of material. But there is a danger: he may read *one* article in some magazine and give an oral carbon copy of it before a class, many of the members of which have probably read the same article. If the sole source of material for your talk is a magazine article, then for the sake of individuality, at least tell your listeners the source of your talk and then give them your reaction to the article.

Most audiences are not particularly interested in what you have read, how well you have memorized it, or how much of it you can recall; but they are interested in your opinion of what you have read—what *you* think of it. Does the article give an unbiased presentation, is it fair, is it comprehensive, is it logical, is it reasonable, is it supported by the facts? Only by your answers to questions like these do you justify your use of a printed article as a sole source of material for a talk. Your talk should spring from, and not consist of, the content of the article. The question you should ask yourself is, "What do *I* have to contribute to this topic?"

After you have selected a topic that interests you and have obtained from the many sources the material for your talk, after you have decided what your purpose is to be—to inform, entertain, stimulate, convince, or actuate—the next problem is to organize the material. Good talks, like good written papers, must have order. They must have a framework which supports them, just as the skeleton supports the human body. In most talks the material can be organized in outline form, which aids the speaker in presenting his material and his audience in following his thought. The most common outline forms are the complete-sentence outline and the topical outline. The first of these serves best in the preparation of a talk; the second is to be preferred for use in presenting a talk. Material to be outlined may take one of several orders of arrangement, among which the most common are the chronological, the spatial, the selective, and the logical.[2]

Having secured the material, determined your purpose, decided on the order of organization for your talk, and made an outline, you still have to decide how to begin and close your speech. Consider first the introduction. Stated in its simplest form, the chief aim of an introduction is to secure the attention of the audience, to arouse an interest in the subject, and to show the relevancy of the subject to the occasion. In beginning a speech, avoid such trite expressions as "I am going to talk today about . . ."; "My subject is . . ."; "The topic selected by me is . . ."; or "I'm reminded of a story." Do not start any speech on the dead level of mediocrity. Remember that your speech should strike fire at the first stroke of the verbal flint.

Let us look at some examples of speeches well begun, introductions that meet the criteria set forth. A British-born student attending an American university, endeavoring to show the necessity of American aid to war-torn Europe, began by saying, "We here tonight are living in an uncongested city of 25,000

---

[1] See *Harbrace Handbook,* Section 33b, for specific information on the use of the library.

[2] For information on outlining and on orders of arrangement, see *Harbrace Handbook,* Sections 32b-32f and 31b(1), respectively.

population, spread over approximately sixteen square miles. Two hundred miles to our south is a city of 300,000, with which most of you are familiar. Visualize an area as large as this small city completely destroyed in the very heart of that larger city and you will understand the condition of my home city in England following World War II. Imagine the helplessness and hopelessness of the people in a city of 300,000 inhabitants with its business or industrial center blotted out." By thus referring to familiar physical surroundings, the speaker made his introduction graphic and prepared the way for the acceptance, even support, of his argument for American aid as a means of preventing desperate peoples from falling a prey to perilous "isms." Another student speaker, whose purpose was to convince his hearers that they should learn to play golf, began: "I am here to tell you why every one of you should learn to play golf. 'Golf,' you say; 'what are you talking about? Why, that's an old man's game!' Now, that's where you fall into error. It's not an old man's game and I want to prove it to you." Here's still another good introduction. The speaker used a startling statement: "Even while I am speaking to you tonight fifty people will die of cancer. That's right, cancer will claim fifty lives in the next five minutes." Or, to go outside the classroom, let us examine the introductory statement of a radio address by Fred A. Hartley, Jr., who at the time was Congressman from New Jersey. The purpose of the address was to show that every individual, even if he pays no income or real-estate tax, is a taxpayer. He began by saying, "This talk concerns your pocketbook." With this commonplace but personal introductory reference the speaker captured his hearers' interest at once and continued to make lively and challenging a topic often tedious with details and laden with dull statistics.

When you prepare the introduction to your talk see that it meets the criteria of a good beginning.

Now let us see what the conclusion of a speech should accomplish. Again, stated in the simplest terms, the purpose of the conclusion is to round off the talk, summarize the material, appeal for action on the part of the audience, challenge the audience. In closing a speech, avoid such hackneyed statements as

"I see my time is up, so I'll quit"; "If I had time I could say much more"; "Last but not least"; or "I guess that's all I have to say." Like the distance runner who paces himself so as to have a surge of speed to carry him to the finish line, build your speech so that it closes strong.

Let us consider briefly some good conclusions of speeches. Patrick Henry closed his famous speech with this challenging statement, "I know not what course others may take, but as for me, give me liberty, or give me death." In a less dramatic situation but with a sincerity of sentiment, Robert Ingersoll closed the eulogy he delivered at his brother's funeral with this summary sentence: "There was, there is, no gentler, stronger, manlier man." A person need not be an orator of national renown to bring his talk to an effective conclusion. Here are some good examples from student speeches. A sophomore closed his talk on a phase of education with this statement, which combined a summary with an appeal for action: "If you believe the schools of this state need better facilities, if you agree that the state has the money to provide them, then you will support this minimum school program." A talk on a proposal to change a specific provision of the student government constitution was concluded with these words: "We have examined the causes of failure in our present constitution, we have weighed the advantages and the disadvantages of the proposed change, we have found that there is much to gain and nothing to lose. Let's vote for the amendment." Plan to bring your talks to a strong conclusion. Remember: let the last impression you make upon your audience be a favorable and enduring one.

Making the Body Aid in Speaking

Let us visit a class in any college or university and observe the students while a discussion is in progress. Let us watch some students who are engrossed in the discussion, each eager to have his say: their animation is obvious. The play of facial expression, the sparkle in the eyes, the movements of the head and the body, the gestures of the hands—all illuminate, illustrate, emphasize, and punctuate what is being said. Each student speaks with his entire body, and that fact largely accounts for his effectiveness.

Now let us ask one of them to stand, come to the front of the room, and enlarge on what he has been saying. All too often the student seems to undergo a metamorphosis. His body becomes stiff, his face masklike, his hands seem glued to the edges of the desk. For some unexplainable reason, now that he is standing before the class (as he puts it, "making a speech"), he seems to feel that his body has suddenly become a hindrance. His physical frame, the muscles he used to advantage when participating in the class discussion, now loom as a barrier between him and his attempt to communicate effectively. This should not and need not be.

The use of the body while speaking is normal, as is shown in the behavior of children. Observe any group of normally uninhibited children from six to twelve years of age when they are on the playground or the athletic field or in a class meeting. Watch them speak; literally, *watch* them *speak*. What do they do? They twist about, wave their arms, jump to their feet, smile, frown, grimace, scowl, pout—in short, run the gamut of bodily activity and facial expression. And you say to yourself, "That is good; it is effective." And it *is* effective: effective because it is free from artificiality or affectation; effective because it is genuine and normal; effective because it aids in conveying meaning. Such was the now-petrified speaker when he was just a few years younger.

Society, through its customs and traditional modes of behavior, tends to exert pressure on the individual and force him to the common level of the group. He naturally shrinks from scorn, cringes under ridicule, wilts at public laughter, does not dare to be different; in short, he tries to conform to the group and be as inconspicuous as possible. This desire for anonymity leads him to suppress his natural tendency to use bodily action when speaking. Yet when he is so aroused that he is eager to justify his point of view, or enthusiastic over the material he is presenting, or angry in defending himself under questioning, he uses his body in his speaking. He becomes, once again, a normal speaker. If you have come under the curb of convention, so to speak, then become yourself once again and speak as you once spoke, using your body to help you speak.

There is another reason why the beginning speaker should use bodily action. Most speaking, and certainly the best speaking, has a foundation in feeling. To be effective a speaker must feel that what he is saying is worth saying well, is worth listening to, is a matter of importance. Recognizing as his first goal the necessity of securing and holding the attention of his audience, he should bring to the occasion some feeling—enthusiasm or sympathy or indignation or whatever is appropriate. Genuine feeling should permeate his very being, physical, mental, emotional. That is, the speaker should summon to his aid all his resources; he should seek to acquire the habit of speaking with his whole body.

If you have ever seen a moving picture showing Franklin D. Roosevelt speaking, you must have detected in the set of his body, in the expression of his face, and in the tone of his voice an undercurrent of feeling that permeated the man. Every fiber of the man's being was in his utterance; he was tremendously effective. Every talk you make should have a similar foundation—a foundation built on genuine feeling. A spirit of enthusiasm should be evident in all talks: you should sound enthusiastic, look enthusiastic, feel enthusiastic.

The speaker who refuses to let his body aid him in expressing his feeling soon finds that he has suppressed the feeling. Rather than an indignation that is evident throughout his whole being, what he shows, if he stands physically inert, with muscles lax and face immobile, is mere mild disapproval or complete indifference. The speaker's action, or lack of it, may weaken, warp, or even contradict his words. Give physical vent to your feelings, not in a wild, unrestrained fashion but in the manner of a sensible, cultured person.

Sometimes, when you seem to be tense, you will find that this tension expresses itself in your emotions, causing a feeling of uneasiness to come over you. The more tense you become physically, the tighter you become emotionally, and vice versa. The best way to free yourself from the effects of this circular response pattern is through the use of bodily action. Even before you get up to speak, move your fingers and your hands, wiggle your toes, start working off the excessive bodily tensions. When it is time for you to speak, move briskly to the appropriate place, swinging the arms freely as you walk. Before you actually start speaking, it may even be advisable to busy your hands for a few moments arranging your notes. Release the bodily tensions by physical action. Do not remain a slave to these tensions; free yourself.

It is a commonplace that action should aid in conveying the meaning of the speaker. Suppose you are describing a rectangular object whose dimensions are twelve by eighteen inches. A descriptive bit of hand action shows the shape and the approximate dimensions. When you state that an object is about five feet high, at the same time indicate the height. In telling a story, simulate the action of an individual, and show increased tension or excitement, at least in part, by the tension or physical set of your body. You may say at a certain point in the narrative that one of the characters was wringing his hands. Do so with your own hands. In argumentative speaking you may wish to drive home a good point; drive it home with action that serves to emphasize the idea. In practically all speaking situations bodily action can aid in conveying the meaning. And the test to apply to any and all bodily action is this: Does it aid in conveying your meaning?

One of the best ways to indicate a transition in thought is to change your position. Do not be content with a slight shuffle to one side; actually walk, taking several steps. Action helps not only to secure but also to direct the attention of your listeners.

Sometimes beginners have the notion that the way to improve their use of action is to apply mechanical exercises. Nothing could be further from the truth. Prearranged bodily activity—such as planning at certain points in a talk to move one or two steps to the right or left; to raise the right hand or thrust out the forefinger of the left hand; to look upward, out the window, or at the floor—is mechanical and meaningless. Such gestures are artificial; they do not spring from a genuine desire to communicate; they may actually become amusing to the audience.

Animation, one of the requisites of good action, simply means showing signs of life. The speaker who employs good action has taken the first step in making a lively presentation. The sparkle of his eye, the way in which he walks, the alertness of his entire body—all say to the observer that this man is alive. Today we are all familiar with animated cartoons. An outstanding characteristic of these is action, movement; whatever else they may lack they do not want for animation. In speaking, it is better to err on the side of too much than of too little action and animation. Your instructor can easily apply what little restraint may be needed if your enthusiasm carries you beyond the bounds of good action, that is, if your bodily movements tend to draw attention from what you are saying to what you are doing. But you yourself should constantly remember that, as a speaker, you must be alert physically as well as mentally.

A Final Note of Challenge

You have finished a brief study of the principles underlying good speaking and some suggestions for making those principles effective in practice. To apply them is important. But the application of the principles may not make you a good speaker. A good speaker is, first of all, one who, when he calls upon himself, finds somebody at home. Or, to paraphrase Emerson, one should strive to be not merely a good speaker but a good man speaking effectively. In the final analysis, your speaking will be a reflection of your character.

This is a day of high specialization. Standards are prescribed for those engaged in every occupation or profession—barbers, plumbers, lawyers, doctors, teachers, engineers. One of the earliest professional codes originated about 2,500 years ago when Hippocrates, a famous physician of ancient Greece, gave the medical profession an admirable code of ethics. To this date the Hippocratic oath, administered to those about to enter upon the practice of medicine, may be found in doctors' offices throughout the world. Citizens of a democracy, where public speaking plays so large a part in molding public opinion, would no doubt profit greatly by some improved standards for speakers. To this end, Professor Brigance suggests that each person who wishes to make public addresses, after having passed a prescribed test, be certified to speak in public only after he has taken a required Hippocratic oath for speakers, pledging that he will never speak in public unless he has prepared himself with something worth saying and has put it in a form that can be comprehended; that whenever he appears before an audience he will think of its welfare and not of his own pride; that he will not mumble or fidget or otherwise evade or shirk his duty; and that he will present his ideas with such sincerity, earnestness, and consideration for the audience that none can fail to hear or comprehend.[3]

This is indeed a high ideal. You have begun its attainment. Your continued effort can help bring this ideal to full fruition in your experience as a speaker.

Postscript: Reading Aloud

In ancient and medieval times, when nearly everyone was illiterate, most instruction was given orally by the clergy, the scholar, or the minstrel. With the advent of printing, there was an immediate increase in literacy; and being able to read became, after a time, synonymous with being able to read silently. Today most reading is silent and private: students studying in their room; members of the family seated in the living room, each absorbed in his newspaper, magazine, or book; commuters riding on train or bus with their faces hidden by newspapers. Since schools have emphasized for the past several years the necessity of improving the speed and the comprehension of silent reading, little oral reading is done in the public schools and even less in the colleges and universities.

And yet, oral reading has an increasingly important place in social and intellectual life. Many of you belong to one or more clubs whose work is largely done by committees. It may often fall to your lot to give the report for a committee; this report is usually written and read aloud to the larger group whose understanding of it will depend upon your ability to convey clearly the ideas expressed in the report. You may be, or may become, the secretary of an organization. A good secretary takes accurate and adequate notes of the proceedings, writes them up in acceptable English, and reads them aloud to the members at the next meeting of the organization. It is also a duty of the secretary to read aloud the letters

3 For a full text of a Hippocratic oath for speakers, see William Norwood Brigance, *Speech Communication*, New York: F. S. Crofts & Co., 1947, p. 8.

and other written communcations that are sent to the organization. Some of you may be preparing for the teaching profession or the ministry, both of which require much oral reading. A few of you may become actors (professional or amateur), radio announcers, sportscasters, or news commentators—activities in which ability in oral reading is certainly of prime importance. Then there is the perennial experience of reading to children, from which the adult may derive a great deal of pleasure and satisfaction as he observes the joy of the child listener.

If you consider that at least two types of literature, drama and poetry, are written to be read aloud, you, as college students, will again be impressed with the importance of oral reading. The essence of the dramatic form is dialogue; the effect of poetry depends in no small measure on the merging of sound and sense. Only when the printed words have projected into them the sound of the reader's voice do they become alive and full of meaning. If you are to derive from literature the full degree of pleasure that is there, you must learn to read aloud with understanding and feeling. The effective oral reader blends thought, language, voice, and body into a harmonious whole.

The first step in becoming a good oral reader is to get beyond the word-recognition and word-calling stage. When a child reads "I-see-the-cat" with equal time intervals between words and a sameness of pitch, he is failing to read ideas. Similarly the college student who reads in a methodical manner "Four-score-and-seven-years-ago" is still performing on an elementary reading level. Ideas are usually expressed by word groups, not by words used singly. Even the group of words "Four score and seven years ago" expresses one idea which is part of a much larger and more important idea expressed in these words of President Lincoln: "Four score and seven years ago, our fathers brought forth on this continent a new nation, conceived in liberty, and dedicated to the proposition that all men are created equal." When read as a group, these words express a complete idea.

The second step in improving oral reading is to increase your knowledge of the meaning of words. While it is true that frequently you can guess the meaning of a word from its context, this does not necessarily follow. In the sentence "He is an expert in ballistics," if you think that *ballistics* is related to *ballet* or *ball,* you have completely missed the meaning. In the sentence "He is skilled in histrionics," if you associate *histrionics* with *history,* you have likewise failed to comprehend the meaning expressed. Again in the sentence "He is an indefatigable worker," knowing what the *indefatigable* means gives the key to the idea.

In addition to knowing the meaning of words, you must know how to pronounce them. Hesitating, stumbling, struggling over the pronunciation indicate not only lack of preparation but also the level of the reader's education. If in the last sentence in the preceding paragraph the word "indefatigable" is pronounced *in-de-fa-tīg'a-ble,* the result would probably be a supercilious smile or a look of pained embarrassment on the part of the informed listener. At times shifting the accent in a word from one syllable to another may so change the sound of the word that it becomes ludicrous or even unrecognizable; for example, *su-per-flu'ous* for *su-per'flu-ous, discip'line* for *dis'ci-pline,* om-ni-po'tence for *om-nip'o-tence.* Mispronunciations embarrass the reader and confuse or amuse the listener.

In oral reading it is important to realize that the idea conveyed depends upon the word stressed. The meaning of "I am telling you to go," for example, will vary as the stress shifts from one word to another.

I am telling you to go. (I, no one else)
I *am* telling you to go. (No doubt about it)
I am *telling* you to go. (Not writing or telegraphing)
I am telling *you* to go. (You, not the others)
I am telling you to *go.* (Don't delay, don't argue)

A similar technique in improving oral reading is to make important words or ideas stand out by pausing before we speak them. For example, in *Hamlet* the old man Polonius in the course of advising his son Laertes, who is about to go on a journey, closes with these words,

This above all: to thine own self be true,
And it must follow, as the night the day,
Thou canst not then be false to any man.

The punctuation and the sense of the selection indicate that a pause at the colon will serve to give the added emphasis needed to the ideas that are to follow. Similarly a pause after "true" gives the preceding idea a better chance to impress itself upon the hearer. At times a pause accompanied by a lowering of the pitch of the voice may serve to indicate that the material read is subordinate or incidental. In the sentence "The owner of the car, Gordon—whose first name I have forgotten, and it is unimportant anyway—reported the accident to the policeman," the reading of the portion set off by dashes with a lowered pitch of the voice indicates that it is parenthetical and not a necessary part of the main thought.

A word of caution is needed, however: vocal techniques are not to be applied mechanically; the idea to be expressed must always be the governing factor. The reader thinks the author's thought and re-creates the idea in its intellectual setting as he reads the material aloud. Therefore the reader must, at the outset, determine the mood or the spirit of the selection. Lincoln's Second Inaugural Address was given at a sobering time in American history; the occasion was serious, solemn, dignified; and the thought expressed, as is evident from the concluding paragraphs, grips one with its undertone of dedication and devotion.

Fondly do we hope, fervently do we pray, that this mighty scourge of war may soon pass away. Yet, if God wills that it continue until the wealth piled by the bondsman's two hundred and fifty years of unrequited toil shall be sunk, and until every drop of blood drawn with the lash shall be paid with another drawn with the sword; as was said three thousand years ago, so still it must be said, "The judgments of the Lord are true and righteous altogether."

With malice toward none, with charity for all, with firmness in the right, as God gives us to see the right, let us strive on to finish the work we are in, to bind up the nation's wounds, to care for him who shall have borne the battle and for his widow and orphans, to do all which may achieve and cherish a just and a lasting peace among ourselves and with all nations.

For a marked contrast in mood to this address consider this passage from Samuel L. Clemens's speech on "New England Weather."

Yes, one of the brightest gems in the New England weather is the dazzling uncertainty of it. There is only one thing certain about it, you are certain there is going to be plenty of weather—a perfect grand review; but you never can tell which end of the procession is going to move first. You fix up for the drought; you leave your umbrella in the house and sally out with your sprinkling-pot, and ten to one you get drowned. You make up your mind that the earthquake is due; you stand from under and take hold of something to steady yourself, and the first thing you know, you get struck by lightning.

These are great disappointments. But they can't be helped. The lightning there is peculiar; it is so convincing! When it strikes a thing, it doesn't leave enough of that thing behind for you to tell whether—well, you'd think it was something valuable, and a Congressman had been there.

And the thunder. When the thunder commences to merely tune up, and scrape, and saw, and key up the instruments for the performance, strangers say: "Why, what awful thunder you have here!" But when the baton is raised and the real concert begins you'll find that stranger down in the cellar, with his head in the ash-barrel.

It is also desirable when reading aloud to show changes in mood or character, usually indicated by bodily sets and vocal variations. This is particularly applicable in the case of dialogue. The speakers are different, have individual characteristics, ideas, ideals, mentalities, and emotions. The speech of the easygoing, slow-thinking person necessitates a reading manner that suggests this type. The reader would indicate this by relaxation in his own body and voice. On the other hand, the speech of an alert, energetic, enthusiastic person calls for tension in the body and voice of the reader.

Try reading aloud the moving scene which closes *Death of a Salesman*. Differentiate the characters—Charley, a middle-aged man who is the Lomans' neighbor; Biff, the Lomans' athletic but incompetent older son; Happy, their shrewd but unscrupulous younger son; Linda, Mrs. Loman, the type of the devoted wife. Willy Loman, the Salesman, has just been buried.

CHARLEY. It's getting dark, Linda.
(LINDA *doesn't react. She stares at the grave.*)
BIFF. How about it, Mom? Better get some rest, heh? They'll be closing the gate soon.
(LINDA *makes no move. Pause*)

HAPPY (*deeply angered*). He had no right to do that. There was no necessity for it. We would've helped him.
CHARLEY (*grunting*). Hmmm.
BIFF. Come along, Mom.
LINDA. Why didn't anybody come?
CHARLEY. It was a very nice funeral.
LINDA. But where are all the people he knew? Maybe they blame him.
CHARLEY. Naa. It's a rough world, Linda. They wouldn't blame him.
LINDA. I can't understand it. At this time especially. First time in thirty-five years we were just about free and clear. He only needed a little salary. He was even finished with the dentist.
CHARLEY. No man only needs a little salary.
LINDA. I can't understand it.
BIFF. There were a lot of nice days. When he'd come home from a trip; or on Sundays, making the stoop; finishing the cellar; putting on the new porch; when he built the extra bathroom; and put up the garage. You know something, Charley, there's more of him in that front stoop than in all the sales he ever made.
CHARLEY. Yeah. He was a happy man with a batch of cement.
LINDA. He was so wonderful with his hands.
BIFF. He had the wrong dreams. All, all, wrong.

A final suggestion for improving oral reading is to observe the explicit cues that the author gives in descriptive words that precede the speech of a character: such words and phrases as "hesitatingly," "after a long pause," "speaking rapidly," "whispering," "with words tumbling over one another," "screaming," "angrily," "sympathetically," "belligerently," "softly," "soothingly," "pompously," "precisely," "puffing like a locomotive." Note, for example, how, in the following passages from *Huckleberry Finn*, body and voice cues are given to the reader.

"Why he . . ." I stopped. I reckoned I better keep still. She run on, and never noticed I had put in at all.
Then she took off the hank and looked me straight in the face, but very pleasant, and says: "Come, now—what's your real name?"

He set there a-mumbling and a-growling a minute and then he says—"Ain't you a sweet-scented dandy, though?"

The duke had to learn him over and over again, how to say every speech; and he made him sigh, and put his hand on his heart, and after a while he said he done it pretty well; "only," he says, "you mustn't bellow out *Romeo!* that way, like a bull— you must say it soft and sick, and languishy, so— R-o-o-meo! that is the idea. . . ."

Mary Jane straightened herself up, and my, but she was handsome! she says: "*Here* is my answer: She hove up the bag of money and put it in the king's hand. . . ."

Sometimes, on the other hand, the cues are only implied in the dialogue itself. In *Hamlet,* Act III, Scene 2, though there are no explicit cues given, one can be quite sure how Shakespeare intended the lines to be read.

HAMLET. Speak the speech, I pray you, as I pronounced it to you, trippingly on the tongue; but if you mouth it, as many of your players do, I had as lief the town-crier spoke my lines. Nor do not saw the air too much with your hand, thus, but use all gently; for in the very torrent, tempest, and, as I may say, the whirlwind of passion, you must acquire and beget a temperance that may give it smoothness. O, it offends me to the soul to hear a robustious periwig-pated fellow tear a passion to tatters, to very rags, to split the ears of the groundlings, who for the most part are capable of nothing but inexplicable dumb-shows and noise. I could have such a fellow whipped for o'erdoing Termagant. It out-herods Herod. Pray you, avoid it.

FIRST PLAYER. I warrant your honour.

HAMLET. Be not too tame neither, but let your own discretion be your tutor. Suit the action to the word, the word to the action; with this special observance, that you o'erstep not the modesty of nature. For anything so overdone is from the purpose of playing, whose end, both at the first and now, was and is, to hold, as 't were, the mirror up to nature; to show virtue her own feature, scorn her own image, and the very age and body of the time his form and pressure. Now this overdone, or come tardy off, though it make the unskilful laugh, cannot but make the judicious grieve; the censure of the which one must in your allowance o'erweigh a whole theatre of others. O, there be players that I have seen play, and heard others praise, and that highly, not to speak it profanely, that, neither having the accent of Christians nor the gait of Christian, pagan, nor man, have so strutted and bellowed that I have thought some of nature's journeymen had made men and not made them well, they imitated humanity so abominably.

And in poetry, of course, there are seldom any explicit directions as to how the lines should be read, but there are two general prin-

ciples which the reader may find helpful to keep in mind: observe the punctuation marks, perhaps even more closely than in prose, and be governed by the sense of the poetry regardless of the break in the lines. Note, for instance, that observing these principles as one reads the first stanza of Robert Frost's "Stopping by Woods on a Snowy Evening" facilitates an understanding of these quiet lines.

> Whose woods these are I think I know.
> His house is in the village though;
> He will not see me stopping here
> To watch his woods fill up with snow.

And, in the following stanza of Alfred Noyes's "The Highwayman," the reader need only to consider the content of the lines to recognize their effective onomatopoeia and telling rhythm. These qualities, if such a stanza is read properly, in turn intensify the excitement and suspense of the passage.

> Over the cobbles he clattered and clashed in the
>   dark inn-yard,
> And he tapped with his whip on the shutters, but
>   all was locked and barred;
> He whistled a tune to the window, and who should
>   be waiting there
> But the landlord's black-eyed daughter,
>   Bess, the landlord's daughter,
> Plaiting a dark red love-knot into her long black
>   hair.

Thus far some of the basic principles in oral reading have been considered and some points on preparing to read aloud have been given. When reading aloud you will doubtlessly be more effective if you can put some or all of the following practical techniques into use:

1. Relax but be sufficiently alert to give the appearance of confidence in yourself and of interest in what you are doing.

2. Face your hearers squarely with the weight of your body about equally distributed on both feet, hips level, chest up.

3. If there is a speaker's stand, place the material to be read on it. If not, hold the book in both hands at a comfortable distance from your eyes. Do not hold the book so that it obstructs the eye-level contact you have with the audience.

4. Read in a manner that is genuinely communicative. Get the sense of the selection

across to the listener. Read with enough volume to be easily heard. Look up occasionally from the printed page.

5. Observe the punctuation marks, which are guides to the sense of the selection.

6. When reading the words of a character do not be afraid to "let yourself go" a little; suggest the individual with bodily set, possibly gesture, certainly facial expression and voice.

DONALD E. BIRD *Fundamentals of Listening*

The Importance of Listening

One way to measure the importance of listening is to find out how much time one spends each day in the role of a listener. One group of college freshmen kept a daily log of the time they spent reading, writing, speaking, and listening, dividing conversation and discussion time equally between listening and speaking. The results were as follows: listening, 42 per cent; speaking, 25 per cent; writing, 18 per cent; and reading, 15 per cent. Results of similar experiments in other colleges varied somewhat, but in every case listening consumed the greatest amount of time. Apparently, you spend more time listening than you do speaking, reading, or writing. Although it does not follow that listening is three times as important as reading and twice as important as writing, it is evident that an activity that takes up so much time warrants consideration and study.

It might be worthwhile for you to take a closer look at your listening activities. A daily record of time spent listening in conversation, listening in the classroom, listening to radio, television, and motion pictures, and listening to formal talks, announcements, and directions would give you some information on the relative frequency of various kinds of listening situations.

Most of what you know and believe, you have learned by listening. From the beginning of school through college more of your education is acquired by listening to teachers and students than by any other means. The grades you get in most of your classes depend upon your skill as a listener as much as or more than they do upon your skill as a reader or writer.

One study of the relative importance of reading and listening in college classes by college freshmen indicated that they considered listening more important than reading in 41 per cent of their courses. In 43 per cent of their courses they considered listening and reading equally important, and in only 16 per cent did they rate reading as more important than listening. The explanations they gave for their judgments revealed that many teachers spend much time explaining and illustrating the main ideas of the course in the classroom and base their tests largely upon these ideas.

Radio, television, and motion pictures are an important part of your daily life. Through these media you are constantly being bombarded with words intended to stir your emotions and shape your opinions. Accurate and critical listening is essential to intelligent response to these media.

The Prevalence of Poor Listening

Evidence and observation indicate that most college students are poor listeners. They jumble directions, distort ideas, remember unimportant details, misunderstand opinions, misjudge evidence, take inadequate notes, and are unable to find the central idea, all because they do not know how to listen.

A recent survey revealed that only 27 per cent of a group of freshman students could identify the main points in a lecture, and only 18 per cent could locate the inferences correctly. When these freshmen answered questions about stories to which they had listened, 75 per cent of them responded correctly to 33 per cent or less of the items. No more than half of a freshman group could identify the point of view expressed in a short controversial statement.

If you are a poor listener, it may be because you have never given the matter any consideration. You have never studied listening in school, and you have probably assumed that listening just happens whenever words are being spoken, that it is an involuntary process like breathing. A look at some of the listening experiences in your daily life will reveal how false these assumptions are.

Have you ever suddenly become conscious that you are not listening to someone who is speaking to you—that your mind is occupied with irrelevant thoughts or that you are watching the movement of his lips or the way he squints his eyes? It is an embarrassing awareness, and you probably give yourself a mental shake and concentrate on tuning in the speaker. Perhaps he finishes talking and you become aware that you have not the slightest notion of what to say in response.

Do you ever deliberately affect attention in conversation, smiling and nodding your head while impatiently waiting for the speaker to finish? Perhaps you have learned the trick of reliving in your imagination some exciting experience you have had; the interest on your face and the sparkle in your eye encourage the speaker without subjecting you to the tedium of listening. Are you quickly bored by conversation unless it is about you or your special interests? If you are frequently guilty of these faults—and everyone is sometimes—you are a poor listener.

What happens in class when the teacher is talking? Do you take notes? What do you put down, and how do you decide what to put down? Do you think about what the teacher is saying before putting his words on paper? Do you take the same kind of notes in all classes? How useful are the notes weeks later; are they a jumbled mass of details, topics, generalizations, and meaningless words? If they are, you are a poor listener.

When the speaker tells you the way he thinks about a problem, what do you do? Do you get angry and excited if he attacks your ideas? Do you criticize his delivery or the color and design of his tie? Are you bored by any serious talk about any subject beyond your immediate world of personal concerns? If so, you are a poor listener.

Poor listening is common and is probably the undetected cause of much misunderstanding, unhappiness, and conflict. The tiff with your roommate, the falling out with your girl or boy friend, angry words with your parents, the *F* you received in biology—all may be due, in part at least, to faulty listening.

The Process of Listening

If you want to become a better listener, the first thing you need to do is to become aware of the importance of listening and your own need for improvement. Then, you are ready to examine the process of listening.

Hearing is the first phase of the process of listening. Your ears receive the sound waves created by the spoken utterance and transform them into auditory impulses. Interestingly enough, it appears that one need not have perfect hearing in order to be a good listener. Experiments seem to indicate that some hearing loss does not significantly diminish listening ability but rather that persons who have some hearing loss and who are aware of it listen better because they try harder.

As the previous section above points out, hearing may occur without listening. *Attention* is necessary for listening. When the speaker says, "May I have your attention, please?" he is recognizing that unless you try to listen, his words will be spoken in vain. Attention is a mental readiness to receive the message and is accompanied by a physical alertness. You are "at-tension," for you are exerting mental and physical energy as you direct your thinking toward understanding and interpreting the incoming message. Attention operates like a "make-and-break" electrical circuit; brief periods of attention alternate with brief periods of rest or recovery. Attention is tiring; there seem to be definite limits to the length of time an adult can listen to a single source of stimulation, such as a speaker. It has been estimated that 75 per cent of the average adult audience can give adequate attention during the first fifteen minutes of a talk, but only 50 per cent maintain a high level of attention during the next fifteen minutes. Only 25 per cent continue to give optimum attention throughout a forty-five-minute talk, and any remarks beyond forty-five minutes are so much wasted energy on the part of the speaker.

Perception is the process by which the listener "decodes" the message he is getting from the speaker. It happens so rapidly as to be apparently instantaneous, but probably a process of identification and recognition goes on. Let us look at a simple example on a nonverbal level. At ten o'clock each morning in our town the whistle at the power plant is blown, not only to indicate the hour but also to predict the weather. When I hear the sound, I identify it as the sound of a whistle, and because of its particular loudness and timbre, I recognize it as the power-plant whistle. I also understand that it is now ten o'clock, and I set my watch accordingly. If my knowledge also includes acquaintance with the code, I am able to understand what the particular kind of blast means. Three short blasts indicate rainy and colder weather ahead, and one long blast indicates that it will be fair and warmer. By an analogous process you recognize words, phrases, and sentences. You search for the meaning of the words and units of thought by relating the speaker's ideas to similar ideas in your past experience. You try to create in your own mind a reasonable facsimile of the idea which was in the speaker's mind.

Listening is complicated by the fact that meaning is conveyed not only by the spoken words themselves but also by how they are spoken, and when and where and to whom they are spoken. Therefore, as in the case of the whistle, perception probably occurs at various levels, depending upon the knowledge and experience of the listener and his ability to discern the implications of all the factors involved.

Evaluation is the stage of listening that involves the application of judgment to the ideas perceived. You are not content to understand. You also make a judgment about the adequacy of the evidence, the value of the information, the validity of the conclusion. In other words, you decide whether the idea is good or bad, whether it is one to remember or forget, whether it should be put in your notes or discarded.

Response or reaction is an inevitable outcome in the process of listening, whether implicit or explicit, immediate or delayed. In conversation the listener's reaction is likely to be immediate; in listening to a lecture it is likely to be delayed. In a sense, you talk to yourself about what the speaker is saying, you

formulate questions you would like to ask, you plan the reply you would like to make, or you store away certain ideas to be contemplated at your leisure.

In other words, successful listening is a complex process requiring energy and skill. It does not simply happen when you are quiet and another person is talking. It is neither passive, like receiving a blow on the head, nor automatic, like the operation of a vending machine when a coin is put in the slot. You listen because you want to listen, and you listen effectively when you know how to get the most out of what you hear.

Visual cues are important not only as helps in determining meaning but as a means of focusing attention. One does not actually need to observe the color of the speaker's tie or his mannerisms and features. To do so is distracting. But seeing the speaker or at least looking in his direction seems to make listening more effective.

Factors Which Influence Listening Effectiveness

Let us examine some of the many factors which influence listening effectiveness. The good listener is conscious of these factors. He knows that some of them provide cues to the meaning of what is said or motivate his listening; others are distractions which impede listening.

The speaker. We are generally conscious of delivery factors in the speaking-listening situation; in fact, we are probably too sensitive to them. We become speech critics rather than listeners seeking information and ideas. The physical appearance, mannerisms, and dress of the speaker can be distractions; the poor listener dwells on them and the good listener ignores them.

The rate of speaking becomes a distraction when it is much slower or much faster than normal. Inflection, emphasis, pauses, and gestures usually help you get the intended meaning of the message; however, overuse or exaggeration of any technique of delivery makes it a distraction, diverting the listener's attention from the ideas being expressed to the techniques being used.

The better the speaker, the better the listening is likely to be, but the well-motivated, trained listener gets the message regardless of the quality of the speaking. In fact, it is re-assuring to know that the skill of the speaker does not make a great deal of difference if you know how to listen. The world is full of poor speakers who have interesting ideas and useful information to share with us.

The speech. In what is said as well as how it is said lie roadblocks to understanding or aids to listening. If the words are unfamiliar, if the phrases are trite, or if the ideas are vague, the good listener has difficulty, and the poor listener is lost. Attention to the speaker's use of transitional expressions, to his repetition of important points, illustrations of main ideas, and enumeration of reasons makes listening easier, as these factors help the listener to re-construct the speaker's thought structure.

The subject of a speech does not seem to make much difference to the listener, but he is strongly influenced by its difficulty. You can read and understand more difficult material than you can listen to effectively. Material which, as a junior in high school, you could read and understand with some difficulty is equally difficult for you now when presented as listening material.

The situation. Listening often occurs at a time and place and in circumstances not of the listener's choosing; therefore, most listening situations contain real and imagined distrac-tions, which the poor or reluctant listener seizes upon as excuses for not listening.

Sitting where you can see and hear the speaker without strain makes it easier to pay attention and therefore helps your listening. The people about you may encourage you by their interest and attention, or they may make listening almost impossible by their noise and restlessness.

Other possible sources of irritation in the listening situation may be ventilation, tem-perature, outside noises, humidity, seats, light-ing, time of day, weather, acoustics, and even the decoration and architecture of the room. Consciousness of any of these factors may easily block your listening, especially if you are disinclined to listen.

The listener. Less obvious and most power-ful are the factors in you, the listener. Personal worries and concerns will claim your atten-tion the moment you cease to direct your

thinking toward the incoming message. A prac-tice group of college freshmen reported that they were diverted from listening by thoughts of "vacation, marriage, French test last hour, research paper to be written, letters, lake, com-ing week end, illness of father." The good listener is able to set aside such personal con-cerns while listening. Other factors in the lis-tener identified by the practice group as causes of poor listening were: "not interested in the subject, prejudices, previous ideas, previous experiences, questioned statement, statement made me angry, wondered about application to me, heard it before."

The Principles of Effective Listening

Your listening will be more effective if you know the principles of good listening and how to apply them.

The listening experience begins when you first know that you are to be in a listening situation and continues beyond the listening act itself so long as you reflect upon or discuss what you have heard. Probably you have never stopped to observe that the success of your listening in your class is influenced by your attitudes and actions before you come to class and that the "proof of the pudding" is in what you subsequently do with what you hear.

Preparing to listen. The good listener gets ready to listen by finding out something about the speaker and the subject or by calling to mind what he has previously read and heard about them. He tries to sit where he can see and hear the speaker easily, and he does what he can to eliminate or adjust to the obvious distractions about him. He sets aside any nega-tive or indifferent attitudes toward the speaker or the subject matter. In other words, he listens with an open mind. If the situation requires, he is ready to take notes.

Understanding the ideas of the speaker. The primary task in most listening situations is to find or to formulate the central idea, which embraces the meaning and purpose of what is being said. Some of the clues to the central idea are structural. It is often presented as a thesis in the introduction and restated in the conclusion. It may be repeated in various ways during the talk and may be prefaced by phrases such as this: "Now you can see from all that I have said that. . . ." Often the speaker will help the listener by emphasizing the central idea or by pausing before and after it.

After determining the speaker's central idea, the good listener tries to find the main supporting ideas. They may be enumerated, stated in question form, anticipated by leading remarks, or stated as topic sentences beginning parts of the talk. Voice volume, intensity, and pauses may help to identify these main ideas. Try always to distinguish what is relevant from what is irrelevant to the general purpose of the talk, fact from opinion, and detail from generalization.

Some listeners reconstruct the speaker's outline in their minds by identifying the introduction, the main divisions of the talk, and the conclusion. The danger in this approach is that the result may be, like many a student outline, a list of topics rather than statements of ideas.

Equally as important as the main ideas but less easily detected are the implicit meanings in a speech: the speaker's purpose (frequently not stated), the inferences to be drawn from his remarks, and the significance of what he leaves unsaid. At this point we can only try to make intelligent guesses based on what seems to lie behind the words or is hinted in voice and manner.

Evaluating the ideas of the speaker. The good listener seeks first to understand and then to evaluate. He asks himself such questions as these: Are the speaker's facts accurate and complete? Is his reasoning sound? Is his opinion based upon evidence and is the evidence adequate? Do the facts he gives support his conclusion? Do the details he presents support his generalizations?

The good listener checks the opinions and assertions of the speaker against his past knowledge and experience in an effort to judge their soundness and accuracy. The poor listener tends to accept the speaker's statements as true or false on the basis of whether he agrees with them rather than on the basis of the evidence presented and the logic employed. He is inclined to be quite sure of their truth if the speaker states them emphatically and with dramatic appeal. He unquestioningly accepts facts and conclusions because of the way they are said or the reputation of the speaker.

When the speech is over, he is unable to decide whether what was said was worthwhile or not.

Responding to the ideas of the speaker. The good listener responds to what he hears. Response may be in the form of notes. Good notes are the product of an understanding-evaluating process, not a matter of writing down exactly what the speaker says. Notes should be a record of the ideas—generalizations and significant details—which you, the listener, have understood and judged to be important. They should be in sentence form and should use familiar words, not in unrelated topics or meaningless phrases. Probably the best notes are those which are reworked soon after the listening experience, although few students seem to find time for reorganization and restudying of the notes they take in class.

The poor listener tries to write down what the speaker says without thinking about the ideas, asks no questions, is unresponsive during listening, and is unable to discuss or restate the ideas of the speaker afterwards. The pattern of response by the poor listener begins like this: "I enjoyed the talk," "Wasn't it awful?" or "Isn't he a handsome man?" In response to the question of what was said he continues, "Oh, he talked about China," "He told a good story," or "He didn't say anything new." We ask for one main idea—just one—and this is what he says: "Oh, I can't remember," "He told us many interesting things," or "I don't know, but he was a good speaker."

Applying the Principles of Effective Listening

Poor listeners can become good listeners, and good listeners can become better listeners by applying the principles of effective listening in their daily listening experiences. Here are some things which you can do to become a better listener:

In general. Make an analysis of your listening habits. When and where are you a listener, and what do you do when you listen? How frequent and important is your listening in conversations, in the classroom, at speeches, and in radio–television–motion-picture situations?

In conversations. 1. Find a reason for listening that is strong enough to sustain your attention.

2. Watch the speaker, trying not to think about his appearance, his mannerisms, or your feelings about him.

3. Before responding to a statement of opinion, restate it in your own words and ask the speaker if you have understood him correctly. Do not give your opinion on the issue until you have satisfied him that you understand his point of view.

4. Show the speaker that you are listening by your actions while listening as well as by your subsequent reply. React to what he says with appropriate facial expressions, head movements, and encouraging words.

5. Relate your response to the remark just made in words and content. Introductory phrases such as "That's right," "I see what you mean, but . . . ," or "I agree with you that . . ." indicate that you have been listening. Help to build the conversation by relating your remark to the one before it.

6. Try writing down a conversation word for word. Examine it for evidences of poor listening, such as disconnected remarks and obvious misunderstandings.

7. If the conversation involves directions and specific details which are to be acted upon, repeat them and ask the speaker to correct any inaccuracy.

In the classroom. 1. If note taking is in order, take down significant details and important generalizations. State them in your own words and in complete sentences. Compare your notes with those of another student in the same class; discuss the differences. Suit the method to the course; probably in biology most of the notes will be details, and in history most of the notes will be generalizations. Rework your notes soon after class, omitting details which in light of the entire lecture are not significant and formulating additional generalizations in accordance with the details.

2. If at all possible, ask questions and make comments to check on your understanding of the ideas and to practice restating them in your own words. Mulling over the ideas with the teacher and your classmates helps your comprehension.

3. Listen to your classmates' questions and comments. If one of the other students has not

made his point clear, try putting the same ideas in your own words. In class discussion, talking and listening among students are often more fruitful than talking and listening to the teacher.

At a speech. 1. Find a strong personal reason for listening to the speaker—one that will hold you to your job as a listener for the duration of a long talk.

2. When practical, take notes on your listening problems in a speaker-audience situation. When your mind wanders, put down where and why. When you react to an emotional word, idea, or mannerism, put down the circumstances and your reaction.

3. Prepare a listening-experience report on the speech. Include a statement of the central idea, main supporting ideas, and your reactions to the ideas. If possible, have the speaker check your report.

4. Summarize the talk for persons who have not heard it; write about it in a letter. Concentrate on stating ideas and your reactions to them, not on the speaker and how you liked or disliked him.

5. Discuss the speech with friends who have also heard it. Compare your understanding of the central idea with theirs. Try to arrive, as a group, at a statement of the central idea and the supporting main ideas, and at a consensus as to the validity and significance of what was said.

6. Listen to many kinds of speakers, in many different situations, talking on many different subjects. Make reports on these speaking situations.

Radio, television, and motion pictures. 1. Listen to discussion programs of various kinds—news commentators, newscasters, interview programs, and forums.

2. Compare the analysis of the same news events by different news commentators. Listen for motive, inference, and use of emotional language.

3. Discuss the ideas in a radio or television commentary or a serious movie. Use one such program or movie as a basis for group discussion.

For a check list by which you can make a self-analysis of your listening behavior, see the *Exercise Manual.*

part four

A Preface to Writing

Good writing, like good speaking, is the effective communication of thoughts and feelings. In general communication is effective (1) when the writer knows what he has to say, that is, when he knows his subject; (2) when the writer knows how to arrange his material on the subject, that is, when he knows how to give structure to his ideas; and (3) when he knows how to present his ideas in language, that is, when he is in command of an appropriate style.

We can recognize these three traits of good writing almost immediately. For example, in "Painting as a Pastime" (p. 110), Winston Churchill talks about the hobby of painting. We realize that he knows his *subject* from the ideas and facts actually presented in his essay. He discusses his own personal experience as a painter. He gives his reasons for painting and the several steps necessary to master the essentials of the art. He compares the technique of painting with that of a military operation and shows how amateurs can derive pleasure and relaxation from painting.

Churchill's mastery of his subject is expressed in an orderly arrangement of ideas. He first wins our attention by pointing out the importance of mental change for men and women who live intensely busy lives. Then he discusses a variety of hobbies before developing the central idea of his essay, namely, the special value of painting—". . . For they [the painters] shall not be lonely. Light and colour, peace and hope, will keep them company to the end, or almost to the end, of the day." This central idea is then explained by presenting the reasons why painters are happy people. These reasons are well chosen and carefully linked together.

Finally, the style is clear, varied, graceful.

Thus, the essay as a whole is stamped with all the marks of the good writer—knowledge of the subject, a clear arrangement of ideas, and a style that is lucid, vivid, and entertaining.

Two Ways of Becoming a Good Writer

Good writing such as Winston Churchill's does not come easily. One may recognize good writing and state the basic principles that underlie it without being able to produce it. But behind every good writer lie many years of experience in observing facts and details of human life, in exploring ideas in the realms of science, literature, and philosophy, and in thinking a subject through to its essential meaning.

Hence a beginning student needs to be patient with himself. He cannot suddenly know all he should in order to write well about an important subject, a book, an author, a philosophical idea. He must study a subject carefully, listen, read, think. He must begin over again, read more widely, revise his thoughts, rearrange his plans, constantly correct his language. Good writing is based on continuous growth in knowledge, reflection, and writing.

But we cannot wait to write until we are experts on a subject. Writing itself is a means by which we come to know a subject, evaluate our knowledge of it, and refine our style. Indeed, good writing is an *end;* writing as well as we can is a *means* to that end.

Two of the best ways of achieving the end of good writing have already been placed before you in *College English.* The first is the *analysis* of effective prose on subjects within your range of interest and ability. To read the essays in Part I carefully is to discover the principles that underlie the choice of a particular subject, the type of analysis used in explanation and reasoning, the arrangement of the various parts of the whole piece in relation to a central theme, the use of a particular style. In other words, these essays, together with the biographies and fiction in Part II, may be analyzed, or broken down, in order to see how they are composed. This analytic process develops your knowledge of the art of writing.

The second way of becoming a good writer, *synthesis*—that is, putting things together—is closely related to analysis. Analysis breaks down what is already composed; synthesis, or composition, puts together what is not yet composed.

Obviously composition is the more pressing task for the beginning writer. In analyzing the work of another writer, Churchill's "Painting as a Pastime," for instance, he studies a work that is already composed. A reasonable amount of application enables him to discover the purpose of the work, its central idea, its method of development, its meshing of thought and style. But in composing his own thoughts on a subject of his own choice, the beginning writer climbs uphill all the way. Unless a topic is assigned by an instructor, he begins with preliminary questions such as "What should I write about?" "How long should my composition be?" "What do I intend to say?" After that he must construct some kind of outline. Finally he has the difficult job of putting his sentences in a logical order and of choosing the most exact and vivid words to make his purpose, or central idea, plain.

Now, just as the readings in *College English* help you to cultivate the habit of analysis—the first way to become a good writer—so the *Harbrace Handbook* helps you plan and write your own compositions. The basic rules are all there—what to do and what not to do with the word, the sentence, the paragraph, and the whole composition.

Reread Sections 31-33 of the *Harbrace Handbook*. Note how the handbook refers constantly to the elements of rhetoric—the selection and study of the subject, the analysis

of the subject, the arrangement (outline) of the whole composition, the details of paragraph and sentence structure and of diction. In the following pages the assumption is made that the student is aware of and knows how to make use of the contents of the *Harbrace Handbook*.

The handbook, however, is primarily concerned with the principles of writing in general rather than with the particular forms of discourse (see Sections 31-33). The following chapter attempts to show how the principles of good writing may be applied to the four forms of discourse—exposition, argument, description, and narration—and to the principal types of writing that most college students and graduates are expected to use in their academic, social, and professional lives.

The Forms of Discourse

Theoretically, prose composition may be divided into four forms of discourse—exposition, argument, description, and narration. Is this division a mere convenience? Does it really conform to the practice of good writers today?

At first glance, many of the essays in Part I appear to contain two or more forms of discourse. For instance, Virginia Woolf's "Beau Brummell" (p. 42) describes the subject, relates some incidents of his life, and explains his character. E. B. White's "Here Is New York" (p. 46) is also descriptive and narrative as well as explanatory. In "Faith in Science" (p. 138) I. I. Rabi seems first merely to explain his subject and then to attempt to convince his readers that they too should have faith in science. In "The Road to Peace" (p. 179) Ralph Bunche's exposition moves from explanation to argument. In fiction, too, in Stephen Crane's "The Open Boat" (p. 366), for example, the descriptive element is just as important as the narrative element. Again, G. B. Shaw's drama *Pygmalion* and Arthur Miller's *The Death of a Salesman* contain dialogue that is expository or argumentative rather than narrative or dramatic in character. Although it is true that writers rarely employ one form of discourse exclusively, the student should, for several reasons, study the separate forms of discourse.

First, most effective compositions have a

single dominant shape or character; they are primarily expository, argumentative, descriptive, or narrative. This is to say that good writing has a specific *purpose* or aim. Good writing explains an idea (exposition) or convinces the reader of the truth of a proposition or thesis (argument), or depicts in words the realities that strike the senses (description), or relates a series of incidents (narrative). When a writer intermingles one form of discourse with another, as was shown above, his specific aim—his governing purpose—compels him to emphasize one form of discourse rather than another. If he failed to do so, his essay or article would lack unity of purpose and hence unity of impression. It would not be effective writing.

The second reason flows from the first. In order to combine several forms of discourse successfully a writer must know what each form is meant to do. A good writer, conscious of his main purpose, chooses that form of discourse that is the proper vehicle of his purpose. In Frederick Lewis Allen's essay "The Spirit of the Times" (p. 208) the main purpose is exposition of the idea contained in the title. Mr. Allen does not directly or explicitly argue for or against the spirit of the times. Why? Because argument would distract his readers from his main point, an explanation of the contemporary spirit. Like all good writers, Mr. Allen knows that argument is not meant simply to explain an idea or a subject, but to convince the reader of the truth or falsity of a proposition.

To illustrate a mistaken use of the forms of discourse, let us suppose that I propose to *convince* you (argument) that college athletics contribute to the intellectual growth of the student. This proposition is debatable. To prove it I must define the terms *college athletics* and *intellectual growth* and then give reasons for the truth of my proposition. Suppose again that, instead of following this procedure, I choose to relate my own personal experiences as a football player (narration). Even if, in the course of my personal narrative, I recount football incidents that were related to my intellectual growth, it is extremely unlikely that I would convince you of the truth of the proposition. You might believe my story, even be interested in it. But it would remain at best but a single testimony. It would be less calculated to convince you than it would be to arouse your interest or feelings. I would have aimed at conviction and achieved something else. Such confusion of purpose produces effective writing only accidentally if at all.

The third reason for study and practice of the various forms of discourse is perhaps the most important of all. Each form of discourse has its own appropriate structure and style. In each the general principles of structure—unity, coherence, emphasis—are applied in a slightly different way. In argument, for instance, unity is determined by the logical process of the reasoning, whereas in literary description unity proceeds from the dominant impression the author wishes to convey, and in fictitious narrative from the effect the writer aims to produce. The principle is the same, but the application is different.

There is, too, a marked difference in the tone and style of the various forms of discourse. A writer of exposition normally views his subject calmly and objectively and speaks primarily to the reason. On the other hand, a writer who argues to influence the decision or conduct of his reader frequently writes in a style made vivid by his convictions and his feelings.

To sum up, we study and practice the four forms of discourse because we thereby help ourselves (1) to clarify the purpose of writing and thus to attain the chief end of rhetoric, effective writing, and (2) to adapt the general principles of structure and style to the different forms of written and spoken discourse.

We shall now study in order exposition, argument, description, and narration.

Exposition

Exposition is a form of discourse that explains. Its purpose is to clarify a subject. The subject may be an idea, such as a scientific principle, a historical fact, such as Lincoln's address at Gettysburg, a significant aspect of character, such as the formative influences on George Washington, or an operation, such as the disposal of atomic waste. Indeed anything that needs clarification is a proper subject of exposition.

Hence exposition is the commonest form of discourse. It is the mode of speech adopted in most lectures and textbooks, in encyclopedia articles, and in informative writing in general. The questions proposed in final examinations almost always demand exposition: "Explain the circumstances that led up to the War of 1812." "Discuss the effect of the frontier on American life." "Show how the characters in Mark Twain's *Huckleberry Finn* are related to the main theme." All these questions call for exposition.

Obviously one cannot explain what one does not know. You might be a first-rate writer in the sense that you employ good grammar, command a wide vocabulary, and have a knack of stringing sentences together. But this skill does not guarantee that you can write anything worthwhile about a subject that you do not know. The essential condition of good exposition then is the knowledge of the subject. (To check up on the means of investigating a subject, consult the *Harbrace Handbook,* Section 33.)

Of equal importance, however, is the ability to analyze a subject that you have chosen or been directed to explain. Experience has already shown you that a mass of facts, even when neatly recorded on index cards under various heads, does not organize itself into a clear, purposeful composition. Facts must be weighed, sifted, analyzed if you are to discover their true value, just as an assayer weighs, sifts, and refines mineral ore to obtain the copper, silver, or gold it contains. In other words, method, as well as matter, is important.

But what methods of analysis should be used? How is a subject made clear? There are many possible methods, five of which will be briefly considered here—definition, exemplification, cause and effect, comparison and contrast, and process.

Definition. A writer makes a subject clear by *defining* its terms, the words that contain the key ideas of the subject. A scientific definition of a term sets it apart from other terms by stating the class to which the term belongs and the special characteristics that distinguish it from other members of the class. Thus, for example, a student in contemporary civilization may well be asked to explain the term *empiricism.* As a first step in his exposition he might say that *empiricism* (the term to be defined) is a doctrine (the class) that all knowledge is derived from experience (the difference that distinguishes *empiricism* from all other doctrines).

This definition of *empiricism* may of course be expanded in a number of ways. The writer may point out when empiricism began, or he may identify individual authors associated with the doctrine, and so on. Indeed many essays are really extended definitions. Often the writer begins his essay with a strict definition and then expands his answer by developing his ideas according to one or more of the other methods listed below. For example, in "The Language Line" (p. 75) Susanne K. Langer first defines what she means by a *symbol,* a *sign,* and a *thing,* the key terms in her essay, and then modifies and distinguishes the meanings of these terms in her subsequent discussion. This essay is an extended definition.

Exemplification is a specific, concrete illustration or proof of a general principle or idea. It is perhaps the most frequent method of analysis in expository discourse. In exposition we are never called upon to explain concrete, specific objects or things; we describe them. But a general principle, such as the psychological law of association or the idea of democracy, normally requires explanation. These general, or abstract, subjects are rarely understood even when they are strictly defined. The reader needs to see how the principle works out in practice or how the idea manifests itself in actual life. Hence, we typically say, "Democracy, for example, the form of government practiced in the United States," or "a lyric poem, such as Shelley's 'Ode to the West Wind.' "

A good example is *direct* and *cogent.* It is *direct* when it brings the details of a subject before your eyes: ". . . no matter where you sit in New York you feel the vibrations of great times and tall deeds," writes E. B. White in "Here Is New York" (p. 46). "Great times," "tall deeds"—these general terms are immediately illustrated by specific references to the funeral of Rudolph Valentino, the execution of Nathan Hale, the murder of Stanford White, and other events of interest or importance.

An example is *cogent* when, in itself or as a link in a series of examples, it tends to prove the truth of a given statement. In "Radio, TV, and the Common Man" (p. 174) Gilbert Seldes supports his statement "Supply comes first in this business and creates its own demand" by a good single instance, one that represents many others, and perhaps calls these other instances to mind.

A few months ago *Time* published a letter from a reader in Nigeria which gives a perfect, though extreme, instance of this principle. The writer said: "In the Gold Coast one movie owner possesses only two features, 'King Kong' and 'The Mark of Zorro.'. . . On Mondays, Tuesdays, and Fridays he has packed them in for years with the former; [the other three weekdays he shows the latter] . . . On Sundays there is always a surefire double feature—'King Kong' and 'The Mark of Zorro.' " I submit that this enterprising exhibitor began by satisfying an unspecific demand for entertainment, then created an audience for a specific kind of entertainment, and finally prevented an audience for any other kind of entertainment from coming into existence.

In many situations, however, a single example is insufficient to indicate the truth of a statement. The writer must adduce a series of instances, all interconnected, to demonstrate his general statement. Accordingly, in "The Unwritten Rules of American Politics" (p. 217) John Fischer attempts to prove that the principles of majority rule (concurrent majority) and sectional compromise operate not only in Congress but also in other American political institutions. In the context of the whole essay, the series of examples below is a compelling demonstration of the truth of his general statement.

Calhoun's principles of the concurrent majority and of sectional compromise operate just as powerfully, though sometimes less obviously, in every other American political institution. Our cabinet, for example, is the only one in the world where the members are charged by law with the representation of special interests—labor, agriculture, commerce, and so on. In other countries, each agency of government is at least presumed to act for the nation as a whole; here most agencies are expected to behave as servants for one interest or another. The Veterans' Administration, to cite the most familiar case, is frankly intended to look out for Our Boys; the Maritime Board is to look out for the shipping industry; the National Labor Relations Board, as originally established under the Wagner Act, was explicitly intended to build up the bargaining power of the unions.

Even within a single department, separate agencies are sometimes set up to represent conflicting interests. Thus in the Department of Agriculture under the New Deal the old Triple-A became primarily an instrument of the large-scale commercial farmers, as represented by their lobby, the Farm Bureau Federation; while the Farm Security Administration went to bat for the tenants, the farm laborers, and the little subsistence farmers, as represented by the Farmers Union.

Underlying the method of exemplification is the logical relationship of the genus and species. A genus is a whole or class consisting of two or more species or parts which, though distinct, are united because of their common, that is, generic, qualities. Thus, the term *science* is a genus that comprises the species *physics, biology,* and *chemistry.* What we say of the genus or whole must be true of its species or parts. For example, if we say that science is a body of organized knowledge, it must also be true that physics, biology, and chemistry are, individually, bodies of organized knowledge. A good example, then, is a species of its genus, or a specific illustration of a general statement.

Cause and effect. We frequently hear the words "Why?" and "What are the results?" A freshman may say, "I understand what Mr. Stoke means by *College Athletics* [see p. 131] (definitions) and I recognize his specific allusions (exemplification), but why did college athletics come into being in the first place? Surely, there is some reason for their place in American education." Or we might hear it said on the same subject, "What are the results? College athletics may be wrong in some ways, but they do some good."

The questions "Why?" and "What are the results?" are simply common-sense references to the method of analysis known as cause and effect. We sometimes analyze a subject by discovering its causes, or by describing its effects, or by doing both because both methods help to show us just what our subject is. Let us take *cause* first.

A *cause* is the reason why something exists. The subject *White House*, for instance, is the result of a number of factors. Most important are the so-called *efficient* causes. The architect or designer, Daniel Hoban, was chiefly responsible for the official residence of the President of the United States. Cooperating with him were various artisans and laborers. Their work, together with that of their successors, contributed to the total effect. Hoban, the artisans, and the laborers were the efficient causes.

But the *White House* is also made up of *material* things—wood, brick, and plaster—materials given a special *form*, design or shape, by the architect and the artisans. Hence, among the many causal factors are the *material* and the *formal* causes. Moreover, the artisans used certain instruments in constructing the White House. Surely the tools they used are at least secondary, or *instrumental*, causes. Then, too, the White House would never have existed unless it had a purpose, unless the people of the United States through their Congress had communicated to the architect their desire for a Presidential residence at once worthy of the national dignity and simple enough for republican tastes.

The knowledge of these and other factors that make up the total cause of the effect—the *White House*—are evidently helpful ways of understanding and explaining the subject. In a large-scale analysis, each aspect of cause might well require a whole chapter. Even a short analysis would certainly reveal many details that might be overlooked in external description, or even in an impressionistic sketch.

Another example of causal analysis is found in Samuel Eliot Morison's "The Young Man Washington" (p. 282). In this essay, the author investigates the factors in Washington's youth that account for his character in later life. What causes transformed "the passionate young man into an effective man"? Not his heredity or his parents, not book learning or formal religion, the author concludes, but mainly a stoic philosophy learned through personal friendship with the Fairfaxes, the experiences of farming, surveying, and soldiering on the frontier.

We may also describe a subject in terms of its effects. Some subjects, for instance, sorrow, laughter, joy, and fear, are frequently too complex for causal analysis. We are compelled, therefore, to show what they do, what effect they produce. In this manner William McDougall defines the true theory of laughter:

We find the key to the true theory [of laughter], if we ask—What does laughter do for us? What are its effects or consequences? Well, obviously we enjoy laughter; it does us good to have a good laugh. The fact is notorious. And when we feel depressed and moody, we welcome and seek the situations, objects, or persons that will make us laugh. Laughter prevents (for the moment at least) gloomy thinking and melancholy brooding, no matter how it is induced. How does it achieve this beneficial effect? In two ways—one purely physiological, the other more psychological. Physiologically its immediate effect is to stimulate the respiration and the circulation, to raise the blood pressure, and to send a fuller stream of blood to the head and brain; as we see in the ruddy face of the hearty laugher. Psychologically it works by breaking up every train of thinking and every sustained activity, bodily or mental. . . .[1]

So, too, along with his definitions and examples, James L. Mursell, in "The Miracle of Learning" (p. 19), explains his subject by showing the effects of the will to learn, its triumph over fatigue and over age (Paragraphs 21-22).

Sometimes both cause and effect are employed together. One of the most famous instances of this occurs in Edmund Burke's *Bristol Oration*, in which he shows that the Repeal of the Act of 1699 was good both in its causes and its effects. After describing the particular features of this act Burke presents his cause-and-effect analysis in the manner described in the table below. Note that the subject is at once the effect of good causes—hence good for that reason—and in itself the cause of good effects—hence good for another reason.

[1] Reprinted from *Scribner's Magazine* for March, 1922, p. 360, by permission of Anne McDougall.

CAUSES ⟶	SUBJECT ⟶	EFFECT
1. Excellence of men who made the law	Repeal of the Act of 1699	1. Good effects in England
a. Sponsor: Sir George Saville		2. Good effects in Ireland
b. Seconder: Mr. Dunning		3. Good effects abroad
c. Ratifiers: King, both houses, all clergy of all sects		
2. Noble purpose of the bill		
3. Justice of its provisions		
4. Expedience of its provisions		

Comparison and contrast. You can show

> A subject in its form and fit
> By setting it against its opposite;
> Jack is more or less like Jim
> And Tom's the contrary of Tim;
> Comparison the likeness shows
> Unlikeness in the contrast glows.

We do explain our views to others by putting our subject side by side with other subjects that are in the same class. In ordinary conversation we are continually saying something like this, "You've never been to Atlantic City. . . . Well, it's something like Coney Island. . . ."

The purpose of stressing the likeness or unlikeness of a subject with subjects that are closely related to it is to sharpen understanding. What makes a good comparison or contrast? A good *comparison* or *contrast,* like the good example, is either an illustration or a proof. It illustrates when it explains a relatively unfamiliar idea by virtue of its similarity, or dissimilarity, with a relatively familiar idea. Thus, in "The Language Line" (p. 75) Susanne Langer illustrates her ideas on the animal mind (the unfamiliar idea) by comparing it to a telephone exchange (the familiar idea).

The animal mind is like a telephone exchange; it receives stimuli from outside through the sense organs and sends out appropriate responses through the nerves that govern muscles, glands, and other parts of the body. The organism is constantly interacting with its surroundings, receiving messages and acting on the new state of affairs that the messages signify.

In the next paragraph the author contrasts the human mind with the animal mind by turning her metaphor in another direction. Note how Mrs. Langer first denies the validity of the comparison between the human mind and a telephone exchange and then affirms a second comparison between the human mind (the less familiar idea) and a great projector (the more familiar idea).

But the human mind is not a simple transmitter like a telephone exchange. It is more like a great projector; for instead of merely mediating between an event in the outer world and a creature's responsive action, it transforms or, if you will, distorts the event into an image to be looked at, retained, and contemplated. For the images of things that we remember are not exact and faithful transcriptions even of our actual sense impressions. They are made as much by what we think as by what we see. It is a well-known fact that if you ask several people the size of the moon's disk as they look at it, their estimates will vary from the area of a dime to that of a barrel top. Like a magic lantern, the mind projects its ideas of things on the screen of what we call "memory"; but like all projections, these ideas are transformations of actual things. They are, in fact, *symbols* of reality, not pieces of it.

Comparison and contrast may also be used to reason as well as to illustrate. In "College Athletics" (p. 131) Harold W. Stoke argues that college athletics, as presently conducted, are incompatible with education. As proof he contrasts athletics with education and compares athletics with public entertainment.

Process. Definition explains what a subject is; exemplification sets forth specific details about a subject; cause and effect answer the questions "Why?" and "What are the results?"; comparison and contrast show how a subject is like and unlike subjects in the same class. *Process* is a method of analysis that answers the question "How does something work?"

This method is particularly valuable when a subject is dynamic rather than static. The practical operation of a general idea (how democracy works), the development of a historical concept (how the middle classes rose), the analysis of events that lead up to a problem (how the Salk Vaccine test was handled or mishandled)—a subject of this kind is best treated by tracing each successive step in its development.

Process is sometimes used by itself, frequently with other methods of analysis. Thus, in "Riveting a Skyscraper" (*Harbrace Handbook,* Section 32g) the writers are exclusively concerned with describing how rivets are prepared in the furnace, passed to the catcher, then placed and secured with the aid of the bucker-up and the gun-man. In "The Birth of an Island" (p. 156), on the other hand, Rachel Carson shows how islands gradually come into being, survive for a time, and then disappear, and she also explains the scientific laws behind the process. She intermingles process with causal analysis.

Good process analysis accounts for all the essential steps in the development of an idea, the application of a principle, or the meaning of an event. "Riveting a Skyscraper" is particularly clear in its account of each successive step in an event. Another outstanding example of process analysis occurs in Albert H. Marckwardt's "What Is Good English" (p. 79). The purpose of this essay is to define an idea—good English. But, as the author points out in Paragraph 4, he must first clear up some erroneous ideas about linguistic liberalism. To do so he proposes first to show "how [process] and why [causal analysis] this change of attitude [from linguistic purism to linguistic liberalism] came about." In the succeeding paragraphs (5-17) he summarizes the history of grammar from the eighteenth century to the present. He shows how the linguistic purists assumed that standards never changed. His second step (Paragraphs 7-8) shows how the nineteenth-century concept of historical change influenced the ideas on language in the direction of linguistic liberalism. Finally in Paragraphs 9-17 he explains how liberal grammarians approach the problem of standards today. His historical survey (process), combined with an analysis of causes, helps to clear up his idea on what is good English.

How to combine methods of analysis. We have just sketched five methods of analysis frequently employed by writers in exposition.

Except in short compositions, however, these methods are rarely used alone. Most subjects require virtually all the methods, for, as we have seen, one leads to another. A definition is supported by an example, a comparison suggests a contrast, cause and effect are mingled with process, and process usually helps to define a subject. The essays in Part I of this book employ whatever methods are most likely to make the subject clear to a given audience.

The following analysis of Robert U. Jameson's "How to Stay in College" (p. 3) will make this interrelationship clear.

ANALYSIS OF "HOW TO STAY IN COLLEGE"

1. *Purpose.* Is there a discernible purpose? Mr. Jameson's aim, revealed in the title, is to show students, particularly freshmen, how to stay in college. But the purpose, *explaining how to stay in college,* is intimately linked with explaining the reasons why students fail. The student can know how to stay in college only if he can analyze the causes of failure, take the necessary measures to prevent failure, and adjust himself to the demands of college life. This purpose is made most explicit in the last two paragraphs of the essay.

2. *Subject.* To achieve his aim the author talks throughout of the causes of failure and, by contrast, of the causes of success. His central idea is: students fail because they are not adjusted to college life. The subject is appropriate for the general reader as well as for the two and a half million college students in the United States.

3. *Arrangement.* A brief introduction in the first four paragraphs and a brief ending in the last two paragraphs frame the main section of the essay. In the main section of the essay the author shows the causes of failure in this order:

a. Students are not adjusted to the demand for original thinking.

b. They are inadequately trained in reading.

c. They do not know how to study or how much to study.

d. They are inadequately trained in composition.

e. They are poorly advised by their families.

f. They overemphasize social life.

g. They do not grasp the true purposes of a college education.

4. *Methods of development.* In general Mr. Jameson's method of discourse is expository, that is, he states and explains. At times, however, as in his concluding paragraphs, he introduces an argu-

ment, that is, he reasons from proposition to proposition. The chief method of analysis is causal analysis, but examples, definition, and contrast are also frequently employed.

5. *Style.* As in most expositions directed to a general rather than a learned audience, the style aims at simplicity and clearness. The *words* are notably concrete. Note particularly the profusion of names and terms denoting specific facts. Abstract terms, such as *college education,* are defined; definitions are supported by concrete examples. Consider, too, the comparative brevity of the *sentences* and *paragraphs,* the frequent use of the question-and-answer technique, the use of down-to-earth quotations from students and professors. All these factors help to clarify the basic problem by using language in a manner the reader can readily understand.

It is worth noting that Jameson's style, addressed to readers of the *Saturday Evening Post,* is much simpler and more colloquial than that of James L. Mursell and John S. Dickey, whose essays, "The Miracle of Learning" (p. 19) and "Conscience and the Undergraduate" (p. 26) first appeared in the *Atlantic Monthly.*

Argument

Argument is a form of discourse that aims to convince the reader of the truth of a given proposition. As we have already seen, exposition sometimes is indirectly argumentative: it does not always merely state and explain facts; it occasionally reasons from one statement to another. "If what I have just explained is true, then, it follows. . . ." Some such language is inescapable even in the purest exposition.

In argument, however, the element of reasoning is the direct, immediate, essential element. "I want you to believe that John Smith is a good husband, because, as I shall show, he is faithful, generous, and forgiving." That sentence differs sharply from explanatory remarks on the same subject, such as, "John invariably goes and comes from home at regular hours, provides for his family generously, rarely grows sullen under the pressures of domestic life." The first sentence gives reasons, and promises to develop these reasons, for believing the statement that John Smith is a good husband. The second sentence merely states facts that are not necessarily proposed as reasons or means of convincing the reader that John is a good husband.

A good argument is one that provides convincing reasons—reasons that serve as proof. When we argue convincingly we make our reader agree with us. To do this honestly requires us to get the facts straight, to produce our evidence, to make our theory plain, to introduce pertinent authorities or witnesses. For the fact, or theory, or evidence that provides the *content* of argument is not taken for granted. We do not argue about the obvious. It goes without saying, then, that the first condition of good argument is the reliability of our evidence.

Just as in exposition, the subject must be examined and developed according to the various methods of analysis, and the reasons must be made clear. This is done by organizing our arguments or proofs in two different ways—deduction and induction.

The kinds of argument. In *deduction* we reason from premises to a conclusion, that is, from two statements, one general and one particular, so connected that a third statement or conclusion necessarily follows. In algebraic formula, deduction goes this way:

$$A = B$$
$$C = A$$
$$C = B$$

Note that the third statement, or conclusion, follows from the two preceding statements. Or, to put it in the form of a syllogism:

All animals (A) require food (B).
But a fox (C) is an animal (A).
Therefore a fox (C) requires food (B).

In *induction* we argue from a series of particular statements *sufficient in number and in cogency* to establish reasonable grounds for a general statement or conclusion. In T. H. Huxley's language,

Suppose you go into a fruiterer's shop, wanting an apple—you take one up, and, on biting, you find it is sour; you look at it, and see that it is hard, and green. You take up another one and that too is hard, green, and sour. The shopman offers you a third; but, before biting it, you examine it, and find that it is hard and green, and you immediately say that you will not have it, as it must be sour, like those that you have already tried.

Nothing can be more simple than that, you think, but if you will take the trouble to analyse and trace out into its logical elements what has been done by the mind, you will be greatly surprised. In the first place, you have performed the operation of induction. You found, that, in two experiences, hardness and greenness in apples went together with sourness. It was so in the first case, and it was confirmed by the second. True, it is a very small basis, but still it is enough to make an induction from; you generalize the facts, and you expect to find sourness in apples where you get hardness and greenness. You found upon that a general law, that all hard and green apples are sour; and that, so far as it goes, is a perfect induction.[2]

In both kinds of argument reasons are given for a conclusion. In deductive argument the conclusion derives from the logical connection between two premises; in inductive argument the conclusion derives from the strength of the evidence contained in the particular facts.

As Huxley observes, deduction and induction are not totally separated methods of reasoning. Frequently the conclusion of an induction becomes the basis of a deduction, as he demonstrates below:

Well, having got your natural law in this way, when you are offered another apple which you find is hard and green, you say, "All hard and green apples are sour; this apple is hard and green, therefore this apple is sour." That train of reasoning is what logicians call a syllogism, and has all its various parts and terms—its major premise, its minor premise, and its conclusion. And, by the help of further reasoning, which, if drawn out, would have to be exhibited in two or three other syllogisms, you arrive at your final determination. "I will not have that apple." So that, you see, you have, in the first place, established a law by induction, and upon that you have founded a deduction, and reasoned out the special conclusion of the particular case.

The same reciprocal relationship between deduction and induction may be observed in the speech "The Ancient Classics in a Modern Democracy" (p. 782). Here, Samuel Eliot Morison aims to convince his audience that the ancient classics, Greek and Latin, have a place in a democracy. His argument, chiefly deductive, may be expressed formally in complete syllogisms, although Morison, like most argumentative writers, does not explicitly state his major premises. One such deduction is this:

Whatever is needed to develop the in-

2 From Letter III, On Our Knowledge of the Causes of the Phenomena of Organic Nature, 1863.

tellect (A) deserves a place in a modern democracy (B). (This general statement, or major premise, is implied.)

But Latin and Greek (C) are needed to develop the intellect (A). (This minor premise is stated.)

Therefore Latin and Greek (C) deserve a place in a modern democracy (B). (This is the conclusion.)

You will note, however, that the minor premise in this deductive process—Latin and Greek are needed to develop the intellect—is supported by five particular statements. (See sentence outline, p. 781.)

Fallacies in argument. A fallacy is a flaw in the reasoning process. In deduction, for example, it is essential to establish the connection between two propositions ($A = B$; $B = C$) so that the conclusion ($A = C$) is necessarily implied. If we said $A = B$, $C = D$, we could not say $A = D$. There is no such connection between A and D as there is between A and C by virtue of their common identification in the middle term C. Note how the figures below explain this point.

A and C are connected by their common *situation* within the compass of B.

Note the difference, however, in this figure:

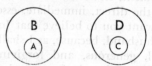

A is connected with B and C with D; but there is no connection between the pairs A, B and C, D. Hence, to say that $A = D$ is to assert a *non sequitur,* that which does not follow.

There are many possible fallacies in deductive reasoning, but all of them have this in common—the conclusion does not follow (*non sequitur*) from the premises that are given as reasons. The error is in the use of one or all of the three terms (ambiguity, for instance) or in the specious connection between the terms, as has been shown above.

In induction the essence of our reasoning is to establish a general truth by an examination of the particular truths that go to make it up. Thus to prove that poetry in general is characterized by exceptionally vivid language we might show how this characteristic is present in Shakespeare, in Milton, in Keats, and so on. But we may err here if we state exceptional cases rather than representative particulars, or if our individual examples do not converge on the same general point, or if we do not use a sufficient number of examples to establish the probability of our general statement.

The external form of argument. Argument then differs from exposition in its emphasis on reasoning. It also tends to differ from exposition in its outward form, in the way it is usually presented.

Each element in an argumentative essay or speech is shaped to achieve the central purpose—conviction or persuasion. Hence, the *beginning,* especially in formal argument, is likely to be more elaborate than the beginning of an exposition. Here, a writer explains his purpose, introduces his subject, defines his terms, and sets forth his central thesis or proposition. When the argument is long, he frequently announces the main divisions or headings that he will develop.

The *middle* section of an argument contains the proof of his proposition. This proof is normally set forth in the clearest, most coherent, and emphatic order—often concluding, as in the climax of a drama, with the most forceful argument. Frequently the writer follows the positive proof with a refutation (denial, distinction, or retort) of the principal objections against his proposition.

The *end* of an argument not only sums up the main points but also appeals directly for the audience's consent to the proposition or even for its decision to act in accordance with the author's views.

Thus argument, from beginning to end, attempts to change the audience's mind. The style as well as the arrangement conforms to this purpose.

The language of argument, particularly in a speech, establishes a direct contact with the audience, underlines the connections between statements, stirs the emotions by vigorous and often figurative language, and constantly prods

the audience to act. Let us see how Samuel Eliot Morison does this in his commencement address at Wooster College on the important subject "The Ancient Classics in a Modern Democracy."

The sentence outline below indicates the general line of the development. Read this outline first. In the marginal comment on the speech (pp. 782-85) the special characteristics of the argument are stressed.

SENTENCE OUTLINE OF "THE ANCIENT CLASSICS IN A MODERN DEMOCRACY"

Beginning: Statement of Purpose and Central Concept
  I. The classics, Latin and Greek, deserve a place in a modern democracy. (1-18)
    A. The classics will make for true democracy—a leveling up.
    B. The classics formed Thomas Jefferson, an ideal democrat.
    C. The classics have a practical value.

Middle: Development of Argument
  II. Latin and Greek are needed to develop the intellect. (19-34)
    A. Latin develops conciseness of thought and expression.
    B. Greek aids precise expression of complicated thought.
    C. Latin and Greek are logical in contrast to uninflected languages.
    D. Latin and Greek help the modern American to organize his speech into literature.
    E. Latin and Greek, with Mathematics, are unrivaled in the training of youthful minds in accurate and original thought.
  III. Latin and Greek are vital to the understanding of the best of English and modern European literature. (35-39)
  IV. Latin and Greek are important to future scientists. (40-44)
  V. Latin and Greek are useful to students of the social sciences. (45-53)
    A. Latin classics help us to know history by revealing the significance of the Roman Empire, which in turn reveals the significance of medieval and modern history.
    B. Greek historians, such as Thucydides, help us to know ourselves.
      1. They warn of the consequences of power politics and demagoguery.
      2. Greek history, as well as Roman history, was a guide of our forefathers.

VI. The classical training of our early leaders (along with their religious faith and their political heritage from Great Britain) accounts for the amazing success of the young American Republic. (54-71)
  A. Their classical background helped our early leaders to know what they were doing.
  B. It was partly responsible for the phenomenal accomplishments of our early leaders.
  C. A majority of the signers of the Declaration of Independence and of the framers of the Federal Constitution were classically trained men.
  D. These men were governed by the ideal of Greek virtue and Roman honor.

End: Summary of Argument
VII. The classics are necessary in America today. (72-81)
  A. America needs an intellectual aristocracy in a political democracy.
  B. The classics, working hand in hand with Christianity, provide the only means of cultivating an intellectual aristocracy.

The Ancient Classics in a Modern Democracy [3]

by Samuel Eliot Morison

1. It is often said that the classics are all very well for an aristocratic society, but are not to be cultivated in a democracy, because other things are more important for the average boy, and because their acquisition marks off those so educated as a separate caste. 2. Now, let us admit at once that other things are more important nowadays for the average American, who will end his formal education at the age of sixteen or eighteen. . . . 3. But it seems to me a perverted logic to deny the classics to *some* because they are beyond attainment for *all*. 4. Yet that is what many progressive educators today advocate. 5. They would keep school studies so easy, so elementary, that no child in full possession of his faculties would fail . . . , while providing nothing to challenge the admiration and stimulate the ability of a gifted young person. 6. This leveling down is the inversion of true democracy, which implies a leveling up.

Morison challenges the logic of progressive educators and prepares the ground for his own position

7. Thomas Jefferson never expected education to produce equality; on the contrary: "It becomes expedient for the publick happiness," he wrote, "that those persons, whom nature hath endowed with genius and virtue should be rendered by a liberal education worthy to receive, and able to guard the sacred deposit of the rights and liberties of their fellow citizens; and that they should be called to that charge without regard to wealth, birth or other accidental condition or circumstance." 8. In other words, Jefferson's educational object was to create an intellectual aristocracy, by taking the most gifted young men, irrespective of their parents' wealth or social station, and giving them a liberal education—an education of which the classics and ancient history were the core—that they might be the more fit to govern America, to embellish her cities with beautiful buildings, and to write a national literature. 9. And in all his schemes of education, the classics were central. 10. He himself was an excellent classical scholar. 11. At the age of fifty-six, when Vice-President of the United States, he wrote "to read the Latin and Greek authors in their original, is a sublime luxury. . . . I thank on my knees, Him who directed my early education, for having put into my possession this rich source of delight; and I would not exchange it for anything which I could then have acquired, and have not since acquired." 12. A young man who visited Jefferson at Monticello when the sage was eighty-two years old recorded that he rode horseback ten or twelve miles a day, spent several hours on the business of the University, and passed his leisure reading Greek. 13. Jefferson is a good enough democrat for me!

Jefferson is cited in favor of the speaker's view.

[3] From *The Ancient Classics in a Modern Democracy* by Samuel Eliot Morison. Copyright 1939 by Oxford University Press, Inc.

14. Yet I am aware that if the classics are to be retained as an investment of democracy, some immediate return, some palpable dividend must be promised. 15. If thus valued, the classics ask for no more than a fair comparison with rival subjects. 16. Is it not a generous estimate to assume that less than five per cent of the boys and girls who are now learning algebra in school will ever find any "use" for it? 17. French is as much a dead language for the average high-school graduate as Latin. 18. He will never hear it spoken or read a page of it again; but let us waive that, and apply the practical test to the ancient languages and literatures.

Here Morison is leading up to his central proposition. He does not state the division of his points. (For the actual division, see outline, pp. 781-82.)

19. In several different ways, Latin and Greek are superb instruments for developing the human intellect. 20. Latin is so concise, and the words so packed with meaning, that it cannot even be translated into another language with equal brevity. 21. That is why the study of Latin helps one to write clear, concise, forceful English prose. 22. And Greek is the most magnificent instrument so far invented for the precise expression of complicated thought, by the human mind. 23. It combines simplicity with flexibility and sensitiveness—the qualities attained in the best English poetry. 24. Both languages are organic, not slipshod like the uninflected modern languages, where so much depends on idiom, or the order of words. 25. A Greek poem, or a passage of good Latin prose, is articulated, functional, and inevitable, like the steel skeleton of a skyscraper; everything is there that is structurally necessary. . . . 26. This logical quality of the ancient languages is such that the very act of translation is an intellectual discipline of the highest order, helping one to counteract the tendency of English to gain emphasis by mere repetition, and to check the sloppiness in which writers not educated in the classical tradition, like Charles Dickens and Gertrude Stein, are prone to indulge. 27. Just as musical theory and counterpoint enable a musician to compose melodies, concertos, and symphonies out of his national folk-song; so Latin and Greek enable an American to organize the common speech of his countryside into enduring literature. 28. Of this I have an example that will surprise you. 29. It was Ernest L. Thayer, one who took A's and B's in his classics course, a graduate *magna cum laude* of my own university, who wrote that classic on the great American game, "Casey at the Bat"!

The speaker does not quote specimens of Latin and Greek poetry. Does this lessen the force of his argument? The method of proof here is cause and effect.

Note the transition from causal analysis *to* contrast *in sentence 26, to* comparison *in sentence 27, and then to* example *in sentences 28-29.*

30. Latin, Greek, and Mathematics are instruments unrivaled by anything invented in twenty centuries of educational experience for the training of youthful minds in accurate and original thought. 31. The analysis involved in translating Latin or Greek into English provides an unconscious training in logic. 32. If in after life your job be to think, four years or more of Latin is the best training you can possibly have. 33. You are learning logic, the art of thinking, without knowing it. 34. And the art of thinking is the key to creative work in science and statesmanship, as in philosophy.

Morison resumes his proof from cause and effect.

35. For understanding the best English literature and modern European literature, the classics are vital. 36. The ancient world was implicit in the writings of Dante, of Chaucer, of Montaigne, of Milton, and of Goethe, to name only a few. 37. They cannot become explicit to us, unless we grasp in some measure the background of their thought. 38. How wretched are those school texts of Milton, with every god and goddess and classical allusion annotated! 39. If we cannot teach our pupils a little Greek and Roman mythology first, better give up Milton and Dryden, Keats and Shelley, and start English poetry with Walt Whitman.

Argument from specific examples *to prove necessity of classics in understanding English literature. Note the exclamatory style of sentence 38, the irony in sentence 39.*

40. For future scientists, the ancient languages are important not merely as a mental discipline, and as a means of recreation, but as the basis of all scientific terminology. 41. After a man has made up his mind to choose a career in medicine, engineering, or applied science, it is usually too late to get a fundamental grounding in Latin. 42. One result of engineers' and scientists' neglecting the classics is a purely parrot-knowledge of their basic terminology, and a blatant misuse of it both in speech and writing. 43. The style of the average American scientific paper nowadays is often so bad that

Argument from contrast: *what happens when scientists neglect the classics. Note, too, how the speaker ridicules the writing of the scientist—an indirect form of* refutation.

even specialists in the writer's own field cannot tell what he is trying to say. 44. Indeed, the only worse English to be found nowadays is written by those "Progressive Educators" who have done their best to kill the classics, and who write dissertations on high-school plumbing in a jargon that may best be described as Pedagese English.

45. Again, the ancient classics are of use as an introduction to the social sciences, and a running interpretation of them. 46. They open a window to your mind from these times to other times, and from this place to all other places. 47. The Roman Empire is a bottle-neck through which the vintage of the past has flowed into modern life. 48. To comprehend in some manner the mentality of Rome is the key to medieval and modern history; and in ancient history you will find many of the current questions of today threshed out in a clean-cut fashion that will help you to comprehend your own age. 49. What a terrible warning Thucydides gives of the consequences of war and power politics and demagoguery! 50. And it will enable you to get under the skin of American history, too. 51. The fathers of our Revolution, the framers of our federal and state constitutions, and the great Senators (note the term) of the nineteenth century were steeped in Roman and Greek History. 52. Antique liberty was a phrase often on their lips, and ever in their hearts. 53. They were closer to the ancients in spirit, Americans as they were, than we are to them.

> Sentences 46 and 47 contain metaphors that are persuasive as well as explanatory.

54. Those men, the founders of our Republic, seemed to know what they were doing, and where they were going, whilst "The *merely modern* man never knows what he is about." 55. Our forefathers were not *merely modern,* even in their own day. 56. Behind them, in the backs of their minds, and before them as a goal there was always the supreme achievement of Judaea in religion, the supreme achievement of Hellas in the good life, and the supreme achievement of Rome in statecraft. 57. They knew what they wanted, in terms of the attainable. 58. Most of our present leaders don't know what they want, except that they want very much to get in power if they are out, or stay in power if they are in.

59. No generation of Americans has ever accomplished so much of permanent good for this country as the generation of 1770. 60. Thirty years saw independence won, a colonial policy—the Northwest Ordinance—worked out, the gateways to the West opened, state constitutions adopted, the Federal Constitution drafted and ratified, federal government placed in successful operation on a scale hitherto unknown, the war debt liquidated, American credit placed higher than that of most European countries, the bases of American foreign policy laid, and finally, a peaceful revolution (the election of Jefferson) effected by the ballot. 61. No American can look back upon the achievements of that generation without pride; and, when we contemplate the mess the world is in today, we can look back not only with pride but with wonder at those men who pledged to the cause of Independence their lives, their fortunes, and their sacred honor.

> An appeal to patriotic pride.

62. Where did they acquire the political maturity that enabled them to perform so admirably these almost superhuman tasks? 63. Partly, no doubt, from the experience in self-government that they had enjoyed as part of [Great Britain]. 64. That nation had a long tradition in self-government, from which we benefited and the ripe experience of which went into our constitutions, our bills of rights, and our political tolerance. 65. Yet, partly, the achievement of our heroic age must be ascribed to the fact that America was a Christian nation, that far from regarding the State as the be-all and end-all of political existence, an entity that could do no wrong, its interest was the supreme good; our founders believed that citizens individually were responsible to God for the acts of the state, that righteousness exalteth a people, and sin is a reproach to any nation.

> The proof from *cause and effect* is again resumed. In sentences 63-65, the speaker admits that other causes helped to produce the political wisdom and philosophical maturity of the founding fathers.

66. And partly, too, the amazing success of the young republic was due to the classical training of her leaders. 67. A majority of the signers of the

Declaration of Independence and of the framers of the Federal Constitution were classically trained college men; and most of the remainder had studied in school more classics than most Americans nowadays learn in college. 68. Our Revolutionary leaders were *not* fitted for responsibility by courses in civics, sociology, and psychology. 69. It was by Plutarch's Lives, the orations of Cicero and Demosthenes, and by Thucydides that the young men of the 1760's learned the wisdom to deal with other men and with great events in the 1770's and 80's. 70. American Revolutionary leaders both North and South, the Adamses and Trumbulls of New England; Hamilton, John Jay, the Morrises and Stocktons of the Middle States; Madison, Mason, and Jefferson of Virginia; and the Rutledges and Pinckneys of South Carolina were prepared for their unexpected tasks by a study of classical culture that broadened their mental horizon, sharpened their intellectual powers, stressed *virtus* and promoted *areté,* the civic qualities appropriate to a Republican. 71. It was of Greek virtue and Roman honor that Thomas Jefferson was thinking when he concluded the immortal Declaration, "We mutually pledge to each other our lives, our fortunes, and our sacred honor."

Proof through example *of the* effects *of classical training.*

72. And so I come to this final argument, that we need the classics because our country needs the intelligent leadership and disinterested service of an intellectual aristocracy—not a plutocracy, or a hereditary ruling caste, but an intellectual élite recruited from the people, as Thomas Jefferson said, "without regard to wealth, birth or other accidental condition or circumstance." 73. It was just such an aristocracy of brains and character that won the United States independence, that secured by diplomacy our free access to the West, that founded our colleges and universities. 74. And it was want of it, in business and in politics, that led to the great depression. 75. Now that we all know that slough in which materialism, unrestrained greed, and untrained leaders brought us, it would seem logical to return to the noble American tradition of Thomas Jefferson: an intellectual aristocracy in a political democracy. . . .

Note the deductive reasoning. The classics produce intelligent leaders; we need intelligent leaders; therefore we need the classics.

76. If educated people simply drift with the current, reject responsibility, and adopt the protective coloring of the mediocre, America may well drift into the gangster state . . . , the negation of democracy, or, at best, will aim no higher than to provide for the needs and desires of the average. 77. Without a leadership imbued with the standards of antique virtue, and trained in the classical tradition, our civilization threatens to become the mirror where the common man contemplates himself, and is pleased at the sight of his imperfections. 78. Now, the only base on which to rebuild an intellectual aristocracy, so far as I can see, is the civilization of the ancient world, working hand in hand with Christianity, as it has done in the universities of Europe and America these six hundred years. 79. Let the autocracies of today . . . , if they wish, delude themselves into believing that they can establish a completely new order divorced from the past, unblessed by God. 80. We, I trust, are wiser than they, and will hold fast to that which is good. 81. To cut loose from our classical background would be to sever the main nerve of modern civilization, to attenuate and impoverish life, and to leave some of man's noblest capacities unused.

Note the abridged syllogism in sentence 76. Major: *If educated people in America drift . . .* Minor *(implied):* But educated people in America are drifting . . . Conclusion: *America may well. . . .*

Summary of main arguments.

This speech was delivered in 1939, when Russia and Germany were temporarily allies.

The metaphors, the parallel constructions, the climax, the periodic structure—all contribute to the vigor and suspense of this concluding passage.

Description

Description is the form of discourse that presents the physical details of a subject. Hence, it appeals primarily to our senses: sight, hearing, taste, touch, and smell. It answers the question—how does the subject (a house, person, landscape, tree) appear to the beholder?

It is employed by all of us in some fashion to conduct our daily business. "A white stucco house, on a level green plot, surrounded by maple and pine trees, adjacent to a brook . . ." reads the real estate announcement. "Wanted: John Jones, height 6', weight 200 lbs., scar over left eye, thick brown hair, muddy complexion, rasping voice . . ." goes the police circular. "A smooth pillow, of rough grain texture, stuffed with aromatic pine cones, suitable for den or divan" states the advertisement.

In scientific writing description is frequently the first step in analysis. The ambulance surgeon presents details concerning the patient's appearance, reaction to touch, and so on; the biologist describes the skeleton, the organic structure, and the tissues of a particular species.

In literary discourse, however, description provides more than accurate technical information. The essayist, the narrator, the fiction writer all attempt to create a vivid, dominant impression of the subject rather than merely to state a series of accurate particulars. To do this the writer establishes a well-defined point of view, selects salient details, fuses these details into a meaningful whole.

In "On the Blue Water" note how Ernest Hemingway employs these features of description.

In the first place, the Gulf Stream and the other great ocean currents are the last wild country there is left. Once you are out of sight of land and of the other boats you are more alone than you can ever be hunting and the sea is the same as it has been since before men ever went on it in boats. In a season fishing you will see it oily flat as the becalmed galleons saw it while they drifted to the westward; *white-capped* with a fresh breeze as they saw it running with the trades; and in *high, rolling blue hills* the tops blowing off them like snow as they were punished by it, so that sometimes you will see *three great hills of water* with your fish jumping from the top of the farthest one and if you tried to make a turn to go with him without picking your chance, one of those breaking crests would *roar down in on you with a thousand tons of water.* . . .

In the first two sentences Hemingway establishes his point of view. In emotional terms, he regards the ocean as a vast, lonely wilderness. In technical terms, he describes it from the angle of vision of a fisherman in a small boat. In the third sentence he picks out a few significant details (italicized in the quota-

tion)—all of which *suggest* the wildness and vastness of the ocean, its contrasting moments of quiet and storm.

Stephen Leacock's description of Mark Twain, in the passage below, also illustrates the impressionistic character of artistic description. The details of Sam Clemens's appearance create a general impression of vital energy and extreme individuality.

At the time when Sam Clemens abandoned mining and betook himself definitely to journalism (August 1862), he was twenty-six years old. He was a robust-looking young man with a mop of sandy hair turning to auburn and a blue eye filled with life and intelligence. In his infancy he had been a puny child, but the outdoor life of farm and bush and river had done its work and had presently endowed him with that deep-seated energy and vital power which is the birthright of the frontiersman.

As a young and rising pilot he had liked to make himself in point of dress a mirror of fashion. As a miner he did the exact opposite, outdoing his fellows in the careless roughness of his dress and the lazy slouch of his walk. He possessed, and accentuated by use, a slow and drawling speech. In short, he tried to make himself a "character," and succeeded to the full measure of his wish. A large part of his popularity and his local reputation in his Nevada days sprang from the attraction of this easy and careless manner and appearance. Second nature though it became, there was beneath it an eager and a restless mind, filled in his mining days with the fever of the search for gold, dreaming of fortune. At times even his robust health, broke under the strain of the intensity of his pursuit of fortune.

The structure of description. The pattern of description is determined by two factors—the nature of the subject and the attitude of the writer. A fixed or static subject, such as a city or a landscape, almost always imposes a spatial order in description. We view such a subject from the right or left, from near to far, from bottom to top. "Cross Creek," writes Marjorie Kinnan Rawlings, "is a bend in a country road. . . . We are four miles west of the small village of Island Grove, nine miles east of a turpentine still, and on the other sides we do not count distance at all, for the two lakes and the broad marshes create an infinite space between us and the horizon."

William Bartram, an early American naturalist, also used a spatial order to frame his picture of the same St. Johns River country described by Mrs. Rawlings. Note how Bartram, in the italicized phrases, establishes the order of his description.

From this promontory, looking *eastward* across the river, I beheld a landscape of low country, unparalleled as I think; *on the left* is the east coast of the little lake, which I had just passed; and from the orange bluff *at the lower end* the high forests begin, and increase in breadth *from the shore of the lake,* making a circular sweep *to the right,* and contain many hundred thousand acres of meadow; and this grand *sweep* of high forests *encircles,* as I apprehend, at least twenty miles of these green fields, interspersed with hummocks or islets of evergreen trees, where the sovereign magnolia and lordly palm stand conspicuous. The islets are high shelly knolls, on the sides of creeks or branches of the river, which wind about and drain off the superabundant waters that cover these meadows during the winter season.[4]

Some subjects of description, however, are seen in movement rather than in a fixed position. A description of the sun's course or a trip to the moon, as in "Weekend on the Moon" (p. 86), requires a shifting point of view in which the subject is seen now from one angle, now from another, or in successive moments.

The order of description may also be determined by the subjective response of the writer. His mental attitude, as well as the place or vantage point from which he views his subject, gives form to his description. Hence, some writers compose their pictures in impressionistic patterns. Bryan MacMahon describes the lion-tamer by saying that "his nose was pointed to make his profile a shallow isosceles triangle with the vertex on the tip of his nose" (pp. 320-21). Hawthorne sees a mountain as a great stone face. To Robert Louis Stevenson, Monterey, California, is a giant fishhook. Imaginative patterns of this kind often make a stronger and more pleasing impression on the reader than the impersonal objective notation of appearances.

Extended description is normally tied into the framework of narrative. Thus, in describing a house the writer might first show how it appears from the front. "As I walked up the path I noticed. . . . Inside I observed. . . .

4 From *Travels through North and South Carolina, Georgia, East and West Florida,* 1791.

Going upstairs. . . . From the garden it appeared. . . ." Huck's description of the Grangerford House in Chapter 17 of *Huckleberry Finn* (pp. 449-51) is an excellent example of extended description.

Narration

Narration is a form of discourse that recounts what happened. It tells a story in terms of the *persons* or *characters* who act at a certain *time,* in a certain *place,* in a certain *manner,* and for certain *motives.* "James Moody," the newscast goes, "yesterday heaved his mother-in-law into Central Park Lake because she complained that the sun was too hot." This brief, single incident contains the essentials of narrative: it tell *what* happened, *who* acted, *when, where, how,* and *why* the incident occurred.

In extended narratives, such as newspaper articles, "reportage," historical and biographical essays, adventure stories, and autobiographies the problem of telling a meaningful story is much more complex. Characters and events are intertwined. It then becomes necessary to present incidents in a way that makes sense—to unite parts into a meaningful whole. Just as the writer of exposition must clarify a subject by analysis, so the narrator must bring out the meaning of an action by presenting incidents in an orderly manner, with due regard for pace, proportion, and climax.

The structure of narration. In general all good narratives observe two orders—chronological order and logical order. The first kind of order needs little explanation. All action occurs in time. To make any action clear we must recount it in the order of its occurrence, from the first incident to the last. Not to do so would be to invite chaos. We could not tell the story of the Civil War accurately by jumbling together Appomatox, Bull Run, and Gettysburg.

Important as chronology is, it does not necessarily bring out the meaning of an action. Take, for example, this recent piece of news. "The President left the hospital at 9 A.M. He flew to Washington, arriving at 4 P.M. Crowds welcomed him at the airport." The chronology is clear. The sentences tell a story. How much more meaningful, however, is the statement below.

"The President, cured of the heart ailment that disabled him for the last two months, left the hospital at 9 A.M. He flew to Washington, arriving at 4 P.M. Grateful because of his return to active duty, crowds greeted him at the airport."

The second statement observes time order, but it also establishes a logical connection between events. The President left the hospital *because* he was cured. Crowds welcomed him *because* his return allayed their anxiety. We read here a *connected* story—one in which the several incidents are interrelated.

In every good narrative, then, there are two ways of achieving unity—the use of chronological order, which establishes a clear sequence of events in time, and the concomitant use of logical order, which establishes the logical sequence of events. Let us show just what we mean by these two orders by referring to the extended narrative, "Annapurna—The Third of June" (p. 104).

Beginning, middle, end. Even a cursory reading of Maurice Herzog's narrative reveals a definite chronological order. Save for occasional flashbacks, the events occur successively throughout a single day. The chronicle, complete and orderly, begins at dawn of June 3 and ends in the early evening. But within this chronological order a logical order operates as well. Events do not merely *succeed* each other in time; they flow from each other necessarily. *From* an initial situation (the beginning), the decision to try to reach the summit of Annapurna, the action moves *through* the complications and trials of climbing up and down the peak (the middle), *to* the successful return (the end).

Hence, *beginning, middle,* and *end* are not merely tape-measure terms designating respectively the first few paragraphs, the paragraphs in between, and the concluding paragraphs; they are qualitative terms, too, in that *beginning* signifies the initial cause of an action, *middle* signifies the cause in operation, and *end* signifies the effect or result of the action.

Pace, porportion, climax. Order, we have observed, assures unity in narrative. Coherence is attained by establishing links between the several incidents through connective phrases and transitions, and by the consistent handling of point of view. (For a discussion of point of view, see "The Short Story: Introduction," pp. 297-98, and *Harbrace Handbook,* Section 27h.) Emphasis is given to narrative by appropriate pace, proportion, and climax.

Pace is the rate of movement of the action. A good narrative *moves* steadily toward its goal. Sometimes it races in a swift succession of incidents set forth in brief, vivid sentences, as in Alfred Noyes's ballad, "The Highwayman" (p. 697); sometimes it winds slowly, like Paul Horgan's Rio Grande, through banks of description and exposition. A right pace is not necessarily fast or slow. Rather it is adjusted to the subject itself.

Proportion is the relative weight given to the various incidents of the narrative. Less important incidents are usually treated briefly, while the more important scenes are expanded or intensified. In "A Clean, Well-Lighted Place" (p. 379), for instance, Ernest Hemingway gives most space to the two paragraphs ("It was late . . . 'Good night,' the other said") that bring out the theme of the story. The other incidents are related in the barest possible fashion.

Climax is the building of interest by tension and suspense. It means, too, the points of highest interest, the peaks of our tension and suspense, the moments before our fears and hopes are finally resolved.

Pace, proportion, and climax owe as much to style as they do to careful arrangement. A narrative moves and engages our attention by the selection of details *and* by the use of image-making words—words that make the reader feel that he is actually in the midst of the action. Moreover, language whose rhythm simulates the movement of the story creates in the reader a sense of immediate participation in what is being told.

After the preface of a book comes the contents—the substance. Just so, after this preface to writing, you come to the job itself. Remember the caution at the beginning of this essay: you cannot expect to become a great writer, or even a good writer, on your first try. But if you are willing to work hard on your writing, you can achieve clear and effective expression of your thoughts.

part five

Harbrace College Handbook

FOURTH EDITION

By

JOHN C. HODGES *University of Tennessee*

In consultation with

Francis X. Connolly *Fordham University*

▶ To the Instructor

The *Harbrace College Handbook* is both a guide for the individual writer and a text for use in class. It presents its subject matter in a readily usable form, and thus lightens the instructor's task of reading student papers.

Numbers. The book contains only thirty-five major sections, or numbers, referring to errors commonly made in writing. These include (as has been shown by a comprehensive examination of student writing) everything to which instructors normally refer in marking papers. But other errors less frequently made have not been overlooked. They are subordinated logically to the thirty-five primary numbers and may be found readily by reference to the back end papers or to the detailed Index. If an instructor wishes to have any of these subordinate errors conveniently before his students, he can have them added in the blanks provided on the chart inside the back cover. With some college students Sections 1-18 may be needed only for review or for occasional reference.

Symbols. Instead of the simplified list of numbers, the instructor may, if he prefers, use the corresponding symbols. Most of these symbols are well known to English teachers; they are entered on the back charts.

General Plan. The sections on **Sentence Sense** (1) and **Grammatical Terms** (35) are general sections. The former may be used, whenever needed, as an introduction to the other sections; the latter should be used throughout as a glossary of terms. For correction of specific errors, students will normally be referred to Sections 2-34.

Drill Materials. Exercises are provided both for the major sections and for many subsections, and there are also general exercises applicable to two or more sections. Many of these exercises consist of lively paragraphs instead of conventional groups of unrelated sentences. Many other exercises are of a positive type, in which the student is asked not to correct errors but to compose good sentences to illustrate the principle involved. Some classes may need very little of the drill materials; others may need all of it, or even additional exercises such as those in the *Exercise Manual for College English: The First Year,* Revised Edition (keyed to the *Harbrace College Handbook,* Fourth Edition).

Contemporary Usage. This Fourth Edition of the *Harbrace Handbook* attempts to describe the usual practice of good contemporary writers, and to state that practice as simply as possible. The "rules" are to be interpreted as principles, or descriptions, derived from usage; and they have authority only to the extent that they describe usage. In the illustrations throughout the book, labels such as RIGHT and WRONG indicate what might be expected and what is usually avoided in standard written English.

Acknowledgments. Any English handbook must owe a debt to linguistic scholarship too extensive to be acknowledged in detail. Fortunately this scholarship is now very active. Among the many individuals who have generously offered suggestions for making this handbook more usable, the author wishes especially to thank Professors Francis X. Connolly (Fordham), Robert R. Gross (Bucknell), Gerald A. Smith (Maryland), Grover C. Smith, Jr. (Duke), Francis Lee Utley (Ohio State), and Walter R. Whitney (Maine). For important contributions to Section 33 (**Library Paper**), the author is grateful to Mr. John Dobson and Miss Eleanor Goehring, of the Library Staff (Tennessee), and to Miss Ruby Jean Harris and Mr. Jack Howard Wilson (Tennessee).

Finally, the author is indebted to Professor Bain Tate Stewart and other members of the Freshman Staff at the University of Tennessee for many helpful suggestions. He wishes to express particular thanks to Mr. Roy F. Montgomery, who has prepared most of the new exercise materials.

▶ To the Student

Numbers or Symbols. A number or a symbol written in the margin of your paper indicates an error and calls for a correction. If a number is used, turn directly to the corresponding boldface number at the top of the page in the *Handbook*. If a symbol is used, first consult the alphabetical list of symbols inside the back cover to find the number to which you should turn.

Ordinary References. The ordinary reference will be to the boldface number or symbol standing at the head of one of the thirty-five sections of the *Handbook*. The statement in large boldface at the beginning of each section covers the section as a whole. One of the statements in smaller boldface within the section will usually be needed for the correction of your specific error. Study the section to which you have been referred—the whole of the section if necessary—and master the specific part of the section that explains your error. To prove that you have found the specific principle needed for the correction, write the appropriate letter (**a, b, c,** etc.) after the number or symbol supplied by your instructor. An *ex* written by the instructor after a number or symbol calls for the writing out of the appropriate exercise.

Specific References. Whenever your instructor wishes to refer you to a specific part of a section, he will add the appropriate letter to the boldface number or symbol.

EXAMPLES   **2c** (*or* **frag-c**), **18b** (*or* **sp-b**), **28d** (*or* **ref-d**).

General References. At times your instructor may give you a very general reference from which you are to determine and correct your error. For example, the symbol **gr** will refer you to the whole division on GRAMMAR, in-cluding Sections **1-7**; the symbol **m** to the division on MECHANICS, Sections **8-11**; the symbol **p** to the division on PUNCTUATION, Sections **12-17**; and so forth. An obvious error may be called to your attention by the symbol **x**, and general awkwardness by the symbol **k**.

Diagraming. To supplement the explanations, simple diagrams are used occasionally. These diagrams are often limited to parts of sentences—in order to concentrate your attention on the immediate problem and to prevent your becoming more interested in complicated lines than in grammatical relationships.

Additional Help. Some of the principles treated in English handbooks can be mastered only by students who understand the fundamentals of the sentence. A well-developed "sentence sense" is especially helpful in the mastery of Sections **2** (**Sentence Fragment**), **3** (**Comma Splice**), **6** (**Agreement**), **12** (**The Comma**), **14** (**The Semicolon**), **21** (**Wordiness**), **23** (**Unity**), **24** (**Subordination**), **25** (**Coherence**), **26** (**Parallelism**), and **30** (**Variety**). If you have difficulty in understanding these sections, you should first master the fundamentals of the sentence treated in Section **1** (**Sentence Sense**), and then turn again to the principle immediately involved. If you fail to understand any term of grammar used in the *Handbook,* consult the alphabetical list in Section **35** (**Grammatical Terms**).

Revision. After you have mastered the principle underlying the correction of each error, you should make careful revision in the manner recommended by your instructor. One method of revision is explained in Section **8** (**Manuscript Form and Revision**), pages 830-31.

Exercises. The exercises are to be written out on paper, not marked in the book.

▶ Contents

GRAMMAR

▶ Sentence Sense

1 Master the essentials of the sentence as an aid to clear thinking, effective writing, and intelligent reading.

Mastery of sentence sense—a recognition of what *makes* a sentence, and of the proper relationships between its several parts—is your key to good writing and reading. If you lack sentence sense, you cannot effectively communicate your own thoughts, nor effectively and fully comprehend the statements of others.

Sentence sense is prerequisite to the intelligent use of this handbook, especially Sections **2** (Sentence Fragment), **3** (Comma Splice), **6** (Agreement), **12** (The Comma), **14** (The Semicolon), **21** (Wordiness), **23** (Unity), **24** (Subordination), **25** (Coherence), **26** (Parallelism), and **30** (Variety).

The student who lacks a well-developed sentence sense can only with difficulty recognize and avoid the sentence fragment—that is, the failure to complete a thought in the normal fashion of good writers. He will be prone to make comma splices—that is, to link main clauses with only a comma between them—simply because he cannot recognize main clauses; to make errors in agreement because he cannot determine verbs and associate them with their subjects; to misuse the comma because he lacks the ability to distinguish such parts of the sentence as main and subordinate clauses, adverb clauses, adjective clauses, compound predicates, and phrases. Once he has learned how to analyze his sentences, he can make them more effective by applying the principles underlying unity, subordination, coherence, parallelism, and sentence variety. Any student who does not understand the usual and normal construction of the sentence should develop his sentence sense and then study the sections of the handbook concerned with his particular difficulties.

1a Learn to recognize verbs.

The verb ("He *ran* fast"; "you *are* late") is the heart of the sentence. Without a verb any group of words ("after a while," "no advice from anyone," "all waiting for the signal") is only a sentence fragment. A verb is a word (or a group of words) that expresses action, indicates a state of being, or asserts something. It is used (1) in making a statement, (2) in asking a question, or (3) in giving a command.

1. The rain *falls* gently.
2. *Are* you happy?
3. *Walk* carefully.

The verb may consist of one word (as in the three sentences above) or a group of two, three, or four words. The group, called a *verb phrase,* comprises the verb and the auxiliary words often required in English to show inflection; the group is just as much a verb as the single word.

1. The man *will work* faithfully.
2. The man *has been working* faithfully.
3. The man *should have been working* faithfully.

The words that make up a verb phrase are often separated.

1. It *is* not *raining.*
2. It *will* almost certainly *rain* tomorrow.

A verb may be combined with the adverb *not,* or with a contraction of *not.*

1. He *cannot go.*
2. He *can't go.*
3. It *isn't* cold.
4. He *doesn't know.*

The student who can find the verb (or verb phrase) and can separate it from other elements has gone a long way toward acquiring sentence sense.

► EXERCISE 1. For each of the following sentences supply an appropriate verb (or verb phrase). Then compose five sentences of your own and underline each verb (or verb phrase).

1. Steve _____ _____ in Baltimore in 1926. 2. His parents _____ six other children, all younger than he. 3. When Steve _____ thirteen, his father _____ _____ in a shipyard accident. 4. With the life-insurance money, Steve's mother _____ to keep the children in school; for she _____ the value of education and _____ _____ _____ any sacrifice to see them graduated. 5. After high school Steve _____ the Navy; and during his last year in service, he _____ his oldest sister to college. 6. When he _____ _____ his period of enlistment, he _____ at the same college. 7. It _____ there that I first _____ this brother and sister. 8. I _____ never _____ two finer people.

► EXERCISE 2. Underline the fourteen verbs and four verb phrases in the following sentences. Do not underline verbals—participles, gerunds, and infinitives. (For a discussion of verbals, which are derived from verbs but are not regular verbs, see below under 1d.)

1. Jim angrily called himself a fool, as he had been doing all the way through the woods, for allowing Fred to talk him into this mad idea. 2. What were ghosts and family legends to him, in this year of grace and nuclear fission? 3. He had mysteries enough of his own, of a highly complex electronic sort, to occupy him through the rest of a lifetime. 4. But to be plodding along here, like the Mississippi schoolboy he had been a dozen years before, on a ghost chase in the middle of the night, was preposterous. 5. It was an outrage to everything he stood for; it was lunacy. 6. It was—he swallowed the truth like a bitter pill—frightful! 7. The legend and the ghost had been a horror to him as a child; and they were a horror still. 8. Standing at the edge of the weed-choked, briar-tangled slope, on the top of which the decayed mansion waited evilly, he felt almost sick. 9. The safe, sure things of every day had become distant, childish fantasies. 10. This

grotesque night and whatever, ghoulish and monstrous, inhabited it were clammily, horribly real.

► EXERCISE 3. Underline the thirteen verbs and the four verb phrases in the following sentences.

1. Driving his oxen in the face of the dust storm was a wearying task. 2. He buried his face deep in his scarf. 3. Stumbling, he almost fell. 4. "Keep on," he said to himself. 5. His wife called from the wagon, her voice muffled by the roaring storm and by the flapping of the canvas. 6. Finally he made out what she was saying. 7. "Don't you think that we ought to stop?" she said. 8. "No," he shouted back. 9. There would be time to stop when they reached water, when he could do something for the stumbling oxen, whose anguished bellowing seemed to reproach him. 10. He hoped then to rest, to sleep.

► EXERCISE 4. Underline the twenty-seven verbs or verb phrases in the following sentences.

1. When Falstaff wishes to persuade Mistress Ford of the honesty of his love, he disclaims all likeness to "these lisping hawthorn buds that come like women in men's apparel and smell like Bucklersbury in simple-time." 2. "Simples" are herbs of which medicines are compounded. 3. They were formerly an item of trade in the grocery business. 4. And grocers, as a chronicler of London writing in 1598 tells us, were then to be found mostly in Bucklersbury. 5. There were two men from Stratford who were partners in a grocery business in London during Shakespeare's time, and their shop was located in Bucklersbury. 6. One of the partners was Richard Quiney, whose brother Thomas was later to become the husband of Shakespeare's younger daughter, Judith. 7. A rather extensive correspondence among the Quineys and some of their family connections in Stratford and London during 1598 frequently mentions Shakespeare and indicates that he was involved with them in several business transactions. 8. More often than not, the transactions were small loans which one or another of his fellow townsmen sought of him, indicating that they regarded him as a person of some means, able and willing to be of service to his friends in their minor emergencies. 9. As H. B. Wheatley has pointed out, there seems no doubt that Shakespeare had occasion to visit the business house of his grocer friends in Bucklersbury. 10. There seems likewise no reason to doubt that it was the familiar fragrance of the stocks of herbs there which supplied him with the figure of comparison Falstaff used in his love-making.

Note: Ask a competent person to check the accuracy of your spotting of verbs. If you can mark the verbs accurately, you are ready to take up the next exercises. If not, mark verbs in other lists of sentences (such as the exercises at the end of this section) and get assistance in checking the accuracy of your work. Many students confuse verbs with participles, gerunds, and infinitives, which are treated below under **1d.**

1b   Learn to recognize the subjects (and objects) of verbs in sentences.

A sentence is a unit of expression that may stand alone. It is followed in speaking by a pause and in writing by a period, a question mark, or an exclamation point. Regularly it has both a verb (called the *predicate*) and its subject, or at least these are implied.[1] In the following sentences the subjects are in *italics* and the predicates (verbs) are in **boldface.**

Men	**work.**
Some *men* on farms	**work** long hours during the summer.
[*You*]	**walk** carefully

The subject and the words associated with it ("Some men on farms") are called the *complete subject;* the predicate and the words associated with it ("work long hours during the summer") are called the *complete predicate.*

In order to find the subject, simply ask, in connection with the verb, "Who or what?" In the sentences listed above, who or what *work? Men* work. Who or what *walk? You* walk. No matter how long or how involved the sentence is, the subject can readily be found—if the verb has first been recognized.

The *airplane,* having reached Miami after a long flight from South America, **circles** the city before landing at the airport. [Who or what *circles?* The *airplane* circles.]

It is sometimes helpful to make a diagram, or to form a mental picture, of the subject and its verb, thus:

airplane	circles

Any student who can bring the subject and verb together in this way should have little

trouble in making the two "agree" (see Section 6); for example, *airplane* **circles,** *airplanes* **circle.**

The subject of an interrogative sentence is more readily located when the sentence is recast in the form of a statement.

Has the *last* of the deserters **surrendered?**
The *last* of the deserters **has surrendered.**

A sentence may have a compound subject (*Mary* and *Jane* **played**), a compound predicate (*Mary* **sang** and **played**), or both compound subject and compound predicate (*Mary* and *Jane* **sang** and **played**).

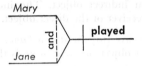

[Sentence with a compound subject]

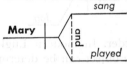

[Sentence with a compound predicate]

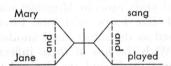

[Sentence with a compound subject and a compound predicate]

► EXERCISE 5. Diagram (or point out) the subject and predicate in each of the following sentences. Note that some of the subjects and predicates are compound.

1. Looking out from the attic window, Jim and Ben could see the cattle grazing on the range and hear the bleating of the calves. 2. There were two herds, one of Herefords and one of Angus. 3. Was anything more beautiful than such a sight on a clear, spring morning? 4. Jim opened the window and sniffed the air. 5. Quietly, joyfully his eyes embraced the scene: the woods on the left, the creek in the foreground, the range beyond, the corral and bunkhouse on the right. 6. He looked and thought. 7. A thing like this should last forever. 8. If not forever, then it should last for a very long time. 9. Home and the ranch meant a

---

[1] For a discussion of incomplete sentences, which do not bulk large in written English, see page 806. In this book the word *sentence* will refer to the regular, or complete, sentence.

great deal to him that morning. 10. He counted it a golden moment, a golden day, to be treasured against the coming deficit of time.

Some verbs have "objects." A word or group of words that receives the action of a verb is called its *object.*

1. The boy hit the *ball.* [*Ball* is the object of *hit.*]

boy	hit	ball

2. The boy trained the *dog.* [*Dog* is the object of *trained.*]

Note: Sometimes a sentence has both a direct object and an indirect object. The indirect object states the receiver of the direct object.

> The boy gave [to] the *dog* a *bone.* [*Dog* is the indirect object of *gave; bone* is the direct object.]

boy	gave	bone
	\ dog	

Word Order. In modern English the subject and the object can be determined by the normal order of words in the sentence. A thousand years ago our language was highly inflected, like Latin, with one form of the noun used as the subject and another as the object. With the loss of these inflections we have come to depend on the order of the words to distinguish between subject and object, as in "The dog killed the bear" and "The bear killed the dog." The meaning of these sentences is unmistakable because of our typical language pattern: subject—verb—object.

▶ EXERCISE 6. In the following sentences underline the nineteen subjects once, the twenty-one verbs (or verb phrases) twice, and check the fourteen direct objects of verbs (or verb phrases). Diagram the first three sentences which contain direct objects to show subject, verb, and object.

1. Henry drove up to the gas station. 2. He honked his horn. 3. "Shall I fill her up?" asked the attendant. 4. Henry indicated his assent. 5. He watched the fuel gauge as it fluttered from empty to full. 6. The gasoline pump stopped whirring. 7. "Shall I check your oil?" 8. The attendant grinned at him through the windshield. 9. He lifted the hood and, after fussing with the oil stick and radiator cap, he closed the hood. 10.

"You don't need any oil, but your carburetor is leaking and the points should be cleaned." 11. Henry, anxious to get home, waved a five-dollar bill as a signal that he would discuss the question of major repairs at some other time. 12. As soon as he had pocketed the change, he started the engine, stepped on the gas, and soon rounded the corner on two wheels.

▶ EXERCISE 7. Compose ten complete sentences and underline each verb or verb phrase twice and each subject once. Check each object of a verb.

1c   Learn to recognize all the parts of speech.[2]

Words are usually classified into eight "parts of speech" (one could just as well say "parts of writing") according to their uses in the sentence.

Names	*Uses in the sentence*
1. VERBS	Indicators of action or state of being
2. NOUNS (substantives)[3]	Subjects, objects, complements
3. PRONOUNS (*I, you, he,* etc.)	Substitutes for nouns
4. ADJECTIVES	Modifiers of nouns
5. ADVERBS	Modifiers of verbs, adjectives, adverbs
6. PREPOSITIONS (*at, for, in,* etc.)	Words used before substantives to relate them to other words in the sentence
7. CONJUNCTIONS (*and, for, but,* etc.)	Connectives
8. INTERJECTIONS (*oh! alas!* etc.)	Expressions of emotion (without grammatical relationship to the rest of the sentence)

Note how the use of each italicized word below determines its part of speech. Many words can be used as several different parts of speech.

The *sail* is torn. [Noun—a substantive]

[2] For definitions of substantives, complements, and the eight parts of speech, see Section **35.**

[3] The word *substantive* is a general term to cover nouns and any words (or groups of words) that are used as nouns. Pronouns, the chief noun-substitutes, function just as nouns do and need little separate attention except that some pronouns have different forms for subjects and objects. Other substantives are phrases and clauses, which are treated below under **1d.**

It is torn. [Pronoun—a substantive, substituting for the noun *sail*]

I *sail* tomorrow. [Verb—indicator of action]

The *sail* hook is used in sailmaking. [Adjective—modifier of the noun *hook*]

He walks *fast*. [Adverb—modifier of the verb *walks*]

He walks *very* fast. [Adverb—modifier of the adverb *fast*]

This is a *fast* train. [Adjective—modifier of the noun *train*]

A *fast* is sometimes a religious observance. [Noun—subject of the verb *is*]

Fast when you should. [Verb—predicate of *you* understood]

For is usually a conjunction or a preposition. [Noun—subject of the verb *is*]

I rested, *for* I was tired. [Conjunction—connecting the subordinate clause *I was tired* with the main clause *I rested*]

I worked *for* him. [Preposition—showing the relation of the substantive *him* to the verb *worked*]

Oh is commonly used as an interjection. [Noun—subject of *is*]

Oh, I do hope you will go. [Interjection—expression of emotion]

Adjectives and **adverbs** are usually placed in the sentence near the words they modify, and in diagrams they are attached to these words. In the following sentences the adjectives are in boldface and the adverbs in italics.

The *exceedingly* **tall** man walked *very rapidly.*

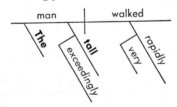

The *predicate adjective,* which helps to complete the meaning of the verb and also to describe the subject, is diagramed thus:

The man is old. (He is an old man.)

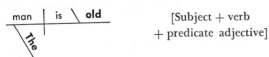

[Subject + verb + predicate adjective]

The common **prepositions** are *across, after, as, at, before, between, by, for, from, in, in front of, in regard to, of, on, over, to, together*

with, under, up, with. In the following sentence the prepositions are in italics.

The poems *by* Burns express *with* great force his love *of* liberty.

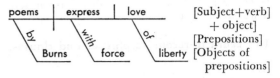

[Subject+verb] + object]
[Prepositions]
[Objects of prepositions]

Note: The preposition may follow, rather than precede, the noun or pronoun, and be placed at the end of the sentence. At times a sentence is most idiomatic or emphatic with the preposition at the end.

UNNATURAL   *For* what are you waiting?
NATURAL   What are you waiting *for?*
NATURAL   We live *by* faith.
NATURAL   (*and more emphatic*)   Faith is what we live *by.*

Conjunctions fall into two classes: (1) the co-ordinating conjunctions (*and, but, or, nor, for,* and sometimes *so* and *yet*), used to connect words or phrases, or clauses that are of equal rank; and (2) the subordinating conjunctions (such as *after, because, if, since, till, when, where, while*), used to connect subordinate clauses with main clauses. In diagrams, conjunctions are usually placed on broken lines drawn between parts connected by the conjunctions.

When the weather permitted, boys *and* girls played on the lawn *and* walks *and* even in the street.

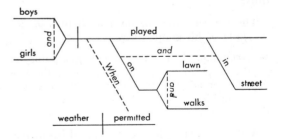

An **interjection** is followed by an exclamation point when the emotion expressed is strong, otherwise by a comma. In diagrams the interjection is set off by itself to indicate its grammatical independence of the rest of the sentence.

Oh, I can hardly believe it.

Oh		[Interjection]
I	can believe	[Subject + predicate]

▶ EXERCISE 8. Compose and diagram ten sentences to illustrate all the parts of speech.

1d   Learn to recognize phrases and clauses.

Phrases

A phrase is a group of related words, without subject and predicate, used as a substantive (called a *noun phrase*) or a modifier (called an *adjective phrase* or an *adverb phrase*). A phrase is connected to the sentence by (1) a preposition—and therefore called a *prepositional phrase,* (2) a participle—called a *participial phrase,* (3) a gerund—and called a *gerund phrase,* or (4) an infinitive—and called an *infinitive phrase.*

Prepositional phrases are commonly used as adjectives or as adverbs. In the following sentences the adjective phrases are in **boldface** and the adverb phrases in *italics.*

The boy **with the dog** lives *on a farm.*

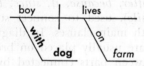

In this sentence *dog* is said to be the object of the preposition *with,* and *farm* the object of the preposition *on.*

Prepositional phrases often come in groups, thus:

The boy **with the dog on a leash** lives *on the farm* **of his grandfather.**

▶ EXERCISE 9. In Exercise 3, page 796, point out all the prepositional phrases, classifying them as adjective or adverb. (If you prefer, do this exercise by making a simple diagram for each prepositional phrase.)

Verbals. Participles, gerunds, and infinitives are derived from verbs and are therefore called *verbals.* They are much like verbs in that they have different tenses, can take subjects and objects, and can be modified by adverbs. But they are not verbs, for they cannot serve as the heart of a sentence: they cannot

make a statement, ask a question, or give a command. Compare the following:

The boy *ate* an apple. Did he *eat* it? *Eat!* [Verbs in complete sentences]

The boy *eating* the apple . . . [Participle (present)—an adjective modifying *boy*]

Eating an apple, the boy . . . [Participle (present)—an adjective modifying *boy*]

The apple *eaten* by the boy . . . [Participle (past)—an adjective modifying *apple*]

Eating an apple is good for the health. [A gerund serving as a noun]

To eat an apple . . . [Infinitive—in a sentence fragment. All verbals are, by themselves, only fragments of sentences.]

Note that the gerund *eating,* like the present participle *eating,* ends in *-ing* and that the two are to be distinguished only by the use in the sentence: the participle is the adjective and the gerund is the noun.

The boy *eating* the apple is happy. [Participle—an adjective]

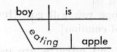

Eating is enjoyable. [Gerund—a noun]

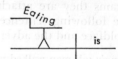

Note that the gerund *eating* in the sentence above is a single word, not part of a phrase. All verbals may be used thus or may be used with related words as parts of a verbal phrase.

▶ EXERCISE 10. In Exercise 3, page 796, point out all participles, showing the noun or pronoun modified by each participle. Point out each gerund in this exercise and show its use in the sentence. (If you prefer, do this exercise by making a simple diagram for each participle and each gerund.)

Infinitive phrases are used as substantives and as modifiers, and may be diagrammed thus:

To eat watermelons is enjoyable. [Infinitive phrase used as the subject]

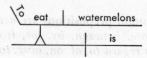

He began *to open the box*. [Infinitive phrase used as the object of the verb]

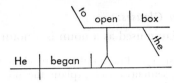

He enlisted *to become an aviator*. [Infinitive phrase used as an adverb]

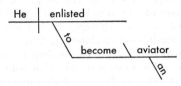

▶ EXERCISE 11. In Exercise 3, page 796, point out each infinitive phrase and show its use in the sentence. (If you prefer, do this exercise by making a simple diagram for each infinitive.)

▶ EXERCISE 12. In the following sentences point out the participial, gerund, and infinitive phrases and show how each is used as an adjective, an adverb, or a noun. (If you prefer, do this exercise by making a simple diagram for each verbal.)

1. Eddie and Cliff had nearly everything they needed to build their diving float. 2. They had spent the whole morning in rolling the eight oil drums from Cliff's back yard down to Eddie's. 3. Now the problem was to find some lumber. 4. Eddie, ransacking his brain, finally thought of a supply. 5. Mr. Kelly had torn down an old barn last fall to build a garage. 6. Going around his paper route only yesterday, Eddie had seen the leftover boards, still piled there and overgrown with weeds. 7. But getting them now, before the Donovan boys found them too, was the important thing. 8. "Get on your feet, boy, and stop wasting our time." 9. Cliff, nudged into movement by a front bicycle wheel, obediently got up. 10. Away they wheeled, pedaling as if the devil himself were after or the Donovans ahead of them. 11. It would be hard to say which might be worse. 12. Coming up to the site, the boys were happy to find the boards safe underneath the weeds.

Clauses

Anyone who can point out verbs and their subjects can also point out clauses, for a clause is simply part of a sentence containing a verb and its subject. There are two kinds of clauses:

1. Subordinate (also called *dependent*) clauses.
2. Main (also called *independent* or *principal*) clauses.

1. SUBORDINATE CLAUSES

A subordinate clause cannot stand alone. It depends upon the rest of the sentence (the main clause) for its meaning, and it is normally introduced by a subordinating conjunction or by a relative pronoun (*who, whom, which, what, that, whoever,* etc.).[4] Subordinate clauses are used as adverbs (called *adverb clauses*), as adjectives (called *adjective clauses*), or as nouns (called *noun clauses*).

EXAMPLES   *When it rains,* the work stops. [*When it rains* is a subordinate clause preceding the main clause; it is an adverb clause because it modifies the verb *stops.*]

We can employ all *who will come*. [*Who will come* is a subordinate clause following the main clause; it is an adjective clause because it modifies the pronoun *all*.]

Whoever will come will be welcome. [*Whoever will come* is a noun clause, subject of the verb *will be*.]

(a) Adverb Clauses:

Any clause that modifies a verb, adjective, or adverb is an adverb clause. In the following exercise, each subordinate clause modifies the verb of the main clause. Therefore the subordinate clause serves as an adverb and is called an *adverb clause.*

▶ EXERCISE 13. Bracket the adverb clauses in the following sentences.

1. While he was shaving, Mr. Baker began to think of the day ahead. 2. He always began his day's work before he got to the office, though usually it was not this long before. 3. After he got on the train, he nearly always began planning his day. 4. And sometimes he began before the train arrived, if it was a minute or two late. 5. But this morning, as he was shaving the tender place under his chin, details of the day's work began to go clicking through his mind. 6. When he was falling off to sleep last night, he had been reciting these same details. 7. Since he had first been

---

[4] The relative pronoun is sometimes omitted, as in the following sentences: He knew [that] he was going. We respect men [whom] we can trust.

made head accountant, he couldn't remember having brought the job home with him. 8. Whenever anything wasn't as usual with him, he naturally wondered. 9. But suddenly he remembered; while he was rinsing his razor under the hot water, he smiled cheerfully. 10. Today, unless they broke a years-long habit, the state auditors would show up. 11. And because this time he had worked extra carefully to have the books ready for them, he could look forward happily to their coming. 12. Because of all this, after he had finished shaving and while he dressed and listened for his wife's call to breakfast, he was still smiling.

Note the connecting words (subordinating conjunctions) used in these twelve sentences to relate the adverb clauses to the main clauses: *while* (three times), *before* (twice), *though, after* (twice), *if, as, when, since, whenever, unless,* and *because.* Other subordinating conjunctions commonly used to introduce adverb clauses are *although, as soon as, how, in order that, so that, than, till, until, where,* and *why.*

▶ EXERCISE 14. Compose five sentences containing adverb clauses introduced by subordinating conjunctions not used in Exercise 13. Bracket each adverb clause.

(b) Adjective Clauses:

Any clause that modifies a noun or a pronoun is an adjective clause. Adjective clauses are frequently introduced by a relative pronoun such as *who, which,* or *that,* which also serves as the subject of the subordinate clause.

Each subordinate clause in the following exercise modifies a noun or pronoun. In other words, it serves as an adjective. Therefore it is called an *adjective clause.*

▶ EXERCISE 15. Bracket the adjective clauses in the following sentences.

1. William was not at the corner where he usually took the bus. 2. The bus driver, who knew all his regular passengers, commented about it to one of those getting on. 3. The passenger remembered something that William had said one day about beginning his vacation in the middle of the week. 4. That sounded reasonable to the driver, who after all had a schedule to maintain. 5. Edging the big bus back into the traffic that was streaming by, he mentally put William on his "absent with leave" list for the next two weeks.

▶ EXERCISE 16. Compose five sentences containing adjective clauses and bracket the clauses.

(c) Noun Clauses:

Any clause used as a noun is a noun clause.

▶ EXERCISE 17. Bracket the noun clauses in the following sentences and explain the use of each clause.

1. The repairman said that he would have to take the typewriter in to the shop. 2. What it needed most of all was to be junked. 3. But he remembered that his customer had a sentimental fondness for this old machine. 4. And he had long ago learned that a battered, used-up piece of machinery could be to some people what politics, wife, or religion were to others. 5. What one man loved, other men had to pretend to respect. 6. The repairman wondered whether that saying was in the Bible. 7. He decided that it was.

▶ EXERCISE 18. Compose five sentences containing noun clauses.

2. MAIN CLAUSES

A main clause (an independent part of a sentence) has both subject and verb and is not introduced by a subordinating conjunction. A main clause does not modify anything. [It can stand alone as a simple sentence.]

EXAMPLE   When it rains, *the work stops.*

The work stops is a main clause; it (1) has both the verb *stops* and its subject *work* and (2) is not introduced by a subordinating conjunction. Therefore it can stand alone as a complete sentence: *The work stops. When it rains* has both a verb and its subject, but it cannot stand alone because it is introduced by the subordinating conjunction *when.*

▶ EXERCISE 19. Point out the main clauses in Exercises 13 and 15.

1e   Learn to recognize types of sentences.

Sentences are classified according to the number and kind of clauses they contain, as (1) simple, (2) compound, (3) complex, or (4) compound-complex.

A **simple sentence** is a sentence made up of one main clause.

EXAMPLE   The work stops.

A **compound sentence** is a sentence made up of two (or more) main clauses.

EXAMPLE   The work stops, but the tools are kept in readiness.

A **complex sentence** is a sentence made up of one main clause and at least one subordinate clause.

EXAMPLE   The work stops when it rains.

A **compound-complex sentence** is a sentence made up of two (or more) main clauses and at least one subordinate clause.

EXAMPLE   The work stops when it rains, but the tools are kept in readiness.

▶ EXERCISE 20.   In the following compound (or compound-complex) sentences point out the subject and the verb of each main clause and bracket the subordinate clauses. (If you prefer, do this exercise by making simple diagrams as indicated below.)

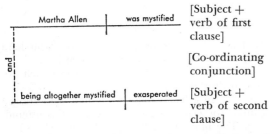

Martha Allen	was mystified	[Subject + verb of first clause]
		[Co-ordinating conjunction]
being altogether mystified	exasperated	[Subject + verb of second clause]

1. Martha Allen was altogether mystified; and being altogether mystified exasperated her.   2. Not two minutes ago she had put down her thimble with her sewing, and now the thimble had utterly disappeared.   3. She turned back to the kitchen to look; but she knew for certain that she wouldn't have worn the thimble to the kitchen.   4. So back again to her sewing she came; and now the scissors were gone!   5. Just then a flapping outside the window made her look out, and there was the children's pet crow flying up to the dead limb in the locust tree.   6. He scrambled about awkwardly in landing, and then Martha saw what was causing his trouble—and her trouble too.   7. Blackie had flown off with her scissors; and that explained the missing thimble as well.   8. In fact, Martha would be much surprised if Blackie wasn't accountable for a great deal of recent mischief; for she remembered now that her thimble and scissors were far from the first of such losses suffered by the household.

▶ EXERCISE 21.   Classify each of the following sentences (selected from the August 6, 1955, issue of *The New Yorker*) as (1) simple, (2) complex, (3) compound, or (4) compound-complex. Be prepared to justify your classification by an analysis of the sentence.

1. Once a month, the local Civil Defense people like to raise a terrible hullabaloo by turning on all their air-raid-warning sirens—seven hundred and six of them.

2. At most meetings, each of the powers was represented at the council table by eleven or twelve persons, and there were seldom fewer than thirty or thirty-five additional staff people—members either of the secretariat or of the middle echelons of the delegations—in the chamber.

3. A big, voluble man in his forties, he works surrounded by books, filing cabinets, tapes, tape recorders, cameras, pictures, a home developer, a huge record turntable, and an impressive loud-speaker.

4. When I decided to make this trip, I applied to the Guggenheim people for a grant, and got it.

5. While Sprott was blowing away on his harmonica, a friend of his named Harry Rutledge suddenly sprang up and did a buck dance, which is something you never see any more, and the cabin began to go up and down like a ship in a swell.

6. When a big blue convertible with the top up came around the corner at the end of the dusty street, all three looked up.

7. She thought it better not to offer to help with getting supper; instead, she watched and took it easy.

8. His shore home, a local show place, is planted thickly with shrubs that provide excellent covert for a man ducking the public view.

9. He went ahead to explain that his own experience with money was wholly a matter of spending it.

10. Aldrich was at this time twenty-seven himself, but he had an air so paternal, as a result of his precocious achievements, that men twice his age often came to him for advice.

11. Before the dessert arrived, Aldrich had sealed an oral contract with Reed that gave him an excellent salary and a nice percentage of Reed's future gross profits.

12. This summer theatre had been established in 1927 in a structure that had run the gamut of human usefulness.

13. The Provincetown structure also had proved to be injudiciously placed; having been built on a wharf, it departed Provincetown and drifted off to sea one windy afternoon during a high tide.

14. Although Sylvia promises to love him for eternity, she soon goes off and marries somebody else.

15. At the time, it might reasonably have been asked where in the world today the heads of the greatest powers on earth could hope to assemble in privacy and seclusion.

▶ EXERCISE 22. Compose ten sentences and classify each sentence as (1) simple, (2) complex, (3) compound, or (4) compound-complex. Write at least two sentences of each type.

▶ EXERCISE 23. Analyze the following sentences (selected from *Fortune*) according to instructions given for Exercise 21.

1. That the United States could well afford to switch some of its production to defense seemed clear.

2. The pioneering days, whether territorial or industrial, are over; and although many deny that the United States has reached maturity, all agree that it is out of its infancy.

3. There is pleasant talk, as the elections draw nearer, of tax reduction.

4. Surveying the dismal option before the British electorate, the London *Economist* recently called for a new party to represent "the extreme center."

5. The experience in Pittsburgh, where industry finally helped the city back into the light after a century of smoggy darkness, is an example of what can be performed when business puts itself behind a civic effort.

6. Generally speaking, therefore, it can be said that the medical services of the United States, while adequate, or nearly so, in certain wealthy areas of the country, fall in other areas far below any standard that an American could conscientiously defend.

7. The test of the dynamic businessman is how much he is doing with what he has to work with.

8. The talent for self-examination is another intangible asset.

9. Like his perfumes, he is a volatile essence in a small, stylish package.

10. As the motorist emerges from the Holland Tunnel, Jersey City proudly puts its worst foot forward.

11. There is nothing particularly sententious to say about this city street, except that it is lacking in the amenities.

12. Looking backward through an autumn haze of imperfect memory, he catches seductive glimpses of a world that never was, a world that nonetheless he wants desperately to return.

13. Conservatism may be defined as the system of thought and habit opposed to innovation in the institutions and mores of our established society.

14. A true conservative must have "a sound sense for the pace of historical change."

15. Looked at from the long view of history, the American capitalist, however "sound" his views on politics, family, or religion, has been the most marvelous agent of social change the world has ever known.

▶ EXERCISE 24. Compose ten varied sentences and analyze them as directed by the instructor.

▶ EXERCISE 25. Analyze the following sentences of the Gettysburg Address as directed by the instructor.

1. Fourscore and seven years ago our fathers brought forth on this continent a new nation, conceived in liberty, and dedicated to the proposition that all men are created equal.

2. Now we are engaged in a great civil war, testing whether that nation, or any nation so conceived and so dedicated, can long endure.

3. We are met on a great battlefield of that war.

4. We have come to dedicate a portion of that field as a final resting place for those who here gave their lives that that nation might live.

5. It is altogether fitting and proper that we should do this.

6. But in a larger sense we cannot dedicate, we cannot consecrate, we cannot hallow this ground.

7. The brave men, living and dead, who struggled here, have consecrated it far above our power to add or detract.

8. The world will little note, nor long remember, what we say here; but it can never forget what they did here.

9. It is for us, the living, rather to be dedicated here to the unfinished work which they who fought here have thus far so nobly advanced.

10. It is rather for us to be here dedicated to the great task remaining before us, that from these honored dead we take increased devotion to that cause for which they gave the last full measure of devotion; that we here highly resolve that these dead shall not have died in vain; that this nation, under God, shall have a new birth of freedom, and that government of the people, by the people, for the people shall not perish from the earth.

▶ Sentence Fragment

2   Do not carelessly write a sentence fragment—a phrase or a subordinate clause—as if it were a complete sentence.

Caution: Can you distinguish between phrases and clauses, and between main and subordinate clauses? Until you can do so, you are likely to write careless sentence fragments. You may need to master the fundamentals of the sentence treated in Section 1, **Sentence Sense,** especially **1d,** before you can understand Section 2.

A sentence fragment—a phrase or a subordinate clause—should not be set off as if it were a complete sentence. The fragment should be (1) included in the sentence, that is, attached to the main clause, or (2) rewritten to form a sentence by itself.

WRONG   He registered for the summer session. Hoping thus to graduate ahead of his class. [We have here one sentence and one fragment, a participial phrase.]

RIGHT   He registered for the summer session, hoping thus to graduate ahead of his class. [Participial phrase included in the sentence]

RIGHT   He registered for the summer session. By this means he hoped to graduate ahead of his class. [Participial phrase made into a sentence]

WRONG   He registered for the summer session. Because he hoped thus to graduate ahead of his class. [We have here one sentence and one fragment, a subordinate clause.]

RIGHT   He registered for the summer session because he hoped thus to graduate ahead of his class. [Subordinate clause included in the sentence]

RIGHT   By registering for the summer session, he hoped to graduate ahead of his class.

RIGHT   He registered for the summer session. By this means he hoped to graduate ahead of his class. [Subordinate clause made into a sentence]

A TEST FOR SENTENCE COMPLETENESS

The sentence fragment is characterized by its incompleteness of meaning. This incompleteness is usually obvious; however, it may be tested (1) by searching for the verb and its subject and (2) by determining whether this verb and subject are introduced by a subordinating conjunction. If the supposed sentence does not have a verb and its subject, it may be identified at once as a phrase. *Hoping thus to graduate ahead of his class,* for example, has no verb. *Hoping* is a participle and *to graduate* is an infinitive, but there is no verb. Even when both verb and subject are present, they may be introduced by a subordinating conjunction and thus constitute a subordinate clause. *Because he hoped to graduate ahead of his class* has the verb *hoped* and the subject *he.* But since these words are introduced by the subordinating conjunction *because,* the group of words is a subordinate clause—still a sentence fragment.

Make a diagram, or at least form a mental picture, of the core of each sentence: its subject + its verb (predicate). Then if you find that subject and verb are not introduced by a subordinating conjunction such as *because, since, if,* or *when,* you may be reasonably sure that the sentence is grammatically complete. (For logical completeness see Section 23.)

He registered for the summer session.

He	registered
		[Subject + verb]

The diagram shows subject and verb, and there is no subordinating conjunction: the sentence is complete.

2a   Do not carelessly write a phrase (participial, prepositional, or infinitive) as a complete sentence.

WRONG   I made little progress. *Finally giving up all my efforts.* [Participial phrase]

RIGHT   I made so little progress that I finally gave up all my efforts. [Fragment included with the sentence]

RIGHT   I made little progress. Finally I gave up all my efforts. [Fragment made into a sentence]

WRONG   Soon I began to work for the company. *First in the rock pit and later on the highway.* [Prepositional phrases]

RIGHT   Soon I began to work for a company, first in the rock pit and later on the highway. [Fragment included with the sentence]

WRONG   He will have an opportunity to visit his home town. *And to talk with many of his old friends.* [Infinitive phrase]

RIGHT   He will have an opportunity to visit his home town and to talk with many of his old friends. [Fragment included with the sentence]

2b   Do not carelessly write a subordinate clause as a complete sentence.

WRONG   A railway control board should be constructed with care. *Because from this board trains are moved through a system of tracks and switches.* [Subordinate clause]

RIGHT   A railway control board should be constructed with care, because from this board trains are moved through a system of tracks and switches. [Fragment included with the sentence]

WRONG   I had some definite ideas about college. *Although I had never before been on a college campus.* [Subordinate clause]

RIGHT   I had some definite ideas about college although I had never before been on a college campus. [Fragment included with the sentence]

2c   Do not carelessly write as a complete sentence any other fragment, such as an appositive or a member of a compound predicate.

WRONG   My father was born in Cartersville. *A little country town where everyone knows everyone else.* [Appositive]

RIGHT   My father was born in Cartersville, a little country town where everyone knows everyone else.

WRONG   At school Paul ran into many new problems. *Such as handling his pocket money and choosing his friends.* [Appositive]

RIGHT   At school Paul ran into many new problems, such as handling his pocket money and choosing his friends.

WRONG   William was elected president of his class. *And was made a member of the National*

Honor Society. [Detached member of a compound predicate]

RIGHT   William was elected president of his class and was made a member of the National Honor Society.

Note: At times sentences may be grammatically incomplete and yet clear because omitted words can be readily supplied by the reader. Such elliptical expressions occur in commands, in exclamations, and in questions and answers, especially in dialogue. But these expressions are not real fragments since the completion is unmistakably implied.

COMMANDS   Come nearer. [You come nearer.]
Open the door. [You open the door.]
Please enter. [You will please enter.]

EXCLAMATIONS   Too bad! [That is too bad!]
What a pity! [What a pity it is!]

QUESTIONS AND ANSWERS   Why did he go? Because his friends were going. [He went because his friends were going.]
"Will you play with me? A lot?" ["Will you play with me a lot?"]
"Perhaps." ["Perhaps I will."]

Real fragments are sometimes used intentionally by professional writers, especially in fiction. In the following passages, from Aldous Huxley,[1] the intentional fragments are in italics.

"He wasn't a gorilla. *Just the cutest little baboon.* And the garbage wasn't garbage. It was ice cream. *A genuine strawberry and fish-guts sundae.*"

From corned beef hash Pamela turned to the latest starlet. *Five feet five and a half. One hundred and seventeen pounds.*

But such fragments are employed consciously, for rhetorical effect, by experienced writers. And besides, such fragments are not common in expository writing emphasized in college. Students are usually advised to learn the fundamentals of English composition and the accepted style of expository writing before permitting themselves the liberties taken by experienced craftsmen.

▶ EXERCISES ON THE SENTENCE FRAGMENT

A. Test each of the following for sentence completeness as suggested on page 805. As an aid in your analysis underline each verb (*not* verbal) in a

[1] "Voices," *Atlantic Monthly,* July, 1955, pp. 35, 42.

main clause twice and its subject once, and bracket each subordinate clause. Write *C* after each numbered item which contains no fragment. Attach each fragment to an existing sentence or make it into an independent sentence.

1. There were no eclipses visible in England in 1604 and 1606. Although there were three in 1605.

2. The festival beginning on the twentieth of June and continuing through the month of July.

3. It was all I could do to keep my mouth shut. Finally I did speak out.

4. Since the party was made up of twelve men, nine of whom had been members of the previous year's expedition.

5. The hydraulic lift raises the plows out of the ground. And lowers them again.

6. I had a feeling that some sinister spirit of evil brooded over the place. A feeling that I could not analyze. But that was impossible to disregard or reason away.

7. Our stay at the Halcombs' cottage was altogether delightful. Except for the mosquitoes, which nothing seemed to discourage.

8. To watch Dempsey in the ring was to watch a perfectly engineered machine operated with exact precision.

9. To anyone who knew him in 1840, it would have seemed ridiculous beyond belief. To predict that one day this rawboned frontier lawyer would be President of the United States.

10. The time when you are young and enthusiastic. That's when you should work. Leave dreams to old men.

11. This was the nightmare that haunted her, the dread of the inevitable surrender.

12. I am often told to do things I don't like. Such as getting out of bed.

13. He was still angry with me. His eyes glaring fiercely.

14. He killed three ducks with one shot. Against the law of averages but possible.

15. She dressed exactly like the Hollywood starlets. Since she wanted to become one of them herself.

B. Identify each fragment; determine whether it falls under the rule for **2a, 2b,** or **2c;** then make the appropriate correction. Write *C* in place of each numbered item which contains no fragment.

1. I knew that he was asking for trouble. As soon as I heard of his buying that motorcycle.

2. He let me believe that I had first chance at the job. But without definitely committing himself.

3. Unless I can get a lower birth, I prefer to go by coach.

4. By noon we already had our bag limit. More birds than we had ever seen during the first half of the season.

5. That lion was in just about as bad a spot as a lion can be in. Until his faithful little friend the mouse came along and found him there.

6. Andy was here just a minute ago. You may find him in the poolroom next door.

7. There is my pride, my joy, and my dependable money-maker. That herd of fat black Anguses.

8. At least he stays sober on the job. Which is more than I can say for the last agent we had here.

9. Early in life he decided upon a simple philosophy. From which grew all his subsequent opinions.

10. Sheriff Nolan took no deputy along with him. Believing that he could handle the prisoner easily enough alone.

11. Let's take a ten-minute break. But see that you don't make it twenty.

12. Wilson is one of the most capable men we have. Besides being one of the most even-tempered.

13. The painter asked us to be careful about touching the walls. Since it would take all night for the paint to harden.

14. Doc Potter is exactly what you said he would be. A thoroughly profane and thoroughly entertaining old reprobate.

15. He picked up the revolver by thrusting a pencil into its muzzle. In order to avoid smearing any prints which might be on it.

C. Follow directions given under A or B, or under both A and B, as your instructor may direct. In writing your revision, omit the numbers.

1. Very late in *The Merry Wives of Windsor,* Shakespeare introduces an incident which is altogether extraneous to either of the plot lines in the play. 2. And which advances the action in no way whatsoever. 3. Bardolph in a very brief scene with the Host announces that "the Germans" desire three of the Host's horses. 4. So that they may go to meet "the Duke," who is to be at court on the next day. 5. The Host seems to know so little of these Germans that he must ask if they speak English. 6. A highly improbable ignorance on his part, for in his next lines he states that they have been already a week at his tavern. 7. But he lets them have the horses. 8. Insisting, however, that they must pay for them. 9. Two scenes later Bardolph returns to the tavern with the report that the villainous Germans have handled him roughly on the road. 10. Thrown him into a puddle, and run off with the horses. 11. Immediately

on his heels, in come first Sir Hugh and then Dr. Caius. 12. With rumors confirming Bardolph's assurance of the evil character of the Germans. 13. So that the Host is at last alarmed. 14. He is convinced now that the Germans have indeed cozened

him of a week's board bill. 15. And stolen his horses in the bargain.

[See other exercises on sentence fragments at the end of Section 3.]

▶ Comma Splice and Fused Sentence

3 Do not carelessly link two main clauses with only a comma between them (comma splice), or, worse, without any punctuation (fused sentence).

Caution: If you cannot recognize main clauses, study Section 1, Sentence Sense, especially 1d, before trying to apply the following instructions to your writing.

COMMA SPLICE The current was swift, he could not swim to shore. [Two main clauses linked only by a comma]
FUSED SENTENCE The current was swift he could not swim to shore. [Omission of the comma makes an even worse error than the comma splice.]

Note: The fused sentence is corrected in exactly the same way as the comma splice. Hence all the methods of correction given below apply equally to comma splices and fused sentences.

3a Usually the comma splice is best corrected by some method of subordination.[1]

WRONG The current was swift, he could not swim to shore. [Comma splice]
RIGHT Since the current was swift, he could not swim to shore. [First main clause changed to a subordinate clause]
RIGHT The current was so swift that he could not swim to shore. [Second main clause changed to a subordinate clause]
RIGHT Because of the swift current he could not swim to shore. [First main clause changed to a prepositional phrase]
RIGHT The swiftness of the current prevented his swimming to shore. [The two main clauses changed to one simple sentence]

[1] See also Section 24, Subordination.

3b Sometimes the comma splice is best corrected by some method of co-ordination.

Co-ordination is preferable when the writer wishes to give equal weight to the ideas in the two main clauses. If these ideas are sufficiently independent, the clauses may be made into separate sentences.

WRONG The hunting instinct in man is deep, it is universal. [Comma splice]
RIGHT The hunting instinct in man is deep. It is universal. [Each main clause made into a sentence] —NEW YORK TIMES MAGAZINE

WRONG Hiking is great fun, you should try it. [Comma splice]
RIGHT Hiking is great fun. You should try it. [Each main clause made into a sentence]

If the ideas in the main clauses are closely related, the clauses may be separated (1) by a semicolon instead of a comma or (2) by a comma + a co-ordinate conjunction (*and, but, or, nor,* or *for*).

WRONG He dared not retract, money and fame were at stake. [Comma splice]
RIGHT He dared not retract; money and fame were at stake. [Main clauses separated by a semicolon]

—SATURDAY REVIEW OF LITERATURE

WRONG I thought about that, I found the answer. [Comma splice]
RIGHT I thought about that, and I found the answer. [Main clauses separated by a comma + *and*] —ATLANTIC MONTHLY

WRONG He kept no old friends, he made lots of shiny new friends. [Comma splice]

RIGHT He kept no old friends, but he made lots of shiny new friends. [Main clauses separated by a comma + *but*]   —ATLANTIC MONTHLY

3c *Caution:* **Do not let a conjunctive adverb, a transitional or a parenthetical expression, or a divided quotation trick you into making a comma splice.**

When a conjunctive adverb (such as *accordingly, also, anyhow, besides, consequently, furthermore, hence, however, indeed, instead, likewise, moreover, nevertheless, still, then, therefore, thus*) or a transitional expression (such as *for example, in fact, namely, on the contrary, on the other hand, that is*) is used to connect main clauses, a semicolon is commonly used between the clauses.

WRONG The two teams line up for the kickoff, then comes the thrill. [Comma splice]

RIGHT The two teams line up for the kickoff; then comes the thrill. [Semicolon used instead of comma]

RIGHT The two teams line up for the kickoff, and then comes the thrill. [Co-ordinating conjunction supplied]

WRONG The story was not true, however, it was interesting. [Comma splice]

RIGHT The story was not true; however, it was interesting. [Semicolon used instead of comma]

RIGHT The story was not true, but it was interesting. [Co-ordinating conjunction substituted]

WRONG Bears in the park are very tame, in fact, they will eat food from one's hands. [Comma splice]

RIGHT Bears in the park are very tame; in fact, they will eat food from one's hands. [Semicolon used]

Divided Quotations:

WRONG "Your answer is wrong," he said, "correct it."

RIGHT "Your answer is wrong," he said. "Correct it."

WRONG "What are you looking for?" she asked, "may I help you?"

RIGHT "What are you looking for?" she asked. "May I help you?"

Exceptions: Short co-ordinate clauses in series, parallel in form and unified in thought, may be separated by commas:

RIGHT I came, I saw, I conquered.

ALSO RIGHT I came; I saw; I conquered.

The comma is also used to separate a statement from the echo question and sometimes to set off a main clause when subordination is implied:

You can come, can't you? [Statement echoed by question]

I must confess, [that] I did not want to go. [Implied subordination of the second clause]

Main clauses separated only by commas are fairly common in some informal types of writing. Occasionally examples are found in more formal writing, chiefly when there is a balance or contrast between the clauses.

But this was better, this was much more satisfying.   —ALDOUS HUXLEY

The English of those days did not paint broadly, they filled in with deft touches.

—BONAMY DOBRÉE

They were unprepared, their people were divided and demoralized.   —WALTER LIPPMANN

But the immature writer is much more likely to produce an ordinary comma splice than an effective sentence of this sort. He will do well to make sure that main clauses in his sentences are separated (1) by a comma + co-ordinate conjunction or (2) by a semicolon.

▶ EXERCISES ON THE COMMA SPLICE

A. Determine which of the following sentences contain comma splices. As an aid to your analysis (1) underline each verb of a main clause twice and its subject once, (2) bracket each subordinate clause, and (3) place an inverted caret (v) between main clauses, drawing a wavy line under the co-ordinating conjunction (if any) that connects the main clauses. Write *C* after each sentence that needs no revision. Correct each comma splice in the appropriate way.

1. Some athletes strive for mere delight in competition, Jim Thorpe was one of these.

2. There used to be alligators in that lake, I remember seeing them when I was a boy.

3. "This is the way you do it," he explained, "you step on the clutch and the brake and press the starter."

4. We were lucky in our choice of a day for the trip, though it had been raining at bedtime, the weather cleared during the night.

5. There was no coffee, no bacon, no bread, and the milk had begun to sour, therefore my breakfast consisted of marmalade and four limp crackers.

6. Walt calls that place of his a "farm," "weed patch" would describe it better.

7. Jay was the fastest first baseman I ever saw, if his batting eye had been a little better, he could have gone all the way up.

8. The hut was built to house eight men, nevertheless, there were sixteen in it when I arrived.

9. The large table is always reserved for Mr. Mansfield and his guests, but his secretary has just phoned that he will not be able to come today.

10. I wouldn't carry that gun into the house loaded, son, you're not going to shoot anybody in there, are you?

11. Jefferson's political views became more and more democratic, but his opponents did not cease reminding him of his wealth.

12. Typhus used to kill far more soldiers than warfare itself did, however, this disease is little heard of now.

13. Washington Irving was one of the first American writers to exploit local legends, by writing "Rip Van Winkle," he helped to start America's folklore tradition.

14. To earn money by baby-sitting, a co-ed must know the rudiments of domestic science, for example, she should know how to warm a bottle and burp the baby.

15. Florida depends upon tourists for much of its income, visitors spend many millions at hotels, restaurants, race tracks, and "palaces" of entertainment.

B. Revise each comma splice (or fused sentence) by some method of subordination. Write *C* in place of any sentence that needs no revision.

1. Frantically I wound and jerked the starting cord a tow of gravel barges was bearing directly down upon me.

2. Sheila has her mind made up, nothing you can say will change it.

3. We have enough bricks we can build a barbecue pit.

4. I spoke of the Rufus Kane matter to Chief Kelly, he recalled the case quite clearly.

5. The plaster hardens rapidly it should not be mixed in large quantities.

6. When you come to a red brick church across from a filling station, turn left and go exactly one block.

7. There is a roadside market on the Maryville highway you can buy all the berries you want there.

8. At farrowing, her pigs weighed slightly over three pounds apiece, this is a little above average weight.

9. We do not plan to come back in the fall, therefore we are giving up our apartment.

10. One man was digging at the bottom of the well, the other stayed at the top to haul up the loose dirt.

C. Revise each comma splice (or fused sentence) by the method that seems most appropriate. Be ready to explain and justify the method used. Write *C* in place of any sentence that needs no revision. (Some students may find it helpful to analyze the sentences as directed in Exercise A.)

1. Let me know at least a week before you expect to be here, I will need that long to get your cabin ready.

2. You must first preheat your oven then you put your rolls in to bake.

3. The winters here are quite mild, however I cannot say the same for the summers.

4. I could have sworn I had an extra pair of shoelaces in this drawer, I surely can't find them now.

5. I have never been able to understand why there is no traffic light on this corner.

6. "Don't unsaddle him," George called from the doorway, "I'll want to ride down after the mail in a minute or two."

7. The Santa Gertrudis is an American breed of cattle, it was developed to combine the heat-resistance of the Brahma with the meat-producing qualities of the Shorthorn.

8. In 1728 William Byrd was a member of a party of surveyors, they were charged with the task of determining the proper boundary between Virginia and North Carolina.

9. The bay was far too rough to venture upon, therefore we decided to walk around by land.

10. The Red Cross opened its blood bank to the survivors, as a result, many lives were saved.

D. Copy from a book or magazine (1) five sentences in which main clauses are separated by a semicolon and (2) five sentences in which main clauses are separated by a comma + a co-ordinating conjunction.

► EXERCISES ON THE SENTENCE FRAGMENT AND COMMA SPLICE

E. Test the following for sentence fragments and comma splices (or fused sentences) and make appropriate corrections. Write *C* in place of any numbered item that needs no revision.

1. International misunderstanding is a great calamity, however there is advantage to those who fish in troubled waters.

2. There is probably no more efficient fund-raising device in the United States than a clear-eyed, neatly uniformed Boy Scout who is patriotically seeking adult help in doing his daily good turn.

3. It was the kind of day to inspire an adventure a warm wind blew across the lake.

4. Dine at the Campus Cookery. Where the beans taste like caviar.

5. A lifeboat wallowed alongside the raft, grappled for the lifeboat, and finally made it fast.

6. A few hundred feet out in the lake, drifting away in the offshore wind, was a derelict canoe.

7. The teacher's friendliness impressed me. Nothing like that having been expected.

8. Night and cold closed down on the field, thus we could search no longer.

9. On top of the hill is a windmill, after you pass that, you will see the town in the valley below.

10. The peasants remember many periods of inflation, therefore they prefer to keep their produce rather than exchange it for paper currency.

11. "You will soon be needed," he said, "how long will you be gone?"

12. Edgar Allan Poe attended West Point, there he was not a success.

13. Just to stand up in the face of life's problems. That takes courage.

14. Certainly there is no reason for our becoming panicky, on the other hand, there is no reason for our failing to take due precautions.

F. Follow directions given under E.

1. Under the law the Speaker of the House is next to the Vice-President in line of succession he precedes the Secretary of State.

2. The silver iodide smoke ascends into the clouds, this causes condensation, and thus artificial rainfall is produced.

3. Hour after hour Coast Guard boats methodically zigzagged over the area, sweeping the water with searchlights.

4. Learn to recognize the need for good manners philosophers say that good manners are the outward signs of good morals.

5. Arizona is blessed with a fine climate, therefore many sanatoria are located there.

6. Strange-sounding names and faraway places. Travel brings you to them.

7. Some students claim that Walt Whitman is the best American poet, their opinion of his works, however, is far too favorable, according to the admirers of Lowell, Longfellow, Whittier, and Emily Dickinson.

8. Some of the most beautiful scenery in Canada is in the Maritime Provinces. The forests, the rivers, and the sea in combination.

9. There is some pessimism about our steel supply, since the resources of the Mesabi Range have been depleted, there is no comparable source of iron ore in the United States.

10. I hope to learn English in one year. Since I am now living with people who speak the language.

11. "Don't sell your freshman textbooks," Jim advised, "they will be helpful throughout the rest of your college course."

12. I came here for two reasons. To see you and to be seen by you.

G. Rewrite the paragraph, correcting each fragment and comma splice by the method that seems most suitable. Be ready to explain and justify the method used. (Not all the sentences in the exercise are faulty ones.) In making the revision, omit the numbers.

1. When Boyd and Nancy were preparing to move to Pennsylvania. 2. Nancy asked me if I knew anybody who would want a cigar box full of cat bones. 3. These were the dismantled parts of a cat skeleton. 4. Which she had used in teaching a science course in the local school. 5. I told her that I would be delighted to have them. 6. Feeling quite sure that the day would come when I should find them useful. 7. In this way one former cat, retired from teaching, found a home with me, then I went on my vacation, and while I was away, my landlady decided to refinish the floor of my room. 8. I suppose I should count it among my blessings. 9. That I wasn't around to hear what she had to say about the miscellaneous gear I have accumulated during my residence here. 10. But she was very kind about it all. 11. And had nothing to say when I came back. 12. Except that she hoped I liked the new floor. 13. The floor was quite elegant, her rearrangement of my goods and chattels is a puzzle that I haven't yet altogether untangled. 14. I am still finding, in all sorts of odd places, things that I had long ago forgotten. 15. But search as I will, I cannot find those cat bones, I wish I had the nerve to ask what she did with them.

H. Follow directions given under G.

1. At half-past nine that morning I went out and got into the car. 2. Intending to drive across town to Fielding's Garden Shop to see about some tulip bulbs I had ordered. 3. The traffic had just cleared. 4. Letting me turn left at the main intersection, then I first heard the siren. 5. It made me think of an air raid. 6. And of a bomb that

might drop right on top of me. 7. A bomb couldn't have done any more to me than that fire truck did. 8. Does anybody want to buy the gearshift knob of what was once an automobile? 9. I'll ask the nurse to get it, the ambulance driver had to take it away from me. 10. When he hauled me in here. 11. It seems that I thought it was a tulip bulb. 12. One that I had to plant.

▶ Adjectives and Adverbs

4 Distinguish between adjectives and adverbs and use the appropriate form.

Adjectives and adverbs modify—that is, they make clearer and more specific—the meaning of other words. Adjectives modify nouns; adverbs modify chiefly verbs, adjectives, and other adverbs. In the following sentences the adjectives are in **boldface** and the adverbs are in *italics*.

Boys like toys.   [No modifiers]
Young boys *usually* like **colored** toys.
Very **young** boys *almost always* like *brightly* **colored** toys.

FORMS OF ADJECTIVES AND ADVERBS

A good dictionary shows the appropriate form for adjective or adverb, but only the use to which the word is put in the sentence determines whether the adjective or the adverb form is required. The dictionary shows, for example, that the form *beautiful* is used only as an adjective and *beautifully* only as an adverb: The **beautiful** woman sang *beautifully*. In this sentence *beautiful* is the required form as modifier of the noun *woman*, and *beautifully* is the required form as modifier of the verb *sang*.

Although the *-ly* ending is the usual sign for the adverb, the dictionary shows that a few words in *-ly* (such as *manly, saintly, womanly*) are adjectives. A few others in *-ly* (such as *only, early, cowardly*) may be either adjectives or adverbs, and the same is true for a considerable number of common words not ending in *-ly* (such as *far, fast, late, little, near, right, straight, well*).

Adjective	*Adverb*
The **early** bird gets the worm.	He rose *early* to go to work.
He came on a **late** train.	He came *late*.
I have **little** energy.	He was a *little* ambitious.
He is **well**. He feels **well**.	He works *well*. He plays *well*.

▶ EXERCISE 1. Compose sentences to illustrate each of the following words (1) as an adjective and (2) as an adverb: *only, cowardly, far, fast, near, right, straight.*

Most adjectives and adverbs have distinct forms which must be used with care.

4a Use the adverb form for modifiers of verbs, adjectives, and other adverbs.

(1) Modifiers of verbs

WRONG   His clothes fit him *perfect*. [The adjective *perfect* cannot modify the verb *fit*.]
RIGHT   His clothes fit him *perfectly*.

WRONG   One can drown in a pool as *easy* as in a lake. [The adjective *easy* cannot modify the verb *can drown*.]
RIGHT   One can drown in a pool as *easily* as in a lake.

WRONG   He ran *good* for the first half mile. [The adjective *good* cannot modify the verb *ran*.]
RIGHT   He ran *well* for the first half mile.

(2) Modifiers of adjectives

WRONG   The farmer has a *reasonable* secure future. [The adjective *reasonable* cannot modify the adjective *secure*.]

RIGHT   The farmer has a *reasonably* secure future.

WRONG   The plane was a *special* built fighter.

RIGHT   The plane was a *specially* built fighter.

COLLOQUIAL [1]   *Most* all men

STANDARD   *Almost* all men

COLLOQUIAL (or DIALECTAL)   It's *real* hot.

STANDARD   It's *really* (or *very*) hot.

(3) Modifiers of adverbs

COLLOQUIAL   She was *most* always late.

STANDARD   She was *almost* always late. [*Almost* is the regular adverb.]

4b   As a rule use the adjective form after *is*, *was, seems, becomes,* and the verbs pertaining to the senses (*feel, look, smell, sound, taste*).

RIGHT   The man is *old*. [*Old* is an adjective modifying *man:* The man is an *old* man.]

RIGHT   The girl was *excited*. [An *excited* girl]

RIGHT   The town seems *deserted*. [A *deserted* town]

RIGHT   The Indian became *hostile*. [A *hostile* Indian]

RIGHT   The boy felt *lonesome*. [A *lonesome* boy]

RIGHT   The flower smells *sweet*. [A *sweet* flower]

RIGHT   The milk tastes *sour*. [The *sour* milk]

RIGHT   The woman looked *angry*. [An *angry* woman]

RIGHT   I feel *well*. [*Well,* the form for either adjective or adverb, is here the adjective meaning "not sick." The adjective *good* should not be used with this meaning.]

Exception: The modifier is an adverb when it refers to the action of the verb.

RIGHT   The blind beggar felt *cautiously* along the wall. [The adverb *cautiously* qualifies the verb *felt*.]

RIGHT   The woman looked *angrily* at him. [The adverb *angrily* qualifies the verb *looked*.]

Note: A modifier following a verb and its direct object is an adjective when it refers to the object rather than to the action of the verb.

[1] For the distinction between colloquial and standard usage see Section **19**.

RIGHT   Dig the hole *deep*. [*Deep* is an adjective: *deep* hole.]

RIGHT   The hole was dug *deep*. [*Deep* hole]

RIGHT   Dig *deeply* into the ground. [*Deeply* is an adverb modifying the verb *dig*.]

4c   Standard English tends to prefer the adverb in *-ly*.

Some adverbs have a form identical with that of the adjective (*loud, quick, slow*) and also another form in *-ly* (*loudly, quickly, slowly*). For such adverbs, standard English generally prefers the form in *-ly*. The shorter form is very common in commands: "Drive slow," "Move quick," "Speak loud."

STANDARD   He shouted as *loudly* as he could. The sword hung *loosely* at his side.

4d   Use the appropriate forms for the comparative and the superlative.

In general the shorter adjectives (and a few adverbs) form the comparative degree by adding *-er* and the superlative by adding *-est;* the longer adjectives and most adverbs form the comparative by the use of *more* (*less*) and the superlative by the use of *most* (*least*). Some adjectives, such as *good* and *bad,* and some adverbs, such as *well* and *badly,* have an irregular comparison. But these are among our common words and are seldom confused.

	Positive	Comparative	Superlative
ADJECTIVES	warm	warmer	warmest
	tired	more tired	most tired
	good	better	best
	bad	worse	worst
ADVERBS	warmly	more warmly	most warmly
	well	better	best
	badly	worse	worst

(1) Use the comparative degree for two persons or things.

RIGHT   Today is *warmer* than yesterday.

RIGHT   James was the *taller* of the two boys. [The superlative is occasionally used in such sentences, especially in informal speaking and writing.]

(2) Use the superlative degree for three or more persons or things.

RIGHT   Today is the *warmest* day of the year.

RIGHT   William was the *tallest* of the three boys.

Usage tends to ignore the fact that such adjectives as *round, square, perfect,* and *unique* express a complete thing or idea and are therefore logically incapable of comparison.

ILLOGICAL This hoop is *rounder* than that.
LOGICAL This hoop is *more nearly round* than that. [Preferred by some careful writers.]

4e Avoid any awkward or ambiguous use of a noun form as an adjective.

Although many noun forms (*boat* race, *show* business, *opera* tickets, etc.) are used effectively, especially when no appropriate adjective is available, such forms should be avoided when they are either awkward or ambiguous.

AWKWARD The man sometimes forgets his *gentleman* habits.
BETTER The man sometimes forgets his *gentlemanly* habits. [The regular adjective form substituted]

AMBIGUOUS Recently I was involved in a *race* argument.
BETTER Recently I was involved in an argument *concerning race* (or *about racing*).

► EXERCISES ON ADJECTIVES AND ADVERBS

A. In the following sentences choose the standard form of the modifier within parentheses. Justify your choice by a simple diagram or by analysis of the sentence. Use your dictionary to distinguish between standard and informal usage.

1. The plans, (beautiful, beautifully) drawn, were presented in all their (careful, carefully) elaborated detail.
2. The (older, oldest) of the two brothers had the (brighter, brightest) red hair, but the (smaller, smallest) one (easy, easily) outnumbered him in freckles.
3. We sold the house at a (considerable, considerably) higher price than we had paid for it.
4. His (nightmare, nightmarish) tales made me feel (glum, glumly).
5. Now you pull (steady, steadily) on the knob until I lock the door.
6. (Most, almost) all students fall short of their possibilities; I (sure, surely) have.
7. I want someone who can do the work (prompt and efficient, promptly and efficiently) and still behave (courteous, courteously) toward the customers.

8. Do you realize how (bad, badly) your mother will feel if you do not work (steady, steadily) or (serious, seriously) enough?
9. The horse trotted (rapid, rapidly) and won the race (easy, easily).
10. Dave is (uncommon, uncommonly) light on his feet for such a (heavy, heavily) built man.
11. It was a (fair, fairly), warm day in April.
12. It was a (fair, fairly) warm day in April.
13. Mr. Porter was so excited that he could not play his part (good, well).
14. Visitors to the cavern never fail to comment upon the (awful, awfully) quiet of the place.
15. It is (awful, awfully) dark in there.
16. The wind blew (fierce, fiercely) and the snow fell (continuous, continuously) all the long night.
17. The next few weeks passed very (rapid, rapidly).
18. I am afraid that the good woman is (some, somewhat) confused.
19. Under our new (department, departmental) arrangement, Mr. Willoughby's time is taken up almost wholly with (administration, administrative) work.
20. If you study (consistent, consistently) and (regular, regularly), you should overcome (most, almost) any handicap.

B. Rewrite the following sentences to provide the proper adjectives or adverbs in accordance with standard English usage. Write *C* for each sentence that needs no revision.

1. Henry, I do wish you wouldn't stop so sudden.
2. We began to eat more often and plentiful, and everything went along smooth for a while.
3. I can't tell which smells more sweetly, the roses or the honeysuckle.
4. I have tried both brands, and I still can't decide which I like best.
5. He rang the bell loud; loudly it sounded through hall and yard.
6. William, the oldest of the two brothers, always got along good with his studies.
7. Uncle Ben spends all his leisure time working in the garden.
8. If you want to catch him, you had better be quick about it.
9. We felt sure we had acted quick enough.
10. The boys played good last Saturday and won the game very easy.
11. Remember, if you do bad in this test, you may not have another chance.
12. Timmy felt sleepily under his pillow to see if the tooth was still there.

13. If you didn't snore so noisy, you wouldn't keep waking yourself up.

14. Without careful study no student can make good grades consistently.

15. A good hog has short legs and a reasonable wide body.

16. The author pictures the scene so vivid

that the reader is eager to know what happens next.

C. Compose sentences in which each of the following words is used (1) as an adjective and (2) as an adverb: *well, near, daily, even, ill, fast, hard, high, straight.*

▶ Case

5 Use the proper case form to show the function of each noun or pronoun in the sentence as subject, possessor, or object.[1]

Nouns have a common form for the subject (*boy, dog*) and the object (*boy, dog*) and a distinctive form only for the possessor (*boy's, dog's*).

The *boy* (subject) bought the *dog* (object).
The *dog* (subject) followed the *boy* (object).
The *boy's* (possessor) dog; the *dog's* (possessor) collar

Six of our common pronouns have one form for the subject (*I, he, she, we, they, who*), another for the possessor (*my* or *mine, his, her* or *hers, our* or *ours, their* or *theirs, whose*), and a third form for the object (*me, him, her, us, them, whom*). Therefore these pronouns must be used with special care.

NOUN

	Subjective	Possessive	Objective
SING.	boy	boy's	boy
PL.	boys	boys'	boys

PRONOUN

Singular

	Subjective	Possessive	Objective
1.	I	my, mine	me
2.	you	your, yours	you
3.	he, she, it	his, her, hers, its	him, her, it

[1] The subject is said to be in the subjective or nominative case, the possessor in the possessive or genitive case, and the object in the objective or accusative case.

PRONOUN (Cont.)

Plural

	Subjective	Possessive	Objective
1.	we	our, ours	us
2.	you	your, yours	you
3.	they	their, theirs	them
SING. PL.	who	whose	whom

Note on appositives: An appositive has the same case as the noun or pronoun with which it is in apposition.

RIGHT   We—*John* and *I*—are responsible for the damage. [The appositives *John* and *I* are in the subjective case, in agreement with *we.*]

RIGHT   The damage was caused by us—*John* and *me.* [The appositives *John* and *me* are in the objective case, in agreement with *us.*]

Subjective Case

5a   Use the subjective case for subjects of verbs. See 5g for subjects of infinitives.

RIGHT   *He* is old. *She* is kind. *They* work diligently.

In certain types of sentences care must be taken to prevent mistaking the subject for the object:

(1) Do not allow the subjective who (whoever, whosoever) to be incorrectly changed to whom (whomever, whomsoever) by a following parenthetical expression such as I think or he says. (Note that such parenthetical expressions may be omitted without destroying the sense of the sentence.)

WRONG   She is a very dependable person *whom* I think will prove worthy of every trust.

RIGHT   She is a very dependable person *who* I think will prove worthy of every trust.

who	will prove

WRONG   Jones is a man *whom* we know is dependable.

RIGHT   Jones is a man *who* we know is dependable.

(2) The subject of a noun clause is always in the subjective case, even when the whole noun clause is the object of a verb or a preposition.

WRONG   Employ *whomever* is willing to work.

RIGHT   Employ *whoever* is willing to work. [*Whoever* is the subject of *is willing*. The object of *employ* is the whole clause *whoever is willing to work*.]

WRONG   He had respect for *whomever* was in power.

RIGHT   He had respect for *whoever* was in power. [The complete clause, not merely the pronoun *whoever*, is the object of the preposition *for*.]

(3) Use the subjective case after the conjunction *than* or *as*, if the pronoun is the subject of an implied verb.

RIGHT   He is older than *I* [am].

RIGHT   He is as wise as *they* [are].

RIGHT   He likes you better than *I* [like you].

RIGHT   He likes you as well as *I* [like you]. (See 5f(3) for the use of the objective case after *than* or *as*.)

▶ EXERCISE 1.   Compose ten sentences to illustrate the appropriate use of pronouns in the subjective case as explained in 5a(1),(2),(3). Underline each pronoun in the subjective case and explain why it is properly used.

5b   Use the subjective case for the predicate (subjective) complement.

RIGHT   It is *I* (*he, she, we, they*).

Note: Informal usage accepts *It is me* (*It's me*) but not *It is him* (*her, us, them*).

▶ EXERCISE 2.   Select from your reading ten sentences to illustrate the various uses of pronouns in the subjective case.

Possessive Case

5c   Use the apostrophe to form the possessive of nouns and indefinite pronouns, but not the possessive of personal pronouns (*my, mine, your, yours, his, hers, its, our, ours, their, theirs*) nor of the relative-interrogative pronoun *whose*.[2]

Apostrophe carelessly omitted:

WRONG   my *sons* wife; both *sons* wives; *everyones* wife

RIGHT   my *son's* wife; both *sons'* wives; *everyone's* wife

Apostrophe wrongly used:

WRONG   Virtue is *it's* own reward. The hat is *her's*.

RIGHT   Virtue is *its* own reward. The hat is *hers*.

Remember that the possessive *it's* or *her's* or *our's* or *their's* is just as incorrect as *hi's*—an error no one would make. Of course *it's* is correct as a contraction of *it is*: "*It's* cold today."

5d   A pronoun immediately preceding the gerund is usually in the possessive case.

RIGHT   My brother approved of *my* (*her, our, your, their*) going to the fair.

When a pronoun (*this, that*) has no common possessive form, or when either a noun or a pronoun is separated from the gerund, the use of the possessive would be awkward or incorrect.

RIGHT   I cannot approve of *this* (*that*) being done.

RIGHT   The chance of *anyone* in the party *falling* out was remote.

Nouns immediately preceding the gerund are often in the possessive case, but they are also common in the objective case, especially when the emphasis falls on the noun rather than on the gerund.

[2] See further details for forming the possessive case under Section 15.

RIGHT   I was pleased by *John's* asking me to dinner.

RIGHT   Just imagine *Mary* being on time. [Emphasis on *Mary*]

COLLOQUIAL   Just imagine *him* being on time.

5e   An of phrase is sometimes preferred to the possessive in 's.

(1) For inanimate objects

UNUSUAL   The house's roof; the wall's surface; the property's value

BETTER   The roof of the house; the surface of the wall; the value of the property

Note: Usage justifies many exceptions, especially to indicate time or measure (*month's leave, day's work, hour's delay, year's end, stone's throw*) or personification (*love's song, pity's sake, mercy's plea*).

(2) To avoid awkwardness

RIGHT   The wagon *of the boy* who lives next door was stolen (not "The boy's wagon who lives next door . . ." or "The boy who lives next door's wagon . . .").

RIGHT   As soon as the tourists were assembled, the officers examined the papers *of each* (not *each's*). [Some of the indefinite pronouns— such as *each, any, all, some, most,* and *few*— are not used with *'s.*]

Objective Case

5f   Use the objective case for the object of a verb, a verbal, or a preposition.

RIGHT   All of *us* (not *we*) students gave *him money.* [*Us* is the object of the preposition *of; him* is the indirect object of the verb *gave; money* is the direct object of the verb *gave.*]

RIGHT   By opposing *him* we offended *her.* [*Him* is the object of the verbal *opposing; her* is the object of the verb *offended.*]

(1) Who and whom

Informal English is tending more and more to avoid the use of the objective *whom,* except when it comes immediately after a preposition; but in formal writing *whom* is still generally used for the objective case.

WRONG   For *who* did you vote? [*Who* immediately follows the preposition *for,* of which it is the object.]

RIGHT   For *whom* did you vote?

RIGHT   *Whom* did you vote for? [Somewhat formal]

RIGHT   *Who* did you vote for? [Informal use of *who* when it does not follow the preposition]

FORMAL   The artist and the model *whom* he loved had a quarrel. [*Whom* is the object of *loved.*]

INFORMAL   The artist and the model he loved had a quarrel. [*Whom* is avoided.]

(2) Pronouns following the conjunction and

WRONG   Last summer my father took Tom and *I* on a camping trip.

RIGHT   Last summer my father took Tom and *me* on a camping trip. [*Me* is an object of the verb *took.*]

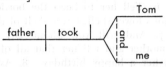

WRONG   This is a secret between you and *I.*

RIGHT   This is a secret between you and *me.* [*Me* is an object of the preposition *between.*]

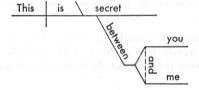

(3) Pronouns following the conjunctions than or as

Use the objective case when the pronoun following *than* or *as* is the object of an implied verb.

RIGHT   He likes you better than [he likes] *me.*

RIGHT   He likes you as well as [he likes] *me.*

(See 5a(3) for use of the subjective case after *than* or *as.*)

5g   Use the objective case for the subject, the object, or the complement of an infinitive.

RIGHT   *Whom* do you think *him* to be? [*Whom* is the complement and *him* the subject of the infinitive *to be. Him to be whom* is the object of the verb *do think.*]

RIGHT   He asked *me* to help *him.* [*Me* is the subject and *him* the object of the infinitive *to help.*]

► EXERCISES ON CASE

A. In the following passage select the word in parentheses that is in the proper case and give the reason for your choice.

1. Miss Adams, will you ask (whoever, whomever) calls for me while I'm away to talk to Dr. Knight instead? 2. There is one patient (who, whom) I believe may phone—a Mrs. Abell—but Dr. Knight can take care of her as well as (I, me). 3. It was (she, her) who phoned just now about her little (boys, boy's, boys') foot. 4. And if Mrs. Watson comes in about the (twins, twins') prescription, that is (theirs, their's, theirs') on the corner of my desk. 5. Caution her that (its, it's) to be given exactly according to directions and that she must report promptly on (them, their) showing any skin reaction. 6. Tell her to keep the bottle on the (refrigerator's lower shelf, lower shelf of the refrigerator). 7. And will you phone Dr. (Browns, Brown's) mother and tell her that all of (we, us) here wish her a happy birthday. 8. Ask her in (whose, who's) care we should address letters to him now.

B. In the following passage, choose between the pronouns in parentheses and justify your choice.

1. Sheriff Comstock, to (who, whom) I introduced myself, had on his desk the records of the three men (who, whom) he believed were capable

of committing a burglary such as that in East Dover Heights. 2. His deputy, Abe Phillips, with (who, whom) I had worked on the Berryman jewel theft a few years earlier, came into the office.

3. "(Whoever, Whomever) we find out did this job, it won't be Joey Piper," Phillips said. 4. "I've just talked to the superintendent of Davis Polyclinic, (who, whom) tells me that Joey has been there for three weeks, in a plaster cast up to his waist."

5. "You'd better get (whoever, whomever) is out that way on the case to check on Joey," the sheriff said. 6. He turned to me. "Between you and (I, me), I wouldn't trust Joey Piper's dead body in a lead coffin. 7. You must get me to tell you sometime about the troubles we have had—Joey and (I, me)."

8. "You think it mightn't be (he, him) out at Davis?" I suggested.

9. "I think that (whoever, whomever) takes Piper for granted is a fool," he said.

10. The sheriff turned to his deputy. "Abe, (who, whom) do you think should check on Piper out at Davis? . . . Flamm? Good. Have Flamm get me a complete case history, along with X rays of all Joey's injuries. 11. (They, Them) should be new X rays—made today."

12. Sheriff Comstock moved the Piper file to one side. "Well," he said, "(he, him) we can forget for a while. 13. But even if Piper is clear, that still leaves you and (I, me) two others (who, whom) are just as capable of this sort of job as (he, him)."

► Agreement

6   Make every verb agree in number with its subject; make every pronoun agree in number with its antecedent.[1]

Caution: Can you easily distinguish verbs and relate them to their subjects? Can you readily find the antecedents of pronouns? Until you can do so, you may continue to have difficulty with agreement. If necessary, master first the fundamentals of the sentence treated in Section 1, Sentence Sense, especially 1a, 1b, and

1 For other kinds of agreement see Section 27.

1c; then study Section 6.

Singular subjects require singular verbs; plural subjects require plural verbs. Pronouns agree with their antecedents (the words to which they refer) in the same way. Note that in the subject the *s* ending is the sign of the plural, that in the verb it is the sign of the singular.

RIGHT   The *engine runs* smoothly. [Singular subject—singular verb]

RIGHT   The *engines run* smoothly. [Plural subject—plural verb]

RIGHT   The *woman* washes *her* clothes. [Singular antecedent—singular pronoun]

RIGHT   The *women* wash *their* clothes. [Plural antecedent—plural pronoun]

Make a diagram, or at least form a mental picture, of each subject and its verb

$$\left(\;\; \frac{\text{engine} \;\;\big|\;\; \text{runs}}{} \qquad \frac{\text{engines} \;\;\big|\;\; \text{run}}{} \;\;\right)$$

and of each antecedent and its pronoun (*woman* ← *her, women* ← *their*). This practice will make it easy to avoid errors in agreement.

6a   Make every verb agree in number with its subject.

(1) Do not be misled (a) by nouns or pronouns intervening between the subject and the verb or (b) by careless pronunciation of nouns ending in *st*.

WRONG   The *recurrence* of like sounds *help* to stir the emotions.

RIGHT   The *recurrence* of like sounds *helps* to stir the emotions.

WRONG   His *interest* were many and varied. The *Communist are . . . Scientist are . . .*

RIGHT   His *interests were* many and varied. The *Communists are . . . Scientists are . . .*

Most writers feel that the number of the subject is not changed by the addition of parenthetical expressions introduced by such words as *with, together with, as well as, no less than, including, accompanied by.*

RIGHT   *John,* together with James and William, *was drafted* into the Army.

RIGHT   *Thomas,* like his two brothers, *was* often in debt.

(2) Subjects joined by *and* usually take a plural verb.

RIGHT   A hammer and a saw *are* useful tools.

RIGHT   Mary, Jane, and I *were* tired after our morning's work.

Exceptions: A compound subject referring to a single person, or to two or more things considered as a unit, takes a singular verb.

RIGHT   My best friend and adviser *has gone.* [A single individual was both friend and adviser.]

RIGHT   The tumult and the shouting *dies.*—KIPLING. [Two nouns considered a single entity]

Each or *every* preceding singular subjects joined by *and* calls for a singular verb.

RIGHT   Each boy and each girl *is* to work independently.

RIGHT   Every boy and girl *has been urged* to attend the play.

(3) Singular subjects joined by *or, nor, either . . . or, neither . . . nor* usually take a singular verb.

RIGHT   Neither the boy nor the girl *is* to blame for the accident.

RIGHT   Either the man or his wife *knows* the exact truth of the matter.

When the meaning is felt to be plural, informal English occasionally uses the plural verb: "Neither she nor I *were* dancing, for we felt weary."

If one subject is singular and one plural, the verb usually agrees with the nearer.

PERMISSIBLE   Neither teacher nor pupils *are* in the building.

PERMISSIBLE   Neither pupils nor teacher *is* in the building.

PERMISSIBLE   Either you or I *am* mistaken.

BETTER   Either you *are* mistaken or I *am.*

(4) When the subject follows the verb (as in sentences beginning with *there is, there are*) special care is needed to determine the subject and to make sure that it agrees with the verb.

RIGHT   According to the rules, there *are* to be at least three *contestants* for each prize.

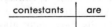

$$\frac{\text{contestants} \;\;\big|\;\; \text{are}}{}$$

RIGHT   There *are* many possible *candidates.*

RIGHT   There *is* only one good *candidate.*

Before a compound subject the first member of which is singular, a singular verb is sometimes used: "In the basement there *is* a restaurant, which serves delicious food, and a poolroom and two barber shops."

Note: The expletive *it* is always followed by a singular verb: "It *is* the *woman* who suffers." "It *is* the *women* who suffer."

(5) A relative pronoun used as a subject takes a plural or singular verb to accord with its antecedent.

RIGHT   *Boys* who *work* . . . A *boy* who *works* . . .

RIGHT   Mary is among the *students* who *have done* honor to the college. [*Students* is the antecedent of *who.*]

RIGHT   Mary is the only *one* of our students who *has achieved* national recognition. [*One,* not *students,* is the antecedent of *who.* The sentence means, "Of all our students Mary is the only *one* who *has achieved* national recognition."]

(6) *Each, either, neither, another, anyone, anybody, anything, someone, somebody, something, one, everyone, everybody, everything, nobody, nothing* regularly take singular verbs.

RIGHT   Each *takes* his turn at rowing.
RIGHT   Neither *likes* the friends of the other.
RIGHT   Someone *is* likely to hear the signal.
RIGHT   Everyone *has* his prejudices.
RIGHT   Nobody *cares* to listen to worries.

None is plural or singular, depending upon the other words in the sentence or in the immediately surrounding sentences (the context) which condition its meaning.

RIGHT   None *are* so blind as those who will not see.
RIGHT   None *is* so blind as he who will not see.

(*Any, all, more, most,* and *some* are used with plural or singular verbs in much the same way as *none.*)

(7) Collective nouns (and numbers denoting fixed quantity) usually take singular verbs because the group or quantity is usually regarded as a unit.

RIGHT   The whole family *is* concerned. [The common use: *family* regarded as a unit]

RIGHT   The family *have gone* about their several duties. [Less common: individuals of the family regarded separately]

RIGHT   A thousand bushels *is* a good yield. [A unit]

RIGHT   A thousand bushels of apples *were crated.* [Individual bushels]

RIGHT   One third of the crop *was ruined.* [A fraction followed by a singular object in the *of* phrase is usually singular]

RIGHT   One third of the peaches *were ruined.* [A fraction followed by a plural object in the *of* phrase is usually plural]

RIGHT   The public *is* aroused. [A unit]

RIGHT   The public *have been* warned. [Regarded as a group of individuals]

RIGHT   The number in the class *was* small. [*The number* is regularly taken as a unit.]

RIGHT   A number of the class *were* sick. [*A number* refers to individuals]

RIGHT   The data is sound. [A unit]

RIGHT   The data *have been* carefully *collected.* [Individual items]

(8) A verb usually agrees with its subject, not with its predicate noun.

RIGHT   His chief support *is* his brother and sister.
RIGHT   His brother and sister *are* his chief support.

But such sentences are often better recast so as to avoid the disagreement in number between subject and predicate noun.

BETTER   His support came chiefly from his brother and sister.

(9) Nouns plural in form but singular in meaning usually take singular verbs. In all doubtful cases a good dictionary should be consulted.

Regularly singular: esthetics, civics, economics, linguistics, logistics, mathematics, measles, mumps, news, physics, semantics

RIGHT   Mathematics *is* exact. The news *is* good.

Regularly plural: oats, pliers, scissors, trousers

RIGHT   Pliers *are* useful. The trousers *are* new.

Means and *headquarters* may be either singular or plural. Some nouns ending in *-ics,* such as *acoustics* and *statistics,* are considered singular when referring to an organized body of knowledge and plural when referring to activities, qualities, or individual facts.

RIGHT   Acoustics *is* an interesting study.
RIGHT   The acoustics of the hall *are* good.

RIGHT   Statistics *is* a science.
RIGHT   The statistics *were* easily *assembled.*

(10) A title of a single work or a word spoken of as a word, even when plural in form, takes a singular verb.

RIGHT   *Twice-Told Tales was written* by Hawthorne.

RIGHT   The New York *Times has* a wide circulation.
RIGHT   *They is* a pronoun.

▶ EXERCISE 1.   In the following sentences, find each verb and relate it to its subject. Then rewrite each sentence to secure agreement of subject and verb. Justify every change. Write *C* in place of each sentence that needs no revision.

1. The King's eldest son and heir apparent were then only six years old.
2. Do each of you know where to go if the alarm should sound?
3. This book, a collection of recent articles published by the editor and others, give you a comprehensive view of a many-sided question.
4. There come to my mind now three men who might have qualified, but none of the three was given the chance.
5. Everybody one met in the streets that summer were excitedly talking about Essex's homecoming.
6. The significance of words are taught by simply breaking them up into suffixes, prefixes, and roots.
7. A majority of delinquent children are from broken homes.
8. A simple majority is sufficient to elect a candidate to office.
9. Application exercises for each chapter enables the student to practice the principles which the various chapters set forth.
10. His one ambition was to get well and get back to work.
11. His aging parents and the provision he might make for them were his one principal concern.

▶ EXERCISE 2.   Rewrite the following *correct* sentences as directed. Change verbs to secure agreement and make any additional changes required for good sentence sense.

1. Certain portions of our collection are kept in an underground, air-conditioned vault and are never placed on exhibit. [Insert *One* before *Certain.*]   2. Each piece in the exhibit has to be carefully dusted and polished once a day and then put back in place. [Change *each piece* to *the pieces.*]   3. I might mention that this particular specimen has a distinguished place in history. [Change *this* to *these.*]   4. Our staff takes great pride in the efficient cataloguing system which we have developed here. [Insert *members* after *staff.*]   5. In this room is my assistant, who is cataloguing a newly arrived shipment. [Change *assistant* to *assistants.*]   6. One of our research parties has just returned from the field and is to be meeting with the directors during the remainder of the week. [Change *One* to

Two.]   7. A detachment of four men has been left behind to maintain a permanent camp at the excavation site. [Omit *A detachment of.*]   8. Eaton Murray, the leader of the expedition and an especially capable man, is among the four. [Insert *John Wade* after *and.*]   9. Neither of the others is known to us here. [Change *is known* to *are unknown.*]   10. Both, however, were selected for particular abilities which they have shown. [Change *they* to *he.*]

6b Make each pronoun agree in number with its antecedent.

A singular antecedent (the word to which a pronoun refers) takes a singular verb and is also referred to by a singular pronoun; a plural antecedent takes a plural verb and is referred to by a plural pronoun.

(1) In standard [2] English use a singular pronoun to refer to such antecedents as *man, woman, person, one, anyone, anybody, someone, somebody, everyone, everybody, each, kind, sort, either, neither, no one, nobody.* See also 6a(6).

WRONG   An outstanding trait of primitive *man* was *their* belief in superstitions.
RIGHT   An outstanding trait of primitive *man* was *his* belief in superstitions.

STANDARD   Each of the sons had planned to follow *his* father's occupation.
COLLOQUIAL   Each of the sons had planned to follow *their* father's occupation.

STANDARD   Everybody stood on *his* chair.
COLLOQUIAL   Everybody stood on *their* chairs.

(2) Two or more antecedents joined by *and* are referred to by a plural pronoun; two or more singular antecedents joined by *or* or *nor* are referred to by a singular pronoun. If one of two antecedents joined by *or* is singular and one plural, the pronoun usually agrees with the nearer. See also 6a(2),(3).

RIGHT   Henry and James have completed *their* work.
RIGHT   Neither Henry nor James has completed *his* work.
WRONG   When a *boy or girl* enters college, *they* find it different from high school.
RIGHT BUT CLUMSY   When a *boy or girl* enters college, *he or she* finds it different from high school.

[2] See pages 870-71 for the distinction between standard and colloquial English.

BETTER   When *boys and girls* enter college, *they* find it different from high school.

RIGHT   Neither the *master* nor the *servants* were aware of *their* danger. [The plural *servants* is the nearer antecedent.]

RIGHT   Neither the *servants* nor the *master* was aware of *his* danger.

(3) Collective nouns are referred to by singular or plural pronouns depending on whether the collective noun is considered singular or plural. See also 6a(7).

Special care should be taken to avoid making a collective noun *both* singular and plural within the same sentence.

WRONG   If the board of directors *controls* the company, *they* may vote themselves bonuses. [*Board* is first singular with *controls,* then plural with *they.*]

RIGHT   If the board of directors *control* the company, *they* may vote themselves bonuses. [Made plural throughout as demanded by the last half of the sentence]

RIGHT   If the board of directors *controls* the company, *it* may vote itself a bonus. [Last half of the sentence changed to agree with the first]

► EXERCISE 3.   In the following sentences select the pronoun in parentheses that agrees with its antecedent in accordance with standard English usage. Note also any pronouns that would be acceptable in conversation or familiar writing but not in formal writing.

1. The foreman unlocked the shed and everybody went in and got (his, their) tools.   2. Each man, and Charlie too, left (his, their) lunch pail inside.   3. Roy and Dave were tearing out concrete forms, and (he, each, they) took a section apiece and went to work.   4. One or another would yell for the helpers to clear away the salvage lumber (he was, they were) tearing out.   5. The helpers were supposed to pile the lumber outside the foundation, where Andy was cleaning (it, them) up and stacking (it, them) for re-use.   6. Every few minutes someone would call out for the water boy to bring (him, them) a drink.   7. The crew was small, but (its, their) thirst was large.   8. Charlie, the water boy, had all he could do to keep (it, them) satisfied.   9. "If anybody here ever drank water when (he was, they were) off the job," he grumbled, "I'd be proud to shake (him, them) by the hand."   10. But nobody volunteered (his, their) hand to be shaken.   11. Every minute, instead, somebody new would be yelling for water, and

Charlie would trudge off toward (him, them).   12. It was either Roy or Dave who was whooping for (his, their) ninetieth drink when the noon whistle blew.   13. Nobody was so ready to stop where (he was, they were) as Charlie.   14. "Whoever wants a drink knows where (he, they) can get it," he let it be known, and emptied his bucket out on the ground.

► EXERCISE 4.   In Exercise 3 make changes as directed below and then complete the sentence so as to secure agreement of pronoun with its antecedent. In Sentence 1, change *everybody* to *the workmen.* In 4, change *One or another* to *Both.* In 9, change *anybody here* to *these men.* In 11, change *somebody new* to *two or three more.*

► EXERCISE ON AGREEMENT

In the following passage correct each italicized word which needs correcting. Explain whether the correction is necessary to secure agreement between (1) subject and verb or between (2) pronoun and antecedent. Justify each italicized word which you would leave as it is.

1. Everybody, I suppose, is entitled to *their* own opinion about Major McIntyre and the Confederate gold.   2. Anyhow, there *is* all sorts of opinions to be heard if a person has patience enough in *their* being to hear them all.   3. This wagonload of gold, most of it in bars, *were* being moved from the capital to keep *them* from being captured when the capital fell.   4. Or at least, so one of the stories *go.*   5. Some *says* that there *was* two wagonloads and that Abel or one of the younger McIntyre boys *were* driving the second one.   6. And some few of us *haven't* decided to put any belief in the tales at all.   7. But nearly everybody else *are* agreed that the gold got this far, because while it was being moved, one or another of the McIntyre brothers *were* captured and shot at the family home near here.   8. You can still see the ruins of the house, which *were* burned after the soldiers had ransacked it.   9. All the family *were* deeply involved in the war and couldn't afford to risk *their* lives by staying where *they* could easily be found.   10. So the house had been standing empty when the Major, or Abel, *were* captured there that night.   11. All the McIntyre slaves but one *were* scared off when the soldiers surrounded the place, and this one couldn't say which of the brothers *was* captured.   12. He saw someone dragged out and shot and *their* body thrown back into the burning house, but there *wasn't* enough left of the body afterward to tell whose it was.   13. And neither the Major nor Abel nor the gold *were* ever seen again.

▶ Tense

Mood; *Shall* and *Will*

7 Use the appropriate form of the verb.

Tense

7a   Use the appropriate tense form.

Tense, from the Latin word meaning "time," refers to changes in the form of the verb to indicate the time of the action. But tense and time do not always agree. The present tense, for example, is by no means limited to action in the present time. It may be used also to recall vividly the events of the past, as in the "historical present," or to refer to future action: "I leave for Chicago tomorrow morning." English verbs have six tenses.

1. PRESENT—present action: "He *sees* me now"; customary action: "He *sees* me daily"; and other uses such as: "Napoleon *opens* the campaign brilliantly" [historical present, used instead of the past tense]; "I start my vacation a week from Friday" [used instead of the future tense]; "Some early philosophers knew that the earth *is* round" [timeless truth, expressed in the present even when the main verb is in the past].

2. PAST—past action not extending to the present: "He *saw* me at the game yesterday."

3. FUTURE—action at some time after the present: "He *will see* me next month in New York." The future is frequently expressed by the phrase *is going to*: "He *is going to see* me next month in New York."

4. PRESENT PERFECT—past action extending to the present: "He *has seen* me many times."

5. PAST PERFECT—past action completed before some indicated time in the past: "My friend *had seen* me before the game started." "I *had* already *decided* to talk with him before I left the house." [Sometimes put in the simple past tense: "My friend *saw* me before the game started." But note that "I *decided* to talk with him before I left the house" would be a change of meaning.]

6. FUTURE PERFECT—action to be completed before some indicated time in the future: "He *will have seen* me again before my departure tomorrow." [Commonly put in the simple future tense: "He *will see* me again before my departure tomorrow." The future perfect tense is seldom used.]

These six tenses are built on three forms, called **principal parts**: (1) the present stem (infinitive)—*see, use,* (2) the past tense—*saw, used,* and (3) the past participle—*seen, used.* Most English verbs, like *use,* are **regular**; that is, they form both the past tense (*used*) and the past participle (*used*) by adding *-d* or *-ed* to the present stem (*use*). Other verbs, like *see,* are **irregular** because they change the present stem (*see*) to form the past tense (*saw*) and the past participle (*seen*). It will be noted below that the present stem is the basis for both present and future tenses; the past, for the past tense alone; and the past participle, for the present perfect, past perfect, and future perfect tenses.

In addition to the simple verb forms illustrated above, English uses a "progressive" form to show action in progress and a "do" form for (1) emphatic statements, (2) questions, or (3) negations.

SIMPLE FORM   I see, he sees; I saw, he saw; I am seen.

PROGRESSIVE FORM   I am seeing, he is seeing; I was seeing, he was seeing; I am being seen.

"DO" FORM   (1) I do see, he does see; I did see, he did see.

(2) Does he see her? Did he see her?

(3) He does not see her. He did not see her.

Principal Parts

The writer usually knows the tense needed to express his ideas. He can determine the correct form of this tense by consulting his dictionary for the principal parts of the verb. In the dictionary every irregular verb is listed by

CONJUGATION OF THE VERB *TO SEE*
(Principal Parts: *see, saw, seen*)

INDICATIVE MOOD [1]

Active Voice		*Passive Voice*	

PRESENT TENSE

Singular	*Plural*	*Singular*	*Plural*
1. I see	we see	I am seen	we are seen
2. you see	you see	you are seen	you are seen
3. he (she, it) sees	they see	he (she, it) is seen	they are seen

PAST TENSE

1. I saw	we saw	I was seen	we were seen
2. you saw	you saw	you were seen	you were seen
3. he saw	they saw	he was seen	they were seen

FUTURE TENSE

1. I shall see	we shall see	I shall be seen	we shall be seen
2. you will see	you will see	you will be seen	you will be seen
3. he will see	they will see	he will be seen	they will be seen

PRESENT PERFECT TENSE

1. I have seen	we have seen	I have been seen	we have been seen
2. you have seen	you have seen	you have been seen	you have been seen
3. he has seen	they have seen	he has been seen	they have been seen

PAST PERFECT TENSE

1. I had seen	we had seen	I had been seen	we had been seen
2. you had seen	you had seen	you had been seen	you had been seen
3. he had seen	they had seen	he had been seen	they had been seen

FUTURE PERFECT TENSE (seldom used)

1. I shall have seen	we shall have seen	I shall have been seen	we shall have been seen
2. you will have seen	you will have seen	you will have been seen	you will have been seen
3. he will have seen	they will have seen	he will have been seen	they will have been seen

SUBJUNCTIVE MOOD

Active Voice	*Passive Voice*

PRESENT TENSE

Singular: if I, you, he see   if I, you, he be seen
Plural: if we, you, they see   if we, you, they be seen

PAST TENSE

Singular: if I, you, he saw   if I, you, he were seen
Plural: if we, you, they saw   if we, you, they were seen

PRESENT PERFECT TENSE

Singular: if I, you, he have seen   if I, you, he have been seen
Plural: if we, you, they have seen   if we, you, they have been seen

PAST PERFECT TENSE

(Same as the Indicative)

---

[1] Such terms as *mood, indicative, subjunctive,* and *voice* are explained in Section 35, **Grammatical Terms.**

IMPERATIVE MOOD

PRESENT TENSE

see   be seen

PARTICIPLES

PRESENT TENSE

seeing   being seen

PAST TENSE

seen   been seen

PRESENT PERFECT TENSE

having seen   having been seen

INFINITIVES

PRESENT TENSE

to see   to be seen

PRESENT PERFECT TENSE

to have seen   to have been seen

GERUNDS

PRESENT TENSE

seeing   being seen

PRESENT PERFECT TENSE

having seen   having been seen

---

its infinitive or present stem; for example, *see*. Then follow the past tense (*saw*), the past participle (*seen*), and the present participle (*seeing*). *See, saw,* and *seen* are the principal parts from which the writer can readily derive the proper form for any of the six tenses. For regular verbs (such as *use*) the past tense and the past participle, when not given, are understood to be formed by adding *-d* or *-ed*.

WRONG   The boy *seen* where the bullet had entered. [Past tense needed; the dictionary gives *saw* as the correct form.]

RIGHT   The boy *saw* where the bullet had entered.

WRONG   I *use* to live in the country. [Past tense needed]

RIGHT   I *used* to live in the country.

► EXERCISE 1.   Some verbs are frequently confused because of similarity in spelling or meaning. Master the principal parts of the following verbs. Then compose sentences (three to illustrate each verb) in which each verb is correctly used (1) in the past tense, (2) in the present perfect tense, and (3) in the present tense (progressive form, using the present participle).

Present stem (infinitive)	Past tense	Past participle	Present participle
lie (to recline)	lay	lain	lying
lay (to cause to lie)	laid	laid	laying
sit (to be seated)	sat	sat	sitting
set (to place or put)	set	set	setting

WRONG   He *layed* (or *laid*) down on the bed. [Past tense of the intransitive verb *lie* needed]

RIGHT   He *lay* down on the bed.

WRONG   He *lay* the book on the table. [Past tense of the transitive verb *lay* needed]

RIGHT   He *laid* the book on the table.

RIGHT   The book is *lying* (not *laying*) on the table.

WRONG   He *set* in the chair. [Past tense of the intransitive verb *sit* needed]

RIGHT   He *sat* in the chair.

RIGHT   He *set* the bucket on the table. [Transitive]

RIGHT   The man is *sitting* (not *setting*) in the chair.

► EXERCISE 2.   Principal parts of other difficult verbs are listed below. *Add the principal parts of all verbs that you have used incorrectly in your writing.* Then master the whole list and compose sentences to illustrate the correct use of each principal part (as assigned, perhaps in groups of ten, by the instructor).

Present stem	Past tense	Past participle
begin	began	begun
bid (offer)	bid	bid
bid (order)	bade	bidden
bite	bit	bitten, bit
blow	blew	blown
break	broke	broken
bring	brought	brought
burst	burst	burst
catch	caught	caught
choose	chose	chosen
come	came	come
dive	dived, dove	dived
do	did	done
drag	dragged	dragged
draw	drew	drawn
drink	drank	drunk
eat	ate	eaten
fall	fell	fallen
flee	fled	fled
fly	flew	flown
forget	forgot	forgotten, forgot
freeze	froze	frozen
get	got	got, gotten

Present stem	Past tense	Past participle
go	went	gone
grow	grew	grown
know	knew	known
lead	led	led
lose	lost	lost
raise	raised	raised
ride	rode	ridden
ring	rang, rung	rung
rise	rose	risen
run	ran	run
see	saw	seen
shrink	shrank, shrunk	shrunk, shrunken
sing	sang, sung	sung
speak	spoke	spoken
spring	sprang, sprung	sprung
steal	stole	stolen
swim	swam	swum
swing	swung	swung
take	took	taken
tear	tore	torn
write	wrote	written

Sequence of Tenses

7b   **Make a verb in a subordinate clause or an infinitive or a participle agree logically (naturally) with the verb in the main clause.**

1. *Verbs*

RIGHT   The audience rises as the speaker *enters*. [The present *enters* follows the present *rises*.]

RIGHT   The audience *rose* as the speaker *entered*. [The past *entered* follows the past *rose*.]

RIGHT   I *have ceased* worrying because I *have heard* no more rumors. [The present perfect follows the present perfect.]

RIGHT   I *believed* (or *had believed*) that the letter *had* (not *has*) *been lost*. [The past perfect in the subordinate clause follows the past or past perfect in the main clause.]

RIGHT   I *believe* (or *will believe, have believed*) that the letter *has* (not *had*) *been lost*. [The present perfect in the subordinate clause follows present, future, or present perfect in the main clause.]

RIGHT   You *will find* that he *will have done* well. [The future perfect in the subordinate clause is used only with the future in the main clause.]

POOR   I *hoped* that I *could have gone*.

BETTER   I *hoped* that I *could go*. [In the past time, indicated by *hoped*, I was still anticipating going.]

POOR   When I *was* at camp four weeks, I *received* word that my father *had died*.

BETTER   When I *had been* at camp four weeks, I *received* word that my father *had died*. [The past perfect *had been* or *had died* indicates a time prior to that of the main verb *received*.]

2. *Infinitives*

Use the present infinitive to express action contemporaneous with, or future to, that of the governing verb; use the perfect infinitive for action prior to that of the governing verb.

RIGHT   I was happy *to find* (not *to have found*) you at home. [The finding and the happiness were contemporaneous.]

RIGHT   I hoped *to go* (not *to have gone*). I hope *to go*. [Present infinitives. At the time indicated by the verbs I was still hoping *to go*, not *to have gone*.]

RIGHT   I should like *to have lived* in Shakespeare's time. [Perfect infinitive—expressing time prior to that of the governing verb. Simpler: I wish I had lived in Shakespeare's time.]

RIGHT   I should have liked *to live* (not *to have lived*) in Shakespeare's time. [Present infinitive—for time contemporaneous with that of the governing verb]

3. *Participles*

Use the present participle to express action contemporaneous with that of the governing verb; use the perfect participle for action prior to that of the governing verb.

RIGHT   *Walking* along the streets, he met many old friends. [The walking and the meeting were contemporaneous.]

RIGHT   *Having walked* all the way home, he found himself tired. [The walking was prior to the finding.]

Caution: Do not confuse gerunds and participles.

RIGHT   After *walking* home he found himself tired. [Gerund]

RIGHT   *Having walked* (not *After having walked*) home, he found himself tired. [Participle. *After* would be redundant.]

Subjunctive Mood

7c   **The subjunctive mood is still required in a few types of expressions, and may be used in others.**

The subjunctive mood has been largely displaced by the indicative. Distinctive forms for the subjunctive occur only in the third person singular of the present tense (*I demand that he* **see** *a physician* instead of the indicative *he sees a physician*) and in the verb *to be* as indicated by boldface below.

Present indicative

I am	we are
you are	you are
he is	they are

Present subjunctive

if I **be**	if we **be**
if you **be**	if you **be**
if he (she, it) **be**	if they **be**

Past indicative

I was	we were
you were	you were
he was	they were

Past subjunctive

if I **were**	if we were
if you were	if you were
if he (she, it) **were**	if they were

The subjunctive is regularly used (1) in *that* clauses of motions, resolutions, recommendations, orders, or demands and (2) in a few idiomatic expressions.

RIGHT   I move that the report *be* approved.

Resolved, that dues for the coming year *be* doubled.

I recommend (order, demand) that the prisoner *be* released.

I demand (request, insist) that the messenger *go* alone.

If need *be; suffice* it to say; *come* what may; etc. [Idiomatic expressions in which the subjunctive is fixed]

Most writers prefer the subjunctive in contrary-to-fact conditions and in expressions of doubts, wishes, or regrets.

STANDARD   If the apple *were* ripe, it would be delicious. [Subjunctive]

COLLOQUIAL   If the apple *was* ripe, it would be delicious. [Indicative]

RIGHT   If the apple *is* ripe, I will eat it. [The indicative is regularly used in conditions not contrary to fact.]

STANDARD   The man looks as if he *were* sick. [Subjunctive]

COLLOQUIAL   The man looks as if he *was* sick. [Indicative]

STANDARD   I wish that he *were* here. [Subjunctive]

COLLOQUIAL   I wish that he *was* here. [Indicative]

▶ EXERCISE 3.   Choose the proper form for the subjunctive mood in the parentheses below.

1. We insist that he (be, is) punished.
2. I wish that James (was, were) here.
3. We have talked of a trip to Madrid as though it (was, were) impossible.
4. Present-day problems demand that we (be, are) ready for any emergency.
5. "A good idea," one of the members said, "but I propose that the suggestion (be, is) tabled for the present."
6. Our purpose, (suffice it, it suffices) to say, is to win the confidence of our patrons.
7. If there (was, were) time, I could finish my report.
8. We ought to refuse consideration of this idea lest the prospective trip to Europe (prove, proves) too much a distraction to our immediate business.
9. "If this (be, is) treason, make the most of it."
10. I demand that he (make, makes) an explanation.
11. I wish he (was, were) present to explain his continued neglect of his duties.
12. If he (was, were) here, he might explain everything to our full satisfaction.
13. The principal urged that everyone (stay, stays) until the end of the meeting.

▶ EXERCISE 4.   Compose five sentences in which the subjunctive is required. Compose three other sentences in which either the subjunctive or the indicative may be used, giving the indicative (colloquial) form in parentheses.

Shifts in Tense or Mood

7d   Avoid needless shifts in tense or mood.[2]

WRONG   He *came* to the river and *pays* a man to ferry him across. [Contradictory use of tenses within one sentence]

RIGHT   He *came* to the river and *paid* a man to ferry him across.

INCONSISTENT   It is necessary to restrain an occasional foolhardy park visitor lest a mother

[2] See also Section **27, Shifts in Point of View.**

bear *mistake* his friendly intentions and *supposes* him a menace to her cubs. [Mood shifts improperly from subjunctive to indicative within the compound predicate.] But females with cubs *were* only one of the dangers. [A correct enough sentence if standing alone, but here inconsistent with present tense of preceding one, and therefore misleading] One *has* to remember that all bears *were* wild animals and not domesticated pets. [Inconsistent and misleading shift of tense from present in main clause to past in subordinate clause] Though a bear *may* seem altogether peaceable and harmless, he *might* not remain peaceable and he is never harmless. [Tense shifts improperly from present in introductory clause to past in main clause.] It *is* therefore an important part of the park ranger's duty *to watch* the tourists, and above all *don't* let anybody try to feed the bears. [Inconsistent. Mood shifts needlessly from indicative to imperative.]

IMPROVED It is necessary to restrain an occasional foolhardy park visitor lest a mother bear *mistake* his friendly intentions and *suppose* him a menace to her cubs. But females with cubs *are* only one of the dangers. One *has* to remember that all bears *are* wild animals and not domesticated pets. Though a bear *may* seem altogether peaceable and harmless, he *may* not remain peaceable and he is never harmless. It *is* therefore an important part of the park ranger's duty *to watch* the tourists and above all not *to let* anybody try to feed the bears.

▶ EXERCISE 5. In the following passage correct all errors and inconsistencies in tense and mood and any other errors in verb usage. Write *C* in place of any sentence which is satisfactory as it stands.

1. Across the Thames from Shakespeare's London lay the area known as the Bankside, probably as rough and unsavory a neighborhood as ever laid across the river from any city. 2. And yet it was to such a place that Shakespeare and his company had to have gone to build their new theater. 3. For the Puritan government of the City had set up all sorts of prohibitions against theatrical entertainment within the city walls. 4. When it became necessary, therefore, for the Company to have moved their playhouse from its old location north of the city, they obtain a lease to a tract on the Bankside. 5. Other theatrical companies had went there before them, and it seemed reasonable to have supposed that Shakespeare and his partners would prosper in the new location. 6. Apparently the Puritans of the City had no law against anyone's moving cartloads of lumber through the public streets. 7. There is no record that the Company met with difficulty while the timbers of the dismantled playhouse are being hauled to the new site. 8. One difficulty the partners had foresaw and forestalled, and that is the effort that their old landlord might make to have stopped their removing the building. 9. Lest his presence complicate their task and would perhaps defeat its working altogether, they waited until he had gone out of town. 10. And when he came back, his lot was bare, the building's timbers were all in stacks on the far side of the river, and the theater is waiting only to be put together. 11. It is a matter of general knowledge that on the Bankside Shakespeare continued his successful career as a showman and went on to enjoy even greater prosperity after he had made the move than before.

Shall *and* Will

7e Observe such distinctions as exist between *shall* (*should*) and *will* (*would*).

(1) Use *should* in all persons to express an obligation (in the sense "ought to") or a condition.

RIGHT I (You, He, We, They) *should* (i.e., *ought to*) help the needy.
RIGHT If I (you, he, we, they) *should* resign, the program would not be continued.

(2) Use *would* in all persons to express a wish or a customary action.

RIGHT *Would* that I (you, he, we, they) had received the message!
RIGHT I (You, He, We, They) *would* spend hours by the seashore during the summer months.

Shall is generally used for the first person in asking questions (*Shall* I enter?), and it is often used in all persons for special emphasis. Except for these uses of *shall,* and for the use of *should* to express an obligation or condition, informal English tends to use *will* and *would* in all persons.

(3) Some careful writers distinguish between *shall* and *will*:

(a) By using *shall* in the first person and *will* in the second and third to express the simple future or expectation (I *shall* plan to stay; he *will* probably stay).

(b) By using *will* in the first person and *shall* in the second and third to express determination, threat, command, prophecy, promise, or willingness (I *will* stay; you and he *shall* stay).

(c) By using in a question the same form expected in the answer (*Will* you stay? Expected answer: I *will* stay).

▶ EXERCISE 6. Select the form in parentheses that is consistent with contemporary usage. Justify your choice.

1. To save time we (should, would) fly to the coast.

2. No totalitarian tyrant (will, shall) treat us with contempt.

3. (Will, Shall) I go on the early train?

4. Very often during those years we (should, would) go to the country for relaxation.

5. At school we learn what we (should, would) do throughout life.

▶ EXERCISE 7. Compose five sentences to illustrate the chief distinctions in the use of *shall, should,* and *would.* Explain the meaning of each sentence.

MECHANICS

▶ Manuscript Form and Revision; Syllabication

8 Put your manuscript in acceptable form. Make revisions with care.

8a Use the proper materials.

(1) Paper. Unless you are given other instructions, use standard theme paper, size 8½ by 11 inches, with lines about half an inch apart, and write only on the ruled side of the paper. (The usual notebook paper, even if it is the standard size, should not be used because the narrow spaces between lines make for hard reading and allow insufficient space for corrections.) For typewritten papers use the unruled side of the theme paper; or, if you prefer, use regular typewriter paper, size 8½ by 11 inches.

(2) Ink. Use black or blue-black ink.

(3) Typewriter. Submit typewritten papers only if you do your own typewriting. Use a black ribbon and make sure that the type is clean.

8b Arrange your writing in clear and orderly fashion on the page.

(1) Margins. Leave sufficient margins—about an inch and a half at the left and top, an inch at the right and bottom—to prevent a crowded appearance. The ruled lines on theme paper indicate the proper margins at the left and top.

(2) Indention. Indent the first lines of paragraphs uniformly, about an inch in longhand and five spaces in typewritten copy.

(3) Paging. Use Arabic numerals—without parentheses or period—in the upper right-hand corner to mark all pages after the first.

(4) The Title. Center the title on the page about an inch and a half from the top or on the first ruled line. Leave the next line blank and begin the first paragraph on the third line. In this way the title will be made to stand off from the text. Capitalize the first word of the title and all succeeding words except articles and short conjunctions and prepositions. *Do not put quotation marks around the title or underline it* (unless it is a quotation or the title of a book), and use no period after the title.

(5) Poetry. Quoted lines of poetry should be arranged and indented as in the original. In typing, use single spacing. (See also Section 16a.).

(6) Punctuation. Never begin a line with a comma, a colon, a semicolon, or a terminal mark of punctuation; never end a line with opening quotation marks, brackets, or parenthesis.

(7) Endorsement. Papers are endorsed in the way prescribed by the instructor to facilitate handling. Usually papers carry the name of the student, the date, and the number of the theme.

8c Write legibly, so that your writing may be read easily and accurately.

(1) Spacing for Legibility. Adequate space between lines and between the words in the line is essential to easy reading. In typewritten copy use double space between lines. Single-spaced copy is difficult for the instructor to read and even more difficult for the student to revise. Leave one space for a comma or semicolon, one or two after a colon, and two or three after a period, a question mark, or an exclamation point. In longhand make each word a distinct unit: join all the letters of a word and leave adequate space in the line before beginning the next word.

(2) Shaping for Legibility. Shape each letter distinctly. Avoid flourishes. Many pages of manuscript, though artistic and attractive to the eye, are almost illegible. Dot the *i,* not some other letter nearby. Cross the *t,* not the adjoining *h* or some other letter. Make dots and periods real dots, not small circles. Let all capitals stand out distinctly as capitals and keep all small letters down to the average of other small letters. Remember that you will not be present to tell the reader which letters you intend for capitals, which for small letters.

8d Revise the manuscript with care.[1]

(1) Revising the paper before submitting it to the instructor. If time permits, the writer should put the paper aside for a day or more after completing his first draft. Then he will be able to read the paper more objectively, to see what parts need to be expanded, what to be excised. If extensive revisions are necessary, he should make a completely new copy to submit to the instructor. If only a few changes are needed, the paper may be handed in—after corrections have been made—without rewriting. The changes should be made as follows:

   (a) Draw one line horizontally through any word to be deleted. Do not put it in parentheses or make an unsightly erasure.

   (b) In case of a short addition of one line or less, place a caret (∧) in the line where the addition comes and write just above the caret the part to be added.

[1] For marks used in correcting proofs for the printer see *Webster's New Collegiate Dictionary,* pp. 1208-09, or *The American College Dictionary,* Text Edition, p. xxxv.

Check List for Revision

1. Have I stated my central idea clearly, and have I developed it adequately in the paper? (See Section 32.)

2. Is the manuscript form correct? (See Section 8.)

3. Are grammar and mechanics correct? (See Sections 1-7; 9-11.)

4. Is the punctuation correct? (See Sections 12-17.)

5. Is the spelling correct? (See Section 18.)

6. Is the diction standard, exact, concise? (See Sections 19-22.)

7. Are the sentences as effective as possible? (See Sections 23-30.)

8. Are the paragraphs properly developed? (See Section 31.)

9. Does the outline follow exactly the final version of the paper? (If not, revise the outline to fit the paper. See Section 32.)

10. What do my answers to the foregoing questions show my chief defects to be? (Review intensively the sections of this book which deal with your defects. Observe the same procedure for additional defects noted by your instructor.)

(2) Revising the paper after the instructor has criticized it. The best way to learn to write is by correcting one's own errors. Corrections made by another are of comparatively little value. Therefore the instructor points out the errors but *allows the student to make the actual revision for himself.*

The instructor usually indicates a necessary correction by a number or a symbol from the handbook marked in the margin of the paper opposite the error. For example, if he finds a fragmentary sentence, he will write either the number **2** or the symbol **frag.** The student should then find in the text the specific part (**a, b,** or **c**) of Section **2** that deals with his error, should correct the error in red, and write the appropriate letter after the instructor's number or symbol in the margin. (See the example paragraph on the next page.)

The comma. After the number **12** in the margin the student should take special care to supply the appropriate letter (**a, b, c,** or **d**) to show why the comma is needed. The act of inserting a comma teaches little; understanding why it is required in a particular situation is a definite step toward mastery of the comma.

The following page reproduces a student paragraph and shows, in the first column, the instructor's markings (for grammar and other details) and, in the second column, the same

Marked by the Instructor—with Numbers

3   Making photographs for newspapers is hard work,

12   it is not the romantic carefree adventure glorified

in motion pictures and fiction books. For every

18   great moment recorded by the stareing eye of the

camera, there are twenty routine assignments that

28   must be handled in the same efficient manner. He

must often overcome great hardships. The work con-

24   tinues for long hours. It must meet the deadline.

At times he is called upon to risk his own life to

2   secure a picture. To the newspaper photographer,

getting his picture being the most important thing.

Marked by the Instructor—with Symbols

cs   Making photographs for newspapers is hard work,

⌐/   it is not the romantic carefree adventure glorified

in motion pictures and fiction books. For every

sp   great moment recorded by the stareing eye of the

camera, there are twenty routine assignments that

ref   must be handled in the same efficient manner. He

must often overcome great hardships. The work con-

sub   tinues for long hours. It must meet the deadline.

At times he is called upon to risk his own life to

frag   secure a picture. To the newspaper photographer,

getting his picture being the most important thing.

Corrected by the Student—in Red

3b   Making photographs for newspapers is hard work ; /

12c   it is not the romantic, carefree adventure glorified

in motion pictures and fiction books. For every

staring
18d   great moment recorded by the ~~stareing~~ eye of the

camera, there are twenty routine assignments that

28c   must be handled in the same efficient manner. ~~He~~
The
newspaper photographer must often overcome great
~~must often overcome great hardships. The work con-~~
24a   hardships and work long hours to meet the deadline.
~~tinues for long hours. It must meet the deadline.~~

At times he is called upon to risk his own life to

is
2a   secure a picture. To the newspaper photographer,

getting his picture ~~being~~ the most important thing.

---

cs-b   Making photographs for newspapers is hard work ; /

⌐/c   it is not the romantic, carefree adventure glorified

in motion pictures and fiction books. For every

staring
sp-d   great moment recorded by the ~~stareing~~ eye of the

camera, there are twenty routine assignments that

The
ref-c   must be handled in the same efficient manner. ~~He~~
newspaper photographer must often overcome great
~~must often overcome great hardships. The work con-~~
sub-a   hardships and work long hours to meet the deadline.
~~tinues for long hours. It must meet the deadline.~~

At times he is called upon to risk his own life to

is
frag-a   secure a picture. To the newspaper photographer,

getting his picture ~~being~~ the most important thing.

---

paragraph after it has been corrected by the student. These corrections should be in red to make them stand out distinctly from the original paragraph and the markings of the instructor. (For three student papers, with the instructor's comments on content and organization, see pages 936-38 at the end of Section **32**. The content, or subject matter, of a paper is first in importance, but a paper must also stand the test of the "Check List" on page 830.)

8e   Keep a record of your errors to check the improvement in your writing.

A clear record on a single sheet of paper will show at a glance the progress you are making from paper to paper. In each paper try to avoid mistakes already pointed out. Master the spelling of any word incorrectly spelled in order to avoid misspelling it a second time. *Be sure that you have made, and that you understand fully, every correction on* *your last paper before you write the next.* If you follow this plan consistently throughout the year, your writing will show marked improvement.

One simple but useful way to record your errors is to write them down in the order in which they occur in each paper, grouping them in columns according to the seven major divisions of the handbook as illustrated below. In the spaces for Paper Number 1 are recorded the errors from the student paragraph above.

RECORD OF ERRORS

Paper No.	Grammar 1—7	Mechanics 8—11	Punctuation 12—17	Words Misspelled 18	Diction 19—22	Effectiveness 23—30	Larger Elements 31—34
1	3b 2a		12c	Staring		28c 24a	
2							

In the spelling column appears the misspelled word with the correct spelling, and in other columns the section number with the letter to indicate the specific error made.

8f Divide words only between syllables (parts naturally pronounced as separate units of the word), and never set off a syllable made up of a single letter. (For hyphenated words see Section 18f.)

If the writer leaves a reasonable right-hand margin, he will seldom need to divide words, especially short ones. The reader will object less to an uneven margin than to a number of broken words.

WRONG ignit-ion, sentin-el [Words not divided between syllables. Whenever you are uncertain about the proper syllabication of a word, consult a good dictionary.]

RIGHT ig-nition (*or* igni-tion), sen-tinel (*or* sentinel)

RIGHT can-ning, com-mit-ting [Double consonants are usually divided except when they come at the end of a simple word: kill-ing.]

WRONG enjoy-ed, gleam-ed, watch-ed, remember-ed [Never confuse the reader by setting off an -*ed* pronounced as part of the preceding syllable.]

WRONG e-nough, a-gainst, e-vade [The saving of space is not sufficient to justify the break. Begin the word on the next line.]

WRONG man-y, show-y, dyspepsi-a [The final letter can be written as readily as the hyphen.]

WRONG fire-eat-er, mass-pro-duced, Pre-Raphael-ite

RIGHT fire-eater, mass-produced, Pre-Raphaelite [Divide hyphenated words only where the hyphen comes in the regular spelling.]

▶ EXERCISE. With the aid of your dictionary, write out the following words by syllables, grouping (1) those that may properly be divided at the end of a line, and (2) those that may not be divided: *affection, against, alone, combed, decadent, erase, immense, levy, looked, nature, rainy, thought, through, transient, treaty, troller, trolley, vary, veiled, walked, weary, willing, willow, wily, windy.*

▶ Capitals

9 Capitalize words in accordance with general usage. Avoid unnecessary capitals.

9a Capitalize proper names and, generally, derivatives of proper names and abbreviations of them.[1]

1. SPECIFIC PERSONS OR PLACES: Milton, Miltonic, California, Californian, Cal.; the South (referring to a specific section of the country); the Orient, an Oriental custom
2. ORGANIZATIONS OF ALL KINDS: Rotarians, Quakers, the Standard Oil Company, the Republican

Party, Communist (a member of the Communist Party), the Senate, the Air Service, the United Nations, the Atomic Energy Commission, the Freshman Class (*but* a freshman)

3. RACES, PEOPLES, AND LANGUAGES: Caucasian, Indian, Negro, Dutch, Norwegian, Pole, Polish, Spanish.
4. DAYS OF THE WEEK, MONTHS, SPECIAL DAYS: Friday, June, Christmas, Easter, Labor Day.
5. HISTORICAL PERIODS, EVENTS, OR DOCUMENTS: the Dark Ages, the Stone Age, the Spanish War, the Revolution, the Magna Carta, the Declaration of Independence

[1] In general, abbreviations are capitalized or not according to the capitalization of the word abbreviated. One important exception is *No.* for *number.* For a more detailed discussion of capitalization of words and abbreviations see the *Style Manual* of the United States Government Printing Office, 1953, pp. 17-50, or *A Manual of Style,* the University of Chicago Press, 1949, pp. 23-45. Capitalization of individual words may well be

checked in a good dictionary, such as *The American College Dictionary* or *Webster's New World Dictionary* (in the main vocabulary) or *Webster's New Collegiate Dictionary* (in the main vocabulary and also in a special section, pp. 998-1007).

6. WORDS PERTAINING TO DEITY: God the Father, the Lord, the Saviour, the Trinity, the Almighty, the Creator

7. PERSONIFICATIONS:

Can Honor's voice provoke the silent dust,
Or Flattery soothe the dull cold ear of Death?
                                              —GRAY

8. ADJECTIVES DERIVED FROM PROPER NOUNS: Southern or Western (referring to the South or the West, specific sections of the country), an English ship, an Italic custom (but italic type because this common adjective is no longer closely associated with the source). In case of doubt, consult a recent dictionary.

9b   Capitalize titles preceding the name, or other words used as an essential part of a proper name.

RIGHT Mr. Brown, Judge White, King George, Aunt Mary

(1) Titles immediately following the name, or used alone as a substitute for the name, are capitalized only to indicate pre-eminence or high distinction: Dwight D. Eisenhower, President of the United States; the President of the United States; the President. On the other hand, ordinary titles are usually not capitalized; William Smith, president of the First National Bank; the president of the bank.

(2) Words denoting family relationship (*father, mother, brother, aunt, cousin*) are generally capitalized when used as titles or alone in place of the name, but not when preceded by a possessive: Brother William; Sister Mary; [2] Mary, my sister; my brother; my sister; a trip with Father; a trip with my father; a letter from Mother; a letter from my mother.

(3) Such words as *college, high school, club, lake, river, park, building, street, pike, county, railroad,* and *society* are (except in newspapers) usually capitalized when they are an essential part of a proper name, but not when used alone as a substitute for the name: Knox College, the college; Central High School, the high school; Madison Street, the street; the Pennsylvania Railroad, the railroad.

▶ EXERCISE 1. In the following sentences supply capitals wherever needed. State the reason for the use of each capital.

[2] This rule also applies to names of members of religious orders.

1. Very gradually the prince's position changed. 2. He began to find the study of politics less uninteresting than he had supposed. 3. He read blackstone, and took lessons in english law; he was occasionally present when the queen interviewed her ministers. 4. At lord melbourne's suggestion he was shown all the despatches relating to foreign affairs. 5. Sometimes he would commit his views to paper, and read them aloud to the prime minister, who, infinitely kind and courteous, listened with attention, but seldom made any reply. 6. An important step was taken when, before the birth of the princess royal, the prince, without any opposition in parliament, was appointed regent in case of the death of the queen. 7. Stockmar, owing to whose intervention with the tories this happy result had been brought about, now felt himself at liberty to take a holiday with his family in coburg. 8. But his solicitude, poured out in innumerable letters, still watched over his pupil from afar. 9. "Dear prince," he wrote, "I am satisfied with the news you have sent me. 10. Mistakes, misunderstandings, obstructions, which come in vexatious opposition to one's views, are always to be taken for just what they are—namely, natural phenomena of life, which represent one of its sides and that the shady one." [3]

▶ EXERCISE 2. Copy the following sentences, supplying capitals wherever needed. State the reason for the use of each capital.

1. We invited judge green to meet uncle henry at the cosmos club to make plans for the annual community chest drive.

2. This club meets every monday in the madison state bank building on walnut street.

3. We invited mother and aunt bertha to attend our class play at parker high school.

4. Both my mother and my aunt had graduated from the same high school.

5. Before the end of the summer, perhaps during july, the president of the first national bank will take a vacation in florida.

6. The pacific ocean was discovered in 1513 by a spaniard named balboa.

7. When I returned to my work after labor day, I met mr. morgan, president of the liberty trust company.

8. The sussex riding club has bought a large tract of land near sand lake.

[3] Adapted from *Queen Victoria*, by Lytton Strachey, copyright, 1921, by Harcourt, Brace and Company, Inc.; renewed, 1949, by James Strachey. Reprinted by permission of the publishers.

9. The president of this club is also president of the second national bank.

10. We are expecting father and uncle robert to visit us during the easter vacation.

11. After William was graduated from westview high school, he entered simpson college.

12. This high school has sent more than one hundred of its graduates to harvard during the past twenty years.

13. As soon as mother met uncle james, she told him that she had seen major white at the claiborne county fair.

14. Young northerners are sometimes advised to settle in the south or in the west, and many of them do go south or west.

9c In titles of books, plays, student papers, etc., capitalize the first word and all succeeding words except articles (*a, an, the*) and short conjunctions or prepositions.

RIGHT *Crime and Punishment, To Have and to Hold, Midnight on the Desert, The Man Without a Country* [A conjunction or preposition of five or more letters (*without*) is usually capitalized.]

9d Capitalize the pronoun *I* and the interjection *O* (but not *oh*).

RIGHT If *I* forget thee, *O* Jerusalem, let my right hand forget her cunning. —PSALMS

9e Capitalize the first word of every sentence (including quoted sentences and direct questions) and the first word of every line of poetry.[4]

RIGHT He said, "The work is almost finished."

RIGHT He said that the work was "almost finished." [A fragmentary quotation does not begin with a capital.]

RIGHT The question is, Shall we go?

RIGHT But I was one-and-twenty,
No use to talk to me. —HOUSMAN

Capitals after the colon. A quoted sentence after the colon regularly begins with a capital, but other sentences are usually not capitalized if they are closely related to the preceding clause. For examples see Section 17d.

[4] Except poetry originally printed without initial capitals.

9f Avoid unnecessary capitals.

Many students err in using too many rather than too few capitals. If you have a tendency to overuse capitals, you should study the five principles treated above (**9a, b, c, d, e**) and use a capital letter only when you can justify it.

WRONG He went farther South for the winter. [Mere direction—*south, southwest, north, east*—is not capitalized.]

RIGHT He went south for the winter, *or* He lived in the South during the winter.

RIGHT Winter, spring, summer, and autumn are the four seasons. [Names of the seasons are usually not capitalized.]

RIGHT I studied History 2, geography, Spanish, and mathematics. [It is preferable to capitalize the name of a study only when it is specific—*History 2*—or when it is derived from a proper name—*Spanish.*]

RIGHT I went to high school, to college, to the library (*or* to Dover High School, to Oberlin College, to Wade Memorial Library).

RIGHT Gum arabic; italic type. [Words from proper nouns that have acquired general meanings are not capitalized. When in doubt, consult your dictionary.]

▶ EXERCISE 3. Indicate which of the capitals in the following sentences should be changed to small letters and which small letters changed to capitals. State your reasons.

1. According to traditions now perhaps forever impossible to verify, Shakespeare wrote *The merry Wives Of Windsor* at the desire of queen Elizabeth, who commanded that it be finished in a fortnight and that it show Falstaff in Love. 2. One may believe these Tales or not, as he chooses. 3. but suppose they are true. 4. Two weeks is an uncomfortably short time, and a Dramatist pressed to fill such an order would quite imaginably summon up every short cut in his Bag of Tricks to meet the deadline. 5. First a plot of some sort must be pieced together, with falstaff in it, in love. 6. But suppose that done, or at least begun. 7. Now if the dialogue were in Prose, some writing time might possibly be saved. 8. And if here and there another Character besides Falstaff, already created for another Play, could be worked in, there might be an added saving. 9. Lines might be written, too, in a wild skimble-scamble of Rant, Cant, Jargon, and Malapropism; to have the mouths of half the characters filled with such Nonsense might

be overdoing it, but that would have to be risked. 10. And if, to piece out the Plot with Incident, the Ragbag of recent gossip—windsor gossip especially—were tumbled out and ransacked, a play of sorts might conceivably be rigged out in time.

11. Any or all of these short cuts might do to try— Still assuming, of course, that the traditions are correct and that by Hook or by Crook a play was going to have to be ready within the Fortnight as ordered.

▶ Italics

10   Italicize (underline) titles of publications, foreign words, names of ships, titles of works of art, and words spoken of as words. Use italics sparingly for emphasis.

In longhand or typewritten papers, italics are indicated by underlining. The printer sets all underlined words in italic type.

TYPEWRITTEN   In David Copperfield Dickens writes of his own boyhood.

PRINT   In *David Copperfield* Dickens writes of his own boyhood.

10a   Titles of separate publications—such as books, bulletins, magazines, newspapers, musical productions—are italicized (underlined) when mentioned in writing.

Occasionally quotation marks are used instead of italics for titles of separate publications. The usual practice, however, reserves quotation marks for short stories, short poems, one-act plays, articles from periodicals, and subdivisions of books. See Section **16b**.

RIGHT   *David Copperfield* opens with a chapter entitled "I Am Born."

RIGHT   Many people still enjoy Mark Twain's *Roughing It.* [Note that the author's name is not italicized.]

RIGHT   We read *The Comedy of Errors,* which is based on the *Menaechmi* of Plautus. [An initial *a, an,* or *the* is capitalized and italicized only when it belongs to the title.]

RIGHT   Mozart's *Don Giovanni;* Beethoven's *Fifth Symphony.*

RIGHT   He pored over *Time,* the *Atlantic Monthly,* the *Saturday Evening Post,* and the *New York Times* (or: New York *Times*). [Italics are not

commonly used for articles standing first in the titles of periodicals, and sometimes not used for the name of the city in the titles of newspapers. Many periodicals omit all italics for titles, but students are usually cautioned against this informal practice.]

10b   Foreign words and phrases not yet Anglicized are usually italicized (underlined).

Such words are indicated in *Webster's New Collegiate Dictionary* by parallel bars (||), and in *Webster's New World Dictionary* by a double dagger (‡), immediately before the words; in *The American College Dictionary,* by the italicized name of the language immediately after the words.

RIGHT   She had a *joie de vivre* distinctly her own.
RIGHT   Mexico is sometimes called the land of *mañana.*
RIGHT   The *Weltansicht* of despots is often discolored by their ambitions.

▶ EXERCISE 1. With the aid of your dictionary list and underline five foreign words or phrases that are generally written in italics. List five other foreign words or phrases (such as "apropos," "bona fide," "ex officio") that no longer require italics.

10c   Names of ships and aircraft and titles of works of art are italicized (underlined).

RIGHT   The *Queen Mary* and the *Princess Elizabeth* sailed from New York.
RIGHT   Rodin's *The Thinker* stands in one of the Parisian gardens.

10d Words, letters, or figures spoken of as such or used as illustration are usually italicized (underlined). (See also 16c.)

RIGHT   The article *the* has lost much of its demonstrative force. In England an *elevator* is called a *lift*. [Sometimes quotation marks ("the," "elevator," "lift") are used instead of italics.]

RIGHT   The final *e* in *stone* is silent.

RIGHT   The first *3* and the final *o* of the serial number are barely legible.

► EXERCISE 2.   Copy the following sentences, italicizing (underlining) as necessary.

1. Galsworthy's The Man of Property, In Chancery, and To Let were published separately as novels between 1906 and 1921, before they were issued in one volume entitled The Forsyte Saga.

2. To Let was completed in September, 1920, before Galsworthy sailed from Liverpool on the Empress of France to spend the winter in America.

3. Galsworthy's novels have been reviewed in such periodicals as Harper's Magazine, the Saturday Review of Literature, and the New York Herald Tribune.

4. According to Greenough and Kittredge, in their book entitled Words and Their Ways in English Speech, "it is more natural for us to say divide (from L. divido) than cleave (from A.S. cleofan); travel than fare; river than stream; castle than burg; residence than dwelling; remain than abide; expect than ween; pupil or scholar than learner."

5. A Manual of Style, published by the University of Chicago Press, recommends that such Latin words or abbreviations as vide, idem, ibid., and

op. cit. be italicized when used in literary references.

10e As a rule do not use italics (underlining) to give special emphasis to a word or a group of words. Do not underline the title of your own paper.

Frequent use of italics for emphasis defeats its own purpose and becomes merely an annoyance to the reader. This use of italics has been largely abandoned by good contemporary writers. Emphasis on a given word or phrase is usually best secured by careful arrangement of the sentence. See Section 29.

Note: A title is not italicized when it stands at the head of a book or an article. Accordingly, a student should not italicize (underline) the title standing at the head of his own paper (unless the title happens to be also the title of a book).

► EXERCISE ON ITALICS

Copy the following passage, underscoring all words that should be italicized.

1. I was returning home on the America when I happened to see a copy of Euripides' Medea. 2. The play was of course in translation, by Murray, I believe; it was reprinted in Riley's Great Plays of Greece and Rome. 3. I admire Medea the play and Medea the woman. 4. Both of them have a quality of atrocitas which our contemporary primitivism misses. 5. Characters in modern plays are neurotic; Medea was sublimely and savagely mad.

► # Abbreviations and Numbers

11 In ordinary writing avoid abbreviations (with a few well-known exceptions), and write out numbers whenever they can be expressed in one or two words.

Abbreviations

11a In ordinary writing spell out all titles except Mr., Messrs., Mrs., Mmes., Dr., and St. (saint, not street). Spell out even these titles when not followed by proper names.

WRONG   The Dr. made his report to the Maj.

RIGHT   The doctor (*or* Dr. Smith) made his report to the major (*or* to Major Brown).

In informal writing *Hon.* and *Rev.* may be used before the surname when it is preceded by the Christian name or initials, never before the surname alone.

WRONG   Hon. Smith, Rev. Jones

RIGHT   Hon. George Smith, Hon. G. E. Smith, Rev. Thomas Jones, Rev. T. E. Jones

RIGHT   (more formal)   The Honorable George Edward Smith, the Reverend Thomas Everett Jones, the Reverend Mr. Jones

For forms of address in writing or speaking to officials and other dignitaries of church and state see *Webster's New World Dictionary,* pages 1717-19.

11b   In ordinary writing spell out names of states, countries, months, and days of the week.

WRONG   He left Ia. on the last Sun. in Jul.
RIGHT   He left Iowa on the last Sunday in July.

WRONG   James will go to Mex. in Oct.
RIGHT   James will go to Mexico in October.

11c   In ordinary writing spell out *Street, Road, Park, Company,* and similar words used as part of a proper name.

WRONG   The procession moved down Lee St. between Central Pk. and the neon signs of the Ford Motor Co.
RIGHT   The procession moved down Lee Street between Central Park and the neon signs of the Ford Motor Company.

Avoid the use of & (for *and*) and such abbreviations as *Bros.* or *Inc.* except in copying official titles: A & P; Goldsmith Bros.; Best & Co., Inc.; Doubleday & Company, Inc.

11d   In ordinary writing spell out the words *volume, chapter,* and *page* and the names of subjects.

WRONG   The notes on chem. are taken from ch. 9, p. 46.
RIGHT   The notes on chemistry are taken from chapter 9, page 46.

Many abbreviations not acceptable in the text are preferable in footnotes. See Section 33.

11e   In ordinary writing spell out Christian names.

WRONG   Jas. Smith, Geo. White
RIGHT   James Smith, George White

Permissible Abbreviations: In addition to the abbreviations mentioned in 11a, the following are permissible and usually desirable.

1. *After proper names:* Jr., Sr., Esq., and degrees such as D.D., LL.D., M.A., M.D.

RIGHT   Mr. Sam Jones, Sr., Sam Jones, Jr., Thomas Jones, M.D.

2. *With dates or numerals:* A.D., B.C., A.M., P.M. (*or* a.m., p.m.), No., $

RIGHT   In 450 B.C., at 9:30 A.M.; in room No. 6; for $365

WRONG   Early this A.M. he asked the No. of your room. [The abbreviations are correct only with the numerals.]
RIGHT   Early this morning he asked the number of your room.

3. *For names of organizations and government agencies usually referred to by their initials:* DAR, ECA, GOP, RFC, TVA, WAC

4. *In general use, but often spelled out in formal writing as indicated in parentheses:* i.e. (*that is*), e.g. (*for example*), viz. (*namely*), cf. (*compare*), etc. (*and so forth*), vs. (*versus*)

Note: Use *etc.* sparingly. Never write *and etc.* The abbreviation comes from *et cetera,* of which *et* means *and.*

Special Exceptions: Many abbreviations are desirable in footnotes, in tabulations, and in certain types of technical writing. In such special writing the student should follow the practice of the better publications in the field. If he has any doubt regarding the spelling or capitalization of any abbreviation, he should consult a good dictionary such as *Webster's New Collegiate Dictionary* (in a special section, pages 998-1007) or *The American College Dictionary* or *Webster's New World Dictionary* (in the main vocabulary).

Numbers

11f   Although usage varies, writers tend to spell out numbers that require only one or two words; they regularly use figures for other numbers.

RIGHT   twenty years; a sum of four dollars; fifty thousand dollars; a million dollars

RIGHT after 124 years; a sum of $2.27; only 187 votes; exactly 4,568,305 votes [Note the commas used to separate millions, thousands, hundreds.]

Special Usage Regarding Numbers:

1. *Use figures for dates.*

RIGHT May 1, 1951; 1 May 1951; July 12, 1763

The letters *st, nd, rd, th* should not be added to the day of the month when the year follows; they need not be added even when the year is omitted.

CORRECT May 1, July 2.

When the year is omitted, the day of the month may be written out.

CORRECT May first, July second

Ordinal numbers to designate the day of the month may be written out or expressed in figures.

CORRECT He came on the fifth (*or* 5th) of May.

But the year is never written out except in very formal social announcements or invitations.

2. *Use figures for street numbers, for pages and divisions of a book, for decimals and percentages, and for the hour of the day when used with* A.M. *or* P.M.

RIGHT 26 Main Avenue, 460 Fourth Street
RIGHT The quotation is from page 80.
RIGHT The bar is .63 of an inch thick.
RIGHT She gets 10 per cent of the profits.
RIGHT He arrived at 4:30 P.M.

3. *Be consistent in spelling out or using figures. Normally use figures for a series of numbers.*

RIGHT The garden plot was 125 feet long and 50 feet wide and contained an asparagus bed 12 feet square.
RIGHT He earned $60 weekly, spent $15 for room rent, $17.50 for board, $12 for incidentals, and saved $15.50.

4. *Normally spell out any numeral at the beginning of a sentence. If necessary, recast the sentence.*

WRONG 25 boys made the trip.
RIGHT Twenty-five boys made the trip.
WRONG 993 freshmen entered the college last year.
RIGHT Last year 993 freshmen entered the college.

5. *The practice of repeating in parentheses a number that is spelled out (now generally reserved for legal and commercial writing) should be used logically if at all.*

ILLOGICAL I enclose twenty ($20) dollars.
LOGICAL I enclose twenty (20) dollars.
LOGICAL I enclose twenty dollars ($20).

▶ EXERCISE ON ABBREVIATION AND NUMBERS

A. Correct the abbreviations and numbers in the following letter. Where necessary, substitute a word or phrase for abbreviations improperly used. Justify all corrections.

1. Dear Rev. Peabody 2. I left the State Ref. and arrived at home last Sat. A.M. 3. The family, etc., were very kind, as you said they would be. 4. Early tomorrow I'm going to 27 Jackson Blvd. to tell the Dr. how sorry I am. 5. I'll pay him the $475 I stole as soon as I have the $.

B. Consult your dictionary to find out what the following abbreviations mean.

1. R.F.D.	7. B.C., B.C.	12. ex lib
2. AAA	8. i.e.	13. AAF
3. A.D., A.D.	9. A.A.U.P.	14. Ph.C.
4. chm.	10. P.H.	15. D.V.
5. S.P.C.A.	11. viz.	16. C.I.F.
6. UNESCO		

C. In the following sentences correct all errors in the use of abbreviations and numbers.

1. My father moved to Cal. about 10 years ago.
2. He is now living at sixty-five Sandusky St. in Frisco.
3. Geo. Washington, our first Pres., was born in seventeen hundred and thirty-two.
4. When he was 20 years old, he inherited Mt. Vernon from his half bro.
5. He assumed command of the Continental armies in Cambridge, Mass., on Jul. 3, 1775.
6. 125 men were stationed in the mts. to serve as guides.
7. These one hundred and twenty-five men have been in service for nearly 5 years.
8. Our class in math. did not meet last Wed.
9. Do you know the No. of the prof's office?
10. Rev. Williams will preach next Sun.

PUNCTUATION

▶ The Comma

12   Use the comma where it is demanded by the structure of the sentence.

The many different uses of the comma may be grouped under a very few principles and mastered with comparative ease by anyone who understands the structure of the sentence.[1] These principles, which cover the normal practice of the best contemporary writers, are adequate for the needs of the average college student. He may note that skilled writers sometimes employ the comma in unusual ways to express delicate shades of meaning. Such variations can safely be made by the writer who has first learned to apply the following major principles:

a. To separate main clauses joined by *and, but, or, nor,* or *for.*
b. To separate an introductory clause (or a long phrase) from the main clause.
c. To separate items in a series (and co-ordinate adjectives modifying the same noun).
d. To set off nonrestrictive and other parenthetical elements.

Main Clauses

12a   Main clauses joined by one of the co-ordinating conjunctions (*and, but, or, nor, for*) are separated by a comma.[2]

[1] *Caution:* Mastery of the comma is almost impossible for anyone who does not understand the structure of the sentence. If a student cannot readily distinguish main clauses, subordinate clauses, and the various kinds of phrases, he should study Section **1, Sentence Sense,** especially **1d,** before trying to use this section. (Mastery of Section 12 will help to eliminate one of the two most common errors in the average student paper.)

[2] *Yet* is occasionally used as a co-ordinating conjunction equivalent to *but.* Informal writing frequently

[If the conjunction is omitted, the main clauses must be separated by a semicolon—or broken into distinct sentences and separated by a period. See Sections **3** and **14.**]

RIGHT   Other ages have produced inspiring discussions of the nature of the good life, but the people of the twentieth century have not been satisfied with reflection and discussion.
—SUMNER H. SLICHTER

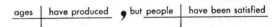

RIGHT   The ranchmen from the valley in the foothills rode in on saddles decorated with silver, and their sons demonstrated their skill with unbroken horses.   —JOHN STEINBECK [3]

Caution: Do not confuse the compound sentence (two main clauses) with the simple sentence (one main clause) containing a compound predicate.

RIGHT   The ranchmen rode with their families into the little town and encouraged their sons to demonstrate their skill with unbroken horses.

| ranchmen | rode and encouraged | [No comma before *and*]

Even more objectionable than the comma between parts of the compound predicate would be the use of a comma before a conjunction which joins merely two words (*men* and *women, white*

uses *so* as a co-ordinating conjunction, but careful writers usually avoid the *so*-sentence by subordinating one of the clauses.

[3] "Always Something to Do in Salinas," *Holiday,* June, 1955, p. 58.

and *black*) or two phrases (*out of the pan* and *into the fire, to see* and *to believe*).

At times the comma is used to set off what seems to be merely the second part of a compound predicate, or even a phrase. Closer examination usually discloses, however, that such a word or phrase is actually a regular main clause with some words "understood." Note, for example, the following sentences, in which the implied matter is inserted in brackets:

There is no other way for the world's living standards to be raised to anything like our level, and [there is] no other way to link or merge the economies of the free nations.   —FORTUNE

The number of high school graduates has been increasing since 1890 about thirteen times as fast as the population, and the number of college graduates [has been increasing] six times as fast.
     —THE ATLANTIC MONTHLY

We are proud of this tradition, and [we are] not [proud] without good cause.   —FORTUNE

Exceptions to 12a:

1. *Omission of the comma:*

When the main clauses are short, the comma is frequently omitted before *and* or *or*, less frequently before *but*. Before *for* the comma is needed to prevent confusion with the preposition *for*. (In colloquial style, especially in narrative writing, the comma is frequently omitted even when the clauses are longer.)

RIGHT   The brown earth turned dark and the trees glistened.   —JOHN STEINBECK

2. *Use of the semicolon instead of the comma:*

Sometimes the co-ordinating conjunction is preceded by a semicolon instead of the usual comma, especially when the main clauses have internal punctuation or reveal a striking contrast. See also Section 14a.

RIGHT   It was childish, of course; for any disturbance, any sudden intruding noise, would make the creatures stop.   —ALDOUS HUXLEY [4]

RIGHT   The visit will have had a certain ritualistic value; but it will not have brightened the man's life, caught his fancy, stirred his soul, or fired a brand-new passion.   —WALTER KERR [5]

[4] "Voices," *Atlantic Monthly,* July, 1955, p. 33.
[5] "Killing Off the Theatre," *Harper's Magazine,* April, 1955, p. 55.

▶ EXERCISE 1.   In each of the following sentences find the main clauses. Then explain why the main clauses should be (1) separated by a comma, (2) separated by a semicolon, or (3) left without any punctuation.

1. The governor proclaimed a state of civil emergency for the water supply was dangerously low.   2. The days passed, and the drought grew steadily worse.   3. The state fire marshal ordered all parks closed but forest fires broke out in spite of all precautions.   4. City-dwellers watched their gardens shrivel and die, and industrial workers were laid off as electric-power output failed.   5. But perhaps the worst afflicted were the farmers, for there was no hope of saving their crops and even their livestock had to be sold on a glutted market or else left to die in the fields.

6. Our first night at the camp I remember very well for I thought I should never live to tell the story.

7. The bus stopped and the children got off.

8. It was a difficult year but I managed to graduate with my class.

9. It was a difficult year, filled with interruptions, new instructors, and shifting schedules, but I budgeted my time so carefully that I was able to hold my place on the team and also to graduate with my class.

▶ EXERCISE 2.   Compose six sentences (two to illustrate each type) in which main clauses are (1) separated by a comma, (2) separated by a semicolon, and (3) left without any punctuation.

Introductory Clauses

12b   A subordinate clause (or a long phrase) preceding the main clause is usually followed by a comma.

RIGHT   *Although I am not a member of the club,* I know much of its history. [Subordinate clause preceding the main clause]

RIGHT   *At the critical moments in this sad history,* there have been men worth listening to who warned the people against their mistakes.
     —WALTER LIPPMANN [6]

Introductory phrases containing a gerund, a participle, or an infinitive, even though short, must often be followed by a comma to prevent misreading.

RIGHT   *Before leaving,* the soldiers demolished the fort.

[6] "The Decline of Western Democracy," *Atlantic Monthly,* February, 1955, p. 33.

RIGHT   *Because of his effort to escape,* his punishment was increased.

Short introductory prepositional phrases, except when they are transitional expressions (such as *in fact, on the other hand,* and especially *for example, generally speaking, in the light of these facts*), are seldom followed by a comma.

RIGHT   *During the night* he heard many noises.
RIGHT   *Within the next few days* I hope to leave.
RIGHT   *In fact,* I hope to leave tomorrow. [Transitional expression]

Many writers omit the comma after short introductory clauses, and sometimes after longer ones, when the omission does not make for difficult reading. In the following sentences the commas may be used or omitted at the option of the writer:

When you arrive(,) you will find me waiting for you.
When *he* comes to the end of the lane(,) *he* should turn to the left. [When the subject of the introductory clause is repeated in the main clause, the comma is usually unnecessary.]
If we do not go(,) we may be sorry.

Adverb clauses following the main clause. Each introductory clause illustrated above is an adverb clause—i.e., it modifies the verb of the main clause. When the adverb clause *follows* the main clause, the comma is usually omitted. (*Example:* The comma is usually omitted *when the adverb clause follows the main clause.*) But such clauses are set off by a comma if they are nonrestrictive or loosely connected with the rest of the sentence, especially if the subordinating conjunction seems equivalent to a co-ordinating conjunction.

RIGHT   Henry is now in good health, although he has been an invalid most of his life. [*Although* is equivalent to *but.*]
RIGHT   He stayed until Sunday, when he packed his trunk and went home. [*When* is equivalent to *and then.*]

▶ EXERCISE 3.   In each of the following sentences find the main clause and identify the preceding element as a subordinate clause or a phrase. Then determine whether to use or omit a comma after the introductory element. Justify your decision.

1. In order to pay his way through college, George worked at nights in an iron foundry. 2. During this time, he became acquainted with all the company's operations. 3. At the end of four years' observation of George's work, the foundry owner offered George a position as manager. 4. Although George had planned to attend medical school and enter his father's profession, he found now that the kind of work he had been doing had a far greater appeal for him. 5. Without hesitation, he accepted the offer.

Items in Series

12c   Words, phrases, or clauses in a series (and co-ordinate adjectives modifying the same noun) are separated by commas.

(1) Words, phrases or clauses in a series

RIGHT   The room is *bright, clean, quiet.* [Form *a, b, c*]
RIGHT   The room is *bright, clean,* and *quiet.* [Form *a, b,* and *c*]
RIGHT   The room is *bright* and *clean* and *quiet.* [Form *a* and *b* and *c.* Commas are omitted when *and* is used throughout the series.]
RIGHT   He walked *up the steps, across the porch,* and *through the doorway.* [Phrases in a series]
RIGHT   We protested *that the engine used too much oil, that the brakes were worn out,* and *that the tires were dangerous.* [Subordinate clauses in a series]

The final comma is often omitted, especially by newspapers, when the series takes the form *a, b,* and *c.* But students are usually advised to follow the practice of the more conservative books and periodicals in using the comma throughout the series, if only because the comma is sometimes needed to prevent confusion.

CONFUSING   The natives ate beans, onions, rice and honey. [Was the rice and honey a mixture?]
CLEAR   The natives ate beans, onions, rice, and honey; *or* The natives ate beans, onions, and rice and honey.

(2) Co-ordinate adjectives

RIGHT   a *clean, quiet* room; a *bright, clean, quiet* room; a *keen, watchful* man. [*Clean* and *quiet* are co-ordinate—that is, of equal grammatical rank—and modify the same noun, *room.*]
RIGHT   a *clean* and *quiet* room; a *bright* and *clean* and *quiet* room; a *keen* and *watchful* man.

[The adjectives are co-ordinate, as shown by the easy substitution of *and* for the comma.]

RIGHT   a *deep, malevolent* satisfaction.

                      —ALDOUS HUXLEY [7]

The comma is omitted between adjectives not truly co-ordinate, as when the second adjective is thought of as a part of the noun.

RIGHT   a *quiet* dining room [*Dining room* has the force of a single noun, like *bedroom. Quiet* and *dining* are not co-ordinate; instead, *quiet* modifies *dining room.*]

RIGHT   a *keen* old man; *beautiful* blue eyes; *ambitious* young men [*Old man, blue eyes,* and *young men* have the force of single nouns. *And* cannot be used between the adjectives.]

But in "young, ambitious men" or "blue, beautiful eyes" the adjectives are co-ordinate, as shown by the possibility of writing "young *and* ambitious men" or "blue *and* beautiful eyes."

Caution: A comma is not used between the adjective and the noun.

WRONG   a clean, quiet, room.

RIGHT   a clean, quiet room.

▶ EXERCISE 4.   In the following sentences distinguish each series and each group of co-ordinate adjectives, inserting commas where needed. Justify each comma used.

1. Do you remember Pete Moore and that old battered lunch pail he used to carry?   2. He would go past our house every morning wait on the corner for his ride hand his lunch pail up to one of the men on the truck then climb up himself and go rolling away.   3. Year after year—spring summer fall and winter—Pete and his lunch pail would wait on that corner.   4. And every year they both got a little older a little more battered a little nearer used up.   5. My brothers my sisters and I used to make bets about which would wear out first.   6. Then one awful day we heard the blast at the plant saw the sky black with smoke and watched the streets fill with frightened hurrying people.   7. That day was the end of old Pete of his battered lunch pail and of the jokes we made about them.

▶ EXERCISE 5.   Compose six sentences to illustrate punctuation of co-ordinate adjectives and different types of items in series.

[7] "Voices," *Atlantic Monthly,* July, 1955, p. 33.

12d   Nonrestrictive clauses (or phrases) and other parenthetical elements ("interrupters") are set off by commas. Restrictive clauses (or phrases) are not set off.

To *set off* means to put a comma after a parenthetical element at the beginning of a sentence, before a parenthetical element at the end, and both before and after one within a sentence. *Caution:* When two commas are needed to set off a parenthetical element within the sentence, as in the third and sixth sentences below, the omission of one of the two commas is usually more objectionable than the omission of both.

EXAMPLES   *My friends,* we have no alternative.
We have no alternative, *my friends.*
We have, *my friends,* no alternative.

He said, "The story has been told."
"The story has been told," *he said.*
"The story," *he said,* "has been told."

(1) Nonrestrictive clauses and phrases are set off by commas. Restrictive clauses and phrases are not set off.

Adjective clauses introduced by *who* or *which* are nonrestrictive (set off by commas) when they merely add information about a word already identified. Such clauses are parenthetical; they are not essential to the meaning of the main clause and may be omitted.

My mother, *who is visiting me,* is on her way to New York.
Henry Smith, *who is lazy,* will lose his job.
Florence, *which he visited next,* was then torn by rival factions.

Adjective clauses introduced by *who, which,* or *that* are restrictive (not set off by commas) when they are needed for identification of the word they modify. Such clauses limit or qualify the meaning of the sentence and cannot be omitted.

A mother *who does not love her son* is unnatural.
A boy *who is lazy* deserves to lose his job.
The city *that he visited next* was Florence.

Anyone who has difficulty in distinguishing between restrictive and nonrestrictive clauses should read aloud the illustrative sentences above, noting the lack of pause before restrictive clauses and the definite pauses setting off nonrestrictive clauses. The "pause" test may prove helpful, but a more conclusive test is to read the sentence without the clause.

NONRESTRICTIVE CLAUSE Our newest boat, *which is painted red and white,* has sprung a leak. [The *which* clause, adding information about a boat already identified, is parenthetical. It is not essential to the main clause, *Our newest boat has sprung a leak.*]

NONRESTRICTIVE PHRASE Our newest boat, *painted red and white,* has sprung a leak.

RESTRICTIVE CLAUSE (NO COMMAS) A boat *that leaks* is of little use. [The clause *that leaks* is essential to the meaning of the main clause.]

RESTRICTIVE PHRASE (NO COMMAS) A boat *with a leak* is of little use.

NONRESTRICTIVE CLAUSE My new car, *which is parked across the street,* is ready. [Clause adding information about a car already identified]

NONRESTRICTIVE PHRASE My new car, *parked across the street,* is ready.

RESTRICTIVE CLAUSE (NO COMMAS) The car *which is parked across the street* is ready. [Clause essential to the identification]

RESTRICTIVE PHRASE (NO COMMAS) The car *parked across the street* is ready.

Sometimes a clause (or phrase) may be either restrictive or nonrestrictive; the writer signifies his meaning by the proper use of the comma.

NONRESTRICTIVE He spent hours caring for the Indian guides, who were sick with malaria. [He cared for all the Indian guides. All of them were sick with malaria.]

RESTRICTIVE (NO COMMA) He spent hours caring for the Indian guides who were sick with malaria. [Some of the Indian guides were sick with malaria. He cared for the sick ones.]

▶ EXERCISE 6. In the following sentences determine whether each clause (or phrase) is restrictive or nonrestrictive. Set off only the nonrestrictive clauses (or phrases).

1. The James Lee who owns the bank is a grandson of the one who founded it.
2. James Lee who owns this bank and five others is one of the wealthiest men in the state.
3. The coach called out to Higgins who got up from the bench and trotted over to him.
4. Higgins had an ankle which sometimes gave him trouble.
5. The coach who chewed on cigars but never lighted them threw one away and reached for another.
6. Anyone who saw him could tell that something was troubling him.
7. All banks which fail to report will be closed.
8. All banks failing to report will be closed.
9. The law permitted banks to borrow money from the Federal Reserve Banks which were twelve in number.
10. Henry betrayed the man who had helped him build his fortune.
11. James White who had helped Henry build his fortune died yesterday.
12. My father hoping that I would remain at home offered me a share in his business.

▶ EXERCISE 7. Compose and punctuate five sentences containing nonrestrictive clauses or phrases. Compose five sentences containing restrictive clauses or phrases and underline the restrictive elements.

(2) Nonrestrictive appositives, contrasted elements, geographical names, and items in dates and addresses are set off by commas.

Note that most appositives may be readily expanded into nonrestrictive clauses. In other words, the principle underlying the use of commas to set off nonrestrictive clauses also applies here.

APPOSITIVES AND CONTRASTED ELEMENTS

RIGHT Jesse, *the caretaker,* is a good fellow. [The appositive *caretaker* is equivalent to the nonrestrictive clause *who is the caretaker.*]

RIGHT Sandburg, *the biographer of Lincoln,* was awarded the Pulitzer Prize. [The appositive is equivalent to the nonrestrictive clause *who is the biographer of Lincoln.*]

RIGHT My companions were James White, *Esq.,* William Smith, *M.D.,* and Rufus L. Black, *Ph.D.* [Abbreviated titles after a name are treated as appositives.]

RIGHT The cook, *not the caretaker,* will assist you. [The contrasted element is a sort of negative appositive.]

RIGHT Our failures, *not our successes,* will be remembered.

RIGHT Trade comes with peace, *not with war.*

Appositives are usually nonrestrictive (parenthetical), merely adding information about

a person or thing already identified. Such appositives are set off by commas. But when an appositive is restrictive, commas are usually omitted.

RIGHT The poet Sandburg has written a biography. [*Sandburg* restricts the meaning, telling what poet has written a biography.]

RIGHT His son James is sick. [*James,* not his son *William*]

RIGHT William the Conqueror invaded England in 1066. [An appositive that is part of a title is restrictive.]

RIGHT The word *malapropism* is derived from Sheridan's *The Rivals.*

RIGHT Do you refer to Samuel Butler the poet or to Samuel Butler the novelist?

Note: The "pause" test and the "omission" test will prove helpful. See pages 842-43.

▶ EXERCISE 8. Copy the following sentences, using commas to set off contrasted elements and nonrestrictive appositives. Underline restrictive appositives.

1. When the three-master *Pharaon* put into Marseilles on February 28, 1815, she was commanded by nineteen-year-old Edmond Dantes not her captain but her first mate. 2. When M. Morrel the owner heard that the old captain had died at sea, he promised the post to Edmond, who went off gaily to see his father and his beloved the Catalan girl Mercedes. 3. Meantime Danglars the supercargo an offensive man of twenty-six who disliked Dantes was informing M. Morrel that Edmond had stopped at the Isle of Elba on the voyage. 4. Edmond found that his father had lived on almost nothing for three months, having paid the tailor Caderousse some money which Dantes owed. 5. The youth then hurried to the beautiful Mercedes, whom he found with her cousin Fernand Mondego a twenty-one-year-old fisherman. 6. While Edmond and Mercedes made hurried preparations for their marriage, Fernand and Danglars plotted together. 7. They wrote an anonymous letter to Ferard de Villefort the deputy *procureur de roi* saying that Dantes was carrying a letter from Napoleon to the Bonapartists in Paris.[8]

▶ EXERCISE 9. Compose ten sentences to illustrate the punctuation of appositives and contrasted elements.

[8] Adapted from *Plot Outlines of 100 Famous Novels,* ed. Roland A. Goodman by permission of Garden City Books. Copyright, 1942, by Doubleday & Company, Inc.

GEOGRAPHICAL NAMES, ITEMS IN DATES AND ADDRESSES

RIGHT Pasadena, California, is the site of the Rose Bowl. [*California* may be thought of as equivalent to the nonrestrictive clause *which is in California.*]

RIGHT My friends live near the Charles River at 24 Radcliff Road, Waban 68, Massachusetts. [Postal zone numbers are not separated by a comma from the name of the city.]

RIGHT Tuesday, May 8, 1956, in Chicago; 8 May 1956; May, 1956, in Boston *or* May 1956 in Boston. [Commas are often omitted when the day of the month is not given, or when the day of the month precedes rather than follows the month. Students are usually advised not to follow the less conservative practice of dropping the comma after the year, as in "May 8, 1956 in Chicago."]

▶ EXERCISE 10. Copy the following sentences, inserting commas where they are needed.

1. Their son was born on Friday June 18 1954 at Baptist Hospital Knoxville Tennessee.
2. Manuscripts should be mailed to the Managing Editor 109 Parrington Hall University of Washington Seattle 5 Washington.
3. He was inducted into the Army at Fort Oglethorpe Georgia on 30 September 1942.
4. William Congreve was born in Bardsey England on January 24 1670.
5. The accident occurred in De Soto Parish Louisiana on Monday September 9 1950.
6. Please send all communications to 383 Madison Avenue New York 17 New York.

(3) Parenthetical words, phrases, or clauses (inserted expressions), words in direct address (vocatives), absolute phrases, and mild interjections are set off by commas.

PARENTHETICAL EXPRESSIONS

As a matter of fact, the term "parenthetical" is correctly applied to everything discussed under **12d**; but the term is more commonly applied to such expressions as *on the other hand, in the first place, in fact, to tell the truth, etc., however, that is, for example, I hope, I report, he says.* The term would apply equally well to expressions inserted in dialogue: *he said, he observed, he protested,* etc.

RIGHT You will, *then,* accept our offer?
RIGHT *To tell the truth,* we anticipated bad luck.

RIGHT   The work is, *on the whole,* very satisfactory.

RIGHT   "We believe," *he replied,* "that you are correct."

RIGHT   We believe, *however,* that you should go. [When *however* means "nevertheless," it is usually set off by commas. But when *however* means "no matter how," it is not parenthetical and is therefore not set off by commas: "The trip will be hard *however* you go.]

Some parenthetical expressions causing little if any pause in reading are frequently not set off by commas: *also, too, indeed, perhaps, at least, likewise,* etc. The writer must use his judgment.

RIGHT   I am *also* of that opinion.

RIGHT   He is *perhaps* the best swimmer on the team.

RIGHT   Your efforts will *of course* be appreciated; *or,* Your efforts will, *of course,* be appreciated.

DIRECT ADDRESS

RIGHT   Come here, *Mary,* and help us.

RIGHT   I refuse, *sir,* to believe the report.

RIGHT   This, *my friends,* is the whole truth.

ABSOLUTE PHRASES [9]

RIGHT   *Everything being in readiness,* we departed promptly.

RIGHT   He ran swiftly, *the dog in front of him,* and plunged into the forest.

RIGHT   I fear the encounter, *his temper being what it is.*

MILD INTERJECTIONS

RIGHT   *Well,* let him try if he insists.

RIGHT   *Ah,* that is my idea of a good meal.

[Strong interjections call for the exclamation point. See Section 17c.]

12e   Note: Occasionally a comma, though not called for by any of the major principles already discussed, may be needed to prevent misreading.

Use 12e sparingly, if at all, to justify your commas. In a general sense, nearly all commas are used to prevent misreading or to make reading easier. Your mastery of the comma

[9] See Section 35, Grammatical Terms.

will come through the application of the more specific major principles (**a, b, c, d**) to the structure of your sentences.

CONFUSING   Inside the room was gaily decorated. [*Inside* may be at first mistaken for the preposition.]

CLEAR   Inside, the room was gaily decorated. [*Inside* is clearly the adverb.]

CONFUSING   After all the conquest of malaria is a fascinating story.

CLEAR   After all, the conquest of malaria is a fascinating story.

► EXERCISES ON THE COMMA

A. Copy the following passage, using commas to set off appositives, parenthetical expressions, words in direct address, absolute phrases, and mild interjections.

1. Gentlemen shall I tell you what you have done? 2. You have sent me a man broken in spirit to an untimely grave. 3. Ah do not think that I shudder at the thought of the grave. 4. On the contrary I welcome it. 5. Even as a hurt child to the arms of a comforting mother I fly to it as my only refuge. 6. My wound being what it is where else should I fly? 7. Man and boy have I not served you on bloody fields of battle and in the halls of the Congress itself? 8. Is this then to be the mark of your gratitude? 9. Must I after a life of selfless service hear my dearest friends question my integrity in this manner? 10. Can it be possible I ask myself that those friends would even listen to the foul slanders spread by my opponent?

B. Copy the following passage, inserting all commas needed.

1. After a night spent in fever and sleeplessness I forced myself to take a long tramp the next day through the hilly country which was covered with pine woods. 2. It all looked dreary and desolate and I could not think what I should do there. 3. Returning in the afternoon I stretched myself dead tired on a hard couch awaiting the long-desired hour of sleep. 4. It did not come; but I fell into a kind of somnolent state in which I suddenly felt as though I were sinking in swiftly flowing water. 5. The rushing sound formed itself in my brain into a musical sound the chord of E-flat major which continually re-echoed in broken forms; these broken chords seemed to be melodic passages of increasing motion yet the pure triad of E-flat major never changed but seemed by its con-

tinuance to impart infinite significance to the element in which I was sinking. 6. I awoke in sudden terror from my doze feeling as though the waves were rushing high above my head. 7. I at once recognized that the orchestral overture to the *Rheingold* which must long have lain latent within me though it had been unable to find definite form had at last been revealed to me.

—RICHARD WAGNER

[*See the general exercises on the comma and the semicolon following Section* 14; *on capitals, italics, and all marks of punctuation following Section* 17.]

▶ Superfluous Commas

13   Do not use superfluous commas.

If you have a tendency to use unnecessary commas, consider every comma you are tempted to use and omit it unless you can justify its use by one of the principles treated under Section 12.

Another way to avoid unnecessary commas is to observe the following rules:

13a   Do not use a comma to separate the subject and its verb, the verb and its object, or an adjective and its noun.

WRONG   Rain at frequent intervals, is productive of mosquitoes. [Needless separation of subject and verb]

RIGHT   Rain at frequent intervals is productive of mosquitoes.

Note, however, that a comma before the verb sometimes makes for clarity when the subject is heavily modified.

EXAMPLE   Rain coming at frequent intervals and in sufficient amounts to fill the ponds, the cisterns, and the many small containers near the house, is productive of mosquitoes.

In the following sentences the commas in parentheses should be omitted:

He learned at an early age(,) the necessity of economizing. [Needless separation of verb and object]

The book says(,) that members of the crew deserted. [Indirect discourse: needless separation of verb and object]

He was a bad, deceitful, unruly(,) boy. [Incorrect separation of adjective and noun]

13b   Do not use a comma to separate two words or two phrases joined by a coordinating conjunction.

In the following sentences the commas in parentheses should be omitted:

The poem has nobility of sentiment(,) and dignity of style.

The players work together(,) and gain a victory. [Compound predicate: *and* joins two verbs.]

He had decided to work(,) and to save his money. [*And* joins two infinitive phrases.]

13c   Do not use commas to set off words or short phrases (especially introductory ones) that are not parenthetical or that are very slightly so.

In the following sentences the commas in parentheses should be omitted:

On last Monday(,) I went to a baseball game.

Maybe(,) he had a better reason for leaving.

The center passes the ball(,) through his legs(,) to a man in the backfield.

In our age(,) it is easy to talk(,) by wire(,) to any continent.

13d   Do not use commas to set off restrictive clauses, restrictive phrases, or restrictive appositives.

In the following sentences the commas in parentheses should be omitted:

A man(,) *who hopes to succeed*(,) must work hard. [Restrictive clause]

A man(,) *disinclined to work*(,) cannot succeed. [Restrictive phrase]

That man(,) *Jones*(,) will outwit his opponents. [Restrictive appositive]

13e   Do not put a comma before the first item of a series, after the last item of a series, or after a conjunction.

In the following sentences the commas in parentheses should be omitted:

I enjoy the study of (,) history, geography, and geology. [Needless comma before the first item of a series. A colon here would be even worse—since there is no formal introduction. See **17d**.]

History, geography, and geology(,) are interesting subjects.

I enjoy these subjects, but(,) for others I have less appreciation.

Field work is required in a few sciences, such as(,) botany and geology.

▶ EXERCISE ON SUPERFLUOUS COMMAS

In the following passages (adapted from Francis Parkman) some of the commas are needed and some are superfluous. Strike out all commas that would usually be omitted in good contemporary writing. Justify each comma that you allow to stand.

1. In opening this plan of treachery, Pontiac spoke rather as a counselor, than as a commander. 2. Haughty as he was, he had too much sagacity to wound the pride of a body of men, over whom he had no other control, than that derived from his personal character and influence. 3. No one was hardy enough to venture opposition to the proposal of their great leader. 4. His plan, was eagerly adopted. 5. Hoarse ejaculations, of applause, echoed his speech; and, gathering their blankets around them, the chiefs withdrew, to their respective villages, to prepare for the destruction of the unsuspecting garrison.

1. The twelve canoes, had reached the western end of the Lake, of St. Peter, where it is filled, with innumerable islands. 2. The forest was close, on their right; they kept near the shore, to avoid the current, and the shallow water, before them, was covered with a dense growth of tall bulrushes. 3. Suddenly, the silence was frightfully broken. 4. The war-whoop rose, from among the rushes, mingled, with the reports of guns, and the whistling of bullets; and several Iroquois canoes, filled, with warriors, pushed out, from their concealment, and bore down upon Jogues and his companions. 5. The Hurons, in the rear, were seized with a shameful panic. 6. They leaped ashore; left canoes, baggage, and weapons; and, fled into the woods. 7. The French, and the Christian Hurons, made fight; for a time; but, when they saw another fleet of canoes approaching, from the opposite shores, or islands, they lost heart, and those escaped, who could.

▶ The Semicolon

14   Use the semicolon (a) between two main clauses not joined by *and*, *but*, *or*, *nor*, or *for* and (b) between co-ordinate elements containing commas. (Use the semicolon only between parts of equal rank.)

Caution: Your understanding of this section will depend upon your ability to distinguish clauses and phrases, main clauses and subordinate clauses. You may need to master Section **1, Sentence Sense,** especially **1d** and **1e**, before studying Section **14.**

14a   Use the semicolon between two main clauses not joined by one of the simple

co-ordinating conjunctions (*and, but, or, nor, for*).

RIGHT   The semicolon is a much stronger mark of separation than the comma; it is almost as strong as the period. [The use of a comma in such a sentence would be a *comma splice.* See Section **3**.]

RIGHT   With educated people, I suppose, punctuation is a matter of rule; with me it is a matter of feeling. But I must say I have a great respect for the semicolon; it's a useful little chap. —ABRAHAM LINCOLN

RIGHT We didn't abolish truth; even we couldn't do that. —WILLIAM FAULKNER [1]

Conjunctive adverbs (such as *accordingly, also, anyhow, besides, consequently, furthermore, hence, however, indeed, instead, likewise, moreover, nevertheless, still, then, therefore, thus*) cannot be used in place of co-ordinating conjunctions. Thus, in accordance with the rule, main clauses joined by these adverbs should be separated by the semicolon.

RIGHT I carried a letter of introduction with me; therefore I had no difficulty in getting an interview. [But usually such sentences are better revised according to the principles of **Subordination**, Section 24: Since I carried a letter of introduction with me, I had no difficulty in getting an interview.]

Explanatory expressions (such as *for example, in fact, namely, on the contrary, on the other hand, that is*) are similar in use to conjunctive adverbs; that is, main clauses joined by them are usually separated by the semicolon.

RIGHT He is coming today; in fact, he is due here now.

Note: Such conjunctive adverbs or explanatory expressions as *therefore* and *in fact,* when used after the semicolon, are or are not followed by a comma, depending on how parenthetical the writer feels them to be. See Section 12d (3).

Co-ordinating conjunctions between main clauses are often preceded by a semicolon (instead of the usual comma) if the clauses have internal punctuation or reveal a striking contrast. See also Section 12a.

RIGHT American education may be sometimes slapdash and fantastic, with its short-story and saxophone courses, its strange fraternities and sororities, its musical-comedy co-ed atmosphere, its heavily solemn games departments; but at least it has never departed from the fine medieval tradition of the poor scholar. —JOSEPH PRIESTLEY

[1] "On Privacy," *Harper's Magazine,* July, 1955, p. 36.

14b The semicolon is used to separate a series of equal elements which themselves contain commas.

This use of the semicolon makes for clarity, showing the reader at a glance the main divisions, which would otherwise be obscured by the commas.

RIGHT Her best friends were Laura Bagley, her sorority sister; John Bagley, Laura's brother; and James White, the president of the class. [Semicolons separating a series of nouns]

RIGHT It is well known that Mr. Fadiman is an exceedingly clever, witty, and nimble writer; that he has read widely and remembered well; and that he is wonderfully adept at communicating his appreciation to others. [Semicolons separating a series of noun clauses] —CHARLES J. ROLO [2]

RIGHT He is not cantankerous, sour, spiteful, parochial, or fanatical; not arrogant, patronizing, or reactionary; not sanctimonious, glibly inspirational, nice-Nellyish, or mushy. [Semicolons separating a series of adjective groups] —IBID.

14c *Caution:* Do not use the semicolon between parts of unequal rank, such as a clause and a phrase or a main clause and a subordinate clause.

WRONG A bitter wind swept the dead leaves along the street; casting them high in the air and against the buildings. [Main clause; phrase]

RIGHT A bitter wind swept the dead leaves along the street, casting them high in the air and against the buildings.

WRONG I hope to spend my vacation in Canada; where I enjoy the fishing. [Main clause; subordinate clause]

RIGHT I hope to spend my vacation in Canada, where I enjoy the fishing.

▶ EXERCISES ON THE SEMICOLON

A. Copy the following sentences, inserting semicolons where they are needed. Do not allow a semicolon to stand between parts of unequal rank. Write *C* in place of each sentence that needs no revision.

1. We first knew the Martinellis in St. Louis; when they were living next door to us.

[2] From "Reader's Choice" by Charles J. Rolo, *Atlantic Monthly,* July 1955. By permission.

2. Mac goes around in par now, he has trimmed several strokes off his game since we played together last.

3. I hear it said by the people hereabouts that the old mansion is haunted, in fact, there are some who swear that it is.

4. Hank had dismantled his motor; intending to give it a complete overhaul for the following week's races.

5. He is fairly even-tempered most of the time, and you should have no difficulty getting along with him but whatever you do, don't ever let him get you into a political argument.

6. He lamented that he had no suggestions to offer, however, he spent the next forty minutes offering them.

7. It's all right for you to be here, I crashed this party myself.

8. I went to the address you gave me; if your brother lives there, he lives upstairs over a vacant lot.

9. In our unit at that time there were Lieutenant Holmes, who was a criminologist by profession and a university lecturer on penology, Captain Sturm, in peacetime a U.S. Steel executive, two old majors, previously retired and now still writing their memoirs, Lieutenant Colonel Beale, a Mississippi cotton planter, and Colonel Quincy, who was, I think, some sort of tycoon in the peanut butter industry.

10. If you expect me to be here in time, or even to get back at all; you had better send somebody to help me.

B. From your reading, copy any five sentences in which the semicolon is properly used. Explain the reason for each semicolon.

C. Compose five sentences to illustrate the proper use of the semicolon.

[See also the general exercises immediately following; also the general exercises following Section 17.]

▶ GENERAL EXERCISES ON THE COMMA
   AND THE SEMICOLON

A. Commas are used correctly in the following sentences. Explain each comma by writing above it the appropriate letter from Section 12: a, b, c, or d. [Instead of using these letters for this and the following exercises, you may prefer to use meaningful abbreviations: m (main clauses), i (introductory clauses, phrases), ser (series), c-ad (co-ordinate adjectives), nonr (nonrestrictive), app (appositives, etc.), par (parenthetical).]

1. After crossing the river we built no more fires, for we were now in hostile Indian country.

2. Having nothing very important to do, I simply did nothing at all.

3. Well, all I have to say is that you didn't try very hard.

4. If he says he'll be there, he'll be there.

5. The smith straightened up, the horse's hoof still between his knees, and then he bent back to his work.

6. Although there are a few adjustments yet to be made, the main part of the work is finished, and the next few days should see it completed altogether.

7. The panting, tormented bull lowered his head for another charge.

8. The doctor, after a brief examination of the patient, gave orders to have him prepared for surgery.

9. The kit contains cement, balsa, paper, and instructions for assembly.

10. You will, I suppose, be back tomorrow.

11. The old opera house, which has stood unused for years, will finally be torn down.

12. Our class meets at ten on Mondays, Wednesdays, and Fridays.

13. The Executive Mansion is located at 1600 Pennsylvania Avenue, Washington, D. C.

14. To tell the truth, I am not quite sure where I was on November 18, 1955.

15. It was a long, hot, tiresome trip, and I was sorry that I had promised to go.

B. Explain each comma used in Section 1, Exercise 21. Follow the directions given under A.

C. Explain each comma used in Section 1, Exercise 23. Follow directions given under A.

D. Explain each comma used in Section 1, Exercise 25. Follow directions given under A.

E. In the following sentences insert all necessary commas and semicolons. Then explain each comma by writing above it the appropriate letter from Section 12: a, b, c, or d (the abbreviations suggested in Exercise A).

1. Yes if you feel that you must go I hope you will not delay longer.

2. There is so far as I can see no reason why you should not.

3. If I were in your position however I would be extremely cautious about believing what I heard.

4. Taking everything into consideration I believe that Robinson should have a better season this year than ever before however you understand that this is only an opinion and that I reserve the right to

amend it after I have seen him work out a few times.

5. After we wash the dishes we must wash the towels.

6. There were four letters for Marion but not a single one for me.

7. Two or three scrawny mangy-looking hounds lay sprawled in the shade of the cabin.

8. Have I your permission sir to continue?

9. While Frank was unpacking the cooking gear and Gene was chopping firewood I began to put up our shelter Phil meanwhile had gone down to the lake to try to get a few bass for our supper.

10. A small Christmas tree would cost very little perhaps we should buy one.

11. After perhaps an hour or so of waiting they may go away but don't expect them to go far and don't think they aren't still watching.

12. Bales of cotton hogsheads of sugar and salted meats barrels of flour and cases and crates of goods of every kind imaginable crowded the busy landing as far up and down the river as the eye could reach.

13. In complete disregard of the machine-gun bullets which were nipping through the grass tops all around us Jerry wriggled on his belly all the way out to where I was put a tourniquet on my leg and then began dragging me back to the shelter of the ditch.

14. "Tim you old reprobate" he shouted "it's good to see your ugly face again."

15. If I am expected to arrive by eleven o'clock someone should volunteer to wake me up otherwise I shall probably sleep until noon.

▶ The Apostrophe

15 **Use the apostrophe to indicate the possessive case (except for personal pronouns), to mark omissions, and to form the plurals of letters and figures.**

15a Do not carelessly omit the apostrophe in the possessive case of nouns and indefinite pronouns.

(1) If the ending (either singular or plural) is not in an *s* or *z* sound, add the apostrophe and *s*.

RIGHT   The man's hat; the boy's shoes; a dollar's worth; today's problems [Singular]

RIGHT   Men's hats; women's dresses [Plural]

RIGHT   One's hat; another's coat; someone's shirt; anybody's room [Indefinite pronouns—singular]

(2) If the plural ends in an *s* or *z* sound, add only the apostrophe.

RIGHT   Ladies' hats (hats for ladies); boys' shoes (shoes for boys); the Joneses' boys (the boys of the Joneses); three dollars' worth

RIGHT   Farmers' (*or* Farmers) Co-operative Society [The names of organizations frequently omit the apostrophe. *Cf.* Teachers College.]

(3) If the singular ends in an *s* or *z* sound, add the apostrophe and *s* for words of one syllable. Add only the apostrophe for words of more than one syllable unless you expect the pronunciation of the second *s* or *z* sound.

RIGHT   James's book; Moses' law; Xerxes' army; Hortense's coat

(4) Compounds or nouns in joint possession show the possessive in the last word only. But if there is individual (or separate) possession, each noun takes the possessive form.

RIGHT   My father-in-law's house; my fathers-in-law's houses; someone else's hat

RIGHT   Helen and Mary's piano [Joint ownership]

RIGHT   Helen's and Mary's clothes [Individual ownership]

Although usage sanctions the apostrophe with compounds to indicate possession, an *of* phrase is frequently more pleasing: the house of my father-in-law; the car of the president of the bank (the president of the bank's car). For the use of an *of* phrase with inanimate objects see Section **5e**.

▶ EXERCISE 1. Copy the following, inserting apostrophes to indicate the possessive case:

1. everybodys business
2. the girls (*sing.*) coat
3. the girls (*pl.*) coats
4. Williams book
5. a months pay
6. two months pay
7. a turkeys nest
8. two turkeys nests
9. a fairys wand
10. fairies wands
11. the childs toys
12. the childrens toys

► EXERCISE 2. Rewrite the following as possessives with the apostrophe:

1. the home of my neighbor
2. homes of my neighbors
3. a book for a boy
4. books for boys
5. the car of my sister
6. the cars of my sisters
7. the ideas of a woman
8. the ideas of women
9. the boat of Robert and Jim
10. the boats of Robert and Jim (individual possession)
11. the hat of the lady
12. the hats of the ladies

15b Do not use the apostrophe with the personal pronouns (*his, hers, its, ours, yours, theirs*) or with the relative-interrogative pronoun *whose*.

WRONG He met *hi's* friend. [An error no one would make]

RIGHT He met *his* friend.

WRONG Virtue is *it's* own reward. [Fully as wrong as *hi's*. *It's* means "it is."]

RIGHT Virtue is *its* own reward.

WRONG her's, hers', it's (possessive), its', our's, ours' your's, yours', their's, theirs', who's (possessive), who'se

RIGHT hers, its (possessive), it's (meaning "it is," as in "It's cold today"), ours, yours, theirs, whose, who's (meaning "who is" as in "Who's going to the game?")

15c Use an apostrophe to mark omissions in contracted words or numerals.

RIGHT Can't; didn't; he's (he is); it's (it is); you're; o'clock (of the clock); the class of '55 (1955)

Caution: Place the apostrophe exactly where the omission occurs: *isn't, haven't* (*not* is'nt, have'nt).

15d Use the apostrophe and s to form the plural of letters, figures, symbols, and words referred to as words.

RIGHT Congreve seldom crossed his *t*'s, his *7*'s looked like *9*'s, and his *and*'s were usually *&*'s.

Note: This apostrophe is sometimes omitted when there is no danger of ambiguity: the *1930*'s, or the *1930*s; two *B*'s and three *C*'s, or two *B*s and three *C*s.

► EXERCISES ON THE APOSTROPHE

A. Write the possessive singular and the possessive plural of each of the following words.

1. goose	7. lawyer	13. brother-in-law
2. father	8. princess	14. fox
3. lackey	9. jockey	15. genius
4. milkman	10. witch	16. army
5. other	11. mouse	17. Brooks
6. family	12. sailor	18. Morris

B. Copy the following sentences, inserting necessary apostrophes and omitting needless or faulty ones. Correct spelling if necessary. Underline each possessive once and each contraction twice.

1. Who's going to do the dishes? Who's turn is it?
2. The choice is our's to make, not your's.
3. Shes writing copy for a new program on one of the local station's.
4. On Thursday's the childrens' department does'nt open.
5. That boys one of the worlds' worst; whats he doing now?
6. Its a ladys' world despite the saying's to the contrary.
7. *Ifs, buts,* and *maybes* wont satisfy a young swains ardent proposal.
8. Its not her's to give away.
9. They have'nt said the property is theirs'.
10. I did'nt go to sleep until after two oclock.
11. I cant go on Monday's and you wont go on Friday's.
12. Its a mans right to see that he gets his dollars worth.
13. Theyre not coming to see Freds' new house.
14. The books format is it's best feature.
15. Who'se idea was it? It must have been your's.

▶ Quotation Marks (and Quotations)

16 **Use quotation marks to set off all direct quotations, some titles, and words used in a special sense. Place other marks of punctuation in proper relation to quotation marks.**

Quotations usually consist of (1) passages borrowed from the written work of others or (2) the direct speech of individuals, especially in conversation (dialogue).

Caution: Be careful not to omit the second set of quotation marks: the first set, marking the beginning of the part quoted, must be followed by another set to mark the end. Note that the verb of saying used with a quotation is always outside the quotation marks and is regularly set off by commas.

WRONG   "I have no intention of staying, he replied.

RIGHT   "I have no intention of staying," he replied.

WRONG   "I do not object, he said, to the tenor of the report."

RIGHT   "I do not object," he said, "to the tenor of the report." [Two parts are quoted. Each must be enclosed, leaving *he said* outside of the quotation marks.]

16a   Use double quotation marks to enclose direct (but not indirect) quotations; for a quotation within a quotation, use single marks.

RIGHT   He said, "I have no intention of staying." [Direct quotation—the exact words spoken]

RIGHT   He said that he had "no intention of staying." [Direct quotation of a fragment of the speech]

WRONG   He said "that he had not intended to stay." [Indirect quotation—should not be enclosed in quotation marks]

RIGHT   He said that he had not intended to stay.

RIGHT   "It took courage," the speaker said, "for a man to affirm in those days: 'I endorse every word of Patrick Henry's sentiment, "Give me liberty or give me death!" ' "—WILLIAM

LEWIN. [Note that a quotation within a quotation is enclosed by single quotation marks; one within that, by double marks.]

(1) Long quotations (not dialogue). Quoted passages of ten or more lines [1] are usually set off from the other matter, without quotation marks, by means of smaller type. In typewritten papers such quoted passages are single-spaced and indented, as in the example on page 957 below. [2]

(2) Poetry. Quoted lines of poetry are sufficiently marked by the verse form without the aid of quotation marks. But poetry must be quoted line for line, not written as prose.

(3) Dialogue (conversation). Written dialogue represents the directly quoted speech of two or more persons talking together. Standard practice is to write each person's speech, no matter how short, as a separate paragraph. Verbs of saying, as well as closely related bits of narrative, are included in the paragraph along with the speech.

RIGHT   "You remember Kate Stoddard, Mother?" Georgia asked. "This is Kate to pay us a little visit."

Mrs. Stanton rocked and closed her eyes. "What's everybody shouting for?" she asked.

"Sit down, Kate," Georgia said.

[1] Recommended by "The MLA Style Sheet," *Publications of the Modern Language Association of America,* LXVI (April, 1951), pp. 9-10.

[2] When quotation marks—instead of the usual smaller type or indention—are used for a passage of two or more paragraphs, the quotation marks come before each paragraph and at the end of the last; they do not come at the end of intermediate paragraphs.

Mrs. Stoddard pulled a chair close to Mrs. Stanton. "Well, I will, but I can't stay. I came for a reason."

"We paid our yearly dues," Georgia said. "I don't know what makes you say that," Mrs. Stoddard said. "I don't think you've ever known me to solicit *personally*. I came about quite another matter. I wanted you to look at this." She fished in her bag and brought out the diary, which she held out rather grudgingly to Georgia. "Be careful of it! It's quite old!"   —SALLY BENSON [3]

In the last paragraph, note that although a narrative passage interrupts the dialogue, the speaker is Mrs. Stoddard throughout.

▶ EXERCISE I. Compose five sentences to illustrate the proper use of double and single quotation marks.

16b Use quotation marks for minor titles (short stories, one-act plays, short poems, articles from magazines) and for subdivisions of books.

RIGHT   The February, 1955, issue of the *Atlantic Monthly* contains a short story entitled "The Portrait" by Wolf Mankowitz, a poem called "Winter Leaves" by Claire McAllister, and an article on "The Decline of Western Democracy" by Walter Lippmann.

RIGHT   Stevenson's *Treasure Island* is divided into six parts, the last of which, called "Captain Silver," opens with a chapter entitled "In the Enemy's Camp."

Note: Quotation marks are sometimes used to enclose titles of books, magazines, and newspapers, but italics are usually preferred. See Section 10a.

▶ EXERCISE 2. Compose five sentences showing use of quotation marks with minor titles and subdivisions of books.

16c Words used in a special sense are sometimes enclosed in quotation marks.

RIGHT   The printer must see that quotation marks are "cleared"—that is, kept within the margins.

RIGHT   "Sympathy" means "to suffer with." [Also right: *Sympathy* means *to suffer with*; *Sympathy* means "to suffer with." See also Section 10d.]

[3] From "Spirit of '76" by Sally Benson. Originally published in *The New Yorker*, December 25, 1954.

16d Do not overuse quotation marks.

Do not use quotation marks to enclose titles of themes or to mark bits of humor. In general do not enclose in quotation marks common nicknames, well-known phrases and technical terms, or slang used in informal writing. Above all, do not use quotation marks for emphasis.

NEEDLESS PUNCTUATION   "Old Hickory" was wrought up over the loss of his friend.
BETTER   Old Hickory was wrought up over the loss of his friend.

16e In using marks of punctuation with quoted words, phrases, or sentences, follow the arbitrary printers' rules by placing:

(1) The period and the comma always within the quotation marks.
(2) The colon and the semicolon always outside the quotation marks.
(3) The dash, the question mark, and the exclamation point within the quotation marks when they apply to the quoted matter only; outside when they refer to the whole sentence.

RIGHT   "I will go," he insisted. "I am needed." [Comma and period always inside quotation marks]

RIGHT   He spoke of his "old log house"; he might have called it a mansion. [Semicolon (and colon) always outside quotation marks]

RIGHT   He asked, "When did you arrive?" [Here the question mark applies only to the part of the sentence within quotation marks.]

RIGHT   What is the meaning of "the open door"? [Here the question mark applies to the whole sentence.]

RIGHT   The captain shouted, "Halt!" [Here the exclamation point applies only to the quotation.]

RIGHT   Save us from his "mercy"! [Here the exclamation point applies to the whole sentence.]

▶ EXERCISE 3. Compose six sentences to illustrate the proper placing of the period, the comma, the colon, the semicolon, the dash, the question mark, and the exclamation point in relation to quotation marks.

▶ EXERCISE ON QUOTATION MARKS AND QUOTATIONS

Insert quotation marks where they are needed in the following sentences. Then rewrite the passage, following standard procedures for paragraphing of dialogue and omitting sentence numbers.

1. Young Herman Ponsonby-Jett's countenance was an open page, one upon which might be read a tale of contending emotions. 2. Your countenance, Herman, his Uncle Rodney observed, is an open page, one upon which may be read a tale of contending emotions. 3. Oof, Herman seemed to assent. 4. Or perhaps it was nff. 5. Did you say oof? 6. Or was it nff? 7. The acoustics in here aren't all they might be, considering the club dues one pays. 8. Oof, Herman clarified the matter. 9. Thank you. 10. Oof it is. 11. I like to take care of these little things as they arise. 12. Keeps the picture sharp and clear, so to speak. 13. Am I to gather that the picture at present is not one which sends you into transports of delight? 14. Nff. 15. Not even the faulty acoustics could obscure Herman's meaning. 16. There ought to be a manual published to help the troubled soul out of its plights in times like these—a book with some such chapter as How To Notify a Former Beloved That She Has Been Supplanted, Uncle Rodney said. 17. Herman's silence said eloquently that he found little more solace in what ought to be than in what was. 18. Have you thought of addressing a note to the erstwhile fairest, beginning, let us say, When in the course of human events? 19. Nff; the young man's discourse seemed to be running lately to nff's. 20. Your discourse, young man, seems to be running lately to nff's, remarked Uncle Rodney, ever alert to a gathering trend. 21. I may assume, then, that you had thought of the note and dismissed it as unfeasible? 22. Herman's reply suffered an encounter with the acoustics, concerning which his uncle forebore to comment. 23. Uncle Rodney went on, I deplore our society's abandonment of the art of composing verse. 24. This might be an occasion for sending 'round a few stanzas—perhaps in the manner of Dowson's To Cynara, with the refrain going I shall be true to you, Rosabella! in my fashion. 25. He cast a tentative eye Hermanward. 26. Or, he continued, you could always face the young lady candidly and make a clean—that is, deliver the tidings in so many words, the manly way. 27. I wonder, though, if at these times any of us is really a man at all—or what we are. 28. Mice, said Herman.

▶ The Period and Other Marks

17 Use the period, the question mark, the exclamation point, the dash, the colon, parentheses, and brackets in accordance with accepted usage.

The Period (.)

17a Use the period after declarative and mildly imperative sentences, after indirect questions, and after most abbreviations. Use the ellipsis mark (three spaced periods) to indicate omissions from quoted passages.

(1) Use the period to mark the end of a declarative sentence, a mildly imperative sentence, or an indirect question.

DECLARATIVE They changed the rules.
MILDLY IMPERATIVE Change the rules. Let's change the rules.

INDIRECT QUESTION He asked whether the rules had been changed.

(2) Use periods to follow most abbreviations.

RIGHT Mr., Dr., M.D., etc., i.e., A.D., B.C., A.M., P.M., viz., Jr.

Periods are not used after such contractions as *I've, can't, 2nd, 15th* and usually not with such abbreviations of national or international agencies as *ECA, FBI, NATO, TVA, UN, WAC.* If you have any doubt about the punctuation of a given abbreviation, consult a good dictionary such as *Webster's New Collegiate Dictionary* (in a special section, pages

998-1007) or *The American College Dictionary* or *Webster's New World Dictionary* (in the main vocabulary).

(3) Use the ellipsis mark (three spaced periods) to indicate omissions from quoted passages.

Three spaced periods are used to mark an omission of one or more words within the quoted passage. If the omission ends with a period, this period precedes the usual ellipsis mark to serve as the normal end of the sentence.

RIGHT   "The fundamental justification for poetry on the stage . . . lies in the play itself, in the illusion the play undertakes to create. . . . To go far one must go by art."
—ARCHIBALD MAC LEISH [1]

The Question Mark (?)

17b   Use the question mark to follow direct (but not indirect) questions.

RIGHT   Who started the riot? [Direct question]

RIGHT   He asked who started the riot. He asked whether the riot had been quelled. [Indirect questions, followed by periods]

RIGHT   Did he ask who started the riot? [The sentence as a whole is a direct question despite the indirect question at the end.]

RIGHT   "Who started the riot?" he asked.

RIGHT   He asked, "Who started the riot?"

RIGHT   You started the riot? [Question in the form of a declarative sentence]

RIGHT   You told me—did I hear you correctly?— that you started the riot. [Interpolated question]

RIGHT   To ask who started the riot is unnecessary. [Indirect question, requiring no question mark]

RIGHT   Did you hear him say, "What right have you to ask about the riot?" [Double direct question followed by a single question mark]

RIGHT   Did he plan the riot, employ assistants, and give the signal to begin? *Or:* Did he plan the riot? employ assistants? give the signal to begin? [Question marks used between the parts of the series cause full stops and throw emphasis on each part.]

[1] "The Poet as Playwright," *Atlantic Monthly*, February, 1955, p. 52.

OTHER USES

A question mark (within parentheses) is used to express the writer's uncertainty as to the correctness of the preceding word, figure, or date: "Chaucer was born in 1340(?) and died in 1400." But the question mark is not a desirable means of expressing the author's wit or sarcasm.

QUESTIONABLE   "This kind(?) proposal caused Gulliver to take refuge in nearby Blefuscu." [Omit the question mark. If the context does not make the irony clear, either revise your sentence or give up your attempt to strike an ironic note.]

Courtesy questions common to business letters may be followed by question marks but are usually followed by periods: "Will you (= Please) write me again if I can be of further service."

Caution: Do not use a comma or a period after a question mark.

WRONG   "Are you ready?," he asked.
RIGHT   "Are you ready?" he asked.

The Exclamation Point (!)

17c   Use the exclamation point after an emphatic interjection and after a phrase, clause, or sentence to express a high degree of surprise, incredulity, or other strong emotion.

RIGHT   What! I cannot believe it! How beautiful! [*What* and *how* often begin exclamations.]

RIGHT   Oh! you have finally come! (*Or:* Oh, you have finally come!)

RIGHT   March! Halt! Get out of this house! [Sharp commands—vigorous imperatives]

RIGHT   Forbid it, Almighty God! I know not what course others may take, but as for me, give me liberty, or give me death!
—PATRICK HENRY

Caution 1: Avoid overuse of the exclamation point. Use a comma after mild interjections, and end mildly exclamatory sentences with a period.

RIGHT   Well, you are to be congratulated.

Caution 2: Do not use a comma or a period after the exclamation point.

WRONG "Halt!," cried the corporal.
RIGHT "Halt!" cried the corporal.

► EXERCISE 1. Compose ten sentences to illustrate the chief uses of the period, the question mark, and the exclamation point.

► EXERCISE 2. Copy the following passage, supplying needed periods, question marks, exclamation points, and commas—in proper relation to quotation marks. See 16e.

1. "Now Jane" said Mrs. Colonel Wugsby turning to one of the girls "what is it" 2. "I came to ask ma whether I might dance with the youngest Mr. Crawley" whispered the prettier and younger of the two 3. "Good God Jane how can you think of such things" replied the mamma indignantly 4. "Haven't you repeatedly heard that his father has eight hundred a year which dies with him 5. I am ashamed of you 6. Not on any account" 7. "Ma" whispered the other who was much older than her sister and very insipid and artificial "Lord Mutanhed has been introduced to me 8. I said I *thought* I wasn't engaged ma" 9. "You're a sweet pet my love" replied Mrs. Colonel Wugsby tapping her daughter's cheek with her fan "and are always to be trusted 10. He's immensely rich my dear 11. Bless you" 12. With these words Mrs. Colonel Wugsby kissed her eldest daughter most affectionately and frowning in a warning manner upon the other sorted her cards —CHARLES DICKENS

The Colon (:)

17d Use the colon after a formal introductory statement to direct attention to what is to follow. Avoid needless colons.

The colon and the semicolon, notwithstanding the similarity of the names, differ greatly in use. The semicolon (see Section 14) is a strong *separator* almost equal to a period, and is used only between equal parts. The colon is an *introducer,* calling attention to something that is to follow. It has the meaning of *as follows.*

(1) The colon may direct attention to an appositive (or a series of appositives) at the end of a sentence, to a formal list or explanation, or to a long quotation.

RIGHT All her thoughts were centered on one objective: marriage. [A dash or a comma, which might be used instead of the colon, would be less formal.]

RIGHT We may divide poems into three classes: narrative, lyric, and dramatic. [A dash might be used instead of the colon; because of the following series a comma would be confusing.]
RIGHT At any rate, this much can be said: The Council is not the vital organ it is supposed to be. —THE ATLANTIC MONTHLY
RIGHT Competition in the steel industry is described by one of the Corporation's competitors as follows: "Your ability to win when competition for business gets tough comes in the entire setup of your operation, the quality of your management, . . . and so on. You have to play a judgment game. This is no 2-cent poker." —FORTUNE

(2) The colon may separate two main clauses when the second clause explains or amplifies the first.

RIGHT Webster definitely undervalued the area: with prime ribs at 85 cents a pound, any acreage that can fatten steers has its purpose. —NEW YORK TIMES MAGAZINE
RIGHT We have one chance for escape: we may retreat through the mountain pass. [The second clause explains the first.]
RIGHT The case for fly-fishing can be briefly put: First, trout fishing is a sport—one of the finest man knows. —NEW YORK TIMES MAGAZINE

[For capitalization after the colon see Section 9e.]

(3) The colon may direct attention to a business letter following the salutation, to the verse following the Biblical chapter, or to the minute following the hour.

EXAMPLES Dear Sir:
Matthew 6:10; 9:30 A.M.

(4) Avoid needless colons.

When there is no formal introduction or summarizing word, the colon is usually a needless interruption of the sentence.

NEEDLESS All her thoughts were centered on: marriage.
BETTER All her thoughts were centered on marriage.
NEEDLESS Three kinds of poems are: narratives, lyrics, and dramas. [Awkward separation of verb and its complement]
BETTER Three kinds of poems are narratives, lyrics, and dramas.

▶ EXERCISE 3. Compose ten sentences to illustrate the various uses of the colon.

The Dash (——)

17e   Use the dash to mark a sudden break in thought, to set off a summary, or to set off a parenthetical element that is very abrupt or that has commas within it.

[For a comparison of the dash, the comma, and parentheses, see Section 17f. On the typewriter the dash is made by two hyphens without spacing before or after.]

(1) Use the dash to mark a sudden break in thought.

RIGHT   But you think that I——

RIGHT   We shall need——let's see, what shall we need?

RIGHT   He was now at peace——in his grave.

(2) Use the dash to set off a brief summary.

RIGHT   We need three tools——hammer, saw, and chisel.

RIGHT   A hammer, a saw, and a chisel——all these we shall need.

(3) Use dashes to set off a parenthetical element that is very abrupt or that has commas within it.

RIGHT   He will return——can you believe it?——a major.

RIGHT   He stood up——small, frail, and tense—— staring toward things in his homeland.

—NORA WALN

Caution: The dash should be used sparingly in formal writing. It is more in keeping with an informal style, but even there it becomes ineffective when overused.

Parentheses   ( )

17f   Use parentheses (1) to enclose figures, as in this rule, and (2) to set off parenthetical, supplementary, or illustrative matter.

Parentheses, dashes, commas—all are used to set off parenthetical matter. Parentheses set off parts loosely joined to the sentence and tend to minimize the parts thus set off. Dashes set off sharply abrupt parts and tend to emphasize them. Commas are the mildest, most commonly used separators and tend to leave the parts more closely connected with the sentence. Parentheses and dashes should be used sparingly, only when commas will not serve equally well. (For the use of the comma to set off parenthetical matter, see Section 12d; for the use of the dash, see Section 17e.)

RIGHT   Dashes are used (1) to mark breaks, (2) to set off summaries, and (3) to set off parenthetical elements. [Parentheses enclose figures used to enumerate items.]

RIGHT   Mr. Brown's horses (the best, no doubt, in the whole state) were exhibited at the fair. [Dashes would be used if the writer wished to emphasize the parenthetical matter.]

RIGHT   It is strange (as one reviews all the memories of that good friend and master) to think that there is now a new generation beginning at Haverford that will never know his spell.

—CHRISTOPHER MORLEY

When the sentence demands other marks of punctuation with the parenthetical matter, these marks are placed after the second parenthesis. The comma is never used before the first parenthesis.

Caution: Do not use parentheses or brackets to indicate deletions. Draw a line through any word that you wish to delete.

▶ EXERCISE 4. Compose ten sentences to illustrate the various uses of the dash and parentheses.

▶ EXERCISE 5. Copy the following sentences, supplying colons, dashes, or parentheses where needed. Justify each mark of punctuation used.

1. I quote now from my opponent "I am wholly opposed to wasteful spending but why go into that?"

2. This organization needs more of everything more money, brains, initiative.

3. Our course embraced three projects first, the close reading of Shakespeare's tragedies; second, the writing of critiques on various aspects of these tragedies; and third, the formulation of a tentative theory of tragedy.

4. Two questions well worth asking yourself every day are these What must I do? Have I done it?

5. If our potential enemies I need not be specific insist upon slandering America's good name, we have recourse to two methods of reply words and action.

6. "Dearest" his voice broke and he could say no more.

Brackets [ ]

17g   Use brackets to set off corrections or interpolations made in a quotation by the person using the quotation.

RIGHT   At the office he found a note from the janitor: "Last night i [*sic*] found the door unlocked." [A bracketed *sic* (meaning *thus*) tells the reader that the error appears in the original—is not merely a misprint.]

RIGHT   Every man who loved our vanished friend [Professor Gummere] must know with what realization of shamed incapacity one lays down the tributary pen.   —CHRISTOPHER MORLEY

► EXERCISE 6.   Compose three sentences to illustrate the proper use of brackets.

► GENERAL EXERCISES ON CAPITALS, ITALICS, AND MARKS OF PUNCTUATION

A. Copy the following sentences, entering all necessary capitals, italics (underlining), and marks of punctuation. Change unnecessary capitals to small letters. Justify each change made. Write *C* in place of each correct sentence. (If so directed by your instructor, explain each change by writing above it the appropriate number and subhead.)

1. As for macaulay's point of view everyone knows it was the whig one.   2. In reality this is simplifying too much but however we may describe it there can be no doubt that macaulays vision was singularly alien to the england of the latter years of the seventeenth century like Gibbon, like michelet like the later carlyle he did not to put it succinctly understand what he was talking about. 3. Charles II James II that whole strange age in which religion debauchery intellect faction wit and

brutality seethed and bubbled together in such an extraordinary olla podrida escaped him.   4. He could see parts of it but he could not see into the depths and so much the better he had his point of view.   5. The definiteness the fixity of his position is what is remarkable.   6. he seems to have been created en bloc   7. His maner never changed as soon as he could write at all at the age of eight he wrote in the style of his history   8. The three main factors in his mental growth the clapham sect cambridge holland house were not so much influences as suitable environments for the development of a predetermined personality.   9. Whatever had happened to him, he would always have been a middle-class intellectual with whig views. 10. It is possible however that he may actually have gained something from holland house.[2]

B. Follow directions given under A.

1. "Well Babbitt crossed the floor slowly ponderously seeming a little old   2. "I've always wanted you to have a college degree."   3. he meditatively stamped across the floor again   4. "But I've never now for heavens sake dont repeat this to your mother or shed remove what little hair ive got left but practically ive never done a single thing Ive wanted to do in my whole life   5. I dont knows Ive accomplished anything except just get along 6. I figure out I've made about a quarter of an inch out of a possible hundred rods.   7. Well maybe youll carry things on further I dont know but I do get a kind of sneaking pleasure out of the fact that you knew what you wanted to do and did it   8. Well those folks in there will try to bully you and tame you down.   9. Tell em to go to the devil Ill back you   10. Take your factory job if you want to dont be scared of the family no nor all of zenith nor of yourself the way Ive been   11. go ahead old man the world is yours"   12. arms about each others' shoulders the babbitt men marched into the living-room and faced the swooping family.[3]

[2] Adapted from *Literary Essays*, by Lytton Strachey. Reprinted by permission of Harcourt, Brace and Company, Inc.

[3] Adapted from *Babbitt*, by Sinclair Lewis, copyright, 1922, by Harcourt, Brace and Company, Inc.; renewed, 1950, by Sinclair Lewis. Reprinted by permission of the publishers.

SPELLING

▶ Spelling

18 **Spell every word according to established usage as shown by a good dictionary.**[1]

When one of your misspelled words is pointed out, do not guess at the correct spelling or ask a friend. Consult the dictionary for the correct spelling and write it down in your INDIVIDUAL SPELLING LIST. By keeping a list of all the words you misspell throughout your first college year, and by analyzing and mastering these words as they are called to your attention, you can make steady improvement in your spelling.

The college student cannot count upon much, if any, class time devoted to spelling. Correct spelling is his individual responsibility. If he will follow the program outlined in this section, he can improve his spelling tremendously. *Ignorance of the correct spelling of ordinary words is now, and will probably continue to be, the one universally accepted sign of the uneducated man.*

In order to fix the correct spelling of the word in your memory, use the following:

THE EYE Look carefully at the word (1) as it appears in the dictionary and (2) as you write it *correctly* in your spelling list. Photograph the word with your eye so that you may visualize it later.

THE EAR Pronounce the word aloud several times, clearly and distinctly, in accordance with the phonetic spelling in the dictionary. Note any

difference between the pronunciation and the spelling. Careful pronunciation and an awareness of the difference between spelling and pronunciation help in the spelling of many words.

THE HAND After you are sure of the correct picture and the correct pronunciation, write the word several times—at least once by syllables carefully pronounced. See the correct picture of the word and listen to your pronunciation of it as you write it down. Writing out the word is definitely helpful to many persons as the final step in fixing the correct spelling in the memory.

18a Do not allow mispronunciation to cause misspelling.

▶ EXERCISE 1. In the four lists below determine which words you tend to mispronounce—and to misspell.

(1) Careless omission

Pronounce this first list distinctly, making it a point *not to omit* the italicized letters.

accident*a*lly	*g*eography
ar*c*tic	govern*m*ent
bound*a*ry	li*a*ble
can*d*idate	library
carry*i*ng	literature
consid*e*rable	occasion*a*lly
fam*i*ly	prob*a*bly
Feb*r*uary	quan*t*ity
gen*e*rally	reco*g*nize

---

[1] Careful study of Section **18** will help to eliminate one of the two most common errors in the average student theme.

representative
sophomore
strictly
temperament
used

usually
valuable
veteran
visualize

(2) Careless addition

Pronounce this second list distinctly, making it a point *not to add* any syllable or letter.

disastrous
drowned
elm
entrance
genuine
grievous
handling
height

hindrance
lightning
mischievous
remembrance
similar
suffrage
umbrella

(3) Careless change

Pronounce this third list distinctly, making it a point *not to change* letters, particularly letters in italics.

accumulate
accurate
cavity
divide
existence
formerly
introduce
mathematics

optimistic
particular
prejudice
preparation
privilege
temporary
then (*not* than)

(4) Careless transposition of letters

Pronounce this fourth list distinctly, making it a point *not to transpose* italicized letters.

cavalry
children
hundred

irrelevant
perhaps
perspiration

prefer
prescription
preserve

Add to your INDIVIDUAL SPELLING LIST any of the words in the four lists that you have a tendency to misspell. (If there is no class test on these word lists, or on other lists in Section 18, students may pair themselves outside of class to test one another.)

18b   Distinguish between words of similar sound and spelling, and use the spelling demanded by the meaning.

▶ EXERCISE 2. Study the following list, perhaps ten word groups at a time, to improve your ability to select the word needed to express your meaning. With the aid of your dictionary compose a sentence to illustrate the correct use of each word. Add to your INDIVIDUAL SPELLING LIST any word that you tend to misspell.

accent, ascent, assent
accept, except
advice, advise
affect, effect
all ready, already
all together, altogether
allusive, elusive, illusive
altar, alter
berth, birth
born, borne

its, it's
know, no
later, latter
lead, led
lessen, lesson
lose, loose
moral, morale
of, off
passed, past
peace, piece

capital, capitol
choose, chose
cite, sight, site
coarse, course
complement, compliment
conscience, conscious
council, counsel, consul
decent, descent, dissent
desert, dessert
device, devise

personal, personnel
plain, plane
precede, proceed
presence, presents
principal, principle
prophecy, prophesy
quiet, quite
respectfully, respectively

dual, duel
dyeing, dying
fair, fare
formally, formerly
forth, fourth
freshman, freshmen
hear, here
holy, wholly
instance, instants
irrelevant, irreverent

right, rite, wright, write
sense, since
shone, shown
stationary, stationery
statue, stature, statute
there, their, they're
threw, through
to, too, two
weak, week
weather, whether
whose, who's
your, you're

18c   Distinguish between the prefix and the root.

The root is the base to which prefix or suffix is added. Take care not to double the last letter of the prefix (as in *disappear*) when it is different from the first letter of the root or to drop the last letter of the prefix when the root begins with the same letter (as in *immortal* and *unnecessary*).

dis- (prefix) + appear (root) = disappear
grand- + daughter = granddaughter
im- + mortal = immortal
un- + necessary = unnecessary

18d   Apply the rules for spelling in adding suffixes.

[For more detailed rules consult *Webster's New International Dictionary*, Second Edition, pages lxxix-lxxx or *Webster's New Col-*

legiate *Dictionary*, pages 1195-97 (1949), 1145-47 (1953).]

(1) Drop the final e before a suffix beginning with a vowel but not before a suffix beginning with a consonant.

Drop the final *e* before a suffix beginning with a vowel.

bride	+ -al	=	bridal
combine	+ -ation	=	combination
come	+ -ing	=	coming
fame	+ -ous	=	famous
plume	+ -age	=	plumage
precede	+ -ence	=	precedence
prime	+ -ary	=	primary

Retain the final *e* before a suffix beginning with a consonant.

care	+ -ful	=	careful
care	+ -less	=	careless
entire	+ -ly	=	entirely
place	+ -ment	=	placement
rude	+ -ness	=	rudeness
stale	+ -mate	=	stalemate
state	+ -craft	=	statecraft
sure	+ -ty	=	surety

Some Exceptions: due, duly; awe, awful; hoe, hoeing; singe, singeing. After *c* or *g* the final *e* is retained before suffixes beginning with *a* or *o*: notice, noticeable; courage, courageous.

▶ EXERCISE 3. Explain in each case why the final *e* should be dropped or retained.

1. confine + -ing		6. love + -ly
2. confine + -ment		7. peruse + -al
3. arrange + -ing		8. like + -ness
4. arrange + -ment		9. like + -ing
5. love + -ing		10. like + -ly

(2) Double a final single consonant before a suffix beginning with a vowel (a) if the consonant ends a word of one syllable or an accented syllable and (b) if the consonant is preceded by a single vowel. Otherwise, do not double the consonant.

drop, dro*pp*ing [In a word of one syllable preceded by a single vowel. But preceded by a double vowel: *droop, drooping*.]

admit, admi*tt*ed [In accented syllable, preceded by a single vowel. But in unaccented syllable: *benefit, benefited*.]

▶ EXERCISE 4. Note the importance of the last rule in forming the present participle and the past tense

of verbs. Example: *regret, regretting, regretted*. Supply the present participle for each of the following verbs, justifying the spelling by the rule: *appear, compel, differ, kidnap, occur, plan, profit, remit, scoop, ship*.

(3) Except before a suffix beginning with i, final y is usually changed to i.

defy	+ -ance	=	defiance
happy	+ -ness	=	happiness
mercy	+ -ful	=	merciful
modify	+ -er	=	modifier
modify	+ -ing	=	modifying	[Not changed before *i*]

Note: Verbs ending in *y* preceded by a vowel do not change the *y* to form the third person singular of the present tense or the past participle: *array, arrays, arrayed*. Exceptions: *lay, laid; pay, paid; say, said*.

▶ EXERCISE 5. Explain why the final *y* has, or has not, been retained before the suffixes of the following words: *alloys, craftiness, employed, employs, fanciful, fancying, studied, studying, volleys, volleying*.

(4) Form the plural by adding s to the singular, but by adding es if the plural makes an extra syllable.

boy, boys; cap, cap*s*
bush, bush*es*; match, match*es* [The plural makes an extra syllable.]

Exceptions:

   a. If the noun ends in *y* preceded by a consonant, change the *y* to *i* and add *es*: *sky, skies; comedy, comedies*. But after a vowel the *y* is retained and only *s* is added: *joy, joys*.
   b. If the noun ends in *fe*, change the *fe* to *ve* and add *s*: *knife, knives*.
   c. If the noun ends in *o* preceded by a vowel, add *s*: *radio, radios*.

For other plurals formed irregularly, consult your dictionary.

Note: Add *'s* to form the plurals of letters, signs, and figures. See also **15d** above.

▶ EXERCISE 6. Supply plural forms for words listed below. If words are not covered by the rules given under **18d**, consult your dictionary.

cup	army	foot	passer-by
wife	cameo	son-in-law	room
box	marsh	valley	leaf
child	ox	alumnus	goose
key	sheep	radius	mouse

18e Apply the rules for spelling to avoid confusion of *ei* and *ie*.

When the sound is *ee,* write *ie* (except after *c,* in which case write *ei*).

		(after *c*)
chief	pierce	ceiling
field	relief	conceit
grief	wield	deceive
niece	yield	perceive

When the sound is other than *ee,* usually write *ei.*

eight	heir	sleigh
foreign	neighbor	weigh
height	reign	vein
deign	feign	stein

Exceptions: Either, neither, financier, leisure, seize, species, weird.

► EXERCISE 7. Write out the following words, filling out the blanks with *ei* or *ie.* Justify your choice for each word.

bes—ge	dec—t	fr—ght	r—gned	s—ve
conc—ve	f—nd	pr—st	s—ne	th—f

Hyphenated Words

18f Hyphenate words chiefly to express a unit idea or to avoid ambiguity. (For division of words at the end of a line, see Section 8f.)

A hyphenated word may be either a new coinage made by the writer to fit the occasion, or two words still in the process of becoming one word. In the latter case a recent dictionary will assist in determining current usage. Many words now written as one were originally separate words and later hyphenated in the transitional stage. For example, *post man* first became *post-man* and then *postman.* More recently *basket ball* has passed through the transitional *basket-ball* to *basketball.* The use of the hyphen in compounding is in such a state of flux that authorities often disagree. Some of the more generally accepted uses are listed below.

(1) The hyphen may be used to join two or more words serving as a single adjective before a noun.

[The dictionary ordinarily cannot help with this use of the hyphen. The writer joins recognized words to coin a new unit idea to fit the occasion.]

RIGHT   A well-paved road, a know-it-all expression, a bluish-green dress

But the hyphen is omitted when the first word of the compound is an adverb ending in *-ly* or when the words follow the noun.

RIGHT   A slightly elevated walk, a gently sloping terrace
RIGHT   The road was well paved.
RIGHT   His expression suggested that he knew it all.
RIGHT   The dress was a bluish green.

(2) The hyphen is used with compound numbers from twenty-one to ninety-nine.

RIGHT   twenty-two, forty-five, ninety-eight, one hundred twenty, one hundred twenty-six

(3) The hyphen is used to avoid ambiguity or an awkward union of letters or syllables between prefix or suffix and root.

RIGHT   His re-creation of the setting was perfect.
RIGHT   Fishing is good recreation.

RIGHT   He re-covered the leaky roof.
RIGHT   He recovered his health.

RIGHT   micro-organism, re-enter, semi-independent, shell-like, thrill-less, sub-subcommittee

(4) The hyphen is used with the prefixes *ex-, self-, all-,* and the suffix *-elect.*

RIGHT   ex-governor, self-made, all-American, mayor-elect

► EXERCISES ON SPELLING

A. First on the GENERAL SPELLING LIST
B. Then on your INDIVIDUAL SPELLING LIST

The general list of words most frequently misspelled is made up of 654 (651 + *it's, too, two*) common words that everyone needs in his business and social life. The list is drawn, by kind permission of Dean Thomas Clark Pollock, from his recent study of 31,375 misspellings in the written work of college students.[2] In the list as given below the words *its, it's* and *to, too, two* are treated as word groups; all other words are listed individually, usually omitting any word that is spelled the same as a part of a longer word. For example, the list

[2] See Thomas Clark Pollock, "Spelling Report," *College English,* XVI (November, 1954), 102-09; and Thomas Clark Pollock and William D. Baker, *The University Spelling Book,* Prentice-Hall, Inc., New York, 1955, pp. 6-12.

includes *definitely* but not *definite*, *existence* but not *exist*, *performance* but not *perform*. Each of the first hundred words in the general list below was misspelled more than forty-three times (or more than an *average* of forty-three times in the case of words grouped in Dean Pollock's report). The letters which caused the greatest difficulty are indicated by italics.

A. With the aid of your dictionary study the words in the general list in small units (perhaps fifty words at a time) until you feel sure (1) of the meaning and (2) of the spelling of each word. Then without the aid of your dictionary test yourself by writing sentences in which each word is correctly used and spelled. Add to your INDIVIDUAL SPELLING LIST each word that you tend to misspell.

GENERAL SPELLING LIST

I. *The Hundred Words Most Frequently Misspelled* [3]

1. accommodate	21. define	41. mere	60. prevalent	80. separation *
2. achievement	22. describe	42. necessary	61. principal	81. shining
3. acquire	23. description	43. occasion *	62. principle	82. similar *
4. all right	24. disastrous	44. occurred	63. privilege *	83. studying
5. among	25. effect	45. occurring	64. probably	84. succeed
6. apparent	26. embarrass	46. occurrence	65. proceed	85. succession
7. argument	27. environment	47. opinion	66. procedure	86. surprise
8. arguing	28. exaggerate	48. opportunity	67. professor	87. technique
9. belief *	29. existence *	49. paid	68. profession	88. than
10. believe *	30. existent *	50. particular	69. prominent	89. then
11. beneficial	31. experience		70. pursue	90. their *
12. benefited	32. explanation	51. performance	71. quiet	91. there *
13. category	33. fascinate	52. personal	72. receive *	92. they're *
14. coming	34. height	53. personnel	73. receiving *	93. thorough
15. comparative	35. interest	54. possession	74. recommend	94. transferred
16. conscious	36. its (it's)	55. possible	75. referring *	95. to * (too,* two *)
17. controversy	37. led	56. practical	76. repetition	96. unnecessary
18. controversial	38. lose	57. precede *	77. rhythm	97. villain
19. definitely	39. losing	58. prejudice	78. sense	98. woman
20. definition	40. marriage	59. prepare	79. separate *	99. *write*
				100. *writing*

II. *The Next 551 Words Most Frequently Misspelled*

101. absence	121. accurately	141. affect	160. another	180. arrangement
102. abundance	122. accuser	142. afraid	161. annually	181. article
103. abundant	123. accuses	143. against	162. anticipated	182. atheist
104. academic	124. accusing	144. aggravate	163. apologetically	183. athlete
105. academically	125. accustom	145. aggressive	164. apologized	184. athletic
106. academy	126. acquaintance	146. alleviate	165. apology	185. attack
107. acceptable	127. across	147. allotted	166. apparatus	186. attempts
108. acceptance	128. actuality	148. allotment	167. appearance	187. attendance
109. accepting	129. actually	149. allowed	168. applies	188. attendant
110. accessible	130. adequately	150. allows	169. applying	189. attended
111. accidental	131. admission		170. appreciate	190. attitude
112. accidentally	132. admittance	151. already	171. appreciation	191. audience
113. acclaim	133. adolescence	152. altar	172. approaches	192. authoritative
114. accompanied	134. adolescent	153. all together	173. appropriate	193. authority
115. accompanies	135. advantageous	154. altogether	174. approximate	194. available
116. accompaniment	136. advertisement	155. amateur	175. area	195. bargain
117. accompanying	137. advertiser	156. amount	176. arise	196. basically
118. accomplish	138. advertising	157. analysis	177. arising	197. basis
119. accuracy	139. advice	158. analyze	178. arouse	198. beauteous
120. accurate	140. advise	159. and	179. arousing	199. beautified

[3] An asterisk indicates the most frequently misspelled words among the first hundred. The most troublesome letters for all 654 words are indicated by italics.

200. beautiful
201. beauty
202. become
203. becoming
204. before
205. began
206. beginner
207. beginning
208. behavior
209. bigger
210. biggest
211. boundary
212. breath
213. breathe
214. brilliance
215. brilliant
216. Britain
217. Britannica
218. burial
219. buried
220. bury
221. business
222. busy
223. calendar
224. capitalism
225. career
226. careful
227. careless
228. carried
229. carrier
230. carries
231. carrying
232. cemetery
233. certainly
234. challenge
235. changeable
236. changing
237. characteristic
238. characterized
239. chief
240. children
241. Christian
242. Christianity
243. choice
244. choose
245. chose
246. cigarette
247. cite
248. clothes
249. commercial
250. commission
251. committee
252. communist
253. companies
254. compatible

255. competition
256. competitive
257. competitor
258. completely
259. concede
260. conceivable
261. conceive
262. concentrate
263. concern
264. condemn
265. confuse
266. confusion
267. connotation
268. connote
269. conscience
270. conscientious
271. consequently
272. considerably
273. consistency
274. consistent
275. contemporary
276. continuous(ly)
277. controlled
278. controlling
279. convenience
280. convenient
281. correlate
282. council
283. counselor
284. countries
285. create
286. criticism
287. criticize
288. cruelly
289. cruelty
290. curiosity
291. curious
292. curriculum
293. dealt
294. deceive
295. decided
296. decision
297. dependent
298. desirability
299. desire
300. despair
301. destruction
302. detriment
303. devastating
304. device
305. difference
306. different
307. difficult
308. dilemma
309. diligence
310. dining

311. disappoint
312. disciple
313. discipline
314. discrimination
315. discussion
316. disease
317. disgusted
318. disillusioned
319. dissatisfied
320. divide
321. divine
322. doesn't
323. dominant
324. dropped
325. due
326. during
327. eager
328. easily
329. efficiency
330. efficient
331. eighth
332. eliminate
333. emperor
334. emphasize
335. encourage
336. endeavor
337. enjoy
338. enough
339. enterprise
340. entertain
341. entertainment
342. entirely
343. entrance
344. equipment
345. equipped
346. escapade
347. escape
348. especially
349. etc.
350. everything

351. evidently
352. excellence
353. excellent
354. except
355. excitable
356. exercise
357. expense
358. experiment
359. extremely
360. fallacy
361. familiar
362. families
363. fantasies
364. fantasy
365. fashions
366. favorite

367. fictitious
368. field
369. finally
370. financially
371. financier
372. foreigners
373. forty
374. forward
375. fourth
376. friendliness
377. fulfill
378. fundamentally
379. further
380. gaiety
381. generally
382. genius
383. government
384. governor
385. grammar
386. grammatically
387. group
388. guaranteed
389. guidance
390. guiding
391. handled
392. happened
393. happiness
394. hear
395. here
396. heroes
397. heroic
398. heroine
399. hindrance
400. hopeless
401. hoping
402. hospitalization
403. huge
404. humorist
405. humorous
406. hundred
407. hunger
408. hungrily
409. hungry
410. hypocrisy
411. hypocrite
412. ideally
413. ignorance
414. ignorant
415. imaginary
416. imagination
417. imagine
418. immediately
419. immense
420. importance
421. incidentally
422. increase

423. indefinite
424. independence
425. independent
426. indispensable
427. individually
428. industries
429. inevitable
430. influence
431. influential
432. ingenious
433. ingredient
434. initiative
435. intellect
436. intelligence
437. intelligent
438. interference
439. interpretation
440. interrupt
441. involve
442. irrelevant
443. irresistible
444. irritable
445. jealousy
446. knowledge
447. laboratory
448. laborer
449. laboriously
450. laid
451. later
452. leisurely
453. lengthening
454. license
455. likelihood
456. likely
457. likeness
458. listener
459. literary
460. literature
461. liveliest
462. livelihood
463. liveliness
464. lives
465. loneliness
466. lonely
467. loose
468. loss
469. luxury
470. magazine
471. magnificence
472. magnificent
473. maintenance
474. management
475. maneuver
476. manner
477. manufacturers
478. material

479. mathematics	514. pamphlets	550. psychology	585. simple
480. matter	515. parallel		586. simply
481. maybe	516. parliament	551. psychopathic	587. since
482. meant	517. paralyzed	552. psychosomatic	588. sincerely
483. mechanics	518. passed	553. quantity	589. sociology
484. medical	519. past	554. really	590. sophomore
485. medicine	520. peace	555. realize	591. source
486. medieval	521. peculiar	556. rebel	592. speaking
487. melancholy	522. perceive	557. recognize	593. speech
488. methods	523. permanent	558. regard	594. sponsor
489. miniature	524. permit	559. relative	595. stabilization
490. minutes	525. persistent	560. relieve	596. stepped
491. mischief	526. persuade	561. religion	597. stories
492. moral	527. pertain	562. remember	598. story
493. morale	528. phase	563. reminisce	599. straight
494. morally	529. phenomenon	564. represent	600. strength
495. mysterious	530. philosophy	565. resources	
496. narrative	531. physical	566. response	601. stretch
497. naturally	532. piece	567. revealed	602. strict
498. Negroes	533. planned	568. ridicule	603. stubborn
499. ninety	534. plausible	569. ridiculous	604. substantial
500. noble	535. playwright	570. roommate	605. subtle
	536. pleasant	571. sacrifice	606. sufficient
501. noticeable	537. politician	572. safety	607. summary
502. noticing	538. political	573. satire	608. summed
503. numerous	539. practice	574. satisfied	609. suppose
504. obstacle	540. predominant	575. satisfy	610. suppress
505. off	541. preferred	576. scene	611. surrounding
506. omit	542. presence	577. schedule	612. susceptible
507. operate	543. prestige	578. seize	613. suspense
508. oppose	544. primitive	579. sentence	614. swimming
509. opponent	545. prisoners	580. sergeant	615. symbol
510. opposite	546. propaganda	581. several	616. synonymous
511. optimism	547. propagate	582. shepherd	617. temperament
512. organization	548. prophecy	583. significance	618. tendency
513. original	549. psychoanalysis	584. simile	619. themselves

620. theories	
621. theory	
622. therefore	
623. those	
624. thought	
625. together	
626. tomorrow	
627. tragedy	
628. tremendous	
629. tried	
630. tries	
631. tyranny	
632. undoubtedly	
633. unusually	
634. useful	
635. useless	
636. using	
637. vacuum	
638. valuable	
639. varies	
640. various	
641. view	
642. vengeance	
643. warrant	
644. weather	
645. weird	
646. where	
647. whether	
648. whole	
649. whose	
650. yield	
651. you're	

B. *Analyze your* INDIVIDUAL SPELLING LIST *to learn why you misspell words and how you can most readily improve your spelling.*

Spelling is an individual matter. No two persons make exactly the same errors in spelling. Therefore it is important that you compile and master your INDIVIDUAL SPELLING LIST. Once you analyze this list to determine why you misspell words, you can concentrate on the part of Section 18 (a, b, c, d, e, or f) that treats your difficulty.

When each misspelled word is first called to your attention, consult your dictionary and copy down the correct spelling as directed at the opening of Section 18. Then write out the word by syllables, underline the trouble spot, and indicate why you misspelled the word, by using the letter **a** (omission, addition, change, or transposition), **b** (confusion of words similar in sound), **c** (failure to distinguish prefix from root), **d** (confusion of *ei* and *ie*), **e** (error in adding suffix), **f** (error in hyphenation), or **g** (any other reason for misspelling). See the examples on page 866.

EXAMPLES:

Word (correctly spelled)	Word (spelled by syllables)—with trouble spots underlined	Reason for error
1. candidate	can di date	**a** (letter omitted)
2. athlete	ath lete	**a** (letter added)
3. prejudice	prej u dice	**a** (letter changed)
4. marriage	mar riage	**a** (letters transposed)
5. among	a mong	**b** (confused with *young*)
6. its	its	**b** (confused with *it's*)
7. misspell	mis spell	**c** (prefix not distinguished)
8. bridal	brid al	**d** (drop final *e* before vowel)
9. careful	care ful	**d** (retain final *e* before consonant)
10. duly	du ly	**d** (exception to the rule)
11. occurred	oc curred	**d** (before a vowel double final single consonant after a single vowel in accented syllable)
12. merciful	mer ci ful	**d** (change final *y* to *i* except before *i*)
13. believe	be lieve	**e** (*ie* when the sound is *ee*)
14. receive	re ceive	**e** (*ei* when the sound is *ee* after *c*)
15. forty-five	forty-five	**f** (hyphen with compound number)

DICTION

▶ Good Use—Glossary

19 When in doubt about the meaning of a word, consult a good dictionary. Select the word most appropriate to the occasion. In standard writing employ only words in general and approved use.

Words are the coinage of thought, the medium by which men exchange ideas. To possess a large and varied vocabulary is to possess intellectual wealth. This wealth is not the private property of the few, but a common fund from which anyone may draw as much as he needs. The treasury of language is a good dictionary.

19a Use only a good dictionary, and be sure to use it intelligently.

A good dictionary of the English language is based upon the scientific examination of the writing and speaking habits of the English-speaking world; it records the origin, development, and changing use of words. Any dictionary is reliable only to the extent that it is based on usage. There can be no perfect dictionary, as Dr. Johnson recognized long ago. Among the full or unabridged dictionaries, the following are especially useful:

Webster's New International Dictionary. Second Edition; Springfield, Massachusetts: **G. & C.** Merriam Company, 1934, 1950.

New Century Dictionary. 2 vols. New York: D. Appleton-Century Company, 1948.

New Standard Dictionary. New York: Funk & Wagnalls Company, 1947.

A New English Dictionary on Historical Principles. 10 vols. and Supplement. Oxford: Clarendon Press, 1888-1933. (A corrected reissue in twelve volumes and one supplementary volume appeared in 1933 under the title *The Oxford English Dictionary.*)

Most students must consult these large dictionaries in the library. But even if a student possesses a large dictionary, he will still find indispensable, for more convenient use, one of the smaller dictionaries on the college or adult level, such as the following:

> *American College Dictionary* (Text Edition, 1948)
> *New College Standard Dictionary* (1947)
> *Webster's New Collegiate Dictionary* (1956)
> *Webster's New World Dictionary* (1953)

Note: Dictionaries are usually kept up to date by frequent slight revisions, sometimes with supplementary pages for new words. Long periods elapse between thorough revisions.

Intelligent use of a dictionary requires some knowledge of its plan and special abbreviations as given in the introductory matter. Let us take, for example:

ex·pel (ĭk spĕl′), *v.t.,* **-pelled, -pelling. 1.** to drive or force out or away; discharge or eject: *to expel air from the lungs, an invader from a country.* **2.** to cut off from membership or relations: *to expel a student from a college.* [ME *expelle(n),* t. L: m. *expellere* drive out] —**ex·pel′·la·ble,** *adj.* —**ex·pel′ler,** *n.* —**Syn. 2.** oust, dismiss.

ex·pel′ (ĕks·pĕl′; ĭks-), *v. t.;* EX·PELLED′ (-pĕld′); EX·PEL′LING. [L. *expellere, expulsum,* fr. *ex* out + *pellere* to drive.] **1.** To drive or force out; to eject. **2.** To cut off from membership in or the privileges of an institution or society; as, *to expel* a student from college. — **Syn.** See EJECT. — **ex·pel′la·ble,** *adj.*

ex·pel (ik-spel′), *v.t.* [EXPELLED (-speld′), EXPELLING], [ME. *expellen;* L. *expellere; ex-,* out + *pellere,* to thrust, drive], **1.** to drive out by force; make leave; eject. **2.** to dismiss or send away by authority; deprive of rights, membership, etc.: as, he was *expelled* from school because of misconduct. —*SYN.* see **eject.**

(1) Spelling and pronunciation. The spelling of *expel* (by syllables separated by a dot) is given first, with pronunciation indicated (within parentheses) immediately following. The sound of each letter is shown by the key to pronunciation at the bottom of the page or on one of the inside covers. *Webster's* (*Webster's New Collegiate Dictionary*) gives two acceptable pronunciations for the first syllable; *ACD* (*American College Dictionary*) and *WNWD* (*Webster's New World Dictionary*) give only one. The accent on *expel,* as shown by the mark (′), falls on the last syllable.

(2) Grammatical information comes next: *v. t.* classifies *expel* as a "verb, transitive"; the words in boldface (*ACD*) or in small capitals (*Webster's* and *WNWD*) give the forms for the past participle and the present participle; other parts of speech formed from the base word are listed toward the end of the entry.

(3) Meanings (including synonyms and antonyms). Two separate meanings of *expel* are shown after the numbers 1 and 2. In *Webster's* and in *WNWD* such definitions are arranged in the historical order of development, thus enabling the reader to see at a glance something of the history of the word. *But he should note that the meaning which developed first, and is consequently placed first, may no longer be the most common.* For example, *Webster's* and *WNWD,* in defining *prevent,* begin with the original but obsolete meaning "to anticipate" and come later to the present meaning "to hinder." The *ACD,* which puts the most common meaning first, begins with "to hinder" and comes later to the obsolete meaning. With *expel,* as with many words, the meaning that first developed is still the more common of the two.

The meaning is made clearer by comparing the word with other words of similar meaning (synonyms, abbreviated Syn.) or opposite meaning (antonyms, abbreviated Ant.). The *ACD* lists for *expel* the two synonyms *oust* and *dismiss; Webster's* and *WNWD* refer to another word *eject* under which a very helpful special paragraph compares *expel* with *eject* and other synonyms.

For more detailed information about *expel* the student may consult one of the unabridged dictionaries in the library. In *Webster's New International Dictionary* the entry for this word is more than twice as long as that in the *Collegiate* or the *ACD,* and includes a quotation from Spenser to illustrate the use of the word. *The Oxford English Dictionary,* the most detailed of all dictionaries of the English language, quotes some fifty English writers of the past five or six hundred years to show the exact meaning of *expel* at each stage of its history. The following passage (about one third of the complete entry) illustrates the method used by the *OED.*

Expel (ekspe'l), *v.* Forms: 4-5 expelle, 6-7 expell, 6- expel. [ad. L. *expell-ĕre,* f. *ex-* out + *pellĕre* to drive, thrust: cf. COMPEL. OF. had *espellir,* and in 15th c. *expeller.*]
1. *trans.* To drive or thrust out; to eject by force. Const. *from* (rarely *out of*) also with double obj. (by omission of *from*).
a. With obj. a person, etc.: To eject, dislodge by force from a position; to banish from, compel to quit, a place or country.
c1489 CAXTON *Sonnes of Aymon* xx. 446 Reynawde and his brethern were thus expelled out of it [mountalban]. 1532 MORE *Confut. Tindale* Wks. 810/2 God .. expelled those heretikes and scismatikes out of heauen. 1577 tr. *Bullinger's Decades* (1592) 838 The Apostles receiued power from the Lord..that they should expell and cast them [the devils] out. 1628 HOBBES *Thucyd.* (1822) 8 The Bœotians ..expelld Arne by the Thessalians seated themselues in that Country [Bœotia]. c1710 C. FIENNES *Diary* (1888) 266 Such a State takes Care..to Expel him their Dominions by proclamation. 1749 WEST tr. *Pindar's Olympic Odes* xii. 36 Sedition's Civil Broils Expell'd thee from thy native Crete. 1754 HUME *Hist. Eng.* I. xi. 229 He sent .. two knights..to expel them the convent. 1863 FR. A. KEMBLE *Resid. Georgia* 31 Bidding the elder boys..expel the poultry.
b. With a material thing as obj.: To drive out from a receptacle, etc. by mechanical force; to discharge, send off (*e.g.* a bullet from a gun, † an arrow from a bow); to drive off or dislodge (a substance) from a chemical compound, mixture, solution, etc. Also, † *To expel forth.*
1669 STURMY *Mariner's Mag.* v. xii. 80 The Shot is .. expelled with no other thing, than by the Air's exaltation. 1695 WOODWARD *Nat. Hist. Earth* III. (1723) 151 It [water] is usualy expelled forth in vast Quantities. a1700 DRYDEN (J.), The virgin huntress was not slow T'expel the shaft from her contracted bow. c1700 IMISON *Sch. Art* I. 74 Expelling the water into the bason. 1807 T. THOMSON *Chem.* (ed. 3) II. 394 Alcohol..absorbs about its own weight of nitrous gas, which cannot afterwards be expelled by heat. 1838 — *Chem. Org. Bodies* 168 Not capable of being expelled by a stronger base. 1860 MAURY *Phys. Geog. Sea* xi. § 512 If still more heat be applied .. the air will be entirely expelled. 1878 HUXLEY *Physiogr.* 77 The matter .. thus expelled from the powder by heat.

From the *Oxford English Dictionary* by permission of The Clarendon Press, Oxford. Copyright 1933.

(4) Origin; development of the language. The origin of the word—also called *derivation* or *etymology*—is shown in square brackets, as in the *ACD:* [ME. *expelle(n),* t. L.: m. *expellere* drive out]. This bracketed information means

that *expel* was used in English during the Middle English (ME.) period, A.D. 1100-1500, with the spelling *expelle(n);* that it was taken from (t.) Latin (L.) and is a modification of (m.) the Latin word *expellere* meaning "to drive out." *Webster's* does not give the Middle English form of *expel,* but it does break down the Latin source *expellere* into *ex* "out" + *pellere* "to drive." The original Latin, meaning "to drive out," supplies the basic definition of the English word. Frequently the origins of words give special insight into meanings. *Automobile,* for example, originally signified "self-moving"; *to sympathize* was "to suffer with"; *to telegraph* was "to write far off." Any student who wishes to get at the heart of a word cannot afford to ignore its origin.

Common prefixes (such as *ex-,* out, *ad-,* to, *circum-,* around, *de-,* from or down, *dis-,* from, *inter-,* between, *pre-,* before, *re-,* back, *sub-,* under, *sur-,* over, and *trans-,* across), suffixes (such as *-able,* capable of being, *-age,* amount of, *-al,* pertaining to, *-ation,* act of, *-ic* or *-ical,* like, *-ile,* of or suited for, *-ish,* of the nature of, *-ive,* given to, *-ous,* full of, and *-ty* or *-ity,* state of), and combining forms (such as *tele-,* far off, *grapho-,* writing, and *phono-,* sound) are listed separately in the dictionary and are well worth study because they make up a part of the meaning of many English words.

The bracketed information given by a good dictionary is especially rich in meaning when associated with the historical development of our language. English is one of the Indo-European (IE.) [1] languages, which apparently had at one time, thousands of years ago, a common vocabulary. In the recorded Indo-European languages, many of the more familiar words are remarkably alike. Our word *mother,* for example, is *mater* in Latin (L.), *meter* in Greek (Gk.), and *matar* in the ancient Persian and in the Sanskrit of India. Our pronoun *me* is exactly the same in Latin, in Greek, in Persian, and in Sanskrit. Words in different languages which apparently go back to a parent language are called *cognates.* The large numbers of these cognates make it seem probable that at one time, perhaps three thousand years

[1] The parenthetical abbreviations for languages here and on the next few pages are those commonly used in the bracketed derivations in dictionaries.

before Christ, the Indo-Europeans lived in one region and spoke a common language. By the opening of the Christian era they had spread themselves over Europe and as far east as India. Of the eight or nine language groups into which they had developed (see the inside back cover of the *WNWD* or the entry "Indo-European languages" in *Webster's*), English is chiefly concerned with the Greek (on the eastern Mediterranean), with the Latin (on the central and western Mediterranean), and with the Germanic (in northwestern Europe), from which English is descended.

Two thousand years ago the Greek, the Latin, and the Germanic each comprised a more or less unified language group. After the fall of the Roman Empire in the fifth century, the several Latin-speaking divisions developed independently into the modern Romance languages, chief of which are Italian, French, and Spanish. Long before the fall of Rome the Germanic group was breaking up into three groups: (1) East Germanic, represented by the Goths, who were to play a large part in the last century of the Roman Empire before losing themselves in its ruins; (2) North Germanic, represented by Old Norse (ON.), or Viking, from which we have modern Danish (Dan.) and Swedish (Swed.), Norwegian (Norw.) and Icelandic (Icel.); and (3) West Germanic, the direct ancestor of English, Dutch, and German.

The English language may be said to have begun about 450 A.D. when Jutes, Angles, and Saxons, West Germanic tribes, began the conquest of what is now England and either absorbed or drove out the Celtic-speaking inhabitants. The next six or seven hundred years are known as the Old English (OE.) or Anglo-Saxon (AS.) period of the English language. The fifty or sixty thousand words then in the language were chiefly Anglo-Saxon, with a small mixture of Old Norse words as a result of the Danish (Viking) conquests of England beginning in the eighth century. But the Old Norse words were so much like the Anglo-Saxon that they cannot always be distinguished.

The transitional period—about 1100 to 1500 —from Old English to Modern English is known as Middle English (ME.). Changes already under way were accelerated by the Nor-

man Conquest beginning in 1066. The Normans or "Northmen" had settled in northern France during the Viking invasions and had adopted the Old French (OF.) in place of their native Old Norse. The Normans, coming over to England by thousands, made French the language of the King's court in London and of the ruling classes (both French and English) throughout the land while the masses continued to speak English. But the language that emerged toward the end of the fifteenth century had lost most of its Anglo-Saxon inflections and had taken on thousands of French words (derived originally from Latin). The language, however, was still basically English, not French, in its structure. The marked and steady development of the language (until it was partly stabilized by the beginning of printing in London in 1476) is suggested by the following passages, two from Old English and two from Middle English.

Hē ǣrst gescēop   eorðan bearnum
He first created   for earth's children

heofon tō hrōfe,   hālig scippend.
heaven as a roof,   holy creator.
[From the so-called "Hymn of Cædmon." Middle of the Old English Period.]

Ēalā, hū lēas and hū unwrest is þysses middan-
Alas! how false and how unstable is this mid-

eardes wēla. Sē þe wæs ǣrur rīce cyng and
world's weal! He that was before powerful king and

maniges landes hlāford, hē næfde þā ealles landes
of many lands lord, he had not then of all land

būton seofon fōt mǣl,
but seven foot space.
[From the *Anglo-Saxon Chronicle*, A.D. 1087. End of the Old English Period.]

A knight ther was, and that a worthy man,
That fro the tyme that he first bigan
To ryden out, he loved chivalrye,
Trouthe and honour, fredom and curteisye.
[From Chaucer's Prologue to the *Canterbury Tales*, about 1385.]

Thenne within two yeres king Uther felle seke of a grete maladye. And in the meane whyle hys enemyes usurpped upon hym, and dyd a grete bataylle upon his men, and slewe many of his peple.
[From Sir Thomas Malory's *Morte Darthur*, printed 1485.]

▶ EXERCISE 1. With the aid of your dictionary select the five words in the passage from Malory's *Morte Darthur* that were taken into English—after the Norman Conquest, of course—from the Old French. Copy both the Old French word and the Latin source (if given). (Note that in this passage from Malory all words of one syllable are from Anglo-Saxon. The preposition *upon* may be a combination of two Anglo-Saxon words, *up* and *on,* but more probably it was taken from the Old Norse during the Danish invasions of Britain during the ninth century.)

Although Sir Thomas Malory wrote nearly five hundred years ago, we can still read his *Morte Darthur* with relative ease. William Caxton, who printed Malory's book in 1485, observed that "our language as now used varieth far from that which was used and spoken when I was born." The books he was printing, with millions that have followed since, have helped greatly to stabilize the language.

A striking feature of Modern English (since 1500) is its immense vocabulary. Old English used perhaps fifty thousand words, very largely native Anglo-Saxon; Middle English used perhaps a hundred thousand, many taken through the French from Latin and others directly from Latin; and now our unabridged dictionaries list over half a million. To make up this tremendous word hoard, we have borrowed most heavily from the Latin, but we have drawn some words from almost every known language. English writers of the sixteenth century were especially eager to interlard their works with words from Latin authors; and as Englishmen pushed out to colonize and to trade in many parts of the globe, they brought home new words as well as goods. Modern science and technology have drawn heavily from the Greek. The result of all this borrowing is that English has become the richest, most cosmopolitan of all languages.

In the process of enlarging our vocabulary we have lost most of our original Anglo-Saxon words. But the eight or ten thousand that are left make up the most familiar, most useful part of our vocabulary. Practically all of our simple verbs, our articles, conjunctions, prepositions, and pronouns are native Anglo-Saxon; and so are many of our familiar nouns, adjectives, and adverbs. Every speaker and writer uses these native words over and over, much more frequently than the borrowed words. If every word is counted every time it is used, the percentage of native words runs very high, usually between 70 and 90 per cent. Milton's percentage was 81, Tennyson's 88, Shakespeare's about 90, and that of the King James Bible about 94. English has been enriched by its extensive borrowings without losing its individuality; it is still fundamentally the *English* language.

▶ EXERCISE 2. Note the origins of the words on a typical page (or on several typical pages) of your dictionary. Copy down examples of words derived from (1) Anglo-Saxon; (2) Old French or Latin through Old French; (3) Latin directly; (4) Greek through Latin; (5) Greek directly; (6) other languages.

(5) Dictionary labels—levels of usage. An unabridged English dictionary attempts to define the half million or more words that have been used by English writers during the Modern English period (since about 1500). The better abridged dictionaries for adults—such as *Webster's, ACD,* or *WNWD*—list between 100,000 and 150,000 words. The dictionary uses labels (*Colloq., Slang, Dial., Obs., Archaic, Eccl., Naut.,* etc.) to show the standing or special use of a word. Any word, or any meaning of a word, that does not have one of these labels is said to be "standard," that is, it belongs to the general vocabulary and may be used whenever appropriate to the writer's meaning and style. Labeled words, or labeled meanings of words, should be used with appropriate care as suggested below in the "Outline for Dictionary Labels" and treated further under **19 b, c, d, e, f, g,** and **h** on pages 873-74.

Note that none of the three entries illustrated on page 867 gives a label before either of the two meanings for *expel.* Thus we see that the word is fully standard. But let us note *Webster's* entry for *impose,* shown on page 871, in which three of the meanings are labeled.

For the transitive verb *impose* seven different meanings are given, of which the first, second, fifth, and sixth are unlabeled and therefore standard. The third, labeled *Eccl.,* is a technical word in ecclesiastical usage; the

im·pose' (ĭm·pōz'), *v. t.* [F. *imposer*, fr. *im-* in + *poser* to place.] **1.** To subject (one) *to* a charge, penalty, or the like. **2.** To lay as a charge, duty, command, etc.; hence, to levy; inflict; as, to *impose* burdens or a penalty. **3.** *Eccl.* To lay on (the hands), as in confirmation. **4.** *Archaic.* To place; deposit. **5.** To pass or palm off; as, to *impose* inferior goods on a buyer. **6.** To obtrude; as, to *impose* oneself upon others. **7.** *Print.* To arrange in order on a table of stone or metal (**imposing stone** *or* **table**) and lock up in a chase. — *v. i.* **1.** To impress oneself or itself, esp. obnoxiously; presume; as, to *impose* upon good nature. **2.** To practice tricks or deception; — with *on* or *upon.* — **im·pos'er** (-pōz'ẽr), *n.*

By permission. From Webster's New Collegiate Dictionary
Copyright, 1949, 1951, 1953
by G. & C. Merriam Co.

fourth, labeled *Archaic,* is antiquated—no longer used in ordinary writing; and the seventh, labeled *Print.,* is a technical term used in printing. Neither of the two meanings of the intransitive verb *impose* is labeled, and therefore both are standard.

OUTLINE FOR DICTIONARY LABELS

(*a*) *Standard words*—not labeled by the dictionary.

(Used freely to suit the purpose and style of the writer—usually the commonest word that will express the exact meaning.)

FORMAL   He has none. It is impossible. We should consider the essentials.

INFORMAL   He hasn't any. It's impossible. Let's consider essentials.

(*b*) *Colloquialisms*—labeled *Colloq.*

(Used freely in conversation and in very informal writing.)

EXAMPLES   *hasn't got* any. It's *no go.* Let's get down to *brass tacks.*

(*c*) *Slang*—labeled *Slang.*

(Used only with special care, and never in formal writing.)

EXAMPLES   He has been *done in* (for *done away with* or *killed*). The speech was all hooey (for *nonsense*).

(*d*) *Dialectal words* (*localisms, provincialisms*) —labeled *Dial., Scot., South African,* etc.

(Generally avoided in writing because the words may be known only in a limited region.)

EXAMPLE   The sheep were kept in a kraal (for *enclosure*).

(*e*) *Illiteracies* (*vulgarisms*)—labeled *Illit.* or *Vulgar* (if included in the dictionary at all.

(Always avoided except to illustrate illiterate speech in written dialogue.)

EXAMPLE   He ain't got none.

(*f*) *Obsolete and archaic words*—labeled *Obs., Archaic.*

(No longer used, but retained in the dictionary to explain older writings.)

EXAMPLE   Edward was he *hight* (for *called*).

(*g*) *Technical words*—labeled *Law, Med.*[2] (medicine), *Naut.* (nautical), *Phar.* (pharmacy), *Surg.* (surgery), *Zool.* (zoology), etc.

(Generally limited in use to writing or speaking for specialized groups.)

EXAMPLE   The *hyperemia* (for *increase in blood*) in the left arm is difficult to explain.

(*h*) *Poetic words*—labeled *Poetic.*

(Avoided in general writing and speaking.)

EXAMPLE   The man sat oft (for *often*) in the moonlight.

The labeling or classification of words is often difficult, for the language is constantly changing and many words are on the borderline, as between slang and colloquial or between colloquial and standard; and it is to be expected that good dictionaries will frequently differ in classifying such words. Although classes of words (especially standard, colloquial, illiterate) are commonly referred to as "levels," we are not to think of one class as always higher or better than another. Actually any one of the eight classes may be the best for a given occasion. Even the illiterate word is best when the writer is trying to illustrate the speech of the uneducated. Technical language is often best in speech and writing addressed to those in one's profession. The occasion and the purpose of the writer or speaker will determine the best words to select. The standard (unlabeled) words which make up the bulk of the English vocabulary are usually best for general writing and, along with colloquialisms, for polite conversation. Our standard words range from the very learned to the very simple and are adequate for the most dignified or the most informal style.

2 The *WNWD* writes "in *law*," "in *medicine*," etc., and thus avoids abbreviations.

► EXERCISE 3. Classify according to the labels of your dictionary the thirty-three words beginning with *hunky*.

Example: The thirty-three words in *Webster's New Collegiate Dictionary* preceding *hunky* (beginning with hummingbird) may be classified as indicated below. *Italics* indicates that a word belongs in the class in respect to one or more, but not all, of its meanings.

a. STANDARD (not labeled) hummingbird, *hummock, humor,* humorist, humoristic, *humorous, hump,* humpback, humpbacked, humped, humph, humpy, humus, Hun, *hunch,* hunchback, hunchbacked, hundred, hundredfold, hundred-percenter, hundredth, hundredweight, hung, *Hungarian,* hunger, hungeringly, hunger strike, *hungry,* hunks

b. COLLOQUIAL hunch, hunk

c. SLANG *hump, Hungarian*

d. DIALECTAL *hummock, hump,* hunkers

e. ILLITERATE (None listed)

f. OBSOLETE (OR ARCHAIC) *humor, humorous, hunch, Hungarian,* hungerly, *hungry*

g. TECHNICAL *humor,* humoresque, *humorous, hundred*

h. POETIC (None listed)

► FURTHER EXERCISES ON THE USE OF THE DICTIONARY

► EXERCISE 4. What were the original meanings of the following words?

adjective   conjunction   dialogue   monarchy
aristocracy   democracy   emperor   oligarchy

► EXERCISE 5. What were the original meanings of the following words? What meanings developed later?

amateur   inspiration   nebulous   sanguine
doom   knave   proper   Yankee

► EXERCISE 6. List synonyms for each of the following words. (From synonyms and antonyms you may find that your dictionary should be supplemented by a book of synonyms such as *Roget's International Thesaurus*, New York, 1936, which is available also in a pocketbook size.)

act   change   fight   see
anger   eat   go   think

► EXERCISE 7. List antonyms for each of the following words.

awkward   clever   gallantry   quiet
clear   fast   greed   study

► EXERCISE 8. Study the following pairs of words in your dictionary (in the special paragraphs, if any, that compare and contrast the pairs) and write sentences to illustrate the shades of difference in meaning.

cause—reason   position—situation
freedom—liberty   push—shove
help—aid   valid—sound

► EXERCISE 9. Determine the preferred American spelling of the following words: *connexion, gypsy, labour.* Which of the following words should be written separately, which should be written solid, and which should be hyphenated?

cropeared   girlscout   heartfelt   toiletwater
cubbyhole   heartbroken   heartfree   vestpocket

► EXERCISE 10. Determine the pronunciation for each of the following words. Which of the words change the accent to indicate a change in grammatical function?

absent   exquisite   Montaigne   vehement
contest   impious   object   Viet-Nam

► EXERCISE 11. Classify each of the following words as a verb (transitive or intransitive), a noun, an adjective, an adverb, a preposition, or a conjunction. Give the principal parts of each verb, the plural (or plurals) of each noun, and the comparative and superlative of each adjective or adverb. (Note that some words are used as two or more parts of speech.)

bad   drag   often   since   stratum
bite   into   sheep   sing   tomato

► EXERCISE 12. Which of the following words are always capitalized? Which are capitalized only for certain meanings?

easter   italic   platonic   spanish
italian   liberian   roman   stoical

► EXERCISE 13. Divide the following words into syllables.

analytic   laboriously   vindictive
indistinguishable liberty   vocabulary
industrious   supplement

► EXERCISE 14. Get from your dictionary specific information about each of the following. Note the source of information as (a) general vocabulary, (b) list of abbreviations, (c) gazetteer, (d) biographical list, or (e) appendix.

Annam	Escorial	*vive le roi*
Connecticut College	Melpomene	WAC
Esau	Louis Pasteur	

19b   Colloquialisms are generally avoided in standard (formal) writing.

Colloquial words or expressions (labeled *Colloq.*) are appropriate to conversation and to informal writing. For these purposes colloquialisms often give a desirable tone of informality. But colloquial expressions tend to bring a discordant note into expository or other formal types of writing and should usually be avoided in formal writing.

COLLOQUIAL   The cabin was very *homey*.
STANDARD   The cabin was very *homelike*.

COLLOQUIAL   The man never had a fair *show*.
STANDARD   The man never had a fair *chance*.

COLLOQUIAL   The boys gave a good *show*.
STANDARD   The boys gave a good *performance*.

Contracted forms (*won't, I'd, she'll, hasn't*) are perfectly proper in informal writing and equally proper in all but the most extremely formal speech. But they are to be avoided in formal expository writing. Write them out—*will not, I would, I had,* etc.

INFORMAL   *It's* really too bad that *he's* been detained and *can't* be here for our opening.
FORMAL   *It is* really too bad that *he has* been detained and *cannot* be here for our opening.

▶ EXERCISE 15. Consult your dictionary for *colloquial* meanings of the following words: *brass, dig, fizzle, kick, way.* For each word compose a sentence in which the word is used with the colloquial meaning. Then in each sentence substitute a standard word with the same meaning.

19c   Slang and jargon should be used sparingly if at all in standard speech and writing.

Slang, according to *The American College Dictionary,* is "language of a markedly colloquial character, regarded as below the standard of cultivated speech." Some slang words have a pungent quality: *slob,* which derives from an Irish word for *mud,* along with *jive,*

goop, and *jitter,* may soon join *mob, van, sham,* and *banter* as standard members of the English language. But much slang is trite and tasteless, and is used in an ineffective attempt to mask an inadequate vocabulary. Some people describe everything as "swell" or "lousy," when they really want to say *excellent, generous, satisfying, distinguished,* or *contemptible, foolish, inadequate.*

The objection to slang, then, is not based upon arbitrary *don'ts,* but upon slang's habitual alliance with lazy thinking. Slang is the sluggard's way of avoiding the search for the exact, meaningful word.

For the same reason *jargon*—language which is meaningless, or at least very confusing except to a special group—should be avoided. Almost every trade or occupation has its own jargon. A man with recent military experience might write the following jargon about his first day in college:

The mustering-in was snafu, and the old man blew his top.

This sentence would be easily understood by his army friends; other readers might require a formal statement:

The registration was confused, and the dean lost his temper.

A particularly confusing type of jargon is found in much government writing.[3]

BUREAUCRATIC JARGON   All personnel functioning in the capacity of clerks will indicate that they have had opportunity to take due cognizance of this notice by transmitting signed acknowledgment of receipt of same.
IMPROVED   All clerks will acknowledge in writing the receipt of this notice.

19d   Dialectal words should generally be avoided.

Dialectal words (also called *localisms* or *provincialisms*) should normally be avoided in speaking and writing because they are often meaningless outside the limited region where they are current. Speakers and writers may, however, safely use dialectal words known to the audience they are addressing.

[3] Bureaucratic jargon is also wordy. See Section **21a**.

DIALECT   He filled the *poke* with potatoes.
STANDARD   He filled the *bag* with potatoes.

DIALECT   The *highhole* has flown away.
STANDARD   The *flicker* has flown away.

DIALECT   I *reckon* he will come.
STANDARD   I *suppose* he will come.

19e   Illiteracies and improprieties should be avoided.

Illiteracies (also called *vulgarisms*) are the crude expressions of uneducated people, usually not listed in the dictionary.

ILLITERATE   He *ain't* going.   *They's* no use asking him.
STANDARD   He *isn't* going.   *There's* no use asking him.

An *impropriety* is a good word used with the wrong sense or function.

WRONG   I *except* your invitation. [Wrong meaning]
RIGHT   I *accept* your invitation.
ILLITERATE   (or COLLOQUIAL)   She sang *good*. [Wrong function—adjective used as adverb]
STANDARD   She sang *well*.

19f   Obsolete, archaic, or obsolescent words should be avoided.

All dictionaries list words (and meanings for words) that have long since passed out of general use. Such words as *parfit* (perfect), *ort* (fragment of food left at a meal), *yestreen* (last evening), *waxen* (to grow or become) are still found in dictionaries because these words were once the standard vocabulary of great authors and must be defined for the modern reader.

Some archaic words—like *wight, methinks,* and *quoth*—have been used for purposes of humor. Modern practice tends to label such usage as juvenile.

19g   Technical words should be avoided in nontechnical speaking and writing.

When you are writing for the general reader, avoid all unnecessary technical language. Since the ideal of the good writer is to make his thought clear to as many people as possible, he will not describe an apple tree as a *Malus pumila* or a high fever as *hyperpyrexia*. (Of course technical language, with its

greater precision, is highly desirable when one is addressing an audience that can understand it.)

Sometimes, however, even though the dictionary labels words as technical expressions (*electron* and *atomic theory,* for example), the words are well enough known to justify their general use.

19h   Avoid (1) "fine writing," (2) "poetic" expressions, and (3) unpleasing combinations of sound.

(1) Avoid "fine writing."   "Fine writing" is the unnecessary use of ornate words and expressions. It is generally fuzzy and repetitious; it tends to emphasize words rather than ideas. A simple, direct statement like "From childhood I have looked forward to a journey" can become by fine writing something like this: "From the halcyon days of early youth I have always anticipated with eagerness and pleasure the exciting vistas of distant climes and mysterious horizons."

(2) Avoid "poetic" expressions.   Genuine poetry has its very proper place, and the vivid language of simile and metaphor enriches even colloquial prose. But the sham poetry of faded imagery (*eye of night* for *moon*) and inappropriate expressions like *oft, eftsoons, 'twas,* and *'neath* are misplaced in the usual prose style.

(3) Avoid unpleasing combinations of sound.   Good prose has rhythm, but it does not rhyme. If you write, "In foreign relations, the western nations are subject to dictation," you distract the reader's attention from your meaning. Equally offensive to the average reader is the awkward combination of consonants, as in "Some people shun the seashore."

▶ EXERCISES ON USAGE

A. In the following list check any sentence that requires no revision, even for standard writing. Write *Colloq.* for each sentence approved for informal use only. Label each violation of good usage. Then rewrite all sentences (except those checked) to make them conform to standard English.

1. If I had of known you was coming, I would of waited longer.

2. Everyone suspicioned the old man of stealing our apples.

3. The ad in the paper was sort of hazy.

4. The sifting snow screened our view of the highway.

5. George was not dumb, though he looked like he was.

6. The profs dished out more than we could take.

7. Has your neighbor done sold his house?

8. The boy had a keen desire to win the game.

9. You do things different from anybody I know.

10. We filled the bucket with H_2O.

11. The poor man was in a sad fix.

12. I suppose that your findings are correct.

13. "You are goofy," I yelled. "Now scram!"

14. I am terribly aggravated with your doings.

15. Ten miles is all the farther that I can live away from my store.

B. Rewrite the following passage in standard informal English.

1. I know, Dean, I'm over a barrel good this time. 2. You wouldn't of made all this hullabaloo if you wasn't plenty peeved. 3. So I'm on the hook. 4. Well, I won't try to put the monkey on somebody else's back—pass the buck, that is. 5. I done what the prof says I done, and I can't say as I blame him for being some aggravated over it. 6. I guess I'd be doing flips if I was him. 7. And, like I say, you maybe got a right to be provoked with me too, especially after that hassle with the law over the parking meters last winter. 8. But I never painted up them nickel nabbers, Dean, honest I didn't. 9. The cops just hauled me in because, the way the papers been riding City Hall, they had to put the snag on somebody and I sort of happened to be handy. 10. I was clean as Monday's wash on that deal, Dean. 11. Still, you've got the whole thing on the poop-sheet there—I mean on my record—and that's as black an eye as I need, especially with this Zo lab rhubarb on

top of it. 12. I guess that little ruckus sounded pretty bad by the time it got to the top brass. 13. But it wasn't any worse as a lot of things you never hear a peep about. 14. Sure, I know us guys had no business horsing around like that, but you know how guys are. 15. So when them two caught me logging a little sack time before lab and started putting frogs up my britches legs and then tipped my chair over backward—I told you I'd pay for that busted chair, didn't I, Dean, even if I didn't bust it myself. 16. Well, when I come up with my pants full of frogs and there was this cat barrel I like to have fell in, I just grabbed me a cat and heaved it. 17. How'd I know the prof was going to barge in right then and get it smash in the smush? 18. I know it don't sound too funny to hear tell it, but I wisht you'd a seen him. 19. Honest, Dean, you'd a laid right down and died.

C. Rewrite the following passages of bureaucratic, legal, or academic jargon [4] in simple standard English.

1. It is obvious from the difference in elevation with relation to the short depth of the property that the contour is such as to preclude any reasonable developmental potential for active recreation.

2. Verbal contact with Mr. Blank regarding the attached notification of promotion has elicited the attached representation intimating that he prefers to decline the assignment.

3. Voucherable expenditures necessary to provide adequate dental treatment required as adjunct to medical treatment being rendered a pay patient in in-patient status may be incurred as required at the expense of the Public Health Service.

[4] Quoted, by permission, from Stuart Chase's *Power of Words*, Harcourt, Brace and Company, New York, 1953, pp. 250-53.

▶ Glossary of Usage

19i   Consult this list to determine the standing of a word or phrase and its appropriateness to your purpose.[5] (If the word you are looking for is not included, or if you need more information about any word in the list, consult a good dictionary—preferably one of the unabridged dictionaries in the library.)

[5] Before attempting to use this list, the student should read pages 873-74 above for distinctions between STANDARD (both FORMAL and INFORMAL) and COLLOQUIAL (19b), SLANG (19c), DIALECTAL (19d), ILLITERATE or VULGAR (19e), OBSOLETE and ARCHAIC (19f), TECHNICAL (19g), and POETIC (19h).

A, an. Use *a* before a consonant sound, *an* before a vowel sound. Examples: *a* band, *a* well, *a* yard, *a* unit [*y* sound], *a* one [*w* sound], *a* hammer, *a* history; *an* apple, *an* olive, *an* hour [silent *h* before the vowel]

Accept, except. Do not confuse. The verb *accept* means "to receive." *Except* means "to exclude."

RIGHT   Mary accepted (*not* excepted) an invitation to dinner.

RIGHT   They excepted (*not* accepted) Mary from the invitation.

Ad. Colloquial shortening of *advertisement.* Use the full word in standard speech and writing.

Affect, effect. Do not confuse. *Affect* (a verb) means "to influence." "The attack affected the morale of the troops." *Effect* is both a verb and a noun. As a verb it means "to bring to pass." "The medicine effected a complete cure." As a noun *effect* means "result." "The effect of the medicine was instantaneous."

Aggravate. Means "to intensify, to increase." "Lack of water aggravated the suffering." Colloquially it means "to irritate, exasperate, provoke, annoy."

COLLOQUIAL   He was extremely aggravated by the delay.

STANDARD   He was extremely annoyed by the delay.

Agree to, agree with. One agrees *to* a plan but *with* a person.

A half a. Redundant. See **Half a, a half, a half a.**

Ain't. An illiterate or dialectal contraction. In conversation and in informal writing the following contractions may be used: *I'm not, you (we, they) aren't, he (she, it) isn't.* In formal formal writing the words are usually written out: *I am not,* etc.

Alibi. Colloquial for *excuse.* Standard English accepts the word only in its technical legal sense.

Allude, refer. Do not confuse. *Allude* means "to refer to indirectly." "When he mentioned dictators, we knew that he was alluding to Hitler and Mussolini." *Refer* means "to mention something specifically." "I refer you to the third act of *Hamlet.*"

Allusion, illusion. Do not confuse *allusion,* "an indirect reference," with *illusion,* "an unreal image or false impression."

Already, all ready. *Already* (one word) means "prior to some specified time, either present, past, or future." "By noon the theater was already full." *All ready* (two words) means "completely ready." "I am all ready to go."

Alright. Incorrect spelling. Use *all right.*

Also. A weak connective. *And* is a better connective. "I met Harry and Tom (*not* also Tom)."

Altogether, all together. *Altogether* (one word) means "wholly, thoroughly, in all." "The report is altogether true." *All together* (two words) means "in a group, collectively." "The packages were all together on the table."

Alumnus, alumna. *Alumnus,* a male graduate; *alumni,* two or more male graduates. *Alumna,* a female graduate; *alumnae,* two or more female graduates. *Alumni,* male and female graduates grouped together.

A.M., P.M. (also *a.m., p.m.*). Use only with figures. "He came at 10:00 A.M. (*not* in the A.M.) and left at 4:00 P.M." "He came in the morning and left in the afternoon (*not* in the P.M.)."

Among, between. *Among* always implies more than two. "Joseph's brethren divided the spoils among them." *Between* literally implies only two. "I divided the cake between John and Mary." But *between* is used for more than two to indicate a reciprocal relation. "A treaty was concluded between the three nations."

Amount, number. Use *amount* to refer to things in bulk or mass, *number* to refer to countable objects. "A large amount of grain; a number of watermelons."

An, a. See **A, an.**

And etc. Never place *and* before *etc.* The *and* is redundant since *etc.* is an abbreviation of *et* (and) + *cetera* (other things).

And which, but which. Do not thwart subordination by inserting *and* or *but* before a subordinate clause. "Law enforcement is a current problem which (*not* and which) is hard to solve." "The college needs new dormitories which (*not* but which) cannot be erected until funds are provided." But *and* or *but* may be used before *which* to join two *which* clauses. "Law enforcement is a problem which is current and which is hard to solve."

Ante-, anti-. *Ante-* means "before," as in *antebellum.* *Anti-* means "against," as in *anti-British.* The hyphen is used after *anti-* before capital letters and before *i,* as in *anti-imperialist.*

Anyone, everyone, someone. Distinguish from *any one, every one, some one. Anyone* (one word) means "any person, anybody." *Any one* (two words) means "any single person or thing." Similarly with *everyone, someone.*

Anyways. Dialectal for *in any case, anyway.*

STANDARD   I may not get the pass I have requested, but I am planning to go anyway (*not* anyways).

Anywheres. Illiterate for *anywhere.*

Apt. See **Likely, liable, apt.**

Around. Colloquial in the sense of "about, near."

> COLLOQUIAL To come around noon; to stay around the house.
>
> STANDARD To come about noon; to stay near (*or* about) the house.

As. (1) Generally avoid *as* in the sense of "because." *For* or *since* is usually clearer.

> VAGUE He worked steadily as the day was cool.
>
> CLEARER He worked steadily, for the day was cool.

(2) In standard English do not use *as* in place of *that* or *whether.*

> COLLOQUIAL I feel as I should go.
>
> STANDARD I feel that I should go.

(3) In negative statements careful writers prefer *so . . . as* to *as . . . as.* "I am not so strong as I used to be." "He will go only so far as he is forced to go."

See also **Like, as, as if.**

At. Redundant and usually illiterate in such sentences as the following:

> REDUNDANT Where does he live at? Where are you at now?
>
> IMPROVED Where does he live? Where are you now?

At about. *About* is preferable.

> WORDY He arrived at about noon.
>
> BETTER He arrived about noon.

Awful. Colloquial in the sense of "very bad, ugly, shocking."

> COLLOQUIAL The suit was awful.
>
> STANDARD The suit was very ugly.

Awhile, a while. Distinguish between the adverb *awhile* and the article and noun *a while.* "Rest awhile before leaving." "Rest for a while (*not* awhile) before leaving."

Bank on, take stock in. Colloquial expressions for *rely on, trust in.*

Because. Do not use *because* to introduce a noun clause.

> POOR Because he was sick was no excuse.
>
> BETTER The fact that he was sick was no excuse, *or* His sickness was no excuse.

See also **Reason is because.**

Being as, being that. Substandard for *since, because.*

Beside, besides. Do not confuse. *Beside* is a preposition meaning "by the side of." "Sit beside me." *Besides,* used chiefly as an adverb, means "in addition to." "We ate apples and other fruit besides."

Better. See **Had better, had rather, would rather.**

Between, among. See **Among, between.**

Bunch. Colloquial for *group of people.*

> COLLOQUIAL A bunch of boys, a bunch of farmers
>
> STANDARD A group of boys, a group of farmers; a bunch of carrots

Bust, busted, bursted. Illiterate forms of the verb *burst,* which uses the same form for all its principal parts: *burst, burst, burst.*

But, only, hardly, scarcely. These words, negative in implication, should not be used with another negative.

> POOR He didn't have but one hat.
>
> BETTER He had but one hat; *or,* He had only one hat.

> POOR He wasn't sick only three days.
>
> BETTER He was sick only three days.

> POOR I don't hardly (scarcely) know.
>
> BETTER I hardly (scarcely) know.

But what. Colloquial for *that.*

> COLLOQUIAL He had no doubt *but what* he would succeed.
>
> STANDARD He had no doubt *that* he would succeed.

But which, and which. See **And which, but which.**

Calculate. Colloquial or dialectal for *think, guess, plan.*

Can, may. In formal usage *can* denotes ability and *may* denotes possibility or permission. The use of *can* to denote permission is colloquial.

> COLLOQUIAL Can I go?
>
> FORMAL May I go?

Can't hardly. A double negative in implication. Use *can hardly.* See **But, only, hardly, scarcely.**

Case, line. Often used in wordy expressions. Say "Jones had good intentions," not "In the case of Jones there were good intentions." Say "Get some fruit," not "Get something in the line of fruit."

Cause of. Do not say that the *cause of* something was *on account of.* Complete the expression with a predicate noun or a noun clause.

> LOGICAL The cause of my inability to work was a bad headache (*not* on account of a bad headache). [Predicate noun]
>
> LOGICAL The cause of my inability to work was that I had a bad headache. [Noun clause]

Censure, criticize. See **Criticize, censure.**

Common, mutual. That thing is *common* in which two or more share equally or alike, as in "a common purpose." That thing is *mutual* which is reciprocally given and received, as in "mutual assistance."

Company. A colloquial expression for *guests, visitors, escort.*

Compare to, compare with. "One object is *compared with* another when set side by side with it in order to show their relative value or excellence; *to* another when it is formally represented as like it." (*Webster's*)

> RIGHT He compared the book with the manuscript.

> RIGHT He compared the earth to a ball.

Complected. Dialectal or colloquial for *complexioned.*

> STANDARD He was a light-complexioned (*not* light-complected) man.

> STANDARD He was a man of light complexion.

Considerable. An adjective; colloquial as a noun; illiterate as an adverb.

> COLLOQUIAL He lost considerable in the depression.

> STANDARD He lost a considerable amount of property during the depression.

> ILLITERATE He was considerable touched by the girl's plea.

> STANDARD He was considerably touched by the girl's plea.

Continual, continuous. *Continual* means "occurring in steady, rapid, but not unbroken succession." "The rehearsal was hampered by continual interruptions." *Continuous* means "without cessation." "The continuous roar of the waterfall was disturbing."

Could of. Illiterate corruption of *could have.*

Criticize, censure. In standard English, *criticize* means "to examine and judge as a critic," not necessarily "to censure." *Censure* means "to find fault with" or "to condemn as wrong."

Cunning. Means "shrewd." Colloquial for *attractive.*

Cute. Colloquial for *clever, shrewd, attractive, petite.*

Data, strata, phenomena. Plurals of *datum, stratum, phenomenon.* "These data, these strata, these phenomena, this stratum, this phenomenon." *Stratum* and *phenomenon* have alternative plurals in *s.* The singular *datum* is seldom used. The plural *data* is often construed as a collective noun taking a singular verb: "This data is new."

Date. Colloquial for *appointment, engagement; to make an appointment.*

Deal. Colloquial or commercial term for *transaction, bargain.*

Didn't ought. See **Had ought, hadn't ought, didn't ought.**

Differ from, differ with. Do not confuse. *Differ from* means "to stand apart because of unlikeness." "The Caucasian race differs from the Mongolian race in color, stature, and customs." *Differ with* means "to disagree." "On that point I differ with you."

Done. The past participle of the verb *to do. I do, I did, I have done. Done* is illiterate for *did* or for the adverb *already.*

> ILLITERATE He done well.

> RIGHT He did well.

> ILLITERATE He has done sold the dog.

> RIGHT He has already sold the dog; *or,* He has sold the dog.

Don't. A contraction for *do not,* but not for *does not.*

> WRONG He don't smoke. [He do not smoke.]

> RIGHT He doesn't smoke. [He does not smoke.]

> PROPER CONTRACTIONS I don't, we don't, you don't, they don't. [do not]

He doesn't, she doesn't, it doesn't. [does not]

Due to. A prepositional phrase beginning with *due to* is universally approved as an adjective modifier, as in "His tardiness was due to an accident," in which the prepositional phrase modifies the noun *tardiness.* There is increasing use of *due to* in adverbial constructions, as in "Due to an accident he arrived late," in which the prepositional phrase modifies the verb *arrived.* But for this adverbial construction many writers prefer *because of* or *on account of.* "Because of an accident he arrived late."

Each other, one another. Used interchangeably. Some writers prefer *each other* when referring to only two, and *one another* when referring to more than two.

Effect, affect. See **Affect, effect.**

Elegant. Means *polished, fastidious, refined.* Used colloquially for *delicious, good.*

> STANDARD This food is delicious (*not* elegant).

Emigrate, immigrate. *Emigrate* means "to leave a place of abode for residence in another country." *Immigrate* means "to come for permanent residence into a country of which one is not a native."

Enthuse. Colloquial for *to make enthusiastic, to become enthusiastic.*

> COLLOQUIAL She enthuses over anything.

> STANDARD She becomes enthusiastic about anything.

Equally as good. The *as* is redundant. Say "equally good" or "as good as."

Etc. See **And etc.**

Every bit. Colloquial for *entirely, in every way.*

Everyone, anyone, someone. See **Anyone, everyone, someone.**

Everywheres. Dialectal for *everywhere.*

Exam. Colloquial shortening of *examination.* For formal purposes, use the full word.

Except, accept. See **Accept, except.**

Expect. Colloquial if used to mean "suppose."

> COLLOQUIAL   I expect the report is true.
> STANDARD   I suppose the report is true.

Farther, further. *Farther* is often preferred to express geographic distance. "They went even farther the next day." *Further* is regularly preferred to express the meaning "more, in addition." "Further reports came."

Faze. Colloquial for *worry, disconcert.*

Fellow. Colloquial for *man.*

Fewer, less. *Fewer* refers especially to number. "Fewer than twenty persons attended." *Less* refers especially to value, degree, or amount. "The suit costs less than the overcoat."

Fine. The adjective *fine* is much overused as a vague word of approval. Choose an expression to fit the meaning exactly.

> *Fine* is colloquial or dialectal when used as an adverb meaning "well, excellently."

> COLLOQUIAL   She plays the organ fine.
> STANDARD   She plays the organ well.

Flunk. Colloquial for *fail.*

Folks. Colloquial for *parents, relatives, persons of one's own family.*

Former. Refers to the first named of two. Not properly used when three or more are named.

Foul up. Colloquial for *confuse, entangle, bungle.*

Funny. Colloquial for *strange, queer, odd.* In standard usage funny means "amusing."

Further, farther. See **Farther, further.**

Gent. Illiterate (or humorous) for *gentleman, man.* "The store advertises men's (*not* gents') suits."

Gentleman, lady. Generally preferable: *man, woman.* Use *gentleman, lady* when your purpose is to distinguish persons of refinement and culture from the ill-bred. Use the plural forms in addressing an audience: "Ladies and Gentlemen."

> QUESTIONABLE   Lady preacher, saleslady, lady clerk, cleaning lady, ladies' colleges
> BETTER   Woman preacher, saleswoman, woman clerk, cleaning woman, women's colleges

Get, got. The verb *to get* is one of the most useful words in standard English. It is common in such good idioms as *get along with* (someone), *get the better of* (someone), *get at* (information), *get up* (a dance), *get on* (a horse), or *get over* (sickness). But *get* or *got* is also used in expressions that are colloquial or slangy.

Examples (with standard equivalents in parentheses):

> COLLOQUIAL   He has got to (is obliged to, must) go.
> This work gets (puzzles, irritates) me.
> The bullet got (killed) him.

Good. Not generally recognized as an adverb.

> QUESTIONABLE   He reads good. He works good.
> STANDARD   He reads well. He works well; *or,* He does good work.

Gotten. Past participle of *get,* the principal parts of which are *get* (present), *got* (past), *got,* or *gotten* (past participle). In England *gotten* is now archaic, but in the United States both *got* and *gotten* are in general use.

Grand. Avoid the vague colloquial use of *grand* to mean "excellent." Select the exact word to fit the meaning.

> LOOSE   We had a grand trip.
> BETTER   We had a delightful (pleasant, exciting) trip.

Guy. Slang for *man, boy, fellow.*

Had better, had rather, would rather. Good idioms used to express advisability (with *better*) or preference (with *rather*). *Better* is a colloquial shortening of *had better.*

> COLLOQUIAL   He better listen to reason.
> STANDARD   He had better listen to reason.

Had of. Illiterate for *had.*

> ILLITERATE   I wish I had of gone.
> STANDARD   I wish I had gone.

Had ought, hadn't ought, didn't ought. Illiterate combinations.

> ILLITERATE   He hadn't ought to have gone.
> STANDARD   He ought not to have gone.

Half a, a half, a half a. Use *half a* or *a half,* but avoid the redundant *a half a.*

> REDUNDANT   He worked a half a day.
> STANDARD   He worked half a day.
> STANDARD   He worked a half day. [Perhaps more formal and more specific]

Hardly. See **But, only, hardly, scarcely.**

Healthful, healthy. *Healthful* means "giving health," as in "healthful climate, healthful food." *Healthy* means "having health," as in "healthy boy, healthy woman, healthy people."

Help but. See **Cannot help but.**

Himself, myself, yourself. See **Myself, himself, yourself.**

Hisself. Illiterate for *himself.*

Homey. Colloquial for *homelike, intimate.*

Honorable, Reverend. See **Reverend, Honorable.**

If, whether. Some writers prefer *whether* to *if* after such verbs as *say, learn, know, under-*

stand, doubt, especially when followed by *or.* "I did not know whether he would ride or walk."

Illusion, allusion. See **Allusion, illusion.**

Immigrate, emigrate. See **Emigrate, immigrate.**

Imply, infer. See **Infer, imply.**

In, into. Do not confuse. *In* indicates "location within." "He was in the room." *Into* indicates "motion or direction to a point within." "He came into the room."

In-, un-. See **Un-, in-.**

Incredible, incredulous. *Incredible* means "too extraordinary to admit of belief." *Incredulous* means "inclined not to believe on slight evidence."

Individual, party, person. *Individual* refers to a single person, animal, or thing. *Party* refers to a group, never to a single person (except in colloquial or legal usage). *Person* is the preferred word for general reference to a human being.

> COLLOQUIAL He is the interested party.
> STANDARD He is the interested person.

Infer, imply. *Infer* means "to arrive at through reasoning." "From his statement I infer that he will resign." *Imply* means "to hint or suggest." "His statement implies that he will resign."

Ingenious, ingenuous. *Ingenious* means "clever, resourceful," as "an ingenious device." *Ingenuous* means "open, frank, artless," as "ingenuous actions."

In regards to. Use either of the correct idioms, *in regard to* or *as regards.*

Invite. Slang when used as a noun.

Its, it's. Do not confuse the possessive *its* and the contraction *it's* (= *it is*).

Just. Colloquial for *completely, simply, quite.*

> COLLOQUIAL He was just tired out.
> STANDARD He was completely tired out.

Kind, sort. Singular forms, modified by singular adjectives.

> COLLOQUIAL OR ILLITERATE I like these kind (*or* sort) of shoes.
> STANDARD I like this kind (*or* sort) of shoes.

Kind of, sort of. Loosely colloquial when used as an adverb to mean "somewhat, rather, after a fashion."

> COLLOQUIAL I was kind of (sort of) tired.
> STANDARD I was somewhat tired.

> COLLOQUIAL I kind of (sort of) thought you would go.
> STANDARD I rather thought you would go.

Kind of a, sort of a. Omit the *a* in standard writing.

> STANDARD What kind of (*not* kind of a) car does he drive?
> What sort of (*not* sort of a) car does he drive?

Lady, gentleman. See **Gentleman, lady.**

Later, latter. Do not confuse. *Later* is the comparative of *late* and means "more late." *Latter* refers to the last named of two. If more than two are named, use *last* or *last-mentioned* instead of *latter.*

Lay, lie. Do not confuse. See Section 7a, page 825.

Lead, led. Present tense and past tense of the verb. Do not confuse with the noun *lead* (pronounced *led*), the name of the metal.

Learn, teach. *Learn* means "to acquire knowledge"; *teach* means "to impart knowledge." "She taught (*not* learned) him his lesson."

Leave, let. Do not use *leave* for *let. Leave* means "to depart from"; *let* means "to permit." But "Leave (*or* Let) me alone" is a standard idiom.

> SLANG I will not leave you go today.
> STANDARD I will not let you go today.

Less, fewer. See **Fewer, less.**

Let's us. *Let's* is the contraction of *let us.* Therefore *Let's us go* is redundant for *Let's go. Let's don't stay* is redundant for *Let's not stay.*

Lie, lay. Do not confuse. See Section 7a, page 825.

Like, as, as if. Use *like* as a preposition; use *as* or *as if* as a conjunction. *Like* is much used colloquially as a conjunction, but this use is generally avoided in standard writing.

> STANDARD He worked like a man. Do as (*not* like) I do. It looks as if (*not* like) it might rain.

Likely, liable, apt. Standard writing tends to use *likely* to express mere probability; to use *liable* to suggest, in addition, the idea of harm or responsibility. "My friends are likely to arrive tomorrow." [Mere probability] "The boy is liable to cut his foot with the ax." [Probability + the idea of harm] "The hotel will not be liable for stolen property." [Responsibility] *Apt* implies a predisposition or dexterity. "He is apt to worry." "He is an apt pupil." [Associate *apt* with *aptitude; liable* with *liability.*] In colloquial usage *likely, liable,* and *apt* are interchangeable.

Line, case. See **Case, line.**

Locate. Colloquial for *settle.*

> STANDARD He settled (*not* located) in Texas.

Lose, loose. Do not confuse. *Lose* means "to cease having." *Loose* (verb) means "to set free." *Loose* (adjective) means "free, not fastened."

Lot, lots of. Colloquial for *much, many, a great deal.*

Lovely. Avoid the vague colloquial use of *lovely* to mean "very pleasing." Select the exact word to fit the meaning.

Mad. Means "insane." Colloquial for *angry*.

May be, maybe. Do not confuse the verb form *may be* with the adverb *maybe,* meaning "perhaps." "He may be waiting for my letter." "Maybe he will come tomorrow."

May, can. See **Can, may.**

May of. Illiterate corruption of *may have*.

Mean. Colloquial for *ill-tempered, indisposed, ashamed.*

Might of. Illiterate corruption of *might have.*

Mighty. Colloquial for *very*.

Most. Standard English does not recognize the adjective *most* as a substitute for the adverb *almost.*

> COLLOQUIAL   The trains arrive most every hour.
> STANDARD   The trains arrive almost every hour.
> STANDARD   The trains are most crowded during the holidays. [*Most* is correctly used as an adverb to form the superlative.]

Must of. Illiterate corruption of *must have*.

Mutual. See **Common, mutual.**

Myself, himself, yourself. Properly intensive or reflexive pronouns. "I myself will go; I will see for myself." In general *myself* is not a proper substitute for *I* or *me;* but it is substituted colloquially (1) for *I* after comparisons with *than* or *as* ("Everyone worked as well as myself") or (2) for *me* when it is the second member of a compound object ("He allowed my brother and myself to go home").

Nice. In formal writing, means "precise" or "exact." Do not overwork *nice* as a vague word of approval. Find an exact word.

> VAGUE   It was a nice day.
> SPECIFIC   It was a bright (mild, sunny) day.

No account, no good. Colloquial for *worthless, of no value.*

No place. Colloquial for *nowhere*.

Nowhere near. Colloquial for *not nearly*.

Nowheres. Dialectal for *nowhere*.

Number. See **Amount, number.**

O, Oh. Interjections. *O* is used especially in very formal direct address, is always capitalized, and is never followed by any mark of punctuation. "O God, deliver us!" *Oh* is used to express grief, surprise, or a wish, and is followed by a comma or an exclamation point. "Oh, I hope so."

Of. See **Could of, Had of, Ought to of.**

Off of. *Of* is superfluous. "He fell off (*not* off of) the platform."

One another, each other. See **Each other, one another.**

Only. See **But, only, hardly, scarcely.**

Other times. Use *at other times*.

Ought. See **Had ought.**

Ought to of. Illiterate corruption of *ought to have.*

Out loud. Colloquial for *aloud*.

Outside of. Colloquial in the sense of "except."

> STANDARD   Except (*not* outside of) James, nobody went with him.

Party, person, individual. See **Individual, party, person.**

Per. Used especially in commercial writing. In standard English some authors use *per* only with Latin words, such as *diem, annum.*

> COMMERCIAL   His salary was four thousand dollars per year.
> STANDARD   His salary was four thousand dollars a year.

Per cent (or percent). Means "by the hundred." Use only after a numeral: "10 per cent, 20 per cent." In other situations *per cent* is colloquial for *percentage*. "A large percentage, a small percentage." Do not overwork *percentage* for *portion, part.*

Person, party, individual. See **Individual, party, person.**

Phenomena. Plural of *phenomenon*. See **Data, strata, phenomena.**

Phone. Colloquial shortening of *telephone*. Use the full word in formal writing.

Photo. Colloquial shortening of *photograph*. Use the full word in standard writing.

Piece. Dialectal for *short distance*.

Plenty. Colloquial when used as an adverb.

> COLLOQUIAL   It is plenty good enough.
> STANDARD   It is quite good enough.

P.M., A.M. See **A.M., P.M.**

Practical, practicable. *Practical* means "useful, sensible," not "theoretical." *Practicable* means "feasible, capable of being put into practice." "The sponsors are practical men, and their plans are practicable."

Prefer. Not to be followed by *than*, but by *to, before, above, rather than.*

> UNIDIOMATIC   I should prefer that than anything else.
> IDIOMATIC   I should prefer that to anything else.

Principal, principle. Distinguish between *principal,* an adjective or noun meaning "chief" or "chief official," and the noun *principle,* meaning "fundamental truth."

Proposition. Properly "a thing proposed." Colloquial with the meaning "a project involving action, venture, difficulty."

> STANDARD The mine was a paying venture (*not* proposition) from the first.

Quite. An adverb meaning "entirely, positively." Used colloquially to mean "to a great extent, very."

> COLLOQUIAL The lake is quite near.
> STANDARD The lake is rather near.
> STANDARD His guess was quite wrong.

Quite, quiet. Do not confuse. *Quite* is an adverb meaning "entirely." *Quiet* is an adjective meaning "calm."

Quite a few, quite a bit, quite a little, quite a good deal. Colloquial for *a good many, a considerable number, a considerable amount.*

Raise, rear. Some writers prefer *rear* to *raise* in the sense of "bringing up children." "He reared (*not* raised) the boy from infancy."

Raise, rise. See **Rise, raise.**

Real. Colloquial or dialectal for *very* or *really.*

> STANDARD She was very (*not* real) brave.

Rear. See **Raise, rear.**

Reason is because. Formal English usually completes the construction *The reason is (was)* with a *that* clause or recasts the sentence.

> COLLOQUIAL The reason why he missed his class was because (*or* on account of) he overslept.
> STANDARD The reason why he missed his class was that he overslept.
> STANDARD He missed his class because he overslept.

Reckon. Colloquial or dialectal for *think, suppose.*

Refer. See **Allude, refer.**

Respectfully, respectively. Do not confuse. *Respectfully* means "in a manner showing respect." "Yours respectfully." *Respectively* means "each in the order given." "The President respectfully paid tribute to the Army, Navy, and Air Force, respectively."

Reverend, Honorable. To be followed by the first name, the initials, or some title of the person referred to as well as the surname. See Section 11e.

Right. Colloquial or dialectal as an adverb meaning "very, extremely."

> STANDARD I am very (*not* right) glad to see you.

Right along. Colloquial for *continuously.*

> STANDARD The clock struck continuously (*not* right along).
> I knew it all the time (*not* right along).

Rise, raise. Do not confuse. *Rise* is an intransitive verb. "I rise every morning." "I rose at four o'clock." "I have risen at four o'clock for many months." *Raise* is a transitive verb. "I raise vegetables." "I raised vegetables last year." "I have raised vegetables for many years."

Said. The adjective *said,* meaning "before-mentioned," should be used only in legal documents.

Same, said, such. Except in legal documents, not used as substitutes for *it, this,* or *that.*

> QUESTIONABLE When said coat was returned, same was found to be badly torn.
> BETTER When this coat was returned, it was found to be badly torn.

Say. Colloquial for *give orders.*

> COLLOQUIAL The teacher said to go home.
> STANDARD The teacher told us to go home.

Says. Illiterate for *said.*

> ILLITERATE He says to her, "I am tired."
> STANDARD He said to her, "I am tired."

Scarcely. See **But, only, hardly, scarcely.**

Seldom ever, seldom or ever. Unidiomatic expressions for *seldom if ever, hardly ever.*

Should of. Illiterate corruption of *should have.*

Show. Colloquial for *play, opera, motion picture.*

Sight. Colloquial for *a great deal.*

> STANDARD "He left a great deal (*not* a sight) of money."

Sit, set. Do not confuse. See Section 7a, page 825.

So. An overworked word. Do not overwork *so* to join co-ordinate clauses.

> COLLOQUIAL The work had tired him, so he did not begin his journey the next day.
> STANDARD Since the work had tired him, he did not begin his journey the next day.

In clauses denoting purpose, *so that* it usually preferred to *so.*

> QUESTIONABLE He came early so he might see a friend.
> BETTER He came early so that he might see a friend.

Some. Slang when used as an intensive. "He is making an excellent (*not* some) race."

Someone, anyone, everyone. See **Anyone, everyone, someone.**

Someplace. Colloquial for *somewhere.*

Somewheres. Illiterate for *somewhere.*

Sort. See **Kind, sort.**

Sort of. See **Kind of, sort of.**

Sort of a. See **Kind of a, sort of a.**

Strata. Plural of *stratum.* See **Data, strata, phenomena.**

Such. Note carefully the use of *such* in the dictionary. When *such* is followed by a relative clause, the proper relative is *as*. "I shall give such aid as I think best." When *such* is completed by a result clause, it should be followed by *that*. "There was such a rain that we could not drive." Avoid the weak and vague use of *such*. "We had a good (*not* such a good) time."

Such, same, said. See **Same, said, such.**

Sure. Colloquial for *surely, certainly*.

> STANDARD This is certainly (*not* sure) a quiet place.

Sure and. See **Try and.**

Suspicion. Dialectal when used as a verb in place of *suspect*.

> DIALECTAL I did not suspicion anything.
> STANDARD I did not suspect anything.

Swell. The adjective is slang for *excellent, first-rate*.

> STANDARD Our last symphony concert was first-rate (*not* swell).

Take and. Dialectal or illiterate.

> STANDARD He knocked (*not* took and knocked) the ball over the base line.

Take stock in. See **Bank on, take stock in.**

Tasty. Colloquial for *savory* or *tasteful*.

Teach. See **Learn, teach.**

Terrible, terribly. Colloquial for *extremely bad*.

That. Used colloquially as an adverb.

> COLLOQUIAL I can approach only that near.
> STANDARD I can approach only so near.

Theirselves. Illiterate for *themselves*.

These kind, these sort. See **Kind, sort.**

This here, that there, these here, them there. Illiterate expressions. Use *this, that, these, those*.

Try and, sure and. Colloquial for *try to, sure to*.

> STANDARD Try to (*not* and) calm yourself.
> Be sure to (*not* and) come early.

Ugly. Colloquial for *ill-tempered*.

> STANDARD He was never in an ill-tempered (*not* ugly) mood.

Un-, in-. Do not confuse. The prefix *un-* (from AS. *un-*, not) is used regularly with words derived from Anglo-Saxon (*undo, untie*); *in-* (from L. *in-*, not) is used with either Anglo-Saxon or Latin derivatives. (But distinguish *in-*, not, from the other Latin prefix *in-*, in or into, as in *inbreed, induct*.)

United States. When used as a noun, always *the United States*, with the article.

Used to could. Illiterate or facetious for *used to be able*.

Very. Some careful writers avoid using *very* to modify a past participle that has not yet established itself as an adjective. They insert some appropriate adverb—such as *much, greatly, deeply*—between *very* and the past participle.

> QUESTIONABLE His singing was very appreciated.
> BETTER His singing was very greatly appreciated.

Wait on. Means *to attend, to serve*. Colloquial for *wait for*.

> STANDARD "I waited for (*not* waited on) him to begin."

Want. Cannot take a clause as its object.

> ILLITERATE I want that he should have a chance.
> STANDARD I want him to have a chance.

Want in, out, down, up, off, through. Dialectal for *want to come in* or *get in, out, down, up, off, through*.

Ways. Colloquial for *distance*.

> STANDARD A long distance (*not* ways).

Where. Improperly used for *that*.

> POOR I saw in the newspaper where the strike had been settled.
> BETTER I saw in the newspaper that the strike had been settled.

Where at. Illiterate.

> ILLITERATE Where is she at?
> STANDARD Where is she?

Which, who. Use *who* or *that* instead of *which* or *what* to refer to persons. "Mr. Jones was the man who (*not* which) helped me."

While. Do not overuse this conjunction. In general do not substitute *while* for *and, but, though*, or *whereas*.

Who, which. See **Which, who.**

Worst kind, sort, way. Dialectal for *very much*.

Would of. Illiterate corruption of *would have*.

Would rather. See **Had better, had rather, would rather.**

You all. A Southern colloquialism for *you* (plural).

You was. Illiterate for *you were*.

Yourself, myself, himself. See **Myself, himself, yourself.**

▶ Exactness

Idiom; Freshness

20 Select words that are exact, idiomatic, and fresh.

A word is exact when it expresses the precise idea or conveys the emotional suggestion intended by the writer. By this definition the measures of a right word will be the purpose of the writer, the subject he has selected, and his attitude toward his subject and his readers.

20a Consult a good dictionary for the exact word needed to express the idea.

Before you use a word, know exactly what it means. Do not confuse words that are similar in spelling or meaning. Above all, train yourself to be specific.

WRONG The bell rang *continually* for five minutes.
RIGHT The bell rang *continuously* for five minutes.

WRONG He *contributes* his success to sound preparation.
RIGHT He *attributes* his success to sound preparation.

WRONG She seemed scarcely *conscience* of what she was doing.
RIGHT She seemed scarcely *conscious* of what she was doing.

VAGUE *The thing about it is* that we are destitute.
SPECIFIC *The truth of the matter* is that we are destitute.

▶ EXERCISE 1. Review the first twenty word groups in the list of similar words in Section 18, Exercise 2, consulting your dictionary as necessary to make sure that you can use each word with its exact meaning.

▶ EXERCISE 2. Review in the same way the second twenty word groups in the list.

▶ EXERCISE 3. Review in the same way the third (last) twenty word groups in the list.

Be careful to use the right conjunction to express the exact relation between words, phrases, and clauses.

WRONG There were other candidates, *and* he was elected.
RIGHT There were other candidates, *but* he was elected. [*And* adds or continues; *but* contrasts.]

WRONG I read in the paper *where* you had arrived.
RIGHT I read in the paper *that* you had arrived.

(1) *Denotation and Connotation.* Select the word with the denotation and connotation proper to the idea you wish to express.

The denotation of a word is what the word actually points to. (Thus *cow* stands for the milk-giving quadruped.) The connotation of a word is what the word suggests or implies. (Thus *cow,* when applied to a human being, suggests awkwardness.) Connotation includes the aura of emotion or association that surrounds some words. For example, *street, avenue, boulevard, lane, place, alley, promenade, prospect* all denote much the same thing to a postman. But to various readers, and in various contexts, each word may have a special connotation. *Street* may suggest city pavements; *avenue,* a broad passageway bordered on each side by trees; *boulevard,* a broad highway; *lane,* a rustic walk; *place,* a secluded corner in a large city; *alley,* a city slum; *promenade,* a street for the display of elegance, fashion, and so forth; *prospect,* an avenue commanding a splendid view. Similarly, *highway, road, route, drive, trail, concourse, path, turnpike*—all denote a passage for travel, but each word carries a variety of connotations.

A word may be right in one situation, wrong in another. *Female parent,* for instance, is a proper expression, but it would be very inappropriate to say "John wept for the death of his female parent." *Female parent* used in this sense is literally correct, but the connotation is wrong. The more appropriate word, *mother,* not only conveys the meaning denoted by *female parent;* it also conveys the reason why John wept. The first expression simply implies a biological relationship; the second is full of imaginative and emotional suggestions.

▶ EXERCISE 4. Distinguish between the denotation and the connotation of the following pairs of words. Select phrases from your reading to illustrate proper usage of the words.

cabin–hut	joy–felicity
dirt–soil	palace–mansion
fire–conflagration	steed–nag
foggy–murky	wealth–opulence
healthy–robust	

▶ EXERCISE 5. Show why the italicized words in the following sentences, although literally correct, might be inappropriate because of their connotations.

1. Miss Kincaid's exotic costume won the admiration of everyone at the party, and even the hostess remarked several times how *outlandish* she looked.
2. For the *enlightenment* of the other ladies, Mrs. Bromley measured upon her *belly* the area of her recent operation.
3. Robin Roberts *excogitated* each pitch.
4. Homer squeezed a quantity of *chlorophyllaceous extrusion* onto his toothbrush.
5. The army *scampered* home at full speed.
6. The librarian catalogued her books with *dauntless* energy.
7. We are building our new home on the rim of a most delightful little *gulch.*
8. Heifetz *tucked* his *fiddle* under his chin.

▶ EXERCISE 6. Explain the denotations and connotations of the italicized words in the following selections. Note how context in some instances intensifies the connotative power of a simple, everyday word; in other instances, it determines which of several differing connotations the word will carry. For each italicized word substitute a word of nearly the same denotation and consider its relative effectiveness in the sentence.

1. My good *blade* carves the *casques* of men.
                                          —TENNYSON
2. Thy soul was like a star and dwelt *apart.*
                                          —WORDSWORTH
3. O what can *ail* thee, knight at arms,
   Alone and *palely* loitering?   —KEATS
4. They also serve who *only* stand and *wait.*
                                          —MILTON
5. The barge she sat in, like a *burnished* throne,
   Burned on the water.   —SHAKESPEARE

6. He had a thin *vague* beard.   —BEERBOHM
7. It was a chill, *rain-washed* afternoon. —SAKI
8. He had *flaxen* hair, *weak* blue eyes, and the general demeanor of a saintly but timid *codfish.*
                                          —P. G. WODEHOUSE
9. By *midnight,* the *peace* of *Christmas,* a special *intimate* kind of *wonder,* had *descended* upon them.   —PAUL HORGAN
10. A little man, dry like a chip and agile like a monkey, *clambered* up.   —CONRAD
11. A Poor *Relation* is the most *irrelevant* thing in Nature, a piece of *impertinent correspondency,* an odious *approximation.*   —LAMB
12. But in a larger sense we cannot *dedicate,* we cannot *consecrate,* we cannot *hallow* this ground.
                                          —ABRAHAM LINCOLN

▶ EXERCISE 7. Substitute more suggestive, homely words for the italicized expressions in the following sentences.

1. The family *came together* around the *chimney place* at Christmas.
2. Tex Gray was a *herder of cattle* for a *stockman.*
3. The old *servant* sang a *song* to the *infant.*
4. The salesman *presented* a *plausible appearance.*
5. The *flowers* on the trellis reminded her of her *farmhouse* home in Kentucky.

(2) Concreteness. Select the specific word instead of the vague word.

Avoid vague generalities. General expressions are necessary in science, literature, and philosophy, as the common use of such terms as *deduction, empiricism, diction, style* testify. But the purpose of most writing is to communicate specific observations and practical instructions. Consequently the safest rule is— Be as specific as you can.

Instead of writing *went* consider the possibility of *rode, walked, trudged, slouched, hobbled, sprinted.* When you are tempted to say a *fine* young man, ask yourself whether *brave, daring, plucky, vigorous, energetic, spirited,* or *loyal* would not be more appropriate. Do not be satisfied with the colorless *ask* when you can choose among *beg, pray, entreat, beseech, implore.* The word *try* is ineffective in most situations when *struggle, fight, battle, strive* are available.

The test for the specific word is contained in six words—*who, what, where, when, how, why.* Notice how the following sentences are improved by asking the questions Who? What? Where? When? How? or Why? about one or more elements in the sentence.

VAGUE　The Dean spoke about student life and that sort of thing. [*Who* spoke about *what?*]

IMPROVED　Dean Jones spoke about the social advantages of the student union.

VAGUE　My brother is going away to have a good time. [*Where* is he going? *How* will he have a good time?]

IMPROVED　My brother is going to Gatlinburg in the Smoky Mountains, where he plans to fish and hunt for a few weeks.

VAGUE　All the columnists are commenting on the high cost of living. [*Who* are commenting? *Where* did comment appear?]

IMPROVED　In the July 12 issue of the New York *Herald Tribune,* Walter Lippmann, George Sokolsky, and Robert Ruark discussed the recent advance in food prices.

VAGUE　The Army team finally advanced the ball. [*How* did they do it?]

IMPROVED　Adams, the Army quarterback, received the ball from center Jim Hawkins, retreated to his ten-yard line, and threw a pass to left-end Smith, who was tackled on the Army thirty-five-yard line.

VAGUE　I think the speech was biased. [*Why?*]

IMPROVED　Mr. Jones began his speech without any attempt to support his statement that the policies of the Republican administration were a "total denial of the American way of life."

► EXERCISE 8.　Substitute specific or emphatic words for general words in the sentences below.

1. The officer made a bad mistake.
2. My father looked at the report.
3. The author's criticism of Blake's work is very good.
4. The journey was made to obtain information concerning various aspects of the North American Indians.
5. It is my prime desire to like all my classes.

(3) Vividness. Use figurative language whenever needed to create vividly the required imaginative or emotional impression.

A figure of speech is the use of a word in an imaginative rather than in a literal sense. The two chief figures of speech are the simile and the metaphor. A *simile* is an explicit comparison between two things of a different kind or quality, usually introduced by *like* or *as:* "He sprang on the foe like a lion." A *metaphor* is an implied comparison: "He was a lion in the fight." (See sentences 2, 5, 8, and 10, in Exercise 6 above, for other examples of simile and metaphor.)

Other figures of speech are personification, metonymy, synecdoche, litotes, and hyperbole. To say that our college is an alma mater (fostering mother) is to *personify* an institution. In the words of *The American College Dictionary,* we often use "the name of one thing for that of another to which it has some logical relation" (*metonymy*), such as *scepter* for *sovereignty.* Synecdoche, which is similar to metonymy, puts a part for the whole or the whole for a part, as *fifty head* for *fifty cattle.* *Litotes* is the name for understatement, as in the remark, "Picasso is not a bad painter." *Hyperbole* is deliberate overstatement or fanciful exaggeration: "The waves were mountains high."

A false sense of simplicity still blinds many contemporary writers to the importance of figurative language in everyday communication. Metaphors and similes are not, as is commonly supposed, merely the ornaments of poetry and old-fashioned oratory. They are essential to certain kinds of physical description and to the expression of feelings and states of mind. When a husband slumps into his chair after a hard day's work and says to his wife, "Thank goodness I'm out of that squirrel cage!" *squirrel cage* is not an ornamental word or an elegant variation. It is a very useful, although unoriginal, metaphor. His wife might respond with another figure of speech by saying, "I played bridge at the Women's Club. It was *suffocating.*" Both figures, *squirrel cage* and *suffocating,* are more effective than the conventional terms *job* and *dull.* Both terms express exactly how the man and his wife felt. The husband's work was confining and active; the wife's bridge game was unbearably dull.

Metaphor and simile are especially valuable because they are concrete and tend to point up essential relationships that cannot otherwise be communicated. (For faulty metaphors see Section 23c.)

▶ EXERCISE 9. Test the exactness and force of the metaphors and similes in the following sentences by attempting to state the same ideas literally.

1. Man is a wild beast, carnivorous by nature, and delighting in blood.   —TAINE

2. That luncheon party . . . was the beginning of a new epoch in my life, but its details are dimmed for me and confused by so many others, almost identical with it, that succeeded one another that term and the next, like romping cupids in a Renaissance frieze.

     —EVELYN WAUGH, *Brideshead Revisited*

3. The fortnight at Venice passed quickly and sweetly—perhaps too sweetly; I was drowning in honey, stingless.   —EVELYN WAUGH

4. The prince became flame to refute her.

     —HENRY JAMES, *The American*

5. His face was like a human skull, a death's-head spouting blood.   —HAZLITT

6. The soul is placed in the body like a rough diamond and must be polished or the luster of it will never appear.   —DEFOE

7. Napoleon was the French Revolution on horseback.

8. O full of scorpions is my mind, dear wife.

     —SHAKESPEARE, *Macbeth*

9. She was as graceful as a sow on ice.

10. The cloud emptied its bellyful of rain.

20b   Use the exact idiom demanded by English usage.

Idioms are short, homely, vigorous expressions that grow up with a language and are peculiar to it. Such idioms as *for many a year, to center around,* or *to strike a bargain* cannot be analyzed or justified grammatically; and yet usage has made them the very heart of the language, suitable for either formal or informal occasions. The unabridged dictionaries treat many idiomatic phrases. See, for instance, the idioms built around *go* and listed after this word in your dictionary. (Note that an idiom—like a word—may be classified as *standard, colloquial, dialectal,* or *slang.*) Writers should be careful to use the exact phrasing for each idiom, not some unidiomatic approximation such as those listed below.

Unidiomatic	Idiomatic
accuse with	accuse of
acquitted from	acquitted of
all the farther	as far as
angry at	angry with

Unidiomatic	Idiomatic
authority about	authority on
buy off of	buy from
comply to	comply with
desirous to	desirous of
die with	die of
equally as bad	equally bad
identical to	identical with
in accordance to	in accordance with
in search for	in search of
in the city Denver	in the city of Denver
in the summer 1947	in the summer of 1947
in the year of 1947	in the year 1947
independent from	independent of
off of	off
prior than	prior to
remember of	remember
seldom or ever	seldom if ever, seldom or never
superior than	superior to
treat on	treat of
vie against	vie with
wait on	wait for

▶ EXERCISE 10. In the following sentences make the idioms conform to standard English usage. If you are not sure whether a given phrase is idiomatic, consult an unabridged dictionary. Write *C* in place of each sentence that needs no revision.

1. The steamer collided against the tug.
2. Mother is vexed at Robert.
3. Your hat is identical to Jane's.
4. I finished high school in the year of 1946.
5. I shall try to comply to your request.
6. The destitute have need of help.
7. Divide up the apples among the children.
8. The child was born in the city Miami.
9. Robert has gone in search for a secondhand car.
10. I bought my car off of the man next door.
11. We plan on going to the seashore.
12. The boy soon became independent from his family.
13. The small child was unequal for the task.
14. She was oblivious to the presence of her friend.
15. I am glad the ordeal is over with.
16. I was not to be taken in by such trickery.
17. Mary seldom or ever misses a class.
18. The boy fell off of the pier.
19. He returned a week ago yesterday.
20. I was sick of a cold.

▶ EXERCISE 11. Consult an unabridged dictionary to determine what prepositions are idiomatically used with *agree, charge, compare, consist, deal, differ,* and *part.* Use each of these verbs correctly in two sentences, each with a different preposition.

▶ EXERCISE 12. In an unabridged dictionary study the idiomatic phrases treated under *catch, put, set, tie,* and *win.* Select three different idioms formed with each verb, and illustrate each idiom in a sentence.

20c Select fresh expressions instead of trite, worn-out ones.

Nearly all trite expressions were once striking and effective. *A bolt from the blue, acid test,* and *social whirl* are, in themselves, effective expressions. What you may not know is that excessive use has made them trite. They are now stock phrases in the language, automatic clichés that have lost their effectiveness.

To avoid trite phrases you must be aware of current usage. Catch phrases and slogans pass quickly from ephemeral popularity into the Old Words' Home. Glittering political shibboleths like *grass roots, pulse of public opinion, forgotten man, century of the common man* are notoriously short-lived. Commercial advertising also bestows its *kiss of death* on an honorable phrase. When a mattress company bids you *sleep in peace* or promises a *midsummer night's dream* on their *airy fairy beds,* when blankets are publicized as *soft as down* or *gentle as a baby's breath,* mark the italicized words as lost to good usage for your generation at least.

Some expressions, however, survive the wear of repeated usage. Proverbs, epithets from great writers like Shakespeare, quotations from the Bible will probably live until the English language dies out completely.

▶ EXERCISE 13. Construct sentences which contain acceptable substitutes for twenty of the hackneyed expressions listed below. In your sentences include within brackets the hackneyed expressions you replace. Be careful not to replace one hackneyed expression with another.

Some Hackneyed Expressions

a long-felt want
abreast of the times
after all is said and done
agree to disagree
all work and no play

along this line
as luck would have it
beat a hasty retreat
better late than never
bitter end

Some Hackneyed Expressions (Cont.)

blushing bride
brave as a lion
brilliant performance
briny deep
budding genius
busy as a bee
by leaps and bounds
center of attraction
cold as ice
depths of despair
do justice to the occasion
doomed to disappointment
easier said than done
equal to the occasion
exception proves the rule
fair sex
fast and furious
filthy lucre
glittering generalities
goes without saying
green as grass
green with envy
heart's content
in all its glory
iron constitution
it stands to reason
last but not least
light fantastic
method in his madness
monarch of all I survey
Mother Earth
motley crowd

nipped in the bud
no sooner said than done
none the worse for wear
on the ball
partake of refreshments
poor but honest
powers that be
promising future
psychological moment
reigns supreme
royal reception
sadder but wiser
scratch the surface
sleep of the just
slow but sure
staff of life
stern realities
straight from the shoulder
sturdy as an oak
sumptuous repast
sweat of his brow
table groaned
this day and age
to the bitter end
too full for utterance
too funny for words
tower of strength
watery grave
wee small hours
where ignorance is bliss
white as a sheet
work like a Trojan
worse for wear
wreathed in smiles

▶ EXERCISE 14. Bring to class a list of hackneyed expressions used in a newspaper or magazine.

▶ OTHER EXERCISES ON EXACTNESS

A. Construct sentences to illustrate one of the exact meanings of each of the following words:

latent	judgment	reflection
opinion	equivocal	distinguish
aspire	flexible	enchanting
affiliation	dense	handsome
universal	conclusion	temper
	tense	

B. Improve the following sentences by correcting errors in idiom and by introducing words that are exact and unhackneyed.

1. I shall neither go or send an explanation.

2. We waited on Jane more than an hour.

3. I read a story where a poor man became a millionaire.

4. The poor man was in the depths of despair.

5. William would not except the appointment.

6. John could not leave without he finished his work.

7. Frank looked very funny when I told him that he had failed.

8. He made an illusion to his former position.

▶ Wordiness and Useless Repetition

21   Avoid wordiness. Repeat a word or phrase only when it is needed to gain force or clearness.

Wordiness is an offense against exact usage. The exact word or expression says all that is necessary (see Section 20), neither too little (see 22) nor too much. We say too much:

a. When we use words or phrases that add nothing to the meaning.
b. When we use an unnecessarily elaborate sentence structure.
c. When we repeat words and phrases carelessly.

21a   Omit words or phrases that add nothing to the meaning.[1]

Note how the following sentences are improved by the omission of the bracketed words.

1. The [architectural] design of the White House is basically [the same as] that of the Duke of Leinster's palace in Dublin.

2. [Architect] James Hoban, the designer of the White House, was a native of Dublin.

3. [It was] in 1792 [that] the cornerstone of the White House was laid.

4. The White House is [such] an impressive building, and [so] much in the spirit of its century.

5. The [usual] consensus [of the majority] is that George Washington did not cut down the cherry tree.

6. Thomas Jefferson was more democratic [to a greater degree] than most of his contemporaries.

7. When Andrew Jackson became President of the United States, the banks were close to [the point of] bankruptcy.

8. [The reason why] we honor Lincoln [is] because he saved the Union.

[1] Bureaucratic jargon, called "gobbledygook," is often extremely wordy. See the examples on page 875.

9. John Adams was very different [in various ways] from his predecessors.

10. The Federalist party was soon connected [up] with the new Republican movement.

SOME WORDY PHRASES As a [usual] rule; at ten P.M. [in the evening]; big [in size]; circulated [around]; combined [together]; co-operate [together]; first time [in my life]; Halloween [evening]; [important] essentials; [joint] partnership; meet [up with]; modern colleges [of today]; my [own] autobiography; round [in shape]; small [in size]; ten [in number]; total effect [of all this]; where . . . [at]; yellow [in color]

▶ EXERCISE 1. Strike out unnecessary words from the following sentences. Write C in place of each sentence that needs no revision.

1. It happened that my brother was stronger than I had expected him to be.

2. On our list are the names of many wealthy and influential citizens.

3. The marble columns were gray in color.

4. Mr. McConn divides into three groups, or classes, the students of today who go to modern colleges.

5. As a usual rule the legislature is filled with lawyers.

6. It was during the Renaissance that a very large number of words, many of them terms of scholarship, were then taken from the Latin.

7. My chief aim is to make life easier for the farmer.

8. After the play was over with, we walked home together.

9. I wish to refer you back to the first page.

10. We pondered in our minds how we might descend down to the bottom of the canyon.

21b If necessary, revise the structure of the sentence to avoid wordiness.

Caution: In order to understand 21b you may need to review Section 1, **Sentence Sense,** especially pages 800-02.

An idea may be expressed in one of the four primary units of composition: a sentence, a clause, a phrase, or a word. Sometimes we waste many words in trying to make an idea clear. Note in the following series of examples how the fundamental idea (printed in italics) becomes successively sharper as the expression grows less wordy.

> *The mist hung like a veil.* It obscured the top of the mountain. [Full sentences used to express the idea]
> The mist *hung like a veil* and obscured the top of the mountain. [Part of a compound predicate]
> The mist, *which hung like a veil,* obscured the top of the mountain. [Subordinate clause]
> The mist, *hanging like a veil,* obscured the top of the mountain. [Participial phrase]
> The mist, *like a veil,* obscured the top of the mountain. [Prepositional phrase]
> The mist *veiled* the top of the mountain. [Word]

All of these sentences are acceptable, but they are not equally effective. Although any one of them may, at times, meet the special needs of the writer, the least wordy will normally be the most effective.

Practice reducing sentences to the simplest and shortest form, as in the following examples:

WORDY Another thing is good health. It is one of our great blessings. It may be had through proper diet and exercise. Rest is also desirable. [Four simple sentences—25 words]
BETTER The great blessing of good health may be had through proper diet, exercise, and rest. [Reduced to one simple sentence—15 words]

WORDY A new addition has been built at the side of the house, and this addition has been developed into a library. [Compound sentence—21 words]
BETTER An addition, built at the side of the house, has been developed into a library. [Reduced to a simple sentence containing a participial phrase—15 words]

WORDY When the Indians made tools, they used flint and bone. [Complex sentence—10 words]
BETTER The Indians made tools of flint and bone. [Reduced to a simple sentence—8 words]

WORDY There were six men who volunteered. [Complex sentence—6 words]
BETTER Six men volunteered. [Reduced to a simple sentence—3 words]

▶ EXERCISE 2. Revise the structure of the following sentences to correct wordiness.

1. Personally I believe it was the Spaniards rather than the Indians who first brought horses and ponies to America.
2. If any workers were disgruntled, they made their complaints to the man who was in charge as manager.
3. My uncle was a tall man. He had a long nose. Over his right eye he had a deep scar.
4. The grass was like a carpet. It covered the whole lawn. The color of the grass was a deep blue.

21c Avoid careless or needless repetition of a word or phrase.

Use repetition only to attain greater clearness (see 22b, 22c, 26b, 31b(3)) or emphasis (see 29e).

CARELESS Since the committee has already made three general *reports,* only the *report* dealing with promotions will be *reported* on today.
BETTER Since the committee has already made three general reports, it will submit today only its recommendations on promotions.

CARELESS It is *impossible* to ask me to do the *impossible.*
BETTER You cannot expect me to do the impossible.

Use a pronoun instead of needlessly repeating a noun. Several pronouns in succession, even in successive sentences, may refer to the same antecedent noun, so long as the reference remains clear.

NEEDLESS When Mr. Bevan temporarily lost his place in the Parliamentary party on that memorable day there were many people who thought that *Bevan* would be subsequently expelled from the party. After three weeks of fury and alarm, *Mr. Bevan* was saved by about the tenth of a gnat's eyebrow—that is to say, a compromise resolution was passed by only one vote. Thus for the first time in four years *Bevan's* enemies were defeated on a major issue and Mr. Bevan remains within the fold.

CORRECT   When Mr. Bevan temporarily lost his place in the Parliamentary party on that memorable day there were many people who thought that *he* would be subsequently expelled from the party. After three weeks of fury and alarm, *he* was saved by about the tenth of a gnat's eyebrow—that is to say, a compromise resolution was passed by only one vote. Thus for the first time in four years *his* enemies were defeated on a major issue and Mr. Bevan remains within the fold.

—HUGH MASSINGHAM [2]

▶ EXERCISE 3.   Revise the following sentences to avoid careless repetition.

1. In 1923 Ruth batted .393, and he batted .378 the next year.
2. While driving, a good driver always takes care to obey the driving laws of the state he is driving through.
3. The practice of helping one's neighbors for the enjoyment of it is a very common practice.
4. In the last act of the play we find the explanation of the title of the play.
5. Early in the morning we set out for Jones

[2] From "The Labor Party: A Study in Schizophrenia" by Hugh Massingham, *The New York Times Magazine,* May 15, 1955. Reprinted by permission of the author and the publisher.

Beach so that we could enjoy all the pleasures that that great playground affords.

▶ EXERCISE ON WORDINESS
AND USELESS REPETITION

Rewrite the following passage to eliminate wordiness and useless repetition.

1. Samuel Clemens (Mark Twain) was born in 1835 at Florida, County of Monroe, State of Missouri; but while he was still quite young, his family moved to Hannibal, a small Mississippi River town, where Samuel as a boy spent the days of his youth, and he grew up to young manhood there.   2. In 1853 Samuel Clemens left this small Mississippi River town of Hannibal to see something of the world.   3. In his itinerant wandering during the next four years which followed, Clemens worked at the printing trade in printing shops of various cities in the East and Middle West from the Mississippi to the Atlantic seaboard.   4. In Cincinnati, Ohio, in the year of 1857 Clemens took passage on a river steamboat bound down the river for New Orleans, Louisiana.   5. On this trip down the river Clemens met the pilot who steered the boat, named Mr. Horace Bixby, who agreed for the sum of five hundred dollars in money to teach young Clemens (Mark Twain) the art of piloting boats up and down the river.   6. One may read of Mark Twain's experience as a cub pilot apprentice in his book which he wrote about it and called *Life on the Mississippi.*

▶ # Omission of Necessary Words

22   Do not omit a word or phrase necessary to the meaning of the sentence.

Most faulty omissions in student writing may be traced to carelessness. To avoid such errors, proofread all compositions before submitting them to your instructor.

EXAMPLES   We have learned the importance ᴧ using perfume. [Careless omission of the preposition *of*]
    John had been there only ᴧ moment ago. [Careless omission of the article *a*]
    I wish I ᴧ been able to play football at ᴧ University. [Careless omission of *had* (a part of the verb) and of the article *the*]

22a   Do not omit an article, a pronoun, a conjunction, or a preposition that is necessary to make your meaning clear.

(1) Omitted article or pronoun

RIGHT   A friend and helper stood at his side; *or,* His friend and helper stood at his side. [The friend and helper are the same person.]
RIGHT   A friend and *a* helper stood at his side; *or,* His friend and *his* helper stood at his side. [To show that the friend and the helper are different persons, the article *a* or the pronoun *his* must be repeated.]

(2) Omitted conjunction

CONFUSING They noticed the young men who made up the crew were eager to start. [*Young men* can be momentarily mistaken for the object of *noticed*.]

BETTER They noticed *that* the young men who made up the crew were eager to start.

Note: The conjunction *that* is frequently omitted as an introduction to clauses when the omission is not confusing.

EXAMPLE He said he would go.

(3) Omitted preposition

AWKWARD The school burned down my last term.

BETTER The school burned down *during* my last term.

AWKWARD Mardi Gras he went to New Orleans.

BETTER *For* Mardi Gras he went to New Orleans.

Note: Some idiomatic phrases indicating time or place regularly omit the preposition. *Examples: Next summer* he will go to camp. They arrived *last week.* He will come *home.*

22b Do not omit a necessary verb or a necessary auxiliary verb.

AWKWARD The play is good and the characters interesting. [Singular *is* may be used with singular *play* but not with plural *characters*.]

BETTER The play is good and the characters *are* interesting. [The correct verb is supplied for *characters*.]

AWKWARD He never has and never will be an enemy of his country. [*Be* is the correct auxiliary for *will* but not for *has*.]

BETTER He never has *been* an enemy of his country, and he never will be. [The correct auxiliary is supplied for *has*.]

22c Do not omit words necessary to complete comparisons (or other constructions).

CONFUSING The equipment of a soldier is heavier than a sailor. [Did the soldier's equipment weigh more than an individual sailor?]

CLEAR The equipment of a soldier is heavier than *that* of a sailor.

CLEAR A soldier's equipment is heavier than a sailor's.

CONFUSING The scenery here is as beautiful as any other place. [Comparison of things not capable of comparison]

CLEAR The scenery here is as beautiful as *it is at* any other place.

CONFUSING I admire Shakespeare more than Goethe.

CLEAR I admire Shakespeare more than *I* admire Goethe; *or,* I admire Shakespeare more than Goethe *did.*

Note: Incomplete comparisons are a particularly common fault in advertising copy.

INCOMPLETE This filter tip screens out 50% more harmful tar products. [What two things are being compared?]

COMPLETE This filter tip screens out 50% more harmful tar products than a tea strainer would. *Or:* This filter tip screens out 50% more harmful tar products than it does bugs and flies. [Probably no advertiser would make either of these statements, but at least they do contain some definite information—which the incomplete comparison does not.]

INCOMPLETE You will agree that Crumpet Creek Dairy products are definitely better. [Better than what? Ditch water?]

COMPLETE You will agree that Crumpet Creek Dairy products are definitely better than ever before. *Or even:* You will agree that Crumpet Creek Dairy products are definitely better than ditch water.

Note, however, that once a frame of reference has been established, an intelligible comparison may be made without explicit mention of the second term of the comparison.

RIGHT It is not to be inferred that of this poetical vigor Pope had only a little, because Dryden had more [*than Pope had* is clearly understood without its being stated]; for every other writer since Milton must give place to Pope; and even of Dryden it must be said, that, if he has brighter paragraphs [*than Pope has* again is clearly enough understood], he has not better poems. . . . If the flights of Dryden . . . are higher, Pope continues longer on the wing. If of Dryden's fire the blaze is brighter, of Pope's the heat is more regular and constant. —SAMUEL JOHNSON

INCOMPLETE I have always preferred living in Chiengmai. [Preferred it to what?]

IMPROVED Though Bangkok is by far the larger place, I have always preferred living in Chiengmai.

INCOMPLETE   When you first see Dr. Zeiss, you will be surprised at how different he is. [Different from whom or what?]

IMPROVED   When you first see Dr. Zeiss, you will be surprised at what an unusual person he is. *Or:* When you first see Dr. Zeiss, you will be surprised at how much he has changed.

INCOMPLETE   He is as old, if not older, than his cousin.

IMPROVED   He is as old *as his cousin,* if not older.

Standard writing avoids such intensives as *so, such,* and *too* without the completing clause.

COLLOQUIAL   I was so tired. She had such beautiful eyes. He was not too much interested in the lecture.

STANDARD   I was so tired that I could not sleep. *Or:* I was extremely tired. She has such beautiful eyes that everyone admires them. He was not especially interested in the lecture.

▶ EXERCISE ON OMISSIONS

Rewrite the following sentences, supplying all words that are needed to make the meaning clear and unambiguous. Write *C* in place of each sentence that needs no revision.

1. Our new Hampton shirts last much longer.
2. Jim's wife and mother stood beside him at the trial.
3. You are as good as, if not better than, anyone else.
4. The prisoner had been hiding some place near Detroit.
5. He writes about the days he had neither food nor shelter.
6. William is so different from the others.
7. The lawyer had to prove whatever the witness said was false.
8. The spillway allows the water at the dam be kept at the same level.
9. He was so manly and so brave although only six years old.
10. I protested that I could not come.

EFFECTIVE SENTENCES

▶ Unity and Logical Thinking

The fundamental qualities of an effective sentence are unity, coherence, emphasis, and variety. Unity and coherence help to make a sentence logical and clear. Emphasis makes it forceful. Variety lends interest. Usually every good sentence contains all these equally necessary qualities of style. But for the purpose of study we may consider each quality separately. In this section and the next we shall present some of the problems of unity.

23   Avoid bringing into the sentence unrelated ideas or too many details. Complete each thought logically.

A sentence is unified when all its parts contribute to one clear idea or impression. In such a sentence, thought and expression are one, parts unite to form a perfect whole, and we say: "Here it is. We cannot alter a clause, a phrase, or even a word without disturbing the clarity of thought or the focus of the impression." Such a sentence is like a pane of clearest glass; we look through it, unconscious of its existence. But when an idea is not clear or an impression is somewhat fuzzy, the sentence becomes like a wall that stands between us and what the writer is trying to say.

We have already noted that a sentence lacks unity when it is a fragment (see Section 2), contains a "comma splice" (see 3), or is incomplete (see 22). We shall now note that a sentence also lacks unity:

a. When it combines unrelated ideas.
b. When it has excessive detail.
c. When it is mixed, obscure, or illogical.

23a Unrelated ideas should be developed in separate sentences. (If the ideas are are related, they should be expressed in such a way that the relationship is immediately clear to the reader.)

UNRELATED Mr. Smith is my teacher and he has a large family.
IMPROVED Mr. Smith is my teacher. He has a large family. [Ideas given equal importance]
IMPROVED Mr. Smith, my teacher, has a large family. [Unity secured by subordination of one idea. See Section 24.]

UNRELATED The birds are numerous and the cherries seldom ripen. [Relationship not immediately clear]
IMPROVED The numerous birds pick most of the cherries before they ripen.

UNRELATED Ireland has a deep culture, but the country is out of the path of general travel. [Unity thwarted by a gap in the thought]
IMPROVED Ireland has a deep culture, but this culture is insufficiently appreciated because the country is out of the path of general travel.

► EXERCISE 1. Rewrite the following sentences to point up the implied relationship between the ideas.

1. The stocks continued to drop, and the war was not far off.
2. He came into the room, and immediately the situation explained itself.
3. Lee fell back on Richmond, so that Stuart was forced to retreat.

► EXERCISE 2. Rewrite the following sentences to achieve unity.

1. Mollusks which yield pearls are widespread, and pearl fishing is carried on in many parts of the world.
2. The foreman, speaking in gruff tones and seldom smiling, wore a gray coat.
3. Birds migrate to the warmer countries in the fall and in summer get food by eating worms and insects which are a pest to the farmer.

23b Excessive detail should not be allowed to obscure the central thought of the sentence.

Such detail, if important, should be developed in separate sentences; otherwise it should be omitted.

OVERLOADED When I was only four years old, living in an old Colonial house, little of which remains today, I could already walk the two miles that separated the house from the railroad station.
BETTER When I was only four years old, I could already walk the two miles between my house and the railway station. [If the writer considers other details important, he may write another sentence to include them: I was living in an old Colonial house, little of which remains today.]

OVERLOADED In 1788, when Andrew Jackson, then a young man of twenty-one years who had been living in the Carolinas, still a virgin country, came into Tennessee, a turbulent place of unknown opportunities, to enforce the law as the new prosecuting attorney, he had the qualities in him which would make him equal to the task.
BETTER In 1788, when Andrew Jackson came into Tennessee as the new prosecuting attorney, he had the necessary qualifications for the task.

OVERLOADED AND WORDY I have never before known a man who was so ready to help a friend who had got into difficulties which pressed him so hard. [Avoid this house-that-Jack-built construction: who . . . who, etc.]
BETTER I have never before known a man so ready to help a friend in trouble.

► EXERCISE 3. Recast the following sentences to eliminate excessive detail.

1. The boat, considered seaworthy ten years ago, but now in need of paint and repairs, as is so often true of things that should be discarded, moved out into the bay.
2. The captain asked for a volunteer, and the soldier picked up his pack, which weighed thirty pounds, and asked if he might go.
3. A course in business methods helps the young man to get a job in order that he may prove whether he is fitted for business and thus avoid postponing the test, as so many do, until it is too late.

Be careful to note that length alone does not make a sentence ineffective. Most good writers compose long sentences, sometimes of paragraph length, without loss of unity. The use of parallel structure, balance, rhythm, careful punctuation, well-placed connectives can bind a sentence into perfect unity. Observe the effective repetition (indicated by italics) in Winston Churchill's famous sentence:

We shall go on to the end, *we shall fight* in France, *we shall fight* on the seas and oceans, *we shall fight* with growing confidence and growing strength in the air, *we shall defend* our Island, whatever the cost may be, *we shall fight* on the beaches, *we shall fight* on the landing grounds, *we shall fight* in the fields and in the streets, *we shall fight* in the hills; *we shall never surrender,* and even if, which I do not for a moment believe, this Island or a large part of it were subjugated and starving, then our Empire beyond the seas, armed and guarded by the British Fleet, *would carry on the struggle,* until, in God's good time, the New World, with all its power and might, steps forth to the rescue and the liberation of the old.   —WINSTON CHURCHILL [1]

In the following sentence Henry James maintains unity by balancing the "grand hotel" with the "small Swiss pension." (Italics have been added.)

The shore of the lake presents an unbroken array of establishments of this order, of every category, *from the "grand hotel" of the newest fashion,* with a chalk-white front, a hundred balconies, and a dozen flags flying from its roof, *to the small Swiss pension of an elder day,* with its name inscribed in German-looking lettering upon a pink or yellow wall and an awkward summerhouse in the angle of the garden.
          —HENRY JAMES, *Daisy Miller*

23c Mixed, obscure, or illogical constructions should be avoided.

(1) Do not mix figures of speech by changing too rapidly from one to another.

MIXED   This rebellion must be checked before it boils over. [Figure of spirited horse being reined in + figure of liquid becoming overheated]

BETTER   This rebellion must be checked before it gets out of control (*or* runs away). [Figure of spirited horse carried throughout]

(2) Do not mix constructions. Complete each construction logically.

MIXED   Because he was sick caused him to stay at home. [An adverb clause, a part of a complex sentence, is here mixed with the predicate of a simple sentence.]

CLEAR   His sickness caused him to stay at home. [Simple sentence]

CLEAR   Because he was sick he stayed at home. [Adverb clause retained; main clause added to complete the complex sentence]

MIXED   A sonnet *is when* a poem has fourteen lines. [Avoid the *is when* or *is where* construction. A *when* clause, used as an adverb, cannot be substituted for a noun.]

LOGICAL   A sonnet is a poem of fourteen lines.

MIXED   To banish *is where* a person is driven out of his country. [Adverb clause misused as a noun]

LOGICAL   To banish a person is to drive him out of his country.

(3) Make each part of the sentence agree logically with the other parts.

Often a sentence which contains no grammatical error is nevertheless absurd because of failure in logical agreement.

ILLOGICAL   Many of the men were refusing to reenlist and were returning home to their family. [It is almost impossible to suppose an army in which *many of the men* share among them only one family.]

LOGICAL   Many of the men were refusing to reenlist and were returning home to their families. [This is a far more likely statement of what the men were actually doing.]

ILLOGICAL   George is a better player than the others are. [There is no logical basis for comparison; although George is *a player,* the others are not *a player,* but *players.*]

BETTER   George is a better player than any one of the others.

▶ EXERCISE 4.   In each sentence select the parenthetical word or phrase which logical expression of the thought requires, and give reasons for your choice.

1. (A new wing was, New wings were) added to the building in 1923 and 1949.
2. Do you men realize that your (career depends, careers depend) upon the work you are doing now?

3. The page preceding (each chapter, the chapters) contains an appropriate illustration.

4. Their (temperament was, temperaments were) as nearly alike as any two men's could have been.

5. Every evening this week we have had (a fire, fires) in our fireplace.

6. Besides that, we have needed an extra blanket on (each bed, the beds).

7. Upon completion of their (enlistment, enlistments) the men will be given travel pay to their (home, homes).

8. The Empire State Building is taller than (any, any other) building in New York.

9. The Empire State Building is taller than (any, any other) building in New Orleans.

10. Tourists are not permitted to bring their (camera, cameras) inside the area.

11. Does each of them understand the nature of (his assignment, their assignments)?

12. You children may take off your (mask, masks) now and come into the dining room for refreshments.

(4) Do not use the double negative.

ILLITERATE   I don't want none.

STANDARD   I don't want any.

ILLOGICAL   The driver couldn't hardly miss the way.

LOGICAL   The driver could hardly miss the way.

(5) Do not make illogical, poorly reasoned statements.

The final test of good writing is the soundness of its reasoning. You should make sure that all your sentences are well thought out and contain no fallacies in reasoning. Three fallacies that often occur in writing and speaking are (1) drawing an inference that does not follow from the evidence (called a *non sequitur*, "it does not follow"): "He's an honest boy; he'll make a success at anything he tries"; (2) obscuring the issue by reference to the man involved (called *argumentum ad hominem*, "argument to the man"): "He's a radical; his arguments against the assessment are worthless"; or especially (3) making a hasty generalization—jumping to a conclusion without a sufficient number of instances or examples: "None of my children will drink coffee; children don't like coffee."

▶ EXERCISES ON UNITY AND LOGICAL THINKING

A. Revise the following sentences as necessary to make them unified, logical, and clear.

1. Of course the other car was at fault: the driver was a woman.

2. The late President Franklin D. Roosevelt was a victim of infantile paralysis, and he founded the National Foundation for Infantile Paralysis in 1938 in order to support scientific research as well as to give aid to thousands of sufferers.

3. The average farm wage for the calendar year 1910 was $21.22, including board, a small sum indeed compared with the monthly wage of $96.00 in 1947, although prices have also gone up at the same time.

4. You can't do but one thing at a time, so buckle down and consider your job of studying as better than a wage earner.

5. Alaska is a country for future colonization, and the people from the Dust Bowl have gone there to live.

B. Use the following unified and logical sentences as models for sentences of your own. Do not imitate slavishly. Aim to reproduce the design or structure of the model sentence, not to copy the details. Especially be careful to avoid repeating expressions no longer in common use.

1. MODEL SENTENCE   The human mind is capable of being excited without the application of gross and violent stimulants.—WORDSWORTH
   TOPIC   The human heart

   EXAMPLE   The human heart may be moved to deepest sympathy for human suffering without giving way to excessive sentimentality.

2. MODEL SENTENCE   It is a truth universally acknowledged, that a single man in possession of a good fortune must be in want of a wife.   —JANE AUSTEN
   TOPIC   A poor widow

3. MODEL SENTENCE   He who would be a courtier under a king is almost certain to be a demagogue in a democracy.
      —JAMES FENIMORE COOPER
   TOPIC   A thief in low and high society

4. MODEL SENTENCE   I hate to see a load of bandboxes go down the street, and I hate to see a parcel of big words without anything in them.   —HAZLITT
   TOPIC   The excessive use of cosmetics

▶ Subordination (An Aid to Unity)

24 **Determine the most important idea of the sentence and express it in the main clause. Put lesser ideas in subordinate clauses, phrases, or words. Use co-ordination only for ideas of equal importance.**

Note: Can you distinguish readily between phrases and clauses, between main clauses and subordinate clauses? Until you can do so you will have difficulty in understanding Section 24. If necessary, master first the fundamentals of the sentence treated under Section 1, **Sentence Sense,** especially **1d,** and then study **Subordination.**

The principle of subordination is of great importance in composition, since it is one of the best means of achieving sentence unity. The ability to discriminate between the main idea and the dependent idea is also a mark of maturity. As we develop the power of expression we discard *short, choppy sentences,* or a series of *brief main clauses connected by* "*and,*" in favor of the more precise complex sentence in which our ideas are properly subordinated.

A child will express himself somewhat like this:

I walked down the road. I saw a bird. It was in a tree. It was singing. [Short, choppy sentences—subordination lacking]

At a slightly older age the child might say:

I walked down the road, and I saw a bird, and it was in a tree, and it was singing. [*And*-sentence—subordination lacking]

A mature writer will express in the main clause of his sentence the idea he wishes to stress and will subordinate all other ideas by reducing them to a subordinate clause, a phrase, or a word.

As I walked down the road [subordinate clause], I saw a bird [main clause] singing [word] in a tree [phrase].

If the singing of the bird is more important than the seeing of the bird, the sentence might read:

A bird was singing in a tree as I walked down the road.

24a **In general a related series of short, choppy sentences should be combined into longer units in which the lesser ideas are properly subordinated.**

CHOPPY This is a wreck. It was formerly the stately Industrial Exhibition Hall. It is preserved deliberately as a reminder and symbol.
BETTER This wreck, formerly the stately Industrial Exhibition Hall, is preserved deliberately as a reminder and symbol. —ROBERT TRUMBULL [1]

CHOPPY Thousands of buildings met the same fate. This alone is now being preserved. It marks the center of the explosion. It is being preserved as a symbol. It symbolizes our wish that there be no more Hiroshimas.
BETTER "Of the thousands of buildings that met the same fate, this alone, marking the center of the explosion, is now being preserved to symbolize our wish that there be no more Hiroshimas." [2]

CHOPPY He stood there in his buckskin clothes. One felt in him standards and loyalties. One also felt a code. This code is not easily put into words. But this code is instantly felt when two men who live by it come together by chance.
BETTER As he stood there in his buckskin clothes, one felt in him standards, loyalties, a code which is not easily put into words, but which

[1] "Hiroshima—Ten Years After," *The New York Times Magazine,* July 31, 1955, p. 5.
[2] *Ibid.* (From a bronze plaque at the entrance of the building.)

is instantly felt when two men who live by it come together by chance.   —WILLA CATHER

CHOPPY   I was a little refreshed. I went up into the country. I resolved to deliver myself up to the first savages I should meet. I also resolved to purchase my life from them by some bracelets, glass rings, and other toys which sailors usually provide themselves with in those voyages. I had some of these trinkets with me.

BETTER   When I was a little refreshed, I went up into the country, resolving to deliver myself to the first savages I should meet, and purchase my life from them by some bracelets, glass rings, and other toys which sailors usually provide themselves with in those voyages, and whereof I had some about me.
    —JONATHAN SWIFT, Gulliver's Travels

► EXERCISE 1.   Combine the following short sentences into longer sentences in which ideas are properly subordinated.

    1. The miller was a large man.   2. He weighed well over two hundred pounds.   3. He wore a red beard.   4. It was thick and broad and was shaped like a spade.   5. On his nose grew a wart.   6. Red bristles sprouted out of the wart.   7. This miller was a quarrelsome man.   8. He was proud of his bull-like strength.   9. He missed no chance to display it.   10. He especially liked to show off by tearing down doors.   11. He would jerk them off their hinges.   12. He could also butt them to pieces with his head.   13. Sometimes there was no door convenient.   14. Then he would get attention in other ways.   15. He was a loud-mouth.   16. He always had a story ready to tell.   17. His stories were ones he had picked up in barrooms.   18. Usually they were filthy.   19. It didn't matter that decent people were nearby.   20. He would tell his story anyhow.   21. He had to make a noisy display of himself in one way or another.   22. He never ran out of ways of doing it.   23. He might not be able to find a door to wreck.   24. People sometimes wouldn't listen to his stories.   25. He played a bagpipe.   26. His behavior had its reward.   27. It kept him from being a very well-liked man.

24b   Do not write and, so, or but sentences when one idea should be subordinated to another. Use co-ordination only for ideas of equal importance. (See also 30c.)

INEFFECTIVE   The weather was hot and (or so) I stayed at home. [Two main clauses]

BETTER   Because the weather was hot [subordinate clause] I stayed at home.

ACCEPTABLE   The offer was tempting, but I did not accept it. [Co-ordination used to stress equally the offer and the refusal]

USUALLY BETTER   Although the offer was tempting, I did not accept it. [Stress on one of the two—the refusal]

INEFFECTIVE   North Dakotans are sturdy and industrious, and they are mostly of Scandinavian and German stock, and they are working during this time of no immediate crisis on a promising plan to prevent future dust bowls.

BETTER   Sturdy and industrious, mostly of Scandinavian and German stock, North Dakotans are working during this time of no immediate crisis on a promising plan to prevent future dust bowls.   —TIME [3]

INEFFECTIVE   I had always wanted to go to college, and I had always wished to become an engineer, and so I enrolled at the Carnegie Institute of Technology.

IMPROVED   Because I had always wanted to enter college and prepare myself to become an engineer, I enrolled at the Carnegie Institute of Technology.

IMPROVED   I enrolled at the Carnegie Institute of Technology to achieve my double purpose of attending college and becoming an engineer.

► EXERCISE 2.   Revise the following sentences to subordinate the less important ideas.

    1. Campanella has a good batting record, so pitchers treat him with respect.

    2. We had just reached the bend in the road on our way home, and we saw a truckload of Boy Scouts crowded off the highway by an oncoming car.

    3. First he selected a lancet and sterilized it, and then he gave his patient a local anesthetic and lanced the infected part.

    4. Father Latour was at a friend's house, and he saw two fine horses, and he induced the owner to part with them.

    5. I graduated from high school, and then I worked in a bank, and so I earned enough to go to college.

The conjunctive adverbs however, therefore, and consequently are often used in transitions when subordination would be preferable. Main clauses linked by these conjunctive adverbs can usually be combined and the proper relationship indicated by a subordinat-

[3] August 8, 1955, p. 16.

ing conjunction. Subordinating conjunctions express such relationships as cause (*because, since*), concession (*although*), time (*after, before, since, whenever, while, until*), place (*where*), or condition (*if, unless*).

CO-ORDINATION   I became increasingly uneasy; however, I kept my seat.

SUBORDINATION   Although I became increasingly uneasy, I kept my seat. [Subordination is usually better.]

CO-ORDINATION   Fred knows almost nothing about farming; therefore I do not expect him to enjoy much success.

SUBORDINATION   Since Fred knows almost nothing about farming, I do not expect him to enjoy much success.

► EXERCISE 3.   Write twelve sentences to illustrate the twelve subordinating conjunctions listed above. Let each conjunction introduce a subordinate clause in which you express an idea of less importance than that in the main clause.

24c Do not place the main thought of the sentence in a subordinate clause (or construction).

FAULTY   When we have made a good soldier out of a rookie, he has learned how to march, use his weapons, and respond to commands.

BETTER   When a rookie has learned how to march, use his weapons, and respond to commands, we have made a good soldier out of him.

FAULTY   William was only a substitute pitcher, winning half of his games.

BETTER   Although William was only a substitute pitcher, he won half of his games.

FAULTY   The rising water broke the dam, when the town was doomed.

BETTER   When the rising water broke the dam, the town was doomed.

► EXERCISE 4.   Revise each of the following sentences to give prominence to the main thought.

1. The insects eat the plant off just below the soil, stopping all growth.

2. I was at a lecture when our house burned down.

3. The man was asleep while his comrades planned to rob him.

4. One day I was musing on the pleasures of being idle when the thought struck me that complete idleness was hard work.

5. A cow kicked over a lantern, thus causing one of the world's great fires.

► EXERCISE ON SUBORDINATION

Revise the following passage to achieve proper subordination.

1. I was walking down the street when I found a purse containing fifty dollars. 2. It was just noon. 3. Thousands of people were on the streets. 4. I could not find the owner. 5. I went into the neighboring stores, and I inquired of the shopkeepers whether anyone had lost the money, and I approached the policeman with the same question. 6. No one could say who had lost the money, and so I thought I was the rightful owner, having found the purse myself. 7. But my father did not approve my keeping the purse. 8. He asked me to advertise it. 9. He said I might use the daily paper. 10. Next day I ran an advertisement in the paper, and now a week has passed and I have had no answers, and so I think the money is really mine.

► Coherence: Misplaced Parts; Dangling Modifiers

25 Avoid needless separation of related parts of the sentence. Avoid dangling modifiers.

Note: Can you distinguish readily the various modifiers, the several parts of the sentence? Until you are able to do so, you may have difficulty in understanding Section 25. If necessary, master first the fundamentals of the sentence treated in Section 1, **Sentence Sense**, especially **1d**, then study **Coherence**. See also **Modifier** and **Modify** in Section 35, **Grammatical Terms.**

The meaning of an English sentence depends largely on the position of its parts. Usually these parts—especially the words, phrases, and subordinate clauses serving as modifiers—can be placed in various positions; and they should be placed to give just the emphasis or meaning desired. Note how the meaning in the following sentences changes according to the position of the modifier *only:*

She said that she loved *only* him. [She loved no one else.]

She said that *only* she loved him. [No one else loved him.]

She said *only* that she loved him. [She said nothing else.]

Normally the modifier should be placed as near the word modified as idiomatic English will permit.

Misplaced Parts

25a Avoid needless separation of related parts of the sentence.

(1) In standard written English, adverbs such as *almost, also, only, just, ever, before, even,* or *merely* are regularly placed immediately before the words they modify.

In spoken English, which tends to place these adverbs before the verb, ambiguity can be prevented by stressing the word to be modified.

AMBIGUOUS IN WRITING I *only* delivered the parcel.
Does *only* modify *parcel* or *delivered?*
CLEAR I delivered *only* the parcel.

AMBIGUOUS He is *just* asking for a trifle.
CLEAR He is asking for *just* a trifle.

AMBIGUOUS Every soldier can*not* become a general. [Literally, no soldier can.]
CLEAR *Not* every soldier can become a general. [Some soldiers can.]

► EXERCISE 1. Place the adverbs in the following sentences immediately before the words they modify.

1. Some contemporary poets hardly show any interest in making their poems intelligible.
2. I only bet on the horse to take third place.
3. He took the penny home and polished it almost until it looked like new.
4. The man was only willing to sell a part of the farm.

5. He even works during his vacation.

(2) Phrases should be placed near the words they modify.

MISPLACED The boy says that he means to leave the country *in the first stanza.*
CLEAR The boy says *in the first stanza* that he means to leave the country.

MISPLACED He played a great part in the war with Mexico *as a statesman.*
CLEAR *As a statesman* he played a great part in the war with Mexico.

MISPLACED Heated arguments had often occurred *over technicalities in the middle* of a game.
CLEAR Heated arguments *over technicalities* had often occurred *in the middle of a game.*

► EXERCISE 2. Recast the following sentences to correct undesirable separation of related parts. Explain exactly what ambiguity each separation causes in each sentence.

1. King Arthur decided to punish those who opposed him for very good reasons.
2. The ship was stripped for action and ready for battle within an hour.
3. Romeo received word that Juliet was dead from another messenger.
4. The engineering work was a thing of beauty on all the large buildings.
5. He tells how Lincoln collected fees that his clients did not pay among other things.

(3) Clauses, especially relative clauses, should be placed near the words they modify. (See also 28a.)

AMBIGUOUS I placed the chair in the corner of the room *which I had recently purchased.* [The relative clause seems to modify *room.*]
CLEAR I placed in the corner of the room the chair *which I had recently purchased; or,* In the corner of the room I placed the chair *which I had recently purchased.*

AMBIGUOUS I saw the horse stop at the edge of the precipice *that had raced ahead.*
CLEAR I saw the horse *that had raced ahead* stop at the edge of the precipice.

(4) Avoid "squinting" constructions—modifiers that may refer either to a preceding or to a following word.

SQUINTING I agreed *on the next day* to help him.
CLEAR I agreed to help him *on the next day.*
CLEAR *On the next day,* I agreed to help him.

SQUINTING The tug which was whistling *noisily* chugged up the river.

CLEAR The whistling tug chugged *noisily* up the river.

CLEAR The tug whistled *noisily* as it chugged up the river.

(5) Avoid awkward splitting of infinitives or needless separation of subject and verb, and of parts of verb phrases.

AWKWARD You should now begin *to,* if you wish to succeed, *hunt* for a job.

IMPROVED If you wish to succeed, you should now begin *to hunt* for a job. [In general avoid the "split" infinitive unless it is needed for smoothness or emphasis.]

AWKWARD *I,* knowing all the facts, *want* to be excused.

IMPROVED Knowing all the facts, *I want* to be excused.

AWKWARD There stood the wagon which we *had* early last autumn *left* by the barn.

IMPROVED There stood the wagon which we *had left* by the barn early last autumn.

Dangling Modifiers

25b Avoid dangling modifiers.

Dangling [1] modifiers are verbal phrases (participial, gerund, infinitive) or elliptical clauses which do not refer clearly and logically to some word in the sentence. When these constructions come at the beginning of a sentence, they must refer to the subject of the sentence, as in the following examples:

PARTICIPLE *Taking* our seats, *we* watched the game.

GERUND After *taking* our seats, *we* watched the game.

INFINITIVE *To watch* the game, *we* took our seats.

ELLIPTICAL CLAUSE *When only a small boy,* I went with my father to Denver. [*I was* is implied in the elliptical clause.]

(1) Avoid dangling participial phrases.

DANGLING *Taking* our seats, the game started. [*Taking* does not refer to *game,* nor to any other word in the sentence.]

IMPROVED *Taking* (or *Having taken*) our seats, *we* watched the opening of the game. [*Taking* refers to *we,* the subject of the sentence.]

[1] The term "dangling" is applied especially to incoherent verbal phrases and elliptical clauses. But any misplaced word, phrase, or clause dangles in the sense that it is hanging loosely within the sentence.

IMPROVED *After we had taken our seats,* the game started. [Participial phrase expanded into a clause]

DANGLING The evening passed very pleasantly, *eating* candy and *playing* the radio. [*Eating* and *playing* refer to nothing in the sentence.]

IMPROVED *We* passed the evening very pleasantly, *eating* candy and *playing* the radio. [*Eating* and *playing* refer to *we,* the subject of the main clause.]

(2) Avoid dangling gerund phrases.

DANGLING On *entering* the stadium, the size of the crowd surprises one. [*Entering* does not refer to any word in the sentence.]

IMPROVED On *entering* the stadium, *one* is surprised by the size of the crowd. [*Entering* refers to *one,* the subject of the sentence.]

(3) Avoid dangling infinitive phrases.

DANGLING *To write* well, good books must be read. [The understood subject of *to write* should be the same as the subject of the sentence.]

IMPROVED *To write* well, a *student* must read good books. [*To write* refers to *student,* the subject of the sentence.]

DANGLING *To run* efficiently, proper oiling is needed.

IMPROVED *To run* efficiently, the *machine* must be properly oiled.

Exceptions:

1. Participles, gerunds, and infinitives designating a general truth rather than the action of a specific person or thing may be used without relation to the main clause.

RIGHT Taking everything into consideration, the campaign was successful.

RIGHT To sum up, we all agreed to support the major.

RIGHT To judge from reports, all must be going well.

2. "Absolute" phrases, which consist of a noun or pronoun followed by a participle, are grammatically independent of the rest of the sentence and need not refer to its subject.

RIGHT *The game having ended,* we went home.

RIGHT *No one having objected,* the motion was passed.

(4) Avoid dangling elliptical clauses (or phrases).

An elliptical clause—that is, a clause with an implied subject and verb—"dangles" unless the implied subject is the same as that of the main clause.

DANGLING When only a small boy (or At the age of nine), my father took me with him to Denver. [*I was* is implied in the elliptical clause.]

IMPROVED When I was only a small boy (or When I was nine years old), my father took me with him to Denver. [Elliptical clause expanded]

IMPROVED When only a small boy (or At the age of nine), *I* went with my father to Denver. [Subject of the main clause made the same as the implied subject of the subordinate clause]

DANGLING Prepare to make an incision in the abdomen as soon as completely anesthetized.

IMPROVED Prepare to make an incision in the abdomen as soon as the patient is completely anesthetized.

► EXERCISE 3. Rewrite the following sentences to eliminate dangling modifiers. Write *C* in place of each sentence that needs no revision.

1. Anticipating no such difficulties as later developed, there was no provision in the Constitution for the admission of a new state as a slave state or as a free state.
2. After sitting there awhile, it began to snow.
3. By selecting the judges from both parties, the decisions are likely to give general satisfaction.
4. To grow good tomatoes, the vines should be supported by stakes.
5. Entering Chicago from the west, a whole network of stockyards is the first thing seen.
6. Darkness having come, we stopped for the night.
7. The meeting was adjourned by standing and repeating the pledge.
8. Having taken his seat, we began to question the witness.

9. In drawing up any system of classification, it is likely that there will be some overlapping.
10. Vaccination to prevent smallpox is required before entering the United States from a foreign country.

► EXERCISE 4. Many dangling modifiers may be eliminated by alternate methods. Revise at least half of the faulty sentences in Exercise 3 by a different method from that used in the first revision of the sentences.

► EXERCISE ON COHERENCE

Rewrite the following sentences to make them coherent. Write *C* in place of each sentence that needs no revision.

1. He was enchanted by the roast beef, causing him to tip the waiter inordinately.
2. That statement I do not find it possible to believe at this stage of the argument.
3. We found the house with no trouble after reaching Westwood.
4. After reaching Westwood, locating the house was no trouble.
5. She decided to most mischievously split her infinitives.
6. Being in a hurry to get away on our trip, our automobile was not overhauled.
7. The decision having been made, everyone was happy.
8. Having a broken arm and nose, I thought the statue was very ugly.
9. John and Robert had ridden several days without sleep in the rain.
10. While wondering about this phenomenon, the sun sank from view.

► Parallelism (An Aid to Coherence)

26 Parallel ideas should be expressed in parallel structure. Misleading parallels should be avoided.

Note: Can you distinguish readily the parts of speech, phrases and clauses, main clauses and subordinate clauses? Until you are able to do so you will have difficulty in understanding Section 26. If necessary, master first the fundamentals of the sentence treated in

Section 1, **Sentence Sense,** especially 1c and 1d; then study **Parallelism.**

26a For the expression of co-ordinate (equal) ideas a noun should be paralleled with a noun, an active verb with

an active verb, an infinitive with an infinitive, a subordinate clause with a subordinate clause, and so forth.

AWKWARD   Let us consider the *origin* of engineering and *how engineering has progressed.* [Noun paralleled with a subordinate clause]
BETTER   Let us consider the ‖ *origin* and
‖ *progress* of engineering.
[Noun paralleled with noun]

AWKWARD   *Walking* and *to swim* are good exercise. [Gerund paralleled with infinitive]
BETTER   ‖ *Walking* and
‖ *swimming* are good exercise.
[Gerund paralleled with gerund]

AWKWARD   As a young man he *had been* in Africa, *fighting* in Greece, and *following* his general to India. [Verb paralleled with participles]
BETTER   As a young man he ‖ *had been* in Africa,
‖ *had fought* in Greece, and
‖ *had followed* his general to India.
[Verb paralleled with verbs]

AWKWARD   He retired *respected* by his associates, *admired* by his friends, and *his employees loved him.* [Participles paralleled with a main clause]
BETTER   He retired ‖ *respected* by his associates,
‖ *admired* by his friends, and
‖ *loved* by his employees.
[Participle paralleled with participles]

RIGHT   The dogmas ‖ of the quiet past
are inadequate ‖ to the stormy present.
—ABRAHAM LINCOLN
[Prepositional phrase paralleled with prepositional phrase]

RIGHT   To say ‖ *that* the character of real men cannot be completely known,
that their inner nature is beyond our reach,
that the dramatic portraiture of things is only possible to poetry,
is to say ‖ *that* history ought not to be written.   —J. A. FROUDE
[Clause paralleled with clauses]

▶ EXERCISE 1.   Indicate parallelism in the following sentences by an outline similar to that used above.

1. The example of this social pariah should have commended itself to Mr. Froude, for whom it is not enough that this woman should be made to suffer for a crime of which she was innocent—not enough that inhuman men should mock her infirmities in that awful moment—not enough that in her preparation for death she should be denied the consolations of her own faith—not enough that a religious bigot should be ordered to thrust himself between the victim and her Maker—not enough that she should receive vociferous assurance that her damnation was certain.   —JAMES MELINE

2. Wit is a lean creature with sharp inquiring nose, whereas humor has a kindly eye and comfortable girth.   —CHARLES S. BROOKS

3. We have seen the necessity of the Union, as our bulwark against foreign danger, as the conservator of peace among ourselves, as the guardian of our commerce and other common interests, as the only substitute for those military establishments which have subverted the liberties of the Old World, and as the proper antidote for the diseases of faction, which have proved fatal to other popular governments, and of which alarming symptoms have been betrayed by our own.   —JAMES MADISON

▶ EXERCISE 2.   Revise the following sentences to give parallel structure to co-ordinate ideas.

1. These illustrations will enable you to differentiate unintentional killing and killing with intent to kill.
2. Mr. Smith is fair in his grading but never giving anyone more than he earns.
3. The story is vivid, interesting, and one that appeals to every person.
4. His duties are cleaning up the cabins and to look after the boats.
5. She spends all her time shopping and on her studies.

26b   Whenever necessary to make the parallel clear, repeat a preposition, an article, an auxiliary verb, the sign of of the infinitive, or the introductory word of a long phrase or clause. (See also Section 22c.)

AWKWARD   I admire Tennyson *for the ideals* in his poems but not *his style.*
IMPROVED   I admire Tennyson ‖ *for the ideals* in his poems but
‖ not
‖ *for* his style.

AWKWARD   In the wreck the circus lost *a camel* and *elephant*.

IMPROVED   In the wreck the circus lost || *a camel* and || *an elephant*

OBSCURE   He explained *that* the advertising campaign had been successful, business had increased more than fifty per cent, and additional capital was sorely needed.

CLEARER   He explained || *that* the advertising campaign had been successful, || *that* business had increased more than fifty per cent, and || *that* additional capital was sorely needed.

▶ EXERCISE 3.   Copy the following sentences, inserting the words needed to bring out the parallel.

1. The sentences are difficult to understand, not because they are long but they are obscure.

2. The child learns in nursery school to take his turn, to respect the rights of others, and take care of his materials.

3. They would lie on the battlefield for hours and sometimes days.

26c Correlatives (*either . . . or, neither . . . nor, both . . . and, not only . . . but also, whether . . . or*) should be followed by elements that are parallel in form.

POOR   He was not only *kind* but also *knew* when to help people in trouble. [Adjective paralleled with verb]

BETTER   He was || *not only kind* || *but also helpful* to people in trouble.

POOR   I debated whether *I should give* the beggar money or *to offer* him food. [Subordinate clause paralleled with infinitive]

BETTER   I debated || *whether to give* the beggar money || *or to offer* him food.

26d Caution: Do not use parallel structure for sentence elements not parallel in thought. Never use an awkward or unidiomatic expression for the sake of a parallel. Lack of parallel structure is preferable.

MISLEADING   Our meetings were held on Friday afternoon, on Saturday morning, and on Saturday afternoon we started home.

CLEARER   Our meetings were held on Friday afternoon and on Saturday morning. On Saturday afternoon we started home.

MISLEADING   He discovered that the farm is well adapted to cotton and that it yields a bale to the acre. [Parallel structure used for ideas not co-ordinate]

CLEARER   He discovered that the farm is well adapted to cotton, yielding a bale to the acre.

▶ EXERCISES ON PARALLELISM

A. Copy the following sentences, using parallel structure to express parallel ideas. Write *C* in place of each sentence that needs no revision.

1. He had long wondered whether he should go into his father's business or to start a small business of his own.

2. William is a boy with a good mind and who has the highest principles.

3. Someone has said that Americans cannot enjoy life without a TV set, an automobile, and a summer cottage.

4. My friend told me that the trip would be delayed but to be ready to start on Friday.

5. To learn to balance a ball, playing musical instruments, and riding horseback are some of the tricks a sea lion can perform.

6. A sea lion watches carefully the action of his fellows and how they obey their trainer.

7. He was quiet and in a serious mood after the talk.

8. He took up drinking, gambling, and killed several people.

B. In the following sentence note how Newman develops the parallel between health and general education. Underline the words which bring out the parallelism. (This is an exceptional case of an exceedingly long sentence—203 words—which is maintained in perfect balance.)

Again, as health ought to precede labour of the body, and as a man in health can do what an unhealthy man cannot do, and as of this health the properties are strength, energy, agility, graceful carriage and action, manual dexterity, and endurance of fatigue, so in like manner general culture of mind is the best aid to professional and scientific study, and educated men can do what illiterate cannot; and the man who has learned to think and to reason and to compare and to discriminate and to analyze, who has refined his taste, and formed his judgment, and sharpened his mental vision, will not indeed at once be a lawyer, or a pleader, or an orator, or a statesman, or a physician, or a good landlord, or a man of business, or a soldier, or an engineer, or a chemist, or a geologist, or an antiquarian, but he will be placed in that state of intellect in which he can take up any one of the sciences or callings I have referred to, or any other for which he has a taste or special talent, with an ease, a grace, a versatility, and a success, to which another is a stranger.   —JOHN HENRY NEWMAN

C. With Newman's structure as a guide, some students may wish to construct a shorter sentence on a subject such as the following: The game of football and the game of life; the course of a river and the course of history; military training and college education.

▶ Point of View   (An Aid to Coherence)

27   Avoid needless shifts in point of view.

Sudden and illogical shifts in point of view tend to obscure the meaning and thus cause needless difficulty in reading.

27a   Avoid needless shifts in tense. (See also 7c.)

SHIFT   The boy *closed* his book and *hurries* away to the playground. [A shift from past tense to present tense]

BETTER   The boy *closed* his book and *hurried* away to the playground. [Both verbs in the past tense]

Note: When the historical present is used, as in summarizing plots of narratives, care will be needed to avoid slipping from the present tense into the past tense. *Example:* "Romeo *goes* in disguise to a Capulet feast, *falls* in love with Juliet, and *marries* her secretly. Just after his wedding he *is drawn* into a quarrel with the Capulets and *is banished* (not *was banished*) from Verona."

27b   Avoid needless shifts in mood.

SHIFT   First *rise* to your feet and then you *should address* the chairman. [A shift from imperative to indicative mood]

BETTER   First *rise* to your feet and then *address* the chairman. [Both verbs in the imperative mood]

27c   Avoid needless shifts in subject or voice.

A shift in subject often involves a shift in voice. A shift in voice nearly always involves a shift in subject.

SHIFT   James liked fishing, but hunting was also enjoyed by him. [The subject shifts from *James* to *hunting*. The voice shifts from active to passive.]

BETTER   James liked fishing, but he also enjoyed hunting. [One subject only. Both verbs active.]

SHIFT   Mary took summer courses, and her leisure hours were devoted to tennis. [The subject shifts from *Mary* to *hours*. The voice shifts from active to passive.]

BETTER   Mary took summer courses and devoted her leisure hours to tennis. [One subject only. Both verbs active.]

SHIFT   Paul hurried up the mountain path and soon the laurel came in sight. [The subject shifts from *Paul* to *laurel*.]

BETTER   Paul hurried up the mountain path and soon caught sight of the laurel. [One subject only]

27d   Avoid needless shifts in person. (See also 28c(3).)

SHIFT   *We* have reached a point where *one* ought to face the possibility of a great and sudden change. [A shift from first to third person]

BETTER   *We* have reached a point where *we* ought to face the possibility of a great and sudden change.

SHIFT   *Students* will find the University Book Shop a great convenience. *You* need not leave the campus to purchase any school supplies *you* may need. [A shift from third to second person]

BETTER   *The student* will find the University Book Shop a great convenience. *He* need not leave the campus to purchase any school supplies *he* may need.

27e   Avoid needless shifts in number. (See also agreement of pronoun and antecedent, Section 6b.)

SHIFT   *One* should be thoughtful of *their* neighbors. [A shift from singular *one* to plural *their*]

BETTER   *One* should be thoughtful of *one's* neighbors.

SHIFT   The United Nations *deserves* encouragement. Indeed, *they deserve* much more than that. [If *United Nations* takes a singular verb (*deserves*), it must not be referred to by a plural pronoun (*they*).]

BETTER   The United Nations *deserves* encouragement. Indeed, *it deserves* much more than that.

27f   Avoid needless shifts from indirect to direct discourse.

SHIFT   My friend asked whether I knew the coach and will he be with the team. [Mixed indirect and direct discourse]

RIGHT   My friend asked whether I knew the coach and whether he would be with the team. [Indirect discourse]

RIGHT   My friend asked, "Do you know the coach? Will he be with the team?" [Direct discourse]

27g   Maintain the same tone or style throughout the sentence.

INAPPROPRIATE   Analysis of the principal obstacles to harmony in the United Nations reveals that Russia and her satellites refuse to *play ball* with the rest of the world. [A shift from formal to colloquial style. Substitute *co-operate,* or a similar word, for the italicized expression.]

INAPPROPRIATE   After distributing the grass seed evenly over the lawn, rake the ground at least twice and then *gently bedew it* with fine spray. [The italicized expression is too "poetic" in a sentence with a prosaic purpose. Substitute *water it lightly.*]

INAPPROPRIATE   A big *jazzy* moon bathed the sea in *mellow* light. [*Jazzy* and *mellow* clash. Substitute *harvest* for *jazzy.*]

INAPPROPRIATE   It seemed to Juliet, as she gazed down from the balcony, that Romeo's face was

as white as *the underside of a fish.* [The italicized expression clashes with the romantic beginning of the sentence.]

27h   Maintain a consistent perspective throughout the sentence (and also throughout the larger elements of discourse).

FAULTY PERSPECTIVE   From the top of the Washington Monument, the government offices seemed to be so many beehives, and the workers droned at their tasks behind long rows of desks. [The perspective shifts from the monument to the interior of government buildings.]

CONSISTENT PERSPECTIVE   From the top of the Washington Monument, the government buildings seemed to be so many beehives, and it was easy to imagine the workers droning at their tasks behind long rows of desks.

ILLOGICAL   *Standing in the valley,* I could see our troops at the crest of the hill and, on the other side of the ridge, the enemy in full retreat.

LOGICAL   *From the airplane* I could see our troops at the crest of the hill and, on the other side of the ridge, the enemy in full retreat.

▶ EXERCISE ON POINT OF VIEW

Revise the following paragraph to avoid all needless shifts. If necessary, expand the paragraph.

1. From behind the desk the shopkeeper emerged and comes toward me.   2. He is a heavyset man, and his brown tweed coat was badly worn.   3. An assistant gave me a chair and leaves the room, but not before he had welcomed us and even told me where one might find lodging.   4. "First, look around in this vicinity and then you should find a comfortable place in a nearby hotel," he says.   5. I hurried out of the shop and soon the hotel comes into view.   6. Be thankful for suggestions when offered you.   7. It usually helps one.

▶ Reference of Pronouns   (An Aid to Coherence)

28   Make every pronoun refer unmistakably to a definite antecedent.
(For agreement of pronoun and antecedent see Section 6b.)

One of the principal obstacles to clear and immediate understanding is the faulty use of pronouns. *He, she, it; who, which, what; this,* *that; the same, such,* etc. can have meaning only if the antecedent noun is immediately obvious to the reader. Hence the writer should place all pronouns as close as possible to the antecedent. If, having done this, he finds that the reference of the pronoun is still not obvious, he should repeat the antecedent or use a synonym for it. If repetition proves awkward, he should recast his sentence.

28a Avoid ambiguous reference. Construct the sentence in such a way that the reader can easily distinguish between two possible antecedents.

AMBIGUOUS   John told William that he had made a mistake. [Who made the mistake?]

CLEAR   John said to William, "You have made a mistake."

CLEAR   John said to William, "I have made a mistake."

CLEAR   In talking to William, John admitted that he had made a mistake.

AWKWARD   The books were standing on the shelf which needed sorting. [See also 25a(3).]

BETTER   The books which needed sorting were standing on the shelf.

AMBIGUOUS   It is hard for men to like many people who enjoy solitude. [See also 25a(3).]

CLEAR   It is hard for men who enjoy solitude to like many people.

28b Avoid remote reference—reference to an antecedent (1) too far removed from the pronoun or (2) so placed in a subordinate construction that it is not central in the mind of the reader.

Make your meaning immediately clear to the reader. Save him the annoyance of searching about for the antecedent.

REMOTE   The *lake* covers many acres. Near the shore water lilies grow in profusion, spreading out their green leaves and sending up white blossoms on slender stems. *It* is well stocked with fish. [The pronoun *it* is too far removed from the antecedent *lake*.]

IMPROVED   . . . The *lake* is well stocked with fish. [Repetition of the antecedent *lake*]

VAGUE   He sat by the little window all day and worked steadily at his translating. *It* was too small to give much light. [Temporarily confusing: antecedent of *it* not clear until reader finishes the sentence]

CLEAR   He sat by the little window all day and worked steadily at his translating. The *window* was too small to give much light. [Repetition of the noun]

REMOTE   When *Johnson's* club was organized, *he* asked Goldsmith to become a member. [Reference to antecedent in the possessive case]

IMPROVED   When *Johnson* organized his club, *he* asked Goldsmith to become a member.

Caution: As a rule avoid pronoun reference to the title of a theme, or to a word in the title.

AWKWARD   *He* and I enjoyed hiking. [The first sentence of a theme entitled, "Hiking with My Brother"]

BETTER   My *brother* and I enjoyed hiking.

28c Use broad reference, if at all, only with discretion.

Informal English allows much latitude in the use of antecedents that must be inferred from the context. Even standard English accepts the general idea of a clause as an antecedent when the reference is unmistakable. But students who overuse *this, that, it,* or *which* to refer to the general idea of the preceding clause or sentence may be advised, as a means of insuring greater clarity, to make each of their pronouns refer to a specific substantive.

(1) Avoid reference to the general idea of a preceding clause or sentence unless the meaning is clear and unmistakable.

VAGUE   William was absent from the first performance, which caused much comment. [*Which* has no antecedent.]

CLEAR   William's absence from the first performance caused much comment. [Pronoun eliminated]

VAGUE   The story referred to James, but Henry misapplied it to himself. This is true in real life. [*This* has no antecedent.]

CLEAR   The story referred to James, but Henry misapplied it to himself. Similar mistakes occur in real life.

VAGUE   When class attendance is compulsory, some students feel that education is being forced upon them. This may cause them to dislike college. [*This* has no antecedent.]

CLEAR   When class attendance is compulsory, some students feel that education is being forced upon them. This feeling (*or* this compulsion) may cause them to dislike college.

(2) As a rule do not refer to a noun not expressed but merely inferred from some word.

VAGUE   My mother is a music teacher. It is a profession I know nothing about.

CLEAR   My mother is a music teacher, but the teaching of music is a profession I know nothing about.

VAGUE   He wanted his teachers to think he was above average, as he could have been if he had used it to advantage.

CLEAR   He wanted his teachers to think he was above average, as he could have been if he had used his ability to advantage.

(3) In standard (formal) writing avoid the use of the indefinite it, you, or they. Especially avoid the you habit.

AWKWARD   If a person breaks the law, you may be arrested. [See also **27d**.]

COLLOQUIAL (or STANDARD)   If you break the law, you may be arrested. [Colloquial when *you* means "anyone"; standard when *you* is addressed to a specific person or persons]

STANDARD   If anyone breaks the law, he may be arrested. *Or,* Anyone breaking the law may be arrested.

COLLOQUIAL   In France *they* could not understand William.

STANDARD   In France William could not be understood.

AWKWARD   In the book *it* says that many mushrooms are edible.

IMPROVED   The book says that many mushrooms are edible.

Note: The pronoun *it* is correctly used in such idiomatic expressions as *it seems, it is cold, it is raining, it is useless to go,* and *it is five miles to town.*

28d   Avoid the confusion arising from the repetition in the same sentence of a

pronoun referring to different antecedents.

CONFUSING   Although *it* is very hot by the lake, *it* looks inviting. [The first *it* is the indefinite pronoun; the second *it* refers to *lake*.]

CLEARER   Although it is very hot by the lake, the water looks inviting.

CONFUSING   We should have prepared for our examinations earlier. *It* is too late to do *it* now.

CLEARER   We should have prepared for our examinations earlier. It is now too late to prepare.

▶ EXERCISE ON REFERENCE OF PRONOUNS

Reconstruct the following sentences as necessary to correct faults in reference. Write *C* in place of each sentence that needs no revision.

1. Howard was more intelligent than the average student, but he did not use it properly.

2. I did not even buy a season ticket, which was very disloyal to my school.

3. Her ladylike qualities were reflected in the graciousness of her manner. This was apparent in her every act.

4. Package wrapping has always been my job, because they say that I can do it better than anyone else.

5. When building roads the Romans tried to detour around valleys as much as possible for fear that flood waters might cover them and make them useless.

6. If you are taken to the courthouse, they will fine you.

7. In the article it states that the inland sea is salt.

8. Our language is rich in connectives which express fine distinctions of meaning.

▶ Emphasis

29   Select words and arrange the parts of the sentence to give emphasis to important ideas.

Emphasis, expressing an idea as strongly as possible, is the third of four fundamental qualities of a good style: unity, coherence, emphasis, and variety.

As our ideas vary in importance, so our expression should vary in stress. Short factual statements and routine description or narration cannot always be varied for emphasis without doing violence to the natural order of the English language. It would be absurd for a policeman to describe a prisoner in this fashion: "Red was his hair, blue were his eyes, and on his nose sat a great brown wart." But in most types of writing, sentences may be rearranged to achieve emphasis without sacrificing naturalness of expression.

Emphasis may be gained through the use of concrete words and figurative language (Section 20), through economy of language (Section 21), and through the subordination of less important ideas (Section 24). We may also emphasize ideas:

a. By placing important words in the important positions at the beginning and end of the sentence.
b. By changing loose sentences into periodic sentences.
c. By arranging ideas in the order of climax.
d. By using the active instead of the passive voice.
e. By repeating important words.
f. By putting words out of their usual order.
g. By using balanced construction.
h. By abruptly changing the sentence length.

29a Gain emphasis by placing important words at the beginning or end of the sentence—especially at the end. Whenever possible tuck away in the middle of the sentence parenthetical expressions and other elements of minor importance.

WEAK   The colonel will bluntly refuse, in all probability. [The weakest part of the sentence is given the most emphatic position—the end.]
EMPHATIC   In all probability the colonel will bluntly refuse. [Strong end]
EMPHATIC   The colonel, in all probability, will bluntly refuse. [Most emphatic—strong beginning and end]

WEAK   He became an archbishop in his later years, however.
EMPHATIC   In his later years, however, he became an archbishop.

WEAK   Fallacies as gross as these may easily be detected by all men who can see an inch before them.
EMPHATIC   All men who can see an inch before them may easily detect these gross fallacies.
—DRYDEN

► EXERCISE 1.   Gain emphasis by rearranging the parts of the sentences.

1. He had little success, but he was a tireless worker, if we may believe the reports.

2. The old man withdrew into his cabin for some good reason we must suppose.

3. He may become an expert accountant by a study of business methods at home.

4. A trailer saves hotel expense and can be moved about from place to place readily.

5. However, he could not redeem himself, in my opinion.

29b Gain emphasis by changing loose sentences into periodic sentences. (Section 29b is an extension of 29a.)

A sentence in which the main clause is either placed at the end or completed at the end is called *periodic;* one that makes a complete statement and then adds details is called *loose.* Both types of sentences are effective. The loose sentence, more commonly used, makes for informal writing and easy reading. But the periodic sentence, by holding the reader in suspense and reserving the main idea until the end, is more emphatic. Note the difference in tone in the following sentences.

LOOSE   Practice daily if you want to become a good pianist. [A clear sentence]
PERIODIC   If you want to become a good pianist, practice daily. [More emphatic]

LOOSE   History has proved amply that mere numbers may be defeated by smaller forces who are superior in arms, organization, and morale.
PERIODIC   That mere numbers may be defeated by smaller forces who are superior in arms, organization, and morale is amply proved by history.

Caution: Do not overuse the periodic sentence to the point of making your style unnatural. Variety is desirable. See Section 30.

► EXERCISE 2.   Change the following loose sentences into periodic sentences. Note the gain in emphasis.

1. I attended his wedding, many years ago, on a beautiful June afternoon, in a little village near Cincinnati.

2. He returned to the camp when he found that he could be of no further assistance.

3. It was no concern of mine that he neglected his studies.

4. The workers were afraid to return until the dam had been repaired.

5. It never entered his mind to be dissatisfied

with his dreary lodgings, to resent the purposeless-
ness of his job, or to revolt against the complacent
ignorance of his associates.

► EXERCISE 3. Examine typical pages from several
prose writers (Swift, Newman, Conrad, or others)
to determine the proportion of loose and periodic
sentences.

29c   Gain emphasis by arranging ideas in the order of climax.

UNEMPHATIC   We could hear the roar of cannon,
the shrieks of the wounded, and the crash of
falling timbers.

EMPHATIC   We could hear the roar of cannon, the
crash of falling timbers, and the shrieks of the
wounded. [Climax reached in "shrieks of the
wounded"]

UNEMPHATIC   We have been spurned with contempt by the throne. Our supplications have
been disregarded, and our remonstrances have
produced additional violence and insult. Our
petitions have been slighted.

EMPHATIC   Our petitions have been slighted; our
remonstrances have produced additional violence and insult; our supplications have been
disregarded; and we have been spurned, with
contempt, from the foot of the throne!
                                        —PATRICK HENRY

Note: A striking arrangement of ideas in reverse
order of climax, called anticlimax, is sometimes
used for comic effect.

Not louder shrieks to pitying heav'n are cast,
When husbands, or when lap-dogs, breathe their
last.   —POPE

► EXERCISE 4. Arrange the ideas of each sentence
in what you consider to be the order of climax.

1. He left the city because of ill health, failure
in business, and the loss of his club membership.

2. His confident manner, his knowledge of men,
and his friendliness made him the logical man for
the office.

3. Something must be done at once. The commission is faced with a deficit.

4. Give me death or give me liberty.

5. I gathered together the souvenirs of college
days: my diploma, a textbook on mathematics, my
fraternity pin, and a battered book bag.

29d   Gain emphasis by using the strong ac-tive voice instead of the weak passive voice.

WEAK   His grave was dug by his teeth.
STRONGER   He dug his grave with his teeth.

WEAK   Honey was gathered by the bee as it flitted
from flower to flower.
STRONGER   The bee, flitting from flower to flower,
gathered honey.

Exception: If the receiver of the action is more
important than the doer, the passive voice is more
effective.

EMPHATIC   Wheat is grown in Kansas.
EMPHATIC   Any person who attempts to escape will
be shot.

► EXERCISE 5. Substitute the active for the passive
voice.

1. As the station is reached, the train is seen
coming around a curve.

2. On her head was worn a beautiful green hat.

3. Paul was hesitant to enter the room, for he
saw that a poster was being made by Jane.

4. On Sunday afternoon many fishermen may
be seen trying their luck.

5. It was decided by the members that the meetings were to be held at their homes.

6. When the play was brought to an end, the
actors were greeted with a loud burst of applause
by the audience.

7. It is greatly feared by the citizens that adequate punishment will not be meted out to the
lawbreakers by the jury.

29e   Gain emphasis by repeating important words.

Note the great difference between the careless repetition in Section 21c and the effective
repetition in the following passages.

EMPHATIC   . . . *wet* roads, *wet* fields, *wet* housetops; not a *beautiful,* scarcely a *picturesque*
object met my eyes along the whole route; yet
to me, *all* was *beautiful, all* was more than
picturesque.   —CHARLOTTE BRONTË

EMPHATIC   There is *no mistake;* there has been *no
mistake;* and there shall be *no mistake.*
                                    —DUKE OF WELLINGTON

EMPHATIC   . . . that government of the *people,*
by the *people,* for the *people,* shall not perish
from the earth.   —ABRAHAM LINCOLN

EMPHATIC   If it's *against the law* in the corner
saloons, it is *against the law* in the country
club, too.   —ADLAI STEVENSON

[See also the quotation from Winston Churchill in
Section 23b.]

► EXERCISE 6. From your reading, copy three passages in which emphasis is gained by the repetition
of an important word or phrase.

29f   Gain emphasis by putting a word or phrase out of its natural order.

EMPHATIC   *Trust* her I dare not.

EMPHATIC   *Never* did I think he would return alive.

EMPHATIC   *Mutter* she does at times, but it is in solitary places that are desolate as she is desolate, in ruined cities, *and when the sun has gone down to his rest.*—DE QUINCEY. [Note how the italicized words are deliberately placed out of a natural order.]

Caution: This method of securing emphasis, if overused, will make the style distinctly artificial. And of course the order of the parts of the sentence should never be such as to make for ambiguity. (See **25a.**)

► EXERCISE 7.   Copy from your reading and bring to class five passages in which emphasis is secured by putting a word or phrase out of natural order.

29g   Use balance to gain emphasis.

A sentence is balanced when identical or similar grammatical structure is used to express contrasted ideas. A balanced sentence uses parallel structure (see Section **26**) and emphasizes the contrast between parts of similar length and movement. Overuse of balance seems especially artificial.

UNBALANCED   It is human to err, but to forgive is divine.

BALANCED   To err is human, to forgive divine.
                                                    —POPE

BALANCED   You had better talk trifles elegantly to the most trifling woman, than coarse inelegant sense to the most solid man: you had better return a dropped fan genteelly, than give a thousand pounds awkwardly; and you had better refuse a favor gracefully, than grant it clumsily.   —CHESTERFIELD

BALANCED   The notice which you have been pleased to take of my labours, had it been early, had been kind; but it has been delayed till I am indifferent, and cannot enjoy it; till I am solitary, and cannot impart it; till I am known, and do not want it.
                       —SAMUEL JOHNSON (to Chesterfield)

BALANCED   Fools talk about each other, ordinary men about things, wise men about ideas.

► EXERCISE 8.   Copy from your reading and bring to class five examples of the balanced sentence.

► EXERCISE 9.   Copy all examples of balanced structure from Lincoln's Gettysburg Address (at the end of Section **1,** page 804).

► EXERCISE 10.   Use balanced sentences to show the contrast between the following: men and women, youth and age, success and failure.

► EXERCISES ON EMPHASIS

A. Rewrite the following sentences as necessary to give greater emphasis. Write *C* in place of each sentence that needs no revision.

1. The chairman will give his report after the meeting has been called to order.

2. The soldiers were outnumbered two to one, as you may have heard.

3. It was no fault of hers that the program was a failure.

4. If you cannot come, say so, by all means.

5. The zero hour had come. Already the armies were marching.

6. On the other hand, he had done the best he could, according to his story.

7. At any time I shall be ready, no matter how late the hour is.

8. He saw much to interest him: the Statue of Liberty, the art galleries, the tall buildings, and the crowds on the street.

B. The following sentences are unemphatic statements of certain general truths which are stated emphatically in well-known epigrams and proverbs. Rewrite each sentence to give emphasis. Aim particularly for *conciseness.* Then compare your sentence with the original epigram or proverb.

1. The most appropriate name for woman is "Frailty."

2. If you take care in your work at the beginning, you will save yourself nine times the trouble later on.

3. Americans are willing to spend millions of dollars for defense armament, but they will not give one cent to appease an unjust aggressor.

4. Some people know how much a thing costs in dollars and cents, but they have no estimate of its human or moral value.

▶ Variety

30 Vary the length and the structure of your sentences to make your whole composition pleasing and effective.

Note: Can you distinguish readily between main clauses and subordinate clauses, clauses and phrases, compound sentences and compound predicates? Until you are able to do so you will have little success in learning how to vary your sentences. If necessary, master first the fundamentals of the sentence treated in Section 1, **Sentence Sense,** especially **1d;** then study **Variety.**

Except for the loose, stringy sentences in 30c, this section deals only with *good* sentences. Throughout Section 30 you are cautioned against monotonous repetition of any one type of sentence, not because these sentences are grammatically wrong, but because they do not combine to form a pleasing and effective pattern. Even the best sentence can become boring if it follows a long series of sentences similar in design.

Comparison of the two passages in the following example will illustrate the value of variety. The sentences in these parallel passages are equally correct, and the diction is the same. But one passage is made up entirely of simple or compound sentences. The other passage contains a varied sentence structure which is much more effective.

NOT VARIED	VARIED
I had not time to be of help. The wrestler dropped at last, and Alan leaped back to get his distance. He ran upon the others like a bull, and he roared, and he went along. They broke before him like water, and they turned, and they ran. One fell against another in their haste.	But I had not time to be of help. The wrestler dropped at last; and Alan, leaping back to get his distance, ran upon the others like a bull, roaring as he went. They broke before him like water, turning, and running, and falling one against another in their haste. —ROBERT LOUIS STEVENSON

30a Usually avoid a series of short, simple sentences. Vary the length. (See also Section 29h.)

CHOPPY I settled back to my place. I recharged the three pistols. I had fired them earlier. I kept watch with both eye and ear.

IMPROVED I settled back to my place, recharging the three pistols I had fired, and keeping watch with both eye and ear.
—ROBERT LOUIS STEVENSON

30b Avoid a long series of sentences beginning with the subject.

This type of sentence, like all others discussed in Section 30b, is good. It should be at the command of every writer. In fact, the best writers begin about half their sentences with the subject—far more than in any other one way.[1] But some students use this kind of beginning almost exclusively. To avoid overuse, they should vary the subject-first beginning:

(1) Chiefly by opening with an adverb or an adverb clause.

SUBJECT *The injured man* lay beside the road and waited patiently for help. [Beginning with the subject—an excellent method that should be used for perhaps half of one's sentences but not for nearly all of them]

ADVERB *Patiently* lying beside the road, the injured man waited for help.

ADVERB CLAUSE *While the injured man was waiting for help,* he lay patiently beside the road.

(2) By opening with a prepositional or a participial phrase.

PREPOSITIONAL PHRASE *Beside the road* lay the injured man, waiting patiently for help.

[1] In a study of sentence beginnings George Summey, Jr., *American Punctuation,* New York, 1949, pp. 166-71, finds 53 per cent with subject, 28 per cent with adverb or adverb clause, 9 per cent with co-ordinating conjunction, leaving 10 per cent for all other types of beginnings.

PARTICIPIAL PHRASE *Lying beside the road,* the injured man waited patiently for help.

(3) By opening with a co-ordinating conjunction such as *but, and, or, nor,* or *yet.*

Effective sentences can often begin with a co-ordinating conjunction, but only when the conjunction shows the proper relation of the sentence to the preceding sentence.

CO-ORDINATING CONJUNCTION *But* the injured man, lying beside the road, waited patiently for help. [The *but* makes a contrast with something in the preceding sentence, such as, "The young woman wept and wrung her hands."]

CO-ORDINATING CONJUNCTION *And* the injured man, lying beside the road, waited patiently for help. [The *and* makes a simple addition to the preceding sentence.]

► EXERCISE 1. Compose a good sentence that begins with the subject. Then revise the sentence to vary the beginning in as many ways as you can.

► EXERCISE 2. In a piece of prose assigned by your instructor, classify the beginnings of the sentences into the types designated above.

30c   Avoid the loose, stringy compound sentence. (See also 24b.)

The ineffective compound sentence may be improved:

(1) By using a subordinate clause.

AIMLESSLY COMPOUND The Mississippi River is one of the longest rivers in the world, and in the springtime it often overflows its banks, and many people are endangered.

IMPROVED The Mississippi River, which is one of the longest rivers in the world, often endangers many people during the springtime by overflowing its banks.

(2) By using a compound predicate.

AWKWARD He put on his coat, and next he picked up his hat and cane, and then he hurried from the house.

BETTER He put on his coat, picked up his hat and cane, and hurried from the house.

(3) By using an appositive or other modifiers.

COMPOUND The town had a population of three thousand, and a tornado struck it, and it was practically demolished.

IMPROVED The town, with its three thousand people, was struck by a tornado and practically demolished.

COMPOUND He was the mayor of the town, and he was a genial fellow, and he invited the four young boys into his study.

IMPROVED The mayor of the town, a genial fellow, invited the four young boys into his study.

(4) By using phrases.

COMPOUND The streets were icy and we could not drive the car.

IMPROVED Because of the icy streets we could not drive the car.

COMPOUND You will reach your destination tomorrow, and then you can take a long rest.

VARIED After reaching your destination tomorrow, you can take a long rest.

30d   Learn how to vary the conventional subject–verb sequence by occasionally separating subject and verb by words or phrases.

SUBJECT–VERB The auditorium is across from the park and it is a gift of the alumni. [A loose compound sentence]

VARIED The auditorium, across from the park, is a gift of the alumni.

SUBJECT–VERB The crowd sympathized with the visitors and applauded every good play. [A good sentence]

VARIED The crowd, sympathizing with the visitors, applauded every good play.

Caution: Avoid awkward or needless separation of subject and verb. See 25a(5).

30e   Learn how to vary the usual declarative statement with an occasional question, exclamation, exhortation, or command.

STATEMENT We will fight to the end.

QUESTION Who of us will not fight to the end?

EXCLAMATION Imagine our nation not fighting to the very end!

EXHORTATION Let us fight, then, to the very end.

COMMAND Fight on, fellow citizens, fight to the end.

LARGER ELEMENTS

▶ The Paragraph

31 Make paragraphs unified and coherent; develop them adequately.

A paragraph is a distinct unit of thought—usually a group of related sentences, though occasionally no more than one sentence—of an essay, a story, or a chapter. Just as chapters mark the chief divisions of books, paragraphs mark the chief divisions of chapters. The paragraph has two functions in a composition. First, it is a physical break in the page that allows the reader to rest his eyes. Second, it is a logical break, which allows the reader to collect his thoughts. It serves as a signpost of an approaching curve in the avenue of thought; or it warns him that he must take a new avenue of thought. It announces a new time, place, person, or thing in the course of a narrative, a different point of view in description, a new step in an exposition, or an advance in argument. If the paragraph served only the former, physical function, the writer would need only to chop his composition up into blocks of convenient length. But because of the second function the writer must consider the paragraph as a unit of thought and organize it accordingly around a central idea. Indeed, the paragraph might be defined as a group of sentences related to a central thought.

Length. Expository or argumentative paragraphs in current books and magazines are usually from 50 to 250 words in length, with the average perhaps 100 words. Paragraphs tend to run longer in books and shorter in the narrow columns of newspapers. Shorter paragraphs are more frequent in narrative writing, especially dialogue, in which each speech is paragraphed separately.

Indention. The first lines of paragraphs are indented uniformly, about one inch in longhand and five spaces in typewritten copy.

31a Give unity to the paragraph by making each sentence contribute to the central thought.

A paragraph is said to have unity when each sentence contributes to the central thought. Any sentence that fails to contribute violates the unity of the paragraph and should be omitted. The central thought is usually expressed in a *topic sentence,* often the first sentence of the paragraph, though it may come anywhere within the paragraph. Sometimes it is not expressed at all but merely implied.

In the following unified paragraphs the central idea, when expressed, is indicated by italics.

1 *A cornfield in July is a sultry place.* The soil is hot and dry; the wind comes across the lazily murmuring leaves laden with a warm, sickening smell drawn from the rapidly growing, broad-flung banners of the corn. The sun, nearly vertical, drops a flood of dazzling light upon the field over which the cool shadows run, only to make the heat seem the more intense.

—HAMLIN GARLAND

[Topic stated first]

2 From time to time the American economic system has been solemnly declared on the verge of ruin because of protective tariff, because of free

trade, taxation policies, the abandonment of gold, labor unions, trusts, foreign agitators, Wall Street manipulators—what a list of total calamities could be compiled since 1900! Yet the American economy in sober fact, save for small setbacks in 1907 and 1921, and the large one in 1929, has grown like a green bay tree, to become today the wonder and envy of the world. The helpful indexes have gone up—population, production, output of inanimate energy, output per man hour, literacy, health, longevity—all up, while the curves of disease, slum-dwelling, poverty, have gone down. More than half of all American farmers are now enrolled in conservation districts, with the result that we are even beginning to save our soil. This comparison is given not to show that American economic problems are solved, only that *the facts have consistently belied the predictions of the economists.*
—STUART CHASE [1]

[Topic stated last]

3   A man in cuffless shirt-sleeves with pink arm-garters, wearing a linen collar but no tie, yawned his way from Dyer's Drug Store across to the hotel. He leaned against the wall, scratched a while, sighed, and in a bored way gossiped with a man tilted back in a chair. A lumber-wagon, its long green box filled with large spools of barbed-wire fencing, creaked down the block. A Ford, in reverse, sounded as though it were shaking to pieces, then recovered and rattled away. In the Greek candy-store was the whine of a peanut-roaster, and the oily smell of nuts.
—SINCLAIR LEWIS [2]

[Topic implied: *Such were the activities in Main Street.*]

▶ EXERCISE 1.   Point out, or supply, the topic sentences for paragraphs 6 and 15 on the following pages, or for other paragraphs assigned by your instructor.

Note the lack of unity in the faulty paragraph below. All the sentences are about Michigan in general, but they do not develop any specific topic.

[1] From *Power of Words,* copyright, 1953, 1954, by Stuart Chase. Reprinted by permission of Harcourt, Brace and Company, Inc.

[2] From *Main Street* by Sinclair Lewis, copyright, 1920, by Harcourt, Brace and Company, Inc.; renewed, 1948, by Sinclair Lewis. Reprinted by permission of the publishers.

FAULTY PARAGRAPH

Michigan is a hunter's paradise. Deer, quail, and other kinds of wild game abound in the piny woods of the upper peninsula. Michigan has perhaps more coast line than any other state in the Union, being practically surrounded by Lake Superior, Lake Michigan, and Lake Huron. Along the coast almost every cove affords an ideal location for vacation camps. The lakes that fashion the state into two peninsulas, the upper and the lower, abound in fish which are eagerly sought by fishermen for pleasure or profit.

[The topic shifts from (1) *hunter's paradise* to (2) *coast line* providing sites for *vacation camps* and then to (3) *fishermen.* Each of these ideas might well be developed in a separate paragraph. Another remedy would be to supply a topic sentence, such as *Michigan is a paradise for the lover of the out-of-doors,* to which each of the ideas might be made to contribute.]

IMPROVED PARAGRAPH

4   *Michigan is a paradise for the lover of the out-of-doors.* Made up of two peninsulas, the upper and the lower, it probably has more coast line than any other state in the Union. In the waters of Lake Superior, Lake Huron, and Lake Michigan, which practically surround the state, teem fish, eagerly sought by fishermen for pleasure or profit. Here every cove affords an ideal location for vacation camps. Anyone who prefers hunting to fishing can find deer, quail, and other kinds of game in the piny woods of the upper peninsula. Surely Nature was in an extravagant mood when she created Michigan.

31b   Give coherence to the paragraph by so interlinking the sentences that the thought may flow smoothly from one sentence to the next.

A paragraph is said to have coherence when the relationship between sentences is clear, when the transition from one sentence to the next is easy and natural. The reader should be able to follow the thought without difficulty. In order to secure this coherence, this easy flow of the thought from sentence to sentence, the writer should rely first of all on (1) arrangement of the sentences in a clear order, and then on the use of (2) pronouns referring to the preceding sentence, (3) repeated words or ideas, (4) transitional expressions, and (5) parallel structure.

(1) Arrange the sentences of the paragraph in a clear, logical order.

There are several common, logical ways to order the sentences in a paragraph; the choice of an appropriate order depends upon the writer's purpose and the nature of his material. Perhaps the simplest and best order is "time" order.

POOR ARRANGEMENT OF SENTENCES

After the death of Saul, David ruled Israel for forty years. Once he incurred the king's anger and was driven ignominiously from court. As a shepherd lad he had lived in the hills of Judea. He had vanquished the mighty Philistine with his slingshot. The sad-faced Saul was charmed with his songs. He was the sweetest singer in all Israel.

[Confused time order]

ORDERLY SEQUENCE OF SENTENCES

5 David, the shepherd lad who lived in the hills of Judea, was the sweetest singer in all Israel. It was he who charmed the sad-faced Saul with his songs. It was he, too, who vanquished the mighty Philistine with his slingshot. Later he incurred the anger of Saul and was driven from court. But upon Saul's death David came back and ruled Israel for forty years.

[David's (1) *youth in Judea,* (2) *experiences with Saul,* and (3) *reign over Israel*]

This paragraph about David is made clearer by rearrangement in time order. Narrative paragraphs lend themselves naturally to such arrangement, and other types of paragraphs often have a time element that makes possible and natural a chronological arrangement. For example, in explaining a process—how something is done or made—the writer can follow the process through, step by step, from beginning to end. The following paragraph uses time order in explaining the difference between soaps and detergents.

6 Soaps and detergents have a "split personality" molecular structure, having one end that wants to dissolve in oil and the other end compatible with water. This can be seen by pouring mineral oil and water into a glass, and adding first some sodium-hydroxide (lye) solution, and then some salad oil, such as corn or olive oil. The

sodium hydroxide will mix with water, and the salad oil will mix with mineral oil, but the oil and water layers still won't mix. However, if soap is added, the two layers can be mixed to form a milky emulsion. Soap combines in one molecule the fatty structure of the salad oil with the sodium from the sodium hydroxide, and shares the solubilities of the two minerals. —J. P. MULLEN [3]

Sentences that have no evident time order can sometimes be arranged in "space" order, in which the paragraph moves from east to west, from west to east, from the near to the distant, from the distant to the near, from the left to the right, etc. This order is used especially for descriptive paragraphs. Note the movement from east to west in the following paragraph:

7 In New England woods the fiddlehead ferns were unfolding, and blankets of wisteria spread over the houses. Outside Santa Fe, ribbons of green laced the brown adobe on the flatlands, and here and there the full-flowering lilacs formed purple buttons. On riverbanks of the Northwest, wild rhododendrons, spiraling up to thirty feet, were spreading red and pink and white blooms two hands wide. *Spring was full-blown in the United States, and the nation's prevailing mood seemed to be as bright as its blossoms.* —TIME [4]

[One comprehensive sweep from New England in the extreme northeast to Santa Fe in the mid southwest and then on to the great Northwest, with the topic stated in the last sentence]

Another good arrangement of sentences is in order of "climax," according to which the least important idea is stated first and the others in order of increasing importance, as in the following paragraph:

8 A black spot on the bright surface of the nation had been a huge, jagged patch of drought, spreading over large areas of the west, south and southwest. But last week, on much of the parched land, rain fell. At Hale Center, Texas, clouds that swept up from the gulf dumped six inches of rain in two hours. In other Texas cities, men and women stood and let the rain soak them to the

[3] From "How Modern Detergents Work" by J. P. Mullen, *Popular Mechanics,* August 1955.
[4] Reprinted by permission of *Time* Magazine; copyright Time Inc. 1955.

skin, while children played in the swirling waters of overflowing gutters. The day after Secretary of State Dulles made his television report on international affairs, the top headline in the Omaha *World-Herald* exulted: RAINS UP TO 3 INCHES SOAK STATE'S DRY AREA.   —TIME [5]

[The first two sentences, taken together, state the topic: *The drought areas have been relieved by rains.* The last three sentences, developing the topic, rise to a climax: (1) *The rain fell in torrents;* (2) *the people were so happy that they "let the rain soak them to the skin";* and (3) *the rains even stole the headlines from the most significant world affairs.*]

Sometimes the movement within the paragraph may be from the general to the particular, from the particular to the general, or from the familiar to the unfamiliar. A paragraph may begin with a general statement which is then supported by particular details, or, reversing the process, it may begin with a series of details and conclude with a summarizing statement. Note the movement from the general to the particular in the following paragraph:

9   In the ten years we have been married, I have yet to see Maurine act deviously. Although caginess is presumed to be a prerequisite for politics, she has marched to the top of the ballot by blurting out exactly what is in her mind. When she was asked to back a bill allocating a portion of dog-racing revenues for 4-H clubs, Maurine scolded her constituents for tying a worthy cause to pari-mutuel gambling. The special interests which she has offended would terrify most politicians—utility companies, dairy farmers, the Bar-Tenders' Union, the fairs in all thirty-six Oregon counties, slot-machine operators, the Farm Bureau Federation, even the American Legion.

                        —RICHARD L. NEUBERGER [6]

[The first sentence states the topic: *Maurine never acts deviously.* The second sentence begins the development with a general statement about her positive action. The third sentence shows specifically how she faced up to the 4-H clubs, and the fourth lists other special interests defied in the same way.]

[5] Reprinted by permission of *Time* Magazine; copyright Time Inc. 1955.

[6] From "My Wife Put Me in the Senate," *Harper's Magazine,* June 1955.

Paragraphs 6, 7, 8, and 9 above illustrate four of many possible types of clear sentence arrangement within the paragraph. Any order of sentences, or any combination of orders, is satisfactory so long as it makes the sequence of thought clear. Proper arrangement of the sentences is the first, the basic, step to insure good transitions from sentence to sentence. All other steps presuppose that the sentences have first been arranged in the clearest possible order.

► EXERCISE 2.   Analyze paragraphs 16 and 17 below to determine the order used.

(2) Link sentences by means of pronouns referring to antecedents in the preceding sentences. (See also Section 28.)

In the following paragraphs italics are used to indicate the pronouns serving as links between sentences. Such pronouns should usually come near the beginning of the sentence if they are to be of much use in paragraph coherence.

10   There is still a good book to be written about the legend of the heroic West and the cowboy. The author would have to be a social philosopher as well as an historian. The legend has not been with us long. That West has had a very short history. *It* did not begin until the 'sixties, and *its* Homeric age was over before the century ended. *It* was created by a passing set of economic circumstances, by cheap open grazing-land in the Southwest, and good prices on the hoof in Kansas City. *It* could not survive the invention of barbed wire. Yet what a legend *it* has created!   —J. B. PRIESTLEY [7]

11   The crew are divided into two divisions, as equally as may be, called the watches. Of *these* the chief mate commands the larboard, and the second mate the starboard. *They* divide the time between them. . . .   —RICHARD HENRY DANA, JR.

► EXERCISE 3.   Underline the pronouns used to link sentences in paragraphs 21 and 33, or in any others assigned by your instructor. Check the antecedent (in a preceding sentence) to which each pronoun refers. Underline the pronouns used to link sentences in your last theme.

[7] From *Midnight on the Desert.* By permission of the author.

(3) Link sentences by repeating words or ideas used in the preceding sentences.

In the next paragraph below, note the repetition of the key word *cowboys,* or *cowboy,* as one method of linking the sentences. In paragraph 13 an idea is repeated by means of a summarizing word.

12 It was here in Arizona that I first met cowboys. Many of these *cowboys* now spend more time taking parties of ranch guests out for a morning ride than they do in rounding up cattle. Nevertheless, they are genuine *cowboys*. As a rule they have known nothing but ranch life, and they have all the accomplishments of the legendary *cowboy,* except perhaps that famous marksmanship with a Colt. When not at work they practice for forthcoming rodeos or entertain themselves, and you, with that melancholy music, those long lugubrious strains, for which all men who lead an active openair life seem to have a strange passion. Sedentary men may need gay cynical little tunes, but the *cowboy,* the sailor, the soldier, and their kind ask for nothing better than a gloomy ballad of true love cut short by early death. The *cowboy,* who is a man of tradition, keeps the traditional tone in song, an odd and rather nasal little tone, which would drive any singing-master mad but somehow pleases the rest of us. —J. B. PRIESTLEY [8]

13 The steward is the captain's servant, and has charge of the pantry, from which every one, even the mate himself, is excluded. These *distinctions* usually find him an enemy in the mate. . . . —RICHARD HENRY DANA, JR.

[*Distinctions* repeats an idea rather than a word.]

► EXERCISE 4. In paragraphs 26 and 30, or in any others assigned by your instructor, underline each word or idea that is repeated in order to link the sentences within the paragraph. In your last theme underline words or ideas that are repeated as a means of linking sentences.

(4) Link sentences by using such transitional expressions as the following:

ADDITION moreover, further, furthermore, besides, and, and then, likewise, also, nor, too, again, in addition, equally important, next, first, secondly, thirdly, *etc.,* finally, last, lastly

[8] From *Midnight on the Desert.* By permission of the author.

CONTRAST but, yet, and yet, however, still, nevertheless, on the other hand, on the contrary, after all, notwithstanding, for all that, in contrast to this, at the same time, although this may be true

COMPARISON similarly, likewise, in like manner

PURPOSE to this end, for this purpose, with this object

RESULT hence, therefore, accordingly, consequently, thus, thereupon, wherefore

TIME meanwhile, at length, immediately, soon, after a few days, in the meantime, afterward

PLACE here, beyond, near by, opposite to, adjacent to, on the opposite side

SUMMARY, REPETITION, EXEMPLIFICATION, INTENSIFICATION to sum up, in brief, on the whole, in sum, in short, as I have said, in other words, to be sure, as has been noted, for example, for instance, in fact, indeed, in any event

EXAMPLES

It is the unpunctual who are the slaves of time, which constantly rushes them to and fro with whips and scourges. *Further,* unpunctual persons are unmannerly. —ARNOLD BENNETT

[Note also the repetition of the word *unpunctual* as an aid to coherence.]

It was also in the great hall of the palace of the Olympian king that the gods feasted each day on ambrosia and nectar, their food and drink, the latter being handed round by the lovely goddess Hebe. *Here* they conversed of the affairs of heaven and earth. . . . —THOMAS BULFINCH

[Note also the use of the pronoun *they* as an aid to coherence.]

They fought with more pertinacity than bulldogs. . . . *In the meanwhile* there came along a single red ant. . . . —HENRY DAVID THOREAU

► EXERCISE 5. In paragraphs 25 and 27, or in any others assigned by your instructor, underline all transitional expressions used to link sentences within the paragraph. In your last theme underline all transitional expressions used to link sentences.

(5) Link sentences by means of parallel structure— that is, by repetition of the sentence pattern.

Note how the following paragraph is made coherent by the parallel structure of the last four sentences.

14   In the minds and in the ideals of Americans we have untouched natural resources that need developing just as much as the material treasures still tucked away in unused patents, in undeveloped river valleys, and in the atomic nuclei. For the next war, if one is still required to iron out national vanities, we shall need not so much manpower as brain power and alertness. For the continuing fight against disease, we shall need trained technical skills and unlimited resources in laboratory equipment and service. For the advancement of knowledge generally, we need a deliberate plan to free contemplative men for quiet and respected contemplation. For the realization of "fuller and more fruitful employment and a fuller and more fruitful life" we need a National Science Foundation and a country-wide awareness that governmental support for knowledge-research is henceforth basic in the national policy.

—HARLOW SHAPLEY [9]

▶ EXERCISE 6.   In paragraphs 10 and 21, or in any others assigned by your instructor, point out instances of parallel structure used to link sentences within the paragraph. Can you find instances in your own writing?

We have observed that easy transition from sentence to sentence within the paragraph depends on clear arrangement of the sentences and then on linking these sentences by means of pronouns, repeated words or ideas, transitional expressions, and parallel structure. Usually several of these aids to coherence are found in a single paragraph. In the following paragraph the linking devices are italicized and explained in brackets. Note that the order is from the general to the particular.

15   *They* [pronoun: transition from the preceding paragraph] haven't any ideological principles, or if they have, they don't show. *Their* [pronoun: reference to *they*, subject of previous sentence] only commitment as far as I can see is the well-being of the whole island. *They* [pronoun: reference to *their* and *they* in last two sentences] are not tied up in either Marxian or free-enterprise straitjackets. *They* [pronoun: reference to *they* of last sentence, with some parallel structure] can think without looking it up in the book; they are flexible and mentally free to think

[9] From "Status Quo or Pioneer," *Harper's Magazine,* October 1945.

out what needs to be done. If business can meet a *need* [repetition of *needs*], fine. *But* [transitional expression: contrast with last sentence] *if business cannot* [parallel with *if business can*], then let the government do it, or a co-operative, or a non-profit association. The main thing is to get *it* [pronoun: reference to *it* in the last sentence] done. *They* [pronoun: reference to *they* in preceding sentences] have achieved what you once called "ideological immunity."   —STUART CHASE [10]

▶ EXERCISE 7.   In paragraphs 19, 20, and 21 below, point out all devices used to insure easy transition from sentence to sentence.

(6) Transitions between paragraphs.

Transitions from one paragraph to the next are even more necessary than those between sentences within the paragraph. The reader takes it for granted that all sentences in one paragraph are on the same topic. But the paragraph break signals a new topic or a new phase of the preceding one, and the reader wants to know at once what the new one is to be. In the three connected paragraphs (16, 17, and 18) below, note how each opening sentence ties in with the preceding paragraph and also indicates the direction in which the new paragraph is to go.

16   In Philadelphia, the advantage of a small car was recently illustrated in a court of law. A baffled cop had dragged before a magistrate the owners of two MGs which had both been parked in the motor space designed for a single vehicle. It was the view of the cop that this arrangement resulted in an illicit mulcting of the city at the rate of a dime an hour. The magistrate disagreed; he commended the drivers for their ingenuity.

17   Another and no less precious asset arises not so much from size as from lighter and differently distributed weight. A small car is supremely handy in icy weather. It is almost never trapped by snow or mud, and it will almost never lose traction on a slippery grade. Its skids are rare and gentle. And its driver can enjoy the soul-satisfying experience of wending his way up a steep and snowy hill at an even speed among big cars which have skidded into the gutter or which lie helplessly athwart the highway.

[10] From *Power of Words,* copyright, 1953, 1954, by Stuart Chase. Reprinted by permission of Harcourt, Brace and Company, Inc.

18   For many of the more than a million Americans who own two or more cars, these and other advantages have dictated the choice of a small car as a supplement to the basic big car. The combination of, say, a station wagon and an MG provides a nice balance between capacity and chic and provides an escape from the status of a two-car family with all the financial and social implications it involves. A small car doesn't seem to be *exactly* a car; its sheepish owner can treat it as a gadget and explain that it costs next to nothing to operate.

—LAURENCE LAFORE, R. W. LAFORE, AND
R. W. LAFORE, JR.[11]

The topics of the three paragraphs may be stated thus: (16) *Ease of parking small cars was recently illustrated in Philadelphia.* (17) *The light weight of small cars is especially advantageous in icy weather.* (18) *The small car needs hardly to be considered a "second" car.* The opening sentence of paragraph 16 refers, by *advantage,* to the previously discussed ease of parking small cars and also leads up to the illustration to be used in the paragraph. The next paragraph begins with *another . . . asset,* showing at once that an additional advantage of small cars is to be pointed out (at the same time that *another* calls attention to the one just discussed). And *these and other advantages* in the opening sentence of paragraph 18 ties in with what has preceded while leading to what is to follow.

▶ EXERCISE 8.   Analyze for transitions between paragraphs the seven paragraphs of "Riveting a Skyscraper" in Section 32, pages 934-35.

31c   Develop the paragraph adequately. Supply enough information to satisfy the reader but avoid excessively long paragraphs.

(1) Supply enough information to satisfy the reader.

Avoid short, inadequately developed paragraphs. A topic sentence is not in itself a paragraph. In ordinary writing a very short paragraph is sometimes used for emphasis or for transition between longer paragraphs. But a *series* of paragraphs each less than fifty

[11] From "The Small Cars: Fun on Wheels," *Harper's Magazine,* March 1955.

words in length (except in dialogue and other special types of writing) suggests inadequate development of the thought. If such choppy paragraphs deal with the same topic, they should be combined into one or more longer paragraphs. If not, each paragraph should be given adequate development.

PARAGRAPHS THAT SHOULD BE COMBINED

The line of demarcation between capitalism and socialism is sharp and clear.

Capitalism is that form of organization in which the means of production—and by that is meant the machine and the funds required to utilize the machine—are controlled by private individuals or by privately owned organizations.

Under a socialistic regime the control of the means of production, the control of capital—for even socialists concede the need for capital—is by the group. Under capitalism the profits accrue to the private individual; under socialism, to the group.

[These three short paragraphs, read together, actually make one unified paragraph of ninety words and should be so written. Taken separately, the paragraphs are short and choppy; together they form a paragraph of average length developing with a clearly stated topic sentence: *The line of demarcation between capitalism and socialism is sharp and clear.*]

PARAGRAPHS THAT SHOULD BE EXPANDED

During his first term of office President Roosevelt introduced many laws to promote national recovery. These laws covered all phases of the national life.

[The reader wants to know specifically what some of these laws were.]

My father had an interesting life. I remember the time he began to tell us about the incidents of his boyhood on a Texas ranch.

[Obviously some of the incidents should be related.]

The football game was much more like a movie than like real life. The most improbable things happened.

[Some of the improbable happenings should be mentioned, and the implied contrast between the movies and real life elaborated.]

Each of these short paragraphs begins with a promising topic sentence and then stops before supplying enough information to satisfy the reader. In other words, the paragraphs are not adequately developed.

Methods of Paragraph Development

Analysis shows that good paragraphs may be developed by many methods and by innumerable combinations of methods. No one method, or combination of methods, is better than another except as it happens to fit the needs of a given paragraph. The experienced writer is probably unaware of the method he is using. But even though the particular method of development makes little difference, it is highly important that the development be full enough to satisfy or convince the reader. The inexperienced writer can learn how to fill out his own paragraphs by studying the methods of professional writers. One very common method of paragraph development is by listing the particulars and details suggested by the topic sentence (in italics in the following paragraph).

PARTICULARS AND DETAILS

19 *My aunt was a tall, hard-featured lady, but by no means ill-looking.* There was an inflexibility in her face, in her voice, in her gait and carriage, amply sufficient to account for the effect she had made upon a gentle creature like my mother; but her features were rather handsome than otherwise, though unbending and austere. I particularly noticed that she had a very quick, bright eye. Her hair, which was gray, was arranged in two plain divisions, under what I believe would be called a mobcap; I mean a cap, much more common then than now, with sidepieces fastening under the chin. Her dress was of a lavender color, and perfectly neat, but scantily made, as if she desired to be as little encumbered as possible. I remember that I thought it, in form, more like a riding habit with the superfluous skirt cut off, than anything else. She wore at her side a gentleman's gold watch, if I might judge from its size and make, with an appropriate chain and seals; she had some linen at her throat not unlike a shirt collar, and things at her wrists like little shirt wristbands. —CHARLES DICKENS

[Details of features and dress fill out the picture of the stern but not ill-looking person of the topic sentence.]

▶ EXERCISE 9. Supply specific details to complete one of the following: (1) The sergeant was stern without being cruel. (2) His expression advertised his sense of humor. (3) Our cook was in almost perpetual emotion.

20 *The captain, in the first place, is lord paramount.* He stands no watch, comes and goes when he pleases, and is accountable to no one, and must be obeyed in everything, without a question, even from his chief officer. He has the power to turn his officers off duty, and even to break them and make them do duty as sailors in the forecastle. Where there are no passengers and no supercargo, as in our vessel, he has no companion but his own dignity, and no pleasure, unless he differs from most of his kind, but the consciousness of possessing supreme power, and, occasionally, the exercise of it. —RICHARD HENRY DANA, JR.

[The paragraph lists particulars or details in which the captain is indeed "lord paramount," as stated in the topic sentence.]

▶ EXERCISE 10. Develop a paragraph by listing some important details in support of one of the following topic sentences: (1) The sergeant is the backbone of the army. (2) The dean is an important administrative officer. (3) The modern farmer is a scientist.

21 *My second great fortune was Lily Bess Campbell, professor of English literature at the University of California in Los Angeles.* She taught me to think exactly, to say the precise truth as nearly as I could perceive it. She taught me that there is vitality in logic, that there is logic in humor and in beauty, that in humor the greater the truth the funnier, that in lyricism the more consistent and clear the more moving. She made me brief a Shelley ode as though it were a legal argument. She taught me that a sentence was organic with bones and sinews and for this reason had life, that the power of logic was a passionate power and that Euclid and Grammar were one. And for the first time I recognized Pattern, which is Law as well as Magic. —AGNES DE MILLE [12]

[The paragraph lists nine particulars in which Professor Campbell proved to be a "great fortune." Note that in this paragraph and in paragraphs 19 and 20, the order of development is from the general to the particular.]

[12] From "The Valor of Teaching" by Agnes de Mille, *Atlantic Monthly*, June 1955.

INSTANCES OR EXAMPLES

22   *It is important to remember that, in strictness, there is no such thing as an uneducated man.* Take an extreme case. Suppose that an adult man, in the full vigor of his faculties, could be suddenly placed in the world, as Adam is said to have been, and then left to do as he best might. How long would he be left uneducated? Not five minutes. Nature would begin to teach him, through the eye, the ear, the touch, the properties of objects. Pain and pleasure would be at his elbow telling him to do this and avoid that; and by slow degrees the man would receive an education which, if narrow, would be thorough, real, and adequate to his circumstances, though there would be no extras and very few accomplishments.

                     —THOMAS HENRY HUXLEY

[The topic sentence is developed by the one example, admittedly extreme, of a hypothetical modern Adam.]

► EXERCISE 11.   Develop one of the following sentences by an example in the manner suggested by Huxley's paragraph: (1) No man is wholly fearless. (2) Even an illiterate man can be wise.

23   To those who did not know the U.S. or who did not look closely, the mood of May 1955 might be mistaken for fatuous euphoria. *But beneath the glass surface there was a deep undercurrent, a persistent concern for country.* In Kentucky's Pennyroyal, where farmers were just finishing their tobacco-setting, a middle-aged farm wife apologized for paying too little attention to world affairs, then demonstrated that she had a remarkably clear understanding of what has been going on. "There seems to be a little less fear around," she said. "Fear's sort of lost its power. I thought it was pretty good that Mr. Dulles seemed to have gained what he's been struggling so hard for. He's been trying so hard for footing and he seems to have got it."   —TIME [13]

[The first sentence makes the transition from the preceding paragraph. The topic sentence (the second) is developed by the one example of the Kentucky farm wife.]

24   Disregarding the words and observing any considerable segment of economic behavior, *it is immediately apparent that activities are mixed,* sometimes inextricably tangled. The Tennessee Valley Authority, for instance, is owned by the federal government, but encourages new private enterprise throughout the Valley, sells much power to private power companies, co-operates closely with state and local governments. Great corporations take on functions closely resembling governmental powers, as Peter Drucker has pointed out, while many private businesses are subsidized by governments—for example, trucks on the highways.   —STUART CHASE [14]

[The topic sentence is developed by several examples.]

25   *Perhaps the most extraordinary quality the Mohammedan religion developed in Jolo is its fanaticism.* For years, no Moro would attend school for fear of "invisible conversion" to Christianity. As recently as 1940 the students of one of the schools killed all their non-Moro teachers for no reason that the authorities were ever able to discern. And even today, some people of Jolo will not ride in a car, simply because Christians introduced automobiles to the island. It is also a problem for Moros to go to the hospital, because, according to their reasoning, if they died, a Christian would touch them, and this is not to be borne.

                     —FAUBION POWERS [15]

[The topic sentence is developed by four instances or examples, each in a separate sentence.]

► EXERCISE 12.   Select a suitable topic sentence and develop a paragraph; use several instances or examples.

COMPARISON OR CONTRAST

26   *France offers the world a picture the very opposite of England.* The words of English diplomacy are fuzzy, confusing and, all too often, meaningless; the vigor of English diplomacy springs from the way Englishmen understand each other and stand united in purpose without need of wordy persuasion. French diplomacy speaks in lucid, clear analysis, but it speaks for a people divided from village roots to sovereign assembly. Even France's diplomats are divided; it is doubtful whether ten out of a hundred of the profes-

[13] Reprinted by permission of *Time* Magazine; copyright Time Inc. 1955.

[14] From *Power of Words,* copyright, 1953, 1954, by Stuart Chase. Reprinted by permission of Harcourt, Brace and Company, Inc.

[15] From "The Land-Locked Pirate of the Pacific," *Harper's Magazine,* June 1955.

sionals at the Quai d'Orsay are wholeheartedly agreed that their government's support of European Union makes sense.

—THEODORE H. WHITE [16]

[The topic sentence is developed by contrasting England (in one long sentence) with France (in two long sentences).]

27   *In all the countries of Europe I have visited there is a patent difference between metropolises and smaller towns.* In the provinces of France, or Austria, or Germany you notice the difference in every shop window, in every coffee house, in the universities themselves. When, for instance, you go from Paris to Lille or to Orleans or to Bordeaux the dresses, the books, the furniture you see in the windows will lag some months if not years behind those you were used to seeing in Paris. The hotels and restaurants will be more modest, uncomfortable, and rather shabby. Universities will lack the stimulating élan of the Sorbonne. *Nothing of this kind distinguishes Madison from, let us say, New York or Chicago.* Here you see just the same merchandise in the windows as in New York, the same neon lights, the same pictures in the same movie theaters, you read the same columns and comics in the local papers as in those of New York, and the university with its splendid installations, its rich library, its almost luxurious Students' Union certainly does not fall behind any university I saw in New York, though it is smaller.   —PAUL SCHRECKER [17]

[The implied topic sentence, derived from the two italicized sentences, is: In Europe but not in America, there is a patent difference between metropolises and smaller towns. European conditions (in three sentences following the first italicized sentence) are contrasted with American conditions (in one very long sentence following the second italicized sentence). Note that instances or examples are used to develop the separate parts of the contrast.]

▶ EXERCISE 13.   Develop by contrast one of the following topics: (1) the service in a lunch wagon and in a hotel dining room; (2) the dialogue of a motion picture and the dialogue of Shakespeare; (3) the architecture of the Washington Monument

[16] From *Fire in the Ashes: Europe in Mid-Century* by Theodore H. White, by permission of William Sloane Associates. Copyright 1953 by Theodore H. White.

[17] From "American Diary," *Harper's Magazine*, July 1944.

and of the Lincoln Memorial; (4) the relative effectiveness of radio and television.

28   It is because of this universality of athletic sports that *English training is briefer and less severe.* The American makes, and is forced to make, a long and tedious business of getting fit, whereas an Englishman has merely to exercise and sleep a trifle more than usual, and this only for a brief period. Our oarsmen work daily from January to July, about six months, or did so before Mr. Lehmann brought English ideas among us; the English 'varsity crews row together nine or ten weeks. Our football players slog daily for six or seven weeks; English teams seldom or never "practice," and play at most two matches a week. Our track athletes are in training at frequent intervals throughout the college year, and are often at the training table six weeks; in England six weeks is the maximum period of training, and the men as a rule are given only three days a week of exercise on the cinder-track. To an American, training is an abnormal condition; to an Englishman it is the consummation of the normal.

—JOHN CORBIN [18]

[The topic sentence is developed by the five following sentences, each of which contrasts American and English methods of training athletes. The first states the contrast in general terms; the second deals with rowing; the third with football; the fourth with track; and the fifth makes a general summarizing contrast.]

Note that the last three paragraphs illustrate two different ways of making the contrast. In paragraphs 26 and 27 one side of the contrast is completely developed and then the other; in paragraph 28 both sides are contrasted in each sentence. Either way is good, and so is a combination of the two.

▶ EXERCISE 14.   Develop one of the topics given in Exercise 13 according to the method used in paragraph 28.

DEFINITION

29   *Well, what I mean by Education is learning the rules of this mighty game.* In other words, education is the instruction of the intellect in the laws of Nature, under which name I include not

[18] From *An American at Oxford*, Houghton Mifflin Company, 1902.

merely things and their forces, but men and their ways; and the fashioning of the affections and of the will into an earnest and loving desire to move in harmony with those laws. For me, education means neither more nor less than this. Anything which professes to call itself education must be tried by this standard, and if it fails to stand the test, I will not call it education, whatever may be the force of authority or of numbers upon the other side. —THOMAS HENRY HUXLEY

[The topic sentence, a definition of education, is further defined and explained by the other sentences in the paragraph.]

30 *A guaranteed annual wage is money paid by an employer to people for all or some part of a year in which they are not making products.* The payments are part of the manufacturer's cost and hence part of the consumer's cost. If the manufacturer has ten employees but work for only eight, he must nevertheless recover in the price he gets for his product the payments he makes to his employees for hours they did not work, or he must go out of business. This is true of any employer, whether he has ten or ten thousand employees. —LELAND HAZARD [19]

[The topic sentence defines "guaranteed annual wage," and the remaining sentences serve to refine and clarify this definition.]

31-32 *The Romancer is an artist who deliberately sets out with the intention of representing life as it is not—as he would like it to be, perhaps, and as on rare and heroic occasions it is, when the fire of humanity burns at its highest and hottest.* He represents a world which is like our own, in a sense, but unlike it in the respect that it is infinitely more exciting, more vigorous, more interesting, more profound—more beautiful, in fact, with that beauty which the perceptive eye realizes in nature as in art. The Romancer arrives at this effect by a deliberate selection of qualities and characteristics, by a deliberate heightening of certain values and depressing of others. He does not aim at the development of character, but at the presentation of sentiment, and his characters become, not inconsequent and inconsistent human beings, but types of qualities.

The Realist, on the other hand, aims at presenting life as it is, and character as it develops. He is not afraid, as the Romancer is, of depicting any emotion that might be misinterpreted in a well-bred person. He does not wish to emphasize the

[19] From "Can We Afford a Guaranteed Wage?" by Leland Hazard, *Atlantic Monthly*, March 1955.

driving force of the world, but he wishes to show, in a panoramic kind of way, how lives as a matter of fact do work themselves out, how they triumph, how they collapse. Of course, the Realist has to use selection too, because one cannot treat life in the mass; but his aim is not to represent either life at a high level, or life at a low level. He tries to give the true flavor of it, with its broken hopes, its successes that are often more hollow than its failures, its stolid complacencies, its meaningless sufferings, its baffling mysteries. But the essence of the Realist's art is that he has no preconceived idea of what life ought to be or might be; his one aim is to present it as it is. —A. C. BENSON

[This pair of paragraphs exemplifies both definition and comparison and contrast. Each begins with a topic sentence which defines the subject of the paragraph. The definition is then supported by details.]

▶ EXERCISE 15. Define one of the following sets of opposites in two paragraphs modeled on paragraphs 31 and 32 above: (1) the Easterner and the Westerner; (2) the leader and the follower; (3) the typical male undergraduate and the typical co-ed; (4) the English major and the pre-medical or engineering student.

MISCELLANEOUS PARAGRAPHS

Many good paragraphs are developed not by any one specific method but by a combination of methods. Some good paragraphs almost defy analysis. The important consideration is not the specific method used but the adequacy of the development.

33 I have heard rumors of visitors who were disappointed. The same people will be disappointed at the Day of Judgment. In fact, the Grand Canyon is a sort of landscape Day of Judgment. It is not a show place, a beauty spot, but a revelation. The Colorado River, which is powerful, turbulent, and so thick with silt that it is like a saw, made it with the help of the erosive forces of rain, frost, and wind, and some strange geological accidents; and all these together have been hard at work on it for the last seven or eight million years. It is the largest of the eighteen canyons of the Colorado River, is over two hundred miles long, has an average width of twelve miles, and is a good mile deep. It is the world's supreme example of erosion. But this is not what it really is. It is, I repeat, a revelation. The Colorado River made it, but you feel when you are there that God gave the Colorado River its instructions. It is all Bee-thoven's nine symphonies in stone and magic light. Even to remember that it is still there lifts up the heart. If I were an American, I should make my remembrance of it the final test of men, art, and policies. I should ask myself: Is this good enough to exist in the same country as the Canyon? How would I feel about this man, this kind of art, these political measures, if I were near that Rim? Every member or officer of the Federal Government ought to remind himself, with triumphant pride, that he is on the staff of the Grand Canyon.

—J. B. PRIESTLEY [20]

▶ EXERCISE 16. Pick out the topic sentence in paragraph 33. By what method is this topic sentence developed?

34 I wonder why American towns look so much alike that I sometimes mix them up in my memory. The reference to the standard influence of mass production whose agents are the traveling salesman, the mail-order houses, the five-and-ten cent stores, the chain stores, the movies, is not sufficient. If you stay two days in Bologna and in Ferrara, or in Arles and in Avignon, you will never mix them up in all your life. But it may well happen that after you spend two days in St. Louis and in Kansas City the images of these towns soon merge into one. I think the real reason for this is that these towns have not yet had time enough to individualize and to crystallize visible local traditions of their own. Physiognomically speaking, children are much less differentiated from each other than grown people.

—PAUL SCHRECKER [21]

▶ EXERCISE 17. Notice how paragraph 34 has been developed by asking the question *why*. Develop a paragraph by asking yourself: (1) why you really came to college; (2) why you go to the movies; (3) why you prefer your favorite magazine; (4) why you enjoy college football games.

35 After Colonel Carter was gone home I went to work on my new horse. The old one, the pony, I used only for business: to go to fires, to see my friends, run errands, and go hunting with my new shotgun. But the game that had all my attention was the breaking in of the colt, the beautiful cream-colored mare, who soon knew me—and my pockets. I carried sugar to reward her when

she did right, and she discovered where I carried it; so did the pony, and when I was busy they would push their noses into my pockets, both of which were torn down a good deal of the time. But the colt learned. I taught her to run around a circle, turn and go the other way at a signal. My sisters helped me. I held the long rope and the whip (for signaling), while one of the girls led the colt; it was hard work for them, but they took it in turns. One would lead the colt round and round till I snapped the whip; then she would turn, turning the colt, till the colt did it all by herself. And she was very quick. She shook hands with each of her four feet. She let us run under her, back and forth. She was slow only to carry me. Following Colonel Carter's instructions, I began by laying my arm or a surcingle over her back. If she trembled, I drew it slowly off. When she could abide it, I tried buckling it, tighter and tighter. I laid over her, too, a blanket, folded at first, then open, and, at last, I slipped up on her myself, sat there a second, and as she trembled, slid off. My sisters held her for me, and when I could get up and sit there a moment or two, I tied her at a block, and we, my sisters and I, made a procession of mounting and dismounting. She soon got used to this and would let us slide off over her rump, but it was a long, long time before she would carry me.   —LINCOLN STEFFENS [22]

▶ EXERCISE 18. The topic sentence of paragraph 35—"But the game that had all my attention was the breaking in of the colt, etc."—is developed chiefly by giving details in time order. In like manner expand one of the following topics: (1) how I spent all my time training my hound; (2) how I shot my first deer; (3) how we won the football game; (4) how I got my first job; (5) how I cooked my first dinner.

▶ EXERCISE 19. Indicate an appropriate method of developing each of the following topic sentences:

1. The school is the servant of the individual, the family, and the community.

2. The guaranteed annual wage has aroused much controversy.

3. There is more than one reason why the college student should study English.

4. My roommate has helped me to understand myself.

5. The changing aspects of the seasons are as stimulating as they are restful.

[20] From *Midnight on the Desert* by J. B. Priestley. By permission of the author.

[21] From "American Diary," *Harper's Magazine*, July 1944.

[22] From *The Autobiography of Lincoln Steffens*, copyright, 1931, by Harcourt, Brace and Company, Inc.

6. The companionship of man and animals contains secrets as important as the companionship of man and man.

7. A circus has many mouths to feed.

8. Before talking about democracy we should at least say what democracy is not.

9. If you don't trust my judgment about the value of reading, let me quote a few authorities.

10. Some men think our great cities are monuments of progress; others say they are symptoms of social disease.

11. You can solve most problems by taking a walk.

12. Intelligence means the ability to discriminate.

13. The farmer has recently acquired great popular esteem.

14. To be self-reliant one must know one's predominant weakness as well as one's predominant strength.

15. Three men showed me the true meaning of patriotism.

16. The ability to think and the ability to write are closely allied.

17. Soil erosion is a menace to national security.

18. When the storm was over we all set to work in earnest.

19. It is necessary to read *Hamlet* at least three times.

20. Railroads are a romantic element of the industrial age.

▶ EXERCISE 20. Select a topic sentence and develop a paragraph by one or more of the following methods:

1. Particulars and details
2. Instances or examples
3. Comparison or contrast
4. Definition

(2) Avoid excessively long paragraphs.

In current writing, paragraphs seldom run to more than two or three hundred words, and the average is much shorter, perhaps not more than one hundred words. Whenever a writer finds that he needs more than 250 words to develop his central thought, he should, if possible, divide his material into two or more paragraphs. Let us notice, for example, how we may divide the following long paragraph, which Richard Steele wrote more than two hundred years ago when readers were less hurried than those of our generation.

36 1. When a good artist would express any remarkable character in sculpture, he endeavors to work up his figure into all the perfections his imagination can form, and to imitate not so much what is, as what may or ought to be. 2. I shall follow their example, in the idea I am going to trace out of a fine gentleman, by assembling together such qualifications as seem requisite to make the character complete. 3. In order to do this I shall premise in general, that by a fine gentleman I mean a man completely qualified as well for the service and good as for the ornament and delight of society. 4. When I consider the frame of mind peculiar to a gentleman, I suppose it graced with all the dignity and elevation of spirit that human nature is capable of. 5. To this I would have joined a clear understanding, a reason free from prejudice, a steady judgment, and an extensive knowledge. 6. When I think of the heart of a gentleman, I imagine it firm and intrepid, void of all inordinate passions, and full of tenderness, compassion, and benevolence. 7. When I view the fine gentleman with regard to his manners, methinks I see him modest without bashfulness, frank and affable without impertinence, obliging and complaisant without servility, cheerful and in good humor without noise. 8. These amiable qualities are not easily obtained; neither are there many men that have a genius to excel this way. 9. A finished gentleman is perhaps the most uncommon of all the great characters in life. 10. Besides the natural endowments with which this distinguished man is to be born, he must run through a long series of education. 11. Before he makes his appearance and shines in the world, he must be principled in religion, instructed in all the moral virtues, and led through the whole course of the polite arts and sciences. 12. He should be no stranger to courts and to camps; he must travel to open his mind, to enlarge his views, to learn the policies and interests of foreign states, as well as to fashion and polish himself, and to get clear of national prejudices, of which every country has its share. 13. To all these more essential improvements he must not forget to add the fashionable ornaments of life, such as are the languages and the bodily exercises most in vogue; neither would I have him think even dress itself beneath his notice.

A careful reading shows that this whole paragraph of 404 words develops Steele's concept of the ideal gentleman. The paragraph has unity; except for the excessive length, there would be no reason for dividing it. Fortunately it can (like most overlong paragraphs) be divided into shorter paragraphs, each developing a specific part of the general topic. Steele's long paragraph can be divided, without any rewriting, into three good paragraphs as follows:

FIRST PARAGRAPH (sentences 1-3) The method to be used in depicting the ideal gentleman and a general definition of him.

SECOND PARAGRAPH (sentences 4-7) The ideal gentleman's specific qualities of mind, heart, and manners.

THIRD PARAGRAPH (sentences 8-13) The education needed to develop these qualities.

If the long paragraph were thus divided into three, it would be much easier for the reader, both for his eye and for his comprehension. And each paragraph would be well unified, with good transitions from one to the other. Note especially the excellent transition to the third paragraph: "These amiable qualities are not easily obtained; neither are there many men that have a genius to excel this way."

▶ Planning and Writing the Whole Composition

The four units of composition, in an ascending order, are (1) the word—Sections 19-22, (2) the sentence—Sections 23-30, (3) the paragraph—Section 31, and (4) the whole composition—Section 32. Words make up the sentence, sentences make up the paragraph, and paragraphs make up the whole composition.

32   Arrange and express your ideas effectively.

It has long been a convention of rhetoric to divide all writing into four main types—exposition or explanation, the most common kind of nonfiction writing and the kind most frequently written by college students; argument, similar to exposition but written with the intention of convincing rather than simply explaining; narration; and description. Very seldom is description written independently. Usually it is only part of a composition in which one of the other types dominates. In fact, few compositions are a single form of discourse. Most are mixtures with one form predominant. Thus, a paper on "How to Drive a Car" would be primarily exposition but would also contain bits of description (perhaps of the steering mechanism) and narration (perhaps an anecdote about the author's first drive). Whatever form of discourse a paper may take, it does not fall into order by chance. *Order is the result of careful planning.*

32a   Choose an appropriate subject and limit it properly.

A subject is appropriate:

1. If it appeals to you, or if you can develop an interest in it as you work on it.
2. If it is acceptable to the intended reader.

A subject is properly limited:

1. If you know enough about it or can learn enough in a reasonable period. (Subjects that require extensive reading should be reserved for the library paper. See Section 33.)
2. If the topic is not too broad to treat in the time or space at your command. "Amateur Photography" might be a satisfactory title for a paper of several thousand words; but if you must limit yourself to several hundred words, you will do better with "Developing a Film" or "The Growth of My Interest in Photography."

Let us suppose that you have chosen (or have been assigned) the subject, "My Home Town—Rushville," for a paper of five hundred words. Obviously, you cannot cover everything to be said about your town in five hundred words. You must therefore find a more limited topic. You may be particularly interested in the town's industry, but "The Industries of Rushville" is still too broad for your short paper. So you concentrate on a single industry—perhaps the chief industry, paper making. Your topic then becomes "The Paper Industry in Rushville."

Central Idea. At this stage you will find it helpful to set down, in a single sentence, a central or controlling idea for your paper, such as "Paper manufacturing in Rushville is an interesting process" or "The prosperity of Rushville depends chiefly upon its paper industry" or "The paper industry in Rushville is not an unmixed blessing." This statement, in a single sentence, of the central or controlling idea helps to limit the subject and especially helps determine the items to be included in the outline. If the central idea is not determined in the process of limiting the subject, it should be written out before the outline is completed and then used to test the contents of the outline.

If you wish later to write another paper on your home town, you may use as your central idea "Rushville has a good school system" or (more limited) "Rushville has a well-rounded high-school program." If you wish to convince your readers of the need for action—that is, if you wish to write an argument—you may use a central idea like one of these:

1. Rushville should have a technical night school.
2. Rushville should authorize bonds for new school buildings.

If you wish to interest your readers in the history of your home town, you will choose a central idea suitable for a narrative:

1. The early settlers in Rushville had many difficulties with the Indians.
2. Rushville had a minor but interesting part in the Civil War.

If your purpose is to give a vivid picture of Rushville and its surroundings, you might select a central idea that lends itself to description, such as "Rushville has an interesting setting in the mountains."

Your home town, then—and many other subjects, for that matter—may suggest good topics for your papers, whether you wish to explain (exposition), to convince (argumentation), to narrate events (narration), to describe (description), or to combine two or more of these forms of discourse. The four forms should be used either separately or freely in combination, according to the demands of the topic. A combination of exposition and description might be used, for example, in a paper with one of these central ideas.

1. Colonel Brown is our most distinguished citizen.
2. Old Tony is the most colorful individual in Rushville.

Each of the suggestions listed below is a suitable subject for a student paper. Some of the suggestions, as worded, may provide the exact title you need for your paper. In all likelihood, however, you will wish to limit the subject to the scope of your experience and to sharpen the wording for use as a title. (For the proper capitalization of titles, see Section 9c.)

Suggestions for Written Work

HOME AND THE INDIVIDUAL

1. My home town
2. Being an elder brother (*or* elder sister, only child, etc.)
3. My favorite author (*or* book, poem, magazine, newspaper, radio program, television program, etc.)
4. My hobby and why I like it (hiking; photography; collecting stamps, old glass, coins, books, furniture, etc.)
5. Learning to swim (*or* play tennis, ride horseback, sail a boat, ride a bicycle, skate, play the saxophone, etc.)
6. The efficient or attractive kitchen (*or* bathroom, living room, bedroom, playroom, etc.)
7. Color schemes (*or* draperies, period furniture, etc.) in interior decorating
8. Milk (meat, vegetables, etc.) in the diet
9. Changes in men's (women's) clothing
10. Peacetime draft and its effect on the individual

SCHOOL AND COLLEGE

1. Differences between school and college
2. Freshman Week
3. College slang

4. Earning one's way
5. My first field trip
6. The course I find most practical (or difficult, interesting, etc.)
7. The student union
8. Campus politics
9. My roommate
10. My room at college
11. The writing laboratory
12. Using a microscope
13. Are examinations fair?
14. The honor system
15. How to be a cheerleader
16. What makes school spirit?
17. Why I am going to college
18. Duties of the quarterback (or halfback, fullback, etc.)
19. What is sportsmanship?
20. Life in a dormitory (or fraternity house, sorority house, etc.)

HISTORY, ECONOMICS, AND SOCIOLOGY

1. What do our taxes buy?
2. Peacetime military conscription
3. The third term for President
4. The State of Israel
5. The Monroe Doctrine today
6. Our Foreign Aid Program
7. The guaranteed annual wage
8. The Iron Curtain
9. How to appraise a used car
10. Socialized medicine
11. Today's teen-agers
12. The National Park Service
13. Reforestation
14. Causes of juvenile delinquency
15. Living in a housing development
16. Radio and television advertising
17. The parole system
18. Unemployment insurance
19. Sharecroppers
20. The right to strike (or compulsory arbitration)

SCIENCE AND MEDICINE

1. Atomic submarines
2. Wild plants and their uses in medicine
3. The prevention of forest fires
4. Vitamins from plants
5. Color television
6. Chemical warfare on insects (or DDT, etc.)
7. Yeasts and vitamins
8. Migration of wild ducks and geese
9. Blood plasma
10. Beneficial bacteria
11. Synthetic diamonds
12. Nylon (or rayon, dacron, etc.)

13. Amateur photography
14. The Salk vaccine
15. What is food allergy?
16. Penicillin (or streptomycin, aureomycin, sulfathiazole, etc.)
17. Space flight
18. Coal, the raw material of many products
19. Uses of uranium
20. Plastic surgery

FARM AND MACHINE

1. Soil erosion
2. How to grow tomatoes (or asparagus, strawberries, celery, dahlias, mushrooms, chrysanthemums, etc.)
3. Wild life on the farm
4. The apple, from tree to consumer
5. New car designs
6. Good seeds make good crops
7. Judging cattle
8. Making a tobacco bed
9. Curing tobacco
10. The work of the 4-H Club (or home demonstration work, etc.)
11. Frozen foods
12. Newsprint from Southern pine
13. Electricity in the modern home
14. Air conditioning every home
15. Soilless farming
16. Electric (or gas) refrigeration
17. Mining coal (or lead, copper, zinc, etc.)
18. Building a skyscraper (or road, canal, dam, ship, etc.)
19. The most wonderful machine I know
20. Advantages of living on a farm (or in the city, in a small town)

► EXERCISE 1.   Select one subject from the preceding "Suggestions for Written Work," limit it as necessary to make it a suitable topic for an expository paper of five hundred words, and write a single sentence expressing the central idea for the paper. Choose a suitable title for the paper.

► EXERCISE 2.   Follow directions given under Exercise 1, substituting "argumentative" for "expository."

► EXERCISE 3.   Follow directions given under Exercise 1, substituting "narrative" for "expository."

32b   Develop the outline during the preparation of the paper. (See also 33c.)

The outline is the blueprint of the composition. Just as the carpenter or the engineer follows his blueprint implicitly in order to avoid costly structural blunders, so the writer—especially the student writer—follows his outline carefully so that he may arrange his ideas effectively.

But blueprints can be changed and improved, and so can outlines. The writer should make the outline his helpful tool; he should not become its slave. He should keep the outline a growing, developing plan which he will not hesitate to change at any stage of his composition whenever he hits upon a way to improve it. He will naturally try to perfect his outline before he starts to write the paper, but the actual writing will almost certainly suggest a few desirable changes in the arrangement of details.

The first step in the preparation of an outline is the jotting down of ideas on the topic. The student should not hesitate to jot down a long list of ideas; and he should jot them down rapidly, without much concern for the proper order. When he begins to classify his ideas, he will find it easy to reject needless ones; he may find also that he needs to supplement his knowledge by further observation or reading.

Suppose, for example, a student has selected subject No. 18 under "Farm and Machine" on page 929, "Building a Skyscraper," and has limited this subject to "Riveting a Skyscraper." From his observation of riveters at work, or from his reading on the process of riveting, he may jot down the following items:

1. Throwing the rivets
2. The gun
3. Noise of the gun
4. The catcher and his can
5. The bucker-up and his dolly bar
6. Work of the gun-man
7. The furnace
8. Skill required in heating
9. The rivet boy's duties
10. Danger from dropped rivets
11. Danger to the riveters
12. Co-operation of the gang
13. The alignment of the holes for the rivet
14. The inserting of the heated rivet
15. The complicated task of completing the work
16. Silence of the gang during the work

On inquiry or further reading, additional information may be added, such as:

17. Essential unity of the gang
18. Replacements
19. Experience required
20. Insurance rates for members

At this point—if he has not done so before—the writer should set down in one sentence the central idea of his proposed paper. For a short paper on "Riveters" this controlling idea might well be: "Riveting requires skillful work under dangerous conditions." Such a statement of the scope and purpose of the paper will often suggest, as we have already observed, items to be discarded and others to be added.

The next step in putting together an outline is the grouping, or classification, of the miscellaneous items under a few main headings. A little thought will show that general information about the gang should be gathered under one heading, and that material on the three steps in the actual process of riveting ought to be grouped under other headings. The general information would logically come first, the three steps next. Thus there would be the following main headings:

I. Skillful co-ordination of a riveting gang of four.
II. Preparation of the rivets.
III. Passing of the red-hot rivets.
IV. Securing the rivets in place.

Arrangement of the miscellaneous details under these four headings, with further additions during the writing of the paper, gives the final outline as it appears on page 931.

32c   Make an outline of the type specified by your instructor.

The types of outlines most commonly used are (1) the topic outline, (2) the sentence outline, and (3) the paragraph outline. Many persons prefer the sentence outline because the use of complete sentences forces the writer to express himself with greater clarity. Topic outlines and sentence outlines have the same parts and the same groupings; they differ only in the fullness of expression. In the paragraph outline no effort is made to classify the material into major headings and subheadings: the topic of each paragraph is simply listed in the order in which it is to come.

Topic Outline:

RIVETING A SKYSCRAPER

CENTRAL IDEA   Riveting requires skillful work under dangerous conditions.

I. Skillful co-ordination of a riveting gang of four

  A. Unity of the gang
  B. Replacements of members
  C. Necessity for skill, judgment, and experience

II. Preparation of the rivets

  A. Delivery to the furnace
  B. Precarious position of the furnace
  C. Work of the heater
    1. His equipment
    2. His skill

III. Passing of the red-hot rivets

  A. Need for throwing
  B. Receptacle used by the catcher
  C. Dangerous position of the catcher
  D. Skill of the catcher
  E. Silence during the whole process

IV. Securing the rivets in place

  A. Alignment of the holes
  B. Insertion of the rivet
  C. Precarious work of the bucker-up
  D. Hard work of the gun-man
    1. Use of the heavy gun
    2. Concussion and vibration
    3. Assistance from the catcher
    4. Interchange with the bucker-up

Sentence Outline:

RIVETING A SKYSCRAPER

CENTRAL IDEA   Riveting requires skillful work under dangerous conditions.

I. Riveters work in well co-ordinated, skillful gangs of four.

  A. The gang works as a unit.
  B. Replacements are made by an overlapping of service.
  C. The gang must have skill, judgment, and experience.

II. The rivets must be prepared under difficult conditions.

  A. The rivets are brought to the furnace by the rivet boy.
  B. The furnace stands in a precarious position.

C. The heater must have specialized equipment and skill.

  1. He must have special clothing and tongs.
  2. He must have skill in order to heat the rivets properly.

III. Passing the rivets from the furnace to the place where they are used is an exacting and dangerous process.

  A. Rivets must be thrown, sometimes under difficult conditions.
  B. The catcher receives them in a battered tin "cup."
  C. He stands in a dangerous position.
  D. Only his skill in catching red-hot rivets insures the safety of the persons below.
  E. The whole process of passing rivets is conducted silently and methodically.

IV. Securing the rivets in place requires the exercise of great strength, dexterity, and co-operation.

  A. The gun-man and the bucker-up align the holes from dangerous positions.
  B. The catcher inserts the red-hot rivet.
  C. The bucker-up braces himself with his dolly bar against the end of the rivet.
  D. The gun-man has the heaviest work.
    1. He must handle the heavy gun.
    2. He must endure great concussion and vibration.
    3. He usually is assisted by the catcher.
    4. He sometimes passes the gun to the bucker-up.

Paragraph Outline:

RIVETING A SKYSCRAPER

CENTRAL IDEA   Riveting requires skillful work under dangerous conditions.

1. Riveters work in well co-ordinated, skillful gangs of four men.
2. Rivets must be heated with care.
3. The red-hot rivets must be thrown to the place where the riveting is being done.
4. The catcher, standing in a dangerous position, must have great skill.
5. The whole process of throwing and catching the rivets is carried on in silence.
6. The catcher, the gun-man, and the bucker-up co-operate in securing the rivet in place.
7. The work of the gun-man is the hardest.

32d   Make sure that the outline covers the subject, that it treats of everything promised in the title.

An adequate outline is essential to a successful composition. The major headings (I, II, III, etc.) must be sufficient in number and in scope to satisfy the expectation aroused by the title. And each of these major headings must, in turn, be covered by its subheads just as the title is covered by the major headings. These subheads, however, should not be unduly detailed.

WRONG   (titles not adequately covered by the major headings)

Geology of the United States
I. States east of the Mississippi
II. Texas

History of the United States
I. Period before 1800
II. Period from 1800 till 1860

RIGHT   (titles properly covered)

Geology of the United States
I. States east of the Mississippi
II. States west of the Mississippi

History of the United States
I. Period before 1800
II. Period from 1800 till 1860
III. Period since 1860

It would also be proper to leave the main headings unchanged and to alter the titles to agree, thus: "Geology of Texas and the States East of the Mississippi" and "History of the United States before the Civil War." In the same way the student can revise the title of his paper, thus limiting it further, if he finds that his original topic cannot be covered adequately in the allotted space. The title and the major headings of the completed outline must have the same scope.

32e   Make sure that the parts of the outline are logically arranged.

Logical arrangement is second in importance only to adequacy. If the outline is disorganized and ineffective, the paper that follows it will also be disorganized and ineffective. (See also Section 31b.)

(1) Do not scatter your ideas.

Related ideas should be brought together. As the student begins his outline he ought to jot down as many ideas on the topic as possible, hastily, without regard to order. But then he must group these under two or more major headings. Compare the first hasty jotting down of ideas on "Riveting a Skyscraper" (page 930) with the groupings in the finished outline.

(2) Arrange the parts in a natural, easy order.

The problem of arrangement within the paper as a whole is much the same as that within each separate paragraph. (See pages 916-17.) The nature of the subject will suggest an appropriate arrangement, such as time order, space order, or order of climax.

(3) Do not allow headings to overlap.

Overlapping often occurs when a writer attempts a division according to more than one principle.

WRONG   (overlapping)

History of the United States
I. Period before 1800   [Time]
II. The South   [Space]
III. Negroes   [Group]

RIGHT   (division according to a single principle)

History of the United States
I. Period before 1800   I. The North
II. Period from 1800 till 1860   II. The South
III. Period since 1860   III. The West

I. Indians and original settlers
II. Negroes
III. Immigrants

(4) Do not co-ordinate any heading that should be subordinated. Do not subordinate any heading that should be co-ordinated.

WRONG

History of the United States before the Civil War
I. Period before 1800
A. Period from 1800 till 1860
II. The War of 1812
III. The Monroe Doctrine

RIGHT

History of the United States before the Civil War
I. Period before 1800
II. Period from 1800 till 1860
A. The War of 1812
B. The Monroe Doctrine

[sic] such as this — word similarity after the word, of the material of concrete typeware

(5) Do not allow single headings or subheadings to stand anywhere in the outline.

Headings and subheads stand for divisions, and a division denotes at least two parts. Therefore, each outline must have at least two main headings, I and II. If it has a subhead marked A, it must also have a B. If it has a subhead marked 1, it must also have a 2.

ILLOGICAL

History of the United States

I. Period before 1800

If the history continues after 1800 the outline should indicate it by another major heading. Otherwise the title should read, "History of the United States before 1800."

32f Check the outline for the formal details of (1) notation and indention and (2) parallel structure.

(1) In the outline use consistently one system of notation, and indent headings to indicate degrees of subordination.

Any intelligible system of notation is acceptable. The one used for the complete sentence outline and the topical outline in Section 32c is in very common use and may well be adopted. This system, it will be noted, is as follows:

I. . . . . [Used for major headings]
  A. . . . . [Used for subheadings of the first de-
  B. . . . . gree]
    1. . . . . . [Used for subheadings of the second
    2. . . . . . degree]

Seldom will a short outline (or even a longer one) need subordination beyond the first or second degree. If it does, it may use "a," "b," "c," etc., for the third degree and (1), (2), (3), etc., for the fourth degree.

The indention, as well as the notation, should indicate the degree of subordination. Major headings (I, II, III, etc.) should be indented equally, subheadings of the first degree (A, B, C, etc.) should be indented more, and subheads of the second degree (1, 2, 3, etc.) should be indented still more. If a heading or subheading runs beyond the end of the line, it is given "hanging indention," as in the sentence outline above.

(2) Give parallel structure to parallel parts of the outline to make clearer the co-ordination of the parts. (See the full discussion of parallel structure under Section 26.)

WRONG

II. Preparation of the rivets
  A. Delivering to the furnace [Participle or gerund as the core of the topic]
  B. Precarious position of the furnace [Noun]
  C. The heater works hard [Sentence]
    1. His equipment [Noun]
    2. Skillful [Adjective]

RIGHT

II. Preparation of the rivets
  A. Delivery to the furnace [Noun]
  B. Precarious position of the furnace [Noun]
  C. The work of the heater [Noun]
    1. His equipment [Noun]
    2. His skill [Noun]

The major headings (I, II, III, etc.) should be expressed in parallel structure, as should each group of subheads. But it is unnecessary to strive for parallel structure between different groups of subheads; for example, between A, B, C under I and A, B, C under II. Parallel structure is no problem in the complete sentence outline, for parallelism is insured by the requirement of complete sentences.

32g Write the paper from the outline.

Once you have checked your outline to make sure that it covers the subject (see **32d**), is logically arranged (**32e**), and has proper notation, indention, and parallel structure (**32f**), you are ready to write the paper. You simply write a series of effective paragraphs, with good transitions between them (see **31**), to cover all items in the outline, taking up each item in the order in which it comes in the outline. The actual writing of the paper will probably suggest a better arrangement for some of the details. If so, the proper changes should be made in the outline so that the finished paper and the outline will agree fully.

(1) The paragraphs in relation to the outline. Although the paragraphs must develop the headings (including the subheadings) of the outline in the exact order in which they come in the outline, there is no rule regarding the number of these headings a paragraph may cover. In a general way, however, the writer is limited by the need to make each paragraph a unit and to keep it from being unduly long or short. Let us notice, for example, how the seven paragraphs of "Riveting a Skyscraper" below and on page 935 are related to the topic outline (see page 931). The writer could secure unity for his first paragraph by treating only A ("Unity of the gang") under I, or by treating A, B, and C together since these three form a unit under I ("Skillful co-ordinating of a riveting gang of four"). The deciding factor is usually the number of words needed for adequate treatment. Since only 235 words are required to treat A, B, and C together, a single paragraph is used. Similarly, the second paragraph of 215 words covers the whole of II. But since 420 words are needed to cover III, the writer uses three paragraphs. The first—130 words—covers A and B (throwing and catching the rivets), the second—202 words—covers C and D (the catcher's dangerous position and skill), and the third—88 words—covers E (the silence of the gang). It is possible to use A and B together in the same paragraph only because they form a unit, and the same is true of C and D. The last two paragraphs of the article cover IV, the first—168 words—covering A, B, and C as a unit, and the second—155 words —covering D.

▶ EXERCISE 4. Note that the following article on "Riveting a Skyscraper" follows the exact order of the topic (or sentence) outline. Note also how much of the article is covered by each heading and subheading, and indicate in the margin of the article the point at which the treatment of each begins.

RIVETING A SKYSCRAPER [1]

The most curious fact about a riveter's skill is that he is not one man but four: "heater," "catcher," "bucker-up," and "gun-man." The gang is the unit. Riveters are hired and fired as gangs, work in gangs, and learn in gangs. If one member of a gang is absent on a given morning, the entire gang is replaced. A gang may continue to exist

[1] Reprinted by special permission from the October 1930 issue of *Fortune* Magazine; © 1930 by Time Inc.; all rights reserved under International and Pan-American Copyright Conventions.

after its original members have all succumbed to slippery girders or the business end of a pneumatic hammer or to a foreman's zeal or merely to the temptations of life on earth. And the skill of the gang will continue with it. Men overlap each other in service and teach each other what they know. The difference between a gang which can drive 525 inch-and-an-eighth rivets in a working day and a gang which can drive 250 is a difference of co-ordination and smoothness. You learn how not to make mistakes and how not to waste time. You learn how to heat a rivet and how not to overheat it, how to throw it accurately but not too hard, how to drive it and when to stop driving it, and precisely how much you can drink in a cold wind or a July sun without losing your sense of width and the balance of a wooden plank. And all these things, or most of them, an older hand can tell you.

The actual process of riveting is simple enough—in description. Rivets are carried to the job by the rivet boy, a riveter's apprentice whose ambition it is to replace one of the members of the gang—which one, he leaves to luck. The rivets are dumped into a keg beside a small coke furnace. The furnace stands on a platform of loose boards roped to steel girders which may or may not have been riveted. If they have not been riveted there will be a certain amount of play in the temporary bolts. The furnace is tended by the heater or passer. He wears heavy clothes and gloves to protect him from the flying sparks and intense heat of his work, and he holds a pair of tongs about a foot-and-a-half long in his right hand. When a rivet is needed, he whirls the furnace blower until the coke is white hot, picks up a rivet with his tongs, and drives it into the coals. His skill as a heater appears in his knowledge of the exact time necessary to heat the steel. If he overheats it, it will flake, and the flakes will permit the rivet to turn in its hole. And a rivet which gives in its hole is condemned by the inspectors.

When the heater judges that his rivet is right, he turns to face the catcher, who may be above or below him or fifty or sixty or eighty feet away on the same floor level with the naked girders between. There is no means of handing the rivet over. It must be thrown. And it must be accurately thrown. And if the floor beams of the floor above have been laid so that a flat trajectory is essential, it must be thrown with considerable force. The catcher is therefore armed with a smallish, battered tin can, called a "cup," with which to catch the red-hot steel. Various patented cups have been put upon the market from time to time, but they have made little headway. Catchers prefer the ancient can.

The catcher's position is not exactly one which a sportsman catching rivets for pleasure would choose. He stands upon a narrow platform of loose planks laid over needle beams and roped to a girder near the connection upon which the gang is at work. There are live coils of pneumatic tubing for a rivet gun around his feet. If he moves more than a step or two in any direction, he is gone; and if he loses his balance backward he is apt to end up at street level without time to walk. And the object is to catch a red-hot iron rivet weighing anywhere from a quarter of a pound to a pound and a half and capable, if he lets it pass, of drilling an automobile radiator or a man's skull 500 feet below as neatly as a shank of shrapnel. Why more rivets do not fall is the great mystery of skyscraper construction. The only reasonable explanation offered to date is the reply of an erector's foreman who was asked what would happen if a catcher on the Forty Wall Street job let a rivet go by him around lunch hour. "Well," said the foreman, "he's not supposed to."

There is practically no exchange of words among riveters. Not only are they averse to conversation, which would be reasonable enough in view of the effect they have on the conversation of others, but they are averse to speech in any form. The catcher faces the heater. He holds his tin can up. The heater swings his tongs, releasing one handle. The red iron arcs through the air in one of those parabolas so much admired by the stenographers in the neighboring windows. And the tin can clanks.

Meantime the gun-man and the bucker-up have prepared the connection—aligning the two holes, if necessary, with a drift pin driven by a sledge or by a pneumatic hammer—and removed the temporary bolts. They, too, stand on loose-roped boards with a column or the beam between them. When the rivet strikes the catcher's can, he picks it out with a pair of tongs held in his right hand, knocks it sharply against the steel to shake off the glowing flakes, and rams it into the hole, an operation which is responsible for his alternative title of sticker. Once the rivet is in place, the bucker-up braces himself with his dolly bar, a short heavy bar of steel, against the capped end of the rivet. On outside wall work he is sometimes obliged to hold on by one elbow with his weight out over the street and the jar of the riveting shaking his precarious balance. And the gun-man lifts his pneumatic hammer to the rivet's other end.

The gun-man's work is the hardest work, physically, done by the gang. The hammers in use for steel construction work are supposed to weigh around thirty pounds and actually weigh above thirty-five. They must not only be held against the rivet end, but held there with the gun-man's entire strength, and for a period of forty to sixty seconds. (A rivet driven too long will develop a collar inside the new head.) And the concussion to the ears and to the arms during that period is very great. The whole platform shakes, and the vibration can be felt down the column thirty stories below. It is common practice for the catcher to push with the gun-man, and for the gun-man and the bucker-up to pass the gun back and forth between them when the angle is difficult. Also on a heavy rivet job the catcher and the bucker-up may relieve the gun-man at the gun.

(2) Effective beginnings and endings. Seldom does a short paper need a formal introduction or conclusion. Usually it is wise to begin promptly and to end as soon as the last topic has been adequately treated. Even when some part of the outline is to serve as an introduction or conclusion it should not be called merely "introduction" or "conclusion" but should be given a more informative heading.

Note the lack of any formal beginning or ending in the effective short article (see above) on "Riveting a Skyscraper." The longer library paper on "The French Horn: Its Development and Use" (see pages 953-62) also begins promptly with a striking fact that arouses the reader's interest at the same time that it starts the development of the topic. The last paragraph rounds out the paper by emphasizing the great improvement in the French horn since its humble origin. The last paragraph serves as a brief and effective conclusion, but it is not called "conclusion" in the outline.

▶ EXERCISES ON PLANNING (OUTLINING) AND WRITING

A. Make (1) a topic outline, (2) a sentence outline, and (3) a paragraph outline on the subject used for Exercise 1 above. Then check your outlines with the principles set forth in 32d-f.

B. Write a 500-word paper based on the topic outline prepared for Exercise A.

C. Revise the paper written for Exercise B, using the check list on page 830. Follow through on one point at a time. (After you have had more experience in writing and revising, you may be able to check most of these points at one reading.

Student Papers—with Analyses

(1)   COFFEE

A definition might be given to coffee that would explain what this drink does to a person's system. I would define coffee as a drink that contains caffeine and is drunk in the early morning to soothe a person's shattered nerves.

Another interesting fact about coffee is that no matter how high the price may go, a person will always pay the required amount. If coffee does lift in price, people at first grumble about how they are not going to pay the price. But a little later you might hear the same person asking a friend to have a cup of coffee with him.

Coffee outranks all other beverages in demand. A great many people drink whiskey, wine, and beer, but they will always choose a cup of coffee after they have taken a few drinks of some alcoholic beverage to dispose of their hangover.

Coffee, along with smoking cigarettes, is an essential drink to nervous people, to people who drink alcoholic beverages, and most of all to husbands whose wives are expecting babies. Nervous people take this drink to soothe their nerves and stimulate themselves. People who drink take it to rid themselves of hangovers. And husbands who are pacing the floor because their wives are expecting babies must have a cup of coffee in their hand to keep themselves from chewing their fingernails off up to their elbows. Therefore, coffee is the essential drink in our everyday environment.

Comment on Content and Composition: Your paper shows some planning, but not nearly enough. As a first rough draft it might have served very well for development into a good paper. But you have left it full of inconsistencies.

In paragraph 1 you propose to define coffee according to what it does to a person's system. But you never do. Instead you describe it as a beverage "drunk in the early morning to settle a person's shattered nerves." That is what it is *supposed* to do to the *nerves*. We never are told what it *does* to the *system*.

But paragraph 2 immediately disregards the "early morning" and "shattered nerves" limit you put on coffee drinking and shows two friends—ob-

viously later in the day—drinking coffee, not for shattered nerves, but apparently out of mere sociability. Furthermore, you begin the paragraph with the words "another interesting fact." No interesting fact has preceded it.

Paragraph 3 may be consistent enough with the morning-nerves limit; but look at the way you have stated the matter. Has the alcohol been taken to dispose of the hangover?

In paragraph 4 your phrasing suggests that smoking cigarettes is also "an essential drink." Further on you imply (if your first-paragraph description still holds) that the birth pangs of expectant fatherhood occur only in the early morning. And your last sentence indicates that early morning every day finds us in a state either of shattered nerves, postalcoholism, or maternity-corridor vigilance.

Surely these states do occur. But you yourself must know that they are accountable for very little of the coffee an average coffee drinker consumes in his lifetime. Yet you indicate that they are *the* causes. You need to pay more attention to the logical consistency of your entire paper.

Suggestions for Improvement: Concentrate on a central idea for the whole paper. You might be able to use the concluding statement that you have here; but modify it, since *essential* is too strong a word to fit the facts. Then choose a more specific title—one which contains or suggests the central idea of the paper and no more. Next eliminate anything you have written that is not a development of the central idea: paragraph 2 will probably have to go. Make an outline of what you have left. You will probably see that the outline needs revising. Revise it; and then rewrite the paper.

(2)   IGNORANCE IS BLISS

Have you ever been to a mountainous country and noticed how happy the people are? That is usually because they have had very little schooling and are just too dumb to get along in the outside world. They are happy just sitting around the porch on the general store and shooting the breeze. Their homes as a rule are old weather-beaten shacks and the furniture is that which has been handed down from their grandparents. These people enjoy that life and are not educated enough to strive for any better things in life. You will always find them laughing, talking, and joking. "What is wrong with this life?" you ask. Well, if they were not quite so ignorant, they might have a longer life span and a much cleaner life. People in big cities are not half as happy-go-lucky as the mountaineers, but they have very nice homes and much cleaner habits.

I can't help noticing the unfriendly attitude of the teachers and students. Everyone seems to be in too much of a hurry to ever speak. I have never seen so many sour faces in all my life. This fact seems to prove my statements and goes as further evidence to prove that ignorance is bliss. You have to have a lot of knowledge to get into a college, and it seems that people in a university would be called an educated group. The people in college are always worried about getting ready for a big test, and if they fail it they are downhearted. They never seem happy. But the mountaineers are always happy and never seem to worry about a thing. Therefore ignorance must be bliss.

Comments: Your paper breaks off in the middle, where suddenly you begin to discuss college people without any indication of a reason for the shift. You need to provide some sort of transition. Furthermore, although you mention three groups—mountaineers, people in big cities, and college people—you neglect altogether to develop any discussion of the middle group.

Your arguments suffer from the two faults in logic known as "begging the question" and "false cause."

An argument "begs the question" when it assumes as already proven that which it sets out to prove. You set out to prove that ignorance is the cause of bliss. Yet, without proving it, you make the initial assumption that mountaineers are happy "usually *because* they have had very little schooling and are just too dumb to get along in the outside world."

An argument uses "false cause" when, finding two facts to exist simultaneously, it assumes without sufficient evidence that one is the cause of the other. You produce no evidence to show that, when ignorance and bliss are found together, the one has caused the other.

Actually the facts which common experience shows—your own experience included, if you would only examine it—are that some ignorant mountaineers are altogether miserable and that some college people are quite happy. Bliss, therefore, does not require ignorance to produce it; and bliss may be entirely lacking where ignorance is plentifully present.

This same analysis can be applied to your argument concerning college people.

Suggestions for Improvement: The only assumptions which the facts will support are that among mountaineers many who are happy are also ignorant and that among college people who are in pursuit of learning many are also miserable. And the only safe conclusion is that there *may* therefore be some relationship between ignorance and bliss.

Rewrite the paper with these cautions in mind; provide a suitable transition to introduce your second argument; and eliminate mention of city people unless you are going to develop an additional argument using their circumstances as supporting evidence.

(3) ATHLETICS: MORE WORK THAN PLAY

Athletics to the average participant may be more work than play. The star acquires a love for the game because he is given recognition for his playing and people look up to him as a marvel. But to the average athlete the steady grind of practice soon becomes old. He works and plays hard, but all his efforts are in vain because the star is getting all the recognition for the whole team's work.

When people watch a football game, they watch the man with the ball. Most of them never see the vicious block which was thrown by one of the linemen. And when the paper comes out the day following the game, the back who ran the touchdown is given all the credit. But nothing is said about the lineman who threw the block which set up the touchdown. The back receives the glory; and glory is the "play" that comes from athletics.

The man who does all the handling of the ball is getting the play from the game; the man who is there only to aid the player with the ball to score is doing only work. Football, for a man who never gets his hands on the ball, will then be nothing but work, if he is not given recognition for his playing.

The man who gets recognition after a hard-fought game does not mind the next week's practice, because he may repeat himself in the next game and again he may receive much glory. The boy who is not mentioned will be exactly the opposite; he will hate the week's practice that is to follow. The practice will be all work and no play.

The best example of a boy who works hard on a team and receives no recognition is the center on a football team. He makes the pass to the back, who runs his heart out for the glory. The backfield man will get his glory when the writing concerning the game comes out in the paper. But the center is never mentioned for his precision passes to the backs.

This unfairness could be remedied if the newspaper writers, coaches, and spectators would let it be known in some way that they knew the noncarrying man on the team had played a great game and that he was also responsible for the winning of the game. Athletics then would automatically become more play than work. But as it is at the present time, athletics for most players is more work than play.

Comments and Suggestions for Improvement: This paper begins well and ends well. It is only in the middle part that it is somewhat less than satisfactory.

Good as your beginning is, however, it would improve the paper as a whole if you would indicate, both in your title and very early in your first paragraph, that you are going to discuss football particularly and not athletics generally.

Your second and fourth paragraphs make good use of devices of paragraph development: the second introduces concrete examples to bear out the more generalized comments made earlier; and the fourth very effectively uses the element of contrast.

But there is little if anything said in your third paragraph that is not adequately said elsewhere. Your paper would gain rather than lose if you omitted this paragraph altogether.

Likewise, your fifth paragraph does over again what is already sufficiently done in your second. You make exactly the same point, using the center as an example, as you had already made using the blocking lineman. The fifth paragraph can be eliminated as well as the third.

Then, with a very slight transition furnished to lead into your final paragraph, you will have a well and compactly built argument. As your paper stands now, it is slowed down by the surplus it is carrying. Condition it down; work some of the fat off it. That is about all it needs.

(For the use of numbers or symbols in the correction of errors in grammar, mechanics, punctuation, spelling, etc., see Section 8, page 830.)

▶ Library Paper

33 Learn how to use the library as you prepare a library paper.

In writing the usual expository paper, as explained in Section 32, you have already faced some of the problems of the library paper (also called a research, a reference, or a term paper)—that is, a paper based on materials to be found in the library, with references to the sources of information. You have, for example, already considered the problems of finding and limiting a subject (32a), of making an outline (32b-f), and of writing the paper from the outline (32g). Your only new problems will be (1) finding in the library the needed sources of information and listing these in a bibliography; (2) taking notes from which the paper can be written; and (3) using footnotes to show the exact sources of information.

Section 33 treats these new problems in some detail (and the other problems briefly) by following through the five steps in the preparation of a library paper:

a. Selecting and limiting the subject. (See pp. 938-39.)
b. Preparing the bibliography. (See pp. 939-47.)
c. Making the outline. (See pp. 947-48.)
d. Taking notes. (See pp. 948-50.)
e. Writing the paper—with footnotes. (See pp. 950-53.)

Each of these steps is illustrated in the preparation of a sample library paper, which is then given in full at the end of the section.

33a Select and limit the subject. (Follow the general suggestions given under Section 32a.)

Let us suppose that a student is interested in the general field of music and has limited his subject to the orchestra. But since this is still a subject broad enough for a book, he decides to limit himself further to one of the many instruments in the orchestra, selecting the one in which he has a special interest— the French horn. This topic is sufficiently limited for adequate treatment in a paper of two or three thousand words, the length most frequently used for library papers.

▶ EXERCISE 1. List three general fields in which you have some interest. Then by process of limitation derive three topics (1) which are suitable for library papers of two or three thousand words each and (2) in which you have a special interest. The subject headings and the cross references in the card catalogue or the *Readers' Guide* (see **33b** below) may suggest subjects and possible limitations of them.

33b Prepare the bibliography (and learn your way about the library).

The bibliography lists sources of information—such as books, pamphlets, and articles— from which the student will draw the material for his paper on the French horn. Throughout his college career he will be called upon to write papers for which he will need to prepare bibliographies. To teach the student how to get needed information readily from the library is perhaps the chief purpose of the library paper. As he begins his search, he tries to determine whether he can find enough material on his specific topic and, if so, writes down the most promising titles, thus making up a preliminary bibliography. (Later he will probably drop from the list some books and articles that prove of little value, and will add useful references as he discovers them. The final bibliography will include only those works that help in the writing of the paper—usually those cited in the footnotes.)

Keys to the Library

The chief keys to information in the library are (1) the card catalogue, (2) the indexes to periodicals, and (3) the general reference books.[1]

[1] Although the card catalogue and the periodical indexes are the chief keys to the library, the student

(1) Learn how to use the card catalogue.

The card catalogue is the index to the whole library. It lists all books and all bound magazines, whether they are housed in the

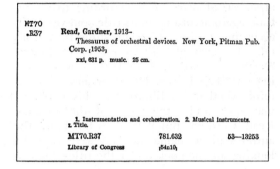

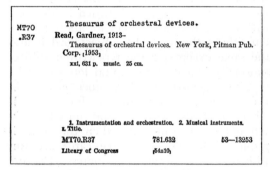

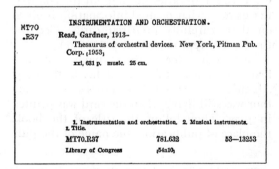

stacks, on the open shelves of the reference room, or in any other part of the building. In many libraries one general card catalogue lists all books owned by the university and indicates whether the book is kept in the general library or with some special collection in another building.

may find it best to start with reference books, especially with articles in general encyclopedias which give a brief survey of his topic, often including a short bibliography.

Usually the card catalogue consists of cards 3 x 5 inches in size, arranged alphabetically in drawers. These may be "author" cards, "title" cards, or "subject" cards; for in most libraries each book is listed in its proper alphabetical place—once according to its author, again according to its title, and yet again according to its subject or subjects. Let us take, for example, *Thesaurus of Orchestral Devices,* by Gardner Read. If the student writing on "The French Horn" wishes to determine whether his library has this book, he may look under the name of the author—Read, Gardner. But if he does not know the author's given name, he may save time by looking for the book under the title—*Thesaurus of Orchestral Devices.* This is given on what is called a title card, which is identical with the author card except for the typewritten title at the top. The subject card is also the same except for the typewritten subject (normally in red or in capital letters) at the top. The typewritten call number,[2] usually in the upper left-hand corner, shows exactly where the book is shelved and must be written out on a "call slip" when the book is requested for use. All three cards are furnished by the Library of Congress as a convenience for libraries throughout the country. Let us note what printed information is given on these carefully prepared cards. (See the three cards reproduced on page 939.)

First comes the author's name, surname first, followed by the date of his birth, 1913. Absence of a second date shows that the author was still living when the card was printed in 1953. Then follow the title of the book, the place of publication, the name of the publisher, and the date. The brackets around this date indicate that the year of publication does not appear on the title page but has been supplied from some other source, usually the copyright date on the back of the title page. The next line shows that the book contains 21 prefatory pages followed by 631 pages, that it contains musical scores, and that it is 25 centimeters high. The lines some distance below suggest that, in addition to the author and title cards, the book should have two subject cards. (Only the first of the two subject cards is reproduced here.) The next line furnishes the Library of Congress call number for the book, then the Dewey Decimal classification number, and finally the number by which the card may be ordered from the Library of Congress. The last line names the publisher of the card (Library of Congress) and gives a special code number.

Of the three kinds of cards, the reader will probably begin by consulting the subject cards. Since a book may be listed under any one of various subjects, depending upon its primary interest, he should not be discouraged if he fails to find all he wants under the first subject consulted. He should look, next, under related subjects. Works not listed under "Agriculture" may appear under "Farming," or "Gardening," or "Soils." Especially helpful are the cards giving cross references to other subjects under which the reader should look. Under "Agriculture," for example, might appear a card reading "Agriculture, see also Agronomy." Works not listed under "Vitamins" but nevertheless important to that subject might appear under "Nutrition," or "Foods," or "Diet." The student

[2] From the Library of Congress system for the classification of books. In the United States most libraries use either this system or the Dewey Decimal system. The Library of Congress uses the following main classes:

A	General Works	J	Political Science	R	Medicine
B	Philosophy, Religion	K	Law	S	Agriculture
C	History	L	Education	T	Technology
D	Foreign History	M	Music	U	Military Science
E, F	American History	N	Fine Arts	V	Naval Science
G	Geography, Anthropology	P	Language and Literature	Z	Library Science, Bibliography
H	Social Sciences	Q	Science		

The Dewey Decimal system has the following main classes:

000	General Works	200	Religion	500	Natural Science	800	Literature
100	Philosophy	300	Sociology	600	Useful Arts	900	History
		400	Philology	700	Fine Arts		

writing the paper on "The French Horn" may find works not listed under "French horn" or "Horn" under "Musical instruments," "Wind instruments," or "Instrumentation and orchestration." Even so general a subject as "Music" might list books that treat of the French horn. And of course the student should not overlook the cross reference (*see also* cards) at the end of the subject cards on the plain subject "Music," where he will probably find many cross references to such subjects as "Bands," "Concertos," "Jazz music," and "Opera."

THE ORDER OF THE CARDS

It is not enough, especially in a large library, to know that the cards are arranged alphabetically. Hundreds of cards may be listed under a single heading such as "England," "Lincoln," or "Washington." The reader who knows the principle of arrangement will save much time in finding what he wants.

Cards for subjects. Cards on a single subject are arranged alphabetically according to the name of the author, which appears on the line immediately below. Subdivisions of a subject are usually arranged alphabetically.

EXAMPLE Michigan
  Michigan—Agriculture
  Michigan—Biography
  Michigan—Constitutional convention
  Michigan—University

But subdivisions of history are arranged chronologically.

EXAMPLE Mexico—History—Conquest, 1519-1540
  Mexico—History—Spanish colony, 1540-1810
  Mexico—History—Wars of Independence, 1810-1821
  Mexico—History—European intervention, 1861-1867

Names or titles beginning with abbreviations. Abbreviations are usually filed as if they were spelled out. Instead of *Mc* look for *Mac;* instead of *Dr.* look for *Doctor;* instead of *St.* look for *Saint;* etc.

"Short before long." In the catalogue a short word followed by other words always comes before a longer word of which the short

word is a part. *Post office* comes before *Postage.*

EXAMPLE Post
  Post office
  Postage
  Postal

(1) Person, (2) place, (3) title. When the same word names a person or place or begins a title, the order is: person, place, title.

EXAMPLE Lincoln, Abraham [Person]
  Lincoln, Nebraska [Place]
  Lincoln and Seward, by Gideon Welles [Title]

(1) Books by a person, (2) books about a person. Books written by a person come first; books written about a person follow. Various editions of an author's work are listed chronologically with collections first and single words second in alphabetical order.

EXAMPLE Shakespeare, William. Works
  Shakespeare, William. Hamlet
  Shakespeare, William. Macbeth
  Shakespeare, William. A Life of William Shakespeare, by Sidney Lee

(1) Saints, (2) popes, (3) kings, (4) others. Saints, popes, and kings are listed in this order by their first names, followed by the surnames of other persons. Kings are listed by countries.

▶ EXERCISES ON USE OF THE CARD CATALOGUE

Use the card catalogue of the library to do the following exercises. In Exercises A-E, investigate either 1, 2, or 3 as directed by your instructor. (The assignments are varied, and may be varied even further by the instructor, to avoid undue wear on any one book.)

A. Does the library have a copy of one of the following:
  1. *Uranium and Atomic Power,* by Jack A. DeMent
  2. *Peace of Soul,* by Fulton J. Sheen
  3. *Patterns of Culture,* by Ruth Benedict
[You should answer this question by looking in the card catalogue either under the author or under the title. You should look under both before deciding that the book is not in the library, for sometimes a card may be misplaced or temporarily removed. Note that librarians do not italicize titles and that they capitalize only the words that would be capitalized in ordinary writing.]

B. How many books by (1) Jack A. DeMent, (2) Fulton J. Sheen or (3) Ruth Benedict does the library have?

[Look for the author cards. Distinguish between author and subject cards. Do not count the same book twice.]

C. Find the card for the book you are investigating under the subject indicated as follows:

1. For *Uranium and Atomic Power* under "Uranium"

2. For *Peace of Soul* under "Apologetics—20th Cent."

3. For *Patterns of Culture* under "Society, Primitive"

How many cards does the library have under this subject heading? Are there subheadings? [If the cards are very numerous, estimate the number instead of counting them.]

D. Find the card for the book you are investigating under the subject indicated as follows:

1. For *Uranium and Atomic Power* under "Radioactivity"

2. For *Peace of Soul* under "Catholic Church—Apologetic Works"

3. For *Patterns of Culture* under "Anthropology"

How many cards does the library have under this subject heading? Do you find any subheadings?

E. Find the card for the book you are investigating under the subject indicated as follows:

1. For *Uranium and Atomic Power* under "Atomic Bomb"

2. For *Peace of Soul* under "Conversion"

3. For *Patterns of Culture* under "Zuni Indians"

Are there any subheadings? Are there any cross references to other subjects?

F. List a few of the subheadings under "Education." In what order are they arranged? List a few of the subheadings under "U.S.—History." In what order are they arranged?

G. Does your library classify its books according to the Dewey Decimal system or the Library of Congress system?

(2) Learn how to use indexes to periodicals.

A periodical is a magazine or newspaper. Magazines are usually issued weekly, biweekly, monthly, or quarterly; newspapers, daily or weekly. For the convenience of those who wish to consult the recent issues, magazines are often kept for a few months or possibly a year on open shelves or racks; then they are bound into volumes, each of which commonly includes the issues of six months or a year. These bound volumes may be kept on the open shelves in the reference room, in a special periodical room, or in the stacks. The general card catalogue lists all periodicals in the library and often indicates where each may be consulted. But a more convenient special card catalogue to periodicals is often kept in the reference room or periodical room, or at the circulation desk.

Contents of periodicals are listed in periodical indexes (printed volumes) which are kept continually up to date. These printed indexes do for articles in periodicals what the card catalogue does for books in the library: an article can be found under author, subject, or title (in some cases). And subjects such as "French horn," "Wind instruments," "Musical instruments," or "Music," with the many cross references, can be followed through just as in the card catalogue. The chief indexes are mentioned below, with the years covered by each.

INDEXES TO PERIODICALS

GENERAL

Poole's Index. 1802-1906.
Nineteenth Century Readers' Guide. 1890-1899.
Readers' Guide. 1900—.
Book Review Digest. 1905—.
International Index. 1907—.
New York Times Index. 1913—.

SPECIAL

Agricultural Index. 1916—.
Art Index. 1929—.
Bibliographic Index. 1937—.
Catholic Periodical Index. 1930—.
Dramatic Index. 1909—.
Education Index. 1929—.
Engineering Index. 1884—.
Index Medicus. 1879-1926; *Quarterly Cumulative Index Medicus.* 1927—.
Index to Legal Periodicals. 1908—.
Industrial Arts Index. 1913—.
Music Index. 1949—.
Psychological Index. 1894-1936.
Public Affairs Information Service. 1915—.
Technical Book Review Index. 1917-1929; 1935—.

See also the indexes to the various abstracts, such as *Biological Abstracts,* 1926—, *Chemical Ab-*

stracts, 1907–, and *Psychological Abstracts,* 1927–.

These indexes are compiled as soon as possible after the periodicals appear. The *Readers' Guide* (an index to over one hundred magazines of general interest) is only a few weeks behind the appearance of the articles. From time to time the issues of the *Readers' Guide* indexes covering single months or short periods of a few months are combined into longer units, and finally into a volume covering more than a year. The earlier volumes cover as many as five years, as will be seen from the following list.

Readers' Guide

I	1900–1904
II	1905–1909
III	1910–1914
IV	1915–1918
V	1919–1921
VI	1922–1924
VII	1925–1928
VIII	1929–June, 1932
IX	July, 1932–June, 1935
X	July, 1935–June, 1937
XI	July, 1937–June, 1939
XII	July, 1939–June, 1941
XIII	July, 1941–June, 1943
XIV	July, 1943–April, 1945
XV	May, 1945–April, 1947
XVI	May, 1947–April, 1949
XVII	May, 1949–March, 1951
XVIII	April, 1951–March, 1953
XIX	April, 1953–February, 1955

A reader wishing to find all references to a given subject listed by the *Readers' Guide* would have to look through each of the larger volumes and the smaller ones covering the most recent months or month. Usually he is concerned only with articles that have appeared during a certain period, and he looks accordingly in the volumes covering that period.

▶ EXERCISES ON INDEXES TO PERIODICALS

Do the following exercises as a means of learning how to use indexes to periodicals. (The dates may be changed to avoid undue wear on any one reference book.)

A. On a rough drawing of the floor plan of the reference room (or periodical room) indicate where the indexes to periodicals may be found. Indicate also the locations of any special list or catalogue of periodicals and any unbound or bound periodicals that may be kept in the room.

B. Pick any volume of the *Readers' Guide* from IV through XIX and see how many articles on the League of Nations are listed in it. Are more listed for the period 1919-1921 or for the period May, 1949–March, 1951?

C. Investigate 1 or 2 or 3 as directed by your instructor. Do both indexes list the same articles?

1. How many articles on "Plastic coating" are listed by the *Readers' Guide* for April, 1953–February, 1955? How many by the *Industrial Arts Index* for 1954 only?

2. How many on "Silicones" by the *Readers' Guide* for April, 1951–March, 1953? How many by the *Industrial Arts Index* for 1952 only?

3. How many on "Transistors" by the *Readers' Guide* for May, 1949–March, 1951? How many by the *Industrial Arts Index* for 1950 only?

D. Investigate 1 or 2 or 3 as directed by your instructor. Do both indexes list the same articles?

1. How many articles on "Skunks" are listed by the *Readers' Guide* for May, 1945–April, 1947? How many by the *Agricultural Index* for October, 1945–August, 1948?

2. How many on "Airplanes in insect control" by the *Readers' Guide* for July, 1943–April, 1945? How many by the *Agricultural Index* for October, 1942–September, 1945?

3. How many on "Hybridization" by the *Readers' Guide* for July, 1939–June, 1941? How many by the *Agricultural Index* for October, 1939–September, 1942?

E. Consult the *New York Times Index* to determine the date of the conferring of knighthood on Prime Minister Winston Churchill (or any other significant event assigned by your instructor). [Since all important newspapers report events on the same day, the *New York Times Index* is a useful guide to all newspapers.]

(3) Learn how to find and use reference books.

Dictionaries, encyclopedias, atlases, and other books especially helpful for reference are usually kept on the open shelves of the reference room, where students may use them directly without the trouble of having them brought from the stacks. Each of these books is listed in the card catalogue, and the call number will often aid in finding the book. The student should learn the general location of the chief classes of reference books in order that he may turn to them without loss of time. For a detailed list of such books, with a short description of each, he should consult Constance M. Winchell's *Guide to Reference Books*.[3] A few of the more important reference books are listed below (with abbreviated entries).

GENERAL DICTIONARIES (UNABRIDGED)

Century Dictionary and Cyclopedia. 12 vols. 1911.
Dictionary of American English. 4 vols. 1938-1944.
New Standard Dictionary. 1947.
Oxford English Dictionary. 12 vols. and supplement. 1933. Originally issued as *A New English Dictionary*. 10 vols. and supplement. 1888-1933.
Webster's New International Dictionary. 1934, 1950.

SPECIAL DICTIONARIES

Allen, F. S. *Allen's Synonyms and Antonyms*. 1938.
Crabb, George. *Crabb's English Synonyms*. 1945.
Fowler, H. W. *Dictionary of Modern English Usage*. 1926.
Horwill, H. W. *Dictionary of Modern American Usage*. 1935.
Partridge, Eric. *Dictionary of Slang and Unconventional English*. 1950.
Roget's Thesaurus of Words and Phrases. 1947.
Webster's Dictionary of Synonyms. 1942.
Wentworth, Harold. *American Dialect Dictionary*. 1944.
Wright, Joseph. *English Dialect Dictionary*. 6 vols. 1898-1905.

GENERAL ENCYCLOPEDIAS

Collier's Encyclopedia. 20 vols. 1949-1951.
Columbia Encyclopedia. 1950, 1953.
Encyclopedia Americana. 30 vols. 1955.
Encyclopædia Britannica. 24 vols. 1954.
Lincoln Library of Essential Information. 1950, 1953.
New International Encyclopaedia. 27 vols. 1922-1930.

SPECIAL ENCYCLOPEDIAS

Adams, J. T. *Dictionary of American History*. 6 vols. 1940.
Bailey, L. H. *Cyclopedia of American Agriculture*. 4 vols. 1907-1909.

---

[3] Seventh ed., 1951, with supplements.

Bryan's Dictionary of Painters and Engravers. 5 vols. 1903-1905.
Catholic Encyclopedia. 17 vols. 1907-1922. New edition, 1936–.
Encyclopædia of the Social Sciences. 15 vols. 1930-1935.
Grove's Dictionary of Music and Musicians. 9 vols. 1954.
Harper's Encyclopedia of Art. 2 vols. 1937.
Hastings, James. *Dictionary of the Bible*. 5 vols. 1898-1902.
Hastings, James. *Encyclopaedia of Religion and Ethics*. 13 vols. 1911-1927.
Hutchinson's Technical and Scientific Encyclopedia. 4 vols. 1935-1936.
Jewish Encyclopedia. 12 vols. 1925.
McLaughlin, A. C., and A. B. Hart. *Cyclopedia of American Government*. 3 vols. 1914. Reprint, 1949.
Monroe, Paul. *Cyclopedia of Education*. 5 vols. 1911-1913.
Monroe, W. S. *Encyclopedia of Educational Research*. 1950.
Munn, Glenn G. *Encyclopedia of Banking and Finance*. 1949.
Thompson, O. *International Cyclopedia of Music and Musicians*. 1949.
Thorpe, Sir Thomas. *Dictionary of Applied Chemistry*. 9 vols. 1937-1949.
Universal Jewish Encyclopedia. 10 vols. 1939-1943.
Van Nostrand's Scientific Encyclopedia. 1947.

ATLASES AND GAZETTEERS

Collier's New World Atlas and Gazetteer. 1953.
Columbia Atlas, ed. John Bartholomew. 1954.
Columbia Lippincott Gazetteer of the World. 1952.
Encyclopædia Britannica World Atlas. 1954.
Hammond's Ambassador World Atlas. 1954.
Rand-McNally Commercial Atlas. 1950.
Times (London) *Atlas of the World*. 5 vols. 1955.
Webster's Geographical Dictionary. 1949.

YEARBOOKS– CURRENT EVENTS

American Yearbook. 1910-1919. 1925–.
Americana Annual. 1923–.
Annual Register. 1758–.
Britannica Book of the Year. 1938–.
Information Please Almanac. 1947–.
New International Year Book. 1907–.
Statesman's Year-Book. 1864–.
Statistical Abstract of the United States. 1878–.
University Debaters' Annual. 1915–.
Whitaker's Almanack. 1869–.
World Almanac. 1868–.

BIOGRAPHY

Current Biography. 1940—.

Dictionary of American Biography. 20 vols. and index. 1928-1937. Supplement.

Dictionary of National Biography. (British.) 24 vols. Indexes and supplements. 1937-1939 reprint.

International Who's Who. 1935—.

Kunitz, S. J. *American Authors, 1600-1900.* 1938.

Kunitz. *American Authors of the Nineteenth Century.* 1936.

Kunitz and H. Haycraft. *Twentieth Century Authors.* 1942. Supplement, 1955.

Kunitz and H. Haycraft. *British Authors before 1800.* 1952.

Webster's Biographical Dictionary. 1943, 1953.

Who's Who. 1848—.

Who's Who in America. 1899—.

LITERATURE

Apperson, G. L. *English Proverbs and Proverbial Phrases.* 1929.

Baker, E. A. *Guide to the Best Fiction.* 1932.

Bartlett's Familiar Quotations. 1955.

Bateson, F. W. *Cambridge Bibliography of English Literature.* 4 vols. 1941.

Brewer's Dictionary of Phrase and Fable. 1953.

English Association. *Year's Work in English Studies.* 1920—.

Gayley, C. M. *Classic Myths in English Literature and in Art.* 1939.

Granger, Edith. *Index to Poetry and Recitations.* Fourth ed., 1953.

Harper's Dictionary of Classical Literature and Antiquities. 1897.

Hart, James D. *Oxford Companion to American Literature.* 1948.

Harvey, Sir Paul. *Oxford Companion to Classical Literature.* 1937.

Harvey, Sir Paul. *Oxford Companion to English Literature.* 1946.

Millett, Fred B., J. M. Manly, and Edith Rickert. *Contemporary British Literature.* 1935.

Millett, Fred B. *Contemporary American Authors.* 1940.

Modern Humanities Research Association. *Annual Bibliography of English Language and Literature.* 1920—.

Sears, Minnie Earl, and Marian Shaw. *Essay and General Literature Index,* 1900-1954.

Spiller, Robert E., and others. *Literary History of the United States.* 3 vols. 1948.

Stevenson, B. E. *Home Book of Quotations.* 1947.

Trent, W. P., and others. *Cambridge History of American Literature.* 4 vols. 1917-1921.

Ward, A. W., and A. R. Waller. *Cambridge History of English Literature.* 15 vols. 1907-1927.

▶ EXERCISES ON REFERENCE WORKS

Do the following exercises as a means of locating some of the more important works of reference and of acquainting yourself with them.

A. Draw the floor plan of the reference room of your library, indicating the location of the most important books of reference. Indicate, for example, the locations of (1) unabridged dictionaries, (2) general encyclopedias, (3) atlases, and (4) the *Dictionary of National Biography* or some other collection of short biographies.

B. Trace the history of one of several words assigned by your instructor (such as *starve, mustard, answer, lady, tobacco*) and quote several passages to illustrate various uses of the word. [Consult the *Oxford English Dictionary.*]

C. When the new Congress convened in 1953 or in 1955 (or in any year assigned by your instructor) what were the respective strengths of the political parties in the two legislative houses? Official census data of late 1952 or 1953 (or any other year assigned) showed what estimated population for the United States? [Consult one or more of the yearbooks.]

D. Locate in atlases several good maps of either (1) Formosa, (2) Kenya, or (3) Bikini. State where you find each map.

E. Look up in a general encyclopedia the article on "Engraving," "Isotopes," or "Franciscans." Then look up the same subject in the appropriate special encyclopedia. Name the two encyclopedias in which the articles are found and indicate very briefly the relative usefulness of the articles.

Bibliographical Form

(4) Follow accepted usage in organizing your bibliography.

While the student is learning how to use the card catalogue, the periodical indexes, and general reference books, he should write out the titles that seem most promising for his library paper. He should put each item on a separate card (3 x 5 or 4 x 6 inches in size) so that he can readily drop or add a card and can arrange the list alphabetically without copying. He should write in ink and follow *exactly* and consistently the bibliographical form he is directed to use. The form illustrated by the models below (and by the footnote forms on pages 950-52) is based on the revised style sheet of the Modern Language Association (MLA). Note that the author's name, when given, always comes first; otherwise the title.

MODEL BIBLIOGRAPHICAL ENTRIES

BOOKS

Anderson, Virgil A. *Training the Speaking Voice.* New York: Oxford University Press, 1942.[4]

Duverger, Maurice. *Political Parties.* Translated from the French by Barbara and Robert North. New York: John Wiley & Sons, Inc., 1954. [A translation]

Hervey, George F., and Jack Hems. *Freshwater Tropical Aquarium Fishes.* London: Batchworth Press, 1952. [Two authors]

Johnson, R. U., and C. C. Buel, editors. *Battles and Leaders of the Civil War.* 4 volumes. New York: The Century Company, 1887-88. [Edited work]

McConnell, F. J., and others. *The Creative Intelligence and Modern Life.* Boulder: The University of Colorado Press, 1928. (University of Colorado Semicentennial Series, 1877-1927. Vol. V.) [A book by more than two authors; also a book in a series]

Prescott, William Hickling. *History of the Reign of Philip the Second, King of Spain.* Edited by John Foster Kirk. 3 volumes. Philadelphia: J. B. Lippincott & Company, 1871. [Author and editor]

Scott, Sir Harold. *Scotland Yard.* New York: Random House, 1955.

MAGAZINES AND NEWSPAPERS

Curti, Merle. "Intellectuals and Other People." *American Historical Review,* LX (January, 1955), 259-282.

Menard, Henry W. "Fractures in the Pacific

[4] Note that the entry falls into three units separated by periods: (1) the author's name; (2) the title; (3) the facts of publication—place, publisher, date. Another common bibliographical form uses commas between all parts, thus:

Anderson, Virgil A., *Training the Speaking Voice,* New York, Oxford University Press, 1942.

Menard, Henry W., "Fractures in the Pacific Floor," *Scientific American,* CXCIII (July, 1955), 36-41.

Floor." *Scientific American,* CXCIII (July, 1955), 36-41.

Salisbury, Harrison E. "Farm Goals Cited by Soviet Official." New York *Times,* August 24, 1955, p. 1 ff.[5]

"Will the Credit Medicine Be Enough?" *Business Week* (August 13, 1955), pp. 26-28.

ENCYCLOPEDIAS

"Jackson, Andrew." *Encyclopædia Britannica,* 1954, XII, 851-853.

Lee, Edwin A. "Vocational Education." *Encyclopedia Americana,* 1950, XXVIII, 160-161. [A signed article]

BULLETINS AND PAMPHLETS

Standards of Practice for Radio Broadcasters of the United States of America. Washington: The National Association of Radio and Television Broadcasters, 1954.

Velvetbean Caterpillar, The. Dept. of Agriculture, Bureau of Entomology and Plant Quarantine Leaflet No. 348. Washington: Government Printing Office, 1953.

UNPUBLISHED THESIS

Blair, Carolyn L. "Browning as a Critic of Poetry." M.A. thesis, University of Tennessee, 1948.

The models given above, with hanging indention, show the proper form for the entries in the final bibliography, which is to be written out and submitted as a part of the library paper. On the separate bibliography cards, the same form may be used; or the author, title, and facts of publication may be written on separate lines as in the following specimen. (The library call number in the lower

Scott, Sir Harold.
Scotland Yard.
New York: Random House, 1955.

HV
8198
L753
1955

[5] Note that page numbers are preceded by *p.* for *page.* The initials *p.* and *pp.* are not used when the volume number in Roman numerals precedes the date in parentheses, as for the first two items under "Magazines and Newspapers."

left-hand corner will save the trouble of looking in the card catalogue again when the book is needed.)

The form of the bibliographical models given above (referred to as MLA style) is commonly used by books and periodicals in languages and social sciences. Scientific periodicals tend to use boldface Arabic numerals for the volume number and to place the date at the end. Indexes to periodicals employ a compact form, but one not commonly used in books or periodicals and consequently not suitable as a model. The card catalogue is also unsuitable as a guide, since it capitalizes only the first word and the proper names in book titles and publication data.

Whatever bibliographical form a writer adopts, he should give due heed to the three divisions of each entry: the author's name (if it is given), the title, and the facts of publication. He should take great pains to be consistent, each time using commas, periods, italics (underlining), and quotation marks exactly as they are called for by his model. This model will usually be suggested by the periodical, the organization, or the department for which the paper is being written. If the instructor does not specify a form, the student may adopt the commonly used form illustrated above. The items may be classified in some logical way, such as "Books" and "Periodicals," or arranged in a single alphabetical list, as in the bibliography on page 962.

► EXERCISE 2.   Prepare a preliminary bibliography of at least ten items on the topic selected for your library paper. Include, if possible, two books, two general reference books, and two articles from periodicals.

33c   Prepare the outline.

[Follow the general directions given under Section **32b-f.** But the outline for the library paper will need even more change and development than the outline for the ordinary exposition. For you must write down at least a few tentative headings of an outline to guide your first note-taking; and then the extensive reading and note-taking required to find material for the paper will show many ways to develop the headings into a complete outline.]

After completing a preliminary bibliog-

raphy and a minimum of general reading on his subject (an encyclopedia article and parts of one or two other works may suffice), the student writing on "The French Horn" will make a preliminary outline that will give direction to his investigation. This tentative outline will enable him to discard irrelevant material from his bibliography and to begin spotting valuable passages on which he will want to take notes. There is nothing but frustration in store for anyone who attempts to take notes without knowing what he is looking for.

The student should be careful, however, not to become a slave to his preliminary outline. For although the outline will direct his reading, his reading will almost certainly suggest ways in which the outline may be improved. No outline should be regarded as complete until the research paper has been finished. As the student takes notes, he will probably revise his original outline frequently, adding subheads to it, changing subheads to major headings, perhaps dropping some headings entirely. After some general reading, he might make out an outline such as the following:

First Preliminary Outline

THE FRENCH HORN

I. History of the horn
   A. Early horns
   B. Modern horns
II. Characteristics of the French horn
III. Musical scores featuring the French horn
IV. Noted players of the French horn—Dennis Brain, etc.
V. The French horn in the twentieth century

With this rough and incomplete outline as a guide, the student is ready to begin his note-taking (see **33d** below). While reading and taking notes he will write into the first outline each desirable addition or change as it occurs to him. He will soon drop Topic III, "Musical scores," on discovering that it is too technical for his paper; and he may decide to omit IV, "Noted players," on the grounds that he can write a better paper by limiting himself to "The French Horn: Its Development and Use." At this point, while the outline is still fluid, it will be helpful to the student if he can make a precise statement, in a single sentence, of the central or controlling idea of his paper, such as: "The French horn has evolved from a humble origin and has won a secure place in modern orchestras." After a few days the developing outline might look somewhat as follows:

Second Preliminary Outline

THE FRENCH HORN: ITS DEVELOPMENT AND USE

CENTRAL IDEA   The French horn has evolved from a humble origin and has won a secure place in modern orchestras.

I. Origin and development of the instrument

  A. Early horns
    1. Roman
    2. Saxon
  B. Seventeenth- and eighteenth-century horns
  C. Nineteenth-century horns

II. Characteristics of the instrument

  A. Dimensions
  B. Quality of tone

III. The French horn in orchestras

  A. Seventeenth century
  B. Eighteenth century
  C. Nineteenth century
  D. Twentieth century

33d   Take notes.

After the student has done enough broad reading on his subject to make a first tentative outline, he is ready (as we have already observed) to begin note-taking. He should learn how to find and evaluate useful passages with a minimum of time and effort. Seldom will a whole book, or even a whole article, be of use as subject matter for any given research paper. To find what is needed for his paper, the student writing on "The French Horn" must turn to many books and articles, rejecting most of them altogether and using from others only a section here and there. He cannot take the time to read each book carefully. He must use the table of contents of the

book and its index, and he must learn to scan the pages rapidly until he finds the passages he needs.

One important consideration always is the reliability of the source. Does the author seem to know his subject? Does he have an official position that implies competence? Do others speak of him as an authority? Is he prejudiced? Is the work recent enough to give the information needed?

The best and most common way to take notes is to use cards or paper sheets of uniform size, usually 3 x 5 or 4 x 6 inches. Each card contains a single note with a heading keyed to significant words in the outline—not to the notation (IA, II, IIIC, etc.), which is especially subject to change. If the research paper is to use the customary footnotes, each card must also show the source of the note and the exact page or pages of the source.

Let us suppose that the student preparing the library paper on "The French Horn" has spotted the three passages quoted below and on the following page. Compare each of these passages with the note taken from it.

In *Saxon* times horns were used by the huntsmen and in battle, and carried by the peaceful traveler as well, to make known his presence. An ancient law stated that "if a man come from afar or a stranger go out of the highway, and he neither shout or blow a horn, he is to be accounted a thief, either to be slain or to be redeemed." [6]

> Early horns - Saxon
> The early Saxons used horns in the hunt, in battle, and in traveling. According to ancient law any stranger or anyone off the highway was required to cry out or sound his horn to insure himself against being slain or taken for ransom as a thief.
> Edgerly, p. 263.

(For the use of this note in the finished library paper, see footnote 8, page 955.)

[6] Beatrice Edgerly, *From the Hunter's Bow* (New York, 1942), p. 263.

Thus we find the ancient Romans in the centuries immediately preceding our era with a varied assortment of what we would call "Military Brass."[7]

> *Early horns - Roman*
>
> *The ancient Romans were using brass horns as early as the first century B. C.*
>
> *Forsyth, p. 68.*

(For the use of this note in the finished library paper, see footnote 5, page 955.)

It became apparent, however, that the most valued attribute of the horn—its characteristic warmth and dark beauty of tone—could not be supplied by the high-pitched B♭ horn, whatever else it had to recommend it. Today this problem seems to have reached a workable solution with the invention of the double horn.[8]

> *Characteristics - tonal quality*
>
> *The quality of the French horn most valued is "its characteristic warmth and dark beauty of tone."*
>
> *Piston, p. 233.*

(For the use of this note in the finished library paper, see footnote 27, page 958.)

The first two notes above are carefully written abbreviations of their sources, expressed by the student in his own phraseology. Since the words are his own, he is free to write them in his paper just as they stand or to adapt them further when he uses the note. A comparison of the notes with the finished paper shows that he adapts the first note but uses the second one exactly as written. The last note of the three is taken partly in the words of the original since the student wishes to quote from the passage.

Quotations. Very seldom should a student write a note that is merely a quotation. Too many quotations in the library paper suggest a lack of mastery of the subject. And besides, the more a student quotes, the less practice he gets in composition. A quotation must be a very telling and important one before a student is justified in using it in his paper. Occasionally, however, a student will discover such a passage. When he does, he should take down the passage verbatim—that is, write every word, every capital letter, every mark of punctuation exactly as in the original. Then he should enclose the quoted passage in quotation marks. When a note-taker quotes, he should quote accurately. When he is not quoting, he should use his own phraseology, getting entirely away from that of the original.

Plagiarism. Any failure to acknowledge borrowed material is a serious offense called plagiarism. If a borrowed idea is expressed in the writer's phraseology, a footnote reference to the sourse is sufficient. If it is in the phraseology of the source, it should be put in quotation marks and also acknowledged in a footnote. Usually any conscious quotation (except well-known or proverbial passages) of three or four connected words or more should be placed in quotation marks.

▶ EXERCISE 3. Use the fifth paragraph of the model library paper at the end of Section 33 to write a short note of fewer than forty words. [Be careful to avoid the phraseology of the source. Write two or three effective sentences to express the gist of the paragraph.]

▶ EXERCISE 4. Use the same paragraph to write a longer note, perhaps three-fourths the length of the source. [Avoid entirely the phraseology of the source. Include more details than the shorter note of Exercise 3 permitted. Make the sentences as effective as you can.]

▶ EXERCISE 5. Make a paraphrase of the first paragraph of the library paper. [Avoid entirely the phraseology of the source. A paraphrase is approximately the same length as the source and should be expressed in equally effective sentences.]

[7] Cecil Forsyth, *Orchestration* (New York, 1947), p. 68.

[8] Walter Piston, *Orchestration* (New York, 1955), p. 233.

▶ EXERCISE 6. Read carefully the paragraph by Harlow Shapley reprinted on page 919. First write, in a single sentence, the central idea of the paragraph. Then write a note half as long as the paragraph. Finally write a note approximately as long as your source. [Avoid entirely the phraseology of the source. Choose your words carefully. Give variety to your sentences.]

33e Use the outline, the bibliography, and the notes to write the library paper.
(Follow the general suggestions given under Section 32g.)

After the outline has been made as complete as possible and after a large number of notes have been taken—notes covering every major section of the outline and every subsection—the student is ready to begin writing. He will arrange his notes in the order of the outline and then use them as the basis of his paper, section by section. Naturally he will have to expand some parts, to cut others; and especially will he need to provide transitional sentences and even transitional paragraphs. He must write the material in the best way he can—in his own style, in his own words.

Since the bulk of the material consists of notes which the student has taken down from others, he should, of course, give proper credit. To do so, he makes use of footnotes. The number needed will vary with the paper. Every quotation must have its footnote, and so must all the chief facts and opinions drawn from others. Usually from two to six footnotes per page will be needed for proper documentation of the average library paper.

The footnote form used for making the first reference to a source (the primary footnote) is similar to, but not identical with, the bibliographical entry: The footnote has a normal paragraph indention; the author's name comes in normal order with surname last; commas replace periods between author, title, and facts of publication; and the exact page of the source is given. When the same title is referred to a second time (a secondary footnote), the entry is much briefer. Below are shown the forms that might be taken by a single title as it appears in (1) the bibliography, (2) the first footnote reference, and (3) the second or any later footnote reference.

1. BIBLIOGRAPHICAL ENTRY

Forsyth, Cecil. *Orchestration*. New York: The Macmillan Company, 1947.

[See the bibliography for the completed library paper, page 962.]

2. PRIMARY FOOTNOTE

[5] Cecil Forsyth, *Orchestration* (New York, 1947), p. 68.

[The form for the first reference to this book. See the library paper, footnote 5, page 955.]

3. SECONDARY FOOTNOTES

[25] Forsyth, p. 117.

[The form for any later reference to this book—provided it is not cited in the footnote *immediately* preceding. See footnote 25, page 958.]

[26] *Ibid.*

[The form for reference to the same book, and the same page, cited in the footnote *immediately* preceding. See footnote 26, page 958.]

[38] *Ibid.,* p. 77.

[The form for reference to the same book, but not the same page, cited in the footnote immediately preceding. See footnote 38, page 959.]

If the bibliography contains a book by Cecil Forsyth and one by William Forsyth, a secondary reference would be "C. Forsyth" or "W. Forsyth." If there are two books by the same author, the title of each is cited.

ABBREVIATIONS

Some abbreviations used in footnotes are as follows (those from Latin usually written in italics):

c. or *ca. (circa)*	about *(ca.* 1550)
cf. (confer)	compare [The English *see* is more common.]
ch., chs.	chapter, chapters
ed.	edited by, edition, editor
f., ff.	and the following page, pages
ibid. (ibidem)	in the same place
l., ll.	line, lines
loc. cit. (loco citato)	in the place cited

ms., mss.	manuscript, manuscripts
n.d.	no date given
n.p.	no publisher given
op. cit. (opere citato)	in the work cited
p., pp.	page, pages
rev.	revised
tr., trans.	translated by
vol., vols.	volume, volumes

MODEL FOOTNOTES—PRIMARY FORMS

complete citation used only once

BOOKS

[1] Virgil A. Anderson, *Training the Speaking Voice* (New York, 1942), p. 11.

[2] Maurice Duverger, *Political Parties,* trans. from the French by Barbara and Robert North (New York, 1954), p. 114. [A translation]

[3] George F. Hervey and Jack Hems, *Freshwater Tropical Aquarium Fishes* (London, 1952), p. 44. [Two authors]

[4] R. U. Johnson and C. C. Buel, eds., *Battles and Leaders of the Civil War* (New York, 1887-88), I, 9. [Edited work; also a work in several volumes]

[5] General James Longstreet, "Our March Against Pope," in *Battles and Leaders of the Civil War,* ed. R. U. Johnson and C. C. Buel (New York, 1887-88), II, 516. [Contributing author in an edited work]

[6] F. J. McConnell and others, *The Creative Intelligence and Modern Life,* University of Colorado Semicentennial Series, V (Boulder, Colo., 1928), pp. 29-30. [A book by more than two authors; also a book in a series]

[7] William Hickling Prescott, *History of the Reign of Philip the Second, King of Spain,* ed. John Foster Kirk (Philadelphia, 1871), III, 87.

[8] Sir Harold Scott, *Scotland Yard* (New York, 1955), p. 101.

MAGAZINES AND NEWSPAPERS

[9] Merle Curti, "Intellectuals and Other People," *American Historical Review,* LX (January, 1955), 279-280.

[10] Henry W. Menard, "Fractures in the Pacific Floor," *Scientific American,* CXCIII (July, 1955), 36.

[11] Harrison E. Salisbury, "Farm Goals Cited by Soviet Official," New York *Times,* August 24, 1955, p. 1. [A signed news story]

[12] Louisville *Times,* June 4, 1938, p. 16. [An unsigned news story]

[13] "Will the Credit Medicine Be Enough?" *Business Week* (August 13, 1955), pp. 26-27. [An unsigned magazine article]

ENCYCLOPEDIAS

[14] "Jackson, Andrew," *Encyclopædia Britannica,* 1954, XII, 853. [An unsigned encyclopedia article. The title here is given as "Jackson, Andrew" because it is found listed alphabetically under *J* and not under *A* in the encyclopedia.]

[15] Edwin A. Lee, "Vocational Education," *Encyclopedia Americana,* 1950, XXVIII, 160. [A signed encyclopedia article. Note the variant spellings: *Encyclopædia* for the *Britannica; Encyclopedia* for the *Americana.*]

BULLETINS AND PAMPHLETS

[16] *Standards of Practice for Radio Broadcasters of the United States of America* (Washington, 1954), p. 18.

[17] *The Velvetbean Caterpillar,* Department of Agriculture, Bureau of Entomology and Plant Quarantine Leaflet No. 348 (Washington, 1953). p. 3.

UNPUBLISHED THESIS

[18] Carolyn L. Blair, "Browning as a Critic of Poetry" (M.A. thesis, University of Tennessee, 1948), p. 41.

MODEL FOOTNOTES—SECONDARY FORMS

The secondary footnotes follow the order in which the works cited appear in the listing of Model Footnotes—Primary Forms.

BOOKS

[19] Anderson, p. 11.   [20] Duverger, pp. 113-114. [It is permissible to place extremely short footnotes two, and even three, on a line, so long as there is no appearance of overcrowding.]

[21] Hervey and Hems, p. 41.

[22] Johnson and Buel, I, 5.

[23] Longstreet, II, 515.

[24] McConnell and others, p. 28.

[25] Prescott, III, 125.

[26] Ibid. [Same work, same volume, and same page as in footnote immediately preceding]

[27] *Ibid.,* II, 94-95. [Same work (Prescott's), but a different volume]

[28] *Ibid.,* p. 95. [Same work, same volume, but only one page this time]

[29] *Ibid.,* III, 125. [Same work, but back to a volume not cited in the *immediately* preceding footnote]

[30] Scott, p. 133.

[31] Prescott, III, 127. [An *ibid.* here would refer to Scott's work, not Prescott's.]

[32] Scott, p. 133.

MAGAZINES AND NEWSPAPERS

[33] Curti, p. 279.   [34] Menard, p. 39.   [35] Salisbury, p. 1.

[36] Salisbury, "Farm Goals Cited by Soviet Official," p. 1. [This is the form that would have to be used if Salisbury had furnished more than one of the sources included in your bibliography.]

[37] Harrison E. Salisbury, p. 1. [This is the form that would have to be used if another author also named Salisbury were included in your bibliography.]

[38] Louisville *Times*, p. 16. [Proper if only one article from this newspaper is used. If more than one are used, the secondary form is the same as the primary. See footnote 12.]

[39] "Will the Credit Medicine Be Enough?" p. 27.

ENCYCLOPEDIAS

[40] "Jackson, Andrew," pp. 851-852. [It is possible that a research paper may use articles with identical titles from several different encyclopedias. In that case, the proper secondary footnote form would be as follows (footnote 41).]

[41] "Jackson, Andrew," *Encyclopædia Britannica*, pp. 851-852. [The year of publication and the volume number are cited in your primary footnote and need not be repeated here.]

[42] Lee, p. 160.

BULLETINS AND PAMPHLETS

[43] *Standards of Practice for Radio Broadcasters of the United States of America*, p. 17.

[44] *The Velvetbean Caterpillar*, p. 3.

UNPUBLISHED THESIS

[45] Blair, p. 38.

Final Outline and Paper, with Footnotes.
After the student has written the first draft of his paper on "The French Horn," complete with footnotes, he will read it over carefully, correcting all errors in spelling, mechanics, and grammar, and making sure that the arrangement is logical and that the writing is as clear, concise, and pleasing in style as he can possibly make it. He will probably rewrite some sentences, strike out others, and add still others. His outline, which has developed steadily throughout the note-taking and the first draft of the paper, should now be in its final form. It has served primarily, of course, as a guide to the writing of the paper; but it will also serve, if copied in its final stage, as a guide to the contents of the paper.

With his first draft corrected and revised, and with his outline put in its final form, the student will write the final draft of his paper. He will use a typewriter if possible; if not, he will use pen and ink, taking pains to write legibly and neatly.

Final Bibliography. We have already noticed that the student assembles a preliminary bibliography early in his research. As he pursues his investigation, he eliminates some items and adds others. Not until he has completed his paper can he know the items that should make up his final bibliography. Now, with his writing completed, he may look through his footnotes. Every book or article appearing even once in a footnote belongs in his bibliography. His instructor may ask him to include everything that he has examined, whether he has actually used it in his writing or not. In that case his bibliography may have, instead of a dozen items, as many as fifty or a hundred. But, on the whole, the best practice is to include only items which have actually been used. Once the student has determined the items that should be included, he can easily arrange the bibliography cards and copy them, either in one alphabetical list or in a classified list.

The completed library paper consists of four units:

1. Title page, giving title, author's name, instructor's name, and course number, and also place and date of writing.
2. Outline, serving as the table of contents (numbered with small Roman numerals if it occupies more than one page).
3. Text of the paper, with footnotes.
4. Bibliography, on a separate page or pages numbered with the text (with Arabic numerals).

Students are often asked to submit, along with the completed paper, the materials used in the preparation of the paper: (1) one of the preliminary outlines, (2) the notes, on cards, (3) the rough draft of the paper, with footnotes, and (4) the bibliography, on cards.

The Sample Library Paper. In the preceding part of this section you have observed how a student has prepared, step by step, a library paper on the French horn. Gradually he limited his subject to the topic, "The French Horn: Its Development and Use," with the central or controlling idea: "The French horn has evolved from a humble origin and has won a secure place in modern orchestras."

As you come to read the completed paper on the following pages, note the adequate development of this central idea in twenty-seven paragraphs covering the three major divisions of the outline. The paper begins without any separate or formal introduction, with (I) the origin and development of the French horn, giving thirteen paragraphs to this important part of the topic. Next come (pages 957-59) four paragraphs on (II) the characteristics of the instrument, then the final ten paragraphs on (III) the use of the horn in orchestras. The last paragraph rounds out the paper by referring to the remarkable progress of the French horn "since its conch-shell beginning." But this final paragraph is still chiefly concerned with the secure place won by the horn in the modern orchestra. Therefore the author lets the paragraph come under the third major division of his outline instead of providing a fourth division: conclusion.

Adequate documentation is provided by 52 footnotes. Of these, numbers 1, 2, 4, 5, 9, 10, 11, 14, 24, 27, 28, 31, 33, 35, 50, and 51 (one for each of the 16 items in the bibliography) are primary footnotes—that is, first references to the source. The 36 other footnotes are secondary—that is, second or later references to the source—and in addition, footnote 33 includes both a secondary and a primary footnote.

By checking any or all of the 52 footnotes with the source, the reader can test the accuracy of the documentation and observe the methods used. To make such checking easier for footnotes 5, 8, and 27, the sources of these footnotes are quoted above on pages 948-49 along with the three notes taken by the student. A comparison of the source, the note taken, and the material used in the completed paper shows (1) that credit is carefully given in each instance for the material used, (2) that the phraseology is that of the author, not the source, except in the one instance (footnote 27) in which quotation marks are used, and (3) that the passage in quotation marks follows the source *exactly*.

The French Horn: Its Development and Use

By Jack Howard Wilson

A Freshman Library Paper
Prepared for Professor Stewart
English 113, Section 36

Knoxville
The University of Tennessee
May 9, 1955

1. Title Page
2. Outline -(used as T. of Contents)
3. Body of paper
4. Bibliography

-1-

Sentence Outline

OUTLINE

<u>Central Idea</u>: The French horn has evolved from a humble origin and has won a secure place in modern orchestras.

I. Origin and development of the instrument
   A. Early horns
      1. Shells and animal horns
      2. Biblical horns
      3. Roman <u>cornua</u>
      4. Saxon and medieval horns
   B. Innovations of the seventeenth and eighteenth centuries
   C. The valve horn of the nineteenth century

II. Characteristics of the instrument
   A. Dimensions of the instrument
   B. Quality of tone
   C. Difficulties of performance

III. Use of the instrument in orchestras
   A. Seventeenth century
   B. Eighteenth century
   C. Nineteenth century
      1. Beethoven and his contemporaries
      2. Brahms
      3. Tchaikovsky
   D. Twentieth century

The ancestors of the modern French horn may be traced back to the earliest days of man, when conch shells picked up from the seashore were used for horns.[1] Other primitive horns were made from the horns of cattle, oxen, and deer. These instruments of prehistoric times--which could sound but one or two rough, indefinite tones[2]--may be classified properly as noise makers, for the sounds they made were not musical.

One of these early horns, the Hebrew ram's horn or <u>shophar</u>, is still used in Jewish temple rites. This very pure-sounding horn is mentioned in the Bible over one hundred times. The priests blew on the shophar when the walls of Jericho tumbled down.[3] Another forerunner of the French horn found in the Bible is the cornet mentioned by Daniel as the first instrument in King Nebuchadnezzar's orchestra. "Cornet" is the rendering in the King James Version, but the Revised Standard Version is probably more accurate in the translation "horn," since the

---

[1] Beatrice Edgerly, <u>From the Hunter's Bow</u> (New York, 1942), p. 4.

[2] "Horns," <u>Encyclopaedia Britannica</u>, 1954, XI, 750.

[3] Edgerly, p. 144.

-2-

Oriental orchestras of those days probably began playing with a call or flourish from
the horn. The other instruments followed, each playing individually.[4]

The ancient Romans were using brass horns as early as the first century B. C.[5]
These _cornua_ (the Latin word for "horns") were of three types: (1) the _tuba_,
a straight trumpet; (2) the J-shaped _lituus_ carried by horse soldiers; and (3) the
buccina, a curved brass horn that wound around the player's body.[6] These horns were
not used as musical instruments, but they were excellent for sounding fanfares.[7]

Saxon England used the animal horn in hunting, and in battle to rally troops or
frighten the enemy. For a stranger or any man off the main highway, it was a means
of identification. Such a person was supposed to cry out or sound his horn to show
that he was not a thief. If he did not properly identify himself to residents,
he ran the risk of being slain.[8]

The nobles of the Middle Ages had little to do but fight and hunt. At first
they used animal horns (as in Saxon England) to signal their soldiers and hunting
companions. Later they discovered that they could get more and clearer tones from
a brass horn. The hunting horn that was developed for them was a marked
improvement over the animal horn, but it was still very simple. It was a circular
tube carried with the arm through the coil and the weight on the shoulder. It
produced a few more tones than the animal horn.[9]

Although the hunting horn of the Middle Ages immediately preceded the hand
horn, the two horns bore only faint resemblance to each other. The bell (the mouth
of a wind instrument from which the sound comes) of the hunting horn was held on a
level with, or slightly above, the player's head.[10] In a picture from Galpin's
Old _English_ _Instruments_ _of_ _Music_, the circular horn has a funnel-shaped bell.
England took the lead in developing the hunter's horn that was to become
the French horn in seventeenth-century France.[11]

----

[4]Curt Sachs, _The_ _History_ _of_ _Musical_ _Instruments_ (New York, 1940), pp. 83-85.

[5]Cecil Forsyth, _Orchestration_ (New York, 1947), p. 68.

[6]Edgerly, pp. 135-136.   [7]"Horns," XI, 750.   [8]Edgerly, p. 263.

[9]George W. Andrews, editor, _Musical_ _Instruments_, IV, in _The_ _American_ _History_
and _Encyclopedia_ _of_ _Music_, W. L. Hubbard, editor-in-chief, 10 volumes
(New York, 1908), IV, 143.

[10]Kathleen Schlesinger, "Horns," _Encyclopaedia_ _Britannica_, 1911, XIII, 701.

[11]Karl Geiringer, _Musical_ _Instruments_ (New York, 1945), p. 81.

-3-

We cannot be positive about the details of this change. We do know that the hunter's horn was used in an undeveloped form in the early seventeenth century. A century later it had become the hand horn, with a lengthened tube and a narrow, partly cylindrical bore. Its cup-shaped mouthpiece had been replaced by a funnel-shaped one. No longer did it sound like a bugle or a piercing trumpet. It had a smooth, mellow sound similar to the modern French horn. Thus, by the end of the seventeenth century the horn had undergone many changes and improvements.[12]

In the middle of the eighteenth century Hampel of Dresden increased the number of notes possible for the French horn by inventing the practice of stopping. He had tried to soften its blaring sound by using a mute, but this had lowered the pitch of the notes. When he inserted his hand into the bell as a mute, he discovered that he could then produce many intermediate tones otherwise unobtainable on a natural horn.[13] Although these stopped tones were odd-sounding, the practice of stopping spread, and the horn gradually gained a place in the orchestra. But many musicians strongly objected to the admission of a rough and unrefined instrument which had so recently been a huntsman's horn.[14]

Composers, however, approved this orchestral newcomer, and the horn assumed a prominent position in French orchestras. Because these orchestras accompanied the French ballet popular in eighteenth-century England, the English began to call the hand horn "the French hunting horn." The "hunting" part was later dropped, and the name "French horn" has been accepted in most countries.[15] Today, some patriotic musicians of other countries refer to it simply as the "horn."

In the second half of the eighteenth century much attention was given to the improvement of the French horn. To increase its range, U-shaped crooks were inserted into the middle of the instrument; the result was the "inventions-horn."[16] Another type, the natural horn, differed from the inventions-horn in that the crooks were inserted at the end nearest the mouthpiece. By making the crooks of various lengths, these newer horns could be changed to play in any key. The disadvantage was that both types required some time to change crooks. A composer writing for either instrument had to give it several measures' rest if he wrote a change of key.[17]

_____

[12]Sachs, p. 384.   [13]Andrews, p. 66.

[14]Arthur Elson, Orchestral Instruments and Their Use (Boston, 1922), p. 211.
[15]Forsyth, p. 69.   [16]Geiringer, pp. 175-176.   [17]Andrews, IV, p. 126.

-4-

Charles Clagget, an Englishman, secured a British patent in 1788 for a third
type of French horn that he thought would end this problem. He united two horns
(one in D, one in E flat), and he put separate openings for a mouthpiece in each horn.
This gave the player eighteen open tones and many stopped ones. The player transferred
the mouthpiece from one horn to the other to play the necessary notes. The invention
did not prove popular; most players continued to use the earlier types. The
nineteenth century saw Clagget's idea carried even further. "Omnitonic" horns that
played in every key were produced. The player chose his key by manipulating a small
dial, but this instrument was too heavy, and the action of the dial was too slow.[18]

Then in 1815 came the solution to the problem of increasing the notes of a French
horn. Blühmel of Silesia and Stölzel of Berlin applied the valve principle to the
French horn. Others improved on their system, but all of these improvements involved
either piston or rotary valves. Sachs' explanation of the valve's action is one of the
clearest and simplest:

> The piston has an up-and-down action. When in rest, the piston
> disconnects the additional crook and allows the wind to pass directly
> through the main tube. When the piston is pressed down, on the contrary,
> the direct passage is barred, and the wind is forced to make the detour
> through the additional crooks before re-entering the main tube.
> In rotary valves, connection and disconnection are effected by a
> revolving cylinder. The player, however, does not need to make a
> rotary movement; he presses a key, the vertical motion of which is
> transformed into rotation.[19]

The invention of valves was the most important single step in the development
of the French horn. In a musical instrument valves have three functions: (1) they
enable a performer to produce the notes of a complete scale; (2) they enable him to
transpose the key; and (3) they correct faults or imperfections in the timbre.
The three valves on a French horn may be used in a variety of combinations to supply
all the tones of the chromatic scale.[20]

The four main parts of the modern French horn are the body, crooks, mouthpiece,
and slides. The body is a tube, approximately seven and one-third feet long, coiled
in a circular manner. At the end of this tube is a bell with a diameter of eleven or
twelve inches. Its crooks can be inserted or taken out to vary the length of the
tube and the pitch and key.[21] The various types of horns and the rarely played
"Wagner tubas" are the only brass wind instruments that use a funnel-shaped mouth-

---

[18]Sachs, p. 426.   [19]Ibid., pp. 426-427.

[20]Andrews, pp. 66-67.   [21]"Horns," XI, p. 749.

-5-

piece.[22] The tuning slides are U-shaped tubes which can be pulled out or pushed in to
tune the instrument exactly.[23] Unlike the crooks, they are permanent parts of the
horn. The old natural horn produced open and stopped tones. The open sounds produced
by the old natural horn were beautiful and sonorous, but the closed sounds were dull
and rough.[24] On the valve horn, all tones are open. It has incorporated the best
features of the hand horn instead of merely replacing it.[25]

Many people have tried to describe the tone quality of the French horn.
Although they hear suggestions of different sounds, almost all agree that its timbre
is unusually beautiful. Forsyth says that "the Horn differs materially from all other
Brass instruments. It is, indeed, at a higher artistic level altogether."[26] Walter
Piston writes of the horn's "characteristic warmth and dark beauty of tone."[27]
Mason describes its tone quality as "unforgettable"[28] and believes that it has varied
and unlimited possibilities. When played loudly, the horn is sonorous and blaring;
yet it may be mysterious or poetic in soft passages. Andrews points out that this
"genial instrument" adds warmth to an orchestra when used in pairs.[29]

Men will go on trying to capture these beautiful tones and put them down on
paper, but there are some things that will never be adequately described. The master
of nineteenth-century orchestration, Berlioz, speaks with authority and feeling on
this subject: "The horn is a noble and melancholy instrument. . . . It blends easily
with the general harmony; and the composer--even the least skilful--may, if he choose,
either make it play an important part, or a useful but subordinate one."[30]

Because the French horn has a difficult range of four octaves,[31] it is practically
impossible for a player to alternate high and low notes or parts. For the sake of
convenience, horn music is written in four parts. The first and third horn players
execute the high parts; the second and fourth, the low parts. Thus most horn players

---

[22]Forsyth, p. 89.   [23]"Horns," XI, p. 749.

[24]Hector Berlioz, A Treatise upon Modern Instrumentation and Orchestration,
trans. from the French by Mary Cowden Clarke (London, 1858), p. 130.

[25]Forsyth, p. 117.   [26]Ibid.

[27]Walter Piston, Orchestration (New York, 1955), p. 233.

[28]Daniel Gregory Mason, The Orchestral Instruments and What They Do (New York,
1909), pp. 70-71.

[29]Andrews, pp. 85-86.   [30]Berlioz, p. 140.

[31]Gardner Read, Thesaurus of Orchestral Devices (New York, 1953), p. 90.

-6-

specialize in either high- or low-range playing.[32] Even the first and third horn
players have difficulty playing high passages for any length of time because their
lips must be extremely tense to play high notes. A French horn player must be a
musician with an excellent ear, and he must have his tone definitely in his mind
before he can produce it.[33] No other brass instrument is as demanding as the
French horn.

The use of some form of the horn in orchestras can be traced as far back as the
seventeenth century. Cavalli and Lulli, Italian composers and conductors, used the
natural horn in some of their operas. Toward the end of the century, Reinhard Keiser,
the founder of the German opera, employed two horns in one of his works. Handel
continued to improve the horn part in his scores.[34]

In the eighteenth century the hand horn came into more general use. Bach wrote
horn parts for several cantatas. Horns also sounded salutes to royal figures or
depicted pastoral scenes.[35] In 1757 Gossec wrote obbligato parts for two horns and
two clarinets in two operatic arias, and thus for the first time the horn was played in
the Paris orchestra.[36] During this period Haydn and Mozart regularly employed two
French horns in their orchestras.[37] It is interesting to note, however, that none of
these earlier composers made much use of stopped tones.[38]

Beethoven devoted more attention to the horn than had any previous composer.
Most of his symphonies contained elaborate horn parts in spite of the limitations of
the hand horn. He used almost as many stopped tones as open ones. The wide and
difficult ranges of his horn parts and his love of high horn passages make his
treatment of the instrument unique.[39]

Beethoven's contemporaries and later composers took a hint from this German
genius. Weber was a master at original, poetic, and complete use of the French horn.
The horns seem to speak in his three best works, Oberon, Euryanthe, and Der
Freischütz.[40] In Der Freischütz he obtains round, full, pure horn tones by writing

---

[32]Piston, p. 227.

[33]Andrews, p. 127; "Young Man with a Horn," Time, LXII (July 6, 1953), 38-39.

[34]Schlesinger, "Horns," XIII, 704.

[35]Charles Sanford Terry, Bach's Orchestra (London, 1932), pp. 46-47.

[36]Elson, p. 211.   [37]Forsyth, p. 120.   [38]Ibid., p. 77.

[39]Ibid., pp. 121-123.   [40]Berlioz, p. 140.

-7-

open tones for horns in F and C.[41] He uses as many as eight horns in his opera, _Preciosa_.[42] Schubert and Mendelssohn wrote sparingly but effectively for the horn. At times Wagner produced lavish horn parts. His "Ride of the Valkyries" demands eight horns,[43] and in the first act of _Tannhäuser_ he wrote for sixteen horns.[44] Some composers used the stopped tones of the natural horn to emphasize special effects. In Gounod's _Faust_ they depict evil. Wagner gets some baleful and effective tones in _Götterdämmerung_. In Massenet's "Angelus" from _Scènes Pittoresques_, the horn represents an old, cracked village bell. Berlioz employs the horn and the harp to imitate a full-toned bell in his _Harold in Italy_.[45]

The composers already mentioned wrote largely for the hand horn. Many nineteenth-century composers disliked the new valve horns. They knew that the difference intended by earlier composers between open and closed sounds might be neglected by players of the new instruments.[46] At first the orchestras ignored valve horns because of their imperfections. But by 1850 they were used as much as the hand horns, and near the end of the century, the valve horns triumphed.[47] However, their orchestral parts have remained characteristically the same as those of the limited natural horn.[48]

Of the later nineteenth-century composers who wrote for the valve horn, Tchaikovsky and Brahms stand out as exponents of the French horn as a solo instrument.[49] Brahms had played it in his early days at Hamburg. He had come to love it and showed his feeling for the instrument by writing important parts for it in such works as his _First Orchestral Serenade_, _First_ and _Second Symphonies_, and _Second Piano Concerto_. He even wrote a trio for piano, violin, and French horn, but this beautiful work is rarely played because of the unusual combination of instruments.[50]

Tchaikovsky used the horn for solos, accompaniment, and sustaining harmony. Of the horn part in Tchaikovsky's _Fifth Symphony_ Huneker gives a picturesque description: "But what an impassioned romance the French horn sings in the second movement! It is the very apotheosis of a night of nightingales, soft and seldom

---

[41]Mason, pp. 67-68.   [42]Forsyth, p. 132.   [43]Elson, p. 215.

[44]Forsyth, p. 132.   [45]Elson, pp. 217-218.   [46]Berlioz, p. 141.

[47]Geiringer, p. 228.   [48]Forsyth, p. 127.   [49]Mason, p. 73.

[50]Walter Niemann, _Brahms_, trans. from the German by Catherine Alison Phillips (New York, 1941), pp. 271-272.

-8-

footed dells, a soft moon and dreaming tree-leaves. Its tune sinks a shaft into your heart and hot from your heart comes a response. . . ."[51]

Entering into the twentieth century, we find many changed conditions in the musical world. The greatest musical composers of our period write vocal, not instrumental, music. There are a number of good composers, but we have no twentieth-century Brahms, Beethoven, or Bach. In the best of our instrumental music--in the scores of Stravinsky, Hindemith, and Bartók--we find the French horn securely holding its place and receiving attention in almost every arrangement.[52]

The repertoires of our modern symphony orchestras consist largely of eighteenth- and nineteenth-century music. There are generally in any symphony orchestra five or six versatile horn players who can play melody, accompaniment, or sustaining harmony equally well. In the popular-music or dance band, the French horn is usually in the background and rarely gets a chance to solo. Exceptions to this practice are made by the bands of Hugo Winterhalter and Mitch Miller, which quite often feature the French horn. Leroy Anderson, composer of semi-classical music, favors the French horn in his compositions. Almost any high school band has two French horn players, but four is a more usual number, and five or six horns are not uncommon. The number of horns in college bands, as in high school bands, depends on the size of the organization. While the horn is of little value in a marching band, it is virtually indispensable to a concert band.

The French horn has made remarkable advances since its conch-shell beginning. It has become a respected member of most musical organizations. Because of its unique tonal quality, it is used as a solo instrument for special effects. And it makes a very pleasing contribution to any band or orchestra, whatever part it plays. We wonder how the many musicians who have contributed in earlier centuries to the development and use of the French horn would feel if they could see and hear it in its modern form. They would be surprised, no doubt, but the surprise would be a pleasant one.

---

[51]James Huneker, _Mezzotints in Modern Music_ (New York, 1905), pp. 121-122.

[52]Read, p. 90.

BIBLIOGRAPHY

Andrews, George W., editor. Musical Instruments, IV, in The American History and
    Encyclopedia of Music, W. L. Hubbard, editor-in-chief. 10 volumes. New York:
    Irving Squire, 1908.

Berlioz, Hector. A Treatise upon Modern Instrumentation and Orchestration.
    Translated from the French by Mary Cowden Clarke. London: Novello and
    Company, 1858.

Edgerly, Beatrice. From the Hunter's Bow. New York: G. P. Putnam's Sons, 1942.

Elson, Arthur. Orchestral Instruments and Their Use. Boston: The Page Company,
    1922.

Forsyth, Cecil. Orchestration. New York: The Macmillan Company, 1947.

Geiringer, Karl. Musical Instruments. New York: Oxford University Press, 1945.

"Horns." Encyclopaedia Britannica, 1954, XI, 749-750.

Huneker, James Gibbons. Mezzotints in Modern Music. New York: Charles Scribner's
    Sons, 1905.

Mason, Daniel Gregory. The Orchestral Instruments and What They Do. New York:
    H. W. Gray Company, 1909.

Niemann, Walter. Brahms. Translated from the German by Catherine Alison Phillips.
    New York: Alfred A. Knopf, 1941.

Piston, Walter. Orchestration. New York: W. W. Norton & Company, 1955.

Read, Gardner. Thesaurus of Orchestral Devices. New York: Pitman Publishing
    Corporation, 1953.

Sachs, Curt. The History of Musical Instruments. New York: W. W. Norton &
    Company, 1940.

Schlesinger, Kathleen. "Horns." Encyclopaedia Britannica, 1911, XIII, 697-706.

Terry, Charles Sanford. Bach's Orchestra. London: Oxford University Press, 1932.

"Young Man with a Horn." Time, LXII (July 6, 1953), 38-39.

▶ Letters

34 Letters should follow the forms prescribed by usage.

Business letters are preferably typewritten on one side only of sheets 8½ by 11 inches in size. These sheets are folded either (1) once horizontally and twice in the other direction to fit an envelope about 3½ by 6½ inches in size or (2) twice horizontally to fit an envelope about 4 by 10 inches in size.

Personal letters and social notes are commonly written by hand on note paper—a four-page sheet to be folded once horizontally for insertion in a matching envelope; or on club paper—a sheet about 7¼ by 11 inches, to be folded twice horizontally to fit a matching envelope 3¾ by 7½ inches. Both sides of the sheets may be used.

34a Business letters should follow pre-scribed usage with respect to the six essential parts:

(1) **Heading.**
(2) **Inside address.**
(3) **Salutation (or greeting).**
(4) **Body of the letter.**
(5) **Complimentary close.**
(6) **Signature.**

MODEL BUSINESS LETTER

1 {
1288 Catawba Street
Columbia 2, Missouri
May 3, 1955
}

2 {
Mr. J. W. Rice
Editor of the Rushville News
122 East Market Street
Rushville, Missouri
}

3   Dear Sir:

    Mr. Erskine Freeman, of your City Room, has mentioned to me your regular practice of employing two student reporters every summer. I am now majoring in journalism at the University of Missouri, and I should like, therefore, to apply for one of those positions for this next summer.

    By the end of this college year I shall have completed three quarters of the university program in journalism. Included in this work are two courses in reporting and one in copyreading. Before I began my college work, I had served four years as sports editor of my high school newspaper, where I learned some of the fundamentals of page make-up. Last year I was awarded the Missouri Press Association Scholarship for journalism.

    I have permission to refer you to my employer of the last three summers:

4   Mr. George Armour
        Armour Drug Store
        Rushville, Missouri

and to the professors under whom I have taken courses in journalism:

        Dr. James D. Turner
        Professor of Journalism
        University of Missouri
        Columbia, Missouri

        Dr. John M. Cain
        Assistant Professor of Journalism
        University of Missouri
        Columbia, Missouri

    I shall be in Rushville after June 6 and should appreciate an opportunity to call at your office for an interview at your convenience.

5   Very truly yours,

6 {
Donald Burke
Donald Burke
}

(1) The heading must give the full address of the writer and the date of the letter.

The heading is usually blocked as in the model, but it may be indented.

BLOCKED   860 Fremont Street
             Bessemer, Alabama
             March 22, 1946
[End punctuation is regularly omitted with the blocked heading.]

INDENTED   860 Fremont Street
              Bessemer, Alabama
               March 22, 1946
[End punctuation is usually omitted with the indented heading.]

Either of these forms may be used. The important thing is to be consistent—to adopt one form and to use it throughout the heading, the inside address, and the outside address.

If there is a letterhead (which supplies the address), the date may be written either under the letterhead or flush with the right margin, as in the heading of the model business letter shown below.

(2) The inside address (identical with the address to appear on the envelope) must give the name and the full address of the person to whom the letter is written.

The inside address must be consistent with the heading. That is, it must be (1) blocked, or (2) indented in accordance with the form adopted for the heading. The inside address is typed flush with the left margin about four spaces lower than the heading.

(3) The salutation (or greeting) should be consistent with the tone of the letter and with the complimentary close.

The salutation is written flush with the left margin two spaces below the inside address and is followed by a colon. The following salutations are used:

For men
Dear Sir:
My dear Sir: [More formal]
Dear Mr. Smith:
My dear Mr. Smith: [More formal]
Gentlemen:

For women
Dear Madam:
My dear Madam: [More formal]
Dear Mrs. Smith:
My dear Mrs. Smith: [More formal]
Ladies:

Note: The masculine salutation is used to address an organization or an individul whose name the writer does not know.

For the proper form of salutation in letters to government officials, ecclesiastical dignitaries, etc., see *Webster's New International Dictionary,* Second Edition, pp. 3012-14; *The American College Dictionary,* Text Edition, p. xxxiii; *Webster's New World Dictionary,* pp. 1717-19.

In salutations and addresses, abbreviations are generally disapproved except for *Mr.*

(plural, *Messrs.*), *Mrs.* (plural, *Mmes.*), and *Dr.*

> Donald Burke
> 1288 Catawba Street
> Columbia 2, Missouri
>
>
> Mr. J. W. Rice
> Editor of the Rushville <u>News</u>
> 122 East Market Street
> Rushville, Missouri

(4) The body of the letter should follow the principles of good writing.

Typewritten business letters are usually single-spaced, with double spacing between paragraphs. All paragraphs (1) should be indented equally, as in the model business letter (p. 963), or (2) should begin flush with the left-hand margin. The subject matter should be well organized and paragraphed, but the paragraphs will frequently be shorter than in ordinary writing. The style should be clear and direct. Indirect, abbreviated, or outdated phrasing should be avoided.

INDIRECT   Your kind favor . . . Your esteemed favor . . .
BETTER   Your letter . . .

INDIRECT   I beg to inform you that we have . . . I beg to send . . . Permit us to report that we now supply . . . I wish to apply . . .
BETTER   We have . . . I send . . . We now supply . . . I apply . . .

ABBREVIATED   Yours of the 5th instant . . . Hope to have . . . Enclose check for six dollars.
BETTER   Your letter of May 5 . . . We hope to have . . . I enclose a check for six dollars.

OUTDATED   Hoping to receive . . . Wishing you success . . . Trusting you will be pleased . . .
BETTER   We hope to receive . . . We wish you success . . . I trust you will be pleased . . .

(5) The complimentary close should be consistent with the tone of the letter and with the salutation.

Ordinary business letters addressed to strangers beginning with the usual *Dear Sir,*

etc., should close with *Yours truly, Yours very truly,* or *Very truly yours.* Professional letters, or business letters addressed to an individual with such an opening as *Dear Mr. White,* may well close with the more friendly *Yours sincerely, Sincerely yours, Sincerely, Faithfully yours,* or *Cordially yours.*

(6) The signature should be written by hand directly below the complimentary close.

If the name does not appear in the letterhead, it may be typed just below the signature. Ordinarily, neither professional titles nor degrees should be used with the signature, but the writer's official capacity may be indicated:

WRONG   *James M. Smith, LL.D.*
PERMISSIBLE   *James M. Smith*
              President

A married woman should sign her own name (*Mary Hughes Black,* not *Mrs. John K. Black*). In business letters her status is indicated by the use of parentheses as follows:

CORRECT   *Mary Hughes Black*
          (*Mrs. John K. Black*)
CORRECT   (*Mrs.*) *Mary Hughes Black*

34b   Personal letters and informal social notes follow in general the form of business letters.

Friendly letters usually omit the inside address. If it is included, it may be placed either at the beginning or at the end of the letter flush with the left margin.

The salutation is usually followed by a comma instead of the more formal colon. As in the business letter, the salutation should be in keeping with the complimentary close and with the tone of the letter. A letter beginning with *Dear Mr. Brown* may close with *Sincerely yours, Yours sincerely,* or *Cordially yours.* A more familiar salutation and complimentary close may be justified by the intimacy of the correspondents.

The body of the letter will vary greatly with the occasion and with the personality of the writer. An easy, informal style is best.

34c Formal social notes—announcements, invitations, answers to invitations—follow very definite conventions.

For the rare occasions when formal notes are required, engraving or handwriting (not typing) is the rule. Formal notes are always written in the third person. They have no inside address, no salutation, no complimentary close, and no signature. The writer's street address and the month and the date may be placed below at the left. Every word (except the street number and the abbreviations *Mr., Mrs.,* and *Dr.*) is spelled out in full. Acceptances and regrets follow the form of the invitation closely, repeating the hour and date to insure understanding. The verb used in the reply is always in the present tense.

▶ EXERCISES ON LETTERS

A. Write the following business letters:

1. Request the circulation manager of your newspaper to send your paper to a new address.
2. Ask the manager of a New York hotel to reserve a room for you.

3. Call the attention of your representative in the city government to some needed repairs in a street near your home.
4. Apply for a position that you are competent to fill. Be sure to include the following: (a) a brief description of the job desired—be specific; (b) your qualifications, including age, schooling, and experience; (c) at least three references—people who know you well and are able to evaluate your ability; (d) a request for an interview. See the model business letter on page 963.
5. Explain to your employer why you must resign your position at the end of the year.

B. Write the following personal letters:

1. Invite a friend to spend a week end in your home.
2. Accept an invitation to spend a week end with a friend.
3. Answer a friend's inquiry about the course in dramatics (or chemical engineering, astronomy, political science, etc.) in your college.
4. Congratulate a friend in another college on his election to some class office (or on any other honor).
5. Introduce a friend to one of your former classmates who lives in a different city.

▶ Grammatical Terms

35 Consult the following list as needed for explanations of grammatical terms.

Absolute. An absolute expression is one that is grammatically independent of the rest of the sentence. Usually it consists of a noun or pronoun followed by a participle, a construction often called the **nominative absolute.**

The game having ended, the crowd went home.

Abstract noun. See **Noun.**

Active voice. See **Voice.**

Adjective. A word (one of the eight parts of speech) used chiefly to modify (*i.e.,* describe or limit) nouns.

Descriptive adjective: *honest* man, *white* pony, *blue* sky, *waving* flag.

Limiting adjective: *my* book, *its* nest, *his, her, our, your, their* property (possessive); *that, this* house, *these, those* apples (demonstrative); *whose* cap? *which* coat? *what* dress? (interrogative); the boy *whose* dog was lost (relative); *one* pear, *three* plums, *first* robin, *third* sparrow (numerical); *a* street, *an* avenue, *the* park (article).

See also Section 4, Adjectives and Adverbs.

Adjective clause. A subordinate clause used as an adjective.

The man *who is honest* will succeed.

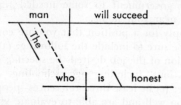

[The clause, equivalent to the adjective *honest,* modifies the noun *man.*]

Adverb. A word (one of the eight parts of speech) used chiefly to modify (*i.e.,* qualify or limit) a verb, an adjective, another adverb, or even a sentence as a whole. An adverb indicates time (*now, then, today*), place (*here, there, outside*), manner (*calmly, quickly, clearly*), or degree (*very, somewhat, only*).

Stand *here.* [*Here* modifies the verb *stand.*]

Stand beside the *very* old clock. [*Very* modifies the adjective *old.*]

Stand *very* quietly. [*Very* modifies the adverb *quietly,* which modifies the verb *stand.*]

Certainly you may be seated. [*Certainly* modifies the sentence as a whole.]

See also Section 4, **Adjectives and Adverbs.**

Adverb clause. A subordinate clause used as an adverb.

I shall leave the house *after she comes.*

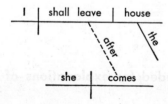

[The adverb clause *after she comes* modifies the verb *shall leave* and indicates time. Adverb clauses may also indicate place, manner, cause, purpose, condition, concession, comparison, or result.]

Antecedent. The name given to a word or group of words to which a pronoun refers.

This is the *man who* came to the house. [*Man* is the antecedent of the relative pronoun *who.*]

When *John* and *Mary* came, *they* told us the facts in the case. [*John* and *Mary* are the antecedents of the personal pronoun *they.*]

Appositive. A noun or any other substantive set beside another substantive and denoting the same person or thing. See also Section 12d(a).

Dr. Smith, our *dentist,* is visiting *England,* his native *country.* [*Dentist* is in apposition with *Dr. Smith,* and *country* is in apposition with *England.*]

Article. Articles are usually classed as adjectives. The definite article is *the.* The indefinite articles are *a* and *an.*

Auxiliary. A verb that is used to form various tenses of other verbs. *Have, may, can, be, shall, will, must, ought,* and *do* are the common auxiliaries.

I *shall* go.
He *was* sent away.
He *has been* promoted.

Case. The inflectional form of a noun (*man's*) or pronoun (*he, his, him*) to show such relations as subject (subjective case—*he*), possession (possessive case—*man's, his*), or object (objective case—*him*). For nouns the position in the sentence is the only indication of subjective and objective case. "The man (subjective) killed the lion." "The lion killed the man (objective)."

See also Section 5, **Case.**

Clause. A group of words that contains a verb and its subject and is used as a part of a sentence. A clause may be main (independent, principal) or subordinate (dependent).

(1) A main (independent, principal) clause can stand by itself as a simple sentence.

The moon rose and *the stars came out.* [Two main clauses, either of which can stand by itself as a simple sentence.]

(2) A subordinate (dependent) clause cannot stand alone. It is used as a noun, an adjective, or an adverb.

That he will run for office is doubtful. [Noun clause: a subordinate clause used as the subject of the sentence.]

See also Section 1d, **Sentence Sense.**

Collective noun. See **Noun.**

Colloquial. Appropriate for conversation and informal writing rather than for formal writing.

Common noun. See **Noun.**

Comparison. The change in the form of an adjective or adverb to indicate degrees of superiority in quality, quantity, or manner. There are three degrees: positive, comparative, and superlative.

EXAMPLES

Positive	Comparative	Superlative
good	better	best
high	higher	highest
quickly	more quickly	most quickly

See also **Inflection**.

Complement. A word or words used to complete the sense of the verb, the subject, or the object. The complement may be an object, a predicate noun, or a predicate adjective.

OBJECTS

John gave the *boy* a *book*. [*Book* is the direct object; *boy* is the indirect object.]

PREDICATE NOUNS

Samuel was a good *child*. [The predicate noun *child*, referring to the subject *Samuel*, is also called the **predicate complement**, the **subjective complement**, or the **predicate nominative**.]

He called the man a *hero*. [*Man* is the direct object. The noun *hero*, referring to *man*, is called the **objective complement** or the **predicate objective**.]

PREDICATE ADJECTIVES

The boy is *obedient*. [The predicate adjective *obedient*, referring to the subject *boy*, is also called the **subjective complement** or the **predicate complement**.]

Jack colored the egg *blue*. [*Egg* is the direct object. The predicate adjective *blue*, referring to *egg*, is also called the **objective complement** or the **predicate objective**.]

Complete predicate. See **Predicate**.
Complex sentence. See **Sentence**.
Compound sentence. See **Sentence**.
Compound-complex sentence. See **Sentence**.
Concrete noun. See **Noun**.
Conjugation. A grouping of verb forms to indicate tense, voice, mood, number, and person. See the conjugation of the irregular verb *to see* in Section **7**. See also **Inflection**.
Conjunction. A word (one of the eight parts of speech) used to connect words, phrases, or clauses. There are two kinds, co-ordinating conjunctions and subordinating conjunctions.

(1) **Co-ordinating conjunctions** connect words, phrases, and clauses of equal rank: *and, or, but, for, either . . . or, neither . . . nor*.

(2) **Subordinating conjunctions** connect subordinate clauses with main clauses: *if, al-* *though, since, in order that, as, because, unless, after, before, until, when, whenever, where, while, wherever*, etc.

Conjunctive adverb. An adverb which serves also to connect or relate main clauses: *however, therefore, nevertheless, hence, then, besides, moreover, thus, otherwise, consequently, accordingly*, etc.

Construction (Syntax). The grammatical functions of words, phrases, or clauses in the sentence.

Co-ordinate, co-ordinating. Of equal rank. For example, two nouns, two subordinate clauses, or two main clauses.

Copula (Copulative verb, linking verb). A verb used to express the relation between the subject and the predicate noun or predicate adjective. "He *is* merry." The chief copulative verbs are *be, become, seem, appear* and verbs pertaining to the senses.

Declension. See **Inflection**.
Demonstrative adjective. See **Adjective**.
Demonstrative pronoun. A pronoun that points out. "*This* is good; *that* is bad."
Dependent clause. See **Clause**.
Descriptive adjective. See **Adjective**.
Diagraming. An arrangement of words on lines to show relationships within the sentence. Various forms are used. Any form is serviceable if it helps the student to understand the sentence. A diagram is only a means to an end, not an end in itself. One form of diagraming in common use is illustrated below.

The very feeble woman carefully placed the cakes on the shelf.

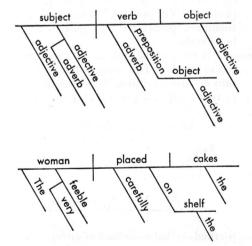

To decide was difficult.

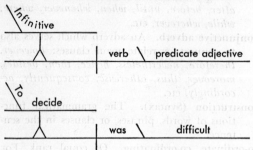

See other diagrams under **Adjective clause,
Adverb clause, Gerund, Modify, Noun clause,
Sentence,** and especially in Section 1, **Sentence
Sense.**

Direct address (Nominative of address, vocative).
A noun or pronoun used parenthetically to
direct a speech to a definite person.

I hope, *Mary,* that you will go. *Mary,* close
the door.

Direct object. See **Object.**

Ellipsis (Elliptical expression). An expression
grammatically incomplete but clear because
omitted words can be readily supplied.

Mary is prettier than Helen (is pretty).
Whenever (it is) possible, you should take
exercise.

For the ellipsis mark in quoted passages, see
Section 17a(3).

Expletive. *It* or *there* used merely as an introductory word or filler.

It is true that he is not coming.
There were few men present.

Finite verb. A verb or verb form that makes a
complete assertion and may thus serve as a
predicate. "The sun *rose.*" "The sun *is rising.*"
Infinitives, participles, and gerunds are not
finite verbs.

Gerund. A form of the verb used as a noun and
ending in *-ing.* The gerund should be carefully distinguished from the present participle
(a verbal adjective), which also ends in *-ing.*

Swimming is enjoyable.

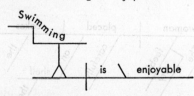

[Gerund—verbal noun used as subject]

The boy *swimming* against the current was exhausted.

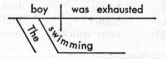

[Present participle—verbal adjective modifying the noun *boy*]

Since the gerund is a noun, it may function
as subject (as in the sentence given above),
as object of a verb ("I enjoy *swimming*"), as
object of a preposition ("By *swimming* he
reached shore"), as a predicate noun ("My
chief recreation is *swimming*"), or as an appositive ("My chief recreation, *swimming,* has
some disadvantages"). The gerund, like a
noun, may be modified by an adjective: "*Skillful* swimming saved his life."

But the gerund shows its verbal origin by its
ability to take an object ("Swimming the
horse across the stream was difficult") or to be
modified by an adverb ("By swimming *rapidly*
he escaped").

Gerund phrase. See **Phrase.**

Idiom. An expression in good use that is peculiar
to a language. (Idioms sometimes violate
established rules of grammar, but are nevertheless sanctioned by usage.

I have known him for *many a year.*
Do you *remember saying that* you were tired?

Indefinite pronoun. See **Pronoun.**

**Independent clause (Main clause, principal
clause).** See **Clause.**

Independent element. Any word or group of
words that has no grammatical connection
with the rest of the sentence.

DIRECT ADDRESS I hope, *William,* that you can
go.

DIRECTIVE EXPRESSION The whole family, *we
hope,* will come.

ABSOLUTE EXPRESSION *Darkness having come,*
he slipped away.

INTERJECTION *Ah,* this is the sport I enjoy.

Indirect object. See **Object.**

Infinitive. A form of the verb commonly preceded
by *to* and used as a noun, an adjective, or an
adverb. After certain verbs the *to* is often
omitted: "He helped *(to) make* the kite." "He
dared not *(to) go* away."

USED AS A NOUN

To walk was a pleasure. [Subject]

He began *to open the box.* [Object of verb]

Her wish was *to see him leave.* [Predicate noun]

He was about *to leave.* [Object of preposition]

USED AS AN ADJECTIVE

I have work *to do.* [*To do* modifies the noun *work.*]

USED AS AN ADVERB

He enlisted *to become an aviator.* [The infinitive modifies the verb *enlisted.*]

The infinitive shows its verbal origin by its ability to take a subject ("I asked *him* to go"), to take an object ("I wanted to pay *him*"), or to be modified by an adverb ("I asked him to drive *slowly*"). Note that the subject of the infinitive is in the objective case.

Infinitive phrase. See **Phrase.**

Inflection. A change in the form of a word to show a change in meaning or in relationship to some other word or group of words. The inflection of nouns and pronouns is called **declension:** *man, man's, men, men's; I, my, me,* etc. The inflection of verbs is called **conjugation;** that of adjectives and adverbs is called **comparison.**

Intensive pronoun. See **Pronoun.**

Interjection. A word (one of the eight parts of speech) expressing emotion and having no grammatical relation with other words in the sentence. "*Oh,* I can hardly believe it." "*Whew!* That was a narrow escape."

Interrogative pronoun. See **Pronoun.**

Intransitive. See *Verb.*

Irregular verb. See **Strong verb.**

Limiting adjective. See **Adjective.**

Linking verb. See **Copula.**

Main clause (Independent clause, principal clause). See **Clause.**

Modifier. Any word or group of words that describes or qualifies another word or group of words. See **Modify.**

Modify. To describe or qualify the meaning of a word or group of words. In a diagram modifiers are attached to the words they modify.

A very old man hobbled slowly along the road.

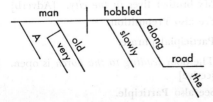

[*A* and *old* modify *man; very* modifies *old; slowly* and *along the road* modify *hobbled; the* modifies *road.*]

Mood (Mode). The form of the verb that is used to indicate the manner in which the action is conceived. English has indicative, imperative, and subjunctive moods. See Section 7.

The **indicative mood** states a fact or asks a question.

The sun *is* shining.
Is the sun shining?

The **imperative mood** gives a command or makes a request.

Release the prisoners.
Walk carefully.

The **subjunctive mood** expresses a doubt, a condition contrary to fact, a wish or regret, a concession, a supposition.

I wish that Mother *were* here.
If I *had* my way, you would not go.
If I *should be gone,* wait for me.

Nominative. Equivalent to **Subjective.** See **Case.**

Nominative absolute. See **Absolute.**

Nominative of address. See **Direct address.**

Nonrestrictive modifier. A nonessential modifier. A phrase or clause which could be omitted without changing the essential meaning of the sentence.

The airplane, *which is now being manufactured in large numbers,* is of immense commercial value.

See also **Restrictive modifier.**

Noun. One of the eight parts of speech, the name of a person, place, thing, quality, etc.

Nouns are used as:

(1) SUBJECTS OF VERBS: The *dog* barked.

(2) OBJECTS OF VERBS, VERBALS, OR PREPOSITIONS: He opened the *door* to let the *dog* into the *house.*

(3) PREDICATE NOUNS: She was his *secretary.*

(4) APPOSITIVES: Mr. Brown, our *neighbor,* is sick.

(5) NOMINATIVES OF ADDRESS: *Mary,* will you help us?

(6) PREDICATE OBJECTIVES (OBJECTIVE COMPLEMENTS): He called the man a *traitor.*

Nouns are classified as:

(1) COMMON OR PROPER.

A **common noun** is the name applied to any one of a class of persons, places, or things: *man, woman, city, state, chair, bed.*

A **proper noun** is the name applied to a specific individual, place, or thing: *Henry Ford, Jane Addams, New Orleans, Texas, the Parthenon, the Washington Monument.*

(2) COLLECTIVE.

A **collective noun** is a name applied to a group: *band, flock, jury, army.* See Section 6a(7) and 6b(3).

(3) CONCRETE or ABSTRACT.

A **concrete noun** names something that can be perceived by one or more of the senses: *water, trees, man, river.*

An **abstract noun** names a quality or general idea: *love, ambition, hate, pity.*

Noun clause. A subordinate clause used as a noun. It may be used as subject, direct object, appositive, predicate nominative, object of a preposition.

Whoever comes will be welcome. [Subject]
I hope *that he will recover.* [Object of the verb]

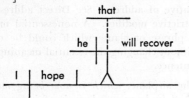

The hope *that he might win* upheld him. [Appositive]
This is *what I asked for.* [Predicate nominative]
I shall spend the money for *whatever seems best.* [Object of the preposition *for*]

Number. The change in the form of a verb, a noun, or a pronoun to designate one (*singular*) or more than one (*plural*).

Object. A noun or pronoun (or a phrase or clause used as a noun) that receives the action of a transitive verb or follows a preposition.

Direct object. Any noun (or its equivalent) that receives the action of a transitive verb.

He raked *leaves.* [Noun]
He supplied *whatever was needed.* [Clause used as a noun]

Indirect object. Any noun (or its equivalent) that receives indirectly the action of the verb.

He gave *me* an apple. [*Apple* is the direct object, *me* the indirect object, of the verb

gave. It is usually possible to substitute for the indirect object a prepositional phrase with *to.*]

Object of a preposition. Any noun (or its equivalent) following a preposition. See **Preposition.**

He walked into the *house.* [*House* is the object of the preposition *into.*]

Objective complement. See **Complement.**

Participial phrase. See **Phrase.**

Participle. A form of the verb used as an adjective. "The *rising* sun, a *concealed* weapon, a *lost* opportunity." The present participle, which ends in *-ing,* should be carefully distinguished from the gerund (a verbal noun), which also ends in *-ing.* (See **Gerund.**) The past participle ends in *-ed, -d, -t, -en, -n,* or makes an internal change.

PRESENT PARTICIPLES concealing, losing, rising, singing.
PAST PARTICIPLES concealed, lost, risen, sung.

Parts of speech. The eight classes into which grammarians group words according to their uses in the sentence: *verb, noun, pronoun, adjective, adverb, conjunction, preposition,* and *interjection.* Each of these is discussed separately in this section. It is important to note that *part of speech* is determined by function. The same word is often used as several different parts of speech.

Passive voice. See **Voice.**

Person. Changes in the form of verbs and pronouns which indicate whether a person is speaking (first person), is spoken to (second person), or is spoken about (third person).

FIRST PERSON *I* see the boy.
SECOND PERSON Can *you* see the boy?
THIRD PERSON *He* sees the boy.

Personal pronoun. See **Pronoun.**

Phrase. A group of related words which lacks subject and verb and is used as a single part of speech.

Prepositional phrase:

The man *with red hair* is my brother. [Adjective]
My brother lives *in the city.* [Adverb]
See also **Preposition.**

Participial phrase:

The door *leading to the porch* is open. [Adjective]
See also **Participle.**

Gerund phrase:

Reckless driving along the highways is responsible for many wrecks.   [Substantive]
See also **Gerund.**

Infinitive phrase:

To err is human.   [Substantive]
See also **Infinitive.**

Verb phrase:

He *has been employed* for a year.   [Verb]

Predicate.   The part of the sentence comprising what is said about the subject. The **complete predicate** consists of the verb (the **simple predicate**) along with its complements and modifiers.

He *runs* through the house.   [*Runs* is the simple predicate; *runs through the house* is the complete predicate.]

Predicate adjective, predicate complement, predicate nominative, predicate noun, predicate objective.   See **Complement.**

Preposition.   A word (one of the eight parts of speech) used to show the relation of a noun (or noun-equivalent) to some other word in the sentence.

He ran *with* the team.   [The preposition *with* shows the relation of the noun *team* to the verb *ran*.]
The bird is *in* the tree.
The man walked *into* the house.
The man *of* the house is absent.

Prepositional phrase.   See **Phrase.**

Present tense.   See **Tense.**

Principal clause (Main clause, independent clause).   See **Clause.**

Principal parts.   The forms of any verb from which the various tenses are derived: (1) present stem (infinitive), (2) past tense, and (3) past participle.

EXAMPLES

see	saw	seen
take	took	taken
love	loved	loved

Pronoun.   A word (one of the eight parts of speech) used instead of a noun.

Personal pronouns: *I, you, he, she, it.*
See the declension under Section **5, Case.**

Interrogative pronouns: *who, which, what.*

Relative pronouns: *who, which, that.*

Demonstrative pronouns: *this, that, these, those.*

Indefinite pronouns: *each, either, any, anyone, some, someone, one, no one, few, all, everyone,* etc.

Reciprocal pronouns: *each other, one another.*

Reflexive pronouns: *myself, yourself, himself,* etc.

You hurt *yourself.*
He ruined *himself.*

Intensive pronouns: *myself, yourself, himself,* etc.

I *myself* will go.
You *yourself* should go.

Proper adjective.   An adjective formed from a proper noun, as *Spanish* from *Spain.*

Proper noun.   See *Noun.*

Reciprocal pronoun.   See **Pronoun.**

Reflexive pronoun.   See **Pronoun.**

Regular verb.   See **Weak verb.**

Restrictive modifier.   An essential modifier. A phrase or clause which cannot be omitted without changing the essential meaning of the sentence.

Men *who are industrious* will succeed.

See also **Nonrestrictive modifier.**

Sentence.   A unit of expression that may stand alone. A complete sentence contains a verb (predicate) and its subject, with or without modifiers. (For the incomplete sentence see page 806.) Sentences are classified structurally as (1) simple, (2) compound, (3) complex, or (4) compound-complex.

(1) **Simple sentence.**   A sentence containing one main clause but no subordinate clauses.

Birds fly.   [Simple sentence]

Birds and bats fly.   [Simple sentence with compound subject]

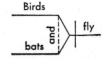

Birds and bats swoop and fly. [Simple sentence with compound subject and compound predicate]

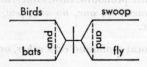

(2) **Compound sentence.** A sentence containing two or more main clauses but no subordinate clauses.

The moon rose and the stars came out.

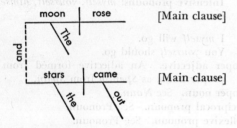

[Main clause]

[Main clause]

(3) **Complex sentence.** A sentence containing one main clause and one or more subordinate clauses.

Birds fly when they are startled.

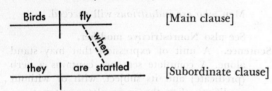

[Main clause]

[Subordinate clause]

(4) **Compound-complex sentence.** A sentence containing two or more main clauses and one or more subordinate clauses.

Engines roared overhead and a bomb fell where we had stood.

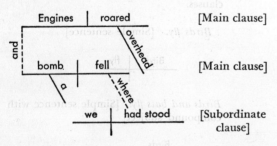

[Main clause]

[Main clause]

[Subordinate clause]

Simple predicate. See **Predicate.**

Simple sentence. See **Sentence.**

Strong verb (Irregular verb). A verb that forms its principal parts by vowel change: *ring, rang, rung; see, saw, seen.*

Subject. The person or thing (in a sentence or a clause) about which an assertion is made.

The *dog* barked at the car.

Subjective. See **Case.**

Subjective complement. See **Complement.**

Subjunctive. See **Mood.**

Subordinate clause. A dependent clause. See **Clause.**

Substantive. Any word or group of words used as a noun. Substantives may be nouns, pronouns, phrases (especially gerund or infinitive phrases), or noun clauses.

Syntax. Sentence structure. See **Construction.**

Tense. Change in the form of the verb to indicate the time of the action. There are six tenses: *present, past, future, present perfect, past perfect, future perfect.* (See also Section 7.)

Transitive. See **Verb.**

Verb. A word or word group (one of the eight parts of speech) used to assert action, being, or state of being.

Transitive verb. A verb with a receiver of the action (object) to complete its meaning. See **Object.**

The boy *sold* his bicycle.
The boy *has sold* his bicycle.

Intransitive verb. A verb without a receiver of the action to complete its meaning.

The boy *fished* in the stream.
The boy *has been fishing* in the stream.

Verb phrase. See **Phrase.**

Verbal. A word derived from a verb but used as a noun or adjective (and sometimes as an adverb). See **Infinitive, Gerund, Participle.**

Vocative. See **Direct address.**

Voice. Distinction in the form of the verb to indicate whether the subject of the verb acts (**active voice**) or is acted upon (**passive voice**). See Section 29d.

Weak verb (Regular verb). Any verb that forms its principal parts by adding *-ed, -d,* or *-t* to the infinitive: *love, loved, loved; sweep, swept, swept.*

[Numbers in **boldface** refer to rules ; other numbers refer to pages. An *ex* indicates that appropriate drill exercises are included. A colon is used after each boldface number to indicate that the following pages refer to the rule or the part of the rule concerned. An *n* indicates reference to a footnote.]

Reading Material

Innocents Abroad – Mark Twain
A Tree Grows In Brooklyn – Betty Smith
The Robe – Lloyd Douglas
The Nazarene – Sholem Asch
The Apostle – Sholem Asch

Rue St. Idonore
Rue de l'Arbre Sec

GRAMMAR

1 ss Sentence Sense
a Recognizing verbs
b Recognizing subjects (and objects)
c Recognizing all parts of speech
d Recognizing phrases and clauses
e Recognizing types of sentences

2 frag Fragment
a Phrase
b Subordinate clause
c Other fragments

3 cs Comma Splice and Fused Sentence
a Subordination
b Co-ordination
c Caution: Conjunctive adverb, etc.

4 ad Adjectives and Adverbs
a Modifiers of verbs, adjectives, adverbs
b After words pertaining to senses, etc.
c Preference for adverb in -ly
d Comparative and superlative
e Awkward noun form as adjective

5 ca Case
a Subject of verb
b Predicate complement
c Possessive noun, pronoun
d Possessive with gerund
e Of phrase
f Object of verb, etc.
g Object, etc., of infinitive

6 agr Agreement
a Subject and verb
  (1) Intervening word
  (2) Subjects joined by and
  (3) Subjects joined by or, etc.
  (4) Subject following verb
  (5) Relative pronoun
  (6) Each, either, etc.
  (7) Collective nouns
  (8) Predicate noun
  (9) Plural form, singular meaning
  (10) Title of book, etc.
b Pronoun and antecedent
  (1) Antecedents such as *man*, *one*, etc.
  (2) Antecedents joined by *and*; by *or*
  (3) Collective nouns as antecedents

7 t Tense (Mood; *Shall* and *Will*)
a Appropriate tense forms
b Sequence of tenses
c Subjunctive mood
d Needless shifts in tense or mood
e Distinctions between *shall* and *will*

MECHANICS

8 ms Manuscript
a Proper materials
b Arrangement on page
c Legibility
d Revision
e Record of errors
f Syllabication

9 cap Capitals
a Proper names
b Titles preceding name, etc.
c Titles of books, etc.
d I and O
e Beginning of sentence, etc.
f Unnecessary capitals

10 ital Italics
a Titles of publications
b Foreign words and phrases
c Names of ships, etc.
d Words, etc., used as such
e Overuse for emphasis

11 ab Abbreviations and Numbers
a Titles
b Names of states, etc.
c Street, road, etc.
d References to volume, page, etc.
e Christian names
f Usage regarding numbers

PUNCTUATION

12 , The Comma
a Main clauses
b Introductory clauses, phrases
c Series; co-ordinate adjectives
d Nonrestrictive elements
e Misreading

13 O Superfluous Commas
a Subject and verb, etc.
b Words, phrases joined by *and*
c Slight parenthesis
d Restrictive elements
e First item of series, etc.

14 ; The Semicolon
a Main clauses
b Elements containing commas
c Caution: Misuse with parts of unequal rank

15 ap The Apostrophe
a Indicating possession
b Misused with personal pronouns
c Marking omissions
d Forming plurals of letters, etc.

16 " " Quotation Marks
a Direct quotations
b Titles
c Special words
d Overuse
e Position with other marks

17 . The Period and
a . Period
b ? Question mark
c ! Exclamation point
d : Colon
e — Dash

Other Marks
f ( ) Parentheses
g [ ] Brackets

SPELLING

18 sp Spelling
a Mispronunciation
b Similar words
c Prefix and root
d Suffixes
e Confusion of *ei* and *ie*
f Hyphenated words

DICTION

19 g Good Use
a Use of dictionary
b Colloquialisms
c Slang and jargon
d Dialectal words
e Illiteracies
f Obsolete and archaic words
g Technical words
h Fine writing, etc.
i Glossary

20 e Exactness
a Exact words
b Idioms
c Fresh expressions

21 w Wordiness and Useless Repetition
a Needed omission
b Needed revision
c Useless repetition

22 ^ Omission of Necessary Words
a Article, pronoun, etc.
b Verb
c Completion of comparisons, etc.

EFFECTIVE SENTENCES

23 u Unity and Logical Thinking
a Unrelated ideas
b Excessive detail
c Mixed, obscure, or illogical constructions

24 sub Subordination
a Short, choppy sentences
b And sentences
c Subordination of main thought

25 coh Coherence
a Misplaced parts
  (1) Adverbs (2) Phrases (3) Clauses
  (4) "Squinting" constructions
  (5) Split infinitives, etc.
b Dangling modifiers

26 || Parallelism
a Parallel form
b Repetition of preposition, etc.
c Correlatives
d Caution: Misleading parallel

27 pv Point of View
a Tense
b Mood
c Subject or voice
d Person
e Number
f Indirect and direct discourse
g Tone or style
h Perspective

28 ref Reference of Pronouns
a Ambiguous
b Remote antecedent
c Broad
d Repeated pronoun with different antecedents

29 emp Emphasis
a Position
b Periodic sentence
c Order of climax
d Active voice
e Repetition
f Unusual order
g Balance

30 var Variety
a Length
b Beginning
c Avoiding compound sentences
d Subject-verb sequence
e Statement